Mason & McCall Smith's

LAW &
MEDICAL ETHICS

Tenth Edition

G. T. LAURIE LLB PhD FRSE
FMedSci FRCP(Edin)

Professor of Medical Jurisprudence at the University of Edinburgh

S. H. E. HARMON Esq.
BA LLB LLM PhD FHEA

Lecturer in Regulation and Risk at the University of Edinburgh

G. PORTER LLB LLM

Lecturer in Medical Law and Ethics at the University of Edinburgh

OXFORD
UNIVERSITY PRESS

OXFORD
UNIVERSITY PRESS

Great Clarendon Street, Oxford, OX2 6DP,
United Kingdom

Oxford University Press is a department of the University of Oxford.
It furthers the University's objective of excellence in research, scholarship,
and education by publishing worldwide. Oxford is a registered trade mark of
Oxford University Press in the UK and in certain other countries

© Oxford University Press 2016

The moral rights of the authors have been asserted

Seventh edition 2005
Eight edition 2010
Ninth edition 2013

Impression: 3

Public sector information reproduced under Open Government Licence v2.0
(http://www.nationalarchives.gov.uk/doc/open-government-licence/open-government-licence.htm)

Published in the United States of America by Oxford University Press
198 Madison Avenue, New York, NY 10016, United States of America

British Library Cataloguing in Publication Data
Data available

Library of Congress Control Number: 2015956653

ISBN 978-0-19-874751-2

Printed in Great Britain by
Bell & Bain Ltd., Glasgow

Mason & McCall Smith's
LAW & MEDICAL ETHICS

'It would not be correct to say that every moral obligation involves a legal duty; but every legal duty is founded on a moral obligation.'

LORD CHIEF JUSTICE COLERIDGE
in *R* v *Instan* [1893] 1 QB at 453

FOREWORD

We need no reminder of the major advances in the physical world around us which have been made in the last half-century. However, we often fail to appreciate the comparable intellectual changes to which we have been subject. Prominent among these is the steady introduction of the decimal system into all phases of our lives. As a consequence, the figure '10' has achieved a special and fundamental significance and publication of the tenth edition of this book seems a particularly apposite moment at which to review its underlying philosophy.

Moreover, the public and legal reaction to law and medical ethics has changed pari passu. It was not until the fifth edition that the increasing disassociation between modern medical law and criminal law was appreciated and acted upon—the apparently insoluble issue of abortion always excepted—while the rejection of US law and its substitution by European law as a template for UK law, has steadily increased.

It seems right that these movements should be reflected in general in the authorship—out with the old, in with the new! These sea changes are acknowledged in this foreword to the tenth edition, which has been kindly requested by the new panel of authors who will introduce a younger, and more contemporary, attitude to our subject.

One of the incremental basic changes over the years has lain within that of the link between medical and other legal disciplines. I have already commented on the weakening of this link between the medical and criminal disciplines and it seems to me that we can, now, rightly detect a comparable alteration in the currently strong association between medical and family law as the latter, in particular, is inexorably replaced by human rights law and ethics—often as guided by the European courts. We can see this by way of three examples of well-known cases.

The problem of abortion has already been raised and it is to be noted that the focus of the issue has altered from being a matter of the taking of human life to one of the woman's human rights to a state-funded abortion service.[1] Somewhat similarly, IVF, which once formed a bastion of family law is now fully accepted and has been reduced to a question of whose rights are involved in demanding treatment for infertility.[2] Third, the determination to end one's life has now passed from being a matter of homicide and the criminal law to one of the human rights of the individual to end his or her life.[3] Human rights law is, however, a fragile discipline which is liable to misappropriation; the question still open is whether this assumed transformation of legal relationships is to be seen as a good or bad development.

The foreword to a book is no place in which to discuss the rights and wrongs of its content and I would not attempt to do so. Rather, I see it as an integral challenge for the new cohort of authors and I look forward to seeing the results of their researches.

---

[1] *Tysiąc* v *Poland* (2007) 45 EHRR 42; [2007] 1 FCR 666.
[2] *Evans* v *United Kingdom* [2008] 46 EHRR 34.
[3] *Nicklinson* v *Ministry of Justice* [2015] AC 657.

Best of luck to one and all! The surface of the road to understanding may be changing, but we must hope that *Law and Medical Ethics* continues to ensure that its signposts are correct and are pursued.

J. K. Mason
Edinburgh, 2015

PREFACE

The advent of the tenth edition of *Law and Medical Ethics* is a cause for both celebration and regret. As to the former, we are delighted that the book continues as the longest-standing textbook in the field examining the laws in the UK, and it will forever be known as *Mason and McCall Smith's Law and Medical Ethics*, even although—as a matter of regret—both founding authors have now left the writing team. Alexander McCall Smith's last contribution was to the sixth edition before he went on to 'greater things', as they say, in the fiction world. And, since the one thing that never changes is change itself, this is the first edition without the grandfather of this book, John Kenyon Mason, whose enthusiasm for the subject has been the single most powerful force behind its success. Notwithstanding our loss of Ken as a co-author in this edition, we are delighted that he has provided us with a foreword and much encouragement to complete this update.

As is customary in any new edition to a textbook, we must reflect on the period since the last edition and comment on milestone changes. On this occasion, however, the shifts have been seismic for a number of reasons, and we wager that this period will come to be seen as the end of an era in medical law and ethics. As well as the legal developments that we highlight below, we have witnessed the departure of notable doyens and doyennes from the medico-legal community: just as Ken Mason has retired in Edinburgh, so John Harris has retired in Manchester. In Glasgow, Sheila McLean has bid her farewells to the academy, and we were very pleased to be involved in the production of her Festschrift: Ferguson and Laurie (eds), *Inspiring a Medico-legal Revolution: Essays in Honour of Sheila AM McLean* (Ashgate, 2015). In similar fashion, and with equal respect for a career's worth of contributions, Margot Brazier's work has been celebrated in Stanton, Devaney, Farrell, and Mullock (eds), *Pioneering Healthcare Law: Essays in Honour of the Work of Margaret Brazier* (Routledge, 2015). Put simply, the discipline will never be the same.

The same can be said of the changes that have occurred in the law, particularly with respect to the role of the Supreme Court. Its decision in *Montgomery* v *Lanarkshire Health Board* (2015) has swept away the last vestiges of the decision of its former self as the House of Lords in *Sidaway* (1985) and concerning the legal rule on what patients are entitled to be told about their own medical care. The dominance of the defining feature of medical law as a sub-discipline within tort and delict—the *Bolam* test—has been incontrovertibly undermined as a result. And in *Nicklinson* v *Ministry of Justice* (2014), the Supreme Court has sent as clear a message as possible to Parliament that matters must also change on the law of assisted suicide. Nonetheless, legislatures on both sides of the border have struggled, and failed, to achieve agreement on legal reform. In other areas, we have witnessed a revival of long-standing issues, such as the return of legal interest in non-voluntary, non-therapeutic sterilisations, and an increased interest in the regulation of surrogacy prompted by international challenges from reproductive tourism. Where once medical law was dominated by case law, many areas have come to be governed by statute. Here too, these statutory reforms—now well established—have been subject to review, and a notable example is the Mental Capacity Act 2005, which passed its tenth birthday with the production of this tenth issue.

Just as these developments might be seen as the next generation of issues in medical law, so too we must welcome the next generation of scholars. *GTL*: speaking personally, it is a real pleasure to welcome Shawn Harmon and Gerard Porter as co-authors on this edition. In turn, our triumvirate would like to extend its gratitude to Murray Earle for his continued contribution to Chapter 3 on EU dimensions, and to Elisabeth Davis who has supported all of us with her excellent research assistance across all chapters of the book. This was made possible by generous funding from Edinburgh Law School, for which we also extend our thanks.

All of the people involved in the production of this edition are former students and/or colleagues of Ken Mason. We are confident that he will be proud of his legacy of instilling a passion for medical law. We are also tentatively hopeful that he will be proud of this first foray without him.

G.T.L.

S.H.

G.P.

Edinburgh, October 2015

NEW TO THIS EDITION

- Discussion of duties of care to families around genetic information—*ABC* v *St George's NHS Trust*
- The emergence of the tort of misuse of private information in *Vidal-Hall* v *Google Inc*
- The Human Fertilisation and Embryology (Mitochondrial Donation) Regulations 2015
- The implications of the Care Act 2014
- Discussion of the Royal College of Paediatrics and Child Health, Making Decisions to Limit Treatment in Life-limiting and Life-threatening Conditions in Children (2015)
- The UK Supreme Court on best interests and the Mental Capacity Act 2005 in *Aintree University Hospitals NHS Foundation Trust* v *James and Others*
- Developments in the processes for validity of Do Not Attempt Resuscitation Orders (DNARs)
- The Supreme Courts of Canada and the United Kingdom on assisted suicide in *Carter* v *Canada (Attorney General)* (2015) and *Nicklinson* v *Ministry of Justice* (2014)
- Judicial consideration of prosecutorial discretion in health-related matters in *Nicklinson* v *Ministry of Justice* (2014) and *R* v *Golding* (2014)
- The use of declaratory relief in mental health cases—*Nottinghamshire Healthcare NHS Trust* v *RC* (2014)—and best interests—*A NHS Foundation Trust* v *X* (2014)
- Discretionary powers of the Mental Health Tribunal—*G* v *Scottish Ministers* (2014)
- Discussion of IP claims in relation to human material at the ECJ—*Brüstle* v *Greenpeace* (2012) and *International Stem Cell Corp* v *Comptroller General of Patents* (2015)—and in the US Supreme Court—*Association for Molecular Pathology* v *Myriad Genetics, USPTO et al.* (2013)
- The Human Transplantation (Wales) Act 2013 with its new opt-out approach to transplantation
- Discussion of the new Health Research Authority, of Regulation (EU) No 536/2014 on clinical trials on medicinal products for human use, which comes into effect in May 2016, and of the 2013 version of the Helsinki Declaration
- Reflections on the legal and ethical challenges posed by brain death and post-mortem pregnancy in light of the High Court of Ireland's decision in *P.P.* v *Health Service Executive* [2014]
- Discussion of parental decision-making and the child's best interests following the High Court decision in *Re Ashya King* [2014]
- Consideration of the effectiveness of the medical product liability regime in response to the Poly Implant Prothèse (PIP) breast implant scandal
- Analysis of the doctor's legal duty to ensure that patients are aware of the 'material risks' entailed in a recommended course of treatment—and to advise of reasonable alternative treatments—after the Supreme Court decision in *Montgomery* v *Lanarkshire Health Board* [2015]

CONTENTS

TABLE OF CASES

TABLE OF UNITED KINGDOM LEGISLATION

TABLE OF LEGISLATION—OTHER JURISDICTIONS

TABLE OF EUROPEAN AND INTERNATIONAL INSTRUMENTS

Regulations

TABLE OF UNITED KINGDOM
STATUTORY INSTRUMENTS

1

MEDICAL ETHICS
AND MEDICAL PRACTICE

1.01 This book is concerned with a vital debate that has captured the imagination of people throughout the world—that is, as to how we should deal with the remarkable advances in medicine and human biology that may well change the way in which we see ourselves as human beings. But the debate is also concerned with the more day-to-day issues of the role of law in medical practice, with the moral and legal contours of the doctor–patient relationship and with the obligations that we owe to each other in matters of (public) health. It has an academic side to it—bioethics and medical law are recognised components of the curricula of many universities and colleges—but it also involves legislators, policymakers, national bioethics committees, and, increasingly, the public itself. It is, of course, inevitable that such an issue should give rise to a burgeoning literature consisting of both general and specialised material.[1]

1.02 The importance and intensity of the public moral conversation about bioethics and medical law are explained in part by the very nature of their subject matter. This is an area of concern which touches upon people's most intimate interests. It deals with matters of human reproduction and human mortality—or sex and death—both of which have traditionally involved our religious convictions and have provoked intense emotions. Increasingly, medical technological advances allow us to manipulate the state of human health from transplantation to genetic modification and on to (de)selection of traits such as deafness or even gender. In addressing these issues, the debate raises many fundamental questions. What is it to be a person? What is the value of human life? How, if at all, should we attempt to influence the future biology of the species through the use of new knowledge?

1.03 There is no shortage of conviction on any of these issues. Most major cultural or religious traditions have firm views on such matters and are frequently prepared to assert them as being valid for all; indeed, much of bioethics is informed by such traditions. Those who approach the subject from the viewpoint of individual freedom, or of human rights, will argue just as vigorously that issues of this sort lie clearly within the confines of individual moral action. The antagonism between these two positions is sometimes intense and it often seems as if there is little prospect of common ground.[2] Yet, insofar

---

[1] The literature on bioethics is now greater than its counterpart in any other area of applied ethics. Constraints of space prevent more than a few examples of the genre but, of the general works available, T L Beauchamp and J F Childress, *Principles of Biomedical Ethics* (7th edn, 2012) has established itself as a classic. A useful starting point for many readers will be the various compilations which have been made, including P Singer and A M Viens (eds), *The Cambridge Textbook of Bioethics* (2008). A complementary companion to our own text is T Hope, J Savulescu, and J Hendrick, *Medical Ethics and Law* (2nd edn, 2008).

[2] R Ashcroft, 'The troubled relationship between bioethics and human rights' in M Freeman (ed) (2008) *Law and Bioethics*, ch 3.

as we have to live in a community, we are obliged to identify what is permissible and what is not—and this implies the involvement of the law. So we do need, for example, a law concerning artificial reproduction because, unless the law pronounces on the issue, society can be seen to be endorsing a non-interventionist approach which allows for unrestricted freedom of choice. In some cases, this may be what society actually wants but, in others, it will not represent the communal position, which also deserves protection. To take another example, euthanasia and physician-assisted suicide remain prohibited in the vast majority of jurisdictions despite numerous challenges before the courts and attempts to introduce enabling legislation. But the fact that a growing number of jurisdictions now do permit assisted dying illustrates the complexities with which this book is concerned; shifting social and moral attitudes make medical law a constantly developing discipline.

1.04 Inevitably, then, the law is drawn repeatedly into the debates—especially so when there is a conflict of individual interests or a clash of individual and community interests— and is catalysed by moral issues. It is pointless to attempt to disengage the moral from the legal dispute. When we talk about legal rules, we are inevitably drawn into a discussion of moral preferences seeking the legitimacy and sanction of law and legal institutions.

1.05 Thus, we often find ourselves engaged in debating not what the law is but what it should be. This requires us to engage in moral evaluation and this, in turn, raises the question of how we are to identify what is at stake, in individual and societal terms, and how we should proceed. This is no easy task, living, as we do, in a pluralist, secular age. And despite a burgeoning number of international legal instruments purporting to embody universal ethical values,[3] their success in providing us with answers to the dilemmas thrown up by modern medicine remains open to question. We are forced, therefore, to turn to the identification of the ethical basis for the practice of medicine itself.

A BASIS FOR MEDICAL ETHICS

1.06 It should not be thought that ethics is necessarily about discovering what is 'right'. Rather, ethics is a system of principles or values that assist in decision-making. Ethics allows us to justify a particular course of action by reference to wider, socially accepted norms or values. Bioethics, then, is the branch of moral philosophy concerned with the ethical issues that arise out of medical practice, life sciences, and a range of other interventions involving humans and animals. Ethics comes into play when we are faced with a dilemma: that is, when we can see two or more possible and justifiable paths to take over any difficult decision. Arguing by reference to ethical principles or concepts helps us to decide which path is the better one; note, however, this also means that we may legitimately disagree over which path to take. In this sense, then, there may be more than one 'right' answer. A 'wrong' answer would be to take a path when we cannot justify doing so—it would be unethical to do so. But what, then, is at hand to assist in ethical decision-making in medicine?

---

[3] Most notably see UNESCO, Universal Declaration on Bioethics and Human Rights (2005) and also the Council of Europe, Convention on Human Rights and Biomedicine (1997).

THE HIPPOCRATIC INFLUENCE

1.07 For the origins of our current medical practice—with its emphasis on the one-to-one relationship between doctor and patient within the confines of the home, surgery, or hospital—we must look to Greece where, even by 500 BC, the acceptance of disease as 'an act of God' was being questioned and, consequently, the originally strong influence of the priest/physician had waned; a predominantly religious discipline had been taken over by the philosophers who, through the processes of logical thought, observation, and deduction, transformed the concepts of medicine. Inevitably, this led to the formation of schools involving the close association of practitioners, paternalism, and the elements of a 'closed shop'; a code of intra-professional conduct evolved, heralding the dawn of what has become known as medical etiquette. In addition, the new concepts dictated that the physician went to the patient rather than the patient to the temple. A standard of practice relevant to the new ideals was required and has survived as the Hippocratic Oath.

1.08 While Hippocrates remains the most famous figure in Greek philosophical medicine, he was not alone and it is probable that the Oath predates his own school. It therefore indicates a prevailing ethos rather than a professorial edict and it is still regarded as the fundamental governance of the medical profession. Much of the preamble relates to medical etiquette and is clearly outmoded—very few ageing medical professors now anticipate social security by way of the generosity of their students! This, however, is not our concern here—and it is to be distinguished clearly from medical ethics. As to the latter, the Oath lays down a number of guidelines. First, it implies the need for coordinated instruction and registration of doctors—the public is to be protected, so far as is possible, from the dabbler or the charlatan. Second, it is clearly stated that a doctor is there for the benefit of his patients—to the best of his ability he must do them good and he must do nothing which he knows will cause harm. This is reflected in modern times in the principles of beneficence and non-maleficence, which we discuss in more detail later. Third, euthanasia and abortion are proscribed; the reference to lithotomy probably prohibits mutilating operations (castration) but has been taken by many to imply the limitation of one's practice to that in which one has expertise. Fourth, the nature of the doctor–patient relationship is outlined and an undertaking is given not to take advantage of that relationship. Finally, the Oath expresses the doctrine of medical confidentiality.

1.09 In fact, the Hippocratic Oath did not become an integral part of ethical teaching until well into the Christian era; it lapsed with the decline of Greek civilisation and was restored with the evolution of university medical schools. It is doubtful if any British medical school now requires a reiteration of the Oath at graduation but, avowed or not, all doctors would admit to its persuasive influence. The language of the Oath is, however, archaic and a modernised version was introduced by the World Medical Association as the Declaration of Geneva.[4] This was last amended at Divonne-les-Bains, France in 2006 and provides the basis for several national and international codes.[5]

1.10 We have seen that Greek medicine was essentially a private matter and, indeed, its mode of practice was scarcely attuned to the needs of public health. For the origins of this, we must turn to the Judaeo-Christian influence which, certainly in the Jewish tradition, expressed itself most powerfully in accepting that the rights of the individual must sometimes be

---

[4] World Medical Association, Declaration of Geneva (1948, as amended).

[5] Including the International Code of Medical Ethics which was adopted in 1949 and most recently updated in 2006.

sacrificed for the good of the community—there was strong emphasis, for example, on the isolation of infectious cases, including those of venereal disease, the regulation of sewage disposal, and the like—and the principles of public health medicine were born. As we have already noted, the fact that medicine was dominated by religion turned out to be mutually advantageous. Much of this attitude passed to the Christians, who were also forced into the group lifestyle, and were fortified by the concepts of equality, charity, and devotion to the less fortunate—concepts which should still underlie the ethical practice of medicine in Christian countries. It is unsurprising that, during the Dark Ages, medicine was virtually kept alive in the monasteries, which provided the template for the voluntary hospitals of later years.

RELIGIOUS THEORIES

1.11 Today, there is a plethora of theories on hand that are designed to help us to justify difficult decisions. Many modern accounts of medical ethics are, however, strangely silent as to the importance of religious theories of medical ethics—the element of surprise stemming from the fact that medicine and religion have been intertwined from the earliest times when, as we have seen, priests were also recognised as physicians. As a direct result, religious theories historically constitute a major element of thinking in medical ethics and their influence continues to be felt in all corners of the subject, even if only tacitly. The common feature of such theories is a vision of man as involved in a dialogue with a divine creator, or possibly a spiritual force, as to the way in which the human body should be treated. This vision may manifest itself in an insistence on ritualistic practices, for example, in relation to burial. Such examples should not, however, be dismissed as an exercise of power based on superstitious reverence—many religious practices, especially those of orthodox Judaism, are, in fact, based on sound principles of public health. It may, on the other hand, be expressed at a higher level of abstraction, fashioning a view of the sanctity of human life which is capable of resolving a whole raft of practical issues. The Judaeo-Christian religious tradition has had the greatest impact in the Western world and is one which continues to influence much of the contemporary debate.[6]

1.12 Religiously based medical ethics have a clear sense of fundamental values. In the Christian tradition, these include not only a belief that human life is a divine gift which cannot be disposed of by mortals but also a strong attachment to the importance of monogamous, enduring marriage. These values are translated into practical rules in the shape of an antipathy to euthanasia and abortion—an antipathy that amounts to prohibition in orthodox Roman Catholic thinking—and of a belief that various forms of intervention in human reproduction are morally wrong. Inherent in many of these traditions is a strong sense of the *natural*, which proposes a teleology for man. In the light of this, it is often seen as wrong to interfere with the manifest destiny which has been prepared for humanity. This may result in the rejection of an everyday medical issue such as sterilisation just as much as it might lead to a blanket refusal to contemplate interference in the genetic endowment of mankind.

1.13 It would be wrong to assume that those who approach medical ethics from a religious viewpoint are uncritical and authoritarian in their moral thinking. Indeed, many of the more sensitive contributions to the literature of medical ethics have been made by those

---

[6] For informative insights see P Morgan and C Lawton (eds), *Ethical Issues in Six Religious Traditions* (2nd edn, 2007).

who approach the subject from this background. And sometimes it is only such a voice which will raise awkward, and yet very important, questions. The debate on euthanasia provides an instance of this in the form of the serious and persistent questioning provided by John Keown.[7] An historic example is the Protestant theologian, Paul Ramsey, whose work anticipated many of the questions which have since become the staple of contemporary debate in medical ethics.[8]

THE CURRENTS OF MEDICAL ETHICS

1.14 As we have seen, ethical discourse is concerned with the search for justification for our actions. An ethical dilemma arises when two or more courses of conduct may be justifiable in any given set of circumstances, possibly resulting in diametrically opposed outcomes. How, then, do we know what is the 'right' thing to do?[9] Various means may be employed to argue for an ethical resolution to a dilemma and morality is but one such means. Morality may be individual or communal, in that it reflects a core set of values by which individuals or communities abide. As we discuss later, morality may even be a simple question of intuition and, on this criterion alone, it is difficult to argue that an individual's personal value system is 'wrong'. Ethics, on the other hand—while informed by moral debate and argument—usually operate within an established framework of values which serves as a reference from which to conduct the debate about the basis on which an action can or cannot be justified. Thus, for example, Beauchamp and Childress have long championed the utility of 'principlism' as a way to this end.[10] In brief, they hold that ethically appropriate conduct is determined by reference to four key principles which must be taken into account when reflecting on one's behaviour towards others. These are:

(i) the principle of respect for individual autonomy (i.e.—individuals must be respected as independent moral agents with the 'right' to choose how to live their own lives);

(ii) the principle of beneficence (i.e.—one should strive to do good where possible);

(iii) the principle of non-maleficence (i.e.—one should avoid doing harm to others); and

(iv) the principle of justice (i.e.—people should be treated fairly, although this does not necessarily equate with treating everyone equally).

While principlism is by no means universally accepted as the lingua franca of ethics[11]—and indeed has been criticised as embodying too much of a North American perspective[12]—it does, nonetheless, provide a very good example of how ethical discourse requires reflection and justification of our actions by reference to accepted values and mores.[13] More

---

[7] In particular by way of *Euthanasia Examined* (revised 1997), *Euthanasia, Ethics and Public Policy* (2002), and *Debating Euthanasia* (2011 with Emily Jackson). See the discussion of euthanasia at Chapter 18.

[8] See e.g. P Ramsey, *The Patient as Person* (2nd edn, 2002).

[9] See generally M J Sandel, *Justice: What's the Right Thing to Do?* (2010).   [10] N 1.

[11] For an excellent collection of papers on the 'virtues' and 'vices' of principlism, see J Savulescu et al., 'Festschrift edition of the Journal of Medical Ethics in honour of Raanan Gillon' (2003) 29(5) J Med Ethics. See also T Walker, 'What principlism misses' (2009) 35 J Med Ethics 229.

[12] S Holm, 'Not just autonomy: The principles of American biomedical ethics' (1995) 21 J Med Ethics 332 and T Takala, 'What is wrong with global bioethics? On the limitations of the four principles approach' (2001) 10 Camb Q Healthc Ethics 72.

[13] See, J S Gordon, O Rauprich, and J Vollmann, 'Applying the four-principle approach' (2011) 25 Bioethics 293.

'European' perspectives are offered by authors who concentrate on notions such as 'dignity' and 'solidarity', thus highlighting ethical concerns that may not be captured by an individualistic frame of reference.[14]

1.15 At a broader level of abstraction, contemporary medical ethics can be seen as a tapestry in which an array of philosophical theories interweave with one another. The two strands of deontological and consequentialist thought are, however, particularly evident. Deontological theories focus on the rightness or wrongness of an act in itself. They are not so much concerned with the consequences which that act will have; rather, they are concerned with identifying those features of the act which mark it as morally acceptable or otherwise. The classical exposition of such a theory is that by Kant, who stressed that every person must be treated as an end in him- or herself, rather than merely as a means to an end. Thus, the essential message of Kantian moral teaching is that we should not use others but should respect their integrity as individuals. Many modern theories of autonomy find their roots in this background and, as we shall see later, autonomy has come to be associated closely with the liberal individualism which has exerted a massive influence on the philosophical climate surrounding medico-legal debate in the last few decades. An irony, however, is that many Kantians emphasise that the core message of their philosophy concerns the *obligations* that we owe to others while, at the same time, many contemporary conceptions of autonomy insist on the atomistic *rights* of individuals to decide for themselves, all the while ignoring the impact of those decisions on the broader community.

1.16 Critics of deontological theories of morality, particularly of those in the Kantian mould, often stress what is seen as a rigidity of approach. The 'strict' Kantian does not give sufficient weight, it is said, either to human intuitions as to what is right at the time or to the virtues such as wisdom, compassion, and fairness, which contribute to living a life of 'human flourishing' (*eudaimonia*).[15] An alternative, and more flexible, approach might be one which was more sensitive to the human feelings involved in any moral dilemma and one which also paid more attention to the consequences which flow from our actions. One such approach is that adopted by utilitarianism, a philosophy which has played a major role in the medical debate and which is regarded by many as underpinning modern ethical medicine.

1.17 Utilitarians are accustomed to being misrepresented by those who believe that utilitarianism is a philosophical theory that started, and ended, with the work of Jeremy Bentham. Classic utilitarianism of the Benthamite school held that the test of the morality of an action was the extent to which it promoted good consequences (pleasure) or bad (pain). The utilitarian measure of good is, therefore, the maximisation of happiness, although modern utilitarians, in particular, would stress that this does not necessarily lead to unrestricted hedonism. Modern utilitarianism acknowledges the importance of rules in identifying moral goals and, in this way, prevents the happiness of the many from overshadowing the rights of the few. Preference utilitarianism, a further modification of the classical theory, allows for the judging of the good of

---

[14] R Houtepen and R ter Meulen R (eds), 'Solidarity in Health Care' (2000) 8(4) Health Care Analysis, Special Issue and H Ten Have and B Gordijn (eds), *Bioethics in a European Perspective* (2001). Also see Nuffield Council on Bioethics, *Solidarity: Reflections on an Emerging Concept in Bioethics* (2011).

[15] A Campbell, 'The virtues (and vices) of the four principles' (2003) 29 J Med Ethics 292. Also see S Holland, 'The virtue ethics approach to bioethics' (2011) 25 Bioethics 192.

individuals according to their own values, a position perhaps best expressed in modern bioethics through the work of Peter Singer.[16]

1.18 Liberal individualism leans towards a utilitarian or consequentialist approach, in that it measures the effect of a decision on individuals. To the liberal individualist, the good which society should pursue is the fulfilment of the individual. The ideal society is, then, one in which people make their own decisions as far as is possible and 'creates themselves'. In this way, the individual exercises and enhances his or her autonomy—how autonomy is used is not a major concern to the liberal individualist, so long as it is not used in a way that unduly restricts others from exercising their own autonomy.

1.19 This is the near antithesis of the last variation on ethical theory that we propose to mention—that is the communtarian ethos which is gaining ground as something of a counterweight to the almost relentlessly increasing reliance on personal autonomy as the cornerstone of both medical ethics and medical law.[17] Communitarianism visualises the community as the integral unit in which autonomy is expressed not so much on an egocentric base but, rather, as a state that is modified by a sharing of values with those of the group in which the individual operates; such values include but are not restricted to solidarity, social justice, and a focus on the obligations we owe to others (as opposed to the rights we can claim for ourselves). Put in practical terms, the acceptability of an action is to be judged by the goodness or badness of its effect not on an individual per se but on persons as interdependent units of society—in short, it recognises John Donne's aphorism that no man is an island.[18] The critic will, immediately, ask what is a community?— and the simple answer is that group of persons who are significantly affected by an action or a decision. In some senses, a well-tuned concept of communitarian ethics can draw on elements of deontological *and* utilitarian thinking whereby the emphasis is both on the obligations that we owe to those around us as well as on the consequences of our individual decisions.[19] This is no truer than in the context of public health, as we explore in Chapter 2. While principlism and rights-based arguments might work well in the confines of the doctor–patient relationship, arguably different values are at stake, and, so, different ethical paradigms are required when we are talking about the health of the community, and this potentially includes the global community.[20]

1.20 We have to admit to our, at least, partial adherence to community ethics. Nevertheless, a book such as this must recognise the undoubted fact that autonomy is by far the most significant value to have influenced the evolution of contemporary medical law, at least in the context of the therapeutic relationship. The concept which has dominated the control of medical practice more than any other in the last half-century is the insistence that individuals should have control over their own bodies, should make their own decisions

[16] Singer's contribution to contemporary applied ethics has been considerable. In the field of bioethics, he is associated with challenges to the traditional sanctity of human life view; on which, see his *Rethinking Life and Death* (1994) and more generally *How Are We To Live?* (1997).

[17] '...it would seem to me a matter of deep regret if the law has developed to a point in this area where the rights of a patient count for everything and other ethical values and institutional integrity count for nothing': *R v Collins, ex p Brady* (2001) 58 BMLR 173 per Kay J.

[18] See M Daly (ed), *Communitarianism: A New Public Ethics* (1994) and A Etzioni, 'On a communitarian approach to bioethics' (2011) 32 Theor Med Bioeth 363.

[19] For an interesting defence of communitarianism against principlism see D Callahan, 'Principlism and communitarianism' (2003) 29 J Med Ethics 287.

[20] H Ten Have, 'Global bioethics and communitarianism' (2011) 32 Theor Med Bioeth 315; John Coggon and Swati Gola (eds), *Global Health and International Community: Ethical, Political and Regulatory Challenges* (2013).

relating to their medical treatment, and should not be hindered in their search for self-fulfilment. The acknowledgement of autonomy has served to discredit medical paternalism in almost all its forms and has led to the promotion of the patient from the recipient of treatment to being a partner, or even client, in a therapeutic project—and this change has been reflected in the rapid development of the legal and political regimes by which medical treatment is now regulated in the United Kingdom (UK).

1.21 In one sense, the philosophical apotheosis of autonomy has brought liberation. It has enhanced the freedom of those whose vulnerability, physical or mental, may have exposed them to insensitive treatment or even to exploitation; it has imparted dignity to the lives of those who might, otherwise, have felt themselves to be powerless in the face of the articulate and the professional. Yet, from another view, the acceptance of a particularly individualistic sense of autonomy as the benchmark of the good has led us to ignore other values, and this may have negative effects.[21] The communitarian approach tells us that, even if self-fulfilment does shine through the development and the exercise of autonomy, there is a social dimension to life which is potentially equally enriching. Autonomy must be qualified by the legitimate interests and expectations of others, as well as by economic constraints. Autonomy is not an absolute.[22] In the medical context, the claims of autonomy must be moderated so as to accommodate the sensitivities of others, including those of the doctor—who is, after all, also an autonomous agent.[23] It may be that respect for individual autonomy points in the direction of allowing voluntary euthanasia—but another moral agent has to administer the drug that ends life, and that person may be affected by the task. Furthermore, in order to protect the vulnerable, it is possible that we may have to deny assisted suicide for patients who have the capacity to request it.[24] Personal autonomy must also be measured against the needs of society as a whole. In an ideal world, a sick person should be able to demand the treatment of his or her choice. A moment's reflection, however, is enough to show us that this is an impossible goal. Society itself demands a just distribution of resources and this cannot be achieved in an ambience of unrestricted 'rights'—put another way, we can only realise our autonomy within the framework provided by society.[25]

1.22 Even so, the concept of rights has many proponents and, like autonomy, rights theory plays an important part in contemporary ethical debate. Yet the language of rights may also become unduly assertive and combative and may hinder, rather than promote, moral consensus.[26] This is not to decry the importance of rights. Many of the central ethical

[21] The conflict between individual autonomy and, say, society's interest in the preservation of life is illustrated in the Israeli Patient's Rights Act 1996 which allows for non-consensual treatment in certain circumstances. See M L Gross, 'Treating competent patients by force: The limits and lessons of Israel's Patient's Rights Act' (2005) 31 J Med Ethics 29—'there are no grounds for respecting a patient's less-than-informed refusal of treatment'.

[22] G Laurie, 'The autonomy of others: Reflections on the rise and rise of patient choice in contemporary medical law' in S McLean (ed), *First Do No Harm: Law, Ethics and Healthcare* (2006), ch 9.

[23] Discussed in G M Stirrat and R Gill, 'Autonomy in medical ethics after O'Neill' (2005) 31 J Med Ethics 127. See also M Brazier, 'Do no harm: Do patients have responsibilities too?' (2006) 65 CLJ 397.

[24] This was the basis of the decision of the European Court of Human Rights in *Pretty* v *UK* (2346/02) [2002] 2 FLR 45; (2002) 35 EHRR 1; (2002) 66 BMLR 147.

[25] See A V Campbell, 'Dependency: the foundational value in medical ethics' in K V M Fulford and G J M Gillett (eds), *Medicine and Moral Reasoning* (1994).

[26] In the view of some philosophers, rights can be reduced to principles which form the real content of morality. For a sceptical view, see R Frey, *Rights, Killing and Suffering* (1983); to be contrasted with L W Sumner, *The Moral Foundation of Rights* (1987) and with the outstanding contribution of K Cronin in *Rights and Christian Ethics* (1992). More recently, see Ashcroft, at n 2, for a sceptical view of rights where he describes them as derivate rather than fundamental moral concepts.

positions defended in this book can be couched in terms of rights. Once again, however, rights-talk is peculiarly suited to an individualistic moral tradition and conflicts of rights tend to lead to moral impasse. Most discussion centres on the rights of the patient—but has the doctor no rights when choosing treatment in accordance with his Hippocratic principles and his training? At one time the former Master of the Rolls, Lord Donaldson, expressed this unequivocally when he said:

> [I cannot, at present, conceive of any circumstances] in which the court should ever require a medical practitioner to adopt a course of treatment which in the bona fide clinical judgment of that practitioner is contraindicated as not being in the best interests of the patient.[27]

This position may no longer hold as strongly as it once did with the advent of increasing judicial intervention in medical decision-making, especially in the context of disabled neonates, as we discuss further in Chapter 15. By the same token, we should not lose sight of the fundamental duty of the doctor described by Lord Donaldson as being to treat the patient in accordance with his own clinical judgement[28]—which opens the way to an alternative dialogue through the language of *obligations*. The way to a satisfactory doctor–patient relationship is perhaps not through the confrontational profession of rights but, rather, through a realisation of the obligations incumbent upon each side to work towards the ideal.

AUTONOMY AND PATERNALISM

1.23 The paternalist acts for the benefit of another, or in the other's best interests, without the specific consent of the person for whom he acts. Until a few decades ago, the practice of medicine was unquestionably paternalist—at least in parts—and many of those involved might have been surprised to discover that their practices could be considered morally objectionable. Thus, patients were often treated without adequate explanation of what was involved or significant facts about their illness were kept from them. It was, for example, common not to pass on information if it was thought that the knowledge would cause distress, and psychiatric patients could be subjected to treatments without any concern as to their views or preferences. Such practices are now largely regarded as unethical in modern Western medicine,[29] and are consequently rare. Yet examples still occur and surfaced, for instance, at the turn of the century in disclosures of the unauthorised retention of tissues from paediatric post-mortem examinations. Certainly, a proportion of the pathologists involved in these practices did not ask for the permission of the parents, but at least some of these failed to do so because they wished to protect the parents from distressing facts. To quote from the President of the Royal College of Pathologists:

> No one ever had enthusiasm for discussing the detailed autopsy process with recently bereaved relatives, and it was always more comfortable to draw a veil over it. But that veil meant that relatives did not know what was going on ... Strip away [the extraneous factors] and there remains the inescapable and uncomfortable fact that in the past post-mortem organ retention has been a prime example of professional paternalism.[30]

---

[27] *Re J (a minor) (wardship: medical treatment)* [1992] 2 FLR 165 at 172; (1992) 9 BMLR 10 at 17.

[28] Ibid.

[29] Compare a Western view: R J Sullivan, L W Menapace, and R M White, 'Truth-telling and patient diagnoses' (2001) 27 J Med Ethics 192 with: D F-C Tsai, 'Ancient Chinese medical ethics and the Four Principles of biomedical ethics' (1999) 25 J Med Ethics 315. Generally, see S Bok, *Lying: Moral Choice in Public and Private Life* (1999).

[30] J Lilleyman, 'From the President' (2001) Bull R Coll Path No 114, p 2.

1.24 Even so, while an unqualified rejection of paternalism in medicine might satisfy some proponents of autonomy, it would undoubtedly, at the same time, cause avoidable harm. Paternalism is acceptable in principle—and, indeed, necessary in practice—where the person who is the object of such action is incapable of making his or her own decision.[31] An intervention in such a case will be justifiable if the disabling condition is either permanent or cannot be expected to lift in time for the person in question to decide for him or herself. The advantages of any intervention must, however, significantly outweigh the disadvantages which would otherwise accrue and the intervention itself must carry a reasonable prospect of success. This is essentially a test of reasonableness, which involves a careful assessment of motives for action and a balancing of interests. To achieve this balance, it may be necessary to take into account not only the patient's past views—when these are knowable—but also to consider what are likely to be his or her future views.

1.25 The principal subjects of medical paternalism are likely to be children, the psychiatrically ill, and the unconscious.[32] The medical treatment of children who are too young to make up their own minds provides a common and clear case of justified medical paternalism. Indeed, at times, the medical professional is called upon to protect the interests of a child against the wishes of his or her parents as to the appropriateness, or otherwise, of medical treatment.[33] Notwithstanding, the paternalist must take into account in this context the fact that capacity increases with growing maturity; caution must, therefore, be exercised in acting paternalistically towards teenagers. Paternalism in relation to the psychiatrically ill may be justified on the grounds that there is a mental disability which incapacitates the patient to the extent that he or she cannot understand that treatment may be required; it is, then, reasonable to assume that the patient will endorse what has been done once recovery has occurred. This latter justification—the appeal to subsequent approbation—may also be invoked in the treatment of the unconscious. The anticipated agreement may well be forthcoming in the majority of cases, but the treatment of those who are unconscious after an attempt at suicide may be more difficult to justify. The doctor who treats such a person is clearly acting paternalistically and might argue either that the attempt at suicide could have resulted from a mental illness (and could, therefore, be treatable without consent), or that the patient will later endorse the treatment. But what about the case where the patient has made it clear in advance that suicide is what he or she wants and is the result of rational consideration?[34] In practice, such patients are often treated, although it is difficult to fit that into the category of justified paternalism.

1.26 As in all areas of medical practice, room must remain for clinical discretion to be exercised by the doctor. There will be cases where minor acts of paternalism aimed at preventing distress to those who are anxious will be an ethically justifiable thing to do. The law might be expected to recognise this at the same time that it recognises and protects the right of individual autonomy. In short, paternalism and autonomy are not mutually exclusive: the task of medical ethics and of medical law is to balance the two in a way which enhances individual dignity and autonomy but which does not inhibit the exercise of discretion in the marginal case. The task for the health care professional is to apprise

[31] For a detailed account of paternalism in all its forms, see E Buchanan and D W Brock, *Deciding for Others: The Ethics of Surrogate Decision Making* (1990).
[32] For a suggestion of its unwarranted extension to pregnant women see C Gavaghan, ' "You can't handle the truth": Medical paternalism and prenatal alcohol abuse' (2009) 35 J Med Ethics 300.
[33] Consider, for example, the treatment of children of Jehovah's Witnesses.
[34] We will see later that there is also a hazard that the patient's life may be reprieved but only in a disabled state.

him or herself of the full armoury of ethical tools for appropriate decision-making with respect to the interests and needs of the immediate patient.

INTUITIONS AND EXPERIENCE

1.27 There are grounds, then, for doubting the practicality or effectiveness of applying a broad deontological brush to medical ethics. Each case is unique, and its individual features may change with each consultation. In supporting this approach, some moral philosophers have stressed the importance of imagination as a means of navigating our way through the moral landscape.[35] This moral imagination may, to an extent, rely on metaphors rather than on rules—which, in turn, points to a role, even if a circumscribed one, for moral intuitions. Intuition may have a limited appeal as a basis for moral philosophy but it should not be wholly discounted and this, for the reasons already given, is especially so in the field of health care.[36] Intuitions may point in the direction of a value which may not always be articulated formally but which may nonetheless be very important.

1.28 Our own view is that medical ethics are perhaps not best served by a rigid attachment to an undiluted vision of patient autonomy—but neither were they well served by the paternalistic philosophy of the past. What is required is an openness to the complexity of moral decisions, and an awareness of the sensitive contexts in which such decisions must be taken. Different contexts might require different ethical approaches; compare, for example, the doctor–patient relationship with concerns about public health. An understanding of the tensions is not necessarily something that philosophers can teach or lawyers prescribe. The insights of cognitive science, and of psychology in general, increasingly recommend a model of moral reasoning which gives a large role to learned moral responses. These moral abilities—if one may call them that—are acquired through education within a particular ethos and through hands-on experience in dealing with people and their suffering. There is all the difference in the world between, say, the experienced nurse who has spent years working in a hospice setting and the layperson who approaches the issue of end-of-life decisions from an entirely theoretical perspective. A moral response which discounts the validity of the insights of the former would be unlikely to be helpful. Those involved in caring for patients are moral beings who must be encouraged to develop and express their sense of the moral demands of a particular situation. There is not necessarily one right answer to the dilemmas which they encounter, and this should perhaps be recognised more extensively than it is today. There may be two, or even more, right answers depending on the people involved and the circumstances. In the end, it is as much the virtues of the decision-maker, as someone who displays qualities such as wisdom, compassion, truth-telling, fairness, and justice, as the existence of philosophical theory that creates the appropriate environment in which ethical decision-making should take place.[37]

1.29 The way in which we make sense of an ethical or legal problem is often the first step to its resolution. Consider this advice from the Nuffield Council on Bioethics:

> There is no set method for addressing an ethical issue. However, there are some generally accepted guidelines which can be applied to an issue. As a starting point for any

[35] See M Johnson, *Moral Imagination: Implications of Cognitive Science for Ethics* (1993); L May, M Friedman, and A Clark (eds), *Mind and Morals: Essays on Ethics and Cognitive Science* (1996).
[36] For expression of this view, see T B Brewin, 'How much ethics is needed to make a good doctor?' (1993) 341 Lancet 161.
[37] For an introduction see D C Russell (ed), *The Cambridge Companion to Virtue Ethics* (2013).

discussion, it is essential that information is accurate and from an objective and reliable source. It is also important to be able to distinguish between facts and opinions. Clarity of terms and expressions is crucial ...

An important part of any ethical inquiry is to examine the implications of holding a particular view. Drawing up a list of the arguments on both sides, both for and against an idea, can help to focus discussion. A further step is to analyse the basis for these arguments. The conclusions of an argument must be defensible, so it is important to look for gaps, inadequacies, fallacies or unexpected outcomes. Having assessed the validity and persuasiveness of all the arguments, a decision may be reached or it may be apparent that more information is needed.[38]

1.30 From this, and what has been said previously, we can offer the following toolkit: **Your checklist to difficult decision-making**:

(1) **Get the facts straight**: separate the relevant from the irrelevant and facts from opinions.

(2) **Identify your approach to the problem**: schools of thought come in handy here.

(3) **Identify the pros & cons of your approach.**

(4) **Consider the counter-arguments and the possible challenges to your position.**

(5) **What conclusions do you reach: are these defensible?**

The crucial point is that the particular 'answer' that is eventually pursued can be justified within a recognised and accepted ethical and moral framework. A moral straitjacket is hardly helpful. Having said which, we should perhaps go on to examine the practical environment in which health carers set about their work.

THE ORGANISATION OF MODERN MEDICINE

1.31 Probably the single most important feature which distinguishes the 'modern' in modern medicine is the importance attached to experimentation and research,[39] and it was this change in emphasis which dictated most urgently that medical practice should be subject to central control.

1.32 The age of medical research can be said to have begun with the Renaissance and, since that time, the practice of medicine has become increasingly scientifically based. New dimensions are, thus, introduced and new dilemmas posed. It is obvious that scientific medicine cannot improve without extensive research while, on the other hand, that process tends to turn medical practice into a series of problem-solving exercises—a diversion which, even now, stimulates, at the same time, some of medicine's severest critics and its admirers.

1.33 Perhaps the first practical effect of the scientific approach was to convince doctors that they have an expertise worth preserving and, as early as the sixteenth century, we find the establishment of the Royal College of Physicians of London, together with a general tightening of the rules governing the practice of surgery.

---

[38] See the Nuffield Council on Bioethics at http://www.nuffieldbioethics.org/ under Further Information.
[39] For a monograph which eloquently analyses this, see R Tallis, *Hippocratic Oaths: Medicine and its Discontents* (2004).

1.34 As organisation proceeded, fortune began increasingly to depend upon fame, and fame, in its turn, upon academic superiority over one's colleagues; from all accounts, British medicine in the eighteenth and early nineteenth centuries was not the happiest of professions. Even so, it was not so much medical ethics, as they are understood today, that were found wanting but, rather, medical etiquette or intra-professional relationships. Something had to be done to ensure the status of the profession and this need was first met by the formation of the British Medical Association (BMA) in 1832. Insofar as the BMA is, today, a non-affiliated registered trade union,[40] its primary function has traditionally been the protection of doctors' interests. Clearly, such an interested party could not satisfy the public need for control of a profession with such power and it was largely due to the lobby of the BMA itself that the General Medical Council (GMC) was established by the Medical Act 1858. The current statutory regulation of the medical profession is found in the Medical Act 1983 which has, in turn, been substantially amended.[41]

1.35 We make no attempt here to overview the administrative law concerning medical practice in detail.[42] What follows is no more than a précis of what we consider to be the main aspects which fall under the rubric of 'law and medical ethics'. With this in mind, it is appropriate to begin with an overview of the GMC, which is the basic regulatory authority of the medical profession.[43]

THE GENERAL MEDICAL COUNCIL

1.36 The GMC is a statutory and charitable body entrusted with protecting, promoting, and maintaining the health and safety of the public by ensuring proper standards in the practice of medicine. The main ways in which the GMC strives to achieve these goals are discussed below. As background, it is important to note that the functions and the day-to-day operations of the GMC have been subject to criticism, and adjustment, almost since its inception. There is no doubt that the number of high-profile, individual instances of alleged misconduct that were exposed at the end of the twentieth century caused sufficient public disquiet to provide solid grounds for extensive review—and revision—of the existing system for control of the medical profession.[44] Given that the preservation

---

[40] Trade Union and Labour Relations (Consolidation) Act 1992. The distinction between a trade organisation and a regulatory body such as the GMC was emphasised in *General Medical Council v Cox* (2002) *The Times*, 16 April, in which it was held that the GMC was not a trade organisation for the purposes of the Disability Discrimination Act 1995, s 13.

[41] Medical Act 1983 (Amendment) Order 2002 (SI 2002/3135); Health and Social Care Act 2008 and General Medical Council (Fitness to Practise and Over-arching Objective) and the Professional Standards Authority for Health and Social Care (References to Court) Order 2015/794.

[42] For that, the reader is referred to the seminal work by J Montgomery, *Health Care Law* (2nd edn, 2002).

[43] We appreciate that it could be more appropriate to speak in terms of 'health care ethics' but that would be to extend the scope of this chapter to unreasonable length. The reader should understand that we are concentrating on the medical profession as being typical of the health care professions as a whole. The others have their own councils but, by and large, their governance is similar to that of the GMC.

[44] Aside from regular reports of individual errors, a number of major incidents were disclosed which resulted in public investigations. Among these are included the standards of paediatric cardiac surgery at Bristol: Report of the Public Inquiry into Children's Heart Surgery at Bristol Royal Infirmary 1984–1995 (Cm 5207, 2001); the retention of organs at Alder Hey Hospital: The Royal Liverpool Children's Inquiry Report (HC 12, 2001); the retention of organs in Scotland: Final Report of the Independent Review Group on Retention of Organs at Post-mortem (Scottish Exec, 2001). The GMC, despite its urgent restyling, itself came under savage attack in what was, essentially, an investigation into a mass murder: Dame Janet Smith, The Shipman Inquiry 5th Report, Safeguarding Patients: Lessons from the Past—Proposals for the Future (2004) (Cm 6394).

of the National Health Service (NHS) is now a major topic in the mind of the electorate, it is unsurprising that the ruling political parties have exerted relentless pressure on the profession's leaders to bend to the prevailing mood. There is no doubt that many of the changes that have been effected are essential to the delivery of high-quality health care; the concomitant result, however, has been the increase of political control at the expense of the profession's self-regulatory powers.[45]

The Investigative Function

1.37 We start with the investigative—or 'disciplinary'—function of the GMC because, based on the now discarded concept of 'serious professional misconduct', this has, perhaps, always been its activity which has occasioned the most interest. It is also an area where a sea change in attitude has occurred—misconduct is now regarded as but one possible cause of unfitness to practise.[46] Other grounds are deficient professional performance, a conviction for, or caution following, a criminal offence, adverse physical or mental health, insufficient knowledge of English, and, finally, a determination by a body responsible for the regulation of the health or social care professions in the UK that fitness to practise is impaired. The broadening of scope is exemplified by the relevant title in the Medical Act 1983 being altered from 'Professional Conduct and Fitness to Practise' to 'Fitness to Practise and Medical Ethics'.[47]

1.38 The GMC is currently dealing with rising numbers of fitness to practise complaints from patients and the public. This increase is said to stem from societal changes, such as patients being generally more assertive and less deferential to doctors.[48] Complaints are normally reviewed within seven days. Some will not proceed further (e.g. because they fall outside the criteria for taking action against a doctor) but others will trigger a formal investigation.

1.39 The committee system, which includes an Interim Orders Panel,[49] an Investigation Committee, and a Fitness to Practise Panel, had previously resulted in the GMC's governing body—the Council—being both investigator and adjudicator. This was a source of concern ever since the publication of the Shipman Inquiry.[50] In order to address this issue, Parliament approved the establishment of the Medical Practitioners Tribunal Service (MPTS) in 2011. The MPTS and its panellists provide a fully independent adjudication service that is separate from the investigatory role of the GMC. A 2014 Department of Health Consultation paper recommended placing the MPTS on a statutory footing. Consultation responses indicated strong support for the proposal, which would require amendments to both the Medical Act 1983 and the NHS Reform and Healthcare Professionals Act 2002.[51] A draft amendment Order that would accomplish these changes was published alongside the consultation paper.

---

[45] See a critical leading article in the BMJ: D P Gray, 'Deprofessionalising doctors?' (2002) 324 BMJ 627. It is fair to say, however, that some of the more draconian proposals have been modified or abandoned.

[46] Medical Act 1983, s 35C(2).   [47] Medical Act 1983, Part V.

[48] J Archer et al., *Understanding the Rise in Fitness to Practise Complaints from Members of the Public* (2014). Available at: http://www.gmc-uk.org/about/research/25233.asp

[49] The function of which is not to investigate complaints against doctors but, rather, to take action for the protection of the public in advance of the complaint being proved. The effect of a suspension order, which can be imposed for 18 months and is renewable with the agreement of the High Court, can be devastating and the potential power of the interim order panel is, in our view, little short of horrifying. Its authority lies in the Medical Act 1983, s 41A. See the wide-ranging article: P Case, 'Putting public confidence first: Doctors, precautionary suspension, and the General Medical Council' (2011) 19 Med L Rev 339.

[50] N 44. See, for example, Department of Health, *Trust, Assurance and Safety: The Regulation of Health Professionals in the 21st Century* (2007).

[51] Department of Health, *The General Medical Council and Professional Standards Authority: Proposed Changes to Modernise and Reform the Adjudication of Fitness to Practise Cases* (2015).

1.40 A Fitness to Practise Panel comprises medical and non-medical people appointed by the MPTS. The GMC is usually represented at a Fitness to Practise hearing by a barrister, and the doctor may also attend with legal representation.[52] Both sides are allowed to call and cross-examine witnesses. The standard of proof required before the panel is the civil standard.[53] If the Panel decides that the alleged facts have been proven and the doctor's fitness to practise is impaired, then a range of sanctions can be applied. These are: taking no action; accepting undertakings offered by the doctor that will protect patients and the wider public interest; placing conditions on the doctor's registration; suspending the doctor's registration; or, erasing the doctor's name from the Medical Register so that they can no longer practise. A warning may be issued in cases where a doctor's fitness to practise has not been found to be impaired but where there has been a significant departure from standards of Good Medical Practice.

1.41 A doctor whose fitness to practise has been found impaired can appeal against the decision. The appeal is made under s 40 of the Medical Act 1983 (as amended) and the papers must be filed at the appropriate court, which depending on the doctor's registered address, would be the High Court for England and Wales, the Court of Session in Scotland, or the High Court in Northern Ireland. As a result, there has been something of a steady flow of cases in which the findings of Fitness to Practise Panels (FPPs) have been modified on appeal and there is some evidence that the courts are anxious to rein in the punitive role recently adopted by FPPs.[54] Panel decision can also be appealed on the grounds that they are unduly lenient and fail to protect the public.[55] The Professional Standards Authority is able to initiate such appeals, and following Government approval the GMC has also been granted the same right. The BMA has expressed concern about this development, highlighting the severe emotional toll that GMC investigations can take on doctors, as well as the problem of 'double jeopardy' that arises if a doctor cleared of wrongdoing by the MPTS is required to face a second round of legal proceedings in court.[56]

The Educational Function

1.42 Another important way in which the GMC exerts control over the profession is through setting standards for medical education and training. The GMC establishes benchmarks for undergraduate and postgraduate students in terms of knowledge, skills, and behaviours. At undergraduate level, university medical schools set the curricula for teaching and assessing students and the GMC monitors universities to ensure that the desired standards are maintained. At postgraduate level, the standards for the two-year Foundation Training programme and further specialty training are also set and overseen by the GMC, but with the curricula developed by the UK's Academy of Medical Royal Colleges. Furthermore, the GMC also approves the relevant training programmes that

---

[52] For some surprising empirical data, see J Cash, 'UK doctors commonly face fitness to practise hearings without legal representation' (2014) 348 BMJ g2850.

[53] Health Care Act 1999, s 60A inserted by Health and Social Care Act 2008, s 112.

[54] E.g. *Patel* v *General Medical Council* [2012] EWHC 3688 (Admin); *Bawa-Garba* v *General Medical Council* [2015] EWHC 1277 (QB). See also, C Dyer, 'David Southall: Anatomy of a wrecked career' (2012) 344 BMJ e3377.

[55] Section 29 of the National Health Service Reform and Health Care Professions Act 2002.

[56] BMA, 'GMC gains right to appeal fitness-to-practise decisions' 26 March 2015. Available at http://bma.org.uk/news-views-analysis/news/2015/march/gmc-gains-right-to-appeal-fitness-to-practise-decisions.

lead to the award of a Certificate of Completion of Training (CCT), which is a prerequisite for registration and practice as a GP or Specialist.[57]

Maintaining the Medical Register

1.43   Maintaining the official List of Registered Medical Practitioners (LRMP) remains a basic function of the GMC. The LRMP is now available as a searchable, online resource that gives details of doctors' reference numbers and gender, the year and place of doctors' primary medical degrees, status on the register, including whether doctors hold a licence to practise, date of registration, entry on the GP and Specialist Registers, and any publicly available fitness to practise history since October 2005.[58]

1.44   The purpose of the register has traditionally been to protect the public from those who have not undergone recognised training; unlike the practice of dentistry, no specific offence lies in an unqualified person practising medicine in the UK—the offence has always been that of pretending to be a registered medical practitioner[59] or of usurping functions which are statutorily limited to registered practitioners—such as prescribing 'prescription only' medicines. This, however, is arguably the function of the GMC that has undergone the greatest metamorphosis in the upheaval of the last few years and registration no longer provides an indefinite entitlement to practise medicine—an additional licence to practise is required.[60]

1.45   This is to be granted on first registration but, thereafter, is subject to revalidation, a procedure whereby the practitioner's continuing fitness to practise is evaluated every five years, with annual appraisals in between. The process of revalidation came into effect from December 2012 and is still evolving. Earlier misgivings about the possible consequences for doctors about whom concerns are raised have largely dissipated. The process encourages, inter alia, reflection on the GMC's core guidance for doctors, 'Good Medical Practice'. Revalidation, therefore, appears more aligned with the GMC's educational role than its investigative function. A large number of doctors have already undergone appraisals and emerged unscathed, with only a tiny proportion of doctors identified as needing retraining. These results have split opinion, with some interpreting them as an indicator that the revalidation process is too lax,[61] while others suggesting they demonstrate that revalidation is an unnecessary administrative burden.[62]

WHISTLEBLOWING

1.46   In the context of the NHS, 'whistleblowing' refers to NHS staff reporting concerns about safety, malpractice, or wrongdoing that may threaten patient safety or undermine public

---

[57] The CCT is awarded in compliance with Directive 2005/36/EC, which aims to harmonise the recognition of professional qualifications within the EU. The certificate confirms satisfactory completion of specialist training which satisfies the requirements of Art 25 of the Directive (or Art 28 for general practice).

[58] http://www.gmc-uk.org/doctors/register/LRMP.asp

[59] Medical Act 1983, s 49. It is now, similarly, an offence to falsely claim to hold a licence to practise (Medical Act 1983, s 49A inserted by the 2002 Order).

[60] General Medical Council (Licence to Practise and Revalidation) Regulations Order of Council 2012 (as amended).

[61] L Donelly, 'Alarm over doctors check with 99.3 per cent pass rate' *The Telegraph*, 10 May 2015.

[62] A Matthews-King, 'Revalidation identifies fewer than 1% of GPs needing remediation' *Pulse*, 6 August 2015.

confidence in the health service. The NHS Constitution was amended in 2012 to include an expectation that NHS staff will report concerns as early as possible.[63] This can be done through a number of channels, including locally through designated persons within an institution, with the GMC (if the concerns relate to a doctor), or via the national whistle-blowing helpline.

1.47 An employee who discloses in good faith, inter alia, that the health or safety of an indi-vidual has been, is being, or is likely to be endangered is now protected from recrimi-nation by the Employment Rights Act 1996, ss 43A–M.[64] Protection of the individual is, of necessity, subject to a number of qualifying conditions which include following a prescribed procedure. Nevertheless, examples of serious problems in the treatment of some whistleblowers have been laid bare in Sir Robert Francis' 2015 *Freedom to Speak Up* review.[65] This report, which followed from the Public Inquiry into unacceptable standards of treatment at hospitals under the Mid Staffordshire NHS Trust, made a number of recommendations to improve support for staff who raise concerns. These include the appointment of local and national whistleblowing guardians, training for staff on how to raise concerns and protect others who do so, and assistance for whistleblowers to find alternative employment. The Government has accepted all of the recommendations in principle. The great majority would commend these further reforms. Not only is frankness in the investigation of both ethical and clinical error to the advantage of the patient,[66] but it is also important that the spectre of 'closed ranks' does not undermine the public's faith in the health care professions. At the same time, the ill-effects of a potential rebound towards defensive practice cannot, or should not, be ignored.

ADVERTISING

1.48 The importance of the overall relationship between the medical profession and the pub-lic cannot be overstated. The established primacy of the cult of patient autonomy and patient choice has carried with it a parallel claim to a right to personal assessment of one's doctor's expertise and quality—aided by a large number of 'league tables' and mortality records. This has added a new dimension to the GMC's traditional attitudes to advertising by the medical profession. There is little doubt that the original restrictions were based on a fear of competitive doctors 'touting' for patients; the advent of the NHS virtually elimi-nated any need for them and the antipathy of the GMC was steadily relaxed.

1.49 Resolution of the position was, however, catalysed by the reference of the GMC's ban to the Monopolies and Mergers Commission, who held that the rule forbidding

---

[63] NHS, *The NHS Constitution for England* (2012, as updated 2015).
[64] Inserted by Public Interest Disclosure Act 1998, s 1 (as amended).
[65] Sir Robert Francis QC, *Freedom to Speak Up: An Independent Review into Creating an Open and Honest Reporting Culture in the NHS* (2015).
[66] This was the purpose behind the National Patient Safety Agency, the function of which was to set up a system for mandatory reporting and collation of incidents and 'near-misses' on a national scale. The Agency, however, has now been abolished: Health and Social Care Act 2012, s 281. Its functions have been transferred to the NHS Commissioning Board: NHS Commissioning Board Authority (Functions of the Authority) (Amendment) Directions 2012. See also the reinvention of the Health and Social Care Information Centre (2012 Act, s 252).

advertising in the press by general practitioners was against the public interest[67] and the GMC's advice currently reads:

> When advertising your services, you must make sure the information you publish is factual and can be checked, and does not exploit patients' vulnerability or lack of medical knowledge.[68]

LEGAL INTERVENTION IN MEDICINE

1.50 The early twenty-first-century picture of medical practice is one of rapidly advancing technology which is effected in a strongly research-orientated environment and which exists within an increasingly hedonistic and materialistic society. Society, for its part, demands more and more esoteric methodology, and personal involvement in medical care is encouraged at all levels. The law, however, moves more slowly than either the medical or public mores. Thus, the general rules of doctoring are being developed within a moral framework which is constantly being restructured by contemporary society while, at the same time, doctors frequently find themselves operating in an atmosphere of legal uncertainty. All of this promotes confrontation within the triangular relationship of medicine, society, and the law;[69] a major purpose of medical jurisprudence as it evolves is to break down any barriers of latent hostility.

1.51 Whether the law has a right to impose morality is a well-known and controversial issue in jurisprudence but, for present purposes, we argue that the public conscience, as embodied in the law, provides a useful guide to medical ethics. As Hoffmann LJ once put it persuasively:

> I would expect medical ethics to be formed by the law rather than the reverse.[70]

This, however, is not to say that the law should dictate to the profession and, particularly, not that it should dictate by means of restrictive statute. Effectively, we are merely pointing out that medicine must operate within broadly stated legal rules—such as those embodied in the common law—and, as Lord Scarman classically indicated,[71] the law must be flexible in the absence of parliamentary direction.

1.52 The crucial question, then, is that of determining the *extent* to which medical decisions should be the object of legal scrutiny and control. At one extreme there are those who hold that the medical profession should be left to regulate itself and that it alone should decide what is acceptable conduct. According to this view, intervention by the law is too blunt a way of tackling the delicate ethical dilemmas which doctors have to face: the individual must confront and resolve the day-to-day ethico-legal issues of medical practice—and it is a truism that no two patients present precisely the same problems in diagnosis and management.

---

[67] Interestingly, the Court of Appeal subsequently upheld that the recommendation did not render the GMC's position unreasonable (*Colman*, para 1: n 50).

[68] General Medical Council, *Good Medical Practice* (2013), para 70.

[69] Lord Woolf identified five main areas of dissatisfaction involving all three parties in 'Clinical negligence: What is the solution? How can we provide justice for doctors and patients?' (2000) 4 Med Law Internat 133.

[70] In *Airedale NHS Trust* v *Bland* [1993] 1 All ER 821 at 858; (1993) 12 BMLR 64 at 103.

[71] In *Gillick* v *West Norfolk and Wisbech Area Health Authority* [1986] AC 112; [1985] 3 All ER 402, HL.

1.53 The contrary view denies that there is any reason why doctors alone should regulate their relationship with their patients. In this view, reserving to the medical profession the right to decide on issues, say, of life and death, is an improper derogation from an area of legitimate public concern and an encroachment by clinicians into what is, properly, social policy. According to the proponents of this opinion, the law, even if it is an imperfect and often inaccessible weapon, is at least one means of controlling the health care professions in the interests of the community as a whole. In the event, modern conditions are such that the courts cannot avoid involvement in decisions that are essentially matters of medical ethics rather than of law; as a result, they are increasingly prepared 'to adopt a more proactive approach to resolving conflicts as to more traditional medical issues'.[72] The reasons for this are several and, in many ways, indeterminate. We suggest, however, that it is in large part due to the rise of the culture of rights and the impact this has had on the non-acceptability of paternalistic practices. In essence, there have been fundamental adjustments in the doctor–patient relationship—and the relationship between law and medicine is also changing.

1.54 The relationship between the law and medicine had, over the years, effectively settled into a classical domestic state in which mutual trust had been, occasionally, interspersed with outbursts of disaffection. Certainly, the law has, traditionally, been content to allow doctors as free a hand in carrying out their duties as is possible. Nonetheless, as Lord Woolf cogently pointed out in a non-judicial capacity,[73] times change—including as to the distribution of domestic chores—and can change rapidly if the conditions are ripe. Thus, we have Lord Brandon holding, some 25 years ago:

> ... [T]he lawfulness of a doctor operating on, or giving treatment to, an adult patient disabled from giving consent will depend not on any approval or sanction of a court but on the question whether the operation or other treatment is in the best interests of the patient concerned.[74]

Within ten years, however, the Court of Appeal was unanimously limiting the powers of the doctor beyond matters of clinical judgement and, at the same time, delineating the relative powers and responsibilities of the doctors and the judges:

> [I]n determining the welfare of the patient, the *Bolam*[75] test [of the acceptability of a doctor's actions] is applied only at the onset to ensure that the treatment proposed is recognised as proper by a responsible medical opinion skilled in delivering that particular treatment ... In deciding what is best for the disabled patient the judge must have regard for the patient's welfare as the paramount consideration. That embraces issues far wider than the medical ... In my opinion *Bolam* has no contribution to make to this second and determinative stage of the judicial decision.[76]

In effect, this retreat from *Bolam* is but part of a steady shift of judicial and societal concern away from the duties of the medical profession and its relocation under the umbrella

---

[72] Lord Woolf, 'Are the Courts Excessively Deferential to the Medical Profession?' (2001) 9 Med L Rev 1.

[73] N 72.

[74] *Re F* [1990] 2 AC 1 at 56, sub nom *F v West Berkshire Health Authority* (1989) 4 BMLR 1 at 8, HL.

[75] *Bolam v Friern Hospital Management Committee* [1957] 2 All ER 118; (1957) 1 BMLR 1. We discuss the *Bolam* test, which judges the propriety of a doctor's action by way of the standards of the medical profession itself, in detail in Chapter 5. Both the Lord Chief Justice of England (nn 72 and 87) and the Lord Chancellor (Lord Irvine of Lairg, 'The Patient, the Doctor, their Lawyers and the Judge: Rights and Duties' (1999) 7 Med L Rev 255) see its modification as central to the development of a medical jurisprudence.

[76] *Re SL (adult patient) (medical treatment)* [2001] Fam 15, (2000) 55 BMLR 105 at 119 per Thorpe LJ.

of patients' rights[77]—though whether or not this serves to harmonise doctor–patient relationships is open to discussion. The advent of the Patient Rights (Scotland) Act 2011 is unusual in that it is the first attempt in the UK jurisdictions to give statutory expression to the growing phenomenon of autonomy in health care provision articulated overtly as patients' rights. The Act includes, for example, the right that health care be 'patient focused, have regard to the importance of providing the optimum benefit to the patient's health and wellbeing, and allow and encourage the patient to participate as fully as possible in decisions relating to the patient's health and wellbeing'.[78] While this might do no more than articulate entitlements that have been developing over the years in the courts, this sea change is emblematic of the shift of power that has occurred in the discipline of medical jurisprudence.

1.55 It has to be said, however, that the courts are also willing to recognise their position in relation to the legislature in face of the speed of evolution of modern technology—as Lord Browne-Wilkinson put it: 'Existing law may not provide an acceptable answer to the new legal questions [raised by the ability to sustain life artificially].'[79] He went on to question whether judges should seek to develop new law to meet a wholly new situation and to suggest that it was a matter which required society, through the democratic expression of its views in Parliament, to reach its decisions on the underlying moral and practical problems and then reflect those decisions in legislation—and, in this, he was strongly supported by Lord Mustill.[80] In other words, the House of Lords, at least, is anxious that society, as the third point in the triangle of policy decision-makers, should take its full share of responsibility for the ethico-legal directions we are following.

1.56 Even so, as we have already noted, statute law is a cumbersome tool for control of an area of what is ostensibly public law but which is, in practice, heavily influenced by considerations of patients' private lives.[81] This has led to a pattern of legislation whereby the day-to-day implementation of policy has been left to regulatory authorities with, more recently, an increasing lay involvement.[82] Its overall impact remains difficult to measure. What we view with greater suspicion is the parallel politicisation of modern medicine—populism is a very doubtful formulator of morality.

---

[77] See, in particular, the seminal case of *Chester v Afshar* [2004] 4 All ER 587, HL (para 4.130). See also G Laurie, 'Personality, privacy and autonomy in medical law' in N Whitty and R Zimmermann (eds), *Rights of Personality in Scots law: A Comparative Perspective* (2009), ch 10.

[78] Patient Rights (Scotland) Act 2011, s 3.

[79] In *Airedale NHS Trust v Bland* [1993] 1 All ER 821 at 878; (1993) 12 BMLR 64 at 124.

[80] (1993) 12 BMLR 64 at 135.

[81] We discuss this paradox in more detail in J K Mason, 'Particularity and Medical Law' in Z Bańkowski and J MacLean (eds), *The Universal and the Particular in Legal Reasoning* (2007).

[82] Albeit that the recent review of health-related authorities (and the subsequent cull of many), suggests yet another political shift in the management of medicine and life science development: see Department of Health, *Liberating the NHS: Report of the Arms-Length Bodies Review* (2010). Inter alia, this has seen many authority functions moving to the Care Quality Commission (CQC) and has led to the abolition of entities such as the Health Protection Agency and National Information Governance Board (Health and Social Care Act 2012, Parts 2 and 10). A consultation on the proposal to transfer functions from the Human Fertilisation and Embryology Authority (HFEA) and the Human Tissue Authority (HTA) to the CQC and the recently established Health Research Authority resulted in a decision not to abolish the HFEA and the HTA but rather to conduct a fundamental review of functions, see Department of Health, Government response to the consultation on proposals to transfer functions from the HFEA and HTA, 25 January 2013, para 69.

THE DOCTOR'S POSITION

1.57 The fact that the courts are prepared to assist doctors in coming to their ethical decisions—and have shown this by the steadily extended use of their declaratory powers[83]—is laudable and helpful. But it does not compensate in toto for the fact that doctors often still have to work in a 'legal vacuum' in which, without such pre-emptive assistance, they may be uncertain as to whether or not they face the prospect of a civil action or, again in the words of Lord Mustill, they take the risk of having to validate their conduct after the event in the context of a trial for murder.[84]

1.58 One effect of this can be to distort people's behaviour through the fear of litigation or prosecution. One may then be concerned, not with doing what one feels to be right, but with what one feels to be the safest thing to do. Doctors in the UK may be particularly fortunate in this respect as, notwithstanding the changes of direction that we have discussed, the courts remain inherently reluctant to interfere in clinical matters. Although, with acceptance of the absolute right of a patient to refuse treatment,[85] and the rise and rise of self-determination, the fear could be that, if anything, the pendulum has swung too far in favour of autonomy, adherence to which may, in too many cases, be tantamount to abandonment of one's patients rather than respect for them as persons.

1.59 Moreover, one must question whether the adversarial system of apportioning justice (or blame) is the right route to follow if there is to be a decision in the event of disagreement between doctor and patient or, more often, between doctor and surrogate decision-maker. The concept of winners and losers provides an uneasy foundation for the solution of sensitive and complex ethico-legal problems but one looks in vain for a suitable alternative. Certainly, the vision of a bed-side consultation, as evidenced in *Re B*,[86] has its attractions but it would be ingenuous in the extreme to suppose that it could take the place—or even partly take the place—of a full court hearing in every similar case.

1.60 Even so, try as one may to avoid the issue, there is no doubt that the intrusion of the law into the doctor–patient relationship, essential as it may be in some instances, leads to a subtle but important change in the nature of the relationship. Trust and respect are more likely to flourish in one which is governed by morality rather than by legal rules and the injection of formality and excessive caution between doctor and patient cannot be in the patient's interest if it means that each sees the other as a potential adversary—as Lord Woolf said, in a non-judicial capacity: 'My cure … involves a change of culture as to litigation resulting from medical care.'[87]

1.61 Where, then, does the doctor stand today in relation to society? To some extent, and perhaps increasingly, he is a servant of the public, a public which is, moreover, widely—though not always well—informed on medical matters. The competent patient's inalienable rights to understand his treatment and to accept or refuse it are now well established

---

[83] See, for example, Practice Note (Family Division: Incapacitated Adults: Declaratory Proceedings) [2002] 1 All ER 794; [2002] 1 WLR 325.

[84] In *Airedale NHS Trust v Bland*, [1993] AC 789.

[85] *Re T (adult: refusal of medical treatment)* [1992] 4 All ER 649, (1992) 9 BMLR 46.

[86] *Re B (adult: refusal of medical treatment), sub nom Ms B v An NHS Hospital Trust* [2002] EWHC 429; (2002) 65 BMLR 149.

[87] Lord Woolf, 'Clinical negligence: What is the solution?' (2000) 4 Med Law Internat 133 at 134.

and society is encouraged to distrust professional paternalism. The talk today is of 'producers and consumers' and the ambience of the supermarket is one that introduces its own stresses and strains.[88]

1.62 It is, moreover, in many ways extraordinary that the provision of a national health service, which one would have thought should, above all other services, be free of bias, has, in recent years, become one of the main political issues that determines the voters' intentions in the UK.[89] As a result, more and more extravagant claims—and, more significantly, promises—are made with little regard for the fallibility and limitations of those who must implement them. Like it or not, only one person can be the best thoracic surgeon in the country; the rest can only carry on doing their personal best which no amount of 'hype' or sanction can improve.

1.63 Unless the humanity of both health carers and patients is appreciated by both sides and is not exploited in the political arena, the resulting disappointment, again on both sides, may well lead to a relationship of conflict—or of mutual suspicion—which is in the interests of neither doctor nor patient. What is needed is one of mutual understanding in which doctors acknowledge the interests of patients and patients, for their part, reciprocate this respect while appreciating the pressures, both physical and mental, under which a health carer must work. The public has also to understand the broader issues in medicine. The profession must experiment and research if it is to improve its art and many would hold that a slight loss of autonomy on the part of patients is a small price to pay for a useful advance in therapeutic skills. The profession must also teach, or there will be no doctors to serve future generations; some loss of confidentiality can be looked upon as a return for the best treatment and the best investigative facilities. Clearly, these opposing attitudes cannot be reconciled so long as they are polarised or if the claims of one party are accepted to the exclusion of the other. A middle way, based on respect and trust,[90] must be found and this is the function of medical jurisprudence which we attempt to express in the chapters which follow.

[88] For discussion, see J K Mason, 'Medicine, doctors and patients: The changing face of society in the health care field' in M Jeeves (ed), *Human Nature* (2006), ch 5.4.

[89] The Chairman of the BMA is on record as stating that the NHS has become 'the Punch and Judy show of British politics': L Eaton, 'Politicians Must Stop Exploiting Patients' (2002) 325 BMJ 6.

[90] For the importance of trust, see O O'Neill, *Autonomy and Trust in Bioethics* (2002).

2

PUBLIC HEALTH AND
THE STATE–PATIENT
RELATIONSHIP

INTRODUCTION

2.01 As we have pointed out in Chapter 1, medical practice encompasses more than a simple, private doctor–patient relationship. All of us and the state have an interest in the well-being of individuals and communities, and both (individuals and the state) have obligations to the community. The state, in particular, has a basic duty, grounded on both the social contract and, increasingly, on the demands of the human rights regime, to protect its citizens from harm. From a health perspective, this means protecting individuals and communities from the ravages of disease. As such, the medical profession must be heavily involved in what can be termed 'public health', as are a range of other non-medical public bodies.

2.02 This public role nuances the doctor's private relationships, necessitating a consideration of how our concepts of medical ethics are altered when engaged in public health supporting measures,[1] which tend to fall into two overlapping categories—health promotion and health protection (or disease prevention and control), both of which are discussed below. There is much that we can do to promote our own health for the sake of ourselves and our significant others; we can eat more healthily, exercise, and avoid alcohol and drugs. But when our state of health slips our control, or if it becomes a threat to others, then personal action can be superseded by the need for government action aimed at protecting the community, even when this entails threats to the rights of the immediately affected individual. The important relationship, then, is no longer that between doctor and patient but rather that between patient and state, and the many actors in between.

2.03 The role of the law is to police the boundaries of these relationships, and to ensure that reasonable justifications for state actions that encroach on individual rights are offered and are well founded, a function that is complicated by the fact that threats to public health can appear quickly and with potentially devastating regional and global effects. The advent of H1N1 in Mexico in April 2009, for example, was declared a global pandemic by the World Health Organization (WHO) within months of its detection in humans.[2] And while the responses to the outbreak of Ebola in West Africa in 2014 was much

---

[1] For a classic treatment of the issues, see M Brazier and J Harris, 'Public health and private lives' (1996) 4 Med L Rev 171. See also Nuffield Council on Bioethics, *Public Health: Ethical Issues* (2007); L Gostin, *Public Health Law: Power, Duty, Restraint* (2nd edn, 2008); J Coggon, *What Makes Health Public?* (2012); and L Gostin, *Global Health Law* (2014).

[2] On 11 June 2009, the WHO declared H1N1 to be the first flu pandemic in 41 years.

criticised,[3] it too was declared a global health emergency, with coordinated efforts following therefrom. The importance of legal preparedness, therefore, cannot be overstated, and action is required at each of the national, regional, and international levels.[4]

HUMAN RIGHTS AND MEDICAL LAW

THE INTERNATIONAL SETTING

2.04   At the outset, it is important to acknowledge that the relatively young discipline of medical law has emerged against a background of universal human rights as embodied in a wide range of international treaties, covenants, agreements, and guidelines.[5] Taken together, these instruments endorse a view of the world which has as its central focus the primacy of the human being. Flowing from this are a number of direct and collateral rights which, it is declared, all humans possess.[6] In the health care context, it is frequently asserted that these include the right:

- to be respected and treated with dignity;
- to the highest attainable standard of physical and mental health and associated right to health care;
- to consent to and refuse medical interventions;
- not to be subjected to medical or scientific experimentation without consent;
- to equality under the law;
- to protection against arbitrary interference with privacy or with the family;
- to enjoy the benefits of scientific progress and its application; and
- to special protection if you are in a class of vulnerable persons.

2.05   This is an impressive array of rights, but it is important to note that they are not all of the same genre. Rights of non-interference (negative rights), such as the right to consent and refuse and the right to protection of one's privacy, are different from rights of entitlement (positive rights), such as the right to the highest attainable standard of health. The consequences of giving effect to positive rights are generally thought to be more far-reaching

---

[3] S Harmon, 'In Search of Global Health Justice: A Need to Reinvigorate Institutions and Make International Law' (2015) Health Care Analysis 1–24, DOI 10.1007/s10728-015-0296-9.

[4] On regional action, see Decision No. 1082/2013/EU of the European Parliament and of the Council, 22 October 2013 on Serious Cross-Border Threats to Health, which is meant to improve preparedness across the EU and strengthen the capacity to coordinate response to health emergencies. For more, see http://ec.europa.eu/health/preparedness_response/policy/decision/index_en.htm, and see European Commission, *Public Health: Improving Health for All EU Citizens* (2014).

[5] E.g. the Universal Declaration of Human Rights (1948), the European Convention for the Protection of Human Rights and Fundamental Freedoms (1950), the European Social Charter (1961), the UN Convention on the Elimination of All Forms of Racial Discrimination (1965), the International Covenant on Civil and Political Rights and the International Covenant on Economic, Social and Cultural Rights (1966), the UN Convention on the Rights of the Child (1989), the UNESCO Universal Declaration on the Human Genome and Human Rights (1997), the Council of Europe Convention on Human Rights and Biomedicine (1997), with its Additional Protection on the Prohibition of Cloning Human Beings (1998), Additional Protocol on Organs and Tissues of Human Origin (2002), Additional Protocol on Biomedical Research (2005), and Additional Protocol concerning Genetic Testing for Health Purposes (2008), and the various UNESCO instruments, including the UNESCO Universal Declaration on Bioethics and Human Rights (2005).

[6] See generally J Griffin, *On Human Rights* (2008).

than those respecting negative rights, especially in economic terms, and this has a direct correlation on the likelihood of such rights being respected or protected by states. As will become clear, there is a significant difference between the state–citizen and the doctor–patient relationship, and this is all the more obvious when rights are asserted and rights discourses relied on. Indeed, as suggested in Chapter 1, the assertion of 'patients' rights' may be antithetical to the establishment and maintenance of a healthy and productive therapeutic relationship, an antithesis that is more pronounced and problematic in the public health context.

2.06 In any event, while the rhetoric of rights has been a powerful motivator for international bodies and international legal instrument-making, many states do little more than pay lip-service to these instruments,[7] and continue to implement domestic laws in breach of their provisions.[8] The problem is that international instruments often represent an ideal; they are ethically justified and contain sound principles and provisions (at least from a Western perspective), but the lawyer who is concerned with turning rights into realities may see them as largely aspirational documents.[9] States which agree to their provisions and sign up to their terms rarely do so with a view to making substantive changes in domestic law. Either it is argued that laws are adequate as they stand, or reservations are taken if the consequences of signing are too great, yet political expediency dictates a show of commitment. Not only is there a substantial lack of volonté to be bound by their terms, but there is also a pitiful lack of effective mechanisms to ensure enforcement by aberrant states. This is not to decry the usefulness of these instruments—they have an intrinsic value in that they can influence the form of further developments, and can guide a path through the ethical and legal mire that must be negotiated if further measures are to be instituted.

2.07 The United Nations Educational, Scientific, and Cultural Organization (UNESCO), in particular, has made its Bioethics Programme a priority, producing a range of instruments, including the Universal Declaration on Bioethics and Human Rights (2005). UNESCO's International Bioethics Committee (IBC) sees its role as a standard-setter, and its instruments aim 'to provide a universal framework of principles and procedures to guide States in the formulation of their legislation, policies or other instruments in the field of bioethics'. The ambition of UNESCO and other organisations is to promote respect for human dignity and protect human rights by ensuring respect for the life of human beings, and fundamental freedoms, consistent with international human rights law;[10] indeed, the obligation to respect the 'inherent dignity of the human person' has pride of place as the first of the Declaration's general principles. But therein lie many of the problems and challenges that such an instrument faces.[11] It is said, for example, that Japanese culture does not recognise a notion of 'human dignity', at least not in the way that it is understood in the West. In what sense, then, can this truly be a *universal*

---

[7] By June 2015, only 29 of the 47 Member States of the Council of Europe had ratified the Convention on Human Rights and Biomedicine (1997). The UK was not one of them.

[8] E.g. the UK has passed laws (e.g., the Human Fertilisation and Embryology (Research Purposes) Regulations 2001, and the Human Fertilisation and Embryology Act 2008) that permit uses of human embryos in clear contravention of Art 18(2) of the Convention on Human Rights and Biomedicine.

[9] See generally S Gevers et al. (eds), *Health Law, Human Rights and the Biomedical Convention: Essays in Honour of Henriette Roscam Abbing* (2005).

[10] See E Wicks, 'The meaning of "life": Dignity and the right to life in international human rights treaties' (2012) 12 HRL Rev 199.

[11] I De Melo-Martin, 'Human dignity in international policy documents: a useful criterion for public policy' (2011) 25 Bioethics 37.

instrument? Moreover, the term 'human dignity' itself begs the question of what exactly this means and who enjoys it?[12] It is telling that the Declaration makes no specific mention of the position of the human embryo. Is this a 'person' within the terms of the instrument?[13] The omission is undoubtedly driven by political expediency because there are few issues that give rise to global disagreement like the question of the moral (and legal) status of the embryo; the reality is that truly sensitive issues often remain unaddressed because the greatest challenge for drafters is to reach consensus. The final version of the Declaration is a considerably watered-down version of the original report of the IBC on the possibility of a universal agreement on bioethics which contemplated, inter alia, issues as broad-ranging as abortion, euthanasia, and intellectual property rights.[14] None are considered in the final document, and that may be for the best.[15] One need only consider the machinations at the United Nations (UN) in the attempt to elaborate an International Convention Against the Reproductive Cloning of Human Beings[16] to understand how fraught the international political process can be.[17]

2.08   At the present, then, the most effective impetus for change remains the implementation of laws at the national level,[18] and this is most clearly demonstrated in the UK by the passing of the Human Rights Act 1998, which incorporated the European Convention on Human Rights (ECHR) into domestic UK law in October 2000.[19] It is easy to envisage how the ECHR's Articles might have a significant influence on patient rights and the practice of medical law. Key provisions of the ECHR embody rights that affect areas at the core of the medical discipline:

- Art 2 (the right to life);
- Art 3 (the prohibition on torture, and cruel and inhuman treatment);
- Art 5 (the right to liberty of the person);
- Art 8 (the right to respect for private and family life);
- Art 9 (the right to freedom of thought, conscience, and religion);
- Art 10 (freedom of expression, especially where this is likely to conflict with other rights such as those to privacy);
- Art 12 (the right to marry and found a family); and
- Art 14 (the prohibition on discrimination in the protection or exercise of these rights).

[12] See H Schmidt, 'Whose dignity? Resolving ambiguities in the scope of "human dignity" in the Universal Declaration on Bioethics and Human Rights' (2007) 33 J Med Ethics 578.
[13] For a comparative account, see E Bernat, 'Which beings should be entitled to human rights?' (2008) 9 Med Law Int 1.
[14] International Bioethics Committee, *Report of the IBC on the Possibility of Elaborating a Universal Instrument on Bioethics* (SHS/EST/02/CIB-9/5 (rev 3)), June 2003.
[15] See R Andorno, 'Global bioethics at UNESCO: In defence of the Universal Declaration on Bioethics and Human Rights' (2007) 33 J Med Ethics 150, and D Gunson, 'Solidarity and the Universal Declaration on Bioethics and Human Rights' (2009) 34 J Med Phil 241.
[16] The General Assembly of the UN established an Ad Hoc Committee to address the issue in 2001 (Resolution 56/93 of 12 December 2001). The debate and the various standpoints can be seen at: http://www.un.org/law/cloning/.
[17] G Annas and R Isasi, 'Arbitrage, bioethics and cloning: The ABCs of gestating a United Nations Cloning Convention' (2004) 35 Case Western Reserve J Int Law 397.
[18] D Benatar, 'Bioethics and health and human rights: A critical review' (2006) 32 J Med Ethics 17.
[19] For commentary on the European dimension, see J Marshall, 'A right to personal autonomy at the European Court of Human Rights' (2008) Europ HR Law Rev 337.

2.09 Throughout this book we examine the jurisprudence and assess the ways in which the recognition of these rights has, or has not, changed this area of the law. It is salutary, however, to note that initial predictions of wide-sweeping changes have not in the main been borne out in practice.[20] It has been established, for example, that the right to life does not imply a correlative right to die,[21] that the withdrawal of feeding and hydration from severely incapacitated patients precipitating their death can still be justified in their best interests,[22] and that so-called dangerous persons can continue to be subjected to a medical control system which can do nothing for them by way of treatment.[23] In some areas the courts have declared that the ECHR rights add nothing to domestic law,[24] while in others the change has simply been a shift in argumentation from an interests- to a rights-based approach, leaving the outcome largely unaltered.[25] And, in the background, we have the European Court of Human Rights (ECtHR) in Strasbourg which, inter alia, continues to refuse to extend ECHR protection to the fetus.[26]

THE DOMESTIC SETTING

2.10 The Human Rights Act 1998 protects UK citizens and residents against the acts or omissions of public authorities that contravene their rights, and the institutions of the NHS are paradigm examples of such authorities.[27] Other examples include the Human Fertilisation and Embryology Authority, the Human Tissue Authority, the Medicines and Healthcare Products Regulatory Agency, and the National Institute for Health and Clinical Excellence. The 1998 Act, which, as noted above, has incorporated the provisions of the ECHR, has perhaps had its most profound influence in the realm of judicial review, where procedural safeguards relating to treatment decisions have been subjected to very close scrutiny, and in many cases, have been strengthened.[28]

2.11 The ECtHR, for example, has taken a stand in favour of the rights of parents who disagree with the medical assessment of their child and on the proper course of action to be taken. In *Glass* v *United Kingdom*,[29] the ECtHR held not only that a decision to treat a child against his parents' wishes constitutes an interference with his right to respect

---

[20] See e.g. BMA, *The Medical Profession and Human Rights* (2001). Cf, G T Laurie, 'Medical law and human rights: Passing the parcel back to the profession?' in A Boyle et al. (eds), *Human Rights and Scots Law: Comparative Perspectives on the Incorporation of the ECHR* (2002).

[21] *R (on the application of Pretty)* v *DPP* [2002] 1 AC 800; confirmed in the ECtHR as *Pretty* v *United Kingdom* (Application 2346/02) [2002] 2 FCR 97. But see *R (on the application of Nicklinson)* v *Ministry of Justice* [2015] AC 657 (UKSC) for shifts in attitude on this.

[22] See *NHS Trust A* v *M, NHS Trust BvH* [2001] 1 All ER 801; (2000) 58 BMLR 87, and more recently, *NHS Trust* v *I* [2003] EWHC 2243 (Fam).

[23] *A* v *The Scottish Ministers*, 2001 SC 1, confirmed by the Privy Council at 2001 SLT 1331.

[24] *Re Wyatt (a child) (medical treatment: parents' consent)* [2004] Fam Law 866.

[25] See *Campbell* v *Mirror Group Newspapers Ltd* [2004] 2 WLR 1232 (HL), which concerned an alleged breach of the medical confidentiality of Naomi Campbell by publication of details of her addiction therapy. Lord Hope remarked, at para 86, that, while the language of the action had now changed from a balance of public interests to a balance of Article rights, he doubted whether 'the centre of gravity has shifted'.

[26] *Vo* v *France* [2004] 2 FCR 577. For comment, see J Mason, 'What's in a name? The vagaries of *Vo* v *France*' (2005) 16 CFLQ 97.

[27] See J Wadham and H Mountfield, *Blackstone's Guide to the Human Rights Act 1998* (1999).

[28] See *R (Wilkinson)* v *RMO, Broadmoor Hospital Authority* [2002] 1 WLR 419 (procedural requirements regarding forced treatment of detained persons). Several other decisions relating to the treatment of the mentally ill are discussed in Chapter 13.

[29] *Glass* v *United Kingdom* [2004] 1 FCR 553. For comment, see R Huxtable and K Forbes, '*Glass* v *UK*: Maternal instinct v Medical opinion' (2004) 16 CFLQ 339.

for private life under Art 8(1), but that the failure to seek court authority for the action in the face of conflict means that there was insufficient justification for the treatment. Procedurally, then, the message is clear: court involvement in contested cases is mandatory if patients' rights are to be fully protected. Although this does not give parents a 'right' to have their every wish respected, it does limit the authority of health care professionals to manage a case on their uncontested view as to what are the patient's best interests.[30]

2.12 Similarly, in *M A K and R K v United Kingdom*, there was a violation of human rights when a child was examined and a blood sample taken, without parental consent, on suspicion of abuse. Crucially, this was before a proper medical assessment of the child to reveal the truth that she suffered from a rare skin condition.[31] At the same time, we must remember that human rights protection is not limited to patients. Professionals, too, can claim procedural safeguards, especially when their professional conduct is under scrutiny.[32]

2.13 Beyond the specific rulings, the details of which we explore in later chapters, the human rights perspective offers a framework within which to consider the evolution of medical law as well as a benchmark against which to test its development.[33] It is trite to say that human rights are fundamental rights, but it is rarely the case that such rights are absolute. Thus, while human rights instruments identify protections that are considered to be of core value to our society, these do not deserve protection at any cost. Exceptions are possible. The starting point is, however, that fundamental rights should be protected and the onus is on those who would interfere with such rights to justify any interference. Some human rights, such as the right to liberty (Art 5, ECHR), only permit exceptions from a restricted and limited list, while other rights, such as Arts 8 (right to respect for private life) and 10 (freedom of expression), permit a range of exceptions which are subject to the watchwords of necessity and proportionality. Justification in such cases is a three-prong test, as follows.

2.14 (i) *In accordance with the law.* This means that measures must have a basis in domestic law; the law must be adequately accessible and foreseeable and with sufficient precision for individuals to know how it operates; there must be sufficient protection from arbitrary decisions and clarity of the scope of discretion. Whether these criteria are met depends on all circumstances in a given context. In *Evans v United Kingdom*,[34] for example, the ECtHR (Grand Chamber) held that the provisions of the Human Fertilisation and Embryology Act 1990 were perfectly clear that the disposal of frozen embryos would be dealt with through a system of informed consent (see further 8.80). Contrariwise, in *R (on the application of Purdy) v DPP*,[35] the failure of the public prosecution service to

---

[30] Other examples of courts contemplating procedural safeguards include *D v An NHS Trust (medical treatment: consent: termination)* [2004] 1 FLR 1110 (legitimacy of proceeding with an abortion involving an incompetent adult woman) and *R (on the application of Khan) v Secretary of State for Health* [2003] 4 All ER 1239 (patient death potentially at the hand of state agents must be investigated promptly and publicly to ascertain the true cause).

[31] [2010] 2 FLR 451; [2010] 51 EHRR 14.

[32] See e.g. *Threlfall v General Optical Council* [2004] All ER (D) 416 (QB) (breach of Art 6 because inadequate reasons given by General Optical Council for finding of serious professional misconduct); cf, *Abu-Romia v General Medical Council* [2003] EWHC 2515.

[33] L Gable, 'The proliferation of human rights in global health governance' (2007) 35 J Law Med Ethics 534.

[34] *Evans v United Kingdom* (2008) 46 EHRR 34.   [35] [2010] 1 AC 345.

articulate with sufficient clarity the factors that are relevant in deciding whether to prosecute assisted suicide led to public guidance.

2.15 (ii) *Legitimate aim.* This means that the measure must further one of the social aims articled in the ECHR. The health of individuals and others, social welfare, and the prevention of disorder or crime are all legitimate aims. In *Pretty* v *United Kingdom*,[36] for example, it was legitimate for the state to argue for its continued prohibition on assisted suicide on the grounds of protecting the lives and welfare of vulnerable persons. Notwithstanding, the *Pretty* case was seminal in that it was the first time the ECtHR gave full effect to the protection of autonomy under the Art 8 right to respect for private and family life. The term 'autonomy' does not appear in the ECHR.

2.16 (iii) *Necessary in a democratic society.* This means that the measure must show that it addresses a 'pressing social need', that its operation is proportionate, and that the reasons advanced for its existence are 'relevant and sufficient'. It is the obligation of authorities to demonstrate that they meet these criteria. Thus, in *Enhorn* v *Sweden*,[37] the state lost because it could not show that the compulsory detention of an individual living with HIV was necessary in order to prevent the spread of the disease.

2.17 Ultimately, the impact of human rights discourse on the discipline of medical law, including public health, turns on the willingness of the courts to be open towards an ethos of human rights.[38] This will best be achieved if they consider the bigger picture— that is, take into account the values that are more fundamental than the particular rights that are articulated in the ECHR and the 1998 Act, and which underpin these instruments. This calls for a more holistic approach to the role of giving effect to human rights. Values such as respect for human dignity and self-determination then emerge as principles that guide the interpretation of individual rights.[39] But this raises questions about how such values will be used to interpret the ECHR rights. Medical lawyers spend much of their time calling for the courts to take responsibility away from the medical profession and to assume it themselves; on the other hand, some have expressed the fear that the system will 'lead to a major shift in power from the executive and legislature to the judiciary'.[40]

2.18 Despite these concerns, as noted above, few rights under the ECHR are absolute; most allow for justifiable interferences, sometimes in the name of the wider community. While 'autonomy' per se is not explicitly mentioned in the ECHR, it is now widely accepted that it forms part of the penumbra of rights enjoying protection, most notably as part of the respect due to private and family life under Art 8(1). Art 8(2), however, provides for legitimate interferences with private and family life when this is 'necessary in accordance with the law' and in the furtherance of certain interests that include public safety, the economic well-being of the country, the protection of health and morals, or the protection of the rights of others.

---

[36] N 21.   [37] (2005) 41 EHRR 30.

[38] S Choudhry and H Fenwick, 'Taking the rights of parents and children seriously: Confronting the welfare principle under the Human Rights Act' (2005) 25 OJLS 453.

[39] See D Beyleveld and R Brownsword, *Human Dignity in Bioethics and Biolaw* (2001), and recent cases such as *Elberte* v *Latvia*, Case No. 61243/08, 13 January 2015 (ECtHR).

[40] Sir N Lyall, 'Whither Strasbourg? Why Britain should think long and hard before incorporating the European Convention on Human Rights' [1997] EHRLR 132, at 136.

HEALTH PROMOTION: IMPROVING
THE HEALTH OF THE COMMUNITY

GENERAL AND INTERNATIONAL CONTEXT

2.19 As noted above, there is much that we can do to promote our own health for the sake of ourselves and our significant others, and indeed for the community. And both the state and the community have an interest in encouraging us to make decisions that support health and productivity. States now take much more interest in the health of their citizens. This may simply be a matter of sound investment, or it may be an economics-driven policy designed to avoid greater and longer-term costs dealing with a chronically ill population. Either way, states spend vast sums of money trying to persuade or coerce their citizens into healthier lifestyles.

2.20 Despite pursuing legitimate state objectives of educating and encouraging the public in good health practices, these programmes can be very controversial, particularly given the retreat from paternalism and the rise of autonomy. To what extent, for example, is it justifiable for a government to require the wearing of seatbelts? And what about state action aimed at promoting the future health of children? Has the government the right to control meals taken to school in the interests of an anti-obesity programme?[41] Importantly, the state is at a double disadvantage. Not only is the focus on individual rights and protections greater now than ever before, which makes such programmes politically charged, but many public health issues—whether of a health promotion or health protection character—are blind to national borders, making individual state action ineffective or potentially counterproductive in any event.

2.21 Consider tobacco, a worldwide industry with powerful protagonists. Tobacco is estimated to have killed some 100 million people in the twentieth century; more than AIDS, tuberculosis, and malaria combined, and it is rising as a cause of preventable deaths.[42] What measures should states take to reduce the ill-effects of tobacco use? Is it appropriate to ban smoking in public places?[43] What other measures might states take, and how might they need to coordinate? In fact, tobacco is one of the health issues for which states have taken international legal action. The Framework Convention on Tobacco Control 2003 (FCTC), adopted by consensus by the World Health Assembly, has been signed by some 177 states.[44] According to Art 3, the FCTC's objective is to protect people, including future generations, from the social, environmental, economic, and health consequences of tobacco consumption and exposure. Its guiding principles include provision of good public information (something the industry stymied for years), building cooperation, and promoting civil society engagement (Art 4). The FCTC addresses demand reduction through pricing and taxation (Art 6), tobacco ingredients (Art 9), packaging, labelling, education, and advertising (Arts 10–13), and

---

[41] In relation to this, the European Commission's Audiovisual Media Service Directive imposes on Member States a responsibility to encourage media service providers to develop codes of conduct regarding inappropriate advertising of foods and beverages: Directive 2007/65/EC of 11 December 2007, Art 3e(2).

[42] WHO, *Report on the Global Tobacco Epidemic 2011: Warning about the Dangers of Tobacco* (2011).

[43] It could be argued that, since smoking is a powerful anxiolytic, the prohibition of smoking in a mental hospital is a rights infringement of persons compulsorily detained, despite being good public health medicine. Interestingly, this has been specifically rejected: *R (E) v Nottinghamshire Healthcare NHS Trust, R (N) v Secretary of State for Health* [2009] EWCA Civ 795.

[44] WHO, *History of the WHO Framework Convention on Tobacco Control* (2009).

illicit trade (Arts 15–16), and it tackles the critical issue of promoting viable alternatives for tobacco farmers, workers, and sellers (Arts 17–18).

UK CONTEXT

2.22   As public health programmes reach deeper into our private lives, the subtlety with which they are promoted increases.[45] In the UK, the establishment of the Behavioural Insights Team in the Cabinet Office was heralded as a more libertarian form of paternalism in encouraging citizens to act in their own health interests. Behavioural insights work on the basis of evidence from psychology and behavioural economics to understand better how people make choices and to influence them accordingly.[46] The paradigm example is placing salads and other healthy options in the front sections of a buffet on the understanding that people tend to fill their plates with what they first see.[47]

2.23   While such so-called 'nudge' policies and practices are thought to be a more acceptable, and effective, form of public health promotion, they still represent, for many, a questionable exercise of paternalism by the 'nanny state'.[48] Their legitimacy turns largely on perspective—is one's own health simply a matter of individual choice, or do we owe a responsibility to ourselves and to others to ensure that we remain as healthy as possible? The communitarian will favour the latter; the libertarian will tend towards the former. This, however, might have significant implications as to access to health care in the face of scarce resources—is the smoker less entitled to coronary bypass surgery than the non-smoker? We discuss this and similar sensitive issues in Chapter 11. For now, we need only note that states take more interest in their public's health than ever before and this means that, when set against the unprecedented rise in autonomy, the tensions inherent within public health law are now more acute than ever before.

2.24   The idea of 'facilitating choice' is certainly more palatable than 'manipulative behaviour', but to the extent that choice is predicated on information, one of the biggest challenges for governments is ensuring that misinformation does not become the primary driver for citizens' behaviour. A Scottish Executive Consultation Paper noted that the BSE (bovine spongiform encephalopathy) and MMR (measles, mumps, and rubella) controversies highlighted the need for health agencies to pay as much attention to assessing public perceptions about risk and communicating with the public as they do investigating hazards and controlling exposures.[49]

2.25   The so-called MMR controversy related to the perceived risks associated with the MMR vaccine which was introduced in the UK in 1988. A fear developed that the vaccine caused autism in children.[50] This provoked a crisis of confidence among British parents, many of whom began to refuse the vaccine for their children. Matters came to a head—in the courts

---

[45] Department of Health, *Choosing Health: Making Healthier Choices Easier* (2004).

[46] CabinetOffice:http://www.cabinetoffice.gov.uk/resource-library/applying-behavioural-insight-health.

[47] See the seminal work of R Thaler and C Sunstein, *Nudge: Improving Decisions about Health, Wealth and Happiness* (2009).

[48] For comment, see T Marteau et al., 'Changing behaviour through state intervention: When does acceptable nudge become an unacceptable shove?' (2009) 337 BMJ 121.

[49] Scottish Executive, *Health Protection in Scotland: A Consultation Paper* (2002) para 23.

[50] The original paper which sparked the controversy was A Wakefield et al., 'Ileal-lymphoid-nodular hyperplasia, non-specific colitis, and pervasive development disorder in children' (1998) 351 Lancet 637. Evidence to the contrary includes K Madsen et al., 'A population-based study of measles, mumps and rubella vaccination and autism' (2002) 347 New Eng J Med 1477; and H Honda, Y Shimizu, and M Rutter, 'No effect of MMR withdrawal on the incidence of autism: A total population study' (2005) 46 J Child Psychol

at least—with the case of *Re C (welfare of child: immunisation)*[51] in which two estranged fathers sought court orders to ensure that their children were inoculated despite the mother's disagreement. The Court of Appeal confirmed the trial judge's approach, which was to consider the best interests of the children, first, from the medical and, then, from a non-medical perspective. Sedley LJ stated that such an approach could admit a variety of possibilities, including support for a parental view that medical intervention was not appropriate. In the instant cases, however, the scientific evidence relied upon by the mothers to demonstrate the dangers of the vaccine was held to be untenable. In contrast, the effectiveness of the vaccine was shown to be high and side effects rare.[52] Orders were issued that the children should be vaccinated. Similarly, in *F v F (MMR Vaccine)*,[53] an estranged father wanted his adolescent daughters immunised contrary to the custodial mother's and the children's wishes. The court considered the welfare of the minors, the risks of vaccination, the relationship between the children and their parents, and the naïvety of their view, and issued orders for vaccination as being in their best interests.[54]

2.26 The decision may be contrasted with that of the Irish Supreme Court in *North Western Health Board v W (H)*[55] in which the Court considered an action brought by a local health board against parents who had refused a 'heel prick' test for their son—a simple blood test aimed at screening for some treatable conditions, including phenyl-ketonuria (PKU).[56] It is a routine practice in respect of all newborns. The parents resisted, however, because of the 'assault' on their son that the prick would represent. The Supreme Court upheld the right of the parents to refuse, relying on the Irish constitutional right to 'family autonomy' which, it was held, should be protected against undue interference by the state. As in the English courts, the notion of the child's best interests was a central consideration; the difference came in how, and by whom, these were to be determined.[57] There is, also, a wider social interest to be gained from the long-term storage and use of the cards upon which these blood spots are kept—so-called Guthrie cards. In the UK, these have now been kept for more than 40 years, beginning at a time when informed consent was anathema. Can or should such collections be used for the greater public good? Their social value can be found both as a research resource and as a forensic collection. The issues are manifold and the answers to the questions raised are far from obvious, but their existence raises once again the delicate balance between individual and collective interests.[58]

Psychiat 572. Dr Wakefield was ultimately struck from the medical register: General Medical Council, Fitness to Practise Panel Hearing, 24 May 2010, Andrew Wakefield, Determination of Serious Professional Misconduct. Cf, a colleague also involved had his registration ultimately reinstated: *Walker-Smith v GMC* [2012] EWHC 503; [2012] 126 BMLR1.

  [51] [2003] 2 FLR 1095 (CA). For more, see E Cave, 'Adolescent Refusal of MMR Inoculation: *F (Mother) v F (Father)*' (2014) 77 Mod Law Rev 630.

  [52] For comment, see K O'Donnell, '*Re C (Welfare of Child: Immunisation)*: Room to refuse? Immunisation, welfare and the role of parental decision-making' (2004) 16 CFLQ 213.

  [53] [2013] EWHC 2683 (HC).

  [54] See also *Re B (a child: immunisation)* [2003] 2 FCR 156 (CA) (medical evidence must be 'clear and persuasive'), *C v A (a minor)* [2011] EWHC 4033 (Fam).

  [55] [2001] IESC 70.

  [56] PKU is a debilitating brain condition which—if detected early—can be avoided by simple dietary changes; otherwise, affected victims can suffer profound disability.

  [57] For commentary, see G Laurie, 'Better to hesitate at the threshold of compulsion: PKU testing and the concept of family autonomy in Eire' (2002) 28 J Med Ethics 136.

  [58] A public consultation was held in 2005 on the storage and use of newborn babies' blood spot cards: see IOE, *Case study on the impact of IOE research into communication about neonatal blood spot screening* (2011), available at http://www.ioe.ac.uk/Research_Expertise/IOE_RD_A4_BSS_0711_p1_1.pdf. The importance of this kind of evidence becomes all the more pressing with the launch of undertakings like the Life Study in 2013, which is the latest of many new large-scale birth cohort projects: see http://www.esrc.ac.uk/research/

2.27 As to the existing law, these cases demonstrate important points—such as the extent of parental rights over their children—to which we shall return in due course. For present purposes, they illustrate that there is no clear line between health promotion and health protection measures. However, it is the extent to which any given measure can be classified under the latter heading—at least at the community level—that determines the degree of paternalistic or coercive state interference that is involved. Whether it is justified must, then, be argued on the particularities of the case; as demonstrated above, any intervention that interferes with individual human rights can be justified only when it can be shown to be a necessary and proportionate response to the harm that is to be avoided.

HEALTH PROTECTION: HANDLING THREATS TO THE COMMUNITY

GENERAL AND INTERNATIONAL CONTEXT

2.28 The health landscape is ever changing. Tuberculosis (TB), once considered to be under control, has persisted in developing nations, and is now increasing in prevalence. While malaria remains the number one killer communicable disease worldwide, the prospect of virus transfer to humans from other species (zoonoses) has increased, and is highlighted by SARS (sever acute respiratory syndrome),[59] and by swine flu (H1N1).[60] Risks are potentially exacerbated by the prospect of xenotransplantation (using animal organs or tissues),[61] and bioterrorism (the deliberate release of biological agents).[62] In short, the health interests of the community can sometimes be so strong—or the threat to its health so great—that even compulsory action against the bodily integrity and freedoms of individuals can be defended.[63]

2.29 However, public health measures should not be taken as a form of unqualified utilitarianism whereby the public good always trumps individual freedoms. Rather, robust health protection programmes should always require the state to justify every measure and intervention, the interventions should be 'proportionate' and 'necessary' in the circumstances (i.e., no other reasonable means are available to achieve the same justifiable ends), and there should be full respect for the rights of individuals who are not implicated in the immediate health threat.[64] For example, state agencies must remain bound by data

---

our-research/life-study/. For more, see G Laurie et al., Guthrie Cards in Scotland: Ethical, Legal and Social Issues (2014), available at http://www.gov.scot/Publications/2014/01/7520.

[59] C Hooker, 'SARS as a "Health Scare" ' in S Ali and R Keil (eds), *Networked Disease: Emerging Infections in the Global City* (2008) 123–37.

[60] G Neumann et al., 'Emergence and pandemic potential of swine-origin H1N1 influenza virus' (2009) 459 Nature 931.

[61] D Louz et al., 'Reappraisal of biosafety risks posed by PERVs in xenotransplantation' (2008) 18 Reviews in Medical Virology 53. We discuss this further in Chapter 17.

[62] This has become an obsession of national security agencies: S Pooransingh and J Hawker, 'Are we prepared for a deliberate release of a biological agent?' (2006) 120 Public Health 613.

[63] L Lee et al., 'Ethical justification for conducting public health surveillance without patient consent' (2012) 102 Am J of Pub H 38.

[64] The human rights dimension of detention measures for people living with infectious disease were addressed in *Enhorn v Sweden* (2005) 41 EHRR 30. Sweden was found to be in violation of its obligations under the ECHR, not because it had legalised measures to detain people who posed a risk to others, but because these measures had not been deployed as a last resort. Sweden had failed to strike a fair balance between the need to ensure that infection (HIV) did not spread and the applicant's right to liberty. For comment, see R Martin, 'The exercise of public health powers in cases of infectious disease: Human rights implications' (2006) 14 Med L Rev 132.

protection measures which ensure that patient personal information will be used on a strict need-to-know basis.[65]

2.30 To reiterate, health risks threaten us as a global community, not merely as individuals. Responsive state agencies exist in most jurisdictions, but responses cannot simply be local given the nature of the problem. International efforts and coordination are essential to effective strategies. The WHO's International Health Regulations 2005 (IHR)[66] establish 'an agreed framework of commitments and responsibilities for States and for WHO to invest in limiting the international spread of epidemics and other public health emergencies while minimising disruption to travel, trade and economies'.[67] Notwithstanding, while acknowledging that the WHO and the IHR may play an important role in surveillance and outbreak reporting, and in providing a framework for tackling a public health emergency, as is often the case in international law, there is little that can be done against a refractory state; effective action must begin and be maintained at the state level.

UK CONTEXT

2.31 Major reforms to public health powers have occurred in the past.[68] One particularly important one was the abolition of the Health Protection Agency, a UK-wide body whose remit was to anticipate, identify, and rapidly respond to infectious disease threats and other health dangers. It was abolished by s 56 of the Health and Social Care Act 2012, with the aim of providing more transparent, responsible, and accountable service in public health. The result is that legal and practical responses to infectious diseases remain divided along jurisdictional lines within the UK, with responsibility in Scotland falling to Health Protection Scotland, established in 2005,[69] and responsibility in England and Wales falling to Public Health England, established in 2013 to bring together public health specialists from more than 70 organisations into a single public health service.[70]

2.32 The Civil Contingencies Act 2004 continues to have UK-wide application; it modernised the law to reflect contemporary emergencies (e.g., terrorist threats, environmental degradation, and pandemics) (ss 1 and 19), and imposes on authorities the responsibility of assessing risks and making plans for the assessment, mitigation, and prevention of emergencies (s 2). It is now the key piece of legislation that governs legal authority to act in a 'true' emergency, empowering authorities and other actors to intervene in response thereto, but it is crucial to note that the Act offers emergency powers only as a last resort, and only when existing legislation is insufficient to respond to the situation in an effective way (ss 21 and 23).[71] This means that, first, we must consider existing public health laws.

---

[65] See e.g. Health Protection Agency, *Safeguarding the Confidentiality of Patient Information while Protecting Public Health* (2008).

[66] WHO, *International Health Regulations (2005)*, 2nd edn (2008), and see http://www.who.int/ihr/en/.

[67] For comment on the role of the WHO, see S Harmon, 'International public health law: Not so much WHO as why, and not enough WHO and why not?' (2009) 12 Med Health Care and Philos 245.

[68] The Health and Social Care Act 2008 reformed the Public Health (Control of Diseases) Act 1984 for England and Wales, while in Scotland the law is found in the Public Health etc. (Scotland) Act 2008.

[69] See http://www.hps.scot.nhs.uk/about/index.aspx.

[70] See https://www.gov.uk/government/organisations/public-health-england/.

[71] For comment, see G Laurie and K Hunter, 'Mapping, assessing and improving legal preparedness for pandemic flu in the United Kingdom' (2009) 10 Med Law Internat 101.

2.33 The prevailing public health legislation in the UK is the Public Health (Control of Disease) Act 1984, which was substantially amended by the introduction in 2008 of a new Part 2A, which establishes general rules and broad powers for Justices of the Peace in response to reports by a Local Authority's 'Proper Officer'. These powers are exceptionally wide as regards both 'persons' and 'things', and, as to the former, run from admission to hospital, through attending training sessions, to abstaining from specified work. Associated Regulations specify both the diseases of interest and the precise powers available to control them.[72] In doing so, they categorise diseases as 'notifiable'; a notifiable disease is one which a registered medical practitioner is legally bound to report to relevant authorities or face summary conviction and fine.[73] Indeed, the most important feature of the Act, from the point of view of the doctor–patient relationship, is the statutory obligation to notify authorities about the existence of certain diseases as they occur. In addition to being the lynchpin on which the control of infectious disease depends, it has obvious significance for confidentiality in medical practice, which is discussed in detail in Chapter 6. (And it is to be noted that local authorities may, themselves, add to the list of notifiable diseases.) Whereas questions remained as to whether the old legislation applied to pandemic flu or other new and emerging conditions, the amended 1984 Act defines a public health threat broadly: 'Any reference to infection or contamination is a reference to infection or contamination which presents or could present significant harm to human health.'

2.34 As this Act and its various Regulations should make clear, effective health protection for the community depends on a number of factors which include early detection, rapid and effective intervention and control, and ongoing surveillance. Central to these is the proper flow of information between those responsible for implementing the public health agenda. In the present context, the Health and Social Care Acts 2008 and 2012 in England and the Public Health etc. (Scotland) Act 2008 can be contrasted. The English legislation does little more than empower the Minister to make such regulations as he sees necessary to cover a multitude of potential public hazards, and in doing so, he or she may incorporate international agreements or arrangements such as recommendations from the WHO within the regulations. The rationale behind the provisions is to allow the Minister to take action according to the circumstance prevailing at the time rather than in respect of a predetermined set of conditions. The interests of the individual are preserved so far as is compatible with public safety—in general, for example, any action taken must be proportionate to the extent of the risk involved. In particular, regulations may not include provisions requiring an individual to undergo medical treatment—including immunisation—nor may health protection regulations create an offence punishable by imprisonment.[74]

2.35 We could also bring an ethical evaluation to bear on these and other legal measures. For example, the Nuffield Council on Bioethics has highlighted the importance of precaution when dealing with threats to public health.[75] It references a European Commission

[72] See the Health Protection (Local Authority Powers) Regulations 2010/657, the Health Protection (Part 2A Orders) Regulations 2010/658, the Health Protection (Notification) Regulations 2010/659, and the Health Protection (Notification) (Wales) Regulations 2010/1546. For guidance on the operation of the framework, see DOH, Health Protection Legislation Guidance (2010), and DOH, *Health Protection and Local Government* (2012).

[73] The list of notifiable diseases for England is set out in the Public Health (Control of Disease) Act 1984, as amended, and its associated regulations, particularly the Health Protection (Notification) Regulations 2010/659, and for Scotland in Sch 1 of the 2008 Act.

[74] This, of course, says nothing about the criminal law—see infra.

[75] Nuffield Council on Bioethics, *Public Health: Ethical Issues* (2007).

Communication on the precautionary principle, which identifies five elements for consideration when developing responses to public health emergencies:

- scientific assessment of risk, acknowledging uncertainties and updated in light of new evidence;
- fairness and consistency;
- consideration of costs and benefits of actions;
- transparency; and
- proportionality.[76]

The Council prefers the term 'precautionary approach' in addressing public health threats and advocates an intervention ladder which offers a way of thinking about possible government action and appreciating the associated consequences for civil liberties. This ranges across options from 'doing nothing' and monitoring a situation, to 'enabling choice', 'guiding choice', 'restricting choice', and, ultimately to 'eliminating choice'. As the intervention becomes more intrusive, so the need for justification becomes more compelling.[77] We have argued elsewhere that a Civil Liberties Impact Assessment should accompany all contingency plans with particularly close attention paid to the points at which escalation of action will take place.[78]

Public Health Protection: Disease Notification (HIV/AIDS)

2.36   Many lessons for the future are to be learned from experiences of the past and, to this extent, it still remains valid to consider the legal responses to one of the greatest public health threats of modern times: infection with the Human Immunodeficiency Virus (HIV).[79] HIV/AIDS emerged in the UK in 1981. The virus attacks the human immune system leaving the individual exposed to any number of opportunistic diseases. In 2014, some 35 million people worldwide were living with the virus.[80] The hysteria which met the advent of HIV/AIDS has calmed somewhat as a result of public education campaigns and the development of anti-retroviral drugs which can slow the progress of the disease,[81] but significant public health issues remain; in particular, over access to those drugs, most especially in developing countries.[82] Numerous countries also continue to

---

[76] European Commission, *Communication from the Commission on the Precautionary Principle*, COM (2000) 1.
[77] N 75, paras 3.37–3.38 and Box 3.2.   [78] N 71.
[79] HIV is a virus that attacks the immune system leaving it incapable of dealing with further assault. Acquired Immune Deficiency Syndrome (AIDS) refers to a state when the individual's immune system is compromised beyond a certain degree. There is international disagreement about the point at which AIDS should be diagnosed. Indeed, recent trends are away from the use of the term altogether. For more on legal responses, see J Chalmers, *Legal Responses to HIV and AIDS* (2008).
[80] UNAIDS Factsheet 2014, available at: http://www.unaids.org/en/resources/documents/2014/20140716_FactSheet_en.pdf.
[81] *IB v Greece*, No 552/10, Judgment 3 October 2013 (dismissal of asymptomatic employee due to HIV+ status is stigmatising and contrary to private life under Arts 8 and 14) represents an all-too-common scenario. Indeed, stigma is considered a big issue, though it has also been presented as a potentially salutary public health tool: M Hartlev, 'Stigmatisation as a Public Health Tool against Obesity: A Health and Human Rights Perspective' (2014) 21 Euro J Hum Rights Law 365.
[82] See G Annas, 'Detention of HIV positive Haitians at Guantanamo—Human rights and medical care' (1993) 329 New Eng J Med 589, and Commission on Intellectual Property Rights, *Integrating Intellectual Property Rights and Development Policy* (2002), ch 2. More recently, see UN Secretary General, *Future of the AIDS Response: Building on past achievements and accelerating progress to end the AIDS epidemic by 2030*, A/69/856, 6 April 2015.

impose restrictions on entry, stay, residency, and access to adequate care for people living with HIV, all of which contributes to the continuing stigma associated with the disease.[83] HIV/AIDS has come to represent the paradigm pandemic affecting humanity on a global scale; its spread has been greatly facilitated by modern travel, the absence of a cure makes the prospect of infection particularly significant, and ignorance and misunderstanding about the disease and its pattern of spread led to calls for draconian measures to be taken against affected groups (and in some cases against groups that were thought to be at 'high risk').[84]

2.37   Although HIV/AIDS has tended to dominate headlines and capture public attention, HIV has never been treated as notifiable in the UK.[85] The reasoning behind this decision reveals one of the fundamental tensions associated with notification of diseases—that is, that its compulsory nature effectively requires practitioners to breach patient confidentiality. Concern with HIV infection has traditionally related not to the nature of the disease itself—which is less easily spread than hepatitis, and constitutes a lesser threat to global health[86]—but rather to the social stigma that surrounded it. The fear was that patients would perceive a forced breach of their confidentiality as a significant threat to their interests and would not return for care; in turn, other infected persons might refuse to come forward—thus, health authorities would be left with no effective means by which to monitor the disease. We see, then, that this policy was originally justified on both private and public grounds. It has not been borne out in practice, however, with labs and clinics voluntarily passing on statistics (on an anonymous basis) to authorities.

2.38   Even so, the case of HIV illustrates the sensitivity of the situation when a new disease emerges and we are uncertain as to what we are dealing with. A major difference between HIV and something like H1N1 is that HIV is actually difficult to spread while H1N1 can be passed on through casual contact. In terms of legal preparedness, the question is—should the law provide specifically for measures to address the particular nature of a particular condition, or should it set up a framework of action which empowers relevant agents to act in response to emergencies? Each approach has its pros and cons, and UK legislation is something of a synthesis.

[83]   See *Kiyutin* v *Russia* [2011] ECHR 439 (violation of Arts 8 and 14 for refusal of residence permit to HIV+ foreigner), *AB* v *Russia*, No 1439/06, Judgment 14 Oct 2010 and *Logvinenko* v *Ukraine*, No 13448/07, Judgment 14 October 2010 (inadequate medical assistance to detainees), and *Centre of legal resources on behalf of Valentin Campeanu* v *Romania*, No 47848/08, pending (insufficient medical treatment for mentally disabled HIV+ person). And see M Weait, 'Unsafe law: health, rights and the legal response to HIV' (2013) 9 Int JLC 535, for a scathing critique of the role of law in perpetuating stigma and discrimination.

[84]   G Annas, 'Detention of HIV positive Haitians at Guantanamo—Human rights and medical care' (1993) 329 New Eng J Med 589. And see *IB* v *Greece*, No 552/10, Judgment 3 October 2013 (dismissal of asymptomatic employee due to HIV+ status is stigmatising and contrary to private life under Arts 8 and 14).

[85]   Specific legislation for HIV/AIDS was introduced in the AIDS (Control) Act 1987 which requires regular reporting by a health authority on the incidence of HIV/AIDS within its area. This is not the same as notification, which requires the reporting of the name, age, sex, and residence of each infected person. The Act was repealed in Scotland by the Public Health etc. Act 2008, Sch 3 and in England and Wales by the Health and Social Care Act 2012.

[86]   Hepatitis B is 100 times more infectious than HIV, and an estimated 3 per cent of the world's population are infected with Hepatitis C: see Hepatitis Foundation International, at http://www.hepatitisfoundation.org/HEPATITIS/Hepatitis-overview.html.

Public Health Protection: The Criminal Law (STIs)

2.39 Discussion of the state's protection of public health would be incomplete without mention of the role of the criminal law—rules are ineffective in the absence of penalties for their transgression.[87] In most circumstances, disease transmission is not a matter of choice; it is not, therefore, something that can rightly be subject to deterrence. But this is not always true. A person with TB may be the unfortunate victim of nature, but what if he wantonly transmits the bacillus to another through contact that is more intimate than purely social?[88] Such considerations will apply particularly to sexually transmitted infections (STIs), which require unique circumstances for their transmission—circumstances which can be brought about, or avoided, through individual action. It is therefore meaningful to consider STIs as a prime example when discussing whether the criminal law has a role to play in encouraging people to behave responsibly in respect of public health.

2.40 The landmark English case is *R v Clarence*,[89] in which a husband with gonorrhoea infected his wife in the knowledge, and his wife's ignorance, that he had the condition. Clarence was prosecuted—and convicted—under ss 20 and 47 of the Offences Against the Person Act 1861 (inflicting grievous bodily harm and actual bodily harm respectively). There was no suggestion that he intended to infect his wife, and it was accepted that she would not have consented to sexual intercourse if she had known the truth. His convictions were, however, reversed on appeal, largely on the grounds that (i) successful prosecution depends on some direct and intentional wounding to the body of the victim and these are not present in the case of reckless infection, and (ii) consent of a wife to sexual intercourse was a given; the only factors that would vitiate it would be fraud as to the nature of the act in question or as to the identity of the actor and neither applied in the instant case. This unrealistic precedent stood for more than a century and distorted the jurisprudence as a result. Thankfully, it has now been overturned.[90]

2.41 There have been a number of attempts in Commonwealth jurisdictions to circumvent the evidential difficulties left by *Clarence*,[91] but the case law has led to inconsistent results. The first successful prosecution for reckless transmission of HIV in the UK is the unreported Scottish case of *Kelly* v *HM Advocate*,[92] where the relative flexibility of Scots law allowed for a charge of 'culpably and recklessly engaging in sexual intercourse to the danger of a woman's health and life'.[93] The essential legal issues for reckless transmission were laid out in *R* v *Dica*,[94] and this still represents the current legal position in England and Wales.

---

[87] S Mathiesson, 'Should the law deal with reckless HIV infection as a criminal office or a matter of public health?' (2010) 21 King's LJ 123.

[88] We are, for example, happy to criminalise the unfortunate person who continues to drive knowing his or her eyesight to be defective.

[89] (1889) 22 QBD 23.

[90] The 'given' as to intra-marital consent to sexual intercourse was rejected in *R* v *R* [1992] 1 AC 599. For Scotland, see *Stallard* v *HM* Advocate 1989 SCCR 248. For consent in HIV infection generally, see *R* v *Konzani* [2005] 2 Cr App R 14. On the difficulties, see L Cherkassky, 'Being informed: the complexities of knowledge, deception and consent when transmitting HIV' (2010) 74 J Crim L 242.

[91] The New South Wales Crimes Act 1900, as amended, includes an offence of causing grievous bodily disease at s 36. The moral obligations are, of course, a distinct matter: see R Bennett, H Draper, and L Frith, 'Ignorance is bliss? HIV and moral duties and legal duties to forewarn' (2000) 26 J Med Ethics 9.

[92] (2001) High Court of Justiciary, Glasgow, 23 February.

[93] More recently, see *HM Advocate* v *Mola* 2007 SCCR 124 which deals with what has to be shown as a matter of fact in determining someone's recklessness towards infecting their partner with a sexually transmitted disease.

[94] [2004] 3 All ER 593.

This case involved the prosecution under s 20 of the Offences Against the Person Act 1861 of an HIV+ defendant for having infected two partners. This route, as we have seen, has caused logical and doctrinal problems because (i) there is no 'assault' on the victim in the sense of physical violence to the victim's body, and (ii) authority suggested that consent to such an 'assault' was irrelevant for criminal purposes.[95] But here the court held that so long as all the other elements of an s 20 offence were present, infection with disease could constitute a crime. Moreover, consent is only irrelevant in circumstances where there is actual intention to harm. In cases involving recklessness, however, the consent of the victim to running the risk of infection could be a complete defence. The central issue is not consent to sexual intercourse but rather consent to run a known risk by engaging in unprotected sexual intercourse.

2.42   *R* v *Konzani*[96] confirmed that the nature of the consent in question is informed consent and that a genuine, albeit mistaken, belief that a partner has consented to sexual intercourse will allow the defence to operate. This may turn, for example, on whether a diagnosis of HIV has been confirmed. *Konzani* has been criticised, however, for not accepting that engagement in unprotected sex might, in itself, be seen as consent for the purposes of the defence.[97] While this and other cases send clear messages about personal responsibility,[98] questions remain as to where the line between intention and recklessness should be drawn.[99] In *R* v *Golding*,[100] a case of reckless transmission of herpes, the Court of Appeal reiterated that a person with an STI who has sexual intercourse with a partner, not intending deliberately to infect her, but knowing that she is unaware of his condition, may be guilty of recklessly inflicting grievous bodily harm, and there is no necessity for an assault to have been committed. Ultimately, the Director of Public Prosecutions (DPP) bears a responsibility to decide carefully which messages to send to the community for adjudication.[101]

PUBLIC HEALTH, PHYSICIANS, AND SECURITY

2.43   Political violence is all around us and the doctor cannot wholly dissociate herself from this; society occasionally demands questionable practices from its doctors. An international attempt to define her position can be found in the Declaration of Tokyo,[102] which

---

[95]   *Clarence*, para 2.21 and *R* v *Brown* [1994] 1 AC 212.   [96]   [2005] 2 Cr App R 14.

[97]   M Weait, '*R* v *Konzani*: Knowledge, autonomy and consent' [2005] Crim LR 763 at 765. See also S Ryan, 'Reckless transmission of HIV: Knowledge and culpability' [2006] Crim LR 981.

[98]   In Canada, see *R* v *Mabior* [2012] SCC 47 (relevance of viral loads and of testimony that partners would not have consented to intercourse had they known of HIV status), and see *United States* v *Gutierrez*, No 13-0522, 23 February 2015, USCA (Armed Forces) (aggravated assault against defendant not sustainable because chance of infection too low to constitute likelihood of death or grievous bodily harm).

[99]   M Brazier, 'Do no harm: Do patients have responsibilities too?' (2006) 65 Cambridge LR 397. On the effect of consent in the context of contact sports, see *R* v *Barnes* [2005] 2 All ER 113.

[100]   [2014] EWCA Crim 889. See also *R* v *Peace Marangwanda* [2009] EWCA Crim 60 wherein the defendant pleaded guilty to reckless transmission of gonorrhoea to two minors as a result of poor hygiene (as opposed to sexual contact as originally alleged). This decision has been criticised for, inter alia, its apparent acceptance of a duty to protect against disease transmission in the absence of awareness of the risk of transmission.

[101]   L Francis and J Francis, 'Criminalizing health-related behaviours dangerous to others? Disease transmission, disease facilitation and the importance of trust' (2012) 6 Crim Law and Philos 47–63.

[102]   The spirit of the Declaration of Tokyo is also expressed in the United Nations Declaration of Human Rights, Art 5 and, domestically, in the Human Rights Act 1998, Sch 1, Art 3 which allows for no derogation.

shows well the difficulties of operationalising ethical codes—definitions of principle can only be interpreted in the mind of the individual. Who is to define a degrading procedure? Is it self-evident that the well-being of an indiscriminate terrorist bomber is as valuable as that of his potential victim? Given that unethical physiological measures are used in detention and interrogation,[103] might it not be that a doctor's presence, although disapproving, could be to the benefit of the subject? And, one might ask, by what right can the doctor command complete clinical independence when, in some circumstances, she may be ignorant of the widespread affect her decision may have on others?[104] The motivation of the Declaration of Tokyo is impeccable in condemning the excesses of politically motivated punishment and torture, but it fails in its general purpose because it was drafted with that rather narrow end in view.[105]

2.44 There has always been something of an armed truce between the medical profession and the police as to confidentiality. The anxiety engendered here has been summed up:

> Although doctors in general wish to cooperate with the police, they must be sure that any information divulged in confidence will not be used in court unless they are aware at the time of interview that that information might be so used.[106]

At times, medical authorities will agree access procedures to govern requests from the police for sight of patient information,[107] but the default position, both with respect to physical samples and patient data, is that an appropriate court order should be sought and served before any access is given.

2.45 However, the impact of human rights law has to be fed into such equations, as demonstrated by the case of *S and Marper* v *United Kingdom*.[108] Here the ECtHR held that the blanket policy in England and Wales of retaining DNA profiles and samples indefinitely when taken from persons without their consent and who had not been convicted of a crime was an unjustified breach of their human rights. Mere retention, even without use, was held to be an interference with the right to respect for private life because of the possible implications that future uses could have for individuals. While a lawful policy for obtention and retention could be developed, it must be proportionate to the pressing social need under scrutiny (pursuant to the three-part test articulated in paras 2.14–2.16 above). As a result of *Marper* and other cases,[109] the Protection of Freedoms Act 2012 was enacted. It should ensure that more than 1 million innocent persons' samples and data are removed from the database, and that future samples taken on arrest for a minor offence are destroyed where there is no charge or conviction.[110] Since then, it has been held that the police policy of retaining indefinitely materials and data obtained from adults convicted of a recordable offence, though an interference with Art 8 ECHR, was,

[103] For which there is considerable evidence: D Summerfield, 'Fighting "Terrorism" with T torture' (2003) 326 BMJ 773.

[104] S Arie, 'Doctors need better training to recognise and report torture' (2011) 343 BMJ d5766.

[105] P Polatin and J Modvig, 'Helping to stop doctors becoming complicit in torture' (2010) 340 BMJ c973.

[106] The problem is discussed further in Chapter 6.

[107] Scottish Government and the Association of Chief Police Officers Scotland, *Information Sharing Between NHS Scotland and the Police* (2008).

[108] *S and Marper* v *United Kingdom* (2009) 48 EHRR 50.

[109] Such as *S* v *United Kingdom* [2009] 48 EHRR 50 (ECtHR) (retention of fingerprints and DNA of suspects is a disproportionate interference with Art 8 rights).

[110] For more serious offences, those charged but not convicted will have samples retained for three years with a single extension period of two further years (on application to a District Judge): Part 1 of the 2012 Act, amending Part 5 of the Police and Criminal Evidence Act 1984.

bearing all factors in mind, both justified and proportionate, and within the margin of appreciation extended to domestic authorities.[111]

2.46 The professional relationship between doctors and the police in England and Wales is, to a large extent, dictated by the Police and Criminal Evidence Act 1984. As regards confidentiality, the British Medical Association (BMA)—and other interested groups— succeeded in protecting medical records from the powers of police search by having them classified as 'excluded material'.[112] The doctor, however, remains the holder of the records and is, therefore, entitled to disclose them if he so wishes;[113] on the other hand, in the absence of a court order, he may withhold them even in the face of serious crime.[114] Quite clearly, the law and the professions will, when possible, take a pragmatic approach which includes consideration of the community's interests.[115] As to searches, the leadership of the BMA agreed with those politicians who regarded the legal permit to make searches as 'an oppressive and objectionable new statutory power [which was] a serious affront to a person's liberty'.[116] Many others, including ourselves, would consider drug peddling, with its potential catastrophic effect on people of all ages, as being a crime which merits draconian preventive methods. In the event, the 1984 Act retained the legal right of the authorities to ask for an intimate search, and/or for the taking of an intimate sample, but stipulated that the latter must be performed by a medical practitioner or a registered nurse.[117] This is now modified further by the provisions of the 2012 Act, discussed earlier.

CONCLUSION

2.47 While the human rights paradigm has been important to public health (and medical law more generally), at least from a constitutive perspective, it has not led to social justice fully realised; public health practice has been accused of leaving unaltered the marginalisation of women's health and the health of those in developing countries.[118] Some have argued that public health is in need of a greater, more principled, theoretical, and moral

---

[111] *Re Gaughran's Application for Judicial Review* [2015] UKSC 29.

[112] Police and Criminal Evidence Act 1984, ss 11 and 12.

[113] *R v Singleton* [1995] 1 Cr App R 431; [1995] Crim LR 236. Section 29 of the Data Protection Act 1998 permits the use or disclosure of 'personal data' for the purposes of prevention or detection of crime or the prosecution or apprehension of offenders without observing the normal formalities of the Act (such as informing the subject of any such use or disclosure).

[114] *R v Cardiff Crown Court, ex p Kellam* (1993) 16 BMLR 76. It is to be noted that Evans LJ made this ruling 'with considerable reluctance'.

[115] In the Scottish High Court case of *HM Advocate v Kelly* (2001)—an unreported case of reckless exposure to HIV infection—the police were allowed to breach the anonymity and confidentiality of a research project involving prisoners in order to trace the strain of virus involved. Discussed in S Bird and A Leigh Brown, 'Criminalisation of HIV transmission: Implications for public health in Scotland' (2001) 323 BMJ 1174; J Chalmers, 'The criminalisation of HIV transmission' (2002) 26 J Med Ethics 160.

[116] W Russell, 'Intimate body searches—for stilettos, explosive devices, et al.' (1983) 286 BMJ 733.

[117] Section 62(9) as amended by the Criminal Justice and Police Act 2001, s 80. There have been a number of amendments to the 1984 Act which include increased powers of the police to retain samples and records in certain circumstances even if the donor was acquitted. These have survived a challenge by way of the ECHR: *R (on the application of S) v Chief Constable of South Yorkshire* [2004] 4 All ER 193, HL. Comparable powers are available in Scotland by way of the Criminal Procedure (Scotland) Act 1995, ss 18 and 19 or by obtaining a Sheriff warrant. Further amendments, similar to those in England, are contained in the Criminal Justice (Scotland) Act 2003, Part 8.

[118] See M Fox and M Thomson, 'Realising Social Justice in Public Health Law' (2013) 21 Med Law Rev 278.

foundation if it ever hopes to meet practical needs while also realising human rights and achieving global health justice.[119] In the UK, our concern, as suggested in Chapter 1, is that disproportionate weight will be accorded to individualistic notions of autonomy which undermine public health actions. Autonomy is undoubtedly an important consideration, but it remains just one value in the family of values that underpins and informs this discipline. As this chapter has shown, collective interests and more communitarian values must also enter the fray.[120]

---

[119] N 3, and see P Ruger, 'Good medical ethics, justice and provincial globalism' (2015) 41 J Med Ethics 103, and A Dawson, 'Ebola: what it tells us about medical ethics' (2015) 41 J Med Ethics 107.

[120] R Ashcroft, 'Could human rights supersede bioethics?'(2010) 10 Human Rights L Rev 639.

3

HEALTH RIGHTS AND OBLIGATIONS IN THE EUROPEAN UNION

3.01 The evolution and implementation of policies relating to bioethics and health have traditionally been the responsibility of nation states. The last quarter of the twentieth century, however, saw a gradual shift towards globalisation of law[1] that has strayed beyond the predominance of single state governance. There have been two main consequences. First, those to whom a given principle is directed are not now confined within national borders and, second, those who shape the policies of bioethical practice are no longer drawn from a parochial pool but, rather, from a society that is relatively unconcerned with political boundaries. This is particularly evident within the European Union (EU) where health policy issues fall into four interrelated themes, each of which is affected by economic rules on cross-border activity:

- mobility—for example, cross-border access to health care by EU citizens and the mobility of health care professionals;
- the liberalisation of trade within the internal market—as affects, for example, the pharmaceutical market in the interest of pubic safety;
- the development of new technologies—especially in the fields of biotechnology and medical devices;
- the extension of public health legislation in such fields as the control of the use of tobacco; blood and blood product safety, and the management of medical emergencies, such as the outbreak of the severe acute respiratory syndrome (SARS).

This phenomenon is also evident in the cooperation between the EU and international bodies, such as the World Health Organization (WHO), which has been instrumental in developing 'evidence-based' policy in public health research as part of Strengthening Public Health in Europe (SPHERE).[2] International cooperation has been promoted under the Horizon 2020 framework in the interest of achieving the wider policy objectives of the EU.[3]

---

[1] See generally, I Glenn Cohen, *The Globalization of Health Care Legal and Ethical Issues* (New York: Oxford University Press, 2013).

[2] See: http://www.ucl.ac.uk/public-health/sphere.

[3] See: http://ec.europa.eu/programmes/horizon2020/en/area/international-cooperation.

THE EUROPEAN MARKET FOR HEALTH

3.02   Given the economic basis on which the processes of European integration and EU law are grounded, it is understandable that the discipline of bioethics in the EU is being driven and shaped predominantly by market forces and is, thereby, being framed in terms of rights and values in a European *market for health.* Indeed, one of the key principles in the EU Health Strategy 2008–13 is 'health in all policies'. This was adopted by the 2007 EU Health Strategy 'Together for Health', which supports the overall Europe 2020 strategy.[4] That, in turn, stresses the economic importance of a healthy population.[5] Europe 2020 aims to turn the EU into a smart, sustainable and inclusive economy promoting growth for all—one prerequisite of which is a population in good health.

This principle should be seen in light of the obligation imposed by Article 168 of the Treaty on the Functioning of the European Union (TFEU),[6] to ensure a high level of human health protection in 'all Union policies and activities'. At the same time it should be remembered that the EU itself began as a common market. Thus, for example, health is viewed as an economic priority and EU policies are designed around European integration and harmonisation, anchored in what is referred to as the 'European Social Model'.[7] And the Directorate General Health and Consumers[8] overtly stated that the 'health in all policies' approach should involve 'all relevant policy areas'—these being social and regional policy, taxation, environment, education, and research.

The following section serves as an introductory analysis, not of EU health policy as a whole[9] but, rather, of examples of those elements of EU health policy which contain a significant 'rights' dimension. This dimension is evolving on the basis of what is referred to as 'common values and principles in European Union health systems', such as universality, access to good-quality care, equity, and solidarity,[10] based on the four core principles of EU Health Strategy: shared health values; that health is the greatest wealth; health in all polices; and strengthening the EU's voice in global health.

HEALTH CARE POLICY IN THE EU

3.03   The EU can do only what the Treaties allow it to do, and an EU public health policy is not among its exclusive competencies. Yet that does not in itself mean that the EU and the Council of Europe are not able to influence elements of the public health policies of Member States. As already noted, the EU has adopted health legislation under the TFEU,[11]

[4] http://ec.europa.eu/health/strategy/policy/index_en.htm.
[5] See *Investing in Health*, European Commission, 2013, which 'establishes the role of health as part of the Europe 2020 policy framework': http://ec.europa.eu/health/strategy/docs/swd_investing_in_health.pdf.
[6] See T Hervey and J McHale, *Health Law and the European Union* (2004) ch 3.
[7] See COM(2004) 29 final. *Delivering Lisbon: Reforms for the Enlarged Union.*
[8] Now the Directorate General Health and Food Safety: http://ec.europa.eu/dgs/health_food-safety/.
[9] For which see T Hervey and J McHale, n 6. See also S L Greer, 'Choosing paths in European Union health services policy: A political analysis of a critical juncture' (2008) 18 J Euro Soc Policy 219 and (although it predates the TFEU treaty numbering), E Mossialos, G Permanand, R Baten, and T K Hervey (eds), *Health Systems Governance in Europe* (2010).
[10] See Council of the European Union conclusions on common values and principles in European Union health systems (OJ 2006; C146(01)).
[11] TFEU Art 168 (protection of public health), Art 114 (approximation of laws), and Art 153 (social policy).

including Directives applicable to cross-border health care rights; pharmaceuticals and medical devices; clinical trials; human organs; blood, tissues, and cells; and tobacco control.

3.04 EU powers are distributed among three types, the most common being concurrent or shared powers. In an area of shared competence, a Member State may legislate to the extent that the EU has not done so.[12] While the EU shared competence in health is small, its shared competence in services is large. This has the effect that the EU may use its competence in services to affect health policy at a national level. Two Directives serve to exemplify this mechanism: the Blood Safety Directive[13] and the Tobacco Products Directive.[14] Whereas these Directives sought positive public health outcomes, their constitutional basis was in commerce and trade, albeit by way of manufacturing standards and consumer protection. This is what has been referred to as the EU 'health care law matrix'.[15] Thus, health policy has evolved as an EU policy in its own right, which is designed to 'complement national policies improving public health, preventing human illness and diseases'.[16]

3.05 EU Member States have articulated a rights-based approach to health in terms of non-discrimination[17] and also formal access to health care in a number of different ways—and not only do constitutional arrangements differ but so do values and attitudes regarding bioethics.[18] In the rights context, the Council of Europe and the European Court of Human Rights (ECtHR) are able to cater for these differences because of the 'margin of appreciation' afforded to Member States. This concept was developed by the ECtHR as a mechanism to take into account the cultural diversity of Member States, as it obliges judges to take those differences into account when ruling on a case. As such, the ECtHR afforded Austria a wide margin of appreciation in allowing Austria's prohibition of gamete donation and use for *in vitro* fertilisation.[19] So too, for example, the margin of appreciation afforded a Member State allows that state to prohibit access to abortion services. But the state cannot prohibit free movement of services and of service users to access such services in another Member State. Those freedoms can themselves be framed in terms of

---

[12] Fields of shared competence are social policy, cohesion policy, agriculture and fisheries (excluding the conservation of marine biological resources), environment, consumer protection, transport, trans-European networks, energy freedom, security and justice, and common safety concerns in public health matters.

[13] 2002/98/EC, setting standards of quality and safety for the collection, testing, processing, storage and distribution of human blood and blood components. See also Art 168(4)(b) TFEU. See D Veelke and H Roscam Abbing, 'Patients' right to health protection and quality and safety of blood (products)' (2005) 12 Euro J Hlth Law 153.

[14] 2001/37/EC of 5 June 2001 concerning the manufacture, presentation, and sale of tobacco products. See A McNeill, L Craig, M C Willemsen, and G T Fong, 'Tobacco control in Europe: a deadly lack of progress' (2012) Euro J Pub Hlth [published online 24 January 2012]; and B Asare, P Cairney, and D T Studlar, 'Federalism and Multilevel Governance in Tobacco Policy: the European Union, the United Kingdom, and Devolved UK Institutions' (2009) 29(1) Journal of Public Policy 79–102.

[15] Mossialos et al. (eds), *Health Systems Governance in Europe* (2010), Chapter 2.

[16] See COM(2000) 285 final in conjunction with the public health programmes which are set out in Art 168(4) TFEU.

[17] See e.g. *Zbigniew Maciejewski v the County Police Headquarters Department IV for Employment*, Sentence of 08.02.2006, IV P 467/05 in which a disabled person, who was rejected for a promotion because of the state of his health, brought an action against his employer. The court in Legnica awarded compensation on the basis of the Labour Code which implements Directive 2000/78/EC, which was the first ruling of its kind in Poland.

[18] T Hervey, 'The right to health in EU law' in T Hervey and J Kenner, *Economic and Social Rights under the EU Charter of Fundamental Rights* (2003) 193–222.

[19] *S.H. and Others v Austria*, Application no 57813/00.

Convention rights. In the *Grogan*[20] case, Irish authorities prohibited the distribution of pamphlets containing information on access to abortion services in the United Kingdom (UK). The Court of Justice of the European Union (CJEU) found provision of information on an economic activity did not amount to the provision of services but constituted a manifestation of freedom of expression and was not contrary to Community law.[21] And in *Tysiąc v Poland*,[22] a woman was denied access to abortion services in Poland because the 'therapeutic grounds' had not been satisfied by the risk to her sight from continuing with her pregnancy. While not finding in favour of a right to abortion per se, the ECtHR found that Poland had failed to comply with the positive obligation towards the applicant to respect for private life (ECHR Art 8).

The numbers of those seeking such services in another Member State, and the media attention devoted to the issue, have ensured that the issue remains on the agenda.[23] But more than that, the question has been raised as to whether there should be a harmonisation of reproductive medicine among EU countries.[24] It should, however, be borne in mind that a harmonisation of reproductive medical practices in the interest of public safety is within the competence of the EU, while under the margin of appreciation doctrine, harmonisation of Member States' legal rules applicable to abortion is not among those competencies.

3.06   Further examples of cultural diversity among Member States can be found in some of the more divisive areas of health care law. The right to human dignity that is contained in the German Basic Law[25] provides a useful example of the extent to which a country's past can frame the parameters of reasoning in constitutional terms. There, the paramount protection accorded to human dignity, together with the responses to biotechnological issues from within academic circles and throughout society as a whole, are underwritten by the experience of National Socialism. This also explains the restrictive response to medical research,[26] as well as the regulation of animal experimentation[27] and embryo research[28]—a reaction that is in direct contrast to the position adopted in other EU Member States, notably the UK.[29] Yet here too, the question is raised as to whether

---

[20] Case C-159/90 *Society for the Protection of Unborn Children Ireland Ltd* v *Stephen Grogan and Others* [1990] ECR I-4685; (1991) 9 BMLR 100.

[21] Under Art 10 of the European Convention on Human Rights (ECHR). See also *A, B and C* v *Ireland* [2011] EHRR 2032 and C Staunton, 'As easy as A, B and C: Will *A, B and C* v *Ireland* be Ireland's wake-up call for abortion rights?' (2011) 18 Euro J Hlth Law 205.

[22] *Tysiąc v Poland*. Application no 5410/03 [2007] 1 FCR 666.

[23] See: 'Hundreds of Irish women travel to Netherlands for abortions', *Irish Times* 16 September 2015, indicating that over a seven-year period, as many as 1,500 women travelled to the Netherlands for that purpose. The principles underlying cross-border access to health care are discussed in greater detail from para 3.31 below. In respect of Ireland and abortion services see A Mulligan, 'The Right to Travel for Abortion Services: A Case Study in Irish "Cross-border Reproductive Care" ' (2015) 2(3) Euro J Hlth Law 239–66.

[24] Including abortion, surrogacy, cross-border reproductive care, and disposal of embryos. See: M Flatscher-Thöni and C Voithofer, 'Should Reproductive Medicine Be Harmonized within Europe?' (2015) 22(1) Euro J Hlth Law 61–74.

[25] Art 1(1) of the Basic Law.   [26] *Arzneimittelgesetz* of 19.10.1994 BGBl. I, 3018 at 3040.

[27] See the *Tierschutzgesetz* of 18.8.1986 BGBl. I, 1319.

[28] *Embryonenschutzgesetz* of 13.12.1990 BGBl. I, 2746.

[29] For the position in other EU Member States, see L Matthiesen-Guyader (ed), *Survey on Opinion of National Ethics Committees or Similar Bodies, Public Debate and National Legislation in Relation to Human Embryonic Stem Cell Research and Use in EU Member States* (European Commission, Directorate General Research, Directorate E, Biotechnology, Agriculture and Food, Brussels, July 2004), reproduced at: https://ec.europa.eu/research/biosociety/pdf/mb_states_230804.pdf. See also 7th Framework Programme (2007–13) for Research and Development and human embryonic stem cell research: http://cordis.europa.eu/fp7/understand_en.html. Note that the current Framework Programme for Research and Innovation

there has been somewhat of a convergence of Member States' legal regimes applicable to research using human embryos.[30]

3.07 European cultural diversity is in evidence in the liberal legal and cultural approaches to the 'right to die' to be found in the Netherlands,[31] Belgium,[32] and, latterly, France, where legislation concerning the right to allow to die, or *laissez mourir*, was enacted by the French Senate in April 2005 after lengthy and heated discussions across the country as a whole.[33] This was largely provoked by the *Humbert* case which concerned the death of a young boy, Vincent Humbert, after his mother and his doctor injected him with sodium pentobarbital. Humbert, who had been involved in a car accident and was left severely disabled, had made repeated requests to die, even going as far as addressing a letter to the then President of the Republic asking for euthanasia. Even so, nowhere has the legislation been enacted in terms of the 'right to die' but, rather, in the context of the de-penalisation of euthanasia through amendments to the respective criminal codes.[34]

3.08 The evolution of the French legislation has not only highlighted the complex and diverse approaches to medical treatment at the end of life to be found both within and outside France, but has also underlined the diverse relationships that exist between the church and the state throughout the Union. In the case of Italy, for instance, the Catholic Church is particularly influential in the context of bioethical issues and the making and implementation of policy.[35] Three factors explain the particularly strong relationship between church and state in Italy. First, the historical and cultural heritage of Catholicism in Italy is an integral element of national identity; second, the ecclesiastical authorities are particularly influential among those with public power (e.g., administrators at both regional and national levels of policymaking, Parliament, and the courts); and, third, the legal status of the church is such that it retains considerable privileges,[36] notwithstanding the secularisation of society as a whole as the discussions surrounding the 'right to die' cases, such as *Welby* and *Eluana*,[37] illustrate—as do the debates concerning abortion prior to the general election of 2008.

is Horizon 2020, established under EU reg 1291/2013, which extends to biotechnology and to health policy: http://ec.europa.eu/programmes/horizon2020/. This field is likely to receive further attention due to the 2012 Nobel Prize in physiology or medicine having been awarded for research on stem cells and the 2014 prize having been awarded in Future and Emerging Technologies: http://ec.europa.eu/programmes/horizon2020/en/news/nobel-prize-laureates-future-and-emerging-technologies-fet.

[30] See: N Zeegers, 'Convergence in European Nations' Legal Rules Concerning the Use of Human Embryos in Research?' (2014) 21(5) Euro J Hlth Law 454–72, in which the author concludes that a convergence has taken place and has done so in the direction of a liberalisation of legal rules. On euthanasia and assisted dying, see Chapter 18 of this book.

[31] The Law of 12 April 2001, which entered into force 1 April 2002, amending Arts 293 and 294 of the Dutch Penal Code.

[32] The Law on Euthanasia [*La loi relative à l'euthanasie*], adopted 16 May 2002 which entered into force 20 September 2002 and which exculpates doctors from prosecution under the penal code in the event of having satisfied the conditions set out in the law.

[33] *Le Monde*, 13 April 2005, p 1.

[34] See S Hennette-Vauchez, 'France', in J Griffiths, H Weyers, and M Adams (eds), *Euthanasia and Law in Europe* (2008).

[35] See L Diotallevi, *Religione, Chiesa e Modernizzazione: Il Caso Italiano* (1999).

[36] According to the Italian constitution, Catholicism is not a state religion. However, the Catholic Church retains some privileges which are not available to other faiths due to the special concordatarian (i.e. international) status. See M Ventura, *La laicità dell'Unione Europea. Diritti, mercato, religione* (2001) and C Cardia, *Ordinamenti religiosi e ordinamenti dello Stato* (2003).

[37] Piergiorgio Welby, who suffered from muscular dystrophy, requested the right to die given the advanced state of the disease. Eventually, a judge ruled that Mr Welby had the constitutional right to have his life support machine switched off but doctors would be legally obliged to resuscitate him. The doctor

3.09 Even if it is arguable that Catholicism provides a type of 'shared legacy' across many EU Member States, it is clear that the influence which this legacy exerts on matters of bioethics differs markedly. The difference between the *laicité* which prevails in France is difficult to reconcile with the position in countries such as Italy, Poland, and Spain where the church is more influential.[38] It would be hard to envisage a successful wrongful life claim in Italy or Spain, for example, as it was in the Netherlands as part of the *Kelly* case in 2005 in which the Dutch Hoge Raad, the Netherland's highest court, awarded damages to a severely disabled child.[39]

3.10 At the same time, EU citizens have benefited from the diverse initiatives[40] and approaches to bioethical issues to be found in the Member States. As the case of the 14-year-old Irish citizen who sought to travel to the UK to seek an abortion shows,[41] EU citizens have, to some extent, relied on their rights under EU law to seek help in another EU state that provides treatment which is unavailable in their own state because of the restrictive laws informed by particular moral or religious values.[42]

3.11 Pragmatism is another strong motivator to encourage citizens to travel to other EU Member States where the treatment is of better quality and/or where the waiting lists are shorter. The tightening of legislation concerning access to fertility treatment in Italy was partly inspired by the desire to limit the likelihood of 'medical tourism' by EU citizens who targeted Italy given the hitherto liberal approach enshrined in the Italian legislation.[43] As was the case in *Grogan*,[44] this kind of scenario gives rise to arguments around the legality of advertising for a service that is legal in one country but not in another, and doing so in the country in which the service is illegal.

who switched off the machine defended his actions on the basis that it was not euthanasia but the patient's right to refuse treatment. See BBC, 21 December 2006: http://news.bbc.co.uk/1/hi/world/europe/6199523.stm. The case also gave rise to other claims, such as the case of Giovanni Nuvoli (see *La Repubblica*, 8 February 2007, p 4) and the case of Eluana Englaro (decision no 334 of the Italian Constitutional Court dated 8 October 2008). For commentary on that case, see S Moratti, 'The Englaro Case: Withdrawal of Treatment from a Patient in a Permanent Vegetative State in Italy' (2010) 19(3) *Cambridge Quarterly of Healthcare Ethics* 372–80.

[38] See S Hennette-Vauchez (ed), *Bioéthique, Biodroit, Biopolitique. Réflexions à l'occasion du vote de la loi du 6 août 2004*, (2006).

[39] C03–206, *Leids Universitair Meisch Centrum v Molenaar*, RvdW 2005, 42. On wrongful life more generally, see paras 10.73–10.76 of this book.

[40] See, e.g., the initiative proposed by the European Parliament to create a European organ donor card at: BBC, 22 April 2008 http://news.bbc.co.uk/1/hi/world/europe/7358789.stm, which also proposes the establishment of a European transplant hotline, measures to ensure that all donations are voluntary and altruistic, and mechanisms to ensure the absence of payment between the recipient and the donor. Subsequently, the Commission has published its Action Plan on Organ Donation and Transplantation (2009–15), and the EU has passed Directive 2010/45/EU of 7 July 2010 on standards of quality and safety of human organs intended for transplantation. It also promotes further research in the interest of safety (see the COPE project at http://ec.europa.eu/programmes/horizon2020/en/news/making-more-donated-organs-transplantable).

[41] Case-C 159/90, *Society for the Protection of Unborn Children v Grogan and Others* [1990] ECR I-4685; (1991) 9 BMLR 100, discussed in para 3.05. See also *Open Door Counselling and Dublin Wellwoman Centre v Ireland* (1993) 15 EHRR 244; (1994) 18 BMLR 1 and *Tysiąc v Poland*. Application no 5410/03 [2007] 1 FCR 666, discussed earlier.

[42] The groundbreaking UK case of Mrs Blood who obtained permission to be posthumously impregnated with her husband's sperm in Belgium is in point (see para 3.34).

[43] See the *Legge, 19 Febbraio 2004, n 40 'Norme in Materia di Procreazione Medicalmente Assistita', pubblicata nella Gazzetta Ufficiale n 45 del 24 Febbraio 2004*. See P Crosignani, 'Italy approves controversial legislation on fertility treatment' (2004) 328 BMJ 9.

[44] N 41, ibid.

3.12 EU citizens have accessed other EU health care systems by cutting across EU law altogether and seeking private treatment, thereby avoiding the legal and administrative
mazes which endanger the realisation of their EU rights, particularly as regards fertility
treatment, dental procedures, and hip replacements. There is, however, case law to the
effect that for the purposes of treatment in another Member State, it is not legally significant whether the treating hospital is public or private.[45] Differences in interpretation
concerning cross-border access to health care and a lack of uniformity, coherence, and
consistency[46] led the European Commission to propose a Directive simplifying the rights
of EU citizens seeking medical treatment abroad, including detailed provisions concerning reimbursement.[47] The final Directive became the so-called Patient Rights Directive.[48]

3.13 Access to health care is not explicitly mentioned in the TFEU but derives from the freedom
of movement provisions that it contains and the principle of equal treatment. While there
had been some Community activity in this field since the late 1970s, it was not until the
Treaty of Maastricht[49] that it was recognised as an explicit EU policy (or what is referred
to in EU parlance as a 'competence'), though it has, since then, also arisen in other fields
of competence.[50] The case law that has evolved[51] has tended to regard health as a mere
'by-product' or 'flanking policy'. In other words, it is not health policy per se that can be
seen as having been comprehensively Europeanised but, rather, that Europeanisation has
occurred on a sectoral basis that has affected health care services.

3.14 Further examples of EU legislation include (the list is not exhaustive):

- the Directive concerning medical devices incorporating derivatives of human blood
  and plasma;[52]

- the Directive on the approximation of the laws, regulations, and administrative provisions of the Member States relating to the implementation of good clinical practice
  in the conduct of clinical trials on medicinal products for human use;[53]

- the Directive on setting standards of quality and safety for the donation, procurement, testing, processing, storage, and distribution of human tissues and cells;[54]

---

[45] See para 3.16 and the *Stamatelaki* case.
[46] See M Aziz, *The Impact of Human Rights on National Legal Cultures* (2004), ch 4.
[47] See COM(2008) 414 final.
[48] Directive 2011/24/EU of 9 March 2011 on the application of patients' rights in cross-border health care.
This and the case law on which it is undoubtedly based is discussed further in paras 3.31 et seq.
[49] Art 152 TEU (now Art 168 TFEU).
[50] See, e.g., the Race Directive: Directive 2000/43 [2000] OJ L180/22 which involves harmonisation in the
area of health.
[51] See Case C-238/82 *Duphar BV and Others* v *the Netherlands State* [1984] ECR 523; Case C-158/96
Kohll v *Union des Caisses de Maladie* [1998] ECR I-1931; Case C-120/95 *Decker* [1998] ECR I-1831; and,
more recently, cases C-368/98 *Vanbraekel* and C-157/99 *Geraets-Smits* v *Stichting Ziekenfonds, Peerbooms*
v *Stichting CZ Groep Zorgverzekeringen* [2001] ECR I-5363 and C-372/04 *The Queen, on the application of
Yvonne Watts* v *Bedford Primary Care Trust, Secretary of State for Health* [2006] ECR I-4325. See also the
Irish cases at para 3.10.
[52] Modifying Directive 93/42/EEC of 14 June 1993 concerning medical devices. See also Directive 2002/
98/EC of 27 January 2003 setting standards of quality and safety for the collection, testing, processing, storage, and distribution of human blood and blood components and amending Directive 2001/83/EC.
[53] On 17 July 2012 the Commission COM(2012) 369 final: Proposal for a Regulation of the European
Parliament and of the Council on clinical trials on medicinal products for human use, and repealing
Directive 2001/20/EC. The reforms also raise questions around insurance and the regulation of research-
related injuries. See M A R Avilés, 'Compensation of Research-Related Injuries in the European Union',
(2014) 21 Euro J Hlth Law 473–87.
[54] Directive 2004/23/EC of the European Parliament and of the Council of 31 March 2004.

- pharmaceutical legislation;[55]
- the 'eHealth' initiatives that cover health cards, integrated care records, evidence-based decisions, clinical excellence, health portals, and telemedicine;[56]
- Internet pharmacies and their supply of medical products to buyers located in other Member States;[57]
- the Communication from the Commission to the Council, the European Parliament, the Economic and Social Committee and the Committee of the Regions on the Future of Health Care and Care for the Elderly, guaranteeing accessibility, quality, and financial viability.[58]

3.15 The regulation of tobacco products is a further example of the many faces of EU health care policy which is linked to public health concerns as well as to the aims of the internal market.[59] It has also arisen in the context of parallel imports of pharmaceuticals[60] and the compatibility of mail order sales of pharmaceuticals[61] and whether an initiative amounts to a measure having an equivalent effect to quantitative restrictions (MEQR) on free movement. There is a considerable body of case law on this topic, including the very political issue of fixing a minimum price per unit of alcohol, which may amount to an MEQR.[62]

3.16 Health also arises in a plethora of other EU policy spheres, such as trade and development. Thus, for example, the European Commission has been proactive in calling for changes to the World Trade Organization (WTO) patent rules, so as to ensure that the poorest countries have access to generic drugs. In particular, the EU has formulated several

---

[55] Regulation (EC) No 726/2004 of the European Parliament and of the Council of 31 March 2004 laying down Community procedures for the authorisation and supervision of medicinal products for human and veterinary use and establishing a European Medicines Agency. Other Directives are updated at http://ec.europa.eu/health/documents/eudralex/vol-1/index_en.htm, including 2011/633/EU (information to the general public); 2011/62/EU (falsified medicinal products in the supply chain); 2010/84/EU (pharmacovigilance); 2009/120/EC; 2008/29/EC; 2005/28/EC; 2004/27/EC; 2003/94/EC; 2003/63/EC; 2002/98/EC; and 2001/20/EC on issues ranging from veterinary products to herbal medicines for human use and the establishment of a Community code on medicinal products for human use.

[56] See European Commission Communication of 6 December 2012, 'eHealth Action Plan 2012–2020—Innovative healthcare for the 21st century' (COM(2012)0736) at http://eur-lex.europa.eu/legal-content/EN/TXT/?uri=CELEX:52012DC0736.

[57] See the E-Commerce Directive: 2000/31/EC, the provisions of the Distance Sales Directive 97/7/EC; Directive 2001/83/EC regarding medicinal products for human use; Directive 92/28/EEC on advertising of medicinal products in the EU. See also Case C-322/01 *Deutscher Apothekerverband eV v 0800 DocMorris NV, Jacques Waterval* [2003] ECR I-14887.

[58] COM(2001) 723 final. See also the European Innovation Partnership on Active and Healthy Ageing, which is part of *Europe 2020*: http://ec.europa.eu/europe2020/index_en.htm.

[59] See, e.g., the Tobacco Products Consolidation Directive 2001/37/EC which is aimed at the elimination of national differences regarding the manufacture, presentation, and sale of tobacco products. See also Directive 2003/33/EC as well as the 'Television without Frontiers' Directive 89/552 EEC which prohibits all television which advertises the promotion of cigarettes. These and other directives are available at http://ec.europa.eu/health/tobacco/policy/index_en.htm.

[60] See, e.g., the opinion of Advocate General Ruiz-Jarabo of 1 April 2008 in the case of *GlaxoSmith Kline*, Joined Cases C-468/06 to C-478/06. See: http://curia.europa.eu/en/actu/communiques/cp08/aff/cp080019en.pdf.

[61] In accordance with Arts 28 and 30 of the EC Treaty. See Case C-322/01 *Deutscher Apothekerverband eV v 0800 DocMorris NV, Jacques Waterval* [2003] ECR I-14887.

[62] Under Articles 34 and 35 TFEU. See Case 120/78 *Rewe v Bundesmonopolverwaltung für Branntwein*, known as the *Cassis de Dijon* case, on minimum per unit alcohol pricing.

proposals to the Trade-Related Aspects of Intellectual Property Rights (TRIPS) to enable poor countries that do not have the capacity to produce drugs, to gain access to essential medicines; this was done by proposing a new paragraph in the TRIPS agreement, so that a foreign supplier can provide medicines on the basis of a compulsory licence issued to a developing country in order to address serious public health needs. The European Commission, which is responsible for enforcing its competition policy, has not as yet followed the US trend in extending its regulatory jurisdiction concerning health policy. There have been several incursions, however, and the trend towards the privatisation of health care throughout the EU means that this is increasingly likely to occur,[63] particularly in the context of the pharmaceutical sector.[64] Yet for the purposes of free movement and treatment in another Member State, it is, 'immaterial whether the [treating] establishment in question is public or private'.[65]

3.17 Health is also an issue in the context of life sciences and biotechnology[66] and EU environmental policy.[67] Ever since the Commission Paper on Food Safety, published in 1999, EU health policy has been developed under the aegis of consumer protection[68] and, in particular, regarding food labelling relating to nutritional and functional claims[69] and telecommunications as part of the eHealth policy initiatives.[70] In addition, Community actions on food safety and nutrition are complemented by EU regulations that establish both general principles of food law and the European Food Safety Authority (EFSA).[71] Further examples of the EU regulatory framework in this context include a regulation on novel foods and novel food ingredients,[72] a regulation covering animal food products produced

[63] J T Lang, 'Privatisation of social welfare: European Union competition rules' in M Dougan and E Spaventa (eds), *Social Welfare and EU Law* (2005), 45 et seq. See also S Thomson and E Mossialos, 'Private health insurance and the internal market' in Mossialos et al. n 15, Chapter 10.

[64] On 16 January 2008, the European Commission launched a sector inquiry into competition in the pharmaceuticals sector under Art 17 of reg 1/2003 and conducts inspections at the premises of a number of innovative and generic pharmaceutical companies in order to examine possible infringements of Arts 81 and 82 of the EC Treaty which govern Community rules on restrictive agreements and abuse of dominant market position (now Arts 101 and 102 TFEU).

[65] Case C-444/05 *Aikaterini Stamatelaki v NPDD Organismos Asfaliseos Eleftheron Epangelmation (OAEE)* [2007] ECR I-3185 on the justification for, and proportionality of, restrictions on the freedom to provide services and the reimbursement of the cost of treatment in private hospitals.

[66] See COM(2007) 175 final.

[67] See the *European Environment and Health Action Plan 2004–2010* COM(2004) 461 final, *European Parliament Resolution on a European Environment and Health Strategy* COM(2003) 338, and the Commission *Report on the implementation of the 'European Environment and Health Action Plan 2004–2010'* SEC (2010) 387 final.

[68] COM(1999) 719 final. The relevant Directorate General is DG Health and Food Safety: http://ec.europa.eu/dgs/health_food-safety/index_en.htm.

[69] See Directive 2000/13/EC which outlines rules for the labelling of foodstuffs to enable European consumers to obtain comprehensive information on the content and the composition of food products. For further information see http://ec.europa.eu/health/nutrition_physical_activity/policy/index_en.htm. See Case C-41/02 *Commission of the European Communities v Kingdom of the Netherlands* (the 'Dutch vitamins' case) and Case C-24/00 *Commission of the European Communities v French Republic* (the 'French vitamins' case), on national marketing legislation on the addition of vitamins to foodstuffs, amounting to an MEQR (see para 3.15 on measures having an equivalent effect to quantitative restrictions on free movement).

[70] This link was first raised in 1996 as part of COM(96) 73: the Communication on Universal Service for telecommunications in the perspective of a fully liberalised environment—an essential element of the information society. For further information on eHealth policy see http://ec.europa.eu/health/ehealth/policy/index_en.htm.

[71] Regulation (EC) No 178/2002: http://www.efsa.europa.eu/.

[72] Regulation (EC) No 258/97 that covers food that was not used to a significant degree for human consumption before 15 May 1997.

from a clone,[73] and Directive 2001/18/EC which regulates the deliberate release into the environment of genetically modified organisms (GMOs). Furthermore, the Commission is responsible for an array of public health campaigns such as an EU anti-smoking campaign,[74] nutrition and physical activity,[75] as well as childhood obesity projects in which case two EC Directives prevail.[76] Both are premised on the link between food advertising and childhood obesity. These projects and initiatives demonstrate the operation of the EU health care matrix that makes use of incentive and disincentive mechanisms, using internal market competencies, to affect member state health policy agendas.

3.18 A further development concerns genomics,[77] under the auspices of the Directorate General Research and Innovation. In 2005, the European Commission made a call, as part of the 2005 work plan of the public health programme, for a networking exercise aiming to identify 'public health issues linked to current national practices in applying genetic testing and which, on that basis, contribute to developing best practice in applying genetic testing'.[78] The potential for discrimination by employers and health insurance companies on the basis of individuals' genetic information is one that has been addressed in other jurisdictions,[79] illustrating the need for legislation in this area.[80] Although currently covered by the In Vitro Diagnostic (IVD) Medical Devices Directive, as genetic tests are classified as medical diagnostics under EU law, it is submitted that the EU trend will continue in the direction of specific legislation.[81] Indeed, the Directive has been the subject of a review partly in those terms, following a public consultation in 2011.[82]

[73] Regulation (EC) No 258/97.

[74] With an estimated total smoking-related cost to EU society of €544 billion (2009), the burden of smoking has been recast as one adversely affecting Europe's health care systems and economies: http://ec.europa.eu/health/tobacco/ex_smokers_are_unstoppable/index_en.htm. See also *A study on liability and the health costs of smoking*. DG SANCO (2008/C6/046), 2012: http://ec.europa.eu/health/tobacco/docs/tobacco_liability_final_en.pdf.

[75] In May 2007, the Commission adopted the White Paper, *A Strategy on Nutrition, Overweight, and Obesity-related Health Issues* COM(2007) 279 final and the Plenary meeting of the European Platform for Action on Diet, Physical Activity and Health, Brussels took place on 20 September 2012. See European Commission, Monitoring the activities of the EU Platform on Diet, Physical Activity and Health, Annual Report 2015: http://ec.europa.eu/health/nutrition_physical_activity/docs/eu_platform_2015_report_and_annex1-3_en.pdf. See also the Core Report, *Eurodiet: Nutrition and Diet for Healthy Lifestyles in Europe: Science and Policy Implications* (European Commission, DG Health, reproduced at: http://ec.europa.eu/health/ph_determinants/life_style/nutrition/report01_en.pdf), and A Faeh, 'Obesity in Europe: the strategy of the European Union from a public health law perspective' (2012) 19 Euro J Hlth Law 69.

[76] Directive 84/450/EEC, Directive 89/552/EEC and Directive 2007/65/EC.

[77] See S Boccia, A Brand, H Brand, et al., 'Public health genomics in Europe' (editorial) (2006) 3 Italian J Pub Hlth 4 and http://ec.europa.eu/research/health/genomics/index_en.htm.

[78] The European Society of Human Genetics has published a page on Legal Regulation of Genetic Testing in Europe, albeit regulation by Member States: https://www.eshg.org/270.0.html.

[79] Notably the USA which has enacted a federal law that proscribes genetic discrimination: the Genetic Information Nondiscrimination Act of 2007: HR Res 493, 110th Cong §101(d)(6)(A) (as passed by the House on 29 March 2007). Signed into law on 21 May 2008 under the same name, Act of 2008.

[80] On the interaction of the principles of privacy, non-discrimination, and data protection, with different frameworks and modes of regulation, see A de Paor, 'Regulating Genetic Information—Exploring the Options in Legal Theory' (2014) 21(5) Euro J Hlth Law 425–53.

[81] Note, in this regard, that Directives 2004/113/EC and 2000/43/EC prohibit discrimination on the basis of racial or ethnic origin, under Art 56 TFEU, and that under Art 4(3) of the Patients' Rights Directive 2011/24/EC: 'The principle of non-discrimination with regard to nationality shall be applied to patients from other Member States.'

[82] 98/69/EC, fully implemented in 2003. See House of Commons Library Post Note 407/2012, *Consumer Genetic Testing*: http://researchbriefings.parliament.uk/ResearchBriefing/Summary/POST-PN-407. See 2015/C 226/03 of 10 July 2015 on voluntary harmonised standards under Directive 98/79/EC.

3.19   In sum, the 'rights' dimension of EU health care policy has arisen in a variety of policy contexts. Many of these have been taken up in legislation and have been enforced by the CJEU. Other provisions—such as those devoted to discrimination (racial, ethnic, sexual),[83] equal treatment for EU migrants, the coordination of social security entitlements, and the impact of free movement of services and entitlements to health care in the context of the internal market—are anchored in the Charter of Fundamental Rights.

RIGHTS AND ACCESS TO HEALTH CARE IN THE EU

3.20   The purpose of this section is to outline the legal framework for the rights dimension of health care policy in the EU.[84] Although EU law contains elements of international law, it cannot be understood exclusively in those terms. This is particularly so given that European law has priority over national legal provisions,[85] that European law prevails when it conflicts with national law,[86] and that damages can be obtained for its non-implementation.[87] Thus, unlike international law, EU law creates rights upon which individuals can rely directly.[88] This is because under Art 288 TFEU, regulations are directly applicable in, and directives are binding on, all Member States.[89]

3.21   The language of rights in connection with health care policy in the EU must be qualified from the outset. It is arguably more appropriate to speak in terms of interests which may give rise to a duty unless it is counteracted by conflicting considerations.[90] Put another way, it is preferable to speak of rights to health care in terms of obligations on behalf of those who are entrusted by the state to provide it, due allowance being made for the tension underlying the allocation of finite resources in the face of infinite demand. Even so, the inclusion of rights to health care in constitutions obscures the need for this distinction. Indeed, it goes some way towards encouraging the view that health care rights include justiciable public rights as well as the rights of members of the medical profession to practise in EU Member States.[91]

---

[83]   E.g. Art 19 TFEU taken in conjunction with Art 3 of the anti-racism Directive that includes the prohibition of discrimination in relation to social protection, health care, housing, and education (Directive 2000/43 [2000] OJ L180/22). See E Ellis and P Watson, *EU Anti-Discrimination Law and the EU* (2012). See also the decision of the CJEU concerning the dismissal of a woman in the advanced stage of in vitro fertilisation, in which the Court held that it was contrary to the principle of equal treatment as envisaged by the Directive on the safety and health at work of pregnant workers (Directive 92/85/EEC); Case C-506/06 *Sabine Mayr v Bäckerei und Konditorei Gerhard Flöckner*, judgment of 26 February 2008, [2008] 2 CMLR 27.

[84]   This section was originally drawn from M Aziz, *The Impact of European Rights on National Legal Cultures* (2004), 113–27.

[85]   Case C-6/64 *Costa v ENEL* [1964] ECR 585.

[86]   *Factortame Ltd v Secretary of State for Transport (No 2)* [1991] AC 603. See also cases C-46/93 and C-48/93 *Brasserie du Pêcheur SA v Germany, R v Secretary of State for Transport, ex p Factortame Ltd* [1996] ECR I-1029.

[87]   Cases C-6/90 and C-9/90 *Francovich and Others v Italy* [1992] IRLR 84.

[88]   Case C-26/62 *Van Gend en Loos v Nederlandse Administratie der Belastingen* [1963] ECR 1.

[89]   See A Hinarejos, 'On the legal effects of framework decisions: Directly applicable, directly effective, self-executing, supreme?' (2008) 14 Euro L J 620.

[90]   See J Raz, *The Morality of Freedom* (1986), 166.

[91]   See Council Directive 93/16/EEC of 5 April 1993 to facilitate the free movement of doctors and the mutual recognition of their diplomas, certificates and other evidence of formal qualifications [OJ L165, 07.07.1993] as amended by a host of legislative acts. This area came to be governed by Directive 2005/36/EC as amended by Directive 2006/100/EC and Arts 45 and 49 TFEU. Following a Green Paper consultation

3.22 Data on the migration patterns of doctors across the EU is based on meta-analysis of secondary databases. There is some indication that there is significant mobility, but there is not reliable evidence of any tendencies in the data.[92] The WHO has, however, presented research on the gaps in this knowledge.[93] Some Member States, such as Poland, have monitored the free movement of doctors and dentists by virtue of recording the issue of professional verification certificates, which enable Polish doctors to apply for jobs in other EU Member States.[94]

3.23 Despite improvements in the collection of data concerning the migration of doctors, there is still no way of monitoring evidence of serious professional misconduct or criminal offences across the Union. Article 12 of Directive 93/16/EEC provides that the home Member State is obliged to communicate information on disciplinary action in the case of serious professional misconduct and criminal offences; however, this is limited to cases where disciplinary action has been taken. It is regrettable that the Advisory Committee on Medical Training (ACMT),[95] which was set up to advise the European Commission on medical training, has been effectively suspended since 1999.[96] However, other organisations have to some extent filled the gap—for example, the Standing Committee of European Doctors (CPME),[97] representing the medical associations of 32 European countries, was set up to promote high standards of training in the interest of quality health care.

3.24 Medical activities amount to services and fall under Art 57 TFEU. This has been the position since the judgment in the Joined Cases *Luisi* and *Carbone*.[98] As services, such activities come within the terms of the Services Directive,[99] which aims to facilitate service providers in their exercise of freedom of establishment, while still maintaining high quality of services. The Services Directive is also inextricably linked to freedom to receive services. While services provided to patients under social security benefits

---

in 2011 (COM(2011) 367 final), the Directive was modernised in 2013, with the adoption of Directive 2013/55/EU (to be implemented by 18 January 2016). The aim of this modernisation is to liberalise service provision through the automatic mutual recognition of professional qualifications. According to the European Court of Justice, the mutual recognition of titles and diplomas under European Community law is based on 'mutual trust' between Member States. See Case C-330/03 *Colegio de Ingenieros de Caminos, Canales y Puertos* [2006] ECR-I-801. See also COM(2011) 367 final.

[92] See M A García-Pérez, C Amaya, and Á Otero, 'Physicians' migration in Europe: an overview of the current situation', *Biomed Central*, December 2007, available at http://www.biomedcentral.com/content/pdf/1472-6963-7-201.pdf. See also K Ling and P Belcher, 'Medical migration within Europe: opportunities and challenges' (2014) 14(6) Clinical Medicine 630-2.

[93] See M Wismar, C B Maier, I A Glinos, G Dussault, and J Figueras (eds), *Health professional mobility and health systems: Evidence from 17 European countries*, World Health Organization, 2011. Available at http://www.euro.who.int/en/publications/abstracts/health-professional-mobility-and-health-systems.-evidence-from-17-european-countries. See also J Buchan and G Perfilieva, *Making progress towards health workforce sustainability in the WHO European Region*, World Heath Organization, 2015: http://www.euro.who.int/__data/assets/pdf_file/0005/287456/Making-progress-towards-health-workforce-sustainability-in-the-WHO-European-Region-rev1.pdf.

[94] See: http://www.mz.gov.pl.

[95] Which was set up by Decision 75/364/EEC; OJ 1975 L 167/17.

[96] See COM(99) 177 final in which the Commission proposed the disbandment of the ACMT to the Council.

[97] http://www.cpme.eu/about/

[98] Joined cases 286/82 and 26/83, *Graziana Luisi and Giuseppe Carbone* v *Ministero del Tesoro*, 31 January 1984.

[99] European Parliament and Council Directive 2006/123 EC, OJ 2006 No. L376/36 on services in the internal market.

is for Member States to determine, that will of course be subject to the case law (in particular, *Watts, Smits and Peerbooms, Müller-Fauré*, and *Kohll*) and, latterly, the Patients' Rights Directive.[100]

3.25 The TFEU[101] refers to the obligation of the Union to take into account requirements for, inter alia, '... the guarantee of adequate social protection ... and protection of human health'.[102] A system of coordination of national social security systems, developed under the aegis of regs 1408/71 and 574/72, and now revised by regs 883/2004 and 2008/897,[103] facilitates the free movement of workers. In particular, workers have the right to medical treatment, EU citizens have the right to emergency treatment, and patients can obtain prior authorisation to be treated in Member States other than that in which they are ordinarily resident.[104] Article 35 of the EU Charter of Fundamental Rights provides a right to health care in the sense that: 'Everyone has the right of access to preventative health care and the right to benefit from medical treatment under the conditions established by national laws and practices.' Two main legal implications stem from this provision. First, it is the foundation of the individual entitlements of EU citizens to both medical treatment and to preventative health care. Second, it is the basis for what is referred to as 'mainstreaming',[105] which is to say that it creates an obligation on the EU institutions in the context of policies and activities of the Union.

3.26 Directive 2004/38/EC on the right of citizens of the Union and their family members to move and reside freely within the territory of the Member States, consolidates and simplifies most of the prior secondary legislation regarding free movement.[106] Regarding health, in order for a citizen to be able to benefit from the right of residence, he must show that he has sufficient resources for himself and his family members so as not to become a burden on the social assistance system of the host Member State during his period of residence, and must also have comprehensive sickness insurance cover in the host Member State.[107] Moreover, the Directive restates the right of a Member State to restrict the freedom of movement of EU citizens on the ground, inter alia, of public health.[108]

3.27 The CJEU has developed a principled approach to health rights in the EU, which may be summarised as follows: while EU law does not detract from the powers of the Member States to organise their social security systems, Member States must, nevertheless, comply with European law when exercising their powers.[109] The requirement for prior authorisation of treatment in another Member State constitutes a restriction of the freedom to provide services as contained in the Treaty. Restrictions can, however, be objectively justified on the basis of the protection of the financial balance of the system or on the ground

---

[100] The line of case law is discussed further in para 3.37 et seq and the Patient Rights Directive is discussed further in para 3.42.

[101] See n 4. [102] See Art 9 TFEU. [103] See 2004 OJ L200/1.

[104] Through the use of the European Health Insurance Card introduced in 2004.

[105] See Art 152(1) EC and CHARTE 4473/00 CONVENT 49.

[106] As regards third country nationals, see Directives 2011/98/EU, 2014/36/EU and, 2014/66/EU.

[107] See Directive 2004/38, Art 7(1)(b).

[108] As provided by Art 45(3) TFEU; see also Directive 2004/38/EC, Art 27(1) and, in particular, Art 29(1) which provides that: 'The only diseases justifying measures restricting freedom of movement shall be the diseases with epidemic potential as defined by the relevant instruments of the World Health Organization [sic] and other infectious diseases or contagious diseases if they are the subject of protection provisions applying to nationals of the host Member State.' See http://ec.europa.eu/health/communicable_diseases.

[109] A further analogy is to be found in the field of education where similar principles have been developed. See Case C-9/74 *Donato Casagrande* v *Landeshauptstadt München* [1974] ECR 773 at 12. See also Case C-293/83 *Françoise Gravier* v *City of Liège* [1985] ECR 293 at 19.

of public health—although in practice this burden of proof has, as yet, been rebutted time and time again, and has never been successfully discharged before the Court. Quite the contrary, in fact: the CJEU has found that economic arguments alone cannot justify restrictions on free movement.[110]

3.28 Inevitably, the provision of health care varies widely across the Union. Three sources of finance are available: out-of-pocket payments, voluntary (or private) insurance premiums,[111] and compulsory (or public) contributions through insurance or taxation.[112] Three methods of the provision of health care must also be distinguished: reimbursement, benefits in kind, and, lastly, ownership and management of providers. 'Administrative fragmentation' is accentuated across EU Member States. In Germany, for example, the provision of health care is distributed at federal and state level and through the courts, the insurance funds and their organisations, and the doctors' organisations. The German example is also notable for the absence of centralised control. In the case of Spain, it is the regions that are responsible for the provision of health care but it is the Ministry of Health that determines the overall health budget; the same is true of the UK under devolution. Experiences differ markedly as regards implementation of health care policy, particularly between the regions of the north and south of both Spain and Italy, a situation which, in some Member States, may also arise in relation to the area in which a person lives. This is also the case in Finland, which has witnessed several reforms that have provoked mergers of municipalities which have traditionally had competence concerning the organisation of health services. Whereas decentralisation has tended to provide favourable opportunities for ensuring greater accountability of health services to the local citizens, migration from rural municipalities towards the cities has placed the system under considerable strain.[113] This diversity will be further amplified as a result of enlargement of the Union, which will bring with it a population with a wide range of health profiles and different systems of health care, not to mention levels of resources.[114] The gap is particularly affected by the simultaneous transition to a market economy which has created considerable fiscal problems. In fact, two basic health indicators—infant mortality and life expectancy— reveal that most candidate countries lag well behind the original EU Member States.[115]

3.29 Public health profiles already differ greatly across the Union. Men's life expectancies at birth range from 68.5 years (Lithuania) and 69.3 (Latvia) among accession states to 80.7 (Lichtenstein and Norway) and 80.5 (Iceland) in northern and western states.[116] The survival rates for cancer of the bladder reveal substantial variations among the Member States, with five-year survival rates ranging from 78 per cent in Austria to 47 per cent in

[110] Case C-157/99 *Geraets-Smits* and *Peerbooms*; Case C-385/99 *Müller-Fauré* v *Onderlinge Waarborgmaatschappij OZ Zorgverzekeringen UA* and Case C-372/04 *Watts* v *Bedford Primary Care Trust*.
[111] As in the case of the Netherlands where health insurance funds are private and governed by private law. They are also permitted to have for-profit status. See N Klazinga, 'The health system in the Netherlands' (2008) 14 Eurohealth 8.
[112] Such as, e.g., the centrally collected 'health-contribution' tax set at 8 per cent of taxable income in Denmark; K Vrangbæk, 'The health system in Denmark' (2008) 14 Eurohealth 7.
[113] See U Häkkinen and J Lehto, 'Reform, change and continuity in Finnish health care' (2005) 30 J Hlth Politics Pol Law 79.
[114] See B Merkel and K Kärkkäinen, 'Public health aspects of accession' (2002) 8 Eurohealth 3.
[115] Indeed, the level of spending on health in absolute and percentage terms is significantly less than in the EU Health's share of GDP. In 2012, EU-27 spending on social protection was 19.9 per cent of GDP and on health it was 7.3 per cent. See *Health at a Glance: Europe 2014*, OECD, which indicates a range of per GDP expenditure among Member States, from 11.8 per cent in the Netherlands, to 5.6 per cent in Romania.
[116] European Commission *Eurostat life expectancy at birth* data for 2013, updated September 2013: http://ec.europa.eu/eurostat/tgm/table.do?tab=table&init=1&plugin=1&pcode=tps00025&language=en.

Poland and Estonia.[117] Life expectancy is significantly lower in the new Member States given the high rates of cardiovascular disease and cancer—especially lung cancer—associated with high rates of tobacco and alcohol consumption and low levels of physical exercise.[118] The communist legacy in the new Member States of the Union is such that their health care systems suffer from chronic under-funding; the combination of the difficulties involved in the transition to market economies and associated corruption mean that access to health care is not equal.[119]

3.30 Despite these differences, the EU promotes the coordination of national long-term care policies through what is termed the 'open method of coordination'. This is a voluntary process based on agreed common objectives, which are translated into the national plans of Member State governments. In respect of long-term care, for example, in 2011 the European Commission launched the Pilot European Innovation Partnership on Active and Healthy Ageing (EIPAHA), which aims by 2020 to increase by two years the average healthy lifespan in the EU.[120] While much of the health policy in the EU is guided by the 'health care law matrix' of different actors and initiatives, the EU also seeks to remove barriers to trade. And it is in this area that free movement principles have changed the landscape of inter-state health care provision.

CROSS-BORDER ACCESS TO HEALTH CARE IN THE EU

3.31 Patient mobility in the EU is a growing phenomenon, with its basis in both legislation and judgments of the CJEU. Given what has already been argued on the economic basis of the EU, for the Court to have considered the issue under the terms of the TFEU has meant, in effect, that health care is subject to the rules of the internal market.[121] In the *Kohll*[122] and *Decker* cases,[123] individuals were able to obtain medical treatment in an EU Member State other than the one in which they were resident.[124] In *Kohll*, the Court held that the need to obtain prior authorisation from an institution of the state for treatment in another Member State constituted a restriction on the freedom to provide services

---

[117] EUROCARE 3—Survival of cancer patients in Europe, see: http://www.eurocare.it.

[118] See B Merkel and K Kärkkäinen, 'Public health aspects of accession' (2002) 8 Eurohealth 3 and also COM(2004) 301 final, 17 et seq.

[119] C Lawson and J Nemec, 'The political economy of Slovak and Czech health policy: 1989–2000' (2003) 24 Internat Political Sci Rev 219.

[120] http://ec.europa.eu/health/ageing/policy/index_en.htm. See also COM(2012) 083 final: 'Taking forward the Strategic Implementation Plan of the European Innovation Partnership on Active and Healthy Ageing'.

[121] Art 56 TFEU, which, 'allowed the Court to compensate for the lack of specific rules on cross-border healthcare'. See G Di Federico, 'Access to healthcare in the Post-Lisbon Era and the Genuine Enjoyment of EU Citizens' Rights', Chapter 8, 184, in L S Rossi and F Casolari (eds), *The EU after Lisbon* (Switzerland: Springer International Publishing, 2014). For a useful tabulation of rules governing health care rights under Art 56 TFEU, the Patient Rights Directive and the Services Directives, see S L Greer and T Sokol, 'Rules for Rights: European Law, Health Care and Social Citizenship' (2014) 20(1) Euro L J 66–87, Table 1, 78.

[122] Case C-158/96 *Kohll* v *Union des Caisses de Maladie* [1998] ECR I-1931.

[123] Case C-120/95 *Decker* v *Caisse de Maladie des Employés Privés* [1998] ECR I-1831.

[124] See Art 22(1)(c) reg (EEC) No 1408/71 which allows EU citizens to go to another Member State to receive medical treatment and to obtain reimbursement of the costs at the rates applicable there. Note that this covers public health insurance schemes only. See also reg (EEC) No 574/72.

within the meaning of Arts 59 and 60 (now 56 and 57 TFEU) of the Treaty. It had done so by, in effect, 'making the provision of services between Member States more difficult than the provision of services purely within one Member State'.[125] The Court rejected arguments advanced by the defendants that expenditure control and the 'genuine and actual risk' of upsetting the financial balance of the social security system provided an objective justification. More recently, the Court has ruled on the entitlement to reimbursement based on a lack of resources in the state of residence. In the preliminary ruling in from the Tribunalul Sibiu, Romania in *Elena Petru* v *Casa Judeţeană de Asigurări de Sănătate Sibiu*,[126] the Court of Justice found that the Member State of residence is required to authorise services ordinarily covered by national benefits, where these are unavailable due to a temporary deficiency rather than to a prolonged structural deficiency.

3.32   In *Decker*, the Court of Justice held that social security and the conditions concerning the right or duty to be insured with a social security scheme—as well as the conditions for entitlement to benefits—were matters for each Member State but that they must comply with Community law. It rejected an objective justification based on the grounds of public health and ensuring the quality of medical products. The Court referred to the general system concerning the recognition of professional education and training and to the fact that the spectacles were purchased on prescription from an ophthalmologist, which guaranteed the protection of public health, a position which has been upheld in later case law.[127]

3.33   As already intimated, the issues that arise as a consequence of these cases include, inter alia, the idea of 'medical tourism' by EU citizens seeking the most favourable services, the protectionism of the medical establishment as regards the labour market, and so on.[128] The practice of seeking non-emergency treatment in another Member State has been steadily increasing from its estimated uptake by some 2 per cent of the insured population in the EU in 2000,[129] to figures as high as 40 per cent of German nationals in 2008.[130] Yet this seems still to amount to only 1 per cent of overall public expenditure on health care (around €10 billion)[131]—and this despite the encouragement by some national Member

---

[125]   Case C-158/96 *Kohll* v *Union des Caisses de Maladie* n 122, para 33.

[126]   Case C-268/13, 9 October 2014 *Elena Petru* v *Casa Judeţeană de Asigurări de Sănătate Sibiu, Casa Naţională de Asigurări de Sănătate*, ruling on Art 22(2) of reg 1408/71. For further discussion of this case and the financial dimension of cross-border health services—including pooling of resources and expertise, privacy, and data protection—see H D C Roscam Abbing, 'EU Cross-border Healthcare and Health Law' (2015) 22(1) Euro J Hlth Law 1–12 (Editorial).

[127]   See Case C-368/98 *Abdon Vanbraekel and Others* v *Alliance nationale des mutualités chrétiennes* [2001] ECR I-5382 in which a Belgian social security institution wrongly refused permission to an insured person to seek medical treatment abroad. See also Case C-157/99 *B.S.M. Geraets-Smits* v *Stichting Ziekenfonds VGZ and H.T.M. Peerbooms* v *Stichting CZ Groep Zorgverzekeringen* [2001] ECR I-5509 and Case C-56/01 *Inizan* v *Caisse Primaire d'Assurance Maladie des Hautes-de-Seine* [2003] ECR I-12403. See generally M Fuchs, 'Free movement of services and social security—Quo vadis?' (2002) 8 European L J 536. See also Case C-385/99 *V.G. Müller-Fauré* v *Onderlinge Waarborgmaatschappij OZ Zorgverzekeringen UA and E.E.M. van Riet* v *Onderlinge Waarborgmaatschappij ZAO Zorgverzekeringen* in which standard procedures for obtaining reimbursement for costs of treatment abroad were not followed. Thus, reimbursement was not granted on the basis that the treatment concerned care which was non-urgent (*Müller-Fauré*) or treatment which could have been provided in the country of insurance (*Van Riet*).

[128]   See generally G Di Federico, n 121.

[129]   W Palm, J Nickless, H Lewalle, et al., *Implications of Recent Jurisprudence on the Co-Ordination of Health Care Protection Systems* (2000).

[130]   H Legido-Quigley et al., 'Cross-border healthcare in Europe: clarifying patients' rights', BMJ 2011;342:d296.

[131]   See European Commission MEMO/11/32 of 19 January 2011: http://europa.eu/rapid/press-release_MEMO-11-32_en.doc. See also M Wismar, W Palm, J Figueras, K Ernst, and E van Ginneken (eds), *Cross-border Health Care in the European Union: Mapping and analyzing practices and policies*, World Health

State governments which, as we have already noted, have adopted policies to send patients abroad in order to reduce waiting lists.[132] However, there is evidence to suggest this is because, in practice, patients have been faced with considerable administrative hurdles when attempting to exercise their right to cross-border access to health care, both once they are in another EU Member State for treatment and when they return to their state of origin.[133] In other words, each stage of the process brings not only benefits, but also respective burdens.[134]

3.34 In *Blood*,[135] an English woman resident in the UK was held not to be precluded from travelling to Belgium for fertility treatment by way of insemination with her husband's posthumous sperm donation.[136] The Human Fertilisation and Embryology Authority (HFEA) originally refused to release the sperm so that she could be treated in Belgium; the Court of Appeal, however, held this to be contrary to EU law and in particular to the then, Arts 59 and 60 (freedom to obtain services). The HFEA was unaware of the EC law nexus of the case, electing instead to draw from principles of private international law by maintaining that the plaintiff did not have adequate 'connecting factors' to link her to Belgium.[137]

3.35 The *Blood* case also illustrates the link between health policy and the achievement of the internal market. The so-called 'Tobacco Advertising case'[138] in which the European Court of Justice annulled Directive 98/43 (prohibiting the advertising and sponsorship of tobacco products)[139] on the ground that it did not fall within the scope of the internal market, is a further case in point. The health and the internal market implications of the Directive are inseparable elements. Indeed, health is regarded not as a policy in its own right but in terms of the removal of both barriers to trade and the distortion of competition, which arise as a consequence of differing national laws regarding the restrictions on the advertising and sponsorship of tobacco products. The case highlights the limits of the elastic nature of EU competences,[140] the extent to which health policy is scattered

Organization and the European Observatory on Health Systems and Policies (2011), 223 et seq and Table 9.2. http://www.euro.who.int/__data/assets/pdf_file/0004/135994/e94875.pdf.

[132] Paras 3.10–3.11. See K Lowson, J Mahon, D Wright, P Lowson, S Tatlok, and S Duffy, *Cross Border Healthcare and Patient Mobility: Data and Evidence Gathering*, Department of Health (2010). See also 'EU plans cross-border healthcare' 2 July 2008, reported at: http://news.bbc.co.uk/1/hi/world/europe/7484198.stm.

[133] See M Wismar et al., n 131.

[134] See H Hermans, 'Cross-border health care in the European Union: Recent legal implications of "Decker and Kohll" ' (2008) 6 Journal of Evaluation in Clinical Practice 431, and S Giubboni, 'Free movement of persons and European solidarity' (2007) 13 European L J 360–79. It remains to be seen to what extent administrative barriers to so-called '*inter*operability' of health systems might be circumvented by the introduction of the European Health Insurance Card (E111). See also the Smart Open Services (SOS) initiative which was aimed at removing linguistic, administrative, and technical barriers by making it easier for people to receive medical assistance as part of the health strategy in conjunction with i2010, the EU's policy framework for the information society and media.

[135] *R v Human Fertilisation and Embryology Authority, ex p Blood* [1997] 2 All ER 687; (1996) 35 BMLR 1. The case is discussed in greater detail in paras 8.17–8.19.

[136] The main provisions on medical treatment are to be found in Title III, Chapter 1 of reg (EEC) No 1408/71 (OJ L28, 30.1.1997).

[137] The Authority was also, however, intent on trying to prevent the creation of a precedent as regards access to gametes where express, written consent has not been given by the donor.

[138] C-376/98 *Germany v Parliament and Council (Tobacco Advertising)* [2000] ECR I-8419.

[139] Directive 98/43/EC of the European Parliament and of the Council of 6 July 1998 on the approximation of the laws, regulations, and administrative provisions of the Member States relating to the advertising and sponsorship of tobacco products (OJ 1992 L213, p 9).

[140] See G de Búrca and B de Witte, 'The delimitation of powers between the EU and its member states' in A Amull and D Wincott (eds), *Accountability and Legitimacy in the European Union* (2002), 201–22.

across a host of EU policies, as well as the predominant nature and tenor of the values and principles which inform decisions of the European Court, namely, market and economic integration.

3.36 It is difficult to make assumptions concerning individual Member States as knowledge concerning access to health care services across borders varies.[141] For example, 'Euregios'[142] include health service arrangements as part of their activities.[143] Indeed, some of the regions have even gone as far as to enact measures to ease the administrative burden on patients. A further phenomenon worth noting is the migration of retirees through the E121 scheme,[144] particularly from the northern EU Member States towards the south of Europe, particularly to Spain, France, Portugal, Italy, Greece, and Bulgaria—and, indeed, patient migration from southern to northern regions in Italy. Thus, for example, more than 400,000 UK citizens retired to other EU Member States in 2010. This has given rise to increased awareness in these regions which have had to adapt their health services in order to adjust to both an ageing population and the free movement of citizens.[145] So it is unsurprising that the EU designated 2012 as the 'European Year for Active Ageing'—even more so given the patient rights implications of current demographic changes,[146] and that one of the more commonly sought cross-border treatments is hip replacement surgery. And it is patients' rights that has ultimately become the focus of cross-border health care developments.

3.37 Cases that have come before the court have certain features in common: patients applied for authorisation to seek treatment abroad; that application was refused; the patient sought treatment in another Member State and the patient then sought reimbursement of their out of pocket expenses from the health authority in their Member State of affiliation. *Kohll* and *Decker* were pivotal as part of the evolutionary process of the development of mobility of EU citizens for medical treatment. In *Vanbraekel* and *Geraets-Smits/Peerbooms*,[147] the Court held that the prior authorisation requirement was a restriction of the freedom to provide and to receive services but that, in the case at hand, it could be

---

[141] See para 3.33 and n 134.

[142] Border regions of EU Member States which benefit from a system of mutual recognition of the arrangements for the provision of health care.

[143] As in, e.g., the Meuse-Rhine Region (Belgium, Germany, and the Netherlands), Rhine-Waal (Germany and the Netherlands), Scheldemond (Belgium and the Netherlands), and Hainaut/Nord-Pas-de-Calais (Belgium and France), which benefit from the EU's INTERREG initiative. See Association of European Border Regions (AEBR): http://www.aebr.eu/en/index.php and the 'Final Report of Evaluation of Border Regions in the European Union' (EUREGIO) 2008: http://www.euregio-mr.com/nl/euregiomr?set_language=nl.

[144] Whereby an EU retired citizen may apply to have his or her social rights transferred from the social security system of his or her home country to the 'receiving country'. Furthermore, a lump sum of money agreed upon by the Social Commission on Migrant Workers is also transferred to the central government of the receiving country to cover costs for health care. The citizen receives a national health insurance card in the new country and is thereby integrated into the system. See H Legido-Quigley and D La Parra, 'The health care needs of UK pensioners living in Spain: An agenda for research' (2007) 13 Eurohealth 14.

[145] See generally L Ackers and P Dwyer, 'Fixed laws, fluid lives: The citizenship status of post-retirement migrants in the European Union' (2004) 24 Age Soc 451. For recent statistics see A Rettmann, EU Observer, 10 February 2014 https://euobserver.com/social/123066.

[146] See M Hartlev, 'Healthy Ageing—a Patients' Rights Perspective' (2012) 19 European J Hlth Law 141 and E Rynning, 'The Ageing Populations of Europe—Implications for Health Systems and Patients' Rights' (2008) 15 Euro J Hlth Law 297.

[147] Cases C-368/98 *Vanbraekel* and C-157/99 *Geraets-Smits v Stichting Ziekenfonds, Peerbooms v Stichting CZ Groep Zorgverzekeringen* [2001] ECR I-5363.

objectively justified in the interests of maintaining a balanced medical and hospital service that was available to all and of preventing a social security system becoming seriously undermined—thus confirming the decisions in *Kohll* and *Decker*.

3.38 In *Müller-Fauré*,[148] the plaintiff, a Dutch national on holiday in Germany, had dental treatment over the space of a month without authorisation and applied to her Dutch insurers for reimbursement of the costs of the treatment. The Fund refused on the advice of its advisory dental officer, and the Court found that the argument relied on by the fund—that reimbursement would lead to increased infrastructure cost—did not apply to non-hospital treatment. As such, in respect of non-hospital treatment, the prior authorisation requirement did violate Arts 59 and 60, even if the system is one that provides benefits in kind.[149] The Court held that as regards hospital treatment, the prior authorisation requirement did not violate Arts 59 and 60. Authorisation could be refused only if treatment which is the same or equally effective for the patient could be obtained without undue delay in an establishment which has an agreement with a fund. Undue delay fell to be determined on a subjective basis.

3.39 A variety of issues arise from the case, not all of which can be dealt with here. The implications of the decision as to state sovereignty necessitate the adjustment of both the domestic law and culture of the Member States. In this context, the Court reiterated that, while the sovereignty of the Member States was not undermined, they must adjust their systems of social security in order to accommodate the fundamental freedoms.[150] Although it was untenable to distinguish between medical services based on benefits in kind, and reimbursement, the Court stated that Member States can establish ceilings for reimbursement as long as they are based on objective, non-discriminatory, and transparent criteria. It held that, when assessing the issue of undue delay, national authorities are required to consider 'all of the circumstances of each specific case', which include the nature of the medical condition as well as the degree of pain and the nature of the patient's disability in relation to, for example, his professional activity.[151]

3.40 In its judgment of 16 May 2006,[152] the CJEU upheld Mrs Watts' claim in stating that a patient could apply to seek treatment in another EU Member State if the waiting lists for the treatment sought were such that they could not be justified in relation to an objective assessment of his or her clinical needs in the light of his or her medical condition. Moreover, a refusal to grant prior authorisation cannot be justified by the existence of waiting lists alone. It must also be more subjectively framed in the context of the patient's medical condition.[153] The interventionism by the Court is considerable, to the extent that it engaged in a detailed analysis of how the UK NHS effectively manages its waiting lists. It also addressed the issue of reimbursement in considerable detail,

---

[148] Case C-385/99 *V G Müller-Fauré v Onderlinge Waarborgmaatschappij OZ Zorgverzekeringen UA* and *E E M van Riet v Onderlinge Waarborgmaatschappij ZAO Zorgverzekeringen* [2003] ECR I-4509.

[149] Note that the issue is one of freedom to provide services and no distinction is made between hospital and non-hospital services: see line of case law from *Geraets-Smits* and *Peerbooms* n 147 above to Case 562/10 *Commission v Germany* [2012].

[150] N 148, para 102.   [151] N 148, para 90.

[152] See C-372/04 *The Queen, on the application of Yvonne Watts v Bedford Primary Care Trust, Secretary of State for Health* [2006] ECR I-4325; sub nom *R (on the application of Watts) v Bedford Primary Care Trust* (2006) 90 BMLR 150.

[153] Which is framed in terms of an '... objective medical assessment of the patient's medical condition, the history and probable course of his illness, the degree of pain he is in and/or the nature of his disability at the time when the request for authorisation was made or renewed' (n 152 at para 119).

stating that it must be strictly limited to those costs of medical services inextricably linked to his or her hospital stay.[154]

3.41 Interventionism, however, is not limited to the public sector but also has implications for the private sector. Thus, in *British United Provident Association Ltd (BUPA) and Others*,[155] the Court of First Instance confirmed a decision by the European Commission approving Ireland's risk equalisation system for the private medical insurance sector. The Court considered that the Irish legislation in question was an act of a public authority which retained a wide discretion as to the definition of a service in the general economic interest (SGEI);[156] however, it held that certain minimum criteria must be satisfied, thereby qualifying the competence of Member States regarding the provision of health care within a framework of Community law. The decisions in the European Court of Justice have obvious implications for those with administrative power in the Member States—including the allocation of national resources designed to underpin social solidarity.[157] Clearly, these persons are now constrained by the requirements of European integration.

3.42 The extent of the implementation of these cross-border rights can no longer be assessed with reference to the reported litigation alone, not least because it is of decreasing interest to the Court.[158] In the seventh edition of this book, it was argued that the principles developed by the European Court of Justice would eventually find their way into EU legislation in one form or another.

The Directive on the Application of Patients' Rights in Cross-Border Health Care (the Patients' Rights Directive)[159] now effectively consolidates the principles set out in the case

[154] In keeping with its previous assessment regarding permissible costs; see, e.g., Case C-8/02 *Ludwig Leichtle* v *Bundesanstalt für Arbeit* [2004] ECR I-2641 in which the Court held that a claim for reimbursement of accommodation and other expenses associated with a spa health-cure in another Member State were excessive and unjustified. See also Case C-444/05 *Stamatelaki* v *OAEE*, judgment of 19 April 2007, [2007] 2 CMLR 44.

[155] T-289/03 *British United Provident Association Ltd (BUPA) and Others* v *Commission of the European Communities*, judgment of 12 February 2008, [2009] 2 CMLR 41.

[156] Providers of a Service of General Economic Interest may take advantage of an exception to the strict application of competition rules, under Art 106 TFEU (and Protocol 26 TFEU on the shared values of the EU). Member States enjoy a wide margin of appreciation on whether and how to finance the provision of SGEI. See Commission Decision 2012/21/EU of 20 December 2011 on the application of Art 106(2) (http://eur-lex.europa.eu/legal-content/EN/TXT/?uri=CELEX:32012D0021) and Commission press release 20 December 2011, including frequently asked questions on SGEI, available at http://ec.europa.eu/competition/state_aid/legislation/sgei.html.

[157] See, e.g., C Nedwick, 'Citizenship, free movement and health care: Cementing individual rights by corroding social solidarity' (2006) 43 CML Rev 1645; see also M Dougan and H Stalford (eds), 'The impact of migration on healthcare in the European Union' (2007) 14 MJ 3 Special Issue of the Maastricht Journal.

[158] Even litigation does not provide a comprehensive overview of the implementation of the acquis as many of the cases of the lower courts are unreported. For the economic implications of free movement and health see K Veitch, 'Juridification, medicalisation and the impact of EU law: patient mobility and the allocation of scarce NHS resources' (2012) 20(3) Med L Rev 362–98.

[159] Directive 2011/24/EU of 9 March 2011 on the application of patients' rights in cross-border health care: http://eur-lex.europa.eu/LexUriServ/LexUriServ.do?uri=OJ:L:2011:088:0045:0065:EN:PDF. See M Peeters, 'Free Movement of Patients: Directive 2011/24 on the Application of Patients' Rights in Cross-Border Healthcare' (2012) 19 European J Hlth Law 29. The European Journal of Health Law Volume 21 (2014) is devoted to papers on the implementation of 2011/24 in different Member States, including Finland, Latvia, Spain, Luxembourg, the Netherlands, the Czech Republic, and Greece. In particular, see H Nys, 'The Transposition of the Directive on Patients' Rights in Cross-border Healthcare in National Law by the Member States: Still a Lot of Effort to Be Made and Questions to Be Answered', at 1–14 of that edition. The UK, for example, has implemented the Directive in the National Health Service (Cross Border Healthcare) Regulations 2013 (SI 2013/2269).

law discussed earlier, on the legal bases of the internal market,[160] public health,[161] and SGEI.[162] It will also be applied to existing secondary legislation.[163] The Directive is by its nature a harmonising instrument insofar as it sets out the responsibilities of the Member State of affiliation in respect of the rights afforded to patients seeking cross-border health care,[164] which is defined as any 'health services provided by health professionals to patients to assess, maintain or restore their state of health, including the prescription, dispensation and provision of medicinal products and medical devices'.[165] It should have been transposed into the national legislation of all Member States by 25 October 2013.[166]

3.43 Member States may set up a system of, and criteria for, prior authorisation, subject to the provisions of the Directive. Article 8 sets out the limited types of health care that may be subject to prior authorisation. These provisions do not apply specifically to particular medical treatments, but to certain activities of health care providers. So, for example, prior authorisation may be required for the type of service that would be subject to cost containment, health system efficiency and human resources factors, including care that may require hospital treatment and accommodation and which would be impacted by those kinds of operational factors. The costs of cross-border health care are to be paid directly by the Member State of affiliation to the Member State of treatment, up to the cost that would have been borne by the Member State of affiliation if the service user had received treatment there. A Member State of affiliation may reimburse to a higher or broader degree, but not to a lesser or narrower degree. Provision has also been made setting out the legitimate reasons a state may refuse to grant prior authorisation,[167] including unacceptable risk to the patient or to the general public.

3.44 Further administrative procedures are set out in the Patients' Rights Directive, requiring Member States of affiliation to comply with certain conditions such as reimbursement systems being based on objective, non-discriminatory criteria and that decisions are properly reasoned and subject to review.[168] The Directive also establishes the obligation for Member States to cooperate in the form of 'mutual assistance' to ensure that cross-border access to health care is rendered more accessible, and to set up information mechanisms for patients and 'National Contact Points' responsible for assisting and informing patients about the processes.[169] Provision is made for European reference networks within Member States, and with the support of the European Commission,[170] to facilitate cooperation and improve research and training.

[160] Art 114 TFEU.   [161] Art 168 TFEU.   [162] Art 14 TFEU.

[163] Regulation 1408/71; the recognition of professional qualifications (05/36), the protection of individuals with regard to the processing of personal data (95/46), and information society services (00/31).

[164] Directive 2011/24/EU, Arts 4, 5, and 6. See Roscam Abbing n 126 and Nys n 159, in which Nys notes that there are those who argue that the 'real' intention of the Directive is to harmonise heath care services in ways which the General Services Directive (Directive 2006/123 EC) failed to do.

[165] Directive 2011/24/EU, Art 3(a). It is assumed that off-label prescription of medication is excluded as this arguably falls within the regulation of experimentation or experimental therapy. For an analysis of some of the relevant arguments around the regulation of off-label prescription of medication, see I Vrancken 'Off-label Prescription of Medication' (2015) 22(2) Euro J Hlth Law 165–86.

[166] See H Nys n 159.   [167] Directive 2011/24/EU, Art 8(6).

[168] Directive 2011/24/EU. Art 9, with Member States acting in accordance with Art 6.

[169] This includes eHealth services (Arts 14 and 15), the obligation of recognising prescriptions made in another Member State (Art 11), reporting mechanisms for rare diseases (Art 13) among Member States. The Directive also contains provisions governing the development of European high-quality centres of specialisation as well as measures to collect statistics on cross-border health care.

[170] Directive 2011/24/EU, Art 12.

3.45 The relative novelty of the Patients' Rights Directive is such that its effect cannot yet be evaluated. But to the extent that it is a codification of the jurisprudence that preceded it, we should not expect a shift from the position set out in the line of decisions from *Kohll* to *Watts*. Interest is likely to remain focused at a Member State level, as it is at that level that the Directive has been implemented in domestic law, and that level at which the required administrative procedures and policies are put into effect. The community method that develops the body of EU law, the *acquis communautaire*, is such that health continues to feature prominently on the policymaking agenda. The European Research Area (ERA) is a further case in point.

ETHICS IN SCIENCE AND NEW TECHNOLOGIES IN THE EU

3.46 EU policymakers have increasingly begun to embrace the merits, and indeed the necessity, of an ERA which is able both to stimulate and to generate innovation in research and which will place the EU on a par with the USA, competitively speaking.

COMMITTEES AND COMITOLOGY

3.47 Generally, the EU legislative process relies on the use of committees and what is referred to as 'comitology'—relatively autonomous committees and agencies which are responsible for the collection and generation of specialised information and expertise, as opposed to having direct regulatory functions.[171] A notable example is the European Medicines Evaluation Agency (EMEA) set up by reg 2309/93 EC.[172] The role of the EMEA is controversial, particularly in terms of democratic principles and accountability. Its working methods are obfuscated by the lack of transparency that pervades both national and European channels of policymaking and implementation.

3.48 This process is symptomatic of the 'new governance', which is also known as 'soft law', and is aimed at addressing the 'democratic deficit', which sees the EU as inaccessible to the ordinary citizen because of the complexity of its methods. As a form of governance, soft law is deliberative, consensual, and multilevel. It represents a departure from the strictures of traditional democracy by defining accountability through transparency and scrutiny. The Open Method of Coordination is a form of soft law governance launched in 2004, which became operational in 2006.[173] It is a voluntary process of political cooperation among Member States based on common objectives and indicators, which governments can translate into national plans.

---

[171] See T Christiansen and M Dobbels, 'Non-Legislative Rule Making after the Lisbon Treaty: Implementing the New System of Comitology and Delegated Acts, (2013) 19(1) European L J 42–56. A useful explanatory text is J Blom-Hansen, *The EU Comitology System in Theory and Practice Keeping an Eye on the Commission?* (Basingstoke: Palgrave Macmillan, 2011).

[172] OJ 1993 L214/1.

[173] COM (2004) 304 final, available at http://ec.europa.eu/employment_social/soc-prot/healthcare/com_04_304_en.pdf. See para 3.30 above. Further information is provided by the European Parliamentary Research Service (November 2014) at http://epthinktank.eu/2014/11/05/the-open-method-of-coordination/.

The European Group on Ethics in Science and New Technologies

3.49 The European Group on Ethics in Science and New Technologies[174] has been particularly proactive in advising the Commission concerning the ethics of new technologies[175]—this being as part of a varied selection of EU integration policies and not only those which arise in the context of EU health policy. Briefly stated, the Group on Ethics in Science, which was set up by the European Commission in December 1997, is part of the Group of Policy Advisors which advises the Commission on the ethical aspects of science and new technologies in relation to the preparation and implementation of European legislation or policies.[176] Many of their opinions have been highly influential, although it is difficult to evaluate the full extent of this influence.[177] It is also difficult to assess the extent of their remit, given that EU policymaking in this area is also generated, shaped, and structured by a plethora of both institutional and extra-institutional actors. Their response to stem cell research is a case in point,[178] in that actors in the policymaking process include not only other EU institutions,[179] but also international organisations, patient groups, and other lobbying groups. In practice, it is difficult to distinguish between the rhetoric and the reality of EU policymaking. One cause for concern is that bodies such as the European Group on Ethics in Science and New Technologies serve the ends of EU policymakers who are increasingly being called upon to ensure that the Union is not too remote from the citizen.

3.50 In order for debates concerning bioethical issues in the EU to be conducted throughout the public spheres of the Union, greater openness is required regarding both the status quo and the way in which norms are being generated. Currently, there is an underlying suspicion that the ethics and the legality of health rights and obligations in the EU are being generated and driven by elite actors while, at the same time, participation by society as a whole is excluded.

3.51 The present position regarding stem cell research is an example of what has been argued in the context of EU health policy as a whole—that is, that the generation of ethical and legal norms is being effected under the aegis of the internal market. The approaches to the regulation of stem cell research in the Member States of the EU are varied.[180] This is

---

[174] http://ec.europa.eu/epsc/ege_en.htm

[175] See, e.g., its report of 16 January 2008 on the 'Ethical aspects of animal cloning for food supply' (Opinion No 23), available at: http://stopogm.net/sites/stopogm.net/files/ethicalcloning.pdf. Further bibliographic information is available at http://eucenter.wisc.edu/OMC/open12.html.

[176] The Group was set up in December 1997 to succeed the Group of Advisers on the Ethical Implications of Biotechnology (GAEIB 1991–7).

[177] While the EGE Opinion on patenting human stem cells was considered for guidance by the European Patent Office in its deliberations on the validity of the so-called 'Edinburgh Patent' on cloning technologies, the Opinion was rejected because classic concepts of patent law are misinterpreted and confused: see European Patent Office, Opposition Division, 'Edinburgh' patent (EP 0695351) (July 2002, unreported).

[178] See http://www.euractiv.com, which collects and collates opinions of institutional and extra-institutional actors as part of EU policymaking including in the area of health.

[179] E.g., the various Directorates General of the European Commission and the European Parliament.

[180] For a review of the different legal regimes applicable to medically assisted reproduction and stem cell research among the 28 EU Member States, see F P Busardo et al., 'The Evolution of legislation in the field of medically assisted reproduction and embryo stem cell research in European Union Members' (2014) BioMed Research International at http://dx.doi.org/10.1155/2014/307160. On stem cell research, see also paras 20.42 et seq of this book.

arguably not helped by the absence of a common definition of 'embryo', which, in turn, leads to uncertainty in respect of the permissibility of stem cell research activities.[181]

As regards the EU, competitiveness and the role of industry is stressed in the context of the 7th Framework Programme in the same vein as the 6th Framework Programme.[182] This may be advantageous in the development of the EU's competence on the international stage but, at the same time, it allows the policymakers to be more interventionist than if the framework was dedicated solely to research per se or, indeed, to health policy.[183] The danger then, is that the ethics—and the legality—of research is being generated and driven by a favoured few in the commercial interest while, at the same time, excluding participation by society. In such delicate and sensitive areas, we must beware of the power vested in the relatively faceless persons who make up the many committees scattered at all levels of the European decision-making process. Participation by the European Parliament in the policymaking process regarding health is limited; this is some cause for concern given that it is the only directly elected body among the plethora of EU institutions.[184]

---

[181] Although relating to commercialisation and patentability, see J Mansnérus, '*Brüstle v. Greenpeace*: Implications for Commercialisation of Translational Stem Cell Research' (2015) 22(2) Euro J Hlth Law 141–64 in particular in the present context the broad definition of human embryo in the Advocate General's Opinion (at 149).

[182] See, e.g., Art III-146 to 156 of the Constitution for Europe.

[183] See the decision of the European Court of Justice concerning the Tobacco Directive: *Germany* v *European Parliament and Council*, Case C-376/98 [2000] ECR-I-8419.

[184] See, e.g., its Resolutions on cloning (Resolution of 7 September 2000) and genetics and rights (Resolution of 3 July 2002).

4

CONSENT TO TREATMENT

4.01 The paternalist might argue that there are many examples in medical practice of situations in which treatment is justified in the teeth of the patient's objection. Arguing from such a position—that the patient is failing to appreciate that a particular treatment is in his best interest—the decision of the doctor to impose it is seen as serving the patient's welfare. This, a paternalist would hold, cannot be wrong. Good health and physical comfort are preferable to ill health and physical discomfort: a patient will thus be happier treated than untreated.

4.02 Such arguments can, however, be sustained only in very limited conditions, such as when the patient is in a state of impaired consciousness. Restraining a delirious patient is an instance of justifiable paternalism, as is the action of clearing the air passages of one who is about to choke to death. The intervention is justified by the conviction that this is what the patient would want, were he fully rational, or that sufficient treatment is needed to restore him to a position in which he can make up his own mind.[1]

4.03 The case for imposed treatment can also be couched in social terms. Illness is costly to the community and it could be argued that the individual is not entitled to refuse treatment which may minimise that cost. Moreover, as we have seen in Chapter 2, we must also consider the direct relationship of the individual with the community as a whole, the most obvious example being the person who is suffering from an infectious or otherwise dangerous illness; few would then argue that he should be allowed to refuse treatment if such treatment—or, in the alternative, isolation—is the only way of reducing the consequent risks. Freedom of the individual is, however, a deeply ingrained feature of a civilised society and the universal caveat to the application of imposed treatment is that it should be as non-coercive as is compatible with containment of the threat—a prime example of the human rights concept of proportionality.[2] A coercive society can be administratively effective—but this does not mean it is desirable.

THE LIMITS TO CONSENT

IS CONSENT ALWAYS NECESSARY?

4.04 Based on the strong moral conviction that everyone has the right of self-determination with regard to his or her body, the common law has long recognised the principle that every person has the right to have his or her bodily integrity protected against invasion

---

[1] See, e.g., *Bolton Hospitals NHS Trust v O* [2003] 1 FLR 824; [2003] Fam Law 319 in which it was confirmed that it is lawful to use reasonable force in providing treatment in a patient's best interests when that patient is incompetent.

[2] See M Brazier and J Harris, 'Public health and private lives' (1996) 4 Med L Rev 171.

by others.[3] Only in certain narrowly defined circumstances may this integrity be compromised without the individual's consent—as where, for example, physical intrusion is involved in the carrying out of lawful arrest. In general, however, a non-consensual touching by another may—subject to the principle *de minimis non curat lex*[4]—give rise to a civil action for damages or, in theory at least, constitute a criminal assault.[5]

4.05 Consent can render physical invasion lawful, but the reality of such consent may be closely scrutinised by the law and is, anyway, subject to policy limitations. Consent will not normally render legitimate a serious physical injury; thus, it was held by Swift J in *R v Donovan*:

> As a general rule to which there are well established exceptions, it is an unlawful act to beat another person with such a degree of violence that the infliction of bodily harm is a probable consequence and, when such an act is proved, consent is immaterial.[6]

This being so, it is nevertheless important to note that the degree of harm suffered goes only to the question of damages and does not operate in constituting the tort or delict. Here it is the affront to bodily integrity which makes the conduct actionable and no actual physical harm need arise. In the same way, the motive of the aggressor is irrelevant. Thus, it matters not that the touching is designed to 'help' the person; as a consequence, every touching of a patient by way of medical treatment is potentially a battery. The classic expression is that of Cardozo J:

> Every human being of adult years and sound mind has a right to determine what shall be done with his own body; and a surgeon who performs an operation without the patient's consent commits an assault.[7]

4.06 It is the patient's consent which makes the touching legally innocuous and there is no doubt that surgical intervention is covered by these principles.[8] Theory, then, is quite simple—the reality is somewhat different. Much jurisprudence in common law countries has focused on the consent issue and, as a result, the so-called doctrine of informed consent has assumed a significant role in the medical negligence debate. As will be seen later in the chapter, it is a doctrine which has had a surprisingly uneasy process of development in the medico-legal ambience of the United Kingdom (UK).

---

[3] This is also a human rights issue: In *YF* v *Turkey* (2004) 39 EHRR 34 it was held that physical and psychological integrity of the person is protected by Art 8 European Convention on Human Rights (ECHR) and that compulsory medical intervention is an interference with this right irrespective of whether 'consent' has been obtained. It falls, therefore, to the state to justify any such interference under Art 8(2). Thus, in *K* v *UK* [2010] 2 FLR 451 it was held to be unjustified and disproportionate to take a blood sample and photographs of a child without parental consent when authorities suspected sexual abuse before consulting a health professional on the child's condition.

[4] *Collins* v *Wilcock* [1984] 3 All ER 374 per Goff LJ at 378; *Walker* v *Commissioner of Police of the Metropolis* [2014] EWCA Civ 897; [2015] 1 WLR 312.

[5] In practice, this would be unlikely, although it could be so, particularly when the supposed assault includes an element of indecency. See, e.g., criminal charges for indecent assault for non-consensual touching by a doctor: *R* v *Healy (Timothy John)* [2003] 2 Cr App R (S) 87; and *R* v *Kumar* [2006] EWCA Crim 1946, in which a doctor's appeal against his conviction for indecent assault was dismissed on the basis that the examination he performed, although properly required, was conducted in an inappropriate manner.

[6] [1934] 2 KB 498 at 507: endorsed in *R* v *Brown* [1994] 1 AC 212.

[7] *Schloendorff* v *Society of New York Hospital* 105 NE 92 (NY, 1914).

[8] *A-G's Reference (No 6 of 1980)* [1981] QB 715, [1981] 2 All ER 1057. The Scots equivalent, albeit indirect, lies in *Smart* v *HM Advocate* 1975 SLT 65.

4.07 As a general rule, however, medical treatment, including physical examination, should not proceed unless the doctor has first obtained the patient's consent. This may be expressed or it may be implied, as it is when the patient presents him- or herself to the doctor for examination and acquiesces in the normal routine. This principle applies in the overwhelming majority of cases but there are limited circumstances in which a doctor may be entitled to proceed without this consent. Essentially, these can be subsumed under the heading of 'non-voluntary therapy', which has to be distinguished from involuntary treatment. The latter implies treatment against the patient's expressed wishes; the occasions on which this would be ethical are, indeed, very few, although a case can be made out when the interests of a third party or of society itself are involved.[9] Non-voluntary treatment is that which is given when the patient is not in a position to have or to express any views as to his or her management and these will include, first, when the patient is unconsciousness; second, when the patient's state of mind is such as to render an apparent consent or refusal invalid—both of which can be encompassed under the rubric that the patient lacks capacity; and, finally, when the patient is a minor—that is, lacks capacity by virtue of status.

The Unconscious Patient

4.08 In some circumstances, it is possible to visualise non-voluntary treatment as proceeding with consent, although that consent has not been expressed. Thus, when an unconscious patient is admitted to hospital, the casualty officer may argue that his consent could be implied or presumed on the grounds that if he were conscious he would probably consent to his life being saved in this way.[10] This may be true but, while the majority of patients could be expected to endorse the decision to treat in such circumstances, it is something of a fictitious approach to the problem.[11]

4.09 An alternative route is to apply the necessity principle. It is widely recognised in both criminal and civil law that there are times when acting out of necessity legitimates an otherwise wrongful act. The basis of this doctrine is that acting unlawfully is justified if the resulting good effect materially outweighs the consequences of adhering strictly to the law. In the present context, the doctor is justified, and should not have criminal or civil liability imposed upon him, if the value which he seeks to protect is of greater weight than the wrongful act he performs—that is, treating without consent—*and* there is no other means by which the end can be achieved.

4.10 Thus, necessity will be a viable defence to any proceedings for non-consensual treatment where an unconscious patient is involved *and* there is no known objection to treatment. The treatment undertaken, however, must not be more extensive than is required by the exigencies of the situation—we do well to remember what Lord Devlin said, albeit in a rather different context: 'The Good Samaritan is a character unesteemed in English

---

[9] Hence involuntary treatment is often at issue in the case of psychotic illness—for which see Chapter 13.

[10] In Scotland, this could be expressed as the doctrine of *negotiorum gestio*.

[11] A rather mundane example involved a dental anaesthetist who inserted an analgesic rectal suppository while the patient was anaesthetised in order to minimise the post-operative pain from multiple extractions. He had not discussed this particular treatment before the operation. The General Medical Council found him guilty of serious professional misconduct: see J Mitchell, 'A fundamental problem of consent' (1995) 310 BMJ 43. A far more serious example involved a surgeon who continued with a hysterectomy operation despite discovering the patient to be pregnant, and effectively terminating the pregnancy without consent. This resulted in a severe reprimand by the General Medical Council: GMC Professional Conduct Committee hearing, 27–30 May 2002.

law.'[12] A doctor cannot, therefore, 'take advantage' of unconsciousness to perform procedures which are not essential for the patient's immediate survival or well-being. This was established in two well-known Canadian cases where the courts explored the distinction between procedures that are justified by necessity and those which are merely 'convenient', a distinction which is also applied by the British courts[13] and recognised by professional bodies.[14]

4.11   In the first of these, *Marshall* v *Curry*,[15] the plaintiff sought damages for battery against the surgeon who had removed a testicle in the course of an operation for a hernia. The surgeon's case was that the removal was essential to a successful operation and that, had he not done so, the health and life of the patient would have been imperilled because the testis was, itself, diseased. Taking the view that the doctor had acted 'for the protection of the plaintiff's health and possibly his life', the court held that the removal of the testicle was necessary and that it would have been unreasonable to put the procedure off until a later date. By contrast, in *Murray* v *McMurchy*,[16] the plaintiff succeeded in an action for battery against a doctor who had sterilised her without her consent. In this case, the doctor had discovered during a caesarian section that the condition of the plaintiff's uterus would have made it hazardous for her to go through another pregnancy and he tied the fallopian tubes although there was no pressing need for the procedure to be undertaken. The court took the view that it would not have been unreasonable to postpone the sterilisation until after consent had been obtained, in spite of the convenience of doing it on the spot.

4.12   The principle that emerges from these two cases is that a doctor is justified by necessity in proceeding without the patient's consent if the treatment is necessary in the sense that it would be, in the circumstances, unreasonable to postpone the operation. Postponement of treatment is, however, to be preferred if it is possible to wait until the patient is in a position to give consent. An English example arose in *Williamson* v *East London and City Health Authority*[17] in which the plaintiff consented to removal and replacement of a leaking breast implant. The condition was, however, found at operation to be more serious than had been anticipated and a subcutaneous mastectomy was performed. Although the evidence was conflicting, Butterfield J ruled that consent to such an extensive procedure had not been given. Damages of £20,000 were awarded despite the fact that the court agreed that the operation would have been needed at some time in the future.

4.13   The distinction between necessity and convenience is, nevertheless, often delicately balanced—particularly in the light of the sometimes vague terms of written consent forms. In an unreported Scottish case,[18] the patient signed to the effect: 'I hereby give permission for myself to have a general anaesthetic and any operation the surgeon considers necessary'. The operation proposed was the comparatively simple removal of a

---

[12]   Lord Devlin, *Samples of Law Making* (1962) p 90.

[13]   Per Lord Goff, *Re F* [1990] 2 AC 1, esp at 74–7.

[14]   See British Medical Association, *Medical Ethics Today* (2010) Chapter 15: Emergency situations.

[15]   [1933] 3 DLR 260.

[16]   [1949] 2 DLR 442. For discussion of these cases, see, in particular, Butler-Sloss LJ in the appeal stage of *F* v *West Berkshire HA* [1989] 2 WLR 1025. *Devi* v *West Midlands Regional Health Authority* [1980] C L Y 687 provides an almost exact British parallel.

[17]   (1998) 41 BMLR 85; [1998] Lloyd's Rep Med 6. The case reads as a model moral story as to the importance of filing adequate clinical notes.

[18]   *Craig* v *Glasgow Victoria and Leverndale Hospitals Board of Management* (22 March 1974, unreported) 1st Division. One has to note that this case is more than 40 years old—we seriously wonder if the open-ended nature of the consent would be acceptable today.

supposed branchial cyst but, on exploration, the 'cyst' was found to be a carotid body tumour. Removal of such a mass is a far more difficult procedure and the patient, in fact, sustained paralysis of half his body. The Inner House concluded that permission was not limited by seriousness and that the patient had consented to any operation to the end of removing the swelling: 'Consent must be read as covering any operation considered by the surgeon at the time to be in the patient's interest' (per Lord Robertson). Nonetheless, the three judges concerned could all foresee different conclusions if the operation lay outside the procedure contemplated by the patient. It is less certain that such a decision would be reached south of the border or, say, in the USA, where it has been considered for many years that: 'the so-called authority [of such consent forms] is so ambiguous as to be almost completely worthless'.[19]

Consenting for Mentally Incompetent Persons

4.14 The provision of treatment for a mentally incapacitated adult who cannot consent is possible subject to the terms of s 5 of the Mental Capacity Act 2005 or, in Scotland, by virtue of s 243 of the Mental Health (Care & Treatment) (Scotland) Act 2003 for urgent treatment. The principle that treatment may be provided so long as it is in the patient's 'best interests' drives the law in this area, and we discuss this further later in this chapter.[20] It is also possible for an adult, when capax, to confer lasting powers of attorney on a donee in England and Wales—or on a welfare attorney in Scotland—to take surrogate treatment decisions in the event of he or she losing the mental capacity to do so. Given that such an appointment has been made, the relevant attorney must be consulted before treatment is given. In the event of no such attorney having been appointed, the clear intention of both Acts is that those with a legitimate interest in the welfare of the patient must be consulted and their views taken into consideration.[21]

4.15 In all cases of patients, the conditions underpinning non-consensual treatment will be modified in an emergency—while reasonable steps to satisfy the spirit of the Acts must always be taken, the doctor who deliberately delayed essential treatment in order to comply with the letter would be misinterpreting the law and professional obligation.[22] Furthermore, the recently passed Social Action, Responsibility and Heroism (SARAH) Act 2015—which extends to England and Wales—requires courts to have regard to whether a person was 'acting for the benefit of society or any of its members' when determining the relevant standard of care in negligence cases. The SARAH Act will thus predispose courts to view any mistakes that occur during the provision of emergency assistance in a more forgiving light. Even so, we think it plausible that an emergency

---

[19] *Rogers v Lumbermen's Mutual Cas Co* 119 So 2d 649 (La, 1960). Guidance on obtaining consent is provided both by the General Medical Council and the Department of Health, see for example GMC, *Consent: Patients and Doctors Making Decisions Together* (2008); DH, *Reference Guide to Consent for Examination or Treatment* (2nd edn, 2009).

[20] Mental Capacity Act 2005, s 5. For ideological reasons, the Scottish Act does not say this in so many words—interventions must have the objective 'to benefit' the patient, see Chapter 13 for discussion.

[21] In the 2005 Act, doing so is an integral part of the essential 'best interests' test (s 4(7)). Note that, if there is no such person available, the health carer must consult with an independent mental capacity advocate (2005 Act, s 37).

[22] See n 14. Many states in the USA have enacted 'good Samaritan' legislation aimed at protecting the doctor giving emergency roadside treatment; however, these vary in terms of protection and may not provide liability protection during or after disasters. For Australia see H Gulam and J Devereaux, 'A brief primer on good Samaritan law for health care professionals' (2007) 31 Aust Health Rev 478.

doctor's actions would continue to be evaluated against the benchmark of 'good medical practice' and that the guidelines of the General Medical Council would remain relevant.

Consenting for Minors

4.16   It is a legal truism that proxy consents are truly valid only when the patient has given express authority to another person to give or withhold consent on his or her behalf[23] or when the law invests a person with such power. The most common example of the latter would be that of parent and child and we start from the premise that the common law has always accepted this principle. When proxy consent of this sort is available, the parent must use it reasonably and a third party may be justified in ignoring an unreasonable withholding of consent. Nevertheless, human rights law dictates that specific court authorisation should be sought when there is dispute between a child carer and his or her health care professional.[24]

4.17   Parental control of this nature is confined to the time when the child is incapable of decision-making on both status *and* mental capacity grounds and the position of the 'mature minor' to consent to treatment on his or her own behalf is discussed as a separate issue in some detail later;[25] here, we are concerned only with the immature child. A doctor taking steps to administer life-saving treatment to a minor against the wishes of its parents has traditionally been able to rely upon the common law as discussed earlier, arguing that a parental decision that jeopardises the well-being of their child is, *a priori*, unreasonable. However, a health carer's decision to go against parental refusal must be taken in good faith and in the best interests of a child and be prepared to justify this before a court. Human rights jurisprudence requires the principals to be given full opportunity, including time, to exercise their rights and a degree of latitude as addressed in the European Court of Human Rights (ECtHR) decision in *Glass v United Kingdom*.[26] Here the Court held it to be a breach of the child's human right to respect for his private life—and more specifically his right to bodily integrity—for the hospital trust not to seek court authority to proceed with treatment against his parents' wishes. The Government's argument that the treatment was an 'emergency' could have been valid in justifying proceeding quickly without court intervention (under Art 8(2)), but the facts of the case did not bear this out—there was time to refer the case to the High Court and this should have been done. Procedurally, then, disputes over the care of children should be referred to the courts in all but the most urgent of circumstances. Particular guidance appears in the form of Practice Notes.[27]

4.18   What, then, if such an emergency actually exists? This situation arose in the case of *OT*,[28] which concerned the management of a nine-month-old child with a severe mitochondrial genetic disease which led to severe brain disease. The treating staff were unanimous to the effect that death was inevitable and that continued intensive care was doing no more than escalate the child's suffering; the Trust, accordingly, sought authority to discontinue ventilation immediately. The parents, however, challenged the prognosis and sought continued treatment; in particular—as in *Glass*—they objected to the Trust bringing an

---

[23]   Mental Capacity Act 2005, s 9.
[24]   See *Glass v United Kingdom* (2004) 39 EHRR 341; (2004) 77 BMLR 120.
[25]   See para 4.59.   [26]   N 24.
[27]   Practice Direction (President's Direction on the Representation of Children in Family Proceedings) [2004] 1 WLR 1180; and Practice Direction (CAFCASS Practice Note on the Representation of Children in Family Proceedings) [2004] 1 FLR 1190.
[28]   *Re OT* [2009] EWHC 633 (Fam).

emergency application on the ground, inter alia, that this constituted a breach of their rights and those of their child under Art 8 ECHR insofar as they had been given insufficient time to present their case. The court, however, disagreed, holding that, while it was necessary so far as possible for parents to be in a position to address and respond to an application, emergency applications to the court were not in themselves in breach of a respondent's human rights; moreover, Parker J held that, once it was decided that life-sustaining treatment was no longer in the patient's best interests, its withdrawal constituted a breach neither of Art 2 or Art 8 of the Convention.[29] Weighing up the burdens of continuing treatment against the benefits to the child of ongoing treatment, it was appropriate to make the declarations as sought. In the event, the baby died just hours after the ruling was delivered thus, to an extent, justifying the emergency procedure.

4.19 *Glass* and *OT* combined make it clear that an obligation lies on the *health authority* to seek the advice of the courts in the face of serious disagreement as to the best interests of a child. The route sought will, to an extent, depend on administrative preference. Appeal may be made to the inherent jurisdiction of the court by way of s 100 of the Children Act 1989,[30] or the applicant may seek a specific issue order under s 8.[31] It is also technically possible for the medical advisers to initiate care proceedings.[32] The inherent jurisdiction of the court, which has effectively displaced wardship, and, particularly, its power to make a declaration on a 'best interests' basis, will probably be used in an emergency when speed may be of the essence—as in *OT*. In all other cases, it must be remembered that the courts are ultimate arbiters and they should be approached when impasse becomes inevitable.

4.20 These examples illustrate a number of things about consent. While it is a pivotal concept in the legitimation of medical treatment and patient management, it clearly does not work for all types of patient. Even if it is possible to find a person to provide consent on behalf of another, as demonstrated by these examples, this consent must be tempered by other considerations, most particularly the welfare interests of the principal party. As such, a discussion of consent must necessarily include consideration of the protective duties of the state, the courts, health care professionals and others towards patients. The absolute right of the competent adult patient to consent or refuse medical care is unimpeachable. But the contours of the law that prove most challenging are those that relate to patients who do not fall into this category.

The *Parens Patriae* Jurisdiction and its Aftermath

4.21 The courts have long had a responsibility over vulnerable persons. The *parens patriae*—literally, the 'parent of the country'—jurisdiction derives from the ancient powers of the English monarchy and, at one time, offered a route by which the courts could consent to treatment on behalf of those who were unable to do so.[33] It still survives in a number of countries which draw their legal systems from that of England. These include Australia,

---

[29] See, in confirmation, *An NHS Trust* v *D* [2000] 2 FLR 627, (2000) 55 BMLR 19; *R (on the application of Burke)* v *General Medical Council* [2006] QB 273; (2005) 85 BMLR 1, CA, discussed in Chapter 15. There is now abundant case law relating to negative treatment of both minors and incapable adults which refutes any claim that this course of action is a breach of the Human Rights Act 1998.

[30] E.g. *Re O (a minor) (medical treatment)* [1993] 2 FLR 149.

[31] E.g. *Camden London Borough Council* v *R (a minor) (blood transfusion)* [1993] 2 FLR 757, (1993) 91 LGR 623. This was regarded as the most efficient way.

[32] Children Act 1989, s 31; Children (Scotland) Act 1995, s 57.

[33] For analysis by one of us, see G T Laurie, 'Parens patriae in the medico-legal context: The vagaries of judicial activism' (1999) 3 Edin LR 95.

Canada, Ireland, and the USA, together with Scotland by virtue of its retention of its own legal system after the Act of Union 1707, and it has been used in a number of cases which we consider in this book.[34] The power in England and Wales was withdrawn following the passage of the Mental Health Act 1959 but any need for such a power receded as the 'best interests of the patient' jurisprudential test was developed[35] this, in turn, being founded, albeit derivatively, on the very influential case of Re F.[36] In this sterilisation case, reviewed in detail in Chapter 9, it was clearly stated that a doctor can provide—indeed, is professionally bound to provide—treatment for an intellectually disabled person in the absence of consent so long as that treatment is in the patient's best interests. A subsequent line of decisions has supported that view and, indeed, has extended its scope.[37] The *parens patriae* jurisdiction is, therefore, now of archaic interest only in England and Wales.[38] This is not to say, however, that the court does not have an inherent jurisdiction to protect vulnerable persons, as we discuss later.[39]

4.22 Historically, the best interests of the patient fell to be considered by their doctor, and this was confirmed by the courts through deference to the medical profession, as discussed in Chapter 5. However, there has been a recognisable groundswell of reaction to the *medical* best interests test among the lower UK courts in recent years. Thus, we have Munby J in *A v A Health Authority*[40] stating that an adult's best interests involve a welfare appraisal in the widest possible terms so as to include a range of ethical, social, moral, emotional, and welfare considerations. As authority, he cited Dame Elizabeth Butler-Sloss, President of the Family Court, in *Re A (medical treatment: male sterilisation)*[41] where, indeed, she stressed that, 'In my judgment, best interests encompasses medical, emotional and all other welfare issues'.[42] This was repeated and expanded by the President in *Simms v Simms and Another*,[43] where she was categoric that, 'In a case where an application is made to the court … it is the judge, not the doctor, who makes the decision that it is in the best interests of the patient

[34] See *In Re a Ward of Court* [1996] 2 IR 79; (1996) 50 BMLR 140 (Ireland); *Law Hospital NHS Trust v Lord Advocate* 1996 SLT 848; (1998) 39 BMLR 166 (Scotland); *Re GWW and CMW* (1997) 21 Fam LR 612 (Aus); *Secretary, Dept of Health and Community Services v JWB* (1992) 106 ALR 385 (Aus); *Minister for Health v AS* (2004) WASC 286 (Aus); *Re Eve* [1986] 2 SCR 388 (Canada). In Australia, the jurisdiction allows the courts to overrule competent minors, see P Trowse, 'Refusal of Medical Treatment – A Child's Prerogative' (2010) 10 Queensland U. Tech Law and Justice Journal (2010).

[35] Note the congruence of the 'best interests' test in *Re Y (adult patient) (transplant: bone marrow)* [1997] Fam 110; (1996) 35 BMLR 111 and the very similar *parens patriae* case *GWW*, n 34—both involved donation of bone marrow by an incapax.

[36] *Re F (mental patient: sterilisation)* [1990] 2 AC 1, sub nom *F v West Berkshire Health Authority* [1989] 2 All ER 545.

[37] This has been clarified yet further in the context of abortion and the mentally incompetent patient in *An NHS Trust v D* [2004] 1 FLR 1110, [2004] Fam Law 415. It has been held that 'necessity' here can include situations in which the patient's condition could deteriorate if she were not given protection: see *Re G (an adult) (mental capacity: court's jurisdiction)* [2004] EWHC 2222 (Fam).

[38] Moreover, any lacuna in the provision of health care to incapaces is now covered in the Mental Capacity Act 2005 and the Children Act 1989. See paras 4.24 et seq and Chapter 12.

[39] *DL v A Local Authority* [2012] EWCA Civ 253; [2012] 3 All ER 1064.

[40] [2002] 1 FCR 481, [2002] Fam 213 at para 43.   [41] [2000] 1 FCR 193.

[42] See also, *A Hospital NHS Trust v S and Others* [2003] Lloyd's Rep Med 137; (2003) 71 BMLR 188 at para 47: 'When considering the best interests of a patient, it is … the duty of the court to assess the advantages and disadvantages of the various treatments and management options, the viability of each such option and the likely effect each would have on the patient's best interests and, I would add, his enjoyment of life … any likely benefit of treatment has to be balanced and considered in the light of any additional suffering the treatment option would entail.'

[43] [2003] 2 WLR 1465; [2003] 1 ALL ER 669. For comment, see J Laing, 'Incompetent patients, experimental treatment and the "Bolam test" ' (2003) 11 Med L Rev 237.

that the operation be performed or the treatment be given'.[44] This is undoubtedly true, and while it is always a doctor's duty to act with the requisite standard of care by reference to his or her peers—whether this be in relation to treatment decisions or a judgement about a patient's best interests—that standard is in no way absolute. Thus, in *R (on the application of N) v Doctor M and Others*,[45] where there was a responsible body of medical opinion that a particular course of treatment was *not* in the patient's best interests, the Court of Appeal held that this was 'relevant to the question whether it is in the patient's best interests or medically necessary, but it is no more than that'.[46] It continued, 'The court has to decide in light of all of the evidence in the case whether the treatment should be permitted'.[47]

4.23 This ultimate responsibility for determining best interests not only rests with the courts[48] but it is, now, guided also by the terms of the Mental Capacity Act 2005.[49] While an application to the court is not necessary when issues of capacity and best interests are self-evident, this should be made if there is doubt and/or dispute between interested parties such as family members and health care professionals.[50] Best interests can only be assessed in light of full and accurate medical and non-medical evidence as to the patient's overall condition, and it is accepted that those interests will change as the patient's condition changes.[51] Moreover, it has been stated to be extremely important that the patient be given the opportunity to make representations before any final declaration on treatment is made.[52] This is true even in the context of an (emergency) interim declaration.[53] But doubt has arisen as to the correctness, indeed the legality, of procedures where the incapax person has had no opportunity to make his or her views known or where a declaration has been sought when incapacity has merely been raised as a possibility but not yet established. In *NHS Trust v T*, for example, Charles J sought to question the ongoing validity of judicial activism of recent years[54] as to the procedures to be followed in urgent or borderline cases.[55] In particular, he drew attention to the now well-known case of *Re B*[56] in which damages for assault, albeit nominal, were awarded against health care professionals (HCPs) for continuing treatment against the patient's (subsequently-declared-to-be-competent) wishes even though the HCPs in question acted entirely in good faith and according to what they truly believed to be the best interests of their patient. The clear current guidance—which

---

[44] Ibid, para 46. It should also be noted that the President pointed out that, unlike the instance cases, there was 'no need to investigate the meaning or the extent of the phrase "best interests" in *Re F*', ibid, para 45.

[45] [2003] 1 FLR 667; [2003] 1 FCR 124.   [46] Ibid, para 29.

[47] [2003] 1 FLR 667, citing with approval the ECtHR case *Herczegalvy v Austria* (1992) 15 EHRR 437; (1992) 18 BMLR 48.

[48] For a good example of the step-by-step approach see *R (on the application of PS) v G (Responsible Medical Officer)* [2003] EWHC 2335; [2004] MHLR 1.

[49] See Chapters 12 and 13.

[50] *An NHS Trust v D* [2004] 1 FLR 1110 (termination of pregnancy involving a severely schizophrenic woman was declared to be in her best interests). This is now also a matter of human rights law, see *Glass*, para 4.17.

[51] *A Hospital NHS Trust v S* (2003) 71 BMLR 188 (where the court sanctioned leaving open various medical avenues of treatment depending on how the patient progressed and would not rule out the possibility of kidney transplant on non-medical grounds such as the staff's inability to cope with the patient's behavioural problems related to alternative treatment).

[52] *NHS Trust v T (adult patient: refusal of medical treatment)* [2005] 1 All ER 387.

[53] Ibid; recalling nonetheless, that the terms of a declaration are valid only so long as the patient remains in an incapacitated state and absent any other fundamental change of circumstances.

[54] The guidance in question includes that of the Court of Appeal in *St George's Healthcare NHS Trust v S* [1998] 3 WLR 936 and that in *Re B (adult: refusal of medical treatment)* [2002] 2 All ER 449.

[55] *NHS Trust v T (adult patient: refusal of medical treatment)* [2005] 1 All ER 387 at paras 72–5.

[56] *Re B (adult: refusal of medical treatment)* [2002] 2 All ER 449; (2002) 65 BMLR 149 discussed at para 4.42.

stated that: 'while the question of capacity is being resolved the patient must ... be cared for in accordance with the judgment of the doctors as to the patient's best interests'[57]— might, he thought, no longer protect HCPs from future legal action. As a result, Charles J called for reconsideration of the guidance and of the law's general approach to the problem. We can, therefore, look briefly at the concurrently developing statute law to see how this helps HCPs in their management of the incapacitated adult.

Statutory Reforms

4.24 Reforming measures had been on the horizon in England and Wales since the Law Commission's paper on Mental Incapacity in 1995.[58] Some ten years on, the Mental Capacity Act 2005 scraped through without adequate debate on the dissolution of Parliament despite previous extensive consultation and vacillation over its proposals.[59] The major thrust of the Act is probably aimed at those who have lost capacity through the ageing process and we return to it in Chapter 12. It is clearly relevant, however, to any incompetent who needs treatment for physical disease and some consideration of its terms is, therefore, essential at this point. The Act reflects its Scottish counterpart— the Adults with Incapacity (Scotland) Act 2000—in its general breadth and, importantly, in providing for the appointment of substitute decision-makers (*donees* with a lasting power of attorney)—for which, see para 4.28. There are a number of interesting variations between the two Acts which we will note briefly in para 4.30. For the moment, however, we will concentrate on the Mental Capacity Act, which applies in England and Wales.

4.25 The most important section of the Act for present purposes lies in Part I, which lays out a checklist of issues to be considered in determining best interests, which in turn must be read against a set of guiding principles which underpin the entire instrument. The principles impose, first and foremost, a presumption of capacity and an obligation to assist individuals to make their own decisions as far as it is practicable to do so.[60] The irrational or thought-to-be-unwise decisions of *competent* persons must be respected, reflecting the common law position outlined later. Where incompetence has been established, decisions taken for the person must be in their best interests and in the least restrictive manner, viz, the impact on their rights, freedoms, and interests. Section 4 fleshes out the meaning of best interests. This is defined as an objective test—not one based in substituted judgement—and it requires that *all* factors listed in the clause be weighed in the decision-making process with none having any more importance than any other. Moreover, the incapacitated person should be an integral part of that process so far as it is possible. Consideration should also be given to the likelihood of the person recovering capacity sufficiently to be able to make the decision in the reasonably foreseeable future. Other factors to be considered include: the person's past and present wishes and feelings, their beliefs and values to the extent they might influence their decisions if they had capacity.[61] The

---

[57] *Re B (adult: refusal of medical treatment)* [2002] 2 All ER 449; (2002) 65 BMLR 149, para 100, point (iv).

[58] Law Commission Mental Incapacity (No 231, 1995). For comment at the time, see P Alldridge, 'Consent to medical and surgical treatment—The Law Commission's recommendations' (1996) 4 Med L Rev 129 and P Wilson, 'The Law Commission's Report on mental incapacity: Medically vulnerable adults or politically vulnerable law?' (1996) 4 Med L Rev 227. For comment, M Donnelly, 'Determining best interests under the Mental Capacity Act 2005' (2011) 19(2) Med L Rev 304 and L Hagger, 'The Mental Capacity Act 2005 and mature minors: A missed opportunity?' (2011) 33(2) J Soc Wel & Fam L 157.

[59] See, e.g., Lord Chancellor's Department, *Who Decides? Making Decisions on Behalf of Mentally Incapacitated Adults* (Cm 3803, 1997) and the Government's response *Making Decisions* (Cm 4465, 1999).

[60] Mental Capacity Act 2005, s 1.

[61] We would comment in passing that this comes very close to a substituted judgment approach, yet this approach is expressly eschewed in the Explanatory Notes to the Act, para 28.

views of other parties interested in the incompetent's welfare—to include anyone named by the incapax, carers, any donee of a lasting power of attorney, and any court-appointed deputy—must also be taken into account.

4.26 The obligation, then, is to consult widely and to gather, and use, as much relevant information as possible. Notwithstanding the importance attached to the test, 'best interests' is never defined in the Act—arguably because of the near impossibility of doing so; the task of acting within their limits thus remains one which a decision-maker must justify in each circumstance. The list of circumstances that *must* be considered is the minimum and there is no reason why they should not be extended. Similarly, there is no explicit guidance within the Act itself on *how* balancing of factors should be done.[62] In the meantime, the dicta of Thorpe LJ in *Re A*:

> it seems to me that the first instance judge with the responsibility to make an evaluation of the best interests of a claimant lacking capacity should draw up a balance sheet. The first entry should be of any factor or factors of actual benefit. ... Then on the other sheet the judge should write any counterbalancing dis-benefits to the applicant. ... Then the judge should enter on each sheet the potential gains and losses in each instance making some estimate of the extent of the possibility that the gain or loss might accrue. At the end of that exercise the judge should be better placed to strike a balance between the sum of the certain and possible gains against the sum of the certain and possible losses. Obviously, only if the account is in relatively significant credit will the judge conclude that the application is likely to advance the best interests of the claimant must serve as the best guide for the courts.[63]

4.27 Section 4(8) and (9) attempts to address the concern of Charles J about the interim grey phase where an individual's capacity may be in doubt and yet action is required to protect their interests. These provide, in essence, that it will be lawful to purport to act in a person's best interests when: (i) the actor reasonably believes that the person lacks capacity, and (ii) he reasonably believes that what he does or decides is in the best interests of the person concerned. This, of course, does not absolve such a person of the obligation to comply with the other requirements of the section regarding the factors to be weighed in the balance when deciding what those best interests are.

4.28 Section 9 provides for the appointment of Lasting Power of Attorney,[64] which includes the authority to consent to or refuse medical treatment on behalf of the incapacitated person, subject to two important riders: (i) decisions are subordinated to valid advance directives[65] created by the person in accordance with ss 24–6 of the Act, and (ii) the decision-making power in respect of the administration or withdrawal of life-sustaining care must be expressly provided for in the appointing instrument.[66] The

---

[62] At best, s 6 makes it clear that when restraint is to be used the decision must include an assessment that the action is 'necessary in order to prevent harm' and that it is a 'proportionate response' to the likelihood and seriousness of harm.

[63] *Re A (medical treatment: male sterilisation)* [2000] 1 FLR at 555. Applied in *An NHS Trust v A* [2013] EWHC 2442 (COP) (paras 50–4).

[64] See Adults with Incapacity (Scotland) Act 2000, s 16 for the appointment and duties of the equivalent welfare attorney in Scotland.

[65] The advance directive—or curiously termed 'living will'—is discussed further at para 4.44 et seq.

[66] It should also be noted that certain 'Excluded Decisions' fall outside the authority of any decision-maker under the Act, see Mental Capacity Act, ss 27 and 28. Of relevance in the present context are: (i) any consent under the Human Fertilisation and Embryology Act 1990, and (ii) authority or consent to treat someone for mental disorder (which we discuss in Chapter 13). Furthermore, specific provisions apply in the context of research and the incapacitated person by virtue of ss 30–3 of the Act, on which we say more in Chapter 19.

Court of Protection[67] was created with power to declare acts, proposed acts, or omissions (e.g., a failure to treat) as lawful in respect of a patient's best interests; it is assisted by the Office of the Public Guardian.[68] Many of the declaratory powers and duties previously undertaken by the High Court now come within the province of the new Court of Protection.[69] Notwithstanding, it has been confirmed that the 2005 Act does not usurp the inherent jurisdiction of the court. Thus, in *A Local Authority* v *DL*,[70] the Court of Appeal made it clear that the jurisdiction remains to protect vulnerable persons whose circumstances fall outside the Act. Here the welfare of elderly parents was a concern but the individuals retained mental capacity; their son's influence was, however, tantamount to coercion and triggered the inherent jurisdiction of the court to intervene. The 2005 Act is expressly limited to deal with persons who lack mental capacity, not all vulnerable persons.

4.29   The Mental Capacity Act 2005 has since been amended by the Mental Health Act 2007 (s 50), which introduces 'deprivation of liberty safeguards' by way of ss 4A and 4B of the 2005 Act. These safeguards were established in response to the ECtHR judgment in *HL* v *United Kingdom*.[71] This aspect of mental capacity is, however, concerned with consent only in respect of general care and we return to the case and its sequelae in Chapter 13— this despite the fact that the safeguards apply to persons who are not detained under the Mental Health Act.[72] The complex relationship between the Mental Health Acts, the Mental Capacity Act as amended by the 2007 Act, and the common law in respect of treatment of the incapax requires considerable development and analysis which we cannot attempt in a generalist book such as this.[73]

---

[67] Mental Capacity Act, Part 2, having the same powers as the High Court (s 47(1)).

[68] Mental Capacity Act, ss 57 and 58.

[69] For a very helpful analysis of the relationship between the common law as has developed and the new statute, see G Williams, 'The declaratory judgement: Old and new law in "medical" cases' (2007) 8 Med Law Internat 277.

[70] [2012] EWCA Civ 253; [2013] Fam. 1. For analysis see A Ruck Keene, 'The inherent jurisdiction: Where are we now?' (2013) 3 Eld L J 88; D Lock, 'Decision-making, mental capacity and undue influence: Action by public bodies to explore the grey areas between capacity and incapacity' (2015) 20 J R 42.

[71] (2005) 40 EHRR 32; (the 'Bournewood decision'). For commentary, see K Keywood, 'Detaining mentally disordered patients lacking capacity: The arbitrariness of informal detention and the common law doctrine of necessity' (2005) 13 Med L Rev 108. Also, see the series of articles beginning with S Jackson, 'The deprivation of liberty safeguard: Part 1: Has the Mental Capacity Act 2005 bridged "the Bournewood gap"?' (2012) 42(Mar) Fam Law 319. Also see *Cheshire West and Chester Council* v *P* [2014] UKSC 19; J Stavert, 'Deprivation of liberty and persons with incapacity: The Cheshire West ruling' (2015) 19 Edin L R 129.

[72] The safeguards 'are intended to prevent unlawful detention of people who lack capacity to consent to arrangements for their care or treatment and who need to be deprived of their liberty, in their own best interests and to prevent harm, in either hospitals or care homes' (Explanatory Memorandum to the Mental Capacity (Deprivation of Liberty: Standards Authorisations, Assessments and Ordinary Residence) Regulations 2008 (SI 2008/1858), para 7.1). Pursuant to this section, no person may deprive another person of his or her liberty, except in certain circumstances. These are: (i) if depriving someone of their liberty is giving effect to a relevant decision of the court, defined as 'a decision of the court made by an order under section 16(2)(a) in relation to a matter concerning the person's welfare'; or (ii) if the deprivation is authorised by Sch A1 (hospital and care home residents: deprivation of liberty). Guidance on the deprivation of liberty safeguards is available at: https://www.gov.uk/government/collections/dh-mental-capacity-act-2005-deprivation-of-liberty-safeguards

[73] See *AM* v *South London & Maudsley NHS Foundation Trust* [2013] UKUT 365 (AAC). For discussion see 'Detention under the Mental Health Act 1983: Relationship with the Mental Capacity Act 2005' (2014) 87 R M H L 2. Also see generally G Richardson, 'Mental capacity at the margins: The interface between two Acts' (2010) 18 Med Law Rev 56.

4.30 We have noted earlier that the English Act of 2005 and the Adults with Incapacity (Scotland) Act 2000 differ in some respects that merit comment and, in our view, the key point of departure lies in the fact that, whereas the 2005 Act is committed to the patient's 'best interests' as the benchmark justifying non-consensual medical treatment, the Scottish Ministers shied away from the paternalistic overtones of that test. Rather, the Scottish Law Commission preferred to list a number of factors to be considered before treating an incapable adult and, possibly as a result, the relevant law in Scotland is strongly orientated towards trust in the health care professionals. The 2000 Act grants a 'general authority to treat' for any practitioner primarily responsible for a patient who—in the practitioner's certified opinion—is incapable in relation to a treatment decision. This is an authority to do all that is reasonable in the circumstances 'to safeguard or promote the physical or mental health of the adult'.[74] And, while the Act makes provision for the appointment of proxy decision-makers who should be consulted prior to any action where it is practicable to do so, these persons only have a power to *consent* on behalf of the incapable adult—that is, to accede to medical opinion; there is no correlative power to refuse. If a dispute arises, a second medical officer must be appointed from a list held by the Mental Welfare Commission and his or her agreement with the initial medical opinion provides the legal authority to proceed. The only further action then open to the proxy is to appeal to the Court of Session. The primary carer can also do so in cases where the second medical officer agrees with the proxy.[75] Codes of practice have been issued both for proxy decision-makers[76] and for those authorised to carry out treatment or research under the Act.[77] Deprivation of liberty is also considered, as happens south of the border.[78]

4.31 Reform is currently being discussed in Scotland regarding the Adults with Incapacity (Scotland) Act 2000. In 2014, the Scottish Law Commission released a report[79] advocating amendments to the Scottish Act to ensure human rights compliance in light of the ECtHR decision in *HL* v *United Kingdom* (the *Bournewood* case).[80] Specific recommendations include establishing a legal process to authorise measures preventing an adult from going out of a hospital and a more detailed legal process for the scrutiny of significant restriction of liberty of an adult in a care home or other placement in the community. It is also suggested that the Act should also be amended to provide for a right to apply to the sheriff court for release of an adult who may lack capacity from unlawful detention in certain care settings. There has been some case law that appears to demonstrate the need for reform.[81]

---

[74] 2000 Act, s 47(1) and (2). Note, however, certain treatments such as neurosurgery, sterilisation, and surgical implantation of hormones to reduce sex drive must first receive the approval of the Court of Session, while others such as electro-convulsive therapy, abortion, drugs to reduce sex drive, or other procedures likely to result in sterilisation, must be cleared by the Mental Welfare Commission, see the Adults with Incapacity (Specified Medical Treatments) (Scotland) Regulations 2002 (SSI 2002/275).

[75] We have considered the effect of the statutory requirements elsewhere: G T Laurie and J K Mason, 'Negative treatment of vulnerable patients: Euthanasia by any other name?' [2000] Jurid Rev 159.

[76] Code of Practice for Continuing and Welfare Attorneys under the Adults with Incapacity (Scotland) Act 2000, (March 2011) and Code of Practice for Persons Authorised under Intervention Orders and Guardians under the Adults with Incapacity (Scotland) Act 2000 (March 2011).

[77] Code of Practice for Persons Authorised to Carry Out Treatment or Research Under Part Five of the Act, (May 2010).

[78] A Ward, 'Adults with Incapacity: Freedom and liberty, rights and status – Parts 1 and 2' (2011) 5 SLT 21; (2011) 6 SLT 27.

[79] Scottish Law Commission, *Report on Adults with Incapacity* (2014).   [80] N 71.

[81] *G* v *West Lothian Council* 2014 GWD 40-730. For discussion, see A Eccles, '*G* v *West Lothian Council*, Edinburgh Sheriff Court' (2015) 8 SLT 35.

4.32 It is important to note that the common law still governs the position in emergencies and negative treatment decisions; that is, those relating to the withholding or withdrawal of treatment. This, then, is a convenient point at which to consider the development of the common law approach to refusal of treatment by adults—particularly in the light of the now near sacrosanct regard for the autonomy of the capable adult.[82]

REFUSAL OF TREATMENT BY ADULTS

4.33 *Re T*[83] can be regarded as the index case concerned with refusal of treatment, and was, coincidentally, the first adult Jehovah's Witness case to have come before a British court.[84] A pregnant woman was involved in a car accident and, after speaking with her mother, signed a form of refusal of blood transfusion. Following a caesarian section and the delivery of a stillborn baby, her condition deteriorated and a court order was obtained legalising blood transfusion on the ground that it was manifestly in her best interests; the declaration was upheld by the Court of Appeal. The fundamental decision was to the effect that an adult patient who suffers from no mental incapacity has an absolute right to consent to medical treatment, to refuse it or to choose an alternative treatment[85]—'it exists notwithstanding that the reasons for making the choice are rational, irrational, unknown or even non-existent'.[86] How, then, did the court reach its decision to support the provision of apparently involuntary treatment?

4.34 First, of course, it had to transform involuntary treatment into non-voluntary treatment. This it did by finding that T's mental state had deteriorated to such an extent that she could not make a valid choice as between death and transfusion—and if there was doubt as to how the patient was exercising her right of self-determination, that doubt should be resolved in favour of the preservation of life.[87] But an additional factor of great importance to the doctors was added when it was stated that the effects of outside influence on a patient's refusal have to be taken into consideration; in short, the question of whether the patient means what he or she says has to be posed—and whether the decision was reached independently after counselling and persuasion or whether the patient's will was overborne is a matter to be decided by the doctors. At first glance, this looks suspiciously like opening the door to involuntary treatment—that is, until one comes to Staughton LJ, who said:

> I cannot find authority that the decision of a doctor as to the existence or refusal of consent is sufficient protection, if the law subsequently decides otherwise. So the

---

[82] For a searching appraisal, see S A M McLean, *Consent, Autonomy and the Law* (2010).

[83] *Re T (adult) (refusal of medical treatment)* [1992] 4 All ER 649; (1992) 9 BMLR 46, CA. Not to be confused with the quite exceptional case of *NHS Trust v T (adult patient: refusal of medical treatment)* [2005] 1 All ER 387 where transfusion was refused because the patient thought her own blood was contaminating the transfused blood.

[84] The strength of recognition of the faith was recently confirmed by the ECtHR in *Jehovah's Witnesses of Moscow v Russia* (2011) 53 EHRR 4.

[85] The only possible qualification mentioned by Lord Donaldson—where the choice might lead to the death of a viable fetus—is discussed at para 4.50 et seq.

[86] [1992] 4 All ER 649 at 653; (1992) 9 BMLR 46 at 50, per Lord Donaldson.

[87] For the challenges and disciplinary difficulties of assessing capacity see, P L Schneider and K A Bramstedt, 'When psychiatry and bioethics disagree about patient decision making capacity (DMC)' (2006) 32 J Med Ethics 90, and for the relevance of religious belief, see A M Martin, 'Tales publicly allowed: Competence, capacity and religious belief' (2007) 37 Hastings Cent Rep 33.

medical profession ... must bear the responsibility unless it is possible to obtain a decision from the courts.[88]

4.35 Since this will be possible only rarely in an emergency, *Re T* seems to place a well-nigh intolerable burden on the doctors, not all of whom in the middle of the night will be of consultant status. What, for example, is the young house officer to make of Lord Donaldson:

> what the doctors *cannot* do is to conclude that, if the patient still had the necessary capacity in the changed situation [he being now unable to communicate], he would have reversed his decision ... What they *can* do is to consider whether at the time the decision was made it was intended by the patient to apply in the changed situation.[89]

One of us, at least, is grateful that he is no longer likely to be faced with an uncompleted suicide attempt in a busy casualty department![90] Even the law is undecided on the definition of undue influence[91] and, again, neither Lord Donaldson[92] nor Butler-Sloss LJ[93] made it any easier by including parents and religious advisers among those who might, as a result of their relationship, lend themselves more readily than others to overbearing the patient's will. Now, however, the Mental Capacity Act Code of Practice recognises this possibility; by the same token, the Code counsels that these parties should not be cut out of the capacity assessment or decision-making processes simply by virtue of the fact that they might have influence or even conflicting interests. Their personal views and wishes should not, however, influence the assessment itself.[94] To assist in determining the views and wishes of the patient it is now possible, and often desirable, to appoint an Independent Mental Capacity Advocate.[95]

4.36 The authority of *Re T* was applied shortly afterwards in the very interesting conditions of the case of *Re C*.[96] Despite being a decision at first instance only, the case is, nevertheless, extremely important in that it was the first in which a test for mental capacity was formulated and which is now reflected in the Mental Capacity Act 2005. The case concerned a 68-year-old patient suffering from paranoid schizophrenia who had developed gangrene in a foot while serving a term of imprisonment in Broadmoor. On removal of the patient to a general hospital, a consultant prognosed that he had

---

[88] [1992] 4 All ER 649 at 670; (1992) 9 BMLR 46 at 68. For an excellent analysis of undue influence, see *Centre for Reproductive Medicine* v *U* (2002) 65 BMLR 92; [2002] Lloyd's Rep Med 93; supported on appeal: [2002] EWCA Civ 565, and applied in *Evans* v *Amicus Healthcare Ltd and Others* [2005] Fam 1; [2004] 3 All ER 1025.

[89] [1992] 4 All ER 649 at 662; (1992) 9 BMLR 46 at 60.

[90] See S Davies, 'Suicidal Behaviour—What to do about treatment refusal at 3am' (2010) 341 BMJ c5477; A David, M Hotopf, P Moran, G Owen, G Szmekler, and G Richardson, 'Mentally disordered or lacking capacity? Lessons for management of serious deliberate self harm' (2010) 341 BMJ c4489; G Richardson, 'Mental capacity in the shadow of suicide: What can the law do?' (2013) 9 Int J Law Context 87; D Hubbeling, 'Decision-making capacity should not be decisive in emergencies' (2014) 17 Med Health Care and Philos 229.

[91] The discussion in *Re T* is inconclusive; in the context of financial matters, see *Royal Bank of Scotland* v *Etridge* [2002] 2 AC 773. In the context of contraception, see *A Local Authority* v *A and Another (capacity: contraception)* [2011] 3 All ER 706.

[92] [1992] 4 All ER 649 at 664; (1992) 9 BMLR 46 at 62.

[93] [1992] 4 All ER 649 at 667–8; (1992) 9 BMLR 46 at 65–6.

[94] Department for Constitutional Affairs, Mental Capacity Act 2005: Code of Practice (2007), para 4.49.

[95] Ibid, ch 10.

[96] *Re C (adult: refusal of medical treatment)* [1994] 1 All ER 819; (1993) 15 BMLR 77.

only a 15 per cent chance of survival if the gangrenous limb was not amputated below the knee.[97] The patient, however, refused the operation, saying that he preferred to die with two feet than to live with one. The hospital questioned C's capacity to exercise his autonomy in this way and an application for an injunction restraining the hospital from carrying out the operation without his express written consent was lodged with the court on C's behalf.

4.37 Thorpe J held that C was entitled to refuse the treatment even if this meant his death. Quoting with approval the dicta of Lord Donaldson in Re T, he stated that, prima facie, every adult has the right and capacity to accept or refuse medical treatment. He acknowledged that this might be rebutted by evidence of incapacity but this onus must be discharged by those seeking to override the patient's choice. When capacity is challenged, as in this case, its sufficiency is to be determined by the answer to the question: has the capacity of the patient been so reduced (by his chronic mental illness) that he did not sufficiently understand the nature, purpose, and effects of the proffered medical treatment? This depends on whether the patient has been able to comprehend and retain information, has believed it, and has weighed it in the balance with other considerations when making his or her choice. As Thorpe J said:

> Applying that test to my findings on the evidence, I am completely satisfied that the presumption that C has the right to self-determination has not been displaced. Although his general capacity is impaired by schizophrenia, it has not been established that he does not sufficiently understand the nature, purpose and effects of the treatment he refuses. Indeed, I am satisfied that he has understood and retained the relevant treatment information, that in his own way he believes it, and that in the same fashion he has arrived at a clear choice.[98]

4.38 Several important points arise from this judgment. First, it reaffirms the commitment of the law to the principle of respect for patient autonomy. There is a prima facie presumption of its existence and value which can only be overridden in established circumstances.[99] Furthermore, the particular facts of the case show that incapacity in one or several areas of one's life does not preclude autonomous behaviour in others, nor does it remove the presumption of competence to refuse. Indeed, the injunction obtained by the plaintiff extended not only to the particular operation contemplated by the hospital but to *all* future attempts to interfere with his bodily integrity without his express written

---

[97] This was, however, averted by intervention short of amputation: [1994] 1 All ER 819 at 821; (1993) 15 BMLR 77 at 78–9.

[98] [1994] 1 ALL ER 819 at 824; (1993) 15 BMLR 77 at 82. A similar situation, but one involving a self-inflicted injury, is found in *Re W (adult: refusal of medical treatment)* [2002] EWHC 901, [2002] MHLR 411. Butler-Sloss P held that a psychopathic prisoner with mental capacity on *Re C* terms could refuse treatment even though it might lead to his death. But see: *Trust A v H (an adult patient)* [2006] EWHC 1230 (Fam); [2006] 2 FLR 958, in which the court granted the applicant Trust's declarations to allow them to perform a hysterectomy on a patient who had been detained under the Mental Health Act 1983, s 3, and who suffered from schizophrenia and had delusional beliefs. Although the court confirmed that no medical treatment could be given without the consent of an adult patient who was competent to make decisions, it was clear that in this case the patient did not appreciate the seriousness of her condition and the sense of threat to life that it presented if unalleviated. For a recent case with remarkably similar facts to *Re C*—and the same legal outcome—see *Heart of England NHS Foundation Trust v JB* [2014] EWHC 342 (COP); (2014) 137 BMLR 232.

[99] For an alternative perspective on the relationship between autonomy and best interests, see A Buchanan, 'Mental capacity, legal competence and consent to treatment' (2004) 97 J Roy Soc Med 415.

consent. The significance of this is profound. In effect, it represents the earliest judicial recognition of the validity of advance refusals of treatment[100] which has now been put on a statutory footing under the Mental Capacity Act 2005.[101]

4.39 The judgment in *Re C*, however, suffers from the wideness of its terms and the opportunities for subjective interpretation that it allows. A patient's competence can be successfully challenged if it can be shown that he does not comprehend or absorb information to the extent that he understands it or if he is thought not to believe the information or if he cannot balance this information against other considerations when making his choice. In this way, hurdles are placed in the path of those seeking to exercise their autonomy but, at the same time, it remains uncertain how high they must jump in order to clear these hurdles. For example, the requirement that the patient must actually comprehend the information is not easy to assess—it can depend as much on the amount of information which is given to the patient and the manner in which it is provided as on the capacity of the patient to understand. Yet, the test is not '*Can* the patient understand?' but, rather, '*Does* the patient understand?' This imposes an obligation on medical staff to ensure that actual understanding is reached and this, in itself, is paradoxical given that the treating staff might not want the patient to understand if they disagree with the nature of his or her decision—as in *Re C*. Many of these weaknesses can also be levelled against the Mental Capacity Act which virtually reproduces the common law test.[102]

4.40 Nor is it exactly clear *what* the patient must understand in light of the *Re C* ruling. The decision talks of the 'nature, purpose and effects' of the treatment. This is potentially very broad and can encompass elements ranging from the general aim of the procedure to the risks and the consequences of refusal and beyond. In *A Local Authority* v *A and another*,[103] which involved dispute over consent to contraception, it was held that it had to be shown that the woman was able to understand and weigh up the immediate medical issues surrounding contraceptive treatment including: (1) reasons for contraceptive use; (2) types of contraceptive available and how each is used; (3) advantages and disadvantages of each type; (4) possible side effects and how they can be dealt with; and (5) generally accepted effectiveness of each. The test did not extend to the need to understand the wider implications of bringing up a child.

4.41 Arguably, as Grubb has pointed out, the category of 'autonomous persons' is reduced to only the most 'comprehending' individuals if excessive amounts of information are required to be disclosed and understood.[104] Chapter 4 of the Mental Capacity Act

---

[100] Reaffirmed in *Re AK (medical treatment: consent)* [2001] 1 FLR 129, (2001) 58 BMLR 151.

[101] Mental Capacity Act 2005, s 1(2) (presumption of capacity), and ss 24–6 (advance decisions).

[102] The Mental Capacity Act defines incapacity in s 2 thus: 'a person lacks capacity in relation to a matter if at the material time he is unable to make a decision for himself in relation to the matter because of an impairment of, or a disturbance in the functioning of, the mind or brain'. Section 3 continues that: 'a person is unable to make a decision for himself if he is unable—(a) to understand the information relevant to the decision, (b) to retain that information, (c) to use or weigh that information as part of the process of making the decision, or (d) to communicate his decision (whether by talking, using sign language or any other means)'. A broadly similar functional definition is contained in the Adults with Incapacity (Scotland) Act 2000, s 1(6).

[103] N 91, at para 64. Applied in *A Local Authority* v *K* [2013] EWHC 242 (COP); [2014] 1 FCR 209. Also see *An NHS Trust* v *DE* [2013] EWHC 2562 (Fam); [2013] 3 FCR 343, which concerned a male patient who was found to lack capacity to consent to or refuse a vasectomy. Sterilisation was held to be in his best interests.

[104] See A Grubb, 'Commentary' (1994) 2 Med L Rev 92 at 95.

Code of Practice explores these issues in much greater depth. It offers carers and HCPs worked examples of what it means 'to understand'. Anyone assessing capacity must have a reasonable belief that the person in their care lacks capacity to make relevant decisions about their care or treatment. This means that the carer must have taken reasonable steps to establish the presence or otherwise of capacity with respect to the particular decision that is to be taken and that this is assessed at an appropriate time. It goes without saying that it must also be established that the decision is in the person's best interests.[105]

4.42 The general trend of the common law was ultimately confirmed in *Re B (adult: refusal of medical treatment).*[106] Ms B was a 43-year-old patient who was paralysed from the neck down and sustained only by means of a ventilator. Ms B refused this intervention shortly after it was introduced but she was adjudged incompetent to do so by two psychiatrists in April 2001. She was, however, declared competent by an independent clinician in August of that year and, thereafter, the hospital treated her as such. Nevertheless, her attending physicians refused to remove the ventilator, advocating instead that their patient attend a rehabilitation unit which offered a slim chance of improvement in her condition. Ms B rejected this course of action and repeated her refusal on several occasions. Ultimately, the President of the Family Division attended Ms B's bedside to hear her story. In a poignant ruling, Butler-Sloss P reiterated the fundamental principles that now govern this area, namely, that a competent patient has an absolute right to refuse treatment irrespective of the consequences of her decision, and she issued very clear guidance to health care professionals as to their responsibilities in such cases. These include keeping the patient as involved in the decision-making process as possible, moving to resolve any dispute as promptly as practicable and finding other clinicians to undertake the course of action if the primary carers feel unable to do so.[107] Perhaps most striking of all, notional damages of £100 were awarded in recognition of the technical assault that the health carers had committed by continuing to treat Ms B against her wishes.[108]

4.43 Straightforward as this may seem, these cases have to be read in conjunction with others in which the autonomy of the patient has been overridden and their right to choose for themselves has been denied. We have already drawn attention to the vagueness of the common law in this respect and there is little doubt that much of the uncertainty is perpetuated in statute.[109] This is, then, a suitable place to consider the implications of advance decision-making subsequent to 2007 when the 2005 Act came into force.

---

[105] Mental Capacity Act 2005, s 5(1) and Code of Practice, n 94, and Chapter 5. But note the distinctions between the English and Scottish Acts discussed in para 4.30.

[106] Sub nom *B v NHS Hospital Trust* [2002] 2 All ER 449; (2002) 65 BMLR 149. We return to this case in Chapter 18.

[107] Although note now the reservations of Charles J in *NHS Trust v T*, para 4.23.

[108] For general comment, see Special Clinical Ethics Symposium, 'The case of Ms B' (2002) 28 J Med Ethics 232.

[109] For an assessment of the approach of the 2005 Act to assessing capacity, see M Donnelly, 'Capacity assessment under the Mental Capacity Act 2005: Delivering on the functional approach?' (2009) 29 LS 464; for insights into its application on the ground see A Murrell and L McCalla, 'Assessing decision-making capacity: The interpretation and implementation of the Mental Capacity Act 2005 amongst social care professionals' (2015) Practice DOI: 10.1080/09503153.2015.1074667

ADVANCE DECISIONS AS TO REFUSAL OF TREATMENT

4.44 The legal concept of the advance directive[110] was undefined until the passing of the Mental Capacity Act 2005. Section 24 of that Act now states:

(1) "Advance decision" means a decision made by a person after he has reached 18 and when he has capacity to do so, that if—

(a) at a later time and in such circumstances as he may specify, a specified treatment is proposed to be carried out or continued by a person providing health care for him, and

(b) at that time he lacks capacity to consent to the carrying out or continuation of the treatment,

the specified treatment is not to be carried out or continued.

The Act does not say how the decision is to be expressed. However, prior to the passing of the Act, it was held in *HE* v *A Hospital NHS Trust*[111] that it is not necessary for an advance decision to be in writing in order for it to be valid, while the Act itself now states that revocation or alteration of any such decision can occur other than by written means. This, however, is subject to refusal not being likely to result in death—if that be the case, the directive must be in writing and witnessed.[112]

4.45 An advance decision is invalid if the patient has, subsequently, created a lasting power of attorney in favour of someone else to give or refuse consent to the specified treatment. More controversially, it is invalid if the patient has 'done anything' that is clearly inconsistent with the advance decision remaining his fixed decision.[113] Moreover, an advance decision is not applicable if the treatment is not that *specified* in the decision nor if there are reasonable grounds for believing that 'circumstances exist' which the patient did not anticipate at the time the decision was made. There are, thus, a number of uncertainties that are sufficient to allow the medical attendants to ignore the advance decision or, indeed, to act to the contrary.

4.46 This is important because, while some HCPs may welcome the opportunity to avoid making difficult *professional* decisions in a complex ethical ambience, others will see the advance decision as an interference with their clinical consciences and, in particular, with the medico-legal presumption as to the priority afforded to the preservation of life.[114] The temptation to circumvent the decision may, therefore, be strong.

4.47 Recent case law suggests that this preference towards sanctity of life will be strongly supported by the courts. In *M (Adult Patient) (Minimally Conscious State: Withdrawal of Treatment)*,[115] it was held not to be in a minimally conscious patient's best interests to

---

[110] The words 'advance directive' were generally applied in respect of the common law; the 2005 Act, however, introduces the term 'advance decision'. There is, of course, no reason why one should not make an advance decision to accept treatment in any circumstances; it would not, however, be binding on the medical attendants—see, now, *R (on the application of Burke)* v *General Medical Council* [2006] QB 273; (2005) 85 BMLR 1, CA.

[111] [2003] 2 FLR 408; [2003] Fam Law 733.   [112] Mental Capacity Act 2005, s 25(5) and (6).

[113] In the common law case of *HE*, e.g., the patient's change of religious faith was considered enough to clearly override her prior wishes.

[114] For detailed analysis, see S Michalowski, 'Advance refusals of life-sustaining medical treatment: The relativity of an absolute right' (2005) 68 MLR 958.

[115] [2012] 1 WLR 1653; [2012] 1 All ER 1313. Applied in *St George's Healthcare NHS Trust* v *P* [2015] EWCOP 42, in which—on the facts—the treatment was held to be not overly burdensome and evidence of the patient's values and beliefs prior to loss of capacity pointed towards continuation of treatment.

withdraw artificial nutrition and hydration (ANH) despite considerable evidence from her family that she would not wish to continue with 'this burdensome life with a lack of dignity'. The problem for M was that she had not completed a formal, written advance decision. Accordingly, it fell to the court to consider her overall best interests. It held that all cases of withdrawal of ANH from minimally conscious patients or those in persistent vegetative state must come to court. Any prior statements short of the criteria for an advance decision are merely informal and the court will decide the outcome on a balance sheet assessment. The preservation of life in this carries great weight. In the instance case, M had some positive experiences and it was accordingly determined not to be in her best interests to withdraw care. This begs the serious question of how far a patient must go in expressing their wishes to have them respected, and particularly it raises the serious issue of whether anything short of a ss 24–46 advance decision can be more than 'informal'. For example, in *An NHS Trust v D*,[116] the patient suffered irreparable brain damage and the question arose about the cessation of ANH. This was rejected despite the existence of a signed letter which included, inter alia, the very clear statement: … I refuse any medical treatment of an invasive nature (including but not restrictive to placing a feeding tube in my stomach) if said procedure is only for the purpose of extending a reduced quality of life. This, however, still did not meet the requirements under the Mental Capacity Act for want of a witness and a specific statement that the decision should apply to the specific treatment. In the end, the judge preferred the preservation of life.[117] Something of a contrast is provided by *Nottinghamshire Healthcare NHS Trust v RC*,[118] in which a Jehovah's Witness who suffered from personality disorders which caused him to self-harm signed an advance decision stating that no blood transfusions should be administered to him in any circumstances. The formal requirements for executing an advance decision under the Mental Capacity Act 2005 were found to be satisfied and the patient had capacity at the time it was made. Mostyn J therefore upheld his right to refuse a blood transfusion, notwithstanding the possibility of using s 63 of the Mental Health Act to authorise a transfusion as treatment for the symptom or manifestation of the personality disorders. The duty to save life was subservient to the right to sovereignty over one's own body. Thus, when all legal formalities are satisfied and the patient's wishes and beliefs are clear and constant, advance decisions will be respected.

4.48   Even so, a doctor may make simple errors—in both a positive and negative sense—as to the validity of the patient's decision.[119] It is one thing to say that 'doubt over the continuing validity of an advance directive must be resolved in favour of life unless clear and convincing evidence is offered to the contrary',[120] but this must be balanced against the principle enshrined in s 1 of the 2005 Act that a patient is presumed to have capacity unless the contrary is established. Moreover, the doctor is in double jeopardy as to error.

---

[116] [2012] EWHC 885 (COP).

[117] See also *A Local Authority v E (anorexia nervosa)* [2012] EWHC 1639 (Fam); [2012] 2 FCR 523 which we discuss in full at para 4.85. Here the court held that an advance decision by an anorexic patient to prevent people feeding her was invalid on grounds of incapacity.

[118] [2014] EWCOP 1317; [2014] COPLR 468.

[119] The importance of his or her assessment of the validity of the decision is apparent from the protective terms of s 26(2) and (3).

[120] See *HE*, para 4.44 above at [23] quoting Lord Donaldson MR in *Re T (adult: refusal of treatment)* [1993] Fam 95 at 112.

He or she is liable to an action in battery should he or she mistakenly conclude that the patient was incapax at the time the directive was initiated; by contrast, a failure to treat may be regarded as negligent should that failure be based on an unreasonably mistaken belief that a directive was valid. It has been said that:

> A mistaken assumption that the patient was incompetent when making the advance directive and that his/her refusal was therefore not valid should accordingly only provide a defence in a battery action if the mistake was based on reasonable grounds.[121]

4.49 It is unsurprising that doctors will have recourse to the courts in a number of cases and equally unsurprising that the courts themselves will reach decisions that appear at first glance to be inconsistent. Indeed, in a particularly useful analysis of the jurisprudence, MacLean has argued that:

> In deciding whether to accept a refusal of treatment, the courts will assess the patient's competence on the basis of the *outcome* of the decision that he or she has made. [Emphasis added.][122]

The same author suggests that, rather than protecting the patient's precedent autonomy, the Act is open to criticism for the resulting 'vulnerability of advance directives' and that it (the Act) 'provides patients with a trump that only works when health care professionals and/or the courts are comfortable with the patient's decision'.[123] Recent case law might offer some support to this view. Perhaps the answers must wait on the operation of the Act over the coming years. Once again, the 2007 Code of Practice attempts to put flesh on the bones of the 2005 Act but at the present time this is little more than a gloss on the provisions of the Act as described earlier. An important point that is made about practice, however, is that even if an advance decision is deemed to be invalid or inapplicable, 'healthcare professionals must consider the advance decision as part of their assessment of the person's best interests if they have reasonable grounds to think it is a true expression of the person's wishes'.[124] The case law, however, seems to suggest that expressions of autonomy carry no more weight than any other factor being weighed in the balance. In many ways this goes against the foundational tenets of the legislation which are to give effect to the self-determination of patients as far as is possible. There are also serious practical implications for patients and families if the courts are moving to a position where only a properly executed advanced decision will carry any real weight. Many people will simply not be aware of the formal criteria and might make very clear advance statements in the belief that they will be respected.[125]

---

[121] S Michalowski, 'Trial and error at the end of life: no harm done' (2007) 27 OJLS 257 at 261.

[122] A R Maclean, 'Advance directives and the rocky waters of anticipatory decision-making' (2008) 16 Med Law Rev 1 at 6.

[123] At 22. In fact, the author goes on to infer, albeit indirectly, that the Scottish Act, which accords only presumptive weight to advance decisions, is to be preferred to the English Act which attempts to impose legal imperative.

[124] N 94, para 9.45. For commentary, see M Donnelly, 'Best interests, patient participation and the Mental Capacity Act 2005' (2009) 17 Med L Rev 1.

[125] R Gillon, 'Editorial: Sanctity of life has gone too far' (2012) 345 BMJ e4637; R Heywood, 'Revisiting advance decision making under the Mental Capacity Act 2005: A tale of mixed messages?' (2015) 23 Med Law Rev 81.

REFUSAL OF TREATMENT IN LATE PREGNANCY

4.50   The decision of the Court of Appeal in *Re T* was not without its caveats. Lord Donaldson said:

> An adult patient who ... suffers from no mental incapacity has an absolute right to choose whether to consent to medical treatment, to refuse it or to choose one rather than another of the treatments being offered. *The only possible qualification is a case in which the choice may lead to the death of a viable fetus.*[126]

4.51   This 'possible qualification' was tested in the soon-to-follow decision of *Re S*,[127] in which a health authority applied for a declaration to authorise the surgeons and staff of a hospital to carry out an emergency caesarian section on a 30-year-old woman who was in labour with her third child. The woman refused to submit to a section on religious grounds. The surgeon in charge, however, was adamant that both patient and baby would die without such intervention and, after six days of Mrs S's labour, the health authority sought a judgment from the High Court. The decision of Sir Stephen Brown is approximately one page in length and there is little or no legal argument or analysis in the judgment as to how the declaration was agreed. As the President said:

> I [make the declaration] in the knowledge that the fundamental question appears to have been left open by Lord Donaldson MR in *Re T* ... , and in the knowledge that there is no English authority which is directly in point.

4.52   But it was precisely this lack of precedental authority which provoked major criticism of *Re S* insofar as the case, with all its jurisprudential limitations, bid fair to *provide* that authority. But the problems thus generated were both manifold and manifest. First, the decision was based wholly on the medical evidence. There was no discussion of how the competency of a woman to make such a choice was to be assessed. How would the choice by a woman in S's position be validated? Second, when Lord Donaldson spoke of a 'viable' fetus, he was speaking in relative rather than absolute terms—for viability results from a combination of gestational age and obstetric expertise. At what stage, therefore, would it be regarded as legally acceptable to enforce the operation? Third, we have to ask what importance a court should place on the danger to the life of the woman herself? Strictly speaking, this should have no influence for, as was said in *Re T* and is now confirmed in *Re B*, the right to decide whether to accept treatment persists even if refusal will lead to premature death. Yet we still believe that it is asking a great deal of the health care team to stand by and watch their patient die a painful death and it is probable that such considerations were in the mind of the President when he was confronted with an emergency situation.[128] Finally, the decision depended on very doubtful logic in that it was, and is, well-established law that the fetus in utero has no rights of its own and has no distinct human personality.[129] If, then,

---

[126] [1992] 4 All ER 649 at 652–3; (1992) 9 BMLR 46 at 50, emphasis added.

[127] *Re S (adult: refusal of medical treatment)* [1992] 4 All ER 671; (1992) 9 BMLR 69. This case was decided only two and a half months after *Re T*.

[128] For some judicial sympathy, see Major J dissenting in the Canadian case *Winnipeg Child and Family Services (Northwestern)* v *GDF* [1997] 2 SCR 925: 'Where the harm is so great and the temporary remedy so slight, the law is compelled to act. ... Someone must speak for those who cannot speak for themselves.'

[129] The offence of child destruction is not engaged as the Infant Life (Preservation) Act 1929 requires intention to kill the child-to-be. For analysis see J Keown, 'The scope of the offence of child destruction' (1988) 104 LQR 120. For comparative discussion in the context of a jurisdiction which does protect the right to life of the unborn, see K Wade, 'Refusal of emergency caesarean section in Ireland: A relational approach' (2014) 22 Med Law Rev 1.

we look upon an enforced caesarian as a means of resolving a conflict between a woman who is refusing treatment and a fetus who seeks it, there is, in sporting terms, effectively 'no contest'—there can be no valid reason behind isolating this particular situation as the one occasion on which the fetus achieves legal dominance over its mother. While we have great sympathy with the President in the particular circumstances of *Re S*, it is hard to see his decision as other than logically and legally untenable.

4.53 Nonetheless, it appeared for a time as though *Re S* had, indeed, set a precedent and, despite fierce criticism of the ruling,[130] the English courts went through a phase in which they were prepared to impose caesarean section on unwilling women in the interests of their fetuses—with[131] or without[132] the assistance of the Mental Health Act 1983—and it was not until 1997 that the problem was considered in depth in the Court of Appeal. In *Re MB*,[133] the court ruled adamantly that a woman carrying a fetus is entitled to the same degree of respect for her wishes as is anyone else and reiterated the general principle that a person of full age and sound mind cannot be treated against his or her will without the door being opened to civil and criminal legal consequences. It stressed that circumstances in which non-voluntary treatment is permissible arise only when the patient cannot give consent and when treatment is in the *patient's* best interests. The court has no jurisdiction to declare medical intervention lawful when a *competent* pregnant woman decides to refuse treatment, *even though* this may result in the death or serious disability of the fetus she is bearing. The question of the woman's own best interests *does not arise* in such circumstances. On the facts of the particular case, however, the pregnant woman was declared incompetent because of a fear of needles which had led her to refuse the operation—but, at the end of the day, she consented and a healthy child was delivered.

4.54 This decision clearly places the autonomy of the woman above any interests of the fetus, including an interest in being born alive.[134] Yet, it is important to bear in mind that all of this is subject to the woman being competent when she makes her refusal. If she is not, she must be treated in her best interests. However, it still remains open to speculation how the patient's best interests should be assessed if there is no clear indication of how the mother feels about the birth and, in the final analysis, *Re MB* does little to remove from the medical profession the discretion and power to decide on a patient's capacity to act autonomously—and ultimately, in cases of incapacity, to decide on the patient's best interests.

4.55 This discretion has not been removed although the Court of Appeal's subsequent ruling in *St George's Healthcare NHS Trust* v *S (Guidelines), R* v *Collins, ex p S (No 2)*[135] provided guidance for HCPs called upon to decide on the capacity of a patient to consent to

---

[130] See e.g. A Grubb, 'Commentary on Re S' (1993) 1 Med L Rev 92.

[131] *Tameside and Glossop Acute Services Trust* v *CH (a patient)* [1996] 1 FLR 762; (1996) 31 BMLR 93. For analysis see A Grubb, 'Commentary' (1996) 4 Med L Rev 193. An interesting selection of views is to be found under the general heading 'Caesarian section: A treatment for mental disorder?' (1997) 314 BMJ 1183.

[132] *Norfolk and Norwich Healthcare (NHS) Trust* v *W* [1996] 2 FLR 613; (1996) 34 BMLR 16. The same judge made a similar decision in *Rochdale Healthcare (NHS) Trust* v *C* [1997] 1 FCR 274.

[133] *Re MB (an adult: medical treatment)* [1997] 8 Med LR 217; (1997) 38 BMLR 175, CA.

[134] For consideration of whether a human rights analysis might strengthen the legal position of the fetus, see G T Laurie, 'Medical law and human rights: Passing the parcel back to the profession?' in A Boyle et al. (eds), *Human Rights and Scots Law: Comparative Perspectives on the Incorporation of the ECHR* (2002). For an international perspective see R Copelon et al., 'Human rights begin at birth: International law and the claim of fetal rights' (2005) 13 Reprod Health Matters 120.

[135] [1999] Fam 26; (1998) 44 BMLR 194.

or refuse treatment.[136] The case concerned S, a 36-year-old pregnant woman with pre-eclampsia who was advised that she would require to be admitted. Fully cognisant of the risks, and wishing her baby to be born naturally, S refused. As a consequence, she was seen by a social worker and two doctors and admitted to a mental hospital for assessment. On her transfer to another hospital a declaration was sought and granted to dispense with S's consent and the baby was delivered by caesarian section. S discharged herself and appealed against the declaration. The Court of Appeal upheld its ruling in *Re MB* to the extent that a mentally competent pregnant woman has the absolute right to refuse medical intervention. The actions of the hospital were a trespass and the former declaration was set aside accordingly.[137] Moreover, the court castigated the use of the mental health legislation to treat an otherwise healthy woman:

> The Act cannot be deployed to achieve the detention of an individual against her will merely because her thinking process is unusual, even apparently bizarre and irrational, and contrary to the views of the overwhelming majority of the community at large.

4.56 Thus, the position of the pregnant woman of sound mind has been brought into line with the 'adult of sound mind' referred to in *Re T*. More significantly, the Court of Appeal sought to prevent a repeat of this case and, indeed, others involving the treatment of patients of doubtful capacity, and issued guidelines for future reference extending to ten detailed points, albeit largely concerned with procedure. This was an attempt to provide more certainty for health care professionals faced with the uncertainties thrown up by the common law, although it is noteworthy that the courts consistently shied clear of interfering in clinical matters and were quick to emphasise that the guidelines should not be rigidly adhered to if to do so put the patient's health or life at risk. Indeed, an analysis of the cases shows how fragile, in fact, is the protection provided to the woman's autonomy. MacLean states:[138]

> It is notable that in all of these cases, where the foetus's life was still at stake, the Court declared the caesarean section to be lawful. It was only where the woman could be declared incompetent, or where the fetus had already been delivered, that the court made strong statements supporting self-determination.[139]

4.57 A significant additional feature of *St George's* v *S*, however, lies in its challenge to the use of mental health legislation as a means of legitimising involuntary treatment. A trend in such a use had, in fact, been emerging in the lead up to this ruling, not only in relation to pregnant women, but also in the context of anorexics—whose management is

---

[136] *St George's Healthcare NHS Trust* v *S, R* v *Collins, ex p S* [1998] 3 All ER 673; (1998) 44 BMLR 160. In a later case, *Bolton Hospitals NHS Trust* v *O* [2003] 1 FLR 824, [2003] Fam Law 319, Butler-Sloss followed *Re MB* in re-stating the principles but still finding a woman with post traumatic stress temporarily incompetent due to panic induced by flash-backs. The case adds little to the established jurisprudence.

[137] The case has since been relied upon as authority that the law [is] cautious in imposing duties relative to autonomous acts by persons of full capacity, see *Murphy* v *East Ayrshire Council* [2012] CSIH 47, quoting Lord Hoffmann in *Reeves* v *Metropolitan Police* [2000] 1 AC 360, at 368–69.

[138] N 122, at 4.

[139] The same author quotes a very sensitive expression of relevant judicial insight: 'Whatever emphasis legal principle may place upon adult autonomy with the consequent right to choose between treatments, at some level the judicial outcome will be influenced by the expert evidence as to which treatment affords the best chance of the happy announcement that both mother and baby are doing well'—Lord Justice Thorpe, 'The caesarian section debate' (1997) 27 Fam Law 663.

discussed later.[140] The Mental Capacity Act 2005 emerged against this backdrop but it is notably silent on the challenges thrown up by the pregnant woman. High policy and politics might, of course, have dictated that the broad principle of respect for autonomy meant that no 'special case' should be made, but as these cases demonstrate, principles and practices can easily diverge—albeit for the best of intentions; reinforcement of the pregnant woman's absolute right to refuse through the Code of Practice may have been welcomed on a number of fronts.

4.58 The more recent case of *Re AA*, concerned a pregnant woman detained under s 3 of the Mental Health Act 1983 who suffered from psychotic episodes and had delusional beliefs.[141] Following the approach in *Re MB*, Mostyn J emphasised that the interests of the patient's unborn child were not the court's concern as the child had no legal existence until it was born. Furthermore, despite the patient's detention under the Mental Health Act, the case fell to be decided under the Mental Capacity Act. Evidence demonstrated that the patient lacked mental capacity and that it would be in her best interests for her child to be born alive and healthy. Having paid regard to the principle of least restriction, a caesarean section under general anaesthetic—with reasonable restraint if necessary—was authorised to achieve this safely and successfully. Whilst the outcome and reasoning in *Re AA* is thus in line with earlier cases, its aftermath raised further issues regarding the balance between protecting patient anonymity and freedom of the press[142] as well as consideration of the child's welfare with regards to separation from her biological parents and adoption.[143] In a separate decision shortly after *Re AA*, the Court of Protection issued legal guidance regarding the care of pregnant women who lack, or might lack, mental capacity.[144] The guidance sets out four categories of cases in which applications to the court should be made and the procedures to be adopted. It is intended to clarify and formalise existing practices, rather than to alter the legal position.

MINORS

4.59 Tension between considerations of welfare and autonomy are most acute in the context of minors. While parental authority clearly exists to consent or refuse on behalf of a younger child acting in his or her own best interests, uncertainties arise with the growing independence of a child as she or he becomes their own autonomous person. At what point must law recognise the 'mature minor' and with what consequences for all concerned? Precisely these issues arose in the pivotal case of *Gillick* v *West Norfolk and Wisbech Area Health Authority*.[145] Although the case was primarily concerned with the provision of contraceptives, many of the points made in the majority opinions can be taken as relating to the consent of minors to medical treatment as a whole—indeed, the term '*Gillick* competent' is a central part of medico-legal lore.[146]

---

[140] See para 4.77 and the recent example of *A Local Authority* v *E* [2012] EWHC 1639 (Fam); [2012] 2 FCR 523.

[141] *Re AA (Mental Capacity: Enforced Caesarean)* [2012] EWHC 4378 (COP); [2014] 2 FLR 237.

[142] *Re P (A Child) (Enforced Caesarean: Reporting Restrictions)* [2013] EWHC 4048 (Fam); [2014] 2 FLR 410.

[143] *Re P (A Child) (Enforced Caesarean: Adoption)* [2014] EWHC 1146 (Fam); [2014] 2 FLR 426.

[144] *NHS Trust 1, NHS Trust 2* v *FG (By her litigation friend, the Official Solicitor)* [2014] EWCOP 30; [2015] 1 WLR 1984.

[145] [1986] AC 112; [1985] 3 All ER 402, HL.

[146] *Re R (a minor) (wardship: medical treatment)* [1992] Fam 11; (1992) 7 BMLR 147 at 156, CA, per Lord Donaldson.

4.60 The dominant opinion in the House of Lords[147] was that the parental right to determine whether their minor child below the age of 16 years will have medical treatment 'terminates if and when the child achieves a significant understanding and intelligence to enable him or her to understand fully what is proposed' but, until the child attains such a capacity to consent, the parental right to make the decision continues save only in exceptional circumstances.[148] Despite the general tenor of his judgment, Lord Scarman affirmed that: 'Parental rights clearly exist and do not wholly disappear until the age of majority.' It can be taken as being now accepted that a doctor treating a child should always attempt to obtain parental authority but that, provided the patient is capable of understanding what is proposed and of expressing his or her wishes, the doctor may provide treatment on the basis of the minor's consent alone. The decision to do so must be taken on clinical grounds and, clearly, must depend heavily on the severity and permanence of the proposed therapy. The concurrence of Scots law on this question has scarcely been disputed and is enshrined in s 2(4) of the Age of Legal Capacity (Scotland) Act 1991.

4.61 The court in *Gillick* took the view that it would be a question of fact to be decided in each case whether a child seeking advice had sufficient understanding to give a consent valid in law.[149] An illustration of this is provided by a case in which the court agreed that a schoolgirl aged 15 should be allowed to have an abortion against the wishes of her parents. Butler-Sloss J said: 'I am satisfied she wants this abortion; she understands the implications of it.'[150] Thus, the problem of consent to treatment by minors is, to all intents, settled and is well understood.

4.62 *Re R*[151] was something of a landmark case as it constituted the first time that the question of the relationship between consent to and refusal of treatment by minors was considered. Briefly, the case concerned a 15-year-old girl whose increasingly disturbed behaviour required sedative treatment. However, during her lucid phases—in which she appeared rational and capable of making decisions—she refused her medication and the local authority instituted wardship proceedings, the intention being to seek authority to provide anti-psychotic treatment whether or not she consented. R appealed against an order to that effect which had been obtained.

4.63 The Court of Appeal first made it clear that the powers of the court in wardship were wider than those of parents and that the court could override both consent and refusal of treatment by the ward if that was considered to be in his or her best interests. The court then further distinguished *Gillick* in that it could not be applied to a child whose mental

---

[147] [1985] 3 All ER 402 at 423, per Lord Scarman.

[148] A similar approach by Lord Denning MR in *Hewer* v *Bryant* [1970] 1 QB 357, [1969] 3 All ER 578 was strongly approved and the common law position in Canada, as expressed in *Johnston* v *Wellesley Hospital* (1970) 17 DLR (3d) 139, was also quoted.

[149] A remarkable exposition of the mature minor doctrine, which was acknowledged as originating in the UK, is to be found in the Canadian case of *AC* v *Manitoba (Director: Child and Family Services)* [2009] SCC 30 which employs the device of including a right to self-determination as part of the 'best interests' that must be considered when a refusal of treatment is being considered. These factors must be balanced in association with the severity of the decision when assessing the minor's maturity.

[150] *Re P (a minor)* [1986] 1 FLR 272, 80 LGR 301. The application of *Gillick* to termination of pregnancy has been confirmed in *R (on the application of Axon)* v *Secretary of State for Health* [2006] QB 539 for which, see Chapter 9. For commentary see: R Taylor, 'Reversing the retreat from *Gillick*? *R (Axon)* v *Secretary of State for Health*' (2007) 19 CFLQ 81.

[151] *Re R (a minor) (wardship: medical treatment)* [1992] Fam 11; (1991) 7 BMLR 147.

state fluctuated widely from day to day. But the aspect of the case having by far the most general significance lay in its definition of parental powers. Essentially, Lord Donaldson MR considered that the parental right which *Gillick* extinguished was to *determine* the treatment of a mature minor—and determination was considered to be wider in its implications than a right to consent, insofar as it also included the right of veto. In explanation, Lord Donaldson introduced the concept of consent providing the key to the therapeutic door and of there being, in the case of the mature minor, two keyholders—the minor and her parents; consent by either *enabled* treatment to be given lawfully but did not, in any way, *determine* that the child should be treated.[152]

4.64   *Re R* raised a storm of academic protest that continues today.[153] This was not, primarily, as to the assessment of mental incompetence, which the court considered should be based on the general condition of the patient rather than that at a given moment in time. Rather, the criticism was directed at the retention of the parental right to give consent in the face of the child's refusal—an interpretation of the law which Kennedy described as 'driving a coach and horses through *Gillick*'. But is this, in fact, so? Lord Donaldson's distinction between a parental ability to determine a minor's treatment and to consent to treatment is a legitimate one. Moreover, the Master of the Rolls was, arguably, doing no more than interpreting the statute law of England and Wales. Section 8(1) of the Family Law Reform Act 1969 gives the minor aged 16–18 powers of consent to medical and surgical treatment equivalent to those of an adult. Section 8(3), however, goes on to say:

> Nothing in this section shall be construed as making ineffective any consent which would have been effective if this section had not been enacted.

4.65   It has been widely assumed that this section does no more than confirm the common law right of competent minors to decide these questions for themselves. We have always doubted this, largely because, if this is the correct interpretation, there was never any need for s 8(1)—a view which was endorsed by the absence of any such statute in Scotland prior to the Age of Legal Capacity (Scotland) Act 1991.[154] The better view, in our opinion, is that a parental right to consent on behalf of a child existed before 1969 and that s 8(3) preserves that right in the case of all those below the age of 18; this seems to have been the basis of Lord Donaldson's opinion.[155] The academic response to *Re R* demonstrates, above all, the difficulties which arise when attempting to apply general philosophical principles to particular medical situations. Given R's particular condition, one can well ask, 'What was the court's alternative?' This could only have been to accede to the minor's right to refuse treatment when competent and to treat her when incompetent under the mantle of necessity—and this smacks of a 'cat and mouse' approach which cannot be ethically

---

[152] Lord Donaldson was later to regret his keyholder analogy insofar as keys can lock as well as unlock doors.

[153] Compare S Gilmore and J Herring, ' "No" is the hardest word: Consent and children's autonomy' (2011) 23 Child and Fam L Quarterly 3 and E Cave and J Wallback, 'Minors' capacity to refuse treatment: A reply to Gilmore and Herring' (2012) 20 Med L Rev 423.

[154] The Age of Legal Capacity (Scotland) Act 1991, s 2(4) gives statutory power, which is rather wider even than that envisaged in *Gillick*, to the mature minor under the age of 16 to consent to medical or dental treatment. The section is, however, enabling in that it provides an exception to the general rule that a person under 16 has no capacity to enter into any legal transaction. For the application of the English case law to Scotland, see L Edwards, 'The right to consent and the right to refuse: More problems with minors and medical consent' [1993] JR 52.

[155] (1992) 7 BMLR 147 at 156.

sustainable.[156] It might have been better to confine the ratio to such narrow issues but the Master of the Rolls, albeit with some reservations, consolidated his wider position in the next case—*Re W*.[157]

4.66   *Re W* takes us one step further down the road of consent in that it concerned a 16-year-old girl who, therefore, came within the provisions of s 8(1) of the Family Reform Act 1969 which states:

> The consent of a minor who has attained the age of sixteen years to any ... medical ... treatment which, in the absence of consent, would constitute a trespass to the person, shall be as effective as it would be if he were of full age; and where a minor has by virtue of this section given effective consent to any treatment it shall not be necessary to obtain any consent for it from his parent or guardian ...

4.67   W was suffering from anorexia nervosa and was refusing all treatment despite a rapid deterioration in her health. The Court of Appeal supported an order that she be treated in a specialist unit but, in essence, did so on the clinical grounds that the disease is capable of destroying the ability to make an informed choice—the wishes of the minor thus constituted something which, of themselves, required treatment. In the course of the judgments, however, several general issues were either clarified or reinforced. First, it was reiterated that the court had extensive powers in wardship and that these existed irrespective of the provisions of s 8(1) of the Family Law Reform Act 1969; moreover, Lord Donaldson held that the exercise of the court's power to make a specific issue order did not conflict with those sections of the Children Act 1989 which give a mature minor the right to refuse psychiatric or medical treatment in defined circumstances.[158] All the judicial opinions emphasised that this attitude did not conflict with *Gillick* which was concerned with *parental* powers only. Second, the court disposed in clear terms of the relationship of consent to refusal of treatment with particular reference to the 1969 Act.[159] Lord Donaldson said:

> No minor of whatever age has power by refusing consent to treatment to override a consent to treatment by someone who has parental responsibility for the minor and a fortiori a consent by the court.[160]

Balcombe LJ said:

> I am quite unable to see how, on any normal reading of the words of the section, it can be construed to confer [an absolute right to refuse medical treatment] ... That the section did not operate to prevent parental consent remaining effective, as well in the case of a child over 16 as in the case of a child under that age, is apparent from the words of sub-s (3).[161]

---

[156] For an argument that the provisions of the Mental Capacity Act 2005 to protect autonomy interests should be applied to minors, see V Chico, 'The Mental Capacity Act 2005 and mature minors: a missed opportunity?' (2011) 33 J Soc Wel and Fam L 157.

[157] *Re W (a minor) (medical treatment)* [1992] 4 All ER 627; (1992) 9 BMLR 22. For a comparable Australian case, see *DoCS v Y* [1999] NSWSC 644.

[158] This was clearly restated in *South Glamorgan County Council v W and B* [1993] 1 FCR 626; [1993] Fam Law 398.

[159] For an argument that court powers undermine the concept of 'parental responsibility' see S L Woolley, 'The Limits of parental responsibility regarding medical treatment decisions' (2011) 96(11) Arch Dis Child 1060.

[160] [1992] 4 All ER 627 at 639; (1992) 9 BMLR 22 at 36.

[161] [1992] 4 All ER 627 at 641; (1992) 9 BMLR 22 at 37, 38. Kennedy para 4.64 at 60–1 regarded Lord Donaldson's refusal in *Re R* to accept refusal and consent as twin aspects of the single right to self-determination as bordering on the perverse; this was because he had no stated support. The presence of such support in *Re W* serves to fill the lacuna.

4.68 This is, of course, a legal decision and it is true, as Balcombe LJ himself said, that, in logic, there can be no difference between an ability to consent to treatment and an ability to refuse treatment. It is undoubtedly the case that the courts will seek to respect a mature minor's autonomous wishes in respect of many aspects of his or her life, including matters medical. Thus, for example, in *Torbay Borough Council v News Group Newspapers*,[162] we find Munby J upholding the right of a young woman who was almost 17 to decide for herself whether to disclose the details of her own teenage pregnancy to the press, irrespective of the wishes of her parents. But matters are not so clear-cut when the decision relates to medical *treatment* and when a refusal may involve a serious risk of physical or mental harm, or indeed, death. In such cases, is there not a clear practical distinction to be made? It is reasonable to suppose, paternalistic though it may sound, that a qualified doctor knows more about the treatment of disease than does the average child. Thus, while consent involves acceptance of an experienced view, refusal rejects that experience—and does so from a position of limited understanding.[163] Prognosis is, admittedly, one of the most difficult exercises in medicine but, by and large, the doctor who is advocating treatment will be convinced that the patient's condition can only worsen in its absence. The consequences of refusal are, therefore, likely to be more serious than those of compliance and, on these grounds, refusal of treatment may require greater understanding than does acceptance. In principle, consent and refusal are but reverse expressions of the same autonomous choice; the difference is that the level of understanding at which a choice can be said to be an 'understanding choice' is higher in the latter.[164] We accept, of course, that the same could also be true for most adults. Indeed, as we have seen,[165] just such an approach has been adopted, at least in the case of the incapax, by the courts after the decision of *Re C (adult: refusal of medical treatment)*.[166]

4.69 What is clear from both *Re R* and *Re W* is that, rather like Lord Denning before him, Lord Donaldson was concerned to protect the medical profession from the fire of litigation—his reference in *Re W* to consent providing a flak-jacket for the doctor demonstrates this vividly.[167] It is, therefore, possible to criticise the two decisions as concentrating on this aspect and taking insufficient notice of the developing autonomy of adolescence. Nonetheless, all the speeches in both cases are at pains to emphasise the importance of respecting the minor's wishes—and of giving them increasing value with increasing maturity. They emphasise that those wishes are not binding; but their tenor is such as to establish the concept of the mature minor very firmly in the English medical jurisprudence and to insist that this is breached only in exceptional circumstances. It might, however, be posited that matters have changed with the introduction of the Human Rights Act 1998, and that a failure to respect a refusal by a mature minor would now be a breach of a considerable number of his or her fundamental rights, including those under Arts 2, 3, 5, and 8.[168] We doubt that this is so, and would point to both the doctrine of proportionality—requiring a balance of community and individual

---

[162] [2003] EWHC 2927.

[163] For a specific rejection of this view, see R Huxtable, 'Case commentary: Time to remove the "flak jacket"?' (2000) 12 CFLQ 83.

[164] For a contrary clinico-legal view, see J A Devereux, D P H Jones, and D I Dickenson, 'Can children withhold consent to treatment?' (1993) 306 BMJ 1459.

[165] See paras 4.36 et seq.   [166] [1994] 1 All ER 819; [1994] 1 WLR 290.

[167] For discussion see A Maclean, 'Keyholders and flak jackets: the method in the madness of mixed metaphors' (2008) 3 Clinical Ethics 121.

[168] See A Hockton, *The Law of Consent to Medical Treatment* (2002), paras 8.016–8.021.

interests—and the margin of appreciation that countries enjoy under the ECHR. The English courts have made a concerted effort to demonstrate their desire to find the balance in these cases and there is little in the jurisprudence of the ECtHR that would lead them to upset that delicate equilibrium.

4.70 Nonetheless, the ease with which this balance might be thought to be upset is very clearly illustrated by *Re M (child: refusal of medical treatment)*[169] in which a 15½-year-old girl who had sustained acute heart failure was denied the right to refuse a heart transplant operation. While the High Court emphasised the need to take account of a mature minor's wishes as to her own medical treatment, it also endorsed the legal view that those wishes are in no way determinative. Johnson J was keen that his ruling be very clearly laid out for M to read for herself but, interestingly, he did not, himself, ascertain her views before passing judgment. Instead, these were gleaned by a local solicitor and the Official Solicitor who, together, formed the view that M was overwhelmed by her circumstances. She had said that she did not wish to die. By the same token, she had also indicated that she did not want someone else's heart, nor did she relish the thought of taking medicine for the rest of her life. In the final analysis Johnson J held that it was in M's best interests to receive a new heart and authorised her surgeons to perform the procedure. Whatever one may feel as to its medical merits, this decision must surely represent the outermost reaches of acceptable paternalistic practices. While it seems that she finally acquiesced, was the court really countenancing a forced transplantation if M had continued her resistance? More broadly, we question if it is ethically correct to earmark a scarce and expensive resource for someone who does not want it. There is small wonder that Johnson J expressed concern at the gravity of his decision. A very similar situation arose in the case of Hannah Jones[170] which, at one time, appeared to be running contrary to *Re M*.[171] In the event, however, the issue was not tested as the child changed her mind.[172]

Legal disputes are, necessarily, concerned with those cases where impasse has been reached. Thus, while the categoric refusal of a minor might be overturned as a matter of strict law, the majority of cases ought to proceed in ways that reflect and respect the child's wishes in an environment of care and welfare. There can be little doubt that the ethical and professional obligation involves the promotion of the growing autonomy of minors as far as this is possible, albeit that at times this must concede to the child's overall welfare interests.[173]

4.71 The limit or extent of parental rights to refuse or consent to treatment of their children on non-medical grounds is, however, a different matter and is well exemplified by decision-making on religious or other cultural grounds.[174] This has become a significant factor in an increasingly multicultural society and merits at least brief consideration.

---

[169] [1999] 2 FLR 1097; (2000) 52 BMLR 124.

[170] S de Bruxelles, 'Dying girl Hannah Jones wins fight to turn down transplant' *The Times*, 11 November 2008. Interestingly, it seems that, to date, no court in the USA has permitted a child to refuse medical treatment without parental consent when death is the probable outcome: J F Will, 'My God my choice: The mature minor doctrine and adolescent refusal of life-saving treatment based upon religious beliefs' (2006) 22 J Contemp Hlth L Pol 233. Hannah's parents, however, agreed with her decision to refuse a transplant.

[171] N 169.

[172] S de Bruxelles, 'Change of heart by girl, 14 who fought for the right to die', *The Times*, 21 July 2009.

[173] On the challenges of this kind of approach, see E Cave, 'Maximisation of minors' capacity' (2011) 23 Child and Fam L Quarterly 431; E Cave, 'Goodbye Gillick? Identifying and resolving problems with the concept of child competence' (2013) 34 LS 103.

[174] See the Special Issue of *Medical Law International* edited by J V McHale, 'Health law, faith(s) and beliefs' (2008) 9(4).

Determining the Welfare of the Child: Non-medical Factors

4.72 The welfare of a child is not solely determined by her or his health interests. Indeed, parents will often have strong beliefs and values that they wish to impart to their offspring. An obvious example is religious conviction. Jehovah's Witnesses are a particularly strict Christian sect with strong views about the permissibility of blood transfusions. Given that these procedures are widely required and most commonly used in an emergency situation, refusal of blood transfusion on behalf of a child of Jehovah's Witnesses is probably the commonest situation in the present context and becomes the benchmark for discussion.[175] It must, however, be remembered that there is a variety of religious cultures that impinge on medical practice[176] and, while much of the illustrative material that follows derives from Jehovah's Witness cases, the same principles will apply—and will depend to a large extent on the somewhat nebulous concept of the 'reasonable parent'. Equation of this objective assessment with subjective and sincere religious beliefs lies at the heart of the court decisions in such cases.

4.73 Although there may be little public sympathy for parents who depend upon divine intervention exclusively or refuse on religious or cultural grounds to consent to blood transfusion for a perilously ill child, it would be a mistake to reject their position out of hand. Ignoring deeply held religious convictions is a major change of attitude in a free and diverse society. Such action also entails a significant interference with the principle that parents should have freedom to choose the religious and social upbringing of their children.[177] On the other hand, the objective assessor may well see a difference between endangering life and expressing lesser social concerns; both the courts and the public may well accept the latter while seeing the former as unreasonable parenting. The difference can be summed up in some well-known judicial dicta from across the Atlantic—perhaps the most familiar of these being that of Rutledge J, albeit in a peripheral context: 'Parents may be free to become martyrs themselves. But it does not follow that they are free in identical circumstances to make martyrs of their children.'[178] Similarly, the Supreme Court of Canada has ruled that to allow parents to refuse blood transfusions for their child for religious reasons 'undermines the ability of the state to exercise its legitimate parens patriae jurisdiction'.[179] Indeed, the Court continued: 'As society becomes increasingly aware of the fact that the family is often a very dangerous place for children, the parens patriae jurisdiction assumes greater importance.'[180] The constitutional entitlement of the state to act in a child's best interests, even in the face of both parental and child refusal, has been upheld.[181]

[175] For a comparative view, see S Woolley, 'Children of Jehovah's Witnesses and adolescent Jehovah's Witnesses: What are their rights?' (2005) 90 Arch Dis Child 715.

[176] We have noted elsewhere that the majority of orthodox Jewish dietary restrictions are based on standard public health measures. In 1993, a Rastafarian couple who had refused to allow their diabetic child to be given insulin were convicted of manslaughter—see D Brahams, 'Religious objection versus parental duty' (1993) 342 Lancet 1189. For an easy overview of some apposite situations see S Hollins, *Religions, Culture and Healthcare* (2006).

[177] See, e.g., E E Sutherland, 'A veiled threat to children's rights? Religious dress in schools and the rights of young people' [2009] JR 145.

[178] *Prince* v *Massachusetts* 321 US 158 at 170, quoted in direct context in *People (ex rel Wallace)* v *Labrenz* 104 NE 2d 769 (Ill, 1952).

[179] *B* v *Children's Aid Society of Metropolitan Toronto* [1995] 1 SCR 315 at 433.

[180] But the Supreme Court will not extend the jurisdiction to the child in utero: *Winnipeg Child and Family Services (Northwest Area)* v *G (DF)* [1997] 2 SCR 925.

[181] *AC* v *Manitoba (Director of Child and Family Services)* [2009] 2 SCR 181.

4.74 In this vein, it is unsurprising that it is well-nigh impossible to find a case in the common law jurisdictions where a court has upheld a parental claim to authority to refuse recommended life-saving treatment on behalf of their child purely on the basis of their own religious convictions and, at least in respect of the UK, there is little point in doing more than note examples of the anticipated contrary decisions.[182] In what is a paradigm case, *Re S (a minor) (medical treatment)*,[183] the court ordered transfusion of a four-year-old child against the wishes of his Jehovah's Witness parents despite the fact that treatment was elective and carried only a 50 per cent chance of success; Thorpe J gave the practical advice that the parents could absolve their consciences in that the decision was, by now, out of their hands. Blood transfusion is, from the technical point of view, a comparatively simple form of treatment and, certainly in a reasonably sophisticated health service, should cause significant discomfort to neither donor nor recipient. The same cannot be said for bone marrow transplants yet, even here, the courts are prepared to override parental objection on religious grounds when the life of a child is involved. In *NHS Trust* v *A (a child)*,[184] the court granted the Trust's application for a declaration that a bone marrow transplant should be carried out on the seven-month-old respondent who suffered from a severe genetic defect in her immune system. It was accepted that without the suggested treatment, A would die, probably by the age of one. Medical experts had estimated that the transplant had approximately a 50 per cent prospect of effecting a lasting cure and that she would then have a normal life expectancy; they also considered that there was a 10 per cent risk that the child would die as the result of treatment. The parents resisted a transplant mainly on the grounds that they were convinced the child fell into the latter group, that in any event she would be exposed to undue suffering, and that, should the treatment prove successful, she would be infertile. Complementary to this, as 'practising Christians', they believed that God could and would effect a miraculous cure.[185] Religious objection to treatment in A's case was, therefore, founded on trust in God rather than fear of divine retribution which lies at the heart of the Jehovah's Witness' objections. As a result, Holman J's road to declaring a non-consensual transplant to be lawful was, perhaps, made that much easier.[186]

4.75 We have not, however, considered the less dramatic situation where the general religious dictates of parents demand that life be preserved whenever possible as in the case of orthodox Judaism. For this, we must look to *Re C (a minor) (medical treatment)*[187] in which the High Court refused to respect the wishes of parents, on religious grounds, to continue ventilatory treatment for a 16-month-old child who was suffering from the inevitably fatal condition of spinal muscular atrophy. The significance of *Re C* lies in the attitude of the court in determining the extent to which parental power is subjugated to the clinical judgement of HCPs and, in reaching its decision, the court assiduously followed existing precedents which had eschewed judicial interference with the clinical judgement of HCPs

---

[182] The nearest approach we have discovered in the USA is *In re E G* 549 NE 2d 322 (Ill, 1989) but the minor was aged 17½ and was in agreement with her mother.

[183] [1993] 1 FLR 377.   [184] [2008] 1 FLR 70, (2007) 98 BMLR 141.

[185] There is an interesting paradox in that, while resisting medical advice, A's mother did believe that 'God works through the medical profession' (at [33]).

[186] Holman J also pointed out that, insofar as A was not hospitalised at the time and no order was given, the parents still retained control of the situation (at [2]). Note that he drew heavily on his previous judgment in *A NHS Trust* v *MB* [2006] 2 FLR 319; [2006] Lloyd's Rep Med 323, thus emphasising the close association between consent, refusal, and medical willingness to treat.

[187] [1998] 1 FLR 384; (1997) 40 BMLR 31.

in cases such as this.[188] There was, however, no direct mention in this case of the place for the parents' religious views.[189] *Re C*, thus, opens up new variations on the theme and, for this reason, we defer consideration of its implications until Chapter 15.

Religion and the Mature Minor

4.76 The foregoing could be taken as indicating that the law has very little difficulty in discounting religious beliefs when children's welfare is concerned[190] and this extends to the views of mature minors themselves. Thus, in *Re E*,[191] which involved a 15-year-old otherwise competent boy who was refusing blood transfusion as a Jehovah's Witness, we have Ward J saying: 'I respect this boy's profession of faith, but I cannot discount at least the possibility that he may in later years suffer some diminution in his convictions'—which some would regard as a common-sense direction but, others, as outrageous paternalism. An even more instructive case is the later Jehovah's Witness decision in *Re L (a minor)*[192] involving refusal of blood transfusion by a 14-year-old girl who was described as 'mature for her age'. Sir Stephen Brown P had little hesitation in finding her to be lacking the necessary competence—this on the ground that her limited experience of life 'necessarily limit[ed] her understanding of matters which are as grave as her own present situation'. The courts do seem to have maintained consistency in this field despite the passage of time and the coincident development of young people's rights.[193] Thus, in *Re P (Medical treatment: best interests)*,[194] a hospital sought leave to administer blood to a patient who was an almost 17-year-old Jehovah's Witness if his situation became immediately life threatening. The court granted the application—albeit reluctantly in the light of the young person's religious faith and wishes—holding that his interests, looked at in the widest possible sense (medical, social, and religious), were best served in so doing with the caveat that blood was to be administered only as a last resort if no other treatment was available.

---

[188] *Re J (wardship: medical treatment)* [1991] Fam 33; [1990] 3 All ER 930; *Re J (a minor) (medical treatment)* [1993] Fam 15; [1992] 4 All ER 614; *Re R (a minor) (wardship: medical treatment)* [1992] Fam 11; (1991) 7 BMLR 147.

[189] For an account of the importance of cultural and religious tenets in withdrawal cases, see M F Morrison and S G DeMichele, 'How culture and religion affect attitudes toward medical futility' in M B Zucker and H D Zucker, *Medical Futility* (1997).

[190] See e.g. *In re J (a minor) (prohibited steps order: circumcision)* [2000] 1 FLR 571; (2000) 52 BMLR 82 in which a ritual circumcision at the age of five was considered not to be in the child's best interests. For related discussion in the context of asylum refusal, see *SS (Malaysia) v Secretary of State for the Home Department* [2013] EWCA Civ 888; [2014] Imm AR 170. For counterposing academic views, see S Svoboda, 'Circumcision of male infants as a human rights violation' (2013) 39 J Med Ethics 469; J Mazor, 'The child's best interests and the case for the permissibility of male infant circumcision' (2013) 39 J Med Ethics 421.

[191] *Re E (a minor)* [1993] 1 FLR 386; [1994] 5 Med LR 73. Ward J did say he wished to avoid notions of undue influence. Perhaps, however, feelings are not as strong as they once were: 'of all influences religious influence is the most dangerous and powerful'—*Allcard v Skinner* (1887) 36 Ch D 145; [1886–90] All ER Rep 90 at 99–100, per Lindley LJ, referred to by Butler-Sloss LJ in *Re T* [1992] 4 All ER 649 at 667; (1992) 9 BMLR 46 at 65. *Allcard* was applied in *Pesticcio v Huet* [2004] EWCA Civ 372—though not in respect of religion.

[192] *Re L (medical treatment: Gillick competence)* [1998] 2 FLR 810, sub nom *Re L (a minor)* (1998) 51 BMLR 137. Interestingly, the President would have made the order to treat even if she had been found to be 'Gillick-competent' (at BMLR 140). For overall comment, see C Bridge, 'Religious beliefs and teenage refusal of medical treatment' (1999) 62 MLR 585.

[193] The situation is similar in Australia, thus in *Minister for Health v AS* (2004) WASC 286, the refusal of blood transfusion by a 15-year-old Jehovah Witness was rejected despite being found *Gillick* competent. This is on the basis of the *parens patriae* jurisdiction, see P Trowse, 'Refusal of Medical Treatment – A Child's Prerogative' (2010) 10 Queensland U Tech Law and Justice Journal 191.

[194] [2003] EWHC 2327 (Fam); [2004] 2 FLR 1117.

Other Welfare Considerations

4.77   We have isolated religious conviction as a special aspect of parental proxy consent concerning which it is possible to identify a single jurisprudential response. Elsewhere, however, there are so many variables—including the logic of parental decision-making, the severity of the child's condition, and the consequences of the decision—that it is impossible to discern a pattern. In our view, the principles underpinning the topic derive from the sociopolitical fact that there has been a redefinition of the role of the parents in respect of control of their children and that it is no longer possible to regard them as having an almost absolute power: 'Parental rights to control a child', said Lord Fraser, 'exist not for the benefit of the parent but for the child'.[195] The community interest in the welfare of children is demonstrated in a number of ways, some more draconian than others. Society is prepared, for example, to remove a child from its parents if it is in moral or physical danger—and the child whose life is endangered by parental refusal of consent to medical treatment will receive the same degree of protection as will the battered, or otherwise neglected, child.[196] A few examples will suffice. In *Re C (a child) (HIV testing)*,[197] Wilson J held that, notwithstanding the opposition of both parents who rejected contemporary medical thinking on the causes and treatment of HIV and AIDS, it was overwhelmingly in the interests of the child that her HIV status be known. Accordingly, he ordered that a blood sample should be taken from the child.[198] In the confusingly named *Re C (a child) (immunisation: parental rights)*[199] two fathers consented to the immunisation of their daughters against the wishes of their mothers. After a very long trial, Sumner J decided that the girls' best interests must prevail and, accordingly, he ordered that a programme of immunisation go ahead. The particular interest in this case, however, lies in the fact that the parents disagreed—the court accepted that, otherwise, the parents have a right to choose whether to accept medical advice to have their children immunised.[200] The point to note is that the appropriate benchmark remains the best interests of the patient and this may shift in emphasis according to the purpose for which the test is being undertaken.[201]

4.78   Returning, however, to treatment rather than diagnosis, decisions in favour of parental autonomy are also rare and we are aware of few judicial decisions that are in clear contrast to the general trend. In *Re T (a minor) (wardship: medical treatment)*,[202] the Court of Appeal held that the parents of a child suffering from biliary atresia, a life-threatening liver defect, could legally refuse a liver transplant on behalf of the infant, even though

---

[195] In *Gillick v West Norfolk and Wisbech Area Health Authority* [1986] AC 112; [1985] 3 All ER 402 (see paras 4.59 above et seq). Following Lord Denning MR in *Hewer v Bryant* [1970] 1 QB 357 at 369: 'Parental rights start with the right of control and end with little more than advice.'

[196] The parents of a neglected child may be found guilty of manslaughter. See, on the other hand, *R v Senior* [1899] 1 QB 283.

[197] [2000] Fam 48; [1999] 2 FLR 1004.

[198] Yet, while the principle of law may be well established, this can have little impact on the practical outcome in many circumstances. In the instant case the parents fled the country with the child before the sample could be taken.

[199] [2003] 2 FLR 1095; (2003) 73 BMLR 152, CA also known as *Re B (a child)*. Note that the case was not directly concerned with the MMR (measles, mumps, and rubella) controversy. Followed in *F v F (MMR Vaccine)* [2013] EWHC 2683 (Fam); [2014] 1 FLR. For commentary, see: E Cave, 'Adolescent refusal of MMR inoculation: *F (Mother) v F (Father)*' (2014) 77 MLR 630.

[200] At [356].

[201] J Schweppe, 'Best to agree to disagree: Parental discord, children's rights and the question of immunisation' (2008) Common Law World Review 147.

[202] [1997] 1 All ER 906; (1996) 35 BMLR 63.

there was firmly held medical opinion that a transplant would give the child a number of years of life beyond his current prognosis. We discuss this case in depth later.[203] Suffice it to say here that the significance of the court's ruling from the perspective of the law of consent lies in its willingness, indeed, determination, *not* to equiparate the concept of best *medical* interests with the far broader notion of *overall* best interests—an ideal that now permeates the entire application of the test. The court may, in fact, take the view that parents who object to life-saving treatment for a child could become bad parents and, as a result, his or her childhood may be compromised. Alternatively, the child who is treated contrary to the parent's religion or other deeply held beliefs might come to be regarded as 'tainted' or 'soiled' by the treatment, leading them to reject the child or treat him or her adversely. In such cases, the argument could be put that it is in the child's *overall* best interests *not* to receive the said treatment—and this may go some way to explaining the apparently paradoxical decision in *Re T*.[204]

4.79 Finally, fraught wardship proceedings culminated in the decision in *Re King (A Child)*;[205] a ruling which saw a degree of leeway granted to parents in determining the child's best interests—in quite extraordinary circumstances. Parents sought permission to take their child to Prague to undergo proton therapy; a form of treatment that was then unavailable in the UK. In the parents view, this would be a superior treatment for their son following surgery to remove his brain tumour, as it would cause less radiation and tissue damage to other organs than the conventional radiotherapy offered at the treating hospital. Nevertheless, the NHS Trust was not prepared to recommend or fund travel abroad for proton therapy. The parents subsequently removed their child from hospital without permission and travelled to Spain. The alarm was raised by the local authority, with the result that European arrest warrants were issued for the parents and the child was made a ward of court, requiring him to be presented immediately at the nearest hospital in Spain. The dramatic nature of the case ensured intense media interest.[206] Agreement was eventually reached between the medical teams in the UK, Spain, and the Czech Republic on a treatment plan for proton therapy and evidence of funding was also provided. Baker J authorised the proposal on the grounds that proton therapy was a reasonable course of treatment that was compatible with the child's best interests. The case was not one in which the parents were insisting on a manifestly unreasonable course of treatment. While the outcome and reasoning in this case are consistent with established best interest principles, it could have wider implications by heightening parental expectations regarding entitlement to a preferred course of treatment, possibly leading to increased friction between the domains of child welfare and parental autonomy and that of resource allocation.

---

[203] See Chapter 15.

[204] We would, however, draw attention to the concept of 'family autonomy' which has considerable ethico-political support and is subsumed within the jurisdictions of several communities. An example of this was provided early by the Supreme Court of Ireland which upheld the right of parents to refuse a simple heel-prick test on their new-born child designed to identify the presence of phenylketonuria—an eminently manageable congenital condition which, left untreated, could lead to irremediable brain damage: *North Western Hospital Board v W (H)* [2001] IESC 70. For commentary, see G Laurie, 'Better to hesitate at the threshold of compulsion: PKU testing and the concept of family autonomy in Eire' (2002) 28 J Med Ethics 136. In fact, to decide otherwise could have caused considerable difficulty with Irish constitutional law and it is uncertain whether a UK court would follow the same route.

[205] [2014] EWHC 2964 (Fam); [2014] 2 FLR 855.

[206] 'Brain tumour boy Ashya King free of cancer, parents say', *BBC News*, 23 March 2015.

OTHER VULNERABLE GROUPS

4.80 Returning to a discussion of adults but remaining with the theme of vulnerability, anyone aged over 18 and who is receiving health care is a vulnerable adult and is subject to the Safeguarding Vulnerable Groups Act 2006.[207] Here, however, we intend to take a more restricted view and to consider a group to be vulnerable only when its vulnerability stems from special circumstances conducive to unwarranted coercion either by others or by circumstance, including environment. In this last respect, prisoners constitute a further group which deserves particular mention.

4.81 The status of prisoners has been referred to briefly in Chapter 2. It will be seen from this that it could be held that the incarcerated can never give a valid consent to treatment in that an element of coercion is implicit in the prison doctor–patient relationship. This proposition was considered in *Freeman*,[208] the decision in which greatly restricts this line of argument. The case turned in large measure on its own facts but the suggestion that the position of the prison psychiatrist vis-à-vis his patient voided a general consent was rejected; it was further stated that 'it was not open for it to be argued for the plaintiff that informed consent was a consideration which could be entertained by the courts'. While we believe that this latter opinion derived from a semantic misinterpretation of the concept which is discussed in detail later, the judgment clearly indicates that, in the absence of overt coercion, the restricted circumstances in which a prisoner's consent to treatment is given will be unlikely to affect the validity of that consent in law. An action for trespass is open to those in detention when consent to treatment has not been given[209] but mere negligence in obtaining that consent[210] will not brand the trespass as being coercive or oppressive.

4.82 Bearing in mind the different ambiences of an NHS and a special hospital, all of this must be seen in light of the Court of Appeal decision in *R (on the application of Wilkinson) v RMO, Broadmoor Hospital Authority*,[211] which was one of the first cases to consider the issues in the shadow of the Human Rights Act. In doing so, it emphasised procedural requirements before non-consensual treatment can be embarked upon properly. As Hale LJ said:

> Whatever the position before the Human Rights Act 1998, the decision to impose treatment without consent upon a protesting patient is a potential invasion of his rights under article 3 or article 8. Super-*Wednesbury* is not enough. The claimant is entitled to a proper hearing, on the merits, of whether the statutory grounds for imposing this treatment upon him against his will are made out: i.e. whether it is treatment for the mental disorder from which he is suffering and whether it should be given to him without his consent 'having regard to the likelihood of its alleviating or preventing a deterioration of his condition'.[212]

---

[207] Section 59(1)(d).   [208] *Freeman v Home Office (No 2)* [1984] QB 524; [1984] 1 All ER 1036.

[209] *Barbara v Home Office* (1984) 134 NLJ 888.

[210] See para 4.107 et seq.   [211] [2002] 1 WLR 419; (2001) 65 BMLR 15.

[212] Ibid, para 83. See also, *R (on the application of Wooder) v Feggetter* [2003] QB 219; [2002] 3 WLR 591, CA, in which it was held that adequate written reasons to give a detained patient medication against his will must be produced by a second opinion doctor under the Mental Health Act 1983, and that these should be disclosed to the patient except in the rare circumstances where this would have an adverse effect on his physical or mental health. *Wilkinson* has since been applied in *R (on the application of B) v S* [2005] HRLR 40; [2005] MHLR 347 and *R (on the application of B) v Haddock (Responsible Medical Officer)* [2006] HRLR 40, (2007) 93 BMLR 52, CA. For a discussion of these cases see: P Hope, 'Paternalism or power? Compulsory treatment under section 58 of the Mental Health Act 1983' (2006) J Ment Hlth L 90, and P Bartlett, 'A matter of necessity? Enforced treatment under the Mental Health Act' (2007) 15 Med L Rev 86.

Wilkinson took his case to the European Court of Human Rights but it was ruled inadmissible on all grounds.[213]

4.83 As an example of a valid refusal on the part of a prisoner, we have the judgment in *Secretary of State for the Home Department* v *Robb*,[214] a case which raised the question of whether the decision of a prisoner to go on hunger strike should be respected by the prison authorities. Somewhat unorthodoxly, the court applied a medical law approach to the case, even although the prisoner was not a patient, and upheld the individual's 'right to self-determination', in this case to refuse food. This right has similarly been upheld in the cross-over world of criminals who are detained under hospital orders rather than in prison. In *R (on the application of H)* v *Mental Health Review Tribunal*,[215] a detained patient who had killed his wife sought judicial review of a decision by the Mental Health Review Tribunal not to issue an absolute discharge; he challenged the terms of his conditional discharge which stated that he 'shall comply' with medication prescribed by his responsible medical officer. This phraseology withstood the human rights argument that it interfered with the patient's right to respect for private life, primarily because (i) it did not imply that his right to self-determination was in any way compromised, and (ii) no sanction accompanied the condition if the patient decided not to take the medication. Any pressure on the patient arose 'from the continuing conditional nature of his discharge and not from the condition itself'. Moreover, the Secretary of State could not recall a patient solely on the ground that he had failed to comply with a single condition. In contrast, the attempt by the multiple murderer Ian Brady to starve himself to death was thwarted by the High Court when it refused his application for judicial review of the medical decision to force-feed him on the grounds that his personality disorder made him refuse food and therefore 'feeding' was treatment for his mental condition within the terms of the Mental Health Act 1983.[216] This latter case is better considered in the context of that legislation, and we do so in Chapter 13.

4.84 Another series of cases has similarly sanctioned the force-feeding of persons such as anorexics and depressives who refuse food. The rationale in each case has been that the feeding is *treatment* for the individual's *mental disorder*, this being the sole criterion under the legislation which permits health care professionals to forego consent.[217] Thus, for example, the trial judge in *Riverside Mental Health Trust* v *Fox*[218] held that an adult who was being treated for anorexia nervosa could be force-fed as a part of treatment for her mental condition. The Court of Appeal later overturned this decision but did so on procedural grounds and did not question the validity of the application of the 1983 Act to such a case. As if to endorse this line of reasoning, the Court of Appeal in *B* v *Croydon Health Authority*[219] authorised force-feeding under the 1983 Act of a woman with a borderline personality disorder, and feeding of a depressive and suicidal quinquagenarian was similarly ordered in *Re VS (adult: mental disorder)*.[220] In *Re C (detention: medical treatment)*,[221] an anorexic 16-year-old was detained using the High Court's inherent protective jurisdiction in order

---

[213] Application 14659/02, 28 February 2006.   [214] [1995] 1 All ER 677.

[215] [2007] EWHC 884 (Admin).

[216] *R* v *Collins, ex p Brady* (2000) 58 BMLR 173; [2000] Lloyd's Rep Med 355. For discussion of the implications of this and other UK and US cases for the force-feeding of prisoners held at Guantanamo, see R Easton, 'The power of autonomy' (2013) 157 SJ 36.

[217] In particular, Mental Health Act 1983, s 63.   [218] [1994] 1 FLR 614, (1993) 20 BMLR 1.

[219] [1995] 1 All ER 683, CA. The seminal case of *Re W (a minor) (medical treatment)* [1992] 4 All ER 627 is discussed at para 4.62.

[220] [1995] 3 Med L Rev 292.   [221] [1997] 2 FLR 180; [1997] Fam Law 474.

that she receive 'medical treatment' including, inter alia, force-feeding. This unusual procedure was justified as being in the child's best interests on the grounds that, because it was in her best interests to receive 'treatment' for her condition, it was also a part of those interests that she be detained—using reasonable force if necessary—so that the treatment could be carried out. It is to be noted that this order was not based on the detention provisions of the 1983 Act but, rather, on the common law powers of the High Court—which suggests that this jurisdiction is potentially very wide-ranging. Another interesting point is the use by Walls J of the three-stage test for competency laid down in *Re C (adult: refusal of medical treatment)*.[222] That case concerned the competency of an adult. As we have seen, the capacity of a minor to agree to or refuse medical treatment has relied up until now on the concept of *Gillick* competence, the evaluation of which lies within the discretion of the HCP. This equiparation of the test for competency in adults and minors is, in our view, correct, and adds judicial weight to our earlier argument that refusal of treatment by minors requires a higher standard of competency than does a decision to consent.[223]

4.85 Most recently and against the reforms of the Mental Capacity Act 2005, the Court of Protection was asked in *A Local Authority v E*[224] to declare on the competence of a severely anorexic woman who also suffered alcohol and opiate dependency as well as unstable personality disorder. The request related, in particular, to the validity of an advance decision made under the 2005 Act. If the decision were invalid, this impacted on the question of the patient's best interests in continuing to be fed. On the evidence before it, which included periods of compulsory treatment under the Mental Health Act 1983, the Court held the young woman to be incompetent at the time of making the direction. This was because of her inability to weigh meaningfully the advantages and disadvantages of eating as brought about by her obsessive fear of gaining weight. On a balance sheet assessment, it was in her best interests to be fed, with force if necessary; moreover the Court was satisfied that such a course of action was necessary and proportionate to protect her right to life, and so was not a breach of her human rights. This case should be read with *M (Adult Patient)* (para 4.47) as examples of contemporary judicial attitudes towards vulnerable patients and the relative weight, or not, that is given to their expressions of autonomy. Ms E, for example, had expressed a clear wish not to have further treatment and her parents were also of the view—having lived throughout her experiences—that it would be in her best interests 'to die with dignity in safe, warm surroundings with those that love her' (para 80). The judge, however, found that 'the balance tips unmistakably in the direction of life-preserving treatment' (at para 140).

CONSENT AND ITS SOCIAL CONSEQUENCES

4.86 If a patient proffers his or her arm in response to the proposition from his or her doctor that he or she would 'like to do some blood tests', can it be said that the patient has given valid consent? In one view, consent can be implied by the simple action of the patient, although it most certainly cannot be said to be informed save as to the imminent

---

[222] Para 4.36.

[223] In the context of minors the Scottish courts seem not to agree with us. In *Re Houston, Applicant* (1996) 32 BMLR 93, Sheriff McGown interpreted s 2(4) of the Age of Legal Capacity (Scotland) Act 1991 in respect of a 15-year-old boy suffering from mental illness to mean that capacity to consent encompassed a capacity to refuse and, furthermore, it brings to an end the power of a parent to consent on behalf of the minor.

[224] [2012] EWHC 1639 (Fam); [2012] 2 FCR 52.

venepuncture and extraction of blood. Meaningful informedness would require disclosure of the nature of the intended tests, what these might reveal in terms of diagnosis or illness and, in some circumstances, the consequences of disclosure of the test results both to the patient and/or to the wider community. From an ethical standpoint, however, a doctor might be loathe at this stage to share his or her suspicions of cancer for fear of alarming the patient unnecessarily; by the same token, the patient might be harbouring a blood-borne infection which would pose a risk to medical personnel or others if appropriate precautions could not be taken. When, then, can testing be performed without informed consent?

4.87   Matters are complicated in this area by the possible (adverse) social consequences which can follow from a positive diagnosis of certain types of condition. Sexually transmitted diseases, and particularly HIV infection, carry social stigma and might lead to discrimination or ostracism; there can be insurance and employment implications leading from confirmation of any number of illnesses, while public health considerations relating to highly contagious or infectious diseases might mean that testing must be done as a matter of urgency even when the niceties of informed consent are not possible or practicable.

4.88   What impact should these considerations have on consent practices? Some might point in the direction of seeking explicit informed consent on the basis that the adverse consequences could be so great that patients should be put fully in the picture even before their blood is drawn. Others, however, suggest that the individual's interests are not the trump consideration when the health and lives of others might be at stake. Each case must necessarily be considered on its own facts, weighing the totality and immediacy of the risks involved with the likely consequences of preferring one practice over another. Thus, although tuberculosis is a far greater threat to public health than HIV infection, the social consequences of a positive diagnosis of HIV are potentially much more far-reaching. We do not want to make a special case of HIV in this section, indeed it could be dangerous to suggest this,[225] but the condition serves as a valuable case study to explore the kinds of issues that are in play in deciding whether express consent to testing should be sought.

4.89   The question of whether tests for HIV infection can be undertaken without the express consent of the patient has always been controversial. Even putting the consequences for the patient aside, his or her HIV status might be an issue after a needle-stick injury or blood contamination of medical personnel; the need to know could be urgent, yet the patient might refuse testing. Indeed, in 2002 the Royal College of Surgeons called for the right to test patients for HIV.[226] The legal problems are the same in each instance: does HIV testing exceed the bounds of any consent which the patient has already given to therapeutic or diagnostic investigation? It should be remembered that the risks are very similar, if not greater, for other life-threatening blood-borne diseases, such as Hepatitis B and C, all of which can be grouped under the heading of serious communicable diseases.

---

[225] M F Brewster, 'HIV exceptionalism must end' (2007) 335 BMJ 60. See also, Terrence Higgins Trust, *HIV Home Testing Kits: Time to Legalise and Regulate* (2011). Note that the ban on home testing kits for HIV has been lifted in England, Scotland, and Wales (with a consultation ongoing in Northern Ireland at the time of writing) and the first approved test went on sale in 2015: see Department of Health, *Modernisation of HIV Rules to Better Protect Public* (2013).

[226] A Browne, 'Surgeons demand right to test patients for HIV infection', *The Times*, 29 July 2002, p 3.

4.90 The General Medical Council (GMC), for its part, withdrew its specific guidance on serious communicable diseases in 2006 and instead deals with the issues in its 'Guidance on Consent' and 'Confidentiality' respectively. We cover the issues on disclosure in Chapter 6. As to consent, the Council has this to say:

> Decisions about testing the infection status of incapacitated patients, after a needle-stick or other injury to a healthcare worker, must take account of the current legal framework governing capacity issues and the use of human tissue ... As we understand it, current law does not permit testing the infection status of an incapacitated patient solely for the benefit of a healthcare worker involved in the patient's care.[227]

4.91 This, however, does not say what should be disclosed—or can be withheld—when testing is in the interests of the patient him- or herself and when that person has sufficient capacity. In its guidance on consent, however, the GMC states:

> You should not withhold information necessary for making decisions for any other reason ... unless you believe that giving it would cause the patient serious harm. In this context 'serious harm' means more than that the patient might become upset or decide to refuse treatment ... If you withhold information from the patient you must record your reason for doing so in the patient's medical records, and you must be prepared to explain and justify your decision.[228]

4.92 Advice from such a source carries great ethical weight but it is framed in question-begging terms; for example, 'What information is *necessary* to make a decision?' and 'What counts as *serious* harm?' Does the threat of social stigma qualify? Furthermore, such guidance does not help as to the legality of testing where disclosure is less than full. Here, conflicting advice has been offered to doctors in the UK in the context of HIV. Legal opinion sought by the Council of the British Medical Association was to the effect that, not only was non-consensual testing impermissible but also, to do so, might well constitute an assault;[229] by contrast, the Central Committee for Hospital Medical Services was advised that the doctor may exercise his or her clinical judgement unless the patient asks specifically about HIV testing;[230] finally, the Medical Defence Union obtained an opinion which eliminated the possibility of assault once permission for venepuncture had been given but, nevertheless, thought that, save in exceptional circumstances—as, for instance when the expectation of a positive result was very low—specific consent for HIV should always be obtained.[231]

4.93 It is significant that much has changed in relation to HIV and AIDS since these opinions were proffered. Where once HIV was untreatable, combination therapy now means a near-normal life for people infected with the virus. Moreover, there is less evidence of a special case being made of the disease in law and professional guidance.[232] Practice, however, has still weighed heavily in favour of specific and informed testing and counselling for HIV as opposed to including it in the battery of 'blood tests'; counter-intuitively,

---

[227] At: http://www.gmc-uk.org/guidance/update_serious_communicable_diseases.asp.

[228] GMC, *Consent: Patients and Doctors Making Decisions Together* (2008), paras 16–17.

[229] M Sharrard and I Gatt, 'Human Immunodeficiency Virus (HIV) antibody testing' (1987) 295 BMJ 911.

[230] HMSC, *Advice re HIV Testing* (1988) discussed by C Dyer, 'Another judgment on testing for HIV without consent' (1988) 296 BMJ 1791.

[231] Medical Defence Union, *AIDS: Medico-Legal Advice* (1988). These three opinions are discussed in detail by J Keown, 'The ashes of AIDS and the phoenix of informed consent' (1989) 52 MLR 790; For a more recent US perspective, see E Cowan and R Macklin, 'Unconsented HIV testing in cases of occupational exposure: Ethics, law, and policy' (2012) 19 Acad Emerg Med 1181.

[232] For support for this process, see K M De Cock and A M Johnson, 'From exceptionalism to normalisation: A reappraisal of attitudes and practice around HIV testing' (1998) 316 BMJ 290.

this is potentially damaging to patient interests. It has been argued, for example, that 'HIV exceptionalism' is no longer sustainable and that the practice of requiring specific and relatively lengthy counselling may actually be deterring patients from being tested.[233] The World Health Organization's (WHO) policy already calls for HIV testing to become a routine part of health care provision;[234] it recognises the adverse possibilities attendant to this kind of testing and has called for a 'human rights approach' to HIV testing and counselling, the cornerstone of which remains informed consent.[235]

4.94 For the patient who consults a doctor not knowing of their HIV infection but concerned about their health generally, a position of non-exceptionalism suggests that the patient gives tacit consent to the carrying out of those diagnostic tests that the doctor considers necessary—the patient's consent to each and every test to be performed on a blood sample need not be obtained and it is unreal to speak of 'informed consent' in this context. This is not a unique view—as Dyer has reported: 'some lawyers have suggested that patients with a "perplexing presentation" might be taken to have given an implied consent to any tests designed to find out what was wrong with them'.[236] The essential question is whether any condition (of which HIV is but one example) is of such a nature as to remove it from the scope of those tests to which the patient may be said to consent implicitly. It is true that HIV tests carry major emotional, financial, and social significance; moreover, while the disease process can be contained, the full-blown condition is probably still incurable— which distinguishes the test from one for, for example, syphilis. The same could, however, be said for a hypothetical test which demonstrated the presence of incurable malignant disease and it is certainly true of other blood-borne conditions such as Hepatitis B and C. It would not be necessary for the doctor to obtain specific consent to undertake such a test, yet it could have consequences similar to a test for HIV infection. The question of whether an insurance candidate has had an HIV test can still be asked, and this is also the case for Hepatitis B and C. And, although the Association of British Insurers states in its Best Practice guidelines that insurers should make it clear that 'If the result is negative, the fact of having an HIV test will not, of itself, have any effect on your acceptance terms for insurance',[237] it has been reported that discrimination still occurs.[238]

4.95 We would raise, too, the potential psychological sequelae of an unexpected positive result which do not only relate to the future *health* implications of testing positive. There is no escaping the fact that our society has constructed a stigma around this disease which, even in today's more understanding climate, makes the confirmation of a positive result all the more difficult to accept. Moreover, if such a result comes 'from the blue' when no specific consent was given, the question of the patient's right *not* to know arises.[239]

[233] K Manavi and P D Welsby, 'HIV testing should no longer be accorded any special status' (2005) 330 BMJ 492. See, too, G Bryce, 'HIV testing in primary care' (2009) 338 BMJ b1085.

[234] WHO, *Consolidated Guidelines of HIV Testing Services* (2015).

[235] UNAIDS/WHO, *Statement on HIV Testing and Counseling: WHO, UNAIDS Re-affirm Opposition to Mandatory HIV Testing* (2012). The Statement opines: 'People being tested for HIV must give informed consent to be tested. They must be informed of the process for HTC, the services that will be available depending on the results, and their right to refuse testing. Mandatory or compulsory (coerced) testing is never appropriate, regardless of where that coercion comes from: health-care providers, partners, family members, employers, or others.'

[236] C Dyer, 'Testing for HIV: The medico-legal view' (1987) 295 BMJ 871. D Brahams, 'Human Immunodeficiency Virus and the law' [1987] 2 Lancet 227 shared our view so long as consent to test for HIV infection had not been specifically withheld.

[237] Association of British Insurers, *Statement of Best Practice for HIV and Insurance* (2008) para 3.7.

[238] K Hughes, 'Insurers criticised for attitude to gay men', *The Independent*, 19 April 2008.

[239] Discussed in the context of genetic information in Chapter 7.

These factors certainly constitute grounds for treating the HIV test with special care but it is doubtful if it is a sufficiently powerful argument to exclude absolutely all testing for which no specific consent was given. Nonetheless, the patient could argue that, had he been informed of the doctor's intention, he would not have consented to giving the sample; in such circumstances, an action for negligence might be available under the general terms of the consent doctrine.[240] The critical condition, here, is that he was informed—insurance and comparable complicating factors do not arise if the patient is ignorant of the facts. The professional attitude is summed up by the reported case in which a doctor was found guilty of serious professional misconduct for testing five patients for HIV without consent.[241] The GMC found that there was insufficient clinical evidence of infection in each patient, indicating, perhaps, that matters might be different were it otherwise. However, the practitioner must be prepared to justify his action, both in court and before his peers, in all cases of non-consensual testing, as the most up-to-date version of GMC guidance makes perfectly clear.

4.96 The position of children is somewhat different in that they are victims of circumstances outside their control. Thus, we have *Re HIV Tests (Note)*[242] in 1994—a period when there was no effective treatment for HIV infection—wherein the procedural safeguard was established that 'for the time being', and because of the 'whole range of emotional and psychological and practical problems which bear on the question', it was advised that 'applications to determine whether HIV testing was in a child's best interests should always be considered by the High Court in the first instance'. Only a decade later, however, we have the President of the Family Division's directions executing a 180 turn.[243] Reflecting the growing judicial and medical experience, these now indicate that it is no longer necessary to take a child HIV testing case to the High Court. This will only be so if the inherent jurisdiction of the court is being invoked or if a mature minor is refusing the test and parties seek to override such refusal. Moreover, if all those with parental responsibility agree to testing, and there is no opposition from the child, then no reference to court is required at all. Helpful practical guidance in respect of all minors is now provided by the Department of Health.[244]

4.97 Measures designed to protect health care staff from infection also raise difficult issues, as do measures to protect patients from infection by staff. Would the public interest justify coercive routine testing of some or all health carers? There has been an historical tendency in this direction in the USA,[245] which has been resisted in the UK, by both the government and the medical profession. In practice, it would be an ineffective way of solving a problem which is, to all intents, insignificant. Between 1988 and 2003 there were 28 patient notification exercises in the UK following concerns of infection from health care workers. There was no detectable transmission of HIV from an infected worker despite around 7,000 patients having been tested.[246] It is more than doubtful if it would be morally defensible to spend millions of pounds of health service money[247] on exorcising

---

[240] See para 4.101 et seq.

[241] C Dyer, 'GP reprimanded for testing patients for HIV without consent' (2000) 320 BMJ 135.

[242] [1994] 2 FLR 116; [1994] Fam Law 559.

[243] *President's Direction: HIV Testing of Children* [2003] 1 FLR 1299.

[244] Department of Health, *Children in Need and Blood-Borne Viruses: HIV and Hepatitis* (2004).

[245] M Morris, 'American legislation on AIDS' (1991) 303 BMJ 325.

[246] Department of Health, *HIV Infected Health Care Workers: Guidance on Management and Patient Notification* (2005) para 2.4.

[247] K Tolley and J Kennelly, 'Cost of compulsory HIV testing' (1993) 306 BMJ 1202.

such an ephemeral spectre. Indeed, the tendency in the UK is towards less intervention-ist practices. Thus, following independent scientific advice, the Department of Health announced it 2013 that it would lift the ban on health care workers with HIV being able to carry out certain dental and surgical procedures.[248] Measures relating to treatment, monitoring, and testing will be in place to protect patients.

4.98   The issue of contamination of the health carer has been raised on several occasions by the Royal Colleges of Surgeons of England and of Edinburgh[249] and, indeed, evidence indi-cates that the risk of transmission is greater *from* an HIV-positive patient *to* a health care worker than the reverse. But even then the risks are low. Data to November 2008 indicated that there had only been a total of five documented seroconversions of health care workers exposed to HIV-positive patients in the UK, and none has occurred since 1999. In con-trast, the total number of Hepatitis C seroconversions reported in England between 1997 and 2007 was 14.[250] Once again, this suggests that the debate should be focused on issues of degree of risk and nature of harm rather than on any particular condition. The GMC has stated that testing a patient without consent and purely in the interests of other health workers is unacceptable and probably illegal.[251]

4.99   Random HIV testing, which may be of great epidemiological importance, is less con-troversial but still raises ethical issues.[252] Much of the information that is needed can be best gleaned using blood samples which have been obtained for other purposes but the morality of random testing for a specific condition depends, to a large extent, and as discussed in Chapter 19, on what would be done in the event of a positive result. The inherent dilemmas can be addressed in part by total anonymisation but this only sub-stitutes one potential immorality by another—the knowledge obtained cannot now be used for the benefit of the individual or of his or her contacts. In general, however, the positive advantages of investigation seem to outweigh such objections provided that those tested are informed that their blood may be subjected to anonymised testing of any sort and that they will not be informed of the results. The Unlinked Anonymous Prevalence Monitoring Programme has, in fact, been in operation since 1990, providing a vital ser-vice for public health by generating data which could not be ascertained in any other way. Its work showed that, by the end of 2013, an estimated 107,800 adults were infected with HIV in the UK, 24 per cent of whom were unaware of their infection.[253] Similar results exist for other blood-borne infectious diseases. Such figures are of major value in respect of public health and treatment planning, as well as for further research into diseases and their spread and the cost implications for health care.

4.100   The question of whether it is ethically acceptable to carry out testing of this nature with-out the consent of the donors still remains problematic. There is a strong argument for allowing it on the ground of public interest. In this view, such testing cannot possibly harm the donor of the sample, who may well be unaware that his or her sample is being

[248]   See Department of Health, n 225.

[249]   A Walker, 'Surgeons and HIV' (1991) 302 BMJ 136 and also in 2003, see para 6.31.

[250]   Health Protection Agency, *Eye of the Needle: United Kingdom Surveillance of Significant Occupational Exposures to Bloodborne Viruses in Healthcare Workers* (2008).

[251]   N 227.

[252]   See S Rennie et al., 'Conducting unlinked anonymous HIV surveillance in developing coun-tries: Ethical, epidemiological, and public health concerns' (2009) 6(1) PLoS Med, 20 January 2009, and P de Zulueta, 'The ethics of anonymised HIV testing of pregnant women: a reappraisal' (2000) 26(1) J Med Ethics 16.

[253]   Public Health England, *HIV in the United Kingdom: 2014 Report*.

used in this way. A contrary view—which has been discussed in detail in respect of genetic testing in Chapter 7—is that a wrong is done even if the donor is unaware of it, and that a person who discovers that a personal sample has been used in this way is entitled to feel that his or her privacy has been infringed, irrespective of what protections against de-anonymisation were in place. Moreover, as more and more can be done for individuals infected by diseases such as HIV, there is an ethical case, and potentially a legal duty, to offer feedback when knowledge of infection is generated and when greater harm might be averted through disclosure. On the other hand, care and treatment in respect of blood-borne diseases simply cannot advance if we do not facilitate research and the costs of feedback programmes might be to the detriment of this essential work. Individuals such as pregnant women, genito-urinary clinic attendees, and intravenous drug users are certainly informed of anonymised testing and can opt-out if they so wish. This brings us to our final point for this section: the role consent serves as a means by which we respect individuals and protect their interests. It is, however, possible to achieve these same ends without always relying on consent itself.

PROCEEDING WITHOUT CONSENT: THE CONSEQUENCES

4.101 Failure to obtain consent to medical treatment entitles the patient to sue for damages for the battery that is committed. It is also possible to base a claim on the tort of negligence, the theory being that the doctor has been negligent in failing to obtain appropriate consent. There are important differences between the two forms of action which have given rise to much legal debate.

4.102 An action for battery arises when the claimant has been touched in some way by the defendant and when there has been no consent, express or implied, to such touching. All that the claimant need establish in such an action is that the defendant wrongfully touched him or her. It is unnecessary to establish loss as a result and, therefore, there is no problem as to the causation of damage, which is the unauthorised touching—and the severity of the damage will be reflected in the recompense awarded. By contrast, in an action based on the tort of negligence, the claimant must establish that the defendant wrongfully touched him or her and that the negligence of the defendant in touching him or her without consent has led to the injury for which damages are sought, and which are usually related to the manifestation of an inherent risk in the medical procedure itself. There is, thus, a problem of factual causation to be tackled and, for this reason, the action for battery is an easier option from the claimant's point of view. The measure of damages recoverable will also be different. All direct damages are recoverable in battery whereas only those which are foreseeable and for which it is fair and just to compensate may be recovered in an action for negligence. Thus, an unforeseen medical complication arising from the procedure in question may give rise to something for which damages are recoverable in battery but not in negligence. Clarification of the circumstances in which each action is available was particularly well provided by the Supreme Court of Canada in *Reibl* v *Hughes*[254] and in the first apposite English case of *Chatterton* v *Gerson*.[255]

---

[254] (1980) 114 DLR (3d) 1 at 10, per Laskin CJ. The ruling was applied without modification, inter alia, in *E (D) (guardian ad litem of)* v *British Columbia* (2005) Carswell BC 523, 2005 BCCA 134 (BCCA, 11 March 2005).

[255] [1981] QB 432; [1981] 1 All ER 257. See also *Hills* v *Potter* [1983] 3 All ER 716; [1984] 1WLR 641.

PROCEEDING WITHOUT CONSENT: THE CONSEQUENCES

4.103 An action for battery is appropriate where there has been no consent at all to the physical contact in question. Thus, an action for battery is the suitable remedy if a patient has refused to submit to a procedure but the doctor has, nevertheless, gone ahead in the face of that refusal. Two historic Canadian cases illustrate the typical circumstances. Actions were sustained in *Mulloy* v *Hop Sang*,[256] where the plaintiff's hand was amputated without his consent, and in *Schweizer* v *Central Hospital*,[257] the surgeon performing an operation on the back of a plaintiff whose consent was related to an operation on his toe was held liable for battery. It will be seen in these cases that what the doctor actually did was quite unconnected with the procedure to which the patient had consented. There was no consent to an operation of the 'general nature' of that which was actually performed—thus, they lay within the courts' policy of restricting battery actions to acts of unambiguous hostility.

4.104 Consent is also a matter of fundamental human rights. In *VC* v *Slovakia*, 'consent' to sterilisation was obtained during labour and when the woman was in a state of fear. This was held to be a breach of her right to respect for her private life (Art 8, ECHR) as well as an example of cruel and inhuman treatment (Art 3, ECHR).[258] The relevance of Art 8 was further confirmed and developed in *AK* v *Latvia*,[259] a 'wrongful birth' case brought by the mother of a child with Down's syndrome who complained that due to the negligence of her doctor, she was not given adequate information concerning or a referral for antenatal screening which would have detected fetal abnormalities. In a narrowly focused judgment, the majority of the ECtHR accepted that the applicant's inadequate medical care and the cursory treatment of her subsequent legal action by the Latvian domestic courts were admissible complaints and that Art 8 had been violated in its procedural aspects.

4.105 A claim based on negligence (see further Chapter 5) is apt when the claimant has given his consent to an act of the general nature of that which is performed by the defendant but there is a flaw in this consent and, as a result, there has been no consent to certain concomitant features of the act of which he was unaware. The negligence lies in a failure to apprise the patient of such features as a result of which he has sustained damage; the damage is not due to negligent performance but results from a mishap which, in this instance, was a recognised potential hazard of the procedure. By way of explanation we have Laskin CHC in *Reibl* v *Hughes* who remarked:

> I do not understand how it can be said that the consent was vitiated by the failure of disclosure of risks as to make the surgery or other treatment an unprivileged, unconsented to and intentional invasion of the patient's bodily integrity. I can appreciate the temptation to say that the genuineness of consent to medical treatment depends on proper disclosure of the risks which it entails, but … unless there has been misrepresentation or fraud to secure consent to the treatment, a failure to disclose the attendant risks, however serious, should go to negligence rather than battery.

4.106 Similarly, it was emphasised in *Chatterton* v *Gerson* that an action for trespass to the person is inappropriate once the patient is informed in 'broad terms' of the nature of the procedure and consent is given; an action for negligence is the proper remedy if there is a failure to disclose risks.[260] This, however, is not to say that an action in assault or battery is entirely irrelevant to medical law. In *Appleton* v *Garrett*[261] the High Court awarded both

---

[256] [1935] 1 WWR 714.   [257] (1974) 53 DLR (3d) 494.
[258] [2011] ECHR 1888.   [259] [2014] ECHR 33011.
[260] N 255.   [261] (1995) 34 BMLR 23. See also [1996] 4 Med L Rev 311.

exemplary and aggravated damages against a dentist who had actively deceived patients as to their need for treatment over a number of years. Any consent offered by the patients was vitiated by the fraudulent misrepresentation of the practitioner.[262] The Court held that information had been deliberately withheld and the defendant had acted throughout in bad faith, making an action in battery, rather than in negligence, appropriate. This having been said, there need not be a nefarious purpose behind the touching for an assault to be committed, as the case of *Ms B* shows.[263] However, only notional damages are likely to be awarded in such cases in recognition of the affront to bodily integrity that the unauthorised touching represents.

THE NEGLIGENCE ACTION AND THE VAGARIES OF INFORMATION DISCLOSURE

4.107 When an undisclosed risk arises, the aggrieved patient is, in essence, claiming, 'You did not inform me of the risk which has eventuated; but for your failure, I would not have consented to the procedure; you have failed in your duty of care and, as a result, I have sustained injury'. The problem in negligence actions based on a lack of consent is, therefore, largely that of causation—the court must be satisfied that the defendant's failure to obtain the valid consent of the patient was, in fact, the cause of the patient's injury. To satisfy this requirement, the patient must normally prove that he would not have given his consent had he received the information of which he was allegedly deprived. We explore the whole concept of causation fully in Chapter 5. Here we simply highlight the hurdles faced by a claimant in respect of inadequate information disclosure. The issues have, indeed, been addressed most recently by the Supreme Court in *Montgomery v Lanarkshire Health Board*, wherein the Supreme Court adopted a clear policy line in favour of the patient regarding the standard of care that can be expected from their doctors in terms of disclosure of risks associated with health care.[264] The line of authority began to evolve some time ago and we consider it appropriate to address the question of standard of care before proceeding to causation. In this way the reader can best assess for him- or herself how the law has been developing.

STANDARDS OF CARE AND INFORMED CONSENT

4.108 The discussion in this field centres on the issue of 'informed consent'—a concept which will always remain a classic example of the importation of a medical philosophy from across the Atlantic. Its journey has, in fact, been remarkably slow. Thus, while the first mention of 'informed consent' in the English courts seems to have been as late as 1981,[265] the seed was sown in the USA in 1957 in the case of *Salgo*.[266] Here, the court concluded that the doctor had a duty to disclose to the patient 'any facts which are necessary to form the basis of an intelligent consent by the patient to the proposed

---

[262] Similarly, those who pose as a qualified medical practitioner and elicit consent to touching on this basis are guilty of criminal assault: see *R v Tabassum* [2000] 2 Cr App R 328; [2000] Lloyd's Rep Med 404. On the role of deception, see *R v Jheeta (Harvinder Singh)* [2008] 1 WLR 2582; [2007] 2 Cr App R 34.
[263] Discussed at para 4.42. £100 in token damages was awarded.
[264] [2015] UKSC 11; [2015] 2 WLR 768.
[265] *Chatterton v Gerson* [1981] QB 432; [1981] 1 All ER 257.
[266] *Salgo v Leland Stanford Junior University Board of Trustees* 317 P 2d 170 (Cal, 1957).

treatment'.[267] It is unfortunate that the original terminology 'intelligent consent' was replaced, in a later passage related to therapeutic privilege,[268] by:

> In discussing the element of risk, a certain amount of discretion must be employed consistent with full disclosure of facts necessary to an *informed* consent. [Emphasis added.][269]

Informed consent was later made a requirement for all state-funded research work following a series of allegations that potentially dangerous experiments were being conducted without the consent of the experimental subjects.[270] Silverman maintained that there are, thus, two distinct forms of 'informed consent' and, certainly, this must be so as to the assessment of the quality of the information provided. Such an assessment *must* be prospective in the case of research whereas it can only be retrospective, for example by way of litigation, in respect of day-to-day patient management.

4.109 In either event, informed consent introduced a new element to medical treatment. It is no longer a simple matter of consent to a technical assault; consent must now be based on a knowledge of the nature, risks, consequences, and alternatives associated with the proposed therapy.[271] Bray J's definition has gone relatively unchallenged across the USA but it is still no more than a broad expression of principle. It goes no way to explaining either what counts as informed consent or how we tell that the circumstances surrounding a given event satisfy the requirements.[272] Insofar as it defines a doctor's duties rather than the patient's reaction, the phrase is a misnomer[273] which, we believe, has been applied in medical writing and, indeed, now almost inevitably, in official publications with inadequate exploration of its meaning.[274] Moreover, the phrase is tautologous—to be ethically and legally acceptable, 'consent' must always be 'informed'. It is interesting to note that, although the English text of the Council of Europe's Convention on Human Rights and Biomedicine speaks of 'informed consent' in Art 5, the French text refers merely to 'consentement' *tout simple*.[275]

4.110 The topic recalls the aphorism of Frankfurter J, albeit in a completely different context:

> A phrase begins life as a literary expression; its felicity leads to its lazy repetition; and repetition soon establishes it as a legal formula indiscriminately used to express different and sometimes contradictory ideas.[276]

Thus, we suggest that, when Dunn LJ said in the fundamental House of Lords case of *Sidaway*, 'The concept of informed consent forms no part of English law',[277] he may well

---

[267] Per Bray J.   [268] See para 4.116.

[269] Per Bray J in *Salgo*, n 266, quoted by W A Silverman, 'The myth of informed consent: In daily practice and in clinical trials' (1989) 15 J Med Ethics 6 to whom we are indebted for many of the historical details.

[270] *Surgeon General's Memorandum Clinical Investigations Using Human Subjects* (1966). It is, of course, now an integral part of research on a global scale (see generally Chapter 19).

[271] On this last point, see *Birch v University College London Hospital NHS Foundation Trust* (2008) 104 BMLR 168; *Montgomery v Lanarkshire Health Board* [2015] UKSC 11; [2015] 2 WLR 768.

[272] G R Gillett, 'Informed consent and moral integrity' (1989) 15 J Med Ethics 117.

[273] T K Feng, 'Failure of medical advice: trespass or negligence' (1987) 7 LS 149.

[274] For criticism see, O O'Neill, 'Some limits of informed consent' (2003) 29 J Med Ethics 4; O Corrigan, 'Empty ethics: The problem with informed consent' (2003) 25 Sociology of Health and Illness 768; and M Boulton and M Parker, 'Informed consent in a changing environment' (2007) 65 Soc Sc & Med 2187.

[275] Council of Europe Convention for the Protection of Human Rights and Dignity of the Human Being with regard to the Application of Biology and Medicine (1997), Art 5.

[276] *Tiller v Atlantic Coast Line Railroad Co* 318 US 54 at 68 (1943).

[277] *Sidaway v Board of Governors of the Bethlem Royal Hospital* [1984] QB 493 at 517; [1984] 1 All ER 1018 at 1030, CA.

have been referring to consent based on a subjective patient test[278]—for no one would now deny that 'information' must nowadays be passed from doctor to patient in the UK. Yet, similar disclaimers have been repeated both in England[279] and in Scotland[280]—and have been echoed in Australia[281]—and the legal definition has remained obscured. Indeed, such is the reliance that is now placed on consent to protect and promote interests across the medico-legal sphere, including treatment and research contexts, that it now takes a bewildering variety of forms. These include: informed,[282] broad,[283] open,[284] blanket,[285] generic,[286] specific,[287] implicit/explicit,[288] appropriate,[289] valid, and written consent.[290]

4.111   We cannot hope to do justice to all of these conceptualisations in this chapter. They are revisited at suitable junctures throughout this book. For present purposes, the short-hand of 'informed consent'—meaning valid consent to medical treatment—can be accepted as part of the lore of medical ethics and its repetition among even the highest ranks of judiciary[291] means that we must accept it and consider the basic nature of the information that has to be given in order to validate consent to medical treatment.

What Needs to be Disclosed?

4.112   Looked at from the ethical point of view, the matter is one of self-determination.[292] A person should not be exposed to a risk of harm unless he has agreed to that risk and he or she cannot properly agree to—or, equally importantly, make a choice between—risks in the absence of factual information. The twin problems to be resolved are, therefore, by what general standard should the information be judged and, within that, to what extent must or should particular details be divulged?

---

[278] See para 4.113.

[279] English law does not accept the transatlantic concept of informed consent' per Lord Donaldson in *Re T (adult) (refusal of medical treatment)* [1992] 4 All ER 649 at 663; (1992) 9 BMLR 46 at 61, CA.

[280] '[T]he law ... has come down firmly against the view that the doctor's duty to the patient involves at all costs obtaining the informed consent of the patient to specific medical treatments': *Moyes* v *Lothian Health Board* [1990] 1 Med LR 463; 1990 SLT 444 at 449, per Lord Caplan.

[281] '... nothing is to be gained by reiterating ... the oft-used and somewhat amorphous phrase "informed consent" ': *Rogers* v *Whittaker* (1992) 109 ALR 625 at 633; (1994) 16 BMLR 148 at 156 (High Court of Australia), per Mason CJ et al. For comment, see A Braun, L Skene, and A Merry, 'Informed consent for anaesthesia in Australia and New Zealand' (2010) 38(5) Anaesthesia and Intensive Care 809 for comprehensive and culturally relative perspectives.

[282] A MacLean, 'From *Sidaway* to *Pearce* and beyond: Is the legal regulation of consent any better following a quarter of a century of judicial scrutiny?' (2012) 20 Med L Rev 108.

[283] T Caulfield and J Kaye, 'Broad consent in biobanking: Reflections on seemingly insurmountable dilemmas' (2009) 10 Med L Inter 85–100.

[284] J E Lunshof et al., 'From genetic privacy to open consent' (2008) 9 Nature Rev Genetics 406.

[285] T Caulfield, 'Biobanks and blanket consent: The proper place of the public good and public perception rationales' (2007) 18(2) King's LJ 209.

[286] Ibid.

[287] M Otlowski, 'Tackling legal challenges posed by population biobanks: Reconceptualising consent requirements' (2012) 20(2) Medical L Rev 191.

[288] Ibid.   [289] P Taylor, 'When consent gets in the way' (2008) 456 Nature 32.

[290] For consideration of the legal consequences of these developments, see G Laurie and E Postan, 'Rhetoric or reality: What is the legal status of the consent form in health-related research?' (2012) 20 Med L Rev doi: 10.1093/medlaw/fws031.

[291] See *Chester* v *Afshar*, per Lord Hope at para 57 and Lord Steyn at para 14 who actually states: 'Surgery performed without the informed consent of the patient is unlawful. The court is the final arbiter of what constitutes informed consent.'

[292] For stringent criticism from the ethical perspective, see N C Manson and O O'Neill, *Rethinking Informed Consent in Bioethics* (2007).

4.113   The general standards available are conveniently described as the 'patient standard' and the 'professional standard'. The first of these can be further divided, on the one hand, into the subjective and, on the other, the objective patient standard. The first involves a purely subjective judgement—that is, what would that particular patient have considered to be adequate information? Thus, the extreme of this school of thought would hold that, given a rational patient, the doctor must reveal all the relevant facts as to what he intends to do. It is not for him to determine what the patient should or should not hear. This is clearly open to the abuse of hindsight. It will be only too easy for a claimant, once he has suffered damage, to allege that he would not have given his consent when, in reality, he may well have been quite prepared to do so, even with full knowledge of the risks entailed. The subjective standard is weighted overwhelmingly in favour of the claimant and only a few jurisdictions have accepted it.[293]

4.114   The objective approach, often called the 'prudent patient' test, is to postulate a standard based on a reasonable patient. How much information would the reasonable patient wish to know? This, as with all objective tests, has the disadvantage of being potentially unfair to the claimant. There may be specific circumstances which are unique to the individual and it may well be that he or she genuinely would wish to know the potential affect on them. To apply the objective standard might, then, be equally unsatisfactory: 'if it is Utopian to think one must concentrate on the particular patient, the law should surely be aiming at Utopia'.[294] The reasonable patient test has practical value in that judges are, themselves, potential patients and can, therefore, assess the standard at first hand rather than by proxy; at the same time, this introduces the element of personal prejudice and, in *Maynard*,[295] the trial judge was considered to have been in error in preferring one body of medical opinion to another.

4.115   A third, compromise, possibility exists. The court may opt for an objective approach but qualify it by investing the hypothetical reasonable patient with the relevant special peculiarities of the individual claimant. In this way the edge is taken off the objective test, while the pitfalls of the purely subjective approach are avoided. The courts in Canada vacillated for some time between the alternatives of the objective and subjective approaches.[296] Finally, in *Reibl* v *Hughes*,[297] the Supreme Court came down in favour of the compromise solution. The effect of this is that one's starting point is to determine the extent to which the balance of risks was, medically speaking, in favour of the treatment in question. This allows a decision to be made as to whether a reasonable patient would have consented and, that done, the court can proceed to look at the particular patient's condition. Here the judgment in *Reibl* v *Hughes* emphasised the importance of taking into account the patient's questions to the doctor, as these will demonstrate his or her concerns

---

[293]   The subjective standard was certainly used by the New Zealand Court of Appeal in *Smith* v *Auckland Hospital Board* [1964] NZLR 241, SC; revsd [1965] NZLR 191, NZCA, but there was no argument on the point in this very early case; a clear Antipodean preference for the subjective standard is to be found in the New South Wales Court of Appeal decision: *Ellis* v *Wallsend District Hospital* [1990] 2 Med LR 103.

[294]   K McK Norrie, 'Informed consent and the duty of care' 1985 SLT 289. Or achieving 'the ethical optimum of patient autonomy' as put by M Brazier, 'Patient autonomy and consent to treatment: The role of the law?' (1987) 7 LS 169. These works remain relevant today in the formation of the discipline.

[295]   *Maynard* v *West Midlands Regional Health Authority* [1985] 1 All ER 635; [1984] 1 WLR 634, HL. A rather similar judicial foray into medical decision-making was rejected on appeal in *Gold* v *Haringey Health Authority* [1988] QB 481; [1987] 2 All ER 888, CA. *Maynard* has been widely followed but is now under scrutiny in the light of *Bolitho* v *City and Hackney Health Authority* [1997] 4 All ER 771; (1997) 39 BMLR 1.

[296]   See, e.g., *Male* v *Hopmans* (1967) 64 DLR (2d) 105; *Kelly* v *Haslett* (1976) 75 DLR (3d) 536.

[297]   (1980) 114 DLR (3d) 1.

and will better enable the court to assess what a reasonable patient in the claimant's position would have done. This is now also largely the position adopted in the UK.

4.116   Obviously, there must be some medical assessment of what is or is not significant but, apart from the exclusion of irrelevant material, the patient should be as fully informed as possible so that he or she can make up his or her mind in the light of all the relevant circumstances. This approach most fully satisfies the requirements of self-determination but can be criticised on the grounds that it leaves little scope for the exercise of clinical judgement by the doctor. It is for this reason that even those most dedicated to patient autonomy will allow the doctor the 'therapeutic privilege' to withhold information which would merely serve to distress or confuse the patient.[298] The GMC Guidance advises:

> In deciding how much information to share with your patients you should take account of their wishes. The information you share should be in proportion to the nature of their condition, the complexity of the proposed investigation or treatment, and the seriousness of any potential side effects, complications or other risks.[299]

4.117   This concession applies only to specific items selected by the doctor for specific reasons. It does, however, go beyond the alternative approach to disclosure of information—that is, one based solely on the professional standard.[300] Here, counselling and informing are regarded as an integral part of clinical management; the extent and detail of the information supplied is a matter for decision by the doctor who is, therein, subject to the same duty of care as when prescribing or operating. It follows that, whichever standard is adopted, litigation based on inadequate information must be taken in negligence. Any difference lies in the test to be applied. Given a patient standard, the quality of information will be judged from the viewpoint of the prudent—or, in one formulation, the particular—patient; under the professional standard, it will be that of the prudent doctor.

4.118   The choice between a 'patient standard' and a 'professional standard' is a difficult one for the health carer. There must be respect for the patient's legitimate interest in knowing to what he is subjecting himself but, at the same time, there will clearly be cases where a paternalistic approach is appropriate.[301] In addition, the practicalities of the situation must be borne in mind. Although it might be ethically desirable for patients to be as fully informed as possible, the time spent in explaining the intricacies of procedures could be considerable, particularly if a doctor is expected to deal with remote risks. Doctors—and, particularly, doctors operating in a national health service—simply do not have the time to spend on unduly lengthy explanations of all the ramifications of treatment and many would regard the practice as unnecessarily disturbing for the patient.[302] It has also long

---

[298] For discussion of the ethical and legal considerations, see K Hodkinson, 'The need to know—Therapeutic privilege: A way forward' (2012) 21 Health Care Anal 105.

[299] GMC, n 19, p 5.

[300] This is the standard adopted in New York State by the legislation NY Public Health Law, s 2805-d (2) (2006): see J Dolgin, 'The legal development of the informed consent doctrine: past and present' (2010) 19 Cam Quarterly of Healthcare Ethics 97.

[301] For discussion on patient deception, see R J Sullivan, L W Menapace, and R M White, 'Truth-telling and patient diagnoses' (2001) 27 J Med Ethics 192; M Gold, 'Is honesty always the best policy? Ethical aspects of truth telling' (2004) 34 Internal Medicine Journal 578; and D M Hester and R B Talisse, 'Physician deception and patient autonomy' (2009) 9(Dec) Am J Bioeth 22.

[302] This, and other aspects, have been researched in Sheffield: D D Kerrigan, R S Thevasagayam, T O Woods et al., 'Who's afraid of informed consent?' (1993) 306 BMJ 298 and was found to be unmerited. The study, however, concerned the relatively innocuous repair of inguinal hernia—the authors concede that the results could be different in more serious circumstances.

been pointed out that adherence to a professional standard provides a coherent body of principles;[303] courts that are subject to this standard are, therefore, at least less likely to be inconsistent in their judgment of disputes.

4.119 A final point about the nature of the doctrine of informed consent relates to 'patient understanding'. The focus of the concept is on information given, supposedly to further the autonomy of the patient. But the consequent implication is that the HCP has fulfilled his duty once he or she has proffered the information. Such a narrow interpretation, however, ignores consideration of the patient's ability to assimilate and analyse the information.[304] If it is not also part of the doctor's duty to ensure at least a degree of understanding on the part of the patient, he can discharge his duty by offering information in a way that results in no enhancement of the patient's autonomy—the ethical basis of the doctrine is, accordingly, undermined.[305] An overly technical explanation of a procedure might involve lots of information but equally will do little to advance autonomous decision-making. It is a fallacy to make consent forms longer and more detailed in an attempt to meet the requirements of the law for at least two reasons. First, this is likely to hinder rather than promote patient understanding, and, second, because a signed consent form has, in any case, no binding validity, it merely serves as *some* evidence that consent has been obtained, but this can always be rebutted if contrary evidence demonstrates that the patient was uncomprehending and did not truly provide his or her voluntary assent. This was confirmed by *Williamson v East London and the City Health Authority*.[306] The surgeon maintained that she had explained that an extensive breast operation might be likely. The plaintiff did not accept that she was told this before the operation. The form that was signed related to silicon replacement, but was subsequently altered to read 'Bilateral replacement. Breast prosthesis. Right subcutaneous mastectomy'. There was no evidence that the patient had re-signed the form or initialled the amendments. The judge was satisfied that, on the balance of probabilities, the surgeon did not properly or sufficiently explain her intention to alter the operation.[307]

4.120 The appropriate conclusion to draw from this is that consent must be seen as a process of communication and not as a one-off event.[308] It requires a 'partnership' between HCP and patient in reaching a decision that is right for the patient in his or her circumstances—a process that is increasingly being seen as 'shared decision-making'. This now largely reflects the tenor of detailed guidance provided by both the Department of Health[309] and the GMC[310] as to what patients should be told in order to obtain valid consent. The Department of Health guidance was revised in 2009 to take

---

[303] C Newdick, 'The doctor's duties of care under *Sidaway*' (1985) 36 NILQ 243.

[304] For survey evidence suggesting that detailed descriptions do not confuse or deter, see J R T Greene, 'Effects of detailed information about dissection on intentions to bequeath bodies for use in teaching and research' (2003) 202 J of Anatomy 475. See also, M Dixon-Woods et al., 'Beyond "misunderstanding": Written information and decisions about taking part in a genetic epidemiology study' (2007) 65 Soc Sci & Med 2212 and M E Falagas et al., 'Informed consent: How much and what do patients understand?' (2009) 198(3) Am J Surg 420.

[305] For a very useful example, see *Al Hamwi v Johnston* [2005] Lloyd's Rep Med 309.

[306] (1998) 41 BMLR 85; [1998] Lloyd's Rep Med 6.   [307] See also *VC v Slovakia*, n 258.

[308] For argument to this effect, see Laurie and Postan, n 290.

[309] Department of Health, *Reference Guide to Consent for Examination or Treatment* (2nd edn, 2009). Numerous other documents and guidance—including that for patients—appears on the Department of Health website at: http://www.dh.gov.uk.

[310] GMC, *Consent: Patients and Doctors Making Decisions Together* (2008).

account of developments in legislation and case law and it draws heavily on the position of the GMC as revised in 2008:

> In considering what information to provide, the health practitioner should try to ensure that the person is able to make an informed judgement on whether to give or withhold consent … It is therefore advisable to inform the person of any 'material' or 'significant' risks or unavoidable risks, even if small, in the proposed treatment; any alternatives to it; and the risks incurred by doing nothing …
>
> The GMC … recommends that doctors should do their best to find out about patients' individual needs and priorities when providing information about treatment options. It advises that discussions should focus on the patient's 'individual situation and risk to them' and sets out the importance of providing the information about the procedure and associated risks in a balanced way and checking that patients have understood the information given.[311]

4.121 It is important to note that 'therapeutic privilege' is now treated with a high degree of caution. It should only be exercised in the 'very rare event' that following the guidance will result in serious harm to the patient. All decisions to withhold information must be justified. Importantly, 'The mere fact that the patient might become upset by hearing the information, or might refuse treatment, is not sufficient to act as a justification'.[312]

The Standard of Care Cases

4.122 The recent Supreme Court ruling in *Montgomery v Lanarkshire Health Board* has confirmed that doctors have a legal duty to advise patients of any material risks involved in a recommended treatment, and also of any reasonable alternative treatments.[313] The law in the UK has, however, not always given a clear steer on what is legally required of HCPs. Whatever standpoint one takes on information disclosure, a decision of some court can be found which will endorse one's preferred approach. Within the Commonwealth, there are decisions ranging from the endorsement of the deliberate medical lie to the acceptance of the extreme patient-orientated approach which emphasises complete disclosure of risk.[314] Nevertheless, it is worth recapitulating the reasons given in favour of a shift from the professional standard to the prudent patient standard as set out in an American case in which the onus was transferred.[315] These included:

(i) that conditions other than those that are purely medical will influence the patient's decision;

(ii) that following the whim of the physician is inconsistent with the patient's right to self-determination; and

(iii) that the professional standard smacks of anachronistic paternalism.

In addition, the court in *Largey* specifically ruled out the criticism that the prudent patient test obliges the doctor to list every possible complication of the proposed procedure.

---

[311] Department of Health, n 309, paras 18–19.

[312] N 309, para 20; also see *Montgomery v Lanarkshire Health Board* [2015] UKSC 11 at 85, 91, and 95.

[313] [2015] UKSC 11; [2015] 2 WLR 768.

[314] See R Heywood, 'Subjectivity in risk disclosure: considering the position of the particular patient' (2009) 25 PN 3 and S Harder, 'Medical non-disclosure and hypothetical consent' (2009) 20 King's LJ 435.

[315] *Largey v Rothman* 540 A 2d 504 (NJ, 1988). The prudent patient standard was set in *Canterbury v Spence* 464 F 2d 772 (DC, 1972).

4.123 The starting point for the UK position is found in the complementary cases of *Hunter* v *Hanley*[316] in Scotland and *Bolam* v *Friern Hospital Management Committee*[317] in England, both of which continue to define the essence of 'technical medical negligence' as we outline in more detail in Chapter 5. For the purposes of the present discussion, we need only outline the core *Bolam* dictum thus: 'a doctor is not negligent if he acts in accordance with a practice accepted at the time as proper by a responsible body of medical opinion'.[318] Since it is agreed that actions based on lack of consent to medical treatment should be taken in negligence, it follows that any argument as to what needs to be disclosed in British medical practice hinges upon whether or not the *Bolam* principle applies equally to both diagnosis and treatment *and* to the giving of information.

4.124 That it does so was upheld both in *Chatterton* v *Gerson*[319] and in *Hills* v *Potter*.[320] The acid test, however, came in the seminal House of Lords decision in *Sidaway*,[321] which concerned a neuro-surgeon who had omitted to warn his patient of the 1–2 per cent intrinsic risk of damage to the spinal cord associated with the surgical procedure that he had advised. Although the surgery was performed with proper care and skill, the inherent risk materialised and as a consequence the plaintiff was disabled. A 4:1 majority held that the *Bolam* standard (or a somewhat modified version thereof) was the appropriate legal test, and that the surgeon had acted in accordance with a responsible body of medical opinion when withholding information about the risks involved prior to obtaining Mrs Sidaway's consent to the operation. Lord Diplock pointed out that the doctrine of 'informed consent' had never formed part of English law, and that disclosure of risks may alarm patients and deter them from undergoing treatments that are—in the expert opinion of the doctor—in their best interests. Decisions on whether or not to advise patients of inherent risks and the way in which such warnings should be put constituted an exercise of professional skill and judgement, just as any other part of the doctor's comprehensive duty of care to the individual patient. Expert medical evidence should therefore be used to determine the standard of care regarding the provision of information. Others within the majority were prepared to alter the existing law in certain respects. Thus, Lord Bridge held:

> A judge might, in certain circumstances, come to the conclusion that the disclosure of a particular risk was so obviously necessary to an informed choice on the part of the patient that no reasonably prudent medical man would fail to make it.[322]

while Lord Templeman considered that:

> the court must decide whether the information afforded to the patient was sufficient to alert the patient to the possibility of serious harm of the kind in fact suffered.[323]

4.125 Lord Scarman, however, delivered what was, effectively, a dissenting judgment in which he indicated that: 'it was a strange conclusion if our courts should be led to conclude that our law … should permit doctors to determine in what circumstances … a duty arose to warn'. He found great merit in the US case of *Canterbury* v *Spence*,[324] in which it was

---

[316] 1955 SC 200; 1955 SLT 213.   [317] [1957] 2 All ER 118; [1957] 1 WLR 582.
[318] Per McNair J [1957] 2 All ER 118 at 122.   [319] [1981] QB 432; [1981] 1 All ER 257.
[320] [1983] 3 All ER 716; [1984] 1 WLR 641.
[321] *Sidaway* v *Board of Governors of the Bethlem Royal Hospital* [1984] QB 493 at 517; [1984] 1 All ER 1018 at 1030, CA; affd [1985] AC 871; [1985] 1 All ER 643, HL.
[322] [1985] AC 871 at 900; [1985] 1 All ER 643 at 663, HL.
[323] [1985] AC 871 at 903; [1985] 1 All ER 643 at 665.   [324] 464 F 2d 772 (DC, 1972).

held that, while medical evidence on this matter was not excluded, it was the court which determined the extent of, and any breach of, the doctor's duty to inform. Information includes warning. King CJ, for example, in Australia, specifically instructed that the doctor's duty extends not only to disclose any real risks in the treatment but also to warn of any real risk that the treatment may prove ineffective.[325]

4.126   Two specific aspects of the information issue were confirmed as a result of *Sidaway*. The first is that risks of a certain magnitude must be disclosed. Following *Canterbury*, a risk can be defined as 'material' if a reasonable person in the patient's position, if warned of the risk, would be likely to attach significance to it. Similarly, it is material if the medical practitioner is, or should reasonably be, aware that the particular patient, if warned of the risk, would be likely to attach significance to it.[326] Quite what that means in relation to chance is impossible to assess and, indeed, generalisations may be *inappropriate* because the test relates to the circumstances of the particular case. Moreover, significance in this field is a function not only of incidence but also of severity; as to incidence, it was agreed in *Sidaway* that a risk of 10 per cent of a stroke resulting—as was established in *Reibl* v *Hughes*[327]—was one which a doctor could hardly fail to appreciate as necessitating a warning; but non-disclosure was considered proper in Mrs Sidaway's case when the risk of damage to the spinal cord was of the order of 1 per cent or less. We have to admit to some concern that odds longer than 100:1 might be regarded as immaterial in the eyes of the law.[328] A great deal will, however, hang on the *patient's* requirements as expressed by way of questioning and through genuine communication. We return to this later.

4.127   Second, *Sidaway* confirmed a legal basis for the 'therapeutic' or 'professional' privilege to withhold information that might be psychologically damaging to the patient.[329] This, again, follows the direction in *Bolam*, in which the judge said in his charge to the jury:

> You may well think that when a doctor is dealing with a mentally sick man and has a strong belief that his only hope of cure is submission to electroconvulsive therapy, the doctor cannot be criticised if he does not stress the dangers, which he believed to be minimal, which are involved in the treatment …[330]

This principle continues to receive judicial recognition,[331] and is accepted by the GMC as good medical practice in certain limited circumstances.[332]

4.128   It is also clear from *Sidaway* that, by way of exception to this rule, there must be particularly good reasons, which the doctor would have to justify, for failing to answer such

---

[325]   *F* v *R* (1983) 33 SASR 189, SC. Alternative treatments should also be canvassed—particularly if there is a choice between medical and surgical procedures: *Haughian* v *Paine* (1987) 37 DLR (4th) 624, cited in (1987) 137 NLJ 557.

[326]   Mason CJ et al. in *Rogers* v *Whittaker* (1992) 109 ALR 625 at 634; [1993] 4 Med LR 79 at 83, Aus HC.

[327]   (1980) 114 DLR (3d) 1.

[328]   King JC accepted 200:1 as not being material in *F* v *R* (1983) 33 SASR 189, SC.

[329]   Compare R Mulheron, 'The defence of therapeutic privilege in Australia' (2003) 11(2) J Law Med 201.

[330]   [1957] 2 All ER 118 at 124; [1957] 1 WLR 582 at 590, per McNair J.

[331]   It has been endorsed by the House of Lords (albeit obiter), in *Chester* v *Afshar*, n 347, per Lord Steyn, para 16; *Montgomery* v *Lanarkshire Health Board* [2015] UKSC 11 para 91

[332]   GMC, n 228, para 16: 'You should not withhold information necessary for making decisions for any other reason, including when a relative, partner, friend or carer asks you to, unless you believe that giving it would cause the patient serious harm. In this context "serious harm" means more than that the patient might become upset or decide to refuse treatment.'

questions as the patient puts and that there may, indeed, be a strict obligation to do so.[333] Thus, Lord Bridge held in relation to what has since been dubbed the 'reactive duty'[334], albeit obiter, that:

> When questioned specifically by a patient of apparently sound mind about risks involved in a particular treatment proposed, a doctor's duty must, in my opinion, be to answer both truthfully and as fully as the questioner requires.[335]

Elsewhere we have Mason CJ: 'The fact that the patient asked questions revealing concern about the risk would make the doctor aware that this patient did, in fact, attach significance to the risk'[336]—and, hence, affect its materiality; it was certainly this fact which served to turn a 1:14,000 chance of blindness into a risk which it was found negligent not to disclose in the Australian case of *Rogers* v *Whittaker*.[337]

4.129 The House of Lords' approach in *Sidaway* was subject to strong criticism. Reliance on the *Bolam* standard—even with some modifications—appeared paternalistic and increasingly untenable in the face of the current universal acceptance of a patient's right to decide on his or her own treatment, as evidenced in guidance from the Department of Health and the GMC. The writing was already on the wall some 35 years ago in Canada where, in *Reibl*, it was held:

> [The] scope of the duty of disclosure ... is not a question that is to be concluded on the basis of the expert medical evidence alone ... What is under consideration here is the patient's right to know what risks are involved in undergoing or forgoing certain surgery or other treatment.[338]

4.130 The strongest attack on *Bolam* came from the High Court of Australia where its application to counselling was firmly rejected in the aforementioned *Rogers* v *Whittaker*. The plaintiff had lost most of the sight in her right eye as a child. She was rendered virtually blind after undergoing a surgical procedure on her left eye which was recommended to her by an ophthalmic surgeon. The majority stated:

> There is a fundamental difference between, on the one hand, diagnosis and treatment and, on the other hand, the provision of advice or information to the patient ... Because the choice to be made calls for a decision by the patient on information known to the medical practitioner but not to the patient, it would be illogical to hold that the amount

---

[333] Cf *Blyth* v *Bloomsbury Health Authority* (1985), *The Times*, 24 May; on appeal [1993] 4 Med LR 151. For an interesting survey indicating a widespread lack of interest among patients in asking further questions (at least in respect of anaesthesia) see A Moores and N A Pace, 'The information requested by patients prior to giving consent to anaesthesia' (2003) 58 Anaesthesia 703. Equally, see A S Scheer et al., 'The myth of informed consent in rectal cancer surgery: What do patients retain?' (2012) 55 Dis of Colon and Rectum 970.

[334] For discussion of the so-called 'proactive' and 'reactive' duty to inform in the Australian context, see I H Kerridge and J R McPhee, 'Ethical and legal issues at the interface of complementary and conventional medicine' (2004) 181 Med J Aust 164.

[335] [1985] AC 871 at 898; [1985] 1 All ER 643 at 661, HL.

[336] Mason CJ et al. in *Rogers* v *Whittaker* (1992) 109 ACLR 625 at 631; [1993] at 4 Med LR 79 at 82.

[337] In *Hopp* v *Lepp* [1980] 2 SCR 192, 112 DLR (3d) 67, the Supreme Court of Canada held that in obtaining a patient's consent a doctor must answer any specific questions put by the patient as to the risks involved, and should, even in the absence of questioning, disclose the following: the nature of the proposed intervention, its gravity, any material risks, and any special or unusual risks.

[338] (1980) 114 DLR (3d) 1 at 13.

of information to be provided by the medical practitioner can be determined from the perspective of the practitioner alone or, for that matter, of the medical profession.[339]

and even more trenchantly, Gaudron J:

> even in the area of diagnosis and treatment, there is, in my view, no legal basis for limiting liability in terms of the rule known as 'the *Bolam* test' ... [It] may be a convenient statement of the approach dictated by the state of the evidence in some cases. As such, it may have some utility as a rule-of-thumb in some jury cases, but it can serve no other useful function.[340]

4.131 While appearing to lag behind other jurisdictions, a gradual but definite shift away from the *Bolam* standard in disputes over information disclosure was also occurring in the lower courts in the UK.[341] In *Smith* v *Tunbridge Wells Health Authority*,[342] for example, the failure of a consultant surgeon to inform a 28-year-old man of impotence and bladder dysfunction following an operation to treat rectal prolapse was held to be negligent, despite medical support for the decision. Indeed, it was considered that disclosure of the risk was the *only* reasonable course of action.

4.132 Also of significance was the Court of Appeal decision in *Pearce* v *United Bristol Healthcare NHS Trust*,[343] in which an action in negligence was brought by a couple whose child died in utero almost three weeks overdue. The mother had pleaded with the consultant two weeks after her delivery date either to induce the birth or to carry out a caesarian section, but he advised against it citing the high risks of induction and the long time for recovery from caesarian section. He did not disclose the risks of fetal death in the womb as a result of delay in delivery. In deciding whether the consultant was negligent in this regard, the Court endorsed *Sidaway* as the law and accepted *Bolam* as the relevant test, but also followed Lord Bridge's caveat concerning the need to warn of 'significant risks'. Lord Woolf MR felt that Lord Templeman's views in *Sidaway* best summed up the position, whereby the patient was entitled to such information as was needed to make a balanced judgement in the circumstances. Yet Lord Woolf only generated hope in half-measure, for he went on to apply his test to the facts of the case. In doing so, he concluded that there was no 'significant risk' because 'The doctors called on behalf of defendants did not regard that risk as significant; nor do I'. Moreover, he stated that the consultant could not be criticised when dealing with a distressed patient for not informing her of 'that very, very small additional risk'—one in the order of 0.1–0.2 per cent. In this sense, the risk was 'small' in statistical terms. Even so, there is little doubt that the tenor of debate surrounding these matters was veering to the side of the patient and her right to choose.[344]

---

[339] (1992) 109 ALR 625 at 632; [1993] 4 Med LR 79 at 83. For a full discussion of the case, see D Chalmers and R Schwartz, '*Rogers* v *Whittaker* and informed consent in Australia: A fair dinkum duty of disclosure' (1993) 1 Med L Rev 139 and B McSherry, 'Failing to advise and warn of inherent risks in medical treatment: When does negligence occur?' (1993) 1 J Law Med 5.

[340] (1992) 109 ALR 625 at 635–6; [1993] 4 Med LR 79 at 84. This decision was reaffirmed by the High Court in *Chappel* v *Hart* [1998] HCA 55. However, in *Rosenberg* v *Percival* [2001] HCA 18, a case which was primarily concerned with information and causation, the High Court was not entirely dismissive of *Bolam*; the objection was not so much to the relevance of medical opinion as to its conclusiveness in assessing the necessary extent of disclosure.

[341] For a discussion of the survival of *Bolam* in general in medical negligence actions, see Chapter 5.

[342] [1994] 5 Med LR 334.   [343] (1999) 48 BMLR 118.

[344] The problems involved are explicit in *O'Keefe* v *Harvey-Kemble* (1999) 45 BMLR 74, CA, a case involving cosmetic rather than therapeutic breast surgery. The warnings given were considered insufficient. The

4.133 *Birch* v *University College London Hospital NHS Foundation Trust* concerned a patient who had been informed accurately of the risks involved with catheter angiography and had consented to the procedure, after which she suffered a stroke. The plaintiff argued that the Trust had been negligent in failing to her inform her of an alternative, non-invasive procedure with lower or no risks—an MRI scan.[345] After expressing concern about the continuing uncertain nature of the law on standards of disclosure, Mr Justice Cranston had this to say:

> If patients must be informed of significant risks it is necessary to spell out what, in practice, that encompasses. In this case the defendant informed the patient of the probabilities, the one per cent, and the nature of the harm of this risk becoming manifest, the stroke. But these were the objectively significant risks associated with the procedure which was performed, the catheter angiogram. Was it necessary for the defendant to go further and to inform Mrs Birch of comparative risk, how this risk compared with that associated with other imaging procedures, in particular MRI? … [I]n my judgment there will be circumstances where consistently with Lord Woolf MR's statement of the law in *Pearce* … the duty to inform a patient of the significant risks will not be discharged unless she is made aware that fewer, or no risks, are associated with another procedure. In other words, unless the patient is informed of the comparative risks of different procedures she will not be in a position to give her fully informed consent to one procedure rather than another.[346]

4.134 Much of the fate of informed consent was sealed by the House of Lords' decision in *Chester* v *Afshar*.[347] The bulk of the discussion in that case centred on the issue of causation, and it is therefore discussed in more detail below under that heading. While the House was not in unanimous agreement on causation, there was consensus that the doctor had not fulfilled his duty to warn the claimant of a low risk inherent in the surgical procedure. *Chester*, therefore, signified support for patient autonomy, but the House gave the issue of informed consent surprisingly brief treatment. The ruling did not explicitly alter the standard of care and questions regarding the exact threshold level of risk that would trigger the duty to warn were left unanswered.[348]

4.135 Further clarity has been brought by the recent Supreme Court ruling in the Scottish case of *Montgomery* v *Lanarkshire Health Board*,[349] in which a negligence claim was brought by a mother against a consultant obstetrician in relation to her antenatal care. The mother was diabetic and of short stature. As her baby was likely to be larger than average in size, the risk of shoulder dystocia occurring during 'natural' delivery was 9–10 per cent. The claimant had not been appraised of this fact or advised of the alternative of a caesarean section. In her obstetrician's opinion, providing this information was unnecessary as the likelihood of a grave problem for the baby resulting from shoulder dystocia was very small. The risks of a brachial plexus injury in cases of shoulder dystocia involving diabetic mothers was put at around 0.2 per cent and the risk of cerebral palsy at under 0.1 per cent. Furthermore, the obstetrician held the view that it is not generally in the maternal interest for women to have caesarian sections.

---

problem of the 'significant risk' was well vented in *Wyatt* v *Curtis* (2003) EWCA Civ 1779 where the importance of *Pearce* in this respect was recognised.

[345] [2008] EWHC 2237 (QB), (2008) 104 BMLR 168.
[346] For discussion see R Heywood, 'Medical disclosure of alternative treatments' (2009) 68 CLJ 30.
[347] [2004] UKHL 41; [2005] 1 AC 134.
[348] R Heywood, 'Informed consent through the back door' (2005) 56 NILQ 266.
[349] [2015] UKSC 11; [2015] 2 WLR 768.

4.136 Shoulder dystocia occurred during labour and the baby was deprived of oxygen due to occlusion of the umbilical cord, resulting in serious permanent disabilities. The Outer House of the Court of Session in Scotland rejected the contention that there had been a breach of the duty to inform. This position was upheld on appeal to the Inner House. After close analysis, neither *Pearce* nor *Chester* were interpreted as signifying a change in the law as set out by the majority in *Sidaway*. This meant that the relevant rule to be applied was the *Bolam* standard, unless the proposed treatment entailed a substantial risk of grave adverse consequences—in which case there was a legal duty to inform. Applying that test to the facts at hand, there was no duty to warn the patient of the very small risk of the grave outcome that unfortunately manifested. Furthermore, the claimant had not made any specific enquiries herself as to the risks entailed. The doctor's duty to give full and honest answers was not triggered merely by the expression of general concerns.

4.137 The Supreme Court saw the case differently. The position of the majority in *Sidaway* was said to be 'unsatisfactory'; in as much as it subsumed the doctor's duty to advise the patient of the risks of proposed treatment under the *Bolam* test. Such an approach failed to take account of important social changes that have occurred in the dynamics of the doctor–patient relationship since *Sidaway*. Patients are now widely regarded as persons holding rights, rather than as the passive recipients of the care of the medical profession. GMC guidance advocated supporting patient autonomy in medical decision-making. Furthermore, the important legal development of the Human Rights Act 1998 put increased focus on extent to which the common law reflects fundamental values. On consideration of these and other factors, the Supreme Court was unanimous in rejecting the continued application of the *Bolam* test in this context.

4.138 Subject to refinements by the Court of Appeal in *Pearce v United Bristol Healthcare NHS Trust* and the High Court of Australia in *Rogers v Whitaker*, the view expressed by Lord Scarman in *Sidaway* now prevails. The Supreme Court summarised as follows:

> An adult person of sound mind is entitled to decide which, if any, of the available forms of treatment to undergo, and her consent must be obtained before treatment interfering with her bodily integrity is undertaken. The doctor is therefore under a duty to take reasonable care to ensure that the patient is aware of any material risks involved in any recommended treatment, and of any reasonable alternative or variant treatments. The test of materiality is whether, in the circumstances of the particular case, a reasonable person in the patient's position would be likely to attach significance to the risk, or the doctor is or should reasonably be aware that the particular patient would be likely to attach significance to it.

4.139 The Supreme Court clarified three more matters. First, assessment of materiality of risk cannot be reduced to percentages. It involves a variety of factors besides statistical probability, including the nature of the risk, the effect which its occurrence would have upon the life of the patient, the importance to the patient of the benefits sought to be achieved by the treatment, the alternatives available, and the risks involved in those alternatives. The assessment, therefore, depends on the context and the patient's characteristics. Second, the discharge of the duty to provide information entails a dialogue between doctor and patient, so that the patient is able to exercise autonomy in a meaningful way. Bombarding the patient with technical information that she cannot reasonably be expected to grasp is not consistent with this approach. Third, while a therapeutic exception subsists, it is a limited exception that should not be abused. It is subordinate to the principle that the patient should make the decision whether to undergo a proposed course of treatment: it is not intended to subvert that principle by enabling the doctor to prevent the patient from making an informed choice where she is liable to make a choice which the doctor considers to be contrary to her best interests.

4.140 While *Montgomery* gives emphatically clear directions to HCPs that they must disclose 'material risks' to patients when obtaining consent to treatment, the legal category of 'material risks' remains ambiguous and something of a 'black box'. Perhaps wisely, the Supreme Court has eschewed setting a specific percentage threshold above which risks must be disclosed. At the coalface, however, the resulting legal uncertainties could prompt HCPs to disclose even low inherent risks associated with treatments so as to avoid possible negligence claims.

4.141 The ratio in *Montgomery* has been applied in subsequent cases which do cast some light on the risks that will be regarded by courts as material, as well as the way other contextual factors are taken into account. In *Spencer* v *Hillingdon Hospital NHS Trust*,[350] the claimant had been warned of certain risks associated with surgery to treat an inguinal hernia, but not of the small risks of deep vein thrombosis or pulmonary embolism, which according to expert evidence stood at around 0.7 per cent and 0.9 per cent respectively. Collender J found for the claimant, reiterating that a doctor has a legal duty to take reasonable care to ensure that the patient is aware of any 'material risks' involved in any recommended treatment. The ordinary sensible patient would expect to have been informed of the risks in questions, and would have felt justifiably aggrieved not to have been given the information. Even though the risk was small in many cases, alerting patients to the symptoms would prompt them to seek post-operative medical care if needed, and thus help save lives. The National Institute for Clinical Excellence (NICE) Guidelines are not entirely clear on the categories of patients to which they apply, but on the basis of expert testimony, it was held that modern, safe, and responsible medical practice should be to inform all patients undergoing general anaesthetic of the remote risks of deep vein thrombosis and pulmonary embolism. In another post-*Montgomery* negligence case where the duty to warn was at issue, however, the level of risk was itself disputed.[351] The claimant failed to establish that the risk that her baby might be born suffering from a chromosomal abnormality was around 1–3 per cent. The expert evidence submitted by the defendant NHS Trust was instead preferred, putting the risk at around one in a thousand. Such a remote risk was not regarded by the High Court as material, but rather as a theoretical or background risk that neither the hypothetical reasonable patient nor the actual patient herself would have regarded as significant.

Causation, Informed Consent, and the Future

4.142 Here we move from questions about the standard of care that patients can expect from their doctors to the far more technically complex area of causation where the focus shifts to the patients themselves. Information-disclosure cases can turn on the question of causation: the patient is saying, 'If you had warned me of the risk I would not have consented to run it; I only did so because I didn't know about the risk—the harm (the materialisation of the risk) has been caused by your negligent failure to disclose'. The hurdles are manifold. It may, for example, simply be a question of witness credibility. In both *Smith* v *Salford Health Authority*[352] and *Smith* v *Barking, Havering and Brentwood Health Authority*,[353] the courts refused to accept that the claimants would not have proceeded

---

[350] [2015] EWHC 1058.
[351] *Mrs A* v *East Kent Hospitals University NHS Foundation Trust* [2015] EWHC 1038 (QB); 2015 WL 1651409.
[352] (1994) 23 BMLR 137.   [353] [1994] 5 Med LR 285.

with the respective medical procedures had they been informed of the risks. To be clear, these are not examples of the courts accusing witnesses of lying; rather it is the courts' assessment of the 'facts' of the case that the patients would, on the balance of probabilities, have proceeded even if they had been told.[354]

4.143   Essentially, this is a matter of credibility and likelihood that it is for the court to assess. Rougier J summed up the situation well when he said: 'It is not integrity which is in question but objectivity.'[355] Or, as a Californian court had it: 'Subjectively he may believe [he would have declined treatment] with the 20/20 vision of hindsight but we doubt that justice will be served by placing the physician in jeopardy of the patient's bitterness and disillusionment.'[356]

4.144   In the UK, the complexities have been demonstrated only too well in the House of Lords' case of *Chester* v *Afshar*. Here a young woman found herself in circumstances strangely similar to those of Mrs Sidaway: a surgeon treating the patient for serious back pain failed to disclose a low (1–2 per cent) but serious risk of nerve damage and paralysis inherent in the operation. This manifested itself and the patient sued in negligence claiming that had she been informed of the risk she would not have gone ahead with the operation when she did.[357] It was not established at trial, however, and indeed the plaintiff did not argue, that she would never undergo the operation (and so never run the risk).[358] Moreover, it was accepted that the risk in question was a constant: it was an integral part of the operation in question; it was irrelevant who performed it or when. Thus, a very important issue arose as to whether it could meaningfully be said as a matter of law that the surgeon *caused* the patient's harm. Lords Hoffmann and Bingham were adamant and emphatic in their rejection of the claimant's case. For Lord Bingham, she had not met the basic requirements of the 'but for' test—she had not shown that *but for* the failure to warn she would never have undergone surgery.[359] Lord Hoffmann stated, quite simply, that there was no basis on the ordinary principles of tort law for recovery, and he was not convinced that a special rule was needed in the instant case.[360] But it was precisely on this last point that the three remaining members of the bench took issue with their colleagues.[361] While each acknowledged that, indeed, there could not be recovery on the 'standard rules', they argued, variously, that policy, justice, or the particular nature of decisions relating to one's health and well-being called for a departure from those rules. And, most significantly, common to their arguments was the view that these negligence actions are essentially concerned with protecting the patient's right to choose—that is, her autonomy. They pointed out that each of their Lordships in *Sidaway* recognised this as the basic legal interest at stake; Lord Walker went as far as to emphasise the importance of the growth of autonomy-based arguments over the last 20 years as the basis for justifying an outcome in the claimant's

---

[354]   For a recent Scottish equivalent, see *Murray* v *NHS Lanarkshire Health Board* [2012] CSOH 123.

[355]   In *Gregory* v *Pembrokeshire Health Authority* [1989] 1 Med LR 81 at 86.

[356]   *Cobbs* v *Grant*, 104 Cal Rptr 505 (1972).

[357]   The breach of the requisite standard of care requiring that the information should have been disclosed was not in doubt.

[358]   This contrasts with *Montgomery* v *Lanarkshire Health Board* [2015] UKSC 11, in which the claimant was able to establish on the balance of probabilities that had she been warned of the risks of shoulder dystocia, she would have requested a caesarian section.

[359]   *Chester* v *Afshar*, n 347, para 8.   [360]   *Chester* v *Afshar*, n 347, para 32.

[361]   A lot of support was drawn from the Australian decision in *Chappel* v *Hart* [1999] 2 LRC 341; (1998) 72 ALJR 1344, which dealt essentially with the same issue and where there was also division of opinion among the justices.

favour in the instant case.[362] We speculate tentatively whether this also reflects the motivation for creating a new measure of damages in wrongful pregnancy cases such as *Rees* v *Darlington Memorial Hospital NHS Trust*.[363] Are we moving towards the recognition of a new tort of infringement of autonomy?[364]

4.145 We have stressed throughout this book how fast and far autonomy-based reasoning has come to dominate medical law. As to its influence in information disclosure cases, however, we remain ambivalent. While we disapprove of the enduring role of the *Bolam* test as the measure of the standard of care because of its failure to distinguish between information disclosure and other medically determined treatment scenarios, we find that *Chester* perhaps swings too far in the other direction, allowing obeisance to autonomy to undermine sound legal principle.[365] It is not only justice to the patient that is at stake. Moreover, even if we accept that a patient's self-determination interests have been compromised by a failure fully to inform, we agree with Lord Hoffmann that the resulting harm is more in the nature of solatium—hurt to feelings—than related to the actual physical injury itself.[366] This is important for the significant impact it would have on the measure of damages. But, however one views *Chester*, it does, as we have written in another short appraisal of the case, represent 'an important shift in judicial thinking on questions of causation and has significant implications for the future. It seems, however, that *Bolam*'s place in the relevant law is likely to move regressively towards the rear of the field'.[367]

4.146 Certainly the wind of change is now blowing strongly and the question is no longer, 'Is the doctrine of informed consent coming to the UK?' but, rather, 'What can we do to improve on the American model?'[368] In our view, a start might well be made by dropping the phrase 'informed consent' in favour of 'valid consent'—or, perhaps better, using the word 'understanding', for a competent adult has every right to make a decision which may appear irrational to others. Both are terms which pay due deference to patient autonomy and, at the same time, provide the doctor with a yardstick as to what is expected of him or her.[369] We need to ensure that any spirit of confrontation between the medical profession and the public is halted and abandoned in favour of the concept of what Teff described many years ago as a therapeutic alliance[370] and which is now strongly reflected in the GMC's language of 'partnership' in medical decision-making[371] and, indeed, also in the Supreme Court's decision in *Montgomery*.[372]

---

[362] *Chester* v *Afshar*, n 347, para 92.   [363] [2003] 4 All ER 987.

[364] We discuss this in greater detail in J K Mason, *The Troubled Pregnancy* (2007).

[365] G Laurie, 'Personality, privacy and autonomy in medical law' in N R Whitty and R Zimmermann (eds), *Rights of Personality in Scots Law: A Comparative Perspective* (2009) ch 10.

[366] *Chester* v *Afshar*, n 347, per Lord Hoffmann, para 34 (the physical damage being inherent in the operation and not due to negligence).

[367] K Mason and D Brodie, '*Bolam, Bolam*—Wherefore art thou *Bolam*?' (2005) 9 Edin LR 398.

[368] The various themes that can be accommodated under the umbrella of 'informed consent' are well described in an analysis by A R Maclean, n 282.

[369] The use of other ill-defined terms such as 'effective consent' in the Human Fertilisation and Embryology Act 1990, Sch 3 or 'appropriate consent' in the Human Tissue Act 2004 do little more than compound the difficulties.

[370] Teff, 'Consent in medical procedures: Paternalism, self-determination or therapeutic alliance?' (1985) 101 LQR 432.

[371] GMC, n 228.   [372] Paras 4.135 et seq.

5

LIABILITY
FOR MEDICAL INJURY

5.01 Medical negligence is more than a matter between two parties—it is also a political and serious economic issue. There is concern in both medical and governmental circles over the growing incidence of personal injury actions against doctors and over the cost to the health system of compensating the victims.[1] It is pointed out that medical negligence actions are destructive of trust in a doctor–patient relationship and distort the practice of medicine in an over-cautious direction. From the doctor's point of view, the prospect of being sued in the event of making a mistake is stressful and demoralising—and, in the context of increasing emphasis on 'patient-orientated medicine', the definition of 'mistake' is ever-widening. Legal action is, thus, a very real risk for the medical practitioner and it would be surprising if litigation at this level did not seriously compromise medical morale. Funding bodies might expect to find the picture equally bleak, and the figures are alarming. In 2014–15, the National Health Services Litigation Authority (NHSLA)[2] received 11,497 claims for clinical negligence against National Health Service (NHS) bodies, which shows continued high levels of new claims.[3]

5.02 The Authority paid more than £1.1 billion to patients who had suffered harm in 2014–15, and this is projected to rise to around £1.4 billion in 2015–16. These outlays involve public funds otherwise earmarked for health care. There is long-standing discussion about the need to stem a rising flood, and the reader is referred to the Department of Health's comprehensive document, *Making Amends*, for both a full account of the crisis and a discussion of various reform options both at home and abroad.[4]

5.03 What lies behind this overall increase in litigation? First and foremost, modern medicine is intrusive and the chances of injury are therefore increased: some 5 per cent of the population report deleterious after-effects of medical care.[5] Second, the current social climate encourages expectations of cure. When these are not met, the culture of consumerism—fuelled by a press eager to disclose wrongdoing—advocates the allocation of blame and

---

[1] See generally, Department of Health, *Making Amends: A Consultation Paper Setting Out Proposals for Reforming the Approach to Clinical Negligence in the NHS* (2003).

[2] The NHSLA was established in November 1995 to indemnify English NHS bodies against claims for medical negligence. For further information see NHSLA Factsheet 1, available at: http://www.nhsla.com/.

[3] The Authority's Report and Accounts 2014–15, available on the website.

[4] N 1. See, too, National Audit Office, *Citizen Redress: What Citizens Can Do if Things Go Wrong with Public Services* (HC 21, Session 2004–5, 2005).

[5] Department of Health, *An Organisation with a Memory* (2000). See also the House of Commons Health Committee Sixth Report—Patient Safety (June 2009) ch 3, which states that 'International studies suggest that about 10% of all patients who are admitted to hospital suffer some form of harm'.

the seeking of compensation.[6] Finally, intolerance of error, and denial of the fact that any complex human endeavour will inevitably involve the making of mistakes, means that the public increasingly insists on accountability and, if possible, the pinning of an adverse outcome on some identifiable human agency. The public's tolerance for accidents has been greatly reduced—somebody, somewhere must be made to answer for what has happened.[7]

ALTERNATIVES TO THE NEGLIGENCE SYSTEM

5.04 Even so, the current system for compensating those sustaining injury has come under attack from all quarters.[8] Patients, it is argued, have great difficulty seeking compensation for negligently inflicted medical injury and may face daunting hurdles in the process of suing a doctor. Claims often arise because the patient or family have failed to get any explanation as to what went wrong and, having been offered no apology, may feel that there is no alternative to bringing an action.[9] Both sides—if one should talk of 'sides' in this context—see the current system of compensation for medical injury as being slow, traumatic, and socially expensive, one from which it is often only the lawyers who profit.[10] It is generally accepted that there must be a better way of dealing with this issue—a way which provides reasonably efficient compensation without destroying the doctor–patient relationship and without diverting health-targeted funds from hospitals and patient care into legal fees and damages.

5.05 The question of compensation for medical injury in the United Kingdom (UK) has, in fact, had a number of official airings. It was discussed many years ago as a special issue by the Royal Commission on Compensation for Personal Injury (the Pearson Commission),[11] and Lord Woolf addressed the matter in his wide-ranging investigation into the operation of the system of civil justice. He singled out medical negligence as an area for special consideration on the ground that it was in respect of these claims that civil justice was 'failing most conspicuously'.[12] This failure was demonstrated by a variety of factors, including an unacceptable delay in the resolution of cases and a success rate which was lower than that in other personal injury litigation. The report suggested that the system could be improved by a better complaints procedure and by extending the jurisdiction of the Health Service Ombudsman to include complaints against the clinical expertise of NHS staff, both of which suggestions have been acted upon.[13] Lord Woolf was also concerned to establish what he described as a 'climate of change' that is marked by greater openness. He

---

[6] Cf, Department for Constitutional Affairs, *Tackling the Compensation Culture* (2004), available via http://www.justice.gov.uk; and K Williams, 'State of fear: Britain's compensation culture reviewed' (2005) 25 LS 499. Note that the conclusion of the House of Commons Constitutional Affairs Committee was that no such culture exists: see HCCAC, *Compensation Culture: Third Report of 2005–6*, vol 1, HC 754-1 at 13.

[7] Compare the assessment in A Merry and A McCall Smith, *Errors, Medicine and the Law* (2001). The situation is particularly well discussed by R Tallis, *Hippocratic Oaths: Medicine and Its Discontents* (2004).

[8] Not least from the senior judiciary: Lord Woolf, 'Clinical negligence: What is the solution? How can we provide justice for doctors and patients?' (2000) 4 Med L Internat 133.

[9] Though note that s 2 of the Compensation Act 2006 now makes it clear that the offer of an apology, an offer of treatment, or other redress shall not in itself amount to an admission of negligence.

[10] See generally 'Medical legal costs "excessive and should be capped" ', *BBC News*, 28 June 2015.

[11] Cmnd 7054–1, 1978.

[12] *Access to Justice: Final Report to the Lord Chancellor on the Civil Justice System in England and Wales* (1996) 15.2. See too, Scottish Office Home Department, *Access to Justice: Beyond the Year 2000* (1997). Reforms involving the whole UK were instituted in the Access to Justice Act 1999.

[13] For an overview of the two-stage procedure, see http://www.ombudsman.org.uk/.

suggested that the General Medical Council (GMC) might explore ways of clarifying the responsibilities of the doctor in terms of candour, and he also favoured the wider use of mediation schemes.[14] Later proposals for reform have considered both of these elements.

5.06   An alternative to negligence actions, which commands much support,[15] is to introduce a system of no-fault compensation, which would provide for the making of awards to injured patients irrespective of the requirement of proving fault on the part of medical personnel.[16] Such a scheme has operated in New Zealand since 1974 as part of an overall no-fault compensation scheme and, although it has had its opponents, it has now survived into its fourth decade—albeit in a scaled-down model.[17] In the medical context, however, the New Zealand claimant must still establish that the injury resulted from 'treatment injury', a requirement which has caused difficulties in distinguishing between those conditions which result from the physiological progress of a medical condition and those which are adverse medical events caused by treatment.[18] Thus, it will be seen that such schemes do not do away entirely with all the difficult issues of foreseeability and causation which dog the operation of conventional tort law.[19]

5.07   It is, perhaps, significant that organisations such as the British Medical Association (BMA), whose primary concern as a trade union is for the interests of the profession, have consistently supported the introduction of a no-fault based system into the UK.[20] Under the scheme proposed by the BMA, compensation would be available for medically induced injury but would exclude those injuries which were not avoidable through the exercise of reasonable care. The concept of negligence is, therefore, effectively preserved, although it would undoubtedly be easier to establish; moreover, there would be no inference of 'fault' of quite the same nature as arises in a tort-based system.[21] A no-fault system of compensation has also been advocated by the Royal College of Physicians[22] and such a recommendation was also included in the Report of the Royal Bristol Infirmary Inquiry.[23]

5.08   In Scotland, the No-Fault Compensation Review Group, led by Sheila McLean, recommended in 2011 the adoption of a no-fault scheme in Scotland.[24] The Group laid out what

[14] Pilot mediation schemes were rolled out in England and Wales over three years but only 12 mediations for medical negligence went ahead—11 settled. See L Mulcahy, *Mediating Medical Negligence Claims: An Option for the Future?* (2000).
[15] Although not from the Pearson Commission, n 11, which concluded that there were insufficient grounds for introducing no-fault compensation schemes. Cf, from a medical perspective, W J Gaine, 'No fault compensation systems' (2003) 326 BMJ 997.
[16] An account of various schemes around the world is provided in *Making Amends*, n 1, ch 6.
[17] Criticisms included those of unacceptably low levels of compensation, high cost to the taxpayer, the removal of deterrents to safety practices in the workplace and the gradual reversion to a traditional negligence approach. See K Oliphant, 'Beyond misadventure: compensation for medical injuries in New Zealand' (2007) 15 Med L Rev 357; J M Maning, 'Plus ça change, plus c'est la même chose: Negligence and treatment injury in New Zealand's accident compensation scheme' (2014) 14 Medical Law International 22–51.
[18] For discussion see A Farell, S Devaney, and A Dar, *No-fault Compensation Schemes for Injury: A Review* (2010).
[19] For a trenchant critique of elements of both fault and no-fault-based approaches, see T Douglas, 'Medical injury compensation: Beyond "no fault" '(2009) 17 Med L Rev 30.
[20] BMA, *Report of the BMA No Fault Compensation Working Party* (1987).
[21] The support continues: see BMA, *Medical Ethics Today* (3rd edn, 2012), 869.
[22] *Compensation for Adverse Consequences of Medical Intervention* (1990); also see K M Norrie and R M Hendry, 'No-fault compensation for medical accidents' (2011) 41 J R Coll Physicians Edinb 290.
[23] Royal Bristol Infirmary Inquiry, *Learning from Bristol: The Report of the Public Inquiry into Children's Heart Surgery at the Bristol Royal Infirmary 1984–1995* (2001).
[24] No-fault Compensation Review Group, *Report and Recommendations: Volume 1* (February 2011).

it considered to be essential features of such a scheme, focusing on the cause of harm from medical (in)action rather than proof of fault, and including a need to have an efficient, equitable and affordable scheme. The proposal involves ten recommendations and would cover all medical treatments injuries in Scotland and awards would be based on need (not tariffs). It explores the relationship between the scheme and the right to litigation and would involve an independent appeal process. The Scottish government conducted a consultation on the proposal, announcing in 2014 that it would proceed cautiously and continue to explore the practicalities and cost implications.[25] Public engagement evidence reveals a complex picture of motivations and expectations but this confirms that lack of effective communication is often an important factor leading to break down of trust and the last resort of litigation.[26] Interestingly, as to annual cost for a no-fault scheme in Scotland, the same group opines that:

> Based on a range of plausible assumptions we estimate an upper estimate of £27,014,275 and a lower estimate is £18,357,455. The proportionate increase in public expenditure represented by our upper estimate is considerably lower than that previously estimated for the introduction of a no-fault scheme in England (Fenn et al. 2004).[27]

5.09 It has been predominantly on the grounds of cost that the UK government has not supported the movement and in 1991 a Westminster Private Member's Bill aimed in that direction was defeated.[28] The UK government's attitude has not, however, been one of total inaction,[29] and in 2003 its consultation paper, *Making Amends*, referred to at para 5.02, took the bold step of recommending a *sui generis* system of care and compensation for patients harmed within the NHS; the instrument was in the form of a report from the Chief Medical Officer (CMO) relating only to England and Wales. In line with the government's long-standing antipathy to no-fault compensation, however, this idea was also rejected as a reform option. Basically, four reasons were offered:

(i) a proper no-fault system would be significantly more expensive than the current approach (costing an estimated £4 billion annually);

(ii) payments to patients would have to be substantially lower than at present to keep costs within manageable boundaries;

(iii) problems in differentiating between harm caused by sub-standard care and that occasioned by natural progression of disease would be considerable (as has been experienced in New Zealand); and

(iv) such a scheme does not address broader systemic problems, such as learning lessons from sub-standard practices.

But to us this is essentially just the same old argument about cost. No compensation scheme on its own can tackle operational matters without parallel reforms in the realms of education, training, and openness (e.g., in error reporting). Likewise, problems of

---

[25] The Scottish Government, *Consultation Report – Consultation on Recommendations for No-fault Compensation in Scotland for Injuries Resulting from Clinical Treatment* (2014).

[26] A M Farrell, S Devaney, and A Dar, *Volume III: A Study of Medical Negligence Claiming in Scotland* (2012).

[27] Ibid, paras 1.17 and 3.120 ff.

[28] National Health Service (Compensation) Bill 1991. The case against no-fault compensation is summarised by B Capstick, P Edwards, and D Mason, 'Compensation for medical accidents' (1991) 302 BMJ 230.

[29] The administration of civil justice was, of course, thoroughly considered and overhauled as a result of Lord Woolf's Report, *Access to Justice* (1996). The application to medical negligence is discussed further later.

definition and causation are inherent in any system. The result has been a flurry of administrative activity in England and Wales which led, in the interim, to the NHS Redress Act 2006 and which we discuss in greater detail at para 5.15.

5.10 In fact, it should not be thought that no fault compensation is unknown on British shores. Three schemes currently operate. These are the Industrial Injuries Scheme, the Criminal Injuries Compensation Scheme, and the Vaccine Damage Payment Scheme. The first two function on a tariff system whereby claims are categorised according to the nature and degree of injury sustained and set payments are made accordingly. A medical injury scheme based on this approach, however, was rejected by the CMO as too blunt an instrument to respond accurately and fairly to patients' circumstances and needs. Rather, the government has sought a more holistic approach to the question. The proposed reforming framework is thus designed not only to ensure fair and efficient care and compensation of those injured at the hands of health care professionals (HCPs); it is also aimed at addressing operational issues concerning the nature of the NHS itself and the working practices of its employees. Here the longer-term aim is to reduce the overall instance of clinical error and medically induced harm.

5.11 Limiting medical accidents—if that were possible—would, of course, simultaneously limit their costs, even if no change were made to the system of compensation or to the rules surrounding the bringing of claims. There has been a greatly increased awareness of the scale of medical accidents in recent years and this has been accompanied by a more sophisticated approach to their understanding and prevention.[30] Studies of the occurrence of such events have concluded that the incidence of medical errors is unacceptably high and that many of these errors are potentially avoidable.[31] In the UK, this approach has resulted in a number of initiatives within the NHS, including the setting up of a National Patient Safety Agency (NPSA), the aim of which is to enable safe systems to be installed and to encourage a system of error reporting which will assist in the avoidance of future accidents.[32] Indeed, the reporting of patient safety incidents in England has been mandatory since April 2010.[33] The shift to a safety-orientated approach to medical injury requires the placing of less emphasis on blame, in favour of an approach which encourages safer practices.[34] The proponents of such systems believe that, in the long run, this approach will reduce the level of patient injury and control the cost of medical error far more effectively than will litigation or any system of punishment of those who

---

[30] See, e.g., *Institute of Medicine To Err is Human* (2000), a document which set ambitious targets for the reduction of the number of adverse events resulting in patient injury. This is a US study, and rather different considerations apply in the UK. For a UK perspective, see K G Alberti, 'Medical errors: A common problem' (2001) 322 BMJ 501; L Mulcahy, 'The market for precedent: Shifting visions of the role of clinical negligence claims and trials' (2014) 22 Med Law Rev 274.

[31] On reporting considerations, see W Runciman, A Merry, and A McCall Smith, 'Improving patients' safety by gathering information' (2001) 323 BMJ 298; for more recent discussion see House of Commons Public Administration Select Committee, *Investigating Clinical Incidents in the NHS: Sixth Report of Session 2014–15* (2015).

[32] The National Patient Safety Agency was abolished by s 281 of the Health and Social Care Act 2012. Its patient safety functions go to the NHS Commissioning Board (s 9 of the 2012 Act), with other functions being distributed to other existing bodies.

[33] The direction of official thinking was indicated by the Department of Health document, *An Organisation with a Memory: Report of an Expert Group on Learning from Adverse Events within the NHS* (2000). The NPSA has set up a National Reporting and Learning System (NRLS) which aims to collect reports from health professionals across England and Wales: V Katikrieddi, 'National reporting system for medical errors is launched' (2004) 328 BMJ 481.

[34] House of Commons Public Administration Select Committee, n 31.

make errors. The previous CMO was clearly one such proponent, and key among his recommendations have been measures to reform the law to prevent disclosure of adverse event reporting documents in court[35]—the thinking being that this will encourage more such reporting within the health system. By corollary, he also argued to place a duty of candour on a statutory footing such that HCPs would be required to inform patients if they become aware of a negligent act or omission.[36] The Care Quality Commission (CQC) has put in place a legal duty of candour that applies in England to all registered providers of both NHS and independent health care bodies, as well as providers of social care, from 1 April 2015.[37] Similar developments are in progress in Scotland,[38] Wales,[39] and Northern Ireland.[40] The GMC and Nursing and Midwifery Council (NMC) have also released jointly updated guidance on the implications of this duty for individuals.[41] The impact—if any—that the duty will have on the volume of medical negligence litigation bears careful monitoring over the coming years.

5.12 The proposals for reform envisaged by the CMO in *Making Amends* are composed of four main elements: (i) investigation; (ii) explanation; (iii) care; and (iv) compensation. Following a local investigation of what went wrong and why, there would be provision of an explanation to the patient and an apology from a suitably high-ranking official within the Trust (if appropriate). Thereafter, a 'package' of care and compensation would be put together designed to respond to the patient's particular circumstances. Monetary compensation would only be offered where care needs could not be met by the NHS.

5.13 Such a system is radically different from a negligence-based compensation scheme in both its philosophy and practice. Its focus is very much on improving patient care—both now and in the future—and this end is sought in a very direct fashion that would allow patients and HCPs to cooperate towards common ends. The negligence action is, in contrast, an adversarial process, with each party pitted against the other. Its outcome, if successful for the patient, is a crude monetary payment—only then can proper care be sought. But as we have seen, the competing demands on any reforming measures are great and very politically charged. While there is always the desire to compensate the victim of medical mishap, there are significant financial implications for health services in doing so. Delays are not in any party's interests, and the overarching consideration—certainly for the future—is how to deter repeat errors. It is far from clear, for example, that any deterrent effect arises from the threat of a negligence action. We question whether it is ever possible to deter negligence which, by definition, is *inadvertent* behaviour. Perhaps more likely is the prospect of defensive medicine, which, it is feared, places the parties to the doctor–patient relationship in an adversarial stance.

5.14 This was one of the reasons behind the passing of the Compensation Act 2006 which allows a court in England and Wales to have regard to the implications of requiring particular steps as part of the standard of care if this might: (i) prevent a desirable activity from being undertaken at all, to a particular extent or in a particular way, or (ii) discourage persons from undertaking functions in connection with a desirable activity.[42]

---

[35] *Making Amends*, n 1, Recommendation 13.   [36] *Making Amends*, n 1, Recommendation 12.
[37] Health and Social Care Act 2008 (Regulated Activities) Regulations 2014/2936, reg 20.
[38] Health (Tobacco, Nicotine etc. and Care) (Scotland) Bill (2015), cls 21–5.
[39] Welsh Government, *Health and Care Standards Framework* (2015).
[40] L Donaldson, P Rutter, and M Henderson, *The Donaldson Report: The Right Time, the Right Place* (2014).
[41] GMC and NMC, *Openness and Honesty When Things Go Wrong: The Professional Duty of Candour* (2015).
[42] Compensation Act 2006, s 1.

Similarly, the Act makes it clear that an apology, in itself, will not be taken as an admission of negligence or liability.

5.15   The other important reforming initiative of that year was the NHS Redress Act 2006 which is framed so as to empower the Secretary of State to make regulations and which awaits implementation at the time of writing.[43] It anticipates the proposal in Recommendation 1 of *Making Amends* to introduce an NHS Redress Scheme. Such a scheme will 'provide investigations when things go wrong, remedial treatment, rehabilitation and care where needed, explanations and apologies, and financial compensation in certain circumstances'.[44] The Act relates only to cases involving liabilities in tort arising out of hospital care. The legislation excludes application to primary care services, although the Secretary of State may by regulation specify that certain services are not to be considered primary care services, thus bringing them within the scope of the scheme. It envisages in-tandem development of complaints procedures with compensation packages for claims of £20,000 or less. According to the Department of Health, the Act would provide:

> for a more consistent and open response to patients when things go wrong with their NHS hospital care, placing the emphasis on putting things right for them. It will promote learning and improvement in the NHS, and provide the impetus for wider service improvement.[45]

The Act would also:

> Provide a genuine alternative to litigation for less severe cases, removing the risks and costs of litigation from the patient. It will address the delays that are inherent in the current system and help reduce the general burden of litigation costs ... The reforms will help create a cultural shift within the NHS, moving the emphasis away—where appropriate—from attributing blame towards preventing harm, reducing risks and learning from mistakes. It will provide not only benefits for patients, but an impetus for wider NHS improvement.[46]

It should be noted that the scheme is concerned with: personal injury or loss arising out of or in connection with breach of a duty of care owed to any person in connection with the diagnosis of illness, or the care or treatment of any patient, and in consequence of any act or omission by a HCP.

5.16   How would it work in practice? Here lies the rub because the 2006 Act merely serves as framework legislation leaving the devil and the detail to be implemented by the Secretary of State in secondary legislation. To date, the scheme, as such, has only been implemented to an extent in Wales.[47] In England, matters were stalled by the Conservative-commissioned Young Report[48] on compensation culture in general, and this in turn led to a Ministry of Justice consultation.[49] We leave it to others to assess the pros and cons of the

---

[43] The Act applies to England and Wales only—hence the continuing activity in Scotland described in para 5.08.

[44] Explanatory Notes to the NHS Redress Act 2006, para 4. Available at: http://www.legislation.gov.uk.

[45] Department of Health, *NHS Redress: Improving the Response to Patients* (2005).

[46] Department of Health, *NHS Redress: Improving the Response to Patients* (2005).

[47] National Health Service (Concerns, Complaints and Redress Arrangements) (Wales) Regulations (SI 2011/704); for analysis see V Harpwood, 'Clinical negligence and poor quality care: Is Wales putting things right?' in P R Ferguson and G T Laurie (eds), *Inspiring a Medico-legal Revolution: Essays in Honour of Sheila McLean* (2015).

[48] Lord Young, *Common Sense, Common Safety* (2011).

[49] Ministry of Justice, Solving Disputes in the County Courts: Creating a Quicker, Simpler and More Proportionate System, Consultation Paper CP6/2011.

options,[50] but the ongoing debacle north and south of the border indicates that matters are unlikely to be resolved in a satisfactory manner any time soon.

5.17 As a final point, it is essential to note that the reforms in question are intended to exist in parallel with the common law. There is no suggestion that we abandon 'negligence' as a medico-legal construct. Patients will be free to choose how to seek recompense for harm done. The only caveat is that a choice to take advantage of the NHS scheme will require a patient to sign a waiver indicating that no future action will be pursued in the courts on the basis of the same facts or injury. Thus, irrespective of whether these (or other) reforms are established in the UK, we cannot escape a thorough examination of the negligence action.

THE BASIS OF MEDICAL LIABILITY

5.18 Most claims in respect of medical injury are brought in tort; that is, on the basis of a non-contractual civil wrong. The reason for this is that patients within the NHS are not in a contractual relationship with the doctor treating them. By contrast, there will be a contractual relationship in the private sector where it is, therefore, possible to bring an action for damages in contract.[51] In practice, there is very little difference between the two remedies,[52] although the law of contract may provide a remedy for an express or implied warranty given by a doctor.[53] In a Canadian case, *La Fleur* v *Cornelis*,[54] the court held that a plastic surgeon was bound to an express contractual warranty that he had made to the patient. This warranty arose when he was unwise enough to say: 'There will be no problem. You will be very happy.' This type of case will be comparatively unusual and, for all practical purposes, any discussion of medical negligence can confine itself to liability under the law of torts, in which the first question to be asked is, 'Whom do we sue?'

5.19 A medical injury to the claimant may have been caused by any one or more of the health care personnel who have treated him. Locating negligence may be simple in some cases but, in others, the patient may have to choose the responsible party from a fairly large group, which may include a general practitioner, a hospital consultant, other hospital doctors, and the nursing staff. Locating the specific act of alleged negligence which caused the injury may also involve a considerable degree of disentanglement.

5.20 The claimant may proceed directly against the doctor in question if an allegation is made of negligence on the part of a general practitioner. The general practitioner in the UK is solely responsible for the treatment of his patients and there can be no question of responsibility being imposed on a health authority unless the authority has intervened in the practitioner's treatment of his patient—all partners in a practice may, however, be liable for the actions of one of their number. The general practitioner must have approved indemnity cover,[55] which will normally be by way of membership of a medical defence

---

[50] E Cave, 'Redress in the NHS' (2011) 27 Journal of Professional Negligence 138.

[51] *Pfizer Corporation* v *Ministry of Health* [1965] AC 512 and *Reynolds* v *Health First Medical Group* [2000] Lloyd's Rep Med 240.

[52] For a useful discussion of the distinction between contractual and tortious remedies in this context, see M A Jones, *Medical Negligence* (4th edn, 2008), and CJ Lewis and A Buchan, *Clinical Negligence: A Practical Guide* (7th edn, 2012).

[53] An issue which arose in *Thake* v *Maurice* [1984] 2 All ER 513; revsd [1986] QB 644; [1986] 1 All ER 479.

[54] (1979) 28 NBR (2d) 569, NBSC; discussed by Jones, n 52.

[55] Medical Act 1983 (as amended), s 44C.

society, to whom he will refer any claim against him; the society then advises him and undertakes the defence or settlement of the claim. General practitioners are not covered by the Crown indemnity which applies to hospital doctors unless a claim arises in respect of work undertaken under a health authority contract. A general practitioner will be vicariously liable for the negligence of staff employed by him—nurses, receptionists, etc.—but not for the acts of a locum tenens or a deputising doctor who will, normally, be insured independently.[56]

5.21   The position is different if the alleged negligence occurs after the general practitioner has referred the patient for further treatment within the NHS. If the negligent act is committed by a health service employee, the patient then has the choice of proceeding either against the individual or against the health authority or trust, or against both in a joint action. In practice, many actions are brought against the health authority or trust on the grounds of convenience. The liability of the authority or trust may be based on either of two grounds: (i) the direct duty of a hospital to care for patients; or (ii) the vicarious liability of a health authority for the negligence of its employees.

5.22   There has been some doubt as to whether a hospital owes a non-delegable duty to use skill and care in treating its patients.[57] This has been addressed in some Commonwealth jurisdictions which have a somewhat different form of health care delivery to that existing in the UK. Thus, in the Australian case of *Ellis* v *Wallsend District Hospital*,[58] the majority held that there was a non-delegable duty in those cases where patients were permitted to go directly to the hospital for treatment and advice; no such duty would exist where the hospital merely provided services which a doctor could use to treat his own patients.[59] By contrast, the Ontario Court of Appeal found that the hospital's duty extends no further than employing competent staff.[60] The minority view was, however, that hospitals, to a growing extent, hold out to the public that they provide medical treatment and emergency services—and that the public increasingly relies upon them to do so; Blair JA, in expressing this view, drew upon the evolution of the law in England which he thought supported the view that the hospital could be personally liable for negligent treatment in certain circumstances.[61] The English case of *Wilsher*[62] could have provided an ideal ground to decide the matter but the issue was not raised by the plaintiffs; it was said, however, that:

> I can see no reason why, in principle, the health authority should not be [directly] liable if its organisation is at fault.[63]

5.23   Since then, the door has been pushed to a position which can best be described as 'ajar'. In both *A (a child)* v *Ministry of Defence*[64] and *Farraj* v *Kings Healthcare NHS*

---

[56] There was no vicarious liability for the negligence of a locum tenens in the Canadian case of *Rothwell* v *Raes* (1988) 54 DLR (4th) 193.

[57] For discussion, see A M Dugdale and K M Stanton, *Professional Negligence* (3rd edn, 1998) para 22.20.

[58] (1989) 17 NSWLR 553, CA; confirmed on appeal [1990] 2 Med LR 103.

[59] The matter was also pronounced upon, obiter, by the High Court of Australia in *Commonwealth* v *Introvigne* (1982) 56 ALJR 749 and *Kondis* v *State Transport Authority* (1984) 154 CLR 672; 55 ALR 225.

[60] *Yepremian* v *Scarborough General Hospital* (1980) 110 DLR (3d) 513.

[61] (1980) 110 DLR (3d) 513 at 579.

[62] *Wilsher* v *Essex Area Health Authority* [1987] QB 730; [1986] 3 All ER 801, CA; revsd [1988] AC 1074; [1988] 1 All ER 871, HL, discussed later at para 5.68. The case was applied in *Fairchild* v *Glenhaven Funeral Services Ltd* [2002] UKHL 22; [2003] 1 AC 32.

[63] [1987] QB 730 at 778; [1986] 3 All ER 801 at 833, per Browne-Wilkinson V-C.

[64] [2004] 3 WLR 469; [2005] QB 183; (2005) 82 BMLR 149.

Trust,[65] the courts declined to hold that there was a non-delegable duty, but these can be explicable in that (i) it was the NHS, not the Ministry of Defence, that was responsible for providing health care, and (ii) *Farraj* involved no material discussion one way or the other about the validity of a non-delegable duty and was later overturned on the ground that there was no good reason for extending the general limits of a hospital's duty of care beyond the ambit of medical treatment. In *S v Lothian Health Board*,[66] the court allowed proof before answer on the issue of such a duty on the premise that what is relevant is whether the hospital assumes responsibility for contracted-out services that lead to negligent harm, not whether it had a degree of control over the work done. This has more recently been confirmed by the Supreme Court in *Woodland v Swimming Teachers Association and Others*:

> The true test reflects the factors which suggest that control is important, but has more nuance. I would express it thus. A school or hospital owes a non-delegable duty to see that care is taken for the safety of a child or patient who (a) is generally in its care, and (b) is receiving a service which is part of the institution's mainstream function of education or tending to the sick.[67]

5.24 The question is, then, still open and depends very much on the precise nature of the delegation but it is still of some importance, particularly in respect of staff whose group or personal cover may be less comprehensive than is that of the professions. The issue does, in fact, seem to have been effectively decided in the ratio of *Re R (a minor) (No 2)*. Here it was said:

> Although it is customary to say that a health authority is vicariously liable for breach of duty if its responsible servants or agents fail to set up a safe system of operation in relation to what are essentially management as opposed to clinical matters, this formulation may tend to cloud the fact that in any event it has a non-delegable duty to establish a proper system of care just as much as it has a duty to engage competent staff and a duty to provide proper and safe equipment and safe premises.[68]

If claiming, however, that a safe and proper system has not been provided, it should be argued clearly which elements or features of the said system are thought to be lacking.[69]

5.25 The discussion might be relatively sterile in the case of hospital doctors, the vast majority of whom are direct employees of the NHS. The health authority is, therefore, clearly liable for their negligence under the principle of vicarious liability. This provides that an employer is liable for his employee's negligent acts, provided that the employee is acting within the scope of his employment. It should be borne in mind that the employer may still be held vicariously liable even if the employee acts in direct contradiction of his or her employer's instructions or prohibitions. The vicarious liability of hospitals throughout their hierarchy has been clearly established for half a century[70] and requires no further

---

[65] [2008] EWHC 2468 (QB). The Court of Appeal rejected the trial conclusion that a hospital's non-delegable duty to a patient, if there was one, extended to supervising the quality of tests contracted out to an independent laboratory: [2009] EWCA 1203. For a distinction between contracted-out treatment and investigation, see *M v Calderdale and Kirklees HA* [1998] Lloyd's Rep Med 157.

[66] 2009 SLT 689.   [67] [2013] UKSC 66; [2014] AC 537.

[68] *Re R (a minor) (No 2)* (1997) 33 BMLR 178 at 197, CA, per Brooke LJ—a case including inadequate hospital communications (sub nom *Robertson v Nottingham Health Authority* [1987] 8 Med LR 1).

[69] See *Campbell v Borders Health Board* [2011] CSOH 73.

[70] *Roe v Minister of Health; Woolley v Ministry of Health* [1954] 2 QB 66; *Hayward v Board of Management of the Royal Infirmary of Edinburgh* and *Macdonald v Glasgow Western Hospitals Board of Management* 1954 SC 453.

discussion.[71] If anything, it may be expanding. In *Godden* v *Kent and Medway Strategic Health Authority*,[72] it was held to be an arguable ground of action that a health authority could be held vicariously liable for the acts of a general practitioner who had indecently assaulted and possibly negligently treated his patients.

5.26 The costs, especially to young doctors, of being members of a defence society have increased so dramatically that those who are working in the NHS have had to be subsidised by the authorities (see n 2). Crown immunity has been extended to NHS doctors, dentists, and community physicians since January 1990[73] and, as a result, the entire costs of negligence litigation are now borne by the Health Service itself—though there is, of course, nothing to stop a claimant suing an individual doctor. One consequence is that health authorities may feel obliged to settle cases on the grounds that this is the cheapest, if not the fairest, option; moreover, there is a strong suspicion that compensation for the injured may be bought at the expense of limitations in treatment facilities for other patients—but this is, perhaps, to take too pessimistic a view and, in practice, the load is now spread in that all trusts are encouraged to make use of the mutual insurance offered by the Clinical Negligence Scheme for Trusts operated by the NHSLA.[74] It is to be noted that the scheme as it relates to individual doctors applies *only* to services provided within the NHS; doctors should, therefore, retain cover for any private or 'good Samaritan' work—and, indeed, for medico-legal activity. As we have seen earlier, all negligence litigation involving the NHS is handled by the NHSLA.[75] The Authority itself reports that fewer than 2 per cent of the cases it handles ever end up in court, with the remainder settled out of court or abandoned by the claimant.[76] For those few that do go to court, however, the battle has only just begun.

WHAT CONSTITUTES NEGLIGENCE

5.27 We have flirted with the legal concept of negligence in Chapter 4, where we also outlined briefly the core elements of each negligence action. Once again, these are that the claimant must establish:

   (i) that the defendant owed him a *duty of care*;

   (ii) that there was a *breach* of this duty of care, which amounts to a requirement to demonstrate that the standard of the treatment given by the defendant fell below the standard expected of him by the law; and

   (iii) *because of* this sub-standard treatment the claimant suffered a legally recognised harm (e.g., physical injury or psychiatric illness).[77] This is otherwise known as *causation*: did the defendant's acts or omissions *cause* the claimant's harm?

---

[71] It is also possible to sue the Secretary of State for policy-based operational failures in the delivery of health care: see *Re HIV Haemophiliac Litigation* (1998) 41 BMLR 171.

[72] [2004] EWHC 1629 (QB), [2004] All ER (D) 114 (Jul).

[73] See Department of Health, *HSG (96) 48 NHS, Indemnity Arrangements for Handling Clinical Negligence Claims against NHS Staff* and *Research in the NHS: Indemnity Arrangements* (2005)—for NHS bodies involved in research which involves NHS staff and/or NHS patients, including their organs, tissues, or data.

[74] NHS (Clinical Negligence Scheme) Regulations 1996 (SI 1996/251); repealed by the National Health Service (Clinical Negligence Scheme) Regulations (SI 2015/559).

[75] For more on which see: http://www.nhsla.com/Pages/Home.aspx.

[76] http://www.nhsla.com/Claims/Pages/Handling.aspx

[77] Cf, *Fairlie* v *Perth and Kinross Healthcare NHS Trust* 2004 SLT 1200 (OH) in which 'distress'—in the absence of an identifiable psychiatric or psychological condition or illness—was not considered a legally

If successful in proving all the necessary elements, the claimant is entitled to monetary compensation which is supposed to place him as far as is possible back in the position he would have been in if the negligence had not occurred. Of course, when the harm is something other than financial—as it almost always is in medical cases—the recompense can only ever be a theoretical measure of what the person has lost.

5.28 The concept of medical negligence has experienced a schism over the last quarter of a century. On the one hand, we have the standard line of cases in which there has been a technical failure or misadventure—in other words, those that are associated with medical treatment in one form or another. There has, however, been a rapid growth in accusations of negligence arising before treatment was started—these have become known as information disclosure cases which are based on the rights of the patient to make an informed choice as to his or her treatment—hence, the 'consent-based negligence' action. The principles underlying the tort of negligence are very similar in both situations. Nonetheless, the latter has developed a jurisprudence of its own which is best discussed under the heading of 'consent'—for which, see Chapter 4. Here, for the moment, we confine discussion to the established field of medical misadventure.

5.29 In either situation, a major difficulty for any claimant lies in the burden that falls upon him to prove that the defendant's negligence caused his injury. This is often a difficult task to discharge and, indeed, suggestions have been made that the patient attempting to succeed in an action against a doctor should face a heavier burden in establishing his case than is required in any other personal injury litigation. There is an indication that this occurs in practice insofar as payment is made in some 30–40 per cent of medical cases as compared with 86 per cent in the general run;[78] the figures may, however, conceal more than a simple cause and effect phenomenon. The legal foundation for this view, which was put forward by Lawton LJ,[79] may be tenuous and it was, in fact, strongly opposed in *Ashcroft*;[80] nevertheless, it is certainly true that there has been a degree of policy-based judicial reluctance to award damages against doctors.[81] The clearest examples of this are discussed in the context of wrongful conception/birth cases in Chapter 10.

5.30 At the same time, the courts have not been insensitive to the claimant's difficulties in a medical negligence case. The correctives applied have been the occasional invocation of the principle of *res ipsa loquitur* or, as in *Clark* v *MacLennan*,[82] an attempt to shift the burden of proof to the defendant. The observations of Kilner Brown J in *Ashcroft* on this point are revealing:

> When an injury is caused which never should have been caused, common sense and natural justice indicate that some degree of compensation ought to be paid by someone. As the law stands, in order to obtain compensation an injured person is compelled to allege negligence against ... a person of the highest skill and reputation.[83]

relevant harm. But see, also, *D* v *East Berkshire Community Health NHS Trust; K* v *Dewsbury Healthcare NHS Trust, K* v *Oldham NHS Trust* [2005] UKHL 23; [2005] 2 All ER 443, in which the House of Lords dismissed appeals by three sets of parents who had been falsely accused of child abuse, holding that the parents were not owed a duty of care by the defendant HCPs for psychiatric harm caused by the false allegations, even though they had suffered a recognised form of psychiatric injury.

[78] See Jones, n 52, 275–9.　　[79] In *Whitehouse* v *Jordan* [1980] 1 All ER 650 at 659.

[80] *Ashcroft* v *Mersey Regional Health Authority* [1983] 2 All ER 245 at 247, per Kilner Brown J.

[81] See the Lord Chief Justice, writing extra-judicially: Lord Woolf, 'Are the courts excessively deferential to the medical profession?' (2001) 9 Med L Rev 1.

[82] [1983] 1 All ER 416.　　[83] [1983] 2 All ER 245 at 246.

We return to *res ipsa* later.[84] For now, we begin with a consideration of the first element of the negligence action: is there a duty of care?

DUTY OF CARE

5.31   How do you know if your doctor owes you a duty of care? The answer, in most cases, is disarmingly simple: because he or she *is* your doctor. That is, an automatic legal duty of care arises if a HCP has accepted to treat you, or a general practitioner has accepted you onto his or her files. A duty will also arise in the case of a private patient by virtue of his or her contractual relationship with his or her doctor (or the hospital) and, within a public national health system, the duty arises when the patient presents for treatment and is admitted. It does not follow, of course, that you are entitled to everything that you demand—but this is a question of the *standard* of care that can be expected, and we return to this later.

5.32   Duties in law can be assumed or imposed. The paradigm example of an assumed obligation (of care) is that of contract, where parties voluntarily agree to be bound to each other. As we have noted, however, this is not the legal basis for the operation of the NHS; rather, tort law dictates if and when a duty of care arises. A three-stage test is used. The overarching legal and policy consideration in respect of all duties of care in tort is to ask whether it would be fair, just, and reasonable to impose such a duty in the given circumstances.[85] Furthermore, the relationship between the claimant and the defendant must be sufficiently 'proximate' that harm following the defendant's actions/omissions was 'reasonably foreseeable'.[86] This, in essence, is a question of how directly a claimant might be affected by the behaviour of another. The more direct the likelihood of harm, the more likely it will be that a duty of care will be imposed. This is always, however, subject to the fairness and reasonableness of creating that duty. This can be particularly problematic for relatives who claim that they have been harmed as a result of negligent care of a loved one. Thus, in *Fairlie* v *Perth and Kinross Healthcare NHS Trust*,[87] the argument that a father was owed a duty of care by a health board in respect of the distress he suffered at being accused of abusing his daughter after she underwent allegedly negligent psychiatric treatment was rejected. The court opined that there was nothing to suggest circumstances in which it could be said that the father came at any stage into a special relationship with the attending psychiatrist such that a duty of care would arise.[88] Similarly, in *MK (a child)* v *Oldham NHS Trust*,[89] it was held that disruption to family life occasioned from a prolonged medical and social services investigation of a child's injuries, during which time she was separated from her parents, was not a recognised head of damage in the absence of psychiatric disturbance to the child;[90] nor was there a sufficient degree of proximity between the parents and the defendants to make it fair, just, and reasonable to impose

---

[84]   See paras 5.78 et seq.
[85]   See, principally, *Caparo Industries plc* v *Dickman* [1990] 2 AC 605; also see, e.g., *Kent* v *Griffiths (No 3)* [2001] QB 36; [2000] 2 All ER 474.
[86]   See e.g. *Goodwill* v *British Pregnancy Advisory Service* [1996] 2 All ER 161; [1996] 7 Med LR 129; *Vowles* v *Evans* [2003] 1 WLR 1607, CA.
[87]   2004 SLT 1200 (OH).
[88]   See also, *Sion* v *Hampstead Health Authority* (1994) 5 Med LR 170 and our discussion of the case of *Palmer* v *Tees Health Authority* [1998] Lloyd's Rep Med 447; (1998) 45 BMLR 88 in Chapter 13.
[89]   [2003] Lloyd's Rep Med 1.
[90]   *Reilly* v *Merseyside Regional Health Authority* [1995] 6 Med LR 246 and *McLoughlin* v *O'Brian* [1983] 1 AC 410 applied.

a duty of care as between the parties. While it has been accepted that a duty is owed to the child, the judicial reluctance to extend this to the parents remains; this has now been confirmed at the highest level and as withstanding a human rights challenge.[91]

The Court of Appeal has confirmed in *Simpson* v *Norfolk and Norwich University Hospital NHS Trust*[92] that while a right to recovery for personal injury is a form of property, it is not one inherently capable of assignment unless the assignee has a legitimate interest in pursuing proceedings. This most certainly does not extend to an attempt to make profit from litigation, which would be void as 'savouring of champerty'.

5.33   One thing that is unquestionable is that a public health service owes duties of care to the patients it accepts for treatment—on any analysis it is a fair and reasonable legal position. But is it possible for personnel not to accept patients and so to reject this duty? What of the over-tired houseman who is fed up dealing with the drunks who stagger into the Accident and Emergency Department on a Saturday night after a fight? Can he turn them away? Quite simply, no, he cannot, the reason being that the hospital is holding itself out as offering emergency services, which, self-evidently, is a public statement that it will respond to the public need, however unpleasant that may be.[93] By the same token, it does not follow that any public health care establishment must accept whosoever presents. It is arguably fair and reasonable for a hospital *not* to offer emergency services and to direct patients elsewhere. The same applies to the individual doctor.[94] Whatever one might think of moral obligations, it is no part of the general law in the UK that a doctor must respond to someone in medical need when that person is not already his patient. The doctor need not then raise his hand in response to a request for medical assistance for the airline passenger who has collapsed in the flight.[95] However, a duty of care will clearly arise should he do so and begin to examine the patient and what is then required of him becomes determined by the relevant standard of care. Let us turn, then, to consider the second element of the negligence action, namely, the standard of care, where we seek out what the content of any duty entails.

THE STANDARD OF CARE: THE REASONABLY SKILFUL DOCTOR

5.34   It is apt to continue here with the theme of emergency care. The old, but still relevant, case of *Barnett* v *Chelsea and Kensington Hospital Management Committee*[96] has something of

---

[91]   *JD* v *East Berkshire Community NHS Trust* [2005] UKHL 23; [2005] 2 AC 373 and re-affirmed in *Jain* v *Trent Strategic Health Authority* [2009] UKHL 4; [2009] 1 AC 853. On the impact of human rights developments on duties of care in this area, see K Greasley, 'A negligent blow to children at risk: *MAK and RK* v *United Kingdom (European Court of Human Rights)*' (2010) 73 MLR 1026.

[92]   [2011] EWCA Civ 1149; [2012] QB 640.

[93]   The same applies to the ambulance service where there is a legal duty to respond to a call for help: see *Kent* v *Griffiths* [2000] 2 WLR 1158; [2000] 2 All ER 474. For a discussion of this case see: K Williams, 'Litigation against English NHS ambulance services and the rule in *Kent* v *Griffiths*' (2007) 15 Med L Rev 153. In Scotland, a private law action was confirmed as justiciable in *Aitken* v *Scottish Ambulance Service* [2011] CSOH 49; 2011 SLT 822.

[94]   But see National Health Service (General Medical Services Contracts) Regulations 2004 (SI 2004/291), reg 15(6) with respect to general practitioners who are obliged to provide immediate care after accident or emergency in his/her practice area in core hours.

[95]   Which, of course, also says nothing about the professional perspective on such inaction. See, e.g., GMC, *Good Medical Practice* (2013), para 26, which states: 'You must offer help if emergencies arise in clinical settings or in the community, taking account of your own safety, your competence, and the availability of other options for care'—which, as is so often the case, leaves the decision in the subjective sphere.

[96]   [1968] 2 WLR 422; [1968] 3 All ER 1068.

relevance for each element of the negligence action. As to the role of the casualty officer, the judge had this to say:

> It is not, in my judgment, the case that a casualty officer must always see the caller at his department. Casualty departments are misused from time to time. If the receptionist, for example, discovers that the visitor is already attending his own doctor and merely wants a second opinion, or if the caller has a small cut which the nurse can perfectly well dress herself, then the casualty officer need not be called. However, apart from such things as this, I find the opinion of Dr. Sydney Lockett entirely acceptable. He said ... In my view, the duty of a casualty officer is in general to see and examine all patients who come to the casualty department of the hospital.

The case concerned three workmen who suffered violent illness after drinking tea. They presented to the local cottage hospital, but the doctor was ill himself. The nurse phoned the doctor with the symptoms and he advised that the men go home and see their own doctors. In the event, one of the men died—as it turned out, from arsenic poisoning—and the action was brought by his widow. The court held that the doctor not only owed a duty of care to those who presented to his casualty unit but that, in these circumstances, he should have ensured that the patients were properly examined. Ultimately, however, as we shall see, Barnett's widow did not recover, despite there being a duty of care and despite the ruling that the requisite standard had not been met.

5.35 In this case, the standard was about examining emergency patients. But how are we to know what that standard is across the whole spectrum of medical care? There have been many judicial pronouncements by the courts on the subject. As early as 1838 we find Tindall CJ ruling that:

> Every person who enters into a learned profession undertakes to bring to the exercise of it a reasonable degree of care and skill. He does not undertake, if he is an attorney, that at all events you shall gain your case, nor does a surgeon undertake that he will perform a cure; nor does he undertake to use the highest possible degree of skill.[97]

An echo of this is to be found in *R v Bateman*,[98] where the court explained that:

> If a person holds himself out as possessing special skill and knowledge, by and on behalf of a patient, he owes a duty to the patient to use due caution in undertaking the treatment ... The jury should not exact the highest, or very high standard, nor should they be content with a very low standard.

5.36 Thus, the doctor is not expected to be a miracle-worker guaranteeing a cure or to be a man of the very highest skill in his calling. What standard then is he expected to meet? McNair J provides us with the classic answer to this question in *Bolam v Friern Hospital Management Committee*:[99]

> The test is the standard of the ordinary skilled man exercising and professing to have that special skill. A man need not possess the highest expert skill at the risk of being found negligent. It is a well-established law that it is sufficient if he exercises the ordinary skill of an ordinary man exercising that particular art.

---

[97] *Lanphier v Phipos* (1838) 8 C & P 475 at 478.
[98] (1925) 94 LJKB 791 at 794; [1925] All ER Rep 45, CCA.
[99] [1957] 2 All ER 118 at 121; [1957] 1 WLR 582 at 586.

Nevertheless, he *is* professing a particular skill and, in the further immortal words of McNair J, the test of that skill 'is not the test of the man on the top of the Clapham omnibus because [that man] has not got this special skill'.[100]

5.37 The doctor having that degree of competence expected of the ordinary skilful doctor sets the standard. He is the practitioner who follows the standard practice of his profession—or, at least, follows practices that would not be disapproved of by responsible opinion within the profession; he has a reasonably sound grasp of medical techniques and is as informed of new medical developments as the average competent doctor would expect to be. The circumstances in which a doctor treats his patient will also be taken into account. A doctor working in an emergency, with inadequate facilities and under great pressure, will not be expected by the courts to achieve the same results as a doctor who is working in ideal conditions.[101] This was alluded to by Mustill J in *Wilsher*, where he said that, if a person was forced by an emergency to do too many things at once, then the fact that he does one of them incorrectly 'should not lightly be taken as negligence'.[102]

5.38 The reasonably skilful doctor has a duty to keep himself informed of major developments in practice but this duty obviously cannot extend to the requirement that he should know all there is to be known in a particular area of medicine. In the case of *Crawford v Board of Governors of Charing Cross Hospital*,[103] the plaintiff had developed brachial palsy as a result of his arm being kept in a certain position during an operation. Six months prior to the operation an article had appeared in the *Lancet*, pointing out just this danger but the anaesthetist against whom negligence was being alleged had not read the article in question. The Court of Appeal eventually found in favour of the anaesthetist, Lord Denning stating that:

> it would, I think, be putting too high a burden on a medical man to say that he has to read every article appearing in the current medical press; and it would be quite wrong to suggest that a medical man is negligent because he does not at once put into operation the suggestions which some contributor or other might make in a medical journal. The time may come in a particular case when a new recommendation may be so well proved and so well known, and so well accepted that it should be adopted, but that was not so in this case.[104]

5.39 Failure to read a single article, it was said, may be excusable, while disregard of a series of warnings in the medical press could well be evidence of negligence. In view of the rapid progress currently being made in many areas of medicine, and in view of the amount of information confronting the average doctor, it is unreasonable to expect a doctor to be aware of every development in his field. At the same time, he must be reasonably up to date and must know of major developments. The practice of medicine has, however, become increasingly based on principles of scientific elucidation and report—the so-called 'evidence-based medicine'—and the pressure on doctors to keep abreast of current developments is now considerable. It is no longer possible for a doctor to coast along on the basis of long experience; such an attitude has been firmly discredited not only in medicine but in many other professions and callings.

---

[100] A test approved by the Privy Council: *Chin Keow v Government of Malaysia* [1967] 1 WLR 813.

[101] This is in accordance with the general principle in the law of torts that errors of judgement are more excusable in an emergency: *The Metagama* 1928 SC (HL) 21; the strength of this precedent was confirmed in the non-medical personal injury case of *Morris v Richards* [2003] EWCA Civ 232.

[102] [1987] QB 730 at 749; [1986] 3 All ER 801 at 812.   [103] (1953) *The Times*, 8 December, CA.

[104] (1953) *The Times*, 8 December, CA.

Usual Practice

5.40 The 'custom test'—the test whereby a defendant's conduct is tested against the normal usage of his profession or calling—is one that is applied in all areas of negligence law. The courts have given expression to this test in the medical context in a number of decisions. In the important Scottish case of *Hunter* v *Hanley*, for example, there was a clear endorsement of the custom test in Lord Clyde's dictum:

> To establish liability by a doctor where deviation from normal practice is alleged, three facts require to be established. First of all it must be proved that there is a usual and normal practice; secondly it must be proved that the defender has not adopted that practice; and thirdly (and this is of crucial importance) it must be established that the course the doctor adopted is one which no professional man of ordinary skill would have taken if he had been acting with ordinary care.[105]

5.41 This attractively simple exposition of the law, however, conceals a hurdle at the outset. It may, in many cases, be possible to prove that there is a 'usual and normal practice'— this is particularly so if there are guidelines covering a procedure, a ploy which is increasingly used in UK legislation[106] and which might be seen as being helpful to the claimant.[107] On the other hand, there will obviously be disagreement as to what is the appropriate course to follow in a number of medical scenarios. In some circumstances, the existence of two schools of thought may result in more than one option being open to a practitioner. If this is so, then what are the liability implications of choosing a course of action which a responsible body of opinion within the profession may well reject? Precisely this question arose in *Bolam*,[108] where the plaintiff had suffered fractures as a result of the administration of electro-convulsive therapy without an anaesthetic. At the time, there were two schools of thought on the subject of anaesthesia in such treatment, one holding the view that relaxant drugs should be used, the other being that this only increased the risk. In this case, the judge ruled that a doctor would not be negligent if he acted 'in accordance with the practice accepted by a responsible body of medical men skilled in that particular art'. Negligence would not be inferred merely because there was a body of opinion which took a contrary view.[109] Subsequent cases confirmed this approach. In *Maynard* v *West Midlands Regional Health Authority*, the trial judge had preferred an alternative medical approach to that which had been chosen by the defendant, notwithstanding the fact that this latter course found support in

---

[105] 1955 SC 200 at 206. The rigid simplicity of Lord Clyde's definition was defended in an anonymous article 'Medical negligence: *Hunter* v *Hanley* 35 years on' 1990 SLT 325. *Hunter* was specifically approved by Lord Scarman in *Maynard* v *West Midlands Regional Health Authority* [1985] 1 All ER 635; [1984] 1 WLR 634 and would seem to be the relevant test in Ireland: *Dunne (infant)* v *National Maternity Hospital* [1989] IR 91 per Finlay CJ.

[106] B Hurwitz, 'Legal and political considerations of clinical guidelines' (1999) 318 BMJ 661; A Samanta, M M Mello, C Foster, et al., 'The role of clinical negligence guidelines in medical negligence litigation: A shift from the Bolam standard?' (2006) 14 Med Law Rev 321.

[107] These have not proved to be as productive of litigation as might be expected. For a US perspective see: A I Hyman, J A Brandenburg, S R Lipsitz, et al., 'Practice guidelines and malpractice litigation: A two-way street' (1995) 122 Ann Int Med 450; T K Mackey and B A Liang, 'The role of practice guidelines in medical malpractice litigation' (2011) 13 Virtual Mentor 36.

[108] [1957] 2 All ER 118; [1957] 1 WLR 582.

[109] There is potential conflict here with the existing authority. In *Hucks* v *Cole* (1968) [1993] 4 Med LR 393 it was held that an action that was clearly unreasonable could be negligent despite professional support. For comment, see A Stewart, 'Best interests: towards a more patient-friendly law' (2007) 11 Edin LR 62.

responsible medical opinion; both the Court of Appeal and the House of Lords confirmed that this was an unsatisfactory way of attributing negligence.[110]

5.42 *Bolam* has been the object of sustained criticism from those who object to the implication that the medical profession itself determines what is an acceptable level of care.[111] Critics have persistently argued that doctors themselves should not dictate whether conduct is negligent; this should be a matter for the courts. This has been confirmed—albeit hesitantly—by the House of Lords' decision in *Bolitho* v *Hackney Health Authority*,[112] a case regarded by some commentators as representing a significant nail in *Bolam*'s coffin. *Bolitho* arose out of a failure on the part of a hospital doctor to examine and intubate a child experiencing respiratory distress. Negligence derived from a failure to attend the patient was not disputed; however, the problem of causation still remained. Expert evidence was led by the plaintiff to the effect that a reasonably competent doctor would have intubated in such circumstances. The defendant, however, had her own expert witnesses prepared to say that non-intubation was a clinically justifiable response. The defendant argued that, had she attended the child, she would not have intubated her and her failure to attend would not, therefore, have made any difference to the outcome. The House of Lords accepted the truth of this evidence. The causation issue, here, is important from the jurisprudential aspect insofar as it was made clear that, while the *Bolam* test had no relevance as to the doctor's intention, it was central to the collateral question—would she have been negligent in failing to take action? In other words, *Bolam* was applied to the question of causation when, in reality, the test is concerned only with standards of care. As a result, given that she had responsible support, the action failed on both counts. However, the particular significance of *Bolitho* lies in the House of Lords' support for the Court of Appeal's departure from the certainties of *Bolam*. Rather than accepting a 'body of opinion' simply because it was there, Lord Browne-Wilkinson held that the court must, in addition, be satisfied that the body of opinion in question rests on a logical basis. In particular, in cases involving, as they so often do, the weighing of risks against benefits, the judge, before accepting a body of opinion as being responsible, reasonable or respectable, will need to be satisfied that, in forming their views, the experts have directed their minds to the question of comparative risks and benefits and have reached a defensible conclusion on the matter.[113]

5.43 This appears to be a clear rejection of the *Bolam* rule simpliciter,[114] but it must be read in the light of the strong caveat which Lord Browne-Wilkinson attached:

> In the vast majority of cases the fact that distinguished experts in the field are of a particular opinion will demonstrate the reasonableness of that opinion ... But if, in a rare case, it can be demonstrated that the professional opinion is not capable of withstanding logical analysis, the judge is entitled to hold that the body of opinion is not reasonable or responsible ... I emphasise that, in my view, it will very seldom be right for a judge to reach the conclusion that views genuinely held by a competent medical expert are unreasonable.[115]

---

[110] [1985] 1 All ER 635; [1984] 1 WLR 634. *Maynard* was followed in *Hughes* v *Waltham Forest Health Authority* [1991] 2 Med LR 155, in which the court emphasised that the fact that a surgeon's decision was criticised by other surgeons did not amount in itself to an indication of negligence.

[111] Particularly in the Commonwealth: *Reibl* v *Hughes* (1980) 114 DLR (3d) 1; *Rogers* v *Whittaker* (1992) 109 ALR 625; [1993] 4 Med LR 79. And see, in general, 'information disclosure' in Chapter 4.

[112] [1998] AC 232; [1997] 4 All ER 771, HL.

[113] [1997] 4 All ER 771 at 778; (1998) 39 BMLR 1 at 9.

[114] For an example of weighing the reasonableness and responsibleness of medical opinion post-*Bolitho*, see *M (a child)* v *Blackpool Victoria Hospital NHS Trust* [2003] EWHC 1744 in which an appeal on *Bolitho* terms was rejected.

[115] [1997] 4 All ER 771 at 779; (1998) 39 BMLR 1 at 10.

5.44 Thus, *Bolitho* undoubtedly devalues the trump card which *Bolam* presented to the medical profession, but only in limited circumstances.[116] And, as to that, it is arguably undesirable to undermine the standard test beyond a certain point. *Bolam* provides some protection for the innovative or minority opinion or, indeed, the individual clinical judgement call.[117] If this protection is removed, then the opinion that the cautious practitioner will wish to follow will be that which involves least risk. This may have an inhibiting effect on medical progress: after all, many advances in medicine have been made by those who have pursued an unconventional line of therapy. Such doctors may quite easily be regarded as negligent by a judge given to favouring conventional medical opinion.

5.45 In this respect, we can look to the decision in *De Freitas* v *O'Brien*,[118] which, rather than bolstering a conservative approach in assessing the acceptability of a body of opinion, gives comfort to the so-called 'super-specialist' who may undertake procedures which others might regard as being inappropriate or even too risky. In this case, a spinal surgeon—said to be one out of only 11 such specialists in the country—maintained that the surgery he performed was in line with what his fellow spinal surgeons would have considered clinically justified. The plaintiffs, by contrast, claimed that run of the mill orthopaedic surgeons would not have operated in the circumstances. The Court of Appeal confirmed that the *Bolam* test did not require that the responsible body of opinion be large, thus endorsing the acceptability of acting within limits defined by a sub-specialty. One criticism of the decision in *De Freitas* is that it licenses the taking of risks. Yet, the court clearly retains its ability to declare an opinion to be unreasonable, a power which is firmly endorsed by *Bolitho*.

5.46 The Court of Appeal in *Bolitho* has been hailed as ushering in the 'new-*Bolam*'[119] although there were many who viewed it with a modicum of distrust.[120] It is, therefore, interesting to consider its progress since its birth—and, certainly, the case has attracted its fair share of attention. A few years in its wake, Maclean scoured the databases and unearthed 64 post-*Bolitho* medical negligence cases involving a standard of care[121] and concluded that, prior to November 2001, *Bolitho* was referred to in four cases in the Court of Appeal and in 25 at first instance.[122] There is no way in which all these cases—and those since—could be aired in a book of this size and several of them were 'consent-based' and are considered under that heading.[123] Some do, however, merit mention—if only briefly.

5.47 *Wisniewski* v *Central Manchester Health Authority*[124] seems to us to be the most apposite case in that the 'logic' underlying the expert evidence was specifically considered.

---

[116] For the correct approach for judges when dealing with expert evidence on accepted/acceptable practice, see *A* v *Burne* [2006] EWCA Civ 24.

[117] See e.g. *Zarb* v *Odetoyinbo* [2006] EWHC 2880 (QB); (2007) 93 BMLR 166.

[118] [1995] PIQR P281; [1995] 6 Med LR 108.

[119] A phrase which we would attribute to A Grubb, 'Commentary' (1998) 6 Med L Rev 378.

[120] A most searching review is that of M Brazier and J Miola, 'Bye-bye *Bolam*: A medical litigation revolution?' (2000) 8 Med L Rev 85. See also J Keown, 'Reining in the *Bolam* test' (1998) 57 CLJ 248 and H Teff, 'The standard of care in medical negligence—Moving on from *Bolam*' (1998) 18 OJLS 473.

[121] A Maclean, 'Beyond *Bolam* and *Bolitho*' (2002) 5 Med L Internat 205.

[122] At the same time, there was judgment explicitly by way of the *Bolam* test in eight Court of Appeal and ten High Court cases; the author remarks that 'it would seem that *Bolam* is far from dead'.

[123] See also, R Mulheron, 'Trumping *Bolam*: A critical legal analysis of *Bolitho*'s "gloss" ' (2010) 69 Cam LJ 609 and in the information disclosure context; A MacLean, 'From *Sidaway* to *Pearce* and beyond: is the legal regulation of consent any better following a quarter of a century of judicial scrutiny?' (2012) 20 Med L Rev 108.

[124] [1998] Lloyd's Rep Med 223, CA.

The case concerned a child who was born brain-damaged following 13 minutes' hypoxia during the birthing process; it was alleged that the midwife over estimated her ability and, as a result, the doctor failed to attend in appropriate time. As in *Bolitho*, negligence in relation to non-attendance was not in dispute; the problem, again, lay in causation—and in the two-stage definition of causation developed in *Bolitho* as to what would and should have happened in the absence of negligence. The establishment and the status of a 'responsible body of supporting opinion' were, therefore, of major importance and the conflict is illustrated in two quotations. Thomas J, at first instance, had this to say:

> where analysis of the expert evidence on the facts relating to a particular case shows that a decision made by a doctor and supported by experts cannot be justified as one that a responsible medical practitioner would have taken, then a judge should not preclude himself from reaching [a] conclusion simply because clinical judgment is involved.[125]

However, Brooke LJ said in the Court of Appeal:

> it is quite impossible for a court to hold that the views sincerely held by doctors of such eminence cannot logically be supported at all ... and the views of the defendants' witnesses were views which could be logically expressed and held by responsible doctors.[126]

5.48 The clear inference is that, had the doctor survived the first hurdle as to what he would have done had he attended, *Bolam* would have prevailed and the *Bolitho* exception would not have applied.[127] Logic is, however, a somewhat unusual criterion on which to assess what is, essentially, a matter of clinical judgement and it seems unlikely that the courts will be able to retain control over health care standards if they rely on 'logic' alone.[128]

5.49 It is, therefore, useful to turn to *Marriott*,[129] where a man sustained severe intra-cranial injury allegedly aggravated by his practitioner's failure to refer him back to hospital when his condition deteriorated. The health authority called expert evidence in support of the doctor but the trial judge considered this not to be reasonably prudent and found for the plaintiff. The Court of Appeal dismissed the appeal on two main grounds. First, the Court questioned the acceptability of the evidence for both sides—'it is questionable whether either had given evidence from which it was reasonable to infer that their individual approaches were shared by a responsible body of others in their profession'[130]—a statement which seems to eliminate the single maverick from the *Bolam* equation. Even so, the judge was effectively dismissing the evidence of *both* sides—the Court's opinion suggests that the result might have been different had she chosen one expert's evidence in preference to the other rather than substitute her own analysis. Second, however, the Court affirmed its entitlement to question whether an opinion was reasonably held given an analysis of the risks involved in following that opinion. On the face of things, then,

---

[125] Quoted [1998] Lloyd's Rep Med 223 at 235.   [126] [1998] Lloyd's Rep Med 223, 237.

[127] For the appropriate application of the *Bolam* and *Bolitho* tests in determining what should or should not have been done, see *Gouldsmith* v *Mid-Staffordshire General Hospitals NHS Trust* [2007] EWCA Civ 397.

[128] For a discussion of the 'logical' approach, and the relatively innovative alternative of 'unreasonable risk', see: R Heywood, 'The logic of *Bolitho*' (2006) 22 PN 225.

[129] *Marriott* v *West Midlands Regional Health Authority* [1999] Lloyd's Rep Med 23.

[130] Per Beldam LJ at 27. There is an interesting aside here—does it imply that there is a difference between the *Bolam* and the *Hunter* v *Hanley* tests?

Marriott moves the *Bolitho* test from one of logic to one of reasonableness, which is much more akin to the reasoning applied in other, non-medical standard of care decisions. Unfortunately, the situation is still not clear as, while the Court of Appeal supported the trial judge's approach, it still retained the language of 'logic'. *Marriott* does, however, open an alternative route to the 'new *Bolam*'. *Jones* v *Conwy and Denbighshire NHS Trust*[131] probably encapsulates the tenor of the emerging jurisprudence by collapsing the distinction between logicality and reasonableness in holding that in the absence of a clear bright-line rule about how to proceed in a given set of clinical circumstances—here the decision whether or not to order an immediate CT scan—it was neither illogical nor unreasonable to delay the procedure.

5.50   *Penney* v *East Kent Health Authority*[132] concerned three women who developed cancer of the cervix following a reported negative screening test. As with all screening tests, that for potential cervical cancer inherently involves both false positive and false negative tests, the latter being estimated as occurring in between 5 per cent and 15 per cent of cases examined. It was not, therefore, argued that a false negative report indicated negligence on the part of the screener per se; the issue was confined to what should have been done, in 1993, given the agreed fact that there were abnormalities in the claimants' slides. The health authority maintained that the unusual abnormalities present were open to interpretation and disposal and that the outcome of the case should be decided on *Bolam* principles. The trial judge considered, and the Court of Appeal agreed, however, that the *fact* was that abnormal cells were present which no screener, acting with reasonable care, could have been certain were not pre-cancerous; the slides should, therefore, have been labelled at least as borderline—he found 'the *Bolam* principle ill-fitting to Mrs Penney's case'. It is not easy, however, to see why that should be so in respect of 'excusability'. Pepitt J was clearly conscious of this and further held that, in the event that he was wrong, he would revert to *Bolitho* in that, given the facts, the contention of the health authority's experts that the slides could well have been reported as negative was inconsistent with the accepted principle of 'absolute confidence' and was, consequently, illogical—a conclusion with which it is difficult to disagree.[133] Equally, a failure on the part of a judge to find illogicality (or indeed to have before him explicit findings of fact that would support such a conclusion) will mean that he is not in a position to reject expert medical opinion as unreasonable: see *Ministry of Justice* v *Carter* (CA).[134] It has also been confirmed that a judge is not at liberty to choose between two responsible bodies of medical opinion unless on the basis that one is found to be illogical.[135]

5.51   In addition, we have *Birch* v *University College London Hospital NHS Foundation Trust*.[136] This case is concerned largely with negligence arising from failure to disclose material

---

[131] [2008] EWHC 3172 (QB).   [132] (2000) 55 BMLR 63; [2000] Lloyd's Rep Med 41.

[133] *Lillywhite* v *University College London Hospitals NHS Trust* [2004] EWHC 2452; revsd on appeal [2006] Lloyd's Rep Med 268 was a further case of, this time, radiological misdiagnosis, the main lesson of which seems to be that evidence adduced to refute an allegation of negligence must be that much more convincing when a specific diagnostic question has been posed. *Penney* was considered and approved most recently in *Manning* v *King's College Hospital NHS Trust* [2008] EWHC 1838 (QB); affd [2009] 110 BMLR 175, the gist of which was that a case of doubtful malignancy should not be reported as negative.

[134] *Ministry of Justice* v *Carter* [2010] EWCA Civ 694, at para 22.

[135] *Hannigan* v *Lanarkshire Acute Hospital NHS Trust* [2012] CSOH 152, citing *Honisz* v *Lothian Health Board* (2008) SC 235. Note, although Scottish cases, it is well settled that the position on negligence is the same north and south of the border.

[136] [2008] EWHC 2237 (QB); (2008) 104 BMLR 168.

risks and as such we deal with it more fully in Chapter 4. Nevertheless, on the role of logic in negligence cases, the judge had this to say about *Bolitho*:

> Lord Browne-Wilkinson was indicating that such an opinion is not to be lightly set aside. The body of medical opinion must be incapable of withstanding logical analysis, in other words, cannot be logically supported at all. If there are different practices sanctioned by two bodies of medical opinion, both withstanding logical analysis, there is no basis for a finding of negligence against the doctor choosing one rather than the other. The matter may simply boil down to a different weighing of benefits and risks. If there is no failure to weigh the risks and benefits of each practice the *Bolitho* approach cannot be used to trump *Bolam*, even though the adherence to one body of medical opinion has led to the adverse outcome in the particular case ... Not only am I bound by this view but I conceive it to be eminently sensible: it would be folly for a judge with no training in medicine to conclude that one body of medical opinion should be preferred over another, when both are professionally sanctioned and both withstand logical attack.[137]

5.52 While it is unwise to generalise from a small number of selected cases, the impression gained thus far is that, while the courts are increasingly determined to see that the *Bolam* principle is not extended,[138] they still have an innate reluctance to abandon it in respect of medical opinion.[139] There is a sense that *Bolitho*, although welcome, is being used mainly in a 'back-up' position. What is certain is that *Bolam* can no longer be regarded as impregnable.

Innovative Techniques

5.53 Resort to an innovative therapeutic technique may be appropriate in certain cases but should be made with caution. Whether the use of such a technique could amount to negligence would depend on the extent to which its use was considered justified in the case in question. In assessing this, a court would consider evidence of previous trials of the treatment and would also, no doubt, take into consideration any dangers which it entailed. It is possible that a court would decline to endorse the use of an untried procedure if the patient was thereby exposed to considerable risk of damage.[140] Other factors which might be taken into account would be the previous response of the patient to more conventional treatment, the seriousness of the patient's condition, and the attitude of the patient him or herself towards the novelty and risk. In *Cooper v Royal United Hospital Bath NHS Trust*,[141] the Trust was held to have breached its duty of care to the claimant for abandoning a preferred course of medical care without adequately advising her as to the risks of implementing an alternative method. The standard of care to be applied in such circumstances would be that expected of a doctor who is reasonably competent in

---

[137] (2008) 104 BMLR 168, para 55.

[138] As, e.g., into judging the patient's best interests: *Re S (adult patient: sterilisation)* [2001] Fam 15; [2000] 3 WLR 1288.

[139] See e.g. *Sutcliffe v BMI Healthcare Ltd* (2007) 98 BMLR 211, CA; *C v North Cumbria University Hospitals NHS Trust* [2014] EWHC 61 (QB); [2014] Med LR 189. For critical commentary on post-*Bolitho* obstetric litigation, see R Heywood, 'Litigating labour: Condoning unreasonable risk-taking in childbirth?' (2015) 44 Comm L World Rev 28.

[140] Although, if the only alternative is serious harm or death, then the courts have endorsed the application of highly experimental techniques, see e.g. *Simms v Simms, A v A* [2002] EWHC 2734 (Fam); [2003] 1 All ER 669.

[141] [2005] EWHC 3381 (QB).

the provision of *such treatment*. A doctor should not, therefore, undertake procedures which are beyond his capacity.[142]

5.54 A relevant Scottish case demonstrates the issues.[143] Here, the pursuer had suffered from abdominal pain for more than a year. In something of a last ditch attempt, her doctor prescribed chloramphenicol as a result of which she developed aplastic anaemia from which she recovered only after receiving a bone marrow transplant. She sued her doctor in negligence on the grounds that he could have chosen another drug which was not known to carry the 1:8,000 to 1:30,000 risk of bone marrow dysplasia which was associated with chloramphenicol—it was claimed that the treatment given was, in effect, a 'shot in the dark'. In the event, Lord Johnston was not prepared to hold as negligent a decision which had been carefully arrived at, the doctor having weighed up all the possibilities.[144] Drawing from Lord Browne-Wilkinson in *Bolitho*, the Lord Ordinary held:

> Within the framework of a balanced judgment, I consider that the decision of Dr Todd can be rationally and responsibly supported ... whatever may have been his alternatives. Furthermore, I consider that it should not be categorised even as an error of judgment ... I am prepared to hold that, within the options reasonably available to him ... it was a reasonable course to adopt.[145]

Most recently, in *Walker-Smith* v *GMC*[146] the court recognised that the line between innovative treatment and experimental research is not a bright one and it confirmed, albeit obiter, that the matter falls to be determined by the intention of the HCP. This is important as a matter of which regulatory regime—care or research—governs an intervention.

5.55 A recent attempt to introduce a statutory framework for medical innovation through a Private Member's Bill presented to the House of Lords—the Medical Innovation Bill— was blocked before it could reach debate in the House of Commons.[147] If enacted, the Bill would have added a second system for determining the standard of care for using innovative treatments that would run parallel to the existing (*Bolitho*-modified) *Bolam* test. Under the proposed scheme, a doctor would not be negligent in departing from the existing range of accepted medical treatments for a condition if he or she obtained beforehand the views of one or more appropriately qualified doctors and took full account of the views obtained. Nevertheless, any objections from the consulted qualified doctor(s) could be overridden if the decision to do so was taken 'responsibly'. Many commentators took the view that the ambiguities within the proposed legislation would likely undermine—rather than promote—responsible medical innovation.[148] At the time

---

[142] In *Tomkins* v *Bexley Area Health Authority* [1993] 4 Med LR 235, the patient's lingual nerve was damaged in the course of an operation for the removal of wisdom teeth. Wilcox J observed: 'When fine movements and fine judgments are the order of the day, with surgery being conducted in the confined space of the mouth, a high degree of care is needed.'

[143] *Duffy* v *Lanarkshire Health Board* 1998 SCLR 1142; 1999 SLT 906, OH.

[144] For related discussion of the possible negligence aspects of 'off-label prescription', see R Harding and E Peel, 'He was like a zombie': Off-label prescription of antipsychotic drugs in dementia' (2013) 21 Med Law Rev 243.

[145] As a postscript, Ms Duffy's claim under the Administration of Justice Act 1982, s 8 for remuneration in respect of her sister's marrow donation was also rejected.

[146] [2012] EWHC 503. For comment see P Case, 'Treading the line between clinical research and therapy' (2012) 28 P N 224.

[147] Medical Innovation Bill [HL] 2014–15.

[148] N Hoppe and J Miola, 'Innovation in medicine through degeneration in law? A critical perspective on the Medical Innovation Bill' (2014) 14 Med Law Int 266; cf J Samanta and A Samanta, 'Quackery or quality: The ethicolegal basis for a legislative framework for medical innovation' (2014) J Med Ethics doi:10.1136/ medethics-2014-102366.

of writing, the Medical Innovation Bill has been reintroduced into parliament, and the debate continues as to its merits and drawbacks.[149]

Alternative Medicine

5.56 And what of alternative medicine? By what standard should such practitioners be judged? In *Shakoor v Situ*,[150] a patient died from an 'idiosyncratic' liver reaction after taking nine doses of a traditional Chinese remedy prescribed by a herbal medicinalist. The skin condition from which the patient had been suffering could only be treated by surgery in orthodox medicine. His widow sued in negligence and the issue came down to the appropriate standard of care. The court held that an alternative medical practitioner could not be judged by the standard of orthodox medicine because he did not hold himself out as professing that 'art'; rather, he would be judged by the prevailing standard in his own 'art' subject to the caveat that it would be negligence if it could be shown that that standard itself was regarded as deficient in the UK having regard to the inherent risks involved. In the event, the negligence action failed because the court held that the practitioner had acted in accordance with the standard of care appropriate to traditional Chinese herbal medicine as properly practised in accordance with the standards required in the UK. It should be noted, however, that there is currently no statutory regulation of practitioners who offer herbal and traditional Chinese medicine in the UK, although a consultation was conducted in 2009 on how practitioners of alternative medicines should be regulated.[151] The 2011 Analysis Report lays out arguments for and against regulation in light of the consultation findings.[152] No proposals for law reform were active at the time of writing.

Misdiagnosis

5.57 A doctor is expected by the law to use the same degree of care in making a diagnosis that is required of him in all his other dealings with his patients.[153] A mistake in diagnosis will not be considered negligent if this standard of care is observed but will be treated as one of the non-culpable and inevitable hazards of practice.[154] Liability may, however, be imposed when a mistake in diagnosis is made because the doctor failed to take a proper medical history,[155] failed to conduct tests which a competent practitioner would have

[149] J Miola, 'Bye-bye *Bolitho*: The curious case of the Medical Innovation Bill' (2015) 15 Med Law Int doi: 10.1177/0968533215605667.

[150] [2001] 1 WLR 410; (2000) 57 BMLR 178.

[151] Department of Health, *A Joint Consultation on the Report to Ministers from the DH Steering Group on the Statutory Regulation of Practitioners of Acupuncture, Herbal Medicine, Traditional Chinese Medicine and Other Traditional Medicine Systems Practised in the UK* (2009). Note that a new, voluntary Complementary and Natural Healthcare Council was founded in 2008 under the aegis of the Foundation for Integrated Healthcare; herbalists and acupuncturists have their own organisations.

[152] Analysis Report (2011), available at: http://www.dh.gov.uk/prod_consum_dh/groups/dh_digital assets/documents/digitalasset/dh_124338.pdf.

[153] For a recent example of a medical negligence claim which failed because diagnosis and treatment were found to have been determined correctly, see *Meiklejohn v St George's Healthcare NHS Trust* [2014] EWCA Civ 120; [2014] Med LR 122. For an example of a successful claim—based on negligent failure to diagnose meningitis—see *Coakley v Rosie* [2014] EWHC 1790 (QB).

[154] In *Crivon v Barnet Group Hospital Management Committee* (1959) *The Times*, 19 November, the judge said of misdiagnosis: 'Unfortunate as it was that there was a wrong diagnosis, it was one of those misadventures, one of those chances, that life holds for people.' Courts—and patients—might be less inclined to take such a view today.

[155] *Chin Keow v Government of Malaysia* [1967] 1 WLR 813 (failure to inquire as to the possibility of penicillin allergy); *Coles v Reading and District Hospital Management Committee* (1963) 107 Sol Jo 115 (failure to consider possibility of tetanus).

considered appropriate, or simply failed to diagnose a condition which would have been spotted by a competent practitioner. As a minimum, the doctor must examine his patient and pay adequate attention to the patient's medical notes and to what the patient tries to tell him.[156] Telephone diagnosis or advice is hazardous, especially if the facts as related by the patient are such as to raise in the doctor's mind a suspicion that can only be allayed by proper clinical examination.[157]

5.58 One of the problems in determining whether there has been a mistake in diagnosis turns on deciding what investigative techniques need to be used in a particular case. The answer to this is doubly difficult insofar as the decision is now dictated not entirely by medical intuition. Two factors bear heavily on accurate diagnosis. First, the increasing importance attached to patient choice must, inevitably, lead to a correspondingly increasingly defensive attitude—and all this in the face of budgets that are stretched to the limit. Second, the fragmented nature of modern medicine means that many decisions about appropriate diagnosis and care depend as much on a timely referral than on the skills of an individual doctor.[158] In making his choice of diagnostic options, the doctor must be guided by the *Bolam* test but it will be the 'new *Bolam*'—that is, the test that the courts will read as incorporating an element of 'patient expectation' and also of what might count as a significant factor for the choice of the particular patient.[159] Ordinary laboratory tests must be used if symptoms suggest their use and, here, the situation is eased by the widespread introduction of automated 'battery' testing—the financial implications of doing several rather than a single biochemical analysis are now minimised.

5.59 The use of radiography provides a good example of the problem. Both professionals and the public are aware of the major contribution made by diagnostic radiography to the background radiation in developed countries and of the dangers to the individual of cumulative exposure. At the same time, it is widely stated that only some 1 per cent of radiographs taken of the ankle in casualty departments demonstrate a fracture and, of these, a high proportion would have healed in the absence of identification. The academic will, therefore, remember the archival words of Lord Denning with approval:

> In some of the early cases, the doctor has been criticised for not having taken X-rays with the result that they have sometimes been taken unnecessarily. This case shows that the Courts do not always find that there has been negligence because a patient has not had an X-ray; it depends on the circumstances of each case.[160]

And, indeed, this may sometimes be so. In *Lakey*'s case,[161] the patient fell and it was agreed that she had sustained a fracture of the pelvis when she attended hospital. The casualty officer found no evidence of fracture and, since the patient had been exposed to

[156] *Giurelli* v *Girgis* (1980) 24 SASR 264, discussed in Jones, n 52, 290.
[157] *Barnett* v *Chelsea and Kensington Hospital Management Committee* [1969] 1 QB 428; [1968] 1 All ER 1068; *Cavan* v *Wilcox* (1973) 44 DLR (3d) 42; *Burne* v *A* [2006] EWCA Civ 24 (failure to ask 'closed questions' in arriving at a diagnosis in relation to a child with a known medical condition and history). A number of 'failure to attend' cases have been discussed earlier.
[158] Note that a failure to refer (timeously) can be as much a breach of duty of care as an inappropriate diagnosis, see *Wright (a child)* v *Cambridge Medical Group* [2011] EWCA Civ 669; [2011] Med LR 496.
[159] See *Birch* v *University College London Hospital NHS Foundation Trust* [2008] EWHC 2237 (QB); (2008) 104 BMLR 168; *Montgomery* v *Lanarkshire Health Board* [2015] UKSC 11; [2015] 2 WLR 768.
[160] In *Braisher* v *Harefield and Northwood Hospital Group Management Committee* (13 July 1966, unreported), CA. See H Jellie [1966] 2 Lancet 235.
[161] *Lakey* v *Merton, Sutton and Wandsworth Health Authority* (1999) 40 BMLR 18; [1999] Lloyd's Rep Med 119, CA.

X-irradiation on several previous occasions, he decided against X-ray examination before sending her home; the presence of fracture was, however, confirmed on re-admission. The trial judge found that the original decision was taken after conscious deliberation and was not negligent—a ruling affirmed in the Court of Appeal. Equally, the Court of Appeal has confirmed the importance of first instance findings of fact that it will over-rule only where they are plainly wrong. Disputes over diagnostic procedures can involve differing interpretations of events as between doctor and patient, and the judge is enti-tled to prefer one over another without an obligation to explain in detail his reasons for doing so.[162]

5.60   *Langley* v *Campbell*[163] and *Tuffil* v *East Surrey Area Health Authority*[164] provide old, but still good, examples of successful actions against doctors on the basis of failure to diag-nose correctly the nature of the patient's complaint. In *Langley*, the patient had returned from East Africa shortly before the development of symptoms. The general practitioner failed to diagnose malaria and negligence was found, the judge accepting the evidence of a relative who said that the family had suggested such a diagnosis to the doctor. In *Tuffil*, the patient had spent many years in a tropical climate; the doctor failed to diagnose amoebic dysentery, which proved fatal. This failure to diagnose was held to be negligence on the doctor's part, a finding that would be all the more likely today with increased com-munication and understanding of exotic disease.[165]

5.61   In cases where a doctor is doubtful about a diagnosis, good practice may require that the patient be referred to a specialist for further consideration. It may be difficult for a doc-tor to know when to seek specialist advice—a fact explicitly acknowledged in the case of *Wilsher* v *Essex Area Health Authority*[166]—but in case of doubt, it is certainly safer for a doctor to refer the patient.[167] In *Official Solicitor* v *Allinson*,[168] a general practitioner was found liable in negligence when a patient died from breast cancer after he had examined her and reassured her there was nothing to worry about. His negligence was demon-strated by the failure at least to review his patient's condition within a short period of time given the asymmetry and localised abnormality of the lump in her breast and, on the probable findings at review, for failing to refer her to a specialist.[169]

Negligence in Treatment

5.62   The most important distinction here is that to be made between a medical mistake which the law regards as excusable[170] and a mistake which would amount to negligence.[171] In the former case, the court accepts that ordinary human fallibility precludes liability while, in the latter, the conduct of the defendant is considered to have strayed beyond the bounds of what is expected of the reasonably skilful or competent doctor.

---

[162]   *Burnett* v *Lynch* [2012] EWCA Civ 347.   [163]   (1975) *The Times*, 6 November.
[164]   (1978) *The Times*, 15 March.
[165]   See, e.g., the general work of the Public Health England (https://www.gov.uk/government/organisa-tions/public-health-england).
[166]   [1987] QB 730 at 777; [1986] 3 All ER 801 at 833.
[167]   It is to be noted that access to a second opinion is now a matter of patient entitlement.
[168]   [2004] EWHC 923 (QB).
[169]   For the kinds of factors taken into account in assessing damages with delayed diagnosis, see *Woodward* v *Leeds Teaching Hospitals NHS Trust* [2012] EWHC 2167. For another 'failure to refer' case—this time in the context of allegation of sexual abuse—see *C* v *Cairns* [2003] Lloyd's Rep Med 90. Negligence was not found in the case. We refer to its more interesting confidentiality aspects in Chapter 6.
[170]   See e.g. *E* v *Castro* (2003) 80 BMLR 14. For which, also see the rigid application of the *Bolam* test.
[171]   For discussion, see Merry and McCall Smith, n 7.

5.63   The issue came before the courts most classically in the case of *Whitehouse* v *Jordan*, which still remains the authoritative example.[172] In this case, negligence was alleged on the part of an obstetrician who, it was claimed, had pulled too hard in a trial of forceps delivery and had thereby caused the plaintiff's head to become wedged, with consequent asphyxia and brain damage. The trial judge held that, although the decision to perform a trial of forceps was a reasonable one, the defendant had in fact pulled too hard and was therefore negligent. This initial finding of negligence was reversed in the Court of Appeal and, in a strongly worded judgment, Lord Denning emphasised that an error of judgement was not negligence.[173] When the matter came on appeal before the House of Lords, the views expressed by Lord Denning on the error of judgement question were rejected. An error of judgement could be negligence if it were an error which would not have been made by a reasonably competent professional man acting with ordinary care. As Lord Fraser pointed out:

> The true position is that an error of judgment may, or may not, be negligent; it depends on the nature of the error. If it is one that would not have been made by a reasonably competent professional man professing to have the standard and type of skill that the defendant holds himself out as having, and acting with ordinary care, then it is negligence. If, on the other hand, it is an error that such a man, acting with ordinary care, might have made, then it is not negligence.[174]

In the event, the House of Lords held that there had not, in any case, been sufficient evidence to justify the trial judge's finding of negligence.[175] Further examples of how circumstances can overwhelm a situation and tip the balance in favour of negligence include *Boustead* v *North West Strategic Health Authority*.[176] Here a child suffered brain damage due to hypoxia which was caused by a delay in deciding to opt for a caesarian section. While much of the conduct of the health professionals in managing the childbirth was not judged to be negligent, eventually the failure to perform a caesarian section in light of the growing evidence of fetal distress amounted to a tragic and negligent error of judgement leading to compensation for the child. In *Mugweni* v *NHS London*,[177] brain damage was also in issue arising from a cardiac arrest suffered by a patient during open-heart surgery. The Court confirmed a breach of duty on the part of the anaesthetist for failing to notice early signs of distress, irrespective of the fact that the rest of the team was distracted preparing for the patient's removal. Indeed, particular vigilance was especially required during this time.[178]

5.64   Gross medical mistakes will almost always result in a finding of negligence. Operating mistakes such as the removal of the wrong limb or the performance of an operation on the wrong patient are usually treated as indefensible and settled out of court; hence the paucity of decisions on such points.[179] Use of the wrong drug or, often with more serious

---

[172] [1981] 1 All ER 267; [1981] 1 WLR 246, HL.   [173] [1980] 1 All ER 650 at 658, CA.

[174] [1981] 1 All ER 267 at 281; (1980) 1 BMLR 14 at 30. See a very comparable case in which the obstetrician was found to have pulled on the forceps with a force beyond that which would have been used by a competent practitioner. The difficult issue of causation in cases of neonatal brain damage was also well aired: *Townsend* v *Worcester and District Health Authority* (1995) 23 BMLR 31.

[175] A misjudgment will also be negligent if it is in respect of something 'lying within the area where only a sound judgment measures up to the standard of reasonable competence expected': *Hendy* v *Milton Keynes Health Authority (No 2)* [1992] 3 Med LR 119 at 127, per Jowitt J.

[176] [2008] EWHC 2375 (QB). There appears to have been an element of discrimination in this case by reason of the mother's age.

[177] [2012] EWCA Civ 20.   [178] Note the case failed on causation.

[179] An example is *Ibrahim (a minor)* v *Muhammad* (21 May 1984, unreported), QBD, in which a penis was partially amputated during circumcision; only the quantum of damages was in dispute.

consequences, the wrong gas during the course of an anaesthetic will frequently lead to the imposition of liability, and in some of these situations the *res ipsa loquitur* principle[180] may be applied.

5.65 Many historic cases deal with items of operating equipment being left inside patients after surgery. In these, generally known as the 'swab cases', the allocation of liability is made according to the principle laid down in the locus classicus of the law on this point, the decision in *Mahon* v *Osborne*.[181] In this case, as in subsequent decisions, the courts have shown themselves unlikely to dictate to doctors in a hard and fast way the exact procedure that should be used towards the end of an operation in order to ensure that no foreign bodies are left in the patient. At the same time, however, it is clear that the law requires that there should be some sort of set procedures adopted in order to mini-mise the possibility of this occurring. Overall responsibility to see that swabs and other items are not left in the patient rests on the surgeon; he is not entitled to delegate the matter altogether to a nurse. This point was emphasised in *Mahon* by Lord Goddard, who said:

> As it is the task of the surgeon to put swabs in, so it is his task to take them out and if the evidence is that he has not used a reasonable standard of care he cannot absolve himself, if a mistake has been made, by saying, 'I relied on the nurse'.[182]

5.66 In the later case of *Urry* v *Bierer*,[183] the Court of Appeal confirmed that the patient was entitled to expect the surgeon to do all that was reasonably necessary to ensure that all packs were removed and that this duty required more than mere reliance on the nurse's count.

THE PROBLEM OF THE NOVICE

5.67 The degree of expertise possessed by a medical practitioner obviously depends to a considerable extent on his experience and the argument has been put forward that the standard of competence of a newly qualified doctor will be less than that expected of an experienced practitioner. Although this may be the day-to-day expectation, it is not that of the law. The strict application of the *Bolam* principle[184] would lead the courts to expect the doctor to show that degree of skill which would be shown by the reasonably compe-tent professional. This is an objective standard and it is therefore irrelevant whether the doctor has qualified the day before or ten years before the alleged incident of negligence—it should make no difference to the way in which his conduct is assessed.

5.68 The problem was considered in the case of *Wilsher* v *Essex Area Health Authority*.[185] The plaintiff had been born prematurely and had been admitted to a specialised neonatal intensive care unit. An error was made in the monitoring of arterial oxygen tension and, as a result, extra oxygen was administered by junior hospital doctors. It was claimed that this could have caused the virtually blinding condition of retrolental fibroplasia which

---

[180] See paras 5.78 et seq.   [181] [1939] 2 KB 14; [1939] 1 All ER 535, CA.
[182] [1939] 2 KB 14 at 47; [1939] 1 All ER 535 at 559. Scott LJ, however, qualified this by pointing out that it might be necessary to dispense with normal precautions in an emergency.
[183] (1955) *The Times*, 15 July, CA.   [184] [1957] 2 All ER 118; [1957] 1 WLR 582.
[185] [1987] QB 730; [1986] 3 All ER 801, CA; revsd [1988] AC 1074; [1988] 1 All ER 871. The appeal to the House of Lords was based solely on the problem of causation and the case is revisited under that heading (see para 5.89 et seq). The case was otherwise remitted to another hearing by another judge but it appears to have been settled between the parties.

occurred. It was argued by the defendants that the standard of care expected of the junior doctor was not the same as that of his experienced counterpart. Extensive use, it was said, had to be made of recently qualified medical and nursing staff and it was unavoidable that such staff should 'learn on the job'; it would be impossible for public medicine to operate properly without such arrangements and to do otherwise would, ultimately, not be in the best interests of patients. The judgments in the Court of Appeal are not free of ambiguity. The majority of the judges maintained that the public were entitled to expect a reasonable standard of competence in their medical attendants The decision of Mustill LJ, however, makes it clear that he, at least, was prepared to define the standard of care according to the requirements of the post. An inexperienced doctor occupying a post in a unit which offered specialised services would, accordingly, need that degree of expertise expected of a reasonably competent person occupying that post; the defendant's actual hospital rank—house officer, registrar, etc.—would not be relevant in the determination.

5.69 Glidewell LJ also stressed the importance of applying an objective standard which would not take account of an individual doctor's inexperience. The apparent harshness of this conclusion was, nevertheless, mitigated by his suggestion that the standard of care is very likely to be met if the novice seeks advice from or consults with his or her more experienced colleagues when appropriate. Even so, this apparently simple solution does not answer the question which many juniors may ask, 'How am I to be so experienced as to know when I should be uncertain? And, if, I cannot tell this, am I to ask my seniors before I make any important decision?' These questions effectively force us back to accepting a standard of care test which is based on the doctor of similar experience irrespective of the post in which he operates. Conversely, however, an experienced doctor occupying a junior post would be judged according to his actual knowledge rather than by the lower standard of the reasonably competent occupant of that post—the rationale being that, by reason of his superior expertise, he would be more able to foresee the damage likely to arise from any negligent acts or omissions.[186] It is important to bear in mind that *Wilsher* was very much concerned with specialist units and there is no certainty that the judgments are applicable, say, to the general practitioner insofar as delegation of responsibility, hierarchical organisation, and the like are particular features of hospital practice.

5.70 Hospital authorities cannot, of course, rely too much upon junior employees; the principles of vicarious liability will, by themselves, prevent this. As Lord Denning said in *Jones v Manchester Corporation*:

> It would be in the highest degree unjust that the hospital board, by getting inexperienced doctors to perform their duties for them, without adequate supervision, should be able to throw all the responsibility on to those doctors as if they were fully experienced practitioners.[187]

Once again, this may reflect Lord Denning's particular concern for the practitioner at the coalface and there is little doubt that delegation of responsibility to another can amount to negligence in certain circumstances. A consultant could, for example, be held to be negligent were he to delegate responsibility to a junior in the knowledge that the junior was incapable of performing his duties properly.

5.71 A junior to whom responsibility has been delegated must carry out his duties as instructed by his superior in order to avoid liability. If he chooses to depart from specific

---

[186] See *Wimpey Construction UK Ltd v Poole* [1984] 2 Lloyd's Rep 499.
[187] [1952] 2 QB 852 at 871; [1952] 2 All ER 125 at 133, CA.

instructions, he will be placing himself in a risky position in the event of anything going wrong.[188] At the same time, there may be circumstances in which he is entitled to depart from instructions; obedience to manifestly wrong instructions might, itself, be construed as negligence in some cases.

PROTECTING PATIENTS FROM THEMSELVES

5.72 In certain circumstances, it is part of the duty of care of doctors and nurses to predict that patients may damage themselves as a result of their medical condition.[189] The extent of the duty to safeguard against such damage is problematical and the decisions have not all gone the same way. In *Selfe* v *Ilford and District Hospital Management Committee*,[190] the plaintiff had been admitted to hospital after a drug overdose. Although he had known suicidal tendencies, he was not kept under constant observation and climbed onto the hospital roof while the two nurses on duty were out of the ward; he fell and was injured. Damages of £19,000 were awarded against the hospital.

5.73 By contrast, the plaintiff in *Thorne* v *Northern Group Hospital Management Committee*[191] failed to win an award of damages for the death of his wife who had left a hospital in suicidal mood. In this case, the patient had slipped out of the hospital when the nurses' backs were turned, returned home, and gassed herself. The court took the view that, although the degree of supervision which a hospital should exercise in relation to patients with known suicidal tendencies is higher than that to be exercised over other patients, they could not be kept under constant supervision by hospital staff. A similar view was expressed more recently by the Court of Appeal in *Dunn* v *South Tyneside Health Care NHS Trust*[192] where a bipolar patient on one-hourly observations evaded detection and returned home to consume large quantities of anti-asthma tablets which resulted in severe brain damage. The subsequent negligence action claimed that an observation regime at 15-minute intervals was the appropriate standard of care; moreover, had this been implemented the harm would not have resulted because the police would have been alerted sooner and would have found the patient. The action failed on both counts. The one-hour regime was a reasonable standard of care given the patient's history and mental state on detention and by reference to *Bolam* and *Bolitho*; furthermore, the Court found that it was not an established matter of 'fact' that the police would have intervened to prevent the harm even if they had been alerted earlier.

5.74 In *Hyde* v *Tameside Area Health Authority*,[193] the Court of Appeal overturned a High Court award of substantial damages to a plaintiff who, believing he had cancer, made a suicide attempt in hospital. Not only did the Court take the view that there had been no breach of duty on the part of the defendants, but Lord Denning stressed in his judgment

---

[188] *Junor* v *McNicol* (1959) *The Times*, 26 March, HL.

[189] For the nature and extent of the non-medical duty of care in such cases in respect of people in detention, see *Gary Smiley (through his litigation friend Raymond Smiley)* v *Home Office* [2004] EWHC 240, following *Reeves* v *The Commissioner of Police of the Metropolis* [2000] 1 AC 360.

[190] (1970) 114 Sol Jo 935.

[191] (1964) 108 Sol Jo 484. A similar decision was taken in the Scottish case *Rolland* v *Lothian Health Board* (1981, unreported), OH, per Lord Ross.

[192] [2003] EWCA Civ 878; [2004] PIQR 150. See also the approval of *Hunter* in *McHardy* v *Dundee Hospitals* 1960 SLT (notes) 19.

[193] [1981] CLY 1854, CA; (1986) 2 PN 26, CA.

that there were strong policy grounds why damages should not be awarded in respect of attempted suicide. Nowadays, that would probably be a minority view; the case was, in fact, discussed and doubted in *Kirkham v Chief Constable of Greater Manchester*[194] which involved an appeal to the *ex turpi causa* principle—which may exclude liability where the claimant's act is in some way wrongful. This was, however, rejected. It was held that the award of damages in respect of a suicidal death caused no affront to the public conscience and suicide was no longer a criminal matter.

5.75   Whether suicide when under medical care is a human rights matter was discussed by the House of Lords in *Savage v South Essex Partnership NHS Trust*.[195] This case was brought as an alleged breach of human rights (Art 2—right to life) by the daughter of a woman who had escaped from a mental health institution and took her own life. Although the court questioned the *locus standi* of the daughter in such a case, they, nonetheless, let the case go to trial and, in doing so, clarified some of the parameters of the duty of care with respect to at-risk persons and the relationship with human rights. Thus, per Lord Rodger, there is an overarching obligation to protect lives of patients in hospital, connected to which are ancillary obligations such as employing suitably trained staff and instituting safe working and security practices; failure to do so can lead to a finding of a violation of Art 2. By the same token, if such systems are in place but, nevertheless, a patient kills him- or herself, then it is unlikely that Art 2 will be engaged although it is possible that an action might lie in professional negligence; for example, because a HCP failed to carry out surveillance properly.[196] Thus, while the obligations overlap, they are not entirely the same. More particularly, however, if staff know someone is a 'real and immediate' suicide risk, they must do all that is reasonable to prevent this and failure to do so would result in the possibility of both the breach of duty of care and violation of human rights.

5.76   The Supreme Court has pronounced on the nature and scope of duties of care to voluntary mental health patients and their families in *Rabone and Another v Pennine Care NHS Foundation Trust*.[197] Here the Trust had admitted a depressed patient on a voluntary basis; that is, not subject to the Mental Health legislation, assessed her as a high suicide risk but then allowed her to return home for two days whereupon she killed herself. The novel legal issues that arose were (1) whether a Trust owes a duty of care to protect an informal psychiatric patient in the same way as a sectioned patient in cases where there is a real and imminent risk of suicide, and (2) whether a duty was also owed to the parents of the patient who suffered non-patrimonial loss as a result of their daughter's death. The Supreme Court answered both questions in the affirmative. Thus, it is now clear that duties to voluntary and sectioned patients to be protected from themselves are substantially similar. In practice it means that there should be an assessment of all such patients as to whether there is a real and immediate risk of suicide; if this is found to be the case then, for a voluntary patient, a Trust would be justified in moving to the Mental Health regime to detain the patient, even against their will. The duty to parents arose from Art 2 ECHR—right to life—and they counted as 'victims' under Art 34 of the Convention, as was well established by ECtHR jurisprudence.[198]

---

[194] [1990] 2 QB 283; [1990] 3 All ER 246 and *R v Hickinbottom* [2007] Inquest LR 1.
[195] [2009] 1 AC 681; [2009] 2 WLR 115.
[196] See *Powell v United Kingdom (admissibility) (Application 45305/99)* [2000] Inquest LR 19 ECHR.
[197] [2012] UKSC 2; [2012] 2 AC 72.
[198] See, for example, *Yasa v Turkey* (1998) 28 EHRR 408. For commentary, see M Andenas, 'Leading from the front: human rights and tort law in *Rabone* and *Reynolds*' (2012) 128 LQR 323.

5.77 Note also that in certain circumstances, a negligence claim against a health care provider can be defended partially on the grounds of contributory negligence. A court may reduce the amount of damages awarded if a patient's conduct is seen as irresponsible and contributing to the harm sustained. *Pidgeon* v *Doncaster HA* remains the classic application of the doctrine in the medical sphere.[199] In this case, the patient's cervical smear test had been diagnosed incorrectly as being negative. Nevertheless, the patient had refused to respond to numerous requests from her GP to submit to additional tests that would have indicated pre-cancerous abnormalities. The patient's failure to present for further testing was viewed as blameworthy,[200] and she was held responsible for two-thirds of her injury. The doctrine of contributory negligence has also been invoked to reduce the award of damages in a case of suicide while under police custody.[201] It was held that the deceased had autonomous control over his own actions; responsibility for the suicide would therefore be shared equally between the deceased and the defendant.

RES IPSA LOQUITUR

5.78 Because it may be difficult in many personal injury actions to establish negligence on the part of the defendant, claimants occasionally have had recourse to the doctrine of *res ipsa loquitur*. This doctrine does not shift the onus of proof to the defendant, as is sometimes suggested; what it does achieve is to give rise to an inference of negligence on the defendant's part.[202] If the defendant cannot then rebut this inference of negligence, the claimant will have established his case. It follows from this that it is considerably easier for the claimant to succeed in his claim when *res ipsa loquitur* applies.

5.79 The classic case is that of *Cassidy* v *Ministry of Health*,[203] in which the plaintiff went into hospital for an operation to remedy Dupuytren's contracture of two fingers and came out with four stiff fingers. Denning LJ (as he then was) expressed the view that the plaintiff was quite entitled to say:

> I went into hospital to be cured of two stiff fingers. I have come out with four stiff fingers and my hand is useless. That should not have happened if due care had been used. Explain it if you can.[204]

5.80 The doctrine has been found most useful in cases where damage has occurred in an incident involving machinery or in the context of damage suffered while the claimant was involved in some sort of complex process. It can apply only where the claimant is unable to identify the precise nature of the negligence which caused his injury and where no explanation of the way in which the injury came to be inflicted has been offered by the defendant. The injury itself must be of such a kind as 'does not normally happen' in the

---

[199] [2002] Lloyd's Rep Med 130.

[200] For a contrasting outcome see *P* v *Sedar* [2011] EWHC 1266 (QB), where the patient's failure to present for further testing was not seen as blameworthy because letters had been sent to the wrong address.

[201] *Reeves* v *The Commissioner of Police of the Metropolis*, n 189.

[202] There has been some debate as to the precise effect of *res ipsa loquitur*, but the weight of opinion favours the view outlined here: see *Ng Chun Pui* v *Lee Chuen Tat* [1988] RTR 298, PC.

[203] [1951] 2 KB 343; [1951] 1 All ER 574, CA.

[204] [1951] 2 KB 343 at 365; [1951] 1 All ER 574 at 588. Other medical cases in which *res ipsa loquitur* has applied include: *Saunders* v *Leeds Western Health Authority* (1984) 129 Sol Jo 225; *Cavan* v *Wilcox* (1973) 44 DLR (3d) 42; and *Holmes* v *Board of Hospital Trustees of the City of London* (1977) 81 DLR (3d) 67.

circumstances unless there is negligence. Thus, in a case of neurological damage following difficult aortography,[205] the plea of *res ipsa loquitur* was rejected on the grounds that
the injury sustained was of a kind recognised as an inherent risk of the procedure.

5.81   The doctrine's application in medical cases may still be particularly apt because of the
difficulty that the ordinary claimant sometimes experiences in unravelling the cause of
an injury sustained during technical procedures of which he has little understanding;
indeed, he may well have been unconscious at the relevant time. It may also be seen as a
potential corrective to the tendency of the medical profession to 'close ranks' when one
of their number is accused of negligence. However, it is possibly of less importance in a
climate of increasing openness—or, in today's usage, transparency. It must also be borne
in mind that the courts are generally reluctant to apply the *res ipsa loquitur* principle and
that this is certainly evident in medical negligence cases. As Megaw LJ said:

> [if] one were to accept the view that negligence was inevitably proved if something went
> wrong and it was unexplained], few dentists, doctors and surgeons, however competent,
> conscientious and careful they might be, would avoid the totally unjustified and unfair
> stigma of professional negligence probably several times in the course of their careers.[206]

5.82   An unsuccessful attempt to raise the doctrine of *res ipsa loquitur* was made in *Ludlow* v
Swindon Health Authority,[207] in which it was stressed that the plaintiff had to establish
facts which, if unexplained, would give rise to an inference of negligence. In this case the
plaintiff claimed to have regained consciousness during a caesarian section operation and
to have experienced intense pain. She failed, however, to establish that the pain arose at
a stage during which halothane should have been administered; there was, accordingly,
no inference of negligence in the administration of the anaesthetic. Nevertheless, there
are cases where the injuries sustained by the patient are of such a nature that there is an
inescapable inference of negligence. In *Glass* v *Cambridge Health Authority*,[208] the patient
suffered brain damage as a result of suffering a heart attack under a general anaesthetic.
The court held that this was not an event which normally would be expected to happen
in the circumstances and that the onus therefore transferred to the defendant to provide an explanation of the event which was consistent with the absence of negligence.[209]
The courts' general antipathy to *res ipsa* was re-emphasised in *Ratcliffe* v *Plymouth and
Torbay Health Authority*,[210] a case involving paraesthesia following a spinal anaesthetic.
The plaintiff's appeal was based largely on the trial judge's dismissal of the maxim. In a
very extensive and carefully explanatory judgment, the Court of Appeal affirmed that
it could not be inferred that the untoward symptoms could not have occurred in the
absence of negligence.[211] The courts, it was said, would do medicine a considerable dis-
service if, because a patient suffered a grievous and unexpected outcome, a careful doctor
was ordered to pay him compensation as if the doctor had been negligent:

[205] *O'Malley-Williams* v *Board of Governors of the National Hospital for Nervous Diseases* (1975, unreported), cited in [1975] 1 BMJ 635.
[206] *Fletcher* v *Bench* (1773, unreported), CA cited in [1973] 4 BMJ 117.
[207] [1989] 1 Med LR 104.   [208] [1995] 6 Med LR 91.
[209] See also *Thomas* v *Curley* [2011] EWHC 2103 in which the court found for the claimant on the basis
that, on the balance of probabilities, the defendant had failed to explain how '[the] injury could have been
occasioned in an uncomplicated procedure conducted some distance from the site of the common bile duct
injury other than a want of care...'.
[210] (1998) 42 BMLR 64; [1998] Lloyd's Rep Med 162, CA.
[211] For a similar Scottish ruling, see *T* v *Lothian NHS Board* [2009] CSOH 132.

If the untoward outcome was extremely rare, or was impossible to explain in the light of the current state of medical knowledge, the judge will be bound to exercise great care in evaluating the evidence before making such a finding, but if he does so, the prima facie inference of negligence is rebutted and the claim will fail.[212]

5.83 In effect, and as expressed by Hobhouse LJ, the court pointed out that *res ipsa loquitur* is no more than a convenient phrase to describe the proof of facts which are sufficient to support an inference—based on ordinary human experience with no need for expert evidence— that a defendant was negligent and, therefore, to establish a prima facie case against him.[213]

5.84 We note the apparent paradox that the doctrine of *res ipsa* will be rejected yet negligence be accepted simply because there *is* unassailable evidence of negligence. Thus, in *Hay (Gill's curator bonis)* v *Grampian Health Board*,[214] it was stated that the doctrine can only be used in cases where no explanation for events is available. A variation of this approach was adopted in *Smith* v *Sheridan*[215] where there was little doubt as to the negligence of a doctor during a forceps delivery when he gave a 'hard pull' on the child who suffered serious brain damage as a result. Here, the court rejected the case as an example of *res ipsa loquitur* on the rather confusing, but essentially similar, reasoning that 'it is clear that the defendant must have used excessive force in delivering Jake and was thus negligent in the absence of any other explanation'. It would seem that the basis of this is that, having excluded all other causes on the basis of expert argument, it was probable—perhaps a near certainty—that, despite his protestations, the obstetrician was at fault. Obstetric cases certainly make law and often deal with some of the most complicated circumstances for claimants to prove and for defendants to defend. The terrain is therefore fertile for *res ipsa*-type approaches. This is well illustrated in *Richards* v *Swansea NHS Trust*[216] in which the court held that the considerable delay in performing a caesarean section placed an onus on the Trust to adduce evidence of exculpatory reasons to explain why it took 55 minutes to deliver the child. Its failure to do so led to an inference that there were no such constraints on the management of the case and it followed that the claimant had proven, on the balance of probabilities, a breach of the duty of care owed to him.

5.85 Yet, while the *res ipsa* doctrine is alive and well, it may be treated in a circumspect fashion and given only limited practical effect. The most recent illustration is provided by *Hussain* v *King Edward VII Hospital*,[217] a case involving a patient diagnosed with bladder cancer who underwent a cystoscopy. Following the surgery, he experienced severe pain in his left shoulder and in his submission pleaded *res ipsa loquitor*. Eady J summarised the current status of the doctrine in the following way:

> There is no mystique about the doctrine of res ipsa loquitur. It does not represent a principle of law: nor can it be invoked as giving rise to a presumption of any kind. It is simply a conventional way of saying that the facts, as known to the claimant at the time he pleads his case, give rise in themselves to a prima facie case of negligence. This may or may not be upheld at trial, but at the pleading stage it has the effect of compelling the defendant to respond ... One should never lose sight, however, of the simple fact that the burden of proof remains on the Claimant throughout ... That is why a defendant is only required to show a plausible alternative explanation in order to rebut a prima facie case.[218]

---

[212] Per Brooke LJ at BMLR 80.
[213] *Ratcliffe* was followed in *Gray* v *Southampton and South West Hampshire Health Authority* (2000) 57 BMLR 148; affd [2001] EWCA Civ 855; (2002) 67 BMLR 1, CA.
[214] 1995 SLT 652 (OH).   [215] [2005] EWHC 614; [2005] 2 FCR 18.
[216] [2007] EWHC 487 (QB); (2007) 96 BMLR 180.   [217] [2012] EWHC 3441 (QB).
[218] [2012] EWHC 3441 (QB) at 11–12.

Furthermore, it was emphasised that in medical negligence cases, the plaintiff will need expert evidence to support the assertion that the circumstances relied upon as giving rise to a prima facie case would not ordinarily come about in the absence of negligence. In this instance, the plaintiff was able to make out a prima facie case of negligence, but this was rebutted successfully by the defendant, who demonstrated that reasonable care was applied and that the operation took place routinely and without any untoward incident. Hobhouse LJ's summary of the doctrine remains apt—'Where expert and factual evidence has been called by both sides at a trial, its usefulness will normally have long since been exhausted'.[219]

OPERATIONAL FAILURES

5.86   As we have discussed in earlier sections, reforms to the compensation system are as much about addressing system failures in health care delivery as they are about recompensing patients harmed as a result of those failures. It is, therefore, important to point to other areas of law where such operational oversights are revealed. In *Rabone*, discussed earlier at para 5.76, the failure of the Trust system to prevent a real and imminent risk of suicide was deemed to be a breach of 'operational duty'. Two other cases illustrate the point and suggest that NHS Trusts will be subject to similar scrutiny.

5.87   The role of the coroner in England and Wales is to carry out full and effective inquests into sudden and unexpected deaths, particularly those which give rise to a public interest. This is part of the state's obligation to its citizens and is accordingly also a matter which is subsumed under the umbrella of human rights. Thus, in *R (on the application of Davies) v HM Deputy Coroner for Birmingham*,[220] it was held by the Court of Appeal that the coroner had failed in his duty on behalf of the state under Art 2 (right to life) of the ECHR when he did not invite the jury to consider the care offered to a prisoner. The patient had been a heroin addict who suffered withdrawal symptoms on admission to prison. He was not seen by a doctor, and the nurse who did attend wrongly assessed him as requiring no further medical assistance. He died the next day. The coroner had failed in his duties by not instructing the jury to consider a verdict of *systemic* neglect.

5.88   Very similar circumstances were considered by the ECtHR in *McGlinchey v United Kingdom*.[221] Here, again, an asthmatic heroin addict was admitted to prison with severe withdrawal symptoms. Her weight was inaccurately assessed using scales known to be defective and the medical professional made only an impressionistic assessment of her condition. Out of duty-hours medical cover was thin and, although the patient's condition deteriorated, she was not seen by a doctor over the weekend; she died a few days later. It was argued that the standard of care had been so low as to be a breach of Art 3 ECHR

---

[219]   In *Ratcliffe*, n 213 at BMLR 85.

[220]   [2003] EWCA Civ 1739; *R (Davies)* was subsequently approved by the House of Lords in *R (on the application of Middleton) v HM Coroner for Western Somerset* (also known as *R v HM Coroner for Western Somerset, ex p Middleton, R (on the application of Middleton) v West Somerset Coroner*) [2004] UKHL 10; [2004] 2 AC 182, in which the House of Lords stated that 'there are some cases in which the current regime for conducting inquests in England and Wales, as hitherto understood and followed, does not meet the requirements of the Convention'.

[221]   (2003) 37 EHRR 41; (2003) 72 BMLR 168.

(cruel and inhuman treatment), and, because causation difficulties precluded an action in negligence, the claimant was left with no domestic remedy. The ECtHR upheld the complaint on both of these grounds, namely (i) that the catalogue of systemic omissions and errors demonstrated a breach of Art 3, and (ii) that the non-availability of compensation under domestic law was in violation of Art 13 ECHR (the right to an effective remedy for violation of Convention rights).

CAUSATION

5.89 As if the problems of fault were not enough, it will do the claimant no good to establish negligence on the part of a defendant doctor unless he or she is also able to prove that the damage he has suffered was caused by that negligence. Thus, Mr Barnett's widow (see *Barnett v Chelsea and Kensington Hospital Management Committee*, paras 5.34 et seq) was unable to recover damages for her husband's death from arsenic poisoning even though she proved that her husband was owed a duty of care when he attended the cottage hospital and that it was negligent for the doctor to send him away without examination. Why? Because it is the nature of arsenic poisoning that *even if* Mr Barnett had been examined he would have died anyway, there being no cure or treatment for the condition. In law, therefore, the doctor's negligence did not cause the death.

5.90 Causation issues can be particularly difficult in the medical context because there may be a variety of possible independent explanations for the occurrence of a condition. Thus, if a person brings an action for 'nervous shock', it may well be arguable that the symptoms complained of are those of a psychiatric state which existed before the claimed precipitating event.[222] Some assistance in this respect was provided to the claimant through the Scottish case of *McGhee v National Coal Board*,[223] in which it was held that liability will be imposed if it can be established that the negligence of the defender materially increased the risk of the claimant being damaged in the way in question.[224] Another useful parameter is the 'but for' test: the harm would not have occurred but for the negligent conduct. The challenges are manifold.[225]

5.91 In *Ashcroft v Mersey Regional Health Authority*,[226] the plaintiff underwent a relatively straightforward and commonplace operation to remove granulation tissue—the result of chronic infection—from the ear; she sustained a severe paralysis of the facial nerve. Opinion was divided as to whether the surgeon had negligently pulled too hard on the nerve or whether the injury was an unfortunate accident. In the result, Kilner Brown J

[222] For modern examples, see *Abada v Gray* (1997) 40 BMLR 116, CA (schizophrenia could not be precipitated by a road traffic injury); *Gates v McKenna* (1998) 46 BMLR 9; [1998] Lloyd's Rep Med 405 (it was improbable that taking part in a stage hypnosis programme could precipitate schizophrenia and the possibility was unforeseeable).
[223] [1972] 3 All ER 1008; [1973] 1 WLR 1.
[224] [1972] 3 All ER 1008 at 1011, per Lord Reid; [1973] 1 WLR 1 at 4, per Lord Reid.
[225] See *Bailey v Ministry of Defence* [2009] 1 WLR 1052. For commentary, see S H Bailey, 'Causation in Negligence: What is material contribution?' (2010) 30 Legal Studies 167. See also P Laleng, '*Sienkiewicz v Greif (UK) Ltd and Wilmore v Knowsley Metropolitan Borough Council*: A Material Contribution to Uncertainty?' (2011) 74 Modern Law Review 777; S Steel, *Proof of Causation in Tort Law* (2015).
[226] [1983] 2 All ER 245.

was, with obvious reluctance, unable to shift the burden of proof and found that, on a balance of probabilities, there was no negligence *causing* harm. The correctness of this view was later confirmed in *Wilsher*,[227] where the House of Lords went so far as to reverse the opinion of the Court of Appeal and to order a retrial on the ground that the coincidence of a breach of duty and injury could not, of itself, give rise to a presumption that the injury was so caused: 'Whether we like it or not, the law ... requires proof of fault causing damage as the basis of liability in tort.'[228]

5.92   The difficulty for the plaintiff in *Wilsher* lay in the fact that there were five possible causes for the condition with which he was afflicted. One of these was medical negligence but it could not be established that this *possible* cause actually made a material contribution to the injury. It might have done so, but this fact still required to be proved by the plaintiff. A contrasting outcome was reached in *Bailey v Ministry of Defence*.[229] Again, medical science was unable to establish that 'but for' the negligent treatment the relevant injury would not have occurred, and the court was therefore entitled to apply a modified test for causation. It was deemed sufficient for the claimant to establish on a balance of probabilities that the defendants' lack of care had made a contribution to the injury that was material or something more than negligible. Under this approach, the claimant was able to establish causation.

5.93   These issues are clearly matters of legal policy and justice. Causation is not a strict technical matter which can be 'solved' by the application of quasi-mathematical formulae.[230] Indeed, this is well reflected in two important House of Lords cases. In the non-medical negligence case *of Fairchild v Glenhaven Funeral Services Ltd*,[231] the claimant had suffered multiple exposures to asbestos in the course of working for various employers and could not, strictly, demonstrate *who* then had caused his disease. The court applied *Wilsher* in holding that justice demanded a modified approach to the rules of causation; thus, so long as the claimant could show, on a balance of probabilities, that the wrongdoing of each employer had materially increased the risk to the employee that he might contract the disease, then this would be enough to establish that each employer had materially contributed to it, that is, *each* had caused his loss in legal terms. *Fairchild* was then approved—and, perhaps, expanded—by the House in *Chester v Afshar*.[232] This case involved a dispute about information disclosure and for that reason it is better discussed in Chapter 4. Its relevance for present purposes is to illustrate further the House of Lords' willingness—albeit, in this case, by a majority only—to bend the rules of causation in the name of justice. Here a patient was not told of an inherent risk in a procedure to cure back pain. The risk materialised and the law of causation dictated that she had to prove that if she had known of the risk she would never have had the operation. But the patient

[227] *Wilsher* v *Essex Area Health Authority* [1988] AC 1074; [1988] 1 All ER 871, HL. See, too, a discussion of the scope and effect of the important decision in *Fairchild* v *Glenhaven Funeral Services Ltd and Others* [2003] 1 AC 32; [2002] 3 All ER 305; (2002) 67 BMLR 90 at 393–402.

[228] [1988] AC 1074 at 1092; [1988] 1 All ER 871 at 883, per Lord Bridge.

[229] [2008] EWCA Civ 883.

[230] For recognition of the policy considerations and the difficulty of shifting the onus of prof, see *McGlone* v *Greater Glasgow Health Board* (2011) CSOH 63.

[231] [2003] 1 AC 32; [2002] 3 All ER 305.

[232] [2005] 1 AC 134; [2004] 4 All ER 587. We discuss the case in K Mason and D Brodie, 'Bolam, Bolam—Wherefore Art Thou, *Bolam*?' (2005) 9 Edin LR 398. *Chester* was considered in two cases which address the question of a physician's duty to inform the patient of the risks and benefits of various alternative treatments: *Birch* v *University College London Hospital NHS Foundation Trust* [2008] EWHC 2237 (QB); (2008) 104 BMLR 168, and *Montgomery* v *Lanarkshire Health Board* [2015] UKSC 11; [2015] 2 WLR 768.

did not, and could not, prove that she would *never have* the operation; she only proved that she would not have had it on the day that she did.[233] All five of their Lordships agreed that she should therefore fail on a strict application of the law—but the majority could not accept this outcome and argued that the patient's right to self-determination demanded a remedy. All of the judgments in the case make interesting reading as to how and how far abstract notions such as 'justice' and 'policy' can and should influence the direction of the law. *Chester* is one of the clearest examples we have of this to date but it has been closely mirrored in *Rees v Darlington Memorial NHS Trust*.[234] As a result, we find that our causation rules are now in a state of flux.[235]

5.94 Following the ruling in *Fairchild*, the House of Lords considered another asbestos case: *Barker v Corus UK Ltd*.[236] In this case, their Lordships held that employers who negligently exposed an employee to asbestos, thereby creating a material risk of meso-thelioma, should be severally liable if that risk materialised, but only to the extent of the share of the risk created by their breach of duty. In other words, the attribution of liability would be apportioned according to the relative degree of contribution to the chance of the disease being contracted. The ruling prompted the inclusion of clause 3 to the then Compensation Bill, which enables victims of mesothelioma to receive full compensation from any 'responsible person'. Each responsible person who is successfully sued can then claim contributions from any other responsible person.[237]

5.95 It is undoubtedly the case that these policy-driven decisions are a direct response to the considerable difficulties that claimants can face when attempting to clear the causation hurdle. The problems are well illustrated by the lengthy and complicated litigation over pertussis vaccination. In *Loveday*,[238] the court held that establishing a mere chance that the vaccine might cause brain damage in children did not discharge the obligation on the plaintiff. The problem is, essentially, that of distinguishing between 'association' and 'causation' between two factors and is well reviewed in the context of smoking and car-cinoma of the lung which was considered to be not clearly causative in the Scottish case of *McTear v Imperial Tobacco Ltd*.[239] It is to be noted, parenthetically, that the decision in *Loveday* was not the last word on pertussis vaccine; in *Best v Wellcome Foundation Ltd*,[240] the Supreme Court in Ireland awarded £2.75 million to a young man who had suffered brain damage after its administration. The ground for the award was, however, that the particular batch of vaccine used was sub-standard and should not have been released on the market—future litigants will still have to prove that, on the balance of probabili-ties, their injuries were caused by the vaccine per se. And, in a rather similar causation

---

[233] By contrast, establishing causation was more straightforward in *Montgomery v Lanarkshire Health Board* [2015] UKSC 11; [2015] 2 WLR 768, as it was clear that the plaintiff would have opted for an alternative procedure had she been informed properly of the comparative risks and benefits.

[234] [2004] AC 309; [2003] 4 All ER 987 a 'wrongful pregnancy' case discussed in detail in Chapter 10.

[235] For discussion, see M Hogg, 'Duties of care, causation and the implications of *Chester v Afshar*' (2005) 9 Edin LR 156 and T Clark and D Nolan, 'A critique of *Chester v Afshar*' (2014) 34 OJLS 659.

[236] [2006] UKHL 20; [2006] 2 AC 572.

[237] For an example of litigation under the Compensation Act 2006, see *Sienkiewicz v Greif (UK) Ltd* [2009] EWCA Civ 1159; [2010] QB 370.

[238] *Loveday v Renton* [1989] 1 Med LR 117. Loveday was applied in *Dowson v Sunderland Hospitals NHS Trust* [2004] Lloyd's Rep Med 177, a case involving neonatal stroke.

[239] 2005 2 SC 1, OH. How one regards this case depends very much on whether one is legally or medi-cally trained. For analysis, see B Pillans, 'Smoking kills—Not proven' 2005 SLT 113. The specific interest of *McTear* lies in the weight to be attributed to epidemiological evidence.

[240] [1994] 5 Med LR 81, Ir SC; see D Brahamas, 'Court award for pertussis brain damage' (1993) 341 Lancet 1338; C Dyer, 'Man awarded damages after pertussis vaccination' (1993) 306 BMJ 1365.

problem, both the Court of Session and the House of Lords declared that a judge was not entitled to propound his own theory of a causative link between an overdose of penicillin and deafness; the weight of the evidence in *Kay* was that the causative factor was the meningitis for which the penicillin had been prescribed [241]

5.96 An interesting look at the obverse in vaccination cases was provided by *Thomson* v *Blake-James*.[242] Here, a child developed post-measles encephalitis and the parents sued their general practitioner for having given negligent advice as to vaccination. The child was subject to suspected seizures which, in the practitioner's view, contraindicated vaccination; he did not, however, mention a special protocol for vaccination in such circumstances which had been issued by the then Department of Health and Social Security and, for that and other reasons, the trial judge later found against the first practitioner. Meantime, the parents had moved and had received very similar advice, with additional explanation, from a second practitioner; when they approached a third general practitioner, they informed him they had decided against vaccination. The claims against the second and third practitioners were dismissed at first instance. On appeal, the court distinguished between general and specific advice. Insofar as the vaccination could not, at any rate, be undertaken for several months, Dr Blake-James was providing the former and the court decided that failure to mention alternatives would not necessarily constitute a breach of duty in such circumstances. Moreover, the parents had received further advice from the other practitioners; Dr Blake-James's advice was not, therefore, definitive and was not the cause of the child's disability.

5.97 The increased attention paid in recent years to what might loosely be termed 'psychosomatic' diseases has led to some interesting developments in the field of causation. Repetitive strain injury (RSI)—now more often referred to as task-specific focal dystonia[243]—is one such condition. Medical opinion differs as to whether it is organic or psychiatric in origin or whether it results from a combination of causes. Thus, it is not surprising that litigation has led to some confusing results—ranging from large out of court settlements[244] to judicial comments such as, '[I agree] that RSI is, in reality, meaningless ... Its use by doctors can only serve to confuse'.[245] In what is probably the most important judicial airing of the subject,[246] the House of Lords overturned the Court of Appeal in holding that the fact that the trial judge was unwilling to accept that the plaintiff's condition was simply that of conversion hysteria was not, of itself, sufficient ground to sustain her claim in negligence; it was essential to the success of her case that she proved that her condition had been caused by repetitive movements while typing. If it was impossible to decide what was the cause of the condition from the medical evidence alone, the court was entitled to consider all the other evidence in concluding that the plaintiff had failed to prove her case.[247]

[241] *Kay's Tutor* v *Ayrshire and Arran Health Board* [1987] 2 All ER 417; 1987 SLT 577, HL.
[242] (1998) 41 BMLR 144; [1998] Lloyd's Rep Med 187, CA.
[243] Social Security (Industrial Injuries) (Prescribed Diseases) Regulations 1985 (SI 1985/967), Sch 1, Pt 1, as amended by SI 2012/647. There is nothing to stop an employee suing his employers in negligence despite the fact that the condition sustained is recognised as a work hazard (for which see Social Security Contributions and Benefits Act 1992, s 108(2)).
[244] 'Revenue to pay £79,000 to RSI victim' *The Scotsman*, 19 January 1994, 5.
[245] *Mughal* v *Reuters Ltd* (1993) 16 BMLR 127 at 140, per Prosser J.
[246] *Pickford* v *Imperial Chemical Industries plc* [1998] 3 All ER 462; [1998] 1 WLR 1189, considered in *Newman* v *Laver* [2006] EWCA Civ 1135.
[247] For an instance of an appeal court questioning the trial judge's finding of fact and so changing the outcome as to causation, see *Roughton* v *Weston Area Health Authority* [2004] EWCA Civ 1509.

5.98 Other conditions that raise similar problems include post-traumatic stress disorder,[248] myalgic encephalomyelitis,[249] and the purely psychiatric condition of so-called 'nervous shock'.[250] A full discussion of the law in this area, a proportion of which is based on policy considerations, is beyond the scope of a book of this size.

Loss of a Chance

5.99 An important variation on the causation theme was reintroduced in *Hotson*.[251] Here, the plaintiff was, admittedly, negligently treated following traumatic avulsion of the head of the femur and developed avascular necrosis. However, there was a 75 per cent chance that this lesion would develop even in the event of correct diagnosis and treatment. The trial judge concluded that the matter was simply one of quantification of damages and the Court of Appeal upheld the view that the mistreatment had denied the plaintiff a 25 per cent chance of a good recovery; damages were awarded and reduced accordingly. The House of Lords, however, declined to measure statistical chances[252] and concluded that it was the original injury which caused the avascular necrosis. Lord MacKay expressed the true situation:

> the probable effect of delay in treatment was determined by the state of facts existing when the plaintiff was first presented at the hospital ... If insufficient blood vessels were left intact by the fall, he had no prospect of avoiding complete avascular necrosis whereas if sufficient blood vessels were left intact ... he would not have suffered the avascular necrosis.[253]

Or, as put in *The Times* transcript,[254] what was meant by a chance was that if 100 people had suffered the same injury, 75 would have developed avascular necrosis and 25 would not. Thus, on the balance of probabilities, the plaintiff fell into the larger group—there being no evidence that he was one of the fortunate 25 per cent who could benefit from treatment—and, consequently, his injury could not be attributed to the negligence of the defendants. It would be different if 51 per cent of people sustaining the type of injury which the plaintiff suffered could be treated with, say, a 20 per cent chance of success. Then, on the balance of probabilities, the plaintiff would have fallen into that group of 51 per cent, and, if a hospital negligently failed to offer him the treatment, he would have personally lost that 20 per cent chance of a successful outcome. Whether that 20 per cent loss is something which should attract compensation in the form of 20 per cent damages is left open by the decision in *Hotson*.[255]

5.100 'Loss of a chance' was revisited by the House of Lords in *Gregg* v *Scott*[256] where the whole percentage approach towards such cases was called into question. The facts related to

---

[248] *Frost* v *Chief Constable of South Yorkshire Police* [1999] 2 AC 455; [1998] 3 WLR 1509.

[249] *Page* v *Smith* [1995] 2 All ER 736; (1995) 28 BMLR 133, HL.

[250] *Alcock* v *Chief Constable of South Yorkshire Police* [1992] 1 AC 310; (1991) 8 BMLR 37.

[251] *Hotson* v *East Berkshire Area Health Authority* [1987] AC 750; [1987] 2 All ER 909, HL. A similar claim was dismissed in the early Scottish case of *Kenyon* v *Bell* 1953 SC 125. For discussion, see D T Price, 'Causation—The Lords' "lost chance" ' (1989) 33 ICLQ 735.

[252] Statistical chances and personal chances are quite different matters: T Hill, 'A lost chance for compensation in the tort of negligence by the House of Lords' (1991) 54 MLR 511. The author regrets the fact that the House of Lords appears to leave open the possibility of future successful actions based on a personal loss of chance.

[253] [1987] AC 750 at 785; [1987] 2 All ER 909 at 915.   [254] (1987) *The Times*, 6 July.

[255] For a consideration of *Hotson* and *Bolitho* together, see *Bright* v *Barnsley District General Hospital NHS Trust* [2005] Lloyd's Rep Med 449.

[256] [2005] UKHL 2; (2005) 82 BMLR 52. For comment on the majority ruling and the apparent conflict of the decision with the previous authorities of *Hotson* and *Fairchild*, see J Stapleton, 'Loss of the chance for cure from cancer' (2005) 68(6) *Modern Law Review* 996. An apposite case is *Al Hamwi* v *Johnston* [2005] EWHC 206 (delay in testing for Down's syndrome would have made no difference to choice as to termination).

what must be, sadly, a fairly common occurrence. A patient presented to his doctor with an uncomfortable lump under his left arm. The doctor diagnosed this as benign and reassured the patient such that this was the patient's one and only visit to the general practitioner. In truth, the lump was a malignant tumour for which aggressive treatment was required. This did not commence until some 14–15 months after the initial consultation, by which time the cancer had spread to the patient's chest. It was accepted that the cursory examination of the patient by his general practitioner was negligent;[257] the crux of the matter was whether this had caused a recognised legal harm. In the final analysis, the plaintiff argued that his 'harm' was the loss of the chance of survival for more than ten years,[258] or put slightly differently, the loss of the chance of a more favourable outcome to his prognosis.[259] Statistical evidence[260] indicated that while the plaintiff might have had a 42 per cent chance of still being alive after ten years if there had been no negligence, this chance was reduced to 25 per cent because of the negligence. There was, therefore, a significant drop in his statistical chances as a result of the misdiagnosis, but—crucially—at no point did he enjoy a more-than-50 per cent chance of survival beyond ten years.[261] On a strict application of *Hotson* and the balance of probabilities test, then, the general practitioner did not cause the alleged harm: it was not 'more probable than not' that *but for* the negligence the patient would be alive after ten years. Indeed, the trial judge found that he probably would not be. To put it another way, even without negligence, there would have been a 58 per cent chance that the patient would not survive the decade.

5.101   This outcome was unacceptable to Lords Nicholls and Hope. Lord Nicholls, in particular, argued forcefully that the 'all-or-nothing' approach to what would have happened but for the negligence—that is, the application of the 49/51 per cent rule from *Hotson*—was premised on a falsehood[262] and led to arbitrary and unjust outcomes:

> It means that a patient with a 60 per cent chance of recovery reduced to a 40 per cent prospect by medical negligence can obtain compensation. But he can obtain nothing if his prospects were reduced from 40 per cent to nil.[263]

And Lord Hope opined that the principle on which a patient's loss as a result of negligence is to be calculated—and, presumably, recompensed—is the same whether the prospects were better or worse than 50 per cent.[264]

5.102   The majority, however, rejected the appeal and did so largely to protect the integrity of legal principles. Lady Hale distinguished the House's rulings in *Fairchild* and *Chester* (see para 5.93) as cases:

> dealing with particular problems which could be remedied without altering the principles applicable to the great majority of personal injury cases which give rise to no real injustice or practical problem.[265]

---

[257] Ibid.   [258] Per Lord Hoffmann, [2005] UKHL 2, para 87.
[259] Per Lord Phillips, ibid, para 125. Lady Hale seems to concur on this analysis, para 226. Cf, Lord Hope who denied that this was a 'loss of a chance' case, para 117.
[260] Which was seriously questioned by Lord Phillips, ibid, para 147 ff.
[261] The significance of the criterion of 'survival at ten years' is that this is generally acknowledged in medical circles to amount to a 'cure'. The relevance of this to a legal concept of 'cure' was, however, rejected by Lady Hale, ibid, para 197.
[262] Namely, that 'a patient's prospects of recovery are treated as non-existent whenever they exist but fall short of 50%', ibid, para 43.
[263] Ibid, para 46.   [264] Ibid, para 121.   [265] Ibid, para 192.

She considered the instant case to be an invitation to introduce 'liability for the loss of a chance of a more favourable outcome', but refused to do so for the complexities involved and the consequences that this would have. Those consequences were largely summed up by Lords Phillips and Hoffmann in their view that a departure from *Hotson* would change the basis of causation from *probability* to *possibility*; that is, that some form of recovery would be due if it was shown that it was *possible* that negligence might affect a patient's case. Not only should this be a matter for Parliament, but as Lady Hale put it:

> it would in practice always be tempting to conclude that the doctor's negligence had affected … [the claimant's] chances to some extent, the claimant would almost always get something. It would be a 'heads you lose everything, tails I win something' situation.

And, finally, we have Lord Phillips:

> it seems to me that there is a danger, if special tests of causation are developed piecemeal to deal with perceived injustices in particular factual situations, that the coherence of our common law will be destroyed.[266]

This rejection of the relevance of loss of a chance to claims for clinical negligence has been confirmed by the Court of Appeal in *Wright (a child)* v *Cambridge Medical Group*.[267] This is also an important case because it clarified the respective liabilities of GPs and those to whom patients are subsequently referred. In *Wright* there were serial failures on the part of a GP and then a hospital to diagnose timeously an infant's bacterial superinfection. The GP's failure resulted in a two-day delay in referring the child to hospital, and the hospital's failure added three more days to the debacle by which time the infection had reached the child's hip and resulted in permanent restricted movement. The overarching question was whether the GP's failure to refer was a causative factor given the subsequent negligence of the hospital. In other words, even if the child had been referred on time, would it be the case that the harm would have resulted anyway, and so could the GP be said to have caused harm in their own right? The Court of Appeal found that the trial judge had erred in both fact and law in rejecting the liability of the GP. The cumulative events were a 'synergistic reaction' that did not displace the existing legal principle that every tortfeasor should compensate the injured claimant in respect of that loss and damage for which he should justly be held responsible. The hospital's failures were not so egregious as to overwhelm the causative role of the GP's negligence. Moreover, the harms were separable as a matter of fact: the pain suffered in the two-day delay was different from any pain suffered after. Furthermore, and importantly, a GP cannot escape liability for a failure to refer even if there is subsequent negligence because such a failure will always deprive the patient of an opportunity to be treated properly (at para 61). Finally, the Court revisited the loss of a chance arguments, albeit obiter, confirming their rejection by the House of Lords in *Gregg* v *Scott* and their failure to deliver a suitably responsive system of justice on the balance of probabilities.[268] While the door on the doctrine is not entirely closed in personal injury cases, the Court made it clear that it will be for the Supreme Court to open it any further.

---

[266] [2005] UKHL 2, para 172.   [267] [2011] EWCA Civ 669; [2011] Med LR 496.
[268] 'Loss of a chance' arguments were similarly rejected by the High Court in *Oliver* v *Williams* [2013] EWHC 600 (QB); [2013] Med LR 344 (delayed diagnosis of ovarian cancer).

INJURIES CAUSED BY MEDICAL
PRODUCTS OR DEVICES

5.103   The extensive use of drugs and other medical products in modern medical practice, coupled with the wide variety of available substances and devices, inevitably leads to a high incidence of injuries for which they are held responsible.[269] It has been reported, for example, that 3–5 per cent of all admissions to hospital are due to adverse reactions to drugs, costing the NHS around £500 million a year.[270] The number of persons affected will be small in some instances due to the speedy detection of the dangers and the rapid withdrawal of the products concerned. In others, the scale of the claims may be astronomic, an example being the early series of actions brought against manufacturers of intrauterine devices.[271] For these reasons, the question of compensation becomes an intensely political issue, as it has done in relation to HIV-contaminated blood, certain tranquillisers, and, more recently, measles, mumps, and rubella (MMR) vaccine. The regulation of medicines and medical devices is now controlled by the Medicines and Healthcare Products Regulatory Agency,[272] which was established on 1 April 2003. This body monitors manufacturing standards and approval mechanisms, controls licensing arrangements, and issues rapid warnings when evidence comes to light of a public danger concerning the use of a product or device.[273] It does not, however, have any direct dealings with issues of compensation for harm occasioned as a result of such use.[274]

5.104   Compensation for injury caused by products is now largely regulated in the UK by the Consumer Protection Act 1987.[275] This derives from the EU Council Directive on product liability,[276] the aim of which was to create strict liability for most injuries that were caused by defective products; this policy had long been advocated by commentators on

---

[269]   See, generally, H Teff, 'Products liability' in A Grubb (ed), *Principles of Medical Law* (3rd edn, 2010), ch 18; R Goldberg, *Medicinal Product Liability and Regulation* (2013).

[270]   House of Commons Health Committee, *The Influence of the Pharmaceutical Industry, Fourth Report of Session 2004–2005* (HC 42-I, 2005), 8.

[271]   G R Thornton, 'Intrauterine devices: Malpractice and product liability' (1986) 14 Law Med Hlth Care 4.

[272]   At: http://www.gov.uk/mhra.

[273]   See broadly, E Jackson, *Law and the Regulation of Medicines* (2012). Note that devices are regulated by provisions originating in a series of EU Directives: Directive 90/385/EC relating to active implantable devices, Directive 93/42/EC concerning medical devices, and Directive 98/79/EC on in vitro diagnostic medical devices. Note that in 2012 the European Commission submitted proposals to revise the existing legislation to the European Parliament and the Council.

[274]   It is interesting to speculate as to the Agency's own potential liability for harm caused; e.g., by procedural or operational failures in drug or product approval or withdrawal. No test case has yet emerged. The Agency was, however, criticised by the Parliamentary Health Select Committee for failing to scrutinise licensing data adequately and for insufficient post-marketing surveillance. The Committee called for a fundamental review of the Agency as a result: see House of Commons Health Committee, *The Influence of the Pharmaceutical Industry, Fourth Report of Session 2004–2005* (HC 42-I, 2005). The Department of Health carried out its review of the Agency between October 2008 and March 2009 and published its report and recommendations in September 2009. The report is available at: http://www.dh.gov.uk/en/Publicationsandstatistics/Publications/PublicationsPolicyAndGuidance/DH_104926. See also Department of Health, *Triennial review of the Medicines and Healthcare Products Regulatory Agency* (2015).

[275]   This does not preclude an action in negligence, although one of the reasons for legislative reform was precisely because of the serious limitations that such an action represents for those harmed by defective products: see generally, P R Ferguson, *Drug Injuries and the Pursuit of Compensation* (1996).

[276]   Council Directive 85/374/EEC.

compensation for personal injury.[277] Under the terms of the Act, strict liability is borne primarily by the manufacturer of a defective product, although the suppliers will also be held liable if the manufacturer cannot be identified.[278] Products include the components and raw materials from which a product is made and, in limited circumstances, a doctor may be a supplier of a drug. Despite strong protests from the industry, pharmaceutical products are not exempted from the system of strict liability. A drug will be regarded as defective if it fails to measure up to that degree of safety which 'persons generally are entitled to expect' (s 3(1)).

5.105 In some circumstances, the manufacturer will be able to call on a development risk—or, in US terms, a 'state of the art'—defence.[279] Section 4(1)(e) of the Act provides that the manufacturer will not be liable if it can be shown:

> that the state of scientific and technical knowledge at the relevant time was not such that a producer of products of the same description as the product in question might be expected to have discovered the defect if it had existed in his products while they were under his control.

The aim of this defence is to relieve manufacturers of liability if the existence of a defect was undiscoverable at the time.[280] Expert evidence will be important in deciding whether a manufacturer has attained this goal within the limitation that the Act does not require the highest possible standards. A case in point is the recent breast implant scandal in which the investigating authority concluded that lack of clinical data and poor record keeping on the part of manufacturers meant that the evidence was inconclusive as to the health and safety risks of the implants.[281]

5.106 Is a manufacturer entitled to market a drug which will be beneficial to many but which he or she knows may cause harm to a minority—in other words, is there such a thing as a socially acceptable risk? The traditional approach to this issue is by way of balancing the prospective benefit and risk. In general, sensitive users will have no claim to compensation if it is in the public interest that the drug should be available; much would then depend upon the presentation of the product and the nature of any warnings given. In this respect, s 3(2)(b) of the 1987 Act stipulates that, in assessing what constitutes a defect, consideration must be given to what might reasonably be expected to be done with, or in relation to, the product. For example, it might reasonably be expected that children could gain access to drugs intended for adult use only. It is, however, unlikely that, say, suicide could be reasonably anticipated by the manufacturer. Common sense and notions of general public knowledge and understanding can also have a role to play. Thus, in *Richardson* v *LRC Products*,[282] it was held to be common knowledge that condoms are not fail-safe and

---

[277] D Fairgrieve and G G Howells, 'Rethinking product liability: A missing element in the European Commission's third review of the European Product Liability Directive' (2007) 70 MLR 962.

[278] The European Court of Justice has confirmed that a hospital providing services that use defective products and which ultimately harm a patient would not be considered to be a 'producer' under the Directive and so national remedies making the hospital strictly liable for any such harm would not be precluded: see C-495/10 *Centre Hospitalier Universitaire de Besancon* v *Dutrueux* [2012] 2 CMLR 1.

[279] For a full exposition of the subject, see P R Ferguson, n 275.

[280] C Newdick, 'The development risk defence of the Consumer Protection Act 1987' (1988) 47 CLJ 455. See also C J Stolker, 'Objections to the development risk defence' (1990) 9 Med Law 783.

[281] Scientific Committee on Emerging and Newly Identified Health Risks (SCENIHR), *The Safety of PIP Silicon Breast Implants* (Feb 2012). Department of Health, *Poly Implant Prostheses (PIP) Breast Implants: Interim Report of Expert Group* (Jan 2012) came to the same conclusion.

[282] (2000) 59 BMLR 185.

that a risk of rupture is an inherent part of their use; the happening of such an eventuality did not, therefore, make the product 'defective'.

5.107 The litigation relating to transmission of HIV infection through contaminated blood products was taken in breach of a statutory duty under the National Health Service Act 1977 and in negligence.[283] Although it was for some time in doubt due to the absence of any authoritative interpretation, any argument as to whether strict liability applies to human blood and its derivatives is now settled—blood is a naturally occurring substance which has not been manufactured but which has been won or abstracted, it, therefore, comes within the scope of the Act.[284] Moreover, as we shall see, the production of blood for transfusion is regarded as an industrial process. In terms of the Act, the National Blood Authority would normally be the producer of the 'product'. The application of strict liability to blood transfusion has, inevitably, been considered at greatest length in the USA, where the principle has been applied in some courts but where, in general, transfusion has been looked upon rather as the provision of a service than of a product,[285] thereby attracting potential actions in negligence—which would, of course, still be available outside the Act in the UK.[286] Clark[287] long ago confirmed that the majority of US states have legislated to the effect that the supply of human blood is a service rather than a sale; the introduction of an element of 'sale' perhaps makes the distinction more urgent there than it is in the UK.

5.108 The matter came to the UK courts in the shape of *A v National Blood Authority*.[288] The judgment is a High Court decision only; nonetheless, it is extremely thorough and it is difficult to do it justice in a book of this format.[289] For these reasons, we do no more than attempt to extract the more important points. The case was brought as a class action by a group who had been infected with the hepatitis C virus (HCV) during routine blood transfusion. HCV was discovered in May 1988—although its presence had been suspected since 1975; a test for the presence of the virus was not developed until September 1989 and an improved test was not approved for use in the UK until April 1991. Prior to 1988, however, the occurrence of cases of post-transfusion hepatitis of uncertain origin had prompted the introduction of so-called 'surrogate tests' in the USA in September 1986; these tests did not identify a virus but, rather, the effects of viral contamination or, alternatively, a high-risk lifestyle on the part of the donor. Surrogate tests were not supported, nor introduced, in the UK.

5.109 The group action was brought under the Consumer Protection Act 1987 by the relatively small number of persons who were infected between the coming into force of the Act and the introduction of a screening test for blood in 1989. Claims were lodged notwithstanding the facts that HCV was not identified at the time the claims commenced nor was a screening test available. The defendants agreed that the risk was known but asserted that avoiding the risk was impossible and that it could not be right to expect the unattainable. The public was not entitled to expect 100 per cent clean blood—the most that could be

[283] D Brahams, 'Confidential documents in HIV/haemophilia litigation' (1990) 336 Lancet 805.
[284] 1987 Act, ss 1(2) and 45(1). See, in particular, A M Clark, *Product Liability* (1989) ch 3.
[285] E.g. *Coffee v Cutter Biological* 809 F 2d 191 (1987).
[286] The supply of HIV-infected blood was the subject of common law-based litigation in the Australian case of *H v Royal Alexandra Hospital for Children* [1990] 1 Med LR 297.
[287] Clark, n 284, 62.   [288] [2001] 3 All ER 289: (2001) 60 BMLR 1.
[289] A very full discussion of this case is provided by S Williamson, 'Strict liability for medical products: Prospects for success' (2002) 5 Med L Internat 281. The author believed *A v National Blood Authority* to be the first case to succeed against the producers of a medical product.

expected was that every reasonable precaution had been taken or carried out. In the event, arguments for both sides were based on the Council Directive rather than the 1987 Act— largely on the grounds that the latter *had* to be interpreted so as to be consistent with the former.[290] The issues were, therefore, concentrated on Arts 6 (which defines 'defective') and 7(e) (which describes the 'development risk' defence in much the same terms as s 4(1) (e) of the 1987 Act) of the Directive. It is to be noted that negligence was not a feature of this particular litigation.

5.110   In essence, the court found that the blood was defective, liability being 'defect-based' rather than 'fault-based'; avoidability was not a factor which could be taken into account insofar as it is 'outwith the purpose of the Directive'; the public at large was entitled to expect that the blood would be free from infection; and it was not material to consider whether any further steps could have been taken to avoid or reduce the risk that the blood would be infected. As to Art 7(e), the development risk defence was not available on the grounds that, if there is a known risk, then the producer who continues to produce and supply the product does so at his own risk. The court concluded that it is a lack of opportunity to discover the defect in the particular product that is essential to Art 7(e). Known risks do not qualify, even if they are unavoidable, and the problem came down to whether such 'testing' as was available, but not used, would have been able to identify a risk in an individual bag of blood. The court concluded that, whereas surrogate testing on its own would not, on the balance of probabilities, have done so, the combination of surrogate testing and screening once the virus had been identified would have been effective. A defence under Art 7(e) thus failed. So, as things stand at present, it seems that strict liability means what it says—strict liability; and manufacturers or producers will find it increasingly hard to plead a 'state of the art' defence.

5.111   *A* v *National Blood Authority* was a case fought at an exceptionally high level of responsibility and one wonders how much it will affect the individual doctor or pharmacist.[291] Probably their major concern in respect of strict liability laws lies in the need to ensure that the manufacturer can be adequately identified in order to avoid claims being made against the individual supplier.

5.112   The Group Litigation concerning alleged liability arising from the use of the MMR vaccine developed into a procedural quagmire. The apparently factual basis for the litigation stemmed from an article published in the *Lancet* in 1998 indicating that there may be a causal connection between the vaccine and autism in children.[292] More than 1,000 children allegedly affected in this way were the focus of an ongoing group action which relied on the terms of the Consumer Protection Act 1987 as to the strict liability of the vaccine's manufacturers. It is important to point out in passing that for these families

---

[290] The European Commission had previously lodged a complaint with the European Court of Justice, later dismissed, that the UK's implementation of the 1987 Act did not comply with the Directive: *EC Commission* v *United Kingdom* [1997] ECRI-2649; [1997] All ER (EC) 481.

[291] It is of interest that a leading article in the BMJ stated: 'The only possible response to the judgment must be that the necessity for each transfusion is now carefully weighed up ... and the search for alternatives to allogeneic transfusion intensified'—P P Mortimer, 'Making blood safer' (2002) 325 BMJ 400. Patient demand may also increase the pressure; see e.g. E S Vanderlinde, J M Heal, and N Blumberg, 'Autologous transfusion' (2002) 324 BMJ 772.

[292] The original paper which sparked the controversy was A Wakefield et al., 'Ileal-lymphoid-nodular hyperplasia, non-specific colitis, and pervasive development disorder in children' (1998) 351 Lancet 637. Contrary evidence includes K M Madsen et al., 'A population-based study of measles, mumps and rubella vaccination and autism' (2002) 347 New Eng J Med 1477.

the provisions of the Vaccine Damage Payments Act 1979 were judged to be wholly inadequate. This Act established a strict liability scheme whereby those adversely affected by
vaccines can seek compensation through the Department of Health if it can be shown
that an individual has suffered at least 60 per cent disability as a result of being given the
vaccine.[293] The current payable sum is £120,000. However, this was considered to be an
entirely insufficient sum for the MMR families by which to cover the potentially lifetime
costs of rearing mentally handicapped children. Given that causation must be proved
either way, many sought to take their chances under the 1987 Act.[294] But the main problem for the group litigation was not the law but legal aid (or, rather, its absence). The Legal
Services Commission withdrew funding in 2003 and the decision was upheld on appeal
and survived a judicial review. The litigation petered out shortly thereafter.

5.113   At the time of writing, group litigation is ongoing in the wake of the high-profile Poly
        Implant Prothèse (PIP) breast implant scandal. As is well known, the French company
        PIP had received regulatory approval to manufacture silicone implants and had, indeed,
        become one of the world's largest producers, but an inspection by the French authorities
        in 2010 revealed the company had substituted medical grade silicone in the implants for
        cheaper industrial grade silicone. PIP is now insolvent. More than 1,000 women in the
        UK who received PIP-manufactured implants have joined a group litigation seeking com-
        pensation. The claims are not based under the Consumer Protection Act 1987—which is
        of little assistance due to the manufacturer's insolvency—but instead framed in terms of
        contractual obligations implied by the Sale of Goods Act 1979 (SOGA) and the Supply
        of Goods and Services Act 1982 (SOGSA).[295] The plaintiffs are seeking redress against a
        number of parties, including PIP's UK distributors, the clinics that performed the proce-
        dures, and individual surgeons. The case illustrates the complexities of product liability
        litigation following the demise of a manufacturer and also the challenges for regulatory
        agencies in detecting rare instances of wilful deception by producers.

5.114   Whether we are talking about the common law of negligence, statutory product liability,
        or *sui generis* schemes of strict liability, the problem of causation remains. It is, of course,
        arguable that this is as it should be as a matter of principled justice; but there is also
        the other side of the debate that says that medical causation is of such a specific, highly
        complex, nature that some concessions should be made. We do, indeed, see examples of
        this in cases such as *Fairchild* and *Chester*. But none of this matters if claimants are not
        even afforded their day in court: access to justice and financial support go hand-in-hand,
        taking us from the realm of law to that of politics. The battle must, therefore, be waged
        on many fronts; but in each domain the odds are stacked firmly against the claimant.[296]

CRIMINAL NEGLIGENCE

5.115   Medical negligence is predominantly a civil matter, but a spate of prosecutions in the early
        1990s served to remind doctors that the loss of a patient may sometimes lead to criminal

---

[293]   See further on 'the meaning of 'severely disabled': Regulatory Reform (Vaccine Damage Payments Act
1979) Order 2002 (SI 2002/1592), art 2.
[294]   Recovery under the 1979 Act does not preclude a subsequent action in negligence, but this itself may
be unattractive for reasons we have already outlined.
[295]   Ministry of Justice, *The PIP Breast Implant Litigation*, Ref No. 88, 17 April 2012.
[296]   See also *O'Byrne v Aventis* [2008] UKHL 34; [2008] 4 All ER 881 (HiB vaccine)—stalled for procedural
reasons (primarily identifying the correct defendant manufacturer).

prosecution. Such prosecutions used to be rare; their increase points to heightened interest in the external regulation of medicine and to a diminution in the professional immunity which doctors may previously have enjoyed. In some respects, this process is healthy; in others, it is a matter for regret. The principle that doctors, and indeed all professionals, should be accountable for their failures is entirely acceptable; what is more dubious is that the criminal law, and particularly manslaughter prosecutions, should be the instrument chosen to perform that task. We believe that the concept of criminal liability for negligence involving a breach of duty is, at best, tenuous and that the minimum threshold for the invocation of criminal sanctions should be recklessness. We explore the implications of this later.

5.116   Criminal liability for negligence is effectively limited to prosecutions for manslaughter.[297] The requisite elements are similar to those in the civil law—namely, that there is a duty of care; there is a breach of that duty of care; and the breach amounts to gross negligence. The need for resultant harm is, of course, a given and here it is the death of the patient. The level of negligence which the doctor must have manifested is considerably above that at which civil liability may be incurred. Traditionally it has been defined as 'gross' or 'extreme' negligence and sometimes, somewhat tautologically, as 'criminal negligence'; the essential concern is that it surpasses the civil test, as was stressed in *R v Bateman*:

> In order to establish criminal liability, the facts must be such that ... the negligence of the accused went beyond a mere matter of compensation between subjects and showed such disregard for the life and safety of others as to amount to a crime against the State and conduct deserving punishment.[298]

This, of course, does not answer the question of when conduct goes beyond the compensation level but it is probably impossible to be much more specific. It is clear that what is required is conduct which gives rise to a sense of outrage—or to the conclusion that the accused deserves *punishment* for what he did. Such a conclusion, though, is likely to be articulated in terms of a lack of regard for the patient's welfare or safety—and therein lies the problem. If criminal negligence is defined in terms of a deliberate exposure of the patient to some form of risk, then we are in the realms of recklessness rather than negligence.[299] It is one thing to punish a person for subjective recklessness; it is quite another to punish for objective negligence. In the former case the accused has effectively said, 'I knew of the risk of harm but did not care'; in the latter, he may have been quite unaware of any risk at all—the damage caused may have been the result of incompetence or ignorance, neither of which qualities necessarily deserve criminal punishment.

5.117   The conduct involved in the relevant cases has ranged from, at one extreme, an apparent indifference with all the features of recklessness to mere incompetence at the other. In *Saha and Salim*,[300] two doctors administered an astonishing cocktail of drugs to a remand prisoner who died as a result. They were both convicted and sentenced to a

---

[297] R E Ferner, 'Medication errors that have led to manslaughter charges' (2000) 321 BMJ 1212, was able to find 17 British cases between 1970 and 1999—13 of these arose in the third decade. Seven cases resulted in conviction excluding those where an appeal was successful. Also, see O Quick, 'Prosecuting "gross" medical negligence: manslaughter, discretion and the Crown Prosecution Service' (2006) 33(3) JLS 421.

[298] [1925] All ER Rep 45 at 48; 19 Cr App Rep 8 at 11, per Lord Hewart LCJ.

[299] A difficulty which the courts have acknowledged in those decisions where gross negligence manslaughter appears to have been replaced by reckless manslaughter: *R v Seymour* [1983] 2 AC 493; (1983) 77 Cr App R 21; *Kong Cheuk Kwan v R* (1986) 82 Cr App R 18.

[300] (1992, unreported); see D Brahams, 'Death of remand prisoner' (1992) 340 Lancet 1462.

term of imprisonment. By contrast, the conviction of two young and relatively inexperienced doctors for the manslaughter of a patient to whom they had incorrectly administered cytotoxic drugs was greeted with concern in medical circles and was, in due
course, quashed by the Court of Appeal.[301] Somewhere in between lies the case of *R v
Adomako*,[302] in which an anaesthetist failed to notice the fact that his patient was in
distress when this would have been glaringly obvious to any competent practitioner.
There was conflicting evidence on the question of whether the accused was out of the
theatre at the time; if he had been, and if there had been a failure on his part to make
adequate arrangements for the monitoring of the patient, then that would surely have
amounted to a degree of recklessness which was strongly deserving of punishment. If,
however, he was merely incompetent, it might be more difficult to argue for his conviction of manslaughter—although, undoubtedly, professional sanctions would still be
needed. These cases were heard together on appeal,[303] when it was held that the proper
test in manslaughter cases based on breach of duty was that of gross negligence rather
than recklessness.[304] In contrast to that of the two young doctors, Dr Adomako's appeal
failed. He did, however, carry his case to the House of Lords where his conviction was
upheld.[305] The House considered that gross negligence requires 'an egregious failure' to
exhibit a minimum standard of competence (judged objectively) or a gross dereliction of
care: 'Conduct so bad in all circumstances as to amount to a criminal act or omission.'[306]
It was further clarified that, in cases of manslaughter by criminal negligence involving a
breach of duty, it was a sufficient direction to the jury to adopt the gross negligence test
set out by the Court of Appeal; it was not necessary to define recklessness, although it
was open to the judge to use the word 'reckless' in its ordinary meaning as part of his
exposition of the law.

5.118 Thus, as the criminal law now stands, a grossly incompetent doctor is liable to conviction
despite the fact that there is no element of subjective wrongdoing on his part. This might
well be considered inappropriate.[307] The alternative view is that the law should protect
the public and that prosecution represents one way of controlling those who cannot meet
minimal professional standards. Surely, however, the law should, at the same time, recognise the difference between the reckless and the inadequate practitioner. There is, indeed,
some evidence that the House of Lords was prepared to concede the inherent dangers of
the gross negligence test. Thus, we have Lord MacKay commending the words of the trial
judge in *R v Adomako*:

> You should only convict a doctor of causing death by negligence if you think he did some-
> thing which *no reasonably skilled* doctor should have done [emphasis added][308]

which is a very severe definition.

[301] [1991] 2 Med LR 277.
[302] *R v Prentice, R v Adomako* [1993] 4 All ER 935; (1993) 15 BMLR 13, sub nom *R v Holloway, R v Adomako,
R v Prentice and Sulman* [1993] 4 Med LR 304. See C Dyer, 'Manslaughter verdict quashed on junior doctors'
(1993) 306 BMJ 1432.
[303] (1993) 15 BMLR 13; [1993] 4 Med LR 304.
[304] (1993) 15 BMLR 13 at 21; [1993] 4 Med LR 304 at 310, per Lord Taylor, following *Andrews v DPP* [1937]
AC 576; [1937] 2 All ER 552, HL and *R v Stone, R v Dobinson* [1977] QB 354; [1977] 2 All ER 341.
[305] *R v Adomako* [1995] 1 AC 171; (1994) 19 BMLR 56, HL.
[306] Per Lord Mackay, [1995] 1 AC 171 at 187.
[307] For expansion of this argument, see A McCall Smith, 'Criminal negligence and the incompetent doctor' (1993) 1 Med L Rev 336.
[308] (1994) 19 BMLR 56 at 64–5.

5.119 The ruling in *Adomako* has remained controversial since it was delivered and there have been various attempts to have the House of Lords revisit their decision. Each has failed. The application for appeal was rejected in *R v Mark*, for example, because it was said that the law is perfectly clear and no decision since *Adomako* has questioned its validity.[309] It was, indeed, applied to uphold the convictions of two doctors in *R v Misra; R v Srivastava*[310] in which a patient died after developing a staphylococcal infection following routine surgery. The prosecution arose not because the doctors had failed to diagnose the particular infection, but because they failed to notice that their patient was ill at all, despite his high fever, high pulse rate, and low blood pressure. They did nothing to diagnose his condition until it was too late and the patient succumbed to toxic shock syndrome. The importance of the appeal lay in the questions it raised as to the compatibility of gross negligence manslaughter with the Human Rights Act 1998. Two essential arguments were made: (i) that there was no 'fair trial' (Art 6 ECHR) in such cases because they involve juries that are not required to articulate the reasoning behind their verdict, and (ii) there was a breach of Art 7 ECHR which requires a clear pre-existing criminal offence in law. The argument here was that the English law lacked clarity because of its circularity: the jury should convict if they consider the defendant's behaviour to be 'criminal'; so what is 'criminal' is what the jury considers to be such. Dismissing the appeals, however, the Court of Appeal held that the elements of the offence are very clearly defined in *Adomako* and involve no uncertainty. A doctor can easily be apprised of his obligation to his patients within the limits of the criminal law. Nor is there any valid human rights argument that can call into question the operation of the present jury system: it has, indeed, been accepted as valid by the ECtHR itself. Finally, the Court, once again, refused a request for leave to appeal to the House of Lords.

5.120 As an addendum to the *Misra* case, the NHS Trust was subsequently prosecuted under s 3 of the Health and Safety at Work etc. Act 1974 on an indictment of five charges. In January 2006, the Trust pleaded guilty to an amended charge of failing to adequately manage and supervise the doctors. The Trust was initially fined £100,000, but this was reduced on appeal to £40,000.[311] Potential new avenues of liability have now also arisen through the Corporate Manslaughter and Homicide Act 2007. The offence created in the Act applies to any organisation that owes a duty of care and explicitly covers NHS bodies providing medical treatment.[312] The first prosecution of its kind against an NHS Trust for the criminal offence of corporate manslaughter was initiated in 2015.[313] Penalties under the Act include unlimited fines, remedial orders, and publicity orders.

5.121 But are the criminal courts the appropriate guardians of conditions in the operating theatre? The GMC has been widely criticised in the past for its ineffective control of clinical standards. It now appears prepared to use its newly erupted teeth.[314] It could well be that the better route to the protection of the public from clinical error lies along the development of the investigative and restrictive powers of the GMC and the Royal Colleges, leaving

---

[309] *R v Mark (Alan James)* [2004] EWCA Crim 2490.

[310] [2004] EWCA Crim 2375; (2004) *The Times*, 13 October.

[311] *R v Southampton University Hospital NHS Trust* [2006] EWCA Crim 2971; [2007] 2 Cr App R (S) 9. For a discussion, see J Samanta, 'Charges of corporate manslaughter in the NHS' (2006) 332 BMJ 1404.

[312] A Samuels, 'The Corporate Manslaughter and Corporate Homicide Act 2007: How will it affect the medical world?' (2007) Med Leg J 72.

[313] C Dyer, 'NHS trust is charged with corporate manslaughter over woman's death after emergency caesarean' (2015) 350 BMJ h2181.

[314] See discussion in Chapter 1.

only the subjective wrongdoer where he belongs—in the criminal courts. Algrahini et al. have argued that the new crime of wilful neglect might better protect patients and hold professionals and authorities to account.[315]

5.122   If concern is felt in the UK over the prosecution of, often junior, doctors for causing the deaths of patients, it was amplified in New Zealand where, under the Crimes Act 1961, criminal liability was imposed on a doctor who merely failed to show 'reasonable knowledge, skill and care' in the treatment of his patients. This extraordinarily low threshold of liability was applied in *R v Yogasakaran*[316] and confirmed on appeal.[317] In this case, an anaesthetist had not checked the label on an ampoule of a drug which he injected into a patient. The ampoule was of the appropriate shape and size and was in the right place on the trolley but, for some reason unconnected with the anaesthetist, contained the wrong drug. Presumably, the same result would have been achieved if the anaesthetist had, in fact, read the label but had read it wrongly. Such a common mistake can hardly be seen as justification for convicting a person of a crime which carries with it a very great deal of moral opprobrium—it would surely be better investigated by the Medical Practitioners' Disciplinary Committee. Concerted medical opposition to the use of the criminal law in this fashion led, in fact, to a government-sponsored amendment to the Crimes Act, which required that there should be a major departure from the normally expected levels of care before liability for manslaughter could be imposed.[318] This effectively raised the standard in New Zealand to the gross negligence standard applied elsewhere. Most of the New Zealand doctors or nurses who were found guilty under the old legislation would not be convicted under the new standard.

---

[315] A Algrahini, M Brazier, A Farrell, D Griffiths, and N Allen, 'Healthcare scandals in the NHS: crime and punishment' (2011) 37 J Med Ethics 230. See also, O Quick, 'Expert evidence and medical manslaughter: vagueness in action' (2011) 38 J Law Soc 469.

[316] [1990] 1 NZLR 399.

[317] See D B Collins, 'New Zealand's medical manslaughter' (1992) Med Law 221. The Privy Council refused to consider what it regarded as matters of policy.

[318] Now enacted in the Crimes Act 1961, s 150A, inserted by the Crimes Amendment Act 2011, s 6. On the background, see A Merry and A McCall Smith, 'Medical accountability and the criminal law' (1996) 14 Hlth Care Anal 45 and, by the same authors, 'Medical manslaughter' (1997) Med J Austral 342.

6

MEDICAL CONFIDENTIALITY

INTRODUCTION

6.01 This chapter deals with the protection of patient privacy and the associated potential tensions that arise from the prospect that additional—alternative—value can be produced from use of patient data beyond the confines of the doctor–patient relationship. The starting principle is clear: a general common law duty is imposed on a doctor to respect the confidences of his patients.[1] The nature of this obligation[2]—which applies to all confidential information and not only to medical material[3]—was discussed by the House of Lords in *A-G v Guardian Newspapers Ltd (No 2)*,[4] in which it was affirmed that there is a public interest in the protection of confidences received under notice of confidentiality or in circumstances where the reasonable person ought to know that the information was confidential. In *Hunter v Mann*,[5] the court stated that:

> the doctor is under a duty not to [voluntarily] disclose, without the consent of the patient, information which he, the doctor, has gained in his professional capacity.

In the very significant case of *W v Egdell*,[6] which we discuss in greater detail at paras 6.17 et seq, the court accepted the existence of an obligation of confidentiality between a psychiatrist and his subject, an obligation which counsel submitted was based not only on equitable grounds but also on implied contract. The House of Lords then confirmed in *Campbell v Mirror Group Newspapers Ltd*[7] that details of one's medical circumstances are 'obviously private' and deserving of the full protection of the law of confidence, albeit now subject to the slant afforded to the law by the Human Rights Act 1998, which we

---

[1] This chapter is concerned with confidentiality and not the converse idea of freedom of information. The Freedom of Information Act 2000 gives individuals a right of access to data held by, or on behalf of, public authorities, which include National Health Service (NHS) bodies. Any request for access to personal data, however, is inappropriate under this Act (and should instead be sought under the Data Protection Act 1998: see later); moreover, any request for access to material containing data identifying another individual should be refused if disclosure would breach the data protection principles or the common law duty of confidence: see Information Commissioner's Office, *The Guide to Freedom of Information* (2012) and the House of Lords ruling in *Common Service Agency v Scottish Information Commissioner* (2008) 103 BMLR 190; 2008 SLT 901.

[2] The doctor–patient and priest–penitent relationships were cited as classic examples in *Stephens v Avery* [1988] Ch 449 at 455; [1988] 2 All ER 477 at 482, per Browne-Wilkinson V-C.

[3] The duty to respect confidences is to be distinguished from the (broader) notion of respecting individual privacy although the two are obviously related. Indeed, the House of Lords has confirmed that there is no common law right of privacy in the United Kingdom (UK): see *Wainwright v Home Office* [2003] 4 All ER 969; [2003] 3 WLR 1137, HL; this is not at all the same as saying that privacy interests are not protected.

[4] [1990] AC 109; [1988] 3 All ER 545.

[5] [1974] QB 767 at 772; [1974] 2 All ER 414 at 417, per Boreham J.

[6] [1990] Ch 359; [1990] 1 All ER 835.   [7] [2004] 2 AC 457; [2004] 2 All ER 995.

also consider further later. Added to this, by statute, the processing of 'personal data' is governed by the principles embodied in the Data Protection Act 1998, which, in turn, implements the terms of the respective European Directive. This system is overseen by the Information Commissioner's Office, and indeed there is a plethora of professional organisations and persons part of whose remit is to respect and police the confidentiality of patients' information. These include the General Medical Council (GMC), the British Medical Association (BMA), individuals known as Caldicott Guardians within each Health Authority[8] or Health Board,[9] and the Confidentiality Advisory Group which now operates under the auspices of the Health Research Authority to offer advice on secondary uses of patient data for research and audit.[10] This field is, in fact, in a state of considerable current flux and concern surrounding the legitimate and lawful uses of medical data. A report commissioned by the Ministry of Justice in 2008 concluded:

> [It is necessary] to transform the culture that influences how personal information is viewed and handled; to clarify and simplify the legal framework governing data sharing; to enhance the effectiveness of the regulatory body that polices data sharing; to assist important work in the field of research and statistical analysis; and to help safeguard and protect personal information held in publicly available sources.[11]

THE CONTOURS OF THE LANDSCAPE

6.02 The protection of medical confidentiality is complicated because it is a terrain consisting of, and influenced by, three overlapping spheres of interest: the professions, law and ethics. Indeed, it is difficult to dissociate the two disciplines of law and ethics—thus, we have Lord Coleridge CJ: 'A legal common law duty is nothing else than the enforcing by law of that which is a moral obligation without legal enforcement.'[12] We can, therefore, look not only at what the patient feels is his legal entitlement but also at the ethical requirements of the medical profession itself. Here there are a number of sources from which the doctor can seek guidance. The Hippocratic Oath makes several demands which can scarcely be regarded as binding on the modern doctor; nonetheless, its stipulations as to professional confidentiality are still firmly endorsed. The translation cited in the *sponsio academica* at graduation ceremonials in the University of Edinburgh runs: 'Whatever things seen or heard in the course of medical practice ought not to be spoken of, I will not, save for weighty reasons, divulge.' The Declaration of Geneva (last amended at Divonne-les-Bains, France, 2006) imposes much the same obligation on the doctor, requiring him to 'respect the secrets which are confided in me, even after the patient has died'.

---

[8] NHS England, Confidentiality Policy (2014), available at: http://www.england.nhs.uk/wp-content/uploads/2013/06/conf-policy-1.pdf.

[9] HSC 1999/012: Caldicott guardians. A review of this system was published in 2013, see Dame Fiona Caldicott, Information: To share or not to share? The Information Governance Review (2013), available at: https://www.gov.uk/government/publications/the-information-governance-review. For the government's response, see: Department of Health, Information: To Share or not to Share—Government Response to the Caldicott Review (2013), available at: https://www.gov.uk/government/uploads/system/uploads/attachment_data/file/251750/9731-2901141-TSO-Caldicott-Government_Response_ACCESSIBLE.PDF.

[10] See: Confidentiality Advisory Group, available at: http://www.hra.nhs.uk/resources/confidentiality-advisory-group/.

[11] Ministry of Justice, *Data Sharing Review* (authors Richard Thomas and Mark Walport, 2008).

[12] In *R v Instan* [1893] 1 QB 450 at 453.

6.03 There can be no doubt that confidentiality is taken seriously by lawyers and ethicists alike. Most critics, however, see the concept as being something of a pretence in that bureaucracy, fired by modern administrative technology, is increasingly invasive of the principle; never-ending advances in information technology merely facilitate wider and faster dissemination of patient information, heighten concerns about the risk of unauthorised disclosure, and generally exacerbate the problem.[13] Certainly, patients' records must circulate fairly widely— and among professionals who are less deeply indoctrinated as to confidentiality than are their medical colleagues. But early suggestions that institutions should take over custodian-ship of confidences and impose an overall standard of duty on all who work in health care institutions have now come to represent the position both at common law[14] and by statute.[15] Indeed, sensitivity towards patient confidentiality has probably never been greater, with health authorities and boards holding training sessions for staff at regular intervals.

6.04 Even so, the special position of the doctor is unlikely to change in the foreseeable future and he is currently bound by the authority of, and is subject to the discipline of, the GMC. Subject to certain exceptions, which we discuss further later,[16] the GMC imposes a strict duty on registered medical practitioners to refrain from disclosing voluntarily to any third party information about a patient which he has learnt directly or indirectly in his professional capacity. A breach of this duty will be a serious matter, exposing the doctor to a wide range of potential professional penalties.[17]

6.05 The operation of the Data Protection Act 1998,[18] implementing a 1995 EC Directive,[19] provides further protection for medical information. It is not necessary for the purposes of this book to examine the provisions of the Directive or the Act in any great depth.[20] It

---

[13] See generally, House of Commons Health Committee, *Electronic Patient Record* (HC 422–1, 13 September 2007). More recently, Nuffield Council on Bioethics, The collection, linking and use of data in biomedical research and health care: ethical issues (2015). See more at: http://nuffieldbioethics.org/project/biological-health-data/#sthash.c6hg8Quj.dpuf. Also, G Laurie et al., A Review of Evidence Relating to Harm Resulting from Uses of Health and Biomedical Data (2015), available at: http://nuffieldbioethics. org/wp-content/uploads/A-Review-of-Evidence-Relating-to-Harms-Resulting-from-Uses-of-Health-and-Biomedical-Data-FINAL.pdf.

[14] *A-G v Guardian Newspapers Ltd (No 2)*; para 6.1 imposes a duty on all those who receive confidential information in circumstances which objectively (and reasonably) import a duty of confidence. Communications in a hospital are a paradigm example of this: see *W, X, Y and Z v Secretary of State for Health et al* [2015] EWCA Civ 1034.

[15] Data Protection Act 1998 and the Health and Social Care Act 2012.

[16] See paras 6.10 et seq.

[17] GMC, *Confidentiality: Protecting and Providing Information* (2009), as updated by *Good Medical Practice* (2013). This guidance and related documentation and toolkits are available at: http://www.gmc-uk.org/guidance/ethical_guidance/confidentiality.asp. The guidance was in the process of revision at the time of writing in summer 2015.

[18] The Data Protection Act 1998 came into force on 1 March 2000.

[19] European Directive 95/46/EC on the Protection of Individuals with Regard to the Process of Personal Data and on the Free Movement of Such Data (the Data Protection Directive). There is a general and strong European interest in the subject which is reflected elsewhere in the Council of Europe's Recommendation on the Protection of Medical Data (1997). This recommendation includes not only general principles which should guide national laws on the confidentiality of medical information, but also embraces specific recommendations relating to such matters as storage of data, their transmission across borders, and the use of data in medical research.

[20] For a detailed analysis, see S Pattinson and D Beyleveld, 'Confidentiality and Data Protection' in A Grubb, J Lang, and J McHale (eds), *Principles of Medical Law* (3rd edn, 2010). For a more specialised treatment, see M Taylor, *Genetic Data and the Law: A Critical Perspective on Privacy Protection* (2012). The Data Protection Directive is currently under review towards introduction of a Regulation. For a timely overview and likely consequences, see L Stevens, 'The Proposed Data Protection Regulation and its Potential Impact on Social Sciences Research in the UK' (2015) 1(2) European Data Protection Law Review 97–112.

is sufficient simply to note certain key features.[21] The law protects the privacy rights of individuals in respect of the processing of their personal data. 'Personal data' are defined as 'any information relating to an identified or identifiable natural person; an identifiable person is one who can be identified, directly or indirectly, in particular by reference to an identification number or to one or more factors specific to his physical, physiological, mental, economic, cultural or social identity'.[22] The law regulates the processing of such data by reference to a set of eight principles that ensure, inter alia, that data are only processed when it is fair and lawful to do so, that data are processed and kept only so far as is necessary for the purposes for which they were obtained, that the data are accurate and kept up to date, and that they should not be transferred to any jurisdiction where there are inadequate data protection provisions. A logical first step in determining whether the Data Protection Act applies at all—beyond determining whether data are 'personal data' (discussed later)—is to establish whether data are being 'processed'. The Directive envisages an incredibly wide scope for this term including:

> any operation or set of operations which is performed upon personal data, whether or not by automatic means, such as collection, recording, organization, storage, adaptation or alteration, retrieval, consultation, use, disclosure by transmission, dissemination or otherwise making available, alignment or combination, blocking, erasure or destruction.[23]

6.06 One might think there is little that could be done with data which would not fall within such a definition! Nonetheless, in *Johnson* v *Medical Defence Union Ltd*,[24] the Court of Appeal held that it was not 'processing' for an employee of the Union to carry out a risk assessment of a member based purely on complaints against him (irrespective of whether any complaint was well founded) even when this led to the termination of his membership. There is an important distinction to draw between 'fair processing' and 'fair' decisions. The former is a technical requirement of law that is linked to dealing with information in a 'relevant filing system' and it is to be distinguished from decisions taken by human beings with which one might disagree. Damages were awarded in *Grinyer* v *Plymouth Hospitals NHS Trust* (2011, unreported) for unlawful access to medical records—a sum of £12,500 (exacerbation of pre-existing injury) and £4,800 (loss of earnings). Unlawful processing of personal data can lead to recovery for 'moral damages' for affront to privacy even when there is no pecuniary loss.[25] We discuss this further paras 6.77 et seq.

6.07 The data protection law attempts to categorise information into only two distinct groupings. These are (i) sensitive personal data and (ii) anonymous data. Both are of relevance in the health care setting. Data which are anonymised are not covered by the provisions of the 1998 Act.[26] It is a matter of considerable contemporary debate, however, as to what constitutes 'anonymised' data. In *Common Service Agency* v *Scottish Information Commissioner*,[27] the House of Lords had to rule on a dispute regarding the disclosure

---

[21] For a guide to the Act, see P Carey, *Data Protection: A Practical Guide to UK and EU* Law (2015).
[22] Data Protection Directive, Art 2.   [23] Data Protection Directive, Art 2(b).
[24] [2007] 3 CMLR 9; (2007) 96 BMLR 99.
[25] *Vidal-Hall* v *Google Inc.* [2015] EWCA Civ 311; [2015] CP Rep 28; [2015] 3 CMLR 2.
[26] Advice to Member States on many matters of data protection is available, however, from the Article 29 Data Protection Working Party set up in an advisory capacity under the Directive: available at http://ec.europa.eu/justice/data-protection/article-29/index_en.htm. Relevant Opinions include Opinion No 4/2007 on the concept of personal data and Working Document on the Processing of Personal Data Relating to Health in Electronic Health Records (EHR, 2007).
[27] [2008] UKHL 47; 2008 SLT 901.

of rare incidences of childhood leukaemia in the Dumfries and Galloway postal areas. A request had been made under freedom of information legislation but this would not need to be complied with if the data were 'personal data' which would clearly have been the case if names, ages, and addresses were released. The Commissioner had ruled, however, that the applicant could and should have been provided with data subjected to a process known as 'barnardisation' which can be applied to tables of data involving very small numbers in order to protect individual privacy.[28] Was this sufficient to anonymise the data? The question was unresolved by their Lordships and considered to be a question of fact to be remitted to the Commissioner himself.[29] In legal terms, the position remains unsatisfactory: against which legal standard must an Information Commissioner or any other party determine whether a sufficient level of anonymity is reached? It is well recognised as a matter of practice that a 'spectrum of identifiability'[30] exists with respect to fragments of information about individuals which can be pieced together by a variety of means, and that *absolute* anonymity is elusive if not illusory.[31] Anonymisation is often referred to as a craft. Anonymity and identifiability are, instead, *relative* concepts: '[a]n individual shall not be regarded as "identifiable" if identification requires an unreasonable amount of time and manpower'.[32] Note too, circumstances can change over time—so anonymised data status must be kept under regular review. In contrast, 'sensitive personal data' are defined as data relating to racial or ethnic origin, political opinions, religious or philosophical beliefs, trade union membership, and the processing of data concerning health or sex life.[33] Additional protection is afforded to such data and, as we have seen elsewhere in this book, the primary point of reference is the concept of consent. Thus, consent is the most common and obvious factor to legitimate processing of (sensitive) personal data.[34] However, a wide range of alternative justifications for processing accompanies this protection, of which the following are most pertinent. For example, it is lawful to process sensitive data to protect the vital interests of the data subject or of another person where the data subject is physically or legally incapable of giving his consent.[35] Also, processing is lawful without specific consent if it is required for the purposes of preventive medicine, medical diagnosis, the provision of care or treatment or the management of health care services, and where those data are processed by a health professional subject to the obligation of professional secrecy or by another person also subject to an equivalent obligation of secrecy. Overarchingly, Member States have the power to create exemptions on the basis of 'substantial public interest'.[36] What those public interests are, or may be, is

---

[28] This technique randomly adds 0, +1, or −1 to all values between 2 and 4 in cells of data, and adds 0 or +1 to entries where the value is 1. A cell containing 0 remains unchanged. In this way, it is argued, the data are 'perturbed' and anonymity is protected.

[29] For comment see G Laurie and R Gertz, 'The worst of all worlds? *Common Services Agency v Scottish Information Commissioner*' (2009) 13 Edin LR 330.

[30] For discussion, see W W Lowrance, *Learning from Experience: Privacy and the Secondary Use of Data in Health Research* (2002), pp 29 ff. See more recently, W W Lowrance, *Privacy, Confidentiality and Health Research* (2012).

[31] Information Commissioner's Office, *Anonymisation: Managing Data Protection Risk Code of Practice*, (2012) and H Schmidt and S Callier, 'How anonymous is "anonymous"? Some suggestions towards a coherent universal coding system for genetic samples' (2012) 38 J Med Ethics 304.

[32] Council of Europe, Recommendation R(81)1 on Regulations for Automated Medical Data Banks (1981); Council of Europe, Recommendation R(97)5 on the Protection of Medical Data (1997).

[33] Data Protection Directive, Art 8.

[34] See Article 29 Working Party, Opinion 15/2011 on the definition of consent, (2011) 01197/11/EN WP187.

[35] The Information Commissioner's Office issued useful guidance entitled *Use and Disclosure of Health Data* (2002) in which, e.g., it is stated that 'vital interests' refers to matters of life and death, p 4.

[36] Data Protection Directive, para 6.05, Art 8(4).

discernible in large part from the general tenor of the Directive, which makes special provisions for, among others, national security, the investigation and prosecution of crime, legitimate journalistic activities, and research.[37]

6.08   In this last regard, the law creates a number of important protections for scientific researchers using data obtained from individuals. First, there is no requirement to notify a data subject as to the identity and purposes of those who will process the data, nor of the identity of any further recipients of those data when they have not been received directly from the data subject[38]—a requirement that must, normally, be met.[39] Moreover, EU Member States have a discretion to waive rights of access for individuals in the context of scientific research.[40] Second, the subject access provisions of the Directive do not apply when data are anonymised, for the law is concerned solely with personal data—that is, those from which an individual can be identified.[41] Even so, patients must still be informed when data are to be processed and the purposes to which this is likely to be put unless the research is being carried out on records that are so old that it would involve a disproportionate effort to contact patients in order to obtain their consent.

6.09   The 1998 provisions are all encompassing of identifiable personal information. Consent has a role to play but it does not emerge as a trump card. Indeed, some might argue that the broad and indistinct categories of justifications for processing without consent potentially weaken the protection that is afforded to informational privacy interests. The model, however, is, as always, a search for a balance and few could deny that privacy protection should sometimes bow to other interests. It is often forgotten that the essential purpose of the Data Protection Directive is to legitimate the free flow of information, not to prevent it. The devil is in the detail of determining which interests should be weighed in the balance and how far privacy should be compromised in any given case. The example of research is particularly apt. Some Member States, for example Denmark and Austria, allow research on secondary uses of patient data—that is, uses beyond those for which the data were first obtained—without the need for patient consent so long as the national data protection office gives prior approval.[42] The UK also has mechanisms for allowing research using patient data subject to rigorous review, and we discuss these later. It is to be noted with some regret, however, that a culture of caution has grown up around the workings of the Data Protection Act such that there is a widespread belief that the law now hinders research.[43] In the main, we consider this to be unfounded.[44] If anything fits

---

[37]   See further in England and Wales, the National Health Service Act 2006, s 251, discussed further later.

[38]   Data Protection Directive, para 6.05, Art 11(2).

[39]   For an extensive discussion of the issues and the idea of good governance of research, see N Sethi and G Laurie, 'Delivering proportionate governance in the era of eHealth: making linkage and privacy work together' (2013) 13(2–3) Med L Intl 168, available at: http://mli.sagepub.com/content/13/2-3/168.full.pdf+html.

[40]   Data Protection Directive, Art 13(2).   [41]   Data Protection Directive, Recital 26.

[42]   See the reports of the European Commission Article 29 Data Protection Working Party which is charged with monitoring the data protection provisions throughout Europe: http://ec.europa.eu/justice/data-protection/article-29/index_en.htm.

[43]   J Peto et al., 'Data protection, informed consent and research' (2004) 328 Brit Med J 1029. For an ambitious proposal to tackle this phenomenon, see Academy of Medical Sciences, *Personal Data for Public Good: Using Health Information in Medical Research* (2006). For a pragmatic and principled model, see G Laurie and N Sethi, 'Towards principles-based approaches to governance of health-related research using personal data' (2013) 1 Euro J Risk Reg 43.

[44]   Notwithstanding our own views, the draft proposal for a Data Protection Regulation has caused much consternation about the likely negative impact on (medical) research: Regulation of the European Parliament and the Council on the protection of individuals with regard to the processing of personal data

the case, then it is the common law of confidence, or interpretations of it, which might act in such a way rather than the provisions of the Data Protection Act 1998. This is in part because the common law and statutory provisions must be read together and the two do not offer entirely the same levels of protection. Furthermore, and as is often the case with the common law, the contours of the action for breach of confidence have been shown to be far more flexible than those laid down by instruments of Parliament.

RELAXATION OF THE RULE

6.10 All the classic codes of practice imply some qualification of an absolute duty of professional secrecy. Thus, the Hippocratic Oath has it: 'All that may come to my knowledge ... which ought not to be spread abroad, I will keep secret', which clearly indicates that there are some things which *may* be published. The Declaration of Geneva modifies this prohibition to: 'I will respect the secrets which are confided in me' and the word 'respect' is open to interpretation. The GMC, while always emphasising its strong views as to the rule dictating professional secrecy, still lists a number of specific possible exceptions to the rule which provide a sound basis for discussion.[45]

CONSENT TO PUBLISH

6.11 The first, and most easily recognisable, exception is when the patient, or his or her legal proxy, consents to a relaxation of secrecy. The situation is simple when viewed from the positive angle. A positive consent to release of information elides any obligation to secrecy owed by the person receiving that consent;[46] equally, an explicit request that information should not be disclosed is binding on the doctor save in the most exceptional circumstances—a matter which is of major concern in relation to communicable disease.[47] Note, however, that, even granted the consent of a patient, a health care professional (HCP) is not absolved of fair processing requirements under the Data Protection Act 1998.[48]

and on the free movement of such data (General Data Protection Regulation), Brussels, 25 January 2012, COM(2012) 11 final. Draft Arts 81 and 83 are designed to be more supportive of health-related research using data, and the version approved by the European Council in June 2015 is far more favourable that the initial 2012 proposal. Final agreement could be reached by the end of 2015. Updates can be followed here: https://www.huntonregulationtracker.com/.

[45] *Confidentiality*, n 17. These are grouped under the headings of: (a) disclosures required by law; (b) disclosures with consent; (c) the public interest; (d) disclosures about patients who lack capacity to consent; (e) sharing information with a patient's partner, carers, relatives or friends; (f) genetic and other shared information; and (g) disclosure after a patient's death.

[46] *C v C* [1946] 1 All ER 562. Note that this is an unusual, and old, divorce case.

[47] See paras 6.27–6.39 et seq. The GMC also considers a request by a patient before death to maintain confidentiality after death as an important factor in favour of a strong continuing professional duty: n 17, para 30. For a recent decision upholding confidentiality in a familial dispute about genetic information and putative duties of disclosure, see *ABC v St George's Healthcare NHS Foundation Trust* [2015] EWHC 1394 (QB); [2015] PIQR P18; [2015] Med LR 307. We discuss this further at para 6.51.

[48] For an important contribution as to the conflict of the Act with the public health interest, see J Smith, 'Patient confidentiality and consent to publication' (2008) 337 BMJ 589 and associated commentaries at pp 608–10. The paper also contains some interesting observations on the publication of anonymised case reports. On public interest generally, see MJ Taylor, 'Health research, data protection, and the public interest in notification' (2011) 19(2) Med Law Rev 267.

Sharing Information with Others Providing Care

6.12 The position is not so clear when looked at from the negative aspect—that is, when the patient has neither consented to nor dissented from disclosure—and it may, indeed, be frankly unsatisfactory. How many patients know whether the person standing with the consultant at the hospital bedside is another doctor, a social worker, or just an interested spectator? Would they have consented to their presence if they had been informed? The consultant may be responsible if, as a result, there is a breach of confidence—but this is small consolation to the patient who feels that his or her rights have been infringed. What patient at a teaching hospital outpatient department is likely to refuse when the consultant asks, 'You don't mind these young doctors being present, do you?'—the pressures are virtually irresistible and truly autonomous consent is well-nigh impossible, yet the confidential doctor–patient relationship which began with his general practitioner has, effectively, been broken.

6.13 It is obvious that such technical breaches must be, and generally are, accepted in practice—a modern hospital cannot function except as a team effort and new doctors have to be trained, the return for a technical loss of privacy being access to the best diagnostic and therapeutic aids available.[49] The GMC recognises this in permitting the sharing of information with other practitioners who assume responsibility for clinical management of the patient and, to the extent that the doctor deems it necessary for the performance of their particular duties, with other HCPs who are collaborating with the doctor in his or her patients' management.[50] An implication cannot, however, be taken for granted—especially as to the particular *need* for the information to be imparted. In *Cornelius* v *De Taranto*,[51] for example, the question of whether consent had been given to the referral of a patient to a consultant was disputed; what was clear, however, was that there was no justification for including information in the referral note that had no therapeutic relevance. It was confirmed, moreover, that it is the doctor's responsibility to ensure that those entitled to information appreciate that it is being imparted in strict professional confidence.[52] The doctor's duty is thereby restricted in a reasonable way; it is difficult to see how he can be expected to carry the onus for any subsequent actions by his associates. Once again, common law and the Data Protection Act must be read together. The guidance from the Information Commissioner's Office in respect of using and disclosing health data takes a pragmatic approach in deeming there to be implied consent to processing data for *essential* health services from patients who present for and accept care.[53] While this also applies to the administration of records and to clinical audit, it does not apply to the use of data for clinical research.[54]

---

[49] See, the Code of Practice for contractors to the NHS: Department of Health, *Confidentiality and Disclosure of Information: General Medical Services, Personal Medical Services and Alternative Provider Medical Services Code of Practice* (2013).

[50] *Confidentiality*, n 17, paras 7 and 25–31, although the guidance emphasises the importance of informing patients of the fact that information will be shared for both care and other reasons, such as service planning or medical research.

[51] (2001) 68 BMLR 62, CA.   [52] (2001) 68 BMLR 62, CA.

[53] *Use and Disclosure of Health Data*, n 35.

[54] See also the Article 29 Working Party Opinion on consent, n 34, that states that consent must be freely given, specific, informed, and explicit. If these requirements are not met data cannot lawfully be processed using consent as the legitimating basis. Note, this does not mean that the data cannot be processed, simply that consent cannot be the basis and some other, such as public interest, must be found.

THE PATIENT'S INTERESTS

6.14 It is ethical to break confidentiality without a patient's consent when it is in his or her own interests to do so and when it is undesirable on medical grounds or seriously impracticable to seek such consent. The recipient of the information may be another HCP as earlier, or a close relative or, as in a case where the doctor suspects that the patient is a victim of neglect or physical or sexual abuse, an unrelated third party[55]—but it remains the doctor's duty to make every reasonable effort to persuade the patient to allow the information to be given, and to make clear to the third party that the information is given in confidence. When these situations occur, decisions rest, by definition, on clinical judgement—a properly considered clinical decision cannot be *unethical* whether it proves legally right or wrong and, in the event of action being taken on the basis of breach of confidence, the fact that it was a justifiable breach would offer a complete defence both in the civil courts and before disciplinary proceedings of the GMC.[56] The GMC does, however, stress the need for caution when the patient has insufficient understanding, by reason of immaturity, of what the treatment or advice being sought involves; we return to this aspect later in the chapter.[57]

THE DOCTOR IN SOCIETY

6.15 Insofar as it rests on subjective definitions, the doctor's overriding duty to society represents what is arguably the most controversial permissible exception to the rule of confidentiality. Society is not homogeneous, but consists of groups amenable to almost infinite classification—regional, political, socio-economic, by age, and so on. It follows that what one person regards as a duty to society may be anathema to another. Individual doctors are bound to weigh the scales differently in any particular instance while, in general, all relative weighting must change from case to case—there is, for example, a great deal of difference in respect of confidentiality between being stung by a bee and suffering from venereal disease. While it is clear that no hard rules can be laid down, some aspects of this societal conflict are sufficiently important to merit individual consideration.

6.16 The most dramatic dilemma is posed by the possibility of violent crime. What is the doctor to do if he knows his patient has just committed rape—particularly if there is evidence that this is but one of a series of attacks? Perhaps even more disconcertingly, what if it becomes apparent that his patient is about to commit such an offence? Statute law is helpful here only in a number of negative senses—the Data Protection Act permits the processing of data to assist in the detection and prosecution of crime[58] and legislation establishing professional bodies provided likewise.[59] Common law may appear less clear-cut. There is case law to the effect that the doctor need not even assist

---

[55] For an interesting discussion of possible liability for failure to report suspected abuse, see *C v Cairns* [2003] Lloyd's Rep Med 90, QB. Note too, the GMC Guidance states that:

> If a patient's refusal to consent to disclosure leaves others exposed to a risk so serious that it outweighs the patient's and the public interest in maintaining confidentiality, or if it is not practicable or safe to see patient's consent, you should disclose information promptly to an appropriate person or authority. You should inform the patient before disclosing the information, if practicable and safe, even if you intend to disclose without their consent (n 17, para 55).

[56] On which, see Chapter 1.   [57] See paras 6.44–6.46.   [58] Data Protection Act, s 29.
[59] See *General Dental Council v Savery* [2011] EWHC 3011; (Admin); [2012] Med LR 204.

the police by answering their questions concerning his patients, although he must not give false or misleading information.[60] The obligation on the prosecution to disclose to the defence all unused material which might have some bearing on the offences charged has also caused some difficulty for police surgeons. Generally speaking, an accused gives consent to disclosure of specific information only. Other information may, however, come to light during the course of an examination; once this is in their notes, the police may feel it their duty to include it in their 'disclosure', despite the fact that there is no consent to their so doing. The police surgeon may, therefore, feel it his or her ethical imperative to conceal his or her knowledge—but the decision must, at times, be difficult to make.

6.17 Broadly, the justification for disclosure in such cases rests with the doctrine of the public interest as applied to medicine. This crystallised in the case of *W* v *Egdell*.[61] Here, a prisoner in a secure hospital sought a review of his case with a view to transfer to a regional secure unit. His legal representatives secured a report from an independent consultant psychiatrist that was, in the event, unfavourable to W; as a result, the application for transfer was aborted. W was, however, due for routine review of his detention and the psychiatrist, becoming aware that his report would not be included in the patient's notes, feared that decisions would be taken on inadequate information with consequent danger to the public. He therefore sent a copy of his report to the medical director of the hospital and a further copy reached the Home Office; W brought an action in contract and in equity alleging breach of a duty of confidence. The trial judge, Scott J, considered that, in the circumstances:

> The question in the present case is not whether Dr Egdell was under a duty of confidence; he plainly was. The question is as to the breadth of that duty.[62]

Attention was drawn to the advice of the GMC as to the circumstances in which exception to the rule of confidentiality is permitted. The GMC's guidelines which applied at the time were contained in the so-called '*Blue Book*'. Paragraph 79 stated:

> Rarely, cases may arise in which disclosure in the public interest may be justified, for example, a situation in which the failure to disclose appropriate information would expose the patient, or someone else, to a risk of death or serious harm.

6.18 Scott J based his conclusions on broad considerations—that a doctor in similar circumstances has a duty not only to the patient but also to the public and that the latter would require him to disclose the results of his examination to the proper authorities if, in his opinion, the public interest so required; this would be independent of the patient's instructions on the point.

6.19 The Court of Appeal unanimously confirmed the trial judge's decision to dismiss the action but did so with rather more reservation—particularly as expressed in the judgment of Bingham LJ. The concept of a private interest competing with a public interest was rejected in favour of there being a *public* interest in maintaining professional duties

---

[60] *Rice* v *Connolly* [1966] 2 QB 414; [1966] 2 All ER 649 and more recently *A Health Authority* v *X and Others* [2001] 2 FLR 673; (2001) 61 BMLR 22. But, see the specific position in respect of acts of terrorism, discussed below. The European Court of Human Rights (ECtHR) has confirmed, in contrast, that it is not a breach of the right to respect for private life for national law to require doctors to disclose records to police authorities provided that each person in receipt of the information is under a duty to continue to respect the individual's privacy: *Z* v *Finland* (1997) 25 EHRR 371; (1997) 45 BMLR 107.

[61] [1990] Ch 359; [1990] 1 All ER 835.   [62] [1990] Ch 359 at 389; [1989] 1 All ER 1089 at 1102.

of confidence; the 'balancing' of interests thus fell to be carried out in circumstances of unusual difficulty. Doubts, which we share, were cast on the applicability of the provisions of the *Blue Book* (para 78(b)) to a doctor acting in the role of an independent consultant; disclosure would have to be justified under para 78(g) and, here, it was for the court, not the doctor, to decide whether such a disclosure was or was not a breach of contract. Moreover, there was no doubt that s 76 of the Mental Health Act 1983 showed a clear parliamentary intention that a restricted patient should be free to seek advice and evidence for specific purposes which was to be accepted as confidential. Only the most compelling circumstances could justify a doctor acting contrary to the patient's perceived interests in the absence of consent. Nevertheless, in the instant case, the fear of a real risk to public safety entitled a doctor to take reasonable steps to communicate the grounds of his concern to the appropriate authorities.

6.20 Looked at superficially, it is easy to view *Egdell* as a serious intrusion into the relationship of confidential trust between doctor and patient; it is equally possible to perceive the principle as emerging relatively unscathed. W's case was clearly regarded as extreme and, although we cannot exclude some concern, there is no evidence in the judgment that the courts would condone a breach of confidence on less urgent grounds. The danger, then, is that what is acceptable medical activity—or what are regarded as extreme circumstances—can only be delineated retrospectively. In *R v Crozier*,[63] a psychiatrist called by the accused, concerned that his opinion should be available to the court, apparently handed his report to counsel for the Crown; the now sentenced accused appealed on the grounds that the breach of confidentiality between doctor and patient had denied him the opportunity of deciding whether medical evidence would be tendered on his behalf. The Court of Appeal again thought that there was a stronger public interest in the disclosure of the psychiatrist's views than in the confidence he owed to the appellant; the psychiatrist was found to have acted responsibly and reasonably in a very difficult situation. But what if a doctor acts unreasonably in such circumstances? The damage to the patient is done and he will get little satisfaction from the fact that the doctor is censured; it is surely a thoroughly paternalistic practice that should be carefully restrained.

HUMAN RIGHTS AND THE ACTION FOR BREACH OF CONFIDENCE

6.21 The House of Lords considered the state of the breach of confidence action post-Human Rights Act in *Campbell v Mirror Group Newspapers Ltd*.[64] Although great play was made in the House of Lords that it was the complainer's medical status that was particularly in issue, *Campbell* is not strictly within the common scenario of 'medical confidentiality' insofar as no medical practitioner was involved in its disclosure. However, the case demonstrates a number of important points which would clearly influence the courts' approach to such a breach; it, therefore, merits consideration in depth. The circumstances were that an internationally renowned supermodel accepted that she had previously lied publicly about her being addicted to drugs and did not seek to prevent publication of the fact. She did, however, bring an action in breach of confidence for the publication of additional details of her therapy and of photographs taken of her, covertly, in the street as she left her clinic; it was claimed that these acts interfered with her right to respect for private life (Art 8 of the European Convention on Human Rights (ECHR)). The defendant, in

[63] (1990) 8 BMLR 128.   [64] [2004] 2 AC 457; [2004] 2 All ER 995.

turn, argued the case for freedom of expression (Art 10 ECHR) and for the public interest in publishing the materials in order to correct the claimant's earlier untrue statements.[65] But how were these rights and freedoms to be balanced in the shadow of the Human Rights Act? Lord Hope remarked that the language of the breach of confidence action had now changed from a balance of public interests to a balance of Article rights—but he still doubted whether 'the centre of gravity has shifted'. Furthermore, he considered that the balancing exercise is essentially the same but that it is, now, 'more carefully focused and penetrating'.[66]

6.22 Even so, the focus is now notably on the underlying values that support respect for private life—values based on privacy and personal autonomy—rather than on the need for a confidential relationship, as was previously the case.[67] Second, the focus of such a claim, and the test to be applied as to whether a sound cause of action arises, lies not within the conscience of the receiver of the information but, rather, on the reasonable expectation of privacy that the subject of the information might have.[68] Moreover, we now have a clearer idea of how the process of considering competing claims to control confidential information should be managed. The entire House agreed with Lord Hope that the court must, first, ask if Art 8 is engaged. If it is, then a balance of considerations, applying a proportionality test, is to be undertaken as between the respective claims under Arts 8 and 10.

6.23 In determining whether the threshold has been crossed on Art 8, the court will ask, 'Was the claimant entitled to a reasonable expectation of privacy in all the circumstances?', and this can be answered in one of two ways: (i) was the matter 'obviously private'; or, if it was not, (ii) 'would disclosure be highly offensive to a reasonable person'?[69] If Art 8 interests fall to be protected, then the approach to the balance with other interests is, once again, twofold: (i) does publication pursue a legitimate aim; and (ii) are the benefits achieved by publication proportionate to the harm to privacy?[70]

6.24 Some questions arise from this. First, what is 'obviously private'? In the instant case, the majority held that the details in question, being sensitive medical details, were obviously private, and doubtless many would agree.[71] Other suggested examples include information about personal relationships and finances. Such a visceral test may at first disturb those is search of certainty, yet it reflects our intuitive responses to many privacy claims. The second (alternative) criterion places a far more problematic obstacle in the path of a claimant, requiring that disclosure be '*highly* offensive'—which, again, remains undefined. But the fundamental point is that the relevant perspective is that of the subject

---

[65] Campbell also claimed compensation for violation of the provisions of the Data Protection Act 1998, s 13, to which the defendant claimed the public interest exception under s 32.

[66] *Campbell*, n 64, per Lord Hope, at para 86.

[67] See *A-G v Guardian Newspapers Ltd (No 2)* [1990] AC 109.

[68] On this, see *Murray v Express Newspapers plc* [2008] 3 WLR 1360; [2008] 2 FLR 599.

[69] In articulating this, Lord Hope borrowed from Australian and US concepts; most interestingly, the US approach requires that disclosure also must be of legitimate concern to the public: *Campbell*, n 64 at para 94. He considered the Australian test from *Australian Broadcasting Corporation v Lenah Game Meats Pty Ltd* (2001) 185 ALR 1 which asks whether disclosure would 'give substantial offence to A, assuming that A was placed in similar circumstances and was a person of ordinary sensibilities', *Campbell*, n 64, paras 92–4.

[70] For a recent consideration of 'reasonable expectation' by the Supreme Court (albeit not in the medical context), see *Re JR38's Application for Judicial Review* [2015] UKSC 42; [2015] 3 WLR 155, also citing *R (Catt) v Association of Chief Police Officers of England, Wales and Northern Ireland (Equality and Human Rights Commission intervening)* [2015] UKSC 9, [2015] 2 WLR 664.

[71] Lady Hale points out, however, that not all medical details will necessarily be private: *Campbell*, n 64, para 157. But see now, *W, X, Y and Z v Secretary of State for Health et al* [2015] EWCA Civ 1034.

of the disclosure—in this case, the celebrity. The House of Lords confirmed that public figures are entitled to respect for their privacy, and that the mere fact of being a public figure—even one who has courted publicity—does not automatically create a public interest in publishing private details. Nonetheless, it was also stated that '... a person's right to privacy may be limited by the public's interest in knowing about certain traits of her personality and certain aspects of her private life'.[72] In the final analysis, the House of Lords held that Campbell's privacy had indeed been infringed. While there was a public interest in correcting the celebrity's previous lies,[73] this did not extend to the publication of the additional details about her therapy or the photographs and captions drawing attention to her problems. The balance fell in favour of the appellant because it could not be shown that the publication in question was *in the public interest*.

6.25 Despite this helpful ruling from our then highest court, the common law public interest exception to the duty of confidence remains frustratingly ill-defined. *Egdell* confirms that a threat of physical harm to third parties clearly justifies a breach, as will reasonable assessments by doctors that such a threat may be founded on a person's state of health— an obvious example is the need to report a sick patient to the Driver and Vehicle Licensing Authority (DVLA) regarding his or her fitness to drive. Even this, however, may not be straightforward as is shown by an example reported from New Zealand. There, a bus driver underwent a triple coronary bypass operation and was subsequently certified as fit to drive by his surgeon. His general practitioner, however, asked that his licence to drive be withdrawn and, furthermore, warned his passengers of their supposed danger. The practitioner's activities resulted in a report to the Medical Practitioners' Disciplinary Committee and a finding that he was: 'guilty of professional misconduct in that he breached professional confidence in informing lay people of his patient's personal medical history'. Dr Duncan sought judicial review of this decision. The High Court accepted the propriety of breaching medical confidentiality in cases of clear public interest, but refused the application on grounds which can be summed up: 'I think a doctor who has decided to communicate should discriminate and ensure the recipient is a responsible authority.'[74] Seldom can there have been a case which demonstrates the 'need to know' principle so forcibly.

6.26 Access to patient records in order to carry out internal and external investigations regarding the proper discharge of health care responsibilities can also be justified on this basis[75] and, beyond these specific examples, a few general parameters can be laid down. We recall the classic dictum of Lord Wilberforce in *British Steel Corporation* v *Granada Ltd*[76] in which he drew the crucial distinction between what is *in the public interest* and that which the *public is interested in*—journalists take note! Furthermore, a disclosure

---

[72] *Campbell*, n 64, per Lord Hope, para 120, citing the Supreme Court of Canada in *Aubry* v *Les Editions Vice-Versa Inc* [1998] 1 SCR 59, paras 57–8. See also the ECtHR in *von Hannover* v *Germany* (2005) 40 EHRR 1 and more recently as to public figures and their expectations of privacy *AAA* v *Associated Newspapers* [2012] EWHC 2103 (QB).

[73] *Campbell*, n 64, as per Lord Nicholls at para 24, Lord Hope at para 117, Lady Hale at para 151, and Lord Carswell at para 163.

[74] *Duncan* v *Medical Practitioners' Disciplinary Committee* [1986] 1 NZLR 513 at 521, per Jeffries J.

[75] *A Health Authority* v *X and Others* [2001] 2 FLR 673; (2001) 61 BMLT 22. Statutory obligations of disclosure are, by definition, more clear-cut, as we discuss later. See too *Re General Dental Council's Application* [2011] EWHC 3011 (Admin); [2012] Med LR 204 in which it was confirmed that the Council was lawfully entitled to pass on patient records, even without consent, to its Practise Committee and investigatory body when exploring instances of insurance fraud with respect to its members and patient treatment.

[76] [1981] AC 1096 at 1168.

should only occur where it is *necessary* to achieve the public interest in question, when there is a *reasonable likelihood* that it can do so, and when the disclosure is to those persons or agencies who can further that interest. The onus of justification is placed firmly on the shoulders of the HCP.[77] Within the framework of human rights, the then House of Lords confirmed that the correct approach if an individual's human rights are engaged by conduct involving disclosure of confidential information is to ask (i) whether the disclosure pursues a legitimate aim, such as the protection of the rights and interests of others or freedom of expression, and (ii) whether the benefits achieved by disclosure are proportionate to the harm which might be done by the interference with an individual's privacy rights? If so, then the disclosure will be lawful.[78] In *W v M (An Adult Patient),*[79] the Court of Protection gave guidance on the kinds of factors that should be taken into consideration when determining how far details of medical cases involving vulnerable patients can be reported. The instant case involved the lawfulness of withholding artificial feeding and hydration from a patient in a minimally conscious state, a matter of clear public interest and whose substance we discuss later. For present purposes, the question was how much of the circumstances could be reported. The resultant guidance highlights the following factors: (i) the general rule is that hearings should take place in private unless there is good reason to deviate; (ii) the balance of consideration is as between the right to respect for private life and the right to freedom of expression;[80] and (iii) this could include wider considerations such as whether other Convention rights are engaged (e.g., fair trial), the rights and interests of family members, the nature and strength of evidence of harm, and the fact that the public interest is most often likely only to extend to the general medical issues and not the private circumstances of the patient; equally, there is a public interest in the workings of the Court of Protection being more widely understood. On such a balance, the prohibition against disclosure in the instant case was upheld.[81]

CONFIDENTIALITY AND HIV INFECTION

6.27 The spread of the human immunodeficiency virus (HIV) has given rise to a host of problems related to confidentiality.[82] Sexually transmitted infections are not new to the medico-legal arena, but the HIV/AIDS complex can be set apart for several reasons—prominent among which are its relatively specific sexual connotation, together with its social stigma. Those who are found to be HIV positive may be disadvantaged in a number of practical ways

[77] Medical research is clearly a matter of public benefit but we discuss this as a separate aspect at paras 6.57 et seq.

[78] *Re Attorney General's Reference (No 3 of 1999)* [2009] UKHL 34; [2009] 2 WLR 142.

[79] [2012] 1 WLR 287; [2011] 4 All ER 1295.

[80] Support was given to the dictum of Lord Steyn in this regard in *Re S (A Child) (Identification: Restriction on Publication)* [2004] UKHL 47; [2005] 1 AC 593: 'First, neither article has as such precedence over the other. Secondly, where the values under the two articles are in conflict, an intense focus on the comparative importance of the specific rights being claimed in the individual case is necessary. Thirdly, the justifications for interfering with or restricting each right must be taken into account. Finally, the proportionality test must be applied to each. For convenience I will call this the ultimate balancing test' at para 17.

[81] Cf, *A Healthcare NHS Trust v P* [2015] EWCOP 15; [2015] COPLR 147 ordering disclosure to the press of the identity of an incapacitated individual when a reporting restriction order was applied for, and in the interests of transparency. Note, however, any further disclosure by the press would be a contempt of court if the order were granted.

[82] See Pattenden, *The Law of Professional–Client Confidentiality* (2003), paras 20.28–20.37.

which were noted in Chapter 2 and to which we refer again later.[83] It is reported that one in three people living with HIV/AIDS has experienced discrimination;[84] all serve to fuel the concern which many such persons harbour as to the confidentiality of their status.[85]

6.28 Such concerns attract great sympathy, yet there are also social interests to be considered. The crucial dilemma here is whether relaxation of the confidentiality rule would lead to failure to seek advice and treatment and hence to the spread of the disease, or whether the imposition of absolute secrecy improperly denies others the opportunity to avoid the risk of exposure to infection or to take advantage of the benefits of early therapy where exposure has occurred.[86] Should a sexual partner be told of the risk if the patient him or herself declines to pass on the information? What is the situation if a person known to be infected is employed in circumstances in which he or she might expose others to the virus? The problem of confidentiality cannot, however, be settled by the balancing of conflicting private interests alone—the public health dimension has to be taken into account. HIV/AIDS is not, at present, a notifiable disease as we discuss in Chapter 2[87]—a dispensation which certainly helps to maintain confidentiality. Any public health 'risk' is justified on the ground that, in the conditions of everyday social contact, HIV is transmitted only with great difficulty and in very particular intimate circumstances. As a result, it is government policy, supported by the majority of informed opinion, that any departure from the strictest anonymity in respect of HIV-related information must be subject to intense scrutiny.[88]

6.29 The English courts long ago declared their hand in weighing the balance between a strongly supported public policy in favour of freedom of the press against the need for loyalty and confidentiality with particular reference to the hospital records of people living with HIV. In *X v Y*,[89] the names of two doctors being treated in hospital for AIDS were improperly disclosed; the health authority sought, and obtained, an injunction to prevent their publication by a newspaper. While holding that the health authority had not made out a case for forced disclosure of the source of the information, Rose J stated that such luck a second time was highly unlikely and that prison would be the probable consequence if the informer repeated his or her betrayal of confidence:

> The public in general and patients in particular are entitled to expect hospital records to be confidential and it is not for any individual to take it upon himself or herself to breach that confidence whether induced by a journalist or otherwise.[90]

6.30 The authority's action was not a 'cover-up' operation—the basic reasons underlying absolute confidentiality in AIDS-related cases should be applied irrespective of the patient's calling. The decision can be justified medically on the grounds that the risks of a

---

[83] See generally Chapter 4.   [84] See National AIDS Trust: http://www.nat.org.uk/.

[85] For an annual account of the prevalence of the disease in the UK, challenges, and ongoing concerns about stigma and confidentiality, see Public Health England, HIV: Surveillance, Data, and Management (2015), available at: https://www.gov.uk/government/collections/hiv-surveillance-data-and-management#research-and-analysis.

[86] Although it is too early to speak of a cure, supportive therapy is now very efficient, with prediction that people diagnosed today with HIV will have a life expectancy no different to the general population (assuming appropriate management of the condition), NHS Choices: http://www.nhs.uk/chq/Pages/3106.aspx?CategoryID=118&SubCategoryID=126.

[87] See British HIV Association, *Detention, Removal and People Living with HIV* (2009).

[88] For an early overview of the ethical position which is still valid today, see R Gillon, 'AIDS and medical confidentiality' (1987) 294 BMJ 1675.

[89] [1988] 2 All ER 648; (1992) 3 BMLR 1.

[90] [1988] 2 All ER 648 at 665; (1992) 3 BMLR 1 at 21, per Rose J.

well-counselled physician passing the disease to a patient are, at worst, slightly more than negligible.[91] This is, however, an area in which the media have been insatiable. In the 1990s, a rash of cases occurred in which the names of infected doctors were widely publicised in the press;[92] a number of letters from the health boards concerned testified to the fact that, given that the previous government policy required the boards to notify all patient contacts of such practitioners, it was virtually impossible to preserve anonymity.[93] Matters came to a head in the case of *H (a healthcare worker) v Associated Newspapers Ltd*.[94] This case was unlike any other insofar as the provisions of the Human Rights Act 1998 were in force at the time when the press sought either to name the health authority (N) for which H worked, or to disclose H's specialty and the approximate date when he became HIV positive. A fundamental tension of rights and interests therefore arose between, on the one hand, H's right to respect for his private life (Art 8) and, on the other, the right of the press to freedom of expression (Art 10). The issues were complicated by the fact that H, having received expert advice that the risks of exposure given his discipline were negligible, had challenged the existing government policy[95] that required a health authority to undertake a 'lookback exercise' to identify patients who had come into contact with HIV-positive health workers. He would not, therefore, grant access to his patient records and sought injunctory relief to prevent any disclosure of his identity, discipline, or the name of the health authority for which he worked. In defiance of an order that was given, the *Mail on Sunday* published a story from which clues to H's identity could be gleaned. The injunction was then varied to allow greater disclosure and a challenge was lodged in the Court of Appeal by H and N. In balancing the delicately poised issues surrounding the tensions between Arts 8 and 10, the Court of Appeal found some measure of support for both sides of the argument. First, the Court reiterated the strong public interest in maintaining the confidentiality of health workers infected with HIV—to do otherwise, it was held, would simply deter others from coming forward, and this could be in no one's interests. The injunction against naming H or N was, accordingly, upheld. However, the risk of H being thereby identified was insufficient to justify a continuing restriction on disclosure of his specialty—he was, in fact, a dentist. Such a constraint inhibited the airing of aspects of the debate which were of important public interest. Moreover, the Court recognised the public interest in the new policy guidelines on recontacting patients and, with this in view, ordered that H should hand over his patient records once new guidelines were in place (although these records should not be used without his permission or that of the Court).

6.31 It is interesting to note that, as a result, the government's subsequent guidance supported lookback exercises only in very rare circumstances.[96] A major factor in this decision,

---

[91] This is extremely rare. For example, at the turn of the century there were only two reported instances of patients being infected by health care workers during clinical procedures, and in only one of those was the transmission route clear, see F Lot, J C Seguier, S Fegueux, et al., 'Probable transmission of HIV from an orthopaedic surgeon to a patient in France' (1999) 130 Ann Int Med 1. Since then, only one further case has been officially reported, see Public Health England, The Management of HIV infected Healthcare Workers who perform exposure prone procedures (2014), p 4.

[92] See, e.g., the banner headlines in a quality newspaper: B Christie, 'Hunt for AIDS scare patients' *Scotsman*, 27 May 1993, p 1. It seems that the doctor's name was published by the paper despite the fact that the health board intended to preserve anonymity.

[93] Although this information need not be given 'face to face': *AB v Tameside and Glossop Health Authority* (1997) 35 BMLR 79; [1997] 8 Med LR 91.

[94] [2002] EWCA Civ 195; (2002) 65 BMLR 132.

[95] Health Service Circular Guidance on the Management of AIDS/HIV Infected Health Care Workers and Patient Notification (HSC 1998/226).

[96] Department of Health, *AIDS/HIV Infected Health Care Workers: Guidance on the Management of Infected Health Care Workers and Patient Notification* (2003).

beyond the scientific evidence of negligible risk in most cases, was the disproportionate negative public effect that previous exercises have had by way of unduly distressing sectors of the public. And, once again, the importance of maintaining the confidentiality of those with HIV was recognised.[97] Since then the UK Advisory Panel for Healthcare Workers Infected with Bloodborne Viruses (UKAP) has been established to advise on such matters. Any patient notification exercise would now only be contemplated if there was a viral load above a certain high threshold and on a case-by-case basis after advice from the UKAP.[98]

6.32 Anyone infected with HIV constitutes an undoubted danger to his or her sexual partner(s), although the risk of transmission depends upon the nature of the sexual activity, the frequency and diversity of exposure, good control of infection with antiretrovirals, and the extent to which precautions are taken. Counselling of HIV cases includes such information routinely, and patients are advised as to the need to disclose their status to those whom they might have put at risk of infection. It is unsurprising that there will be some patients who are not prepared to do so nor, indeed, to inform their general practitioners; the doctor is then faced with the problem of whether he or she, him- or herself, should inform those with 'a need to know'.

6.33 The GMC withdrew its specific guidance on serious communicable diseases in November 2006.[99] These complex issues now fall under its general guidance on confidentiality and consent, although the confidentiality guidelines were subject to a public consultation in 2008 and revised in 2009. As part of this process, the GMC issued draft supplementary guidance thus:

> You may disclose information to a known sexual contact of a patient with a serious sexually transmitted disease if you have reason to think that the patient has not informed that person, and cannot be persuaded to do so. In such circumstances you should tell the patient before you make the disclosure, whenever it is practicable and safe to do so. You must be prepared to justify a decision to disclose personal information without consent.... You must not disclose information to anyone, including relatives who have not been, and are not, at risk of infection.[100]

6.34 Thus, passing information to a patient's spouse or other sexual partner in the absence of consent is allowable so long as every effort has been made to persuade the patient to do so and there is a serious and identifiable risk to a specific individual. The GMC concludes that the responsibility for any action taken is entirely that of the individual doctor—which tells us nothing as to how to construct that responsibility.

6.35 Despite the prima facie breach of confidence that such disclosure would entail, a court would almost certainly balance the interests involved and hold that disclosure was

---

[97] Note also, a failure to disclose adequate information with respect to one's risks or past history can lead to removal from the medical register (in this case relating to Hepatitis B infection): see *Saha v General Medical Council* [2009] EWHC 1907 (Admin).

[98] Public Health England, The Management of HIV-infected Healthcare Workers who perform exposure prone procedures (2014), available at: https://www.gov.uk/government/uploads/system/uploads/attachment_data/file/333018/Management_of_HIV_infected_Healthcare_Workers_guidance_January_2014.pdf.

[99] GMC Serious Communicable Diseases (1997).

[100] Available at: http://www.gmc-uk.org/Confidentiality_disclosing_info_serious_commun_diseases_2009.pdf_27493404.pdf. And for a case study example, see: http://www.gmc-uk.org/guidance/ethical_guidance/confidentiality_serious_communicable_diseases.asp.

justified by the intention to protect others from a possibly fatal risk. It is difficult to imagine a court awarding damages to a claimant but there has been no decision directly in point taken in the UK. That having been said, the HCP would need to consider a number of unknown factors in reaching his or her decision to disclose: is there a real ongoing risk of infection—that is, will the partners continue in high-risk behaviour? Do they engage in such behaviour at all? Is the health status of the partner known—that is, does he or she already have the disease? Who has been at risk from whom? Perhaps the partner transmitted the condition to the doctor's patient. Is it excessively paternalistic to interfere in private relations? And, overarchingly, what effect will an unauthorised disclosure have on the primary relationship with the patient? Will this jeopardise care in the long term? The lesson is that no breach of confidence should be incurred lightly and any action to approach a third party must be justified in the clearest of terms. Doubts as to the nature and degree of risks would undoubtedly undermine the case for disclosure. It can be said, then, that, at best, there is a discretion on HCPs to disclose, but not, as yet, a legal duty to do so.[101]

6.36 Conversely, it seems that in some parts of the USA and Canada there is a general common law duty, and sometimes a statutory duty, to inform those at risk.[102] The *Tarasoff* decision,[103] which we discuss in Chapter 13, could be taken as a pointer. An Australian example reveals the complexities. In *PD* v *Harvey and Chen*,[104] the Supreme Court of New South Wales upheld a negligence claim by a woman (PD) against two HCPs who had mismanaged her care and that of her HIV-positive partner. The couple had attended for testing prior to their marriage and each expected that the other would be informed of their respective results. This, however, was prohibited by statute without express patient consent, and they were not told of this legal reality. PD tested negative but her partner (FH) did not—and PD was refused access to FH's results. At no point did either doctor discuss with FH the prospect of informing PD of his status. FH failed to attend a clinic and deceived PD as to his health status; she became HIV-positive. The Court held that the HCPs were negligent for not taking more steps to protect PD. Importantly, however, it was not part of the decision that either doctor should have approached PD to tell her of FH's results—to do so was expressly prohibited by statute. Nonetheless, they could have maintained better communication between themselves as to the state of play and kept fuller records, they could have better informed FH and PD of the realities of risk, they could have pursued FH for non-attendance at the clinic, and, ultimately, they could have reported the case to the Director-General of Health who *did* have the legal authority to communicate the risk to PD without breaching confidentiality. We see, then, that

---

[101] See, however, *Health Protection Authority* v *X* [2005] EWHC 2989, which is discussed in Chalmers, para 2.36, pp 72–4. Here the argument was made that a duty to disclose was incumbent on the Agency to disclose risk to an HIV-positive patient's sex partners; the judge declined to do so for want of 'rigorous adversarial argument'.

[102] In a number of US states, specific statutory provisions have historically sought to impose a duty of disclosure on HIV-positive persons to disclose their status to their partners: see J W Rose, 'To tell or not to tell: Legislative imposition of partner notification duties for HIV patients' (2001) 22 J Legal Med 107. For Canada see, M Vonn, 'British Columbia's "seek and treat" strategy: a cautionary tale on privacy rights and informed consent' (2012) 16 HIV/AIDS Policy and Law Rev 15. Also, Canadian HIV/AIDS Legal Network, *Privacy Protection and the Disclosure of Health Information: Legal Issues for People Living with HIV/AIDS in Canada* (2004) and 2012 guidance: available at http://www.aidslaw.ca. For a Canadian Supreme Court ruling on criminal aspects, see *R* v *Mabior* 2012 SCC 47 and *R* v *DC* 2012 SC 48.

[103] *Tarasoff* v *Regents of the University of California* 529 P 2d 55 (Cal, 1974); on appeal 551 P 2d 334 (Cal, 1976). Decisions following upon this include the contrasting cases of *Brady* v *Hopper* 751 F 2d 329 (1984) and *Peterson* v *State* 671 P 2d 230 (Was, 1983).

[104] [2003] NSWSC 487.

compromising confidentiality was contemplated only as a last resort; the case also makes the point that much can be done in operational terms to protect third-party interests.

6.37 A final curious twist to the topic emerged in the remarkable Californian case of *Reisner*.[105] A young girl had been exposed to HIV infection through the transfusion of tainted blood but neither she nor her parents were informed of this. Some years later she became intimate with a boyfriend, whom she infected with the virus. He raised a successful action for damages against the doctors for their failure to inform her, thereby subjecting him, as a foreseeable victim, to the risk of infection. This decision did not imply that the doctor had a duty to warn and it is not clear how a court might react to a similar situation in the UK where the inference of a duty to care in respect of endangered third parties is difficult to reconcile with existing notions. No duty to warn exists in the absence of a special relationship between the parties and it is difficult to see why the HIV/AIDS situation should constitute an exception to the general common law rule, in both England and Scotland, that there is no duty to rescue.[106] It is, however, possible that a doctor might even be held to have a *duty*—as opposed to mere justification—to warn (or at least protect) a third party *who was also his patient* as, in this case, the relationship could be sufficiently proximate to give rise to a duty of positive action.[107]

6.38 It is impossible to leave the subject of confidentiality in HIV infection without mention of the specific problem of prisons—the environment could have been designed for the spread of the condition and the consequences of disclosure of a positive status could be disastrous for the individual. A policy of confidentiality exists but, clearly, it is difficult to maintain in such a close and controlled environment. There has also been some limited purposeful breaching of confidentiality in respect of a 'need to know' on the part of the staff.[108] Such potentials for disclosure discourage voluntary testing and counselling and serve as barriers to effective public health measures. It has been shown that a guarantee of confidentiality results in a marked increase in identified positive subjects.[109] Such evidence tends to support the general national policy on confidentiality and HIV; at the same time, it cannot be denied that more prisoners are infected than are identified. The issue is, thus, delicately balanced and is, also, closely tied to the use of preventive measures such as the issue of condoms to prisoners—a policy that is only marginally compatible with strict confidentiality; the subject is, however, beyond the compass of this book.[110] In passing we should also note that the ECtHR has declared inadmissible a case from a prisoner who argued that the state's failure to institute a needle exchange programme with respect to HIV infection was a breach of human rights. In *Shelley v United Kingdom*,[111] the state

---

[105] *Reisner* v *Regents of the University of California* 37 Cal Rptr 2d 518 (1995). See, too, *Garcia* v *Santa Rosa Health Care Corp* 925 SW 2d 372 (1996).

[106] For further discussion which remains valid, see A McCall Smith, 'The duty to rescue and the common law' in M Menlowe and A McCall Smith (eds), *The Duty to Rescue* (1993), p 55. Cf, C Gavaghan, 'Dangerous patients and duties to warn: A European human rights perspective' (2007) 14 Euro J Health Law 113.

[107] For a continental European perspective, see B Ketels and T Vander Beken, 'Medical confidentiality and partner notification in cases of sexually transmitted infections in Belgium' (2012) 20(3) Med L Rev 399.

[108] M Beaupré, 'Confidentiality, HIV/AIDS and prison health care services' (1994) 2 Med L Rev, 149. The vexed question of the police's 'need to know' was discussed in J K Mason, 'Recording HIV status on police computers' (1992) 304 BMJ 995.

[109] S A M Gore and A G Bird, 'No escape: HIV transmission in jail' (1993) 307 BMJ 147.

[110] See *R* v *Secretary of State for the Home Department* (1999) *The Times*, 21 July and for a full exposition, admittedly in the context of HCV: *R (on the application of H)* v *Ashworth Hospital Authority* [2002] 1 FCR 206; (2002) 64 BMLR 124.

[111] (2008) 46 EHRR SE16.

had adopted a policy of providing disinfecting tablets but not a full exchange programme and the Court held that it was within the margin of appreciation to do so. While reiterating that prisoners do not forfeit their human rights by virtue of their deprivation of liberty, the Court did nonetheless point out that 'the manner and extent to which they may enjoy those other rights will inevitably be influenced by the context'.

6.39 An example of this, and one which also brings us back to confidentiality, is provided by the Scottish case of *HM Advocate* v *Kelly*.[112] Kelly had given a blood sample while in Glenochil prison as part of a research study into HIV prevalence in the institution. On discovering this, the prosecution sought, and received, a Sheriff warrant to gain access to confidential data from which to prove that the strain of virus with which Kelly was infected was also that contracted by his girlfriend. Serious concern has subsequently been raised as to the impact of such practices on uptake by research subjects in prisons.[113] It is not hard to see how such draconian measures in the name of one public interest may finish by thwarting another. Interestingly, the overall importance of medical confidentiality within the prison ambience has been boosted in the ECtHR. After the issue had run a turbulent course through the domestic courts, the Court held in *Szuluk* v *United Kingdom*[114] that a prisoner's medical correspondence attracted as much privilege as did that with his lawyer—and this despite the fact that, in the particular case, the breach of his Art 8 rights was confined to interference by the prison medical officer. The Scottish have similarly considered prisoners' human rights in *Beggs* v *Scottish Ministers*.[115]

CONFIDENTIALITY WITHIN THE FAMILY

6.40 Wider issues of societal privilege lie within the family; these include intra-familial violence which the doctor may be the first to recognise. The police are, in general, disinclined to interfere in cases of marital violence because of the unsympathetic reception they are likely to get from both sides in so doing. But this may not always be the case, and the doctor cannot be content to watch his patient suffer physical injury and mental trauma either separately or together. In the end, however, it is clear that an adult domestic partner of sound mind is entitled to their autonomy; she or he has the opportunity of reporting to the police or, often more usefully, can have access to one of the many voluntary shelters which operate. She now has considerable protection under the law.[116] All the doctor can effectively do is to advise, and in this he may be able to help by arranging for treatment of the offender—spousal abuse is markedly associated with alcoholism and neurotic symptoms in the abuser partner.

6.41 The position is different in the case of child abuse.[117] Parental autonomy must be forfeited on the grounds of impropriety while the doctor is covered, legally, by the doctrine of necessity, and, professionally, by the advice of the GMC that disclosure is justified in such

---

[112] *HM Advocate* v *Kelly* (23 February 2001, unreported), HCJ.

[113] C Dyer, 'Use of confidential HIV data helps convict former prisoner' (2001) 322 BMJ 633. Where there is not the likely impact on testing, or otherwise, compare S M Bird and A J Leigh Brown, 'Criminalisation of HIV transmission: Implications for public health in Scotland' (2001) 323 BMJ 1174 and J Chalmers, 'The criminalisation of HIV transmission' (2002) 28 JME 160.

[114] (2009) 108 BMLR 190.   [115] [2015] CSOH 98.

[116] Family Law Act 1996, Part IV, as amended and, now, in particular the Domestic Violence, Crime and Victims Act 2004, as also amended by its 2012 counterpart; see also Matrimonial Homes (Family Protection) (Scotland) Act 1981, as amended, and the Protection from Abuse (Scotland) Act 2001.

[117] See most recently Domestic Violence, Crime and Victims (Amendment) Act 2012.

circumstances.[118] By the same token, the courts recognise the fundamental importance in a social care setting of ensuring frankness from parents about what has happened to the child they have allegedly abused; it is within courts' discretion to refuse to order disclosure of reports containing parental statements to the police, and a range of factors have been laid down to consider when assessing such cases.[119]

6.42 In addition to legal problems, however, the doctor faces a clinical dilemma which, although less publicised, is of greater importance. The introduction of registers for infants at risk from violence and the obvious merit in nipping violence in the bud act as servo-mechanisms to one another.[120] There is a real possibility that truly accidental injuries are being misdiagnosed, with a consequent reluctance on the part of parents to seek help for fear of being 'branded';[121] children may, therefore, actually suffer despite the doctor's concern for their safety. A case misdiagnosed as child abuse will cause considerable distress for those accused;[122] but, equally, a missed case which ends in murder can bring great recrimination on the doctor.[123] The concern of the profession as to possible actions for defamation was certainly eased by the decision that a recognised caring authority may refuse to disclose the name of an informant.[124] In the end, however, such a right to or privilege of non-disclosure depends not so much on principles of confidentiality as on what lies in the public interest[125]—or, more particularly, in the child's interests.[126] Equally, the interests of justice mean that the interests of the child are not determinative.[127] Actions for libel and slander over childcare proceedings continue unabated; while absolute privilege does not attach to such sensitive communications, communications between the relevant authorities, in good faith, and with a view to acting in the best interests of the child, attract qualified privilege.[128] Judicial review proceedings challenging a decision to put a child on an 'at-risk' register will rarely succeed.[129] It has recently been established that the principles

---

[118] *Confidentiality*, n 17, paras 53–6. On duties of care around false allegations of abuse, see *JD and Others v East Berkshire Community Health NHS Trust and Others* [2005] UKHL 23.

[119] In *Re C (a minor) (care proceedings: disclosure)* [1997] Fam 76. The Court of Appeal has confirmed that this case remains the leading case in deciding disclosure matters, see *Re H (children)* [2009] EWCA Civ 704. On the public interest in facilitating sharing between agencies, see *Re X (Children) (Disclosure of Judgment to Police)* [2014] EWHC 278 (Fam); [2015] 1 FLR 1218; [2014] Fam Law 961. And in the case of publishing relevant details on fact-finding judgments in care proceedings, see *Wigan BC v Fisher* [2015] EWFC 34.

[120] For professional guidance, see Royal College of Paediatrics and Child Health, *Safeguarding in 2012: Views from the Frontline* (March 2012) as well as a raft of other publications at its website: http://www.rcpch.ac.uk/child-protection-publications. This should be read together with HM Government, *Working Together to Safeguard Children* (2015), available at: https://www.gov.uk/government/publications/working-together-to-safeguard-children--2.

[121] The ECtHR has held that a means of determining allegations of negligence in this respect against local authorities must be available: *Z v United Kingdom* [2001] 2 FLR 612; (2002) 34 EHRR 3, overturning *X and Others (minors) v Bedfordshire County Council* [1995] 2 AC 633; [1995] 3 All ER 353.

[122] See two 'at-risk register' cases: *R v Harrow London Borough Council, ex p D* [1989] 3 WLR 1239; *R v Hampshire County Council, ex p H* [1999] 2 FLR 359. Child protection records can legitimately be held for decades: *R (on the application of C) v Northumberland CC* [2015] EWHC 2134.

[123] In *Z (children) (Application for release of DNA profiles)* [2014] EWHC 1999 the court granted an order that the DNA profiles of children, whose mother had been murdered, could be released to the local authority, to cross-reference with blood found at the scene, to determine if their father committed the crime.

[124] *D v National Society for the Prevention of Cruelty to Children* [1978] AC 171; [1977] 1 All ER 589, HL.

[125] Contrast this with the non-medical case of *Interbrew SA v Financial Times Ltd* [2002] 1 Lloyd's Rep 542 (public interest in discovering iniquity overrode privilege against disclosing sources).

[126] Breach of confidence might, e.g., be needed in order to assist in tracing a missing child.

[127] *Lewisham LBC v D (Local Authority Disclosure of DNA Samples to Police)* [2010] EWHC 1238 (Fam); [2011] 1 FLR 895.

[128] *W v Westminster City Council and Others* [2005] 1 FCR 39.

[129] *R (on the application of A) v Enfield LBC* [2008] 2 FLR 1945; [2008] 3 FCR 329.

applying to (non)-disclosure of information about a child in a care context also apply to the adult who lacks capacity. Thus in *C v C (Court of Protection: Disclosure)*[130] guidance was handed down about the correct approach to disclosure of documents containing personal information in proceedings involving such an adult. The test to be applied is one of 'strict necessity' and the formulation of the question is all-important: not whether it was necessary to see information, but whether it was necessary that they not be seen. Thus, the birth mother of a vulnerable adult was not entitled to see all content of all reports pertaining to her estranged child with whom she now sought contact.

6.43 In *A (A Child) (Disclosure of Third Party Information)*,[131] the Supreme Court laid down the factors to be considered in determining whether the identity of a third party alleging child abuse, X, should be revealed in the entirety of circumstances. X alleged that a father was guilty of abuse of his daughter, as equally he had previously abused X, and that this should be known to the authorities and to the mother as current custodian. X, however, did not wish to be named. The Supreme Court held that the common law position and the human rights analysis aligned: it is a delicate balance of the relevant rights, here being Art 8 of the third party (including the effects of disclosure on her health) as well as the private and family life rights of the affected family, Art 3 of the child (in that the court could not act in a way that would subject her to further abuse), and Art 6 (the importance of a fair trial). In the event, the adverse impact on X was the only material factor against disclosure and this was significant. An order of disclosure fell far short of infringing her Art 3 rights, both because the state was pursuing important public interests and because she was under the supervision and care of a consultant physician and psychiatrist which would mitigate any injury. Moreover, and all other things considered, the disclosure was justified as necessary and proportionate. Every party's Art 8 rights were engaged, and the impact on X did not outweigh or justify the effects of non-disclosure and the interests of a fair trial. This did not mean, however, that X would have to appear in person. Other arrangements could be made, again militating against the strength of her claim.

6.44 Confidentiality between parent and child becomes further involved at teen age. Consent to treatment is discussed in detail in Chapter 4; in the present context, we are concerned only with confidentiality and, particularly, with the doctor's relationship with the family.[132] It is possible to conceive of other medical conditions which a minor might wish to conceal from his or her parents but, in practice, such conditions are likely to be limited to their sexual affairs. It is trite knowledge that young persons of both sexes do have intercourse and the doctor may be confronted by requests as to contraception or abortion by young girls or for treatment of venereal disease by minors of either sex.[133] It is therefore unsurprising that the leading case to address the question of minors' rights to confidentiality—*Gillick*[134]— should concern contraception and has, in fact, been discussed under that head.[135]

---

[130] [2014] EWHC 131 (COP); [2014] 1 WLR 2731; [2015] 1 FCR 135.

[131] [2012] UKSC 60; [2013] 2 AC 66; [2012] 3 WLR 1484.

[132] See J Loughrey, 'Medical information, confidentiality and a child's right to privacy' [2003] LS 510 and R Gilbar, 'Medical confidentiality in the family: The doctor's duty reconsidered' (2004) 18 (2) Internat J of Law, Policy & Fam 195.

[133] On capacity for sexual relations, see *IM v LM* [2014] EWCA Civ 37; [2015] Fam 61; [2014] 3 WLR 409.

[134] *Gillick v West Norfolk and Wisbech Area Health Authority* [1984] QB 581; [1984] 1 All ER 365; on appeal [1986] AC 112; [1985] 1 All ER 533, CA; revsd [1986] AC 112; [1985] 3 All ER 402, HL. For an overview and assessment see S O'Brien, 'Minors and refusal of medical treatment: a critique of the law regarding the current lack of meaningful consent with regards to minors and recommendations for future change' (2012) 7(2) Clinical Ethics 67. Contrast, E Cave 'Goodbye *Gillick*? Identifying and resolving problems with the concept of child competence' (2014) 34(1) Legal Studies 103.

[135] See paras 9.08 et seq.

6.45 The background to the *Gillick* decision is relatively simple, yet it represents the core of the case. As we have already suggested, contraception must be seen as sociologically preferable to abortion; even so, only a few young girls are likely to consent to their parents being told they are 'on the pill' and refusal to supply is unlikely to deter those who want sexual intercourse. On this basis, the doctor who supplies contraceptives on request to a girl under the age of 16 is performing a duty to society.[136] On the other hand, most would agree that parents have a right to know what is happening to their children and should, ideally, give consent to medical treatment irrespective of the minor's capacity to understand the complexities. It is, therefore, apparent that any entitlement to consent carries with it a simultaneous entitlement to confidentiality and vice versa. The House of Lords' solution of the problem is to be found in Lord Fraser's five criteria which have been recapitulated earlier[137] and which can be summarised as granting a right of confidentiality to the mature minor when the exercise of that right was in her best interests. It must, however, be emphasised that, throughout the case, an obligation was firmly imposed on the doctor to attempt to persuade the girl to inform her parents or to allow him to do so—that, in itself, constituting an important qualification of the normal rules of professional secrecy. Thus, despite the case seeming to represent a victory for the autonomy of youth, reliance on *Gillick* can still lead to unease on the part of both the doctor and the patient. On the one hand, the latter cannot know the former's intentions until *after* the consultation; on the other, the doctor must be prepared to justify his decision—but to whom and in what circumstances is left unstated. The decision to respect a minor's right to confidentiality may be a delicate one, and this is particularly so when drugs are prescribed. In one Scottish Fatal Accident Inquiry concerning a 14-year-old girl's death from an overdose of tricyclic antidepressants, a doctor's decision not to inform her parents of her treatment was considered to be perfectly correct. The patient's maturity was held to be such that her desire for confidentiality in relation to her parents had to be respected.[138]

6.46 The jurisprudence concerning the position of children and the proper respect due to their autonomy as to confidences remains disputed. From one perspective, we have the paternalistic stance of the House of Lords being repeated in *Re C (disclosure)*,[139] where the court agreed that it would be lawful to respect the child's wish that her mother not be informed of certain matters during care proceedings, but then expressly noted that the importance of maintaining confidentiality may 'decline' as circumstances change. Autonomy here is relative and subject to the overriding issue of best interests. In contrast, we have Munby J in *Torbay Borough Council v News Group Newspapers*[140] supporting the right of a mature minor (almost 17) to disclose to the press the details of her own teenage pregnancy, with or without parental approval. On one level these cases might seem distinguishable: the first is about maintaining and the second about ending confidentiality. At a deeper level, however, the core issue is how far we are willing to recognise emerging autonomy and whether we will go back on the deal.[141] The answer from the courts seems to

---

[136] Protection from criminal prosecution for a health care professional who acts to protect a child's interests in matters of sexual health or pregnancy is secured by statute: Sexual Offences Act 2003, s 14(2) and (3), and s 73.

[137] See para 4.77.

[138] *Inquiry into the Death of Emma Jane Hendry* (15 January 1998, unreported), Glasgow Sheriff Court.

[139] [1996] 1 FLR 797.   [140] [2004] 2 FLR 949; [2004] Fam Law 793.

[141] *In the Matter of X* [2002] JRC 202 the court upheld the right of the 16-year-old woman to refuse to authorise transfer of tissue from her aborted fetus to the police to determine paternity for the purposes of possible prosecution for unlawful sexual intercourse. This was so despite affidavits from the parents consenting to the procedure. Nonetheless, the court reiterated that its inherent jurisdiction meant that the refusal could be overridden in the child's best interests; in the instance case, however, the court was not convinced that those interests would be served by dismissing the refusal.

be—quite far. In *R (on the application of Axon) v Secretary of State for Health*,[142] the court applied the reasoning in *Gillick* to the confidentiality of abortion advice; furthermore, it rejected any claim that the failure to notify or consult parents in any way infringed their human rights.

6.47 The relationship that is longest established within the core family is that between the spouses—what are their mutual rights as to both the positive and negative aspects of confidentiality? If the treatment is for a medical condition, a married person has the same rights to confidentiality in respect of the spouse as in respect of anyone else and, since the Abortion Act 1967 refers only to medical indications, this must apply to abortion.[143] This can be implied also on legal grounds in that, since the husband has no right of veto either in Great Britain or in the USA,[144] he similarly has no right to information, and it is not hard to think of instances where disclosure of an abortion to the spouse could be construed as being malicious. *A fortiori*, the same reasoning would apply to a decision as to sterilisation (although this might nonetheless provide a ground for divorce).[145]

6.48 The conditions are not quite so clear, however, when treatment of an individual is not primarily based on medical considerations but, at the same time, affects the whole family. The familial nature of much genetic information means that both immediate and not-so-immediate family members may have an interest in knowing, or having access to, a relative's genetic data because of the implications that it might have for their own health or life decisions. We explore this far more fully elsewhere,[146] but the most important point for present purposes is to recognise the challenge which these realities pose to the existing legal regimes for protecting patient privacy. Two examples from the data protection domain illustrate this. First, the European Commission's Article 29 Data Protection Working Group—which is charged with monitoring and recommending necessary changes to European data protection law—has specifically stated that:

> To the extent that genetic data has a family dimension, it can be argued that it is 'shared' information, with family members having a right to information that may have implications for their own health and future life.[147]

But, as to the implications of this, the Group continues:

> The precise legal consequences of this argument are not yet clear. At least two scenarios can be imagined. One is that other family members could also be considered 'data subjects' with all the rights that flow from this. Another option is that other family members would have a right of information of a different character, based on the fact that their personal interests may be affected. However, in both scenarios further options and conditions would have to be considered to accommodate the various conflicts that are likely to arise between the different claims of family members, either to have access to information or to keep it confidential.[148]

---

[142] [2006] 2 WLR 1130; (2006) BMLR 96.

[143] J V McHale and J Jones, 'Privacy, confidentiality and abortion statistics: a question of public interest?' (2012) 38(1) J Med Ethics 31.

[144] Initially confirmed in *Paton v British Pregnancy Advisory Service Trustees* [1979] QB 276; [1978] 2 All ER 987, and in the USA in *Planned Parenthood of Southeastern Pennsylvania v Casey* 112 S Ct 2791 (1992).

[145] See Chapter 9 for further discussion.   [146] G Laurie, *Genetic Privacy* (2002).

[147] Article 29 Working Group Working Document on Genetic Data (2004), pp 8–9.

[148] Article 29 Working Group Working Document on Genetic Data (2004), pp 8–9.

6.49 Data protection law as currently drafted does not accommodate such claims easily.[149] Its focus on the individual as the 'data subject' perpetuates an atomistic view of how rights under the law are to be managed.[150] Nonetheless, recognition of the possible interconnectedness of family claims through genetic data has penetrated the judicial consciousness. In late 2003, the Supreme Court of Iceland adopted a purposive approach to the Icelandic data protection law (which is essentially an adoption of the 1995 EC Directive) in respect of its application to the ambitious Icelandic Health Sector Database (HSD) project. This project—of which we say more in Chapter 7—aims ultimately to link genetic data from the Icelandic people with other records, such as medical and genealogical, so as to create a powerful genetic research resource. The HSD was enabled by legislation from the Icelandic parliament (the Althing) but it has proved to be controversial from the beginning, not least because of its adoption of an opt-out scheme—that is, that all Icelanders are to be included in the project unless they expressly refuse. The case in point arose as an action to prevent transfer to the HSD of a deceased man's medical records to which his daughter laid claim. The enabling legislation provided grounds for such a transfer but no opt-out was available to the relatives of deceased persons. Moreover, the provisions of the data protection law did not apply to deceased persons.[151] The Supreme Court, however, held that personal information relating to the daughter herself could be derived from that of the father because of their genetic connection. Moreover, the Court held that the enabling legislation was unconstitutional because it breached Art 71(1) of the Icelandic Constitution which states that: 'Everyone shall enjoy freedom from interference with privacy, home and family life'—a clear reflection of Art 8(1) ECHR. This was, in part, because the sheer richness of the resource increased the risk that individuals could be identified by linkage. The implications of this ruling could be far-reaching through Europe in at least two respects, namely: (i) the meaning of 'personal data' under European data protection law—do all first generation family members, living or dead, have a say in the management of each other's data?; and (ii) the legality of human genetic databases—how far must researchers go in protecting personal privacy?[152]

6.50 The Article 29 Working Group delivered an Opinion on the meaning of 'personal data' in 2007, designed to assist Member States in the application of the Data Protection Directive. It will be recalled that 'personal data' are those from which an individual is identifiable, directly or indirectly, and includes any information 'relating to' the individual. The Article 29 Group elaborates on this. Information can 'relate to' a person *either* if the 'content' is about the person (for example, medical analysis clearly relates to the patient) *or* if the 'purpose' to which the information is to be put (or likely to be put) will affect a person *or* if the 'result' of use of the information has, or will have, an impact on a person's rights or interests.[153] Importantly, these should be read as alternatives not cumulatively.

---

[149] The draft Data Protection Regulation (2012, and subsequent iterations) does now include 'genetic data' as part of the definition of 'personal data' but does not—at the time of writing—offer any way out of the individualistic impasse. Member States are, however, at liberty to legislate on such data beyond the provisions of the European law.

[150] For discussion, and comment on the Australian position which has attempted to legislate on this point, see G T Laurie and J K Mason, 'Waxing and Waning: The Shifting Sands of Autonomy on the Medico-legal Shore' in C Stanton et al. (eds), *Pioneering Healthcare Law: Essays in Honour of Margaret Brazier* (Routledge, 2015), ch 2.

[151] This is also the case under the Data Protection Act 1998.

[152] For comment, see R Gertz, 'Is it "me" or "we"? Genetic relations and the meaning of "personal data" under the Data Protection Directive' (2004) 11 Euro J Health Law 231.

[153] Compare *Durant* v *Financial Services Authority* [2004] FSR 28 which caused consternation in holding that the individual must be the 'focus' of information before the protections of the Data Protection Act 1998 applied. See now, Information Commissioner's Office, *Data Protection Technical Guidance: Determining What is Personal Data* (2007).

Moreover, the Working Group acknowledges that the same information might relate to different persons but offers no concrete guidance on how this should be handled.[154] Taylor has recently argued that the law ought to recognise the possible claims of multiple data subjects and suggests that the means to resolve conflict can already be found within the Data Protection Directive, viz, through the exemptions from data protection responsibilities such as providing information about data processing to all subjects if this would represent a *disproportionate* and unjustified interference with the fundamental rights and freedoms of the primary data subject.[155] The practical consequence of this is that the law offers little assistance to the HCP acting as data controller: it can accommodate actions both to disclose or withhold information from relatives depending on whether the professional assesses there is just cause.

6.51   Within the UK, such arguments about wider claims arising from the genetic nature of data have recently been rejected by the High Court in *ABC v St George's Healthcare NHS Foundation Trust*.[156] The case involves a disclosure dilemma involving a high penetrant and predictive genetic condition, Huntington's disease, and whether it was lawful to breach confidentiality to a pregnant daughter to reveal a father's condition. We discuss this case fully at para 7.47, but for present purposes it is sufficient to say that the Court held a hard line in ruling (i) the law of confidence affords a discretion to disclose in justifiable circumstances, including the public interest, but imposes no duty to do so, and more particularly, (ii) it was not fair, just, and reasonable to impose a duty of care in negligence on clinicians to disclose in such circumstances.

6.52   Thus, at the end of the day, we must fall back on professional judgement and justification as to what might be a legitimate (or otherwise) interference with a patient's privacy interests. For these reasons it is important to explore the full range of possible interests and considerations at stake.

OTHER SPECIAL GROUPS

6.53   There are many special groups that can be conceived of as raising particular problems in relation to medical confidentiality—those which spring to mind most readily are accused persons, prisoners, and members of the armed forces. Accused persons are legally innocent and therefore have the same rights as any member of the public. The prevailing trend in England and Wales in the context of DNA samples was brought to an end with the ruling from the ECtHR in *S and Marper v United Kingdom*.[157] The argument here was made that there had been incremental encroachment of the law on the private lives of citizens in the name of expansion of the national DNA database.[158] The nadir was reached when it became possible in domestic law for the police to take and retain indefinitely samples and DNA profiles from persons arrested for, but never convicted of, offences. The ECtHR ruled against the UK holding that any retention of DNA material engages the Art 8 right to respect for an individual's private and family life and that the UK's blanket policy of

---

[154]   For discussion, see Pattinson and Beyleveld, n 20.

[155]   M J Taylor, *Genetic Data and the Law: A Critical Perspective on Privacy Protection* (2012), Chapter 5.

[156]   [2015] EWHC 1394 (QB); [2015] PIQR P18; [2015] Med LR 307.

[157]   (2009) 48 EHRR 50. *S and Marper* v *United Kingdom* was not applied in *Gaughran* v *Chief Constable of Northern Ireland* [2015] UKSC 29. The appellant appealed the refusal for judicial review of the indefinite retention of fingerprints, a photograph, and a DNA profile, following a conviction for driving with excess alcohol. This appeal was dismissed stating that this fell within the UK's margin of appreciation.

[158]   For a critical account see Nuffield Council on Bioethics, *Forensic Uses of Bioinformation* (2007).

retention was disproportionate and illegal. The law was accordingly in the Protection of Freedoms Act 2012 that requires destruction of data and samples taken from persons arrested and/or charged but not convicted of a serious offence at the end of a three-year period (with the possibility of one two-year extension). Samples relating to minor offences must be destroyed following acquittal or a decision not to pursue the charge.[159]

6.54 The doctor–patient relationship in respect of prisoners is complicated and confidentiality is best considered as part of the whole spectrum of prison medicine (see Chapter 2).[160] The relationship of medical officers in the armed forces to their individual patients is precisely the same as in civilian practice, with the proviso that the doctor's duty to society is accentuated when this is formulated as a duty to a fighting unit; eventually, the lives of many are dependent upon the health of individuals. There is, thus, a wider justification for disclosure than exists in civilian life and the serviceman has tacitly accepted this in enlisting; nevertheless, the principle of justification remains valid.

6.55 Doctors employed by companies or other institutions to act as medical advisers on staff health also occupy a special position.[161] A workplace doctor who is employed to carry out regular examinations on staff is bound by the terms of his or her contract to deliver information to the employer if this might have a bearing on the employer's business.[162] Moreover, such a doctor is not under a duty of care to a job applicant when assessing suitability for employment, even although it is reasonably foreseeable that the applicant might suffer economic loss if a careless error in assessment leads to the loss of a chance of employment.[163] It must now be stated explicitly before carrying out a pre-employment medical examination, or for fitness to work, that the results of that examination may be communicated to the employer and the written consent of the examinee should be obtained in the light of that information. Likewise, in the case of examinations carried out for insurance purposes, the doctor must obtain the positive agreement of the patient to waive the normal obligations of confidentiality within a 'need to know' formula.[164] In the absence of such agreement, it is unlikely that the doctor engaged in industrial or insurance medicine could justify, on either ethical or legal grounds, a breach of a patient's confidence on the grounds that he, the doctor, owed a duty as an employee to his employer.[165] The BMA has recently issued guidance to GPs about complying with Subject Access Requests (SARs) coming directly from insurance companies. The BMA has been aware of, and concerned about, this practice for quite some time whereby an insurer obtains consent from an applicant to seek access to their full medical record. The concern of the BMA is that this grants disproportionate access relative to the insurer's commercial

---

[159] The distinction between serious and minor offences turns on the meaning of qualifying offence, for which see the 2012 Act, Sch 1, part 1 20D(5) and 20G(15); Sch 1, Part 3, 18E(7).

[160] For a ruling upholding prisoners' human rights to respect for their medical correspondence with a specialist, see *Szuluk v United Kingdom* (2010) 50 EHRR 10.

[161] All medical professionals are now required to follow the Information Commissioner's Employment Practices Code (2011). See also, BMA, The Occupational Physician (2015). For comment, see J Tamin, 'What are "patient secrets" in occupational medicine practice? Privacy and confidentiality in "dual obligation doctor" situations' (2015) Med Law Inter, doi: 10.1177/0968533215587051.

[162] *Kapfunde v Abbey National plc and Daniel* (1998) 46 BMLR 176. See in the sports context, *West Bromwich Albion Football Club Limited v El-Safty* [2005] EWHC 2866 (QB).

[163] Confirmed in *Cheltenham Borough Council v Christine Susan Laird* [2009] EWHC 1253.

[164] At the present time a moratorium is in place in respect of accessing genetic test results, except in the most limited of circumstances; this has been extended on numerous occasions and currently will prevail until at least 2017: see further Chapter 7.

[165] See, generally, *Joint Guidelines from the British Medical Association and the Association of British Insurers* (2010).

needs and could be a breach of the Data Protection Act. The Information Commissioner's Office has agreed that this kind of practice is probably unlawful. Accordingly, the BMA now advises GPs to write to patients on receipt of a SAR from an insurer to reassure themselves—and the patient—of the implications of granting such a request.[166]

6.56 As a corollary, the European Court of Justice, for its part, has held that patients cannot be required to undertake medical tests against their will, nor can these be carried out clandestinely, to further an employer's interest in maintaining a healthy workforce.[167] This would be contrary to the right to respect for private and family life. But the irony is that there is no corresponding right not to be asked questions about one's health; indeed, in *X v Commissioner*, it was held to be legitimate for an employer to draw adverse inferences from a candidate's refusal to disclose health data. The employer could not be obliged to take the risk of recruiting an unhealthy candidate. This is something of a hollow view of privacy protection. It might well be thought that we are entitled to expect better.

FOR THE PURPOSES OF MEDICAL RESEARCH

6.57 Medical research is a matter of significant public interest. Ideally, patient consent to the use of their information in research should be obtained but this is not always possible or practicable.[168] Patient information may be disclosed if necessary for the purposes of a medical research project that has been approved by a recognised ethical committee or other authorising body.[169] The matter is included in the general discussion of medical research in Chapter 19.[170] For the present, we must note the fragility of these approaches and their susceptibility to political change and public disquiet. The delicate nature of the balance of interests has long been appreciated by governmental and regulatory bodies. Thus, we have the Department of Health stating over a decade ago that:

> when the public good that would be served by disclosure is significant, there may be grounds for disclosure [of patient information]. The key principle to apply is that of proportionality. Whilst it would not be reasonable and proportionate to disclose confidential information to a researcher where patient consent could be sought, if it is not practicable to locate a patient without unreasonable effort and the likelihood of detriment to the patient is negligible, disclosure to support the research might be proportionate.[171]

Similarly, the guidelines on medical confidentiality from the GMC emphasise the important public interests in epidemiology, research, and health surveillance that can be gained from further uses of patient data (i.e., uses of information other than those for which they were initially gathered). While stressing that consent from the patient to such uses should normally be sought, the GMC accepts that consent is not always possible or practicable and that it is possible (and justifiable) for doctors to disclose identifiable information to

---

[166] BMA, Focus on Subject Access Requests for Insurance Purposes (2015), available at: http://bma.org.uk/practical-support-at-work/gp-practices/service-provision/subject-access-requests-for-insurance-purposes.

[167] Case C-404/92P *X v Commission* [1994] ECR I-4737.

[168] See Wellcome Trust, *Towards Consensus for Best Practice: Use of Patient Records From General Practice for Research* (2009) and the GMC, *Confidentiality* (2009), n 17.

[169] On the data protection position see the guidance by the Information Commissioner's Office, n 35, ch 3.

[170] For a balanced discussion of the privacy issues see, W W Lowrance, *Privacy, Confidentiality and Health Research* (2012).

[171] Department of Health, *Confidentiality: NHS Code of Practice* (2003), para 34 and *Supplementary Guidance* (2010). See too Department of Health, NHS Information Governance: Guidance on Legal and Professional Obligations (2007), available at: http://systems.hscic.gov.uk/infogov/codes/lglobligat.pdf.

further such a 'positive' public interest so long as certain safeguards are respected. These include the fact that (i) it is necessary to use the information, (ii) it is not practicable to anonymise or code the information, and (iii) a cost–benefit analysis of the benefits/harms of disclosure is conducted. The advice of a Caldicott Guardian or similar expert adviser (e.g., data protection officer) should be sought, and, finally, if existing statutory routes for disclosure can be used then these should be preferred.[172] A review of the Caldicott Guardian scheme in 2013 added a new principle to the existing set, viz, that '…that the duty to share personal confidential data can be as important as the duty to respect service user confidentiality'.[173]

6.58 The Health and Social Care Act 2012 now makes it a clear duty of the Secretary of State to promote research on matters relevant to the health service.[174] The same Act established the Health and Social Care Information Centre which, inter alia, has duties to maintain standards, promote the core function of health services, and to develop a confidentiality code of practice accordingly.[175] All of this builds on statutory provision established by s 251 of the National Health Service Act 2006 which allows the Secretary of State to make provisions for the processing of patient medical data for medical purposes where (i) neither consent nor anonymisation are possible nor practicable, and (ii) when otherwise it would be a breach of confidence so to use those data.[176] The Health Research Authority has responsibility to administer these powers since 2013. Applications and proposals for research uses, together with providing advice on draft regulations are delegated to the Confidentiality Advisory Group (CAG).[177] A similar function has historically been performed in Scotland by the Privacy Advisory Committee (PAC), which was an independent ad hoc body, established in the early 1990s, to advise on these sensitive issues. It was replaced in 2015 by a more widely constituted Public Benefit and Privacy Panel (PBPP), but with much the same remit. The PBPP and the CAG both act in an advisory capacity with respect to the activities outlined earlier. Ultimately, responsibility rests with the Secretary of State in England and Wales and NHS National Services Scotland.

6.59 In England and Wales, Regulations state that:

> Anything done by a person that is necessary for the purpose of processing patient information in accordance with these Regulations shall be taken to be lawfully done despite any obligation of confidence owed by that person in respect of it.[178]

---

[172] GMC, n 17, paras 40–50.

[173] Dame Fiona Caldicott, Information: To share or not to share? The Information Governance Review (2013), available at: https://www.gov.uk/government/publications/the-information-governance-review.

[174] Section 6 of the 2012 Act, inserting s 1E into the National Health Service Act 2006. Note this extends also to Boards and Clinical Commissioning Groups. See also s 111 of the Care Act 2014.

[175] J Grace and M J Taylor, 'Disclosure of confidential patient information and the duty to consult: The role of the Health and Social Care Information Centre' (2013) 21(3) Med Law Rev 415.

[176] These provisions only apply in England and Wales. The Confidentiality and Security Advisory Group for Scotland (CSAGS) produced its report of recommendations in April 2002, *Protecting Patient Confidentiality: Final Report* (2002) and much of this work has been picked up and implemented by the Scottish Health Informatics Programme, funded by Wellcome Trust from 2009–2013: http://www.scot-ship.ac.uk/. SHIP evolved into an element of the UK-wide Farr Institute with much the same remit: http://www.farrinstitute.org/. Wider cross-sectoral data linkage is being promoted by Scottish Government, *Joined-up Data for Better Decisions: Guiding Principles for Data Linkage* (2012) and through its *Data Vision for Scotland* (2014), available at: http://www.gov.scot/Topics/Economy/digital/digitalservices/datamanagement/dmbvfs.

[177] See: http://www.hra.nhs.uk/resources/confidentiality-advisory-group/.

[178] Health Service (Control of Patient Information) Regulations 2002 (SI 2002/1438), reg 4. For comment, see M J Taylor 'Legal bases for disclosing confidential patient information for public health: distinguishing between health protection and health improvement' (2015) 23(3) Med Law Rev 348.

Inter alia, the Regulations allow confidential patient information to be processed with a view to: (i) diagnosing communicable diseases and other risks to public health; (ii) recognising trends in such diseases and risks; (iii) controlling and preventing the spread of such diseases and risks, or (iv) monitoring and managing—(a) outbreaks of communicable disease; (b) incidents of exposure to communicable disease; (c) the delivery, efficacy, and safety of immunisation programmes; (d) adverse reactions to vaccines and medicines; (e) risks of infection acquired from food or the environment (including water supplies); and (f) the giving of information to persons about the diagnosis of communicable disease and risks of acquiring such disease. The Regulations also provide support to Cancer Registries to collect information about incidences of cancer. Note how these terms cover both public health measures and research ends. While, as we have already discussed, the former, at least, can be reasonably easily justified, the extensive discretion of the Secretary of State has been criticised, in general, as giving undue preference to the ill-defined 'public interest' as compared with the individuals' private interests in confidentiality of their medical data.[179] Notwithstanding, the Health and Social Care Act 2012 gave a legal basis for the widespread collection of identifiable patient-level data from GP surgeries for a range of purposes including commissioning of services and medical research. This was to be conducted under the auspices of the *care.data* initiative whereby data would be used in an anonymised form, including—potentially—wider uses by third parties. Where anonymised use was not possible, approval was to be sought from the CAG to authorise identifiable, non-consented uses 'in the public interest'. Leaflets were sent to 26.5 million households, albeit not addressed to individuals. Moreover, this information contained no direct mention of *care.data*. This led to suspension of the service within weeks of its launch in early 2014 after strong professional and patient objections and concerns about potential commercial access. At the time of writing, pilot re-launch schemes are being tried in England, but the associated lessons are salutary ones: no administration should believe when it comes to patient privacy the mere legal authority can necessarily command social legitimacy. Moreover, there is a real and present danger in attempting to borrow 'social licence' from the trust people have in public professionals such as GPs to undertake wider social benefit programmes without serious forethought and robust consultation.[180]

6.60 Trends at common law have been, in some respects, anticipated these reactions. In *R v Department of Health, ex p Source Informatics Ltd*, the Court of Appeal was asked to rule on the legality of disclosing anonymised prescribing data to a firm that wished to sell them to pharmaceutical companies to assist in the marketing of their products.[181] A request was submitted to provide details of general practitioners' prescribing habits, and all data were stripped of patient identifiers before being passed on. Nonetheless, the Department of Health issued a policy statement to the effect that this practice was a breach of patient confidentiality in that there was no provision for obtaining patient

---

[179] D Beyleveld, 'How not to regulate in the public interest' (2001) 2 Genetics L Montr 5; cf, J Higgins, 'Two sides of the fence' (2004) Health Service Journal, 7 October, p 20.

[180] P Carter, G Laurie, and M Dixon-Woods, 'The social licence for research: why *care.data* ran into trouble' (2015) 41(5) J Med Ethics 404.

[181] [2000] 1 All ER 786; (2000) 52 BMLR 65. For criticism of both the trial court's ruling ([1999] 4 All ER 185, (1999) 49 BMLR 41) which was overturned, and that of the Court of Appeal, see D Beyleveld and E Histed, 'Anonymisation is not exoneration' (1999) 4 Med L Internat 69 and 'Betrayal of confidence in the Court of Appeal' (2000) 4 Med L Internat 277.

consent, nor could this be implied from the circumstances in which the information was originally generated. The Court of Appeal held, however, that there could be no breach of confidentiality because, 'The concern of the law here is to protect the confider's personal privacy. That and that alone is the right at issue in this case'.[182] In the Court's view, patient privacy was not under threat because there was no realistic possibility that patient identity could be revealed. Moreover, because the obligation of confidence binds in conscience as an equitable doctrine, and because a reasonable pharmacist's conscience 'would not be troubled by the proposed use made of patients' prescriptions',[183] such treatment of patient information was a fair use and entirely legal. This decision was handed down before the Human Rights Act 1998 came into force, and any such justification today would need to be framed in terms of necessity and proportionality. As it stands, the effect of *Source Informatics* is to reduce the individual's legal interest in his or her own information to no more than that of ensuring that anonymity is maintained. In so doing, other fundamental issues are ignored, including the role of consent in legitimising the uses of information, the concept of reasonable expectations of use, and, ultimately, the importance of maintaining a prima facie respect for confidences. This having been said, there is a tendency to fetishise consent in the medico-legal work as some kind of panacea for perceived ills. The reality is that consent is neither necessary nor arguably sufficient to protect the range of patient interests at stake. While it might be a prima facie indicator of an individual's wishes, it is not an absolute entitlement that the law affords and its utility and desirability must always be considered against other public interests including those in scientifically sound, ethically robust health-related research. Still, the reaction to something like *care.data* suggests that—irrespective of the strict legal position—many people have a strong desire to control what happens to medical data relating to them.[184]

CONFIDENTIALITY AND THE LEGAL PROCESS

6.61 Disclosure of confidential medical information as part of the legal process can be considered in two main categories—statutory and non-statutory. Statutory disclosure presents no problem to the doctor but it is, nevertheless, showing signs of encroachment on traditional values. Thus, the original requirements for reporting by the doctor of infectious disease[185] or industrial poisoning[186] are clearly directed to the good of society. Compulsory notification is also required for statistical purposes[187] and for the protection of individuals by the state.[188] Despite occasional protests on the grounds of 'interference', we feel that most people would accept such regulations.[189]

---

[182] [2000] 1 All ER 797a.   [183] [2000] 1 All ER 796f.

[184] M J Taylor and N Taylor, 'Health research access to personal confidential data in England and Wales: assessing any gap in public attitude between preferable and acceptable models of consent' (2014) 10(15) Life Sciences, Society and Policy 1.

[185] Health Protection (Notification) Regulations (SI 2010/659).

[186] Reporting of Injuries, Diseases and Dangerous Occurrences Regulations (SI 2013/1471).

[187] Abortion Regulations 1991 (SI 1991/499), as amended; Abortion (Scotland) Regulations 1991 (SI 1991/460), as amended.

[188] Misuse of Drugs (Supply to Addicts) Regulations 1997 (SI 1997/1001), as amended.

[189] But some powerful objections can be raised. See, in particular, M Brazier and J Harris, 'Public health and private lives' (1996) 4 Med L Rev 171. Most recently it has been confirmed that local authorities using and sharing information in the discharge of their statutory duties is not a breach of either data protection

6.62 It is to be noted that no immunity is granted to the doctor when a statutory duty is imposed on 'a person' to provide information. Such a situation arises, for example, under s 19 of the Terrorism Act 2000, which places every person under an obligation to disclose to the police information connected with acts of terrorism [190] Opinion is divided, however, as to the working of the Road Traffic Act 1988 when, by virtue of s 172,[191] the doctor must provide on request any evidence which he has which may lead to the identification of a driver involved in an accident. The patient can scarcely expect the doctor to breach confidentiality—were it otherwise, he might well forego essential medical care; yet the doctor's liability under the law has been confirmed.[192]

6.63 There may, of course, be other times when the police would have an interest in access to medical records. Police engaged in the investigation of a serious arrestable offence may obtain a warrant to search for material which is likely to be relevant evidence. Under the Police and Criminal Evidence Act 1984,[193] magistrates cannot, however, issue a warrant to search for 'excluded material', which includes personal records relating to a person's physical or mental health and which are held in confidence; medical records are, therefore, excluded material. However, a constable may still apply to a judge for an order to obtain such records. The Act illustrates some of the difficulties in applying an ethical principle by way of statute. Hospital notes are clearly excluded material and can, therefore, be withheld from the police irrespective of the purpose of their search. Thus, the police cannot obtain them even though their sole purpose is, for example, to establish the whereabouts of a potential murderer at a given time[194]—as Morland J said in *R v Cardiff Crown Court, ex p Kellam*:[195]

> Presumably Parliament considered that the confidentiality of records of identifiable individuals relating to their health should have paramountcy over the prevention and investigation of serious crime.[196]

But one wonders if this was really in the contemplation of the legislature or of those who lobbied them so assiduously. Even so, a doctor who sees it as a public duty to cooperate with the police may produce such records[197]—provided, of course, that he is prepared to justify this later in a court of law or before his peers.

6.64 Other than by regulations, courts of law can compel the disclosure of medical material either through the production of documents or during evidence and cross-examination— a provision that does not apply in several countries of the EU.

---

rules or human rights: *MXA v Harrow LBC* [2014] EWHC 3756. Similarly, sharing on unpaid NHS debt to enforce the UK's immigration sanction scheme is permissible: *R (on the application of W) v Secretary of State for Health* [2014] EWHC 1532.

[190] Exceptions such as exist do not apply to medical practitioners: see Terrorism Act 2000 (Crown Servants and Regulators) Regulations 2001 (SI 2001/192).

[191] As substituted by Road Traffic Act 1991, s 21.

[192] *Hunter v Mann* [1974] QB 767; [1974] 2 All ER 414.

[193] Section 9(1). On the scope of powers of seizure, see the Criminal Justice and Police Act 2001, s 50, and on the international dimension see the Crime (International Co-operation) Act 2003, s 16.

[194] *R v Cardiff Crown Court, ex p Kellam* (1993) 16 BMLR 76. The Court set aside the order to produce the documents 'with considerable reluctance'.

[195] (1993) 16 BMLR 76 at 80.

[196] Compare the position in Scotland at common law and Scottish Government et al., *Records Management: NHS Code of Practice (Scotland)*, Version 2.1 January 2012.

[197] *R v Singleton* [1995] 1 Cr App R 431; [1995] Crim LR 236.

DISCLOSURE OF DOCUMENTS

6.65 A patient contemplating negligence proceedings against a doctor or a health authority will usually need access to his medical records so that his claim can be evaluated by his legal and medical advisers.[198] Those in possession of such records have been enjoined by the courts to act in a spirit of candour and not to resist disclosure—a course of action which might have the effect of delaying the resolution of a dispute and preventing a just outcome.[199] Failure to put one's 'cards on the table' can be met with an order for the discovery of documents under ss 33 and 34 of the Senior Courts Act 1981, as amended. Disclosure may be made to a medical expert or to the applicant's legal advisers. A claimant cannot engage in a general 'fishing expedition' to see whether he has a cause of action—an application must disclose the 'nature of the claim he intends to make and show not only the intention of making it but also that there is a reasonable basis for making it'.[200]

6.66 A person in possession of documents may be entitled to refuse disclosure on the ground that it is not in the public interest to make the documents available.[201] This will rarely arise in medical negligence cases, but the court may have to consider whether disclosure should be denied when there is a public health dimension to a case.[202] This was the position in *Re HIV Haemophiliac Litigation*,[203] where the public interest in question was the confidentiality of policy documents relating to blood products policy. Similarly, in *AB* v *Glasgow and West of Scotland Blood Transfusion Service*,[204] the Court of Session would not order disclosure of the identity of a blood donor in an action resulting from the donation of contaminated blood—the pursuer's right to claim damages was not of such magnitude that it should take precedence over a material risk to the sufficiency of the national supply of blood for transfusion. In contrast, international cooperation between courts ordering access to relevant materials or premises has been greatly facilitated by the adoption of an EU Regulation; thus, in *MMR and MR Vaccine Litigation (No 10); Sayers and Others* v *SmithKline Beecham plc and Others*,[205] the British court deemed it appropriate to request an Irish court to require disclosure of material relevant to the action in respect of adverse consequences of taking vaccines produced in Ireland but administered in the UK.[206]

6.67 Court directions may also be made for the disclosure before trial of expert medical reports which it is proposed to bring in evidence. The exception to this policy once lay in cases involving a suggestion of medical negligence—the rationale being that parties should not have to disclose experts' reports which were directed to establishing liability rather than to the prognosis and quantum of damages.[207] Largely as a result of the unsatisfactory trial in *Wilsher*,[208] alterations were made to the Rules of the Superior Courts so as to bring medical negligence cases into line with others involving personal injury—prior

---

[198] For the converse situation where it was claimed (and rejected) that a patient who raises legal proceedings against his health care professional impliedly waives his right to confidentiality in the relevant medical records, see *Kadian* v *Richards* [2004] NSWSC 382.

[199] *Naylor* v *Preston Area Health Authority* [1987] 2 All ER 353; [1987] 1 WLR 958, CA.

[200] *Dunning* v *United Liverpool Hospitals Board of Governors* [1973] 2 All ER 454 at 460.

[201] *Re EC (disclosure of material)* [1996] 2 FLR 725; [1997] Fam Law 160.

[202] The Senior Courts Act 1981, s 35 allows the court to refuse access in the public interest.

[203] [1990] NLJR 1349; (1998) 41 BMLR 171.   [204] 1993 SLT 36; (1989) 15 BMLR 91.

[205] [2004] All ER (D) 67.

[206] Council Regulation (EC) 1206/2001. For an example of a transatlantic dispute, see *United States of America* v *Philip Morris Inc* [2004] EWCA Civ 330.

[207] *Rahman* v *Kirklees Area Health Authority* [1980] 3 All ER 610; [1980] 1 WLR 1244, CA.

[208] *Wilsher* v *Essex Area Health Authority* [1987] QB 730; [1986] 3 All ER 80, CA; *America* v *Philip Morris Inc* [2004] EWCA Civ 330.

disclosure was to become the norm rather than the exception. In general, *all* the cards must now be put down, not only those obviously concerned with the action; the current view is that the court can deal with problems of confidentiality relating to irrelevant conditions—such as a past history of sexually transmitted infection—by limiting disclosure to the other side's medical advisers who must respect medical confidentiality except where litigation is affected.[209]

6.68 Disclosure of documents and information is, in any case, subject to what is commonly known as 'legal professional privilege'—a doctrine designed to allow the client unfettered access to his advisers.[210] The concept is not without difficulties, of which the doctor should be aware. First, legal professional privilege is tightly defined and is likely to be overridden, whenever this is possible, in the interests of legal fairness.[211] Disclosure of reports which are designed primarily for accident investigation and prevention and only secondarily for the purpose of seeking legal advice is likely to be ordered. It is clear that this gives rise to a conflict of interests. On the one hand, it could be held that the public good of preventive medicine must take second place to the threat of private litigation;[212] on the other, the imposition of professional privilege has, on occasion, been granted only reluctantly in that secrecy is inequitable to the person who suffers medical mishap.[213] Second, while professional privilege is there in order to allow the client to be uninhibited when approaching his or her legal advisers, there is no corresponding privilege to encourage a patient to be equally open in relation to his or her medical advisers.[214] This was demonstrated forcefully in *W* v *Egdell*,[215] where it was concluded that a clear and important distinction was to be made between instructions given to an expert and the expert's opinion given in response to those instructions; the former was covered by legal professional privilege, while the latter was not. We have some difficulty in understanding how a question can be subject to absolute confidentiality while the answer is not; nevertheless, the ruling given at first instance was fully supported in the Court of Appeal. Third, a request for information from a solicitor is not the same as an order of the court even though the conditions—for example, that litigation is in progress—may seem similar; medical practitioners have been found guilty of serious professional misconduct for making such a mistake in good faith but in ignorance. It is worth noting that, while the legal representative may, of course, withhold any documents to which professional privilege applies, the adversary may have the advantage of these if they are disclosed in error

---

[209] Such changes were crystallised as a result of the Woolf report: Lord Woolf, *Access to Justice* (1996) ch 15. For further thoughts, see Lord Woolf, 'Are the courts excessively deferential to the medical profession?' (2001) 9 Med L Rev 1.

[210] On the nature of legal professional privilege, see *Three Rivers District Council* v *Governor and Company of the Bank of England (No 5)* [2004] UKHL 48. While this focuses on lawyers and banker clients the contrast is nevertheless drawn as between doctors and their patients, paras 28 ff.

[211] Professional privilege is, in a sense, a product of the adversarial system of presenting evidence and is less likely to be upheld when proceedings are more akin to inquisitorial. Classic examples of the latter are cases brought under the Children Act 1989 or in wardship proceedings: *Oxfordshire County Council* v *M* [1994] Fam 151.

[212] *Waugh* v *British Railways Board* [1980] AC 521; [1979] 2 All ER 1169. The order to disclose may extend to specific accident report forms which might well be thought to be privileged (*Lask* v *Gloucester Health Authority* (1985) *The Times*, 13 December). Failures, mistakes, and 'near misses' must now be reported to Patient Safety Domain of NHS England, see: https://www.england.nhs.uk/ourwork/patientsafety/.

[213] *Lee* v *South West Thames Regional Health Authority* [1985] 2 All ER 385; [1985] 1 WLR 845, discussed also in 'Disclosure of documents by doctors' (1985) 290 BMJ 1973. See also BMA, *Requests for Disclosure of Data for Secondary Purposes* (2011).

[214] *Three Rivers*, n 210.   [215] [1990] Ch 359; [1989] 1 All ER 1089.

and it is not obvious that privilege has not been waived.[216] Where an order is sought for the disclosure of the medical records of a non-party to a dispute—and we know of only one reported case directly in point—it will be granted only in the most exceptional of circumstances. In *A v X (disclosure: non-party medical records)*,[217] the defendants sought access to the medical records of the brother of the claimant to cast doubt on his claim that the defendant's negligence had brought about psychiatric problems; the implication was that those problems were already manifest in the family. The court refused the order stating that it would only be granted when: (i) the documents for which disclosure is sought are likely to support the case of the applicant or adversely affect the case of one of the other parties to the proceedings; and (ii) disclosure is *necessary* in order to dispose fairly of the claim or to save costs.[218]

6.69 Normally the privilege is seen to operate in an absolute sense, absent an attempt to abuse it for fraudulent purposes. However, in the criminal context, the Court of Appeal has recently confirmed further limits on the privilege in *R v Brown (Edward)* that involved a patient from a high-security psychiatric hospital who had a history of violent attacks against fellow patients and who himself sought ongoing detention in the unit. A request to speak with his lawyer without any security unit staff present was rejected on the basis that 'it will be appropriate to impose a requirement that particular individuals can be present at discussions between an individual and his lawyers if there is a real possibility that the meeting is to be misused for a purpose, or in a manner, that involves impropriety amounting to an abuse of the privilege that justifies interference'.[219] The concern here was the very real risk that the patient would use the opportunity to harm himself or others.

6.70 The doctor in the witness box has absolute privilege and is protected against any action for breach of confidence. The authority of the Earl of Halsbury LC remains undisputed today: the immunity of the witness in court 'is settled in law and cannot be doubted'.[220] This privilege extends to pre-trial conferences and Scottish precognitions,[221] the exception being that a privileged communication must not be made maliciously.[222] Judges may go to great lengths to protect the witness but, when so ordered, the doctor is bound to answer any question which is put to him;[223] refusal to answer in the absence of the court's discretion to excuse a conscientious witness must expose the doctor to a charge of contempt—and the court will take precedence even when there is a statutory obligation of secrecy.[224]

---

[216] *Pizzey v Ford Motor Co Ltd* [1994] PIQR P15, CA. [217] [2004] EWHC 447.

[218] Cf, *S v W Primary Care Trust* [2004] EWHC 2085 where the court ordered disclosure of the records of a child despite concerns on the part of the Trust that it might damage his health interests and that early entries contained sensitive material on his mother. Disclosure was, however, only authorised to legal and medical representatives and to his maternal grandmother as carer.

[219] [2015] EWCA Crim 1328, para 41. [220] In *Watson v M'Ewan* [1905] AC 480 at 486, HL.

[221] On the position regarding pre-trial work generally, see *Raiss v Paimano* [2001] 4 Lloyd's Rep PN 341. For further discussion of the authorities, see *R v Brown*, n 219 above.

[222] *AB v CD* (1904) 7 F 72, per Lord Moncrieff. This is the Court of Session stage of *Watson v M'Ewan*. The same applies in other Commonwealth countries. See *Hay v University of Alberta Hospital* [1991] 2 Med LR 204 (QB, Alberta), in which it was held that the plaintiff had no right to withhold consent to pre-trial discussions by the defendants with his medical attendants.

[223] The exception to this requirement being disclosure of a source of information for which special rules apply (Contempt of Court Act 1981, s 10).

[224] *Garner v Garner* (1920) 36 TLR 196.

PATIENT ACCESS TO MEDICAL RECORDS

6.71 It is still only a few decades since patients have a *right* to see their medical records.[225] An important early development came with the Access to Medical Reports Act 1988, as amended. The reports to which the Act refers are limited to those prepared by a medical practitioner who is or has been responsible for the clinical care of the individual and which are intended for direct supply to the patient's employer, prospective employer, or to an insurance company (s 2). Reports by health professionals who have had only a casual, non-caring professional association with the patient are excluded. Such reports as are included have always been subject to the patient's consent but the applicant must now positively seek such consent and must inform him of his rights to access (s 3). The patient can see the report before it is sent and, unless he has done so, issue of the report must be delayed for three weeks (s 4). He has the right to ask the doctor to alter anything that he feels is inaccurate and he may add a dissenting statement should the doctor refuse to do so (s 5). Access may be withheld if disclosure would cause serious harm to the patient's physical or mental health—or to that of any other person—but, in those circumstances, the patient may withdraw his consent to its promulgation.

6.72 The power of control of his or her medical data provided to the individual by the Access to Medical Reports Act is clearly limited and is confined to a very specific aspect of the doctor–patient relationship. The individual is likely to be far more concerned over dissemination of personal details that are gathered as a result of his or her status as a *patient*. Statutory protection as to the confidentiality of information such as that contained in hospital notes was, for a short time, provided by the Access to Health Records Act 1990. That Act was, however, repealed to a very large extent by, and its contents were assimilated into, the Data Protection Act 1998 which is, now, the main determinant of what may and may not be done with a patient's records.[226] Under the 1998 Act, the 'data subject' has a right to information as to the purposes for which data about him are being processed and the persons who will have access to them.[227] The protection of those about whom information is stored lies in preventing the holding of inaccurate information or of concealing the fact that information is stored at all. As a consequence, a patient has the right, subject to a fee, to be told by the 'data controller'—who could be any health caring body holding records—whether any such information is held and, if it is, to be supplied with a copy of that information.

6.73 Subsequent to the passing of the 1998 Act, further regulations were implemented which deal directly with the management of personal data in the health care context. The Data Protection (Subject Access Modification) (Health) Order 2000 restricts patients' rights over their medical data in a number of respects.[228] For example, the Order provides exceptions to the subject's access rights in the case of personal data consisting of information as to his or her physical or mental condition—which will include most information held by NHS bodies. These are: (i) again, where permitting access to the data would be likely to cause serious harm to the physical or mental health or condition of the data subject or any other person (which may include a health professional); and (ii) where the request for

---

[225] See Information Commissioner's Office, at https://ico.org.uk/for-the-public/health/.

[226] The only significant remnant of the 1990 Act relates to the records of a deceased person (s 3(1)(f)).

[227] There are, of course, some exceptions to this; e.g., medical research uses that do not affect the patient directly and the results do not identify her, see the Information Commissioner's Office Guidance, n 35, ch 3.

[228] The Data Protection (Subject Access Modification) (Health) Order 2000 (SI 2000/413).

access is made by another on behalf of the data subject, such as a parent for a child. In the latter case, access can be refused if the data subject had either provided the information in the expectation it would not be disclosed to the applicant or had indicated it should not be so disclosed, or it was obtained as a result of any examination or investigation to which the data subject consented on the basis that information would not be so disclosed.[229] *Roberts* v *Nottinghamshire Healthcare NHS Trust*[230] is an example of access being denied within the terms of the Order. Given the confidential nature of the proceedings, however, it is impossible to know what the actual basis for the decision was save that the court was satisfied that the Trust gave 'clear and compelling reasons based on cogent evidence that the report should not be released'. This should be contrasted with *RM* v *St Andrew's Healthcare*[231] in which non-disclosure of records to a mental patient was held to be unjustified on the grounds that this would prevent him from knowing he was being covertly medicated and would in turn prevent him from mounting an effective challenge to his continued detention.

6.74   BMA guidance gives support to HCPs who are faced with access requests.[232] This helpfully covers requests for access to both the records of living and deceased persons as well as requests from a variety of actors including parents, children, incompetent persons, next of kin, police, and lawyers. Where access is to be denied, there is clear instruction about the basis upon which this should be justified. We have noted earlier at para 6.55 recent concern by the BMA about insurers using access provisions to secure disclosure of patients' entire medical record, most likely in contravention of the Data Protection Act 1998. This has led to further specific guidance to doctors on how to manage such cases.

6.75   The ECtHR has confirmed that access to records containing personal information is, prima facie, a matter of entitlement under Art 8 of the ECHR and is part of the state's obligation to respect the private and family lives of its citizens.[233] It is not, however, an absolute right and other interests may be in play. For example, in *MG* v *United Kingdom*,[234] the applicant sought access to social service records to confirm his suspicions of childhood abuse at the hands of his father. It was recognised by the Court that the authorities had legitimate concerns about the privacy of third parties in such a case (e.g., the siblings), and that this might be a legitimate reason to deny full access. Notwithstanding this, the absence of an appeal body to challenge a refusal of access constituted a breach of the applicant's human rights. This has now been remedied in the UK whereby the Information Commissioner's Office can hear appeals against denial of access to personal records.[235] In contrast, in *KH and Others* v *Slovakia*,[236] the Court held that the right to respect for one's private and family life must be practical and effective and that there is a positive obligation on the part of states to make available to patients copies of their medical records: '[T]he Court does not consider that data subjects should be obliged to specifically

---

[229]   Before deciding whether these exemptions apply a data controller who is not a health professional must consult the health professional responsible for the clinical care of the data subject; or if there is more than one, the most suitable available health professional. If there is none, a health professional who has the necessary qualifications and experience to advise on the matters to which the information requested relates must be consulted.

[230]   [2009] FSR 4.   [231]   (2010) 116 BMLR 72; [2010] MHLR 176.

[232]   BMA, *Confidentiality and Health Records*, available at: http://bma.org.uk/practical-support-at-work/ethics/confidentiality-and-health-records.

[233]   *MG* v *United Kingdom* [2002] 3 FCR 413.   [234]   *MG* v *United Kingdom* [2002] 3 FCR 413.

[235]   For the human rights dimension more broadly see *MS* v *Sweden* (1999) 28 EHRR 313.

[236]   *KH and Others* v *Slovakia* (2009) 49 EHRR 34

justify a request to be provided with a copy of their personal data files. It is rather for the authorities to show that there are compelling reasons for refusing this facility.'[237]

6.76 The right of access to information about oneself is, then, unassailable. But to what extent is it meaningful to talk about 'my record' or 'my medical notes'? This is common par lance but it has no legal basis. The ownership of the intellectual property contained in a record—that is, the copyright—is held by the person who has created the notes or his or her employer, and not by the subject of those notes. Moreover, the physical notes themselves are owned by the GP practice, health authority, or health board. The patient is therefore unlikely ever to have a successful property claim over his or her records.[238]

THE REMEDIES

6.77 For many years the law was unclear as to the remedies for breach of confidentiality. This was considerably clarified in the House of Lords' decision in *A-G v Guardian Newspapers (No 2)*[239] and again in *Campbell v MGN Newspapers*.[240] A patient can recover damages for improper disclosure of information about his health even if he has suffered no financial loss as a result; this was already implicit from *X v Y*,[241] in which it was said that, 'No one has suggested that damages would be an adequate remedy in this case'—the implication being that they were there for the taking in the absence of a better solution. They might, of course, be only nominal; on the other hand, they might be considerable were it possible to show loss of society, severe injury to feelings, job loss, interference with prospects of promotion, or the like. However, a distinction has to be made between actions in contract and in tort. Thus, in the trial stage of *W v Egdell*,[242] Scott J discarded the possibility of damages for shock and distress—other than nominal—largely on the particular facts of the case but also because it was based on breach of an implied contractual term;[243] the decision had no relevance to an action in tort.

6.78 The question first came before the courts in Scotland over a century ago in two similarly named and well-known decisions, the *AB v CD* cases. In the earlier *AB v CD*,[244] the Court of Session considered an action for damages brought against a doctor who had disclosed to a church minister that the pursuer's wife had given birth to a full-term child six months after marriage. The Court held that there was a duty on the part of the doctor not to reveal confidential information about his patient unless he was required to do so in court or if disclosure were 'conducive to the ends of science'—but, in that case, identification of the patient would be improper. In the second *AB v CD*,[245] the pursuer was seeking a separation from her husband. Having been examined by the defender at the suggestion of her lawyers, she was later examined by the same doctor who was then acting on behalf of her husband. The doctor disclosed to the husband certain information he had obtained in the course of his first examination and the wife argued that this constituted a breach of

---

[237] N 240, para 48. In *RR v Poland* (2011) 53 EHRR 31 it was confirmed that '[c]ompliance with the state's positive obligation to secure to their citizens their right to effective respect for their physical and psychological integrity may necessitate, in turn, the adoption of regulations concerning access to information about an individual's health', at para 188.

[238] In *R v Mid Glamorgan Family Health Services, ex p Martin* [1995] 1 All ER 356; [1995] 1 WLR 110, the court accepted that medical records were owned by the health authority, and a similar view was taken by the High Court of Australia in *Breen v Williams* (1996) 138 ALR 259.

[239] [1990] 1 AC 109; [1988] 3 All ER 545.   [240] N 7.

[241] [1988] 2 All ER 648; (1992) 3 BMLR 1.   [242] [1990] Ch 359; [1990] 1 All ER 835.

[243] Quoting *Bliss v South East Thames Regional Health Authority* [1987] ICR 700.

[244] (1851) 14 D 177.   [245] (1904) 7 F 72.

confidence. Once again, the Court accepted that there was a duty on the part of a doctor not to disclose confidential information about his patient but stressed that not every disclosure would be actionable. As Lord Trayner pointed out,[246] some statements may be indiscreet but not actionable; there might be, for example, an actionable breach if the disclosure revealed that the patient was suffering from a disease which was a consequence of misconduct on his or her part. In fact, disclosure of the background to the illness may be of greater importance than the disclosure of illness itself. [247]

6.79 Qualified privilege should, in the absence of malice or reckless unconcern as to the truth of the statement, be a defence against any action for breach of confidence, as it already is in the law of defamation—qualified privilege in this context being but another expression of the 'need to know' principle. This is the ultimate determinant of ethical disclosure. The profession is not, or should not be, over-concerned with the niceties of intra-professional relationships or of communication in good faith with paramedical or other responsible groups; what really matters is irresponsible gossip—and, here, the ultimate deterrent is the power of the GMC over its members (for which see Chapter 1). Punitive action against a doctor is unlikely to be of material benefit to a wronged patient, but it is still a very effective preventive weapon.

6.80 Injunctory relief—a common remedy in this area of law—is more immediately effective and is one which has been extended considerably in recent years.[248] Given that the real fear at the core of a breach of confidence action is public disclosure of private facts, the 'gagging order' will, in many cases, be more desirable to the claimant than damages—and the utility of this remedy endures, as cases such as *X* v *Y* and *H* v *Associated Newspapers* demonstrate.[249] Often, however, damage has already been done because information has already been made public and, even if it is achieved, victory in a damages action can be pyrrhic: Ms Campbell, for example, received only £3,500 in compensation.[250] Damages are also payable for contravention of the provisions of the Data Protection Act 1998 where a data subject suffers damage or distress. Any such payments have, however, been consistently paltry. In *AB* v *Ministry of Justice*[251] compensation of £2,250 was for distress arising from a breach of the Data Protection Act 1998 concerning processing of information about the claimant's deceased wife. Interestingly, this was awarded even though there was no 'damage' in the sense of a further loss. Moreover, the compensation was separate from the damage from the technical breach, which was awarded only in the sum of £1. Additionally, the enforcement powers of the Information Commissioner's Office have been radically increased to the extent of possible Civil Monetary Penalties up to £500,000. Already, heavy fines have been imposed on NHS bodies for breaches of the law.[252]

---

[246] (1904) 7 F 85.

[247] See, E Reid, 'Breach of confidence: translating the equitable wrong into Scots law' (2014) Jur Rev 1.

[248] *Venables* v *News Group Newspapers Ltd, Thompson* v *News Group Newspapers Ltd* [2001] 1 All ER 908 (indefinite injunction against the entire world in respect of the identification of child killers). Compare the public interest in reporting names of adult family members of child who died as a result of child abuse because of the strong interest in knowing about cases that had previously come to the attention of social services: *Re A (A Child) (Application for Reporting Restrictions)* [2012] 1 FLR 239; [2011] 3 FCR 176.

[249] See *X* v *Y*, para 6.29, and *H (a healthcare worker)* v *Associated Newspapers*, para 6.30.

[250] *Campbell*, para 6.21 above. [251] [2014] EWHC 1847 (QB).

[252] See the example of Brighton and Sussex University Hospitals NHS Trust which was fined £325,000 for selling hard drives on an Internet auction containing personal data of thousands of patients, including those suffering from HIV and other sexually transmitted infections (June 2012).

6.81 We have seen, particularly in *X* v *Y*, that the courts have no great love for the 'media mole' in the hospital and, while there is deep-rooted respect for freedom of the press, there is an equally strong realisation of the need for integrity within the whole of the hospital hierarchy—and not only from those governed by professional codes of conduct; *how* the press comes by its information may be of considerable relevance as to how the courts interpret the media's use of it. Such matters came to a head in the House of Lords in *Ashworth Hospital Authority* v *MGN Ltd.*[253] Here, a newspaper published an article that included verbatim extracts from the medical records of a multiple murderer detained in a secure hospital who was, at the time, engaged in a well-publicised hunger strike. The hospital applied for, and obtained, an order to the newspaper to explain how they obtained their information and to identify any employee of the hospital or intermediary who was involved in its acquisition—and the order was affirmed in the Court of Appeal. The newspaper appealed, largely on the basis of s 10 of the Contempt of Court Act 1981, which holds that no correspondent can be compelled to disclose his sources of information unless it is established that disclosure is necessary in the interests of justice; the order, it was contended, was neither proportionate nor necessary on the facts of the case. The House held, however, that security of hospital records—and particularly those of a security hospital—was of such importance that it was essential that the source should be identified and punished in order to deter similar wrongdoing in the future, that was what made the order necessary, proportionate, and justified. The importance of the hospital informational security as opposed to the privacy concerns of the individual was emphasised in that the fact that the subject himself had been in contact with the press was immaterial to the House's decision. And Lord Woolf could not resist pointing to the fact that the disclosure was made worse by the fact that it had been purchased by a cash payment! From our point of view, perhaps the most important aspect of *Ashworth* lies in its clear message that every member of a hospital's staff is subject to the same duty of confidentiality to the patients.[254] By the same token, the Court of Appeal took the opportunity subsequently to re-enforce the countervailing public interest of maintaining a free press, at least in terms of the procedural safeguards to be followed—in essence, the problem for the courts in such a case is to balance the competing demands of s 10 of the Contempt of Court Act 1981 and, now, the Human Rights Act 1998, Sch 1, Art 10 which defines the right to freedom of expression. *Ashworth* had an important sequel insofar as the named reporter now refused to disclose the primary source of his information; the hospital, which was now anxious to discipline the member of staff responsible for the breach of confidence, accordingly brought an action against the reporter in person, and this came to trial after a prolonged series of summary proceedings.[255] In the event, the trial judge ruled in favour of the journalist and refused to order disclosure—a decision that was confirmed in the Court of Appeal. This case, which can be truly regarded as a saga,[256] is very interesting in providing a wide analysis of the ways in which the s 10/Art 10 balancing exercise can be argued but space prevents further discussion. Suffice it to say that the apparent volte face turned on the precise, and very particular, facts of the case, facts which were altered in the different ambiences of the *Ashworth* and *Ackroyd* hearings. From the point of view of principle, the most important of these, to our minds,

---

[253] [2001] 1 All ER 991; [2001] 1 WLR 515, CA; affd [2002] UKHL 29; [2002] 1 WLR 2033, HL.

[254] It was said, e.g., that a minimum of 200 employees of the hospital had access to the hospital's electronic database: *Mersey Care NHS Trust* v *Ackroyd (No 2)* (2006) 88 BMLR 1 per Tugendhat J at [168].

[255] *Mersey Care NHS Trust* v *Ackroyd (No 2)* (2006) 88 BMLR 1, QBD; (2007) 94 BMLR 84, CA.

[256] For full analysis, see R Sandland, 'Freedom of the press and the confidentiality of medical records' (2007) 15 Med L Rev 400.

is that the element of a pressing social need for disclosure—which is so much a feature of the derogations permitted by Art 10(2)—no longer existed five years after the event.[257] For the rest, the two cases are exemplary of the fact that there is no overarching answer to the medico-ethical dilemma posed by Art 10—each case must be determined on its own facts.[258] As to the law as it now stands, the approach is confirmed as that of the House of Lords in *Ashworth*.[259]

6.82 More recent developments in the realm of remedies demonstrate a strengthening of the position of claimants, especially in light of the disclosure risks arising from the information age. In *Vidal-Hall v Google Inc*,[260] the Court of Appeal confirmed that there exists a tort of 'misuse of private information', entitling claimants to damages under the 'moral damage' as provided within the European Data Protection Directive. Importantly, the Court considered that compensation provisions under s 13(2) of the UK's Data Protection Act 1998 were insufficient to redress the issue at hand, viz, the illegal tracking by a foreign Internet service provider of clients' Internet usage. While no pecuniary damage could be shown, the Court held both that it had jurisdiction in such a case and that it was important that '…data subjects had an effective remedy for a distressing invasion of privacy falling short of pecuniary damage, especially as the Charter of Fundamental Rights of the European Union art.7 and art.8 made specific provision for the protection of personal data'. The claim could proceed on the basis of s 13(1) of the 1998 Act. While this is not strictly a medical case, and it deals with actions outside the UK jurisdiction, this is nonetheless an important decision because it opens the door to 'distress-only' claims, which are very typical in the medico-legal context.

CONFIDENTIALITY AND DEATH

6.83 Final reflection might, appositely, be concerned with death. The Declaration of Sydney says: 'I will respect the secrets which are confided in me, even after the patient has died.' This view is also endorsed by the GMC in its guidance to doctors:

> Your duty of confidentiality continues after a patient has died. Whether and what personal information may be disclosed after a patient's death will depend on the circumstances.[261]

6.84 In practice, this is incapable of fulfilment as to the cause of death since a death certificate, signed by a doctor, is a public document—albeit, available only on payment of a fee for a copy. Our major concerns here, however, are, first, with conditions discovered after death and, second, with the circumstances leading to death. It has, for example, been seriously argued that Lord Moran invited criticism not so much for his disclosures after the death of Winston Churchill[262] as for his failure to draw attention to the physical state of his patient during life.

---

[257] See Sir Anthony Clarke MR (2007) 94 BMLR at [85].

[258] For a consideration of the issues with respect to documents potentially shedding light on the death of Diana, Princess of Wales (and where the order supported release), see [2007] EWHC 2513.

[259] N 253, at [86].   [260] [2015] 3 WLR 409; [2015] 3 CMLR 2.

[261] *Confidentiality*, n 17, paras 70–2, which offer examples of whether disclosure might or might not be justifiable.

[262] Lord Moran, *Winston Churchill: The Struggle for Survival, 1944–1965* (1966).

6.85 In professional ethical terms, there can be no doubt that a post-mortem report merits the same degree of confidentiality as does the report of the clinical examination; insurance companies and the like have an obvious interest in its content but their right to disclosure is the same as the right to discovery of hospital records—in the absence of a court order, consent to disclosure from the next of kin of the deceased is essential. The personal representative of a deceased patient or someone who might have claim arising from their death can request access to the patient's records under the only remaining live provision of the Access to Health Records Act 1990.[263]

6.86 But has the public at large any rights to details of the medical history of the dead?[264] While the principle remains irrespective of personalities, this is essentially a problem of public figures—and it is remarkable how rapidly professional ethics can be dissipated, say, in describing to the media the wounds of President Kennedy or the psychiatric history of the principals in any *cause célèbre*. The former physician to President Mitterrand of France faced professional disbarment, a fine, and up to one year's imprisonment for publishing his book, *Le Grand Secret*, immediately after the President's death in January 1996. The book detailed Mitterrand's long battle with cancer throughout his presidency which had been hidden from the French public. The affair caused a storm of controversy over the appropriate balance between the public's 'right to know' and the individual's 'right to privacy':[265] in the end the French courts followed up an interim injunction on sales with a permanent injunction on publication, the publishers received a hefty fine, and the author was given a four-month suspended sentence. The ECtHR, however, declared France to be in breach of human rights over its reaction to the book, holding that, while the state could defend its laws imposing civil and criminal liability for breach of confidence as 'necessary in a democratic society', the continued ban on distribution of the book no longer met a 'pressing social need' and was disproportionate to the aim pursued; it was, in effect, a breach of the right to freedom of expression.[266] It is easy to say, 'History will out, let it be sooner than later' but it is less easy to decide at what point revelations become history. The ECtHR, however, felt confident that the imposition of a permanent publication ban nine-and-a-half months after the death of the French President was inappropriate.[267]

6.87 Returning to the British perspective, as we saw earlier, the GMC has stated that a duty of confidence persists after the patient's death; whether or not disclosure after death will be improper depends, inter alia, on whether there was any specific requests to keep information confidential, whether disclosure may cause distress to, or be of benefit to, or reveal the identity of the patient's partner or family, and whether the information is already public knowledge or can be anonymised. The GMC does not specify any time limit; a practitioner must be prepared to justify and explain every disclosure. Moreover, a bark in this context carries a bite—no less a person than a former editor of the *British Medical Journal* has been taken to task for reporting information concerning the health of a well-known, albeit controversial, general after his death.[268] Arguments can be made from an ethical perspective that the dead retain interests that are primarily based on reputation

---

[263] 1990 Act, s 3(1)(f).   [264] S E Woolman, 'Defaming the dead' 1981 SLT 29.

[265] A Dorozynski, 'Mitterrand book provokes storm in France' (1996) 312 BMJ 201.

[266] *Plon (Société)* v *France* (2006) 42 EHRR 36 paras 50 ff.

[267] *Plon (Société)* v *France*, n 266, para 53.

[268] S Lock and J Loudon, 'A question of confidence' (1984) 288 BMJ 123 at 125.

and dignity, and that these justify a continued duty of confidence, albeit eventually reduced and limited with the passage of time.[269]

6.88 Respect for the privacy of the dead seems a reasonable requirement—particularly when children or spouses are alive.[270] The Human Genetics Commission, for example, also endorsed the principle. It advocated something akin to a balance of factors similar to that offered by the GMC in determining when, if ever, genetic information can be derived from a deceased person: 'The seeking of DNA information for a good reason may justify the intrusion into the privacy of the dead, whereas seeking it purely for the purposes of sensational disclosure would not provide justification.'[271]

6.89 And so, finally, what of the law? The legal position has long been unclear although it has been argued that, since confidence is, prima facie, a personal matter, the legal duty ends with the death of the patient; contrariwise, it has been suggested that, 'Equity may impose a duty of confidence towards another after the death of the original confider ... the question is not one of property ... but of conscience'.[272] Statute sends equally mixed messages. The provisions of the Data Protection Act 1998 do not apply to information relating to deceased persons, but we have seen that the Access to Health Records Act 1990 continues to apply to the dead and that access is limited to the dead person's personal representative and those with a claim on the estate. The courts, for their part, may apply the principles of medical confidentiality by insisting that an order imposing anonymity in judicial proceedings should remain in force after the subject's death in cases of major sensitivity—such as those involving declarations as to the withdrawal of treatment from the incompetent.[273] Not only does this appear logical but post-mortem publicity may, in turn, raise questions as to the ethics of previous non-disclosure. The law in fact seems to be moving in this direction. The Information Commissioner has taken the view that the common law duty of confidence applies after death and this has been supported by the Information Tribunal.[274]

---

[269] D Sperling, *Posthumous Interests: Legal and Ethical Perspectives* (2008), esp ch 5.

[270] The courts are, however, concerned for a balancing of interests between those of the bereaved and of freedom to publish. See *Re X (a minor) (wardship: restriction on publication)* [1975] Fam 47; [1975] 1 All ER 697, and, at the European level, see the discussion of the rights of Mitterrand's family in *Plon (Société)* v *France*, para 6.86.

[271] Human Genetics Commission (HGC), *Inside Information: Balancing Interests in the Use of Personal Genetic Data* (2002) para 7.28. The HGC was abolished in 2012.

[272] See *Morison* v *Moat* (1851) 9 Hare 241; affd (1852) 21 LJ Ch 248, quoted by R G Toulson and C M Phipps, *Confidentiality* (1996), paras 13–17. However, any action for breach of confidence before the death of the patient could be transmitted to the executor.

[273] *Re C (adult patient: publicity)* [1996] 2 FLR 251—though this may not hold if the public interest dictates otherwise. For the balance of private and public interests and the imposition of anonymity in general, see *Re G (adult patient: publicity)* [1995] 2 FLR 528. See, too, Practice Direction [2002] 1 WLR 325 and *A* v *East Kent Hospitals University NHS Foundation Trust* [2015] EWHC 1038 (QB); [2015] Med LR 262. Cf, the House of Lords has ruled that the anonymity of a dead child and the mother accused of its murder should not be restrained merely to protect the privacy of the surviving child who was not directly involved in the trial: *Re S (a child) (identification: restriction on publication)* [2005] 1 AC 593; [2004] 3 WLR 1129.

[274] See *Bluck* v *The Information Commissioner and Epsom & St Helier University NHS Trust* (2007) 98 BMLR 1. In *Lewis* v *Secretary of State for Health* [2008] EWHC 2196 the court ordered the release of deceased persons to the Redfern Inquiry on nuclear facilities and effects on human tissue. For comment see, K A Choong and J P Mifsude Bonnici, 'Posthumous medical confidentiality: the public interest conundrum' (2014) 1(2) Euro J Comp Law and Governance 106.

CONCLUSION

6.90 Confidentiality remains the undeniable stalwart of the doctor–patient relationship. While its iconic status might be overshadowed at times by the seemingly never-ending development of the role of consent, confidentiality remains the constant that binds patient and doctor together, even when they are in dispute. It marks the contours of the relationship and provides the foundation upon which trust in medical professionals is built. Its importance—and fragility—cannot be overstated, nor should it ever be overlooked.

7

GENETIC INFORMATION AND THE LAW

INTRODUCTION

7.01 The purpose of this introductory section is to outline the nature of genetic disease and to discuss the role of the genetic counsellor in handling personal and familial genetic information. Issues of liability arising from the mishandling of that information are dealt with in Chapter 10; here we explore the challenges posed by the—some would say 'unique'—familial nature of much genetic data. It is, however, perhaps apposite to remind the reader at this early stage of the distinction to be made between genetic and congenital disease. The latter encompasses the whole spectrum of disease which is present at birth; congenital disease may, therefore, be genetic in origin but is not necessarily so. The *extent* of genetically dependent disease, per se, has not increased; its proportionate *importance* has, however, risen, first, as the control of those due to infection has improved. Currently, the proportion of childhood deaths attributable wholly or partly to genetic factors runs at rather more than 50 per cent. Second, it is becoming increasingly clear in the era following the mapping of the human genome— that is, the unveiling of the complete genetic code of the human species—that a genetic component may well operate in many illnesses and conditions. The social, ethical, and legal implications which advances in genetics have for all of us expanded by the day; correspondingly, genetic considerations increasingly breathe new life into the study of medical jurisprudence.

7.02 The rather tired adage that 'information is power' has been rejuvenated with the advent of the so-called 'new genetics'. Developments in genetic medicine over the last few decades now mean that access to genetic information through genetic testing is relatively cheap and easy but, as a result, this has given rise to serious concerns about access to, and the use of, test results.[1] While the sensitivity of medical data is an issue of general concern which we address in the context of confidentiality in Chapter 6, matters are particularly complicated in the context of genetics because of certain features that are said to be particular to genetic information.[2] First, a test result can have implications not only for the individual who has been tested (the 'proband') but also for blood relatives of that person

---

[1] See generally G T Laurie, *Genetic Privacy: A Challenge to Medico-Legal Norms* (2002). At the international level, this has resulted in the Additional Protocol to the Convention on Human Rights and Biomedicine, concerning Genetic Testing for Health Purposes (27 November 2008), being a Protocol of the Council of Europe Convention on Biomedicine and Human Rights (1997).

[2] See the work of the European Commission STRATA Group, *Ethical, Legal and Social Aspects of Genetic Testing: Research Development and Clinical Applications* (2004). On European legal responses, see S Soini, 'Genetic testing legislation in Western Europe—a fluctuating regulatory target' (2012) 3(2) J Community Genet 143, doi: 10.1007/s12687-012-0078-0.

who share a common gene pool.[3] Second, this information can have implications also for *future* relatives, in the sense that many genetic diseases pass vertically through generations and, thus, impact directly on reproductive decisions. Third, genetic test results can disclose a likelihood *of future* ill health in persons who are currently well. Fourth, because, in most cases, testing is carried out by analysing a person's DNA, which remains unchanged throughout their life, genetic testing can be done at any stage from the cradle to the grave—and, indeed, either before or beyond.[4] Thus, a fetus can be tested in utero for a condition such as Huntington's disease which might not manifest itself until middle age.[5] Finally, underlying all of these factors is the perceived benefit which genetic testing can offer in the guise of predictability. This is the 'standard account' of the nature of genetic information which we will challenge in due course (see para 7.28). For present purposes, however, it is important to note that it has significance for two particular classes of subject: first, the unborn (i.e., the frozen embryo or the implanted fetus), who are an increasingly common subject of genetic testing and for whom the consequences can be most severe (i.e., non-implantation of the embryo or termination of the fetus); and second, family members of an individual who has been tested for genetic disease. We will consider the respective positions of these two groups following a discussion of the nature of genetic disease itself.

TYPES OF GENETIC DISEASE

7.03 Something of the order of 99.9 per cent of our genes are positioned on chromosomes which exist in the nuclei of the body's cells in pairs, one member of each pair being derived from each parent. The remainder are to be found within the mitochondria—organelles that exist in the cytoplasm of the cells. Diseases that are reflections of our genetic constitution can, therefore, derive from abnormalities of the chromosomes as a whole or of the individual genes the great majority of which are contained within the chromosomes. The former are of quantitative type—the bulk of or the number of chromosomes is altered while their genetic construction remains unaltered. Typical disease states arise, the classic example being Down's syndrome. Strictly speaking, however, the underlying abnormality is not genetic and such a disease is better considered as being chromosomally derived. The distinction is of more than semantic interest and has serious medico-legal implications;[6] accordingly, we will discuss chromosomal abnormality as a separate entity later.

Nuclear Genetic Disease

7.04 Abnormalities of the individual genes, which are also paired on a parental basis, are qualitative in type—the gene itself 'mutates' into abnormality and will be transmitted in that form; conditions resulting from a single mutation are described as being unifactorial in

[3] On this, see M Brazier, 'Do no harm: Do patients have responsibilities too?' (2006) 65 CLJ 397; and, generally, T Marteau and M Richards, *The Troubled Helix: Social and Psychological Implications of the New Human Genetics* (1996).

[4] For discussion of how genetic tests differ from other medical tests, see House of Lords Science and Technology Committee, *Genomic Medicine* (HL Paper 107.1, 7 July 2009) ch 2.

[5] M A Minear et al., 'Non-invasive prenatal genetic testing: current and emerging ethical, legal, and social issues' (2015) 16 Ann Rev of Genomics and Hum Genetics, 369, doi: 10.1146/annurev-genom-090314-050000.

[6] The main importance of recognising the distinction lies in the fact that abnormal chromosomal conditions, other than in the very specific context of translocation (for which see para 7.13), arise spontaneously and not by way of intergenerational transmission.

origin. Since either of a pair of genes can be donated at random by either parent to their offspring, it is a simple calculation to determine the statistical probability of an infant being so endowed (see Figure 7.1). One gene of the pair may be an 'autosomal dominant' and, should this be a disease-producing mutant, it will express itself as a disease when the pair of genes contains only one which is both abnormal and dominant. Normal natural selection should lead to the eradication of dangerous dominant genes. Such a gene may, however, defy natural selection because it possesses some special attribute. Huntington's disease, for example, persists because the symptoms associated with the responsible gene often do not appear until beyond the time when the subject has attained procreative age—a situation known as late onset genetic disease. Harmful genes may, on the other hand, be 'autosomal recessives' in which case they can persist as 'carriers' but can only express themselves in the absence of a normal partner—that is, when both genes in a pair are similarly recessive mutants. Frank disease will result only if an individual inherits the same two recessive genes—which means that both parents must have been carriers or one was a carrier and the other diseased; this, incidentally, provides the genetic basis for discouraging in-breeding.

7.05   Unifactorial disease may also be 'sex-linked'—or, better, 'X-linked'. Simplistically, this implies that the abnormal gene is present on part of the X chromosome which has no counterpart on the Y chromosome, the possession of which determines maleness. An abnormal recessive X-linked gene will be suppressed in the female by the dominant normal gene on the other X chromosome; it will, however, be free to express itself when coupled in the male XY configuration. Haemophilia is a classic example of such a disease.

7.06   It almost goes without saying that this description of unifactorial disease is grossly simplified. The picture must be painted on a background of penetrance—that is, the ability of the gene to express itself. Some may be so powerful that they cause some symptoms or signs in the recessive state; other, albeit dominant, genes may be virtually expressionless. The degree of penetrance in individuals probably depends mainly on the total genetic environment—that is, the penetrance of a gene will be modified to an extent, by the company it keeps and the ambience in which it exists.

7.07   The result is that very few genetic diseases can be regarded as truly unifactorial. The great majority of genetic disorders result from multifactorial traits which are believed to be the result not only of the effects of one or several genes but also of a combination of genetic

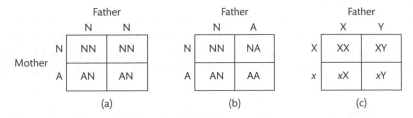

(a) The mother has an abnormal gene (A). If this is dominant, half the children will have the desease; if it is recessive, half the children will be carriers.
(b) Both the mother and the father have one deleterious recessive gene (A); half the children will be carriers and one in four will suffer from the disease.
(c) The mother is a carrier of an abnormal X-linked gene (x); half the male children will have the diesease and half the female children will continue to carry the disease.

Figure 7.1 Unifactorial Disease

and environmental factors. It is, therefore, generally impossible to predict mathematically the occurrence of this commonest type of genetic disorder. Coronary heart disease, for example, is to some extent genetically influenced but the occurrence of symptoms will depend upon a number of uncertain features such as the potential patient's job, diet, recreation and smoking habits, or the genetic control of blood cholesterol levels. The appearance of such conditions, however, lies in the individual's unpredictable future; in respect of defects which can be demonstrated in utero, neural tube defects—spina bifida and anencephaly—are, probably, the most important multifactorial diseases

7.08   Some form of behavioural or remedial surgical treatment is often available for those suffering from multifactorial disease and the same is true for a few unifactorial conditions. But there is no curative treatment for most of the more serious genetic disorders, the control of which then depends on prevention. As the House of Commons Science and Technology Committee pointed out:

> While genetics is likely eventually to transform medicine, it may take some while before treatments based on genetic knowledge become available … [i]n the short term, the most widespread use of medical genetics will be, as now, in diagnosis and screening.[7]

The House of Lords Science and Technology Committee also pointed to the incredible advances that occurred in the last few decades, by 2009 pointing to a '1,000-fold increase in capacity to read a DNA sequence and a 10,000-fold reduction in the cost of DNA sequencing'.[8] Speed continues to increase, while costs fall dramatically to the point where individuals can now seek low-cost sequencing of their own genomic material on the open market.[9] From the clinical perspective, the consequences of this are that geneticists are now making remarkable in-roads to understanding the genetic component of a vast array of common diseases, at both the population and personal level. But, while the House of Lords Science and Technology Committee was confident that this will in due course revolutionise health services, the fact remains that much of the current value of this knowledge remains at the level of diagnosis, screening, and susceptibility risk assessment. This 'public health' objective is a central function of the genetic counsellor; its relative importance, however, poses one of the major ethical problems of modern medicine—and one which is likely to increase for decades to come. We will return to an overview of the problem as a whole when we have outlined a further, and, currently, an incompletely understood, complication of genetic disease—that is, the effect of mutation of DNA in the mitochondrial genes.[10]

Mitochondrial Genetic Disease

7.09   As already stated, some 99.9 per cent of our DNA is derived from the 20,000–30,000 genes contained in the nuclei of our cells. By contrast, the remainder is, effectively, held in 37 operational genes within the mitochondria—of which there are from tens to hundreds of thousands lying in the cytoplasm of the cell. Although the figures appear

---

[7] House of Commons Science and Technology Committee, *Human Genetics: The Science and its Consequences* 3rd Report (6 July 1995) pp 36–7. As the report made clear, *diagnosis* is aimed at the management of individuals; genetic *screening* is the study for specific purposes of populations or their identifiable subsets (e.g. groups at increased risk for particular diseases).

[8] N 4, para 1.3.

[9] See T Caulfield et al., 'Reflections on the cost of "low-cost" whole genome sequencing: framing the health policy debate' (2013) 11(11) PLoS Biol: e1001699. doi:10.1371/journal.pbio.1001699.

[10] Our authority for much of this section is to be found in Nuffield Council on Bioethics, *Novel Techniques for the Prevention of Mitochondrial Disorders: An Ethical Review* (2012).

disproportionate, mitochondrial genes, which are responsible for supplying energy to the cell, exert a profound influence, not only because of their own action but also because of their interaction—both active and passive—with the nuclear genes. Moreover, as suppliers of energy to cells throughout the body, no organs are exempt from the effects of mutant mitochondrial DNA; symptoms may arise anywhere but particularly as a result of malfunction of those cells which utilise maximum energy—of which the brain may turn out to be the most significant.

7.10 Space prevents a full analysis of these potential effects but the reader must have some indication of the main differences between nuclear and mitochondrial genetic disorder. Some general impression can be obtained by visualising the former system as a well-disciplined army and the latter as one that makes its own rules. Thus, the 'load' of mutant mitochondrial DNA does not necessarily indicate the severity of the resulting condition nor does the mother's 'load' predict the effect on her children.[11] Symptoms may appear at any time and in different organs at different times.

7.11 There is, again, no treatment for the condition other than symptomatic and it is possible only to control its perpetuity. Currently, efforts to do so are concentrated on mitochondrial donation by which the nucleus—or chromosomal mass—of a normal egg is substituted by that of the affected woman and the resultant hybrid is used to impregnate her.[12] As things stand, such hybridisation is unlawful,[13] and can involve not only the common assisted reproduction techniques (for which, see Chapter 8) but also more controversial methods such as pre-implantation diagnosis (see para 7.26). Even so, it is now possible for regulations to be made permitting such a process[14] and a research licence for the purpose was issued in 2005.[15] The ethical problems associated with the possible treatments still remain, and include the identity of the resultant child—has he two mothers as sections of the media would maintain?;[16] is the process too close to germ-line therapy for comfort?; what is the legal status of the donor?; what is the extent of risk?; can we inflict an inevitably extensive follow-up regime on any live-born children?, etc. These questions have been the subject of intensive public and parliamentary debate since the last edition of this book. The result was the adoption of new Regulations in 2015, making the United Kingdom (UK) the first country in the world to approve mitochondrial donation.[17]

Chromosomal Disease

7.12 As indicated, chromosomal disease is, essentially, a matter of chromosome overload— a pair may not separate when the primitive 46 chromosome germ cell divides in order to form 23 chromosome gametes, thus leaving one gamete with two chromosomes. The embryo resulting from this gamete will, therefore, have three chromosomes—a condition

---

[11] While male sex cells carry mitochondria, they do not, for uncertain reasons, appear to pass them on to their children (Nuffield Council, n 10 at para 1.10). Therefore, while both sexes may suffer from the disease, transmission is by way of the female partner only.

[12] Alternative techniques involving ovum donation and selective substitution are being studied but there is no advantage in discussing the details here—they are simply illustrated in the Nuffield Report, n 10.

[13] Human Fertilisation and Embryology Act 1990, s 3ZA(2), inserted by HFEA (2008) s 3(5).

[14] Human Fertilisation and Embryology Act 1990, s 35A inserted by the 2008 Act, s 26.

[15] Nuffield Report, n 10 at para 2.2.

[16] The gross discrepancy between the patient's and the donor's contribution to the total DNA load has been noted earlier.

[17] Human Fertilisation and Embryology (Mitochondrial Donation) Regulations (SI 2015/572). See too the statement of the Human Fertilisation and Embryology Authority (24 February 2015): http://www.hfea.gov.uk/9606.html.

known as a trisomy which is further designated by the number allocated to the chromosome involved.[18] There is, therefore, no genetic transmission in the general run of chromosomal disorders: rather, the occurrence of chromosomal abnormalities in the neonate increases markedly with maternal age due, presumably, to increased 'tackiness' in the ageing chromosome's coat. Some 2 per cent of women aged 40, left to uncontrolled pregnancy, will produce a chromosomally defective child, and half of these will be suffering from Down's syndrome; by the age of 45, the risk of trisomy-21 rises to about 3 per cent.[19] It is possible that advanced paternal age may also be a risk factor.

7.13   Thus, trisomy is a chance occurrence which cannot be predicted beyond an estimate of risk. Males with trisomy-21 are commonly sterile but there is the theoretical risk that half the children of a female sufferer will also have the chromosomal defect; in practice, not only is such a pregnancy unlikely but, also, more than half of any affected fetuses would miscarry naturally. However, rather under 5 per cent of Down's syndrome patients are not trisomic but, instead, demonstrate a chromosomal abnormality known as translocation—parts of a chromosome are exchanged for or added to those of its partner prior to the formation of the zygote. This may also occur sporadically but, once it has done so, a carrier state can develop and affect one in three children—passage to later generations is, thus, possible and its occurrence will be independent of maternal age.[20] It will be seen as one goes through this book that this possibility is often overlooked.[21] In summary, then, the management—and the consequent duty of care—rests not so much on the therapist as on the adviser, to whom we should now turn.

GENETIC COUNSELLING AND FETAL TESTING FOR GENETIC DISEASE

7.14   Assessed as an arm of public health, the task of genetic counselling seems easy; in practice, it abounds with practical, ethical, and, inevitably, legal problems and the Nuffield Council on Bioethics chose to make genetic screening the subject of its first report for just such reasons.[22] Modern genetic counselling involves more than merely quoting risks. The ideal is to avoid a directive approach and, rather, to concentrate on the psychological circumstances so that couples can be assisted to make decisions which are right for them rather than right for the scientists.[23] Almost inevitably, however, the counsellor's opinion will be sought and how this is reached depends particularly on whether the counselling is retrospective or prospective—are parents seeking advice because they already have an

---

[18] Thus, the commonest trisomy leading to Down's syndrome is technically known as trisomy-21. Theoretically, an equivalent embryo with a single chromosome should have been produced but a monosomy is incompatible with continued development.

[19] For full analysis of the difficulties involved, see J K Morris et al., 'Comparison of models of maternal age-specific risk for Down syndrome live births' (2003) 23 Prenat Diagn 252, and more recently K Salmeen and M Zlatnik, 'The oldest gravidas: a review of pregnancy risks in women over 45' (2011) 66(9) Obs and Gyn Survey 580, and G de Graaf, F Buckley, and B G Skotko, 'Estimates of the live births, natural losses, and elective terminations with Down syndrome in the United States' (2015) 4 Am J Med Gen Part A 167.

[20] The risk is 1:3 rather than the anticipated 1:4 for unifactorial characteristics because one-quarter of conceptuses will be monosomic and will die in the womb.

[21] A good example is *Al Hamwi* v *Johnston*.

[22] Nuffield Council on Bioethics, *Genetic Screening: Ethical Issues* (1993).

[23] For an excellent modern overview, see E Pergament and D Pergament, 'Reproductive decisions after fetal genetic counselling' (2012) 26 Best Pract Res Clin Obstet Gynecol 517.

affected child or is the need for consultation prior to parenting based on information derived from other sources? Patient–clients who know that genetic disease might affect their family come, in the main, with a degree of preparedness and an appreciation of their future options. The role of the counsellor assumes an entirely different mantle, however, if he is privy to information of which his clients know nothing—perhaps as a result of a confidential discussion with another health care professional (HCP); the question then arises as to whether and how such information should be imparted, and we return to this later.[24]

7.15 In assisting clients towards a particular reproductive decision, the counsellor can virtually never give concrete advice as to having or not having a (further) child. She can take extraneous circumstances—for example, religious or financial status—into consideration but, in the end, she is down to speaking about probabilities. In the case of unifactorial disease, she can give accurate figures—for example, the chances of an overtly affected child are one in four pregnancies if both the mother and father carry recessive deleterious genes.[25]

7.16 In the event of a multifactorial condition, the probabilities can only be derived in an empirical fashion. Even then, the prospects are subject to interpretation. Thus, presented with a child with spina bifida, one can say there is a 10 per cent chance that the couple will have a further child with developmental abnormality; it will sound quite different when expressed as a 90 per cent chance of an unaffected infant. Moreover, 9:1 are acceptable odds to many; others might regard anything less than 99:1 as an unacceptable risk. In the end, the choice rests with the couple and this choice is a product of their ability to understand and the skill of the counsellor. But, as is so often the case, the matter may not be restricted to the confines of the consulting room. In particular, the prospect of undue societal pressure to decide in favour of abortion may be considerable. We return to discuss this at paras 7.88–7.90 in light of our treatment of policy advice and guidance on the matter. The complexities of pre-implantation genetic diagnosis of embryos created for IVF, and the issues surrounding pressures to select a 'healthy' embryo, will be discussed at paras 8.61–8.70.

7.17 Counsellors, for their part, have several advisory options: they can dismiss the risks, they can advise sterilisation of either partner, they can put the options of artificial insemination by donor or of ovum donation—subject, of course, to availability—or they can arrange for a suitably controlled pregnancy coupled with the alternatives of live birth or termination as conditions indicate.

Controlled Pregnancy

7.18 The counsellor may have advised a pregnancy or may be presented for the first time with a couple in which the wife is already pregnant. In either event, should it be felt that a risk exists, he or she now has a considerable technical armamentarium to help in closing the gap between probability and certainty. The methods may be non-invasive or invasive.

Non-invasive Techniques

7.19 X-rays of the fetus are contra-indicated save in an emergency. The modern alternative is visualisation by means of ultrasound which is now used as a routine and which is,

---

[24] See Council of Europe, Genetic Tests for Health Purposes (2012), available at: https://rm.coe.int/CoERMPublicCommonSearchServices/DisplayDCTMContent?documentId=0900001680457fff.

[25] But it has to be remembered that the 'chance' remains constant with every pregnancy—the fact that a couple have three healthy children does not mean that the next one will be affected.

so far as can be told, virtually risk-free;[26] moreover, its use in locating the placenta is an essential prerequisite to amniocentesis or chorionic villus sampling. Ever-increasing technical and interpretative skills have transformed ultrasonography from a fairly crude diagnostic tool to one that is capable of demonstrating not only the sex of the baby and major external abnormalities, such as spina bifida or anencephaly, but also congenital disease of the internal organs, and minor defects such as cleft lip—indeed, the identification of Down's syndrome (discussed later) is often based on the appearance of relatively subtle fetal anomalies[27] and current practice is increasingly directed to computerising their relative 'scores'. The processes of obstetric management and genetic counselling are, therefore, irrevocably entwined and it is important that the woman is aware of the implications, which are similar to those we discuss later under amniocentesis. The clinician who discovers a fetal abnormality as a by-product of management can scarcely conceal his knowledge while the woman, for her part, may be ill-prepared to receive it; the case for 'informed consent' to ultrasonography is strong. It is an interesting psychological side effect of the process that many parents regard the sono-gram as their first 'baby picture'—something which tends to endow the fetus with a recognisable personality; this, in itself, has some influence on the management decision—and may be used with intentions that might not be universally acceptable.[28] More recently, non-invasive whole genome sequencing has become possible.[29] As a diagnostic technique, this is undoubtedly a welcome addition to the clinician's toolbox to inform a woman about her pregnancy; moreover, to the extent that early diagnosis can support effective interventions, this paves the way to more productive fetal medicine. The advance is not, however, without associated ethical and legal concerns. Consider, for example, what should happen with the *whole* genome information if the decision is taken that the fetus should come to term and become a child? Is it permissible to retain this information in light of the newborn's privacy rights? Why should such a wealth of information be stored if only a proportion (or none) is of direct relevance to the child's health? Is retention justified on the off-chance that it might become useful? Given near universal arguments against the blanket screening of newborns,[30] why should this situation be any different?

Maternal Invasion

7.20 Fetuses with neural tube defects—spina bifida or anencephaly—secrete an excess of the protein α-fetoprotein (AFP) into the amniotic fluid and some of this is transferred to the maternal circulation. Testing the maternal serum thus offers a simple and risk-free method of diagnosing neural tube abnormality in the fetus and is very acceptable to mothers. Some 80–90 per cent of cases can be identified in this way and, if necessary, it may be supported by analysing the amniotic fluid for its protein content. Interestingly, the maternal AFP (and oestriol) level is characteristically *decreased* when a woman is carrying a fetus with Down's syndrome. Conversely, other maternal plasma constituents—for

---

[26] Suggestions that ultrasound may predispose, for example, to left handedness seem to have gone unsupported in the decade since they were first mooted.

[27] Ultrasonography of the neck region provides something of the order of an 80 per cent diagnostic rate of Down's syndrome and other trisomies on its own. See F D Malone et al., 'First-trimester or second-trimester screening, or both, for Down's syndrome' (2005) 353 New Engl J Med 2001.

[28] See para 9.85 et seq.

[29] J O Kitzman et al., 'Non-invasive genomic sequencing of a human fetus' (2012) 4 (137) Sci Transl Med 137ra76, doi: 10.1126/scitranslmed.3004323.

[30] See the Human Genetics Commission and the UK National Screening Committee, *Profiling the Newborn: A Prospective Genetic Technology?* (2005).

example, human chorionic gonadotrophin and the protein inhibin A—are raised. Thus, a very effective rate of an antenatal diagnosis of Down's syndrome can be achieved by combining ultrasound and biochemical tests in the first trimester with further biochemical analyses after 14 weeks' gestation—a detection rate of 90 per cent is claimed for the fully integrated test with, equally importantly, a low false positive rate of less than 1 per cent.[31] Many practitioners, however, probably would still wish to offer diagnostic amniocentesis or chorionic villus sampling to women who, despite an equivocal screening test, are aged over 35 years and who are at, generally, higher risk. The introduction of relatively cheap, risk-free, and effective tests raises the possibility of extending routine testing to all pregnant women rather than to the older group alone.[32]

7.21 Even so, it is possible to question the ethical propriety of making available a plethora of tests for conditions, such as Down's syndrome, for which no treatment or cure is available. In these circumstances, the availability of such tests can only be fully justified as facilitating an abortion decision. It is, however, now crystal clear that a patient is entitled to such personal information as is reasonably available; moreover, to withhold information relating to termination of pregnancy is very probably unlawful at both domestic and European level.[33] By contrast with what is, arguably, a dubious justification, it is possible to mount a *strong* ethical argument justifying tests which will identify the probability of illnesses, such as spina bifida, that are likely to expose a child to physical suffering and major surgical interventions. The common ground is that all those involved in the field of prenatal screening would agree that the provision of a test without adequate back-up counselling as to the significance of the results is likely to introduce as much harm as good.

Uterine Invasion

7.22 The commonest invasive techniques for prenatal diagnosis which involve the fetus or its environment are amniocentesis and chorionic villus sampling. The former is technically easier and carries a lesser risk to the pregnancy; despite the theoretical advantages of the latter, amniocentesis is still probably the more popular method of direct investigation in the UK. The process consists of needling the sac surrounding the fetus and withdrawing fluid which contains excretions and metabolites of the fetus together with representative cells; the latter can be grown in culture for chromosomal studies and to detect certain metabolic diseases; the fluid can be used for biochemical analysis as described earlier. Biochemical tests can be made rapidly and can directly diagnose some rare diseases of defective metabolism of the gargoylism type. The onset of 'rhesus disease' can also be detected. But by far the most important test in the present context is that for AFP, by

---

[31] See N J Wald, H C Watt, and A K Hackhaw, 'Integrated screening for Down's Syndrome on the basis of tests performed during the first and second trimesters' (1999) 341 New Engl J Med 461. There is a continuing need for evaluation of the various tests available; a very useful synopsis is to be found in Z Alfrevic and J P Neilson, 'Antenatal screening for Down's syndrome' (2004) 329 BMJ 811. See also B Weisz and C H Rodeck, 'An update on antenatal screening for Down's syndrome and specific implications for assisted reproduction pregnancies' (2006) 12 Hum Repro Update 513. Note that, in the UK, different hospitals may offer tests of varying complexity. The hospital may also levy a charge for tests that its policy does not regard as essential.

[32] See Public Health England, *Fetal Anomaly Screening: Programme Overview* (2013), available at: https://www.gov.uk/guidance/fetal-anomaly-screening-programme-overview. It is, however, possible to raise serious criticisms of the policy: see, e.g., S A M McLean and J K Mason, 'Our inheritance, our future: Their rights?' (2005) 13 Int J Child Rights 255.

[33] *Rand v East Dorset Health Authority* (2000) 56 BMLR 39 per Newman J; *Tysiac v Poland* [2007] 1 FCR 666.

means of which an efficient laboratory can now diagnose all neural tube lesions. Cell culture can indicate the presence of chromosomal disorder in some 10–20 days. In expert hands, the presence of what are termed 'inborn errors of metabolism' can be detected after some six weeks' culture.

7.23   On the face of things, therefore, amniocentesis provides a very powerful means of diagnosing genetic disease but, at the same time, it presents both technical and ethical problems. First, a 'defensive' policy of amniocentesis for all would offer little or no benefit in terms of the proportion of positive results. In practice, it is used selectively on something under 5 per cent of the population and mainly for the diagnosis of chromosomal abnormalities, especially Down's syndrome. As has been discussed, maternal biochemical parameters are widely used in conjunction with the mother's age to calculate a risk score on which a decision to recommend amniocentesis may be robustly based; the majority of hospitals will offer amniocentesis when the risk of having a child with a chromosomal disorder is in the region of 1:200 pregnancies—and, for practical purposes, this involves all pregnant women over the age of 35. Second, there is a risk of miscarriage in close to 1 per cent of investigations[34] and many women reaching the end of fecundity will find this unacceptable. Having decided to test, however, it is best performed at 15–20 weeks pregnancy—although sufficient fluid for testing may be obtained at 12 weeks using sophisticated ultrasonography. An inadequate amount of fluid is obtained in some 5–10 per cent of cases and the test must then be repeated; add to this the time required for effective cell culture and it will be seen that one is, then, close to producing a viable infant—with all the practical and ethical complications involved—in the event that termination of pregnancy is indicated.[35]

7.24   These concerns can be reduced by the use of chorionic villus sampling—or removal and study of the early placental cells; used in conjunction with recombinant DNA techniques, it can revolutionise the diagnosis and management of genetic disease. Chorionic villus sampling suffers in being of no value in the identification of neural tube defects; the incidence of doubtful chromosomal analyses is about four times greater than that following amniocentesis; it is more expensive; and, currently, the risk of miscarriage following the procedure is certainly greater—occurring in some 2–3 per cent of examinations. There is a faint chance that admixture of fetal and maternal blood may initiate 'rhesus' disease in the child. For all these reasons, the early enthusiasm with which the procedure was greeted has waned somewhat. It is probably best reserved for those women who are at greatest risk—and, therefore, most likely to seek a termination involving as little delay as possible—or for cases where there is a single gene defect likely to require diagnosis.

7.25   The evident limitations of invasive diagnostic techniques give rise to their own ethical problems. A raised AFP level does not give a clear indication of the degree of neural tube defect and, although the additional use of high-quality ultrasonography greatly improves the position, the routine abortion of fetuses with any detectable spinal abnormality will result in the destruction of some salvageable—and lovable—children. On the other hand, 10–20 per cent of 'missed' cases will have a severe defect and will require much

---

[34] Although the 'local' incidence, of course, depends to an extent on the skill of the operator. Amniocentesis/CVS remain essential tools in prenatal diagnosis and offer a sensitivity improved by some 10–15 per cent over non-invasive techniques alone: J L Simpson, 'Invasive procedures for prenatal diagnosis: Any future left?' (2012) 26 Best Pract Res Clin Obstet Gynecol 625.

[35] Some of the doctors' dilemmas are resolved by the Human Fertilisation and Embryology Act 1990, s 37(4) which absolves the obstetrician from a charge of child destruction in this context. However, the later the pregnancy, the greater are the risks to the mother in its termination.

corrective surgery. Similarly, the mere presence of the typical chromosomal abnormality does not indicate the likely severity of, say, Down's syndrome in the neonate. There are other problems of interpretation particularly in association with trisomies of the sex chromosomes. Certain arrangements are well known to be associated with severe disease but in others—notably the 'XYY syndrome'—the evidence is by no means clear. XYY boys are said to be prone to vicious behaviour but 'prone' is a very relative concept. Should a doctor, on the one hand, recommend abortion of such a fetus as a 'precaution'? Alternatively, should he inform the parents, allow the pregnancy to run normally, and possibly expose the family unnecessarily to an atmosphere of distrust? What is one to do when one of the other common aberrations of the sex chromosomes—for example, Klinefelter's (XXY) or Turner's (XO) syndrome—is discovered? Such abnormalities are often, but by no means always, associated with a degree of infertility or learning disability. The variations are so many that it is impossible to generalise. The essential point is that patients who request or consent to antenatal *diagnoses* must fully understand the extent of their consent and must be aware of the potential consequent decisions to be made. Some might wish to be apprised of every item of information which has come to light, while others might require to know only of conditions which have a fully understood and significant prognosis; much subsequent searching of conscience can be avoided by preparatory discussion of the issues. At the same time, as we have already intimated, the doctor's or the counsellor's own motivation, prejudices, and failings cannot be discounted. While she may well be operating within the law as it is written, the clinician is still confronted with the moral problems inherent in the interpretation of 'severe handicap' in s 1(1)(d) of the Abortion Act 1967. Antenatal screening and diagnosis, backed by good counselling, seems, at first sight, to be an uncomplicated and thoroughly desirable procedure; it ends, as a Pandora's box of moral uncertainties which we will consider more fully in Chapters 9 and 10.

7.26 Undoubtedly, steady technical improvements are expanding the value of existing aids to genetic counselling thus diminishing the need for developing more direct, and feticidal, techniques such as fetoscopy. Mention must be made, however, of the very different potentials provided by in vitro fertilisation and its adjuncts (for which see Chapter 8). The technique of pre-implantation diagnosis involves removal and genetic analysis of single cells from eight-cell embryos, followed by the selection of such embryos as are found to be normal for implantation. Aside from the many difficulties associated with in vitro fertilisation of itself, the procedure also carries with it many ethical implications (for which, again, see Chapter 8). That having been said, however, it is impossible to ignore either the speed with which this branch of science moves forward or the demand for the techniques available. The range of pre-implantation diagnoses is growing such that it is referable to an ever-widening body of patient–clients. It is now possible to screen for a large number of conditions, including cystic fibrosis, Tay Sachs disease, Duchenne muscular dystrophy, and the haemoglobinopathies—so much so as to raise fears of an incremental return to eugenics and increasing disrespect for the disabled—the proposition seems doubtful, but this is certainly an ethical dimension that cannot be ignored (see further paras 8.61–8.70).[36]

7.27 On the other side of the coin, it is clear that reproduction is an intensely private matter and genetic counsellors should not overemphasise the interests of the state in reducing

---

[36] T S Petersen, 'Just diagnosis? Preimplantation genetic diagnosis and injustices to disabled people' (2005) 31 J Med Ethics 231; A L Bredenoord et al., 'Dealing with uncertainties: Ethics of prenatal diagnosis and preimplantation genetic diagnosis to prevent mitochondrial disorders' (2008) 14 Hum Repro Update 83. For an up-to-date medical account, see P R Brezina and W H Kutteh, 'Clinical applications of preimplantation genetic testing' (2015) 350 BMJ g7611, doi: 10.1136/bmj.g7611.

the incidence of genetic disease; rather, the aim should be to concentrate on the particular circumstances and interests of the parents in wanting a child. The Nuffield Council on Bioethics, the House of Commons Science and Technology Committee, and the British Medical Association (BMA) have all stressed the importance of accepting the ethical principle that screening or testing is justifiable only if based on free and informed consent, and this has been reiterated by the Council of Europe in its Protocol on Genetic Testing. Similarly, in the USA, the National Institutes of Health Task Force on Genetic Testing stated that, '[it] is unacceptable to coerce or intimidate individuals or families regarding their decision about predictive genetic testing'. An older couple, for example, might see a hazardous pregnancy as their last possibility and might prefer to take their chance in the ignorant way of natural parenthood—and they should be allowed to do so. A refusal to accept information must be respected just as much as the desire to receive information. But it has to be admitted that the interests of the state may not stop here, and we return to consider them more fully later.

LEGAL AND ETHICAL RESPONSES
TO THE 'FAMILIAL' NATURE OF GENETICS

7.28   We have already outlined the standard account of genetic information as 'unique', 'predictable', 'certain', and of 'utility to others' in para 7.02. We cannot let this account pass unchallenged, however, because of the important consequences its adoption could have for the future direction of law, policy, and practice. First and foremost, we point to other examples that can be found of non-genetic information which functions in one or more of these ways and we have already mentioned some of these at para 7.02. As the report *Genetics and Health* made clear:

> High cholesterol levels [are] known predictors of cardiovascular disease, and high blood pressure of cerebrovascular disease risk ... [and] ... without recourse to genetic testing familial aggregation [is] discernible not only in the monogenetic disorders but also in a range of common disorders including heart disease, cancers and diabetes.[37]

Moreover, the term 'genetic information' covers a broad spectrum, from highly predictive monogenic disorders through susceptibility genes and on to a simple family history. However, not every class of this information is predictive of future ill health—indeed, many examples of genetic information are no more predictive than is general health information. These factors militate against the argument that genetic data are in some way different from other forms of medical data and, for these reasons, the Human Genetics Commission (HGC) stated that 'we do not feel that all personal genetic information should be treated in the same way in every set of circumstances'.[38] Nonetheless, the debate about how law and ethics should respond to genetic advances has proceeded in large measure on the premise that genetic information is somehow exceptional or 'different'.[39] It is certainly a general perception that genetic information is especially private,[40] and the HGC was established partly in response to this public intuition. Its 2002 report, *Inside*

---

[37]   See, the Nuffield Trust, *Genetics and Health: Policy Issues for Genetic Science and their Implications for Health and Health Services* (2000).

[38]   HGC, *Inside Information: Balancing Interests in the Use of Personal Genetic Data* (2002) para 1.26.

[39]   Cf L O Gostin and J G Hodge Jr, 'Genetic privacy and the law: An end to genetics exceptionalism' (1999) 40 Jurimetrics 21.

[40]   HGC, *Public Attitudes to Human Genetic Information* (2001).

Information, was an attempt to address the public concerns and 'to maintain public trust and confidence that personal genetic information is properly protected'.[41] This remains a very thorough account of the issues that require attention. Its publication reflected both scientific developments in genetics and the policy pressures to make ever more use of genetic information; issues have included the increase in pre-implantation genetic diagnosis, direct-to-consumer genetic testing, and government plans to expand the national DNA database (used for forensic purposes). It is telling, however, that the HGC was wound up in 2012 after a little more than a decade of work. Although this happened as part of the general rationalisation of arm's-length bodies after sweeping government review, it might also be seen as a signal that treating genetic policies differently to other health-related policies is not a prudent way to proceed.

7.29   The belief that genetic data are highly predictive has led a range of persons or bodies to claim an interest in genetic test results.[42] For example, collateral relatives might wish to know if they or their progeny will be affected by disease.[43] Insurers have always taken family history as an index of risk into the assessment of insurance cover but, now, genetic testing offers a seemingly more accurate and more scientific means of predicting liability. Similarly, employers might harbour deep concerns about the future employability of persons likely to be struck down by genetic disease, and the state itself has an undeniable interest in promoting public health by reducing the incidence of genetic disease in its citizens. In light of this range of interests, the potential for conflict over access to, and control of, genetic information is self-evident and it is important to recognise that the impact of a genetic test result on an individual's life might well be felt long before they experience the onset of disease. In its struggle to respond adequately to the dilemmas posed by advances in genetics, the law turns to ethics for guidance.[44] It is, therefore, apposite to consider the nature and strength of the ethical arguments which both support and refute the claims of those in each of the categories and to assess the responses of the law in the light of these.[45]

INDIVIDUAL AND FAMILY INTERESTS IN GENETIC INFORMATION

7.30   The availability of genetic information is appealing because of its perceived utility: 'What does it allow one to do?' Even so, we consider it preferable to begin our inquiry by asking the opposite question, 'What does genetic information *not* allow one to do?' Probably the most important single factor bearing on this debate is that few cures or successful treatments for genetic illnesses exist at present. Thus, except in rare cases, genetic information

[41] HGC, n 38, para 1.25. This report followed the HGC's consultation document, *Whose Hands on Your Genes?* (2000).

[42] For an excellent account, see M J Taylor, *Genetic Data and the Law: Critical Perspectives on Privacy Protection* (2012).

[43] See C Molster et al., 'Australian study on public knowledge of human genetics and health' (2009) 12(2) Pub Health Genomics 84, and L Henneman et al., 'Public attitudes towards genetic testing revisited: comparing opinions between 2002 and 2010' (2013) 21(8) Eur J Hum Genet 793, doi: 10.1038/ejhg.2012.271.

[44] S Soini, 'Genetic testing legislation in Western Europe: A fluctuating regulatory target' (2012) 3(2) J Community Genet 143.

[45] See L Andrews et al., *Genetics: Ethics, Law and Policy* (3rd edn, 2010) and A Buchanan et al., *From Chance to Choice: Genetics and Justice* (2000).

does not necessarily allow us to avoid genetic disease. This is important because it bears on the motivation of those who seek access to genetic testing or test results. Let us begin by considering the claims of the proband and his or her relatives.

7.31 In the absence of treatment or cure, *preparedness* is often cited as the justification for offering or seeking genetic testing. Adults and children can ready themselves, both psychologically and in other ways, for the onset of disease and couples contemplating a family or who have a child on the way can make a more informed reproductive choice in light of all the available facts.[46] Such justification is, however, a double-edged sword for a number of reasons. First, it is by no means clear that pre-emptive knowledge of future ill health is necessarily 'a good thing'.[47] While there are indications that this can be so,[48] there is also a growing body of evidence which suggests that adverse psychological sequelae can flow from such knowledge.[49] For example, Almqvist et al.[50] found that the suicide rate among persons given a positive genetic test result for Huntington's disease was ten times higher than the US average.[51] The Danish Council of Bioethics gave early warning of the possibility of *morbidification*:

> The risk of participants in screening programmes possibly suffering from some form or other of morbidification or the notion of 'falling victim' to some inescapable 'fate' uncovered by the genetic examination in itself furnishes a basis for ensuring the provision of adequate information, counselling and follow-up in connection with such programmes.[52]

---

[46] V English and A Sommerville, 'Genetic privacy: Orthodoxy or oxymoron?' (1999) 25 J Med Ethics 144. Cf T M Marteau and C Lerman, 'Genetic risk and behavioural change' (2001) 322 BMJ 1056.

[47] Knowledge in this context will be relative both as to occurrence and severity of disease.

[48] H Toiviainen et al., 'Medical and lay attitudes towards genetic screening and testing in Finland' (2003) 11 Euro J Hum Gen 565; M R B Hayden, 'Predictive testing for Huntington's disease: Are we ready for widespread community implementation?' (1991) 40 Amer J Med Gen 515. Compare, J Lucke et al., 'The implications of genetic susceptibility for the prevention of colorectal cancer: A qualitative study of older adults' understanding' (2008) 11 Community Genet 283 and M Angrist, 'You never call, you never write: why return of "omic" results to research participants is both a good idea and a moral imperative' (2011) 8(6) Per Med 651.

[49] Cf S van Dooren et al., 'Psychological distress and breast self-examination frequency in women at increased risk for hereditary or familial breast cancer' (2003) 6 Community Genet 235 and Gonzalez et al., 'Short-term psychological impact of predictive testing for Macahdo-Joseph disease: Depression and anxiety levels in individuals at risk from the Azores' (2004) 7 Community Genet 196. See also D B Resnik, 'Disclosure of individualized research results: a precautionary approach' (2011) 18(6) Account Res 382 and D Cragun et al., 'Colorectal cancer survivors' interest in genetic testing for hereditary cancer: Implications for universal tumor screening' (2012) 16(6) Genet Test Mol Biomarkers 493. On developing appropriate support mechanisms, see M den Heijer et al. 'Long-term psychological distress in women at risk for hereditary breast cancer adhering to regular surveillance: a risk profile' (2013) 22(3) Psycho-Oncology 598.

[50] E Almqvist et al., 'A worldwide assessment of the frequency of suicide, suicide attempts, or psychiatric hospitalization after predictive testing for Huntington disease' (1999) 64 Amer J Hum Gen 1293. The authors surveyed 100 centres in 21 countries and gathered data on 4,527 individuals who had undergone predictive genetic testing for Huntington's disease. Of those reviewed, 1,817 people had received a positive result, of whom five had taken their own lives. This extrapolates to 138/100,000 suicides per year, compared with the US average of 12–13/100,000 per year. See also, C Licklederer, 'Mental health and quality of life after genetic testing for Huntington disease: a long-term effect study in Germany' (2008) 146A(16) Am J Med Genet A 2078. Cf, E M Wikler, R J Blendon, and J M Benson, 'Would you want to know? Public attitudes on early diagnostic testing for Alzheimer's disease' (2013) 5(5) Alzheimers Res Ther 43, doi: 10.1186/alzrt206.

[51] While this rate is no greater than that for the symptomatic Huntington's disease population, it is significant that the survey primarily focused on the two years after test results were given. This would tend to indicate that the deaths were more directly related to the disclosure of the genetic information, rather than to some other factors, such as the onset of the disease itself.

[52] Danish Council of Ethics, *Ethics and Mapping the Human Genome* (1993) p 60.

7.32   While it is important to draw a distinction between genetic *testing*, which involves an individual patient being tested in his or her own medical interests, and genetic *screening*, which involves the testing of populations for public health or research reasons, the Danish Council's observation remains valid in both contexts.[53] It is for reasons such as these that the now-defunct Advisory Committee on Genetic Testing (ACGT) issued a code of practice to regulate the availability of 'over-the-counter' genetic testing.[54] The Committee recommended strongly that only tests which reveal carrier status for inherent recessive disorders should be made available outside the National Health Service (NHS) genetic services.[55] Their rationale was that the discovery of carrier status has no direct health implications for the proband. In contrast, the ACGT code suggested that testing for adult onset dominant conditions and X-linked disorders should only be provided in a clinical setting.[56] The importance of full and proper counselling in this context cannot be over-emphasised. The Nuffield Council on Bioethics recognised the rising tsunami of testing provision relating to genetics and whole genome analysis in its 2010 report.[57] Rather than attempt to hold back the tide through regulation, its recommendations focused instead on more and better information for consumers about the likely (and limited) benefits or burdens of testing, save in the case of children where other considerations are in play as we discuss later.[58]

7.33   This kind of response has been mirrored in other bodies. The HGC conducted a public consultation and this resulted in its reports, *Genes Direct* (2003) and *More Genes Direct* (2007)[59] which take as a starting premise that 'the best way of protecting the public is through a combination of legal controls on the sale of tests and professional self-regulation of those who might supply tests'.[60] Thus, the Commission recommended stricter control of the supply of tests but it eschewed the statutory prohibition of some, or all, direct genetic tests. This was largely in recognition of the 'right' to obtain information about oneself and in the belief that the state should not intervene unless there is a risk of harm. By the same token, the Commission felt strongly that there should be more of a commitment to developing genetic services within the NHS so as to elide the possibility that the public would need to seek testing outside that context. Moreover, because of the potential impact of predictive testing, the Commission considered that most such instances should not be offered as direct tests (thereby reflecting the views of the ACGT). The *presumption* should be that such a genetic test is generally unsuitable for supply direct to the public; the onus, therefore, is on those who would seek to offer such a service to convince the regulatory authority that this is acceptable. The HGC also undertook to develop

---

[53] For a comparative survey see, *European Commission Survey on National Legislation and Activities in the Field of Genetic Testing in EU Member States* (2005), updated in part by Soini, n 44.

[54] The first such test made available in the UK was for cystic fibrosis: see ACGT First Annual Report: July 1996–December 1997 (1998).

[55] ACGT, *Code of Practice for Genetic Testing Offered Commercially Direct to the Public* (1997).

[56] ACGT, n 55, p 12.

[57] Nuffield Council on Bioethics, Medical Profiling and Online Medicine: The Ethics of Personalised Healthcare in a Consumer Age (2010) Appendix 1, Recommendations 30–7.

[58] See also Statement of the ESHG on direct-to-consumer genetic testing for health-related purposes (2010) 18(12) Eur J Hum Genet 127 1–3. Most recently, J Cussins, 'Direct-to-consumer genetic tests should come with a health warning' (2015), The Pharmaceutical Journal, available at: http://www.pharmaceutical-journal.com/opinion/comment/direct-to-consumer-genetic-tests-should-come-with-a-health-warning/20067564.article.

[59] HGC, *Genes Direct: Ensuring the Effective Oversight of Genetic Tests Supplied Directly to the Public* (2003) and HGC, *More Genes Direct* (2007).

[60] N 59, p 7.

a voluntary code of practice: *Common Framework of Principles for Direct-to-consumer Genetic Testing Services*. This aims to promote high standards and consistency among genetic test providers at international level. It champions the need that consumers be given simple information about the value and limits of the available tests and possible outcomes, tests for serious hereditary diseases should be accompanied by counselling both before and after testing, and companies must take steps to secure client privacy and to ensure that they have the appropriate consent from the sample source.[61] The House of Lords Science and Technology Committee expressed its support for such a code, opining that it should include a requirement on companies to make public information about the standards they follow and the accreditation required of them nationally.[62] The House of Lords also called upon the Department of Health to publish information on its website about accreditation and quality assurance schemes for companies offering such tests as well as scientific data about the robustness of tests themselves. The difficult problem of policing and enforcing controls over a very fluid and disparate international market remains.[63] This is well illustrated by the debacle over 23andme—the Californian for-profit organisation which has hit headlines around the world for its products related to genetic testing on 100+ disorders and 40+ inherited conditions. The company announced in late 2014 that it intended to begin marketing in Canada and the UK, despite having previously been ordered by the US Food and Drug Administration to discontinue marketing because on serious concerns about the scientific validity of the test results and whether consumers fully understood their implications. The reaction of the ethics community has been somewhat split along neo-liberal and more cautious and suspicious lines.[64] Approval for sale in the UK was allowed under the remit of the Medicines and Healthcare Products Regulatory Agency (MHRA), albeit a spokesman was reported as saying: 'Products used in personal genome services are regulated by MHRA to meet minimum standards. People who use these products should ensure that they are CE marked and remember that no test is 100% reliable so think carefully before using personal genome services.'[65]

7.34   Knowledge of one's own genetic constitution and of possible future ill health can have profound effects on one's sense of 'self'.[66] And, while an individual who seeks out genetic testing might have prepared himself for possible bad news, can the same be said of that person's relatives who might suspect nothing as to the presence of genetic disease in their family? Of high-risk couples, 85 per cent have been reported as having no knowledge of their condition. In such circumstances, information may come to these persons in ways

---

[61] Common Framework of Principles for Direct-to-Consumer Genetic Testing Services (2010). On the importance of consent and counselling, see too Organisation for Economic Co-Operation and Development, *Guidelines for Quality Assurance in Molecular Genetic Testing* (2007) p 13, reiterated in the Additional Protocol to the Oviedo Convention.

[62] N 4, para 6.66.

[63] As the House of Lords pointed out referring to the work of the HGC, 'as most of the companies that offer DCTs are based abroad, the Advertising Standards Agency "has no remit to regulate claims made by companies on their own websites (p 469)", n 4, para 6.62.

[64] Cf, C Siefe, '23andme is terrifying, but not for the reasons the FDA thinks, Scientific American, 27 November 2013, available at: http://www.scientificamerican.com/article/23andme-is-terrifying-but-not-for-reasons-fda/; and R C Green and N A Farahany, 'Regulation: The FDA is overcautious on consumer genomics' (2014) 505(7483) Nature 286.

[65] 'DNA-screening test 23andme launches in UK after US ban', *The Guardian*, 2 December 2014, available at: http://www.theguardian.com/technology/2014/dec/02/google-genetic-testing-23andme-uk-launch.

[66] See M L Underhill et al., 'Living My Family's Story: Identifying the Lived Experience in Healthy Women at Risk for Hereditary Breast Cancer' (2012) 35(6) Cancer Nurs 493 and M Levitt, 'The ethics and impact on behaviour of knowledge about one's own genome' (1999) 319 BMJ 1283.

which may raise issues of confidentiality. Even so, while the prevention of genetic disease may well be seen as admirable community medicine, there are difficulties when the principles are applied to the individual. Should one impose knowledge on someone who has not sought it and who may, perhaps irrationally, be disturbed as a consequence? At what stage should this knowledge be used? It is arguable that premarital advice is preferable to prenatal warning, but to implement such a policy has implications which are scarcely acceptable. On the other hand, has a doctor a moral duty to impose counselling? Here the roles of the genetic counsellor and the HCP assume paramount importance. The general practitioner and other health professional who is in possession of familial genetic information is in a particularly difficult position; he has a general duty of care to all his patients, but a specific duty of confidentiality to the proband. What should he do? It might be asked if there is a legal duty insofar as an action might be brought were parents to discover after the birth of an abnormal child that relevant information had been available but not disclosed,[67] or blood relatives lost out because of non-disclosure of relevant familial health information. Yet, as we discuss in Chapter 6, the practitioner might find himself facing an action for breach of confidence if disclosure was made. In legal terms, the UK has recently had its first legal decision on these issues which we explore at para 7.47 below.[68] First, however, we must consider the ethical arguments to allow us then to assess the direction of legal travel on such thorny issues.[69]

A RIGHT TO KNOW AND
A RIGHT NOT TO KNOW

7.35 The origin of this polemic lies in the fact that various parties have valid claims to the same information because, in essence, it relates to each of them.[70] One could, in the first instance, categorise the strength of any claim to information by straightforward reference to the degree of consanguinity: the chances of a second cousin being affected by the same genetic condition are statistically smaller than those of a first cousin and the strength of

---

[67] G Laurie, 'Obligations arising from genetic information: Negligence and the protection of familial interests' (1999) 11 CFLQ 109. See also R Brownsword, 'An interest in human dignity as the basis for genomic torts' (2003) 42 Washburn LJ 413.

[68] There is some US authority that supports disclosure, see e.g. *Safer* v *Estate of Pack* 677 A 2d 1188 (NJ, 1996), discussed in Laurie, n 1, pp 268–9. See also, K Offit et al., 'The "duty to warn" a patient's family members about hereditary disease risks' (2004) 292 JAMA 1469. For evidence of patient and professional attitudes, see K Kohut et al., 'Should healthcare providers have a duty to warn family members of individuals with an HNPCC-causing mutation? A survey of patients from the Ontario Familial Colon Cancer Registry' (2007) 44 J Med Genet 404, G C Crawford and A M Lucassen, 'Disclosure of genetic information within families: A case report' (2008) 3 Clinical Ethics 7. See also L Black and K A McClellan, 'Familial communication of research results: a need to know?' (2011) 39(4) J Law Med Ethics 605.

[69] For an evaluation of the arguments on both sides, see L Bortolotti and H Widdows, 'The right not to know: The case of psychiatric disorders' (2011) 37(11) J Med Ethics 673.

[70] This has been acknowledged by the Supreme Court of Iceland in a judgment in which the Court held that a daughter had legal standing to control the flow of information held in her deceased father's medical records because, in a certain sense, it also revealed something about her: see R Gertz, 'Is it "me" or "we"? Genetic relations and the meaning of "personal data" under the Data Protection Directive' (2004) 11 Euro J Health Law 231. See, too, the Opinions of the Article 29 Data Protection Working Party which acknowledges that genetic data can 'relate to' more than one individual, raising complex problems of regulation under data protection laws: *Working Document on Genetic Data* (2004) and Opinion No 4/2007 on the concept of personal data. For an argument that existing law can and should take a wider set of genetic interests into account, see M J Taylor, *Genetic Data and the Law: A Critical Perspective on Privacy Protection* (2012) ch 5.

any claim by the former is correspondingly weaker. This is, however, an unsophisticated approach and unhelpful in the case of the nuclear family, where claims to the information are at their strongest. Matters are complicated by the additional problem of deciding what is the best thing to do—to disclose or not to disclose? While few would argue that the risk of genetic disease should be withheld from family members when an effective treatment or cure is available, the motivation for disclosure in the absence of treatment is, once again, called into question. If the aim is to facilitate preparedness, then the HCP must consider the possibility that a relative might not, in fact, wish to know that he might develop a genetic disease for which nothing can be done. Yet, even if the practitioner is confident that a relative would wish to know, he must justify any disclosing action in ethical terms if he is faced with the proband's refusal to authorise release of the information. Current ethical principles are tested to their limits in such circumstances. As Ngwena and Chadwick rightly state:

> what has to be taken into account is the fact that respecting the autonomy of one person may have implications for the autonomy of others. As the Royal College of Physicians argue, 'Blood relatives have an interest in knowing the truth which has nothing to do with influencing their behaviour towards affected individuals in their families, but as a necessary means to finding out the truth about themselves' ... How is the choice between the autonomy of different people made? ... What is clear is that the decision cannot be taken *on autonomy grounds*.[71]

7.36 The ethical principle of respect for patient confidentiality assists the practitioner to a certain degree in that it constitutes one of his primary duties to the proband. Yet release of the information can be justified equally by reference to the principle of non-maleficence if he genuinely believes that harm to relatives (or even their progeny) can be averted through disclosure—neither in ethics nor law is the principle of confidentiality seen as absolute (see Chapter 6). The General Medical Council (GMC) has recognised the issue in the most recent version of its guidance on confidentiality and confirms that disclosure to family members might be justifiable in certain circumstances; ultimately, however, the Council leaves the final ethical decision to the individual practitioner:

> If a patient refuses consent to disclosure, you will need to balance your duty to make the care of your patient your first concern against your duty to help protect the other person from serious harm. If practicable, you should not disclose the patient's identity in contacting and advising others of the risks they face.[72]

This guidance also ignores the possibility of relatives having an interest in not knowing.

7.37 If the avoidance of harm is, indeed, the paramount consideration, then the prospect of harming a relative who might be disturbed by unsolicited information must also be considered. For this and other reasons, we argue elsewhere that the interest or right not to know deserves recognition.[73] Moreover, the basis of this interest lies not in autonomy

---

[71] C Ngwena and R Chadwick, 'Genetic diagnostic information and the duty of confidentiality: Ethics and law' (1993) 1 Med Law Internat 73 at 77.

[72] GMC, *Confidentiality* (2009) para 69.

[73] Generally, Laurie, n 1, esp ch 5. More recently, this argument has been deepened and expanded in G Laurie, 'Recognizing the Right Not to Know: Conceptual, Professional, and Legal Implications' (2014) 42(1) J Law Med and Ethics 53, and G Laurie, 'Privacy and the right not to know: a plea for conceptual clarity' in D Shickle et al. (eds), *The Right to Know and the Right Not to Know: Genetic Privacy and Responsibility* (2014), ch 2.

or confidentiality but, rather, in privacy.[74] Privacy consists of two aspects: informational privacy and spatial privacy. Informational privacy is concerned with the control of personal information and with preventing access to that information by others. An invasion of informational privacy occurs when any unauthorised disclosure of information takes place. Confidentiality is a subset of this privacy interest and is breached when confidential information which is the subject of the relationship is released to parties outside the relationship without authorisation. Informational privacy is wider than this in that it does not require a relationship to exist.

7.38 Spatial privacy protects the individual's sense of 'self'. It recognises the interest which each of us has in maintaining a sense of separateness from others. Our spatial privacy is invaded when others 'invade our space' and this includes invasion of our psychological privacy which occurs, inter alia, when unsolicited information about oneself is received. An interest in *not* knowing about oneself has been recognised by the Convention for the Protection of Human Rights and Dignity of the Human Being with regard to the Application of Biology and Medicine (Oviedo Convention),[75] Art 10(2) of which states:

> Everyone is entitled to know any information collected about his or her health. *However, the wishes of individuals not to be so informed shall be observed.* [Emphasis added.]

Similarly, the UNESCO Universal Declaration on the Human Genome and Human Rights[76] states in Art 5c that:

> The right of every individual to decide whether *or not* to be informed of the results of genetic examination and the resulting consequences should be respected. [Emphasis added.]

And this is now also found in the Additional Protocol on Genetic Testing to the Oviedo Convention, Art 16(3): 'The wish of a person not to be informed shall be respected.'[77]

7.39 However, the efficacy of grounding such a 'right' *solely* in terms of choice is doubtful.[78] The principle of respect for autonomy requires that we see the individual as a 'moral chooser'.[79] In order to choose meaningfully we require full information about the range of options available and the consequences of any particular choice. Unfortunately, this paradigm breaks down in the context of an interest in not knowing genetic information. Here, the choice is about knowledge itself. As Wertz and Fletcher put it:

> There is no way ... to exercise the choice of not knowing, because in the very process of asking 'Do you want to know whether you are at risk ... ?' the geneticist has already made the essence of the information known.[80]

---

[74] Cf R Andorno, 'The right not to know: An autonomy-based approach' (2004) 30 J Med Ethics 435 and G Laurie, 'Commentary' (2004) 30 J Med Ethics 439.

[75] Council of Europe, *Convention for the Protection of Human Rights and Dignity of the Human Being with regard to the Application of Biology and Medicine: Convention on Human Rights and Medicine Oviedo* (1997).

[76] Adopted unanimously on 11 November 1997 in Paris at the Organisation's 29th General Conference.

[77] Council of Europe, *Additional Protocol to the Convention on Human Rights and Biomedicine, Concerning Genetic Testing for Health Purposes* (2008).

[78] Cf J Husted, 'Autonomy and a right not to know' in R Chadwick, M Levitt, and D Shickle (eds), *The Right to Know and the Right Not to Know* (1997) ch 6.

[79] This expression is borrowed from Stanley Benn, who explores the ideas of the 'moral chooser' and 'private life', inter alia, in *A Theory of Freedom* (1988).

[80] D C Wertz and J C Fletcher, 'Privacy and disclosure in medical genetics examined in an ethic of care' (1991) 5 Bioethics 212 at 221.

The principle of respect for patient confidentiality is similarly unhelpful in protecting the interest in not knowing. It is simply not meaningful to talk of a breach of confidence when information about the party to whom the duty is owed is disclosed *to that party*.

7.40 How then is the interest in not knowing to be protected? It is argued in more detail elsewhere that the concept of spatial privacy—which requires that a degree of respect be paid prima facie to an individual's state of separateness or, in this case, state of 'ignorance'—provides a viable mechanism.[81] Spatial privacy can be invaded legitimately, but only if good cause can be shown. The following criteria could be considered for use by any HCP when deciding how to resolve competing claims to genetic information in the familial context:

- the availability of a therapy or cure;
- the severity of the condition and the likelihood of onset;
- the nature of the genetic disease;
- the nature of any further testing which might be required;
- the nature of the information to be disclosed;
- the nature of the request (e.g., testing for the individual's health or for diagnostic purposes for a relative);
- the question of whether disclosure can further a legitimate public interest; and
- the question of how the individual might react if offered unsolicited information (e.g., whether any advance directive has been made).

7.41 It can therefore be argued that a practitioner who is faced with a refusal by a proband to communicate test results to relatives when a cure or effective treatment is available would be justified in disrespecting the proband's wishes in order to protect other family members from harm. He might, however, be rightly less inclined to disclose information about a condition for which nothing can be done and which has relatively mild symptoms. This nuanced approach can be supplemented by taking a hierarchical attitude when testing families—the need to test members of the younger generation can be greatly clarified if the older generations are approached and tested first.[82] The HGC endorsed such a balancing approach:

> Bearing in mind the principle of genetic solidarity and altruism,[83] we take the view that disclosure of sensitive personal genetic information for the benefit of family members in certain circumstances may occasionally be justified. This would arise where the patient refuses to consent to such disclosure and the benefit of disclosure substantially outweighs the patient's claim to confidentiality.

7.42 However, the HGC went on to state that such disclosure should be subject to the provisos that:

> (1) an attempt has been made to persuade the patient in question to consent; (2) the benefit to those at risk is so considerable as to outweigh any distress which disclosure would cause

[81] Laurie, n 1.
[82] See B S Wilfond et al., 'Cancer genetic susceptibility testing: Ethical and policy implementations for future research and clinical practice' (1997) 25 J Law Med & Ethics 243.
[83] These principles remind us that, 'We all share the same basic human genome, although there are individual variations which distinguish us from other people. Most of our genetic characteristics will be present in others. This sharing of genetic constitution not only gives rise to opportunities to help others but it also highlights our common interest in the fruits of medically-based research', see HGC, *Inside Information*, n 38, para 2.11.

the patient; and (3) the information is, as far as possible, anonymised and restricted to that which is strictly necessary for the communication of risk.[84]

Of course, the problem of controlling communication between family members always remains, and a particularly problematic scenario arises when members of the younger generations are tested for a genetic condition and found to be positive. This must mean that one or more parents or grandparents are also affected in some way, yet these persons may have no idea of their condition or may have chosen not to know. It can be very difficult to stem the tidal flow of information within the familial milieu.

7.43 It is in the case of children that an appreciation of these subtleties can be found among legislatures and governments. In the USA, the model Genetic Privacy Act was drafted in 1995 as part of the Ethical, Legal and Social Implications (ELSI) division of the Human Genome Project. This was a piece of model federal legislation designed for possible adoption by individual states. The draft explains the Act's remit:

> the overarching premise of the Act is that no stranger should have or control identifiable DNA samples or genetic information about an individual unless that individual specifically authorizes the collection of DNA samples for the purpose of genetic analysis, authorizes the creation of that private information, and has access to and control over the dissemination of that information.

7.44 The draft Act purports to give an individual from whom a sample is taken (the 'sample source') a number of rights, including the right to determine who may collect and analyse DNA, the right to determine the purposes for which a sample can be analysed, and the right to order destruction of samples. Those who collect samples have a number of corresponding duties. The Act also protects genetic information from a number of potential abuses by third parties, such as the state or employers and insurers, and we return to this later.[85] For present purposes we focus on the provisions of the Act which deal with testing minors for genetic conditions.

7.45 The draft Genetic Privacy Act provides that an individually identifiable DNA sample source shall not be taken from a minor under 16 to detect any genetic condition which, in reasonable medical judgement, does not produce signs or symptoms of disease before the age of 16 unless an effective intervention is available to delay onset or ameliorate the severity of the disease; the said intervention must be made before the age of 16 and written authorisation has to be given by the minor's representative. The rationale behind this has been explained by the authors of the Act:

> There are two reasons for this prohibition on the exercise of parental discretion. First, if someone learns that the child is a carrier of a gene that disposes the child to some condition later in life, this finding may subject the child to discrimination and stigmatization by both the parents and others who may learn of this fact. Second, a child's genetic status is the *child's* private genetic information and should not be determined or disclosed unless there is some compelling reason to do so. [Emphasis added.][86]

---

[84] HGC, *Inside Information*, n 38, para 3.68.   [85] See paras 7.48 et seq.
[86] The Act was drafted by George Annas, Leonard Glantz, and Patricia Roche of the Boston University School of Public Health. A text of the Act and the comments of the authors can be found at: http://web.ornl. gov/sci/techresources/Human_Genome/resource/privacyact.pdf.

Similar sentiments are found in Europe and in legal terms in the Additional Protocol to the Oviedo Convention, Art 10:

> a genetic test on a person who does not have the capacity to consent may only be carried out for his or her direct benefit. Where, according to law, a minor does not have the capacity to consent, a genetic test on this person shall be deferred until attainment of such capacity unless that delay would be detrimental to his or her health or well-being.[87]

A similar professional policy position has been endorsed by the European Society of Human Genetics.[88]

7.46 Domestically, various bodies have considered these issues and produced guidelines which show great sensitivity in respect of genetic information. In particular, the ACGT made an early and strong recommendation that no pre-symptomatic testing for late onset disorders for which there are no clinical treatments should be carried out on minors under 16,[89] and this was endorsed by the HGC.[90] A government review of 2008[91] charted five years' progress noting that the HGC and the UK National Screening Committee had investigated the issues surrounding the prospect of genetic profiling of newborn children. The conclusion of the report, reflecting the arguments outlined here, was that genetic profiling of children on a population basis was both impractical and unacceptable for the foreseeable future.[92]

7.47 And so, what have the British courts made of these kinds of arguments? As indicated above, the first legal case has recently been decided and we introduced this in Chapter 6. Its fully implications are, however, best considered in this chapter because its facts mirror many of the dilemmas outlined above. In *ABC* v *St George's Healthcare NHS*[93] the central legal question was the existence of a duty of care to the daughter of a man suffering from Huntington's disease which, as we have outlined above, is a dominant genetic disorder where the risks to children are 50:50 for each child. In tragic family circumstances, the father had shot and killed the claimant's mother and was being held under the Mental Health Act 1983. The father refused to allow medical staff to tell the daughter of his condition, despite the fact that she attended family therapy sessions with him, and irrespective of the fact that she was pregnant. In the event, the daughter was also

---

[87] This is subject to an important rider in Art 13:

> Exceptionally … the law may allow a genetic test to be carried out, for the benefit of family members, on a person who does not have the capacity to consent, if the following conditions are met: (a) the purpose of the test is to allow the family member(s) concerned to obtain a preventive, diagnostic or therapeutic benefit that has been independently evaluated as important for their health, or to allow them to make an informed choice with respect to procreation; (b) the benefit envisaged cannot be obtained without carrying out this test; (c) the risk and burden of the intervention are minimal for the person who is undergoing the test; (d) the expected benefit has been independently evaluated as substantially outweighing the risk for private life that may arise from the collection, processing or communication of the results of the test; (e) the authorisation of the representative of the person not able to consent, or an authority or a person or body provided for by law has been given; and (f) the person not able to consent shall, in proportion to his or her capacity to understand and degree of maturity, take part in the authorisation procedure. The test shall not be carried out if this person objects to it.

[88] European Society of Human Genetics, 'Genetic testing in asymptomatic minors: recommendations of the European Society of Human Genetics' (2009) 17 Euro J Hum Gen 720.

[89] HGC, *Inside Information*, n 38, para 4.37.   [90] HGC, *Inside Information*, n 38, para 7.6.

[91] Updated in 2013, see N 32.

[92] HGC, *Profiling the Newborn: A Prospective Gene Technology?* (2005).

[93] [2015] EWHC 1394 (QB); [2015] PIQR P18; [2015] Med LR 307.

diagnosed with the condition; because of the ethical practices outlined above—namely, not testing children for late onset disorders—it was not known whether the condition had also been passed to the child. Notwithstanding, it was the argument of the daughter in this case that—had she been informed at a suitable time—she would have taken a test and terminated the pregnancy on the positive diagnosis. Accordingly, she brought an action claiming (a) negligence on the part of the medical professional responsible for her father's care, and (b) violation of her human rights. While the court acknowledged, as we have seen above, that any duty of confidentiality to the father was not absolute, this itself did not impose a *duty* to disclose relevant information to third parties. Rather, any duty would have to be found in the law of negligence. The opinion of the judge in this regard was that there was no analogous precedent to impose a duty in such a case; nor was it fair, just, and reasonable to do so in the circumstances given—as the court saw it—this entirely novel extension of duty and the possible downstream consequences of such a duty, including, for example undermining trust in the doctor–patient relationship and leading to doctors placing undue pressure on patients to allow disclosures. This case was a strike-out application and so at a very early stage. If it is appealed, then other arguments might be brought to bear, including the highly particular nature of the genetic condition and its severity; the nature of public interest in such a scenario set against the reasonableness of the proband's refusal to disclose, and a deep consideration of what, precisely, counts as fair, just, and reasonable within such a fraught family and highly-unusual dynamic. As it stands, the case offers little to engage or advance the ethical arguments.[94]

OTHER PARTIES' INTERESTS IN GENETIC INFORMATION

7.48 A number of parties outside the family context profess an interest in access to genetic information. These include insurers, current and prospective employers, researchers, and the state itself. In this section, the nature of the interests at stake is considered and their respective weights in light of the interests of the proband and his relatives are assessed.[95] The important issue of protection against genetic discrimination is also addressed.

INSURANCE

7.49 The forms of insurance most relevant to genetic testing are life and health insurance. Private health insurance is currently less important in the UK than in other jurisdictions because of the existence of the NHS. Life insurance, however, can be a prerequisite for certain types of loan, including mortgages for the purchase of property. Many individuals also take out life insurance to protect their families in the event of their own premature death and, as we face the growing needs of an increasingly aged population, long-term care insurance is becoming a necessity. In times of financial uncertainty, income-protection

---

[94] For a blog post arguing that the decision is wrong, see R Gilbar and C Foster, 'Do I Have a Right to Access My Father's Genetic Account?', available at: http://blog.practicalethics.ox.ac.uk/2015/05/do-i-have-a-right-to-access-my-fathers-genetic-account/.

[95] See generally, B Godard et al., 'Genetic information and testing in insurance and employment: Technical, social and ethical issues' (2003) 11 Supp 2 Euro J Hum Gen S123.

insurance also becomes a popular option. Insurance thus touches the lives of most of us and its denial can have far-reaching consequences for both individuals and families.

7.50 Genetic information can clearly be important to the insurance industry in order to assess the risk of providing cover at all and to determine the level of premiums if an offer of insurance is made. The nature of the interest at stake is entirely financial, and it is one that the industry may legitimately seek to protect. An insurance contract is an example of a contract *uberrima fides*: of the utmost good faith. In practice, this means that any information having a bearing on the assessment of risk should be disclosed to the insurer; otherwise, the contract can be avoided at any future time. Two possible avenues are open to the insurer in the context of genetic information. First, a request can be made that all test results be disclosed. Second, the insurer can require that the prospective insured undergo genetic testing. In respect of the first of these, it might be argued that this is no different from any other form of medical history. A genetic test result should be disclosed in the same way as one would disclose the removal of a melanoma or a family history of high blood pressure.

7.51 That having been said, concern has been expressed in many quarters that individuals might be deterred from seeking testing if it were to be the case that all test results should be disclosed. As the Science and Technology Committee commented:

> We accept that the insurance industry has collectively tried to deal with genetics in a responsible way; nonetheless we are concerned there is a real danger that people could decide to decline testing, even when such testing would be advantageous to them, because of the possible insurance implications.[96]

Harper has argued that insurers should not be allowed to require disclosure of genetic test results within the ordinary run of life insurance policies.[97] But, even so, the problem remains of deciding whether a family history—as a form of genetic information—should also be excluded in such circumstances. The HGC expressed reservations on this matter, and called for further research.[98] Whether it is right that the increased costs of such a scheme should be passed on to the 'normal' population is probably a matter for Parliament to decide; ultimately, we cannot escape the fact that insurance, as with most social constructs, is a cultural phenomenon. The task, then, is to match the most appropriate legal response to the way in which we wish insurance to operate within our culture. An approach that is biased towards solidarity might be an acceptable price to pay for a gesture of support for those who, through no fault of their own, are likely to find themselves increasingly disadvantaged.[99]

7.52 As a measure of our cultural expectations with respect to genetics and insurance, it is illuminating to consider a MORI poll on public attitudes to human genetic information. This showed that the use of genetic information to set insurance premiums was thought to be the least appropriate of the possible uses of that information. Four out of five respondents said it should not be used for that purpose.[100]

---

[96] Third Report, n 7, para 242.

[97] P S Harper, 'Insurance and genetic testing' (1993) 341 Lancet 224. See, now, P Harper et al., 'Genetic testing and Huntington's disease: Issues of employment' (2004) 3 Lancet Neurology 249.

[98] HGC, *Inside Information*, n 38, paras 7.16–7.18.

[99] There are two basic models of insurance: mutuality and solidarity. The former provides that the contribution of individuals should approximately reflect their level of risk. The principle of solidarity, however, requires that the burden of bearing risks is spread throughout the general body of insured persons.

[100] HGC, *Public Attitudes*, n 40, para 33.

7.53 As to insurers actively requiring prospective customers to be tested, the fear has been expressed that the increased availability of tests will lead to the 'development and pro-liferation of predictive genetic testing'.[101] This is to be deprecated because of the serious implications which it has for the (spatial) privacy interests of individuals required to be tested. An unacceptable degree of coercion is brought to bear in such circumstances which might vitiate any 'consent' to undergo testing. This outcome has not transpired since the fear was first voiced, but rather other means have been used to access infor-mation by insurers, including asking prospective insured persons for consent to the full medical record. Absent the provision of the moratorium discussed below, this insidi-ous practice has caused much concern within the British Medical Association which has issued guidance to its members on how to deal with such requests, including contacting patients to ensure they are fully aware of the consequences.[102]

7.54 The Council of Europe Recommendation on the protection of medical data which are processed automatically, specifically includes genetic information.[103] The Council recom-mends that Member States take steps to ensure that their laws and practices reflect certain key principles embodied in the Recommendation. These provide, among other things, that medical data should, in principle, be collected only by HCPs or their assistants and, in the context of genetic information, this should only be for preventive treatment, diag-nosis or treatment of the data subject, or for scientific research, judicial procedure, or criminal investigation. The collection and processing of genetic data outside these catego-ries should be permitted only for health reasons; it could be allowed in order to predict ill health, but only in the case of an overriding interest and subject to appropriate safeguards defined by law. The drafters of the Recommendation make it clear in the Explanatory Memorandum that:

> a candidate for employment, an insurance contract or other services or activities should not be forced to undergo a genetic analysis, by making employment or the insurance dependent on such an analysis, unless such dependence is explicitly provided for by the law and the analysis is necessary for the protection of the data subject or a third party.[104]

The January 2012 draft of a Data Protection Regulation addresses explicitly, for the first time in this area of law within the European Union, the processing of genetic data.[105] Such processing is unlawful under draft Art 9(1) unless the provisions on lawful processing in draft Art 9(2) are complied with.

7.55 The Nuffield Council on Bioethics has opined that those individuals with a known fam-ily history who decide to take a test and test positive should not be treated by the insur-ance company any differently from other family members—that is, they should still be

---

[101] R Chadwick and C Ngwena, 'The human genome project, predictive testing and insurance con-tracts: Ethical and legal responses' (1995) 1 Res Publica 115.

[102] BMA, Focus on Subject Access Requests for Insurance Purposes (2015).

[103] Council of Europe, *The Protection of Medical Data*, Recommendation No (97) 5 and explanatory memorandum, 13 February 1997.

[104] Council of Europe, *The Protection of Medical Data*, Recommendation No (97) 5 and Explanatory Memorandum, 13 February 1997, para 103.

[105] 'Genetic data' is defined as '...all data, of whatever type, concerning the characteristics of an indi-vidual which are inherited or acquired during early prenatal development', draft Art 4(10) of Proposal for a Regulation of the European Parliament and of the Council on the protection of individuals with regard to the processing of personal data and on the free movement of such data (General Data Protection Regulation), 25 January 2012, COM(2012) 11 final. At the time of writing (summer 2015) discussions towards final adop-tion were proceeding but there was no change to this specific provision.

assessed at the same level of risk as those family members who have not been tested.[106] It was reasoned that, since the industry tends to interpret family history cautiously,[107] 'there is unlikely to be a major difference in insurability between an individual with a family history of a genetic disorder and an individual who has had a positive genetic test result'. By corollary, the Council envisages that those who test negative should benefit from this result and be treated as persons with no family history. In this way the Council hopes that individuals will not be deterred from having genetic tests and also that insurers will not be adversely affected, since they can continue their present practice based on family history. However, the recommendations of the Council are somewhat different in respect of population screening programmes. In such cases the majority of those taking part would not be aware of any family history of disease. The Council considers that:

> If insurers were to demand access to the results of population screening for polygenic or multifactorial disease (for example, for genetic predisposition to breast cancer), and premiums were increased for those who tested positive, many people would clearly be discouraged from participating in such programmes. This could have adverse consequences both for the health of individuals and for the public health,[108]

and it concludes that it is not acceptable for insurers to have access to the results of genetic screening. Furthermore, because of the principle of free and informed consent (discussed in Chapter 4), genetic testing should not be made a prerequisite for obtaining insurance. Thus, it can be seen that the Council is emphatic that genetic testing solely for the purposes of assessing insurance risk is unacceptable—and this is true both for those who have a family history and for those who do not.

7.56   In the absence of clear government guidelines or legislative intervention, the Association of British Insurers (ABI), whose representatives account for 95 per cent of insurance business in the UK, affirmed in 1997 and 1999 that insurers would not require a genetic test as a prerequisite for insurance cover. Moreover, a voluntary Code of Practice, which lays out the principles by which the ABI and its members abide, was developed in 1997. The current version dates from 2014 and will remain in effect until 2019 with a review in 2016.[109] The Code contains details of the Concordat and Moratorium on Genetics and Insurance which is an agreement between the ABI and the government about the industry's use of genetic test results.

7.57   The moratorium instructs members of the industry not to ask for any genetic test results from applicants for any insurance policies of less than £500,000 for life insurance, less than £300,000 for critical illness cover, or paying annual benefits of less than £30,000 for income protection insurance. Above these limits,[110] only tests approved by the government

---

[106] Nuffield Council on Bioethics, *Genetic Screening: Ethical Issues* (1993) para 7.28.
[107] E.g. the Council notes that (para 7.23):

Tables used by the insurance industry show that insurers treat 5% risk of developing Huntington's disease in the same way as a 50% risk: such individuals may be declined insurance or offered insurance at an increased premium, depending on their age at the time of application. Insurance prospects for individuals with a family history of Huntington's disease only improve when the risk is below 5%.

[108] Nuffield Council on Bioethics, *Genetic Screening: Ethical Issues* (1993) para 7.31.
[109] ABI, *Code of Practice for Genetic Tests* (2008).
[110] Previously, only tests approved by the Genetics and Insurance Committee would have been taken into account but the body was only in existence from 1999 to 2009 and only ever approved the test for Huntington's disease in the context of life insurance. In 2009, it reported that it had only received three legitimate complaints in the preceding five years about the use of genetic test results for insurance purposes.

and whose results are relevant to particular insurance products can be used after consultation with independent experts (para 35). Approval will only be possible for conditions that are monogenic, late onset, and highly penetrant (para 17). To date, no such approval has been given as far as we know.

7.58 The House of Lords Science and Technology Committee released its report on Genomic Medicine against this uncertain and ever-changing background. Its primary concern was the prospect that requests might be made for genetic results generated during the moratorium once it comes to an end: this is the so-called 'sunset clause'. Its recommendation was that the government negotiates a new clause in the Code of Practice, Memorandum, and Concordat that would prevent such an eventuality. This is not addressed in the latest version of the Concordat. The Science and Technology Committee was also of the view that a longer term solution must be found that is better than the current approach which simply extends the moratorium further into the future but always for limited periods of time. Any such plans must include adequate monitoring mechanisms of the industry and its use of genetic test results.[111]

EMPLOYMENT

7.59 An employer might have two contrasting reasons for seeking access to genetic information about his employees or future employees. First, there is a financial interest in not employing persons who are likely to become debilitated through disease and so affect profits through days lost. Second, he or she might have a genuine concern that the working environment could affect an employee's health adversely, perhaps by exacerbating an existing condition or by provoking symptoms in an otherwise asymptomatic individual.[112] This concern might relate to the person's health *in se*, and/or to the fear that compensation could be sought by an individual so affected. The propriety of permitting an employer or prospective employer access to genetic information must be addressed in each case. As with the insurance industry, access could be granted either to existing test results or a genetic test could be made a condition of the employment contract. Moreover, a request for genetic information could be made either pre- or post-employment.

7.60 Pre-employment requests for genetic information are the most effective means of reducing costs for the employer. Little expenditure is incurred in obtaining the information; the prospective employee is asked either to reveal existing knowledge or to take a relatively inexpensive test. No future expenditure need be incurred because the employer has no obligation to do so in the absence of an employment contract.

7.61 An employer who seeks genetic information from a current employee is in a very different position. Time and money may have been spent training someone who now cannot do the job, and termination of the employment contract is subject to strict requirements. All of which means that it is very much in the employer's financial interests to seek genetic information from *potential* rather than from *actual* employees. And one might argue that *future* employees can (and should) be excluded from employment if information reveals either the actual presence of, or a predisposition to, genetic disease such as is likely to pose a risk to themselves and/or others if they are employed.

---

[111] N 4, paras 6.41–6.50.
[112] E.g. an environment which is dense with heavy particles is very bad for individuals suffering from or prone to alpha 1-antitrypsin deficiency because this can lead to emphysema.

7.62 This advantage of pre-employment screening was considered further by the Nuffield Council on Bioethics, which stated:

> Employees would, in principle, be empowered to avoid occupations which would increase the risk of ill health and which in the long run might be life threatening. In this way they could protect the economic security of themselves and their families.[113]

7.63 A major difficulty with such an otherwise defensible approach lies in the fact that the accuracy of genetic predictive information is far from assured, and the very factors which concern employers—such as the likely date of onset and degree of affliction—are unlikely to be known. Also, the sensitivity of such information and the apparent public misunderstanding which surrounds genetic information provoke the very legitimate fear that the information could be used to exclude individuals from employment, or to terminate employment, even when they are not affected by disease and are unlikely to be so for some time. The question thus arises as to whether access to genetic information is an acceptable way by which to ensure the interests of employers and of employees or job applicants.[114] The European Group on Ethics has opined that only the present health status of employees should be considered in the employment context.[115]

7.64 A number of bodies in the UK have recognised and appreciated the privacy implications of employer requests for genetic information.[116] Relying heavily on recommendations of the Nuffield Council, the House of Commons Science and Technology Committee recommended a number of years ago that legislation to protect the privacy of genetic information be introduced and be drafted so as to prohibit employers testing for genetic conditions other than those which might put the public at direct and substantial risk. Furthermore, any genetic testing for employment purposes should be strictly limited to specific conditions relevant to the particular employment and samples provided for testing should not be examined for evidence of other conditions.[117] The House of Lords Science and Technology Committee took the opposite view. Its inquiry did not find a sufficient evidence base to warrant legislative intervention—a 2006 report from the HGC found 'no significant evidence of genetic testing occurring in the workplace'—and the uncertain state of the science militates against the routine use of testing in the employment context. Notwithstanding, the House of Lords recommended that the situation be kept under scrutiny.[118] No legislative moves have occurred since.

7.65 Whatever one's view on the need for statutory intervention, the clear message here is that employers' access to genetic information must be justified on the grounds that the knowledge can have a direct bearing on the job of work to be done. In other words, it is unacceptable for an employer to seek access to individual's genetic information simply to further his financial interests. This is especially true when that access is sought in order to identify some *future* risk when that possibility does not affect the individual's current ability to perform his or her work.

---

[113] N 22, para 6.6.

[114] It should be noted, however, that the HGC found no evidence that there is any systematic use of predictive genetic information in employment in the UK: see HGC, *Inside Information*, n 38, para 8.9.

[115] European Group on Ethics Opinion No 18, *Ethical Aspects of Genetic Testing in the Workplace* (2003). For comment see N A Holtzman, 'Ethical aspects of genetic testing in the workplace' (2003) 6 Community Genetics 136.

[116] See Nuffield Council on Bioethics, n 22 above, paras 6.20–6.23, the House of Commons Science and Technology Committee (1995), n 7 above, paras 231–3, and the Human Genetics Advisory Commission The Implications of Genetic Testing for Employment (1999).

[117] Science and Technology Committee Report quoting Memorandum (vol II) p 52.

[118] N 4, paras 6.36–6.40.

7.66 What, however, of the argument that genetic information should be revealed in order to protect the interests of employees and job applicants themselves? The House of Commons Science and Technology Committee concluded that:

> Genetic Screening for employment purposes should be contemplated only where:
>
> (i)   there is strong evidence of a clear connection between the working environment and the development of the condition for which the screening is conducted;
>
> (ii) the condition in question is one which seriously endangers the health of the employee; and
>
> (iii) the condition is one for which the dangers cannot be eliminated or significantly reduced by reasonable measures taken by the employer to modify or respond to the environmental risks.[119]

Importantly, the Committee stressed that 'employees should have the right to decide whether or not to participate in such screening'. It is unclear, however, whether the recommendations are intended to extend both to current employees and job applicants. No convincing argument could be put that this should not be the case, but the Committee only mentions 'employees'. The HGC broadly agreed with this, but emphasised that employers must not demand that an individual take a genetic test as a condition of employment. There must be compelling medical or safety grounds for offering a genetic test in any other circumstances, and this is now part of equality protection, as we see further later.[120] As regards future uses of personal genetic information, the HGC recommended a voluntary undertaking by employers to inform the HGC of any proposals to use genetic testing for health and safety or recruitment purposes and, also, the establishment of a joint committee to monitor developments in genetic testing in this field. All of this is reflected at the European level in the Opinion of the European Group on Ethics, viz: when, in exceptional circumstances, genetic screening is thought to be necessary to guarantee worker health, this is only acceptable if the following conditions are fulfilled:

> (i)   the performance of the test is necessary for guaranteeing the protection of the employee's health and safety or those of third parties;
>
> (ii) there is scientifically proven evidence that the genetic test is valid and is the only method to obtain this information;
>
> (iii) the performance of the test does not prejudice the aim of improving conditions in the workplace;
>
> (iv) the principle of proportionality is respected regarding the motivations involved to perform the test; and
>
> (v)   the principle of non-discrimination is not violated.[121]

7.67 The European Group on Ethics and the House of Lords have both pointed out that there has been far more interest in genetic testing in the employment context in the USA compared with Europe or the UK because employers in the former often contribute to health

---

[119] See n 7 at 233. For a criticism of the Nuffield Council's recommendations, and by implications those of the Science and Technology Committee, see M A Rothstein, 'Genetic discrimination in employment: Ethics, policy and comparative law' in O Guillod and P Widmer (eds), *Human Genetic Analysis and the Protection of Personality and Privacy* (1994).

[120] HGC, *Inside Information*, n 38, generally ch 8.   [121] N 115, paras 2.11–2.12.

insurance as part of the employee's contractual entitlements;[122] there is, of course, concern that US models for health insurance might start to apply in Europe. At present, there is only one example that can be found of genetic screening in the workplace in Europe and this is the screening of British aircrew for the sickle cell gene (which might give rise to susceptibility to low oxygen levels at altitude). But even this was eventually abandoned. Nonetheless, vigilance must remain the watchword. Where pressures to use genetic tests become great and where individual rights and interests are at stake, then we once again enter the discussion about whether law should intervene. The central issue is the spectre of discrimination, and it is to this that we now turn.

DISCRIMINATION

7.68 Perhaps the single most important concern related to genetic information lies in the potential for discrimination that it generates.[123] This is relevant to both the employment and insurance scenarios, yet no specific legal regulation currently exists in the UK to control genetic testing or screening or the uses to which the results can be put.[124] The matter of discrimination must, therefore, be dealt with under the current anti-discrimination laws. The Lisbon Treaty, Art 21, outlaws any discrimination on a range of grounds that includes genetic features as a matter of broad principle of European law.

7.69 More focused efforts have occurred in the USA where the Equal Employment Opportunity Commission (EEOC) settled its first court action in April 2001.[125] The Burlington Northern Santa Fe (BNSF) railway had implemented a programme of genetic testing of previously donated samples without the knowledge or consent of employees to investigate worker claims for injuries based on carpal tunnel syndrome. At least one worker had been threatened with termination of employment for refusing to submit to testing. The settlement ensured that the employer would not directly or indirectly require its employees to submit blood for genetic tests, nor would it analyse any blood previously obtained. The settlement was deemed to be enforceable by the relevant District Court, although the Court in question was at pains to point out that it offered no ruling on the respective arguments of the parties under the Americans with Disabilities Act 1990.[126] The majority of states have, in fact, legislated against genetic discrimination resulting in a patchwork of protection across the country.

7.70 More recently, the US Senate passed the Genetic Information Non-discrimination Act 2008. This federal Act is designed to protect citizens from discrimination in the insurance and employment contexts and to provide a degree of uniform protection that will sit above the myriad state provisions that already exist but which provide a wide variation of measures. Broadly, the legislation prevents health insurers from

---

[122] EGE, n 115, para 1.6, and the House of Lords, n 4, para 6.39.

[123] A failed Discrimination (Genetic Information) Bill was sponsored by Anne Campbell MP in the parliamentary session 1994/95. For discussion of regulation generally, see J Black, 'Regulation as facilitation: Negotiating the genetic revolution' (1998) 61 MLR 621.

[124] This is not to ignore the criminal offence created by the Human Tissue Act 2004, s 45, which concerns non-consensual DNA analysis. The offence is constituted by having material with the intention that the DNA be analysed other than for an 'excepted purpose', such as the detection and prosecution of crime. As such, it is not a device that is fit for purpose to protect against all manifestations of discrimination.

[125] See, also, the Federal Health Insurance Portability and Accountability Act 1996 which has been interpreted as covering genetics in the workplace: see HGC, *Inside Information*, n 38, para 6.36.

[126] United States Equal Employment Opportunity Commission, Press Release, 18 April 2001: http://www.eeoc.gov.

requiring or even requesting genetic information from individuals or their relatives, and from using it in health coverage decisions. Employers are prohibited from using genetic information in decisions relating to the hiring, firing, or promotion of employees, including decisions about their contractual terms. Major limitations on the Act include the fact that protections do not extend to life insurance, disability insurance, or long-term care insurance. Employers with fewer than 15 employees are not caught by the law.[127] The EEOC has reported that more than 1,000 charges of alleged genetic discrimination had been filed as of December 2013.[128] In the same year, the EEOC announced the first settlement of such an action in *EEOC* v *Fabricut Inc* with a fine of $50,000 to a company that asked about family history in a post-offer medical examination; a second suit was also settled in 2014 on similar grounds for $370,000 (*EEOC* v *Founders Pavilion Inc*).[129]

7.71   Anti-discrimination law in the UK has historically been governed by three pieces of legislation: the Sex Discrimination Act 1975, the Race Relations Act 1976, and the Disability Discrimination Act 1995. The protection afforded against discrimination by the 1975 and 1976 Acts is restricted to their precise remits—that is, sexual or racial discrimination. Since many genetic conditions are sex-linked or affect particular ethnic and racial groups, differential treatment of afflicted individuals could amount to discrimination within the terms of these Acts, probably as examples of indirect discrimination. It is not clear, however, how successful such arguments would be, there being no cases on point. More opportunities for redress arose with the advent of the Disability Discrimination Act 1995 which was the first piece of UK legislation to deal directly with discrimination against disabled people. The Act outlawed discrimination in a wide range of fields—such as employment, the provision of goods, facilities and services, the sale and let of property, education, and public transport.

7.72   The Act defined 'disability' and 'disabled persons' in Part I as follows:

1(1)   Subject to the provisions of Schedule 1, a person has a disability for the purposes of this Act if he has a physical or mental impairment which has a substantial and long-term adverse effect on his ability to carry out normal day-to-day activities.

(2)   In this Act 'disabled person' means a person who has a disability.

7.73   In the context of employment, the provisions of the Act ensured that it is unlawful for an employer to treat an individual less favourably than he would treat others for a reason which relates to the individual's disability and when he cannot show that the treatment in question is justified. Discrimination can occur, inter alia, in respect of: (i) the arrangements which an employer makes for the purpose of determining to whom he should offer employment; (ii) the terms in which he offers employment; (iii) his refusal to offer, or deliberate not offering, employment; (iv) his refusal to afford an employee opportunities for promotion, a transfer, training, or receiving any other benefit, or his treating the employee differently in such opportunities; and (v) his dismissal of an employee, or subjecting the employee to any other detriment.

---

[127] For comment on the operation of this law and other state-based provisions, see Presidential Commission for the Study of Bioethical Issues, *Privacy and Progress in Whole Genome Sequencing*, (2012).

[128] See http://www.genome.gov/10002077 (2015).

[129] Summaries of these cases are available at: http://www.genome.gov/10002077. For commentary on the law, see R C Green, D Lautenbach, and A L McGuire, 'GINA, Genetic Discrimination, and Genomic Medicine' (2015) 372 N Engl J Med 397, doi: 10.1056/NEJMp1404776.

7.74 These provisions could clearly go a long way to preventing discrimination against individuals based on information about their genetic constitution—note, particularly, how pre-employment discrimination is also outlawed. However, the question arises as to whether the provisions of the Act extended to persons whose genome contains defective genes which do, or can have, a bearing on their ability to do their job. The crucial term here is *'can have'*. Clearly, persons who are already affected by a genetic condition come within the definition of 'disabled person'. But what of a person who merely has a predisposition to ill health? A literal interpretation of s 1(1) excludes such a person for it speaks of one who *'has a* physical or mental impairment'. The section must, however, be read in conjunction with Schs 1 and 2, which allow for regulations to be made which will clarify the definitions in s 1. In particular, Sch 1, para 8 concerns 'progressive conditions'. The examples given of such conditions are cancer, multiple sclerosis, muscular dystrophy, or infection with HIV. The paragraph provides that someone who suffers from such a progressive condition will be treated as 'disabled' provided that their condition results in an impairment which, at least, has (or had) an effect on their ability to carry out normal day-to-day activities, even if that effect is not a substantial adverse effect. Even so, the individual must still be in some way symptomatic, thus excluding those who have 'merely' a predisposition to disease at the relevant time. This means, by inference, that discrimination against persons in this last category is not unlawful under the Act. This disparity and the question of genetic testing were raised in the parliamentary debates but the Minister in charge stated:

> except in a few well-publicised cases, genetic tests are not as yet a useful indicator of future actual disability. Their inclusion would open up the [Act] to large numbers of people who are clearly not, and may never become disabled ... we cannot wander into a situation whereby, for some reason or another, potentially the entire population could claim protection under the [Act].[130]

7.75 It is certainly true that genetic tests are by no means accurate at present, but that does not mean that such tests cannot be misused by employers and others, nor that they will not be used to exclude people from jobs and other services for irrelevant and irrational reasons. Legislation designed to outlaw discrimination on the grounds of disability should cover *all* forms of discrimination, whether the disability is actual or perceived, current or future. It is arguable that the provisions of the Act as they currently stand are inadequate and are potentially prejudicial to persons likely to develop genetic conditions later in life.

Matters have scarcely been improved under the Equality Act 2010 which absorbed the essential provisions of the 1995 Act.[131] Now 'disabled person' is defined as follows:

> A person (P) has a disability if—
>
> (a) P has a physical or mental impairment, and (b) the impairment has a substantial and long-term adverse effect on P's ability to carry out normal day-to-day activities. A reference to a disabled person is a reference to a person who has a disability.[132]

---

[130] Official Reports, HC, vol 257, col 887 (28 March 1995).
[131] See further, Sch 1, Pt 1 for determination of disability.
[132] Equality Act, s 6(1) and (2). Note, too, that this Act goes far beyond the current legislation, outlawing discrimination on the grounds of age, gender reassignment, marriage and civil partnership, pregnancy and maternity, religion or belief and/or sexual orientation, as well as the current grounds of sex, race, or disability.

This extends the definition but still fails to address our concerns as expressed earlier. Notwithstanding, the Secretary of State might, with advantage, use the powers given under the Acts to expand the definition of disability to cover the specific circumstances of asymptomatic genetic conditions.

7.76 The British position is to be contrasted with that in Australia. The Disability Discrimination Act 1992 covers disability which an individual: (i) has now; (ii) has had in the past (e.g. mental illness); (iii) may have in the future; and (iv) has imputed to him or her. This is eminently sensible since discriminatory practice does not need a founding in fact to exist; indeed, differential treatment founded on a factual basis might even be justified in certain circumstances. Prejudice is another matter. Moreover, these provisions were considered by the Australian Law Reform Commission to be adequate and adaptable to the genetic context; it did not, therefore, recommend the adoption of specific legislation to cover genetics.[133]

7.77 The anomalies in the current UK provisions were summed up by Baroness Jay in the House of Lords speaking last century:

> The paradox which is possible in the present situation is that where genetic counselling, genetic testing and identifying genetic markers is potentially one of the most exciting and liberating developments in medical science at the end of the 20th century, if it becomes the case that people feel that identifying those markers in their own personal situation will lead to discrimination, they will be less likely to take advantage of those extraordinary scientific advances which may help their own condition and in which medical science may be able to help future generations of children.[134]

7.78 An obvious question to arise here is whether there should be genetic-specific legislation. We doubt whether attempts to make a 'special case' of genetics would be productive. We draw attention to the recommendations of the Disability Rights Commission (now the Equality and Human Rights Commission) which, in its first review of the 1995 Act, called for extension of the Act to those with a predisposition to genetic disease.[135] The obvious model here is the Australian experience—one which would in the end avoid the charge of genetic exceptionalism but would provide sufficient protection for all victims of discrimination based on health.[136]

RESEARCH INVOLVING GENETIC MATERIAL

7.79 We lay our cards on the table at this point by admitting our full support for medical research that is scientifically sound, ethically robust, and subject to the rigorous checks and balances that we outline in Chapter 19. To this extent, genetic research is no different from other forms of research in the health care sector although, once again, we find

---

[133] Australian Law Reform Commission, *Essentially Yours* (2003) paras 9.49–9.55.

[134] Official Reports, HL, vol 564, col 1713 (13 June 1995).

[135] Disability Rights Commission, *Disability Equality: Making It Happen—First Review of the Disability Discrimination Act 1995* (2003) p 83. The Commission also recommended specific legislation to prohibit employers and insurers from viewing genetic data save in very restricted circumstances: Disability Rights Commission, *Disability Equality: Making It Happen—First Review of the Disability Discrimination Act 1995* (2003).

[136] For arguments about the need for a European response, see (eds), G Quinn, A de Paor, and P Blanck, *Genetic Discrimination: Transatlantic Perspectives on the Case for a European-level Legal Response* (2014).

that perceptions do not always reflect this reality.[137] The Medical Research Council conducted a survey on public attitudes towards the collection of human biological samples
in October 2000 which found disparate knowledge and understanding of the meaning
and the goals of genetic research.[138] There was considerable evidence of negative associations with this type of work where understanding was lacking[139] and this was so despite
the fact that most people continued to find general medical research to be worthy and
worthwhile.[140] As the report states:

> Underlying these negative associations was a feeling that genetics research can make
> people feel vulnerable about themselves. It was believed to be about seeking to perfect
> the human body, for good or bad ends, and that it could induce concern about individu-
> als' own imperfections … [a]longside this was a feeling expressed by a few that genetics
> research, if put to these sorts of uses, conflicts with the (beneficial) diversity of the human
> race. Though it would be a good thing to attempt to eliminate genetically linked diseases
> and conditions, this is likely to go hand-in-hand with other developments that will make
> it possible to produce 'perfect' people.[141]

7.80   The HGC's People's Panel Quantitative Study of March 2001 revealed similar results.[142]
More than one-third of those surveyed considered genetics research to be 'tampering with
nature' and so unethical. The response of the HGC, in turn, was to recommend that all
genetic research on human non-anonymised tissue samples or bodily material should be
subject to independent research ethics review and that clear policies should be established
by all research bodies for compliance with ethical review.[143] Whether such measures will
succeed in engendering more public trust and confidence remains to be seen.[144] O'Neill
has stated, 'reported public trust in science and even in medicine has faltered *despite*
successes, *despite* increased efforts to respect persons and their rights, *despite* stronger
regulation to protect the environment and *despite* the fact that environmental concerns
are taken far more seriously than they were a few years ago'.[145]

---

[137] For a discussion of trends in genetic research and ethico-legal responses see B M Knoppers and
R Chadwick, 'Human genetic research: emerging trends in ethics' (2005) 6 Nature Reviews Genetics 75 and R E
Ashcroft, 'Human rights and ethics in genomic research: rethinking the model' (2007) 8 Pharmacogenomics
391. Since then, note the establishment of initiatives such as the Global Alliance for Genomics and Health
which '…brings together over 300 leading institutions working in healthcare, research, disease advocacy,
life science, and information technology. The partners in the Global Alliance are working together to create
a common framework of harmonized approaches to enable the responsible, voluntary, and secure sharing of
genomic and clinical data.' See: http://genomicsandhealth.org/.

[138] Medical Research Council, *Public Perceptions of the Collection of Human Biological Samples* (2000).

[139] Medical Research Council, *Public Perceptions of the Collection of Human Biological Samples* (2000),
para 2.2.

[140] Medical Research Council, *Public Perceptions of the Collection of Human Biological Samples* (2000),
para 2.1.

[141] Medical Research Council, *Public Perceptions of the Collection of Human Biological Samples* (2000).

[142] HGC, *Public Attitudes*, pp 20–2. Compare A L Jack and C Womack, 'Why surgical patients do
not donate tissue for commercial research: Review of records' (2003) 327 BMJ 262, and Y Erlich et al.,
'Redefining genomic privacy: trust and empowerment' (2014) 12(11) PLoS Biol e1001983, doi:10.1371/
journal.pbio.1001983.

[143] HGC, *Inside Information*, paras 5.33 and 5.37. E A Whitley, N Kanellopoulou, and J Kaye, 'Consent
and research governance in biobanks: evidence from focus groups with medical researchers' (2012) 15(5)
Pub Health Genomics 232 and C Soto et al., 'Consent to tissue banking for research: qualitative study and
recommendations' (2012) 97(7) Arch Dis Child 632, and J Kaye et al., 'Dynamic consent: a patient interface
for twenty-first century research networks' (2015) 23 Euro J of Human Gen 141, doi:10.1038/ejhg.2014.71.

[144] Laurie (2002), n 1, pp 166–7 and pp 296–8.

[145] O O'Neill, *Autonomy and Trust in Bioethics* (2002) p 11.

7.81 The balance of interests is nowhere more delicately struck than between the concern to protect individuals' rights and the public interest in furthering research.[146] Few would now deny that some compromises must be made with the former in order to secure the latter. Thus, for example, the HGC has supported the view that it is acceptable to seek general consent to future research in cases where there will be anonymisation of data and samples involved in genetic research.[147] Repeated processes of reconsent may not only be impractical but also unnecessarily invasive.[148] Bodies now exist in the separate jurisdictions of the UK to consider whether and when research requests to use patient data for research purposes without consent are legitimate, even with respect to identifiable patient data. In England and Wales, this falls to the Confidentiality Advisory Group (CAG) that operates under the auspices of the Health Research Authority (HRA).[149] This scheme has a permanent statutory basis in England and Wales,[150] but the challenges of navigating data protection and other laws are not trivial. The House of Lords Science and Technology Committee heard evidence of a considerable bureaucratic burden for researchers in the general health context—Department of Health guidance suggests that the area is covered by 43 pieces of legislation, 12 sets of relevant standards, and eight codes of conduct. The Committee, accordingly, called for reduction of this burden, most specifically through clearer guidance from the Information Commissioner's Office on interpreting data protection law.[151] It is a primary function of the HRA[152] to deliver on this call for proportionate governance, and it now has a wider remit both to protect research participant interests and to promote sound research under the Care Act 2014.[153]

7.82 While we agree that regulatory efficiency is a good thing, clearly this cannot come at the expense of adequate protection of patients' rights and interests. The problem is that these rights and interests are constantly subjected to new pressures as genetic and genomic science advances. The following example illustrates this perfectly. An article published in 2008 demonstrated that it was possible to identify individuals whose genomic data had been included in a cohort of anonymised genetic profiles made available to researchers over the Internet.[154] Although this was only possible if the genetic profile of the individual in

---

[146] See generally R Tutton and O Corrigan, *Genetic Databases: Socio-ethical Issues in the Collection and use of DNA* (2004). Also, sometimes there can be a very fine line between research and treatment: see M Parker et al., 'Ethical review of research into rare genetic disorders' (2004) 329 BMJ 288.

[147] HGC, *Inside Information*, n 38, paras 5.18–5.19.

[148] We explore elsewhere the nature and limits of consent and reconsent in the research context: see G Laurie and E Postan, 'Rhetoric or reality: What is the legal status of the consent form in health-related research?' (2012) 20(5) Medical Law Review doi: 10.1093/medlaw/fws031.

[149] Similar functions are performed in Scotland and Northern Ireland by their respective Privacy Advisory Committees. The Scottish entity was replaced in May 2015 by the Public Benefit and Privacy Panel which consolidates the roles of various governance bodies and takes on the dual task of protecting privacy while seeking to further public benefit through research.

[150] See, the NHS Act 2006, s 251 which re-enacted the Health and Social Care Act 2001, s 60 (see now the 2008 Act of the same name and also to be read in conjunction with the equally eponymous 2012 Act). The system provides that the Secretary of State for Health is able to make regulations setting aside the common law duty of confidentiality for the use of identifiable patient data without consent for medical purposes when anonymisation is not possible and consent is not practicable. The overarching consideration then is the promotion of the public interest through access and use of the data.

[151] N 4, paras 6.13–6.30.

[152] See Health Research Authority Regulations (SI 2011/2341) and Health Research Authority (Amendment) Regulations (SI 2012/1108).

[153] S 111.

[154] Homer et al., 'Resolving individuals contributing trace amounts of DNA to highly complex mixtures using high-density SNP genotyping microarrays' (2008) Public Library of Science Genetics J 4:e1000167.

question was already known to those seeking to make the association, this revelation none-theless led international organisations such as the Wellcome Trust and the US National Institutes of Health to close their 'open' systems of sharing data among researchers.

7.83 So how should regulators or those charged with the governance of genetic/genomic sci ence respond to this ever-shifting landscape?[155] The example of UK Biobank[156] raises all of the issues in one project and also offers some potential solutions.[157] This is an ambi-tious long term longitudinal project to follow 500,000 subjects aged between 40 and 69 through various periods of good and ill health, examining genotypic and phenotypic data together with environmental factors to establish the relationships between diseases and genes and the interaction between genes and their environment. In tandem with the development of the scientific protocol, an interim group of advisers worked to create a viable Ethics and Governance Framework to address the various strands of the project; from the role of patient consent to questions of feedback of results; from confidentiality concerns to commercialisation policies. A particular challenge for the group was to oper-ate with ever-moving scientific goalposts, and one of its core recommendations was to establish a permanent Ethics and Governance Council; this was set up in 2004 to monitor and advise UK Biobank over time and especially with respect to participants' interests.[158] The Council acts as an 'ethical mirror' to the funders and researchers involved in the pro-ject. We have suggested elsewhere that this example of reflexive governance is an impor-tant exemplar of how the regulation of (genetic) research must move forward if it is to continue to strike the appropriate balance of considerations outlined earlier.[159] It remains to be seen, however, whether all of these efforts will make UK Biobank and its personnel any more better trusted by the British public.[160]

STATE INTEREST IN GENETIC INFORMATION

7.84 The earlier sections have identified many varied interests in genetic information which are held by both individuals and institutions. Two particular state concerns arise from these interests: an inclination to reduce the financial burden wherever possible and a desire to minimise or eliminate harm to its citizens. The state has a role in protecting and advanc-ing 'the public good'—that is, the collective interests of society as a whole. To what extent, then, can the state legitimately request results of genetic tests or require genetic testing?[161]

[155] For a recent US perspective on the challenges, see the Presidential Commission for the Study of Bioethical Issues, n 127.
[156] This is a joint venture between the Wellcome Trust, the Medical Research Council, and the Department of Health, see: http://www.ukbiobank.ac.uk.
[157] See also M A Austin, S Harding, and C McElroy, 'Genebanks: A comparison of eight proposed inter-national genetic databases' (2003) 6 Community Genetics 37.
[158] Laurie was the Chair of the UK Biobank Ethics and Governance Council from 2006 to 2010.
[159] G Laurie, 'Reflexive governance in biobanking: on the value of policy led approaches and the need to recognise the limits of law' (2011) 130(3) Hum Genet 347.
[160] For some insights into the approach to governance adopted by UK Biobank, see G Laurie, A Bruce, and C Lyall, 'The roles of values and interests in the governance of the life sciences: Learning lessons from the "ethics+" approach of UK Biobank' in C Lyall et al. (eds), *The Limits to Governance: The Challenge of Policy-Making for the New Life Sciences* (2009).
[161] The contrast between permissive and restrictive legislation is highlighted in B M Knoppers and R M Isasi, 'Regulatory approaches to reproductive genetic testing' (2004) 19 Human Repro 2695. More recent dilemmas relate to what should be done with research results: B M Knoppers, M H Zawati, and K Sénécal, 'Return of genetic testing results in the era of whole-genome sequencing' (2015) 16 Nature Review Genetics 553, doi:10.1038/nrg3960.

7.85 One of the most obvious state interests in the health care setting is that of securing public health and, perhaps unsurprisingly, it has been argued that mandatory testing for genetic disorders might halt the spread of genetic disease. Even if little or nothing can be done for those already afflicted, disclosure might prevent the transmission of defective genes to future persons. Set against this, however, is the potential infringement of privacy interests which such practices can represent. We have touched on this earlier at paras 7.37 et seq indicating that various eminent bodies have concluded that patient autonomy and the right to choose should be the overriding consideration. But can it then be argued that the state has a positive interest in *facilitating* individual choice? Certainly, it can adopt a more pastoral role towards individuals by providing them with information which may help them make important life decisions such as whether to have a child if both partners are carriers of, say, cystic fibrosis. Not only does this make individuals more independent as moral choosers but it might also have the desired social end of curtailing the further spread of genetic disease.[162] For example, Ball et al. have noted that this view has been expressed by the Royal College of Physicians:

> [the] Royal College of Physicians report suggests that as long as individuals have the right to decide for themselves whether to bear children it could be argued that such individuals should have access to the fullest possible information, including genetic, pertinent to that decision and therefore this should not be withheld.[163]

7.86 This implies that the state should seek to further its interest in facilitating choice by providing comprehensive screening programmes, a plethora of genetic tests accompanied by suitable counselling services and other support mechanisms, which, controversially, would include access to termination of pregnancy. Cost implications aside, this would certainly further both individual and state interests by making free choice a market commodity. The risk of a conflict of interests would be almost entirely eliminated if such programmes were provided free of any coercive measures.[164]

7.87 It is important at this juncture to note that the ECtHR has ruled on the human rights implications of state-driven genetic testing and profiling practices, albeit in the context of the detection and prosecution of crime. In *S and Marper* v *United Kingdom*,[165] it was held that the blanket policy of the UK to retain DNA profiles and samples indefinitely when taken from persons without their consent and who had not been convicted of a crime was an unjustified breach of their human rights. Indeed, it held that the mere retention of DNA, even without use, was an interference with the right to respect for private life because of the possible implications that future uses could have for individuals. This might raise obvious questions in the health care context especially with respect to collections

---

[162] For sound policy recommendations, see European Society of Human Genetics, 'Populations genetic screening programmes: Technical, social and ethical issues: Recommendations of the European Society of Human Genetics' (2003) 11 Supp 2 Euro J Hum Gen S5.

[163] D Ball et al., 'Predictive testing of adults and children' in A Clarke (ed), *Genetic Counselling: Practice and Principles* (1994) at 77 referring to the Royal College of Physicians of London, *Ethical Issues in Clinical Genetics: A Report of the Working Group of the Royal College of Physicians' Committees on Ethical Issues in Medicine and Clinical Genetics* (1991). The sentiments remain just as valid today.

[164] However, as the Nuffield Council has pointed out (n 22 at 8.11): 'It has been argued that the availability of prenatal screening and diagnosis, together with the termination of seriously affected pregnancies, both reflect and reinforce the negative attitudes of our society towards those with disabilities. Indeed medical genetics may add a new dimension if genetic disorder came to be seen as a matter of choice rather than fate.'

[165] (2009) 48 EHRR 50.

of human samples for which consent has never been obtained. It does not follow that long-term retentions had to cease; it meant that the procedures for governance should be strengthened and clear justifications for use be given—it was for the state to demonstrate that indefinite retention was both a necessary and proportionate interference.[166] Thus, in *Gaughran v Chief Constable of Northern Ireland* the Supreme Court recently held that it was within the state's margin of appreciation to retain biometric data indefinitely upon conviction of a recordable offence.[167] Prospectively, these rulings raise further questions about the lawfulness of requiring population-based screening programmes; the obligation is firmly on the state to show that such measures are both necessary and proportionate to further pressing social needs, and they must be based in transparent and knowable legal terms.

7.88 Ethically speaking, the introducing of population genetic screening programmes has been questioned when no appropriate medical intervention is possible in light of a positive result.[168] No such programmes exist in the UK for adults and the only routine screening of children relates to neonates in respect of treatable conditions such as phenylketonuria, haemoglobin disorders, and hypothyroidism.[169] The availability of a plethora of tests for prenatal or pre-implantation genetic diagnosis has been noted earlier. While this can facilitate parental choices as to the continuance of a pregnancy, it still raises concern that such testing is open to abuse if parents are in any way pressurised to test for a range of conditions and to abort any affected fetuses.[170] Indeed, one has to ask whether the goal of free patient choice is possible, given the fact that, once genetic counselling has been offered and accepted, a likely chain of events has already been set up in the minds of all those involved.[171] Clarke also asks whether the objective is, itself, morally defensible—or have we, for fear of being labelled eugenists, 'fled so far from medical paternalism that we deny ethical responsibility for our professional activities'? Moreover, the whole concept of genetic counselling can be questioned, insofar as it increasingly involves the systematic selection of fetuses and, hence, approaches children as consumer objects subject to quality control.[172]

7.89 The increasing 'need' for genetic counselling can be seen as being based on the increasing number of disorders which can be diagnosed and, as Lippman has said, before long, the definition of fetal imperfection will come to mean any condition which can be diagnosed in utero. The social and economic pressures on a woman to terminate a pregnancy

---

[166] See now the Protection of Freedoms Act 2012 in which England and Wales adopts the existing Scottish approach that has been far less draconian.

[167] [2015] UKSC 29; [2015] 2 WLR 1303; [2015] 3 All ER 655.

[168] Nuffield Council on Bioethics (n 22) at 27. Screening for cystic fibrosis has been introduced more recently in some areas.

[169] See generally, Population Screening Programmes (2015): https://www.gov.uk/topic/population-screening-programmes.

[170] J M Green et al., 'Psychological aspects of genetic screening of pregnant women and newborns: A systematic review' (2004) 8 Health Technol Assess 1.

[171] See, particularly, A Clarke, 'Is non-directive genetic counselling possible?' (1991) 338 Lancet 998. On genetic counselling in general, see the major reference A Clarke, *Genetic Counselling: Practice and Principles* (1994). Not only may the patient accept or reject the advice given but so may her general practitioner: G H de Bock, C J van Asperen, J M de Vries, et al., 'How women with a family history of breast cancer and their general practitioners act on genetic advice in general practice: Prospective longitudinal study' (2001) 322 BMJ 26.

[172] See A Lippman, 'Prenatal genetic testing and screening: Constructing needs and reinforcing inequities' (1991) 17 Am J Law Med 15.

once an abnormality is discovered in her fetus may be such that her autonomous choice is severely prejudiced. These pressures would escalate were the somewhat bizarre suggestion adopted that the cost-efficiency of a genetic counselling service could be gauged by the number of abortions performed.[173] It is astonishing to read, for example, that the House of Commons Science and Technology Committee found that, in Edinburgh, a prenatal test for late onset Huntington's disease would not be offered to a woman who is herself afflicted unless she agrees to terminate if the test proves positive.[174] The rationale was that the child is otherwise burdened by the knowledge of its early death. Yet, such a policy betrays an underlying attitude towards those affected by such a condition and ignores the fact that they can enjoy many happy asymptomatic years of life. One thing is, however, certain: no woman can be forced to destroy her fetus. There is no legislative basis for such a suggestion which has strong overtones of positive eugenics.[175]

7.90 The prospect that parents who choose not to abort a child might come to be seen as irresponsible is deplorable.[176] We agree with the early policy body of the Advisory Committee on Genetic Testing in this regard—the aims of any programme should be clearly articulated, including any public health-related agenda on the part of the state, all programmes should be subjected to strict scrutiny by the UK National Screening Committee (UKNSC) and each programme should be accompanied by impartial pre- and post-testing counselling.[177] While it can be accepted that the state may have legitimate reasons for encouraging individuals to act responsibly in their use of any available genetic information, such encouragement should be offered only in the most moderate of terms. The autonomy and privacy interests of each of us require prima facie respect and this should be borne in mind whenever the introduction of a population screening programme is being considered. It is very difficult to justify any screening programme of children or adults which is unaccompanied by an effective cure or treatment. The strength of the state interest in promoting public health per se is insufficient to justify compromising the interests of individuals in receiving or not receiving genetic information about themselves. The HGC was well aware of these issues and worked with the UKNSC to advise strongly against the routine profiling of the newborn.[178]

GENE THERAPY AND GENE EDITING

7.91 Advances in screening constitute only one aspect of the progress which has been made in human genetics over recent decades. Perhaps more significantly from the scientific point of view, possibilities have opened up for manipulation of the genes of existing and future individuals. It has given rise to considerable bioethical debate.

---

[173] For discussion, and rejection, see A Clarke, 'Genetics, ethics, and audit' (1990) 335 Lancet 1145.

[174] House of Commons Science and Technology Committee, Third Report, para 90.

[175] D J Galton and C J Galton, 'Francis Galton: And eugenics today' (1998) 24 J Med Ethics 99; D J Kevles, 'Eugenics and human rights' (1999) 319 BMJ 435. See also *Emeh v Kensington and Chelsea and Westminster Area Health Authority* [1985] QB 1012 at 1024; [1984] 3 All ER 1044 at 1053, per Slade LJ, CA.

[176] M Grodin and G Laurie, 'Susceptibility genes and neurological disorders: Learning the right lessons from the Human Genome Project' (2000) 57 Arch Neurol 1569.

[177] The National Screening Committee has clear guidance: Evidence and recommendations: NHS population screening (2014), available at: https://www.gov.uk/guidance/evidence-and-recommendations-nhs-population-screening#evidence-review-proces.

[178] HGC, *Inside Information*, n 38, ch 4.

7.92 Gene therapy is one such form of manipulation and this may be of two types—somatic or germ-line. Somatic gene therapy is directed towards the remedying of a defect within the patient and involves the insertion of genetic material which will perform some function which the patient's own genetic material cannot achieve. Germ-line gene therapy can be visualised in two ways: the insertion of genetic material into the pre-embryo, which is pre-emptive treatment of the future being and his or her progeny, or as the insertion of a gene into the germ cells of an individual. The latter therapy has no direct bearing on the individual but is intended to ensure that any subsequent children are born with or without certain characteristics. The scientific techniques involved have spawned considerable—and emotional—debate;[179] indeed, genetic engineering is one of the few modern medical technologies in which study of the moral aspects has preceded the practical realities.

7.93 The ethical implications of somatic gene therapy were considered by the Committee on the Ethics of Gene Therapy—the Clothier Committee—which reported in 1992.[180] The Committee thought that this form of treatment was uncontroversial, if novel, and felt that it gave rise to no new ethical challenges. The Group of Advisors on Ethical Implications of Biotechnology of the European Commission similarly reported in 1994 and encouraged somatic gene therapy at a number of levels, including basic research, clinical trials, and bio-technology.[181] This having been said, the group considered that, because of certain unknown risks associated with the process, research into somatic gene therapy should be restricted to serious diseases for which there is no other effective available treatment. Similar views have been expressed in the USA and in international documents concerned with the bioethics of manipulation of the human genome.[182] We can accept these assessments; the goals of somatic gene therapy are identical to the goals of other forms of treatment and, provided that it does not involve undue risk to the patient or to others, it is as ethically acceptable as is drug therapy or surgical intervention. There may be a need for caution if somatic gene therapy is developed so as to combat behavioural disorders; even then, however, the ethical considerations will be similar to those which already arise from the use of psychotropic drugs or psychosurgery and which are discussed in greater detail in Chapter 13.

7.94 Trials involving gene therapy began in 1990 but suffered a real setback in 1999 when the first death attributable to the technique occurred.[183] Nonetheless, it has been reported in the USA that:

> in the year of the tragedy, ... the National Institutes of Health (NIH) approved a record 91 gene transfer protocols that year, as compared with only 2 in 1990 and 51 in 1998.

[179] See R Iredale, 'Public attitudes to human gene therapy: A pilot study in Wales' (2003) 6 Community Genetics 139. This study showed general support for somatic gene therapy but ambivalence about germ-line gene therapy.

[180] *Report of the Committee on the Ethics of Gene Therapy* (1992).

[181] Opinion of the Group of Advisers on Ethical Implications of Biotechnology of the European Commission, *The Ethical Implications of Gene Therapy* (1994).

[182] In the USA, see *Report and Recommendations of the Panel to Assess the National Institutes of Health Investment in Research on Gene Therapy* (1995). The Council of Europe Convention for the Protection of Human Rights and Dignity of the Human Being with regard to the Application of Biology and Medicine: Convention on Human Rights and Biomedicine states, in Art 13: 'An intervention seeking to modify the human genome may only be undertaken for preventative, diagnostic or therapeutic purposes and only if its aim is not to introduce any modification in the genome of any descendant.' Article 16 of the Universal Declaration on Bioethics and Human Rights (2005) contains the rather anodyne statement that: 'The impact of life sciences on future generations, including on their genetic constitution, should be given due regard.'

[183] E Weiss and D Nelson, 'Teen dies undergoing gene therapy' *Washington Post*, 29 September 1999, p A1.

In 2000, that number dropped to 71, but it edged up to 73 in 2001, according to the NIH's Office of Biotechnology Activities.[184]

In the UK, the Gene Therapy Advisory Committee (GTAC) is the research ethics committee with specific remit to consider ethical approval of clinical trials involving gene therapy.[185] GTAC works with the HRA to deliver the safe exploration of gene therapies, pursuant to a Government White Paper on Genetics in 2003, while also seeking to deliver a proportionate and efficient review service. On a more practical level, the MHRA must approve all gene therapy products for market.[186] In 2007, however, a case arose of a young girl who developed leukaemia as a result of her involvement in a gene therapy trial. GTAC exercised its regulatory role and intervened to close the project.[187] The absorption of GTAC into the HRA has meant that it is now treated akin to other research ethics committees, subject to 60-day approval times and more effective division of labour with four regional entities undertaking review under its auspices.

7.95 The controversial nature of germ-line gene therapy—whether directed to the pre-embryo or to an individual's germ cells—rests on its capacity to change future people. Some such changes will, in themselves, be unobjectionable; it is difficult, for example, to find grounds for objection to preventive medicine which will ensure that the bearers of a serious genetically transmissible disease will not pass the condition on to their children. Such medical practice is no different from other, long-accepted, efforts to eradicate disease within the human population and which, arguably, interfere with the natural order to a comparable degree.

7.96 The difficulty that some have with any form of germ-line therapy is that of the 'slippery slope' which is encountered at a number of points in medical jurisprudence.[188] If we allow germ-line therapy in relation to, say, a seriously debilitating disease, then how are we to prevent its use to eliminate characteristics which we would not, currently, label as a defect but which may be considered undesirable? Rifkin put the problem as follows:

> Once we decide to begin the process of human genetic engineering, there is really no logical place to stop. If diabetes, sickle cell anaemia, and cancer are to be cured by altering the genetic make-up of an individual, why not proceed to other 'disorders': myopia, colourblindness, left-handedness? Indeed, what is to preclude a society from deciding that a certain skin colour is a disorder?[189]

7.97 This is a bleak view of scientific ambitions, but the concern for possible abuse that it expresses has been potent enough to cause a number of governmental or other official bodies to proscribe germ-line gene therapy. The Council of Europe was, initially, sufficiently suspicious to recommend a complete ban on such practices—on the ground of its insult to human dignity—but later modified this to allow germ cell manipulation for

[184] T Ready, 'Gene therapy in recovery phase' (2002) 8 Nature Medicine 429.
[185] Regulation 14(5) of The Medicines for Human Use (Clinical Trials) Regulations 2004—See more at: http://www.hra.nhs.uk/resources/applying-to-recs/gene-therapy-advisory-committee-gtac/#sthash.9y6PPXql.dpuf.
[186] Genetics White Paper (2003), para 6.12.   [187] GTAC, Annual Report (2007/8).
[188] N Holtug, 'Human gene therapy: down the slippery slope' (1993) 7 Bioethics 402.
[189] J Rifkin, Algeny (1983), p 232, quoted in Holtug, 'Human gene therapy: Down the slippery slope' (1993) 7 Bioethics 402 at 405.

therapeutic purposes.[190] UNESCO has not ruled out germ-line therapies *ab initio* in its Universal Declaration on the Human Genome and Human Rights but, rather, prohibits 'practices which are contrary to human dignity'[191] and UNESCO's most recent effort—the Universal Declaration on Bioethics and Human Rights—similarly requires that 'Human dignity, human rights and fundamental freedoms are to be fully respected…'.

The interests and welfare of the individual should have priority over the sole interest of science or society.[192] It also makes specific, if somewhat vacuous, reference to future persons, thus: 'The impact of life sciences on future generations, including on their genetic constitution, should be given due regard.'[193] The debate was opened up again at the national level with the prospect of treatment of mitochondrial DNA disorders, as so well considered by the Nuffield Council in its 2012 report.[194] The Working Party concluded that such techniques are indeed a form of germ-line gene therapy and recommended—in this particular context—that robust oversight and safety considerations could make access to such therapies ethical and justifiable. Moreover, in raising the flag on such techniques as real world prospects of gene therapy, the Council hoped that its ethical reflections would further promote public debate on other techniques or interventions such as those acting on the cell nucleus with heritable effects.

7.98   Germ-line gene therapy is not without its supporters—as Harris has asked, 'Is there anything really wrong in wanting to have a fine child?'[195] The real difficulty lies in distinguishing between eugenically motivated, or enhancement, germ-line manipulation, on the one hand, and truly therapeutic intervention, on the other. It should be necessary to forbid *all* work in this area only if it is felt that the demarcation line can never be held. The faith of the Nuffield Council is based precisely on this point. We agree with the Council and the Human Genome Organisation's Ethics Committee (HUGO) which has called for 'widespread discussion on the appropriateness of the possible future use of gene transfer technology for enhancement and for germ-line interventions'.[196]

7.99   A further irony in the debate is revealed by this quote from Capecchi:

the pressure to initiate germline gene therapy will not likely come from government or dictators with a desire to make a super race, but rather from parents who desire to improve the chances for their biological children to function effectively within our society.[197]

Thus, once again, choice may become the primary policy driver in the advancement of a new field of technology. But the irony to which we allude is this: the post-war development of human rights discourse and the renewed commitment to individualism that this represented was largely driven in response to eugenic practices, albeit at that time at the hands of states. Are eugenic practices any less offensive if they are dressed up in the guise of

---

[190] Council of Europe Recommendation 934 on Genetic Engineering (1982); Recommendation 1100 on the Use of Human Embryos and Foetuses in Scientific Research (1989).

[191] See para 7.3 8, Art 11.

[192] UNESCO, Universal Declaration on Bioethics and Human Rights (2005), Art 1.

[193] UNESCO, Universal Declaration on Bioethics and Human Rights (2005), Art 16.

[194] Nuffield Council on Bioethics, *Novel Techniques for the Prevention of Mitochondrial DNA Disorders: An Ethical Review* (2012).

[195] J Harris, 'Is gene therapy a form of eugenics?' (1993) 7 Bioethics 178.

[196] HUGO, *Ethics Committee Draft Statement on Gene Therapy Research* (2001).

[197] M R Capecchi, 'Human germline gene therapy' in G Stock and J Campbell (eds), *Engineering the Human Germline: An Exploration of the Science and Ethics of Altering the Genes that We Pass to our Children* (2000) pp 31–2.

autonomous choice?[198] Equally, are desires to improve the gene pool through the eradication of disease such a terrible basis for action? Does *choice* bring us back to where we started?[199] Still, choice is meaningless unless the technological possibilities are available. The history of gene therapy indicates these are likely to be incremental for the foreseeable future and this is no bad thing if it allows ethical debate and public attitudes to catch up. The Nuffield Council report probably best sums up the current most ethically defensible position:

> Due to the health and social benefits to individuals and families of living free from mito-chondrial disorders, and where potential parents express a preference to have genetically-related children, on balance we believe that if these novel techniques are adequately proven to be acceptably safe and effective as treatments, it would be ethical for families to use them, if they wish to do so and have been offered an appropriate level of information and support.[200]

7.100 However, as one genetic technology becomes absorbed into the mainstream, a new one surely emerges to take its place on the ethical stage. Current controversy revolves around the prospect of gene editing that arises with the development of new technology in the form of CRISPR-Cas9—a man-made innovation that cuts and splices genetic material in much the same way found in nature. With this possibility have arisen concerns about its actual uses, including the altering of embryo DNA (yet another form of gene therapy),[201] and the creation of inter-species genomic material, giving a new twist to the chimera debate. Future uncertainties have led some to call for a moratorium on these techniques (arguing instead that current interventions should be explored fully first), while yet others reject this position in favour of a moral imperative to pursue such research, partly on the grounds that it could lead to an overall reduction in the number of embryos destroyed in the future.[202] For our part, we suspect the legal and policy response will once again fall back on safety and choice, subject to an initially cautious yet progressive approach that favours exploration. In this respect, this latest technological advance does little to advance our ethical or moral positions. We agree with our colleagues, however, that any such advance must be driven by the imperative to engage society widely and meaning-fully in developing any genuinely defensible response.[203]

CLONING

7.101 The birth of Dolly the lamb in 1997 sparked one of the greatest furores to affect the discipline of medical law and ethics since its beginnings some 40 years ago. Dolly was the first example of an adult vertebrate cloned—that is, genetically copied—from another adult. She was created using a 'fusion' technique whereby the nucleus from an adult cell (in this

---

[198] C Coutelle and R Ashcroft, 'Risks, benefits and ethical, legal, and societal considerations for transla-tion of prenatal gene therapy to human application' (2012) 891 Methods Mol Biol 371.

[199] See, too, A Caplan, G McGee, and D Magnus, 'What is immoral about eugenics?' (1999) 319 BMJ 1284.

[200] N 194 above.

[201] D Cyranoski, 'Ethics of embryo editing divides scientists' (2015) 519(7543) Nature 272, doi:10.1038/519272a.

[202] Compare E Lanphier et al., 'Don't edit the human germ line' (2015) 519 410, doi: 10.1038/519410a and J Savulescu et al., 'The moral imperative to continue gene editing research on human embryos' (2015) 6(7) Protein Cell 476, doi: 10.1007/s13238-015-0184-y.

[203] C Addison and S Taylor-Alexander, 'Gene editing: advising advice' (2015) 349(6251) Science 28 935, doi: 10.1126/science.349.6251.935-a.

case mammarian) was fused with an unfertilised egg from which the nucleus had been removed. This egg was then transplanted into another adult sheep for normal gestation to take place. The benefits of such a technique include the improvement of production of transgenic livestock which can be used to produce therapeutic agents involving human proteins. The development of stem cell technology has since made possible the creation of pluripotent cell lines from undifferentiated human cellular material taken from embryos and deceased fetuses.[204] The potential therapeutic benefits of this form of cloning technique such as the cultivation of replacement cells and tissues for diseased body parts have proved very attractive to researchers and governments alike,[205] leading to the rapid moral and legal acceptance of the practice in many countries.

7.102   These developments, however, also raise the spectre of human cloning, and it is in this regard that much of the controversy has arisen.[206] The prospect that individuals could clone themselves and have children who share precisely the same genetic make-up is, for some, to go too far. There is serious concern that the use of such a technique would alter our perception of what it means to be human. Moreover, many fear that the potential for exploitation is too great and envisage the production of human clones to be used as sources of spare parts.[207] Yet, others have posited that the birth of a clone would distort beyond recognition traditional familial hierarchies and relationships.[208] While many of these fears must be unfounded, we cannot deny that the strength of the reaction to these developments dictates a very cautious approach to the future.

7.103   Initial governmental responses to the birth of Dolly were swift and unanimously condemnatory. The UK government quickly confirmed its position that any work which was designed to produce cloned human beings was unethical and illegal[209]—a matter which we later address further. In the USA, the National Bioethics Advisory Commission (NBAC) reported in June 1997 and concluded that the risks of research into human cloning involving clinical trials were too great and that legislation should be passed to prohibit research into cloning 'complete people'. As a result, the Cloning and Prohibition Bill 1997 was sent to Congress, but the Act was not introduced. Numerous cloning prohibition bills followed in its wake but no federal action has been taken. In August 2001, President Bush announced that research using federal funds to study embryonic stem cells could only be done on stem cell lines or colonies that existed prior to the date of his announcement.[210] This, in effect, precluded federal funding for research into stem cells from cloned human embryos, and one year on it was reported that only three cell lines were available to researchers.[211] Note, that this did

---

[204] For an early account of the science, its promise and the ethical concerns, see European Commission, *Commission Staff Working Paper: Report on Human Embryonic Stem Cell Research* (2003).

[205] For a North American perspective in the immediate aftermath, see Committee on Science, *Engineering and Public Policy Scientific and Medical Aspects of Human Reproductive Cloning* (2002), and for the European position see B Gratton, *Survey on the National Regulations in the European Union Regarding Research on Human Embryos* (July 2002) prepared for the European Group on Ethics in Science and New Technologies to the European Commission.

[206] A fear that gathers some substance when we read R J Boyle and J Savulescu, 'Ethics of using preimplantation genetic diagnosis to select a stem cell donor for an existing person' (2001) 323 BMJ 1240.

[207] For a range of views and arguments see generally (1999) 25 Journal Med Ethics Issue 2.

[208] For a measured proposal, see A L Bonnicksen, 'Procreation by cloning: crafting anticipatory guidelines' (1997) 25 J Law Med & Ethics 273.

[209] Official Reports, HC, col s 615 ff (26 June 1997).

[210] Executive Order on Embryonic Stem Cell Research (2001).

[211] J Gillis and R Weiss, 'Stem cell research not yet booming', *Washington Post*, 6 August 2001, p A01.

not preclude research using private monies—and, indeed, other reports tell of actual attempted reproductive assistance through cloning in the USA and elsewhere.[212] As a matter of national policy, however, one of President Obama's first acts in office was to issue Executive Order 13505 which lifted the federal ban on funding.[213] This resulted, in turn, in the NIH Guidelines on Human Stem Cell Research (2009) which confirm that the NIH will now fund stem cell research, including human embryonic stem cell research (hESC), that is 'ethically responsible, scientifically worthy, and conducted in accordance with applicable law'.

7.104 In Europe, a protocol to the Council of Europe Convention on Human Rights and Biomedicine prohibits the cloning of human beings[214] and the UNESCO Declaration on the Human Genome and Human Rights specifically disallows cloning as being contrary to human dignity.[215] Moreover, incentives to carry out research in this field in Europe have been removed with the passing of the Directive on the Legal Protection of Biotechnological Inventions,[216] Art 6 of which expressly prohibits the granting of a patent for 'processes for cloning human beings'.[217] This has been confirmed by a decision of the European Court of Justice outlawing patenting of inventions that involve the destruction of an 'embryo' at any stage of their development.[218] Most controversy has been created, however, by the UN's attempt to ban cloning. Efforts to agree a binding legal treaty were abandoned in 2004 for lack of consensus over what, precisely, should be banned: should it be all forms of human cloning, should it be only reproductive cloning done with a view to producing a child, and, perhaps most importantly from the research perspective, should embryo stem cell research be allowed to continue? Ultimately, after various proposals for compromise, it was agreed in early 2005 to produce a non-binding declaration whereby Member States are called upon to prohibit 'all forms of human cloning inasmuch as they are incompatible with human dignity and the protection of human life'.[219] This suitably vague wording permits a range of interpretation, and doubtless this facility with be exploited to the full.

7.105 The UK voted against this Declaration. There is, indeed, a strong commitment to research in this field and the UK is a world leader. The Westminster Parliament voted in December 2000 to legalise the creation of embryos purely for research purposes, including stem cell research,[220] while, on the reproduction side, there has been considerable

---

[212] R Dobson, 'Claims of clone pregnancy could threaten US stem cell research' (2002) 324 BMJ 868. See, too, D Cyranoski, 'Stem-cell research: Crunch time for Korea's cloners' (2004) 429 Nature (May) 12.

[213] Presidential Documents, *Removing Barriers to Responsible Scientific Research Involving Human Stem Cells*, Executive Order 13505 of 9 March 2009.

[214] Additional Protocol to the Convention on Human Rights and Biomedicine on the Prohibition of Cloning Human Beings (1998).

[215] Art 11.

[216] Directive of the European Parliament and of the Council on the Legal Protection of Biotechnological Inventions No 98/44/EC of 6 July 1998, published at OJ L213, 30 July 1998, p 13.

[217] It should also be noted that, inter alia, this Art excludes processes for modifying the germ-line genetic identity of human beings from patentability. We discuss this Directive further in Chapter 14.

[218] C-34/10 *Brüstle v Greenpeace eV* [2012] All ER (EC) 809; [2012] 1 CMLR 41.

[219] United Nations, 'Legal Committee recommends UN Declaration on Human Cloning to General Assembly' (Press release GA/L/3271, 2005).

[220] MPs give go ahead for embryo research' *The Times*, 19 December 2000. The House of Lords approved this vote of the House of Commons on 22 January 2001. See now, the Human Fertilisation and Embryology (Research Purposes) Regulations 2001 (SI 2001/188).

dispute over whether a cloned human organism is an 'embryo' for the purposes of the Human Fertilisation and Embryology Act 1990.[221] This has been resolved in favour of a purposive interpretation that brings such an organism within the definition and, therefore, within the Human Fertilisation and Embryology Authority's (HFEA) regulatory regime.[222] Licences for cloning techniques performed to a reproductive end will not be granted; matters are different, however, with respect to therapeutic cloning. The UK's HFEA granted the first licence in Europe to allow therapeutic cloning to produce embryonic stem cells in 2004. Since then, the power of the Authority has been confirmed and extended by the 2008 reforms that we discuss in Chapter 8, and the creation of embryos, both human and admixed, for research purposes and by cloning techniques has similarly been upheld as lawful.[223]

7.106 Is this division between reproductive and therapeutic cloning a distinction without a difference? It is possible, despite the ruling of the House of Lords in *Quintavalle*, to see the moral status of the 'embryo' derived from cloning as being instinctively less equivalent to that of a human being than is that of the embryo resulting from fertilisation;[224] that being so, the preference for therapeutic cloning as a source of stem cells can be justified on deontological as well as utilitarian grounds, while the prohibition on reproductive cloning can be equally defended for the likely harm both to the resultant child and its mother. But, in what can only be described as a surprising move, Baroness Mary Warnock has expressed regret about the absolute nature of the ban on reproductive cloning which has gripped most legislatures.[225] We suspect that the days of the outright prohibition on reproductive cloning are numbered.[226]

7.107 When responding to developments which have consequences as far-reaching as do so many of those subsumed in the discipline of medical law, it is essential that a broad cross-section of views are obtained and, where possible, taken on board. The final response of the law to the advent of cloning remains to be seen—but the means by which the final end is reached can be as important as the reaching of the end itself.

CONCLUSION

7.108 We note in updating the chapter for the current edition that much of the policy response to the prospect and the promise of genetics and genomics was laid down in the early days of debate. Many of the bodies that were initially set up to address the advent of the so-called New Genetics have since been closed down or absorbed into other entities with far

[221] *R (on the application of Quintavalle)* v *Secretary of State for Health* [2002] EWCA Civ 29, [2002] QB 628, (2002) 64 BMLR 72.
[222] *R (on the application of Quintavalle)* v *Secretary of State for Health* [2003] 2 AC 687; [2003] 2 WLR 692. See also J K Mason, 'Clones and cell nuclear replacements: A Quintavalle saga' (2003) 7 Edin LR 379.
[223] S Devaney, 'Regulate to Innovate: Principles-Based Regulation of Stem Cell Research' (2011) 11(1) Med Law Int 53.
[224] J-E Hansen, 'Embryonic stem cell production through therapeutic cloning has fewer ethical problems than stem cell harvest from surplus IVF embryos' (2002) 28 J Med Ethics 86.
[225] M Warnock, *Making Babies: Is There a Right to Have Children?* (2002), pp 102 ff, 'Would the cloning of humans be intrinsically wrong?' Note that only a 'permitted embryo'—i.e., one that has resulted from fertilisation—can be placed in a woman: Human Fertilisation and Embryology Act 1990, ss 3(2) and 3ZA as amended.
[226] A useful overview of the international situation is provided by T Caulfield et al., 'The stem cell research environment: A patchwork of patchworks' (2009) 5(2) Stem Cell Reviews and Reports 82.

wider remits. We suspect this is as much to do with the growing realisation that there is less new about genetics than was first imagined, as it has anything to do with economic expediency. For the most part, this is to be welcomed. Having considered the policy and social issues that arise, much of the current debate returns us to age-old considerations about balances of rights and interests, scientific imperative against patient choice, and fundamental notions of justice. The law's role here need not take on any special mantle to help us resolve the issues as and when they arise.

8

THE MANAGEMENT
OF INFERTILITY
AND CHILDLESSNESS

INTRODUCTION

8.01 We believe that the title of this chapter draws attention to a distinction which is of practical, as well as semantic, importance. Primary infertility is a problem of the production of gametes or of implantation of the embryo. These may be susceptible to hormone therapy—a matter which we barely consider here; ovum or sperm donation then become secondary treatments of childlessness due to unsuccessful treatment of the primary condition. Similarly, the basic in vitro fertilisation (IVF) technique is most commonly used as a treatment of childlessness due to blockage of the fallopian tubes which cannot be corrected by recanalisation therapy. This distinction between infertility and childlessness may seem narrow but it may also be significant in relation to resource allocation. Thus, it could be held that, whereas the treatment of infertility is clearly a medical matter, childlessness can be seen as a social problem which should be funded from a different source.[1] While we do not subscribe to this interpretation, it might serve to justify the relative scarcity of the latter facilities in the National Health Service (NHS).[2]

8.02 Some 10 per cent of marriages or sexual partnerships are said to be infertile and the couple desire children in, at least, a high proportion of these.[3] In addition, there are couples who should give special thought to producing children naturally for genetic reasons, either because one may carry a dominant deleterious gene or because both are known to bear adverse recessive characteristics (see Chapter 7). Again, a couple may be able to conceive a child but the woman is unable to carry it for medical reasons. Opportunities for the adoption of infants remain meagre and, for many years, attention has focused on the elaboration of methods designed either to substitute the gametes of one or other person or to bypass the natural process in other ways.

---

[1] The difficulties of mixing political and clinical decisions have been aired in R E Ashcroft, 'In vitro fertilisation for all?' (2003) 327 BMJ 511.

[2] HFEA, *Fertility Treatment in 2013* (updated to April 2015), indicates that there are now 78 licensed centres offering IVF treatments and 75 providing donor insemination. In 2013, 49,636 women had a total of 61,099 IVF cycles; the comparable figures for DI were 2,379 and 4,611. IVF treatment was funded privately in 57.2 per cent of cases; only 14.8 per cent of DI cycles were paid for by the NHS.

[3] This notional figure, which must be extremely hard to validate, has its basis in *Report of the Committee of Inquiry into Human Fertilisation and Embryology* (Dame Mary Warnock, Chairman, 1984) para 2.1. It may be an underestimate in modern terms: M Freeman, 'Medically assisted reproduction' in A Grubb et al. (eds), *Principles of Medical Law* (3rd edn, 2010), para 14.3, suggests a possible figure of 1:6 couples.

8.03 The legal and moral issues involved have been considered on a worldwide basis since the inception of in vitro reproductive therapy and, in general, the major differences of opinion are determined by attitudes to the respect to be paid to the embryo in vitro. Even so, there are additional procedural variations within the European Union (EU) which contribute to what has been described as a 'procreative tourism'.[4] The United Kingdom (UK) is in some ways atypical in that, while the creation and management of embryos outside the body is tightly regulated, the status of those embryos is, at best, left in a legal limbo. This is largely due to the evolving attitudes of Parliament's own watchdogs which have consistently leant towards the philosophy that medical research—and, hence, medical advancement—should not be restrained unless it can be shown to be positively harmful.[5] Positive harm to an embryo that is destined to die is difficult to establish and we will see later that embryonic research in the UK has extended significantly beyond the limits recommended by the Council of Europe[6] (see Chapter 20). In its way, this leads to a paradox. It is easy to see why a government should be concerned to protect the embryo—possibly the most vulnerable form of human life. It is far more difficult to justify the control of assisted reproduction. Why, it may be asked, should we do so in this particular instance when any attempt to control natural reproduction would probably be condemned out of hand?[7] There is no simple answer, yet that is the way that has been chosen.

THE CONTROL OF ASSISTED REPRODUCTION IN THE UNITED KINGDOM

8.04 The legal response of the UK is to be found in the Human Fertilisation and Embryology Act 1990, as amended by the 2008 Act of the same name. This last legislative endeavour is divided into three parts. Part 1 makes extensive amendments to the 1990 Act,[8] leaving it as the substantive law in this field. Part 2 of the 2008 Act, by contrast, is free-standing and now regulates parenthood in cases involving assisted reproduction.[9] The main concern of Part 3 for the purposes of this chapter is to amend the Surrogacy Arrangements Act 1985.

8.05 The main thrust of the 1990 Act was to establish a Human Fertilisation and Embryology Authority (HFEA) (s 5) which is mandated to supervise and provide information and advice to the Secretary of State about embryos and about treatment services governed by the Act.[10] Perhaps the most important specific function of the Authority in the present

---

[4] M Brazier, 'Regulating the reproduction business?' (1999) 7 Med L Rev 166.

[5] See the highly critical House of Commons Science and Technology Committee Fifth Report *Human Reproductive Technologies and the Law* (HC 7-1, 2005). The report itself was, however, controversial. For commentary, see S A M McLean, 'De-regulating assisted reproduction: Some reflections' (2006) 7 Med L Internat 233.

[6] In particular, the UK has still not ratified the Council of Europe Convention on Human Rights and Biomedicine (1997) of which Art 18(2) is most apropos.

[7] There is a mass of literature on the subject. See, e.g., A Alghrani and J Harris, 'Reproductive liberty: Should the foundation of families be regulated?' (2006) 18 CFLQ 191 and, for an alternative approach, R Brownsword, 'Happy families, consenting couples, and children with dignity: Sex selection and saviour siblings' (2005) 17 CFLQ 435.

[8] For a full analysis, see R Fenton, S Heenan, and J Rees, 'Finally fit for the purpose? The Human Fertilisation and Embryology Act 2008' (2010) 32 J Soc Welf Fam Law 275.

[9] 2008 Act, s 57.

[10] For details, see L Hagger, 'The role of the Human Fertilisation and Embryology Authority' (1997) 3 Med L Internat 1. An interesting appraisal from the lay aspect is given by T Callus, 'Patient perception of the Human Fertilisation and Embryology Authority' (2007) 15 Med L Rev 62. Extensive regulations

context is to maintain a Licence Committee through which four basic types of licence can be issued to clinics approved for the purposes of the 1990 Act—these authorise activities in the course of providing treatment services (s 13, Sch 2, s 1), providing non-medical fertility services (s 13A, Sch 2, s 1A), the storage of gametes and/or embryos (s 14, Sch 2, s 2), and reproductive research (s 15, Sch 2, s 3).[11] In respect of assisted reproductive treatment provided for the public—with which we are primarily concerned in this chapter—the Act, in broad practical terms, prohibits the use, or storage, of gametes and the creation of embryos outside the body unless the clinic is in possession of a licence to do so.[12] Thus, in general, it allows for a flexible development of reproductive art under the control of peer and lay review[13] and, in this respect, probably the most significant development introduced in the 2008 Act lies in the acceptance of the production of embryos containing admixed human and animal DNA—currently for the purposes of research only. This has more recently been extended to research involving mitrochondrial donation.[14]

8.06   In practical terms, the 2008 Act recognises four main categories of 'admixed human embryos':[15]

- Cytoplasmic hybrids—in which a human nucleus is inserted and replaces the nucleus of an animal oocyte which is then stimulated to form an embryo. The scientific need for this procedure is stimulated by the lack of human ova from which to develop human stem cells (for which, see para 20.41). It is to be noted that embryos are being created here rather than being destroyed. The question for the ethicist is, 'Are they the right *type* of embryos?'

- Human–animal hybrid embryos which are created using human eggs and the sperm of an animal or vice versa.[16]

- Human transgenic embryos created by introducing animal DNA into cells of the embryo.

- Human–animal chimeras—human embryos altered by the addition of one or more animal cells.

were introduced in 2007 in order to comply with the stringent requirements of Directive 2004/23/EC of the European Parliament and Council concerning the quality and safety in use of human tissues and cells: Human Fertilisation and Embryology (Quality and Safety) Regulations 2007 (SI 2007/1522). More recently, see Human Fertilisation and Embryology (Quality and Safety) Regulations (SI 2014/2884) and Human Fertilisation and Embryology (Mitochondrial Donation) Regulations (SI 2015/572).

[11] Treatment can also be provided under a 'third-party agreement' which, effectively, covers the use of non-medical—i.e. commercial—fertility services provided by persons licensed to do so. The purpose of this is to allow cooperation with, say, Internet suppliers of sperm (1990 Act, s 2A inserted by 2007 Regulations, reg 7).

[12] Interestingly, the licence holder, or person responsible for the clinic, is not necessarily responsible for criminal activity under the Act by a senior member of the staff: *Attorney-General's Reference (No 2 of 2003)* [2005] 3 All ER 149; [2004] 1 WLR 2062.

[13] The Chairman of the Authority may not be a registered medical practitioner or directly associated with the provision of treatment services; such persons must, however, constitute at least one-third but not more than one-half of the total membership (Sch 1, para 4). The current membership includes appointments from such varied professions as the religious ministry, the law, accountancy, journalism and broadcasting, in addition to health caring.

[14] Human Fertilisation and Embryology (Mitochondrial Donation) Regulations (SI 2015/572).

[15] Inserted into the 1990 Act as s 4A(6).

[16] The same hybrid could be created by combining an animal pronucleus with that of a human pronucleus—the pronucleus being that part of the germ cell which is normally discarded in the formation of the gamete. Generally speaking, the Act governs the use of the pronucleus in the same way as it does that of the nucleus.

So far as is known, there are, currently, no scientific requirements for the creation of admixed embryos of the last three types[17] and it is to be noted that the Act makes a clear distinction between research and therapy in defining admixed embryos.

8.07 In this respect, ss 3, 4, and 4A of the Act define activities which *cannot* and *will not* be licensed. These include: placing in a woman any live gametes or embryos other than those designated as permitted—a permitted gamete being one which is produced by or extracted from a man or woman and whose nuclear or mitochondrial DNA has not been altered, and a permitted embryo being one produced by the fertilisation of a permitted egg by permitted sperm; there must have been no alteration of the DNA of any cell and no cell may be added to it other than by division of the embryo's own cells.[18] The therapeutic use of admixed embryos of any sort is, therefore, not allowed and a licence to do so cannot be issued. Precisely the same restrictions are now placed on any egg or embryo developed with respect to mitochondrial research.[19]

8.08 Of equal, if not greater, significance is the ban on keeping or using an embryo after the appearance of the primitive streak—defined in the Act as equating with not later than 14 days from the day on which the process of creating the embryo began but excluding any time for which the embryo was stored.[20] In this respect, s 1 of the 1990 Act contains some important definitions, which, themselves, show some significant changes following amendment by the 2008 Act. An embryo is now defined, except where otherwise stated, as a live human embryo other than an admixed human embryo, including an egg that is in the process of fertilisation or is undergoing any other process capable of resulting in an embryo.[21] Insofar as the Act governs the creation of an embryo, the definition applies only to the creation of an embryo outside the human body and to those where fertilisation or any other process by which the embryo was created began outside the human body.[22]

8.09 The Authority must also prepare and maintain a *Code of Practice* outlining the proper conduct of activities carried on under licence (s 25). As with all such mandated codes, the code is not legally binding per se—though it may, of course, include provisions that *are* legally binding. The fact that it had been disregarded would, however, count heavily in any criminal or civil actions brought against the offending clinic. Of greater practical importance, the Licence Committee is empowered to vary, revoke, or refuse to renew a licence in the light of any deviations from the provisions of the code (s 25(6)), operating on more routine matters through its Executive Licensing Panel.[23]

---

[17] For an interesting debate on the point in the Committee stage of the Bill, see Official Reports, HC, col 22 (19 May 2008).

[18] 1990 Act, s 3ZA.   [19] N 14 above, reg 10.   [20] s 3(4) as amended.

[21] 1990 Act, s 1(1) as amended by the 2008 Act. This covers the fact that it has been agreed in the House of Lords that an organism produced as a result of cell nuclear replacement is an embryo (see paras 7.105–7.107 for full discussion). But, the restriction on the use of such an embryo imposed by the Human Reproductive Cloning Act 2001 (now repealed) is continued under the amended 1990 Act, ss 3(2) and 3ZA(4) which prohibit the placing in a woman of an embryo other than a permitted embryo.

[22] It will be noted that, as a result, gamete intra-fallopian transfer (GIFT), which involves the introduction of the sperm to the ovum in their natural habitat—the fallopian tube—rather than in the Petri dish, is not subject to licensing unless either the sperm or eggs are donated. Even so, the HFEA is maintaining a watchful eye on the process which carries its own hazards and is now used relatively rarely. By contrast, in zygote intra-fallopian transfer (ZIFT), the preformed zygote is placed in the tube; fertilisation is, therefore, in vitro.

[23] HFEA, *Code of Practice*, 8th edn (updated 2015), available at: http://www.hfea.gov.uk/code.html; http://www.hfea.gov.uk/docs/HFEA_Code_of_Practice_8th_Edtion_(Apr_2015).pdf.

8.10 With that précis completed, we can go on to consider the practical applications of the two Acts when combined so as to govern parenting and assisted reproduction.[24]

INSEMINATION

8.11 Donor insemination (DI)[25] may provide a solution to male infertility, a condition which accounts for roughly 50 per cent of cases of involuntary failure to conceive. In this procedure, semen obtained from a donor is injected into the woman's genital tract; this results in conception in a proportion of cases which is surprisingly low.[26] The husband's or male partner's semen may similarly be introduced by artificial means (AIH or AIP)—a need which might arise from impotence, from inadequate formation of spermatozoa, or from a hostile vaginal reaction to constituents of the semen; treated semen would be used in the last two instances[27] which would, accordingly, require a licence.

ARTIFICIAL INSEMINATION BY THE HUSBAND OR MALE PARTNER

8.12 In general terms, both AIH and AIP are affected by the 1990 Act only tangentially. This derives from the terms of s 4(1)(b) which are that no person shall use the sperm of any man *other than partner-donated sperm which has been neither processed nor stored* (our emphasis) in the course of providing treatment services for a woman except in pursuance of a licence. Both, however, come within the scope of the Act if technical expertise has been involved, in which case the clinic is providing 'basic partner treatment services'. Even then, however, the regulations are less strict—for example, basic partner treatment services do not have to be recorded in the clinic's register of information.[28] Much of the difficulty previously experienced as to the definition of 'partner' is now dispersed in s 1(5) of the 1990 Act which states that, for the purposes of the Act, sperm is to be treated as partner-donated sperm if the donor and the recipient declare that they have an intimate physical relationship. This, however, still begs several questions—in particular, it ignores the duration of that relationship in both pro- and retrospective senses;[29] it is, perhaps, inevitable in such a private field that much still depends on the good sense of those called upon to interpret the Act and its associated Code. In this connection, it is to be noted that

---

[24] For an interesting argument challenging the legal basis of motherhood (currently the woman giving birth to the child), see: R D'alton-Harrison, 'Mater semper incertus est: who's your mummy?' (2014) 22(3) Med Law Rev 357.

[25] Insofar as insemination by donor will virtually always be artificial, we have adopted the modern terminology in preference to the traditional acronym AID. By contrast, artificial insemination by husband or partner must be distinguished from natural insemination and we continue to use the common abbreviations.

[26] The live birth rate was 32.7 per cent in 2012 for the age range 18–34 and success diminishes rapidly with increasing age—it was, e.g., only 13.1 per cent for women aged 40–42 and less than 4.3% above that: (HFEA, *Fertility Treatment in 2013*).

[27] Intra cytoplasmic sperm injection would then be the ideal treatment and its increasing use must contribute to the recent fall in the number of DI cycles provided.

[28] 1990 Act, s 31(2).

[29] One railway company, e.g., laid down two years as a period of partnership qualifying for family rebates: *Grant v South-West Trains Ltd* [1998] All ER (EC) 193; [1998] 1 FLR 839. Twelve months is the applicable period for the purposes of the Civil Partnership Act 2004 (s 17)—but this is a retrospective assessment whereas, in the present context, it is the future intention of the couple which matters to a resultant child.

the problem, such as it is, is a matter of providing treatment—it is distinct from the legal determination of fatherhood, to which we return at para 8.35.[30]

8.13 Finally in this context, it is to be noted that AIH has been refined by the introduction of micromanipulative techniques—in particular, those of intracyto-plasmic sperm injection (ICSI) or sub-zonal insemination (SUZI). In these methods, a single spermatozoon is injected directly into an egg. The sperm can, thus, be preselected and the technique is a valuable adjunct to the management of male infertility due to poor quality of the semen; we are, however, here into advanced techniques which, for more than one reason, can only be performed under licence. It is to be noted that the opportunities for pre-implantation genetic selection—a technique which, although attractive, itself, poses a number of moral issues (discussed further at para 8.62)—are greatly reduced using ICSI or SUZI as compared with standard techniques; this is a matter of particular concern when the quality of the spermatozoon, which is now enjoying a non-competitive existence, is, itself, suspect. As a result, most clinics still adopt a cautious attitude to these techniques.[31] Even so, some 53.1 per cent of all IVF treatments were accomplished by way of ICSI in 2013.[32]

8.14 Leaving aside any aspects of family law which depend upon marital status, and excluding any consideration of the moral value of marriage, it is tempting to conclude that uncomplicated AIH and AIP give rise to no major legal, status or ethical problems of themselves; the procedures will only be regarded as questionable if there is objection to *any* interference with nature in this area. This, however, is something of a simplistic view as AIH can be used for reasons other than compromised fertility in the male and its morality may then be questionable. Pre-eminent among these is the use of AIH as a preliminary to selection of the sex of the conceptus and we discuss this as a separate matter later.

8.15 Otherwise, the major issue raised by AIH lies in the possibility of 'sperm banking' either as an insurance against later sterility due to treatment—for example, radiotherapy for malignant disease—or for use by a woman after her husband's or partner's death as, for instance, when the man is in a high-risk occupation; these possibilities can, obviously, arise in combination. Legally, it could lead to complex problems in relation to probate and succession.[33] In addition, however, absent specific regulations, the child born as a result of posthumous insemination or embryo donation could be, in legal terms, 'fatherless'—a situation which would be, at best, undesirable and, at worst, incompatible with the Human Rights Act 1998.

8.16 Following the recommendations of the McLean Committee,[34] Parliament enacted the Human Fertilisation and Embryology (Deceased Fathers) Act 2003. This has since been repealed but its terms are incorporated in the amended 1990 Act, s 28(5A)–(5I) and are carried through in the 2008 Act, ss 39–41. Essentially, if a child has been carried by a woman as a result of the placing in her of an embryo, or of sperm and eggs, or her artificial

[30] The definition of a 'partner' here is to be compared with that given in the Human Tissue Act 2004, s 54(8) as one of two persons, of either sex, living as partners in 'an enduring family relationship'.
[31] The HFEA requires that they are carried out only by persons who have been appropriately approved: HFEA *Code of Practice* (8th edn, update 2015), para 21.
[32] HFEA, *Fertility treatment in 2013*, n 2.
[33] Although these do not seem insuperable in the USA: *Woodward v Commissioner of Social Security* 435 Mass 536 (2002). The 1990 Act left open the related questions of the man who is reported missing but is, in fact, dead and of the woman who reasonably believes her dead partner to be alive—we think it is likely that legal paternity could be established in either case.
[34] S A M McLean, *Review of the Common Law Provisions Relating to the Removal of Gametes and of the Consent Provisions in the Human Fertilisation and Embryology Act 1990* (1998).

insemination involving the use of a man's sperm after his death, then, subject to a number of conditions—for which, see para 8.17—that man's particulars can be entered as the particulars of that child's father in a register of live or still births.[35] It is interesting that no special relationship is demanded by s 39 of the 2008 Act—the essential element is the man's written consent. Section 40 of 2008 Act also provides for the posthumous transfer of an embryo that was created during a man's life by way of consensual sperm donation (for which, see para 8.17). Here, however, a distinction persists as to the married or unmarried status of the woman in that, if she is unmarried, s 40(2)(b) dictates that the embryo be formed during the course of treatment in the UK by a person to whom a licence applies.[36] In either case, however, the conditions as to posthumous fatherhood apply whether the actual impregnation took place in the UK or elsewhere.[37] It is to be noted that the law as to succession is unaltered—viz, the child will not inherit from its 'father's' estate—and that the purpose of these concessions is strictly limited to providing the resulting child with a traditional birth certificate.

8.17   The conditions validating the grant of the birth certificate are strict. In particular, the woman must elect in writing that the man be treated as the father of the child within 42 days of the birth of the child.[38] Most importantly, the man must have given his written consent to posthumous parenthood before his death. This clearly demands foresight and the problem of consent to assisted reproduction in general was at the heart of the crucial case of Mrs Blood.[39] This also has wider implications and we think it still merits some discussion despite the fact that it has been largely overtaken by the events it catalysed.

8.18   In essence, Mr Blood was the victim of meningitis. When he was in terminal coma, his wife requested, and obtained, a specimen of semen, which she hoped to use for insemination after his death. If it could have been established clearly that he was alive, removal of the specimen could have been seen as treatment for a husband and wife together and, since it was arguably in his 'best interests',[40] there would have been little to stop his wife's immediate AIH.[41] However, therein lies the rub. The team was reluctant to proceed along this road without authority. The imposed delay dictated storage of the specimen—and the legality of storage of gametes under licence depends on the written consent and counselling of the donor. Neither condition could be satisfied. Accordingly, the HFEA held that storage of the specimen and its future use would be unlawful; furthermore, the Authority declined to exercise its discretion to allow the gametes to be exported to another country where treatment could be given in the absence of the donor's written consent.

8.19   Mrs Blood applied for judicial review of this decision but her application was dismissed. The Court of Appeal agreed with the High Court decision to the extent that the HFEA was, effectively, following the will of Parliament. It did, however, conclude that, in failing

---

[35] 2008 Act, s 39.
[36] There is now no reference to 'treatment together'. But since, in either situation, an embryo must be created in vitro, it is a little difficult to see the distinction as being other than one without a difference.
[37] 2008 Act, ss 39(2) and 40(3).
[38] The period is 21 days in Scotland (s 28(5E)). The period can be extended in both jurisdictions with the consent of the Registrar General provided he is satisfied that there are compelling reasons why he should do so (s 28(5F) and (5G)).
[39] R v Human Fertilisation and Embryology Authority, ex p Blood [1997] 2 All ER 687; (1997) 35 BMLR 1, CA.
[40] It is an assault to touch a person who is incapable of consenting unless, among other possibilities, it is in his or her best interests to do so: Re F (mental patient: sterilisation) [1990] 2 AC 1, sub nom F v West Berkshire Health Authority [1989] 2 All ER 545.
[41] Accepted by Lord Woolf in the Court of Appeal [1997] 2 All ER 687 at 696; (1997) 35 BMLR at 23.

to exercise its discretion to facilitate treatment abroad, the HFEA had not been properly advised as to the importance of EC law in relation to cross-border services and had been over-concerned with the creation of an undesirable precedent. The case was, therefore, remitted to the Authority, which exercised its discretion in the light of the further evidence adduced in the Court of Appeal. In the end, then, *Blood*'s main contribution to the jurisprudence was to accelerate the changes to the domestic law that were so clearly desirable.[42] It also showed that we cannot ignore the effect of membership of the EU even in such an intimate sphere as that of reproductive choice—see Chapter 3. In respect of the particular issue under consideration, it is to be noted that posthumous insemination per se is governed by the common law and is not unlawful[43]—indeed, Sch 3, para 2(2) of the original 1990 Act allows for the relevant consent from the man prior to his death. Nevertheless, as we will see later, s 13(5) of the 1990 Act and its associated *Code of Practice* allow the clinics considerable leeway as to the use of available techniques; the indications are that a significant proportion disapprove of at least some aspects of the process—particularly, perhaps, those that infringe the dignity of a dying person or a corpse.[44]

The paramountcy of written consent as the legal touchstone to govern the use of one's gametes was most recently confirmed by the High Court in *R (on the application of IM) v Human Fertilisation and Embryology Authority*,[45] this time in respect of a deceased woman's frozen unfertilised eggs. The parents sought to export the eggs to the USA for use in the mother as a surrogate. They presented evidence of conversations to this effect with their daughter. Notwithstanding, the Court held that the Authority was entitled to refuse to surrender the eggs for want of clear, effective, written, and informed consent. Moreover, the Authority had no discretion to dispense with such a central provision of the legislation.

8.20 A further legal problem could arise were nullity of the marriage to be mooted—as it could well be in some circumstances calling for AIH. Use of the procedure does not constitute consummation of marriage and a decree of nullity can still be obtained if a woman conceives in this way; approbation might, however, preclude the granting of such a decree.[46] Any resulting children would still be regarded as legitimate on the grounds that the parents were married at the time of conception.

---

[42] The generally uncertain nature of the law even since *Blood* is demonstrated by the length of the judgment in *L v Human Fertilisation and Embryology Authority* (2008) 104 BMLR 200. It is, however, clear that no one, not even the court, has the power to waive the consent conditions as to the posthumous use of sperm—and, in particular, recourse to the Human Tissue Act 2004 is precluded. Given, however, that the sperm exists, the HFEA has the authority to allow its export under s 24(4) of the 1990 Act and, as a prerequisite to this, to modify the conditions for storage.

[43] See e.g. *L v Human Fertilisation and Embryology Authority*, n 42 at [76].

[44] For criticism of this last practice in general, see R D Orr and M Siegler, 'Is posthumous semen retrieval ethically permissible?' (2002) 28 J Med Ethics 299. In an unusual case, which is also of interest as to the meaning of 'undue pressure', a clinic actually put pressure on a man to withdraw his consent to posthumous use of his sperm; the court found, with regret, that he had done so: *Centre for Reproductive Medicine v U* [2002] EWHC 36 (Fam); (2002) 65 BMLR 92; [2002] Lloyd's Rep Med 93; the decision was upheld on appeal: [2002] Lloyd's Rep Med 259. More recently, a widow of a man who had clearly given consent to ongoing storage of his sperm after his death was allowed extended storage for use even although the statutory time period had expired. The reasoning was that the do otherwise would be a disproportionate burden on human rights considerations, and also in recognition of the fact that the clinic had failed to inform the husband of changed regulations for storage and to seek his written consent thereto: *Warren v Care Fertility (Northampton) Ltd* [2015] Fam 1; [2014] 3 WLR 1310.

[45] [2015] EWHC 1706 (Admin).

[46] *REL v EL* [1949] P 211; [1949] 1 All ER 141 (see also *G v G* 1961 SLT 324).

8.21 A further application of AIH relates to long-term prisoners whose wives may wish, or need on the grounds of age, to conceive before their release. A significant case was heard in the Court of Appeal[47] in 2001 in which it was held that the justifiable withdrawal of conjugal rights which was inherent in imprisonment could include a denial of access to artificial insemination. However, the principle of proportionality applies and it was held that exceptional circumstances could require the consequences of imprisonment to yield to the European Convention on Human Rights (ECHR);[48] the policy whereby the Secretary of State judges each case on its merits was considered to be neither in breach of the Convention nor irrational or unlawful.[49] In an interesting obiter opinion, Lord Phillips thought that the starting point for exceptional circumstances could be when the founding of a family was prevented absolutely rather than delayed by a refusal to grant facilities for insemination.[50]

8.22 *Mellor* has now been superseded by the case brought by Mr and Mrs Dickson which ran the whole gauntlet of human rights litigation from judicial review to the Grand Chamber of the European Court of Human Rights (ECtHR)—and it was not until this last phase that the UK's wall of resistance to the acceptance of sexual rights for prisoners was, at least partially, breached.[51] Up until then, all the courts, both domestic and European, had followed *Mellor*. The Grand Chamber, however, by a majority of 12:5, held, inter alia, that the UK policy demanded too much of the applicants to prove exceptional circumstances in their case and that, as a consequence, there had been a violation of Art 8 of the Convention. The judgment of the Grand Chamber was very much directed to the instant case and it is at least debatable that it will affect the UK position in general.[52]

Primary Sex Selection

8.23 Public concern has been aroused by the entry into the market place of preconception sex selection of children. Most methods claiming scientific respectability depend upon altering the proportion of male- and female-bearing spermatozoa in the ejaculate and artificial insemination with the processed specimen. Opinions differ as to whether such methods are efficient and to what extent they can be relied upon but the HFEA is clearly concerned as to their effect on the gametes and states that a licensed clinic should not use

---

[47] *R (on the application of Mellor)* v *Secretary of State for the Home Department* [2001] 3 WLR 533; (2001) 59 BMLR 1.

[48] Per Lord Phillips MR at para 45. See now Human Rights Act 1998, Sch 1, Arts 8 and 12. For critical analysis of the case, see J Williams, 'Have the courts got it right?—*The Queen on the application of Mellor v Secretary of State for the Home Department*' (2002) 14 CFLQ 218.

[49] The Court noted that the European Commission on Human Rights had already approved this possibility in *ELH and PBH* v *United Kingdom* (1997) 91 AD & R 61.

[50] At para 68.

[51] *Dickson and Dickson* v *Premier Prison Service Ltd* [2004] EWCA Civ 1477; *Dickson* v *United Kingdom* [2008] 46 EHRR 41, ECtHR, Grand Chamber. The almost predictable indecision of the ECtHR is well caught by M Eijkholt, 'The right to procreate is not aborted' (2008) 16 Med L Rev 284. Mrs Dickson was, in fact, the first unimprisoned wife to plead her case in the courts. Space prevents more than a passing reference to this rather marginal aspect of reproductive medicine. For a very comprehensive review of the case up to and including the ECtHR, see H Codd, 'The slippery slope to sperm smuggling: Prisoners, artificial insemination and human rights' (2007) 15 Med L Rev 220.

[52] An interesting variant has been reported in Australia where a female prisoner aged 45 sought periodic release from custody in order to complete her IVF treatment (see para 8.48) before she became too old to qualify for treatment. The Court held that this came within her rights to humane treatment and respect for her dignity: *Castles* v *Secretary to the Department of Justice* [2010] VSC 310 (Charter of Human Rights and Responsibilities Act (Vic.) 2006).

sperm samples which have been separated for the purpose of sex selection for medical reasons;[53] moreover, due to concerns about the reliability of the technique, sperm that has been subject to gradient density methods of sperm sorting for sex selection should not be used for medical reasons.

8.24 Beyond this, sex selection for non-medical or social reasons has been classed as anything from 'playing God' to offering an acceptable new dimension to family planning. While the latter view cannot be rejected out of hand, it, nevertheless, presupposes that the method is perfected and, in practice, there is bound to be a residue of couples who have been to considerable expense and discomfort to select the sex of their child and who will be bitterly disappointed when their wishes are unfulfilled. It follows that, in contrast to most other forms of reproductive liberty,[54] primary sex selection poses a real threat of distasteful increase in the number of 'social' abortions that might result.[55]

8.25 What calls for analysis is the ethical position in the event that accurate selection was found to be a viable prospect. Discussion is then at two levels—the practical and the deontological. The fact that both are highly culture-dependent—with a very evident East/West divide—deserves emphasis. Thus, at the practical level, it is probably fair to say that pre-conception sex selection would have, at most, a negligible effect on the distribution and status of the sexes in the UK. But this is essentially a Western view and one which might well not be true elsewhere.[56] On the ethical plane, however, it is supposed that even those concerned to minimise any suggestion of embryonic and fetal rights would see 'sperm sorting' as being morally preferable to secondary sex selection by way of pre-implantation embryo selection or abortion—and this would be independent of cultural bias.

8.26 Deontological argument apart, however, the legal limitation of 'gender clinics' to those licensed to undertake the practice is to be advocated on technical and safety grounds alone and this has become the de facto position since the European Directive on Tissues and Cells came into force.[57] As a result of this, s 4(1)(b) now includes partner-donated sperm which has been processed amongst those gametes which cannot be used to treat a woman other than in pursuance of a licence.[58]

[53] HFEA, *Code of Practice* (8th edn, updated 2015), s 10.

[54] D McCarthy, 'Why sex selection should be legal' (2001) 27 J Med Ethics 302 makes a powerful case for the onus being with those who oppose sex selection to show that its restriction would be a restriction of liberty that could not reasonably be rejected. Interesting arguments against sex selection irrespective of the harm principle are provided by S McDougall, 'Acting parentally: An argument against sex selection' (2005) 31 J Med Ethics 601 and, more recently, H Strange and R Chadwick, 'The ethics of non-medical sex selection' (2010) 18 Healthcare Anal 252.

[55] For a very useful review of the arguments from both sides, see H Strange et al., 'Non-medical sex selection: Ethical issues' (2010) 94 Brit Med Bull 7.

[56] The need for control has been, however, questioned by B M Dickens, 'Can sex selection be ethically tolerated?' (2002) 28 J Med Ethics 335; this article also discusses the relationship of sex selection and sexism.

[57] See n 10. Problems of safety do not arise in selection on the basis of a search for Y chromosome material from fetal blood circulating in that of the mother. This is also not without its deprecators: A Tuffs, 'Doctors protest about fetal sex tests in early pregnancy' (2007) 334 BMJ 712.

[58] The HFEA has confirmed that 'processing' includes sperm sorting for social purposes. It is notable that the Council of Europe Convention on Human Rights and Biomedicine (1997) specifically outlaws the use of techniques of medically assisted procreation for the purpose of choosing a child's sex other than for sound medical reasons (Art 14); the UK has not, however, yet ratified the Convention.

DONOR INSEMINATION

8.27   Donor insemination introduces two additional concepts into the management of infertility. First, the procedure escapes the confines of a private matter between two persons in a close emotional relationship; rather, it involves a generally indifferent third party whose contribution lies at the heart of the enterprise. Second, sperm donation inevitably results in the production of a gross excess of gametes and, consequently, to the creation of options for their storage and later use. Ideally, therefore, all forms of DI should be subject to control but, effectively, this is as impossible as is the control of natural insemination. We have seen already that the wording of s 4(1)(b) of the 1990 Act excludes the need for a licence when carrying out AIH or AIP without recourse to storage or processing of the sperm; whether privatised DI is also excluded is, however, less obvious. Section 4(1)(b) equally makes it an offence to use any sperm other than as limited 'in the course of providing any treatment services for a woman except in the pursuance of a licence'. How, then, are we to harmonise this with the evident impossibility of enforcement within, say, a closely knit community? The solution lies in the fact that the section must be interpreted along with the meaning of treatment services which are defined in s 2(1) as 'services provided to the public or a section of the public'. It is widely agreed that, taken together, ss 2(1) and 4(1)(b) combine to exclude 'do-it-yourself' inseminations from the strictures of the Act and that this is irrespective of whether the sperm used is that of a husband, a partner, or an altruistic donor.

8.28   Control of a public insemination programme is, however, both desirable and possible and, to this end, the use of the sperm of a man other than a partner—and, conversely, the use of any other woman's eggs—in providing treatment services is permitted only in pursuance of a licence.[59] Ultimately, the legality and morality of DI and ovum donation[60] depend on the consent of the donors to their use; consent provides the plinth on which control is based and its form is detailed in Sch 3 of the 1990 Act.

Consent to DI

8.29   In summary, so-called 'effective consent' must be in writing and signed and can apply to the use, storage and/or disposal of gametes or of embryos resulting from their use.[61] The obligation of being signed is, however, demitted if the person is incapacitated provided that it is signed at the direction of the incapacitated person; but the concession does nothing for those, say, in the position of Mr and Mrs Blood. Consent to the use or storage of gametes implies consent to the use of any resulting embryo or admixed embryo (Sch 3, para 2(4)). Conversely, gametes cannot be used or received other than in accordance with the terms of an effective consent (Sch 3, para 5) and this extends to the use of any embryo created from those gametes—in which case the consent must be by each 'relevant person' (Sch 3, para 6(3A)); a consent to storage of gametes—which is, itself, governed by the clinic's possession of a 'storage licence' (s 11(b))—can be subject to conditions which must be met and, again, this applies to any embryo so formed (Sch 3, para 8(2)). The 1990 Act now makes provision for storage without consent of the gametes of children below the age of 18 and of incapacitated adults above the age of 16 who are to undergo treatment that is likely to result in significant impairment of their fertility subject to stringent medical

---

[59]   1990 Act, s 4(1)(b).   [60]   See para 8.56.
[61]   Interestingly, it is now open to gamete donors to specify extra conditions for their storage or use, subject to compatibility with the Equality Act 2010. The Act prohibits clinics from discriminating by treating people less favourably because of various protected characteristics. (Cf. the donation of tissues and organs—Chapter 17.) HFEA Chair letter CH(12)01, (2012), 28 January.

conditions as to the need for so doing[62] (Sch 3, paras 9 and 10); lastly, the person giving consent to storage must specify what is to be done with the gametes or created embryos in the event that he or she dies or becomes incapacitated and must specify the maximum period of storage if this is less than the statutory storage period (Sch 3, para 2(2)).[63] In addition, the donor must be given adequate information and must be counselled before consenting to procedures under the Act and particular aspects of counselling are now detailed (Sch 3, paras 3, 4, and 4A and Sch 3ZA). It goes without saying that the conditions surrounding effective consent are everywhere modified so as to accommodate the creation and use of admixed embryos.

8.30   The furore surrounding the case of Ms Evans—for which, see para 8.82—precipitated some relatively radical amendments to the conditions governing modification and withdrawal of consent to the use of gametes and embryos. This is an area that gives rise to particular concern and it is worth summarising the provisions in Sch, 3, paras 4 and 4A in some detail:

- the terms of any consent can be varied or withdrawn by the person giving consent by giving notice to the person keeping the relevant gametes or embryos;
- the terms of any consent to the use of any embryo or admixed embryo cannot be varied or withdrawn once the embryo has been used;
- where the embryo in storage was created for treatment purposes and one of its progenitors gives notice of withdrawal of consent before the embryo is used, the person keeping the embryo must, so far as is reasonably possible, notify each interested person—including a person who was to be treated by the use of the embryo—of that notice;
- then, storage of the embryo remains lawful for 12 months from the day on which notice of withdrawal was received or until each interested person consents to the destruction of the embryo within that time.

These paragraphs are clearly aimed at achieving a reconciliation between two gamete donors who are in dispute; whether, in fact, they do anything more than prolong an unhappy episode is, of course, open to debate—the reader may be better able to form an opinion after considering Ms Evans' case.

DI and the Marital Bond

8.31   Notwithstanding the protective mechanisms enshrined in statute, it must not be forgotten that there are those who might object strongly to DI on the grounds that the basis of the marriage bond is compromised by the wife's pregnancy through another man. It is supposed that the sanctity of marriage is invaded and that, in this respect, DI is little different from adultery. The question of whether DI constitutes adultery in legal terms was first debated in the Scottish case of *MacLennan* v *MacLennan*,[64] where it was determined

---

[62] Including that the person is not only incapacitated at the time but is also likely to regain capacity to consent to storage. Non-consensual storage is subject to a 'best interests' test and the gametes may not be stored after the patient's death.

[63] They cannot, normally, be stored for longer than ten years (1990 Act, s 14(3)). An exception may be made if the person seeking storage was under 45 years of age when the gametes were placed in storage and the other conditions laid down in the regulation have been satisfied. These include the fact that the special circumstances arose after storage began: Human Fertilisation and Embryology (Statutory Storage Period for Embryos and Gametes) Regulations (SI 2009/1582).

[64] 1958 SC 105.

that adultery could not be held to have taken place because there was no sexual contact between the woman and the donor. This approach to the question is now almost certainly acceptable throughout the common law jurisdictions. DI without the consent of the husband could, however, be taken as constituting cruel and unreasonable conduct for divorce purposes. Otherwise, given the consent of both parties, the acceptance of DI can be seen as the fulfilment of the perfectly legitimate desire to have a child.

8.32   This is not to recommend that DI be undertaken lightly. Ill considered donation can lead, inter alia, to the transmission of both genetic and sexually transmitted disease; in addition, it may promote some aspects of eugenic selection that are, at least, of questionable morality. Counselling as to its psychological and legal implications is an integral part of the provision of a public DI service in the UK.[65]

Major Ethical Problems

8.33   It is probably fair to say that the major ethical problems associated with DI have been eliminated from the standard husband and wife or heterosexual partnership situations. It can, however, happen that a single woman requests DI or the request may come from a lesbian couple. The individual doctor who is morally opposed to extra-marital procreation of any sort could attempt to plead the 'conscience clause' embedded in s 38 of the 1990 Act, although the chances of that now happening seem remote. Parliament has, however, now limited objections to providing treatment for such women insofar as ss 43–53 of the 2008 Act allow not only for the application of the terms of the Civil Partnership Act 2004 but also for a homosexual woman to consent to being and to be accepted as a second parent;[66] while this is primarily a matter of family law, the implication is that there is no objection in principle to lesbian parenting. This seems to be the inevitable conclusion in logic[67] once it is appreciated that there is no suggestion that single and lesbian women should be prevented from having children by natural means. While, as we have suggested, the doctor may have his or her own moral code—the matter of strict equality under the law is resolved by the 2008 Act.[68] There remain some concerns, however, as to whether equality is being enjoyed in practice or indeed whether lesbian prospective mothers require their own treatment pathways.[69]

8.34   It is to be noted further that the HFEA's *Code of Practice* originally listed five wide-ranging major factors which clinics should take into account when people seek treatment using donated gametes[70] and, among these, was to consider the resulting child's 'need for a father'. The 8th edition of the Code and the Act, itself, which also originally spoke of the need for a father, are now amended to read 'the need of that child for supportive

---

[65] 1990 Act, s 13(6).

[66] And, in such circumstances, no man is to be regarded as the father (2008 Act, s 45(1)).

[67] Although the 'logic' depends on whether the word 'parent' is interpreted in procreative or social terms. It also leaves open the underlying question of whether NHS resources should be used for non-medical purposes.

[68] Although new permutations of modern family relationships reach the courts regularly. In *T v B* [2010] Fam 193, [2011] 1 All ER 77, the biological mother of a child born to a lesbian couple failed in a claim for financial relief from her partner after they separated.

[69] H Priddle, 'How well are lesbians treated in UK fertility clinics?' (2015) Human Fertility, first online, doi: 10.3109/14647273.2015.1043654.

[70] The 8th edition (updated 2015) still advises a remarkably extensive list of recommended investigations into the proposed patient's (or her partner's) suitability for parenthood—and a correspondingly large breadth of discretion which, one feels, could well lead to reproductive 'shopping-around'.

parenting'.[71] It is worth reminding the reader at this point that, while the Code has no legal force per se, it is produced pursuant to a statutory obligation; renewal of a licence would undoubtedly be prejudiced were its recommendations to be flouted (1990 Act, s 25(6)). The words of the Act are, however, a different matter.[72] As to their actual interpretation, it is a matter of considerable conjecture as to what the 'supportive parenting' provision is actually designed to achieve, how this can be policed, whether (and how) it is invoked, and whether it does little more than provide subjective licence to discriminate against those seeking fertility services.[73]

Legal Considerations

8.35 The statutory definitions of parenthood are covered by both ss 27–9 of the amended 1990 Act and ss 33–47 of the 2008 Act while, at the same time, Sch 6, para 35(3) of the 2008 Act states that both remain 'relevant statutory provisions'.[74] Any potential confusion is, however, eliminated by s 57 of the 2008 Act which makes it clear that this is no more than a matter of timing—the provisions of ss 27–9 of the 1990 Act do not have effect in relation to children born by way of assisted reproduction after the commencement of ss 33–48 of the 2008 Act. Conversely, the relevant sections of the 2008 Act will apply only to children born after their commencement.[75] Accordingly, we use the 2008 statute as our template, noting that not only is much new law introduced but, also, that a number of anomalies which previously existed between England and Wales and Scotland are eliminated.[76]

8.36 Section 35 covers the case of the married woman. In essence, the rule is that, when she has been inseminated with the sperm of a man other than her husband and provided that her husband has consented, her husband will be treated as the father of the child; the donor is covered against withdrawal of consent by the husband by s 41(1).[77] The s 35 rule is voided if the husband can show that he did not, in fact, consent to the procedure. The somewhat confusing terms of s 38(2) and (3) do, however, retain the common law principle of *pater est quem nuptiae demonstrant*; thus, the husband who does not consent to DI will still have to rebut that presumption in an acceptable way. It is to be noted that the statutory provisions will prevail in the event of disagreement between the partners.[78] The somewhat archaic exclusion of hereditary titles, honours, and the like from the general principles attaching to the AID child still applies under s 49(7) and (8) of the 2008 Act.

---

[71] 1990 Act, s 13(5) as amended by 2008 Act, s 14(2)(b). It seems that the courts may have considerable difficulty in the event of a dispute as to care of any children but that the gestational and biological relationship will be significant in assessing the child's best interests: *Re G (children) (residence: same-sex partner)* [2006] 4 All ER 241; [2006] 2 FLR 142, HL. For a specific feminist appraisal of the new wording, see J McCandless and S Sheldon, 'No father required? The welfare assessment in the Human Fertilisation and Embryology Act 2008' (2010) 18 Fem Leg Studies 201.

[72] Accordingly, the current Code contains three main divisions—Mandatory Requirements, HFEA Interpretation of the requirements, and HFEA Guidance. Conformity to the first is mandatory insofar as they express a legal requirement or a condition of licence (*Code of Practice* 8th edn, update 2015).

[73] For discussion, see S Sheldon, E Lee, and J Macvarnish, '"Supportive parenting", responsibility and regulation: the welfare assessment under the reformed Human Fertilisation and Embryology Act (1990)' (2015) 78(3) Mod Law Rev 461, doi: 10.1111/1468-2230.12124, and S E P Walker, 'Potential persons and the welfare of the (potential) child test' (2014) 14(3) Med Law Int 157.

[74] See also Child Support Act 1991, s 26, Case B1 where the sections are regarded as alternatives.

[75] 2008 Act, s 57(1) and (2).

[76] Note that the original 1990 Act is also subject to considerable amendment by way of the European Directives.

[77] There is, of course, nothing to prevent a man claiming paternity under the common law: *X v Y* 2002 SLT 161, Glasgow Sheriff Court. The potential advantages of this to the child were expressed in the pioneer Australian case *Re Patrick* (2002) 28 Fam LR 579.

[78] *Re CH (contact: parentage)* [1996] 1 FLR 569.

8.37 Section 36 of the 2008 Act extends the responsibilities and privileges of fatherhood to a man other than a woman's husband subject, first, to the insemination being carried out in a licensed clinic and, second, to satisfaction of the 'agreed fatherhood' provisions laid down in s 37.[79] The agreed fatherhood conditions are that both the man and the woman concerned have given the person responsible for the treatment notice in writing that they consent to the man's fatherhood and that neither has withdrawn their consent or otherwise altered the agreed conditions of parenthood. Reciprocal protection of the donor when such an agreement is reached is provided by s 38(1) in respect of both married and unmarried couples. It is interesting that s 37 makes no mention of the quality of the relationship or its duration—all that matters is bilateral consent between a man and a woman.

8.38 In *X v St Bartholomew's Hospital Centre for Reproductive Medicine*,[80] the question over paternity of the child born from sperm donation arose because the clinic mislaid the legal documentation. The partner of the woman would not, technically, be the father in the absence of a signed consent form from him. This was missing when the HFEA ordered the clinic to undertake an audit. Notwithstanding, the court declared the man to be the father for legal purposes on the basis that all evidence suggested that it was more likely than not that he has signed the requisite legal forms. The failures of the clinic, while unprofessional, did not invalidate the clinic's legal authority to treat the man's partner.

8.39 Subsequent to this case, another action involving no less than seven applicants seeking declarations of parentage came to the High Court on the basis of the same HFEA audit that had revealed the anomaly in the *X* case, above. The case in question was *In the matter of the Human Fertilisation and Embryology Act 2008 (Cases A, B, C, D, E, F, G, H)*[81] where Sir James Munby P lamented the loss of consent forms or the failure to complete HFEA designate forms in a number of clinics as 'alarming and shocking', revealing a 'deeply troubling picture' of 'great public concern' and 'widespread incompetence'. In a very pragmatic decision, exemplifying the 'Golden Rule' of statutory interpretation par excellence, Sir Munby held that although the regulatory authority had directed that particular consent forms be used, a failure to do so (or their loss) could not, in itself, invalidate what would otherwise be a valid consent. Moreover, the used of a clinic's own internal forms—duly completed—could serve as sufficient evidence of such consent.

8.40 The mischief that the concept of 'agreed fatherhood' is intended to avoid is well illustrated in the unusual early case of *U v W*.[82] In this case, a woman conceived and bore twins as a result of micromanipulation of her ova and the sperm of an anonymous donor, the process having failed when using the semen of her partner. U applied to have her partner declared the father of the twins by virtue of s 28(3)(a) of the 1990 Act.[83] In the process of deciding the meaning of 'treatment together', Wilson J opined:[84]

> what has to be demonstrated is that, in the provision of treatment services with donor sperm, the doctor was responding to a request for that form of treatment made by the woman and the man as a couple, notwithstanding the absence in the man of any physical role in such treatment.[85]

---

[79] Thus, eliminating the obscure phraseology of two persons being 'treated together' as is to be found in the original 1990 Act. For the need for this, see the quandary of Johnson J in *Re Q (parental order)* [1996] 1 FLR 369. Even so, the phrase still appears in the 1990 Act, s 28(3) and (5B)(c).

[80] [2015] EWFC 13; [2015] Fam Law 642.   [81] [2015] EWHC 2602 (Fam).

[82] *U v W (A-G intervening)* [1997] 2 FLR 282; (1997) 38 BMLR 54.   [83] See para 8.35.

[84] (1997) 38 BMLR 54 at 66.

[85] U, in fact, failed in her bid to impose paternity on W because the procedure was not carried out in a clinic licensed in the UK. The restriction was held not to constitute an infringement of the ECHR, Art 59.

And s 36 effectively restates this in a structured fashion.

8.41 The 2008 Act, however, is not yet done as to parenthood as, as we have already intimated, it, inevitably, extends the provisions of the Civil Partnership Act 2004 to assisted reproduction, s 42 enabling a woman in such a partnership to assume the role of parent of a child born as a result of DI. Section 43, however, also allows a woman in a homosexual relationship outside civil partnership to be treated as a parent of a DI child subject to the same, modified, conditions as apply to heterosexual couples that are laid down as agreed female parenthood conditions[86]—and this, again, being without limitation as to the strength of the relationship.[87] Section 46 also extends the civil partnership and intended female parenthood provisions to the posthumous situation. Note that all the arrangements already outlined in relation to fictional, albeit legal, parenthood are subject to the parties not having withdrawn their consents and, in this context, treatment as a couple relates to the time the treatment is provided, not when consent is given.[88] There seems, however, to be little limit to the complexities introduced by the combination of DI and modern attitudes to 'the family'. In *A v B (Contact: Alternative Families)*, the male member of a *ménage à trois* involving a lesbian partnership donated sperm to one of the women and later claimed biological fatherhood. The case is, essentially, a matter of family law but is important insofar as the Court of Appeal refused to apply the general rules as to parentage in the changed circumstances. All such cases are fact specific;[89] the only common factor, irrespective of any prior agreements is the paramountcy of the resulting child's welfare, the assessment of which may change as time passes. This has been confirmed most recently in *JB v KS*[90] where the court granted a parental responsibility order to a man who had donated sperm to a lesbian woman to have a child and on the basis of co-parenting arrangements. While the adult relationship broke down, factors impacting on the child's welfare included evidence of a previously sustainable joint project by the adults, the fact that the man had an enduring relationship, and his financial and emotional commitment to the child.

8.42 Other than in respect of posthumous fatherhood, and posthumous female parenthood,[91] neither the 1990 Act nor the 2008 Act make specific mention as to the registration of the birth of the child but, again, this appears to be clarified by implication. Section 48 of the 2008 Act states that the recognition of a person by the law as the mother, father, or parent of a child under ss 33–47 is 'for all purposes'—and this must include the registration of births and marriages. Near absolute freedom from parental responsibility is conferred on the donor by s 48(2) of the 2008 Act, which, again, refers to exclusion 'for any purpose'.[92]

A comparison of *Blood* and *U v W* provides a nice example of the juggling which can accompany attempts to harmonise domestic and EC law.

[86] Section 44.

[87] As would be expected, a woman is not to be regarded as 'the other parent' merely because of egg donation (2008 Act, s 47). For a review of the legal framework with respect to civil partnerships and biological parentage, see *Re G Children* [2014] EWCA Civ 336.

[88] *Re R (IVF: paternity of child)* [2005] 2 FLR 843, HL. This case, admittedly, refers to the insertion of an embryo but the same principles would apply to DI. It also contains some robust criticism of both the 1990 Act and of the HFEA and is discussed in detail by S Fovargue, '*Re R (IVF: paternity of child)*: Assisting conception for the single infertile' (2006) 18 CFLQ 423.

[89] Per Thorpe LJ: *A v B (Contact: Alternative Families)* [2012] 1 FCR 510 at 23. See also the even more strange *ménage* in *MA v RS (Contact: Parenting Roles)* [2012] 1 FLR 1056.

[90] [2015] EWHC 180 (Fam); [2015] Fam Law 376.

[91] Which are concerned with the registration of the deceased as the father or second parent of a live birth or stillbirth.

[92] It will be seen from what has already been said that the donor could, e.g., be seen as the legal father if he provides a specimen for insemination of an unmarried couple by an unlicensed practitioner.

Provision of Information

8.43 At the time when the 1990 Act was drafted and for many years thereafter, anonymity of the donor was ensured. This was only subject to the licensing authority being obliged to keep a register of identifiable individuals who had been treated, whose gametes had been stored or used, and who were, or may have been, born as a result of treatment services (s 31(2)). However, after a successful human rights challenge,[93] new regulations[94] came into force on 1 April 2005 which allow a person over the age of 18 access to the name, date and place of birth, appearance, and last known address of a donor parent. However, since a change in the regulations cannot be retrospective,[95] the new facility cannot be invoked until 2023 at the earliest.

8.44 We still have our doubts as to the advantages of abandoning the anonymity rule.[96] Certainly, the right to discover the identity of the donor has been recognised elsewhere in Europe,[97] this being based not only on the supposition that a knowledge of one's true parentage is a fundamental right but also that children have a strong psychological urge to acquire this knowledge.[98] Although the latter is now widely regarded as a proven fact, much of the evidence is, inevitably, anecdotal and no comparable study of children born by way of adultery has been, nor can be, made. Moreover, there is also some evidence that hurtful psychological consequences can result from the receipt of such information.[99] The frequently drawn analogy with adoption—in which there is a statutory right to discover a true genetic relationship[100]—is flawed. In the latter situation, some bonding with the true parents may have occurred; there is, at least in the 'stranger' process, no necessary genetic affiliation with either adopting parent; and, pragmatically, disclosure of status is almost certain once the child requires to see his or her birth certificate. The *need* for the DI child to have the same discovery rights as the adoptee is, therefore, by no means self-evident.

---

[93] For the balance between parental anonymity and the child's desire to know, see the ECtHR opinion, and particularly that of the minority, in *Odièvre v France* [2003] 1 FCR 621; (2004) 38 EHRR 871 and commentary by T Callus, 'Tempered hope? A qualified right to know one's genetic origin: *Odièvre v France*' (2004) 67 MLR 658. This was an adoption issue, peculiar to French law.

[94] Human Fertilisation and Embryology Authority (Disclosure of Donor Information) Regulations 2004 (SI 2004/1511).

[95] 1990 Act, s 31(5).

[96] See L Turney, 'The making and breaking of paternity secrets in donor insemination' (2010) 36 J Med Ethics 401.

[97] Anonymity in Europe ranges from absolute in France to a child's right to identify his or her father on reaching maturity in Sweden—a right which still depends, to an extent, on parental discretion. For an interesting review of Swedish donors' attitudes, see K R Daniels, H L Ericsson, and I P Burn, 'The views of semen donors regarding the Swedish Insemination Act 1984' (1998) 3 Med L Internat 117. Surprisingly, opposition to lifting the veil was found as much, if not more so, among the families and doctors as among the donors. In Germany, a need for knowledge of the truth of one's heredity is so much ingrained in the national psyche that laws provide for compulsory examinations in order to obtain the evidence from reluctant parties: §372a of the German Civil Procedure Code (ZPO).

[98] For a look at the overall situation, see R Probert, 'Families, assisted reproduction and the law' (2004) 16 CFLQ 273. The change in the law was heavily influenced by the concept of 'the child's right to personal identity': See I Turkmendag, 'The donor conceived child's "right to personal identity"' (2012) 39 J Law Soc 58.

[99] A J Turner and A Coyle, 'What does it mean to be a donor offspring? The identity experiences of adults conceived by donor insemination and the implications for counselling and therapy' (2000) 15 Human Reproduction 2041.

[100] Adoption and Children Act 2002, s 60; Adoption and Children (Scotland) Act 2007, s 55(4).

8.45 Very few of us ever question our paternity and still fewer will doubt their maternity—for the same regulations apply to ovum donation[101] as to sperm donation; it seems to us that the almost inevitable result of regulating for a few to question their parentage will be to encourage the majority to do so. It is doubtful if the statutory creation of children anxiously awaiting their sixteenth birthday in order to exorcise an implanted suspicion can be to the overall benefit of family relationships.[102] Even so, it must be acknowledged that modern opinion is strongly in favour of early disclosure of true parentage[103]—and this is particularly so in the event of the reason for DI lying in a genetic abnormality in a woman's husband or partner; however, we still believe that the situation is better met by good counselling within a responsible family environment rather than by statutory obligation—and this remains governmental policy.[104]

8.46 Finally, there is always the possibility that the supply of suitable semen specimens will be compromised even further than is currently the case—and the recognition of 'non-medical fertility services' indicates official recognition of the problem. As is to be expected, reports of the effect of the radical policy reversal are conflicting but may not be as negative as was feared.[105] Be that as it may, the Regulations are, here to stay and have been, in fact, strengthened by the inclusion in the revised 1990 Act of extensive provisions for exchange of far-reaching information between the Authority, the donor, and the recipient. Among the more interesting are the right of the resultant young adult (the 'relevant individual') to know how many and the nature of any half-siblings he or she may have (s 31ZA(2)(b)) and to know if he or she may be related to the person whom he or she not only intends to marry but also with whom he or she intends to form a civil partnership or establish an intimate relationship (s 31ZB(2)). The donor, on the other hand, is entitled to know, anonymously, that such inquiries are afoot (s 31ZC) and, should he wish to know, he must be informed as to the number, sex, and age—but not the identity—of any children born as a result of his consensual cooperation (s 31ZD(3)); significantly, a father is specifically further prevented from knowing the identity of his children insofar as the information available under this subsection may not be given if it appears to the provider of the information that doing so may lead to their recognition (s 31ZD(5)). There are also provisions for inter-sibling disclosure of a relationship (s 31ZE) and, throughout the section, disclosure can only be legal if an offer of counselling has been made.

---

[101] See para 8.56 et seq.

[102] Much the same concerns were expressed by J Harris, 'Assisted reproductive technological blunders' (2003) 29 J Med Ethics 205.

[103] For both sides of the question, see C Smart, 'Law and the regulation of family secrets' (2010) 24 Int J Law Pol Fam 397.

[104] HFEA policy on the subject is unequivocal: 'The centre should encourage and prepare patients to be open with their children from an early age about the circumstances of their conception'—HFEA, *Code of Practice* (8th edn, 2015), D20.8. Or, elsewhere: 'The centre should tell people who seek treatment with donated gametes or embryos that it is best for any resulting child to be told about their origin early in childhood' (at D20.7). It would seem that individual clinics could refuse to provide treatment if the patients were adamant in rejecting such advice—see *Code of Practice*, 'Welfare of the child' in general.

[105] Ranging from 'a national crisis' in the more sensational press: E Cook, 'Anonymity law change blamed for chronic sperm donor shortage' *Daily Mail*, 30 July 2006, to the HFEA's estimate that the number of donors rose by 6 per cent in the year following the enforcement of the new legislation: see M Day, 'Number of sperm donors in UK rises despite removal of anonymity' (2007) 334 BMJ 971. For an Australian plea to allow access by children born from donor sperm, see L Horler, 'Sperm donors may want anonymity, but there are real kids out there', *The Guardian*, 17 August 2015, available at: http://www.theguardian.com.

THE INFERTILE OR CHILDLESS WOMAN

8.47 Childlessness due to abnormalities in the man is, as we have seen, largely a matter of the defective formation of spermatozoa. A woman may also suffer from primary infertility but, in addition, she may be beset by anatomical problems which prevent her having children by natural means—of which, blockage of the fallopian tubes is the most common. The proportion of cases due to anatomical abnormality and to infertility resulting from faulty ovum production is approximately 3:2.[106] We do not, here, discuss the purely medical treatment of the latter; its incidental legal and ethical significance is noted briefly later.[107] However, when hormonal treatment has failed, the anovular woman is in the same position as the azoospermic man and may be able to parent a child by way of gamete replacement; ovum donation is a practical routine procedure despite the fact that ova are far more scarce and are more difficult to handle than are spermatozoa. Even so, it is, perhaps fortunately, still impossible to develop a full-term fetus in a laboratory environment. Ovum donation is, therefore, pointless without, at the same time, providing a womb. Both may be contributed by the same woman or they may be available independently. It is these features that underlie the majority of the legal and moral problems which complicate the treatment of the infertile woman. By contrast, childlessness due to various anatomic or physiological abnormalities may be treated according to its specific cause; the nature of the available procedures will become apparent as the chapter progresses.

IN VITRO FERTILISATION (IVF)

8.48 Many reproductive techniques involve the fertilisation of the ovum in laboratory—or in vitro—conditions and the subsequent transfer of the embryo from the Petri dish to the uterus. Strictly speaking, therefore, IVF and embryo transfer (ET) are technical terms applicable to a number of specific treatment regimes. Nevertheless, popular usage generally equates IVF with the particular treatment for childlessness due to blockage of the fallopian tubes and it is in that sense that we use the term in this section.

8.49 Standard IVF treatment involves collection of ova from the wife's abdomen, fertilisation of these with her husband's sperm in the laboratory, and transfer of the resulting embryo to her uterus; the treatment is, therefore, essentially one designed to bypass diseased fallopian tubes. The cycle does, however, involve complex hormonal priming to ensure superovulation. This is important to the process as an excess of subsequent embryos is needed so that a choice can be made so as to ensure that those inserted are normal. A significant collateral advantage is that unused ova can be made available for ovum donation—a process known as 'egg-sharing' to which we return at para 8.56.

8.50 The mean live birth rate depends to an extent on the size and expertise of the treatment centre and is strongly influenced by the age of the woman but, overall, is currently in the order of 24 per cent of treatment cycles using the woman's own fresh eggs; this falls to about 18 per cent when using frozen embryos.[108] Interestingly, however, a live birth rate of 33 per cent is achieved using fresh donor eggs.[109] Thus, while IVF may well be the optional

---

[106] HFEA, *Fertility Facts and Figures – 2008*, fig 4.   [107] See para 8.56.
[108] HFEA, *Fertility Treatments in 2010 – Trends and Figures* (2011).
[109] There is no significant difference in pregnancy or birth rates when either two or three embryos are implanted but the triplet rate is unacceptably high in the latter event. As a result, the HFEA limits the number of embryos inserted to two per cycle and the number of eggs to three save in the case of a woman over

treatment for one of the commonest female causes of childlessness, the expectation of success in current circumstances is never going to be better than about 2:1 against—an important point to be made when counselling childless couples. The pregnancy and live birth rates following IVF show no significant differences when related to the underlying reason for the treatment.[110]

8.51 The rationale of the process corresponds closely to that of AIH and, as such, presents no problems in the field of family law. The genetic and natural parentage of the resulting infant are not disputed. All that has occurred is that a technique has been substituted for a natural process; if any would protest that this is in some way immoral, they would, at the same time, have to contend that the surgical treatment of any disease is similarly immoral. It is, however, apparent that IVF, by definition, involves the creation of an embryo outside the human body. It is a fundamental premise of the 1990 Act that it is unlawful for an unlicensed person to do so; accordingly, IVF therapy can only be undertaken by a licensed practitioner. There is, of course, no technical reason why the sperm must be that of the husband or partner and, in the event of combined male infertility and an impassable female genital tract, donor semen could be used in the same way. In such circumstances, the legal problems and solutions would be comparable to those of DI, which have been discussed earlier.

8.52 All of which clearly depends on there being no error. Standards in UK fertility clinics are very high but, humanity being what it is, occasional mistakes will be made; again, it is in the nature of things that any such errors are likely to be discovered only in unusual circumstances. Such an instance arose in *Leeds Teaching Hospital NHS Trust v A*.[111] Here, a Caucasian couple—Mr and Mrs A—were undergoing IVF treatment together. When twins were born, it was apparent that they were of mixed race and it was established that the sperm used had been provided by a Mr B who was also being treated with his wife. The issue of fatherhood was settled mainly on the basis of the consent requirements in s 28 of the 1990 Act. Clearly, Mr A did not consent to Mr B's sperm being used; he was, therefore, not the legal father by virtue of s 28(2). Section 28(3) was found not to apply to married couples despite some cogent arguments to the contrary; even if it did, the 'fundamental error' vitiated the whole concept of 'treatment together' for the purposes of the 1990 Act.[112] Furthermore, s 28(6), which excludes parenthood in the case of a consenting donor, could not be applied because Mr B did not consent to the use of his sperm. In the end, then, Mr B remained the legal father of the twins by virtue of their genetic relationship. The court also considered the human rights dimension of the case with particular reference to the rights and interests of the children. They would remain within a loving and stable home and their rights could be met by appropriate family or adoption orders—and

40 years of age using her own eggs when three embryos or four eggs may be used. If the eggs or embryos are donated, the limits are two embryos and three eggs irrespective of the age of the donee (*Code of Practice* (8th edn, 2015), paras 7.4–7.6). For further discussion on 'limits' under the law, see J Millbank, 'Numerical limits in donor conception regimes, genetic links and "extended family" in the era of identity disclosure' (2014) 22(3) Med Law Rev 325.

[110] The main factor limiting the success of the treatment is failure of implantation. The report of the House of Commons Science and Technology Committee (n 5) commented, at para 297, on the relatively poor results of IVF in the UK across Europe as measured by the number of embryos required to produce a live birth but was unable to explain it.

[111] [2003] 1 FLR 1091; (2003) 71 BMLR 168.

[112] Per Butler-Sloss P at [37]. There is no reason to suppose that the substitution of the 'agreed fatherhood' conditions of the 2008 Act, s 37 would have altered the reasoning in the case.

these would be proportionate to the undoubted potential infringement of their rights to respect for their family life with Mr and Mrs A.

8.53 There is no doubt that *Leeds* v *A* is an atypical case. Despite the fact that such a situation could arise within the terms of s 28 of the 1990 Act, there was no doubt that Mr A was *not* the father of the twins but all the parties were agreed that they should remain with the family into which they were born.[113] In relation to the question of a child's right to know his or her genetic origins,[114] Butler-Sloss P emphasised that it was not a 'sperm donor' case and that to refuse to recognise Mr B as the twins' biological father would be to distort the truth which, some day, the twins would have to learn. Significantly, she said that, had she been compelled to do so, it would have been possible 'so to construe s 28(3) as to squeeze it into the present situation'.[115]

8.54 The case is another good example of the importance of the particularities of individual cases in the evolution of medical law and may be contrasted with a further 'laboratory error' case that arose more recently in Northern Ireland.[116] Here, donor sperm from a 'Cape-coloured' South African was wrongly used for treatment of a white couple. As a result, dark-skinned twins were born who, at the age of 11, sued the Trust for harm resulting from, inter alia, racist harassment at school. Almost inevitably, the case failed on the grounds that they had sustained no recognisable injury but its implications were, in our view, dealt with very superficially and it, thereby, loses potential significance.[117]

8.55 A final recent case concerned what can only be described as a non-*ménage à trois* in which disputed paternity arose when a woman received both artificial insemination and had sexual intercourse with a third party she had contacted over the Internet for his services as an unpaid sperm donor. In *M* v *F* (*Legal Paternity*),[118] the putative 'donor' challenged legal parentage of the subsequent child arising from the unusual set of circumstances. The woman and her then husband had initially met the donor to discuss arrangements for artificial insemination, but the husband left shortly afterwards. It was accepted on this first occasion that artificial insemination took place, but then on all subsequent meetings the woman and 'donor' had sexual relations. On the birth of the child, the legal dilemma was this: if the child were born from the sexual relations, then the 'donor' would be the legal father; it the child were born from artificial insemination then the provisions of the Human Fertilisation and Embryology Act would determine paternity. To complicate matters, the 'donor' argued that the husband had provided valid consent within the terms of the Act because he had never notified his lack of consent to the other parties. On the facts, it was held that the father was the 'donor' through sexual relations, but on the law the point was clarified that the Act has no such requirement that lack of consent be notified.

---

[113] It has been suggested that any adversarial litigation following a laboratory error would be based on a 'wrongful birth' action (Chapter 10): M Ford and D Morgan, '*Leeds Teaching Hospitals NHS Trust* v *A*—Addressing a misconception' (2003) 15 CFLQ 199.

[114] The device of giving legal parentage to the genetic father and legal responsibility to the social father is applauded in A Bainham, 'Whose sperm is it anyway?' [2003] CLJ 566.

[115] At [58].

[116] *A and B* (*by C, their mother and next friend*) v *A* (*Health and Social Services Trust*) [2011] NICA 28.

[117] For in depth criticism, see S Sheldon, 'Only skin deep? The harm of being born a different colour to one's parents' (2011) 19 Med L Rev 657. Note that although the action was clearly one for wrongful life, it was, for some reason, argued as one for wrongful conception; it was bound to fail in either circumstance (see Chapter 10).

[118] [2013] EWHC 1901.

OVUM AND EMBRYO DONATION

8.56 An alternative therapeutic scenario is that the ovum is donated by another woman. The need might arise as being the only way in which a woman with, say, abdominal adhesions could have children and it might be desirable in the event of a potential mother carrying an X-linked genetic disease (see Chapter 7); about 16 per cent of childlessness for female reasons is due to ovarian failure and the ovaries may be destroyed during, say, treatment for cancer. The procedure is, then, that the donated egg is fertilised by the husband's semen and the embryo then transferred to the wife's womb. The process can, therefore, be looked upon as the female variant of DI.[119] The obvious practical difference is that, whereas spermatozoa are plentiful and easily harvested, ova are scarce and their recovery involves some discomfort and inconvenience to the donor. Thus, the donor must be stimulated hormonally in order to coincide with the recipient's optimal menstrual state and, in many cases, a laparoscopy will be required. The difficulties, then, associated with ovum donation lie not only in the technique but, also, in finding the donors—the process is such that pure altruism generally provides no more than a fraction of the overall requirement. Ova may be obtained from women in the course of other surgery—in particular, during sterilisation. The process is not without risk for the donor;[120] nevertheless, centres in the UK may still pursue such arrangements provided that very strict criteria as to counselling, management, and consent are met.[121] The HFEA has also accepted the more common practice of 'egg-sharing'—in which women who are, themselves, undergoing infertility treatment involving ovarian stimulation donate a proportion of their surplus ova for others to use in treatment, almost always in return for an adjustment in the costs of treatment.[122] Very stringent requirements as to consent are imposed—including a double consent by the egg provider both as an IVF patient and a donor and consent by her male partner; there is no relaxation of the assessment of donors' suitability for parenthood because one or both are receiving payment in kind.[123] Currently, the demand for eggs greatly outstrips their availability and egg-sharing is a near essential component of satisfactory treatment services.

8.57 The difficulties associated with ovum donation or the delayed use of the patient's own ova are compounded by the fact that, in contrast to the storage of spermatozoa and early embryos, cryopreservation of ova is not proven to be entirely risk free in respect of induced chromosomal abnormality;[124] the HFEA has, however, sanctioned the use of stored ova in strictly controlled conditions.[125] An alternative, presently experimental, approach to

---

[119] The HFEA established a National Donation Strategy Group in 2011. It has a wide advisory function and also covers sperm donation. The Group has since launched the 'Lifecycle' initiative to improve sperm and egg donation in the UK: see, http://www.hfea.gov.uk/8350.html.

[120] See S Bewley, L Foo, and P Braude, 'Adverse outcomes from IVF' (2011) 342 BMJ d436.

[121] A woman may now be offered a flat rate of £750 for donating her eggs per cycle: HFEA, *Code of Practice* (2015, s 13). For a flowchart of the egg donation process as of October 2014, see: http://www.hfea.gov.uk/docs/HFEA_The_donation_process_for_egg_donors_LR.pdf. Contrast: sperm donors may be compensated up to £35 per visit to a clinic. For discussion of the regime, see: S Wilkinson, 'Is the HFEA's policy on compensating egg donors and egg sharers defensible?' (2013) 21(2) Med Law Rev 173.

[122] A range of benefits in kind is encouraged. The HFEA also accepts the practice in respect of donating ova for research. The evidence is that egg-sharing does not affect the success rate in donors.

[123] HFEA, *Code of Practice* (8th edn, 2015), Guidance, s 12.

[124] Though it generally found that the success rate using frozen embryos is about half that using fresh embryos.

[125] In particular, frozen eggs are not to be mixed with fresh eggs in any configuration.

the preservation of a woman's procreative capacity is to remove, store, and, later, graft a portion of ovarian tissue. Although it is fair to say that this form of treatment is still in the experimental stage, it is to be noted that germ-line cells come within the definition of gametes and are subject to the same regulation; in addition, centres storing ovarian (or testicular) tissue for transplant purposes are subject to the Human Tissue Authority's *Code of Practice*.[126]

8.58   Once fertilisation by the husband or partner and implantation of a donated ovum has been achieved, however, the natural—though not the genetic—parentage will be reasonably clear. It is difficult to foresee any circumstances in which motherhood would be challenged[127] and, in a patrilineal society, there are fewer objections to an admixture of ovum-derived genes in the family than to those which arise as a result of DI. In any event, the matter was put beyond legal doubt by s 33 of the 2008 Act which holds that a woman who carries a child as a result of the placing in her of an embryo or of sperm and eggs, and no other woman, is to be treated as the mother of the child.

8.59   But what of the similar wife with an infertile husband or partner (or, of course, the infertile, single woman) who wants a child? Such a combination could, theoretically, arise in about one in every 400 marriages or partnerships seeking children. Such a state can be managed by embryo donation whereby an embryo preformed from donated ovum and donated sperm is implanted in the infertile woman. The resultant complications then lie somewhere between those of in vitro fertilisation and those surrounding surrogate motherhood and are best discussed under that heading later. Once again, the 1990 Act, as amended, has cleared the legal air; by virtue of ss 35 and 36 of the amending 2008 Act, the child born of embryo donation is, for all purposes, the child of the carrying mother and her consenting husband or partner.

THE AVAILABILITY OF IVF

8.60   We have discussed some of the moral issues surrounding assisted reproduction under the heading of DI. Very much the same principles apply in the case of the infertile wife. There is, however, one major, and obvious, difference—while DI is a relatively simple process, IVF and its counterparts are both cost- and manpower-intensive. Problems of resource allocation are, thus, superimposed on those of ethical practice. In point of fact, the government aims to provide three free cycles of IVF to women under 40 on a national basis but it is still a matter of aspiration only at the time of writing.[128] The access considerations are different (and more onerous) for women between 40 and 42 when the chances of a live birth fall dramatically: contrast 10–15/100 live births at 42 with 45/100 live births at 22.[129] We are, however, here concerned with the broader question of whether, and in what circumstances, IVF should be available to fertile couples.[130] This involves a consideration of the motives behind the request—and these are many and varied.

---

[126] HFEA, *Code of Practice* (8th edn, 2015), s 25, para T20.
[127] See *Ampthill Peerage* [1977] AC 547, HL, per Lord Simon at 577.
[128] National Institute for Health and Care Excellence (NICE), *Fertility: Assessment and Treatment for People with Fertility Problems* (2013, confirmed for update in June 2015; next review 2017).
[129] N 128, Figure 2.
[130] See E I Kamphuis et al., 'Are we overusing IVF?' (2014) 348 BMJ g252, doi: http://dx.doi.org/10.1136/bmj.g252.

Pre-implantation Diagnosis

8.61 Simplistically, one could classify the possible reasons into medical and non-medical, although we will see that this is not the easy division that might be supposed.[131] In essence, the ethics of embryo selection mirror those of sperm selection which we have discussed earlier save for the fact that we are now dealing with an organism which, *of itself*, has the potential for human development; put at its lowest level, the human embryo is deserving of *some* respect and protection in law.[132] There may be good medical reasons, mainly in relation to the carriage of abnormal recessive genes, which the likely majority of persons would see as justifying appropriate intervention on behalf of otherwise fertile couples; indeed, IVF combined with pre-implantation genetic diagnosis (PGD), may offer the *correct* management.[133]

8.62 Even at this optimum level, however, PGD raises a number of moral difficulties, in particular, the obvious proposition that, in deliberately selecting embryos that are likely to result in disabled infants for destruction, we are open to the charge of denigrating the disabled population in general. The argument runs from, on the one hand, that the procedure should be outlawed on that ground alone to, on the other, that persons carrying defective genes have a duty to ensure that, so far as is possible, they are eliminated from the overall gene pool—a version of so-called intergenerational justice—all of which, in turn, drive us into the wider reaches of reproductive freedom and its legitimate extent.[134] There is now a mass of literature on the subject, the agreement with which is very much a matter of personal morality. Essentially, a balance has to be reached between, on the one hand, the importance of reproductive autonomy and the moral value of *any* human embryo[135] and, on the other hand, the justification for 'risk-taking' in the context of the 'do no harm' principle.[136] But there remain legitimate spaces for disagreement as to what constitutes 'doing harm' in this context.

8.63 Again, however, the 2008 Act clarifies ambiguity to an extent insofar as Sch 2, para 3 to the Act added new sections to Sch 2 of the 1990 Act. Thus, s 1ZA(1)(b) of the latter now allows for the testing of an embryo for a genetic abnormality where there is a particular risk that the embryo may have that abnormality. In addition, the sex of the embryo can be established under para (1)(c) if there is a corresponding risk of a gender-related abnormality. It is to be noted, however, that s 1ZA(2) mandates that an abnormality sought under para (1)(b) must carry with it a significant risk of serious disability in the person affected[137] while,

---

[131] For discussion, see J A Robertson, 'Extending preimplantation genetic diagnosis: Medical and non-medical uses' (2003) 29 J Med Ethics 213.

[132] Warnock Committee at para 11.17.

[133] Special requirements for the provision of information when using PGD are dictated in the *Code of Practice* (8th edn, 2015), Guidance note, and for tissue typing at s 10.

[134] A really helpful analysis is to be found in A Algharani and J Harris, 'Reproductive liberty: Should the foundation of families be regulated?' (2006) 18 CFLQ 191. For a comparative view, see R Mykitiuk, J Nisker, and E Wagner, 'Constructing "health", defining "choice": Legal and policy perspectives on the post-PGD embryo in four jurisdictions' (2008) 9 Med L Internat 45, and most recently J Snelling and C Gavaghan, 'PGD past and present: Is the HFE Act 1990 now "fit for purpose"?' in K Horsey (ed), *Revisiting the Regulation of Human Fertilisation and Embryology* (2015), ch 6.

[135] R Scott, 'Choosing between possible lives: Legal and ethical issues in preimplantation genetic diagnosis' (2006) 26 OJLS 153.

[136] Much depends, of course, on the definition of 'disability'. See J Harris, 'Is there a coherent social conception of disability?' (2000) 27 J Med Ethics 95; 'One principle and three fallacies of disability studies' (2001) 27 J Med Ethics 383; and an alternative: S M Rendal, 'Disability, gene therapy and eugenics—A challenge to John Harris' (2000) 26 J Med Ethics 89.

[137] For a particularly useful analysis of this criterion, see T Krahn, 'Preimplantation genetic diagnosis; Does age of onset matter (anymore)?' (2009) 12 Med Hlth Care Philosoph 187.

under para (1)(c), the abnormality must, at least, affect one sex significantly more than the other. The lawfulness of 'negative selection' of embryos is, thus, acknowledged but considerable difficulty still lies in the interpretation of 'serious' in this context.[138] This is, perhaps, particularly so in the case of chromosomal disease where the clinical and social effect is variable—as in Down's syndrome.[139] In the end, we must depend on the virtue ethics which govern good medical practice and on the guidance provided by the HFEA.[140]

8.64 Even greater moral uncertainty surrounds the extension of pre-implantation diagnosis into the realm of therapy—currently into therapy for an existing sibling who suffers from genetic disability; this involves the production of an embryo that is not only genetically but also tissue-type compatible with the disabled child so that, following its birth, its umbilical stem cells can be used to supply a normal gene for its affected elder sibling. The HFEA's policy of agreeing to license such activity was challenged by way of judicial review—the 'Hashmi case'—and the application was successful.[141]

8.65 The finding was, however, reversed on appeal.[142] The basis for the unanimous decision can be summed up in the words of Lord Phillips who said, in respect of PGD:

> if the impediment to bearing a child is concern that it may be born with a hereditary defect, treatment which enables women to become pregnant and to bear children in the confidence that they will not be suffering from such defects can properly be described as 'for the purpose of assisting women to carry children'.[143]

Which, of course, precipitated the inclusions in the 1990 Act outlined earlier. As to tissue typing, he added:

> No evidence suggests that the wish of a woman to bear a child in order to provide a source of stem cells for a sick or dying sibling was anticipated at [the time the Act was passed]. Such a wish is now the reality,[144]

and the only difference between activities that were already regularly licensed and tissue typing was the nature of the 'desired characteristics' of the embryo. Lord Phillips concluded that IVF treatment that includes PGD constituted 'treatment for the purpose of assisting women to bear children' irrespective of the purpose of the PGD. Once more, this is now incorporated in the 1990 Act.[145]

8.66 There is no doubt that the decision of the Court of Appeal was in line with current popular opinion. Even so, the creation of a number of embryos with the avowed intention of destroying the majority, which is inherent in the IVF process as a whole, is undoubtedly amplified by the use of this procedure and many would doubt its morality on these grounds alone. We feel, however, that it infringes more than 'respect' for the status of the embryo and can also be seen as potentially offending the fundamental Kantian

---

[138] For a very full discussion, see R Scott, C Williams, K Ehrich, and B Farsides, 'The appropriate extent of pre-implantation genetic diagnosis: Health professionals' and scientists' views on the requirement for a "significant risk of a serious genetic condition"' (2007) 15 Med L Rev 320.

[139] The example is analysed in depth by T Krahn, 'Regulating preimplantation genetic diagnosis: The case of Down's syndrome' (2011) 19 Med L Rev 157.

[140] *Code of Practice* (8th edn, 2015), Guidance, ss 10A, 10.5–10.16.

[141] *R (on the application of Quintavalle on behalf of Comment on Reproductive Ethics) v Human Fertilisation and Embryology Authority* [2003] 2 All ER 105; (2003) 70 BMLR 236, QBD.

[142] *R (on the application of Quintavalle) v Human Fertilisation and Embryology Authority* [2003] 3 All ER 257; (2003) 73 BMLR 116, CA.

[143] At para [43].   [144] At para [47].   [145] At Sch 2, s 1ZA(1)(d).

principle that a person should not be used merely as a means—the procedure involves the creation of a child—a person—primarily as a therapeutic tool for the benefit of its sibling.[146] The welfare of the created child must also, and always, be considered. In the absence of suitable cells being available from cord blood, the so-called 'saviour sibling' will be subjected to, at least, bone marrow donation—and this, perhaps, on more than one occasion.[147] The process is highly invasive and may be required long before the new child is able to consent or refuse to cooperate. Psychological pressures in the form of sibling rivalry and disproportionate parental attention may be intense.[148] Further, we are, perhaps, even more concerned with the practical possibility that the therapy provided does not work; attitudes to the new arrival, which will undoubtedly have been loving and caring at its inception, may change to those of acute disappointment[149]—in which case, the provision of IVF cannot be said to have been in the neonate's best interests.[150] There can be few applications of reproductive techniques that merit more intensive counselling or, perhaps, more close consideration of the protection of the 'saviour'. Nevertheless, it is to be noted that the *Hashmi* ruling survived examination in the House of Lords[151] and the great majority of the misgivings discussed earlier are covered in the HFEA's *Code of Practice*.[152]

8.67 A rather more unusual form of procreative planning takes the form of requests for 'positive selection' of embryos with *known* genetic defects, the most widely publicised being that of a lesbian couple suffering from congenital deafness seeking to acquire through IVF a child with a similar disability.[153] It is possible to construct a justification for this on the grounds of procreative autonomy, although on the other side are considerations of intergenerational justice. We will forego argument and take refuge in the revised 1990 Act which states, in paraphrase, that embryos that are known to have a genetic or a chromosomal abnormality that involves a significant risk that a person with that abnormality will

[146] Contrast R Boyle and J Savulescu, 'Ethics of using pre-implantation genetic diagnosis to select a stem cell donor for an existing person' (2001) 323 BMJ 1240, and B Mulvenna, 'Pre-implantation genetic diagnosis, tissue typing and beyond: The legal implications of the *Hashmi* case' (2004) 6 Med Law Internat 163 at 176. See, in general, S Sheldon and S Wilkinson, 'Should selecting saviour siblings be banned?' (2004) 30 J Med Ethics 533—the conclusion being that it should not. Most recently, C Gavaghan, 'Saviour siblings - no avoiding the hard questions' (2015) J Med Ethics, first online: J Med Ethics doi:10.1136/medethics-2014-102605.

[147] For a very helpful transatlantic review, see S M Wolf, J P Kahn, and J E Wagner, 'Using preimplantation genetic diagnosis to create a stem cell donor: issues, guidelines and limits' (2003) 31 J Law Med Ethics 327. For a Commonwealth appraisal, S-N Then, 'The legality of tissue transplants for the benefit of family members in the UK and Australia: Implications for saviour siblings' (2009) 10 Med L Internat 23.

[148] S Holm, 'The child as organ and tissue donor: Discussions in the Danish Council of Ethics' (2004) 13 Camb Q Healthcare Ethics 156. This is part of a wider symposium published in the same issue (2).

[149] The possibility of the parents being able to bring an action in contract or negligence is analysed, and largely dismissed, in V Chico, 'Saviour siblings: Trauma and tort law' (2006) 14 Med L Rev 180.

[150] Shortly after the decision, the HFEA refused a licence for similar treatment to be applied in the case of Charlie Whittaker who was suffering from Diamond-Blackfan anaemia. The reason given was that, while it was possible to ensure that an embryo was not affected by β-thalassaemia, as in the *Hashmi* case, it was not possible to test for Diamond-Blackfan disease. It might well, therefore, not be in the interests of the 'saviour sibling' to be born. Although the reasoning seems hard, it does pay lip service to the fragile Kantian principles. The distinction is forcefully criticised in S Sheldon and S Wilkinson, '*Hashmi* and *Whitaker*: An unjustifiable and misguided distinction?' (2004) 12 Med L Rev 137—and the HFEA changed its mind in 2004.

[151] *R (on the application of Quintavalle)* v *Human Fertilisation and Embryology Authority* [2005] 2 AC 561; [2005] 2 All ER 555—largely on an extended definition of the breadth of the Authority's discretion.

[152] 8th edn, 2015, Guidance, s 10. The whole topic is well summarised in A Alghrani, '"Suitable" to be a "saviour"' (2006) 18 CFLQ 407.

[153] See J Savulescu, 'Deaf lesbians, "designer disability", and the future of medicine' (2002) 325 BMJ 771.

develop a serious physical or mental disability must not be preferred to those that are not known to have such an abnormality and the same goes for gender-related disabilities.[154]

8.68 Non-medical reasons for using IVF are of several types, the extreme being, perhaps, that of sex selection as a matter of parental choice for social reasons.[155] The issue arose as something of a *cause célèbre* in 2000 when a couple wished to ensure the birth of a girl, having lost their only daughter in tragic circumstances.[156] The HFEA was, at the time, ambivalent on the subject and, in this particular instance, no clinic could be found which was willing to undertake the case. The Authority is now, however, firmly opposed—'The law requires that the centre should not, for social reasons: a) select embryos of a particular sex, b) separate sperm samples, or use sperm samples that have been separated, for the purpose of sex selection, or c) participate in any other practices designed to ensure that a resulting child will be of a particular sex.'[157] Yet, it will be seen that the case demonstrates the difficulties of categorisation. If the parents can show that they are suffering from, say, a demonstrable reactive depression as a result of their loss, selective replacement of their child *becomes* a medical treatment and the moral high ground has shifted—though perhaps not far enough to justify disregard for the interests of the resulting child. Even so, there is a tenable case for holding that we should not pass judgement in respect of a personal dilemma which affects no other person.[158]

8.69 Other 'non-medical' reasons for 'fertile IVF treatment' include the early removal of ova and their impregnation for use in later life, thus circumventing the increased risk of chromosomal abnormalities in the child of a late pregnancy, or, second, the wholly hedonistic use of 'womb-leasing' for social reasons. The latter is discussed later.[159] The former is perfectly acceptable practice in the UK. There are, however, practical difficulties. The problems initially introduced by limitations on the storage times for embryos have been alleviated to an extent since the maximum time has been extended to 55 years provided the storage is for treatment purposes, and certain conditions are met; being genuine cases of premature infertility, with the person's written consent, and with a (ten years renewable) medical confirmation from a medical practitioner.[160] Second, the risks of pregnancy itself rise dramatically with age—the maternal mortality rate over the age of 40 is some ten times that in the case of women aged 20–4. Third, the pregnancy rate following embryo transfer deteriorates with age[161] and, finally, the indications are that older women require the implantation of more embryos than do the young in order to achieve the same success rate.[162]

---

[154] Section 13(9) and (10) inserted by s 14(4) of the 2008 Act. Again, of course, this begs the questions of what constitutes 'significant' or 'serious'. It has been suggested that the law is disproportionate and little more than symbolic: J L Scully, '"Choosing disability", symbolic law and the media' (2011) 11 Med L Internat 197.

[155] Purely preferential reasons are criticised, inter alia, on sexist grounds. J A Robertson, 'Extending preimplantation diagnosis: Medical and non-medical uses' (2003) 29 J Med Ethics 213 has pointed out that this applies only to the selection of the sex of a first child.

[156] See e.g. K Scott, 'IVF selection still off limits' *Guardian*, 19 October 2000.

[157] HFEA, *Code of Practice* (8th edn, 2015), s 10D.

[158] It is, of course, equally possible to argue that the deontological problem involved is a matter for public decision.

[159] See para 8.118.

[160] Human Fertilisation and Embryology (Statutory Storage Period for Embryos and Gametes) Regulations (SI 2009/1582).

[161] Though this is irrelevant in the present context as it applies only when using their own fresh eggs.

[162] M G R Hull, C F Fleming, A O Hughes, and A McDermott, 'The age-related decline in female fecundity' (1996) 65 Fertil Steril 783, but contrast far more recently N Gleicher et al. 'The "graying" of infertility services: an impending revolution nobody is ready for' (2014) 12 Reprod Biol Endocrinol 63, doi: 10.1186/1477-7827-12-63.

8.70 There is little doubt that there is a measure of emotional discrimination against the older person seeking treatment that is based on no more than societal conditioning.[163] Have we any moral right to discriminate against an older woman in denying her access to motherhood when we would provide the facilities without qualm to her younger sister in otherwise identical circumstances in which the woman herself is providing the scarce resource—the eggs? The counter-argument depends, to an extent, on the effect on the consequent child and it is not difficult to dream up circumstances in which an 'aged' mother could be seen as a disadvantage to a young child. Nevertheless, given that we would not consider depriving 40-year-old women of natural pregnancy, it seems paternalistic in the extreme to deny them assisted reproductive services on the grounds of age alone. On the other hand, IVF is expensive in terms of NHS resources and becomes increasingly hard to justify in the face of success rates that deteriorate with the age of the patient. It is for this reason that the courts, which are traditionally reluctant to interfere with clinical judgement, have supported at least one health authority's decision not to fund infertility services for women above the age of 35[164]—and, certainly, it is hard to criticise the policy if this is based on sound medical evidence.[165] We might add, in parentheses, that the same will apply to the post-menopausal woman. Quite apart from the fact that, here, we are dealing with ovum donation—and, hence, with a publicly scarce resource—'treatment' in this case is not that of an unfortunate abnormality but is, rather, an interference with the natural order. Paternalism is, thus, excluded from the equation and we are free to concentrate entirely on the resultant child.[166]

Screening in Assisted Reproduction

8.71 As in the case of DI, the well-being of the resultant child is to be taken into consideration before IVF treatment is provided. Here, in contrast to the DI situation, medical involvement in the procedure is essential; it follows that the doctor cannot opt out of judgements, despite the fact that they may involve purely social values. No legally enforceable principles as to selection of candidates for the limited resource have been laid down, but the *Code of Practice* contains a number of conditions, some of which are markedly intrusive, not only as to the welfare of the child but also in relation to each patient and her partner. The centre may make widespread inquiries and, while the patients should be given the opportunity to respond to adverse information, ultimately, treatment may be refused.[167] One might have thought that this could lead to considerable wrangling and 'centre tourism'— 'taking account of' potential risks does not imply reaching a uniform or transparent conclusion. It is, therefore, somewhat surprising that only one apposite case has so far been reported—refusal of treatment being on the grounds that the patient had a history of prostitution and had been rejected as an adopter; the court agreed that the centre was

---

[163] N Gleicher et al., 'Too old for IVF? Are we discriminating against older women?' (2007) 24(12) J of Assisted Repro and Genetics 639.

[164] *R v Sheffield Health Authority, ex p Seale* (1994) 25 BMLR 1. It is to be noted that the HFEA imposes age limits for gamete donors. In respect of treatment, gametes should not be taken from women over 36 and men over 41 (HFEA, *Code of Practice* (8th edn, 2010), Guidance, s 11.2). Gametes must not be taken for treatment (other than the patient's own treatment or treatment of his/her partner), storage, or research from persons below the age of 18 (Guidance, s 11.6).

[165] NICE has recommended that women up to the age of 42 who have been unable to conceive naturally should be offered at least one cycle of IVF within the NHS, n 128, above.

[166] (1994) 308 BMJ 723.

[167] The full list of conditions is to be found in the *Code of Practice* (8th edn, 2015) Guidance, ss 8.2–8.12.

subject to judicial review but the case itself was not considered so questionable as to pro-vide grounds for such judicial intervention.[168]

The Legal Position of the Clinician

8.72 All procedures involving gamete donation carry the risk that the gametes themselves are defective. As we have seen, this is a major justification for controlling the treatment of childlessness. Moreover, all those involving in vitro embryo transfer introduce the additional hazard that the embryo will be damaged either by the hormonal treatment required for superovulation—and this is a real possibility—or during manipulation and that an abnormal fetus will result. Reports of such occurrences in humans are rare and are, inevitably, conflicting;[169] the general impression, however, is that uncomplicated IVF, at least, poses no serious risk.

8.73 A less unlikely cause of litigation would be the negligent selection of already defective gametes or embryos and, here, the ground rules are clear. Section 44 of the 1990 Act inserts s 1A into the Congenital Disabilities (Civil Liability) Act 1976 to the effect that if a child resulting from embryo transfer, the placing in a woman of sperm and eggs or DI[170] is born disabled and the disability results from an act or omission in the course of the selection, or the keeping or use outside the body, of the embryo or the gametes used by a person answerable to the child, then the child's disabilities are to be regarded as damage resulting from the wrongful act of that person and actionable at the suit of the child. This does not apply if one or both parents knew of the risk of their child being born disabled; particular importance is, therefore, likely to attach to the effectiveness of their consent in respect of the information given. Interestingly, this seems to open the door to an action for 'wrongful life'.[171]

UTERINE LAVAGE

8.74 Uterine lavage represents a somewhat unusual extension of the technique of IVF through embryo transfer. In this process, a fertile woman is impregnated with semen; the resultant embryo is washed out of the uterus before implantation and is transferred to the infertile patient. The Warnock Committee looked at the matter from the point of view of the donor and concluded (para 7.5) that the risks were such that the technique of embryo donation by lavage should not be used at that time—and it is still regarded with considerable scepti-cism. The method seems to us to be so comparable to the practice of animal husbandry that there are good policy reasons for its proscription. Nevertheless, the current British

---

[168] *R v Ethical Committee of St Mary's Hospital (Manchester), ex p H (or Harriott)* [1988] 1 FLR 512; [1988] Fam Law 165. The possibility was not foreclosed—the greater part of the argument turned on whether the Committee was purely advisory or whether it had administrative responsibility. The case was also somewhat clouded by allegations of deceit.

[169] A large study from Australia indicated, after careful evaluation of extraneous factors, that there is no significant difference between those conceived by IVF and those conceived naturally. The odds ratio of defect was, however, 1.57 when intratcytoplasmic sperm injection was compared with natural conception; yet this could be no more than a reflection of male infertility per se as ICSI is often the treatment of choice in this form of infertility: M J Davies, V M Moore, K J Wilson, et al., 'Reproductive technologies and the risk of birth defects' (2012) 366 New Engl J Med 1803.

[170] I Kennedy and A Grubb, *Medical Law* (3rd edn, 2000), p 1530 point out that GIFT may not be included by reason of the precise wording of the section. We believe that, should it be questioned, it would be decided on the basis of 'parliamentary intention' as per *R (on the application of Quintavalle) v Secretary of State for Health* [2003] 2 AC 687; [2003] 2 All ER113, HL.

[171] See para 10.53 et seq.

legislation clearly allows for the use of embryos formed in vivo (1990 Act, Sch 3, para 7). They may not, however, be used to bring about the creation of any embryo in vitro or any human admixed embryo in vitro (para 7.4).

THE SURPLUS EMBRYO

8.75 It is inevitable that surplus embryos will be produced whether IVF or ovum donation is being attempted. The status and disposal of such embryos have significance which is independent of the problems of successful implantation.

8.76 Insofar as the embryo has no legal status, the problem can be characterised as purely ethical and one which turns on the *nature* of the embryo. As already noted, the Warnock Committee recommended only that the embryo of the human species should be afforded *some* protection in law. Such prevarication indicates the measure of the moral difficulties involved but is, at the same time, unhelpful. The extreme positions can be summarised as holding either that the embryo is a full human being—in accordance with rigid theologi-cal, perhaps mainly Roman Catholic, doctrine—or, as the pure scientist might claim, it is simply a product of the laboratory, comparable to a culture of human tissue. The indi-vidual must, then, decide on his or her moral stance—does one stand at either extreme or can one establish a tenable intermediate position?

8.77 We have argued previously that there are many acceptable reasons for suggesting that morally relevant 'humanity' is not established until implantation—this being largely on the grounds that it is only at implantation that the embryo achieves a capacity for meaningful development.[172] The acceptance of a 'specific moment' theory as to the acquisition of humanity is, however, by no means universal; an alternative approach suggested by Poplawski and Gillett[173] is to regard the process of becoming a human per-son as 'a progression through a series of linked developmental stages' and to attribute rights to the embryo because it represents a phase in the whole human form. We prefer our view, however, that, in the absence of implantation, there is no continuum and there is no human interaction; moreover, no moral value can be attributed to the embryo by virtue of its potential for personhood—for no such potential exists in the medium of the Petri dish.[174]

8.78 Acceptance of this premise also solves one's moral problems as to embryonic research which, when done well, must be valuable to the community as a whole. Nevertheless, this conclusion cannot be accepted without qualification—at the very least, the embryo must be accorded the respect due to any living human tissue. It could be replied that, in logic, there is no need to control laboratory interference with a research object that one believes has no human status; but there *is* public disquiet over scientific involve-ment in the reproductive process and, on this ground alone, it must be contained within a controlling framework. Most importantly, the moral argument rests upon the limitations of current technology. It is clear that our formula would be inadequate should technology advance to the state of being able to 'grow' fetuses to full term

---

[172] J K Mason, *Medico-legal Aspects of Reproduction and Parenthood* (2nd edn, 1998) p 234. For the argu-ment based on 'ensoulment', see N M Ford, *When Did I Begin?* (1988) pp 56, 171. Perhaps 'humanity' and 'ensoulment' are different expressions of the same thing.

[173] N Poplawski and G Gillett, 'Ethics and embryos' (1991) 17 J Med Ethics 62.

[174] For criticism of this approach, see M Brazier, 'Human(s) (as) medicine(s)' in S A M McLean (ed), *First Do No Harm* (2006).

in vitro; were this to happen, we would be confronted with the production of non-humanised human beings, which would be intolerable.

8.79   For the present, the interests of the embryo/fetus are protected from encroachment by ss 3(3)(a) and 41(1)(b) of the 1990 Act which, in essence, make it a criminal offence, punishable by up to ten years' imprisonment, to keep or use an embryo in vitro, however created, that is more than 14 days old—excluding any time spent in suspended animation while frozen. Even so, this specific time limit can be attacked, mainly on the grounds that a 13-day embryo is no less alive than is one of 15 days' gestation and that it is entitled to the same respect—as is the embryo formed at fertilisation.[175] The counter-argument is that *some* controlled embryonic research is essential if the attack on genetic disease—which may well be the most important single factor dictating morbidity in humans—is to be carried on in a scientifically acceptable way.

8.80   Given that the undeveloped in vitro embryo merits a certain, albeit unspecified, respect, its management presents a dilemma of which there are three major elements. The first is that of the use of and, indeed, the production of embryos for research purposes; this highly emotive issue is discussed in Chapter 20. The second is closely related and concerns the pre-implantation selection of embryos which we have discussed at para 8.61 et seq. Although this raises formidable ethical issues, we have seen that they can be solved—at least at the legal level.

8.81   The third main problem derived from embryonal status relates to the practical problems surrounding the disposal of those that are surplus to immediate therapeutic needs. It is clear that over-production of embryos is inherent in the treatment of infertility by IVF; it is impossible to guarantee receptive wombs for those embryos which remain unused in the individual case and, in many instances involving defective embryos, it would, in our view, be wrong to attempt to implant them all. It follows that any legislation that attempted to criminalise the necessary destruction of embryos would, at the same time, effectively shut the door on this form of treatment and it is, indeed, arguable that, so long as we accept it as morally acceptable, it is logical to accept the production and destruction of embryos for *any* reputable purpose—for example, embryo research.[176] Under the terms of the 1990 Act, the disposal of gametes and embryos depends almost entirely on the consent and, hence, the decision of those donating the gametes. It follows that whether or not an embryo can be used for treatment or research or whether it is to be destroyed at a certain time or in certain circumstances—for example, on the death of the donor—depends upon the agreed consent of the two progenitors and any other 'relevant persons' (1990 Act, Sch 3, para 6).[177] Even after amendment, however, the Act provides no permanent alternative resolution for the condition most likely to cause difficulty—that is, when there is disagreement between the two parties concerned. The need for some such form of legislation in the almost inevitable conflict of judicial interpretation was

---

[175] For a modern recapitulation of the age-old problem, albeit from a transatlantic viewpoint, see N M de S Cameron, 'Pandora's progeny: Ethical issues in assisted human reproduction' (2005–6) 39 Fam LQ 745.

[176] For ourselves, we cannot agree with this without qualification. For discussion, see S Chan and J Harris, 'Consequentialism without consequences: Ethics and embryo research' (2010) 19 Camb Q Hlthcare Ethics 61.

[177] Relevant persons include not only those whose gametes were used to create an embryo (embryo A) but also any persons whose gametes were used in the creation of an embryo that was later used to create embryo A (1990 Act, Sch 3, para 6(3E) inserted by 2008 Act, Sch 3, para 9(5)). The paragraph also makes provision for consent by minors.

foreshadowed in the USA as early as 1989.[178] It was not until 2003, however, that an apposite, and extremely high-profile, case arose in the UK.

8.82 The case of *Evans and Hadley*[179] was complex and was of such intellectual significance that it eventually reached the Grand Chamber of the ECtHR[180]—but, in the end, the issue became, essentially, a matter of statute law, the ethical component being aired, in the main, in the accompanying public debate. In essence, the case concerned two couples who had stored embryos which they had not used successfully before they parted. The women were anxious to become pregnant but both male gamete donors withdrew their consents to storage and subsequent use of the embryos, which meant that they should be allowed to die. In summary, Ms Evans and Mrs Hadley fought their case along two main lines. First, they sought injunctions requiring restoration of their partners' consent and declarations that they could be lawfully treated during an extended period of storage and, second, they applied for a declaration that the restrictions imposed by the 1990 Act were incompatible with the Human Rights Act 1998 by way, particularly, of Arts 8, 12, and 14 of the European Convention. Additionally, Arts 2 and 8 were pleaded in respect of the embryos themselves.

8.83 It seemed that the primary actions were bound to fail in the light of the very clear provisions as to consent embodied in Sch 3 of the 1990 Act and, indeed, this proved to be the case. The court of first instance, backed by the Court of Appeal,[181] disposed of the first and second pleas on the ground of the clear statutory requirements as to consent. Consent had been given to the use of the embryos for treatment of the donors 'together'; treatment together was provided when the embryos were transferred into the woman[182] and, by this time, the couples were no longer together. Thus, there was no effective consent either to storage or use of the embryos by either of the women on their own and, accordingly, the clinic could not store or use the embryos lawfully.[183] Wall J found the human rights aspects of the case to be far more demanding—particularly those governed by Art 8 of the Convention. In the end, he decided that the provisions of Sch 3 to the 1990 Act do interfere with the right to respect for a person's private life but that the infringement applies equally to each gamete donor. Moreover, the court considered that

---

[178] Three very illustrative cases are *Davis v Davis* 842 SW 2d 588 (Tenn Sup Ct, 1992), *Kass v Kass* 696 NE 2d 174 (NY, 1998) and *Marriage of Witten III* 672 NW 2d 768 (Iowa Sup Ct, 2003). They are now only of historic interest and, in the interests of space, we will forego discussion. Virtually every potential scenario was, however, explored.

[179] *Evans v Amicus Healthcare Ltd, Hadley v Midland Fertility Services Ltd* [2003] 4 All ER 903; (2003) 75 BMLR 115, FD. A perceptive article from Australia bridged the gap between the US cases and *Evans*: G Fuscalado, 'Genetic donation: when does consent become irrevocable?' (2000) 15 Human Reproduction 515.

[180] An extensive literature developed around the case: J K Mason, 'Discord and disposal of embryos' (2004) 8 Edin LR 84; A Alghrani, 'Deciding the fate of human embryos' (2005) 13 Med L Rev 244; A Scully-Hill, 'Consent, frozen embryos, procreative choice and the ideal family' (2004) 63 CLJ 47; S Sheldon, '*Evans v Amicus Healthcare, Hadley v Midland Health Services*—Revealing cracks in the "twin pillars"' (2004) 16 CFLQ 437; S Sheldon, 'Gender equality and reproductive decision making' (2004) 12 Fem Leg Stud 303; C Lind, '*Evans v United Kingdom*—Judgments of Solomon: Power, gender and procreation' (2006) 18 CFLQ 576; J Bomhoff and L Zucca, 'The tragedy of Ms Evans: Conflicts and incommensurability of rights, *Evans v the United Kingdom*, Fourth Section judgment of 7 March 2006, Application No 6339/05' (2006) 2 Euro Constit LR 424; T Annett, 'Balancing competing interests over frozen embryos: The judgment of Solomon?' (2006) 14 Med L Rev 425.

[181] [2005] Fam 1; [2004] 2 FLR 766, CA.

[182] See also *Re R (IVF: paternity of child)*, n 88 which disposes of the argument that insertion of the embryo is merely consequential to the mixing of the sperm and eggs.

[183] 1990 Act, Sch 3, para 6(3).

the provisions of the 1990 Act, based as they were on consent of the parties and the inter-ests of the unborn child, were proportionate to the restrictions they imposed. A pos-sible infringement of the rights of the embryo to life was dismissed fairly peremptorily, largely on the ground that it is illogical to attribute a right to life to the embryo when no such right attaches to the fetus.[184] An appeal by Ms Evans was, predictably, dismissed.[185] Thorpe LJ summed up:

> To dilute [the requirement for bilateral consent to implantation] in the interests of propor-tionality, in order to meet Ms Evans's otherwise intractable biological handicap, by mak-ing the withdrawal of the man's consent relevant but inconclusive, would create new and even more intractable difficulties of arbitrariness and inconsistency ... The sympathy and concern which anyone felt for Ms Evans was not enough to render the legislative scheme of Schedule 3 disproportionate.

8.84 The issue was, apparently, so clear-cut that permission to appeal to the House of Lords was refused and Ms Evans struck out alone for the ECtHR,[186] challenging the UK legisla-tion by way of Arts 8, 12, and 14 of the ECHR. Again—and, again, almost inevitably—she failed, mainly on the grounds that the UK's 'bright line' policy lay within a national jurisdiction's margin of appreciation when determining the balance between the con-flicting rights of Ms Evans—not to be prevented from having a family—and those of her partner—not to be forced into unwanted parentage.[187] Moreover, as was confirmed by a 13:4 majority, by the Grand Chamber,[188] certainty in the law was one aspect of fairness which was, of itself, a factor to be considered in the balancing exercise.[189] As a conse-quence of all this, there could be no violation of Art 14.

8.85 *Evans and Hadley* was a generally unpopular decision but there is little doubt that it was the correct legal result given the terms of the statute. Moreover, there is evidence that a similar jurisprudence is developing in Ireland without recourse to statute. The cir-cumstances in *MR v TR*[190] were almost identical to those in *Evans* save that a successful pregnancy had already resulted from the use of three embryos prior to cryopreservation of the remaining three; the marriage broke down subsequent to this, McGovern J held at first instance that, while the status of the embryo in vitro was undefined, it was not an unborn child and, accordingly was not protected under the Constitution of Ireland, Art 40.3.3. Later, and more significantly in the present context, the Supreme Court of Ireland unanimously rejected the woman's appeal both on constitutional and contrac-tual grounds[191]—the latter depending largely on the finding that the husband's consent related only to the first implantation. As to the former, the Court held that the status of the unborn depended on a physical relationship between the embryo and its mother; the

[184] It is arguable that this is paralogic insofar as the absence of fetal rights derives from a possible conflict of interests between the fetus and its mother; no such conflict exists between the embryo in vitro and its pro-genitors. It is, however, clear that a limitation on embryonic rights operates throughout the IVF programme.
[185] *Evans v Amicus Healthcare Ltd* [2004] 3 All ER 1025; [2004] 3 WLR 681.
[186] Application 6339/05, Fourth Section judgment of 7 March 2006: *Evans v United Kingdom* (2006) 43 EHRR 21; [2005] Fam 1.
[187] N 186 at para 65.
[188] *Evans v United Kingdom* (2008) 46 EHRR 34; [2007] 1 FLR 1990; (2007) 95 BMLR 107.
[189] N 188 at para 89. A powerful dissenting opinion was based largely on the fact that the interests of and effects on Ms Evans and on her partner were so disproportionate that the decision could not be compatible with Art 8 or with the Convention's general purposes of protecting human dignity and autonomy.
[190] [2006] IEHC 359. See H Coveney, 'Assisted reproductive technologies and the status of the embryo' (2007) 13 Med-Leg J Ire 14.
[191] *Roche v Roche & ors* [2009] IESC 82; (2009) 114 BMLR 1.

embryo has no constitutional protection until implantation—a surplus embryo in vitro can, therefore, be legitimately destroyed.[192] Interestingly, none of the judgments referred to *Evans*.

8.86 Our main concern with Ms Evans' case lies in the fact that, in this particular area, UK law is founded on the principle of equality between the gamete donors. Yet, it is undeniable that mammalian reproduction is not gender neutral—within the spectrum of assisted reproduction, it is far more difficult for the woman to produce eggs than for the man to produce sperm, the woman must carry the embryo from implantation to birth and it is she who will nurse the neonate. It is because of this disparity of biological contribution that we have suggested in previous editions of this book that, in the event of discord, British legislation should allow for 'a right of management' (akin to a quasi-property claim) to be vested in the person for whom the embryos were intended—that is, the proposed woman recipient.[193] This solution, admittedly, ignores the man's interest in his genetic survival and it opens the door to imposing unwanted financial obligations on him in the future.[194] The former seems a relatively small price to pay for the advantage to women, many of whom, like Ms Evans, will have no more gametes to provide.[195] The latter can be dealt with by legislation—there is little reason why a man who wishes to opt out of an arrangement should not be granted the same legal immunity as that accorded the sperm donor.[196] It is, indeed, to be noted that the powerful dissenting opinion in *Evans* in the Grand Chamber was based largely on the fact that the interests of and effects on Ms Evans and on her partner were so disproportionate that the decision could not be compatible with Art 8 or with the Convention's general purposes of protecting human dignity and autonomy.

8.87 The government's response to *Evans and Hadley* has, as we have noted at para 8.30, been to propose that it will be legal to store embryos for a further period of 12 months after a gamete provider has notified his or her withdrawal of consent to their being used for treatment services.[197] This is clearly a well-intentioned effort to introduce a 'cooling-off period' during which happy relationships might be restored. We have to admit to a suspicion that it is more likely to impose a further year of acrimonious argument.

8.88 In passing, it is to be noted that the power of each gamete donor to decide the fate of the embryo is limited by statute even when they are in accord—stored gametes must be destroyed at the end of ten years as must embryos; regulations may, however, specify circumstances in which the period may be altered in either direction.[198] Thus, safety considerations aside, a limit is set to the difficulties in estate planning and the like that are inherent within a permitted policy of indefinite preservation of embryos.[199]

---

[192] See Denham J at [70]. Interestingly for future cases, two judges (Murray CJ and Denham J) thought that there could be times—e.g., when the woman had no alternative means of having a child (cf. Ms Evans)—when a woman could be entitled to implantation of her embryos absent her partner's consent.

[193] We discuss this further in Chapter 14. A similar—and seemingly unique—attitude has been adopted in the Israeli Supreme Court: *Nachmani v Nachmani* (1996) 5(4) PD 661.

[194] E.g. by way of the Child Support Act 1991.

[195] A Mrs Grant of Inverness was in the same position and her embryos were destroyed on the instructions of her former husband. F Gibb, 'Woman who lost IVF embryos wins change in the law' *The Times*, 20 May 2003, p 2. Other interested parties will, in future, have to be informed whenever possible before unilateral action can be taken: 1990 Act, Sch 3, para 4A(2) inserted by 2008 Act, Sch 3, para 7.

[196] 1990 Act, s 28(6).   [197] 1990 Act, Sch 3, para 4A(4).   [198] 1990 Act, s 14(3), (4), and (5).

[199] The relatively academic problems of succession of 'twin embryos' that are implanted at different times are settled by the elimination of 'storage time' from the age of an embryo (1990 Act, s 3(4)).

THE SURPLUS FETUS

8.89 The management of both infertility and childlessness due to abnormalities in the female provokes the particular problem of multiple pregnancies. Hormone treatment of primary infertility can be over-successful and result in pregnancies involving anything up to sextuplets—and, occasionally, beyond. As to childlessness, the chances of IVF ending in a live birth are improved by the insertion of two to three embryos and the chances of more than one of these then implanting can be as high as 32 per cent of those transfers that result in pregnancy.[200] Few people can afford to bring up several children of the same age at the same time. Moreover, the common scenario of high-order pregnancies which lead to live birth is that the infants are of very low birthweight; they occupy the facilities of a neonatal intensive care unit to a disproportionate extent; the parents face the spectre of their children dying one by one over a period of weeks and those that survive may well be brain-damaged as a result of prematurity.[201] It is for these reasons that the problem of multiple pregnancy and birth has been described as 'the biggest risk of fertility treatment'.[202] Currently, the UK *Code of Practice* decrees that no more than three eggs or two embryos are to be transferred in any one cycle; as an exception to the rule, four eggs or three embryos may be implanted in women over the age of 40 provided the eggs involved are their own.[203] Nevertheless, even triplets[204] may be an unwelcome result of a successful treatment and evidence has been adduced that a multiple pregnancy rate of over 40 per cent arises when more eggs are used in the GIFT process.[205] Moreover, the superfetation of hormone therapy is hard to control. Thus, the clinician may well, though is increasingly unlikely to, be faced with the option of pregnancy reduction in utero.

8.90 This process, which is carried out at or earlier than the 12th week of pregnancy, is generally known as selective reduction of pregnancy, but it has been pointed out that, as

---

[200] Y Khalaf, T El-Toukhy, A Coomarasamy, et al., 'Selective single blastocyst transfer reduces the multiple pregnancy rate and increases pregnancy rate' (2008) 115 Brit J Obs Gynaec 385.

[201] In a particularly publicised case, which one hopes will remain unique, a woman conceived octuplets through a series of adventures and misadventures. She decided to maintain her pregnancy and all eight were stillborn at 19 weeks: leading article 'The death of babies', *Daily Telegraph*, 4 October 1996, p 25.

[202] A Doran (Interim Chief Executive, HFEA), *HFEA Statement on Elective Single Embryo Transfer (eSET) Guidelines*, 3 September 2008 [subsequently referred to as 'SET']. The technique of elective single embryo transfer which ideally involves selection of young, first-time IVF subjects combined with back-up frozen embryo storage is well described by R Cutter et al., 'Elective single embryo transfer: Guidelines for practice' (2008) 11 Human Fert 131. Offering SET to 50 per cent of IVF patients would reduce the twin pregnancy rate for IVF as a whole to less than 10 per cent.

[203] HFEA, *Code of Practice* (8th edn, 2015), Guidance, ss 7.4–7.6. The Authority's right to limit practice in such a way was upheld in the Court of Appeal: *R (on the application of Assisted Reproduction and Gynaecology Centre) v Human Fertilisation and Embryology Authority* [2002] Lloyd's Rep Med 148. It is to be noted that many authorities regard even two embryos as providing an excessive risk—hence the move towards SET (n 202) where only one embryo is implanted but others are frozen and retained as 'back-up' in the event of failure. The difficulty here lies in equating the success rate with the extra economic burden imposed and the procedure involves a careful choice of patient; 'elective', therefore, refers to the choice of patient rather than the choice of embryo. The HFEA now requires documented evidence as to why SET was not adopted in a suitable case (*Code of Practice*, para 7A).

[204] Currently some 1 in 4 IVF pregnancies result in twins or triplets as compared with 1 in 80 in natural pregnancies. The aim is to reduce this to 1 in 10. In *Thompson v Sheffield Fertility Clinic* 2000 WL 33148917, QBD, three embryos were inserted into a woman who had requested that only two be used. She was delivered of triplets and accepted an award of £20,000 for loss of amenity. The case is of additional interest in that it may represent the exception for the birth of a healthy child in breach of contract which was left open as a possibility by the House of Lords in *McFarlane v Tayside Health Board* [2000] 2 AC 59; [1999] 4 All ER 961.

[205] This being one reason why GIFT is being decreasingly used—the pregnancy results of standard IVF are now just as good and without the extra risk.

the individual fetal characteristics are unknown at the time, there is no 'selection' other than that dictated by operative convenience. We prefer the suggested alternative of reduction of multifetal pregnancy—a description which serves to distinguish the process from the truly selective termination which, when combined with chorionic villus sampling, may be used, say, to identify and eliminate fetuses that are genetically compromised. The legality of either practice depends upon additions to the Abortion Act 1967 arising from s 37(5) of the 1990 Act; their morality is inseparable from that of abortion which is discussed in Chapter 9.

SURROGATE MOTHERHOOD

8.91 Surrogate motherhood requires the active cooperation of an otherwise uninvolved woman in the process of pregnancy and birth. It thus introduces a third party into the reproductive process.[206] At its simplest, and as the term is most commonly used, the infertile woman and her husband or partner[207] arrange with another woman that she will carry a child conceived by donor insemination with the husband's semen and will surrender it to its genetic father after birth. The alternative, which also concludes with the return of the infant to the commissioning couple, is that an embryo which is created in vitro from the gametes of a couple is then implanted in the uterus of a 'surrogate'. There are several conceptual reasons for separating the two processes, which are often described respectively as partial and complete surrogacy; we, for our part, find it easier to refer to the latter technique more descriptively as 'womb-leasing'.[208] We return to this subject later but, for the present, we limit discussion to partial surrogacy.[209] The process, as defined, is akin to a pre-emptive adoption with the advantage that the 'adopted' baby shares half its genes with its 'adopting' parents. Since the practical possibility of following the normal process of adoption is decreasing steadily, there is much to be said, theoretically, in favour of surrogate motherhood as a treatment for the woman who is irrevocably childless—indeed, it is the *only* treatment for one who is childless by virtue of being both sterile and without a functional uterus—or otherwise unable to gestate. Yet, when considered as part of the emerging 'reproductive revolution', the great majority of early commentators shied away from accepting it as a means of satisfying an urge to parenthood—why? The reason was summarised many years ago in the classic words of Winslade: 'The practice has a potential for economic exploitation, moral confusion and psychological harm to the surrogate mothers, the prospective adoptive parents and the children.'[210] This view crystallises the debate which surrounded surrogacy when it first came to the attention of British courts some 30 years ago; it is only fair to say, however, that three decades of evolution of society's sexual and reproductive mores have served to restrict controversy to relatively case specific issues. Indeed, the issues have exploded on the global stage, particularly in countries like India where commercial surrogacy is increasingly seen as the norm and attracts considerable numbers of interested parties from around the world. Space does not permit

[206] A helpful one-stop-shop site, including accessible information about the legal position is provide by Surrogacy UK: http://www.surrogacyuk.org/home.
[207] It is trite to point out that the procedures are open to any couple where there is a relationship including, where appropriate, civil partnerships or habit.
[208] The technical term 'in vitro fertilisation surrogacy' is also used.
[209] It is to be remembered that the legal and practical implications of DI will apply.
[210] For an early view that laid down many markers, see W J Winslade, 'Surrogate mothers: Private right or public wrong?' (1981) 7 J Med Ethics 153.

a discussion of the recent drivers of this phenomenon. For this, we refer readers to the following literature;[211] instead, we concentrate on the UK legal position.

STATUTE LAW AND SURROGACY

8.92   Prior to 1990, the only way by which the prospective social parents—the 'commissioning couple'—could achieve their aim was through the medium of adoption and, as we have noted, it is quite reasonable to regard a surrogacy arrangement as a form of adoption—albeit pre-arranged. The terms of the Adoption and Children Act 2002 thus have at least an indirect bearing on surrogacy and, indeed, Parliament clearly intended that it should be so.[212]

8.93   The significant parts of the Adoption Acts for present purposes relate to the prohibition of commercialism within the process—effectively banning 'baby selling'.[213] From the very beginning, therefore, there was a real probability that surrogate motherhood which involved any form of monetary transaction was illegal.[214] Even so, there is much to be said for the view that surrogate motherhood and adoption are quite distinct, albeit closely linked, processes.[215] In the first place, the surrogate mother is not pregnant, nor has she an existing child which she has to abandon at the time the proposition is put to her. Moreover, she is under no pregnancy-related pressures. It is true that surrogacy might be one response to economic need—but the element of urgency that is a hallmark of adoption is still lacking. The nature of any proposed payment is also different in the two cases. In one it can be seen as a matter of purchase of an existing commodity for sale; in the other it is a matter of expenses coupled with payment for services rendered.[216] It is, therefore, clear that legislation as to payment for surrogacy should be distinct from that associated with adoption.

8.94   While we will see later that harmony between the statutory provisions of the Adoption Acts and the practicalities of surrogacy has been virtually achieved with the introduction of the parental order, it is, nevertheless, interesting to see how the courts struggled with the problem when it first presented. *Re an adoption application (surrogacy)*[217] was a remarkably amateurish affair. The principals met casually and the surrogate was impregnated naturally. A fee of £10,000 was agreed. All the principals, the judge said later, were supremely happy. They were also inexperienced and it was not for a further

---

[211] A Donchin, 'Reproductive tourism and the quest of global gender justice' (2010) 24(7) Bioethics 323 and J A Gupta, 'Reproductive Biocrossings: Indian egg donors and surrogates in the globalized fertility market' (2012) 5 Int J of Fem Approaches to Bioethics 25, and J Tobin, 'To prohibit or permit: what is the (human) rights response to the practice of international surrogacy? (2014) 63(2) Intl and Comp Law Q 317.

[212] And also, of course, the Adoption and Children (Scotland) Act 2007. However, for ease of writing, we will refer here only to the 2002 Act.

[213] Adoption and Children Act 2002, s 96 (carrying on the Adoption Act 1976, s 57).

[214] In the first US test, the court agreed on the fundamental right to include a third party in a pregnancy arrangement but excluded the right to carry a child for payment: *Doe v Kelly* 307 NW 2d 438 (Mich, 1981).

[215] I M Mady, 'Surrogate mothers: The legal issues' (1981) 7 Am J Law Med 323; I Davies, 'Contracts to bear children' (1985) 11 J Med Ethics 61. The great majority of citations in this area result from the surge in interest in surrogacy in the early 1980s. The settled dust has only recently been disturbed, but there remains very little recent research. A helpful summary and exception is: C Fenton-Glynn, 'The regulation and recognition of surrogacy under English law: an overview of the case-law' (2015) 27(1) Child and Fam Law Q 83.

[216] R Macklin, 'Is there anything wrong with surrogate motherhood? An ethical analysis' (1988) 16 Law Med Hlth Care 57. For a strongly opposing view, see B Cohen, 'Surrogate mothers: Whose baby is it?' (1984) 10 Am J Law Med 243.

[217] [1987] Fam 81; [1987] 2 All ER 826.

two-and-a-half years that the de facto 'parents' applied for an adoption order. The issue was simply whether this would be valid following the 'payment or reward'.[218] In summary, Latey J held that a surrogacy arrangement would not contravene the Adoption Act so long as the payments made did not constitute an element of profit or financial reward; he thought that the payments in the instant case did no more than compensate for the inconveniences of pregnancy. An adoption order was made. This relatively courageous decision was later followed without qualm.[219] Indeed, the most recent British cases now confirm the paramountcy of the child's welfare in surrogacy cases in general and the granting of parental orders in particular—'it will be only in the clearest case of the abuse of public policy that the court will be able to withhold an order if otherwise welfare considerations support its making'.[220] Thus retrospective payments, clearly beyond 'expenses', to surrogates in the USA[221] and India[222] have been authorised purely on 'welfare' grounds.

8.95 Most recently, the court exercised its discretion[223] in *J v G (Parental Orders)*[224] when granting a parental order to authorise payment in excess of reasonable expenses with respect to a professional surrogate who had been engaged in the USA. The surrogate was paid $56,750 to cover an allowance for unspecified 'incidental expenses', an inconvenience fee for the IVF transfer, and a pregnancy compensation fee. The court justified its action on the basis that the payment was not so disproportionate as to be an abuse of public policy, and because the parties had acted at all times in good faith and with every attempt to comply with parenting laws in the UK.[225]

8.96 The situation in Scotland provides something of an antithesis. In the comparable case of *C v S*,[226] the surrogate, who was unemployed, received £8,000 in expenses but then regretted her decision to give up the child. A parental order (for which, see para 8.99) was, therefore, unavailable on the grounds of lack of consent by the legal mother and the commissioning couple sought to adopt the child a year after its birth. The sheriff, while holding that consent to adoption was being withheld unreasonably, nonetheless refused an adoption order because he considered the monetary transaction breached the terms of the statute;[227] a custody order was granted in lieu. On appeal to the Court of Session, however, it was held that the money had been paid in the expectation of a parental order rather than of adoption; the Act had, accordingly, not been contravened and an adoption order was substituted. While it is unclear to us why a provision for unreasonable withdrawal of consent should be available in respect of an adoption order but not of a parental order, *C v S* serves, at least, to harmonise policy as to the authorisation of 'reasonable' payments in respect of surrogacy on both sides of the border.

---

[218] Adoption Act 1976, s 57(1) which was then in force.

[219] *Re Q (parental order)* [1996] 1 FLR 369. And, more recently: *Re X (Children) (Parental Order: Foreign Surrogacy)* [2009] Fam 71.

[220] *Re L (A child) (Parental order: foreign surrogacy)* [2011] Fam 106; [2011] 2 WLR 1006 per Hedley J at 10, though with some misgivings at 12.

[221] *Re L*, n 220, *Re S (Parental order)* [2010] 1 FLR 1156.

[222] *Re X and Y (Children: foreign surrogacy)* [2012] Fam Law 286.

[223] Section 54(8) of the Human Fertilisation and Embryology Act 2008.

[224] [2014] 1 FLR 297; [2013] Fam Law 972.

[225] For a discussion of 'reasonable expenses' with respect to payments made to an Indian surrogate (being the equivalent of £6,875), see Re *X (A Child) (Surrogacy: Time Limit)* [2015] Fam 186; [2015] 2 WLR 745.

[226] 1996 SLT 1387, sub nom *C and C v GS* 1996 SCLR 837. For practical guidance and commentary on more recent cases, see A Inglis, 'Hagar's baby: surrogacy arrangements' 2014 SLT 105.

[227] Adoption (Scotland) Act 1978, ss 24(2) and 51 then in force.

8.97 Nonetheless, outside the USA, there appears to be a consensus—at least in Europe and Australasia—which condemns, not so much the making of private arrangements but, rather, the blatant commercialisation of childbearing by way of intermediate, profit-making agencies.[228] It is this which underpins the Surrogacy Arrangements Act 1985.[229] The main purpose of the Act is to prohibit the making of a surrogacy arrangement on a profit-making basis.[230] The principals involved are expressly excused from criminal liability (s 2(2)); moreover, payments made to or for the benefit of the surrogate are not regarded as being made on a commercial basis (s 2(3)). Thus far, the measure is broadly acceptable. It is clear that it allows for third party involvement provided no payments are made but it removes the financially motivated entrepreneur from the scene and, at the same time, excludes any suggestion of a criminal ancestry for the resulting children. Some aspects are, however, open to criticism. Few organisations can exist on a purely altruistic platform and amateur action in such a delicate field is beset with pitfalls.[231] This problem is addressed in the amendment to the 1985 Act whereby facilitating the making of a surrogacy arrangement is no longer an offence provided it is a service provided for a non-profit-making body.[232] The concept of a non-profit-making surrogacy organisation is now accepted by statute and we return to this below.

8.98 The concession has, however, to be taken in conjunction with s 1A of the 1985 Act,[233] by virtue of which no surrogacy arrangement is enforceable by or against any of the persons making it.[234] In so legislating, the UK Parliament reflects the majority trend of those countries that have addressed the subject; whether it is the correct approach is open to argument. A surrogate arrangement is clearly a difficult contract to draw up[235]— it must allow for changes of heart on either side, illness in the surrogate, abnormalities in the resultant child, and other imponderables, some of which, such as recourse to an abortion within the terms of the Abortion Act 1967, can be seen as basic rights. The current law, however, is entirely negative and to retain deliberately the uncertainties of a breakable agreement which is not against public policy seems to do little more than reflect a persistent ambivalence in a Parliament which, while unable to follow the

[228] For a critical discussion, see J Hanna, 'Revisiting child-based objections to commercial surrogacy' (2010) 24 Bioethics 341.

[229] This aspect has been the subject of legislation in all jurisdictions. In Australia, see Surrogacy Act 2010 (NSW); Assisted Reproductive Treatment Act 2008 (Victoria); Family Relationships Act 1975 (as amended) (South Australia); Surrogacy Act 2010 (Queensland); Surrogacy Act 2008 (WA); Surrogacy Act 2012 (Tasmania). Distinctions are made, however, between full and partial surrogacy.

[230] Advertising by way of newspapers, periodicals, and telecommunications is proscribed in s 3, the criminal liability resting on the proprietor, editor, publisher, etc. I Kennedy and A Grubb, *Medical Law* (3rd edn, 2000) believed that the Act also criminalises the woman who advertises herself (p 1383).

[231] For ideologists who disapprove of the idea of an experienced agency, it is worth noting that breakdown of surrogacy arrangements is far less common in those clinics which require the intervention of professional expertise. See P R Brinsden, T C Appleton, E Murray, et al., 'Treatment by in vitro fertilisation with surrogacy: Experience of one British centre' (2000) 320 BMJ 924. It is believed that neither the lawyer who advises nor the doctor who merely assists in a pre-arranged surrogacy has committed an offence even if he or she was paid for the service: I Kennedy and A Grubb, *Medical Law* (3rd edn, 2000), p 1381.

[232] 1985 Act, s 2(8A) inserted by Human Fertilisation and Embryology Act 2008, s 59(6).

[233] Inserted by Human Fertilisation and Embryology Act 1990, s 36.

[234] For the practical implications of this, see *Re TT (Surrogacy)* [2011] EWHC 33 (Fam); [2011] 2 FLR 392; [2011] Fam Law 362.

[235] Nevertheless, it can be done; the judicial decision at first instance in the celebrated US case of *Re Baby M* 525 A 2d 1128 (NJ, 1987) was largely based on the law of contract.

German model in outlawing the practice,[236] seems determined to oblate any signs of approval—surrogacy is to be seen as a form of legal liberty.[237]

8.99 Even so, a system which depends upon the vagaries of the courts cannot be satisfactory and some formula must be evolved if the commissioning couple is to have a legal right to receive the child—for the surrogate, at least in the UK, is clearly its legal mother[238] irrespective of whether or not it is the product of her own ovum and, if she is married and conception was via consensual donor insemination, her husband is its father (1990 Act, ss 27 and 28); moreover, neither can simply surrender their parental duties.[239] Section 30 of the 1990 Act, however, offered an alternative to adoption by which the court may, on application, make a parental order, the regulations for which are now to be found in s 54 of the 2008 Act.[240] This currently provides for a child carried by a woman, who is not one of the applicants, as a result of the placing in her of an embryo or sperm and eggs or her artificial insemination to be treated as the child of the applicants provided that the gametes of at least one of the applicants were used to bring about the creation of the embryo.[241] The applicants must be either husband and wife, or civil partners of each other, or two persons who are living as partners in an enduring family relationship;[242] both must be aged over 18 years. Among other conditions, the application must be made within six months of the birth of the child whose home must be with the applicants. Grant of the order is subject to the free consent, given with full understanding, of the surrogate and, where applicable, any other parent of the child— including a man who is the father by virtue of s 35 or 36 of the 2008 Act and a woman who is a parent according to s 42 or 43—if they can be found;[243] moreover, the agreement of the woman who carried the child is ineffective if made less than six weeks after the child's birth. Overarchingly, the court must be satisfied that no money, other than reasonable expenses, has been given or received by the applicants in relation to the surrogacy arrangement other than as authorised by the court. Applications are heard in private and a guardian ad litem is appointed to watch over the child's interests.[244] It

---

[236] *Embryonenschutzgesetz* [Embryo Protection Act] 1990, s 1(1)(vii). Surrogacy is also banned in France (*Code Civil*, art 16–7, 1994) although the courts will sometimes confer civil status on 'surrogate children' when it is to the child's advantage.

[237] The same cannot be said for the courts where an increasingly tolerant approach has been evident for some time.

[238] The interesting thought has been mooted that it might be to the child's advantage to be aware of its wider kinship and that there is no absolute reason why a child should not have two 'mothers': J Wallbank, 'Too many mothers? Surrogacy, kinship and the welfare of the child' (2002) 10 Med L Rev 271—particularly, perhaps, now that the concept of 'second parent' is accepted.

[239] Children Act 1989, s 2(9).

[240] For the avoidance of doubt, s 30 of the 1990 Act ceases to have effect by virtue of the 2008 Act, s 57(3).

[241] In an unusual case, the biological father died between the application and the hearing; it was held that 'the applicants' involved those who made the application: *A v P* [2012] 1 FCR 408.

[242] Note that this is the same criterion as applies to the provision of treatment as opposed to agreed fatherhood which is simply a matter of consent. Presumably, this is to allow some discretion to the clinics and the courts.

[243] Legislation under the 1990 Act, s 30 confined parental orders to husband and wife. Those who were in the other eligible relationships recognised earlier can apply for an order within six months of the 2008 Act coming into force (2008 Act, s 54(11)).

[244] Parental Orders (Human Fertilisation and Embryology) Regulations 1994 (SI 1994/2767); Parental Orders (Human Fertilisation and Embryology) (Scotland) Regulations 1994 (SI 1994/2804), both repealed by the Human Fertilisation and Embryology (Parental Orders) (Consequential, Transitional and Saving Provisions) Order (SI 2010/986). Also, see 2008 Act, s 54(8). The first 'order' was, in fact, made preemptively: *Re W (minors) (surrogacy)* [1991] 1 FLR 385.

is exceptional for a parental order to be refused if these conditions are fulfilled.[245] In *J v G*,[246] Theis J stated that 'the court is only likely to refuse parental orders in the clearest case of the abuse of public policy where otherwise the child's welfare requires the order to be made'.

CASE LAW

8.100 Binding surrogacy contracts can certainly provide cautionary tales—particularly when different jurisdictional systems open the door to 'surrogate tourism'—which now constitutes the most uncertain area related to surrogacy.[247] In *W and B v H (child abduction: surrogacy)*,[248] a British woman entered into a legally binding contract to act as a surrogate in California. The discovery shortly after she was implanted with an egg from an anonymous donor, fertilised by W, that she was carrying twins led to a dispute. She then issued civil proceedings in California, resulting in an order declaring that W and B should have custody of the children at birth, and that the surrogate mother did not have any parental responsibility or rights. She returned to England, changed her mind about the surrogacy, and resolved to keep the children. When she refused to give up the children at birth, the Californian couple brought abduction proceedings under the Hague Convention on the Civil Aspects of International Child Abduction 1980. The judge at first instance decided that, since the children had no permanent home, they could not be abducted and the surrogate was allowed to keep them. The commissioning couple then appealed under the inherent jurisdiction of the court[249] which, then, ordered the summary removal of the children to California—California being the most convenient jurisdiction for the determination on the merits of the future of the twins. The words of Hedley J, who presided at both hearings, deserve repetition as a warning to those who believe that any advance in reproductive technology must, *ispo facto*, be advantageous:

> This case is a tribute to the scientific skills of those involved but its outcome, its cost in terms of human unhappiness let alone its future implications for these children, may serve to caution against an imbalance between our scientific and ethical capacities ... What it will mean to these children as they grow up and try to unravel and come to terms with their origins, no one can say. Much more sad is the fact, as I suspect, that no one has ever considered it.[250]

This last judicial suspicion is difficult to substantiate but, given the almost inevitable absence of any global policy, similar problems are bound to recur and are doing so on a

---

[245] The very great advantages of the parental order system were illustrated by the parallel US cases: *Doe v Doe* 710 A 2d 1297 (Conn, 1998) and *Doe v Roe* 717 A 2d 706 (Conn, 1998), the gist of which was to apply parental rights in the best interests of a child who had been accepted into a family.

[246] [2014] 1 FLR 297; [2013] Fam Law 972.

[247] The Foreign and Commonwealth Office issued guidance in June 2014 on foreign surrogacy and the implications for a child's nationality: https://www.gov.uk/government/uploads/system/uploads/attachment_data/file/324487/Surrogacy_overseas__updated_June_14_.pdf. It is emphasised that, even if a couple's names appear on a local birth certificate of a child born outside the UK, the child will not automatically be entitled to British nationality and application must be made to the Home Office. For discussion, see S Sucker, 'To recognize or not to recognize? That is the question! Motherhood in cross-border surrogacy cases' (2015) 17(2) Euro J Law Reform 257.

[248] [2002] 1 FLR 1008.

[249] *W v H (child abduction: surrogacy)* [2002] 2 FLR 252; [2002] Fam Law 501.

[250] [2002] 1 FLR 1008 at [1].

regular basis[251]—indeed, it has been suggested that 'the biggest challenge to the regulation of assisted conception services ... comes from the fact that the internet has made it very easy for people to access treatments in other countries and to make their own arrangements outside the regulated sector'.[252]

The British Cases

8.101 As to the British domestic cases, judicial attitudes have developed in a relatively untrammelled pattern over the last 30 years. Certainly, we have come a long way since the earliest example of *A v C*,[253] in which Ormrod LJ described a surrogate agreement as 'pernicious and void' and the biological father as being 'a constant reminder of the whole sordid story'—and the Court of Appeal unanimously decreed that the father, who had entered into a surrogacy arrangement for £3,000, should not be allowed to see his son. We doubt, however, if it is now useful to recapitulate the cases in detail; what follows is little more than an *aide memoire* as to those cases which constitute significant milestones on the road to full legal acceptance of the process.

8.102 *Re C (a minor)*[254] was the first truly apposite case to be fully covered. Even so, it was, essentially, a matter of wardship initiated by the local authority. Latey J refused to discuss the rights and wrongs of surrogacy and concentrated solely on the welfare of the child—how she had been born was irrelevant. On these grounds, he gave the commissioning couple care and control while, at the same time, continuing the wardship, thus rejecting suggestions that the commissioning couple were unfit parents because they had entertained a commercial surrogacy arrangement.

8.103 The relationship between surrogacy and adoption, was more directly considered in *Re an adoption application (surrogacy)*.[255] The facts and the outcome—including the liberal stance of the trial judge—have been discussed earlier.[256] *Re P (minors) (wardship: surrogacy)*[257] was the first UK case in which the surrogate declined to hand over the twins she had conceived by a married man. The children were made wards of court and, by contrast, were allowed to stay with their natural mother, the judge being strongly influenced by the degree of maternal bonding that had already arisen. Again, there was no criticism of either the commissioning parents or of the surrogate for having entered into a surrogacy agreement.

8.104 In *Re W*,[258] as noted earlier, the judge was prepared to pre-empt the law in order to ensure bonding of 'womb-leased' twins with their genetic parents. Following this, there was a dearth of new cases until the leading Scottish case of *C v S*[259] which has been discussed already.[260] The marked change in reporting probably does no more than reflect the fact

---

[251] For a light-touch appraisal, see N Gamble, 'The Indian surrogacy industry – and why we need to reform UK surrogacy law' (2012) BioNews 659, 6 June.

[252] E Jackson, 'The future of national regulation of healthcare services in the era of the internet and global travel' (2012), Paper presented to the Mason Institute for Medicine, Life Sciences and Law, 6 June.

[253] (1984) 14 Fam Law 241; [1985] FLR 445. Commentators at the time saw the case as of interest from the DI aspect only.

[254] [1985] FLR 846. [255] [1987] Fam 81; [1987] 2 All ER 826.

[256] See para 8.94. A similar attitude to the rules governing both payment and maternal objection was followed in *Re AW (adoption application)* [1993] 1 FLR 62 and *Re MW (adoption: surrogacy)* [1995] 2 FLR 789; [1995] Fam Law 665. In both cases, the welfare of the child was the determining factor although the decision must have been difficult in the former.

[257] [1987] 2 FLR 421. [258] *Re W (minors) (surrogacy)* [1991] 1 FLR 385.

[259] 1996 SLT 1387, sub nom *C and C v GS* 1996 SCLR 837. [260] See para 8.96.

that surrogacy is now so well established that cases are no longer regarded as meriting report unless there are special circumstances. Even so, there are sporadic newspaper reports of examples which have had a less than happy ending.[261]

8.105 More recent developments have evolved along two, sometimes interrelated, lines. First, cases involving same-sex couples and the legal recognition of civil partnerships, and second, foreign surrogacy arrangements with attendant questions about the nationality of the child. We offer some illustrative cases here that highlight the central issues that have arisen.

8.106 As an opener to the more recent jurisprudence, we have the statement by the Family Division of the High Court in *JP v LP (Surrogacy Arrangement: Wardship)*[262] that given the increasingly common nature of parental order applications, it should be within the ordinary competence of a legal family practitioner to know the particularities of the law and to advise accordingly (as it was solicitors had drawn up an illegal agreement, leading to considerable complications surrounding any parental order including non-compliance with the parental order time limit). As to these time limits, the High Court has taken a purposive approach to the statutory requirement, especially when set against the welfare of the child, and has ruled that the six-month limit is not as hard and fast as the wording of the law seems to imply. Thus, in *Re X (A Child) (Surrogacy: Time Limit)*[263] Sir Munby P granted a parental order for a child born in India in December 2011, even although the child was not brought to the UK until July 2013, and a clear indication given from the surrogate of a wish to surrender parental responsibilities until December 2013. The court held that no one would be harmed by the granting of such an order, and yet considerable harm would be done by not doing so.

8.107 Other developments have included guidance coming from clearly frustrated courts when parties have not thought through the implications of their actions in an attempt to produce a child. In *AB v CT*[264] the facts involved civil partners who had paid £16,000 to an Indian agency (with £2,250 to the surrogate) and who sought a UK parental order some three years after the birth of twins to the surrogate. In allowing the order, the court highlighted the need for couples undertaking surrogacy abroad to seek specialist advice. Prospective parents are strongly urged to establish the necessary legal steps involved in all relevant jurisdictions, and to make any parental order promptly after birth in whichever jurisdiction they might wish to move to (in this case the couple had been living in Australia and then moved to the UK). The court also stressed the importance of maintaining clear lines of communication with the surrogate mother (which had been lost in this case, and so the order was granted in her absence), and finally to maintain honest and accurate records of any sums paid (and the specific purposes). For our part, this case—and many others like it[265]—suggests that the law and the courts are in an intractable bind. The trumping principle of the welfare of the child is sweeping away all detailed attempts in the law to regulate these practices. This having been said, this line of authority should be contrasted

---

[261] In one, the surrogate was thought to be acting on behalf of two families at the same time: C Dyer, 'Surrogate mother refuses to give up baby' (1997) 314 BMJ 250. In another, there were allegations that the surrogate had fabricated an abortion in order to keep the child: D Kennedy, 'Minister hints at change in the law' *The Times*, 16 May 1997, p 2. See also *W v H*, n 249.

[262] [2015] 1 All ER 266; [2015] 1 FLR 307   [263] [2015] Fam 186; [2015] 2 WLR 745.

[264] [2015] EWFC 12; [2015] Fam Law 643.

[265] See, *Re A* [2015] EWHC 1756 (Fam) [child born in South Africa—first case to consider this], and *D v ED (Parental Order: Time Limit)* [2015] EWHC 911 (Fam); [2015] Fam Law 1052 [couple commissioned surrogacy in the USA and were legally advised they would be parents].

with the slightly earlier decision in *AB* v *CD* v *The Z Fertility Clinic*.[266] Although this was not a surrogacy case as such, it involved a same-sex couple and the need for a legal declaration of parenthood with respect to children born through reproductive services. In brief, the formalities of the 2008 reforms that recognise same-sex unions as legal parents had not been complied with. The requisite forms had not been signed or lodged with the clinic prior to commencement of treatment. The judge took a firm, literal line in interpreting the rule, and the partner seeking recognition of parentage was accordingly denied her claim. The justification was the importance of certainty in the law. Moreover, the judge was not persuaded by the argument that public policy required a more accommodating approach, nor by the claim that the decision might otherwise be discriminatory to same-sex couples. In the final event, this case is probably an outlier in light of subsequent decisions. It should be noted, for example, that the final words of the judge were to warn against a continuation of the 'lamentable history of conflict' which would clearly not be in the interests of the children in question.

The US Scene

8.108 Comparative US law is becoming less important on this side of the Atlantic as the UK and Europe develop their own medical jurisprudence. However, surrogacy has traditionally been far more common in the relatively free market of the USA[267] and, as a result, there are lessons still to be learnt from the US common law. It is also true that cases come to public notice only when there is conflict and those such as *Re Baby M*,[268] which demonstrates multiple failings, are instructive—albeit probably atypical.

8.109 In that case, the surrogate, who had agreed to a fee of US$10,000, refused to relinquish her child and, in fact, absconded with it contrary to a court order. When the matter came to trial, the judge concluded, on the one hand, that a valid contract had been made and broken and, on the other, that the state's interest in the welfare of its children dictated that the child be adopted by the commissioning couple. The Supreme Court of New Jersey, however, had no hesitation in overturning this decision.[269] The surrogacy contract was found to be against public policy and, as such, invalid; both the termination of the mother's parental rights and the adoption order were voided. Nonetheless, the Supreme Court could find nothing in law against voluntary, non-commercial surrogacy, provided that the arrangement did not include any clause binding on the surrogate to surrender her baby. As a result, the court was able to dissociate the contractual aspects of surrogacy and the 'best interests' of the child and followed the lower court in awarding custody to the commissioning parents.[270]

8.110 A contrast is seen in the Californian case of *Johnson* v *Calvert*.[271] Here, the surrogate was paid US$10,000 to carry the embryo of a commissioning couple. After gestating for six months, she changed her mind as to handing over the child and the court was asked to decide on its parentage. The trial court held that a surrogate contract was both legal and enforceable and that the commissioning couple were the child's genetic, biological, and natural parents; no parental rights attached to the surrogate. This disposition was upheld

---

[266] [2013] EWHC 1418 (Fam).
[267] It is also subject to much variation as to acceptance. See K Drabiak, C Wegner, V Fredland, and P R Helft, 'Ethics, law and commercial surrogacy: A call for uniformity' (2007) 35 J Law Med Ethics 300.
[268] 525 A 2d 1128 (NJ, 1987).   [269] 537 A 2d 1227 (NJ Sup Ct, 1988).
[270] See G P Smith, 'The case of *Baby M*: Love's labor lost' (1988) 16 Law Med Hlth Care 121.
[271] 851 P 2d 776 (Cal, 1993) discussed by A Grubb, 'Surrogate contract: parentage' (1994) 2 Med L Rev 239.

on appeal. In dismissing a further appeal, the Supreme Court of California held that it was the intention of the parties at the time of making the arrangement which decided a contested suit and, in the present case, the surrogate had done no more than 'facilitate' the procreation of the commissioning couple's child.[272] The Court further stated that surrogate contracts did not violate any existing public policy as to adoption; any payments in the former were, effectively, made for services rendered and not as compensation for the transfer of parental rights. Needless to say, this opinion has been severely criticised as fundamentally misunderstanding the biological realities of the surrogate's contribution.[273]

8.111   The significance of the apparent inconsistency between *Re Baby M* and *Johnson v Calvert* is explained to some extent by *Re Marriage of Moschetta*.[274] Here, the 'parents' of a one-year-old child, born by standard surrogacy, separated and the surrogate then claimed legal parentage. The Court of Appeal was, thus, able to distinguish the case from *Johnson* because there was no conflict as to maternity—the surrogate was both the genetic and the gestational mother and was to be regarded as such. It is, however, to be noted that the Court distinguished the definition of status from the allocation of custody—the latter was governed by the best interests of the child.

Australia

8.112   It is surprising that a surrogacy case was not litigated in Australia until 1998. *Re Evelyn*[275] was an interfamilial, altruistic case that 'went wrong' and resulted, ultimately, in a residency dispute in the Full Court of the Family Court. The final decision was in favour of the surrogate mother, a conclusion based largely, but not entirely, on the assumption that the child's best long-term interests lay in preservation of her natural bonding with her biological mother—this despite the fact that she had lived with the commissioning couple for the first year of her life. Both the trial judge and the Full Court also considered that the ambience of the surrogate's family was preferable for the child.[276] Since then, as we note above, all states and territories have legislated the matter.

The Cases Assessed

8.113   The British cases indicate that the public, as represented by its judiciary, are sympathetic to surrogate motherhood—an attitude which probably derives more from the fait accompli nature of the proceedings than from any basic empathy with the practice. Accordingly, it is very unlikely that a parental order will be withheld in the event of an application by the commissioning parents and consent on the part of the surrogate and the legal father—if there is one. While it would always be possible for the court to override agreement by the parties, it is difficult to see how the motivation of the couple and their almost inevitable

---

[272] The concept of intention was carried a stage further in *In the Marriage of Buzzanca* 72 Cal Rptr 2d 280 (CA, 1998) where a separated couple who had used both a surrogate and a donated embryo were declared the legal parents on the grounds that they initiated the pregnancy. This approach is embedded in statute in several US states—e.g. Florida, Virginia, and New Hampshire.

[273] R B Oxman, 'California's experiment in surrogacy' (1993) 341 Lancet 1468.

[274] 30 Cal Rptr 2d 893 (1994), discussed in detail by A Grubb, 'Surrogate contract: Parentage' (1995) 3 Med L Rev 219.

[275] (1998) FLC 92. The case is examined in depth in M Otlowski, '*Re Evelyn*—Reflections on Australia's first litigated surrogacy case' (1998) 7 Med L Rev 38. The author points out that, despite the varying, but generally antipathetic, attitudes to surrogacy shown by the states' legislatures, non-commercial surrogacy arrangements are now acceptable throughout Australia.

[276] Wallbank, n 238, reiterates that, since a variety of factors were taken into consideration, the case does not establish a legal precedent—particularly as to the sharing of long-term care.

superior material status could be irrelevant to the child's 'best interests'—which is not to say that economic advantage will always take precedence.[277] Insofar as it is possible to apply pre-1990 standards to the present day conditions, the indications are that the prime factor in the court's thinking in the event of disagreement between the parties would be the extent of family bonding—much would depend on where, and for how long, the child was living at the time of adjudication. It is, however, impossible to generalise. The paramount feature lies in the child's best interests. The published cases provide no indication of what would result if the commissioning couple were to refuse to accept the infant; the precise details of each case would, again, be all-important, but it is difficult to see, in general, an alternative to intervention by the local authority by way of care proceedings. The position of the surrogate's husband under the terms of s 35(1) of the 2008 Act might then be problematical.

8.114 While there is no firm evidence on the point, and despite the contrary evidence from the USA, we fancy that British judges would take much the same approach whether the surrogate had incubated her own egg, that of the commissioning woman, or one donated— concern for the welfare of the child, would trump any other arguments. This has, perhaps, been demonstrated in *N (a child)*[278] where there was a deliberate deception on the part of a surrogate mother, as a result of which she had managed to retain care of the child for 18 months before the commissioning father became aware of its existence. The court held that the case represented a classic discretionary balancing exercise[279] by which to determine the best interests of the child. All the options were carefully analysed and, in the end, it was decided that the child would thrive best in the care of his biological father and his wife. Nevertheless, the decision might easily have gone the other way and still have been acceptable.

THE MORALITY OF SURROGATE MOTHERHOOD

8.115 What, then, is so particular about the morality of surrogacy? Clearly, the most important factor lies in the inclusion of a third party to procreation—and in such a way as to provoke not only serious moral but also important socio-political questions—and the latter are, by definition, gender-based. Stripped to its essentials, surrogacy can be viewed from this perspective as being one way of exploiting women for the benefit of men—a matter to which we have alluded earlier. The alternative is to see the outlawing of the practice as downright paternalism which denies a woman a chance to use her body as she pleases. It seems fair to say that the feminist movement is divided in its approach;[280] the argument is one which we will not take further here save to note the difficulties that arise from generalising in personal and individual affairs.

8.116 The second major concern lies in the suggestion that surrogacy is 'baby-selling'.[281] It is possible, however, to maintain that a baby is 'sold' only if persons with no genetic association purchase an infant that is already in being. It seems more logical to regard any monetary transaction in respect of surrogacy as payment for gestational expertise,

---

[277] See e.g. *Re P (minors) (wardship: surrogacy)* [1987] 2 FLR 421.

[278] *N (a child), In the matter of* [2007] EWCA Civ 1053; [2008] 1 FLR 198. It is interesting that, even in 2007, there was some conflict in the Court of Appeal as to the legal fatherhood of the child—see Lloyd LJ at [19].

[279] As regulated by the Children Act 1989, s 1.

[280] For analysis of the extensive literature, see E Jackson, *Regulating Reproduction* (2001), p 291 et seq.

[281] So far as is known, only Israel positively encourages a commercial element in surrogacy arrangements: D A Frankel, 'Legal regulation of surrogate motherhood in Israel' (2001) 20 Med Law 605.

or 'services rendered', and, as the British cases indicate, the critical distinction lies between reasonable recompense and inducement to gestate.[282] The majority of assisted reproduction is centred on private health care and, even within a public health service, there is indirect payment for obstetric expertise. Looked at in this way, either both surrogacy and embryo transfer are 'baby purchasing' or neither is—and there is no suggestion that sophisticated assisted reproductive techniques are immoral on this score.[283] Third, it could be argued that surrogacy increases the chances of an ill-effect on children in general or on the individual resultant child. The former, represented by a fear that children may become 'objects for barter', is valid only so long as surrogacy itself is categorised as objectionable; the premise disappears once it is regarded as a legitimate treatment for childlessness. Any effect on the individual child by way of confusion as to parentage is comparable to that which we have discussed in relation to other forms of assisted reproduction. Whether there is a detriment seems to us to be unproven.

8.117 In favour of surrogacy, it must be remembered that, as already noted, it *is* a treatment for some forms of childlessness. Such cases may be rare, yet to encourage treatment by way of ovum donation for the woman who is childless because of ovarian inadequacy and, at the same time, to forbid surrogacy for the one who has no uterus, smacks of unfair discrimination.

8.118 Surrogacy could, however, be used for purely selfish reasons—for example, a desire to have a child without interference with a career—although the prospect may be given exaggerated importance. Such hedonistic womb-leasing is so comparable to nineteenth-century wet-nursing that 'full' surrogacy as a whole has become suspect.[284] This is unfortunate because there are, in fact, far more conditions in which IVF-linked surrogacy would be the preferred treatment of childlessness than there are those in which standard surrogacy would be indicated. Abnormality of the uterus or other causes of persistent miscarriage are more common than loss of both uterus and ovaries; moreover, womb-leasing is the logical answer to an inability to carry, rather than to conceive, a baby. The other, and obvious, important difference is that, in womb-leasing, the commissioning couple are the genetic parents. Thus, one would imagine that the surrogate, having no such relationship to her fetus, would be less exposed to psychological trauma on surrendering it; the receiving parents are in precisely the same end position as natural coital parents; and the child suffers no 'genetic insecurity'. Certainly, womb-leasing involves the use of high-grade technology, but even this serves to remove some of the intuitive distaste provoked by standard surrogacy. Legislation following the Warnock Committee has not distinguished between partial and full surrogacy; we feel, however, that the better approach lies in favour of clearly separating the two.[285]

---

[282] The court in *Johnson* v *Calvert* 851 P 2d 776 (Cal, 1993) considered many of these points and rejected the suggestion that surrogacy arrangements violated public policy. For further debate, see A van Niekerk and L van Zyl, 'Commercial surrogacy and the commodification of children: An ethical perspective' (1995) 14 Med Law 163.

[283] M Freeman, 'Does surrogacy have a future after Brazier?' (1999) 7 Med L Rev 1 suggested that remuneration is inevitable and is better in the open rather than underground.

[284] Even so, 'womb-leasing' has been allowed in some Australian States where traditional surrogacy has been banned.

[285] Theoretically, womb-leasing should be the preferred surrogacy method for those of the Jewish faith as 'Jewishness' is transferred through the female line. In fact, current Israeli law states that surrogacy is legal in that country only if the ovum does not come from the surrogate: R H B Fishman, 'Surrogate motherhood becomes legal in Israel' (1996) 347 Lancet 756.

8.119 There is, however, one aspect of womb-leasing that merits special attention—that is, the use of intrafamilial surrogates. Not only does this seriously disturb familial relationships but also the procedure opens the door to emotional coercion. It appears to be a practice which should, at least, be carefully regulated if not made unlawful—as it is in many jurisdictions—although not everyone would agree.[286]

THE FUTURE

8.120 The law relating to surrogacy is still in an uncertain state—and, as suggested, is likely to be further confused with the clear growth in 'Internet tourism'—as most of the recent legal cases demonstrate. Many would say that it is right that customs so private as reproductive choice should be allowed to evolve by way of public opinion as represented by the common law. Others, however, would feel that the implications of surrogacy are such that it ought to be controlled by statute and that, as things stand, regulation in the UK is unsatisfactory—and this because it is, largely, both indirect and inconsistent. At present, while IVF-associated surrogacy clearly lies within the framework of the Human Fertilisation and Embryology Act 1990, standard surrogacy does not do so unless it involves donor insemination with manipulation of the sperm[287]—and this leaves an unsatisfactory dichotomy. While very few would now wish to criminalise what is an accepted form of treatment,[288] most would also agree that it must be regulated but that control should be uniform.[289] The recent cases suggest, however, that the formula for successful regulation remains extremely illusive. If a well-intentioned and economically empowered commissioning couple are able to obtain receipt of a child and bring him or her to the UK, the odds are now very much stacked in their favour. And yet, this does not remove the legal precariousness of the strategy. To paraphrase one judge: surrogacy is probably the least satisfactory way to become a parent.

8.121 The fundamental problem lies in the nature of that regulation—is it to be purely negative, as is the current position in the UK, or positive in that statute lays down the conditions under which a surrogacy contract can be legally binding? The overriding difficulty as to the latter, as we see it, lies in the problem of enforcement. Florida is one of the few states of the USA that have addressed the question of parenthood in surrogacy independent of a paternity/adoption process and have done this by way of Pre-planned Adoption Agreements.[290] These include comprehensive requirements of both a positive and negative type. Two requirements are, however, particularly significant in the present context—first, the agreement is not binding until seven days after the birth of the child and, second,

---

[286] In response to an English case involving a post-menopausal woman acting on behalf of her childless daughter, Lady Warnock has been reported as saying 'It is a wonderful idea': D Kennedy, 'Surrogacy attempt divides experts', *The Times*, 3 July 1995, p 8. The baby was successfully delivered by caesarian section.

[287] It has been reported that fewer than one-third of licensed clinics will provide a surrogacy service (Brazier, n 291 at para 6.9). The 2008 *Code of Practice* (update to 2015) states that the HFEA does not regulate surrogacy but gives advice to clinics on counselling as to the law and on the mandatory requirements as to gamete donation (at para 14A). The impression gained is that, while clinics are not barred from taking part in surrogacy, they are certainly not encouraged to do so.

[288] We know of no jurisdiction in the Anglophone world where surrogacy is now outlawed although distinctions may be made between full and partial surrogacy.

[289] The possibility that regulation offends against the Human Rights Act 1998 is discussed by J Ramsey, 'Regulating surrogacy—A contravention of human rights?' (2000) 5 Med L Internat 45. The author concludes that it is unlikely to be so held and we agree.

[290] Florida Statutes 63.212.

it can be terminated at any time by any party. In short, it is difficult to see how such agreements are anything other than dependent on the goodwill of the parties—and this is the position as it stands at present in the UK.

8.122   It was against this background that the Brazier Review Team was set up in 1997, intending to ensure that the law continued to meet public concerns.[291] Briefly, the team recommended, first, that payments to surrogate mothers should cover only genuine expenses associated with the pregnancy and that additional payments should be prohibited in order to prevent surrogacy arrangements being entered into for financial benefit; reasonable expenses should be defined by the Ministers. Second, it was recommended that agencies to oversee surrogacy arrangements should be established and registered by Health Departments which would be required to operate within a *Code of Practice*; an advisory code would be drawn up to provide guidance for the registered agencies and also for those acting in a private capacity. Third, current legislation dealing with surrogacy should be repealed and replaced by a consolidated Surrogacy Act which would address the whole subject rather than specific aspects. In this respect, it was recommended that surrogacy arrangements should remain unenforceable, that the ban on commercial agencies and advertising should remain in force, and that the prohibition should include the operation of unregistered agencies.

8.123   These proposals were carefully researched and have much to commend them; it is a matter for surprise that none has as yet been incorporated into statute law.[292] Nevertheless, we would take issue with some of them. Prominent in this respect is the question of payment—the rejection of which is central to the Brazier position. The concepts of provision of a service and recompense for that service are so closely linked that, save in unusual circumstances, the majority of persons would expect them to go hand in hand. Given that the demand for surrogates will not abate and given that private surrogacy arrangements are not prohibited, we have to agree with Freeman[293] that the effect of prohibiting paid arrangements in the registered field must be to force the process onto the 'back streets', which would be to overturn the whole purpose of regulation. Of perhaps more immediate concern, as we have already intimated, it would take a very great deal of argument to convince us that payments to a surrogate mother are any less moral than payments to an IVF clinician. We support the case for reasonable payments provided these are determined by an overall authority,[294] which we would prefer to see established as a distinct committee of the HFEA rather than as yet another independent quango.

8.124   Finally, we are unrepentant in our antipathy to declaring all surrogacy arrangements unenforceable. Very little attention is paid by commentators to the situation in which the commissioning couple wish to avoid their responsibilities and it is this that, in our opinion, constitutes the main potential mischief attached to surrogate motherhood; it

---

[291] M Brazier (Chair) *Surrogacy: Review for Health Ministers of Current Arrangements for Payment and Regulation* (Cm 4068, 1998).

[292] K Horsey and S Sheldon, 'Still hazy after all these years: The law regulating surrogacy' (2012) 20 Med L Rev 67. See also, K Horsey (ed), *Revisiting the Regulation of Human Fertilisation and Embryology* (2015), ch 8 asking what should be done about surrogacy in the UK?

[293] N 283.

[294] Brazier, herself, wrote a comprehensive review of the role of payments in the treatment of childlessness. While not committing herself, she clearly did not discard controlled payment for surrogacy as an arguable option. It is interesting to compare her analysis with the uncompromising report of the Brazier Committee published only a year before: M Brazier, 'Can you buy children?' (1999) 11 CFLQ 345.

seems to be far preferable to establish the *specific conditions* of an arrangement that are unenforceable rather than to declare it unenforceable as a whole.[295]

8.125 Having said all of which, it is clear that the 2008 Act, particularly in recognising a status for non-profit-making bodies,[296] has gone a considerable way in improving and sanitising surrogate motherhood provision in the UK. A non-profit-making body will now be able to receive payment for initiating negotiations with a view to the making of a surrogacy arrangement or compiling information about surrogacy—for example, listing willing surrogates or prospective commissioning couples; they will also be able to advertise within these parameters. A non-profit-making body will still not be able to *receive payment* for negotiating a surrogacy arrangement. Nevertheless, this seems a fair enough compromise that is roughly in line with changing public attitudes.

8.126 To say so is not, however, necessarily to condone the uncritical acceptance of reproductive surrogacy. We would, in fact, subscribe to a view that the procedure should be unlawful unless it is undertaken for a *bona fide* medical reason, other options having been considered and properly rejected.[297] Effectively, then, we are making a plea for medicalising surrogacy—thus emphasising our view that surrogacy is the treatment of choice for a specific, and limited, group of causes of childlessness and is, therefore, comparable to any other 'treatment services' provided under the general umbrella of the 1990 and 2008 Acts.

CONCLUSION

8.127 We commend the reader who has stayed the course on this circumnavigation of the vagaries of the regulation of reproduction. Baroness Warnock and her committee could scarcely have imagined the multiple dimensions to regulation that would spring from their recommendations for more active legal intervention in the field. But, of course, these are simply driven by the human biological imperative to reproduce; and much like nature itself, people will always find a way.[298] The complexities arise from the fact that, in many respects, the law in this area is caught in a double bind. The idea of the 'right to reproduce'—in the negative sense of not placing obstacles in people's way—is incredibly powerful; there are few arguments or actions that can stand up to it. Moreover, once a new human life is in existence, his or her welfare rightly must take precedence. Legal niceties and fine-grained rules are easily swept aside when set against such considerations.

---

[295] A relatively minor recommendation of the Brazier team was that judges should be unable to authorise otherwise impermissible payments. There will always be exceptional circumstances and the adoption and surrogacy procedures are so close to one another that it should not be possible to play one off against the other. Similarly, there seems no reason why it should not be possible to overrule an unreasonable objection to a parental order such as can be done in relation to an adoption order.

[296] Surrogacy Arrangements Act 1985, s 2(2A) inserted by 2008 Act, s 59.

[297] For a very strongly opposed view, see E Jackson, *Regulating Reproduction* (2001) ch 6.

[298] The prospect of artificial gametes only promises to add to the complexities, see A Smajdor and D Cutas, 'Will artificial gametes end infertility?' (2015) 23(2) Health Care Analysis 134.

9

THE CONTROL OF FERTILITY

INTRODUCTION

9.01 The control of fertility is a chapter heading that covers an exceptionally wide spectrum of medical expertise, medical ethics, and medical law. It can range in social significance from being a purely personal matter—as in the extreme example of abstinence from sexual intercourse—through contraception in its many guises to, at the other extreme, feticide which, in general, is the necessary outcome of abortion. Attitudes to fertility control will vary in parallel with such diversity of effect. At one end of the scale, we have the ultra-conservative ethicist who perceives sexual intercourse and procreation as a unitary function and will, accordingly, object to, say, barrier methods of contraception; somewhere in the middle is the purist who sees any interference with the human body as unethical unless it be for therapeutic purposes and who will condemn ligation of the fallopian tube or vas deferens as being fundamentally wrong; and, at the other end, lies he or she who is committed to the concept that a woman's body is hers to dispose of as she pleases and who advocates abortion on demand. Across the whole spectrum we must also accept that modern fertility control involves more than numerical limitation of the family; it also includes control of the nature of the family which may encompass anything from selection of the sex of one's children to manipulation of the family's genetic pool and it is in this field, in particular, that the seeds of ethical conflict are sown.[1] This perhaps leads to a final observation that fertility control is not simply a matter of private concern—the community has a legitimate and significant interest. Thus, the day may come when the eugenist movement is, once again, recognised as an acceptable expression of public health policy while, even today, there are many who would hold that global population control is essential to planetary survival.

9.02 The latter problems are, however, beyond both the individual's capacity to influence and the remit of this book. Here, we concentrate on the control of fertility as an aspect of what is, essentially, family planning and discussion in this area is dominated by two overarching precepts. On the one hand, we have the fundamental bioethical principle of respect for autonomy (see Chapter 1) which has now established itself as the cornerstone of modern medical jurisprudence in the United Kingdom (UK). It is possible to regard *any* restriction of an adult's lifestyle as an affront to that autonomy and reproductive choice is certainly one of its major components. On the other hand, given that quantitative and qualitative choice of one's offspring must involve rejection of some forms of future life, fertility control confronts both the ethical and legal acceptance of personal autonomy with the essentially communitarian principle that human life should be preserved whenever

---

[1] For a very full consideration of modern reproductive rights from the international perspective, see R J Cooke and B M Dickens, 'Reproductive Health and the Law' in P R Ferguson and G T Laurie (eds), *Inspiring a Medico-legal Revolution: Essays in Honour of Sheila AM McLean* (2015), ch 1.

this is possible. Both ethics and the law must, therefore, compromise and this chapter is structured on our view as to the extent of compromise that is required.

9.03 In essence, this chapter discusses the methods available in what we see as the order in which they will provoke ethical controversy as outlined earlier. There being no actual human life in isolated gametes, contraception stands as the morally most acceptable form of fertility control[2] and a form of 'quality' control that depends on gamete selection will attract less criticism than will one that depends on destruction of embryos. Sterilisation, on the other hand, while it involves prevention rather than loss of life, raises issues of both maim and of consent and has, at least in the past, been the subject of intense debate. Embryocide resulting from contragestation is clearly more open to questioning than is contraception per se but, at the same time, it is less subject to moral objection than is feticide in the form of abortion.[3] Termination of pregnancy itself becomes progressively less acceptable as fetal maturity increases and here the law steps in to regulate and provide some measure of protection for the fetus; finally, that protection becomes complete at birth where, subject to the vagaries of legal and medical necessity (for which, see Chapter 15), neonaticide remains unlawful irrespective of any opposing philosophical attractions.

9.04 What we can derive from the foregoing is that any distinction between contraception, contragestation, termination of pregnancy, and neonaticide, whether it be morally, legally, or even, in a slightly different context, medically based, depends upon the answer to the age-old question which arises at each point in the sequence, 'When does life begin?'

THE CONCEPT OF PERSONHOOD

9.05 The value that we place on human life is intimately linked with respect for personhood but what constitutes personhood is certainly not a matter of scientific fact. Rather, it is an amalgam of legal expedience, cultural variation, and moral supposition; as such, it is likely to be subject to wide and varied interpretation.[4] Thus, the view exemplified, particularly, by the Roman Catholic Church lies at one extreme; this holds that personhood, and its consequent right to protection, exists from the moment of conception—put another way, that the zygote formed from the union of male and female gametes is a 'person'. We suggest that there are comparatively few who would support this extreme view as a matter of legal policy; there are, in fact, relatively good reasons, based, inter alia, on the totipotential capacity of the early embryonic cells, for regarding the pre-implantation blastocyst as being, also, pre-embryonic. We will see, however, that personhood may be one thing but that human life is another; hence, it is possible to argue that, while the zygote may not be a person, there is no logical alternative to regarding it as the first stage in human life—and we return to this aspect at para 9.07. At the other end of the scale, there are those

---

[2] Subject to the possible rejoinder 'abstinence excepted'.

[3] Though it is, perhaps, surprising how seldom the former is used. In one Scottish study, only 12 per cent of women coming for abortion had used contragestative means to avoid their unwanted pregnancy and this is the widespread experience: F Lakha and A Glazier, 'Unintended pregnancy and the use of emergency contraception' (2006) 368 Lancet 1782.

[4] All of which is exemplified in the European Convention on Human Rights (ECHR), Art 2—'everyone's right to life shall be protected by law'. At what point in life is 'one' a 'person'? See B Hewson, 'Dancing on the head of a pin? Foetal life and the European Convention' (2005) 13 Feminist LS 363.

who would equate personhood with intellect and with the power to make decisions.[5] We also reject this extreme, if for no reason other than by way of an intuitive distaste for its natural consequence which would be to deprive even relatively mature infants of a right to be valued as persons.

9.06   So, how is the dilemma to be resolved? Many attempts are made to define the point at which the embryo or fetus is morally entitled to, at least, consideration. Within these brackets, for example, the Jewish rabbinical law sets the time as when pregnancy is recognisable externally;[6] the early Christian moralists were attracted to the evidence of life exhibited by quickening—or perceptible fetal movement;[7] and, in more modern terms, there is a widely accepted tendency to accord full protection to the fetus when it is capable of being born alive. The definitional complications of 'viability' are discussed later.[8] At this point, we would only remark on the well-appreciated fact that the limits of viability in terms of gestation periods will be steadily lowered to the physiological baseline of pulmonary morphology as improved neonatal medicine becomes more widely available. Perhaps as an indirect consequence of this, the law, in its search for certainty, draws a bright line at birth.[9] There is no legal personhood in a fetus but a neonate has all the legal attributes and rights to protection of a 'reasonable creature in being'—and this distinction, as we will see, leads to some anomalous conclusions insofar as it excludes a moral dimension.[10] Recently, this was confirmed as a matter of legal principle by the Court of Appeal in *CP (A Child) v Criminal Injuries Compensation Authority*[11] in which the Court held that because a fetus did not constitute a separate legal person, it could not be the subject of the criminal offence of grievous bodily harm. The facts related to a pregnant woman who excessively consumed alcohol in the knowledge that it could harm her unborn child. Notwithstanding, on the above reasoning, a subsequent claim to compensation by the seven-year-old daughter was unsuccessful.

9.07   An alternative approach, which we endorse, can be couched in terms of potential—a human 'organism'[12] acquires humanity when it has the potential to become a human being. On this basis, the pre-implantation embryo has no potential and implantation, itself, represents the critical moral watershed in human development.[13] This discussion

---

[5] M Tooley, 'A defense of abortion and infanticide' in J Feinberg (ed), *The Problem of Abortion* (1973) and H Kuhse and P Singer, *Should the Baby Live?* (1985); in particular, ch 6. A valuable modern discussion of 'personhood' from a rather different aspect is to be found in M Ford, 'The personhood paradox and the "right to die"' (2005) 13 Med L Rev 80.

[6] A Steinberg, 'Induced abortion in Jewish law' (1980) 1 Int J Law Med 187. Contrast: M Ghaly, 'Human personhood in contemporary Islamic bioethical discourse' (2014) QScience Proceedings: Vol. 2014, The Human Person: Challenges for Science, Religion and Governance, 4, doi: 10.5339/qproc.2014.islamicbioethics.4

[7] See G R Dunstan, 'The moral status of the human embryo: A tradition recalled' (1984) 10 J Med Ethics 38 for a comprehensive review.

[8] At para 9.99 et seq. A Peterfy, 'Fetal viability as a threshold to personhood' (1995) 16 J Leg Med 607 provides a most interesting overview.

[9] See, A K Burin, 'Beyond pragmatism: defending the "bright line" of birth' (2014) 22(4) Med Law Rev 494.

[10] But even this provides no absolute certainty—a fetus in the process of being born is not legally 'born' and requires the specific statutory protection of the Infant Life (Preservation) Act 1929—which does not run to Scotland.

[11] [2014] EWCA Civ 1554.

[12] In the important case *Attorney-General's Reference (No 3 of 1994)* [1998] AC 245; [1997] 3 All ER 936, Lord Mustill was unable to define the status of the fetus and referred to it as 'a unique organism' at AC 256, All ER 943.

[13] This comes very close to the comparable theological position based on 'ensoulment': see N M Ford, *When Did I Begin?* (1988).

has, however, already shown us that, whatever point we may choose as the marker for the acquisition of humanity, it represents no more than a convenient fare-stage in the continuum of early human development; an embryo in the process of implantation is the same embryo once it has become embedded and a fetus in utero is the same fetus whether or not it could survive after parturition.[14] That is, until we revert to the beginning of the journey. Left to themselves, gametes can only die. The only absolute in the saga is that 'human life' as it is generally understood begins with the formation of the human zygote; on this view, the conservative Roman Catholic view represents the only tenable option—the difficulty being that it is also the least practical solution to the question and calls for the greatest degree of intervention by the law.[15] It is, therefore, appropriate to begin our discussion of the control of fertility with discussion of this fundamental procedure—prevention of the formation of the zygote.

CONTRACEPTION

9.08 We have seen that there are few moral objections that can be levelled against contraception. Certainly, it is possible that the use of contraceptives increases casual sexual activity but, other than in connection with children (for which, see para 9.11 et seq), we are not, here, concerned with sexual mores. By far the most important feature in the present context, however, is that, while contraception may inhibit the production of a life that might otherwise materialise—an effect which, as we have already noted, is regarded as morally unacceptable by some—it does not involve the *destruction* of human *life* in any of its forms. Problems of a physical nature, however, arise with many forms of contraception which should, therefore, not be undertaken—and, certainly, not imposed—lightly. For these reasons, a short consideration of the complications is essential to the discussion.

9.09 Although oral hormonally based contraception has been greatly refined over the years, there is little doubt that compounds with a high oestrogen content will predispose to intravascular thrombosis[16] and, the risks of any form of hormonal contraceptive are increased when their use is combined with smoking.[17] Although the evidence is ambiguous, the probability is that the risk of venous thrombosis following the use of the newer progestogen pills is rather higher that when using the earlier preparations.[18] This important

---

[14] S Sheldon, 'The regulatory cliff between contraception and abortion: the legal and moral significance of implantation' (2015) J of Med Ethics, first online, doi: 10.1136/medethics-2015-102712.

[15] It is also very difficult to apply to the in vitro situation. See a short and contentious article, J Burn, 'Can a cell have a soul?' (2008) 336 BMJ 1132 which is of main interest for the correspondence it provoked—in particular, D A Jones, 'Missing the meaning' (2008) BMJ, 16 May.

[16] So far as we are aware, contraceptives have been blamed for death in only one reported case litigated on the point: *Coker v Richmond, Twickenham and Roehampton Area Health Authority* [1996] 7 Med LR 58; the action failed on the grounds that the risks had been properly explained—which probably accounts for the dearth of reports. Similarly, an allegation that a second-generation contraceptive was responsible for a tragic case of brain stem stroke, failed on its facts and on the grounds of causation—an association between the drug and the event could not be shown on the balance of probability: *Vadera v Shaw* (1999) 45 BMLR 162, CA. The case, which has considerable significance in relation to statistical evidence, was discussed by R Goldberg, 'The contraceptive pill, negligence and causation: Views on *Vadera v Shaw*' (2000) 8 Med L Rev 316.

[17] Smoking per se is a potent cause of cardiovascular disease in both sexes.

[18] A distinction must be made between venous and arterial thrombosis; the difference is reversed when considering the latter condition. The annual death rate due to idiopathic venous thromboembolism in users of contraceptives in general is of the order of 1:100,000—L Parkin, D C G Skegg, M Wilson, et al., 'Oral contraceptives and fatal pulmonary embolism' (2000) 355 Lancet 2133. The history and issues to the present

issue has, in fact, been subjected to judicial analysis. It was accepted in a major class action,[19] brought on behalf of seven women who had died from thrombotic disease, that the risk from third-generation contraceptives was some 1.7 times that of the earlier preparations; it had, however, been agreed that the action would fail if the increased risk was less than two times and, as a result, *Schering* takes us no further forward. Against this background of 'risk', it must be remembered that, on a worldwide scale, the risk of death associated with pregnancy is several hundred times that of death associated with contraception. We should also mention that 'depot' preparations may cause menstrual disturbances;[20] and a possible association between contraceptive therapy and various forms of cancer is still debated; it is being increasingly agreed that there is no unacceptable added risk.[21]

9.10 The very effective and widely used interceptive methods are also suspect in that, although any such association is certainly not a simple one, they may cause pelvic inflammation and permanent infertility. The formulation of intra-uterine devices (IUDs) has, however, undergone profound change and, in general, IUDs offer rather better protection against pregnancy than do depot hormonal contraceptives.[22] These are, however, mainly aspects of clinical medicine; they are introduced here only to emphasise that non-surgical contraception also has its pitfalls and cannot be *imposed* without forethought.[23]

CONTRACEPTION AND MINORS

9.11 The provision of contraceptives to minors was once a burning issue;[24] the evolution of, particularly, educational policy has now stripped it of its urgency and the historic case of *Gillick*[25] is probably best discussed under 'Consent' (see Chapter 4). Nevertheless, the dilemma confronting the doctor who is consulted by a female minor requesting contraceptive advice and treatment still merits consideration.[26]

---

day are discussed by S Jick, 'Oral Contraceptives and the Risk of Venous Thromboembolism' in M Harrison-Woolrych (ed), *Medicines for Women* (2015), ch 6.

[19] *X, Y, Z and Others* v *Schering Health Care and Others* (2002) 70 BMLR 88. The report contains a mass of statistical detail and is reviewed in D C G Skegg, 'Oral contraceptives, venous thromboembolism, and the courts' (2002) 325 BMJ 504. Thromboembolism has also been in the courts in relation to airline travel: *Deep vein thrombosis and Air Travel Group Litigation, Re* (2004) 76 BMLR 38, CA—causation was not pursued but it would have been interesting to know how many of the 55 claimants were women 'on the pill'.

[20] D R Bromham, 'Contraceptive implants' (1996) 312 BMJ 1555; see *Blyth* v *Bloomsbury Health Authority* [1993] 4 Med LR 151, CA. Insertion and removal also requires expertise.

[21] For a succinct analysis of the whole field, see O Melrik and T M M Farley, 'Risk of cancer and the oral contraceptive pill' (2007) 335 BMJ 621—'The pill is a safe contraceptive method with respect to cancer' at 622. The US National Cancer Institute (2012) provided a very useful factsheet obtainable at http://www.cancer.gov/about-cancer/causes-prevention/risk/hormones/oral-contraceptives-fact-sheet. The simple answer is that, where there is any increased risk, it is slight and may, in fact, be negative.

[22] Note that the Court of Appeal in *Re S (adult patient: sterilisation)* [2001] 3 Fam 15; [2000] 3 WLR 1288 preferred the use of the Mirena coil to sterilisation (see para 9.46).

[23] The case of *A Local Authority* v *A (capacity: contraception)* [2011] 3 All ER 706, [2011] 2 FCR 553 points also to the practical near-impossibility of enforcing long-term contraception.

[24] See generally, National Institute for Health and Care Excellence (NICE), *Guidelines: Contraceptive services with a focus on young people up to the age of 25* (2014): https://www.nice.org.uk/guidance/ph51.

[25] *Gillick* v *West Norfolk and Wisbech Area Health Authority* [1984] QB 581; [1984] 1 All ER 365; on appeal [1986] AC 112; [1985] 1 All ER 830, CA; revsd [1986] AC 112; [1985] 3 All ER 402, HL.

[26] For some interesting insights from Ireland, see H Cronin, E Duggan, C O'Tuathaigh, and K Doran, 'Attitudes of general practitioners to prescribing contraception to minors – a medico-legal review' (2013) 19(1) Medico-legal J of Ireland 28.

9.12 The practical problem lies in deciding whether the physician should do anything which might facilitate her engaging in sexual activity. If the patient is, say, aged 14 or 15, he or she may well be of the view that that is too young an age for sexual intercourse. This disapproval may rightly be based on the view that sexual activity at such an age may lead to emotional trauma and, more obviously, a risk of disease. On the other hand, a refusal to prescribe contraceptives may ultimately be more damaging to the patient in that sexual activity may result in pregnancy—and giving birth to a child or abortion at such an age are likely to be severely disruptive of the patient's life.[27] Aside from such 'social' considerations, a decision to provide contraception to a minor poses a number of ethical and legal dilemmas for the doctor, including whether he or she can proceed without the consent of the parents (which we discuss in Chapter 4), the nature and extent of his or her obligation of confidence to the minor (which we explore in Chapter 6), and whether he or she attracts any criminal liability as being a party to an offence of sexual intercourse with a minor.

9.13 All these issues were considered in *Gillick*, a controversial case that resulted from the publication of a circular by the Department of Health stating that practitioners could, in strictly limited circumstances, discuss and apply family planning measures to minors without the express consent of their parents; Mrs Gillick sought, inter alia, to have the instruction declared unlawful. In the absence of any binding authority, the trial judge relied heavily on the common law and on the Canadian case of *Johnston*[28] and concluded that a person below the age of 16 was capable of consent to contraceptive therapy provided she was of sufficient mental maturity to understand the implications. The Court of Appeal, however, concentrated on the duties and rights of parents, which it considered to be inseparable. The trial judge's decision was overturned unanimously. The Authority then appealed to the House of Lords which reverted to what might be loosely termed the 'mature minor' principle—and has come to be known as '*Gillick* competence'—and decided against Mrs Gillick by a majority of 3:2.

9.14 We have already discussed *Gillick* in Chapters 4 and 6. Here we need only recall the overall tenor of the judgment as expressed by Lord Scarman:

> If the law should impose upon the process of growing up fixed limits where nature knew only a continuous process, the price would be artificiality and a lack of realism in an area where the law must be sensitive to human development and social change.[29]

9.15 This interpretation has materialised—social mores have altered and *Gillick* represents the law now even more firmly than it did 25 years ago.

At the same time, Lord Fraser laid down his delphic 'five points' in which he said that the doctor would be justified in proceeding with contraceptive advice without the parents' consent or even knowledge provided that he or she was satisfied that:

   (i) the girl would, although under 16, understand the advice;

   (ii) she could not be persuaded to inform her parents or to allow the doctor to inform the parents that she was seeking contraceptive advice;

   (iii) she was very likely to have sexual intercourse with or without contraceptive treatment;

---

[27] The pregnancy rate for women aged 15–17 was reported in February 2015 to be 24.5 conceptions per thousand as of 2013, down 13 per cent from the rates the previous year. In fact, the teenage pregnancy rate is now at its lowest level since 1969, when records began. Figures: Official for National Statistics—http://www.ons.gov.uk/ons/index.html.

[28] *Johnston* v *Wellesley Hospital* (1970) 17 DLR (3d) 139.   [29] [1985] 3 All ER 402 at 421.

(iv) unless she received contraceptive advice or treatment her physical or mental health or both were likely to suffer; and

(v) her best interests required the doctor to give her contraceptive advice, treatment, or both without parental consent.[30]

9.16 Lord Fraser emphasised that the judgment was not to be regarded as a licence for doctors to disregard the wishes of parents whenever they found it convenient to do so and he pointed out that any doctor who behaved in such a way would be failing to discharge his professional responsibilities and would be expected to be disciplined by his own professional body accordingly.[31] The medical response to the House of Lords' decision in *Gillick* was, in fact, generally one of relief and the guidelines of the General Medical Council (GMC) now state that the doctor who considers that the patient lacks capacity to give consent to treatment or disclosure, and who has failed to persuade the patient to allow the involvement of an appropriate third party, may disclose relevant information to an appropriate person or authority if it is essential to do so in the patient's medical interests. This, however, is subject to the incapax having been told of the intention.[32] It is fair to say, then, that Lord Fraser's guidance is still the template for good medical practice.[33]

9.17 The narrowness of the decision in *Gillick* cannot be overlooked—it is noteworthy that, on a simple head count, more judges supported the complainer than opposed her throughout the legal process. But, then, neither can the fact that a new generation has matured since *Gillick* was decided. One has only got to compare the lengthy arguments in *Gillick* with the almost summary dismissal of Ms Axon's application[34] to appreciate the effects of time and custom. It is now fair to say that the sexual connotations of *Gillick* can be relegated to history. The lasting importance of the case is that, by extrapolation, it changed the entire face of adolescent medical treatment in which contraception plays but a minor role.

CONTRAGESTATION

9.18 Certain types of contraception are designed to—or, in practice, do—work after the embryo has formed. They are commonly referred to as interceptive methods or as emergency contraception although this is false nomenclature as conception has already occurred.[35] For this reason alone, there are good reasons for treating them as separate entities and, as we have already pointed out, there are even stronger moral and legal reasons for so doing. We, therefore, think it preferable to speak in terms of contragestational methods of fertility control, the prime examples being the so-called 'morning after' pill[36] and the IUD when it is used for this specific purpose rather than as a barrier. Such methods are,

---

[30] [1985] 3 All ER 402, 413.

[31] The collateral question of the doctor's criminal liability in giving advice on sexual matters to young girls is now settled by the Sexual Offences Act 2003, s 73 whereby a person is not guilty of aiding or abetting childhood sexual activity if, inter alia, the advice given is for the purpose of preventing the girl becoming pregnant.

[32] GMC, *0–18 years: Guidance for all Doctors* (2007) paras 64–9.

[33] For discussion, see R Taylor, 'Reversing the retreat from *Gillick*? *R (Axon)* v *Secretary of State for Health*' (2007) 19 CFLQ 81.

[34] For which, see para 9.121.

[35] Nevertheless, the terminology is in general use and will be well understood.

[36] It has been pointed out that the term 'morning after' implies a spurious sense of urgency; in fact, emergency hormonal contraception need only be instituted within 72 hours of sexual intercourse and there is evidence that this is an over-cautious estimate: A M C Webb, 'Emergency contraception' (2003) 326 BMJ 775.

essentially, designed to prevent the implantation and subsequent development of the embryo and the question arises as to whether they offend against the Offences Against the Person Act 1861 which, as we will see (para 9.59) criminalises the procurement of a miscarriage of a woman.

9.19 The greater part of the relevant discussion, therefore, turns on the interpretation of the word 'miscarriage' and whether this relates only to the *displacement* of the already implanted embryo. For our part, we find it illogical to suggest that there can be miscarriage in the absence of true carriage. In any event, the issue has now been put beyond doubt. It is currently legal for a pharmacist to dispense 'emergency contraception' without a doctor's prescription[37] and an application for judicial review of the relevant order has been dismissed on the grounds that we have outlined earlier—interceptive methods of control of pregnancy, it was said, are plainly excluded from the operation of the 1861 Act.[38]

9.20 A clear legal—and, possibly, moral[39]—distinction is, however, to be made between interception and the use of displanting methods that are specifically designed to displace the implanted embryo—the technique that is euphemistically termed 'menstrual extraction' is a common example of the latter while an IUD may also be used for this purpose; its intended function is, essentially, a matter of timing—was the embryo implanted at the time? These techniques are clearly on the same level as 'medical' methods of termination of pregnancy and we return to them later.

STERILISATION

9.21 The aim of sterilisation is to end the patient's reproductive capability. A number of surgical procedures may be used to achieve this. In males, the most common method is vasectomy, in which the vas deferens is cut and tied.[40] Sterilisation in females is usually achieved by division or clipping of the fallopian tubes, which carry the ova between the ovary and the womb.[41] An important feature of both operations from the legal and ethical standpoint is that they are generally intended to be irreversible; although it may be possible to repair the effects of the operation, prospective attempts to allow for reversibility are likely to result in procedures which fail in their primary purpose. Even so, it is generally assumed that a 'sterilisation operation' will bring a basic human function to an end.[42]

---

[37] The Prescription Only Medicine (Human Use) Amendment (No 3) Order 2000 (SI 2000/3231) came into force in January 2001. There is, then, considerable doubt as to whether the pharmacist who refuses to supply the drug is covered by the 'conscience clause' in the Abortion Act 1967—for discussion, see para 9.110.

[38] *R (on the application of Smeaton)* v *Secretary of State for Health and Others* [2002] 2 FLR 146; (2002) 66 BMLR 59. This provides an exhaustive review of the relevant literature at the time. It has, however, been severely criticised by J Keown, '"Morning after" pills, "miscarriage" and muddle' (2005) 25 LS 296, and also receiving mention in J Montgomery, C Jones, and H Biggs, 'Hidden law-making in the province of medical jurisprudence' (2014) 77(3) Modern LR 343.

[39] For which, see V Satkoske and S Parker, 'Emergency contraception policy: How moral commitments affect risk evaluation' (2010) 9 Law Prob Risk 187.

[40] For discussion of the associated issues, R Barton-Hanson, 'Sterilization of men with intellectual disabilities: whose best interests is it anyway?' (2015) Med Law Inter, doi: 10.1177/0968533215592444.

[41] Modern techniques rely on the body's self defences against foreign bodies to seal the tubes: NICE, *Hysteroscopic Sterilisation by Tubal Cannulation and Placement of Intrafallopian Implants* (2009, IPG 315).

[42] Current methods, however, also allow for reversal of vasectomy—a success rate of up to 40 per cent successful pregnancies is claimed.

9.22 Ethical objections to sterilisation usually focus on this aspect of irreversible interference with the ability to reproduce. Those who object on this ground would argue that the individual may later undergo a change of mind and may wish to return to a position which is probably now closed. They would also stress that the decision to sterilise is one which is taken in the midst of subtle social and personal pressures; the likelihood of the decision being entirely free is, thereby, diminished—yet it is one that cannot easily be retracted.[43] The objection of the Catholic Church is more direct. In Catholic teaching, sterilisation is a mutilation of the body which leads to the deprivation of a natural function and which must, therefore, be rejected unless it is carried out for strictly therapeutic purposes—that is, where it is necessary for the physical health of the patient; the performance of a hysterectomy in the treatment of excessive menstrual bleeding, for example, is admissible.[44] Insofar as it is possible to identify a lay consensus on the matter, it is that sterilisation is an acceptable method of contraception provided that the person undergoing the operation is adequately informed of the implications. Very strong objections may be voiced, however, when there is any question as to the reality of the patient's consent and we return to the subject later.[45]

9.23 The legality of contraceptive sterilisation in the UK is now beyond doubt.[46] It is also clear that the decision is personal to the individual concerned—the doctor owes a duty of care to the patient, not to his or her spouse or partner, and it has been held that the courts would never grant an injunction to stop sterilisation or vasectomy.[47] As to the medical attitude to consent, there is no reason to suppose other than that the BMA still regards the routine search for a partner's agreement as being inappropriate—the decision to be sterilised is one for the individual patient.[48]

NON-CONSENSUAL STERILISATION

9.24 If consensual sterilisation raises ethical misgivings, then non-consensual sterilisation can be seen as a minefield of powerful objection. Neither legislatures nor courts can totally disregard the ghost of the eugenic movement which flourished in the first half of the twentieth century and led to legislative measures in several jurisdictions that provided for the sterilisation of mentally handicapped persons, those suffering from certain forms of genetically transmissible diseases, and even criminal recidivists.[49] Eugenics on a

---

[43] See an excellent letter: E Tuddenham, 'Sterilise in haste: Repent at leisure and at great expense' (2000) 321 BMJ 962.

[44] On a world scale, the attitude of orthodox Islam is just as rigid: D A R Verkuyl, 'Two world religions and family planning' (1993) 342 Lancet 473.

[45] See paras 9.24 et seq.

[46] Many jurisdictions impose a legal age limit. The situation in the UK would be governed by the general rules as to consent (see Chapter 4). Age would be of particular importance depending on whether the operation was regarded as medical treatment or a medical procedure (see para 4.59 et seq).

[47] *Paton v British Pregnancy Advisory Service Trustees* [1979] QB 276 at 280; [1978] 2 All ER 987 at 990, per Sir George Baker P.

[48] BMA Ethics Department, *Medical Ethics Today* (3rd edn, 2012) p 278.

[49] Some 12,500 operations were performed in the USA between 1907 and 1963: Annotation 'Validity of statutes authorizing asexualization or sterilization of criminals or mental defectives' 53 ALR 3d 960 (1973). Comparative later developments in Europe are discussed by A N Sofair and J C Kaldjian, 'Eugenic sterilization and a qualified Nazi analogy: The United States and Germany, 1930–1945' (2000) 132 Ann Intern Med 312. And shades remain—see, e.g., in the Czech Republic, K Krosnar, 'Roma women were unlawfully sterilised' (2006) 332 BMJ 138, although there may have been a reputable medical basis for some of the cases reported.

national scale can, however, now be relegated to history and we are concerned here only with the management of individual cases.[50]

9.25 The root problem of non-consensual sterilisation lies in the fact that it raises starkly the subject of what has been named the basic human right to reproduce—to which we return for general discussion later.[51] The phrase seems to have originated in the US case of *Skinner* v *Oklahoma*[52]—which, in fact, concerned the punitive sterilisation of a man— and has, since, come into common usage throughout the English-speaking world. In the UK, the concept was first articulated in the very significant case *Re D (a minor)*.[53] The minor in this case was an 11-year-old girl who suffered from a rare condition known as Sotos syndrome. Her IQ was roughly 80, a rating which need not necessarily make it impossible for the person in question to cope reasonably well in everyday life or even to marry and raise a child.

9.26 Heilbron J summarised her judgment in this case:

> A review of the whole of the evidence leads me to the conclusion that in a case of a child of 11 years of age, where the evidence shows that her mental and physical condition and attainments have already improved, and where her future prospects are as yet unpredict- able, where the evidence also shows that she is unable as yet to understand and appreciate the implications of this operation and could not give valid or informed consent, that the likelihood is that in later years she will be able to make her own choice, where, I believe, the frustration and resentment of realising (as she would one day) what happened could be devastating, an operation of this nature is, in my view contra-indicated.[54]

9.27 Heilbron J assumed that there was a 'basic human right of a woman to reproduce' and concluded that it would be a violation of that right if a girl were sterilised without her consent for non-therapeutic reasons. *Re D* then remained the English authority for more than a decade and was quoted with approval in the Canadian case of *Re Eve*.[55] *Eve* remains an important case to study because it was exceptionally well argued and, by the time the trial had gone through all its stages, virtually every variant view had been aired and sup- ported in the judgments.

9.28 Eve was a mentally disabled adult whose mother asked that she be sterilised, a major plank supporting the request being that, in the event of Eve becoming pregnant, neither she nor her mother would be able to care for the baby. The Supreme Court was in no doubts as to its having a *parens patriae* jurisdiction through which to authorise sterilisa- tion should the need arise. That power was, however, limited by the principle of its being exercised in the best interests of the girl. In the light of this, the judgment was deeply con- cerned to distinguish between therapeutic and non-therapeutic reasons for sterilisation. La Forest J concluded:

> The grave intrusion on a person's rights and the certain physical damage that ensues from non-therapeutic sterilization without consent ... have persuaded me that it can never

---

[50] The result of a long line of early decisions in the USA can be summarised by *Re Hayes* 608 P 2d 635 (Wash, 1980) in which it was laid down that the courts could authorise sterilisation in the absence of consent so long as, inter alia, the subject was incapable of forming a judgement, was physically capable of procrea- tion, was likely to engage in sexual activity, and there was no reasonable alternative to sterilisation. In the recent unreported Texas case involving Ms Salazar (child abuse) the judge said he was unable to order steri- lisation; interestingly, however, he could impose a ban on pregnancy as a condition of probation: see K Brady, 'Some people just shouldn't have kids!' (2010) 16 Tex Wesleyan L Rev 225.

[51] See para 9.34 et seq.   [52] 316 US 535 (1942).   [53] [1976] Fam 185; [1976] 1 All ER 326.
[54] [1976] Fam 185 at 196; [1976] 1 All ER 326 at 335.   [55] (1986) 31 DLR (4th) 1.

safely be determined that such a procedure is in the best interests of that person ... [I conclude that non-therapeutic sterilization] should never be authorised ... under the *parens patriae* jurisdiction.[56]

He appreciated that there could be difficulty in drawing a line between a therapeutic and a non-therapeutic operation, but was content to emphasise that, 'the utmost caution must be exercised commensurate with the severity of the procedure'. In essence, it was this problem which provoked the apparent conflict between the court in *Eve* and that involved in the comparable English case of *Re B*,[57] which was the first of its kind to reach the then House of Lords.

9.29 It is unfortunate from the comparative aspect that *Re B* concerned a girl aged 17—she would shortly have passed out of the wardship jurisdiction and it was agreed that the *parens patriae* authority no longer applied in England to an adult.[58] A speedy decision was, thus, dictated, and there is no doubt that Lord Hailsham LC, on it being suggested that the girl's progress could well be observed for a year, laid open his defences when he said, 'We shall be no wiser in twelve months than we are now'.[59]

9.30 B was a mentally disabled epileptic with a mental age of five to six years. She had never conceived and was not pregnant but, absent being fully institutionalised, she was in danger of becoming so. Medical opinion—which, in contrast to that given in *Re D*,[60] was scarcely challenged—was that she would either have to be maintained on hormonal contraceptives for the rest of her reproductive life or her fallopian tubes could be occluded—and the court accepted this as being an irreversible procedure; it was common ground that any pregnancy that occurred would have to be terminated.

9.31 In authorising sterilisation, the House of Lords upheld the decisions of both the court of first instance and the Court of Appeal. The basic principle involved was the welfare of the girl; Lord Oliver, in particular, emphasised that there was no question of a eugenic motive, no consideration was paid to the convenience of those caring for the ward and no general principle of public policy was involved. Lord Hailsham LC made some specific comments aimed, in the main, at explaining any apparent variances from other relevant decisions. With particular reference to *Eve*, he said:

> [The] conclusion that the procedure of sterilisation should 'never be considered for non-therapeutic purposes' is totally unconvincing and in startling contradiction to the welfare principle ... [The] distinction [drawn] between 'therapeutic' and 'non-therapeutic' purposes of this operation in relation to the facts of the present case ... [is] irrelevant...[61]

Lord Oliver also found, in effect, that there was no logic in distinguishing prophylaxis from therapy when both were directed to the ward's interest and we would certainly agree with this. It is, however, possible to argue that 'non-therapeutic' in terms of La Forest J's

---

[56] The extant case at the time, *Re K and Public Trustee* (1985) 19 DLR (4th) 255, in which the main therapeutic ground for sterilisation was a phobic aversion to blood which would be accentuated with the onset of the menses, was regarded as 'at best, dangerously close to the limits of the permissible'—this despite the fact that an Appeal Court judge in *Re K* thought that the case should never have come to the court (per Anderson JA at 277). See also the later New Zealand case *Re X* [1991] 2 NZLR 365.

[57] *Re B (a minor) (wardship: sterilisation)* [1988] AC 199; [1987] 2 All ER 206, HL.

[58] See G T Laurie, '*Parens patriae* jurisdiction in the medico-legal context: The vagaries of judicial activism' (1999) 3 Edin LR 96.

[59] [1987] 2 All ER 206 at 212.   [60] N 53.   [61] *Re B* [1987] 2 All ER 206 at 213.

judgment in *Eve* referred only to treatment designed for the benefit of others. If this be so, *Eve* and *Re B* are not greatly in conflict.[62]

9.32 The *Re B* decision was widely criticised in the British academic literature.[63] We wonder, however, whether sufficient attention was paid to the *medical* aspects of the case. There is no doubt that pregnancy *is* contraindicated in some mentally disabled patients or that B was one of them—medically speaking, *Re B* and *Re D* appear to be poles apart. We suggest that the major conceptual difference between *Eve* and *Re B* is that the former generalises on the basis of principle, whereas the latter is determined to particularise on the facts—and we see no objection to the latter line of thinking so long as its pragmatic nature is recognised and its limited scope as a precedent accepted.[64]

9.33 Lord Hailsham, however, also addressed the question of rights[65] and it is this issue that so occupied the commentators at the time. He said:

> The right [of a woman to reproduce] is only such when reproduction is the result of informed choice of which the ward in the present case is incapable[66]

and, again:

> To talk of the 'basic right' to reproduce of an individual who is not capable of knowing the causal connection between intercourse and childbirth ... [or who] is unable to form any maternal instincts or to care for a child, appears to me wholly to part company with reality.[67]

9.34 The concept of a right to reproduce is one which deserves discussion in depth but which, again, we cannot provide in the space available. Put simplistically, it is not easy to envisage a right that requires the cooperation of another person who is under no obligation to provide it; moreover, an absolute right to reproduce would entail access by right to all means of assisted reproduction including surrogate motherhood by way of womb-leasing—and this is clearly untenable.[68] Grubb and Pearl[69] argued very convincingly that the only such right currently recognised in English law is the right to choose whether or not to reproduce—this being grounded in the principle of individual autonomy.[70] Even so, this begs the question as to the rights of a subject who is unable to make a rational choice.

9.35 An alternative approach is to regard the 'right' as one to retain the capacity to reproduce. Although, as has already been pointed out, the proposition has not been tested, such a right, in addition to being directly addressed in Art 12, could well be subsumed within

[62] K McK Norrie, 'Sterilisation of the mentally disabled in English and Canadian law' (1989) 38 Int & Comp LQ 387.

[63] See e.g. S P de Cruz, 'Sterilization, wardship and human rights' (1988) 18 Fam Law 6; R Lee and D Morgan, 'Sterilisation and mental handicap: Sapping the strength of the state?' (1988) 15 J Law & Soc 229; J Montgomery, 'Rhetoric and "welfare"' (1989) 9 OJLS 395—a particularly trenchant attack.

[64] We discuss this matter in general in J K Mason, 'Particularity in medical law' in Z Bankowski and J MacLean (eds), *The Universal and the Particular in Legal Reasoning* (2006).

[65] The problem of rights under the Human Rights Act 1998, Sch 1 may yet arise: see E Jackson, *Regulating Reproduction* (2001) p 57.

[66] [1987] 2 All ER 206 at 213.

[67] [1987] 2 All ER 206, 213. But, for an opposing opinion, albeit at first instance, see *A Local Authority*, n 114.

[68] Per Hale LJ in *Briody v St Helens and Knowsley Area Health Authority* [2002] 2 WLR 394 at 404–5; [2001] 2 FLR 1094 at 1104.

[69] A Grubb and D Pearl, 'Sterilisation and the courts' (1987) 46 CLJ 439. See also Nicholson CJ in the Australian case *Re Jane* (1989) FLC 92–007. The reasoning in this case was very similar to that in *Re B*.

[70] Reproductive autonomy has been re-examined extensively by E Jackson, n 65, esp ch 1.

Art 8 of the Human Rights Act 1998, Sch 1. Any court interference with that right would, then, have to be justified under Art 8(2). How far this could be stretched depends, in our view, upon the definition of reproduction which, surely, cannot be limited and impersonalised to the single aspect of giving birth it must include an element of after-care. Some mentally disabled persons may not be able to supply this, although some can—it is, again, a question of degree and a matter of the individual medical status.[71] The practical significance of this definition reaches it apogee when, as in *Re B*, it is acknowledged that any pregnancy would have to be followed by therapeutic abortion.

9.36 A further, and final, criticism of *Re B* has been based on the suggestion that it, and others like it, are sex discriminatory—'Would the court,' asked Freeman,[72] 'have sterilised a boy of 17?' The answer is certainly, 'No'—and has been shown later to be so[73]—but this only proves the rule.[74] Unfair it may be, but it is a fact of life that reproduction can have no immediately adverse medical effect on a man. There is only one recent case of non-therapeutic sterilisation of a man that we discuss at para 9.54. This does little to detract from the fact that the burden of sterilisation falls squarely on women.

9.37 Two very similar and, in their way, instructive, wardship cases were reported shortly after *Re B*.[75] In both, sterilisation was approved at first instance and neither was appealed. Significantly, however, medical evidence was given at both hearings to the effect that the proposed operation was reversible[76]—in up to 75 per cent of cases, according to the gynaecologists in *Re M* who, in disclaiming the emotive overtones of 'sterilisation', preferred to regard the operation as contraceptive in nature. We suspect that this greatly influenced the judges because the evidence in favour of early sterilisation was less than fully agreed in both cases. Perhaps the most interesting feature of both *Re M* and *Re P* is that they can well be regarded as exemplars of sterilisations which were authorised on social grounds for the benefit of the wards—a matter of protecting their lifestyles—with a strong hint of regard for the benefit of their carers; the decisions were certainly open to criticism.

9.38 Thus far, we have been dealing only with minors concerning whom there was no doubt, at the time, of the courts' authority under the wardship jurisdiction. The problem of the adult who was incapable of consent to treatment was yet to come and was first addressed by Wood J in *T v T*,[77] a case which involved an adult incompetent who was found to be pregnant; medical opinion was consistent that the pregnancy should be terminated under the terms of the Abortion Act 1967 and there was an additional application from the subject's mother for leave to sterilise her at the time of the termination. In the course of a wide-ranging determination, which had to be made in the absence of precedent, Wood J fell back on the expedient of an anticipatory declaration that the performance of the two operations would not be unlawful[78]—a solution which was later approved in the House of Lords in the important case of *Re F*.[79]

---

[71] See L Appleby and C Dickens, 'Mothering skills of women with mental illness' (1993) 306 BMJ 348.

[72] (1987) LSGazR 949.

[73] *Re A (medical treatment: male sterilisation)* [2000] 1 FLR 549; (2000) 53 BMLR 66; [2000] Lloyd's Rep Med 87. This is an odd decision as males with Down's syndrome are characteristically sterile.

[74] But see *An NHS Trust v DE* [2013] 3 FCR 343; [2013] Med LR 446; (2013) 133 BMLR 123.

[75] *Re M (a minor) (wardship: sterilisation)* [1988] 2 FLR 497; [1988] Fam Law 434; *Re P (a minor) (wardship: sterilisation)* [1989] 1 FLR 182; [1989] Fam Law 102.

[76] It was said, in somewhat unusual phraseology: 'The situation to-day is that the operation is not irreversible although it is the current *ethical* practice to tell the patients that it is an irreversible operation' (emphasis added; per Eastham J, *Re P* [1989] 1 FLR 182 at 189).

[77] [1988] Fam 52; [1988] 1 All ER 613.   [78] RSC Ord 15, r 16.

[79] *Re F (mental patient: sterilisation)* [1990] 2 AC 1, sub nom *F v West Berkshire Health Authority* [1989] 2 All ER 545.

9.39 In the end, *Re F* was concerned very largely with court procedure. Nevertheless, it forms the basis for the 'best interests' test which is now such an integral part of British medical jurisprudence; even if only for this reason, it still merits attention. The conditions of *Re B* were, effectively, replicated save that F was now beyond the protection of wardship. The lower courts tended to justify the operation on somewhat negative grounds—for instance, that treatments provided in a patient's best interests lay within the exceptions to the law of battery;[80] that there was nothing incongruous in doctors and others who had a caring responsibility being required to act in the interests of an adult who was unable to exercise a right of choice;[81] or that the performance of a necessary, albeit serious, operation, including an operation for sterilisation, on a patient who could not consent would not be a trespass to the person or otherwise unlawful.[82]

9.40 The correctness of the decision to sterilise F was not challenged in the House of Lords, which was, rather, concerned with the resolution of questions of law and of legal procedure. The House, inter alia, confirmed that the *parens patriae* jurisdiction no longer existed in England, and that, if it were to be recreated, it would be for the legislature to do so. Their Lordships also ruled that the procedure by way of declaration was appropriate and satisfactory in cases of this kind, the court having no power to consent to the operation. Indeed, the most important aspect of the decision for our purposes was to establish that the common law does provide that a doctor can lawfully give surgical or medical treatment to adult patients who are incapable of consenting—provided that the operation or other treatment is in their best interests; it would be in their best interests if, but only if, it was carried out in order to save their lives or to ensure improvement, or prevent deterioration, in their physical or mental health.[83] Logically, this authority would also apply to sterilisation but six reasons were given for requiring special conditions for that operation—including its general irreversibility which would almost certainly deprive the woman of 'what was widely, and rightly, regarded as one of the fundamental rights of a woman, the right to bear a child'.[84]

9.41 At the same time, however, the House of Lords held[85] that whether the 'best interests' test had been met would be judged on *Bolam*[86] principles and it seemed at the time that, having made a bid for judicial supervision, the court, in so stating, effectively handed back control of the decisions to the doctors. The matter has, however, now been resolved and, although it is jumping ahead in time, it should be noted here that the current Practice Direction makes it clear that sterilisation of a person who cannot consent to the operation is one of special types of case that will require the prior sanction of a judge in virtually every instance.[87]

---

[80] Per Scott Baker J citing *Collins* v *Wilcock* [1984] 3 All ER 374 at 378; [1984] 1 WLR 1172 at 1177, per Goff LJ. These were devised, in the main, to cover the exigencies of everyday life and Lord Donaldson MR in the Court of Appeal, however, found this a step too far.

[81] [1990] 2 AC 1 at 18, per Lord Donaldson.   [82] [1990] 2 AC 1, 32 per Neill LJ.

[83] Per Lord Brandon [1990] 2 AC 1 at 55. Note that this definition would now be too narrow to satisfy the terms of the Mental Capacity Act 2005, s 4(2)—see para 4.24.

[84] These historic cases now do little more than emphasise how they effectively implanted the 'best interests' or 'welfare' principle as the governance of English law related to non-consensual treatment in adults. It has now been accepted as the cornerstone of the Mental Capacity Act 2005, ss 1(5) and 4 which would include therapeutic sterilisation. We are uncertain if the same applies to Scotland Adults with Incapacity (Scotland) Act 2000—for discussion see para 4.24.

[85] [1990] 2 AC 1, per Lord Bridge at 52, Lord Brandon at 66–8, and Lord Goff at 78.

[86] *Bolam* v *Friern Hospital Management Committee* [1957] 2 All ER 118; [1957] 1 WLR 582.

[87] *Practice Note (Official Solicitor: Declaratory Proceedings: Medical and Welfare Decisions for Adults who Lack Capacity)* [2006] 2 FLR 373; it is to be emphasised that this note deals only with adults. The other

9.42 The precedent set by *Re F* is that, because the details of each case differ, decisions of this
nature will continue to be made on a case-to-case basis and, with that in mind, it is useful
to follow the fate of some of the cases that have been decided since *Re F*. Two cases were
heard in 1992. *Re HG*[88] concerned a girl aged 17 who was an epileptic and who suffered
from an unspecified chromosomal abnormality; there was no dispute that pregnancy
would be disastrous for her and that long-term hormonal contraception was contraindicated. In making the order, the deputy judge said:

> [My conclusion is that] a sufficiently overwhelming case has been established to justify
> interference with the fundamental right of a woman to bear a child. I am certainly satis-
> fied that it would be cruel to expose [her] to an unacceptable risk of pregnancy and that
> that should be obviated by sterilisation in her interests.[89]

The adult patient in *Re W*[90] was also an epileptic who, again, was at small risk of becoming
pregnant. Nevertheless, sterilisation was held to be in her best interests and a declaration
was granted. A feature of the case was the reliance on *Bolam* as a measure of 'best interests'—an aspect that came in for some criticism.[91]

9.43 The Practice Note[92] relevant at the time, however, specifically advised that a declaration in favour of non-consensual sterilisation should be granted only if there was a real
danger rather than a mere chance of pregnancy resulting—and this was reflected in *Re
LC*.[93] *LC* seems to have been the first case since *Re D* in which sterilisation was refused
in the face of medical opinion. The danger to the woman was, however, not so much
that of pregnancy as of sexual assault—and the latter risk was present irrespective of her
fertility. One notable feature was that the care afforded her was exceptional, and this,
of itself, was thought to provide a good ground for not imposing the risks of a surgical
intervention.

9.44 There was, then, a hiatus in reported cases until 1998, when two further cases were heard.
In the first of these,[94] Johnson J found the circumstances to be indistinguishable from
those in *Re LC* in that the risk of pregnancy was speculative rather than real. This aspect of
the case was independent of any 'right to reproduce' which, it was agreed, was irrelevant
in *Re B* terms.[95] The freedom from risk, however, was, again, due to the care expended by
the woman's parents; it is probably this factor which mainly caused the judge to reach his
conclusion and to follow *Re LC* 'with reluctance'. Thus, it seemed that a group of cases

---

situation is the discontinuation of nutrition and hydration of a person in a vegetative state (see Chapter 15).
For Scotland, see Adults with Incapacity (Specified Medical Treatments) (Scotland) Regulations 2002, Sch 1
(SSI 2002/275). Note that the Code of Practice on the Mental Capacity Act 2005 repeats advice that a court
order is to be obtained in all cases of non-therapeutic sterilisation.

[88] *Re HG (specific issue order: sterilisation)* [1993] 1 FLR 587; (1992) 16 BMLR 50. The case is interesting in
that, for financial reasons, the parents sought a specific issue order under the Children Act 1989, s 8. It was
held that this was an appropriate, albeit not ideal, way of proceeding.

[89] *Re HG (specific issue order: sterilisation)* [1993] 1 FLR 587, 592.

[90] *Re W (mental patient: sterilisation)* [1993] 1 FLR 381; [1993] Fam Law 208.

[91] See I Kennedy, 'Commentary' (1993) 1 Med L Rev 234.

[92] *Practice Note (Official Solicitor: Sterilisation)* [1993] 3 All ER 222; [1993] 2 FLR 222.

[93] *Re LC (medical treatment: sterilisation)* [1997] 2 FLR 258; [1997] Fam Law 604 (judgment in the case
was given in October 1993).

[94] *Re S (medical treatment: adult sterilisation)* [1998] 1 FLR 944; [1998] Fam Law 325.

[95] [1988] AC 199; [1987] 2 FLR 314. See dicta of Lord Oliver and Lord Hailsham in that case. Johnson J did
not, however, feel the same way about the House of Lords' somewhat cavalier attitude to the risks of surgical
operation.

were being separated which depended on the immediacy of the risk of pregnancy. This was confirmed from the other side of the coin in *Re X*,[96] in which the woman concerned actually wanted to have a baby—sterilisation was authorised when it was agreed that she would have been incapable of looking after it.

9.45 All the cases thus far discussed have been related to the incompetent person's way of life or, put another way, to her best social interests. At the same time, however, a line of cases was developing which referred to the subject's medical interests. The solution of some such cases will be obvious—clearly, for example, it would not be essential to obtain court approval before undertaking a hysterectomy in the treatment of carcinoma of the uterus despite the fact that the patient would be rendered infertile as a secondary effect.[97] Difficulty arises when the disability is associated with menstrual excess—a very real problem in the case of the incompetent who may well be confused and disturbed even by normal periods. Sterilisation is, however, a high price to pay for treating what may well have been, in ordinary circumstances, a comparatively simple menstrual disorder or, even, no more than a 'phobia'. In the first such case to come before the British courts, *Re E*,[98] concerning a 17-year-old, Sir Stephen Brown held that no formal consent of the court was necessary and that the parents were in a position to give a valid consent: 'A clear distinction is to be made between an operation to be performed for a genuine therapeutic reason and one to achieve sterilisation.'[99] Sir Stephen's easy assurance in the face of the difficulties encountered in Australia[100] is a little difficult to accept. Nevertheless, in a second case, *Re GF*,[101] which concerned a 29-year-old woman, the President confirmed his opinion and declined to grant a declaration of lawfulness on the grounds that it was unnecessary to do so when an operation was designed to improve the health of the patient. He did, however, lay down the conditions under which no application to the court was needed. These were that two doctors agreed: first, that the operation was necessary for therapeutic purposes; second, that it was in the patient's best interests; and, third, that no practicable less intrusive treatment was available.[102]

9.46 It was this last condition that brought a third significant case to the Family Court—that of *Re Z*,[103] which involved a 19-year-old woman with Down's syndrome. There was essentially no dispute as to the facts that Z suffered from painful and excessive periods and that a pregnancy would be disastrous; however, the experts disagreed as to how these conditions were to be managed—was it to be by way of the insertion of a Mirena IUD (see para

---

[96] *Re X (adult patient: sterilisation)* [1998] 2 FLR 1124; [1998] Fam Law 737.

[97] But circumstances may make it highly desirable to do so. For an illustrative decision, see *DH NHS Foundation Trust* v *PS* (2010) 116 BMLR 142 (carcinoma of the uterus—the special condition being the potential use of force).

[98] *Re E (a minor) (medical treatment)* [1991] 2 FLR 585; (1992) 7 BMLR 117.

[99] (1992) 7 BMLR 117 at 119.

[100] Where the 'menstrual case' has been especially well considered. See, in particular, *Secretary, Department of Health and Community Services (NT)* v *JW Band SMB (Marion's case)* (1992) 175 CLR 218; (1992) 66 ALJR 300. The case was thoroughly explored by N Cica, 'Sterilising the intellectually disabled' (1993) 1 Med L Rev 186. For following cases, see *Re L and M (Sarah's case)* (1993) 17 Fam LR 357 and *P* v *P* (1994) 19 Fam LR 1.

[101] [1992] 1 FLR 293; [1993] 4 Med LR 77, sub nom *F* v *F* (1992) 7 BMLR 135.

[102] Now, it would be necessary to comply with the rigid conditions of the Mental Capacity Act 2005, ss 3, 4, and 5.

[103] *Re Z (medical treatment: hysterectomy)* [2000] 1 FLR 523; (1999) 53 BMLR 53.

9.10) or by hysterectomy? Bennett J, relying on Lord Goff in *Re F*,[104] clarified the position of experts vis-à-vis the court:

> Experts are what they are—experts. They must be listened to with respect, but their opinions must be weighed and judged by the court.[105]

In the end, Bennett J concluded that Z's best interests were served by hysterectomy, the risks of which were offset by the certainty that it would eliminate her periods and would, at the same time, protect her totally from pregnancy; the use of a coil was unacceptably uncertain on both counts.

9.47   The problem of treatment of menstrual 'phobias' has also arisen in Scotland, where it provided a part basis for the first reported case in which sterilisation of an incapax was opposed. In *L, Petitioner*,[106] it was held in the Outer House of the Court of Session that sterilisation of an autistic woman would not be justified only as a way of avoiding pregnancy—other methods of contraception were available although, as we have discussed earlier at paras 9.09 et seq, these had their inbuilt risks. The fact that these would not prevent menstruation, with which she was unable to cope, tipped the balance in favour of sterilisation by way of partial hysterectomy.[107]

9.48   Clearly, then, much will depend on the courts' attitudes to menorrhagia—does it or does it not constitute a disability medical condition which merits treatment in the patient's 'best interests' sufficient to trump the preservation of her reproductive 'rights'? The dilemma was well illustrated in England by the stormy conditions evidenced in *Re S*[108]—the first relevant case to reach the Court of Appeal since *Re F*. Here, the conditions and the problems were very similar to those in *Re Z*, including the fact that alternative methods of treatment were available and had been advocated. Wall J, at first instance, regarded S's menstrual problems as the most important issue and followed Bennett J in *Re Z* in concluding that S's best interests lay in a subtotal hysterectomy rather than in the insertion of a coil—a procedure which, of itself, did not require court approval. Having declared the hysterectomy to be lawful, he then adopted the rather innovative strategy of leaving the choice of treatments to S's mother and her medical advisers in consultation.

9.49   In the event, the Court of Appeal was highly, and perhaps unfairly, critical of this decision, pointing out that the judge had run contrary to unanimous medical opinion; the declaration in favour of hysterectomy was reversed in favour of the insertion of a coil with the option of a further hearing should this not prove an effective remedy. The details of the individual case are not, however, as important as are the wider implications as to the relationship between the *Bolam* test[109] and the 'best interests' test. As Thorpe LJ put it: 'There can be no doubt that the speeches in *Re F* determine that the *Bolam* test is relevant to the judgment of the adult patient's best interests when a dispute arises as to the advisability of medical treatment.' There can, however, be a number of courses which might be followed by responsible doctors; the function of the *Bolam* test is, therefore, of a

---

[104] [1990] 2 AC 1 at 80.   [105] (2000) 53 BMLR 53 at 64.
[106] 1996 SCLR 538. Other, unopposed, sterilisation applications had been granted: A Ward, 'Tutors to adults: Developments' 1992 SLT 325.
[107] It is to be noted that sterilisation of an incapax in Scotland is now statutorily subject to the approval of the Court of Session other than when there is disease of the reproductive organs: Adults with Incapacity (Specified Medical Treatments) (Scotland) Regulations 2002, Sch 1 (SSI 2002/275).
[108] *In re S (adult patient: sterilisation)* [2000] 1 FLR 465; [2000] Fam Law 322; revsd [2001] 3 Fam 15; [2000] 3 WLR 1288.
[109] N 86.

preliminary nature, doing no more than to establish the propriety of the options on offer. By contrast, there can be only one '*best* interest'—and it is the function of the doctor or of the court to establish this as the paramount precondition to providing treatment for the incompetent. Moreover, the welfare of the patient will be decided on more than medical grounds—ethical, social, moral, and welfare considerations must also be weighed in the balance.[110] The *Bolam* test, thus, has no place in the second or determinative phase of what is, effectively, a two-stage test for the lawfulness of non-voluntary treatment. It will have been seen in Chapter 5 that *Bolam* has come under increasing attack as a modern legal principle, most recently by the Supreme Court in *Montgomery* v *Lanarkshire Health Board*;[111] in our view, *Re S* provides a particularly strong barrier to any extension of its application. A final and important comment on *Re S* is to note that the Court of Appeal was unanimous in holding that any interpretation of Sir Stephen Brown's ruling on the need for involvement of the courts in cases such as these[112] 'should incline towards the strict and avoid the liberal'—a form of words which carries a ring of euphemism!

9.50 However, one of the most significant features to be extracted from the cases throughout the Anglophone jurisdictions is their pragmatic acceptance that non-therapeutic or social considerations—which we are happy to see as aspects of preventive or holistic medicine—can properly be prayed in aid of the incompetent, whether she be an adult or a minor. The words of Pashman J in the influential US case of *Grady* provide a suitable coda to the discussion:

> [She] should have the opportunity to lead a life as rewarding as her condition will permit. Courts should cautiously but resolutely help her achieve the fullness of that opportunity. If she can have a richer and more active life, only if the risk of pregnancy is permanently eliminated, then sterilisation may be in her best interests [and] it should not be denied to her.[113]

And it is surprising how often this is forgotten.

9.51 Contraception and sterilisation sit on the same spectrum of interference with reproductive capacity, albeit with one self-evidently far closer to an extreme than the other. Often, however, both options can be in play and sometimes favoured differently by different parties for different reasons. This was the case in *A Local Authority* v *K*[114] which involved a 21-year-old woman with Down's syndrome and learning difficulties (K). Her parents sought medical advice to support their wish that she be sterilised in her own best interests. Her case came to the attention of a Matron for Safeguarding Vulnerable Adults, who sought further medical advice that contraception through the fitting of a coil was the preferable, least restrictive, course of action and so more in line with the woman's best interests. A best interest meeting took place with the Local Authority and all of the parties, and the conclusion was that non-therapeutic sterilisation was not in K's best interests; notwithstanding, the parents then threatened to take K abroad. The instant action was raised by the Local Authority for a declaration on the matter, once the parents gave an undertaking not to remove their daughter from the jurisdiction. To begin, the court relied on *A (Capacity: Refusal of Contraception)*[115] to determine the threshold criteria on the question

---

[110] Per Butler-Sloss P at 3 WLR 1288, 1296. The President also noted that she had expressed similar views in *Re A*, n 73.

[111] [2015] UKSC 11.   [112] N 108.

[113] *In the matter of Lee Ann Grady* 426 A 2d 467 (NJ, 1981) at 486.

[114] [2013] EWHC 242 (COP); [2014] 1 FCR 209; (2013) 130 BMLR 195.

[115] [2010] EWHC 1549 (Fam), [2011] Fam 61.

of K's capacity to take decisions by herself in such matters. Applying the criteria from that case[116] relating to contraception, it was determined that she did not have capacity and therefore the best interest test fell to be considered. The court then took the opportunity to reiterate its role and the appropriate approach in such difficult cases. In stressing the serious nature of non-therapeutic sterilisation, the court reminded the parties of the need for court approval in all such applications (Court of Protection), and for the importance of prior consultation with the Official Solicitor's department. In addition to further procedural safeguards, the court stressed the importance of least restrictive approach as a matter of human right: was sterilisation a necessary and proportionate interference? As to best interests, the court tried to strike a balance between protection and empowerment, and after considering the nature, risks and consequences of both procedures, concluded that sterilisation in this case would be a disproportionate step at the time to achieve contraception for K. It would be lawful to attempt less restrictive methods of contraception than sterilisation.

9.52 We can contrast this ruling with *Mental Health Trust* v *DD*[117] in which sterilisation was preferred over other forms of contraception and justified in the person's own best interests. The case related to D, a 36-year-old woman with Autistic Spectrum Disorder and an IQ of 70. She had six children, aged between six months and 12 years, none of whom had any continuing contact with their mother. D was in a long-term loving and sexual relationship with BC, who had an IQ of 62. This ruling was the culmination of a series of hearing about D's circumstances relating to her sixth pregnancy, and involving questions of her capacity for the use of short-term contraception before, at, and post-delivery of her child. Matters had clearly reached a head, and the court here was concerned, primarily, with D's capacity for to take decisions on long-term contraception/non-therapeutic sterilisation, and the nature of best interests if capacity was found to be lacking. On this very point, the court followed unanimous medical opinion that D lacked capacity both with respect to contraception (following the case of *A* above[118]), and the more serious intervention of sterilisation. The ruling is a good illustration of the careful judicial application of the specific terms of the Mental Capacity Act 2005 to the particular circumstances of a vulnerable person (paras 48–80). As to best interests in this case, the court immediately acknowledged that any proposed intervention would interfere with D's Art 8(1) rights, and so could only be justified in terms of Art 8(2) as necessary and proportionate. Thus— as a matter of broad legal approach—this perfectly mirrors *A Local Authority* v *K*. On the facts, however, the conclusion was radically different. A central concern was the risk of future pregnancies in two senses: first, that D would have yet more children for whom she could not care, but more importantly, that further pregnancies would themselves pose serious risks, including uterine rupture, placenta previa, and a thrombotic event, all of which led the Official Solicitor to suggest a risk of about 70 per cent of a life-threatening event. Against this, the court was cognisant of its statutory duty (s 1(6) of the 2005 Act) to have 'regard' to the less restrictive intervention with respect to impact on a person's rights and freedoms. In doing so, Mr Justice Cobb acknowledged that sterilisation was by no means the least restrictive medical measure, but that best interests admit a wider set

---

[116] These include the ability to weigh up the following factors: (i) the reason for contraception and what it did; (ii) the types of contraception available and their uses; (iii) the advantages and disadvantages of each type; (iv) possible side effects; (v) how easily each type could be changed; and (vi) the generally accepted effectiveness of each type.

[117] For discussion and a comparison with the position in Scotland, see H Gomersall, 'Show some restraint' (2015) 118(Jul) PS 20.

[118] N 114.

of consideration. In particular, he opined that sterilisation would free D from repeated examinations and interventions that would necessarily accompany the use of a contraception coil. And, in a thorough execution of the balance sheet approach that listed the pros and cons of each possible intervention, the ultimate conclusion was that sterilisation was in D's best interests, assisted by 'two factors of "magnetic" importance':

(i) Future pregnancy poses such a high risk to DD's life that the option which most effectively reduces the prospects of this should be preferred; this is one of those exceptional cases where medical necessity justifies the considerable interference.

(ii) Sterilisation is the treatment which most closely coincides with DD's dominant wishes and feelings to be left alone to enjoy a 'normal' life free from intrusion by health and social services (para 113).

9.53 These two cases represent extreme opposite ends of the contraception/sterilisation spectrum, but they confirm the same points of fundamental legal principle. As is fitting the person-centred nature of the best interests test—they each turn on their own particular facts. Nonetheless, whether one agrees that the final step of authorising non-therapeutic sterilisation can *ever* by justified will remain a point of central concern.

9.54 Our final case concerns something that we once thought would never happen—the non-consensual, non-therapeutic sterilisation of an incompetent *male* adult. The case is *An NHS Trust v DE*[119] in which declarations were sought on the lawfulness of such an intervention as being in the best interests of the man, D, who had learning difficulties and lived with his parents. He had a child with a woman in 2009, leading to concerns about his ability to consent to sex;[120] this in turn resulted in him being under constant supervision, and this in turn severely restricted his freedoms. D was very clear that he did not want any more children, and it was accepted that he lacked capacity with respect to decisions about contraceptives. His parents were of the view that it was in his best interests to have a vasectomy, and the case turned on the application from the Trust on (i) his capacity to consent to such a procedure, and (ii) whether this would be in his best interests in the absence of capacity. Having held that there was no capacity, the court's view on best interests was—once again—entirely driven by the particular facts. Relevant considerations here were, first, that D was in a loving relationship with a woman and it was important for him that this continue; it was clear too there was a sexual element that would be supported by this course of action; second, there was a concern that the birth of another child (and its removal) would distress his partner and jeopardise the relationship; third, D himself had been clear that he did not want another child, and fourth, that he wished to remain with his parents while enjoying his previously hard-won independence. All of this led to the view that the only way these options could be guaranteed was by way of a vasectomy. As the court said: '. . . it is both the entitlement and in the best interests of any person with significant disabilities, (whether learning or physical), that they be given such support as will enable them to be as much an integral part of society as can reasonably be achieved' (para 94).

9.55 We would suggest that these more recent decisions demonstrate the all-encompassing nature of the best interests test, particularly assisted by evidence of what vulnerable persons themselves would want. They lead us to question the foundational or near-absolute

---

[119] [2013] 3 FCR 343; [2013] Med LR 446; (2013) 133 BMLR 123.
[120] On the considerations for this category generally, see *Re M (An Adult) (Capacity: Consent to Sexual Relations), Re* [2014] EWCA Civ 37. For wider commentary, see J Herring and J Wall, 'Capacity to consent to sex' (2014) 22(4) Med Law Rev 620.

nature of claims to reproductive liberty, and this can be a difficult nettle to grasp. Equally, the range of protections and safeguards is extensive, and none of these cases departs from the central legal principle of the paramountcy of best interests. Still, we confess to a residual degree of disquiet when the ever-expanding nature of this test seems to know no limits as to which considerations can be added to the mix to (potentially) justify diametrically opposing outcomes.[121]

TERMINATION OF PREGNANCY

9.56 We have included the legal termination of pregnancy, or legal abortion,[122] within this chapter because it is logical to do so—the control of pregnancy *is* an aspect of the control of fertility. This is not to imply, however, that it should, as a consequence, be regarded as a facet of family planning—at best, it should be seen in that context as *failed* family planning. One's attitude must, of course, depend on how far one accepts the concept of existing rights, or interests, of the fetus in the reproductive process which we have outlined in para 9.05 et seq—and this forms a main basis of the discussion that follows.

9.57 As is only too well known, the abortion debate is one that is centred on ethics. Any legal argument is, essentially, confined to how, and to what extent, the ethics should be constrained by the law. The passing of the Abortion Act 1967 did, however, exercise a profound and direct influence on the medical ethos. Once the Act was accepted by doctors, the profession abrogated a main tenet of its Hippocratic conscience—as recently as 1994, the Declaration of Geneva, as amended in Stockholm, was advising: 'I will maintain the utmost respect for human life from its beginning.'[123] The Declaration of Oslo, however, while retaining this moral principle, modified it to accord with modern attitudes: 'Diversity of response to this situation [the conflict of vital interests of the mother with vital interests of the child] results from the diversity of attitudes towards the life of the unborn child. This is a matter of individual conviction and conscience.'[124] This ethical watershed has spilled over to influence the attitudes of doctors towards all aspects of life and death. Modern medicine now clearly accommodates the concept of death as a therapeutic option.

9.58 In the wider context, however, attitudes to abortion depend almost entirely on where the holder stands in respect of, on the one hand, the fetal interest in life and, on the other, a woman's right to control her own body and it is this which perpetuates a near intractable moral conflict with which the law must come to terms—and, until recently, it has singularly failed to do so. An opportunity to define the moral status of the fetus arose in *Attorney-General's Reference (No 3 of 1994)*[125]—a case of fatal fetal injury resulting from an attack on its mother—but the House of Lords' only concession to recognition of fetal interests was to override the Court of Appeal in accepting that the fetus was more than

---

[121] R Barton-Hanson, 'Sterilization of men with intellectual disabilities: whose best interests is it anyway?' (2015) Med Law Inter, doi: 10.1177/0968533215592444.

[122] It is of interest that the Abortion Act 1967 started as the Medical Termination of Pregnancy Bill and many would wish that it had remained so. 'Abortion', in our view, has traditional ties with criminality and, so far as is possible, we avoid the term in the present context. Abortion is, however, so firmly equated in the public mind with the legal termination of pregnancy that it would be perverse not to use the former expression as shorthand; the two terms can be regarded as synonymous so far as this book is concerned.

[123] There is, however, a subtle change of wording from the original 'from the time of conception'.

[124] World Medical Association (as amended 2006).   [125] [1998] AC 245; [1997] 3 All ER 936.

an adjunct of its mother; it then, however, declined to elaborate on what its status was.[126] It is true to say that harm to the fetus *before* birth can be actionable *after* birth; even so, the subsequent live birth is an essential prerequisite;[127] thus, any protection provided by the common law is, essentially, protection of the neonate. An antenatal fetal right to life is recognised in the criminalisation of child destruction (see para 9.60). Again, however, any recognition of fetal interests under this head is indirect insofar as the relevant legislation was enacted primarily so as to close a gap in the law of infanticide. Nowhere is there any mention of feticide as an offence per se and it is against this background that we must consider the development of abortion law in the UK.

THE EVOLUTION OF THE LAW ON ABORTION

9.59 The fundamental law in England and Wales lies in ss 58 and 59 of the Offences Against the Person Act 1861. The Act proscribes procuring the miscarriage of a woman by a third party, self-induced miscarriage, attempted procurement of miscarriage, and supplying the means to do so[128]—it is to be noted that the word 'abortion' appears only in the marginal note to the sections.[129] The Act makes no distinction between criminal and therapeutic activity and, despite frequent scrutiny, these sections have not been repealed. It is, however, important to note that, as a continuum to the discussion in para 9.58, there is still no engagement of fetal interests. Criminalisation of procuring the miscarriage of a woman was undoubtedly intended for the protection of *women's* health—once again, no direct concern for the fetus was shown.

9.60 The first statutory variation is to be found in the Infant Life (Preservation) Act 1929, which introduced the offence of child destruction or causing the death of a child capable of being born alive before it has an existence independent of its mother. There is no offence, however, if the act was done in good faith for the purpose only of preserving the mother's life. This meagre concession, in the main, served only to decriminalise killing the infant in the event of an impacted labour. It was left to the case of *R v Bourne*[130] to temper the legal influence on medical practice in the field. Mr Bourne performed an abortion, with no attempt at secrecy, on a 15-year-old girl who was pregnant following a particularly unpleasant rape. Although Mr Bourne was indicted under the Offences Against the Person Act 1861, Macnaghten J took the opportunity to link the 1861 and 1929 statutes and ruled that, in a case brought under the 1861 Act, the burden rested on the Crown to satisfy the jury that the defendant did not procure the miscarriage of the girl in good faith for the purpose only of preserving her life: the word 'unlawful' in the 1861 Act 'imports the meaning expressed by the proviso in section 1(1) of the Infant Life (Preservation) Act 1929'.[131] The summing-up essentially recognised that a woman's life depended upon her physical and mental health and that an abortion was not unlawful if it was performed

---

[126] For discussion of the case, see M Seneviratne, 'Pre-natal injury and transferred malice: The invented other' (1996) 59 MLR 884. Also J K Mason, 'A Lords' eye view of fetal status' (1999) 3 Edin LR 246.

[127] E.g. *Burton v Islington Health Authority, de Martell v Merton and Sutton Health Authority* [1993] QB 204; [1992] 3 All ER 833; *Hamilton v Fife Health Board* 1993 SLT 624. For discussion see A Whitfield, 'Common law duties to unborn children' (1993) 1 Med L Rev 28.

[128] But limited to some 'thing'—e.g. not by coercion or fraud: *R v Ahmed* [2011] QB 512, CCA.

[129] The distinction, if any, between 'miscarriage' and 'abortion' is of academic interest in relation to pre-implantation methods of contraception. Some writers believe the terms to be interchangeable: see, e.g., I J Keown, '"Miscarriage": A medico-legal analysis' [1984] Crim LR 604. We believe that 'abortion' implies interference whereas miscarriage is a natural misfortune.

[130] [1939] 1 KB 687; [1938] 3 All ER 615.   [131] [1939] 1 KB 687 at 691; [1938] 3 All ER 615 at 617.

because these were in jeopardy.[132] Mr Bourne was acquitted and the law and the medical profession then lived in harmony for many years; the *Bourne* decision was undoubtedly stretched to the limits of interpretation by many doctors but the authorities turned a sympathetic eye.

9.61 But it is never a good thing for any section of the public to flirt with illegality; moreover, there was still no authority for termination of the pregnancy in the event of probable handicap of the potential neonate. The situation was resolved when the Abortion Act was put into law in 1967; despite repeated attack, it remained unchanged until 1990.

9.62 It is interesting to compare the historical attitudes in England with those prevailing in Scotland where procuring a woman's miscarriage has always been a common law offence. The whole subject, including a review of the 1967 Act, occupies less than three pages in *Gordon*.[133] The difference in concern lies in the emphasis laid in Scots law on 'evil intent' as a measure of criminality; there is little doubt that Mr Bourne would have been unlikely to provoke a test case in Scotland. It is, in fact, arguable that there was no need to extend the Act to Scotland; its inclusion was justified in that it removed any doubt as to the limits of therapeutic abortion in that country where, in effect, a policy similar to that recognised in *Bourne* had been openly followed for decades.

The Abortion Act 1967

9.63 The Abortion Act 1967[134] was significantly amended by s 37 of the Human Fertilisation and Embryology Act 1990.[135] In summary, s 1(1) now states that a person shall not be guilty of an offence under the law of abortion when termination is performed by a registered medical practitioner and two registered medical practitioners have formed the opinion in good faith that:

(a) the continuance of the pregnancy would involve risk, greater than if the pregnancy were terminated, of injury to the physical or mental health of the pregnant woman or any existing children of her family; these therapeutic and social grounds, which accounted for 181,216 or 99 per cent of all abortions performed on residents in England and Wales in 2014, are subject to the pregnancy not having exceeded its twenty-fourth week. The remaining justifications are now free of such temporal restriction;

(b) that there is a risk of grave permanent injury to the physical or mental health of the pregnant woman;

(c) that the continuance of the pregnancy would involve risk to the life of the pregnant woman greater than if the pregnancy were terminated. Grounds (b) and (c) together accounted for 252 cases in England and Wales in 2014 (one-tenth of one per cent);

(d) that there is a substantial risk that, if the child were born, it would suffer from such physical or mental abnormalities as to be severely handicapped—1 per cent of the total in 2014 (being 3,099 cases).[136]

---

[132] [1939] 1 KB 687 at 694; [1938] 3 All ER 615 at 619.
[133] G H Gordon, *The Criminal Law of Scotland* (3rd edn, 2010), two volumes and supplements, ch 28.
[134] Hereafter 'the 1967 Act'.   [135] Hereafter 'the 1990 Act'.
[136] Department of Health, *Abortion Statistics, England and Wales, 2014* (June 2015). These figures do not include 5,521 abortions performed on non-residents of England and Wales in 2014. 2013 was the lowest figures since records began in 1969, being 5,469 cases.

9.64 Subsections (b) and (c) are, additionally, not restricted by requiring the opinion of two registered medical practitioners; single practitioners may operate on their own initiative in such circumstances.[137] Termination under the Act may be carried out in National Health Service (NHS) hospitals or in places approved for the purpose by the Minister or the Secretary of State (s 1(3))—in fact, some 67 per cent are now carried out in approved independent sector places under NHS contract albeit 98 per cent are funded by the NHS. The advent of medical methods for the termination of pregnancy[138] has dictated a change in the location rules, which are now relaxed for this purpose.[139]

9.65 As noted, the vast majority of legal terminations are performed under s 1(1)(a) of the 1967 Act for minor therapeutic or social reasons. It is arguable that the risks of an abortion to the health of a woman are always less than those of a full-term pregnancy—particularly if the termination is carried out in the first trimester,[140] and that now at least half the terminations carried out in the UK are 'medical' in nature. Equally, it is obvious that the mental health of a woman who is carrying an unwanted pregnancy must suffer more damage if she is forced to carry her fetus than it would if she were relieved of her burden. Simple economics dictate that a *risk* to the well-being of any existing members of the family is occasioned by the advent of another mouth to feed. The indications are, therefore, that it is impossible for a doctor to perform an abortion in Great Britain[141] that can be shown to have been unlawful, provided that all the administrative conditions are met.[142] As a corollary, the doctor who applies the letter of the law must always be acting in good faith—indeed, possibly the only way in which a termination can be carried out in *bad* faith is when it is done without the woman's consent.[143]

9.66 Apparently paradoxically, this also applies when considering terminations under s 1(1)(d)— the 'fetal abnormality' ground—which one might have thought was there for the benefit of the fetus who may, otherwise, be born in a handicapped condition.[144] Apart from

[137] It is to be noted that s 1(1)(b) contains no comparative element—there simply has to be a risk and it is arguable that pregnancy always carries such a risk even though it is minimal.

[138] Medical abortions, as opposed to surgical abortions, accounted for 51 per cent of the total in 2014 in England and Wales. The proportion of medical abortions trebled between 2004 and 2014—largely due to the availability of abortifacient drug Mifegyne (mifepristone, also known as RU486)—and 2014 was the first year where more medical abortions than surgical abortions took place.

[139] Section 1(3A), inserted by the 1990 Act, s 37(3). But the courts will not sanction any further extension on the basis of semantic wrangling: *British Pregnancy Advisory Service v Secretary of State for Health* [2011] 3 Al ER 1012; (2011) 118 BMLR 172. See K Greasley, 'Medical abortion and the "golden rule" of statutory interpretation' (2011) 19 Med L Rev 314.

[140] Abortion methods are becoming increasingly safe but complication rates still increase with the period of gestation.

[141] The Abortion Act 1967 does not extend to Northern Ireland, where the Infant Life (Preservation) Act 1929 is preserved in the Criminal Justice Act (Northern Ireland) 1945, s 25; conditions as to the latter are unaffected by the Human Fertilisation and Embryology Act 1990, s 37 (see Northern Ireland at para 9.71). The Channel Islands have adopted legislation which is similar to, although rather more strict than, that of Great Britain—e.g. Termination of Pregnancy (Jersey) Law 1997.

[142] One could, in fact, apply much the same reasoning to s 1(1)(c) though this sub-section is plainly intended to cover terminations in late pregnancy when the dangerous toxaemias of pregnancy most commonly arise.

[143] And, even then, the charge would be under the Offences Against the Person Act 1861 rather than under the 1967 Act.

[144] We discuss the question of 'wrongful life' in the following chapter. In fact, the sub-section is probably intended for the protection of the woman who may have to rear a disabled child; fetal 'rights' are not involved. There are relatively few circumstances in which death, rather than a life with disability, could be said with assurance to be in the interests of the neonate—see S Sheldon and S Wilkinson, 'Termination of pregnancy for reason of foetal disability: Are there grounds for a special exception in law?' (2001) 9 Med L Rev 85.

anything else, the prospect of a disabled child is likely to affect a woman's mental health more than if she terminated the pregnancy; from the woman's aspect, there is, therefore, no absolute need for s 1(1)(d)—other than, if necessary, to take advantage of the concession as to the length of gestation. More specifically, the sub-section is, again, open-ended in its phraseology.[145] What is a substantial risk? What is a serious handicap? Neither is defined and each can be interpreted on a wholly subjective basis.[146] As a result, it will be difficult, if not impossible, to demonstrate that a decision to terminate the pregnancy was not taken in good faith. Ms Jepson, who succeeded in obtaining access to judicial review of a termination performed because the fetus had a cleft palate received no sympathy from either the police or the medical profession and the Crown Prosecution Service refused to take action on the ground that the decision had been taken in good faith.[147] It is hardly surprising that we have been able to find only one conviction under the Act[148] and this appears to have arisen mainly because of the way the operation was performed.

9.67 The medical profession as a whole tends to look on the Act as a success and resists any attempt to stiffen its conditions.[149] Circumstances must, however, arise when the proportionality between termination of pregnancy and the severity of the mischief it avoids is so balanced as to make one wonder if the law should not intervene—abortion on the basis of fetal sex selection provides such an example. Most people, we imagine, would instinctively regard it as an abuse of medical skills. Moreover, the clear restrictions on gender-based embryocide[150] must surely imply parliamentary disapproval of the practice. Nevertheless, it cannot necessarily be illegal. Section 1(2) of the 1967 Act specifically states that, in making a determination as to the risk of injury to the woman's or her existing children's health, 'account may be taken of the pregnant woman's actual or reasonably foreseeable environment'. Given the right ethnic ambience—most particularly within Asian and Muslim cultures—there can be no doubt that the birth of a female child could affect a woman's mental health and, possibly, her physical well-being; there is nothing in the Act which limits such risks to those directly associated with the condition of pregnancy; and even a person with a Western background may be mentally disturbed by the thought of a third male (or female) child. A positive argument for sex selection can be based on the concept of procreative autonomy[151] and, it has even been suggested that, once one accepts termination on the grounds of fetal disability, one is logically bound to accept gender-based abortion.[152] While gender-led abortion may not constitute a major problem

---

[145] See: R Scott, 'Interpreting the disability ground of the Abortion Act' (2005) 64 CLJ 388.

[146] For an equally full discussion, see E Wicks, M Wyldes, and M Kilby, 'Late termination of pregnancy for fetal abnormality: Medical and legal perspectives' (2004) 12 Med L Rev 285. The problem also vexes the professionals: Royal College of Obstetricians and Gynaecologists, *Termination of Pregnancy for Fetal Abnormality in England, Wales and Scotland* (2010). The College takes a generally restrictive view.

[147] *Jepson v Chief Constable of West Mercia* [2003] EWHC 3318. See too, S McGuinness, 'Law, reproduction, and disability: fatally "handicapped"?' (2013) 21(2) Med L Rev 213.

[148] *R v Smith (John)* [1974] 1 All ER 376; [1973] 1 WLR 1510, CA.

[149] A study of medical students' attitudes indicated that 62 per cent could be described as 'pro-choice': R Gleeson, E Forde, E Bates, et al., 'Medical students' attitudes towards abortion: A UK study' (2008) 34 J Med Ethics 783. This compares with a study in 2000 which indicated that 82 per cent of general practitioners favoured abortion. The authors question whether this means that attitudes are changing with the times or do so with exposure to medical practice.

[150] See Human Fertilisation and Embryology Act 1990, Sch 2, para 1ZA(1)(b–c) discussed at para 8.61.

[151] J Savulescu, 'Sex selection: The case for' (1999) 171 Med J Austral 373.

[152] J Williams, 'Sex selective abortion: A matter of choice' (2012) 31 Law Philos 125. This depends upon one also accepting that s 1(i)(d) is there for the benefit of the mother.

in our society,[153] it serves to illustrate how wide is the facility for termination within the wording of the 1967 Act.

9.68 The availability of lawful termination has been further extended by s 37(4) of the 1990 Act, which amends s 5(1) of the 1967 Act so as to read:

> No offence under the Infant Life (Preservation) Act 1929 shall be committed by a registered medical practitioner who terminates a pregnancy in accordance with the provisions of this Act.

The criminal associations with 'viability' of the fetus[154] and the living abortus (to which we refer briefly at para 9.106) are, therefore, now almost, although not quite, entirely dispelled.

9.69 There are still some who regard abortion in Great Britain as being unreasonably restricted as compared with other jurisdictions;[155] even so, the scope of the Abortion Act 1967 probably exceeds that envisaged by its originators. The number of terminations carried out in England and Wales rose relentlessly until 1990, when 173,900 abortions were performed on women resident in England and Wales. There was then a steady decrease until a sharp rise occurred in 1996 and, since then, the upward trend has resumed, reaching an all-time high of 198,499 in 2007—but it has now fallen to 184,571 in 2014;[156] the age standardised abortion rate among residents in England and Wales aged 15–44 is now 15.9/1,000 women. The figures for Scotland show a steady rise until peaking to 13,111 in 2009. The numbers have since declined and 11,475 terminations were performed on residents in Scotland in 2014, the lowest reported since 1995; simultaneously, the number of abortions performed on Scottish women in England and Wales has significantly declined.

9.70 The number of terminations provided for non-resident women in England and Wales in 2014 was 5,521—representing 2.99 per cent of the total. 2013 saw the lowest figure since 1969 at 5,469 cases. Clearly, there have been policy changes in other countries in the intervening years and it is worth considering some of these briefly.

THE COMPARATIVE POSITION

Northern Ireland

9.71 We have, thus far, spoken only in terms of Great Britain as far as domestic law is concerned. The position in Northern Ireland is particularly sensitive, due to its close association with the Republic of Ireland. The Abortion Act 1967 does not run to the Province, where the law is governed by the 1861 Act, subject to modification by some important court decisions. In *Re K (a minor)*,[157] it was held that the law lay in the 1861 Act as modified by the charge to the jury in *R v Bourne*;[158] termination of a 13-week pregnancy in a

---

[153] Note that this unconcern reflects a typical Western attitude. In India, e.g., the sex ratio in young children dropped from 945 to 927 girls per 1,000 boys in the decade 1991–2001 despite the existence of criminal sanctions: G Mudur, 'Activists claim proposals to strengthen ban on prenatal sex selection hide inaction' (2008) 336 BMJ 1038.

[154] For review of attitudes to late terminations, see J Savulescu, 'Is current practice around late termination of pregnancy eugenic and discriminatory?' (2001) 27 J Med Ethics 165.

[155] It has been suggested that some 42 per cent of the British public would support the availability of abortion without any reason other than the woman's choice: J Wise, 'British public supports legal abortion for all' (1997) 314 BMJ 627.

[156] 2006 was the first year in which the total number of terminations exceeded 200,000, but the levels have since declined.

[157] *Re K (a minor), Northern Health and Social Services Board v F and G* (1991) 2 Med LR 371.

[158] [1939] 1 KB 687; [1938] 3 All ER 615.

severely handicapped ward of court was authorised. Again, in *Re A*,[159] the court used the reasoning in *Bourne* to apply s 25 of the Criminal Justice Act (Northern Ireland) 1945 to the 1861 Act; a termination was held to be in the handicapped woman's best interests. The overall effect of the law was summarised by the Northern Ireland Court of Appeal in *Family Planning Association of Northern Ireland v Minister for Health and Social Services and Public Safety*[160] as follows:

'... A termination will ... be lawful where the continuance of the pregnancy threatens the life of the mother, or would adversely affect her mental or physical health; The adverse effect on her mental or physical health must be a 'real and serious' one, and must also be 'permanent or long term'; In most cases the risk of the adverse effect occurring would need to be a probability, but a possibility might be regarded as sufficient if the imminent death of the mother was the potentially adverse effect; It will always be a question of fact and degree whether the perceived effect of a non-termination is sufficiently grave to warrant terminating the pregnancy in a particular case.'

9.72 The real-world effect of this is that there is no automatic entitlement to services, even in the case of rape or incest. Moreover, it takes no account of fetal abnormality as a basis for termination. The extent of the difference is seen by the fact that there were 51 terminations of pregnancy in Northern Ireland during 2012/13 and only 23 in 2013/14, compared with the mainland figures quoted above at para 9.69. This explains in large part why, in 2014, 828 Northern Irish women travelled to the mainland for terminations. Notwithstanding, the difficulty of the situation for women seeking access to services has been compounded by the refusal of the Secretary of State in England to pay for women who travel from Northern Ireland; and the reasonableness of this refusal was recently upheld by the Court of Appeal in judicial review.[161] In parallel, a further judicial review of the Northern Irish position was heard in June 2015, brought by a woman who had to travel to the mainland for termination on grounds of fetal abnormality. She was joined by Amnesty International, which has pointed out that the Northern Irish penalties are the highest in Europe.[162] As we go to press, the High Court has confirmed a breach of human rights in the case. This reflects the results of a 2013 consultation which were almost universally condemnatory of the existing position as a throwback to the nineteenth century.[163]

The Republic of Ireland

9.73 The Republic of Ireland, along with Poland and some other countries within the European Union (EU), particularly those with a strong Roman or Orthodox Catholic tradition, confers a constitutional right to life on the fetus while, at the same time, paying due regard to the equal right to life of the mother.[164] Historically, the definitive law on abortion was derived from the UK Offences Against the Person Act 1861 which was incorporated in

[159] *Re A (Northern Health and Social Services Board v AMNH)* (1991) 2 Med L Rev 274.
[160] [2004] NICA 37, para 12.
[161] *R (on the application of A (A Child)) v Secretary of State for Health* [2015] EWCA Civ 771.
[162] M Ritchie, 'Abortion: How Northern Ireland could be forced to ditch its "nightmare" law', *The Telegraph*, 15 June 2015.
[163] 2013 consultation: http://www.dhsspsni.gov.uk/termination-pregnancy-responses-2013.pdf.
[164] Irish Constitution, Art 40.3.3. Similar legislation, with variable exceptions, is to be found in Andorra, Liechtenstein, Malta, and San Marino. Abortion 'on demand at less than 10 weeks' gestation was legalised in Portugal in April 2007.

the Health (Family Planning) Act 1979. This was revisited in 2013 after the tragic death of a woman who was miscarrying but left on a wait-and-see policy by hospital staff.[165] The resultant law was the Protection of Life During Pregnancy Act 2013, whose title alone betrays the core of its priorities. Like the Northern Irish position, it does not make provision for cases of incest, rape, or fetal abnormality. It goes further, however, whereby it is only concerned with a 'real and substantial risk' to a woman's life, not necessarily to her health. Moreover, its access provisions require the input of three medical practitioners to certify that a woman qualifies, and in the case of a suicide risk two of the practitioners must be psychiatrists.[166]

9.74 The Irish position has been difficult to maintain against a European backdrop. In 1991, the Irish High Court sought a ruling from the European Court of Justice (ECJ) on the legality of prohibiting the distribution of information relating to the availability of abortion facilities for Irish citizens in the UK; the answer was that, as a matter of morality, the Irish government was entitled to follow its own public policy.[167] The following year, the Supreme Court of Ireland extended the grounds on which a termination was permissible from circumstances in which there was an inevitable or immediate risk to the life of the mother to those where there was a real and substantial risk to her life—represented in the instant case by the possibility of suicide. In obiter remarks, however, the Court indicated that the right of an unborn child to life would, were the conflict to arise, take precedence over the right of the mother to travel.[168]

9.75 Later in the year, the twin problems of providing information and arranging travel to another jurisdiction were again aired, this time before the European Court of Human Rights (ECtHR),[169] when an injunction of the Supreme Court restraining such counselling was challenged. On this occasion, while agreeing that the purpose of the injunction was to protect the national morality, the European Court decided that the degree of restraint imposed was disproportionate to the aim pursued. Accordingly, Art 10 (freedom of expression) of the ECHR was infringed. Two national referenda supported this view and, as a result, the Regulation of Information Act 1995 was passed and held to be constitutional; the injunctions against the provision of information concerning the availability of abortion in Great Britain were subsequently lifted—subject to there being no advocacy of termination. A further rape-associated case, this time involving a 13-year-old girl, arose in 1997. Here it was confirmed that a 'suicide risk' came within the definition of a substantial risk to the mother's life, by reason of which an abortion carried out in Ireland would not be unlawful; as a result, the girl concerned could leave the country in order to have the termination.[170]

9.76 Following these cases, the government established a powerful working party, which, later, reported to an equally authoritative Committee on the Constitution, in an effort to clarify

[165] R Sanghani, 'Ireland's abortion problem: new report lays bare the horrifying truth', *The Telegraph*, 9 June 2015.
[166] For a prior history see B Daly, 'Braxton Hicks or the birth of a new era? Tracing the development of Irelands' abortion laws in respect of the ECHR jurisprudence' (2011) 18 Euro J Hlth Law 375.
[167] *Society for the Protection of Unborn Children Ireland Ltd v Grogan* [1991] 3 CMLR 849; (1992) 9 BMLR 100.
[168] *A-G v X* [1992] 1 IR 1; (1994) 15 BMLR 104.
[169] *Open Door Counselling and Dublin Well Woman v Ireland* (1993) 15 EHRR 244; (1994) 18 BMLR 1.
[170] *A and B v Eastern Health Board* [1998] 4 IR 464. An interesting feature of the case is that the Health Board applied for, and obtained, authority to arrange a termination against the wishes of the 13-year-old girl's parents; the parents did not, however, appeal the decision.

the law but, although substantial support was given to several proposals, no single course of action for reform could be agreed. A third referendum was called in 2002 but, effectively, it was confined to an attempt to exclude potential suicide as a legal justification for termination of pregnancy.

9.77   *D v Ireland* was something of a groundbreaking case involving the carriage of a fetus with trisomy-18—a particularly lethal chromosomal anomaly but one which did not involve danger to the life of the mother.[171] D, being medically advised that she was not eligible for an abortion in Ireland, was not prepared to go through a legal hearing, and underwent a termination in the UK. On her return, she lodged a complaint with the ECtHR to the effect that existing Irish law as applied to a fatal fetal diagnosis was incompatible with her rights under Arts 3, 8, 10, and 14 of the Convention. The European Court is notoriously anxious to avoid being embroiled in the discourse of fetal rights. Nevertheless, it seemed almost inevitable in the instant case that the court should deem the application inadmissible on the ground that the full range of domestic resources had not been exhausted. To that extent, therefore, the case is comparatively irrelevant. Its significance lies in the government's submission which included the proposition that the domestic courts:

> '...would be unlikely to interpret [the law] with remorseless logic particularly when the facts were exceptional ... [I]t was impossible to foresee that Article 40.3.3 [of the Constitution] clearly excluded an abortion in the applicant's situation in Ireland. Indeed, the tenor of the whole submission demonstrates an almost palpable anxiety for the courts, rather than the politicians, to be given the opportunity to acknowledge the viability of D's case.'

9.78   The saga continued, however—largely as a result of what has been described as legislative inertia and resurfaced in a ECtHR case brought by three women who claimed that their Art 8 rights were infringed due to their being unable to obtain terminations in Ireland despite the ruling in *Attorney General v X*.[172] The case is *A v Ireland*,[173] but in the event, the Court found that the rights of C, who had cancer, were infringed but not those of A and B. The end result was the setting up of yet another expert group and the uncertainty surrounding the legality of abortion in the Republic persisted. The death of Mrs Halappanavar prompted major public outcry and yet another review, but the 2013 Act does not move the abortion law in the Irish Republic beyond the most meagre attempt to comply with these ruling against the state;[174] indeed, some would argue it is now the most draconian in Europe.

9.79   Meantime, the practical effect of the current situation is very telling. In 1982, 3,650 Irish nationals had terminations in Great Britain; by 2003, this figure had risen to 6,320 but

---

[171] ECtHR (Application 26499/02), 28 June 2006. The transcript contains a very detailed analysis of abortion law in Ireland. The case is not to be confused with that involving another 'Ms D' who was carrying an anencephalic fetus. The High Court overruled a decision by the District Court not to authorise her travel for a termination: C Dyer, 'Girl carrying anencephalic fetus is granted right to travel' (2007) 334 BMJ 1026.

[172] *A-G v X* [1992] 1 IR 1; (1994) 15 BMLR 104.

[173] [2011] 3 FCR 244; (2011) 53 EHRR 13. See further, S Palmer, 'Abortion and human rights' (2014) 6 EHRLR 596.

[174] S Donoghue and C-M Smyth, 'Abortion for foetal abnormalities in Ireland; the limited scope of the Irish Government's response to the A, B and C judgment' (2013) 20(2) Euro J Health Law 117.

dropped to 3,752 in 2014—which still represents 68 per cent of all terminations performed on non-resident women.[175]

The USA

9.80 Although the transatlantic experience now has little relevance to the UK, the USA
remains one of the few jurisdictions where abortion remains an active political issue. It is,
therefore, worth taking a brief look at its development.

9.81 In 1973, the Supreme Court was called upon to determine the relationship between
state abortion laws and a woman's rights under the US Constitution. It did so in the
historic twin decisions of *Roe v Wade*[176] and *Doe v Bolton*.[177] The effect of these well-
known cases can be summarised thus: it is an invasion of a woman's constitutional
right to privacy to limit her access to abortion by statute; the expression 'to preserve
the life' of a woman, which previously defined the grounds for a legal termination in
several states, was declared unconstitutionally vague, although 'to preserve the life
or health' was acceptable. It was suggested at the time the decisions were reached
that health is inclusive of convenience and that this effectively allows for abortion on
demand—and although the Supreme Court specifically stated that there was no such
absolute constitutional right, there is no doubt that the result of *Roe* is that abortion
during the first trimester is an inalienable prerogative of the American woman and
is grounded in the right to individual privacy. Nevertheless, the court did give some
weight to the rights of the developing fetus. In the first trimester, the question of termination was to be decided solely between the woman and her physician; during the
second trimester, the state could intervene by reason of its interest in the health of the
mother. After 'viability' of the fetus, which the court assessed as somewhere between
the twenty-fourth and twenty-eighth week of pregnancy, it was agreed that the state
had a compelling interest in the health of the fetus and could, therefore, constitutionally intervene on its behalf excepting when the conditions threatened the life or health
of the mother.

9.82 The decision in *Roe v Wade* has been a subject of controversy ever since it was made.[178]
Aside from the moral issues involved, the most practical objection is that the trimester
rule, which rests upon fluctuating medical expertise and medical technology, is unreli-
able. This was well put by O'Connor J:

> The lines drawn [in *Roe*] have now become 'blurred' … The state can no longer rely on a
> 'bright line' that separates permissible from impermissible regulation.… Rather, the State
> must continuously and conscientiously study contemporary medical and scientific litera-
> ture in order to determine whether the effect of a particular regulation is to depart from
> accepted medical practice.[179]

[175] An interesting attempt to reverse the process and claim that deportation of a pregnant woman
offended Art 40.3.3 insofar as neonatal care was inferior in her country to that in Ireland was unsuccessful. The Article, it was said, was relevant to abortion, not to fetal and neonatal health: *Baby O v Minister for
Justice, Equality and Law Reform* [2002] 2 IR 169.
[176] 93 S Ct 705 (1973).   [177] 93 S Ct 739 (1973).
[178] It is poignant to find that 'Ms Roe' has been converted to the 'pro-life' cause and that, in fact, she never
obtained her own termination: N McCorvey, 'My legal fight helped start a generation of child slaughter and
that makes me weep', *Daily Telegraph*, 20 January 1998, p 4.
[179] In *Akron v Akron Center for Reproductive Health* 462 US 416 (1983) at 455–6.

9.83 There are, however, additional reasons why we should dissociate US attitudes and British thinking in this area. Fundamentally, abortion in the USA is not so much a philosophical issue as it is one of constitutional law. Moreover, the subject has become highly politicised and the composition of the Supreme Court is subject to political adjustment. Thus, the Supreme Court firmly repelled a major attack on *Roe* which was mounted in the mid-1980s[180] but a further sally towards the end of the decade[181] was more successful in that the Court upheld a Missouri statute which certainly limited the availability of abortion.

9.84 In 1992, the Supreme Court was again asked to pronounce on the legality of a state statute—in this case, the Abortion Control Act of Pennsylvania—which created a number of obstacles in the way of abortion 'on demand'.[182] The issues, here, included, on the one hand, the woman's right to bodily privacy and, on the other, the state's interest in the protection of life and a preference for childbirth over abortion. Essentially, *Casey* empowered the state to impose financial, medical, or emotional barriers to abortion provided that these did not become a substantial obstacle, or undue burden, to choosing to terminate a pregnancy; the basic premise of the woman's liberty of conscience and bodily integrity was, in this way, upheld. Even so, some fetal rights were maintained, in that states could restrict abortion of the 'viable' fetus save in relation to a medical emergency threatening the mother. The opinion has been said to please the no lobby and there is every indication that the abortion debate will continue in the USA in an atmosphere of increasing acrimony and increasing subservience to political exigency.

9.85 Indeed, it has done so with a vengeance insofar as South Dakota has enacted the Women's Health and Life Protection Act 2006 which seeks to turn the wheel full-circle and prohibit abortion other than to save the life of the pregnant woman. Moreover, in at least four states, an ultrasound investigation is mandatory before an abortion and there are varying rules as to the amount of information that must be provided to the woman. South Dakota has also used its 'informed consent' law to insist on a standardised form of information as to the significance and dangers of the procedure before termination is undertaken—including a danger of post-abortion suicide.[183] We conclude that US jurisprudence has little to offer that of the UK. As was said in the case of Ms Axon:

> the social and moral values of American society are very different from those which are prevalent in the UK. There is a sensitivity and a controversy regarding the availability of abortion [in the USA] which does not exist on a comparable scale in this country.[184]

The Commonwealth

9.86 Turning to the Commonwealth, the most interesting abortion battles have been waged in Canada where, until the last 25 or so years, control of legal terminations was vested in hospital abortion committees under s 251 of the Criminal Code 1971; in the long-running case of *R v Morgentaler*,[185] however, the Supreme Court held that this section violated the

---

[180] *American College of Obstetricians and Gynaecologists* v *Thornburgh* 476 US 747 (1986).
[181] *Webster* v *Reproductive Health Services* 109 S Ct 3040 (1989).
[182] *Planned Parenthood of Southeastern Pennsylvania* v *Casey* 112 S Ct 2791 (1992).
[183] Rather surprisingly upheld in *Planned Parenthood of Minnesota* v *Rounds* (2012, 8th Circuit CA, 24 July, 09-3231).
[184] *R (on the application of Axon)* v *Secretary of State for Health* (2006) 88 BMLR 96, per Silber J at [37].
[185] [1988] 1 SCR 30.

security and liberty of the pregnant woman. The Chief Justice expressed his reasons for this conclusion as follows:

> Forcing a woman, by threat of criminal sanction, to carry a fetus to term unless she meets certain criteria unrelated to her own priorities and aspirations, is a profound interference with a woman's body and thus a violation of security of the person.[186]

In parallel litigation, the Canadian Charter of Rights and Freedom, Art 7 of which guarantees the 'right to life, liberty and security of the person', was held to be inapplicable to the fetus.[187] It is to be noted that neither the Supreme Court of the USA nor that of Canada will allow a 'trade-off' or balancing act between fetal and maternal rights to life or health—it is the latter which are to be safeguarded.

9.87 The innate tendency towards liberal abortion law is also demonstrated in Australia where, other than in South Australia, the Northern Territories, and Western Australia, which have enabling statutes, the basic law corresponds to that in the Offences Against the Person Act 1861.[188] It is, therefore, particularly interesting to see how case law in the individual states has managed to provide for a very wide availability of apparently 'unlawful' terminations, largely on the basis of the *Bourne* determination.[189] The so-called 'Kirby ruling'[190] suggested that, in the same way as we analyse the position in Great Britain, it would be very difficult to establish that any termination performed by a medical practitioner was unlawful. It seems that no doctors performing abortions had been prosecuted in Australia for some 20 years before two were charged in 1998 with contravention of the Criminal Code of Western Australia. The result was the rapid passage of the Acts Amendment (Abortion) Act 1998 (WA) which established what is probably the most liberal legislative control of abortion in Australia.[191] The grounds included what is virtually abortion on request up to the twentieth week of pregnancy. Interestingly, termination after the twentieth week is rather more restricted than it is in other Australian jurisdictions.

The European Ambience

9.88 There is very little to be gained from consideration of the law on abortion as it is laid down in the individual states around Europe, instructive as it may be.[192] If, as the German experience at the time of reunification taught us,[193] there can be profound disagreement within

---

[186] [1988] 1 SCR 30, at 56 per Dickson CJ. For discussion of this decision, see M L McConnell, 'Abortion and human rights: An important Canadian decision' (1989) 38 ICLQ 905.

[187] *Borowski* v *A-G of Canada* (1987) 39 DLR (4th) 731 (Sask, CA).

[188] Crimes Act (Vic) 1958, ss 65, 66, Crimes Act (NSW), ss 82, 83, Criminal Code 1899 (Qld), ss 224–226 where there is also a statutory defence at s 282.

[189] Originating with the essentially negative case of *R* v *Davidson* [1969] VR 667 (the Menhennitt ruling) which introduced the concepts of necessity and proportionality of termination of pregnancy to offset potential harm; *R* v *Wald* (1972) 3 DCR (NSW) 25 in which the social and economic effects of pregnancy were taken into consideration; for Queensland, see *R* v *Bayliss and Cullen* (1986) 9 Qld Lawyer R 8, *Veivers* v *Connolly* [1995] 2 Qd R 326.

[190] *CES* v *Superclinics (Australia) Pty Ltd* (1995) 38 NSWLR 47 per Kirby AC-J. For Australian law in general, see Victoria Law Reform Commission, *Law of Abortion* (Final report, 2008).

[191] By amendments to the Health Act 1911, s 334 (WA).

[192] Some Member States of the EU, e.g. Denmark, have very liberal abortion laws and the impression is that, with the recent increase in membership of the Union, this will apply to the majority—especially when termination is sought in the first 12 weeks of pregnancy. A helpful account of the laws in 22 European countries, as of January 2015, can be found here: http://www.loc.gov/law/help/abortion-legislation/abortion-legislation.pdf.

[193] The history of German legislation is instructive in that it was developed in the ambience of constitutional drama resulting from reunification of the country; it is, therefore, unique in that, rather than being founded predominantly on religious beliefs, it illustrates how secular socio-political ideologies can influence the debate.

one jurisdiction, how much more is there likely to be between 47 sovereign states within the Council of Europe? Reduced to essentials, however, significant variations between states depend not so much on administrative law as on moral attitudes to fetal interests and it is lack of consensus on this particular point that lies behind the ECtHR's steadfast refusal to pronounce firmly on issues involving fetal well-being. Accordingly, we propose to limit discussion to cases relevant to the problem which have been adjudicated in the European courts and which, as a result, have a direct bearing on the UK.[194] In point of fact, there is surprisingly little definitive European case law,[195] the great majority of the early applications having fallen at the first hurdle of scrutiny by the erstwhile European Commission.

9.89 Perhaps the nearest approach to a positive decision by the latter is to be found in *H v Norway*[196] where the Commission found it did not have to decide whether the fetus 'may enjoy a certain protection under Article 2' but 'did not exclude the possibility'. Otherwise, both the Commission and the Court have been dominated by the realisation that a diversity of opinion is inevitable in a multinational organisation and have, thus, allowed a wide margin of appreciation to the individual jurisdictions—the basic principle being that a fair balance is struck between maternal and fetal interests.[197] More recently, however, an almost perfect case for a full analysis of fetal status presented to the ECtHR in the form of *Vo v France*.[198] Once again, the result was unsatisfactory but most of the problems associated with the definition of 'personhood' that we have discussed earlier were addressed as the case progressed through the French courts; it is, therefore, worth considering in some detail.

The Case of Mrs Vo

9.90 Mrs Vo attended an antenatal clinic at approximately 21 weeks' gestation. Following a series of extraordinary administrative mishaps, the obstetrician negligently perforated the amniotic sac and this resulted in the death of the fetus; Mrs Vo raised actions under both the civil and the criminal law but it is the latter with which we are mainly concerned, the charge against the doctor being that of unintentional homicide. The passage through the courts was turbulent—the main basis for the action lying in Article 16 of the French civil code which provides:

> The law secures the primacy of the person ... and guarantees the respect of every human being from the beginning of life.

The court of first instance noted that the terms 'embryo' and 'human embryo' were undefined in the law and that there was no legal rule to determine the position of the fetus in law. A number of definitions attempted by Members of Parliament were, however, quoted. The following[199] expresses the general tenor:

> It is not yet known with precision when the zygote becomes an embryo and the embryo a f[o]etus, the only indisputable fact being that the life process starts with impregnation.

---

[194] See also the case of *D v Ireland* discussed at para 9.77 and *A v Ireland* at para 9.78.

[195] See D Fenwick, '"Abortion jurisprudence" at Strasbourg: deferential, avoidant and normatively neutral?' (2014) 34(2) LS 214.

[196] Application 17004/90, Commission decision of 19 May 1992.

[197] In the early case of *Bruggemann and Scheuten v Federal Republic of Germany* [1977] 3 EHRR 113 it was held that not every aspect of the regulation of termination of pregnancy constitutes an interference with a woman's private life. The state had not done so by prohibiting abortion on demand. See also one of the, then, relatively rare cases to go to the Court: *Bosso v Italy* (Application 50490/99), ECtHR 2002-VII where the Court was not prepared to interfere with domestic legislation.

[198] *Vo v France* (2005) 10 EHRR 12; (2004) 79 BMLR 71. We have discussed this case at length in J K Mason, 'What's in a name?—The vagaries of *Vo v France*' (2005) 17 CFLQ 97.

[199] Attributed to Professor J-F Mattéi.

Faced with such legal indecision, the court resorted to basic science and declared that a fetus of 21 weeks' gestation was not viable, was not, therefore, a 'human person', and that, accordingly, the offence of unintentional homicide of a 21-week-old fetus was not made out—in short, there was no such offence as feticide.

9.91 The Cour d'Appel, however, reverted to the concept of 'the beginning of life' and also to the truism that viability is an indefinite and uncertain concept[200]—it was, in fact, held to be devoid of all legal effect and that 'elementary common sense', inter alia, dictated that negligence leading to the death of a 20- to 24-week-old fetus should be classified as unintentional homicide. The Cour de Cassation, by contrast, almost inevitably decided that the criminal law provisions must be strictly construed and that the fetus was not a person in law.

9.92 The issue then went to the ECtHR whose decision was eagerly awaited. In the event, however, the majority of the Court[201] addressed the case in terms of abortion law; having done so, it ruled that it had no competence to decide on matters which were essentially the prerogative of individual legislatures. Clearly, the cynic might well say that it is but another example of the refusal of judiciaries to come to terms with the problem of fetal status. It seems to us that there is no insuperable difficulty in harmonising the concept of feticide—of which *Vo* was an undoubted example[202]—with therapeutic abortion, nor does the acceptance of the former threaten the rights of the pregnant woman as to the latter. Rather, acknowledging an offence of feticide serves only to protect the interests of the woman who *wants* to maintain her pregnancy. But this is, admittedly, the easy case. In contrast, the reluctance of the ECtHR and other judicial fora to address the fetal question directly may largely be born of the fear of establishing precedents that cannot then be controlled and which might open dangerous floodgates in the realm of maternal/fetal conflict in circumstances where the woman does *not* want to remain pregnant.[203]

Further Developments

9.93 Other developments, however, indicate that the European courts may be involved in more interests—or 'rights'—than those of the fetus. In *Tysiąc v Poland*,[204] the Court held that, in addition to defining a right to respect for one's private life, Art 8 of the European Convention might also impose positive obligations by which to render such respect effective. Ms Tysiąc had lodged a criminal complaint against the doctor whose report had prevented her from having a termination. The Court held that, in framing the abortion regulations in such a loose way as to make it possible to establish liability on the part of the medical staff while acting within their terms, the Polish state had failed to comply with their positive obligations to secure effective respect for the applicant's

---

[200] For which see para 9.99.

[201] We discuss the historical attitude of the ECtHR towards fetal status in G T Laurie, 'Medical law and human rights: Passing the parcel back to the profession' in A Boyle et al. (eds), *Human Rights and Scots Law* (2002).

[202] The minority opinions in the case are especially useful and concede that the Court could and should have done better.

[203] But the difficulties are not insuperable particularly if consideration is given only to the 'viable' fetus (see para 9.99). For further discussion, see A Plomer, 'A foetal right to life? The case of *Vo v France*' (2005) 5 HRL Rev 311.

[204] Application 5410/03, Judgment of 20 March 2007. For discussion, see N Priaulx, 'Testing the margin of appreciation: Therapeutic abortion, reproductive rights, and the intriguing case of *Tysiąc v Poland*' (2008) 15 European J Hlth L 361; the author shares our difficulty in interpreting the judgment.

private life (at para 129).[205] *Tysiąc* was, admittedly, an atypical case in that the pregnancy posed a real threat to the woman's health which subsequently materialised—there was, therefore, no *conflict* of rights. Nonetheless, the judgment suggests that the ECtHR is likely to adopt an increasingly proactive stance to the termination of pregnancy when domestic legislation imposes significant restrictions on its availability and is, perhaps, veering towards the US concept of access to abortion being a matter of personal privacy. As a result, it is possible that future similar actions will be more likely to succeed in the European courts by arguing that the domestic law is inadequate in protecting against an infringement of a woman's rights under Art 8 rather than that it is incompatible with Convention rights[206]—retrospective measures are inadequate for the task (at [127]). Even so, although Art 8(2) was not mentioned,[207] the judgment as a whole has shades of incompatibility due to lack of clarity as to the consequences and effect of the existing law on the claimant: 'It created a situation of prolonged uncertainty. As a result, the applicant suffered severe distress and anguish' (at [124]). There are distinct similarities with the House of Lords' interpretation of Art 8(2) in the totally unassociated English case of Ms Purdy.[208]

9.94 Finally, the decision in *P v Poland*[209] demonstrates that the ECtHR will strictly hold a signatory state to its own legal obligations. In this case a 14-year-old rape victim decided quickly after discovering she was pregnant to seek a termination. She was in possession of official documentation certifying her eligibility under the law, but was then twice refused a referral, and the second hospital made her see a priest and leaked her details to the national press. Moreover, she was removed from her parents to a juvenile shelter. While the ECtHR acknowledge a state interest in ensuring citizens are fully informed about such life decisions, the removal and the failure to respect confidentiality were simply unjustifiable in human rights terms. A violation of Art 8 had occurred. A state cannot provide legal rights, such as access to abortion, and then arbitrarily impose real limits on the exercise of the same.

SOME SPECIAL ASPECTS OF FETAL STATUS AND TERMINATION OF PREGNANCY

9.95 We have considered fetal status in terms of a continuum at para 9.07. There are, however, points in fetal development which have special legal implications. The first of these is at the very beginning of fetal life.

9.96 So-called interceptive methods of contraception have been discussed within that section at para 9.18. They are to be contrasted with other procedures, in particular menstrual extraction and late insertion of IUDs, when these are performed not for contraceptive purposes but, at least partly, because a pregnancy might exist and before a definitive

---

[205] There is a suggestion that a similar policy is emerging in the UK jurisprudence. In *Rand v East Dorset Health Authority* [2000] 56 BMLR 39, Newman J found that the mere existence of the Abortion Act 1967 was sufficient to impose a duty on an Authority to take steps to ensure that the parents could exercise their choice under the Act (at 57).

[206] As suggested by B Hewson, 'Therapeutic abortion—human right or wrong' (2006) 156 NLJ 1348 based on a comparison of *D v Ireland*, para 9.77, and the preliminary hearing in *Tysiąc*.

[207] Which states, 'There shall be no interference ... with the exercise of this right except such as is in accordance with the law'.

[208] *R (on the application of Purdy) v Director of Public Prosecutions* [2009] 3 WLR 403, HL.

[209] *P v Poland* [2013] 1 FCR 476; (2013) 129 BMLR 12.

diagnosis can be made. In our view, menstrual extraction, which deals with the termination of a problematical implantation, is probably unlawful from two aspects. In the first place it is difficult to see why it is not using an instrument with the intention to procure the miscarriage of a woman 'whether or not she be with child' and, accordingly, transgresses s 58 of the Offences Against the Person Act 1861. In addition, it cannot be rendered legal under the terms of the 1967 Act which is concerned with the assessment of an established pregnancy; in the circumstances of the test, it is impossible to comply with the regulations as to certification.[210] Nonetheless, as we have already suggested, displanting 'contraception' is among those forms of 'after the fact' action to prevent the birth of an unwanted baby which are less likely to offend the public conscience than is frank fetal destruction; it seems illogical that they could be equally liable to censure under the 1861 Act.

9.97 The same considerations apply to the late insertion of an IUD but, so far as we know, only one apposite prosecution has succeeded; the case did, however, concern the insertion of an IUD into a woman who was certainly pregnant.[211] Rather more help can be gained from an unreported case[212] which involved a charge under s 58 of the Offences Against the Person Act 1861 against a doctor who fitted a contraceptive coil to his secretary some 11 days after they had had intercourse. The judge, having heard gynaecological evidence that implantation would not have occurred, withdrew the case from the jury on the ground that the woman could not have been pregnant 'in the true sense of the word'. He is also reported as saying, 'Only at the completion of implantation does the embryo become a fetus. At this stage, she can be regarded as pregnant'.[213] Thus, the question of what would be the result if an IUD were to be fitted after the eleventh day following intercourse still remains open. It seems unlikely that a prosecution would succeed—the difficulty of proving intent would be almost insurmountable. Whatever may be the true situation in England and Wales, it is apparent that a prosecution in these circumstances for the common law crime of procuring an abortion could not succeed in Scotland, where proof of pregnancy is essential to a successful prosecution for that offence. Nonetheless, the possibility of a prosecution for attempted abortion remains open.[214]

9.98 Consideration of early termination techniques must now include 'medical' abortion. There has been surprisingly little overt opposition to the method in Britain[215]—although, by contrast, the introduction of mifepristone in France resulted in pressure sufficient to force the manufacturers to withdraw the product until the government, as a major shareholder, insisted on the resumption of research and clinical evaluation. It is possible to recategorise the process as 'contragestation' rather than abortion.[216] Semantics cannot, however, disguise the fact that the treatment is clearly abortifacient; it can, therefore, be

---

[210] SI 1968/390.

[211] *R v Price* [1969] 1 QB 541; [1968] 2 All ER 282. The conviction was quashed on the ground of a misdirection.

[212] *R v Dhingra* (1991) *Daily Telegraph*, 25 January, p 5. The case was quoted with approval in *Smeaton*, n 39 but it is to be noted that *Smeaton* was not concerned with mechanical displanting methods.

[213] He may have been attentive to the terms of the Human Fertilisation and Embryology Act 1990, s 2(3) which states that '*For the purposes of this Act*, a woman is not to be treated as carrying a child until the embryo has become implanted'. The emphasis is added but the wording could be persuasive in other branches of the law.

[214] *Docherty v Brown* 1996 SLT 325.   [215] See n 217.

[216] R Macklin, 'Antiprogestin drugs: Ethical issues' (1992) 20 Law Med Hlth Care 215 is of particular, albeit now of little more than historical, interest.

administered only within the terms of the 1967 Act.[217] We are concerned that 'medical abortion' will inevitably come to be regarded as a safe form of contraceptive back-up. It overtook surgical abortions for the first time in 2014. The result must be to blur the essential ethical distinction between contraception and abortion; while these two processes may be comparable in that they both *prevent* new life, it is only abortion that can be seen as *taking* life.

Viability

9.99 Elsewhere in the context of fetal life, the law's main concern with gestational age lies in the concept of viability. This is not only a matter of UK jurisprudence; viability is universally regarded as an important milestone—and we have seen to what an extent it worried the French courts in the case of Mrs Vo. It merits more than cursory consideration.

9.100 Viability is something of a legal fiction, originating in the USA, that is designed to define some point at which the state accepts a compelling interest to protect the lives of its unborn citizens. Conceptually, therefore, viability is a term of US constitutional law and it probably has no place in English law, which generally refers, in the same context, to 'capability of being born alive'. 'Live birth' itself, however, remained undefined until the seminal case of *C v S*[218] and this gave rise to some interpretative confusion. A stillborn child is one that did not at any time after being completely expelled from its mother breathe or show any other sign of life[219]—from which it follows that, from the registrar's point of view, the neonate need only have managed one breath, which may well have been unproductive, to have been 'born alive'.[220] Definitions intended for statistical use are not, however, necessarily the same as those to be applied in practice. Thus, on the one hand, the statutory definition has considerable relevance to the investigation of infanticide or child murder.[221] Very different issues are, however, raised in relation to abortion which attracts moral overtones in addition to those of criminality. As Sir John Donaldson MR said in *C v S*,[222] the interpretation of the statutory words 'capable of being born alive' is a matter for the courts—and he contented himself with holding that, in respect of the 1929 Act, a fetus that would be incapable ever of breathing either naturally or with the aid of a ventilator was not capable of being born alive.

9.101 This is a negative conclusion and the obverse decision was reached in *Rance*,[223] which, like its closely analogous case *Gregory*,[224] was a matter of 'wrongful birth' (see Chapter 10). There it was held that a child was born alive if, after its birth, it existed as a live child, that is to say, was breathing and living through the use of its own lungs alone. From the point of view of

---

[217] See, now, the Abortion Act 1967, s 1(3A) (inserted by Human Fertilisation and Embryology Act 1990, s 37(3)) which extends the types of premises in which a legal abortion can be performed.

[218] [1988] QB 135; [1987] 1 All ER 1230.

[219] Births and Deaths Registration Act 1953, s 41; Registration of Births, Deaths and Marriages (Scotland) Act 1965, s 56. It must also be of 24 weeks' or more gestation: Still-Birth (Definition) Act 1992, s 1.

[220] 'Any other sign of life' might include a feebly beating heart. This was the view of the World Health Organization quoted in *C v S* [1988] QB 135 at 142; [1987] 1 All ER 1230 at 1236. For reasons given in the text, we doubt its significance now.

[221] *Attorney General for Northern Ireland v Senior Coroner for Northern Ireland* [2013] NICA 68; [2015] NI 14 ('A coroner would not be acting ultra vires by conducting an inquest pursuant to the Coroners Act (Northern Ireland) 1959 s.14(1) into a stillbirth. The effect of s.18(1) was to extend the definition of "deceased person" to include a foetus in utero then capable of being born alive.').

[222] At QB 151; All ER 1242.

[223] *Rance v Mid-Downs Health Authority* [1991] 1 QB 587; [1991] 1 All ER 801.

[224] *Gregory v Pembrokeshire Health Authority* [1989] 1 Med LR 81.

the law of homicide, therefore, the meaning of being born alive remains as it was decided more than a century ago.[225] 'Live birth' is clearly defined by the capacity to breathe and the confusing phrase 'any other sign of life' is, correspondingly, irrelevant in this context.[226]

9.102 Thus, the concepts of US viability and British live birth are, now, congruent but both have their difficulties. In the first place, both depend upon the medical support available; second, the diagnosis can only be made after the event—a matter of importance in relation to the living abortus (see later). The case of Mrs Rance also demonstrates vividly the unsatisfactory state of the law prior to 1990. Her child was known to be physically abnormal but, by the time the diagnosis was established, the gynaecologists were unable to terminate the pregnancy for fear of transgressing the Infant Life (Preservation) Act 1929. The possibility of the doctor being accused of child destruction under the 1929 Act by way of aborting a 'child capable of being born alive' has now been removed[227] but it is arguable that it has been replaced by additional technical problems and by moral considerations which are, if anything, exaggerated by the 1990 amendments to the 1967 Act.

9.103 Those who support the interests of the fetus have always been concerned to prevent the abortion, or feticide, of those capable of a free existence by lowering the fetal age beyond which termination is impermissible so as to keep in step with the increasing medical capacity to lower the age of 'viability'. They can be said to have succeeded to an extent by having this set at 24 weeks for the relatively slight medical and social reasons described in s 1(1)(a) of the 1967 Act.[228] The offset is that it maybe difficult, particularly in the face of human error, to make a prognosis of serious neonatal handicap within that timescale. Accordingly, the 1990 Act removed the prevailing 28 weeks' legal limit and imposed no other time restrictions on abortions performed by reason of fetal abnormality. Similar de-restriction applies in the event of risk or grave injury to the pregnant woman—and such conditions are likely to arise particularly in late gestation. The *need* for late abortion thus remains and the Act is silent as to what is to be done with a live abortus. It has to be remembered that a living abortus is a creature in being; to kill such a being or to allow it to die without good reason may be murder or manslaughter—and s 37(4) of the 1990 Act absolves the gynaecologist of child destruction only.

9.104 One practical solution is to ensure that no mature abortus is given the opportunity to live. It is possible to attempt this by varying the fluid used in the infusion of the amniotic sac, which may, of itself, be relatively dangerous to the pregnant woman. But the vast majority of late terminations are performed by way of dilatation and evacuation (D&E) of the uterus which incorporates piece-by-piece removal of a well-formed fetus—and it is difficult to visualise a process which offends the Hippocratic and intuitive conscience more directly.[229] This is exemplified by the furore which surrounded 'partial-birth' abortion,

---

[225] *R v Handley* (1874) 13 Cox CC 79.

[226] But it may still have significance in some circumstances. Based on the *C v S* definition, a case can be made out for the disabled Siamese twin in the well-known case of *Re A (children) (conjoined twins: surgical separation)* [2001] Fam 147; [2000] 4 All ER 961 having been stillborn despite the apparent evidence of life. See J K Mason, 'Conjoined twins: A diagnostic conundrum' (2001) 5 Edin LR 226.

[227] 1990 Act, s 37(4).

[228] There have been repeated attempts to lower the age at which a 'social' abortion can be performed still further. The UK government has not, however, supported this in the past: A O'Dowd, 'No evidence backs reduction in abortion time limit, minister says' (2007) 335 BMJ 903. It is arguable that the discussion is misplaced—viability has little fundamental importance in the abortion debate in that abortion destroys human life at any stage of fetal development.

[229] The House of Lords approved the action of the BBC when it prohibited an election broadcast that showed abortions in practice: *R (ProLife Alliance) v British Broadcasting Corporation* [2004] 1 AC 185.

a variation on D&E, in the USA. Here, a Nebraska statute banning the procedure was declared unconstitutional by the Supreme Court,[230] as a result of which, Congress enacted the Partial-Birth Abortion Ban Act 2003. This was, again, struck down by two Circuit Appeal courts but, having undergone a change of personnel, the Supreme Court now upheld the Congressional ban[231] on the grounds that it did not impose an undue burden on the due process right of women to obtain an abortion.

9.105 It was precisely this situation that the 'pro-life'[232] parliamentary lobby sought to avoid and a clause designed to ensure that reasonable steps were taken to assist a mature abortus to live was introduced at a late stage in the debate on the 1990 Bill.[233] The motion was defeated, largely as a result of advice that doctors carrying out terminations after the twenty-fourth week of pregnancy 'would make every conceivable effort ... to make sure the baby was capable of living ... a normal and independent existence'.[234] It seems, however, that times have changed, The Royal College of Obstetricians and Gynaecologists now recommends feticide as a preliminary to all terminations beyond a gestational age of 22 weeks.[235] Feticide has become a routine part of late termination of pregnancy—and this is not only for the reasons discussed later but also to ensure that the fetus suffers no pain in the process.[236]

The Living Abortus

9.106 The obstetrician presented with a live abortus is certainly in a difficult position. On the one hand, he or she has effectively contracted to relieve a woman of her fetus. On the other, there is now an infant who, on any interpretation, is entitled to a birth certificate and, if necessary, a certificate as to the cause of death.[237] Considerations as to the proper use of limited resources must also colour any decision-making. The principles underlying elective non-treatment of a disabled neonate (see Chapter 15) might well apply but, otherwise, we can see no theoretical objection to the view that failure to attempt to sustain a living infant could result in a charge of manslaughter or, in Scotland, of culpable homicide.

9.107 Legal precedents are slender in Great Britain. What few there are, are largely confined to the Coroners' courts and, even then, are inconsistent. In fact, it is the sheer dearth

---

[230] *Stenberg* v *Carhart* 530 US 914 (2000).

[231] *Gonzales* v *Carhart* 550 US 124 (2007). It is to be noted that both decisions were by a 5:4 majority. To emphasise the intensity of the argument, the decision in *Gonzales* was deprecated by the medical profession as being 'the first time the Court has ever held that physicians can be prohibited from using a medical procedure deemed necessary ... to benefit the patient's health': G J Annas, 'The Supreme Court and abortion rights' (2007) 356 New Engl J Med 2201.

[232] It has been pointed out that the wide use of this term is unfortunate in that it implies that the opponents are 'anti-life': S McLean, 'Emotional extremes miss the heart of abortion dilemma', *Scotland on Sunday*, 25 April 2004.

[233] Such a condition has been declared unconstitutional in the USA: *Colautti* v *Franklin* 439 US 379 (1979); *American College of Obstetricians and Gynecologists Pennsylvania Section* v *Thornburgh* 106 S Ct 2169 (1986).

[234] Official Reports (Lords) vol 522, col 1043 (18 October 1990), per Lord Walton at 1050.

[235] RCOG, *Termination of Pregnancy for Fetal Abnormality* (2010, at 29). The Department of Health abortion statistics for 2014 report that: 'In 2014, of the 1,193 abortions performed at 22 weeks and over, 58% were reported as preceded by a feticide and a further 37% were performed by a method whereby the fetal heart is stopped as part of the procedure. 4% of abortions at 22 weeks or beyond were confirmed as having no feticide. For the remaining 12 cases, at the time of publication, we had not been able to confirm whether feticide had been performed' (para 2.43).

[236] M Brazier and E Cave, *Medicine, Patients and the Law* (5th edn, 2011) at 407.

[237] See Lord Wells-Pestell, HL Official Reports (5th series) col 776 (12 December 1974).

of cases which leads us to believe that the living abortus is not a significant problem in practice.[238] This is not so much a matter of the law turning a blind eye as that, as we have already seen, those performing the termination will ensure that the process is, intentionally, feticidal—and within the law, given the current ethical climate, in the UK. Even so, it is hard to defend the position in terms of morality; the living abortus has no such time to plead his or her case as is available to the disabled neonate.

9.108 The discussion, thus far, has failed to recognise that there is, in fact, no certainty that all women seeking a termination of pregnancy also seek the destruction of their fetus—indeed, the longer a woman has carried her fetus, the more likely it is that she would wish to preserve it. McLean, while insisting on the woman's right to control her whole pregnancy, has enlarged this concept and has suggested that attitudes might, with advantage, be overturned and that women might be given encouragement and the *opportunity* to undergo late, and salvageable, abortions.[239] Indeed, one might go further and encourage women to go to term; there is no reason why surviving neonates of either category should not be regarded as parentless infants and offered for adoption on that basis.

OTHER PEOPLE'S RIGHTS

9.109 The rights of those who, of necessity, participate in terminations of pregnancy receive comparatively little attention in the abortion debate as compared with that devoted to the woman and her fetus. Yet, they are of very considerable communitarian importance.[240]

Conscientious Objection

9.110 Section 4 of the Abortion Act 1967 excuses the conscientious objector from participating in treatment by abortion unless that treatment is directed towards the saving of life or of preventing grave permanent injury to the health of the mother.[241] But, while this would seem to be perfectly clear, not everyone would agree as to the doctor's right to such a dispensation—this largely on the grounds that it leads to uncertainty and, perhaps, to discriminatory treatment.[242] This may, in fact, work two ways in that an unfortunate result of s 4 is that some discrimination must be levelled against doctors, and especially those seeking to become gynaecologists, who are unable to accept the wide terms of the 1967 Act. It is to be noted that, while a doctor may, in general, refuse to take part in the abortion procedure, he or she remains under an obligation to advise. The GMC has published

---

[238] Yet, an investigative journalist reported six contemporary cases in which a living abortus was allowed to die and no action had been taken: S-K Templeton and L Rogers, 'Babies that live after abortions are left to die', *Sunday Times*, 20 June 2004, p 1.3. It is fair to say that this view has been regarded as unduly complacent: see Wicks et al., n 146.

[239] S A M McLean, 'Women, rights and reproduction' in S A M McLean (ed), *Legal Issues in Human Reproduction* (1989); see the same author 'Abortion law: Is consensual reform possible?' (1990) 17 J Law & Soc 106.

[240] See the recent (failed) attempt before the European Committee of Social Rights to challenge Sweden's absence of conscientious objection laws for health workers with respect to induced abortion, *Federation of Catholic Families in Europe (Fafce) v Sweden* (2015) 61 EHRR SE12.

[241] Conscientious objection is becoming something of a European political football. The Council of Europe's Parliamentary Assembly has adopted a resolution (but only by a majority of 56:51) affirming the principle but, at the same time, calling for states to ensure it is appropriately regulated: Resolution 1763 *The Right to Conscientious Objection in Lawful Medical Care* (October 2010). The Assembly, however, has only a consultative role. See M Campbell, 'Conscientious objection and the Council of Europe' (2011) 19 Med L Rev 467.

[242] For a very critical review, see J Savulescu, 'Conscientious objection in medicine' (2006) 332 BMJ 294.

supplementary guidance on the specific issue[243] which attempts to balance what are both doctors' and patients' rights. Essentially, if the procedure involved is one to which the doctor has a conscientious objection, he or she must tell the patient of her[244] right to see another doctor and provide the patient with sufficient information to exercise that right.[245] Providing such information is subject to the normal rules of medical negligence; moreover, since in the specific context of abortion, a second referral inevitably delays a termination, the objecting doctor must ensure that arrangements are made, without delay, for another doctor to take over the patient's care in the event that she is unable to make her own arrangements. Moreover, in providing information a doctor should not express disapproval of a patient's lifestyle, choices, or beliefs. It is often forgotten that a doctor's objection to abortion may be Hippocratic rather than, say, religious in origin; whatever its basis, however, the doctor's conscience does not, as we have seen, absolve him or her from treating a woman when the continuation of the pregnancy is life-threatening; consequently, statute can deprive a doctor of his or her rights as well as to specify the entitlement. These considerations apply equally to the nursing staff and other health care workers who have their own professional guidelines.

The Nursing Staff and Others Involved

9.111   The role of the nurse in therapy of all types is becoming more significant; this is exemplified in the sphere of abortion by the widespread use of prostaglandin infusions for induction of premature labour. Nurses have so great a part to play in this process that some doubt was raised as to whether they were, in fact, thus guilty of performing illegal abortions in the sense that they were not 'registered medical practitioners' as required by the 1967 Act; the Royal College of Nursing accordingly sought a declaration to the effect that the advice in a departmental circular[246] stating that, irrespective of the precise action taken, an abortion was legal provided that it was initiated by and was the responsibility of a registered medical practitioner, was wrong in law. The complexities were such that the Royal College lost its case in the High Court, won it in the Court of Appeal, and, finally, lost it in the House of Lords.[247] The result is, therefore, that abortion, no matter how it is performed, is accomplished by way of a team effort and is no different in this respect from any other form of treatment. It is, nevertheless, interesting that, in total, five out of nine judges involved took the view of the nurses.

9.112   We believe that, in general, the sensibilities of the nursing staff are inadequately recognised within the abortion debate. The damage that conscientious objection causes to their career prospects may well be greater than that sustained by doctors—a doctor does not *have* to practise gynaecology but, as Lord Denning emphasised many year ago, nurses are expected to be mobile throughout the hospital system.[248] Moreover, current

---

[243] GMC, *Personal Beliefs and Medical Practice* (2013), available at: http://www.gmc-uk.org/guidance/ethical_guidance/21171.asp. See too J V McHale, 'Faith, belief, fundamental rights and delivering health care in a modern NHS: an unrealistic aspiration?' (2013) 21 Health Care Analysis 224.

[244] Note that the GMC's guidance refers to objection to 'a particular procedure' not just to an intervention for which there is statutory relief. The BMA criticises this open-endedness and suggests that the guidance should be limited to a shortlist of clearly defined procedures.

[245] *Barr v Matthews* (2000) 52 BMLR 217 provides an interesting commentary, including the option of adoption. Alliott J approved an arrangement whereby a conscientious objector immediately referred a termination case to a colleague.

[246] CMO (80) (2).

[247] *Royal College of Nursing of the United Kingdom* v *Department of Health and Social Security* [1981] AC 800; [1981] 1 All ER 545, HL.

[248] [1981] AC 800 at 804–5; [1981] 1 All ER 545 at 555.

methods of termination beyond the twelfth week of pregnancy involve the nursing staff in an uncompromising way—whether it be in the delivery of what is comparable to a premature birth or in counting the fragmented parts of a formed fetus;[249] there can be no doubts as to their *rights* to special consideration even if these are not always respected.

9.113 Valid conscientious objection within the terms of s 4 of the Abortion Act 1967 is, however, limited by a proximity test—that is, that it covers only those involved in the therapeutic team effort. The case of Mrs Janaway, who regarded herself as having been unfairly dismissed following her refusal to type a letter referring a patient for termination of pregnancy, was considered so important that it was taken to the House of Lords.[250] In the event, Mrs Janaway failed at every step, essentially on the grounds that participation in treatment, in terms of s 4, referred to actual participation in treatment administered in a hospital or other approved place. Mrs Janaway's case does not provide the ideal test as she was clearly well distanced from the actual treatment.[251] Even so, the right to conscientious objection is clearly closely circumscribed. In *Doogan* v *Greater Glasgow and Clyde Health Board*,[252] the Supreme Court rejected a claim to s 4 protection by two midwives whose primary duties consisted of coordinating the work of the labour ward.[253] It reiterated the point already made by the House of Lords that the protection only extended to those professionals taking part in the medical treatment itself; it did not extend to those who carried out ancillary, administrative, and managerial tasks which are necessarily, but indirectly, associated with the provisions of termination services.[254] The advent of medical termination also raises the unusual position of the conscientiously objecting pharmacist who is asked to fill the necessary prescriptions; we have previously expressed the view that any proximity test would be satisfied, while acknowledging that much would depend on how the relationship between the pharmaceutical and medical professions is viewed; in light of the recent Supreme Court ruling, however, this might not be so because the court preferred the narrow view of any test, being restricted to '... actually performing the tasks involved in the course of treatment' (para 37).[255]

---

[249] The seminal work, J Glover, *Causing Death and Saving Lives* (reprinted 1986) p 142 points to the effects on the health carers as providing a major moral distinction between, say, contraception and abortion.

[250] *R* v *Salford Health Authority, ex p Janaway* [1989] AC 537, CA; affd sub nom *Janaway* v *Salford Area Health Authority* [1989] AC 537; [1988] 3 All ER 1079, HL.

[251] But see C Foster, 'When two freedoms collide' (2005) 155 NLJ 1624.

[252] [2015] UKSC 68; [2015] AC 640; [2015] 2 WLR 126.

[253] It is interesting that, whereas the 'conscience clause' in the 1967 Act refers to participation in 'any treatment' authorised by the Act, s 38 of the Human Fertilisation and Embryology Act 1990, which 'governs' abortion by way of s 37, refers to participation in 'any activity' governed by the Act. The latter is, arguably, open to wider interpretation.

[254] For comment, see C Beresford, 'Human rights: religion or belief – interference with – healthworkers' (2015) 4(2) Ox J Law and Religion 328, and M Neal, 'The scope of the conscience-based exemption in section 4(1) of the Abortion Act 1967: Doogan and Wood v NHS Greater Glasgow Health Board' (2014) 22(3) Med Law Rev 409.

[255] The philosophical arguments have been aired by D P Flynn, 'Pharmacist conscience clauses and access to oral contraceptives' (2008) 34 J Med Ethics 517. This is from the US view, where the impression is gained that the woman's right to treatment would trump the pharmacist's moral stance in the US courts. Even so, it is reported that four US states have passed legislation to allow pharmacists to refuse to fill prescriptions for emergency contraception and similar draft legislation is in preparation in nearly half the states. By contrast, nine states have 'must fill' policies: V English et al., 'Ethics briefings' (2006) 32 J Med Ethics 743 at 744. More recently, Z Deans, 'Conscientious objections in pharmacy practice in Great Britain' (2013) 27(1) Bioethics 48.

The Father

9.114 The anomalous position of the father in the right to life debate also falls to be considered. It is clear from current worldwide decisions that, insofar as abortion is concerned, he has, for practical purposes, *no* rights. It seems incongruous that this should be so, irrespective of the reason for the abortion, and that it should apply even in cases which do not relate to the health of the mother; a father could not, for example, save the existence of a potentially haemophiliac son. Morally speaking, it seems that the anxious father should, ideally, be entitled to a hearing but this would surely be as far as one could go—it would not be possible to support any legal right to the unacceptable consequences that might attend acceptance of his wishes.

9.115 The English position was established in *Paton*,[256] where it was clearly laid down that a husband cannot by injunction prevent his wife from undergoing a lawful abortion. The decision was upheld by the European Commission on Human Rights; the Commission was, however, clearly worried by the possible complication of fetal 'viability'—the matter was not decided and it remains an area of potential doubt.[257] It was clarified no further in *C v S*,[258] in which the unmarried father's *locus standi* was firmly rejected—and the decision was not appealed—but in which the main thrust of the hearing was to establish that the fetus in question was *not* viable.[259] Any possibility that a Scottish fetus might be able to petition through its tutor—that is, its father—for interdict of any threatened harm has now been excluded. In *Kelly v Kelly*,[260] the Inner House of the Court of Session agreed that a review of the extensive Commonwealth decisions supported the view that the fetus had no rights for the protection of which the remedy of interdict might be invoked. It followed, therefore, that the father, as the guardian of the fetus, had no standing by which to prevent his wife's abortion.[261]

9.116 Attitudes elsewhere in the Commonwealth are generally in agreement. The firm English stance would seem to be accepted in New Zealand but the reasoning there was based more on statute than on common law.[262] It is unlikely that an injunction to prevent a maternally desired abortion would ever be granted in Australia but the position there is, again, complicated—this time by considerations of legality.[263] It is only in Canada that paternal status has achieved a glimmer of recognition. In *Medhurst*,[264] a husband was given standing to seek an injunction against abortion and in *Tremblay*,[265] it was considered that a potential father had as much right to speak on behalf of the fetus as anyone; neither of these cases succeeded beyond this and they probably represent no more than the general willingness of the Canadian courts to grant a *locus standi* to interested parties.[266]

---

[256] *Paton v British Pregnancy Advisory Service Trustees* [1979] QB 276; [1978] 2 All ER 987.

[257] *Paton v United Kingdom* (1980) 3 EHRR 408.   [258] [1988] QB 135; [1987] 1 All ER 1230.

[259] Nor can a father recover for distress on hearing diagnosis of miscarriage, *Wild v Southend University Hospital NHS Foundation Trust* [2014] EWHC 4053 (QB).

[260] 1997 SC 285; 1997 SCLR 749.

[261] *X v United Kingdom* (Application 8416/79) 1980. By contrast, paternal rights as to the neonate have been confirmed by the ECtHR. An unmarried father can veto the adoption of his child: *Keegan v Ireland* (Application 16969/90) (1994) 18 EHRR 342.

[262] *Wall v Livingston* [1982] 1 NZLR 734, NZCA.

[263] *A-G of Queensland (ex rel Kerr) v T* (1983) 46 ALR 275 indicates the difficulties.

[264] *Medhurst v Medhurst* (1984) 9 DLR (4th) 252.

[265] *Tremblay v Daigle* (1989) 59 DLR (4th) 609.

[266] See also *Re Simms and H* (1980) 106 DLR (3d) 435.

9.117 There is every reason to suppose that this worldwide negative attitude to paternal/fetal rights will persist. Nothing can alter the fact that it is the woman who carries the fetus for nine months and whose health is mainly at risk during that time—and it is this factor which explains the difference in legal attitudes to the father's interest in his fetus and in his in vitro embryo which we have discussed at para 8.83. An objecting father may well deserve sympathy but, in the final analysis, a woman's right to control her body must take precedence.

ABORTION AND THE INCOMPETENT

9.118 We have no reason to believe that termination of pregnancy in the mentally incapacitated or minors is to be regarded differently from any other aspect of medical treatment; the principles involved are, therefore, best considered within the whole spectrum of consent, which is addressed in Chapter 4. In respect of minors, the courts will, in the event of conflict, always put the interests of a young mother above those of her fetus—indeed, they *must* do so.[267]

9.119 Specific problems as to confidentiality—and particularly in respect of parental rights and duties—are, however, likely to arise in the unique context of under-age pregnancy. At one time, these caused particular concern in the USA; the matter has now probably been put beyond dispute in *Casey*,[268] where the need for parental consent was confirmed.

9.120 In Britain, the concept of the 'understanding child' has gone unchallenged since it was first mooted by Butler-Sloss J in 1982.[269] There can, however, be no doubt that to perform an operation without parental permission on a child too young to understand the issues—and, hence, to give a valid consent—would constitute an assault. In practice, absent strongly held religious views, it must be very rare for the parents of an unmarried girl below the age of 16 not to consent to termination of pregnancy[270] but the question remains—*must* the parents be informed prior to legal termination of a minor's pregnancy? The Abortion Act itself makes no distinctions as to age.[271] One might suppose that the majority of children who are old enough to *become* pregnant are also old enough to understand the consequences but there are bound to be exceptions. A case in point is *Re X (A Child) (Capacity to Consent to Termination)*[272] where a 13-year-old girl was assessed to be non-*Gillick*-competent on account of her failure to appreciate the consequence of continued pregnancy and childbirth. Notwithstanding, it was deemed to be in her best interests for a termination to proceed, albeit that her supportive wish for this outcome was heavily influential on the assessment. One wonders what would have happened had she objected.

9.121 The other issue that arises here relates to the conditions as to confidentiality laid down in *Gillick*.[273] The circumstances surrounding pregnancy—including termination of

---

[267] Children Act 1989, s 1(1). See the specific criticism of an expert witness in *Re B (wardship: abortion)* [1991] 2 FLR 426 at 431 per Hollis J.

[268] *Planned Parenthood of Southeastern Pennsylvania* v *Casey* 112 S Ct 2791 (1992).

[269] *Re P (a minor)* [1986] 1 FLR 272; (1982) 80 LGR 301.

[270] For a case in which a mother opposed a termination for her 12-year-old daughter, see *Re B (wardship: abortion)* [1991] 2 FLR 426.

[271] In 2014, 2,399 legal terminations were carried out on girls aged under 16.

[272] [2014] EWHC 1871 (Fam); (2014) 139 BMLR 143; [2014] Fam Law 122.

[273] *Gillick* v *West Norfolk and Wisbech Area Health Authority* [1986] AC 112; [1985] 3 All ER 402, HL. The position in Scotland would be covered by the Age of Legal Capacity (Scotland) Act 1991, s 2(4). See Chapter 4 for a full discussion.

pregnancy—and childcare are, however, so unique that, until recently, there have been lingering doubts. These have now been put to rest in *R (on the application of Axon) v Secretary of State for Health*.[274] In that case, the claimant, a divorced mother of five children who had, herself undergone a termination, sought a declaration to the effect that, since a doctor owed no duty of confidentiality to a minor in respect of advice and proposed treatment related to contraception, sexual health, and abortion, he or she could not provide such advice or treatment without the consent of the minor's parents; Ms Axon also sought a declaration that guidelines issued by the Department of Health which failed to acknowledge this exception to the general rule were unlawful. It is hard to see that these claims were anything other than doomed from the start and they were rejected essentially on the ground that, to accept them would involve overturning the House of Lords in *Gillick*. In anticipation of this, the claim was amended, in the alternative, to apply to abortion only and it is this aspect of the case which is of immediate concern to us here.

9.122 Silber J recognised the distinctive aspects of abortion to which we have already alluded and he also accepted that about one-third of terminations in England and Wales involving girls under the age of 16 were carried out without at least one parent being informed (at [83]). In the end, however, he fell back on Lord Fraser in *Gillick* who pointed out that the medical professional was only justified in proceeding without parental consent or knowledge if he or she is satisfied that 'the girl will understand his advice' and on Lord Scarman:[275]

> It is not enough that she should understand the nature of the advice which is being given; she must also have a sufficient maturity to understand what is involved.

In other words, the *Gillick* test is a pliable test that can be adjusted so as to apply to the precise circumstances—the benchmark being that the more intricate or significant in the long term is the treatment to be given, the more mature must be the minor before she can be entrusted with her own destiny. There was nothing in the *Gillick* decision to suggest that it depended on the nature of the treatment under review.[276] Which does not, perhaps, allay one's misgivings as to the unique nature of abortion but which, nevertheless, makes perfect logic so long as *Gillick* represents the relevant law.[277]

9.123 Thus, although the knowledge and agreement of the parents are clearly desirable, a doctor who has made reasonable efforts to induce his patient to confide in her parents and is still faced with an adamant refusal of consent to disclosure and who goes on to terminate a minor's pregnancy would be secure from action in the courts or before the GMC. The trend in medical, legal, and societal attitudes towards children's rights over the last three decades gives added support to this view.[278]

9.124 Almost certainly, many abortions are carried out on the mentally handicapped under the twin cover of good medical practice and legal necessity; authority for termination

---

[274] [2006] QB 539; (2006) 88 BMLR 96.   [275] At [1986] 1 AC 188.

[276] Perhaps the most determinant effect of *Axon* is to quash any attempt to say that *Gillick* was concerned with contraceptive advice alone.

[277] Ms Axon also claimed that her rights under the ECHR, Art 8 were violated by the guidelines but this claim was dismissed in a lengthy judgment which is not directly relevant to this chapter but which merits careful analysis elsewhere. In brief, Ms Axon had no Art 8(1) rights because these only accrued if her daughter was found to be *Gillick*-incompetent.

[278] J Ribot, 'Underage abortion and beyond: developments of Spanish law in competent minor's autonomy' (2012) 20(1) Med L Rev 48.

of pregnancy has probably also been obtained in camera on more than one occasion.[279] Abortion is to be distinguished from, say, sterilisation in that the former is governed by statute which gives sufficient protection to doctors provided they comply with its terms. There is nothing in either the Mental Capacity Act 2005 or the Adults with Incapacity (Scotland) Act 2000 which excludes abortion as a matter on which the designated surrogate can make a decision and, as to a minor, termination of pregnancy falls easily into the ambience of parental decision-making in the case of a *Gillick*-incompetent child. Although a supposed 'right to procreate' is violated by both non-consensual abortion and non-consensual sterilisation, the former does not create the same conditions of permanence as does the latter; a formal declaration of lawfulness by the High Court would, therefore, serve no useful purpose in an uncontested case involving termination of pregnancy.[280] The courts have also confirmed that the proposition-specific nature of any capacity assessment equally applies to termination of pregnancy. Thus, in *Re SB (A Patient) (Capacity to Consent to Termination)*[281] a 37-year-old woman with bipolar disorder and who was detained under the Mental Health Act 1983 was assessed to have sufficient capacity under the Mental Capacity Act 2005 to decide to have an abortion at almost 24 weeks' gestation, despite psychiatric assessment to the contrary. While she suffered from paranoia and delusional thoughts, she nonetheless had given additional sound reasons for desiring a termination that demonstrated her ability to make her own decision on this matter.

REDUCTION OF MULTIPLE PREGNANCY AND SELECTIVE REDUCTION

9.125 The need for a reduction in the number of fetuses carried at one time has been discussed in Chapter 8. Original doubts as to the legality of the process were based mainly on terminological grounds—first on whether the phrase 'termination of pregnancy' in the 1967 Act relates to the pregnancy as a whole and, if this strict interpretation is inappropriate, whether individualised feticide in situ can be regarded as an abortion.[282] Whatever the solution of this interesting academic argument may be, the situation has now been resolved in practice—both selective reduction and reduction of multiple pregnancy in utero are legal when the requirements of the Abortion Act 1967, as amended, are fulfilled in relation to the individual fetus.[283]

9.126 Given that account may be taken of the woman's actual or reasonably foreseeable environment, there is no legal difficulty in justifying pregnancy reduction on the grounds that continuance of a multiple pregnancy would involve a risk of injury to the mental health of the pregnant woman greater than if it was reduced.[284] It might be equally appropriate to plead risk to the physical or mental health of the existing family—particularly if the intended remaining fetus or fetuses were regarded as 'existing children of the family'. Selective destruction of an abnormal fetus is, of course, justified under the serious

---

[279] F Gibb, 'Judge orders abortion on woman, aged 25' *The Times*, 28 May 1987, p 1 records the surprise of a judge when his decision was publicised.

[280] *Re SG (adult mental patient: abortion)* [1991] 2 FLR 329, sub nom *Re SG (a patient)* (1992) 6 BMLR 95; superseding *Re X* (1987) *The Times*, 4 June.

[281] [2013] EWHC 1417 (COP); [2013] 3 FCR 384; (2013) 133 BMLR 110.

[282] For somewhat opposing views, see J Keown, 'Selective reduction of multiple pregnancy' (1987) 137 NLJ 1165; D P T Price, 'Selective reduction and feticide: The parameters of abortion' [1988] Crim LR 199.

[283] Human Fertilisation and Embryology Act 1990, s 37(5) adding to the 1967 Act, s 5(2).

[284] R L Berkowitz, 'From twin to singleton' (1996) 313 BMJ 373.

handicap clause of the 1967 Act. Whether there is tort liability in the event of damage to a surviving fetus is arguable; the probability is that the doctor would not be liable in the absence of negligence in the operation.[285]

9.127   It scarcely needs emphasising that all the foregoing relates to legal justification—the morality of the procedure is open to question. There is, clearly, a difference between reducing a twin pregnancy and reducing one involving sextuplets. To say that both are wrong in that they offend against the principle of respect for human life is to ignore the equally valid argument that ensuring the death of all six fetuses by inaction is, equally, disrespectful; the death of all octuplets following refusal of fetal reduction in an, at the time, *cause célèbre* provides an extreme example. The subject opens up the age-old question of whether it is permissible to use unacceptable means to achieve a desirable end—at which point, one can only retire behind the defence that each case must be judged on its particular merits.

CONCLUSION

9.128   Control of fertility is a matter of profound importance, but it is not an issue that can be settled by appeals to autonomy alone. Even in cases where we are dealing with competent persons, the state can continue to claim an interest in the exercise of such control, especially when another life is involved. In the case of minors and incompetent adults, the best interests test dominates and it might be said, tentatively, that in these contexts the foundational nature of the right to reproduce is giving way to more holistic interpretations of the interests at stake. In all cases, the claims to moral objection by parties not directly involved continue to be diminished unless, perhaps, they can persuade their state to take up their cause. All of these factors conspire to maintain the question of fertility as a central feature of any political landscape.

---

[285] M Brazier, 'A legal commentary' (1990) 16 J Med Ethics 68 in discussion of R P Jansen, 'Unfinished feticide' (1990) 16 J Med Ethics 61.

10

CIVIL AND CRIMINAL LIABILITY IN REPRODUCTIVE MEDICINE

10.01 The medical control of both natural and assisted reproduction requires considerable expertise.[1] Moreover, it is not without risk, not only to the prospective parents but, perhaps especially, to the resultant child. Risks to the former by virtue of the necessary hormonal and invasive techniques employed—at least in the case of the mother—have already been noted. For the purposes of this chapter, however, we are concerned with parental 'risk' only in the quite separate sense that, to some couples, parenthood, itself, may be seen as a risk which they may seek health care assistance to eliminate. Consequently, the birth of a child into the family will be unexpected or uncovenanted[2] and this may well be due to negligence on the part of the relevant health carer. This situation commonly results from a failed sterilisation of either the man or the woman involved and is generally known as a 'wrongful pregnancy'.[3] A variation in which a multiple, or excessively multiple, birth is unwanted is a specific hazard of in vitro fertilisation and the problem has been discussed under that heading.

10.02 It is also, perhaps unfortunately, true that many parents who want a child do not, at the same time, want the responsibilities of caring for one that is disabled. Certainly, save in exceptional circumstances, very few would actively seek a child that most people would regard as disabled;[4] fortunately, however, there are many who would happily adopt such a child. Some couples will have no anticipation of a disabled child; others, whether by virtue of age or family history may be well aware of a potential risk—or, at least, their health

---

[1] Much of the material in this chapter is to be found in greatly expanded form in J K Mason, *The Troubled Pregnancy: Legal Wrongs and Rights in Reproduction* (2007).

[2] The expression 'uncovenanted' was used by Kennedy J in *Richardson v LRC Products Ltd* (2001) 59 BMLR 185, [2000] Lloyd's Rep Med 280 to describe such a situation. In Scots law, the word has been used to describe not so much an unexpected happening as one which was not contemplated by the parties concerned. It is, therefore, apt to describe the results of a failed sterilisation. We believe that it is preferable to use the expression in place of the more commonly used, but distasteful term 'unwanted pregnancy'. This may also be inaccurate—it is a tribute to human nature that the disabled child has come to be greatly loved in nearly all the reported cases.

[3] Many writers use the term 'wrongful conception' rather than 'wrongful pregnancy'. We prefer the latter on the grounds that no damage is sustained by conception; the potential for damage arises only at implantation.

[4] Over a decade ago, a deaf lesbian couple created a stir in deliberately attempting to create a deaf child who would fit into their milieu: N Levy, 'Deafness, culture and choice' (2002) 28 J Med Ethics 284. The ethical arguments for and against such a choice are wide ranging: see the companion article K W Anstey, 'Are attempts to have impaired children justifiable?' (2002) 28 J Med Ethics 28. The question has now been settled by statute: Human Fertilisation and Embryology Act 1990, s 13(8) inserted by the Human Fertilisation and Embryology Act 2008, s 14(4) and has been discussed in Chapter 8.

carers should be so informed. The actual birth of a disabled child may, then, derive from inadequate antenatal care—often associated with genetic counselling or its lack[5]—and result in what is popularly known as a 'wrongful birth'. It goes without saying that the categories may overlap; a wrongful pregnancy, for example, can also result in a disabled child.

10.03   It is clear that, despite the specialised nomenclature, actions for both wrongful pregnancy and wrongful birth are no more than variants of medical liability and negligence and the initiative in commencing legal proceedings lies with the parents or parent. Alternatively, however, the neonate who has been injured in utero may raise an action in negligence against the person he or she regards as responsible for that injury; this may or may not be available and we consider the jurisprudential quality of such an action at the end of this chapter. In the present context, however, neonatal risk is almost entirely that of congenital disease, as a result of which—and depending on its severity—the complainant may plead, effectively, that he or she would be better dead than alive and that he or she is alive only because of mismanagement of his or her gestation.[6] Such a 'wrongful life' action is, therefore, one of a very distinct nature. Wrongful birth and wrongful life actions may be, and often are, raised simultaneously but there is no overlap; they are based on different premises and will be analysed separately. This chapter also provides a convenient place in which to review the legal aspects of fetal injury and of feticide in the form of fetal manslaughter or murder. Finally, we will take the opportunity to overview the status of the fetus by way of considering the particular legal responsibilities of the mother to her child in utero.

10.04   As has already been pointed out, all these legal actions involve a form of negligence.[7] We explore the nature and content of the negligence action—including that of criminal negligence—extensively in Chapter 5; for present purposes, a brief introduction will assist the unfamiliar reader in the discussion that follows. An action in negligence is premised on the notion of a duty of care. That is, it must be shown that the defender in the action—for us, the health care professional—had a duty to provide a certain level of care to his or her patient; the action will be successful if it can be established that this standard of care was not provided and, importantly, that this breach of duty of care caused a recognisable form of harm to the claimant. The benchmark standard in all cases is that of *reasonable care*, which can only be determined in light of all of the circumstances in a given case. While all doctors—and other health carers—will owe a duty to patients for whom they accept general or specific responsibility, the more problematic issue lies in the nature and extent of that duty. Here, we confine discussion to professional duties as they relate to reproductive choice and care.

THE UNCOVENANTED CHILD: THE ACTION FOR WRONGFUL PREGNANCY

10.05   Before discussing the nature of the duty of care in the action for wrongful pregnancy, we must first consider to whom the duty is owed. Clearly, if a man or woman seeks

---

[5] For a discussion of which, see Chapter 7.

[6] For a European overview, see A Ruda, ' "I didn't ask to be born": Wrongful life from a comparative perspective' (2010) 1 JETL 204.

[7] The cases discussed in this chapter, together with others, are very usefully reviewed by V Chico, 'Saviour siblings: Trauma and tort law' (2006) 14 Med L Rev 180.

sterilisation independently, the doctor's duty of care is limited to that man or woman. By contrast, the doctor owes a duty to both partners if they come to him together seeking a limitation of fertility that is of benefit to both. It follows from either premise that the doctor cannot be held liable to a potential present or future sexual partner of his patient of whom he has no knowledge. While this seems to be a relatively simple proposition, it has been the subject of extensive argument in the Court of Appeal. Here, it was confirmed that a woman who became pregnant by a man who had been told three years previously that he need take no contraceptive precautions had no cause of action against those who had given the advice.[8]

10.06 Given, however, that a duty of care has been established, liability for a pregnancy resulting from an unsuccessful sterilisation will not be imposed unless it can be established that the surgeon failed in his or her duty. Such failure can, in turn, be attributable either to incompetent clinical expertise or, and more controversially, to inadequate explanation of the inherent shortcomings of the procedure—in particular, as to the possibility that conception might still occur after the operation due purely to the vagaries of nature.

10.07 As to what constitutes a breach of duty of care, we need, here, only remark that the juris- prudence is still largely governed—albeit with increasing scepticism—by the *Bolam*[9] principle, under which it is held that a doctor's action will not be held to be negligent if it conforms to a practice which would have been adopted by a responsible body of medical opinion. As a result, it has long been supposed that a judge presented with two diver- gent expert opinions as to what was the correct procedure to adopt cannot simply choose which to accept. A distinction has to be made, however, between preferring an opinion— as in the House of Lords case of *Maynard*[10]—and preferring an interpretation of the facts. This was neatly explained in *Fallows* v *Randle*.[11] In this case of failed female sterilisation, the rings occluding the fallopian tubes had either been placed negligently or had slipped off through no one's fault. In preferring the former sequence of events, Stuart-Smith LJ had this to say:

> [The *Bolam* principle] has no application when what the judge has to decide is, on balance, which of the explanations [of failure] is to be preferred. This is a question of fact which the judge has to decide on the ordinary basis of a balance of probabilities.[12]

10.08 We suspect that the majority of actions based on the negligent *performance* of a sterilis- ing operation will generally be of this relatively simple type and that liability may well be acknowledged prior to any hearing. An exception would almost certainly lie when the patient has insisted on a modified operation in the anticipation of reversal at some time in the future[13] but the situation would be far more doubtful were the individual surgeon

---

[8] *Goodwill* v *British Pregnancy Advisory Service* [1996] 2 All ER 161; (1996) 31 BMLR 83.

[9] *Bolam* v *Friern Hospital Management Committee* [1957] 2 All ER 118; [1957] 1 WLR 582.

[10] *Maynard* v *West Midlands Regional Health Authority* [1985] 1 All ER 635; [1984] 1 WLR 634, HL.

[11] (1997) 8 Med LR 160.

[12] (1997) 8 Med LR 160, 165. Moreover, two techniques may each pass the *Bolam* test for professional acceptability but it is for the court to decide which is in the patient's best interests: *Re S (adult patient: steri- lisation)* [2001] Fam 15; [2000] 3 WLR 1288, CA.

[13] As exemplified in the very early twin Canadian cases of *Doiron* v *Orr* (1978) 86 DLR (3d) 719 and *Cataford* v *Moreau* (1978) 114 DLR (3d) 585. Liability for a subsequent pregnancy was not imposed in the former in which the operation had been modified; the surgeon was found to have been negligent in the latter where there were no such extenuating conditions.

to modify his or her technique with this in mind.[14] A relatively specific aspect of negligent sterilisation in women is, however, to be found in a failure to diagnose pre-existing pregnancy at the time of the operation. Error as to missed diagnosis then tends to be piled upon error, each resulting in therapeutic delay; consequently, either the patient finds herself no longer able, often on moral grounds, to consent to a lawful termination or the opportunity to do so is lost due to the lapse of time.

THE UNDIAGNOSED PREGNANCY

10.09   Several such cases are of importance in tracing the development of liability for 'wrongful pregnancy' in the United Kingdom (UK) and are discussed in greater detail later. Typical of these was *Scuriaga* v *Powell*[15] in which a healthy child was born following a negligently performed termination. Although there was no claim for damages in respect of the child's upbringing, Watkins J, at first instance, foreshadowed future developments in saying:

> Surely no one in these days would argue [that damages were irrecoverable] if the child was born defective or diseased. The fact that the child born is healthy cannot give rise to a different conclusion save as to a measure of damages,

and this view was supported in the Court of Appeal.

10.10   In *Venner*,[16] a gynaecologist who accepted the patient's word that she could not be pregnant at the time of the operation was held to be not negligent on the ground that other practitioners would have omitted a precautionary curettage in similar circumstances. Other defendants have not been so fortunate. In the virtually identical case of *Allen* v *Bloomsbury Health Authority*,[17] the authority admitted liability and the only matter in issue was the quantum of damages. In a still later case, damages of over £88,000, which included an element to cover private schooling, were awarded against a gynaecologist who failed to explain to a patient that she might be pregnant at the time of her sterilisation.[18] Interestingly, a diagnostic partial dilatation and curettage was actually performed but, again, no warning was given that the nature of the procedure was not such as to ensure the dislodgement of any fetus that was present. In fact, the patient was several weeks pregnant at the time and did not appreciate the fact until the fifteenth week of gestation—at which point she was unwilling to consent to a termination. Fortunately, the child was healthy. *Groom* v *Selby*[19] is very comparable but, at the same time, raises some unique features; it is considered separately at para 10.29.

---

[14] In *Re M (a minor) (wardship: sterilisation)* [1988] 2 FLR 497, expert evidence preferred to look upon tubal ligation as being 'contraceptive in nature'. The sterilisation was, however, non-voluntary and the argument was based on different premises (see Chapter 9).

[15] (1979) 123 Sol Jo 40. In 2001, a Mrs Nicholls received £10,000 in an out of court settlement when a twin pregnancy was missed at termination; the second child was born healthy—O Wright, '£10,000 for mother who gave birth after abortion', *The Times*, 23 November 2001, p 14.

[16] *Venner* v *North East Essex Area Health Authority* (1987) *The Times*, 21 February.

[17] [1993] 1 All ER 651; (1993) 13 BMLR 47. For a review stimulated by this comparatively early case, see A Mullis, 'Wrongful conception unravelled' (1993) 1 Med L Rev 320—although we believe that the paper was wrongly titled.

[18] *Crouchman* v *Burke* (1998) 40 BMLR 163.   [19] [2001] EWCA Civ 1522; [2002] PIQR P18.

STERILISATION AND INFORMATION DISCLOSURE

10.11 These cases, which embody an element of failure in communication between doctor and patient, lead us naturally to the more common actions in both negligence and in contract which have been based entirely on the grounds of inadequate provision of warning of the possibility of failure of a sterilisation operation. In such cases, the supposed deficit has proved to be no more than a matter of misunderstanding—in effect, providing good examples of the distinction to be made between consent that is based on information and that which is based on understanding of the information, to which we refer at para 10.50. Thus, in the interesting case of *Thake v Maurice*,[20] the issue turned eventually on the definition of the word 'irreversible'—the defendant claiming that it implied no more than that the procedure could not be reversed by surgery while the plaintiff contended that it represented a contract[21] to provide absolute sterility which was beyond recall by nature. After a remarkable volte face between the trial court and the Court of Appeal as to breach of contract—which was accepted in the trial court—it was held on appeal that the surgeon had been negligent in his failure to warn of the possibility of natural reversal of vasectomy. A rather similar case turned on the interpretation of the words on the form signifying consent to operation which stated, 'We understand that this means we can have no children' and which the plaintiffs contended amounted to a representation that the operation was foolproof; the trial judge, however, held that the words merely acknowledged that the intended effect of the operation was that the couple should not have more children and found for the defendants.[22] Such semantic difficulties had been foreseen in the important Australian case of *F v R*[23] when King CJ specifically drew attention to the need not only to warn of the possible complications of surgery but also of the risk of failure in respect of the intended end result. There have been further English cases involving much the same issues[24]—one of which concerned a woman who became pregnant while her husband was producing persistently negative seminal specimens[25]—but these are better discussed together under the heading of consent to treatment.[26]

---

[20] [1986] QB 644; [1984] 2 All ER 513; revsd [1986] QB 644; [1986] 1 All ER 497. It was later said of the trial stage of this case: 'I, for my part, think that ... the less we say about that decision, the better' (per Slade LJ in *Eyre v Measday* [1986] 1 All ER 488 at 492).

[21] Mr Thake was, in fact, a private patient.

[22] *Worster v City and Hackney Health Authority* (1987) *The Times*, 22 June. As a further hurdle, the plaintiffs may have to convince the court that they would have continued contraceptive methods if they had been informed of a risk: *Newell v Goldenberg* [1995] 6 Med LR 371.

[23] (1983) 33 SASR 189, SC.

[24] E.g. *Eyre v Measday* [1986] 1 All ER 488, CA; *Gold v Haringey Health Authority* [1987] 1 FLR 125; revsd [1988] QB 481; [1987] 2 All ER 888.

[25] *Stobie v Central Birmingham Health Authority* (1994) 22 BMLR 135. The case drew attention to the fact that the common law interpretation of paternity may be challenged by way of laboratory tests. The phenomenon is said to occur in about 1:80,000 cases—see J C Smith, D Cranston, T O'Brien, et al., 'Fatherhood without apparent spermatozoa after vasectomy' (1994) 344 Lancet 30.

[26] See Chapter 4. It is possible to discern an incremental shift towards judicial reliance on the patients' understanding rather than on what the surgeon said: *Gowten v Wolverhampton Health Authority* [1994] 5 Med LR 432; *Lybert v Warrington Health Authority* (1995) 25 BMLR 91; [1996] 7 Med LR 71. The relative unfairness of the test was, however, acknowledged in *Al Hamwi v Johnston* [2005] Lloyds Rep Med 309. The importance of proximity in such cases scarcely needs emphasis. By no stretch of the imagination could, say, the Department of Health or its advisers be regarded as being sufficiently proximate to unknown members of the public to be responsible for providing advice on sterilisation: *Danns v Department of Health* [1998] PIQR P226.

10.12 Thus far, we have accepted that a surgeon and/or his or her employers can be liable in the event of a 'wrongful'—that is, tortious—pregnancy. What we have not broached is the *extent* of that liability and it is here that we run into considerable analytical difficulty which has been highlighted in a succession of cases that have arisen in relatively recent years. Even so, we must return to the older examples if only on the grounds that one cannot see where a principle should go without an idea of where it came from.[27]

THE EXTENT OF LIABILITY FOR FAILED STERILISATION

10.13 Damages following a wrongful pregnancy can be sought under two main heads. First, there are those that derive from the pregnancy itself including damages for the pain and suffering of gestation and childbirth together with recompense for loss of earnings or additional expenses resulting from pregnancy and its convalescence—the bases of what can be loosely referred to as 'the mother's claim'. So far as we know, such damages have never been denied in any anglophone jurisdiction. Second, and far more controversial, is the claim for the upkeep of the resulting child until, or even beyond, maturity—and it is here that the law has followed a course of sinewave appearance in the last 40 years or so. Put in simplest terms, the questions at issue have been whether damages for the upkeep of an uncovenanted child should ever be awarded and, if so, whether the condition of the child or its mother should affect the quantum.

10.14 On the face of things, the issue is reasonably clear. A surgeon owes a duty of care to a couple. He has failed in that duty and, as a result, the very circumstance his intervention was intended to avert has, in fact, occurred; ergo, the couple are entitled to restitution.[28] The fact that a child—and, particularly, a healthy child—is involved, however, introduces complications which are more of a moral than a legal nature; in essence, objection to *any* award in such a context is based on the view that a child is a blessing and that the gift of a child should never be regarded as a matter for compensation. The question was fully addressed many years ago in Canada by the court in *Doiron* v *Orr*; the judge stated that he would have been prepared to award damages for mental anguish caused to the plaintiff, but was adamant in his refusal to accept that there could be liability for the cost of bringing up an unsought child:

> I find this approach to a matter of this kind which deals with human life, the happiness of the child, the effect upon its thinking, upon its mind when it realised that there has been a case of this kind, that it is an unwanted mistake and that its rearing is being paid for by someone other than its parents, is just simply grotesque.[29]

And we will see later how this view has weathered the years.

10.15 Such rejection concentrates on the effect which an award might have on the child; in other cases, the focus has been more on the entitlement of the *parents* to damages. Basically, there are four possibilities in the solution of actions for wrongful pregnancy: damages should never be awarded; damages should always be awarded; the

---

[27] Quoting from Lord Mustill in *Attorney-General's Reference (No 3 of 1994)* [1998] AC 245 at 256; [1997] 3 All ER 936 at 944.

[28] See, e.g., Waller LJ in *Rees* v *Darlington Memorial Hospital NHS Trust* [2002] 2 All ER 177; (2002) 65 BMLR 117 at para 44 quoting previous concurrence.

[29] (1978) 86 DLR (3d) 719 at 722, per Garett J.

blessing of parenthood should be offset against the concurrent economic loss and the damages adjusted accordingly; and, finally, a distinction should be made between healthy and disabled children and damages should be awarded only for the *extra* costs involved in the upkeep of the latter.

10.16 Actions for wrongful pregnancy originated in the USA where the courts have taken a less than uniform approach to the problem since the index suit of *Custodio* v *Bauer* in which the normal rules of tort were applied.[30] There are certainly several cases in which redress has been refused, the view having, again, been that parents cannot be held to have been damaged by the blessing of children. At the other extreme, damages have been awarded not only in respect of the pain and suffering involved in an unwanted pregnancy but also to offset the cost of rearing the child to maturity.[31] In summary, while it is probably true to say that the majority of states have allowed recovery for all losses excluding those attributable to bringing up a healthy child,[32] it is, nevertheless, possible to extract virtually any 'solution' to the problems involved by a discriminatory selection of opinions within the various US jurisdictions.[33] It is fair to say that the UK courts could derive little precedental assistance from the US experience when the time came to establish a rule in this country.[34]

10.17 Even so, the validity of the wrongful pregnancy action was upheld in *Udale* v *Bloomsbury Area Health Authority*,[35] in which damages were given for pain and suffering along with loss of earnings following a negligently performed operation; at the same time, an award in respect of the cost of bringing up the child was firmly rejected. In his judgment, Jupp J reiterated that the joy of having the child and the benefits it brought in terms of love should be set off against the inconvenience and financial disadvantages resulting from its birth—'It is an assumption of our culture', he suggested, 'that the coming of a child into the world is an occasion for rejoicing'.[36]

10.18 The Court of Appeal opposed this view in the later case of *Emeh* v *Kensington and Chelsea and Westminster Area Health Authority*;[37] where, in addition, there was a strong rejection of the trial judge's view that the plaintiff's refusal of abortion was so unreasonable as to

---

[30] 251 Cal Rep 2d 303 (1967).

[31] *Lovelace Medical Center* v *Mendez* 805 P 2d 603 (NM, 1991). By contrast, the 'offset rule' was followed in *Sherlock* v *Stillwater Clinic* 260 NW 2d 169 (Min, 1977)—a case that has been widely quoted in the UK courts. This 'balancing' approach was, however, criticised in *Public Health Trust* v *Brown* 388 So 2d 1084 (Fla, 1980): see J H Scheid, 'Benefits vs. burdens: The limitation of damages in wrongful birth' (1984–5) 23 J Fam Law 57. For a comparative review, see A Stewart, 'Damages for the birth of a child' (1995) J Law Soc Scot 298. The argument for full recovery in the USA has been put forcibly by P Baugher, 'Fundamental protection of a fundamental right: Recovery of child-rearing damages for wrongful pregnancy' (2000) 75 Wash L Rev 1205. Also see M Ramsey, 'Wrongful pregnancy and the offset/benefits approach' (2015) 28 Can JL & Jur 129.

[32] The problem of the unhealthy child depends very much on the doctor's expected anticipation of such an outcome: e.g. *Williams* v *University of Chicago Hospitals* 688 NE 2d 130 (Ill, 1997).

[33] For a useful analysis, see *Burke* v *Rivo* 551 NE 2d 1 (Mass, 1990). A jurisprudence was also building up within the Commonwealth. See the intense debate in *CES* v *Superclinics (Australia) Pty Ltd* (1995) 38 NSWLR 47 where the concept of 'offset' was well described by Kirby A-CJ at 77.

[34] See *McFarlane* v *Tayside Health Board*, para 10.20.

[35] [1983] 2 All ER 522; [1983] 1 WLR 1098. Similar sentiments were expressed in an unreported negligence case, *Jones* v *Berkshire Area Health Authority*, first quoted in *Gold* v *Haringey Health Authority* [1986] 1 FLR 125; revsd [1988] QB 481; [1987] 2 All ER 888.

[36] At All ER 531, WLR 1109.

[37] (1983) *The Times*, 3 January; revsd [1985] QB 1012; [1984] 3 All ER 1044, CA.

eclipse the defendant's wrongdoing.[38] Equally significantly, however, the Court of Appeal awarded damages for the cost of rearing the child and rejected the policy objections voiced in *Udale*. Thus, despite the somewhat unsatisfactory nature of the case, *Emeh* became the leading case in England and the practice of allowing damages for the upkeep of an uncovenanted, healthy child was followed in a succession of cases—and these included special damages for the costs associated with any defect and, conspicuously, for the costs of private education when that seemed appropriate.[39] None of these was taken to appeal. Indeed, the only remaining difficulty appeared to lie in the relationship between the two heads of damage—were they distinct or did one flow from the other? The Court of Appeal later held that a wrongful pregnancy is a personal injury which cannot be separated from its consequences.[40]

10.19 Meantime, Scottish policy was evolving independently. Earlier reports are, for the most part, concerned with procedural matters and do not deal with the substantive legal arguments or their outcomes.[41] Two unreported cases,[42] both based on lack of warning of the risk of failure rather than on operative negligence, caught the attention of the media. Both were settled out of court; but the substantial sum of £50,000 was offered in compensation in *Lindsay*,[43] suggesting that the Scottish courts might well recognise the unexpected birth of a healthy child as a suitable matter for 'damages'. This was supported in *Allan v Greater Glasgow Health Board*,[44] in which the court explicitly accepted that there were no grounds—of principle or of policy—to prevent an award of damages for the upbringing of a child born in such circumstances. There is, of course, much force in the argument that such compensation amounts to a rejection of a fundamental value in our society—that of family love. On the other hand, it is implicit that the patient undergoing consensual, non-therapeutic sterilisation does not want any more children and that this may be for economic reasons. It is hard to refute the famous words of Peter Pain J: 'Every baby has a belly to be filled and a body to be clothed.'[45]

The *McFarlane* Case and its Immediate Outcome

10.20 The relatively still waters of cross-border consensus were, however, to be rudely disturbed when this fundamental contradiction was addressed by the entire gamut of appeal courts in *McFarlane v Tayside Health Board*.[46] The facts of the case were relatively standard.

---

[38] Also see *Crouchman v Burke*, n 18, where a woman who would have had an early termination refused one at 15 weeks 'for understandable reasons' (per Langley J at 176). It is now doubtful if a different approach would be adopted in respect of an early abortion.

[39] *Benarr v Kettering Health Authority* [1988] 138 NLJ Rep 179; *Robinson v Salford Health Authority* (1992) 3 Med LR 270; *Allen v Bloomsbury Health Authority* [1993] 1 All ER 651; (1993) 13 BMLR 47; *Crouchman v Burke*, n 18.

[40] *Walkin v South Manchester Health Authority* [1995] 4 All ER 132; (1995) 25 BMLR 108. Which meant, in passing, that actions for wrongful pregnancy would be subject to the Limitation Act 1980, s 11—followed in *Godfrey v Gloucestershire Royal Infirmary NHS Trust* [2003] EWHC 549 (QB). But note the opposite view taken in the British Columbia Court of Appeal in the same year in a case of wrongful birth: *Arndt v Smith* [1996] 7 Med LR 108; (1995) 126 DLR (4th) 705.

[41] *Smith, Petitioner* 1985 SLT 461; *Jones v Lanarkshire Health Board* 1990 SLT 19; 1989 SCLR 542; affd 1991 SLT 714; 1991 SCLR 806; *Teece v Ayrshire and Arran Health Board* 1990 SLT 512.

[42] *Pollock v Lanarkshire Health Board* (1987) *The Times*, 6 January; *Lindsay v Greater Glasgow Health Board* (1990) *The Scotsman*, 14 March.

[43] N 42.

[44] (1993) 17 BMLR 135; 1998 SLT 580, OH. The court found, however, that there had been no negligence in this case. See also *Cameron v Greater Glasgow Health Board* 1993 GWD 6–433, in which damages of £40,000 were agreed; again, however, the action was unsuccessful.

[45] In *Thake v Maurice* [1984] 2 All ER 513 at 526; [1985] 2 WLR 215 at 230. For a very good review of this position, see M Hogg, 'Damages for pecuniary loss in actions of wrongful birth' (2010) 1 JETL 156.

[46] 1997 SLT 211 (1996).

Mrs McFarlane already had four children. Her husband underwent a vasectomy and, in due course, was informed that he could safely resume sexual intercourse without undertaking contraceptive methods. Mrs McFarlane became pregnant some two years later and, together, she and her husband raised an action in negligence.[47] In accordance with established practice, this was in two parts—the 'mother's claim' for pain and suffering during pregnancy and childbirth and the 'parents' claim' for the upkeep of the child until maturity. At first instance, the Lord Ordinary in the Outer House of the Court of Session held that a normal pregnancy culminating in a healthy child was a natural event which could not be regarded as an injury—hence, it could not form a basis for damages. He also decided that the joys of the child's existence wholly compensated the financial cost of its upbringing— he rejected the concept of 'off-set', or a balancing of some benefit against some disadvantage, in that it involved placing a specific value on the life of the child, which he regarded as unacceptable. This decision was reversed in the Inner House, where the Lord Justice Clerk declined to discuss the relationship of pregnancy to personal injury and, rather, addressed the problem in terms of the basic principles of Scots law.[48] *Injuria*, or the wrongdoing, coincided with the *damnum*, or the interference with the person's legal interests, when Mrs McFarlane conceived. *Damnum* was manifested, first, in the adverse effects of pregnancy and childbirth on her bodily integrity and, second, in the pecuniary interests of both parents. An obligation to make reparation arises when there is concurrence of *injuria* and *damnum*—and these conditions were satisfied in the instant case once the pregnancy was established.[49] The Inner House rejected the proposition that the blessing of a child was an overriding benefit, pointing out that the couple were relying on sterilisation in order to avoid the additional expenditure which the birth of another child would entail and, having decided the issue by way of principle, went on to conclude that there was no overriding consideration of public policy which the awarding of damages would contravene.

10.21 Most commentators then assumed that equilibrium between English and Scots law had been re-established but *McFarlane* was appealed to the House of Lords,[50] presumably so as to ensure that this was so. While the House decided by a 4:1 majority that the 'mother's claim' in respect of pain and suffering due to pregnancy and childbirth should stand, the main appeal related to reparation for the costs of bringing up a healthy child was, somewhat surprisingly, upheld unanimously.

10.22 The reasoning behind the rejection of the latter claim, which undoubtedly represented a U-turn in the development of the jurisprudence, has never been easy to unravel, given that the defender's duty of care to the pursuers was admitted and acknowledged by way of the 'mother's claim'; each of the five Lords of Appeal gave different reasons for his decision and there is neither the space nor, now, the need to explore these in detail here.[51] In

---

[47] Interestingly, the course of the case was such that the fact of negligence was neither proved nor disproved before being accepted in a later action.

[48] *McFarlane and McFarlane v Tayside Health Board* 1998 SC 389 at 393; (1998) 44 BMLR 140 at 144.

[49] Reiterated by Lord McCluskey 1998 SC 389 at 398 who went so far as to hold that the right of a married couple to have sexual relations with each other without any likelihood that those relations will result in a pregnancy is a right that the law recognises. The House specifically held that the deliberate continuation of the pregnancy did not affect the chain of causation: cf, Slade LJ in *Emeh v Kensington and Chelsea and Westminster Health Authority*, n 37.

[50] *McFarlane v Tayside Health Board* [2000] 2 AC 59; [1999] 3 WLR 1301.

[51] As with the whole of this chapter, our fuller analysis of the case is to be found in *The Troubled Pregnancy*, n 1. Of the mass of available literature, see L C H Hoyano, 'Misconceptions and wrongful conceptions' (2002) 65 MLR 883; P Booth, 'A child is a blessing—Heavily in disguise, right?' (2001) 151 NLJ 1738. More widely, V Chico, 'Saviour siblings: Trauma and tort law' (2006) 14 Med L Rev 180 and, covering much the same field from a different perspective, N Priaux, *The Harm Paradox* (2007).

summary, Lord Slynn concluded that it would be neither just nor reasonable to impose on the doctor liability for the upkeep of a child until maturity and this is the theme which is adopted most often in the post-*McFarlane* cases;[52] Lord Steyn took refuge in some rather tenuous concepts of distributive justice; Lord Hope thought that, since the benefits associated with a healthy child were incalculable, it was illogical to attempt an assessment of the net economic loss sustained by the child's parents; Lord Clyde was struck by the disproportion between the damages available when based on the full costs of upbringing and the surgeon's degree of culpability; while Lord Millett eventually returned to the reasoning in the index English case[53] in holding that the law must accept the birth of a healthy baby as a blessing, not a detriment.[54]

10.23   In our view, the problem does not lie in the value of a child but is simply that of whether two persons should be compensated if their financial resources are diverted as a result of the negligence of the agent engaged to avert that outcome.[55] Moreover, the House in *McFarlane* deliberately left open the possibility of recompense for the upkeep of an unexpected *disabled* child—since this was, apparently, still available by way of existing precedent, the resulting doubt had to be settled with some urgency. Efforts both to circumvent the decision and to clarify the situation were, therefore, to be expected.

10.24   Attempts to undermine the 'healthy child = no maintenance' rule were disposed of summarily. In *Richardson* v *LRC Products Ltd*[56]—a burst condom case brought under s 3 of the Consumer Protection Act 1987—it was clearly held that the rule applied whether the claim was laid in negligence or in breach of a statutory duty. *Greenfield* v *Irwin (a firm)*[57] was a further case of missed pregnancy rather than failed sterilisation; otherwise, the conditions were very similar to those in *McFarlane*. The plaintiff, however, sought to distinguish her case on the grounds that her loss was consequent on the physical injury of the pregnancy rather than on negligent advice; she also rather ingeniously attempted to demonstrate a difference between expenditure on a child and loss of earnings due to caring for that child. The Court of Appeal found both distinctions to be irrelevant; the suggestion that failure to provide financial support would contravene the Human Rights Act 1998, Sch 1, Art 8—respect for family life— was also dismissed.

10.25   By contrast, attempts to entrench the possible exception for disabled children firmly within the law have, in general, been successful. Unfortunately, the underlying reasoning has been misapplied in that the great majority of cases in which this aspect of *McFarlane* has been followed have been, in fact, instances of wrongful birth and, as indicated at para

---

[52] See *Caparo Industries plc* v *Dickman* [1990] 2 AC 605; [1990] 2 All ER 568.

[53] *Udale* v *Bloomsbury Area Health Authority*, n 35.

[54] Although the matter was discussed in depth only by a minority of the House, a refusal to terminate the pregnancy was very firmly regarded as not constituting a *novus actus interveniens*. The circumstances surrounding 'wrongful pregnancy' are such that a termination could be lawful under the Abortion Act 1967 irrespective of the health of the fetus (see Chapter 9 for discussion).

[55] The decision was, in general, badly received by academic lawyers—e.g. E Cameron-Perry, 'Return of the burden of the blessing' (1999) 149 NLJ 1887; J Thomson, 'Abandoning the law of delict?' 2000 SLT 43; O Radley-Gardner, 'Wrongful birth revisited' (2002) 118 LQR 11. For rare support, see T Weir, 'The unwanted child' [2000] CLJ 238.

[56] N 2. The ruse of attempting to substitute breach of contract for negligence has been summarily dismissed—e.g. *Reynolds* v *Health First Medical Group* [2000] Lloyd's Rep Med 240.

[57] [2001] EWCA Civ 113; [2001] 1 WLR 1279, sub nom *Greenfield* v *Flather and Others* (2001) 59 BMLR 43.

10.43, these have a wholly different genesis; we hope to avoid compounding the confusion and, accordingly, they are considered later in this chapter.[58]

10.26 The only acceptable comparator in our view is *Parkinson* v *St James and Seacroft University Hospital NHS Trust*.[59] Here, a woman gave birth to a disabled child following an admittedly negligent sterilisation operation. Brooke LJ pointed out that parents in a similar position had been able to recover damages for some 15 years following *Emeh*[60] and that both the 'fair, just, and reasonable' test and the principles of distributive justice would be satisfied if the award was limited to the special costs associated with the disability. He was supported in a powerful speech by Hale LJ who was, incidentally, the first female judge to express a view on the *McFarlane* judgment. Hale LJ started from the premise that to cause a woman to become pregnant against her will was an invasion of her bodily integrity; she then listed an impressive catalogue of the consequences of pregnancy which, she insisted, retained an invasive nature despite the fact that they derived from a natural process. She could find nothing unusual, or contrary to legal principle, in awarding damages in such a case on the ground that the caring role—and, hence, the interference with the woman's personal autonomy—persists throughout childhood. The admission of damages limited to the restitution of costs beyond those involved in bringing up a normal child gave no offence to those with disability and simply acknowledged that the costs in the event of disability were greater than in the case of normality—put another way, the 'deemed equilibrium' between the benefits derived from and the costs of maintaining an uncovenanted healthy child that underpins the *McFarlane* decision is distorted to an extent that is determined by the degree of disability in an unhealthy child.[61]

10.27 In our view, however, the importance of Lady Hale's opinion is that her arguments based on bodily invasion can be applied almost verbatim to the birth of an uncovenanted *normal* child and, somewhat paradoxically, this leads one to question the logic of the *Parkinson* decision. It was, in fact, agreed that the child's disability was in no way attributable to a breach of duty on the defendant's part; that being the case, why is liability apportioned in *Parkinson* but not in *McFarlane*? The feeling remains that one or other decision must be wrong.[62] In the event, the tenor of the *Parkinson* judgment leaves a strong impression of the court's dissatisfaction with the superior ruling in *McFarlane*[63] and the decision in the Court of Appeal in the former was not appealed to the House of Lords. Thus, the

---

[58] A fact which was particularly noted by Brooke LJ in *Parkinson* v *St James and Seacroft University Hospital NHS Trust* [2002] QB 266; [2001] 3 All ER 97 at [48]. For a fuller consideration of the post-*McFarlane* cases, see J K Mason, 'Wrongful pregnancy, wrongful birth and wrongful terminology' (2002) 6 Edin LR 46; L C H Hoyano, 'Misconceptions about wrongful conception' (2002) 65 MLR 883.

[59] N 58. It is to be noted that, even so, the child's disability in *Parkinson* (autism) only became apparent during infancy as opposed to at birth. *Taylor* v *Shropshire Health Authority* [1998] Lloyd's Rep Med 395 is a comparable case which pre-dated *McFarlane*; the nature of the disability is uncertain but it was present at birth and, presumably, it could have been detected in utero. Full expenses were allowed subject to a very modest 'offset' for any associated joy and comfort; in fact, had *Taylor* gone to appeal, the case might have provided a better test of the *McFarlane* exception than does *Parkinson*.

[60] N 37.

[61] It is important to note that the apparently attractive concept of 'deemed equilibrium' was rejected in *Rees*, n 68, in both the concurring and dissenting judgments. We do not think that this affects the practical value of Hale LJ's exposition.

[62] Such a lack of a causal link between the doctor's negligence and the child's disability was emphasised in the apposite US appeal case: *Simmerer* v *Dabbas* 733 NE 2d 1169 (Ohio, 2000).

[63] Described by both Gummow and Kirby JJ as a 'rebellion' in *Cattanach* v *Melchior*, transcript, 11 February 2003, p 23. See also Lord Scott in *Rees* v *Darlington Memorial NHS Trust* [2003] 4 All ER 987 at para [143].

extent to which compensation for the unexpected birth of a disabled child is available is not entirely settled—and we will see in the light of later litigation that this may have significant implications.

10.28   Hale LJ's innovative recognition of the invasive nature of the negligence involved in cases of unwanted pregnancy was further expressed in *Groom* v *Selby*,[64] which was tried at first instance before, and at appeal after, the Court of Appeal hearing in *Parkinson*. *Groom* is an unusual case which almost defies classification and is, therefore, somewhat parenthetic to the present discussion. However, it reflects an important aspect of the reaction to *McFarlane*.

10.29   In brief, *Groom* was an instance of the not unusual condition, adverted to briefly earlier,[65] in which a sterilisation is carried out in the presence of an unnoticed pregnancy. Ms Groom later consulted her general practitioner who negligently failed to diagnose her pregnancy until her fetus was so far developed as to make a termination personally unacceptable; a normal infant was born, albeit three weeks prematurely. Thus far, then, the case was an example of an action for wrongful pregnancy of the 'missed' variety. However, some three weeks after birth, the child developed meningitis due to infection by salmonella organisms derived from her mother's birth canal; as a result, she was left with a prognostically uncertain degree of brain damage. *Groom*, therefore, raises an interesting variation on the wrongful pregnancy theme—was the child normal at birth and, thus, subject to the *McFarlane* rule, or was she born disabled as a consequence of negligence during the process of birth? At first instance, Clark J found that 'Megan is not and never has been a healthy child', a proposition that was, in our view justifiably, contested on appeal. Nevertheless, the Court of Appeal upheld the judgment. Brooke LJ summarised the position:

> [The] birth of a premature child who suffered salmonella meningitis through exposure to a bacterium during the normal processes of birth was a foreseeable consequence of Dr Selby's failure to advise the claimant that, although she had been sterilised, she was in fact pregnant.[66]

At first glance, this seems harsh but acceptable in that a fetus is not 'born alive' until it is completely extruded from the mother; the infant's 'injury' here was clearly inflicted during the birth process. Brooke LJ, however, went a stage further and considered that, although the child was apparently healthy at birth:

> it should not stand in the way of our doing justice, in a case like the present, in which a child's enduring handicaps, caused by the normal incidents of intra-uterine development and birth, were triggered within the first month of her life.

He went on to say that the longer the period before the disability is triggered off, the more difficult it may be to establish a right to recover compensation. Whether it is right to undermine the *McFarlane* rule in such indefinite terms remains to be established.[67]

10.30   During the course of her judgment in *Groom*, Hale LJ repeated her view that the costs of bringing up a child who has been born as a result of another's negligence are not 'pure' economic loss but, rather, economic loss consequent upon the invasion of a woman's bodily integrity. Her concept of unavoidable responsibility imposed by motherhood

---

[64] (2002) 64 BMLR 47; [2002] Lloyd's Rep Med 1 at [31], CA.   [65] At para 10.10.
[66] At para [24].
[67] And we cannot help wondering why it was not the obstetric unit who were sued.

was, again, applied when she extended the potential *McFarlane* exception from disability in the resultant child to disability in its mother. In *Rees v Darlington Memorial Hospital NHS Trust*,[68] a healthy child was born following a negligently performed sterilisation operation on a woman who was severely visually disabled. Hale LJ could see no essential difference between compensating for the extra costs of bringing up a disabled child vis-à-vis his or her normal counterpart—as in *Parkinson*—and compensating a woman for the extra costs in supporting a normal child that were dictated by her own disability—thus continuing and extending the concept of a *persisting* injury resulting from 'wrongful pregnancy' that she developed in *Parkinson*. Hale LJ thought that this did no more than put the mother in the same position as her 'able bodied fellows' who, by contrast, had no *need* for additional help in attending to a child's basic needs. Walker LJ, while rejecting the argument based on a 'deemed equilibrium' between the advantages and disadvantages of an uncovenanted normal child, nevertheless agreed that the circumstances of the case were not covered by *McFarlane* and represented a legitimate extension of *Parkinson*. Waller LJ, however, in a dissenting judgment, pointed to the unfairness of compensating a woman by virtue of her physical disability when other mothers in as great a need could not benefit. While many may have considerable intuitive sympathy for the majority in *Rees*, it has to be admitted that the decision raises its own problems. We have, for example, suggested that the courts are well able to judge the additional costs associated with disability in a child; it is, pace Lady Hale's disclaimer, far less easy to assess the *costs* resulting from a degree of disability in its mother. Moreover, we must ask what constitutes disability and what is so special about physical disability? Presumably, *Rees* would extend quite naturally to mental disability and, if so, why not to life's other challenges, including that of economic hardship? Waller LJ found these to be good reasons for dissenting in *Rees*. At the same time, he reminded us that the House in *McFarlane* recognised that a claim for damages for bringing up a healthy child born as a result of the negligence of a surgeon would succeed under the normal rules of tort[69] and there is little doubt that a case that was decided to the contrary on what were, largely, moral principles, provides a less than satisfactory base from which to explore its various implications.

Wrongful Pregnancy in Australia

10.31 Precisely this point was taken up in the important case of *Cattanach v Melchior*,[70] heard in the High Court of Australia shortly after *McFarlane* was decided in the House of Lords. The circumstances in *Cattanach* were comparable to those in *McFarlane* save that the former involved a negligent female sterilisation. Holmes J's comment at first instance set the scene:

> were there a single, distinct line of reasoning to be discerned from either [*McFarlane* or *CES*[71]] I should follow it. However given the divergence of approach, I can see no alternative but to distil from those decisions the reasoning which appeals to me as sound[72]

---

[68] [2002] EWCA Civ 88; [2003] QB 20.

[69] At para [44]. See also Thomson, n 55, for similar criticism.

[70] (2003) 199 ALR 131. Our detailed assessment of the case is available electronically in J K Mason, 'A turn-up down under: *McFarlane* in the light of *Cattanach*' (2004) 1 SCRIPT-ed.

[71] *CES v Superclinics (Australia) Pty Ltd* (1995) 38 NSWLR 47—a similar case in the NSW Court of Appeal that ended as something of a contrived compromise and which was widely quoted in *McFarlane*. Leave to appeal to the High Court was given in *CES* but the case was settled prior to the hearing.

[72] *Melchior v Cattanach* [2000] QSC 285 at para [50].

and she awarded Aus$105,249 for the costs of raising a normal but uncovenanted child.[73] An appeal to the Supreme Court of Queensland was then dismissed and the case was finally heard by a seven-judge panel in the High Court where the deliberations were confined to the single issue of whether a court could award damages which require a doctor who is responsible for the negligent birth of an unintended child to bear the cost of raising and maintaining that child.

10.32 The judgment in *Cattanach* is very long and detailed and, insofar as the result depended on a narrowly split decision, the arguments provide an interesting contrast to those deployed in the unanimous decision in *McFarlane*. This is, however, no place to consider them in detail.[74] In essence, they rested on whether the court should be governed by moral or legal principles—that is, is it wrong that the addition of a much loved, albeit unsought, child to a family should be regarded as a compensatable damage or should the legal principles of tort law be maintained in the face of such moral considerations.

10.33 In the end, the court divided 4:3 in favour of legal principle and, thus, rejected the *McFarlane* rule.[75] The case for allowing the appeal can be summarised in the conclusion to the speech of Heydon J who put it thus:

> The various assumptions underlying the law relating to children and the duties on parents created by the law would be negated if parents could sue to recover the costs of rearing unplanned children. That possibility would tend to damage the natural love and mutual confidence which the law seeks to foster between parent and child. . . . It would permit conduct inconsistent with the duty to nurture children.[76]

10.34 The case for the majority was put most forcibly by Kirby J who was highly critical of the *McFarlane* decision, of which he said, 'the diverse opinions illustrate what can happen when judges embark upon the "quicksands" of public policy, at least when doing so leads them away from basic legal principle'.[77] And, to summarise his position,[78] 'Neither the invocation of Scripture nor the invention of a fictitious oracle on the Underground[79] . . . authorises a court of law to depart from the ordinary principles governing the recovery of damages for the tort of negligence'.

10.35 It is to be noted that, while the most common denominator in the House of Lords' decisions lies in an appeal to justice, fairness, and reasonableness based on *Caparo* principles,[80] *Caparo* currently forms no part of the Australian jurisprudence; it is, therefore, at least possible to see *McFarlane* and *Cattanach* as not being incompatible, at least in precedental terms. Nonetheless, most commentators would have seen two of the highest courts in the Commonwealth as being on a collision course and would wonder if, given the opportunity, the House of Lords might reconsider its position.

---

[73] Relying, in the main, on the case of *Perre v Apand Pty Ltd* (1999) 73 ALJR 1190.

[74] For further discussion, see *The Troubled Pregnancy*, n 1, at pp 126–37. For an Australian analysis, see, in particular, D Stretton, 'The birth torts: Damages for wrongful birth and wrongful life' (2005) 10 Deakin L Rev 310.

[75] Note, however, that shortly after the *Cattanach* decision the Queensland Parliament passed the Justice and Other Legislation Amendment Act 2003, which amends the Civil Liability Act 2003 and prevents a court from awarding damages for the financial costs ordinarily associated with rearing or maintaining a healthy child. This does not prevent courts from awarding damages for costs over and above the ordinary costs of raising a child; e.g., if the child is disabled.

[76] Para [404].   [77] At para [158].   [78] At para [151].

[79] An allusion to Lord Steyn's commuter on the Underground as an assessor of distributive justice in *McFarlane* at AC 59 at 62, SLT 154 at 165.

[80] *Caparo Industries plc v Dickman* [1990] 2 AC 605; [1990] 1 All ER 568.

The Status Quo in the UK

10.36 That opportunity arose when Ms Rees' case was further appealed to a bench of seven judges in the House of Lords.[81] Unfortunately, the House did not analyse *Cattanach* in depth, the general feeling being that the arguments had already been fully rehearsed. At the same time, the decision in *McFarlane* was confirmed unanimously; this, however, was not as a result of further consideration but, rather, on the grounds that it would be improper to reverse a House of Lords' decision within the short period of four years.[82] *Rees*, however, remains a most important case in its own right and, in the event, the House allowed the appeal by a majority of 4:3. Given the narrow majority, it is unsurprising their Lordships' reasons were, again, diverse.[83] The argument rested on whether, on the one hand, it was the exceptional costs dictated by disability in either the child or the parent which attracted recompense or whether the definitive factor was *normality* in the result-ant child. In the event, the latter view held sway.

10.37 Perhaps the most interesting aspect of *Rees* lies in the fact that *McFarlane* was accepted as representing an *exception* to the normal rules of tort by both the majority and minority—thus, renewing concern that justice was, at least, not being seen to be done. Lord Bingham's response,[84] which was followed by the majority, was to make a conven-tional award of £15,000 to all victims of a negligent sterilisation in recognition of the affront to a woman's autonomy imposed by an unwanted pregnancy. Lord Bingham was adamant that this was in no way compensatory but it is difficult to accept this at face value and, clearly, other members of the House—including those who supported the measure—were in some doubt. Lord Steyn, indeed, went so far as to question the power of the courts to make such an award—to do so, he maintained, should be the prerogative of Parliament. For our part, we would prefer to see the 'conventional award' as recogni-tion of a new head of damages—that is, a breach of autonomy or interference with the right to plan one's life as one wishes. This, we believe, would harmonise the apparent conflict between the Inner House of the Court of Session and the House of Lords in *McFarlane* and would be widely recognised as being a fair solution to an intense moral and legal dilemma.

10.38 There is, in fact, some evidence that judicial policy is moving in such a direction.[85] Nevertheless, it does not represent the law as it now is in respect of the 'birth torts' which is that the rule laid down in *McFarlane*—that there should be no compensation for the costs of upkeep of a healthy, uncovenanted child—stands, and it is to be emphasised that it is the state of health of the child that determines the issue.[86] The only modification lies in

---

[81] *Rees* v *Darlington Memorial Hospital NHS Trust* [2003] UKHL 52; [2004] 1 AC 309.

[82] See Lord Bingham at para [7]. Even so, the possibility was open: *Practice Statement (judicial precedent)* [1966] 1 WLR 1234. The cases quoted, however, indicated that even 11 years could be too short an interval.

[83] For a brief appraisal, see C Dixon, 'An unconventional gloss on unintended children' (2003) 153 NLJ 1732. The case is examined in detail in: J K Mason, 'From Dundee to Darlington: An end to the *McFarlane* line?' [2004] JR 365.

[84] At para [8].

[85] See, in particular, *Chester* v *Ashfar* [2005] 1 AC 134; (2005) 81 BMLR 1, a decision involving 'a narrow and modest departure from traditional causation principles' (per Lord Steyn at para 24). For commentary, see G Laurie, 'Personality, privacy and autonomy in medical law' in N Whitty and R Zimmermann (eds), *Rights of Personality in Scots Law* (2009) ch 10.

[86] This was foreseen in *AD* v *East Kent Community NHS Trust* [2003] 3 All ER 1167; (2003) 70 BMLR 230, CA which was heard before *Rees* went to the House of Lords. Here, a woman who was detained under the Mental Health Act 1983 was delivered of a healthy child as a result of supposed negligent supervision. The case is complicated in that the child's grandmother voluntarily undertook charge of the infant. In the end, *McFarlane*, rather than *Rees* at Court of Appeal level, was applied insofar as no 'extra costs' were involved.

the 'conventional' award—if that be the proper description. The persistence of the Court of Appeal ruling in *Parkinson*, however, means that recompense in tort is available for the excess costs imposed by any disability in the resultant child. Lord Bingham indicated that he would give the conventional award to *all* victims of wrongful pregnancy and this leaves some doubt as to the outcome should another case such as that of Mrs Parkinson arise—will both damages for the excess costs of upbringing and the conventional award be given or will one replace the other? To that limited extent, the law in relation to wrongful pregnancy remains uncertain. Were it to be reconsidered, we suspect that the overriding consideration would be to align the decision with those that have evolved from the cases of wrongful birth to which we now turn.

REPRODUCTIVE COUNSELLING AND NEGLIGENCE: THE ACTION FOR WRONGFUL BIRTH

10.39   The parents of an afflicted child may choose to raise an action in negligence against a doctor or antenatal counsellor who has failed either to advise them of the risk of congenital illness in their children or to carry out, and interpret correctly, appropriate diagnostic procedures which would have disclosed abnormality in the fetus. The doctor or counsellor owes them a duty of care in which he or she has been found wanting; the parents may contend that, as a result, they have been deprived of the opportunity to terminate the pregnancy and that they are now faced with the upkeep of a sick or handicapped child. Such an action, brought by and on behalf of the parents, is generally known as one for 'wrongful birth'.[87] Damages may be sought in respect of the distress occasioned by the parents in respect of the existence of the defect in their child and for the extra costs which are entailed in bringing up the child. It should be noted that many of the cases that follow involve instances of genetic or chromosomal disease which has been misdiagnosed or has gone undetected. We refer the reader to the first section of Chapter 7 for a detailed account of the nature of and testing for such disease. For present purposes, however, we are less concerned with the *medical* cause of harm—that is, whether the congenital disability results from a genetic or non-genetic disorder—than with whether the courts consider that the costs of raising an unhealthy child is a *legal* harm when those costs are incurred because of mismanagement of prenatal care.

10.40   The courts in the USA, which can, again, be seen as the pathfinders in this area, experienced something of a rollercoaster ride on their early journey to recognising a legitimate claim for damages for the birth of a handicapped child. In one of the first cases, *Becker v Schwartz*,[88] the New York Court of Appeals allowed a parental claim for damages in respect of the cost of the institutional care of a child suffering from Down's syndrome. The negligence in question was the failure of the doctor to recommend amniocentesis to a 37-year-old mother who, by virtue of her age, had a relatively high risk of bearing a handicapped child. Later, however, the courts found difficulty as to the conflict of interests. On the one hand, there was the question of public policy which should, in theory, favour birth

---

[87] A term which is open to criticism insofar as it implies that the alterative—termination of pregnancy—is necessarily right.
[88] 386 NE 2d 807 (NY, 1978).

over abortion.[89] On the other, the woman's prerogative to control her own body, and the consequent acceptability of termination, have been increasingly recognised since these early days. The widely accepted rule that has emerged is that such claims will succeed.[90] Even so, moral concerns as to the status of fetal life remain as does the legal problem of causation. In *Noccash*,[91] for example, widely based damages were awarded for the birth of an infant with Tay-Sachs disease but costs concerned with the child's funeral were disallowed on the grounds that the fatality was the result of hereditary factors rather than of the defendant's negligence. Other difficulties relate to the fact that pregnancy has been actually sought in these cases. Should the damages awarded then reflect the full costs of rearing a defective child or should they be limited to the difference in financial burden posed by a normal and a handicapped infant? Should they extend to compensation for emotional distress? These questions seem to be very finely balanced in the US courts and legislatures[92] and, while, as has been noted, the majority will accept a wrongful birth action in principle, some state legislatures have enacted laws stating clearly their preference for denying such causes of action.[93]

10.41 The UK courts have, even more clearly, been happy to allow the action—indeed, we suspect that many cases are so clear that they are settled out of court;[94] the early case of *Salih*,[95] involving the congenital rubella syndrome, is apposite in this connection in that liability was admitted without question. In *Gregory v Pembrokeshire Health Authority*,[96] the trial judge found that the doctors' neglect to inform of the failure of an amniocentesis was a breach of the duty of care; the action failed, however, on the ground of causation, the plaintiff being unable to convince the court, or the Court of Appeal, that she would have had a second investigation had she been offered one, far less that she would have aborted her child. In *Anderson v Forth Valley Health Board*,[97] a couple sought damages in respect of the alleged negligence of a health board which led to their two sons being born suffering from muscular dystrophy. The pursuers averred that, had they been referred for genetic counselling and testing, the genetic disorder carried by the wife would have

---

[89] But this argument has been used in the main to counter claims for wrongful life (see para 10.51).

[90] The development of the jurisprudence is discussed in P M A Beaumont, 'Wrongful life and wrongful birth' in S A M McLean, *Contemporary Issues in Law, Medicine and Ethics* (1996) ch 10. For an example, see *Schirmer v Mt Auburn Obstetric and Gynecologic Associates, Inc* 802 NE 2d 723 (2003) where the action was described as a negligence claim that was to be determined by application of common law principles.

[91] *Noccash v Burger* 290 SE 2d 825 (Va, 1982).

[92] Cases discovered which have refused the claim in toto are *Azzolino v Dingfelder* 337 SE 2d 528 (NC, 1985); *Atlanta Obstetrics and Gynecology Group v Abelson* 398 SE 2d 557 (Ga, 1990); and *Grubbs v Barbourville Family Health Center* 120 SW 3d 682 (Ky, 2003). The last is a decision by the Supreme Court of Kentucky; the action failed on grounds of causation and of a fear of reintroducing eugenics into the law; it was also said to be 'at variance with existing precedents both old and new'.

[93] As an example, consider this provision from the Idaho Code §5-334(1): 'A cause of action shall not arise, and damages shall not be awarded, on behalf of any person, based on the claim that but for the act or omission of another, a person would not have been permitted to have been born alive but would have been aborted.'

[94] The status of the wrongful birth action vis-à-vis abortion on both sides of the Atlantic was reviewed in depth by R Scott, 'Prenatal screening, autonomy and reasons: The relationship between the law of abortion and wrongful birth' (2003) 11 Med L Rev 265.

[95] *Salih v Enfield Health Authority* [1990] 1 Med LR 333; on appeal [1991] 3 All ER 400. It is to be noted that, while the trial judge awarded damages which included the basic costs of maintaining a child, the Court of Appeal held that the family had been spared the cost of a normal child and this head of damages was extinguished. But see the most recent apposite case: *FP v Taunton and Somerset NHS Trust* [2011] EWHC 3380 (QB) where the only issue was the quantum—and perpetuation—of damages.

[96] [1989] 1 Med LR 81.   [97] (1998) 44 BMLR 108; 1998 SLT 588.

been discovered and the couple would have chosen to terminate both pregnancies. As it was, no tests were ever offered or carried out, despite the fact that the hospital had been informed of a history of X-linked Duchenne muscular dystrophy among the male members of the wife's family. The children's condition only came to light when one of the boys injured himself in a fall. After a very comprehensive review of the case law, Lord Nimmo Smith held that he could see 'no good reason' not to treat the pursuers as having suffered personal injuries 'in the conventional sense' and he accordingly awarded damages under the heads of both solatium—injury to the feelings—and patrimonial loss. *Anderson* was followed shortly afterwards in England in *Nunnerley* v *Warrington Health Authority*[98]—a case involving admittedly defective genetic counselling; here, the parents were held to be entitled to full compensation for the upkeep of their child up to and beyond his eighteenth birthday.

10.42   The decision of the Scottish courts in *McLelland* v *Greater Glasgow Health Board*[99] should, also, be noted as to the matter of damages for solatium. In this case, a father was, for the first time, awarded damages for the shock and distress he suffered as the result of the birth of a son suffering from Down's syndrome—as in *Anderson*, the hospital had been made aware of a family history suggestive of genetic disease but had failed to offer an amniocentesis. This ruling was unprecedented because it is normally only the mother of the child who will receive damages for pain and suffering. In addition, the claimant must normally prove an element of psychiatric disturbance or illness in order to recover damages for personal injury in the form of 'nervous shock'. In *McLelland*, however, Lord MacFadyen was persuaded that this criterion goes only to the question of the existence of a duty of care; once liability is admitted the question becomes whether there has been material prejudice to a pursuer's interest that is recognised by law. The father had suffered—and would suffer further—shock and distress which he would not have done had the management of the case not been negligent. Accordingly, his claim to solatium was considered sound.[100]

10.43   So far, so good, but the UK courts' attitudes were to be markedly affected by the House of Lords' ruling in *McFarlane* v *Tayside Health Board*,[101] which has already been discussed in some detail. It will be remembered that, while the House rejected the concept of compensation for the undesired normal child, it left open the position were such a child to be born disabled—thus, raising the possibility that the well-established action for wrongful birth might no longer be available or, at best, might only be available in a modified form.[102] This resulted in a rash of cases anxious to settle the matter. This was unfortunate as the two actions—wrongful pregnancy and wrongful birth—are distinct both in concept and practice; to argue the latter in terms of the former can

    [98] [2000] Lloyd's Rep Med 170.   [99] 1999 SC 305; 1999 SLT 543.

    [100] The McLellands, in fact, fell into the *McFarlane* trap (see para 10.20) between the Outer and the Inner Houses. Solatium was still awarded but the 'ordinary' costs of maintaining their child were deducted from the previously awarded full costs at the appeal which was heard after *McFarlane*: *McLelland* v *Greater Glasgow Health Board* 2001 SLT 446. The opinions are both interesting and innovative; in particular, Lord Morison, dissenting, gave good reasons for considering the two actions distinct—an analysis with which we would clearly agree.

    [101] 2000 SC (HL) 1; [2000] 2 AC 59.

    [102] When one applies the reasoning of the individual Lords of Appeal in *McFarlane*, it becomes apparent that that might well have been the case: J K Mason, 'Wrongful pregnancy, wrongful birth and wrongful terminology' (2002) 6 Edin LR 46. For further analysis of the proposition, see G Hughes-Jones, 'Commentary on *Taylor* v *Shropshire HA*' [2000] Lloyd's Rep Med 107.

only confuse the jurisprudence. It is not inappropriate, therefore, to recapitulate some pointers as to the nature of the distinction.

10.44 These include the fact that, although the Health Trust may well be involved in both, the individual defender is likely to be different in the two cases. The surgeon will be accused of negligence in the wrongful pregnancy case while, in wrongful birth, responsibility will probably shift to the laboratory or the genetic counsellor. A more important difference is that, in the former case, the woman did not want a child whereas, in the latter, save in exceptional circumstances—as in *Greenfield*[103]—she wanted a child but not one that was disabled. Third, it is at least arguable that an action for personal injury cannot survive within the context of one for wrongful birth because the pregnancy has been willingly accepted.[104] And, fourth, there can be no question of failure to minimise one's losses or of *novus actus interveniens* by way of refused termination in wrongful birth[105] because the action is best founded on the denial to the woman of the opportunity to invoke that intervention. The basis for compensation is of more than academic interest. To regard the birth of a disabled baby as a personal injury—which constituted the grounds for redress in the early cases—is to raise the wide questions of the sanctity of life and the rights of the disabled. Hence, there is a growing tendency to regard the infringement of a woman's right to self-determination as the primary cause of action.[106]

10.45 Even so, it has to be especially noted that termination of pregnancy raises its own problems in the wrongful birth case by way of causation because, as we have already seen in the case of Mrs Gregory,[107] before she can receive damages, the claimant must convince the court that, given the opportunity, she *would* have terminated the pregnancy under s 1(1)(d) of the Abortion Act 1967. We have alluded to this in Chapter 9 but the problems merit a brief re-statement here. In the first place, it is an unfortunate corollary that the rule encourages dishonesty in the witness.[108] This is, of course, a matter for the court to evaluate but it leads to the second, and more significant, question, 'How does the court approach this task?', given that it is, as likely as not, interpreting a 'hypothetical response to hypothetical advice given at a hypothetical consultation'.[109] And, in essence, this means a choice between an objective and subjective standard. There is really no better way of reaching a conclusion than to consider the reasoning in the important Canadian case of *Arndt v Smith* which, after swaying back and forth, went to a nine-judge bench in the Supreme Court.[110] In the end, a majority of the Supreme Court held that the correct

---

[103] *Greenfield v Irwin (a firm)* [2001] 1 FLR 899. An unusual case of missed pregnancy in which the woman would have opted for termination despite the fact that her child was normal; the judge had, therefore, to follow *McFarlane*.

[104] Nevertheless, Henriques J applied this theory in the Court of Appeal in the wrongful pregnancy case of *Walkin v South Manchester Health Authority* [1994] 1 WLR 1543 per Auld LJ at 1552 in the wrongful birth case of *Hardman v Amin* (2000) 59 BMLR 58 at 64 and concluded that both constituted personal injuries.

[105] Although the House in *McFarlane* specifically rejected such a failure as constituting a *novus actus*—the defence has, effectively, not been available since the trial judge in *Emeh*, n 37, was overruled in the Court of Appeal. Interestingly, a failure to initiate emergency post-coital contraception was so construed in *Richardson v LRC Products Ltd* (2000) 59 BMLR 185 per Kennedy J at 194.

[106] See E Babrinska, 'Wrongful birth and non-pecuniary loss: Theories of compensation' (2010) 1 JETL 171.

[107] N 96.

[108] Referred to as 'scripted ' answering in *Brindley v Queen's Medical Centre University Hospital NHS Trust* [2005] EWHC 2647 (QB) at [214].

[109] Per Nicholls LJ in the Court of Appeal, *Gregory*, n 96, at 86.

[110] (1994) 93 BCLR (2d) 220; (1995) 126 DLR (4th) 705, CA; [1997] 2 SCR 539.

approach lay in a modification of the rule elaborated in *Reibl* v *Hughes*;[111] the court must consider what the reasonable patient in the claimant's circumstances—interpreted in a wide context—would have done if faced with the same situation.

WRONGFUL BIRTH FOLLOWING *MCFARLANE*

10.46 There is little to be gained by a detailed description of the several relevant cases although each introduced some individual observations which should be recorded—the cases have not been disturbed. It can be said, in general, that the pattern developed in *Rand*[112] has been widely accepted and, as a result, the underlying validity of the wrongful birth action has been fully upheld. The extent of the available damages has, however, been modified in the light of *McFarlane* in that the costs of rearing a healthy child must, now, be deducted from the gross costs of caring for one who is disabled.[113]

10.47 *Rand*, a Down's syndrome case, was followed closely by *Hardman* v *Amin*,[114] which involved a child suffering from the congenital rubella syndrome. *McFarlane* was analysed in detail in both and the courts found no difficulty in basing the costs derived on the degree of disability per se; the only rather surprising difference lay in the fact that, whereas the quantum in *Rand* was related to the parents' means and, hence, their economic loss, Henriques J in *Hardman* preferred an assessment made on the basis of the child's needs; the latter is, surely, to be supported.[115] Interestingly, both courts agreed that the mere existence of the Abortion Act 1967 establishes a relationship between the medical advisers and the patient and is sufficient, of itself, to impose liability for the consequences of failure to warn of the likelihood of fetal disability. To complete what is, in effect, a trio of complementary cases, we draw attention to the fully confirmatory example—*Lee* v *Taunton and Somerset NHS Trust*,[116] a case of spina bifida—the main thrust of which, in our view, was to define the extent of the health carers' liability in cases of wrongful birth. As Toulson J put it, the needs of a severely disabled child should be uppermost in everyone's thoughts when investigating the possibility of fetal abnormality; as a consequence, the authorities cannot plead injustice and unreasonableness when a heavy penalty is imposed—the problem which so exercised the minds of the Lords of Appeal in *McFarlane*.[117]

10.48 Finally, and as by way of an epilogue, we draw attention to *Al Hamwi* v *Johnston*,[118] a case which, within itself, illustrates the majority of problems associated with antenatal counselling and actions for wrongful birth. Mrs Al Hamwi already had one normal child and was aged 29 at the time she sought a second. Four of her cousins, a niece, a nephew, and a half-sister all suffered from a rapidly fatal congenital condition which was considered to

---

[111] (1980) 114 DLR (3rd) 1. *Reibl* has always seemed to us to epitomise a common-sense view which is adopted by most courts—even if only *sub silentio*.
[112] *Rand* v *East Dorset Health Authority* [2000] Lloyd's Rep Med 181; (2000) 56 BMLR 39.
[113] T Weir, 'The unwanted child' (2002) 6 Edin LR feared that this might result in the courts 'finding' disability where none exists; we doubt if this would arise in cases of wrongful birth though might be possible in the event of wrongful pregnancy.
[114] [2000] Lloyd's Rep Med 498; (2000) 59 BMLR 58.
[115] For further discussion of these cases—and, indeed, of the whole subject matter of this chapter—see A R Maclean, 'Genes, justice and the law: The disabled child and liability for negligent antenatal diagnosis' [2007/2008] CIL 153.
[116] *Lee* v *Taunton and Somerset NHS Trust* [2001] 1 FLR 419; [2001] Fam Law 103. The availability of a claim based on defective counselling was confirmed in *Enright* v *Kwun* [2003] EWHC 1000; (2003) *The Times*, 20 May.
[117] Applying the well-known principle laid down in *Caparo Industries plc* v *Dickman* [1990] 2 AC 605.
[118] [2005] EWHC 206 (QB); [2005] Lloyd's Rep Med 309.

be Down's syndrome—and she informed the hospital of this. At 11 weeks' gestation she was told by her general practitioner that it was 'too late to have genetic tests'—in itself, a rather strange comment—and it was not until she was 17 weeks pregnant that she was referred for hospital antenatal care where preliminary maternal serum tests were carried out and the question of amniocentesis was raised. The evidence thereafter is less certain but it is reasonably clear that, while she originally wanted the invasive investigation, she had changed her mind at the end of an hour-long consultation.

10.49   She had been informed that the risk of miscarriage following the procedure was 1:100; nonetheless, she believed adamantly that the risk was 75 per cent. She was also told that her blood tests indicated the risk of her carrying a disabled child as being 1:8,396.[119] Mrs Al Hamwi eventually refused amniocentesis and, in due course, gave birth to a child suffering from the familial condition. She sued the practitioner on account of the delay involved in referring her for antenatal screening and the hospital for misinforming her of the hazards of amniocentesis, the combined effect of which was to deny her proper diagnostic facilities and, hence, the opportunity to terminate her pregnancy which she claimed she would have done given the right information at the right time.

10.50   In the event, Simon J dismissed the case against the general practitioner on the factual evidence that the amniocentesis—or the alternative of chorionic villus sampling at another hospital—was not, in practice, delayed or voided by her admitted negligence; accordingly, the breach of duty had caused no damage. As to the hospital, he found that Mrs Al Hamwi had been given appropriate counselling by way of an information leaflet and interview with the obstetrician concerned. He did, however, concede that she may have been confused—and it must be said that all the elements of confusion were there in abundance. In this respect, the judge made some interesting observations, taking the view that to hold that it is the clinician's duty to ensure that the information given to the patient *is understood* is 'to place too onerous an obligation on the clinician'. He continued:

> Clinicians should take reasonable and appropriate steps to satisfy themselves that the patient has understood the information which has been provided; but the obligation does not extend to ensuring that the patient has understood.[120]

It may be that to *ensure* success in achieving 'understanding consent' is an impossible goal in the circumstances. But we still wonder if Simon J's dictum is strictly in accord with modern medical practice. In addition to the specific problems of communication,[121] however, the case illustrates some of the general subjective difficulties in counselling. In this case, we have a devout Muslim[122] being counselled by an equally devout Christian who would no longer perform amniocenteses herself, having been once involved in the miscarriage of a normal fetus.[123] This may be an extreme example but it still raises the

---

[119] The hospital was working on the assumption that the family history was one of Down's syndrome (trisomy-21); the fact that this was affected by a rare translocation type of chromosomal abnormality was discovered only in the postnatal follow-up.

[120] At [69]. J Miola, 'Autonomy ruled OK?' (2006) 14 Med L Rev 108 considered that, in giving preference to informing over understanding, Mrs Al Hamwi was denied an autonomous choice.

[121] Public Health England, *Fetal Anomaly Screening Programmes: Programme Handbook* (2015).

[122] The expert evidence was that the majority of Muslim jurists hold that ensoulment occurs 120 days after conception. Termination after this would be sinful but within the conscience of the woman who could, therefore, consent to a late termination if the fetus was known to be at risk of abnormality. The doctrine of 'darura'—'necessity permits prohibited things'—adds even more flexibility to the rule.

[123] The judge found no evidence of bias but such situations must often be difficult for both sides. In contrast, Morland J, in *Enright* v *Kwun*, n 116, at [30], found that the defendant doctor's approach to counselling had been coloured by his religious beliefs.

question of whether counselling in a fundamentally moral arena can ever be strictly non-directional (see Chapter 7).

WRONGFUL (OR DIMINISHED) LIFE ACTIONS

10.51 The basis of a parental claim for 'wrongful birth' may be clear enough, but it could well be argued that it is misplaced. The parents of a disabled child may be exposed to both emotional and financial hardship but it is the child who suffers from the disablement. The disabled neonate whose existence results from health care negligence can, therefore, legitimately argue that he or she would not be exposed to an impaired existence were it not for that negligence—and that, consequently, he or she is entitled to compensation in tort. An action so based is commonly known as one for wrongful life.

10.52 The purist could—and does—dismiss such an action as being flawed from the start. The function of tort law is to restore the victim of negligence, so far as is possible, to the position he or she would have occupied absent that negligence—and there can be no cause of action in this particular instance insofar as it is impossible to restore someone to the state of pre-existence; moreover, when assessing the difference between an existence and non-existence, we have no known comparator. While we have much sympathy with the logic of such a view, it seems to represent an unduly formalistic way of disposing of what can be seen as a matter of justice. The action for wrongful life faces some barely superable hurdles but, despite its restricted practical importance, it deserves closer consideration as an example of the complex reasoning in this area of law.

WRONGFUL LIFE IN PERSPECTIVE

10.53 As is so common in medical jurisprudence, the history of the wrongful life action can be most simply traced through the US courts. In *Gleitman v Cosgrove*,[124] the plaintiff was born deaf, mute, and nearly blind as a result of his mother's exposure to German measles during pregnancy. The Supreme Court of New Jersey dismissed the plaintiff's claim for damages against the doctors who were alleged to have told the mother that there was no risk of German measles harming her child. The basis for dismissal was that its acceptance would amount to a statement that it was better not to be born at all than to be born handicapped; it was logically impossible, the Court felt, to weigh the value of a handicapped life against non-existence. As it was expressed:

> It is basic to the human condition to seek life and to hold on to it however heavily burdened. If [the plaintiff] could have been asked as to whether his life should be snuffed out before his full term of gestation could run its course, our felt intuition of human nature tells us he would almost surely choose life with defects against no life at all. 'For the living there is hope, but for the dead there is none...'

10.54 A year later, the claim of a child similarly damaged by its mother's illness was rejected on the ground that to allow a claim based on failure to abort the plaintiff would be the antithesis of the principles of the law of tort, which is directed towards the protection of the

---

[124] 296 NYS 2d 687 (1967). The seminal article is H Teff, 'The action for "wrongful life" in England and the United States' (1985) 34 ICLQ 423.

plaintiff against wrongs. The greatest wrong, it was pointed out by the court, is to cause another person's death.[125] In other cases, the courts have chosen to reject the claims of handicapped children on the ground that it is impossible to assess the child's damages.[126]

10.55 There is no indication that the courts, in refusing the children's claims, have intended to limit compensation for this type of negligence. Actions by the parents for emotional shock, expenses incurred in rearing a defective child, and the like have been successful and the trend has been—as explained in *Robak*[127]—to focus on the family as the true object of the claim. This was emphasised in *Prokanik v Cillo*,[128] which was a rare instance of a wrongful life action being accepted; a main reason for so doing was that the parents were time-barred and could not sue on their own behalf. In line with other common law jurisdictions, the US courts will, where it is possible, allow the neonate a suit for prenatal injury while denying one for wrongful life.[129]

10.56 To our knowledge, there is only one straightforward instance of a wrongful life action being allowed in full in the USA.[130] This case was effectively overturned by the Supreme Court of California in *Turpin*,[131] when it adopted the principle of allowing the suit to proceed and accepting a claim to special damages—that is, those incurred as a result of the congenital defects—but not to general damages; the basis for the latter restriction lay in the still insoluble problem of comparing an impaired existence with not being born at all. Any movement towards acceptance of the suit has, however, been arrested and there is now a definite trend in favour of rejecting such claims *in toto*.[132] When the plaintiff in *Bruggeman v Schimke*[133] averred that actions for wrongful life were being increasingly recognised, the court replied that this was simply not true and that any theory sustaining a legal right to be dead rather than to be alive with deficiencies was one completely contrary to the laws of the state.

10.57 If it is possible to define a common thread amongst these cases, it could, perhaps, be summed up in the word 'distaste'. Put brutally, the neonate is saying that death is preferable to a sub-standard life—a claim that not only disturbs the public conscience but is one which is particularly offensive to those concerned for the interests of the disabled and to those who object to the basic concept of therapeutic abortion. It is also potentially offensive to those who might be living with the particular disability. Whether or not this

---

[125] *Stewart v Long Island College Hospital* 296 NYS 2d 41 (1968).

[126] E.g. *Dumer v St Michael's Hospital* 233 NW 2d 372 (Wis, 1975); *Blake v Cruz* 698 P 2d 315 (Idaho, 1984); *Smith v Cote* 513 A 2d 341 (NH, 1986); *Cowe v Forum Group Inc* 575 NE 2d 630 (Ind, 1991). There is no evidence that the widespread antipathy to the wrongful life action is diminishing as is implicit in, e.g., the Kentucky case *Bogan v Altman and McGuire*, (Ky. CA, 22 June 2001).

[127] *Robak v United States* 658 F 2d 471 (1981).

[128] 478 A 2d 755 (NJ, 1984). A similar option was later left open: *Viccaro v Milunsky* 551 NE 2d 8 (Mass, 1990).

[129] E.g. *Cowe v Forum Group Inc* 575 NE 2d 630 (Ind, 1991).

[130] *Curlender v Bio-Science Laboratories* 165 Cal Rptr 477 (1980).

[131] *Turpin v Sortini* 182 Cal Rptr 377 (1982). Also followed in *Harbeson v Parke-Davis Inc* 656 P 2d 483 (Wash, 1983). *Turpin* is, however, a doubtful authority insofar as it was, in our view, an example of the pre-conception tort, for which, see para 10.75.

[132] E.g. *Ellis v Sherman* 515 A 2d 1327 (Pa, 1986); *Proffitt v Bartolo* 412 NW 2d 232 (Mich, 1987); *Cowe v Forum Group Inc* 575 NE 2d 630 (Ind, 1991); *Hester v Dwivedi* 733 NE 2d 1161 (Ohio, 2000).

[133] 718 P 2d 635 (Kan, 1986).

is the reason,[134] it is against this background in the USA that *McKay* v *Essex Area Health Authority*[135] was heard and to which we must still turn for analysis of UK jurisprudence.

The UK

10.58   In this classic case, the mother of the disabled child had been in contact with the rubella virus. The first sample having been mislaid, a second sample of blood was taken and the mother was informed that neither she nor the infant had been infected; however, the infant girl was found to be severely handicapped when she was born. The plaintiffs— who included both the mother and the child—alleged negligence on the part of the defendants in that they either failed to carry out the necessary tests on the blood samples or failed to interpret them correctly. A number of claims were made as a result of this alleged negligence, including one by the child for damages in respect of entry into a life of distress and suffering. While recognising that there was no reason why a mother in such circumstances may not be able to claim in respect of the negligent failure to advise her of her right to choose abortion—that is, to raise an action for wrongful birth—the court was not prepared to recognise any claim by a child to damages for wrongful life.

10.59   The court's initial analysis was in terms of the duty of the doctor. The doctor clearly owes a duty to the fetus not to do anything to injure it, but what duty is owed to a fetus which has been damaged by some agency for which the doctor can bear no responsibility—in this case by the rubella virus?[136] The only duty which the court could see would be an alleged duty to abort the fetus and the question then to be considered was whether there could ever be a legal obligation to terminate a person's existence.[137] As to 'wrongful life', it was held that an *obligation* to abort:

> would mean regarding the life of a handicapped child as not only less valuable than the life of a normal child, but so much less valuable that it was not worth preserving, and it would even mean that a doctor would be obliged to pay damages to a child infected with rubella before birth who was in fact born with some mercifully trivial abnormality. These are the consequences of the necessary basic assumption that a child has a right to be born whole or not at all, not to be born unless it can be born perfect or 'normal', whatever that may mean.[138]

---

[134]   Kirby J in *Harriton* v *Stephens* [2006] HCA 15 at [13] (see para 10.61) suggested that the words 'wrongful life' implicitly denigrate the value of human existence and that, as a result, that label has made judges reluctant to afford remedies in such cases.

[135]   [1982] QB 1166; [1982] 2 All ER 771, CA. The Law Commission had considered the merits of the wrongful life action prior to this Court of Appeal decision in its *Report on Injuries to Unborn Children* (Law Com No 60), and had come to the conclusion that it should not be allowed. The Congenital Disabilities (Civil Liability) Act 1976 was enacted as a result and s 1(2)(b) is said to exclude the right of a child to sue in such circumstances. A good argument can, in fact, be made out that wrongful life actions are not excluded. It can also be argued that such actions are still available at common law: J E S Fortin, 'Is the "wrongful life" action really dead?' [1987] J Soc Welfare Law 306, and, from a rather different aspect, Maclean, n 115. See also the commentary on the US case of *Cowe* v *Forum Group Inc* 575 NE 2d 630 (Ind, 1991): A Grubb [1993] 1 Med L Rev 262. In any event, the infant plaintiff in *McKay* was born before 22 July 1976 and did not come within the ambit of the Act; the issue of the wrongful life action was, therefore, open to the court.

[136]   For this reason, the doctor's liability was rejected in the US case of *Wilson* v *Knenzi* 751 SW 2d 741 (Mo, 1988).

[137]   Ackner LJ's reference at QB 1188, to 'a person ... in utero' is interesting in other contexts. His suggestion that what was an unacceptable duty of care would arise by way of advice to the mother is, in our view, difficult to reconcile with a corresponding duty to the mother to advise her of the possible effects of rubella infection. See Mason P in *Harriton*, n 134 at [109] et seq.

[138]   [1982] 2 All ER 777 at 781, per Stephenson LJ.

10.60   Having declined to find a duty basis of the claim, the court also cavilled at the difficulties of assessing damages in such a case. Here, the impossibility-of-comparison
argument was seen as a strong one: how could a court compare the value of a flawed
life with non-existence or, indeed, with any 'after life' which an aborted child was
experiencing?—the court declined to undertake any judgment on the conflicting
views of theologians and philosophers on the latter aspect. Even having accepted this
conceptual difficulty, Stephenson LJ was of the opinion that it was better to be born
maimed than not to be born at all except, possibly, in the most extreme cases of mental
and physical disability—which provokes the questions, 'What is extremity?' and 'By
what right do the courts take the view that existence is always to be preferred to non-
existence?' The decision is, surely, one which should be left to the handicapped child
by way of an objective substituted judgement—that is, given the degree of disability,
what would the individual child have thought?[139] Even so, although the matter has not
been tested directly, it is very probable that a Scottish court would follow the ruling
in *McKay*.[140]

Developments in the Commonwealth

10.61   The unanimity of opinion in *McKay* meant not only that there was very little debate
but also that the ruling has stood without challenge in the UK for more than 25 years.
Consequentially, if we are to complete our analysis, we must, again, look to the
Commonwealth for recent review of the common law approach to the problem. The
opportunity was taken in the conjoined Australian cases of *Harriton* and *Waller*,[141]
the facts of which are fairly standard in that both children were born with congenital
disability—the one due to the maternal congenital rubella syndrome and the other to
genetic disease. Each asserted that their suffering and consequent financial liability would
not have occurred absent a failure to provide their mothers with sufficient information on
which to found a choice that ensured they would not be born. The judge at first instance
held that the health carers owed no such duty to their mothers and the children then lost
their appeal. The majority opinion of the court was based on a mix of the arguments that
we have already considered in *McKay* together with some which seem to have little basis
in legal principle. Spigelman CJ, for example, said:

> In my opinion, the duty asserted by the Appellants should not be accepted as it does not
> reflect values generally, or even widely, held in the community. [At para 21.]

One wonders how he could possibly know this to be the case and it is difficult to see
why the *absence* of consensus on the matter should *prohibit* the court from seeking an
answer.[142] In our view, however, the main interest in the appeal stage of *Harriton* lies

---

[139]   This was clearly in the mind of counsel for the plaintiffs in a reference to *Re B (a minor) (wardship: medical treatment)* [1990] 3 All ER 927; [1981] 1 WLR 1421.

[140]   *Anderson* v *Forth Valley Health Board* 1998 SLT 588 at 604, per Lord Nimmo Smith, referring to
Lord Osborne in *P's Curator Bonis* v *Criminal Injuries Compensation Board* 1997 SLT 1180, (1997) 44
BMLR 70.

[141]   *Harriton* v *Stephens, Waller* v *James, Waller* v *Hoolahan* [2004] NSWCA 93. For review of the early
stages of the case, see P Watson, 'Wrongful life actions in Australia' (2002) 26 Melbourne U L Rev 736. It is
interesting that causation was scarcely in issue in the case of Keegan Waller—it seems to have been a preconception tort (see para 10.75) which might well have succeeded in the UK under the Congenital Disabilities
(Civil Liability) Act 1976, s 1A.

[142]   There are echoes here of Lord Steyn's commuter on the London Underground in *McFarlane* (see para
10.34) who, the commentators generally agreed, may not be the best lawmaker.

in the powerful dissent of Mason J, President of the Family Division[143] which, in effect, embodies all the arguments in favour of allowing an action for wrongful life. At this point, we draw attention only to his insistence on the commonality of the plea in actions for wrongful birth and wrongful life:

> there is no reason in principle why the medical practitioners' negligence in the advice and treatment they gave the mothers cannot sound in damages being awarded to the [children]. The appellants were born alive and their disabilities were in one sense caused by the negligence of the respective doctors, who omitted to give advice and treatment to the mothers that would have prevented the suffering presently endured by the appellants [at [116]].

the reason being that this is, effectively, the argument that was accepted later by the French and Dutch courts which we discuss later.[144]

10.62 Nevertheless, despite the President's advocacy, an appeal to the High Court of Australia was dismissed by a majority of 6:1.[145] The case was so well argued in the High Court that it will be convenient and most instructive to summarise, first, the majority opinion as expressed by Crennan J:

- the ultimate conclusion is that the nature of the damage alleged in a wrongful life case is not such as to be legally cognisable in the sense required to found a duty of care. That conclusion, in fact, makes it unnecessary to address any other aspects of the suit (at [243]);

- the damage alleged will be contingent on the free will, free choice, and autonomy of the mother (at [248])—the woman cannot be required or compelled to have an abortion;

- the possibility of the child suing its mother for the fact of its existence is to be avoided (at [250]);

- a comparison between a life with disabilities and non-existence for the purposes of proving actual damage is impossible (at [252]);

- a duty of care cannot be stated in respect of damage which cannot be proved and which cannot be apprehended or evaluated by a court (at [254]);

- to allow a disabled person to claim his or her own existence as actionable damage is not only inconsistent with statutes preventing differential treatment of the disabled but it is also incompatible with the law's sanction of those who wrongfully take a life (at [263]);

- to posit that the real test is to compare an actual life with disabilities with a notional life without disabilities—or a 'fictional healthy person'—depends on a legal fiction; life without special pain and disabilities was never possible for the appellants (at [266] and [270]);[146]

- a need for corrective justice—if such is relevant when no one is found responsible— cannot be determinative of a novel claim in negligence (at [275]).

---

[143] Space prevents detailed analysis here but it is essential reading for those interested in the juris-prudence. In fact, the majority of what he said was recapitulated in the High Court of Australia which is considered later.

[144] At para 10.68.   [145] *Harriton* v *Stephens* [2006] HCA 15; (2006) 226 CLR 52.

[146] This 'fiction' also provided the rationale for recognising a legal basis for damages in the groundbreak-ing Israeli case of *Zeitzoff* v *Katz* [1986] 40(2) PD 85. See Amos Shapira, ' "Wrongful life" lawsuits for faulty genetic counselling: Should the impaired newborn be entitled to sue?' (1998) 24 J Med Ethics 369.

In short, 'Life with disabilities,' said Crennan J, 'like life, is not actionable'.

10.63 Against this, we have the very powerful argument put by Kirby J in the minority—albeit one that ultimately does little more than replicate that of Mason P in the court detailed later. Thus, Kirby J's counter argument runs along these lines:

- as to causation in general, the child would not have been born had it not been for the respondent's negligence; consequently, the suffering, expense, and losses of which she now complains would have been avoided;

- 'True, the respondent did not give rise to, or increase, the risk that the appellant would contract rubella. However, he did, through his carelessness, cause the appellant to suffer, as she still does, the consequences of that infection';

- the duty owed by the health carers to take reasonable care to avoid causing prenatal injury to a fetus is sufficiently broad to impose a duty of care on the respondent in this case (at [71]);

- to deny the existence of a duty of care amounts, in effect, to the provision of an exceptional immunity to a tortfeasor—the common law resists such an immunity (at [72]);

- a mere potential for a conflict of maternal/fetal duties will not prevent a duty of care arising (at [74]);

- the respondent owed the appellant a relevant duty of care (at [77]);

- as to the 'unquantifiable' nature of the damage, the courts have had no difficulty in assessing these in relation to the parallel parental claims, nor as to special damages— and, as a result, the 'impossible comparison' argument also falls away[147] (at [87]);

- it is wrong to deny compensation where resulting damage has occurred 'merely because logical problems purportedly render that damage insusceptible to precise or easy quantification';[148]

- both 'general damages for proved pain and suffering and special damages for the needs created by the negligence of the medical practitioner in respect of a fetus in utero are recoverable in an action brought by or for that child' (at [109]).

All of which can be summed up in his comment:

This argument against allowing actions for wrongful life [that 'life' cannot be a legal injury] depends upon a false categorisation of such actions. It is not life, as such, which a plaintiff in a wrongful life action claims is wrongful. It is his or her present suffering as a life in being.[149]

10.64 We have to admit to a preference for the dissent in this case. Nevertheless, it is clear that the action for wrongful life is still unacceptable in the common law jurisdictions and this, in turn, leads to the question of whether the soubriquet of 'wrongful life' does not act to the detriment of the pursuer. Would the results be different were the actions to be brought in

---

[147] To quote Kirby J in full, 'It follows that, by ordinary principles, at least special damages are recoverable in a case such as the present. There is no difficulty in the computation of such damage. In my view, this application of basic principles of law discloses starkly that the impediment to recovery is founded in policy considerations, not law' (at [93]).

[148] Referring to Pollock J in *Procanik*, see n 128. See A Grey '*Harriton v Stephens*: Life, logic and legal systems' (2006) 28 Sydney L Rev 545. See also the English case *Chester* v *Afshar* [2005] 1 AC 134; [2004] 4 All ER 587 for 'adjusting the law' in the name of fairness.

[149] At [118].

negligence per se or would the hurdle of legally cognisable damage still persist? The point arose in the leading Canadian case on the subject—to which jurisdiction we now turn.

10.65   *Cherry v Borsman*, which was heard in the British Columbia Court of Appeal,[150] demonstrates the depth of antipathy which is displayed to the wrongful life action in the Anglo-Saxon courts. Here, a continuing pregnancy following a negligently performed abortion resulted in a severely disabled neonate who, subsequently, brought an action against the obstetrician. The point of present interest is that, while the action was raised in negligence, the defendant sought to categorise it as one for wrongful life—presumably assuming that it would be disallowed on the grounds of precedent. Indeed, as the trial judge said, the admission of negligent post-operative care and the fact that the woman would have had a second abortion had she been aware of her continuing pregnancy, 'do set up a wrongful life action [and], in fact ... almost encourage such an action'.[151] Even so, both the Supreme Court and the Court of Appeal were able to set this aside and to confine the issue to that of negligently causing the neonate's injuries; the issue of the validity of an action for wrongful life was determinedly avoided.[152] Rather, it was held that, insofar as a negligently performed abortion can cause foreseeable harm to the fetus, the practitioner owed a duty to the fetus to prevent that harm; accordingly, causation being inferred, he was liable to the neonate in negligence.

10.66   The case, for which we know of no equivalent, raises some interesting points. Certainly, the inference that the doctor caused the injuries is justified. His intention, however, was to kill the fetus—or, at least, prevent her survival. Given that the law considers the greatest injury to be death, it is a little difficult to see how mitigating that injury can be tortious. The court in *Cherry* was anxious that the disabled neonate should be recompensed and no one could disagree with that aim. We do, however, feel that it would have been achieved more logically by way of an action for wrongful life—insofar as the reason for the child's disabilities was not in dispute, it could, indeed, have been used to demonstrate the importance of causation, or the lack of it, to the generic 'wrongful life' action.[153]

10.67   In practical terms, children who fail in an action for wrongful life are unlikely to be wholly abandoned by the law since an action by the mother for wrongful birth will always be available. We have, however, seen that the effect of *McFarlane* is that recompense will be available only for the *extra* costs imposed by rearing a child who is disabled and, to that extent, the child itself may be indirectly disadvantaged. Moreover, the recompense will be awarded to the mother and is not there to compensate the child for its suffering. There is, therefore, no absolute guarantee that the child will benefit under the existing jurisprudence.[154] These are some of the considerations which led the French

---

[150] (1992) 94 DLR (4th) 487, BC CA.   [151] At 679.

[152] No case has yet succeeded in Australia. The action has also been rejected at first hand in the Roman–Dutch jurisdiction of South Africa: *Friedman v Glickson* 1996 (1) SA 1134, where the coincident claim for wrongful birth was upheld.

[153] The Abortion Act 1967 gives no indication that there is a duty to the fetus to kill it in the most effective way and *Cherry* adds a new dimension to the problem of the living abortus (see para 9.107). Assuming that s 1(1)(d) is there for the benefit of the mother rather than the fetus, would the fetus' condition make any difference? For an interesting discussion, see J Gillott, 'Screening for disability: A eugenic pursuit?' (2001) 27, Supp II J Med Ethics 21 and J Wyatt, 'Medical paternalism and the fetus' (2001) 27, Supp II J Med Ethics 15.

[154] We have also noted the increasing concern of both the US courts and the state legislatures to express their preference for birth over abortion—and this to the extent that not only wrongful life but also wrongful birth actions may be rejected. For a seminal review, see E H Morreim, 'The concept of harm reconceived: A different look at wrongful life' (1988) 7 Law & Philos 3.

courts, bound by the civil law, to counter the trend and become the first European jurisdiction[155] to allow an action for wrongful life.[156]

Wrongful Life in Europe

10.68 In what, for ease of reference, we will refer to here as the *Perruche* case,[157] the familiar scenario arose in which a handicapped child was born following a negligent failure to interpret correctly a pregnant woman's positive tests for rubella antibodies; had she been correctly counselled, she would certainly have terminated the pregnancy. In an action for breach of contract brought on behalf of the parents, the court of first instance found against both the physician and the laboratory; innovatively, however, it also found them liable to the child for the loss caused by his handicap.[158] The Cour d'Appel then followed precedent and, while confirming the decision in favour of Mme Perruche, overturned that in favour of the child on the ground of causation[159]—the arguments being similar to those rehearsed in *McKay*. The case then went through a series of appeals and was eventually referred to the full chamber of the Cour de Cassation which held that causation in the child's case was demonstrated by the mother having been prevented from exercising her freedom to proceed to a termination of the pregnancy in order to avoid the birth of a disabled child; the harm resulting to the child from such handicap was caused by that negligence and he could claim compensation for it. The court was, in addition, anxious to ensure that the child himself was compensated because there was no guarantee that his parents would always support him. This very unusual case[160] not only disturbed the accepted medical jurisprudence in this area but also caused something of a political uproar in France. At heart, the public rejection of the *Perruche* judgment was based on revulsion at the concept of being compensated for being born and came, in the main, from three sources. It was attacked by the anti-abortion lobby by virtue of the stress laid on the woman's right to choose a termination of pregnancy. Disabled support groups protested that it devalued the lives of the imperfect—criticism was especially loud in the case of two allied Down's syndrome decisions and, since persons with Down's syndrome are not suffering and are probably perfectly happy in their

---

[155] For a full account of the European scene, see A Ruda, ' "I didn't ask to be born": Wrongful life from a comparative perspective' (2010) 1 JETL 204. The author concludes that it is a matter of such complexity that it is one for the legislatures rather than the courts. For a similar European overview of the whole topic of this chapter, see B Steininger, 'Wrongful birth and wrongful life: Basic questions' (2010) 1 JETL 125.

[156] We have found only one previous jurisdiction that has accepted the infant plaintiff's cause when confronted with the problem *de novo*: *Zeitzoff* v *Katz* (n 146). See J Levi, 'Wrongful life decision in Israel' (1987) 6 Med Law 373; A Shapira, ' "Wrongful life" lawsuits for faulty genetic counselling: Should the impaired newborn be entitled to sue?' (1998) 24 J Med Ethics 369.

[157] *X* v *Mutuelle d'Assurance du Corps Sanitaire Français et autres* (2000) JCP 2293. The case is discussed in detail, and the decision disapproved, by T Callus, ' "Wrongful life" a la francaise' (2001) 5 Med Law Internat 117. It is carefully analysed, and again disapproved, by T Weir, 'The unwanted child' (2002) 6 Edin LR 244 where the German position is also considered. An extensive review of the Anglo-French situation is to be found in A Morris and S Saintier, 'To be or not to be: Is that the question? Wrongful life and misconceptions' (2003) 11 Med L Rev 167.

[158] Tribunal de Grande Instance, Evry, 13 January 1992.

[159] Casse Civ 1, 26 March 1996, Bull Civ, 19910.1.1510.

[160] A similar judgment was handed down in 2001 in the case of L, a child with Down's syndrome. See M Spriggs and J Savulescu, 'The Perruche judgment and the "right not to be born" ' (2002) 28 J Med Ethics 63. For great help, see A M Duguet, 'Wrongful life: The recent French Cour de Cassation decisions' (2002) 9 Euro J Hlth Law 139.

own environment, this particular resentment can be well appreciated.[161] Most power-fully, the medical profession rebelled and, indeed, went on strike at the thought of being compelled to be always right in their prenatal screening.

10.69   The furore was sufficient to force the government into emergency legislation. As a result, one cannot, in France, treat the mere fact of being born as constituting damage. The par-ents of a child born with disability which remained undiagnosed during pregnancy due to a *serious* professional fault can claim compensation for harm suffered by them person-ally but not for expenses attributable to the child's being disabled—these will be covered through the social services.[162] Thus, the French government has gone one stage further than the House of Lords in *McFarlane* and has outlawed damages for the upbringing of an uncovenanted child whether that child be healthy or disabled.[163] Moreover, not only is an action for wrongful life no longer available but neither is one for wrongful birth. So, in the end, the ruling of the Cour de Cassation had an effect opposite to that which was intended and it was only a matter of some two years before the matter was again raised—this time in the Netherlands.[164]

10.70   In what we will call, again for ease of reference, the *Molenaar* case,[165] a midwife failed to heed indications for diagnostic amniocentesis and a child was born suffering from an unspecified chromosomal abnormality which resulted in severe physical defects and pain. Here, the Court of Appeal in The Hague followed the French courts and awarded damages not only to the parents on the basis of a wrongful birth claim but also to the child in respect of non-pecuniary damage. The Court's reasoning as to the latter took two lines. First, it was proposed that the midwife had a contractual obligation to the pregnant woman and that the unborn child could be considered to be party to that contract.[166] In our view, it is unlikely that such an extended interpretation would be accepted in the UK[167] and The Hague Court was, itself, clearly hesitant on the point. In the alternative, it was held that the health authority was under a legal obligation to look after the interests of the fetus as an independent entity. Here, the Court relied to an extent on the *nasciturus* principle—that is, that a child in utero can be regarded as being alive if it is in his or her interests to do so. The element of causation necessary for a successful action in negligence was supplied by the fact that the birth of the child could have been prevented; the child's suffering was, as a result, a direct consequence of a negligent medical error.[168]

10.71   The difficulty with both these last points lies in the fact that they require that the court should say to the claimant, 'Yes, it would be better had you not been born.' This judgment,

---

[161] For a thorough review of the French response to a third case, see P Lewis, 'The necessary implications of wrongful life: Lessons from France' (2005) 12 Euro J Hlth Law 135.

[162] Law adopted by the French Senate on 19 February 2002. We are indebted to Weir, n 157, for the transla-tion on which this précis is based.

[163] For discussion of a later unsuccessful constitutional challenge, see: C Manaouil, M Gignon, and O Jardé, '10 years of controversy, twists and turns in the Perruche wrongful life claim: Compensation for children born with a disability in France' (2012) 31 Med Law 661.

[164] *X v Y*, The Hague, Court of Appeals, 26 March 2003.

[165] T Sheldon, 'Court awards damages to a disabled child for having been born' (2002) 326 BMJ 784. See also H F L Nys and J C J Dute, 'A wrongful existence in the Netherlands' (2004) 30 J Med Ethics 393.

[166] As had previously been accepted in the unreported 'Baby Joost' case of 8 September 2000. However, this argument was unanimously rejected in Australia in *Harriton*, n 134.

[167] It is not unlike the concept of transferred malice which was rejected in *Attorney-General's Reference (No 3 of 1994)* [1998] AC 245, HL.

[168] Interestingly, in contrast to the *Perruche* case, the court took a determinedly objective view as to the opportunity for termination and causation.

however sympathetic to the motives behind it, would seriously compromise the value of human life which the courts are more usually called upon to endorse. The disabled should be helped and, if possible, compensated for the suffering which their lives may entail, but the moral basis for such compensation should be the desire to make life more comfortable and bearable—not the notion that they should not be in existence at all.

10.72 As a result, *Molenaar* was appealed to the Dutch Supreme Court[169] which considered the case very thoroughly. In the event, the Supreme Court upheld the appeal court and awarded damages for 'material and emotional damage' to both the parents and child—the latter's emotional damage being attributable to the fact that she was born. All the costs of the child's upbringing were awarded together with those resulting from the mother's psychiatric treatment which was necessitated by the birth. To obviate some of the inevitable criticism, it was emphasised that the damages were based exclusively on the fact that 'the midwife made a serious mistake with regard to the fundamental rights of the parents'.[170] Although there have been calls for restrictive legislation as occurred in France, it appears that no further action has been taken.[171]

WRONGFUL LIFE RECONSIDERED

10.73 While we fully appreciate the sensitivities of those who regard the wrongful life action as generally contrary to human dignity and, in particular to the interests of the disabled, we feel, intuitively, that it is wrong to accept an action for wrongful birth and, at the same time, reject one for wrongful life.[172] We suggest that many of the conceptual difficulties associated with the latter would be largely dissipated if, first, s 1(1)(d) of the Abortion 1967—the so-called 'eugenic clause'—were accepted as having been drafted in the fetal, rather than the maternal, interest.[173] The 'right' of the handicapped fetus to abortion is then comparable to the defective neonate's 'right' to refuse treatment; failure to respond to the interests of either, albeit necessarily expressed by proxy, then falls into the ambit of consent-based negligence (see Chapter 5)—in effect, the fetus is saying, 'But for the negligent advice given to me through my parents, I would not have chosen a disadvantaged condition; I now have to be disadvantaged and, therefore, I am entitled to compensation.' Second, we favour abandoning the principle of 'wrongful life' in favour of 'diminished life'; we can then consider the actual suffering that has been caused rather than embark on baseless comparisons.[174] There would have been no suffering in the event of an abortion, there was no abortion as a result of negligence, and it follows that the negligence has produced suffering which should be compensated according to its degree. This carries the practical advantage that the courts can understand and accommodate this form of damage, which also allows for a distinction

[169] LINAR5213, Hoge Raad, C03/206HR, 18 March 2005.
[170] This synopsis is based on a partial translation of the transcript by one of our students, Ms C van Tooren.
[171] A typical Dutch criticism of the *Molenaar* decision is provided by A Hendriks, 'Wrongful suits? Suing in the name of Terri Schiavo and Kelly Molenaar' (2005) 12 Euro J Hlth Law 97.
[172] For further critique, see R Scott, 'Reconsidering "wrongful life in England after thirty years: Legislative mistakes and unjustified anomalies' (2013) 72 CLJ 115.
[173] For discussion, see J K Mason, *Medico-Legal Aspects of Reproduction and Parenthood* (2nd edn, 1998) pp 157–8. It is noteworthy that Stephenson LJ adopted this view in *McKay* (at All ER 780). But, having done so, why disallow 'wrongful life' actions on the ground that they would encourage abortion?
[174] For support of this controversial conclusion, see Kirby J in *Harriton* v *Stephens*, HCA.

to be made between serious and slight defect.[175] Thus, while the legal and philosophical arguments in favour of rejecting the wrongful life action are powerful, they can be challenged.

10.74　Even so, the apparently insurmountable hurdle on the road to acceptance is posed by causation—it is undeniable that, save in exceptional circumstances, such as direct injury,[176] no *person* has caused the disabilities.[177] Yet, in an age when compensation for injury is so widely available, it is difficult to see why the faulty genetic counsellor should be thus protected and intuition, again, urges that equity is, thereby, thwarted—suffering, if not the cause of the suffering, has been created by the negligence and to suffer is to be injured. We have attempted to resolve the impasse by suggesting that, while the genetic counsellor has not caused the disability, he or she has allowed the disabled fetus to survive in the face of a duty to advise as to whether this is in the fetus' best interests; accordingly, he or she is liable to the disabled neonate.[178] While this formula will not satisfy every criticism of the wrongful life action, it would, if accepted, ensure that justice was seen to be done. It is also reflected in the reasoning of both the French and the Dutch courts outlined earlier.

10.75　Before leaving the topic of wrongful life, it should be noted that a comparable action in negligence will be available if the problem of causation can be evaded. Such a situation is accepted in what is known as the 'preconception tort'. As is clear from the phrase itself, the child may, in such an action, claim that there was negligence prior to his or her conception and that this negligence has resulted in he or she being born disabled. An example of such a claim is provided by the US case of *Yeager v Bloomington Obstetrics and Gynecology, Inc*.[179] This concerned a child born suffering from brain damage due to haemolytic disease of the newborn which occurred because the hospital negligently failed to treat rhesus immunisation of the mother during a previous pregnancy; the court held it

---

[175] See also Ackner LJ in *McKay* (at All ER 786): 'Subsection (2)(b) [of the 1976 Act] is so worded as to import the assumption that, but for the occurrence giving rise to a disabled birth, the child would have been born normal and healthy, not that it would not have been born at all'—and that, having disposed of the phrase 'wrongful life', appeared to be acceptable to the court.

[176] As in *Cherry v Borsman*, n 150. Nearer to home, the Congenital Disabilities (Civil Liability) Act 1976, s 1A (inserted by way of the Human Fertilisation and Embryology Act 1990, s 44) allows for an action by a disabled infant when the disability is attributable to wrongful acts or omissions—including embryo selection—arising during the provision of treatment for infertility. This seems indistinguishable from an action for wrongful life, and it is not suggested that there will be any difficulties in the assessment of damages. And why, one wonders, should treatment for infertility be isolated from normal obstetric practice?

[177] This, however, begs the question of the prescription of teratogenic drugs—could a wrongful life action succeed given such a cause? Our feeling is that it should do so but an action in negligence would now be more appropriate. For discussion, see the contrasting Canadian cases *Webster v Chapman* [1998] 4 WWR 335 and *Lacroix v Dominique* (2001) 202 DLR (4th) 121. Unfortunately, the major British case: *S v Distillers Co (Biochemicals) Ltd* [1970] 1 WLR 114; [1969] 3 All ER 1142 led to a compromise solution in which the question of negligence was not argued—but, of course, the Congenital Disabilities (Civil Liability) Act 1976 post-dated the case. There is marginal supporting evidence that actions for wrongful life could have succeeded: see *Claimants Appearing on the Register of the Corby Group Litigation v Corby BC* [2009] All ER (D) 312 (a case of environmental contamination brought under the Environmental Protection Act 1990).

[178] J K Mason, 'Wrongful life: The problem of causation' (2004) 6 Med L Internat 149. This is, essentially, the argument put forward by Mason P in *Harriton*, n 141, at [115].

[179] 585 NE 2d 696 (Ind, 1992). For earlier examples, see *Lazevnick v General Hospital of Monro County Inc* 499 F Supp 146 (Md, 1980); *Jorgensen v Meade-Johnson Laboratories* 483 F 2d 237 (1973); *Renslow v Mennonite Hospital* 367 NE 2d 1250 (Ill, 1977).

to be reasonably foreseeable that subsequent children would be injured as a result.[180] Such a claim would also be competent in English law provided that, at the time of conception, the parents were not aware of the risk that their child would be born disabled. This exemption does not apply if, in an action by the child against its father, it is established that the father knew of the risk while the mother did not.[181]

10.76 The jurisprudential difficulty of the preconception tort lies in the assessment of the relative importance of proximity and a duty of care in attributing negligence. For how many future generations or how many potential siblings is a health carer to be held responsible for a negligent act? The answer can scarcely be based on logic but, pragmatically, it is fair to say that liability for preconception negligence can be, and should only be, imposed if the tortfeasor owed a duty of care to the mother of the damaged child.[182] The concept of the preconception tort also draws attention to its counterpart in the field of human rights—that of intergenerational justice,[183] which suggests that we have a duty to future generations not to harm their prospective parents: 'The present generations have the responsibility of ensuring that the needs and interests of future generations are fully safeguarded.'[184] The issue has also been addressed in the ECtHR where it was strongly indicated that the state may well have a positive obligation to protect the quality of life of those who have yet to be conceived.[185] The subject is, however, large and is only peripheral to the current topic. Nonetheless, it serves to remind us that there is a public as well as a private interest in the health of our future children whether it be genetically or environmentally determined.

WRONGFUL INJURY TO THE FETUS AND FETICIDE

10.77 This discussion of wrongful life also reminds us that the fetus per se receives surprisingly little legal protection. We have seen in Chapter 9 how the law takes a pragmatic view of fetal status and legal personhood—the generally accepted threshold for the emergence of rights is birth. Thus the fetus—as opposed to the child—has no rights as such. It does not follow, however, that those who harm the fetus necessarily enjoy immunity from liability, and we explore this more fully in this section.

10.78 Any protection provided to the fetus by ss 58 and 59 of the Offences Against the Person Act 1861 is no more than derivative of the primary offence which is unlawfully procuring

---

[180] It is significant that even those US states that do not allow an action for wrongful birth will accept one on the grounds of a preconception tort: *Gallagher* v *Duke University* 852 F 2d 773 (4th Circ, 1988) (North Carolina).

[181] Congenital Disabilities (Civil Liability) Act 1976, s 1(4).

[182] A view based largely on the Australian case of *X and Y* v *Pal* (1991) 23 NSWLR 26; [1992] 3 Med LR 195. A very useful discussion of the causation/proximity debate in attributing liability is to be found in the US case *Hegyes* v *Unjian Enterprises, Inc* 234 Cal App 3d 1103 (1991) which was not a case of medical negligence but one which can be easily extrapolated to that genre.

[183] Discussed briefly in the context of reproductive medicine in S McLean and J K Mason, *Legal and Ethical Aspects of Healthcare* (2003) p 124.

[184] UNESCO *Declaration of the Responsibilities of the Present Generations towards Future Generations* (1997), Art 1.

[185] *LCB* v *United Kingdom* (1999) 27 EHRR 212. The case concerned the effect of radiation on future generations rather than genetics but the issues are similar. In the event, the case failed because the government had insufficient knowledge of the potential risk.

the miscarriage of a woman; feticide is no more than its, generally, inevitable correlate. Otherwise, the only direct protection of fetal life in utero is provided by the Infant Life (Preservation) Act 1929 which defines the offence of child destruction or 'destroying the life of a child capable of being born alive'.[186]

10.79 Despite this paucity of statutory protection, it is perfectly clear that the fetus has a general, and strong, interest in not being injured by the wrongful act of a third party. This was first clearly recognised at common law in Canada and in Australia in two important decisions, *Duval* v *Seguin*[187] and *Watt* v *Rama*.[188] The almost universally accepted limitation on this, however, is that, although fetal interests may be established while in utero—or even before conception—they cannot be realised unless the fetus is born alive and attains an existence separate from that of its mother;[189] given this condition, however, 'fetal' rights will accrue as a matter of common law.[190]

10.80 The legal demand for neonatal survival is unequivocal. 'There can be no doubt, in my view', said Sir George Baker,[191] 'that in England and Wales the fetus has no right of action, no right at all, until birth' and the same is equally true in Scotland—Scots law recognises no right of the fetus to continue to exist in its mother's womb.[192] From Canada, we have, 'There is no existing basis in law which justifies a conclusion that fetuses are legal persons'.[193] No suit for wrongful fetal death is recognisable in the UK[194] and we are left with an apparent paradox—as Pace[195] put it many years ago, 'Liability is incurred for negligent injury to the fetus but not—or, at least, not necessarily—for its deliberate destruction'.[196]

10.81 Throughout this book it will be noted that we question the logic behind distinguishing the *moral* value of a fetus of, say, 23 weeks' from that of one of 25 weeks' gestation.[197] In terms of legal rights and responsibilities under the civil law, however, the test of capability

---

[186] The 1929 Act does not run to Scotland although it is very probable that an offence comparable to child destruction exists. But the Canadian courts still deny such protection: see *R* v *Sullivan* (1991) 63 CCC (3d) 97.

[187] (1973) 40 DLR (3d) 666.   [188] [1972] VR 353.

[189] An exception probably lies in the criminal law of California, where an offence of feticide has been established: *People* v *Davis* 872 P 2d 591 (Cal, 1994).

[190] *Burton* v *Islington Health Authority, de Martell* v *Merton and Sutton Health Authority* [1993] QB 204; [1992] 3 All ER 833. The legal concept of a separate existence is further limited in England and Wales in the Congenital Disabilities (Civil Liability) Act 1976, under which the neonate must survive for 48 hours before being able to recover statutory damages in negligence. Recent actions in the USA have been based on product liability legislation. For discussion, F Sohn, 'Products liability and the fertility industry: Overcoming some problems in wrongful life' (2010) 44 Cornell Int L J 145 where it is argued that a products liability approach circumvents many of the objections to the wrongful life action.

[191] *Paton* v *British Pregnancy Advisory Service Trustees* [1979] QB 276 at 279; [1978] 2 All ER 987 at 989; applied in *Re DM* [2014] EWHC 3119 (Fam).

[192] *Kelly* v *Kelly* 1997 SC 285, 1997 SCLR 749, per Cullen LJ-C.

[193] *Borowski* v *A-G of Canada and Minister of Finance of Canada* (1984) 4 DLR (4th) 112 at 131, per Matheson J. See also *Winnipeg Child and Family Services (Northwest Area)* v *G (DF)* (1997) 3 SCR 925.

[194] For a thorough review of the situation, see A Whitfield, 'Common law duties to unborn children' (1993) 1 Med L Rev 28.

[195] P J Pace, 'Civil liability for pre-natal injury' (1977) 40 MLR 141.

[196] Or, as was said in *Amadio* v *Levin* 501 A 2d 1085 (Pa, 1985): 'To deny a stillborn recovery for fatal injuries during gestation while allowing such recovery for a child born alive would make it more profitable for the defendant to kill the plaintiff than to scratch him.' The tone in that case, indicates not so much a shift in jurisprudential reasoning as a search for punitive sanctions against the person who negligently destroys the child in utero—a form of expression of an intrinsic concern for the status of the fetus.

[197] For judicial approval, see Balcombe LJ in the Court of Appeal in *Re F (in utero)* [1988] Fam 122; [1988] 2 All ER 193.

of being born alive makes sense.[198] A stillbirth may have been fatally harmed but it cannot be recompensed; it seems reasonable to suppose that justice has been done so long as its mother can be recompensed for the injury she has received through the loss of her infant.[199] The question remains, however, as to whether the criminal law should be invoked as a direct means of fetal or maternal protection or as a punitive response to serious negligence.[200]

FETICIDE

10.82 In addition to its intrinsic interest, the criminal counterpart to fetal injury merits further consideration insofar as it is integral to the analysis of judicial attitudes to fetal status. There can be no doubt that, insofar that it was a pioneer case in which a woman was alleging criminal responsibility on the part of a doctor for the loss of her child, the case of *Vo v France*[201] in the ECtHR had all the ingredients to make it the most important recent case that has relevance to UK jurisprudence in that field. The fact that it did not so develop can be attributed to the fact that the European Court chose to see it as a test of abortion legislation—and we have already discussed the case under that heading.[202] For present purposes, it needs only to be pointed out that the basic matter in contention was the significance of the gestational age of the fetus. Although the Cour d'Appel took the view that it was immaterial and that 'as a matter of elementary common sense' the negligent killing of a 20–24-week-old fetus should be regarded as unintentional homicide, both the trial court and the Cour de Cassation considered that this depended on whether the child in utero was or was not viable in the US sense.[203] Since it was determined that the child was not viable, there was no criminal offence—in short, there was no offence of feticide, at least in France, and the European Court, by a majority, declined to comment.[204] We must, therefore, turn for guidance, with little greater success, to the relevant UK authority—*A-G's Reference (No 3 of 1994).*[205]

---

[198] For a very clear, general, discussion, see A Peterfy, 'Fetal viability as a threshold to personhood' (1995) 16 J Leg Med 187.

[199] Damages to the mother have been given for a stillbirth resulting from negligent treatment: *Bagley v North Herts Health Authority* [1986] NLJ Rep 1014. Damages in respect of bereavement under the Fatal Accidents Act 1976 were expressly disallowed on the ground that the negligence had caused the child to die in utero. See also *Grieve v Salford Health Authority* [1991] 2 Med LR 295, where only the quantum of damages for negligence leading to stillbirth was considered. Whether this is an adequate response by the law remains open to question. In the more recent case of *Less v Hussain* [2012] EWHC 3513 (QB); [2013] Med LR 383, the claimant was unable to establish causation.

[200] It seems that, while 'wrongful fetal death' statutes are in place throughout the USA, judicial interpretation varies—in general, most states operate a 'viability' limitation with recovery available only to the viable fetus.

[201] Application 53924/00 (2005) 40 EHRR 12, (2004) 79 BMLR 71.

[202] See chapter 9. For further analysis, see K O'Donovan, 'Taking a neutral stance on the legal protection of the fetus' (2006) 14 Med L Rev 115.

[203] For discussion of this point, see A Plomer, 'A foetal right to life? The case of *Vo v France*' (2005) 5 Human Rights L Rev 311.

[204] The dissenting opinions, however, examined the issue in detail and concluded that a fetus should be protected under Art 2 ECHR. It is to be noted that the concept of feticide appears to be further developed in the USA than elsewhere; at least 38 states have legislation related to 'fetal homicide' and recognition of a right to protection extends to the fetus of any age in 19 of these (data provided by National Conference of State Legislatures, March 2015). The discrepancies are, of course, closely associated with attitudes to abortion. The right of South Carolina to make such laws was upheld in *Whitner v State* 523 US 1145 (1998).

[205] [1996] QB 581; [1996] 2 All ER 10, CA.

10.83   In essence, this reference concerned the stabbing of a pregnant woman who gave birth to a severely premature baby two weeks later; it transpired that, contrary to what had been supposed, the fetus had been injured in the assault and the resulting infant died 120 days after birth. The attacker was charged with murder and the trial judge directed an acquittal on the grounds that neither a conviction for murder nor for manslaughter was possible under the existing law. The Attorney-General then sought a ruling from the Court of Appeal, asking whether the crimes of murder or manslaughter could be committed where unlawful injury was deliberately inflicted to a child in utero or to a mother carrying a child in utero, where the child was born alive and died having existed independently of the mother, the injuries in utero having caused or made a substantial contribution to the death; the court was also asked whether the fact that the child's death was caused solely as a consequence of injury to the *mother* could remove any liability for murder or man-slaughter in those circumstances.

10.84   We are concerned here not with the niceties of the criminal law but, rather, with those aspects of the judgment which relate to the legal status of the fetus. In this respect, Lord Taylor LCJ developed a two-stage argument. First, it was held that, in the eyes of the law, the unborn fetus is deemed to be part of the mother—an intention to cause serious harm to the fetus is, therefore, an intention to cause severe injury to a part of the mother; and, second, this being the case, malice directed at the mother can be transferred to the fetus once it is born.[206]

10.85   This decision was greeted by many lay commentators as another step towards the recogni-tion of a fetal right to life. In fact, it is nothing of the kind, insofar as it deprives the fetus of any individual personality it may have enjoyed previously. The concept of an intention directed towards a child capable of becoming a person in being was summarily rejected— as Lord Taylor put it:

> An intention to cause serious bodily injury to the foetus is an intention to cause serious bodily injury to a part of the mother just as an intention to injure her arm or her leg would be so viewed,[207]

thus glossing over several differences, including the not unimportant fact that an arm is incapable of developing into an individual human being. And, in fact, the House of Lords would have nothing to do with that view when the case was referred to them,[208] Lord Mustill believing it to be wholly unfounded in fact.[209] Pointing to the truism that mother and fetus were unique human beings once the latter was born, his Lordship emphasised that the maternal–fetal relationship was one of bond, not of identity. In effect, the fetus was neither a 'person' nor an adjunct of its mother—it was a unique organism. Unfortunately, the House never defined the nature of that unique organism save in the negative sense that it is not, legally speaking, a person in being while in utero—it was confirmed yet again that there is no offence of feticide and there never has been.[210] At the same time:

> For the foetus, life lies in the future, not the past. It is not sensible to say that [the foetus] cannot ever be harmed or that nothing can be done to it which can ever be dangerous ... It

---

[206] For an analysis of this decision, see M Seneviratne, 'Pre-natal injury and transferred malice: The invented other' (1996) 59 MLR 884.

[207] [1996] 2 All ER 10 at 18.

[208] *A-G's Reference (No 3 of 1994)* [1998] AC 245; [1997] 3 All ER 936, HL.

[209] *A-G's Reference (No 3 of 1994)* [1998] AC 245, at 255.

[210] The House did not address the question of deliberate injury to a fetus which dies following a live birth.

may also carry with it the effects of things done to it before birth which, after birth, may prove to be harmful.[211]

Thus, the fetus remains a person-in-waiting—or a thing which will, in due course, become something; *A-G's Reference (No 3 of 1994)* dispels the 'maternal appendage' theory of fetal existence but, in the end, it does nothing to improve or even clarify the legal status of the fetus itself.[212]

10.86 As a result, the problem of whether an offence of feticide is either needed or feasible remains open. Intuition surely tells us that non-consensual feticide, which is a gross infringement of a woman's right to reproduce, ought to be an offence rather than something on which the law turns its back. The offences described in ss 58 and 59 of the Offences Against the Person Act 1861 are concerned with procuring a miscarriage rather than protection of the fetus and the two are not necessarily the same thing while, as already noted, the Infant Life (Preservation) Act 1929 has no relevance to the fetus that is incapable of an independent existence. There is, we believe, a hiatus in the law which could be filled by legislation subject to the terms of the Abortion Act 1967. To provide it would not be to deprive women of the right to determine what is to be done with their bodies but, rather, would operate to the positive advantage of *all* pregnant women.

MATERNAL RESPONSIBILITY FOR FETAL WELL-BEING

10.87 Maternal negligence in respect of the fetus—both tortious and criminal—merits special mention. The Law Commission considered the first of these questions and decided that an action against its mother in respect of damage resulting from her negligence during pregnancy should not be available to a child. It was felt that a claim of this type would compromise the parent–child relationship and might also be used as a weapon in matrimonial disputes. Accordingly, s 2 of the English Congenital Disabilities (Civil Liability) Act 1976 excludes claims by a child against its mother except as to injuries sustained during traffic accidents; here, special policy grounds and the availability of insurance were held to justify the admissibility of such claims.[213] Furthermore, the possibility of a child claiming compensation from the Criminal Injuries Compensation Authority (CICA) as a result of being born with Foetal Alcohol Spectrum Disorder (FASD) was foreclosed by the Supreme Court in 2014.[214]

10.88 This leads us to discussion regarding the extent to which the mother's duty of care towards her unborn child might be held to limit her freedom of personal behaviour during pregnancy. Interest in this aspect of the fetal–maternal relationship reached its peak some 30 years ago.[215] Major attention has since focused on the use of alcohol and other drugs, including tobacco, on fetal morbidity and mortality and there is now virtually irrefutable evidence of their teratogenic effects.[216] The issues of responsibility and liability for any consequent negligent injury have been the subject of widespread debate.

---

[211] *A-G's Reference (No 3 of 1994)* [1998] AC 245, at 271, per Lord Hope.

[212] Which is unfortunate as, in the circumstances prevailing, the mother is being deprived of a child she actively desires. For further commentary, see J K Mason, 'A Lords' eye view of fetal status' (1999) 3 Edin LR 246; also 'What's in a name? The vagaries of *Vo v France*' (2005) 17 CFLQ 97.

[213] The contribution of a seatbelt to injury to the fetus—or to its protection—would be an interesting discussion in many cases, particularly if the placenta was on the anterior uterine wall.

[214] *CP (A Child) v Criminal Injuries Compensation Authority* [2014] EWCA Civ 1554.

[215] See, e.g., J L Lenow, 'The fetus as a patient: Emerging rights as a person' (1983) 9 Amer J Law Med 1.

[216] For review: K O Haustein, 'Cigarette smoking, nicotine and pregnancy' (1999) 37 Int J Clin Pharmacol Therap 417; American Academy of Pediatrics, 'Fetal alcohol syndrome and alcohol-related neurodevelopmental disorders' (2000) 106 Pediatrics 358.

10.89 Scrutiny of the interplay of fetal interests and maternal lifestyle has been nowhere more intense than in the USA, where well over 6,000 children are born each year suffering from FASD and where the occurrence of drug withdrawal symptoms in neonates is very high.[217] There, the state has not only a right but also a duty to protect its children under the *parens patriae* jurisdiction and there is strong support for the view that this extends to an interest in the well-being of the 'viable' fetus. Cases of fetal neglect that have come before the courts have been assessed both under the common law and through the federal and state legislation prohibiting child abuse and neglect; as might be expected, the outcomes have not been entirely consistent and depend, to a large extent, on how the charges were framed and on the states' attitudes to feticide.[218] One example concerned Ms Stewart, who was found to have ingested amphetamines and cannabis before her infant was born brain-damaged. The mother was charged in the criminal court with omitting to furnish necessary medical attendance or other remedial care; the case was dismissed on the ground that there was no statutory basis for the charge. This has been the general fate of most criminal charges.[219] A number of civil actions have, however, been officially reported; these suggest that the fetus enjoys an enhanced standing in such courts and, having been born, may be able to sue on its own behalf.[220]

10.90 The courts in Canada have also appreciated the concept of intra-uterine child abuse and have immediately placed in care and protection neonates who have been subjected seriously to drugs or alcohol during pregnancy.[221] However, the courts will not go so far as to restrict the freedom of a woman to live her life as she would please while she is pregnant. In *Winnipeg Child and Family Services (Northwest Area)* v *G (DF)*,[222] the Supreme Court ruled on a case involving an order which had been granted at first instance requiring that a five-month-pregnant woman who was addicted to glue sniffing be detained in a health centre until the birth of her child. One of the grounds for the order was the *parens patriae* jurisdiction in respect of the fetus. It was argued that this inherent jurisdiction of the courts to protect the vulnerable—normally incapax adults and minors—should be extended to protect the fetus in utero. The Supreme Court refused, however, to sanction such a major change to the law. Noting that this would involve conflicts of fundamental rights and interests and difficult policy issues, the court recognised that the unique relationship which a woman has with her fetus is such that 'the court cannot make decisions

---

[217] The problem is, however, worldwide. Closest to home, approximately 13 per cent of all neonatal discharges from hospital in Scotland demonstrate withdrawal symptoms due to maternal use of drugs of addiction: Scottish Executive, *Written Parliamentary Answers*, 2 May 2001 (Mr Malcolm Chisholm).

[218] See n 215.

[219] E.g. *State* v *Gray* 584 NE 2d 710 (Ohio, 1992); *State* v *Carter* 602 So 2d 995 (Fla, 1992); *Commonwealth* v *Kemp* 643 A 2d 705 (Pa, 1994). In at least one state, however, women who used drugs during pregnancy have been convicted of feticide: *Whitner* v *South Carolina* 492 SE 2d 777 (SC, Sup Ct, 1995). Routine neonatal testing for drugs has been found unreasonable on account of its penal connotations: *Ferguson et al.* v *City of Charleston* 121 S Ct 1281 (2001). US courts may well extend fetal protection on an ad hoc basis—a federal judge insisted on the continued detention of an HIV-positive woman on the ground that she might not seek treatment if released (*Boston Phoenix*, 11 June 2009). For a critical overview, see M Goodwin, 'Fetal protection laws: Moral panic and the new constitutional battlefront' (2014) 102 Calif Law Rev 781.

[220] *Grodin* v *Grodin* 301 NW 2d 869 (Mich, 1981).

[221] *Re Children's Aid Society of Kenora and JL* (1982) 134 DLR (3d) 249; *Re Superintendent of Family and Child Service and McDonald* (1982) 135 DLR (3d) 330.

[222] [1997] 2 SCR 925. See, also, an earlier case, *Re Baby R* (1989) 53 DLR (4th) 69—powers to interfere with the rights of women must be given by specific legislation.

for the unborn child without inevitably making decisions for the mother herself'. Such a power, if it were thought desirable, had to be introduced by the legislature.[223]

10.91 A ruling to the same effect has already been given in England in *Re F (in utero)*,[224] a case in which the local authority sought to make the fetus a ward of court so that it could be protected from its mother, who was leading a nomadic existence and who, shortly before the child was due, again went missing. The application was refused both at first instance and in the Court of Appeal on the ground that, until the child was actually born, there would be an inherent incompatibility between any projected exercise of the wardship jurisdiction and the rights and welfare of the mother. Relying heavily on *Paton*,[225] the Court of Appeal first concluded that the fetus had no individual personality and that, therefore, there could be no jurisdiction in wardship; and, second, it was made clear that, in practice, it would be impossible to follow the principle of the paramountcy of the child's welfare in wardship if that conflicted with the liberty and legal interests of the mother.

10.92 The preferred course of action in such cases has been to make the child a ward of court on its birth.[226] The authority for this is the decision of the House of Lords in *D (a minor) v Berkshire County Council*,[227] in which the court upheld a decision to make a care order in respect of a child born prematurely and suffering from drug dependency. The House held that the words, '[The child's] proper development is being avoidably prevented or neglected', in s 1(2)(a) of the Children and Young Persons Act 1969, referred to a continuing, rather than an instant, situation. Thus, while the court would not go so far as to make a fetus a ward of court, conditions both before birth and in the hypothetical future could be taken into account when assessing a neonate's need for care and control, the important point being that there is a genuine continuum. The decision caused considerable concern; first, on the grounds that its application to family law might be extended to the criminal field and, second, because it denied the drug-addicted mother the right to prove her capacity for motherhood. For ourselves, we see *D (a minor)* as yet another case that was decided on its own facts; there is no reason to suppose that a similar decision would be taken in every instance—only that the remedy is there should it be needed in serious cases.[228]

10.93 In a similar vein, the 'exceptional circumstances' that would justify the forceful separation and removal of a baby from its mother at birth—without informing the mother of that plan in advance—had not been made out in the more recent Family Division ruling in *Re DM*.[229] An expectant mother's behaviour was viewed as posing a risk to her own

[223] For a wide-ranging review of the whole field, see R Scott, 'Maternal duties to the unborn? Soundings from the law of tort' (2000) 8 Med L Rev 1. See also the same author 'Maternal foetal conflict' in R E Ashcroft et al. (eds) *Principles of Health Care Ethics* (2nd edn, 2007).

[224] [1988] Fam 122; [1988] 2 All ER 193. Other Commonwealth jurisdictions have attempted rather similar protection of the viable fetus: *In the matter of Baby P (an unborn child)* [1995] NZFLR 577. The absence of fetal/maternal conflict was a feature of this case in which the mother was taken into care in the interests of the fetus.

[225] *Paton v British Pregnancy Advisory Service Trustees* [1979] QB 276; [1978] 2 All ER 987.

[226] Although, now, it is more likely that, either an appeal would be made to the inherent jurisdiction of the court (Children Act 1989, s 100) or the court would make a specific issue order (Children Act 1989, s 8).

[227] [1987] AC 317; [1987] 1 All ER 20, HL.

[228] The court will certainly use its power. In *Re P (a minor) (child abuse: evidence)* [1987] 2 FLR 467, CA a place of safety order was granted on the day of a child's birth into a family which had a history of sexual abuse.

[229] *Re DM* [2014] EWHC 3119 (Fam).

health and that of her baby. Nevertheless, Hayden J emphasised that a capacitous patient has the right to refuse medical treatment. The kind of anticipatory relief that had initially been sought by the city council should be regarded as draconian and a powerful restriction of a woman's autonomy. The court preferred a less restrictive approach that would keep the mother and baby together in the period immediately following birth. Further applications could then be made to the Family Proceedings Court following the birth as necessary. Any claims for protection vested in the fetus are thus strictly circumscribed. Whether or not one agrees with such a loading of the odds, there is little doubt that it has to be accepted on pragmatic grounds. It would be extremely difficult—if not impossible— to invoke the criminal law so as to control a pregnant woman's smoking, eating, or sexual habits, nor would it be desirable—among other ill-effects, doctors would be turned into police informers.[230] We can also foresee great difficulty in proof of causation: teratogenic effects are maximal in the first trimester of pregnancy and the further in time that the cause is removed from the visible effect, the more difficult it becomes to associate the two.

10.94 Finally, we mention the problem of the mother's duty to her full-term child—and, particularly, the dilemma associated with refusal of caesarean section when that operation is indicated in the fetus' best interests. We do so, however, only to refer the reader to Chapter 4 where the subject is explored in detail. For the present, it need only be said that, while, say, some of the US states might regard such refusal as being contrary to statutory child abuse, or even homicide, provisions,[231] there is now no way in which a surgical procedure can be forced on a mentally competent[232] woman who refuses such treatment in the UK—and this irrespective of the effect on a viable fetus.

---

[230] Various ways in which the interests of the fetus might be given greater protection—including an innovative invocation of the Mental Capacity Act 2005—are unearthed in E Cave, 'Drink and drugs in pregnancy: Can the law prevent avoidable harm to the future child?' (2007) 8 Med L Internat 165, although none is wholly convincing nor, in her view, desirable if they conflict with the best interests of the pregnant woman.

[231] C Marwick, 'Mother accused of murder after refusing caesarian section' (2004) 328 BMJ 663.

[232] But the definition of competence is all-important—see Chapters 12 and 13.

11

HEALTH RESOURCES
AND DILEMMAS
IN TREATMENT

INTRODUCTION

11.01 No resources are infinite. Even if a basic material is widely available, the costs of harvesting, treating, or assembling it put some restraint on its use; moreover, the manpower required for distribution and exploitation of the finished product is also going to be limited. Applying these principles to medicine, it is clear that it is impossible to provide every form of therapy for everyone—some sort of selective distribution is inevitable.

11.02 The massive technological advances of the last century have been such that, in the words of a leading article in *The Times*: 'genuinely world-class universal health care, free to all at the point of need, is no longer realistic'.[1] Costs of all types are rising as is the average span of life—at least in the developed countries.[2] 2015 figures suggest that UK life expectancy is likely to rise to late 80s by 2030.[3] As a result, people need treatment for longer and this is not the 'easy-cure' type appropriate to infectious diseases but is rather a matter of sophisticated care for the results of degenerative change. In addition, members of the public are better informed on medical matters and are better able to assimilate the information they are given; they are subjected to a barrage of information of varying quality on the Internet and, consequently, the choice of treatment is increasingly influenced by the patient's demands, with proportionate erosion of the doctor's discretion—in effect, while the latter may wish to treat on a productivity basis, the former views therapy in terms of feasibility.

11.03 Somehow, a compromise must be achieved between demand and supply; the distribution of scarce resources poses some of the more complex ethical problems of modern medicine and permeates every aspect of its provision. They are not confined to the higher administrative echelons nor to the more esoteric departments of major hospitals. They do, indeed, arise—and are answered subconsciously—every time a GP signs a prescription form.[4]

---

[1] Leading article, 'A quiet revolution', *The Times*, 5 November 2008, p 2.

[2] The World Health Organization estimates for global life expectancy for 2013 are 71 years. Updates can be found here: http://www.who.int/gho/mortality_burden_disease/life_tables/situation_trends/en/.

[3] NHS Choices (April 2015), available here: http://www.nhs.uk/news/2015/04April/Pages/UK-life-expectancy-expected-to-rise-to-late-80s-by-2030.aspx.

[4] The same applies to the distribution of a doctor's time within a hospital; see the discussion in *Garcia* v *St Mary's NHS Trust* [2006] EWHC 2314. J Beswick, 'A first class service? Setting the standard of care for the contemporary NHS' (2007) 15(2) Med L Rev 245.

11.04 Such an example relates to the treatment of individuals. But the ethics of health service distribution can also be considered on a global scale; the problems arising at a
national level occupy an intermediate position.[5] We propose examining these as three
distinct issues.

GLOBAL DISTRIBUTION OF RESOURCES

11.05 It is beyond question that the world's medical resources are distributed unevenly in both
material and human terms. The money to buy the expensive paraphernalia associated
with modern hospital medicine is often not available in the low- to middle-income countries and, often, the infrastructure with which to support patients throughout their illnesses simply does not exist.[6] At the same time, there are inadequate facilities for the local
training of doctors who must, therefore, travel to obtain experience. The result can be a
vicious circle in which doctors accustomed to the sophisticated methods of the developed nations return to their own countries only to depart again dissatisfied with what
they have found; permanent emigration of doctors and, in particular, nurses adds to the
problem. Even less morally acceptable is the practice in some countries of regarding the
developing world as a ready supply of trained health care professionals when needed, only
to withdraw their opportunities for employment when circumstances alter.[7]

11.06 All this occurs in the face of increasingly destructive pandemics of infectious disease, the
effect of which is amplified by a shortage of public health resources. Requests are then
made of developed countries for medical assistance in the form of rapid response and the
supply of cheap drugs[8] or containment strategies.[9] The response, such as it is, is not necessarily entirely altruistic. Along with the development of international travel, we have
created ideal conditions for the spread of such diseases and any action taken at source
may be a matter of self-preservation.[10] Supply of medicines also, of course, comes at a
price; while Western pharmaceutical companies might be well placed to ease the plight in
developing countries, they also need to protect their markets. Thus, the practice of buying

---

[5] See most recently, C Newdick, 'Bioethics Through the Telescope' in PR Ferguson and GT Laurie (eds),
Inspiring a Medico-Legal Revolution: Essays in Honour of Sheila AM McLean (2015), ch 8.

[6] See World Health Organization, The World Health Report 2006 – Working Together for Health (2006),
which includes a ten year proposal to tackle crisis in the global health workforce, available at: http://www.
who.int/whr/2006/en/.

[7] Which led to a clash between the Home Office, by way of its immigration rules, and the Department of
Health through its recruitment policies. The then House of Lords decided that guidance given to National
Health Service (NHS) employers which discriminated against international medical graduates in favour of
UK/European Economic Area nationals was contrary to the current rules under the Immigration Act 1971
and was unlawful: *R (on the application of Bapio Action Ltd) v Secretary of State for the Home Department*
[2008] 1 AC 100; [2008] 2 WLR 1073. See too for a wider range of health-related professionals, *R (on the
application of Alvi) v Secretary of State for the Home Department* [2012] UKSC 33; [2012] 1 WLR 2208; [2012]
4 All ER 1041.

[8] J Frenk and O Gómez-Dantés, 'Globalisation and the challenges to health systems' (2002) 325 BMJ 95.
Note: World Health Organization (WHO), *Macroeconomics and Health: Investing in Health for Economic
Development* (2003).

[9] On the significant challenges of effective response to the Ebola crisis, see E Tartari et al.,
'Preparedness of institutions around the world for managing patients with Ebola virus disease: an infection
control readiness checklist' (2015) 4 Antimicrobial Resistance and Infection Control 201522, doi: 10.1186/
s13756-015-0061-8.

[10] J G Hodge Jr, 'Global and domestic legal preparedness and response: 2014 Ebola outbreak' (2015) 9(1)
Disaster Medicine and Public Health Preparedness 47, doi: http://dx.doi.org/10.1017/dmp.2014.96.

drugs cheaply in one market for importation into developing countries in an attempt to address their public health crises has often been met by the strategic exercise of restrictive intellectual property rights by the manufacturers of the drugs. The tensions have been recognised by the World Trade Organization (WTO) which issued its Doha Declaration in November 2001 in an attempt to reach compromise and agreement on the issues.[11] The Declaration stresses the importance of implementing international intellectual property agreements so as to promote access to medicines and to encourage the development of new ones.[12] Agreement was eventually reached in August 2003, and we have discussed this elsewhere.[13] Its terms, and indeed those of almost any kind of aid provided to countries in need, are, however, heavily politically influenced and, thereby, become a matter beyond the scope of our current discussion.[14] Notwithstanding, the WTO has reported that 'Since the Declaration was adopted in 2001, prices for many treatments have fallen significantly, in part due to generic competition and tiered pricing schemes'.[15] Others offer a less favourable account of progress to date.[16]

THE ALLOCATION OF NATIONAL RESOURCES

11.07 We come closer to personal significance when discussing resource allocation on a national scale and, here, a mass of relevant literature has built up over the years—much of which admits the near impossibility of a wholly just solution. The primary problem, which is essentially political, is to establish what share of the national resources is to be allocated to health—and it is the open-endedness of claims to health care that leads to particular difficulties. Although it is relatively protected, the budgetary allocation for the NHS as a whole cannot escape the economic turmoil that has affected the UK since 2008 and from which the country is only barely recovering. Accounts published for NHS England in June 2014,[17] and covering the period and plans between 2010/11 and 2015/16, showed an extra £16.7 billion spend over the six years. Allowing for inflation, it has been estimated that this is a real rise of 4.4 per cent over the six years—or an average of 0.7 per cent per year in the period. Massive though the net sum still seems, it appears that 'the average real annual increase in spending for the current administration represents the lowest amount since the 1950s'.[18] Even so, the impression is that no matter how much is allocated, claims can never be met in full. In a sense, the government, of whatever colour it happens to be at

[11] For an account of the history and possible future of DOHA, see WTO, *The Road to DOHA and Beyond* (2002). And for a recent review of the literature on the topic, see N Chorev and K C Shadlen, 'Intellectual property, access to medicines, and health: new research horizons' (2015) 50(2) Studies in Comparative International Development 143.

[12] See, too, the separate Declaration on the TRIPS Agreement and Public Health (November 2001).

[13] G Laurie, 'Patenting and the human body' in J Hale et al. (eds), *Principles of Medical Law* (3rd edn, 2010).

[14] For further commentary see F M Abbott and J H Reichman, 'The Doha Round's public health legacy: Strategies for the production and diffusion of patented medicines under the amended TRIPS provisions' (2007) 10 J Int Economic L 921.

[15] WTO: https://www.wto.org/english/thewto_e/coher_e/mdg_e/medicine_e.htm.

[16] G Velásquez, *Guidelines on Patentability and Access to Medicines* (2015), available at: http://www.southcentre.int/wp-content/uploads/2015/03/RP61_Guidelines-on-Patentability-and-A2M_EN.pdf. This publication was published under the auspices of the South Centre (http://www.southcentre.int/), albeit that the views contained therein are personal to the author.

[17] Department of Health, Annual Reports and Accounts 2013-14 (2014), available at: https://www.gov.uk/government/uploads/system/uploads/attachment_data/file/335166/DH_annual_accounts_2013-14.pdf.

[18] The King's Fund, NHS Funding: Past and Future (2014), available at: http://www.kingsfund.org.uk/blog/2014/10/nhs-funding-past-and-future.

the time, is hoisted with its own petard. The NHS has become the paradigm sociopolitical sacred cow of the twenty-first century. Innumerable attempts to change its nature have been made but all have been restricted by the demands of the ballot box. Indeed, counter political movements have occurred in the last few years to halt seemingly endless and fruitless reforms.[19]

11.08 Ideally, resource allocation within the country as a whole should provide equal access to health care for those in equal need and attempts have been made over the years to achieve this by systematically correlating the revenue given to the health authorities with their individual needs. These needs were originally based by the Resource Allocation Working Party (RAWP) on the standardised mortality rates which were taken as representing the underlying morbidity. This, in itself, is open to criticism, as it reflects the needs at hospital level rather than those of the provision of primary care which is particularly affected by external factors such as the degree of social deprivation and other socio-economic factors. Nevertheless, RAWP, as the process was popularly known, appeared to provide an objective, albeit rough, formula which could be readily understood; inevitably, it was subject to criticism but the major discrepancies were ironed out slowly[20] and RAWP was effectively replaced by the so-called weighted capitation formula. This was, again, extensively reviewed by the Advisory Committee on Resource Allocation[21] which, itself, admitted that it is impossible to confront need and inequality in one model; hence, the new formula proposed contains a number of distinct data sources.[22] A truly massive reorganisation was initiated by the Health and Social Care Act 2012,[23] which established the NHS Commissioning Board (NHS CB),[24] the function of which was, essentially, to assist the Secretary of State in the provision of services in accordance with the NHS Act 2006. The NHS CB operated under that name from 1 October 2012 until 1 April 2013 from when it has used the name NHS England.[25] NHS England commissions primary care, specialised services, and more particular services for prisons and the armed forces.[26] The wider NHS commissioning budget is managed by clinical commissioning groups (CCGs) consisting of general practices which are charged with commissioning the best services for the populations in their areas. Space does not permit discussion of the position in the other health systems of the UK, for which the reader is referred to the links in this footnote.[27]

---

[19] See, in particular, the widespread adoption of the slogan 'Hands Off Our NHS' across various parts of the health sector. Equally, the Chairman of the Care Quality Commission has been quoted as suggesting that an attitude of indignation about criticising the NHS has had negative consequences, see D Hannan, '"Hands Off Our NHS": the attitude that led to the horrors of Mid Staffs', *The Telegraph*, 22 December 2013.

[20] For recent policy, see Department of Health, NHS Outcomes Framework 2014 to 2015 at https://www.gov.uk/government/publications/nhs-outcomes-framework-2014-to-2015.

[21] L Eaton, 'London PCTs lose out in proposed formula for funding health care' (2009) 338 BMJ 130 gives a useful summary.

[22] For a critical, admittedly lay, approach, see N Hawkes, 'Resource allocation—it's a jungle out there' (2009) 338 BMJ 139.

[23] Complemented more recently by the Health and Social Care (Safety and Quality) Act 2015.

[24] Section 9, inserting s 1G into the National Health Service Act 2006.

[25] NHS England, Putting Patients First: The NHS England Business Plan for 2013/14 – 2015/16, available at: http://www.england.nhs.uk/pp-1314-1516/.

[26] See generally, NHS Commissioning Board, Commissioning Policy: Ethical Framework for Priority Setting and Resource Allocation (2013), available at: http://www.england.nhs.uk/wp-content/uploads/2013/04/cp-01.pdf. This was under review at the time of writing, see http://www.england.nhs.uk/commissioning/policies/gp/ethical-framework/.

[27] For NHS Scotland (http://www.ournhsscotland.com/our-nhs/nhsscotland-how-it-works), for Wales (http://www.wales.nhs.uk/sitesplus/888/page/69484), and for Northern Ireland (http://www.dhsspsni.gov.uk/index/hss.htm).

11.09 Equity gives way to the dictates of demand when allocation at sub-regional level is considered. This inevitably involves choices and the risk of inequitable decisions is high. The ethical control of resources must be strongly influenced, first, by the broad base of representation on the allocation body and, second, on the willingness of the constituent members not to press their own interests too hard[28]—a process which has been described, and, to an extent, approbated, as shroud waving.[29] The lay influence on the provision of services has always been regarded as being of major importance and this is now a central feature of both operational practice, legal responsibility,[30] and political commitment.[31] Healthwatch England now exists on a statutory basis to act as a 'national consumer champion in health and care'. Its legal powers are designed to ensure that the consumer voice is heard '. . . by those who commission, deliver and regulate health and care services'.[32]

11.10 As to budgets, the clinical commissioning groups exist across the country with the function of arranging for the provision of health services in England.[33] In this role, they are required, inter alia, to seek continuous improvement in the effectiveness, safety and patient experience of the service.[34] Choices of action can never be easy—is it possible to decide the relative importance between, say, strict economy, the avoidance of suffering, or the prolongation of life? Given that there are similar populations in two groups, is it right to take their relative social conditions into consideration? And, if one considers only the medical parameters, how is one to identify the best route to the intended goal? There is a strong economic incentive to apply some sort of 'productivity test' in distributing the resources of society; the question is, 'Is it ethical to do so?' Analysis of the problem raises some stark questions and disturbing answers—particularly, perhaps, in relation to the aged.[35]

11.11 This immediately draws attention to one major difficulty encountered when any such evaluation is influenced by powerful public opinion—that the welfare of unproductive citizens is likely to be regarded as secondary to that of the productive; the mentally handicapped and the elderly are, in fact, in double jeopardy—not only may they be seen as less deserving of resources, but they are less likely to be invited to subscribe to the opinion-making process or be able to do so. Geriatric patients, it is said, would not and should not expect priority over younger patients. Which is true enough—but they *would* expect equal consideration.

11.12 It is probable that, so long as there is a restriction on resources, some principle of maximum societal benefit must be applied and that the individual's right to equity must, at least, be viewed in the light of the general need. In a way, this is inevitable in view of the

---

[28] A problem that was highlighted by the proposal that membership of Scottish Health Boards should depend upon direct election. See *BMA News*, 24 January 2009, p 1.

[29] J Rawles, 'Castigating QALYs' (1989) 15 J Med Ethics 143.

[30] Health and Social Care Act 2012, Part 5, Chapter 1. Community Health Partnerships are established in Scotland: National Health Service Reform (Scotland) Act 2004 inserts s 4A to the National Health Service (Scotland) Act 1978. See: http://www.chp.scot.nhs.uk/.

[31] Radically, see I Torjesen, '£4 billion of extra NHS funding should be allocated to patient centred reforms, IPPR think tank urges' BMJ 2015; 351:h4018.

[32] Health and Social Care Act 2012, s 181 and the Healthwatch website, here: http://www.healthwatch.co.uk/.

[33] National Health Service Act 2006, s 1(I) inserted by Health and Social Care Act 2012, s 10. The duties of the groups are now detailed in the 2006 Act, s 3 as amended and inserted by the 2012 Act, s 13. A distinctly innovative provision is that primary care providers must be members of commissioning groups: 2012 Act, s 28.

[34] 2006 Act, s 14R inserted by 2012 Act, s 26.   [35] Which we discuss in the next chapter.

government's dual objectives of patient satisfaction and economy.[36] Essentially, there are three potential measures of a free health service—comprehensiveness, quality, and accessibility. The realistic situation is that the goal of fully comprehensive, high-quality medical care that is freely available to all on the basis of medical need is unattainable in the face of steadily increasing costs—and the temptation is to lower one standard in favour of the other two.

11.13   The difficulties are formidable because what we are discussing at this level is essentially 'horizontal resource allocation', or priority setting between different types of service, which depends not so much on professional medical assessment and advice as on public opinion and on economic evaluation—and the former, at least, is a fickle measuring instrument. Not only can polls be grossly distorted by the way in which questions are put but also opinion is very subject to political and other extraneous influences—particularly that of the media whose circulations depend on maintaining an aggressive and partisan attitude. However, the emphasis on explicitness—or transparency—in rationing strategies is an important pre-requisite and is evolving rapidly.[37]

11.14   Despite the obvious difficulties in reaching any formula, we see it as self-evident that some form of cost evaluation in health care is essential at the resource-purchasing level, if only to ensure impartiality—pressure groups tend to be bad advocates from the point of view of society as a whole. We agree with those who believe that there are no intrinsic ethical barriers to applying economic considerations to health resource allocation. It should, rather, be accepted that without such control there is likely to be an unethical maldistribution of resources; as Williams once put it, anyone who says no account should be paid to costs is, in reality, saying no account should be paid to the sacrifices thereby imposed on others—and there are no *ethical* grounds for ignoring the effect of an action on other people.[38]

11.15   In addition, however, we must remember that there are more reasons than cost for limiting the availability of drugs and other treatments. A health authority may, for example, believe that a given therapy is useless and, accordingly, refuse to sanction its purchase. Such situations arise most commonly in those conditions for which there is, currently, no effective treatment. Sufferers from multiple sclerosis, for example, will clutch at any straw and will be unimpressed by the need for statistical evaluation of a drug before they can be given the chance to use it.[39] The result of leaving the adoption of a new drug to local opinion must, however, be an inequality of distribution which breeds consumer dissatisfaction.[40] Alternatively, the nature of the condition itself may be questioned—is its alleviation a truly medical matter or is it one of 'lifestyle enhancement' only? Here, we

---

[36] For a concise review, see J Russell, T Greenhalgh et al., ' "No decisions about us without us"? Individual healthcare rationing in a fiscal ice age' (2011) 342 BMJ d3279.

[37] It is to be noted that the deliberations of many of the committees and arms of the National Institute for Health and Care Excellence (NICE, see para 11.19) are held in public (https://www.nice.org.uk/Get-Involved/Meetings-in-public).

[38] A Williams, 'Cost-effectiveness analysis: Is it ethical?' (1992) 18 J Med Ethics 7.

[39] See e.g. *R v N Derbyshire Health Authority, ex p Fisher* (1997) 8 Med LR 327. The Authority was not bound to follow governmental directions but was, at the same time, not at liberty to ignore them.

[40] At the same time, a national policy for the provision of a service may result in local decisions as to collateral economies; uniformity may, as a result, be even further compromised: R Cookson, D McDaid, and A Maynard, 'Wrong SIGN, NICE mess: Is national guidance distorting allocation of resources?' (2001) 323 BMJ 743 and for a Scottish comparison see J A Ford et al., 'NICE guidance: a comparative study of the introduction of the single technology appraisal process and comparison with guidance from Scottish Medicines Consortium' (2012) 2(1) BMJ Open e000671, doi: 10.1136/bmjopen-2011-000671.

could place, for example, assisted reproduction[41] and gender reassignment in the 'grey' area of the black to white scale where we are likely to get different answers from different authorities.[42] At the more extreme, we could consider the supply of sildenafil (Viagra) through the NHS. There are occasions when impotence—as opposed to sexual inadequacy—can be seen as a proper medical concern. But this is a far cry from supplying a drug with no intention other than to improve sexual performance. Consequently, the government foresaw an exceptional demand for sildenafil which could have had an adverse effect, both financial and healthwise, on the rest of the community; accordingly, it issued Circular no 1998/158 which advised doctors not to prescribe sildenafil and health authorities not to support the provision of the drug at NHS expense other than in exceptional circumstances. The circular was, however, declared unlawful in the High Court in that its 'blanket' nature was interfering with doctors' professional judgements.[43] It has, in fact, long been apparent that the courts' inclinations will be to uphold the right of the *individual* patient to individual consideration in the face of attempted 'rationing', but only when it is agreed that it is the treatment of a recognisable *disease* that is in issue; indeed, it has been agreed that it is reasonable to allocate resources on the basis of clinical indications alone.[44]

11.16 Finally, it must, of course, be conceded that societies differ and, while some form of resource rationing is, as we believe, inevitable, no single system will be universally acceptable. Britain has been described as an original sin society[45] in which tribulation in the form of ill health is expected—a view which, incidentally, is becoming less and less acceptable as the years pass. The USA, on the other hand, is seen as a society dominated by consumerism and striving for perfectibility of man; the demand for and the use of medical resources are bound to differ. That being so, it is, perhaps, anomalous that the first experiment in public consensus health care rationing should have had its origins in the USA.[46] As a result of research including extensive public debate, the state of Oregon reached an adaptable prioritised list of treatments which would and would not be available under Medicaid and business-related private insurance arrangements. In effect, Oregon attempted to ration care according to a priority list of services to which more individuals who could not afford private insurance could have access. The overall effect, it has been said, is that the aggregate health status of all the poor is increased, but only by making those who already received Medicaid worse off than they were before rather than other social groups that are better off bearing the burden of sacrifice. The original plan had obvious difficulties—one of which lay in the constantly changing list of priorities

[41] S Redmayne and R Klein, 'Rationing in practice: The case of in vitro fertilisation' (1993) 3306 BMJ 1521 used this as an example in what is still a most valuable overview of the influential features of resource allocation.

[42] Even so, once the condition is classified as a disease, the authority must consider the individual's condition before refusing to fund treatment: *R v North West Lancashire Health Authority, ex p A, D and G* [2000] 1 WLR 977; (2000) 53 BMLR 148. But the Trust is entitled to set its own standards as to, say, the distinction between cosmetic and therapeutic treatment and, if the latter, to prioritise on the need. See *R (on the application of AC) v Berkshire West PCT* (2011) 119 BMLR 135, CA.

[43] *R v Secretary of State for Health, ex p Pfizer Ltd* [1999] Lloyd's Rep Med 289; (2000) 51 BMLR 189.

[44] *R (on the application of Condliff) v North Staffordshire PCT* (2011) 121 BMLR 192; [2011] EWCA Civ 910; [2012] 1 All ER 689.

[45] R Klein, 'Rationing health care' (1984) 289 BMJ 143.

[46] For contrasting views on the current Oregon situation compare: S W Howard et al., 'Oregon's experiment in health care delivery and payment reform: coordinated care organizations replacing managed care' (2015) 40(1) J Health Polit Policy Law 245, doi: 10.1215/03616878-2854919, and A M Chang et al., 'Oregon's medicaid transformation: observations on organizational structure and strategy' (2015) 40(1) J Health Polit Policy Law 257, doi: 10.1215/03616878-2854959.

and the consequent inflation of the basic health care package that was available. Its success or failure also depended to a large extent on extraneous factors such as the strength of the state economy as a whole, which would lead to fluctuation in the number of those covered.[47] We doubt, however, if the Oregon experiment has any direct relevance to the UK. Quite apart from the disparate populations involved, the Oregon plan and the current approach are directed at those who cannot, for financial and other reasons, obtain private medical insurance, whereas the NHS is open to all in the UK as of right.[10] Thus, the experience in New Zealand, which is, so far as we know, the only Commonwealth country to have overtly adopted a rationing policy in a fully tax-funded health system, might be expected to provide a more useful comparator.[49] In point of fact, its somewhat turbulent history seems to do little more than epitomise the inherent difficulties imposed by politicisation of health care.[50]

11.17 New Zealand appears to have rapidly abandoned the Oregon model of a list of treatments that are and are not available—or core services. Instead, the Core Service Committee issued a series of guidelines as to how restricted, publicly funded resources were to be allocated, this being based on the principles that a treatment service should provide benefit, be value for money, be a fair use of public funding, and be consistent with community values. Guidelines were developed for the treatment of specific conditions and the resulting compartmentalisation of resources, of necessity, induced some uncomfortable decisions. The guidelines as to eligibility for treatment of end-stage renal failure, for example, included recommendations that, in usual circumstances, persons aged over 75 should not be accepted for dialysis and that other serious diseases or disabilities that are likely to affect survival or the quality of life would be additional reasons for exclusion. The latter condition clearly opened the door for discrimination on the basis of value-laden judgements which may well be beyond the medical remit.[51]

11.18 The seminal test of the New Zealand guidelines[52] concerned just such a man; W was in end-stage renal failure and also suffered from diabetes and dementia.[53] A decision was taken to discontinue interim dialysis—first, on the grounds that W's moderate dementia left him outside the group of persons considered suitable for inclusion in the treatment

---

[47] For an analysis that indicates that these factors continued: V Alakeson, 'Why Oregon went wrong' (2008) 337 BMJ 900. See also an interesting critique of the US system overall: E J Lamb, 'Rationing of medical care: Rules of rescue, cost-effectiveness, and the Oregon plan' (2004) 190 Amer J Obs Gynecol 1636.

[48] See E D Kinney, *The Affordable Care Act and Medicare in Comparative Context* (2015). For a critical assessment of President Obama's 2010 Affordable Care Act, see J P Geyman, 'A five-year assessment of the Affordable Care Act: market forces still trump the common good in U.S. health care' (2015) 45(2) Int J Health Serv 209, doi: 10.1177/0020731414568505. See too J Quadagno, 'Right-wing conspiracy? Socialist plot? The origins of the Patient Protection and Affordable Care Act' (2014) 39(1) J Health Polit Policy Law 35, doi: 10.1215/03616878-2395172.

[49] For an analysis, see J Manning and R Paterson, '"Prioritization": Rationing health care in New Zealand' (2005) 33 J Law Med Ethics 681.

[50] See R Gauld, 'Health care rationing in New Zealand: Development and lessons' (2004) 3 Soc Pol Soc 235.

[51] For an argument in favour of public involvement based on UK evidence, P Dolan and A Tsuchiya, 'It is the lifetime that matters: public preferences over maximising health and reducing inequalities in health' (2012) 38 J Med Ethics 571, doi: 10.1136/medethics-2011-100228.

[52] *Shortland* v *Northland Health Ltd* [1998] 1 NZLR 433, (1999) 50 BMLR 255.

[53] Richardson P described this as brain damage (at BMLR 256) and his general practitioner as mild dementia. W had expressed a wish to remain alive—cf, the English case of *Re D (medical treatment: consent)* [1998] 2 FLR 22; (1998) 41 BMLR 81 in which it was held that dialysis need not be imposed on a patient who could neither accept nor refuse treatment.

programme but, later, on a purely clinical and 'best interests' standard. The decision was forcefully contested and the matter was ultimately heard by the New Zealand Court of Appeal. There, the Court refused to accept the case as a test of the guidelines, and, hence, as a question of rationing, and determinedly held it to be no more than a matter of the exercise of clinical judgement within good medical practice; accordingly, the decision of the High Court that it was totally inappropriate for a court to attempt to direct a doctor as to what treatment should be given to a patient was upheld.[54] Despite its restricted scope, *Shortland* is still relevant to the 'rationing' debate in that it shows the difficulties inherent in making subjective clinical decisions once general guidelines have been laid down for the use of resources in specific conditions. Once it is established that the state is responsible, to a greater or lesser extent, for the health of *all* its citizens, the overall problem of the use of resources becomes that of balancing public demand against distributive justice. We believe that the imposition of some form of health care rationing is imperative in a free-for-all health economy. To do so, however, involves careful ethical analysis to which we now turn with particular reference to UK experience over the last few decades.[55]

HEALTH CARE ECONOMICS

11.19 The current approach in England and Wales rests on the National Institute for Health and Care Excellence (NICE)[56] which resulted from an amalgamation of the National Institute for Clinical Excellence with the Health Development Agency. The latter's function was, essentially, within the public health sector and, thus, was responsible for the prevention of ill health; the former was established as a special health authority within the NHS in 1999[57] with a remit described as being to carry out such functions in connection with the promotion of clinical excellence in the health service as the Secretary of State may direct.[58] In essence, this wide responsibility crystallised into providing advice and guidance as to what treatments are best for patients on a national scale. With its re-establishment under the Health and Social Care Act 2012 as the National Institute for Health and Care Excellence,[59] the core purposes of NICE have become preparation of standards on provisions of NHS services, public health services and social care in England (s 234), and provision of advice and guidance to the Secretary of State on any quality matter (s 236), while having regard to (i) the broad balance of benefits and costs, (ii) the degree of need of persons, and (iii) the desirability of promoting innovation (s 233). All of this, moreover, must be done 'effectively, efficiently, and economically' (s 233(2)).

---

[54] Salmon J at BMLR 257 relying heavily on *Re J (a minor)* [1993] Fam 15; [1992] 4 All ER 614.

[55] For an excellent collection of essays on the philosophy and practice of rationing, see A den Exter and M Buijsen (eds), *Rationing Health Care: Hard Choices and Unavoidable Trade-offs* (2012).

[56] The UK methodology, while attracting global interest, may, however, be particularly aligned to the almost unique nature of the NHS: N Hawkes, 'NICE goes global' (2009) 338 BMJ 266.

[57] National Institute for Clinical Excellence (Establishment and Constitution) Order 1999 (SI 1999/220, revoked by National Treatment Agency (Abolition) and the Health and Social Care Act 2012 (Consequential, Transitional and Saving Provisions) Order 2013/235 Sch 2(2) para 179 (1 April 2013). Legal authority for NICE is now s 232 of the Health and Social Care Act 2012. NICE's relationship with Scotland is complex. In general, the Scottish Medicines Consortium (SMC) advises NHS Scotland on new and modified drug therapies; NICE advice based on single technology appraisal has no direct status in Scotland. Healthcare Improvement Scotland (HIS), set up by the Public Services Reform (Scotland) Act 2010, alerts Scottish Health Boards to NICE guidance and advises on its applicability in Scotland (http://www.healthcareim-provementscotland.org/our_work/technologies_and_medicines/nice_guidance_and_scotland.aspx). We will confine our observations to NICE—the same ethical principles apply in the case of SMC and HIS.

[58] See now, Health and Social Care Act 2012, Pt 8.   [59] Health and Social Care Act 2012, s 232.

11.20 'Best practice' in this context can be divided into three categories: clinical guidelines, recommendations as to audit and the appraisal of the clinical, and cost-effectiveness of new and existing health technologies and, of these, the last is, by far, the most important from this chapter's point of view.[60] In this respect, the Institute was initially hailed as a rational response to the existing situation, already outlined earlier, whereby individual health authorities determined whether, or in what circumstances, a given treatment would be provided—a system which had come to be popularly known as 'postcode prescribing'. Ideally, NICE's decisions were intended to be based on pure clinical need and efficiency but, inevitably, they had to include consideration of what was best for the health service itself; as we have already seen, scientific value and social value judgements cannot be dissociated in a tax-funded service[61]—the conclusion, as a leading article in *The Times* put it, is that, 'The National Institute for Clinical Excellence is rationing made plain'.[62]

11.21 As a consequence, NICE was, to an extent, living a lie[63] and was subject not only to commercial and political pressures but also to massive influence from the media—it becomes very much easier to approve a new or expensive treatment than to refuse its use.[64] Nonetheless, the importance of such an organisation to the health service is now well established and its decisions were unashamedly moulded to a large extent by their economic effect.[65] At its simplest, this is a matter of deciding what increase in health is likely to accrue from the increased expenditure involved in introducing a new treatment—the so-called incremental cost-effectiveness ratio—and NICE's preferred measure of this is the cost per quality adjusted life year (QALY). We discuss the concept of the QALY as applied to the individual below. Here, it need only be said that, having established for how long a new treatment offers an enhanced quality of life, a commissioning authority will estimate what extra cost this would involve individually and, by extrapolation, what effect this would have on the overall economy of a health service.[66] We will see later that the definition, and use, of special reasons opens a can of worms. It has been suggested that it is not constitutionally appropriate for NICE to set thresholds, this being the function of the purse-holders—that is, Parliament. Rather it should be seeking the optimum threshold, incremental cost-effectiveness ratio, given the available expenditure.[67]

[60] Cf K Syrett, ' "Nice work?" Rationing, review and the "legitimacy problem" in the "New NHS"' (2002) 10 Med L Rev 1 and M D Rawlins, 'National Institute for Clinical Excellence: NICE works' (2015) 108(6) J R Soc Med 211, doi: 10.1177/0141076815587658.

[61] The way in which decisions are taken was detailed by the Institute's current chairman: M D Rawlins and A J Culyer, 'National Institute for Clinical Excellence and its value judgments' (2004) 329 BMJ 224.

[62] Leading article, 'Not a nice habit' *The Times*, 12 April 2002, p 23. It is probably fair to say that NICE was, and particularly 'new' NICE is now, concerned as much with the clinical effect of a treatment as its cost per QALY: J Raftery, 'NICE: Faster access to modern treatments? Analysis of guidance on health technologies' (2001) 323 BMJ 1300.

[63] R Smith, 'The Failings of NICE' (2000) 321 BMJ 1363. J Waxman, 'We need cancer drugs: NICE must go', *The Times*, 8 August 2008 claimed that NICE, itself, was costing £30 million per year.

[64] It has been pointed out that to concentrate on new treatments alone is inflationary: A Maynard, K Bloor, and N Freemantle, 'Challenges to the National Institute for Clinical Excellence' (2004) 329 BMJ 227.

[65] For a very considered view of rationing in modern Britain, see C Newdick, 'Accountability for rationing—Theory into practice' (2005) 33 J Law Med Ethics 660.

[66] M D Rawlins and A J Culyer, 'National Institute for Clinical Excellence and its value judgments' (2004) 329 BMJ 224. And for an assessment of NICE from the early years see Rawlins, n 60 above.

[67] A Culyer, C McCabe, A Briggs, et al., 'Searching for a threshold, not setting one: The role of the National Institute for Health and Clinical Excellence' (2007) 12 J Hlth Serv Res Pol 56. See also J Appleby, N Devlin, and D Parkin, 'NICE's cost effectiveness threshold' (2007) 335 BMJ 358.

11.22 Be that as it may, a pattern has been well established but someone still has to pay the bill. The Darzi review of the health service[68] recommended that patients should, in future, have a legal right to all drugs approved by NICE if a doctor says they are clinically appropriate. The government, however, changed and the Darzi proposals were never implemented in full. Thus, the distribution of selected treatments still varies across the country. The legal position has recently been considered and summed up by the High Court in *R (on the application of Elizabeth Rose) v Thanet Clinical Commissioning Group*.[69] The claimant had been a long-standing sufferer of Crohn's disease and was due to receive chemotherapy which carried a high risk of making her infertile. Her request to access oocyte cryopreservation before the chemotherapy began was repeatedly turned down by her clinical commissioning group (CCG), and this judicial review was heard as a matter of urgency because her treatment could not be delayed for long. The core argument was that the CCG had unlawfully ignored NICE guidance from 2013 that cryopreservation in such cases be offered. Mr Justice Jay pointed to the obligation of the CCG under the NHS Constitution to make rational, evidence-based funding decisions, but equally noted that the regulatory regime under which NICE operates implicitly meant that recommendations in such cases do not have to be followed.[70] Notwithstanding, as a matter of general public law, citing *R v North Derbyshire Health Authority (ex parte Fisher)*,[71] to have due regard to national guidance such as that produced by NICE. In the event, the CCG's only reason for not following NICE was that it disagreed with its scientific basis; this was insufficient on its own and the associated policy was unlawful. Of course, being a judicial review this did not mean that a differently formulated policy could not still deny the treatment, but the standing policy had to fail.

11.23 As something of a quid pro quo, it is to be noted that NICE is also charged with advising as to what is known as disinvestment in the NHS—that is, in identifying those treatments that are no longer cost-effective or are no longer appropriate. This is clearly a logical counterpart to the duty of advising on what is the most effective way of delivering health care. Whether or not it makes any significant difference to the health care budget is, however, still undecided.[72] NICE can still be regarded as a brave attempt to rationalise, and nationalise, our health care allocation decision-making that will still be ongoing by way of the new CCGs. But, in the end, the distribution of resources cannot escape the overall political mastery that characterises the NHS.

11.24 The question: 'What is NICE's, or its equivalent's liability in the event that its advice is faulty?' is, so far as we know, as yet untested. Certainly, decisions are subject to judicial review, as we have seen above, but this is of small consolation to the patient who

---

[68] Lord Darzi, *High Quality Care for All: NHS Next Stage Review Final Report* (Department of Health, 30 June 2008).

[69] [2014] EWHC 1182 (Admin).

[70] The case involves a helpful discussion of the architecture of the regulatory regime, and in particular reg 5 [advice and guidance] which applied in this case, see National Institute for Health and Care Excellence (Constitution and Functions) and the Health and Social Care Information Centre (Functions) Regulations (SI 2013/259). Note, however, as the judge continued: 'This is in contrast to separate regulatory provisions relating to "technology appraisal recommendations" and "highly specialised technology appraisal recommendations", with which relevant health bodies such as CCGs must comply', n 69 above, para 22.

[71] (1998) 10 Admin LR 27; [1997] 8 Med LR 327; (1997) 38 BMLR 76.

[72] S Pearson and P Littlejohns, 'Reallocating resources: How should the National Institute for Health and Clinical Excellence guide disinvestment efforts in the National Health Service?' (2007) 12 J Hlth Serv Res Pol 160. And, more recently, S Garner and P Littlejohns, 'Disinvestment from low value clinical interventions: NICEly done?' (2011) 343 BMJ d4519.

sustains injury as a result of his or her doctor following the wisdom of the Institute, possibly against his or her better judgement. This aspect of the 'legitimacy' of the Institute was addressed in depth by Syrett[73] and the test is certainly a hard one, particularly in that an essentially scientific body is being asked to make what are often moral judgements within a pluralistic society. No NICE decisions are likely to please everyone and the role of the courts in enforcing 'reasonableness' becomes increasingly important. The question is, 'Is legal intervention to be welcomed or distrusted?' At present, successful challenges to NICE's procedures are rare.

THE LEGAL SITUATION

11.25 In much the same way, it is surprising that there have not been more actions brought by patients who feel that the Secretary of State has failed in his or her duty to '... to require the Board to arrange, to such extent as it considers necessary to meet all reasonable requirements' broad provision as part of the health service.[74] But, on reflection, it is probable that the relative paucity of cases results from the extreme improbability of a successful outcome. A further explanation, recently reiterated by the European Court of Human Rights (ECtHR), is that nation states enjoy a wide margin of appreciation in determining how or whether to allocate scarce resources involving social, economic, and health care policy.[75]

11.26 We are left, then, to consider the landmark decisions that exist. The classic action, which set the tone for all later cases, is that of *Hincks*.[76] In that case, patients in an orthopaedic hospital sought a declaration that the Secretary of State and the health authorities were in breach of their duty in that they had been forced to wait an unreasonable time for treatment because of a shortage of facilities arising, in part, from a decision not to add a new block to the hospital on the ground of cost. In dismissing the application, Wien J said it was not the court's function to direct Parliament what funds to make available to the health service nor how to allocate them. The duty to provide services 'to such extent as he considers necessary' gave the Minister a discretion as to the disposition of financial resources. The court could only interfere if the Secretary of State acted so as to frustrate the policy of the Act or as no reasonable Minister could have acted. Moreover, even if a breach was proved, the Act did not admit of relief by way of damages. The case went to appeal[77] where, as might be expected, the judgment turned on the interpretation of 'reasonable requirements'. Lord Denning MR considered this to mean that a failure of duty existed only if the Minister's action was thoroughly unreasonable. It was further thought that we should be faced with the economics of a bottomless pit if no limits in respect of long-term planning were to be read into public statutory duties; the further the advances of medical technology, the greater would be the financial burden placed upon the Secretary of State.

11.27 However, health authorities, under whatever name, are required to balance their individual budgets, thus bringing the decision-makers into closer contact with those affected. Society, now in the guise of Local Healthwatch organisations, has a statutory place in the

---

[73] N 60.   [74] National Health Service Act 2006, s 3B.
[75] *McDonald* v *United Kingdom* (2015) 60 EHRR 1; 37 BHRC 130; (2014) 17 CCL Rep 187. Note, the Court went as far as to point out that the margin is particularly wide when resources are limited, citing *Osman* v *United Kingdom* [1999] 1 FLR 193; (2000) 29 EHRR 245.
[76] *R* v *Secretary of State for Social Services, ex p Hincks* (1979) 123 Sol Jo 436.
[77] *R* v *Secretary of State for Social Services, ex p Hincks* (1980) 1 BMLR 93, CA.

process[78] and, as a corollary, is entitled to judicial review of decisions thought to have been taken improperly. Nevertheless, attempts to extend this privilege to individuals seeking improved access to treatment have foundered consistently on the rock of the reasonableness test inherent in the jurisprudence to date.

11.28 The paradigmatic case is that of *Walker*,[79] which concerned a baby whose surgery had been postponed five times because of a shortage of skilled nursing staff. The trial judge, Macpherson J, deprecated any suggestion that patients should be encouraged to think that the court had a role in cases which sought to compel the authority to carry out an operation that was not urgent; and the Court of Appeal confirmed his refusal of the application for review. Within two months, the same health authority was involved in a comparable case, the only major difference being that the child was possibly in greater immediate danger.[80] Reiterating that, to be so unreasonable as to come within the jurisdiction of the court, the Authority would have had to make a decision that no reasonable body could have reached,[81] Stephen Brown LJ said:

> In the absence of any evidence which could begin to show that there was [such a failure] to allocate resources in this instance...there can be no arguable case...It does seem to me unfortunate that this procedure has been adopted. It is wholly misconceived in my view. The courts of this country cannot arrange the lists in the hospital...and should not be asked to intervene.

11.29 While expressing great sympathy with the parents, Stephen Brown LJ suggested that it might have been hoped that the publicity would bring pressure to bear on the hospital and there is no doubt that this effect could, and on occasion does, materialise—particularly in a life-saving situation. Perhaps the most publicised relevant incident since then has been that of 'Child B', in which funding for an essentially ineffective treatment was refused.[82] This case is discussed in detail later;[83] for the present, it is appropriate only to quote the Chief Executive, who was, as the mouthpiece of the health authority, taken to be responsible for the decision:

> [The] case took on a symbolic importance, helping people to grasp the reality that expectation and demand had now outstripped their publicly funded systems' ability to pay without regard to the opportunity cost.[84]

11.30 The NHS has not, however, been singled out as a test-bed for judicial husbandry. In a case brought under the Chronically Sick and Disabled Persons Act 1970, it was held that the costs of the arrangements and the local authority's resources were proper considerations in assessing whether a person had a need and whether it was necessary to make arrangements to meet it.[85] The case concerned the *removal* of social services

---

[78] Health and Social Care Act 2012, s 181 amending Local Government and Public Involvement in Health Act 2007, s 221.

[79] *R v Central Birmingham Health Authority, ex p Walker* (1987) 3 BMLR 32, CA.

[80] *R v Central Birmingham Health Authority, ex p Collier* (6 January 1988, unreported, available on Lexis).

[81] *Associated Provincial Picture Houses Ltd* v *Wednesbury Corpn* [1948] 1 KB 223 at 229; [1947] 2 All ER 680 at 683, per Lord Greene MR, CA.

[82] *R v Cambridge Area Health Authority, ex p B (a minor)* (1995) 25 BMLR 5; revsd (1995) 23 BMLR 1, CA.

[83] See Chapter 15.

[84] S Thornton, 'The *Child B* case—Reflections of a Chief Executive' (1997) 314 BMJ 1838. Interestingly, reporting restrictions were lifted in order to facilitate a public appeal fund: *Re B (a minor)* (1996) 30 BMLR 10 1.

[85] *R v Gloucestershire County Council, ex p Barry* [1997] AC 584, (1997) 36 BMLR 69, HL.

from a disabled man; some of the difficulties involved are crystallised in the dissenting opinion of Lord Lloyd:

> How can resources help to measure [the man's] need?...It cannot, however, have been Parliament's intention that local authority B should be able to say 'because we do not have enough resources, we are going to reduce your needs'. His needs remained exactly the same. They cannot be affected by the local authority's inability to meet those needs.[86]

Even so, as in the medical cases, the court was not minded to interfere with the intricacies of resource allocation.[87]

11.31　More recently, however, the Human Rights Act 1998 has provided a new arena for the settlement of resource allocation cases. In practice, the Act has had surprisingly little impact on the provision of health services in the UK,[88] and we have already noted above that the ECtHR has confirmed that the margin of appreciation is particularly wide when resources are scarce.[89] Nonetheless, it does, at the very least, require that decisions are made with regard to due process requirements and to claims to equality and proportionality. It is very unlikely that Art 2 of the European Convention on Human Rights (ECHR), which protects the right to life, would ever provide an automatic entitlement to treatment in any particular case;[90] it could, however, prevent the evolution of any policy which denied reasonable access to available resources. In 2006, a Ms Rogers did, in fact, challenge the refusal of her Primary Care Trust (PCT) to fund treatment of her early breast cancer with the currently unlicensed drug Herceptin; this was on the grounds, inter alia, that the refusal offended against Arts 2 and/or 14 of the European Convention as embodied in Sch 1 to the 1998 Act.[91] An application for judicial review was refused at first instance. The Court of Appeal, however, considered that the Trust's *policy*—which involved withholding such treatment unless each patient concerned could demonstrate the existence of 'exceptional personal or clinical circumstances'—was irrational and, therefore, unlawful; Ms Rogers' personal problem was, as a result, not addressed—nor could it be in the context of a judicial inquiry.[92]

11.32　Interestingly, Counsel for Ms Rogers and the court agreed that the case would have been very different had the Trust's policy been founded, at least in part, on budgetary considerations,[93] and this was demonstrated in the very comparable case of Ms Otley[94]

---

[86]　[1997] AC 584 at 599; (1997) 36 BMLR 69 at 96.

[87]　But other considerations—e.g. Disability Discrimination Act 1995, s 49A—must also be taken into account: *R (on the application of W) v Birmingham City Council* (2011) 120 BMLR 134.

[88]　C Foster, 'Simple rationality? The law of healthcare resource allocation in England' (2007) 33 J Med Ethics 404, provides a useful thumbnail sketch of the overall position.

[89]　Para 11.25 above.

[90]　'There is no example in any medical context of Art 2 demanding more of the NHS than domestic law does'—Foster, n 88.

[91]　*R (on the application of Rogers) v Swindon NHS Primary Care Trust* [2006] 1 WLR 2649; (2006) 89 BMLR 211. Analysed with approval by K Syrett, 'Opening eyes to the reality of scarce health care resources?' [2006] PL (Winter) 664.

[92]　In the same vein, the court only ordered that the Trust should review its policy. The case is discussed in an extensive review of judicial policy in similar 'exceptional' cases by C Newdick, 'Judicial review: Low-priority treatment and exceptional case review' (2007) 15 Med L Rev 236. See also *R (on the application of Gordon) v Bromley NHS Primary Care Trust* (2006) EWHC 2462 (Admin) for the importance of clarity in decision-making.

[93]　At [58]; *R (on the application of Murphy) v Salford PCT* [2008] EWHC 1908 (case referred to Primary Care Trust on the grounds of inadequate consideration).

[94]　*R (on the application of Otley) v Barking and Dagenham Primary Care Trust* (2007) 98 BMLR 182.

who was refused funding for treatment of her colorectal cancer with the unlicensed drug Avastin. Here, by contrast, the policy of the Trust—which included consideration of the 'impact of funding on the health of the whole population'—was assessed as being rational and sensible. Even so, Ms Otley's search for treatment was successful in that, first, the Trust's reasons for the *particular* exclusion were flawed and unlawful on *Wednesbury*[95] grounds and, second, that the proposed treatment would have required the allocation of only small resources. Unfortunately, the question of a breach of Art 2 of the Convention was again not addressed directly.[96]

11.33 There is some evidence that these, and similar, cases have made their mark[97] insofar as, from 2009, NICE extended its customary QALY limit as to cost-effectiveness in the case of patients who are not likely to live for longer than 24 months and whose life will, as a result of treatment, be extended by at least three months.[98] We do, however, wonder if this apparent advance in patient care is not being bought at the expense of ethical principles. Whether it is right to approve exceptional expenditure *because* it will be, by definition, limited is, at least, arguable. In summary, whatever the reasoning employed, it has been said that, whether or not a patient is exceptional does not sit comfortably with the axiom that doctors should treat all patients with equal concern.[99] With which we would all agree—but it does nothing to *solve* the problem.

11.34 A couple of decades ago, Klein suggested that it was only a slight exaggeration to say that the demand for health care is just what the medical profession chooses to make it.[100] Which may well be so but, insofar as, in the event of a water shortage, one cannot make a pot of tea without tap water unless one takes the water from the coffee urn, it adds little to the solution of the *overall* problems. What the public needs is not so much a universally acceptable answer but, rather, honesty and openness in assessing the role of NICE and other resource-allocation decision-makers; there is much to be said for the suggestion of an influential Member of Parliament that it be renamed the National Institute of Cost-Effectiveness and Rationing.[101] The first Triennial Review of NICE, published in July 2015, reported that the body is a 'respected, trusted, high-performing organisation'.[102] Most recommendations relate to increased efficiency within the organisation and between other bodies, and notably there is also a Recommendation to consider whether NICE should become the single expert body for clinical and cost-effectiveness appraisals, including the Cancer Drugs Fund and the Joint Commission on Vaccinations and Immunisation.[103]

Whatever the logistics and operational considerations, the concentration of such power in the current or an even larger body such as NICE does not detract from the central

---

[95] N 81.

[96] It has been held that a reasonable rejection of an IFR does not breach Art 8 of the Convention: *Condliff*, n 44.

[97] For an exceptionally well-argued and described case where an appeal against refusal to finance an unapproved cancer treatment was successful, see *R (on the application of Ross) v West Sussex PCT* [2008] EWHC 2252.

[98] National Institute for Health and Clinical Excellence, *Appraising Life-extending, End of Life Treatments* (2009). For discussion see M Collins and N Latimer, 'NICE's end of life decision making scheme: impact on population health' (2013) 346 BMJ f1363, doi: http://dx.doi.org/10.1136/bmj.f1363.

[99] A Ford 'The concept of exceptionality: A legal farce?' (2012) 20(3) Med L Rev 304.

[100] R Klein, 'Dimensions of rationing: Who should do what?' (1993) 307 BMJ 309.

[101] E Harris, 'Cancer treatments need rigorous assessment', *The Times*, 11 August 2008, p 27.

[102] Department of Health, Report of the Triennial Review of the National Institute for Health and Care Excellence (2015), available at: http://www.nice.org.uk/news/article/nice-a-respected-trusted-high-performing-organisation.

[103] N 102 above, Recommendation 5.

question which is, essentially, a matter of economics. The major *ethical* dilemma, however, centres on the consequently imposed limitations on the treatment of the individual and it is to that aspect that we now turn.

TREATMENT OF THE INDIVIDUAL

11.35 In discussing the medical treatment of the individual, we are faced with the patient who is actually at risk. Objectivity is no longer the main arbiter of treatment and is replaced by need—which, in a medical context, can be defined as existing 'when an individual has an illness or disability for which there is an effective and acceptable treatment'.[104] We should, therefore, first exclude from this discussion, and treat as a special case, the patient who is using a scarce resource but who is obtaining no benefit. The most clear example of this is one who is brain-damaged and is being maintained in intensive care—a situation discussed in detail in Chapter 15. We believe that, once treatment is clearly of no avail, it is not only permissible but positively correct to discontinue heroic measures.[105] Leaving that caveat aside, it has been abundantly clear throughout this discussion that access even to *effective* treatments will be limited by their cost—for a limited budget will provide only a limited number of treatment units—and effectiveness is a relative term. As a result, some form of differential treatment is enforced and, in turn, the assessment of relative needs involves value judgements.

11.36 How, then, are those judgements to be made? In practice, many urgent decisions are made instinctively and without the need for profound analysis.[106] Moral agonising is largely reserved for the treatment of chronic, life-threatening diseases, not only because they offer the opportunity for analysis but because they attract the use of expensive resources and will consume these for a long time—at which point the dilemma involves not only the allocation of resources but also their withdrawal. The current position is that the only obligation on Health Authorities is to provide such therapy as is positively recommended by NICE (cf discussion of *R (on the application of Elizabeth Rose) v Thanet Clinical Commissioning Group*); otherwise, individual CCGs are free to delineate those drugs or other aids that it will provide only in exceptional circumstances—essentially 'non-core' procedures which will be detailed in the Local Authority's policy. Application for treatment that is *not*, for whatever reason, routinely available through the NHS is submitted to the relevant CCG by the patient's doctor in the form of an individual funding request—or IFR.[107] The request, of which there are some 30,000 annually in England, is, then, usually referred to a multidisciplinary panel.[108] The panel's decision is subject to a series of appeals and, ultimately, to judicial review with all that that implies in respect of clarity,

---

[104] N Bosanquet, 'A "fair innings" for efficiency in health services' (2001) 27 J Med Ethics 228.

[105] An example is to be found in *Re G (adult incompetent: withdrawal of treatment)* (2001) 65 BMLR 6. It is to be noted, however, that such cases are rarely, if ever, argued on a resource basis.

[106] Cf, D Strech and M Danis, 'How can bedside rationing be justified despite coexisting inefficiency? The need for "benchmarks of efficiency"' (2012) J Med Ethics, first online, doi: 10.1136/medethics-2012-100769, and K Voigt, 'Rationing, inefficiency and the role of clinicians' (2014) 40 J Med Ethics 94, doi: 10.1136/medethics-2012-101236.

[107] At the highest level see, NHS Commissioning Board, Interim Commissioning Policy: Individual funding requests (2013), currently under review and available at: http://www.england.nhs.uk/wp-content/uploads/2013/04/cp-03.pdf.

[108] For an example of one CCG's policy and processes, see: http://www.cambridgeshireandpeterboroughccg.nhs.uk/Exceptional-Cases.htm.

reasonableness, and justice, the basic principle being that each case must be adjudged on its merits—a 'blanket' rule for the treatment of a disease is unlikely to be approved.[109] The treatment of chronic renal disease provides a good example on which to base discussion.

11.37 It is easy to say that enough dialysis machines should be made available to treat all cases of chronic renal failure but, in existing circumstances, this may merely mean that some other financially dependent resource must be curtailed. Costs can be cut by, for example, changing a policy of hospital dialysis to one of home treatment, but the fact of financial restraint is not thereby removed—only its degree is altered. At the same time, the modern patient undoubtedly regards access to high technology medicine as his individual right and such a view is readily tenable when a proven effective countermeasure is available. If the doctor is, perforce, to qualify those rights, his reason for so doing must be beyond reproach and this is seldom easy to demonstrate.

11.38 The case of Mr McKeown in New Zealand[110] is a classic of its type. James McKeown was a man aged 76 in end-stage renal failure. He also had coronary artery disease and prostatic cancer. Given dialysis, his expectation of life was about two years; nevertheless, he clearly failed the relevant consensus guidelines for the treatment of renal failure and the head of the dialysis unit is quoted as saying, 'Given our resources, he had to fit into a group we said no to'. The patient's family then laid a complaint of age discrimination with the Human Rights Commission of New Zealand. As a result, the hospital authorities ordered a clinical review of the case, renal dialysis was started, and Mr McKeown died 18 months later—presumably by way of his malignant disease. How is this case to be evaluated in retrospect? On one view, the treatment, at best, served no more than a doubtfully useful purpose and, at worst, may have deprived a more deserving claimant of therapy. In the alternative, one can hold that dialysis is the appropriate treatment for all persons who have lost their kidney function; all are, therefore, equally entitled to life-saving intervention and their length of survival is immaterial.[111] Our inclination is to adopt the latter stance—but we freely admit that intuition does not solve the underlying dilemma.[112]

11.39 Essentially, the New Zealand system, as discussed earlier, involves allocating resources in terms of triage. Triage is a curiously derived expression meaning, in the present context, the separation of casualties into priority treatment groups. It is basically a military concept which allocates categories of casualty ranging from those whose slight injuries can be managed by self-care to those who cannot be expected to survive even with extensive treatment and who are, therefore, treated on a humanitarian basis only. Triage in this sense is not only good emergency surgical practice but is also ethically acceptable because it is directed to a single discernible end—that is, in military terms, to win the battle. But we are not dealing with a single issue in normal civilian practice. The circumstances of, and the circumstances surrounding, each patient are so disparate that triage, and its underlying principles, cannot be used as a convenient substitute, or subterfuge,

[109] Established in *R v North West Lancashire Health Authority, ex parte A, D and G* [2000] 1 WLR 977; (2007) 53 BMLR 148.

[110] Reported by C M Feek et al., 'Experience with rationing health care in New Zealand' (1999) 318 BMJ 1346.

[111] This was, roughly, the view of J Harris, 'What is the good of health care?' (1996) 10 Bioethics 269 and one which he has elaborated over the years. The question of from whose viewpoint we are to judge the utility, or otherwise, of an 18-month extension of life is discussed in Chapter 15.

[112] For a comparison of the New Zealand and UK positions, see J Manning, 'Exceptional circumstances schemes and the social factors exclusion in healthcare rationing' (2013) 13(1) Ox Uni Comm Law J 75.

for resource allocation; although not everyone would agree, we believe it should be abandoned for present purposes. What, then, does one put in its place?

AVAILABLE MODELS

11.40 There have been many attempts to find a solution[113] but none is satisfactory—all generalisations tend to fail when applied to the particular. We will briefly outline some proposals which have been made and it is, perhaps, easiest to progress from those parameters which we consider to be least appropriate.

11.41 As we have seen, a cost–benefit analysis of some sort is inevitable but care must be exercised in its application, particularly when we are dealing with potentially fatal situations. It needs no profound philosophical discourse to make one appreciate instinctively that it is right to deploy a helicopter to rescue a man on a drifting pleasure raft, despite the fact that his danger is of his own making, despite the expense, and despite the fact that the helicopter is designed to carry ten persons. The immediacy of the situation has placed a very high value on life which it would be immoral to ignore. The value cannot, however, be infinite—otherwise, faced with the choice of saving one man on a raft or ten men in a sinking dinghy, the grounds for any 'value choice' would be equal. Such choices must, however, be very rare in practice. In the chronic situation, as exemplified by dialysis, we are effectively confronted with a one-to-one choice between two individuals; at this point it might be possible to introduce a cost–benefit argument which takes the form of assessing the relative *societal* gain of saving one or the other. In practice, this would invoke the use of some formula such as 'earning capacity x (retiring age—actual age)'. Neither age nor income group should, however, be primary criteria regulating choice per se—it might be that the aged respond less well to treatment than do others[114] but that would be a different consideration—and one which NICE was prepared to acknowledge in that its major consultation document recommended that:

- health should not be valued more highly in some age groups rather than others;
- individuals' social roles, at different ages, should not influence considerations of cost effectiveness;
- however, where age is an indicator of benefit or risk, age discrimination is appropriate.[115]

Although this last passage is not easy to interpret, it clearly allows for some concern for the quality or expectation of life to be thrown into the therapeutic balance as is discussed later.

11.42 The corollary to this line of thought is that scarce resources should be distributed on the basis of the 'deserts' or basic merits of the recipients. The assessment of 'deserts' is commonly taken to apply to the intrinsic worth of the individual subject to society—and we may look at this from the negative or positive aspect. First, such a method of selection inevitably discriminates against those who have some additional disability—whether this

---

[113] Despite its antiquity, the paper by H J J Leenen, 'The selection of patients in the event of a scarcity of medical facilities: An unavoidable dilemma' (1979) 1 Int J Med Law 161 remains a classic analysis. For the present day, see the monograph by C Newdick, *Who Should We Treat?—Rights, Rationing and Resources in the NHS* (2005) and A den Exter and M Buijsen (eds), *Rationing Health Care: Hard Choices and Unavoidable Trade-offs* (2012).

[114] Hence, say, the relative acceptability of denying in vitro fertilisation to older women: *R v Sheffield Health Authority, ex p Seale* (1994) 25 BMLR 1.

[115] NICE, *Social Value Judgements* (2005), Recommendation 6. The second edition of this document is available here: https://www.nice.org.uk/proxy/?sourceUrl=http%3a%2f%2fwww.nice.org.uk%2fmedia%2f C18%2f30%2fSVJ2PUBLICATION2008.pdf. It was under revision at the time of writing.

be physical or mental—which limits their perceived value in a societal sense; this group, however, is, perhaps, better included among those falling to be assessed under the 'medical benefit' test discussed later. The alternative, positive, approach in the event of shortage of facilities for treatment is to select those who offer the greatest contribution to society now and in the future. In our view, allocation tests which attempt to distinguish the 'values' of citizens qua citizens are clearly beyond the capacity or function of the doctor—or, come to that, anyone—and the 'principle' can be dismissed out of hand.

11.43 The one 'deserts-related' issue which is most commonly raised is that of age. It is very widely held that the older a patient is, the less can he or she command equal opportunity in a competition for therapy. The reasons for this differ. Some will rely on the argument 'he's had his innings'[116]—but even this depends, to an extent, on his or her position in the batting order; others, more rationally, will point to the fact that results of treatment are generally better in the young than in the old—but simply because the results of coronary surgery are commonly more satisfactory in the middle-aged patient does not mean that surgery is not worthwhile in the 75-year-old.[117] There is, moreover, a tendency to forget that not every therapy is effective for a full lifespan; it matters not whether the patient treated is aged 20 or 60 if we anticipate that the treatment will result in survival for no more than five years. We suspect that the reason underlying the common assumption is that those responsible for decision-making are below retiring age;[118] it has been said, rightly, that there is often a wide discrepancy between the optimum solution of a problem from the perspective of society as a whole and that of the individual within that society.[119] Some time ago, Lewis and Charny[120] tried, by means of an opinion poll, to establish the points at which the public would be prepared to accept age-based choices.[121] While this was a praiseworthy effort which could, indeed, be copied in the future as the government-inspired lay participation in medical decision-making maintains momentum—e.g. by way of Healthwatch—it is unlikely that a poll involving the elderly alone would reach the same conclusions. Harris's argument,[122] which sees the saving of life as the medical benchmark is at its strongest when we are considering the use of QALYs as a parameter for the assessment of the disposal of scarce resources. The choice between a 20-year-old and an 80-year-old may be straightforward to the outsider. But, at the moment of decision, each patient values his or her life equally—and, as Harris, again, puts it:

> The age-indifference principle reminds us that the principle of equality applies as much in the face of chronological age or life expectancy or quality of life as it does to discrimination on the basis of gender, race, and other arbitrary features.[123]

Which is meat and drink to the moralist but is far less digestible to the cash-strapped economist.

---

[116] An exceptionally lucid review of the model is provided by M M Rivlin 'Why the fair innings argument is not persuasive' (2000) 1 BMC Med Ethics 1, available at: http://www.biomedcentral.com/1472-6939/1/1.

[117] The treatment of the aged is discussed in more detail in the next chapter.

[118] And it probably operates at a subliminal level: K Halvorsen et al., 'Priority dilemmas in dialysis: The impact of old age' (2008) 34 J Med Ethics 585.

[119] P A Lewis and M Charny, 'Which of two individuals do you treat when only their ages are different and you can't treat both?' (1989) 15 J Med Ethics 28.

[120] See n 119.

[121] See more recently, P Dolan and A Tsuchiya, 'It is the lifetime that matters: public preferences over maximising health and reducing inequalities in health' (2012) 38 J Med Ethics 571, doi: 10.1136/medethics-2011-100228.

[122] J Harris, 'Unprincipled QALYs' (1991) 17 J Med Ethics 185.

[123] J Harris, 'It's not NICE to discriminate' (2005) 31 J Med Ethics 373.

11.44 Clearly, the most widely acceptable criterion of selection would be that determined by medical benefit.[124] However, unless one is dealing with a recoverable condition,[125] medical benefit is a relative matter; moreover, prognosis is, at best, uncertain. Medical benefit, although being an essential part of the equation, can never be more than an inspired supposition.

11.45 All 'deserts-based' models are, however, confrontational and we should not forget the alternative proposed by Daniels,[126] which is reminiscent of the standard legal approach to these questions in the UK and which certainly influences the policies of NICE.[127] He advocated a fair, deliberative process of setting limits on difficult decisions where it is impossible to satisfy all parties; the process is typified by clear articulation of criteria for decision-making, transparency at every level, and an overall aim to reach decisions which are acceptable to all reasonable persons because the reasons—and values—behind them are at least understood, even if they are not agreed. This epitomises the search for justice in health care rationing,[128] and is clearly potentially relevant at each of the levels of resource allocation that we have identified; indeed, it seems to accord with current government policy[129] and with the attitude of the courts.[130] Justice must, however, be seen to be done and the majority would, we believe, agree that some form of structured distribution of facilities at micro-allocation level is essential even though equity and efficiency may be difficult to accommodate within the same design.[131]

11.46 Whatever principles are invoked to establish a fair and a preferred method of distribution of resources at patient level, it is impossible to exclude the health economist from decision-making even at the doctor–patient interface. Restricting the availability of expensive drugs inevitably raises questions of professional clinical independence—and, equally, promotes some polarisation of views. Thus, on the one hand, it has been said that to allow clinical problems to be resolved in financial terms is to condone, 'the development by health economists of fairer methods of denying patients treatment'.[132] To which the economist would reply, 'The economic perspective is clear—to maximise health improvements from limited resources by targeting resources at those activities high in the cost-QALY league table'.[133]

---

[124] As was also the implicit choice of the court in *Re J (a minor) (wardship: medical treatment)* [1993] Fam 15; [1992] 2 FLR 165.

[125] Very different considerations, including triage, would apply in respect of the provision of dialysis in the not-improbable circumstance of a large number of people requiring treatment for recoverable renal failure, say, following a building collapse.

[126] The seminal work is N Daniels, *Just Health Care* (1985); see, too, N Daniels and J E Sabin, *Setting Limits Fairly: Can We Learn to Share Medical Resources?* (2002).

[127] J McMillan, M Sheehan, D Austin, et al., 'Ethics and opportunity costs: Have NICE grasped the ethics of priority setting?' (2006) 32 J Med Ethics 127. See *Social Value Judgements*, n 115.

[128] An invaluable analysis was given by R Cookson and P Dolan, 'Principles of justice in health care rationing' (2000) 26 J Med Ethics 323.

[129] For a general overview, see K Syrett, 'Deconstructing deliberation in the appraisal of medical technologies: NICEly does it?' (2006) 69 MLR 869.

[130] The suggestion that a patient was entitled to dictate his or her own treatment which was raised in the trial stage of *R (on the application of Burke)* v *General Medical Council* [2005] QB 424; (2004) 79 BMLR 126 was firmly refuted on appeal [2006] QB 273; (2005) 85 BMLR 1.

[131] For further discussion, see A Friedman, 'Beyond accountability for reasonableness' (2008) 22 Bioethics 101.

[132] J Rawles and K Rawles, 'The QALY argument: A physician's and a philosopher's view' (1990) 16 J Med Ethics 93.

[133] A Maynard, 'Ethics and health care "underfunding"' (2001) 27 J Med Ethics 223.

11.47 It is up to society to define its objectives in an area where successful compromise is hard, if not impossible, to achieve. But, even if we allow the clinician responsibility for the allocation of his expertise unfettered by budgetary restrictions, he must consider the quality of the life he is extending and perhaps the greatest influence in this context over the last few decades has been the introduction of the concept of QALY, which we have already introduced at the national scale earlier.

QALY and the Individual

11.48 The principle of the QALY at this level is simple enough. A year of healthy life expectancy is scored as 1 and a year of unhealthy life as less than 1, depending upon the degree of reduction in quality; while death is taken as zero, a life considered to be worse than death can be accorded a minus score. The 'value' of treatment in terms of 'life appreciation' can then be assessed numerically. Thus far, however, QALYs as applied to the individual seem to be doing little more than expressing the intuitive findings of the competent clinician in a mathematical formula. And, therein lies the rub—for, at the individual level, the 'quality scoring' will still be founded on a 'best interests' assessment made by a third party and the paternalistic element in that assessment has been scarcely modified by the use of numbers. It is, thus, apparent that, at this level, a QALY can only be properly evaluated with the patient's cooperation; it can then be used to decide between two possible treatments for the same condition. Used in this way, QALYs may actually augment the patient's autonomy by explicitly involving him or her in the process of shared therapeutic decision-making.[134] Even so, a note of caution may be sounded as it is not difficult to confuse the objectives. The easy phrase 'not clinically indicated' may mean either that the treatment is not considered to be of overall benefit to the patient or it may imply an inappropriate allocation of resources.[135] The distinction is conceptually important—the doctor and the patient may well be singing from different songbooks.

11.49 There are other more specific objections to QALYs as applied at the individualistic level. Clearly, they operate to the disadvantage of the aged; they measure only the end-point of treatment without considering the *proportional* loss or gain in the quality of life; and there are parameters other than simple health which need to be fed into the equation. Possibly the most important moral criticism is that the QALY sets no value on life per se. Harris considers that we should be saving as many lives, not life years, as possible—a proposition which simplifies the argument by removing it from the ambit of life-saving treatment which should, then, be apportioned only on a 'first come, first served' basis;[136] we also suggest that the customary use of the term 'life-saving', when what is really meant is 'death-postponing', can lead to false reasoning. What this view certainly does, however, is to emphasise that QALYs can never be used to compare the value of 'life-saving' therapies with those which are merely life-enhancing. Indeed, we may well wonder whether we have any right to pronounce on the quality of other people's lives and, hence, whether abstract formulae, whatever their nature, should ever be used to compare the management of individual persons or different disease states. We should be very careful lest we find that we have unwittingly written into the equation a

---

[134] See Chapter 4. See, also, C Charles, A Gafni, and T Whelan, 'Shared decision-making in the medical encounter: What does it mean?' (1997) 44 Soc Sci Med 681.

[135] See T Hope, D Sprigings, and R Crisp, ' "Not clinically indicated": Patients' interests or resource allocation?' (1993) 306 BMJ 379.

[136] For a reiteration of this long expressed view, see J Harris, 'It's not NICE to discriminate' (2005) 31 J Med Ethics 373 and 'NICE is not cost effective' (2006) 32 J Med Ethics 378.

constant such as that the congenitally handicapped are, by definition, possessed of less QALYs than are those with no such inherent deficit.[137]

11.50   In view of these many criticisms, it is not surprising that alternatives to the QALY are being actively sought. In this respect, there is much to be said for the more recent introduction of the 'discrete choice experiment' in which the attributes of a treatment—or those features of a treatment which influence the way in which the therapeutic outcome is achieved   are fed into its evaluation; in other words, the process as well as the outcome is taken into consideration.[138] The use of the word 'choice' indicates the importance attached to patient preference; research along these lines is, therefore, very much in line with current health care policies but, once again, we wonder if this is not just another example of using a slogan to describe good medical practice. Another suggestion has been for QALYs themselves to take a more inclusive, almost holistic, view of 'well-being' rather than medical benefit in making assessment.[139]

11.51   In our view, much of the argument depends not so much on the theory of QALYs as on the conditions in which that theory should be applied. McKie and his colleagues, in a continuing debate with Harris, who is the main antagonist of the system,[140] saw QALYs as a sensitive and egalitarian method of distributing scarce resources among competing individuals.[141] We still doubt if they should be used in this way as it perpetuates the fallacy that 'rationing' involves a conflict of interests. To say that 'the QALY approach is egalitarian because no one's QALYs count for more than anyone else's' takes no note of the fact that, when the chips are down, the QALYs available to each player are unequally stacked.[142] We believe they should be used only as a way of choosing between alternative *therapies*—either for general distribution, which is the function of NICE, or for the treatment of the individual patient which is a matter of clinical judgement.[143]

Random Selection

11.52   Harris's preferred alternative to QALYs as a method for the equitable provision of limited treatments at the coalface lies, essentially, in random selection of patients—or of lottery, or 'first come, first served'—and provides our final model for discussion. Such a policy has the advantage of apparent objectivity and, as we have seen, it could be regarded as the morally desirable choice in the context of potentially fatal disease. It is, however, a bad medical option because it takes no account of the gravity of the patient's condition and no account of 'medical benefit'—it concentrates on justice and ignores 'welfare'; moreover, the sheer length of waiting lists may prevent the most acceptable cases from the physician's point of view from ever obtaining treatment. As an option, it is also socially suspect

---

[137] For something of an ethical defence of inequality, see J Savulescu, 'Resources, Down's syndrome and cardiac surgery' (2001) 322 BMJ 875.

[138] M Ryan, 'Discrete choice experiments in health care' (2004) 328 BMJ 360 quoting M Ryan and S Farrar, 'Eliciting preference for healthcare using conjoint analysis' (2000) 320 BMJ 1530.

[139] M D Adler, 'QALYs and Policy Evaluation: A New Perspective' (2006) 6(1) Yale J of Health Pol, Law & Ethics, available at: http://digitalcommons.law.yale.edu/yjhple/vol6/iss1/1.

[140] J Harris, 'Would Aristotle have played Russian roulette?' (1996) 22 J Med Ethics 209.

[141] J McKie, H Kuhse, J Richardson, et al., 'Double jeopardy, the equal value of lives and the veil of ignorance' (1996) 22 J Med Ethics 204.

[142] On the (non) role of QALYs which seem to support death, see S Barrie, 'QALYs, euthanasia and the puzzle of death' (2015) 41(8) J Med Ethics 635, doi: 10.1136/medethics-2014-102060. Also, J L Pinto-Prades et al., 'Valuing QALYs at the end of life' (2014) 113 Soc Sci & Med 5, doi: 10.1016/jsocscimed.2014.04.039.

[143] For amplification, see K Claxton and A J Culyer, 'Not a NICE fallacy: A reply to Dr Quigley' (2008) 34 J Med Ethics 598 following on M Quigley, 'A NICE fallacy' (2007) 33 J Med Ethics 465.

in that it treats human beings as 'things' and pays no justice to human values and aspirations. And, finally, its acceptance may be a cloak for no more than abrogation of responsibility. Nevertheless, it may be the way of allocating scarce resources that the public prefer and it is, in fact, practised in the form of, say, waiting lists for transplantable organs.

11.53 It is to be noted, collaterally, that, whereas the law as to the failure to provide or the withdrawal of resources from a patient already using them is well established (see Chapters 15 and 17), nowhere is there any authority for such action on the ground of competing medical benefit—that is, that a further latecomer to the scene would be likely to do better. Indeed, there are strong indications that the contrary holds. In *Re J*,[144] Balcombe LJ said:

> I would stress the absolute undesirability of the court making an order which may have the effect of compelling a doctor or health authority to make available scarce resources (both human and material) to a particular child, without knowing whether or not there are other patients to whom the resources might more advantageously be devoted... [It might] require the health authority to put J on a ventilator in an intensive care unit, and thereby possibly to deny the benefit of those limited resources to a child who was much more likely than J to benefit from them.

The implication is clear—there would be little or no legal support for a policy of scarce medical resources based solely on randomisation.

The Contribution of the Patient

11.54 We have thus reached a position where no single parameter seems entirely satisfactory. Gordon,[145] in a discussion of the doctrine of necessity, speaks of it as offending 'against the feeling that no human being has a right to decide which of his fellows should survive in any situation'; but, while most would agree with this proposition in a general sense, doctors cannot opt out of such decisions. Perhaps the major constraining influence lies in the fact that doctors in the NHS cannot be entirely independent insofar as, while the overwhelming majority of practitioners would support its basic philosophy, the service itself is in thrall to the politicians and its operatives must play by the rules.[146] We should, nevertheless, look at some aspects of resource distribution that are problematical or difficult to accommodate within the current ideology.

Payment within the NHS

11.55 We have not, for example, discussed the ability to pay for a resource as a possible criterion of selection. Clearly, this could not operate as a *principle* within the NHS but the opportunity is not foreclosed as private health care is available in parallel with the service and we have hypothesised in previous editions that a modified form of a free market could have its attractions as a way of alleviating scarcity while still retaining moral respectability.[147] Any such policy would be, we admit, difficult to apply with absolute equity but, in certain circumstances, there may be a logical case for including private medicine within the public sector with possible benefit to the latter. As Bosanquet[148] argued, other options for

---

[144] *Re J (a minor) (wardship: medical treatment)* [1992] 2 FLR 165 at 176; (1992) 9 BMLR 10 at 20.

[145] G H Gordon, *The Criminal Law of Scotland* (3rd edn, 2000) vol 1, p 506.

[146] It is noteworthy that the British Medical Association (BMA), while seeking to establish a Board of Governors for the day-to-day running of the NHS, has declared that it would still opt to leave the major policy decisions to the Government: BMA, *A Rational Way Forward for the NHS in England* (2007).

[147] This, indeed, is said to be the motivation behind the Health and Social Care Act 2012.

[148] N 104.

choice and competition are available and it is, perhaps, a failing of modern health economics that these potentially dynamic forces for developing improved and cost-effective programmes have not been explored more fully.

11.56 The issue is exemplified in the provision of expensive drugs—and, in particular, those for the treatment of malignancy which NICE has found to be insufficiently cost-effective to be approved for unlimited use. The arguments have been fierce and raise the question of what has become known as co-payment for drugs. Early in 2008, a Ms Boyle paid some £11,000 for a supply of cetuximab—an anti-cancer drug which her health authority was not prepared to provide. Given that this decision was reached on reasonable grounds as discussed earlier, it could well be justified. The Authority, however, went a considerable step further and refused to finance *any* further treatment, insisting that Ms Boyle was to be treated either in the NHS *or* in the private sector.[149] This seems to be the philosophy of the dog in the manger but, as we have already intimated, an ideological attachment to a monopolistic tax-funded health service is deeply entrenched in the UK psyche at all levels of involvement and it was adopted as government policy—at least in England—because co-payment would create a two-tier service in the NHS, thus going against its founding principles.[150] It is unclear why the person who could afford 'top-ups' but could not afford the full costs of treatment but is prevented from doing so is not as much the victim of discrimination as is one who can afford neither[151] and the decision was strongly opposed by the libertarian lobby.[152] As a result, the government set up a committee to consider the problem which recommended that no patient should lose an entitlement to NHS care they would have otherwise received simply because they opt to purchase additional treatment for their condition[153]—and this recommendation, along with several others devoted to the same problem, was accepted, the main concession to the traditionalists being that the NHS should play no part in the 'topping-up' process.[154] Jackson, in an outstanding review, concludes that 'topping-up', while no doubt inevitable, does little to solve the problem of cancer treatment.[155]

The Responsibility of the Individual

11.57 No discussion of this type would be complete without a passing reference to the responsibility of the individual to avoid the need for medical resources and for the use of such

[149] It was estimated in 2009 that there were some 18 similar cases under review: House of Commons Health Committee, *Top-up Fees*, 4th report of Session 2008–9, para 24.

[150] Department of Health, *A Code of Conduct for Private Practice* (April 2003), para 3.22. The policy was disapproved at the BMA's annual conference and has been criticised in the lay press.

[151] D M Shaw, 'Crocodile tiers' (2008) 34 J Med Ethics 575.

[152] C Dyer, 'NHS faces legal action on payments by patients for private drugs while receiving NHS care' (2008) 336 BMJ 1265. One newspaper report suggested that some 1,300 patients may have been denied 'life-extending' drugs: D Rose, 'Drug pleas rejected for one in four cancer patients', *The Times*, 11 August 2008, p 20.

[153] Report for the Secretary of State for Health by M Richards, *Improving Access to Medicines for NHS Patients* (November 2008), DH-089952[1]. For a somewhat indecisive analysis of the Richards report, see A Weale and S Clark, 'Co-payments in the NHS: An analysis of the normative arguments' (2010) 5 Hlth Econom Pol Law 225.

[154] Department of Health, *Guidance on NHS patients who wish to pay for additional private care* (2009). An interesting suggestion has been made that certain drugs should be ring-fenced as being available by way of co-payment pending a final decision by NICE: I Finlay and N Crisp, 'Drugs for cancer and copayments' (2008) 337 BMJ 2. Stringent conditions are recommended but the authors do not explain, other than on doctrinaire grounds, why co-payment should not be a patient's right.

[155] E Jackson, 'Top up payments for expensive cancer drugs: Rationing, fairness and the NHS' (2010) 73 MLR 399.

resources as they are allocated.[156] The argument that prevention is better than cure has been widely popularised. No one would deny the importance of the theory at all levels but, equally, it is difficult to decide when friendly persuasion ceases and restriction of liberty begins. It follows that a good case can be made out for a right to choose to be unhealthy—and this not only on Kantian but also on utilitarian grounds, for every sudden death in late middle age that is prevented is potentially a long-term occupation of a bed in a psychogeriatric ward; it could well be that the quest for dementia that is inherent in many of the currently popular limitations on habit are remarkably cost-inefficient.

11.58   What does *not* follow is that there is a concomitant right to health resources when the consequences of that choice materialise. It seems that the public have little sympathy for the cavalier approach—in Williams's experience, the least unacceptable reason for discrimination in prioritisation was that the prospective patients had not cared for their own health.[157] In making such value judgements, however, the public are not constrained by principles of justice and professional ethics; the issue can certainly not be so easily dismissed by health care providers. For a fairly stereotypic example, we can look back on an interesting debate in the BMJ as to whether coronary bypass surgery should be offered to smokers.[158] The attitude of the surgeons was conditioned by the poor results obtained in smokers and the fact that they spent longer in hospital. Non-treatment could, therefore, be justified on the grounds that treatment of smokers deprived others of more efficient and effective surgery. An alternative medical view was that non-treatment of symptomatic patients is often less effective in terms of overall cost to society than is surgery, that there are many other 'self-inflicted' conditions which one would not hesitate to treat and that, at least in some cases, smoking is an addictive disease which merits sympathy. A warning was also sounded that, in regarding those who have brought medical ills upon themselves as, somehow, less deserving, the doctor is coming perilously close to prescribing punishment. None of which addresses the powerful communitarian argument that such patients and those treating them are, in fact, acting anti-socially in that they are diverting resources which could be put to better uses in the context of the community as a whole—could, then, limiting the treatment on offer to the irresponsible patient be regarded as good professional ethics?[159] In this respect, we might also take into account the prevalence of recidivism. Reports to the effect that 25 per cent or more of those who have received a cardiac transplant will revert to smoking—and, in doing so, lose five years of life-gain—make depressing reading.[160]

11.59   The difficulty in using personal responsibility as a criterion controlling the use of scarce resources lies not so much in theory as in its practical application. It is rarely possible to attribute ill health solely to irresponsible behaviour; moreover, responsibility is by no means always a matter of free choice—it is almost always influenced to a greater or lesser

---

[156] For an interesting philosophical analysis, see H Schmidt, 'Just health responsibility' (2009) 35 J Med Ethics 21 and associated papers.

[157] N 38.

[158] M J Underwood, 'Should smokers be offered coronary bypass surgery?' (1993) 306 BMJ 1047; J S Bailey, 'Coronary bypass surgery should not be offered to smokers' at 1047; M Shiu, 'Refusing to treat smokers is unethical and a dangerous precedent' at 1048; R Higgs, 'Human frailty should not be penalised' at 1049; J Garfield, 'Let the health authority take the responsibility' at 1050.

[159] Although eschewing the precise problem outlined earlier, Margaret Brazier has made a trenchant case for the recognition of patients' responsibilities within a nationalised health service: M Brazier, 'Do no harm—Do patients have responsibilities too?' (2006) 65 CLJ 387.

[160] P Botha et al., 'Smoking after cardiac transplantation' (2008) 8 Amer J Transplant 866.

extent by the social and physical environment.[161] We see it as impossible and undesirable to attempt a blanket response—whether it be all or nothing—to what is, in effect, an anti-social approach to social care. There seems no reason, however, why it should not be employed as one element in the distribution of resources in an egalitarian health care system.[162] We would accept the view that the patient should be offered the chance when a positive therapeutic advantage—albeit a less than ideal advantage—may be attainable, but that offer could properly be limited according to the limits of that advantage. NICE's own guidance is, unfortunately, relatively non-directive:

> Discrimination against patients with conditions that are, or may be, self-inflicted should be avoided. If, however, self-inflicted cause(s) of the condition influence the likely outcome of the use of an intervention, it may be appropriate to take this into account.[163]

The solution to the problem thus comes down to the 'best interests' of the individual and we believe that this is the route that would be taken by the courts were such a case to be litigated—but the matter would, now, be more probably resolved on *Re S* standards[164] than by reliance on *Bolam*.

Responsibility for Use

11.60 One final possibility that we have not touched upon as yet is that of patients distributing the available resources themselves. Such a system was introduced through amendments to the National Health Service Act 2006. In summary, the Secretary of State is empowered to make regulations under which payments may be made to individual patients as a way of providing the obligatory services detailed in ss 2(1) and 3(1) and paras 8 and 9 of Sch 1 of the 2006 Act (s 12A(1)); Regulations were passed after successful pilot schemes under s 12C.[165] The object is to give the patient choice—and, with it, responsibility—as to how he or she distributes the costs of his or her health care.[166]

11.61 Based on a similar but not identical scheme operating in social care for over 15 years, the results of pilots between 2009 and 2012 suggested that payment in lieu of services were cost-effective, reduced hospital admissions, and improved people health.[167] There are three categories of personal budget—(i) direct to the patient, as the name suggests, (ii) a notional personal budget by which patients may make choices within known constraints, and (iii) third party which is held by, say, his or her general practitioner. Everyone who has received NHS Continuing Healthcare from April 2014 has the right to request any of the categories, and best practice guidelines exist to assist CCGs in the task of deciding who

[161] A very useful discussion, including that of the principle of solidarity in a community, is provided by A N Buyx, 'Personal responsibility for health as a rationing criterion: Why we don't like it and maybe we should' (2008) 34 J Med Ethics 871.

[162] For a consideration of its introduction in Germany: H Schmidt, 'Personal responsibility for health—Developments under the German Healthcare Reform 2007' (2007) 14 Eur J Hlth Care 241.

[163] NICE, *Social Value Judgements* (2005), Recommendation 10.

[164] *Re S (adult patient: sterilisation)* [2001] Fam 15; [2000] 3 WLR 1288, CA—the standard being the overall best interests rather than the medical assessment.

[165] National Health Service (Direct Payments) Regulations 2013 (SI 2013/16/17) as amended by the National Health Service (Direct Payments) (Amendment) Regulations 2013 (SI 2013/2354).

[166] See, NHS England, Guidance on Direct Payments for Healthcare: Understanding the Regulations (2014).

[167] Available in a user-unfriendly format here: https://www.phbe.org.uk/about_the_evaluation.php. A lay guide is available here: http://www.nhs.uk/choiceintheNHS/Yourchoices/personal-health-budgets/Pages/about-personal-health-budgets.aspx.

should receive them.[168] There are, however, few significant reasons why, given adequate protection for the vulnerable, arrangements that have operated successfully within the social services for over a decade should not do so in the NHS;[169] whether or not they are popular remains to be seen.

CONCLUSION

11.62 We appreciate that, at the end of this fairly lengthy discussion, we have come to little in the way of firm conclusions. We have approached the issues from the position of doctor and lawyer and it is, in some ways, comforting to find that philosophers may be in much the same dilemma. Gillon probably summed up the debate correctly when he implied that, provided decisions are made taking into account fundamental moral values and principles of equity, impartiality, and fairness, and provided the bases for decision-making are flexible in relation to the times, then the underlying system is just and is likely to yield just results.[170] Alternatively, we can simply be stoical and acknowledge that: 'to live with circumstances that are unfortunate but not unfair is the destiny of men and women who have neither the financial nor the moral resources of gods and goddesses'.[171]

---

[168] N 26, above.

[169] Department of Health, *Understanding Personal Health Budgets* (May, 2012) But the NHS should learn from the teething troubles of the social services: C Glendinning, N Moran, D Challis, et al., 'Personalisation and partnership: Competing objectives in English adult social care?...' (2011) 10 Soc Pol & Soc 151.

[170] R Gillon, 'Justice and allocation of medical resources' (1995) 291 BMJ 266.

[171] H T Engelhardt, 'Allocating scarce medical resources and the availability of organ transplantation' (1984) 311 New Engl J Med 66.

12

TREATMENT OF THE AGED

INTRODUCTION

12.01 Old age used to present no particular medico-ethical problems—senescence carried with it an increasing susceptibility to infection and the majority of the aged died at home within the family circle, having strayed not too far from their biblical allocation of three score and ten years. However, fewer people die in middle age today,[1] and the physical health of the elderly is steadily improving. As of 2014, some 18 per cent of the population of the United Kingdom (UK) were aged 65 or over.[2] Population ageing is accelerating and life expectancy continues to rise. Consequently, the elderly are growing older, and the very elderly—those over 80—now constitute over 4.5 per cent of the population.[3] This means that people will suffer from chronic and/or degenerative conditions for longer periods (i.e., men will spend 64.2 years, or 81.9 per cent of their lives, and women 66.1 years, or 80.2 per cent of their lives, in good health).[4] This provides more time during which the inevitable wastage of a limited supply of brain cells can occur, which sets the stage for increased numbers suffering from various degrees of dementia; this may be of a primary degenerative type, or it may be secondary to disease of the cerebral vasculature. Long-stay is likely when such patients are admitted to hospital, and so resource allocation issues become critical—currently, persons over the age of 65 occupy some two-thirds of the general and acute hospital beds, and admission rates for those over 65 is three times that for those aged 16–64 years.[5] The result is an escalating annual cost to the National Health Service (NHS) for treating the elderly; the NHS net expenditure represented 8.46 per cent of GDP in 2013, and was £113.3 billion in 2014/15.[6]

12.02 The above throws into sharp relief the problems we are beginning to face, and we are only beginning to address the means by which to tackle them. Those means cannot, however, be determined on the basis of administrative convenience alone, but must also involve both ethical and legal considerations within the overall constraints of national budgets.

---

[1] A newborn boy can expect to live for 78.9 years, and a newborn girl 82.7 years: Office for National Statistics, *National Life Tables 2011–2013* (2014).

[2] World Bank, at http://data.worldbank.org/indicator/SP.POP.65UP.TO.ZS.

[3] Office for National Statistics, *2011 Census, Population and Household Estimates for England and Wales* (2012).

[4] Office for National Statistics, *Health Expectancy at Birth and at Age 65 in the UK 2009–11* (2014).

[5] King's Fund, *Briefing Note: Age Discrimination in Health and Social Care* (2000). In short, there are multiple health imbalances associated with age: T Dixon, M Shaw, et al., 'Hospital admissions, age, and death' (2004) 328 BMJ 1288. And many government initiatives are hoping to alter the imbalances: Department of Health, *National Service Framework for Older People* (2008), and associated progress reports; Law Commission, *Adult Social Care* (2011).

[6] NHS Confederation, Key Statistics on the NHS, at http://www.nhsconfed.org/resources/key-statistics-on-the-nhs.

Successive governments have been aware of the difficulties involved in remediation, not least the uneasy amalgam of health and social services,[7] but successful policies are elusive. Suffice to say, the medical management of the elderly requires a very different, and demanding, approach to medical practice from that associated with 'acute wards', and this chapter is largely devoted to the ethics of bridging that divide and the associated legal attempts to do so.

AUTONOMY, PATERNALISM, AND RESPONSIBILITY

12.03 The conflict between autonomy—or the exercise of choice—and paternalism—or the efforts of others to protect those who they consider to be in need of protection—lies at the heart of modern-day medical jurisprudence, and it is far more complex in the context of geriatric medicine than it is in the relatively straightforward field of consent to surgical treatment by a competent adult. The elderly person is constrained in his or her choice of action by many factors, some of which are endogenous—such as the effects of early dementia—but others of which are extraneous—for example, poverty or social disregard. The impetus to paternalistic decision-making for the aged, no matter how it is ultimately applied, is likely to come from that person's family, and, although it may be minimised in individual cases, it is undeniable that, in general, it is easier to live without the burden of caring for one's ageing parents; children take on the mantle of paternalism when they seek institutional care for their parents, and there is no way in which subjectivity can be wholly eliminated from such action. It is arguable that children have neither a legal nor a moral obligation to support their parents.[8] Regrettable as it may seem, no such obligation has ever existed in English law, and the common law duty which existed in Scotland has been removed by statute.[9]

12.04 Help provided unwillingly is likely to be of doubtful quality,[10] and public awareness of intra-familial abuse of the elderly remains poor.[11] Nonetheless, there is little doubt that

---

[7] In 2008, the Law Commission identified 34 statutes relevant to adult care, noting outdated concepts, stigmatising language, and its potential incompatibility with European Convention on Human Rights (ECHR), all of which gave rise to difficulties in application such as geographical variations in available support, bureaucracy, conflict, and avoidable financial and human costs: Law Commission, *Adult Social Care: Scoping Report* (2008).

[8] N Daniels, 'Family responsibility initiatives and justice between age groups' (1985) 13 Law Med Hlth Care 153; N Daniels, *Am I My Parents' Keeper?* (1988); N Daniels, *Just Health: Meeting Health Needs Fairly* (2008). For commentary, see S Brauer, 'Age rationing and prudential lifespan account in Norman Daniels' (2009) 35 J Med Ethics 27.

[9] Family Law (Scotland) Act 1985, s 1(1)—by non-inclusion of a child/parent obligation to aliment. But this is not universal. A duty to care for one's indigent parents exists, say, in South Africa: P Boberg, *The Law of Persons and the Family* (1991) quoting *Re Knoop* (1893) 10 SC 198. For more on the role of children, see M Szinovacz and A Davey, 'Changes in adult children's participation in parent care' (2013) 33 Ageing & Society 667.

[10] And interestingly, research indicates that elderly people with few children are likely to get better familial support than those with several children: E Grundy and J Henretta, 'Between elderly parents and adult children: A new look at the intergenerational care provided by the "sandwich generation"' (2006) 26 Ageing and Soc 707.

[11] House of Commons Health Committee, *Elder Abuse* (2004); B Penhale, 'Elder abuse in the UK' (2008) 20 J Elder Abuse Neg 151; J Manthorpe, 'The abuse, neglect and mistreatment of older people with dementia in care homes and hospitals in England: The potential for secondary data analysis: Innovative practice' (2015) 14 Dementia 273.

abuse is widespread and that it occurs in various forms—generally agreed as compris-
ing verbal, physical, psychological, sexual, material (e.g., financial), or imposed by way
of neglect or deprivation. A study undertaken jointly by the National Centre for Social
Research and King's College London puts the figure of mistreatment in the home of
those aged over 66 at 2.6 per cent, with women being by far the worse affected;[12] this
is said to be in line with figures from other comparable cultures.[13] It follows that any
attempt to enforce a filial duty of care for the aged would likely exacerbate domestic
violence or neglect, and so undermine the geriatrics' conditions.[14] As a leading article
in *The Times* put it succinctly: 'You cannot legislate for love'.[15] Much of the care of the
elderly, therefore, falls to the medical and social services, and both must be supported
by the law.

FRAGMENTATION, COMPLEXITY,
UNCERTAINTY

A COMPLICATED SYSTEM IN CRISIS?

12.05 While still challenging and (too often) unsatisfactory,[16] medical treatment of the aged
in the UK has, as in all advanced societies, moved a long way since the chronically sick,
including those who were simply homeless, were almost arbitrarily assigned to hospital
wards which have been described as little more than 'human warehouses'.[17] Policy in the
UK is now articulated by the Care Act 2014, which applies in England, the Social Services
and Well-being (Wales) Act 2014, and the Public Bodies (Joint Working) (Scotland) Act
2014, each of which articulate health and social care principles, standards, and expected
outcomes for which NHS Boards and Local Authorities are jointly responsible, and they
impose on those bodies the need to integrate health and social care budgets, and to
strengthen the role of clinicians, care professionals and third and independent sectors in
the planning and delivery of services.[18] However, before examining the new regime, the
practical consequences of which will not be evident for years to come, it is important to
appreciate some of the elements of the pre-existing regime because many aspects of it will
continue under the new regime.

---

[12] M O'Keeffe, A Hills, et al., *UK Study of Abuse and Neglect of Older People: Prevalence Study Report*
(2007).

[13] One review indicates that severe verbal abuse occurred in some 34 per cent of families studied; physical
abuse, however, was relatively uncommon: C Cooper, A Selwood, et al., 'Abuse of people with dementia by
family carers: Representative cross sectional survey' (2009) 338 BMJ 155.

[14] The government approached the problem in 2000 when guidance for the multidisciplinary management of elder abuse was published: Department of Health, *No Secrets* (2000). But only a consultation document followed: Department of Health, *Safeguarding Adults* (2008). See also ADASS guide, *Safeguarding
Adults* (2005). There has been a resurgence of legal interest in the treatment of the elderly: G Ashton, *Elderly
People and the Law* (2nd edn, 2009); J Herring, *Older People in Law and Society* (2009).

[15] Lead, 'Who cares?' *The Times*, 14 January 2009, p 2. The article was associated with a scathing report
on the state of UK nursing homes: S de Bruxelles, 'Care homes: A system in crisis', p 16 and following
days.

[16] M Calnan, W Tadd, S Calnan, et al., '"I often worry about the older person being in that system": exploring the key influences on the provision of dignified care for older people in acute hospitals' (2013) 33 Ageing
and Society 465; M Fine, 'Individualising care: The transformation of personal support in old age' (2013) 33
Ageing and Society 421.

[17] T Howell, 'The birth of British geriatrics' (1983) 13 Geriat Med 791.

[18] See http://www.gov.scot/Topics/Health/Policy/Adult-Health-SocialCare-Integration.

12.06 The simplest form of care was (and remains) sheltered housing—which may be provided by the local authority, housing associations, or as a private venture—but the degree of available supervision is generally so low as to eliminate it as a resort for persons who are anything greatly less than fully independent. Sheltered housing might be the ideal refuge for the elderly person who is subject to abuse and, thereby, among those eligible for priority accommodation.[19] Beyond sheltered housing, it may be possible to arrange for residential care in accommodation which the local authority has the power to provide under the National Assistance Act 1948,[20] though the local authority had no obligation to provide nursing care by a registered nurse in such institutions, which have long been accepting patients whose requirements exceed those for which this method of disposal was designed. Finally, at the encouragement of government, local authorities have been using private homes.[21] 'Care homes', which must be registered under the Care Standards Act 2000, include those which provide board and personal care to those in need of it (residential care homes),[22] and those which, in addition, provide nursing care (nursing homes). The 2000 Act makes no distinction between the two but the nature of the building, the staff requirements, and the like will be reflected in the grant of registration.[23] The extension of private nursing homes, with governmental assistance as to charge, has eased the problem of scarcity of residential accommodation,[24] but the situation is uncertain due to fluctuating closure rates of private homes on economic grounds.[25] The result is that hospital beds tend to be blocked by older patients who cannot be moved—not only are the elderly thus retained in conditions that were not designed for such use, but also those who would benefit are deprived of hospital accommodation.[26]

---

[19] The local authority must maintain a 'housing register' of those qualifying for housing accommodation: Housing Act 1996, s 159. There are strong guidelines as to priority allocation in s 167. 'Vulnerability' as noted in the now repealed Part III of the Housing Act 1985 can only be defined following wide-ranging inquiry: *R v Lambeth Borough Council, ex p Carroll* (1988) 20 HLR 142. For a case on out-of-borough and temporary accommodation of those with support needs, see *Nzolameso v Westminster City Council* [2015] UKSC 22.

[20] This is subject to a directive which covers, in general terms, resident persons over the age of 18 who 'by reason of age, illness, disability or any other circumstance are in need of care and attention not otherwise available to them': Local Authority Circular (93) 10, s 2(1).

[21] Community Care (Residential Accommodation) Act 1992, amending National Assistance Act 1948, s 26.

[22] Personal care essentially means bodily care for those who cannot manage for themselves. The fact that a person is not receiving assistance with bodily functions does not, however, mean that he cannot be in need of personal care: *Harrison v Cornwall County Council* (1990) 11 BMLR 21.

[23] The regulation of care in hospitals and care homes is now the responsibility of the Care Quality Commission established under the Health and Social Care Act 2008, s 1, which abolished the Commission for Health Care Audit and Inspection, the Commission for Social Care Inspection, and the Mental Health Act Commission (see Chapter 13). The Scottish equivalent is the Scottish Commission for the Regulation of Social Care, set up under the Regulation of Care (Scotland) Act 2001.

[24] It appeared at one time that private homes providing care under contract with the local authority were not public bodies within the meaning of the Human Rights Act 1998, s 6. Thus, patients having such care were not covered by the ECHR: *Y L v Birmingham City Council* [2007] 3 All ER 957. This lacuna has now been filled by way of the Health and Social Care Act 2008, s 145. The local authority will also be able to investigate complaints about private 'social carers': Local Government Act 1974, Pt 3A inserted by way of the Health Act 2009, s 35.

[25] At one point, the closure of homes was in the order of 5 per cent per annum: A Netten, J Williams, and R Darton, 'Care-home closures in England: Causes and implications' (2005) 25 Ageing & Society 319.

[26] The Health and Social Care Change Agent Team (CAT) was established in 2002 to advise on the problem. CAT provides a wide range of advice and support as to the care of older people including the Dignity in Care Campaign.

12.07 The government's response, perhaps predictably, was to place responsibility for improvement on the NHS and local authorities. Under the Community Care (Delayed Discharge etc.) Act 2003, the local authority must pay a fine of £100 for every day, beyond two days, that a patient has to remain unnecessarily in an acute hospital bed because a suitable package of care—whether domiciliary or in alternative accommodation—has not been arranged.[27] One of the government's initiatives involved the creation of some 5,000 intermediate care beds together with supported intermediate care places to expedite discharge from hospital, prevent unnecessary admissions, and avoid premature admission to long-term residential care.[28] Intermediate care has, however, come to mean different things to different people, which has led to fragmentation of the service and tensions as to the allocation of human resources.[29] Almost inevitably, the effectiveness of various models—both as to results and costs—remains unclear, and the approach was not beyond criticism ab initio.[30]

12.08 The pressures have led to what many would regard as manifest inequity; so long as the geriatric remains in hospital, her needs are met free through the NHS. The use of a local authority's residential or nursing home, however, is subject to a means test.[31] Effectively, a person who has capital over a specified amount,[32] which includes the value of her own home (but not if a spouse, civil partner, or partner still lives there), has to pay charges in full; the local authority will pay the difference between the person's basic and the actual costs until the person's savings have been reduced to a specified amount; the authority will then pay the full fee.[33] Something of a conflict may, therefore, develop between the local NHS Trusts, who are anxious to clear their bed-space, and the elderly, backed by their families, many of whom would, quite reasonably, wonder why they have been singled out as a group to whom the facilities of a comprehensive socio-medical service are denied when most needed. (It was estimated in 2000 that some 40,000 houses are sold each year in order to finance long-term nursing care.[34]) Local authorities may, and do, claim that their duty of care is limited by the resources available. As a result, policies on the limitation of long-term care are variable—and, in practice, very few will provide nursing care homes; at the same time, the social services cannot find places for an indefinite number of persons discharged from hospital. Thus, not only may the older patient be discharged from hospital prematurely, but also he may be moved from NHS to local authority accommodation with corresponding financial penalty.[35]

---

[27] Admittedly, the government allocated £100 million annually to defray the inevitable costs to local authorities but the probable clash of interests between the two forms of authority—to the disadvantage of patients—is almost self-evident. See a scathing article by D Rowland and A Pollock, 'Choice and responsiveness for older people in the "patient centred" NHS' (2004) 328 BMJ 4. The authors particularly note the curtailment of choice for those with long-term illness.

[28] Department of Health, *National Service Framework for Older People: Modern Standards and Service Models* (2001). Some 10 per cent of all patients over the age of 65 discharged from hospital are discharged to intermediate care while nearly 3 per cent are discharged to residential homes or hospices: 'Dr Foster's case notes' (2004) 328 BMJ 605.

[29] J Glasby, G Martin, and E Regan, 'Older people and the relationship between hospital services and intermediate care' (2008) 22 J Interprof Care 639.

[30] J Evans and R Tallis, 'A new beginning for care for elderly people?' (2002) 322 BMJ 807. I Heath, 'Long term care for older people' (2002) 324 BMJ 1534.

[31] The assessment of whether a person is 'in need' is not resource-dependent. It is only after the need has been established that means affect charging for the services provided: *Robertson (AP) v Fife Council* (2002) 68 BMLR 229 (HL).

[32] National Assistance (Sums for Personal Requirements and Assessment of Resources) (Amendment) (England) Regulations 2009 (SI 2009/597), reg 3.

[33] SI 2009/597, reg 4.   [34] Leading article, 'The age of health' *The Times*, 24 July 2000.

[35] It has been proposed that elderly persons discharged from hospital should receive direct cash payments to provide services that the local authorities' budgets cannot meet: A Vass, 'Elderly patients to receive cash to

12.09 The classic example arose in *R v North and East Devon Health Authority, ex p Coughlan.*[36] A paraplegic woman had been assured of a 'home for life' in a nursing home controlled by the NHS; she applied for judicial review of the health authority's decision to close the home and transfer the residents to local authority care where 'nursing care' would be paid for according to the patients' means. The Court of Appeal considered the concept of 'nursing care' and, while admitting the difficulties involved in the marginal case, distinguished between that which might be expected from an authority providing 'social care' and that which was required by way of a primary health need—in essence, the test was both quantitative and qualitative. The Court considered that the health authority was at fault in imposing eligibility criteria for admission to its nursing home which were so severe as to force the local authority to accept responsibilities for which it was unsuited under the terms of s 21 of the National Assistance Act 1948.[37]

12.10 It can be said that *Coughlan* clarified but did not resolve the inequities of the situation—as it has been said: 'the demarcation between nursing (health) and personal (social) care . . . is "unworkable, unfair and unjust" '.[38] The government launched a number of initiatives intended to adjust these inequalities.[39] Among these, we would highlight that nursing care is now provided free in nursing homes controlled by the local authority; personal care is, however, still means tested.[40] A second major concession is that the value of a person's house is not now counted against his capital assets for the first 12 weeks of residential care, thus allowing the geriatric time for reflection and adjustment[41]—and plans are mooted for repayment to be delayed until after death. Finally, Commissions to oversee the provision of care to those in need have been authorised on both sides of the border.[42] It is also to be noted that the difficulties associated with the placement of elderly people

speed up hospital discharge' (2002) 325 BMJ 179— which seems to be only a different way of distributing the same money. Admittedly, the Government allocated £100m annually to defray the inevitable costs to local authorities but the probable clash of interests between the two forms of authority—to the disadvantage of patients—is almost self-evident.

[36] [2000] 3 All ER 850 (CA). For a brief, see A Loux, S Kerrison, and A Pollock, 'Long term nursing: Social care or health care?' (2000) 320 BMJ 5.

[37] As amended by National Health Service and Community Care Act 1990, s 42. The local authority has a duty, if so directed, to make specific arrangements to promote the welfare of old people who do not qualify under the National Health Service Act and may engage suitable voluntary organisations for this purpose: Health Services and Public Health Act 1968, s 45(3) inevitably due for replacement.

[38] See I Heath, 'Long term care for older people' (2002) 324 BMJ 1534, at 1535. A critical report was commissioned by the Department of Health: M Henwood, *Continuing Health Care: Review, Revision and Restitution* (2004). And, as will be seen, a central feature of the Care Act 2014 is better integration of social and health care provision.

[39] See in particular NHS, *The NHS Plan: The Government's Response to the Royal Commission on Long Term Care* (2000); Department of Health, *National Service Framework for Older People* (2001)—this is a ten-year programme. Full analysis is provided in Department of Health, *Health and Care Service for Older People: Overview Report on Research to support the National Service Framework for Older People* (2008).

[40] A situation that has been described as 'futile and destructive': Heath, n 38. Personal care is, however, free in Scotland: Community Care and Health (Scotland) Act 2002, s 1—defined as being concerned with day-to-day physical [and mental] tasks and needs: Regulation of Care (Scotland) Act 2001, s 2(28). For a comparative review of alternative systems, including compulsory insurance, see (2002) BMJ 1542.

[41] National Assistance (Assessment of Resources) 1992 (SI 1992/2977), Sch 4, para 1A inserted by National Assistance (Assessment of Resources) (Amendment) (No 2) (England) Regulations 2001 (SI 2001/1066), reg 5.

[42] Health and Social Care Act 2008, s 1; Regulation of Care (Scotland) Act 2001, s 1. In England, the amalgamation of the Health Care Commission, the Commission for Social Care Inspection, and the Mental Health Act Commission has resulted in the establishment of the overarching Care Quality Commission. The Scottish equivalent is the Care Commission.

under the care of either the health or local authorities was eased by the introduction of a single assessment process that is governed by strict guidelines.[43]

12.11 Be aware, however, that the care of the disabled elderly is a relatively thankless task, and the number of dedicated 'coalface' staff who are needed to establish perfect conditions within residential and nursing homes is unlikely to be available. Moreover, the practical difficulties faced by an over-worked staff must be fed into the equation when standards are being criticised. Thus, in the conditions of housing supplied by the local authority, injuries due to falls and other mishaps are likely to arise in an unsupervised situation; deaths which occur later, and which may be no more than temporarily associated, are likely to be the subject of inquiry by either the Coroner or the Procurator Fiscal. Many such incidents may be beyond the control of insufficient and inexperienced staff, notwithstanding their dedication; yet, the fear of culpability can rebound to the overall detriment of the patient—'defensive' action by the nurses may result in unnecessary restraint of their charges.[44]

12.12 Overshadowing all this is the effect of the Human Rights Act 1998 on the management of geriatrics in institutional care.[45] A fair and authoritative appraisal of this was published by a Joint Committee of the House of Lords and House of Commons in 2007.[46] While emphasising that care is often of high quality, the Committee noted that 21 per cent of care homes were still failing to meet the minimum standards required of them.[47] The Joint Committee concluded that elder abuse is a serious and severe human rights problem which is perpetrated on vulnerable people who often depend on their abusers to provide them with care,[48] and it identified some common examples of neglect ranging from problems with personal care, through rough handling, to leaving the subjects' sensory aids out of reach.[49] All told, the atmosphere was that of a lack of respect for the privacy, dignity, and confidentiality of old people in care, and the Joint Committee considered protection

---

[43] This was a key element of Department of Health, *National Service Framework for Older People* (2001). See, now, Community Care Assessment Directions 2004, LAC(2004)24 authorised under the National Health Service and Community Care Act 1990, s 47(3).

[44] And is likely to put the carer at risk of being reported to the Independent Barring Board, and barred from further contact with vulnerable adults: Safeguarding Vulnerable Groups Act 2006, s 3(3) (currently under the Care Standards Act, 2000, s 82). See also, Protection of Vulnerable Groups (Scotland) Act 2007.

[45] Whether it is having significant impact is debatable: J Morris, 'Human rights and healthcare: Changing the culture' (2010) 39 Age and Ageing 525. The recent socio-medical picture has been dominated by events in Mid-Staffordshire which were the subject of two major inquiries: Healthcare Commission, *Investigation into Mid-Staffordshire NHS Foundation Trust* (2009), and Department of Health, *Independent Inquiry into Care Provided by Mid Staffordshire NHS Foundation Trust January 2005–March 2009* (2010). Insofar as the matter was really one of hospital administration, and treatment of the elderly was an incidental issue, we do not intend analysing them in detail here.

[46] Joint Parliamentary Committee on Human Rights, *The Human Rights of Older People in Healthcare* (HC 378–1, 2007).

[47] For definition, see Department of Health, *Care Homes for Older People—National Minimum Standards* (3rd edn, 2003). It was reported that 34 per cent of calls to their helpline related to abuse perpetrated by staff, 'that is, through abusive practices that are institutional and passed from one worker to another': Action on Elder Abuse, *Hidden Voices: Older People's Experience of Abuse* (2004). Interestingly, 23 per cent of reports to the helpline concerned care homes where less than 5 per cent of the older population live: this is to be compared with the 5 per cent of calls that concerned hospital settings.

[48] Joint Committee, n 46, para 20, and it pointed out that this may now be a criminal offence: Mental Capacity Act 2005, s 44. Note that Art 2—the right to life—may be claimed to be engaged: *Bicknell v HM Coroner for Birmingham and Solihull* (2007) 99 BMLR 1.

[49] Ibid, para 20.

against this to be a fundamental function of the Human Rights Act.[50] The government subsequently published a memorandum on human rights and health care which is aimed at the institutional carer, and is, of course, not limited to the rights of the elderly,[51] suggesting even before the recent regime reform that human rights will assume a more fundamental basis for care.[52] In the end, it has to be said, it comes back to love: 'Food, shelter and warmth are important but it's lack of someone caring that leads to despair.'[53]

UNCERTAINTY OVER SERVICE AND LIBERTY?

12.13 It has not only been difficult to unravel the various threads of support that are available to the elderly, but it is also often hard to distinguish between age and disability when considering the target for assistance. Not only are disabled persons not always old but also old people are not always disabled to the extent that they need sophisticated interventions. It is this last category of patient—the person whose failing ability to manage their own lives can be attributed to a no-more-specific diagnosis than 'senescence' that we now turn. Assistance in such cases—and, indeed, for those with a specific mental or physical disability—is available by way of rather complex social service legislation which, in general, comes into play only when such disability is severe.[54] In essence, a disability living allowance, divided into care and mobility components, is payable to a person who, inter alia, is so physically or mentally disabled as to require the constant attention of another person by day (or prolonged or repeated attention at night) to assist with his or her bodily functions or for his or her protection from danger.[55]

12.14 This, however, is a book on medical law, and we cannot embark on a detailed analysis of social security legislation. Of greater immediate importance are the ethical problems surrounding those geriatrics who clearly need care and attention but want to retain their independence and resist removal to an institution. The danger, then, is that the 'cussedness' of old age may be designated as mental illness, and it is here that the Mental Health Act 1983 or the Mental Capacity Act 2005 may well come into play (see Chapter 13). Although the person may have no recognisable mental disorder, and may retain capacity as defined in the 2005 Act, his behaviour may yet be so deviant as to give rise to both medical and social concern—and this opens a gap in which socio-medical care can be provided in the person's best interests.

---

[50] Ibid, para 93. Human rights can, however, operate both ways. The current rules for barring abusive carers from further similar work (Care Standards Act 2000, s 82) have been declared incompatible with the 1998 Act, Sch 1, Art 6: *R (otao Wright) v Secretary of State for Health* (2009) 106 BMLR 71—but see n 44.

[51] Department of Health et al., *Human Rights in Healthcare: A Framework for Local Action* (2008).

[52] Of course, the fact that care of the elderly is determined by the personal relationship between the subject and his carers means there will be 'bad apples'. In a six-month period in 2007, 81,043 calls were made to the Care Quality Commission: L Donnelly, 'Thousands of elderly abused in care homes' *Daily Telegraph*, 4 May 2008.

[53] Quoted in Age Concern and Mental Health Foundation, *Promoting Mental Health and Well-being in Later Life* (2006).

[54] The most important of which, in the present context, is the Social Security Contributions and Benefits Act 1992, Part III of which describes the non-contributory benefits that are available.

[55] Social Security Contributions and Benefits Act 1992, ss 64 and 71. These benefits are to be distinguished from carers' allowance which is paid to the carer (s 70) and which is payable only if the person became eligible for care before reaching retirement age (s 70(5)). Some facilities may be available to carers to lighten the load and these will be considered in the light of a 'carer's assessment'. The rights of married daughters to what was, then, invalid care allowance have been upheld by the European Court of Justice: *Drake v Chief Adjudication Officer* [1986] ECR 1995.

12.15   It was in such situations that s 47 of the National Assistance Act 1948 came into play; it allowed the compulsory removal from their homes of persons who are not mentally ill but who are suffering from grave chronic disease or, being aged, infirm, or physically incapacitated, are living in unsanitary conditions, and are unable to devote to themselves, and are not receiving from other persons, proper care and attention. Removal could be effected in the person's own interest, or in order to prevent injury to the health of, or serious nuisance to, other persons. While it was estimated that s 47 was invoked less than some 200 times annually in England,[56] the moral issues underpinning s 47—such as the difficulty of balancing the rights to self-determination and community values—are self-evident, and the provision—particularly its 'bad neighbour' element and the operation of its accelerated procedure—gave rise to significant anxiety.[57]

12.16   As a result, many preferred the exercise of similar powers under other legislative schemes. For example, the emergency provisions within the Mental Health Act 1983, as amended by the Mental Health Act 2007, and the Scottish equivalent—the Mental Health (Care and Treatment) (Scotland) Act 2003—allow a justice of the peace, acting on information from an approved social worker, to authorise police entry and removal to a place of safety (for up to 72 hours) of a mentally disordered person who is at risk and living alone.[58] More important are the powers relating to compulsory admission to hospital for assessment (or emergency assessment) of the person's mental status.[59] The definition of mental disorder is now so wide that it might not be difficult to invoke them in cases where s 47 might have been used—indeed, the Mental Health Act has, in the past, been seen as the preferred route in an emergency.[60] However, committal under the 1983 and 2003 Acts inevitably classifies the elderly and confused as being mentally abnormal—and, to many, that represents a stigma.[61]

12.17   In any event, the unfortunate result has been that, in the majority of run-of-the-mill cases, legal process has been avoided; relatives and others may—and do—resort to pressure of various sorts to ensure compliance, and the elderly person will be 'talked into' abrogating her independent status. Such an ad hoc approach to institutional management of care and restriction of liberty has, unsurprisingly, led to challenge under the Human Rights Act 1998. In *R* v *Bournewood Community and Mental Health NHS Trust, ex p L,*[62] the

---

[56]   P Nair and J Mayberry, 'The compulsory removal of elderly people in England and Wales under section 47 of the National Assistance Act and its 1951 amendment: A survey of its implementation in England and Wales in 1988 and 1989' (1995) 24 Age and Ageing 180. This analysis is old but there is no reason to suppose that the pattern has greatly changed. The Mental Capacity Act 2005, Sch A1 (deprivation of liberty) seems to be ineffective as the person is not in care at the time.

[57]   The use of s 47 has not been challenged under the Human Rights Act 1998, but similar legislation in Europe has been accepted: *HM* v *Switzerland* (Application 39187/98) 2002, European Court of Human Rights (ECtHR).

[58]   See s 135 in England, and s 292 in Scotland, where this can only be done after a mental health officer or a medical commissioner has been refused entry. Section 136, which refers to persons in public places, is being used more commonly as the proportion of patients in community care increases.

[59]   See ss 2 and 4 in England, and ss 44 and 36 in Scotland. For more, see Chapter 13.

[60]   E Murphy, 'What to do with a sick elderly woman who refuses to go to hospital' (1984) 289 BMJ 1435. The use of what is, effectively, a convenient administrative ruse seems to be more morally reprehensible than is the use of the more straightforward s 47.

[61]   In *St George's Healthcare NHS Trust* v *S* [1998] 3 All ER 673 (CA), at 692, Judge LJ stated: 'The [mental health] Act[s] cannot be deployed to achieve the detention of an individual against her will merely because her thinking process is unusual, even apparently bizarre and irrational, and contrary to the views of the overwhelming majority of the community at large.' More recently, see *NHS Trust* v *T (adult patient: refusal of treatment)* [2005] 1 All ER 387.

[62]   [1998] 3 All ER 289 (HL). For more, see Chapter 13.

House of Lords was concerned with the detention of a man on an informal basis—that is to say, without the use of statutory powers of compulsion—for the treatment of a mental disorder. The case went to the ECtHR, which overturned the House of Lords to the effect that informal treatment was compatible with Art 5.1 ECHR.[63] This had implications beyond the boundaries of mental health law insofar as it embraced all disabled persons who were deprived of their liberty—and, particularly in the present context, those in care homes; the *Bournewood* case thus has major significance in relation to the management of the elderly.[64]

12.18 The government's response was to use the Mental Health Act 2007 as a way of introducing a compromise, making it lawful for a hospital or care home to deprive a person of his liberty *only* after obtaining an authorisation from a supervisory body or as a consequence of effecting an order of the Court of Protection on a welfare matter.[65] The identity of the supervisory body depends on who commissions the patient's treatment. Reflecting the close relationship between the medical and social services in this field, it may be the Primary Care Trust in which the relevant hospital is situated,[66] or the local authority in which the patient normally resided or that in which the care home is situated.[67] The grant of an authorisation depends upon the satisfaction of a number of positive assessments related to the requirements for establishing lawfulness, including, and most innovatively, an evaluation of 'best interests' by an independent assessor.[68] The very complex legislation demonstrates not only a statutory acceptance of the close legal association between mental incapacity and mental disorder but also the frequent difficulty of making a clinical distinction.[69] There is, in fact, a groundswell of opinion which believes that the so-called 'deprivation of liberty safeguards' as a whole lack clarity and are likely to be misunderstood.[70]

A NEW APPROACH TO CARE SERVICES

12.19 The above demonstrates just some of the difficulties of the care regime, which exhibits both important ethical challenges and profound practical consequences for the geriatric. As previously noted, however, the Care Act 2014 reforms the situation in England, while the Social Services and Well-being (Wales) Act 2014, and the Public Bodies (Joint Working) (Scotland) Act 2014, apply in those jurisdictions. The emphasis here remains on the English Act, which will impose changes on social services practices in a staged

---

[63] *HL v United Kingdom* (2005) 40 EHRR 32.

[64] For a more recent liberty case in the context of acknowledged incapacity due to mental disability, see *Cheshire West and Chester Council v P* [2014] UKSC 19, discussed infra.

[65] Mental Capacity Act 2005, s 4A as inserted by the Mental Health Act 2007, s 50. The conditions governing the deprivation of liberty in hospitals and homes are detailed in the Mental Capacity Act 2005, Sch A1 inserted by way of the Mental Health Act 2007, Sch 7. In Scotland, see the review by H Patrick, *Autonomy, Benefit and Protection* (2008).

[66] Mental Capacity Act 2005, Sch A1, para 180.   [67] 2005 Act, Sch A1, para 182.

[68] 2005 Act, Sch A1, Pt 3.

[69] For analysis, see G Richardson, 'Mental capacity at the margin: The interface between two Acts' (2010) 18 Med L Rev 56.

[70] A Zigmond, 'Deprivation of liberty safeguards and the Mental Capacity Act' (2009) 338 BMJ 1284, quoting the Parliamentary Joint Committee on Human Rights at 1285. On the difficulty of defining 'deprivation of liberty', see *JE v DE* [2007] 2 FLR 1150, where the restriction on freedom to come and go and the absence of valid consent was considered to be of prime significance. On the intricate interplay between the two Acts, see *J v The Foundation Trust* [2010] 3 WLR 840 (CP).

manner for years to come.[71] It is meant to create a national level of care and support across all councils, promote greater integration and cooperation among service providers, facilitate seamless coverage in the face of mobility, better support carers, and simplify and make more just payment for services.[72] Part 1 is intended to consolidate and modernise existing care and support law. Part 2 gives effect to elements of the government's response to the Mid Staffordshire Public Inquiry, addressing duties and powers of the Care Quality Commission (CQC), which includes reviewing service providers[73] and issuing warnings to local authorities.[74] Part 3 makes changes to the Trust Special Administration regime, and establishes Health Education England and the Health Research Authority as non-departmental public bodies. Part 4 establishes a fund for the integration of care and support with health services, to be known as the Better Care Fund, and makes provision for additional safeguards around dissemination of health and care information.[75]

12.20 At base, and on a universalistic basis (within their catchment), local authorities have a duty to promote the individual's 'well-being'.[76] Well-being is understood as relating to:[77]

(a) personal dignity (including treatment of the individual with respect);

(b) physical and mental health and emotional well-being;

(c) protection from abuse and neglect;

(d) control by the individual over day-to-day life (including over care and support, or support, provided to the individual and the way in which it is provided);

(e) participation in work, education, training, or recreation;

(f) social and economic well-being;

(g) domestic, family, and personal relationships;

(h) suitability of living accommodation;

(i) the individual's contribution to society.

12.21 Central to all its actions in support of this duty is the taking of steps, at first instance, to prevent, reduce, or delay people's needs for care and support.[78] Once needs are established, however, there is a duty to maintain the individual's preferred environment as far as is possible.[79] Thus, s 1(3) stipulates that in exercising its functions, a local authority *must* have regard to:

(a) ... the assumption that the individual is best placed to judge the individual's well-being;

(b) the individual's views, wishes, feelings, and beliefs;

---

[71] See https://www.gov.uk/careandsupport. Indeed, the process of introducing its reforms has been criticised as being too compressed and under-funded: House of Commons Committee of Public Accounts, *Adult Social Care in England* (2014), and L Clements, *The Care Act 2014 Overview* (2015), at http://www.lukeclements.com.

[72] Department of Health, *Care and Support: What's Changing* (2014). And it should be emphasised that it applies to all those in need of social care, and their carers, not just the elderly. For example, it has many provisions dealing with the transition of patients to adulthood.

[73] Care Act, s 91.   [74] Care Act, ss 82–5.

[75] And ss 92–4 articulate a new offence of making available information that is false or misleading.

[76] Care Act, s 1(1).   [77] Care Act, s 1(2).   [78] Care Act, ss 1 and 2.

[79] The importance of recognising a duty to promote and respect the autonomy of the aged was emphasised by K Lothian and I Philp, 'Maintaining the dignity and autonomy of older people in the healthcare setting' (2001) 322 BMJ 668, and is a feature of other social welfare systems: see *Central Association of Carers in Finland* v *Finland* (2014) 58 EHRR SE7.

(c) the importance of preventing or delaying the development of needs for care and support or needs for support and the importance of reducing needs of either kind that already exist;

(d) the need to ensure that decisions about the individual are made having regard to all the individual's circumstances (and are not based only on the individual's age or appearance or any condition of the individual's or aspect of the individual's behaviour which might lead others to make unjustified assumptions about the individual's well-being);

(e) the importance of the individual participating as fully as possible in decisions relating to the exercise of the function concerned and being provided with the information and support necessary to enable the individual to participate;

(f) the importance of achieving a balance between the individual's well-being and that of any friends or relatives who are involved in caring for the individual;

(g) the need to protect people from abuse and neglect;

(h) the need to ensure that any restriction on the individual's rights or freedom of action that is involved in the exercise of the function is kept to the minimum necessary for achieving the purpose for which the function is being exercised.

12.22 In addition, local authorities must, when appropriate, integrate care and support with the provision of health care, and housing is considered a health-related provision.[80] In short, great effort must be taken to provide a more seamless and effective transition from health care to social care and vice versa. Additionally, authorities must provide good information and advice,[81] and in doing so they have a duty of candour, compliance with which is reviewable by the CQC.[82] And there are provisions which structure the assignment of independent advocates to individuals, whether patient or carer, so as to facilitate their involvement in the authority's exercise of its functions.[83] Finally, they must cooperate with local partners in the integration of services, and promote the efficient and effective operation of a market in services.[84]

12.23 With respect to individuals, local authorities must undertake needs assessments to determine eligibility for care services;[85] regulations structure this undertaking in some detail, setting national criteria and a limit on the amount any individual must pay towards their care over their lifetime. Once the authority is satisfied of an individual's needs, it must prepare a support plan and budget, and open an account.[86] It then has a duty to make a variety of suitable arrangements,[87] and s 8 offers an illustrative list of what may be provided to meet those needs, namely:

(a) accommodation in a care home or in premises of some other type;

(b) care and support at home or in the community;

---

[80] Care Act, s 3.
[81] Care Act, s 4. And it is an offence to supply, publish, or otherwise make available information that is required under an enactment or other legal obligation, and the information is false or misleading in a material respect: see Care Act, s 92, and s 93 for penalties. For a case on the quality of information prior to implementation of the Care Act 2014, see *CC* v *KK* [2012] EWHC 2136 (COP), wherein the court cautioned against conflating capacity assessments and judgments about best interests.
[82] Care Act, s 81.   [83] Care Act, ss 67–8.
[84] Care Act, ss 5–7 and 53–7. And we have already seen that private support partners have been an integral aspect of the care environment for years.
[85] Care Act, ss 9–13. The local authority can proceed with an assessment in the absence of a request. Eligibility criteria are addressed in s 13.
[86] Care Act, ss 24–30.   [87] Care Act, ss 18–23.

(c) counselling, advocacy, and other types of social work;

(d) goods and facilities;

(e) information and advice.

Obviously, this list is broadly drafted and admits of all manner of preventive actions such as help with the design of the house and the provision of meals, facilities for recreation, home help, and the like.

12.24 Of course, it must be recalled that resources are not infinite and decisions around the provision of support and care will be informed, in part, by a concern for cost-effectiveness.[88] Having said that, it was previously held that the local authority cannot manipulate the regulations so as to tie an applicant's point of entitlement to assistance to the level of its resources, and there are many cases, both reported and unreported, that confirm this position.[89] There are also times when the local authority *must* give support irrespective of resources.[90] Nonetheless, the fact remains that, subject to the promotion of equality of opportunity, the general rule is that the weighing of resources and demand for services is a matter for council members,[91] and courts are generally loath to interfere with the distribution of public funds.[92]

12.25 In this regard, *R (on the application of D)* v *Worcestershire County Council*,[93] though not involving an elderly person, is informative. In this case, D, a 17-year-old who received 24-hour care in his home, was concerned that the support designed for him would not address his needs, so he applied for judicial review of the local authority's Policy for Determining the Usual Maximum Expenditure for Non-Residential Care Packages, which was meant to reduce the costs of homecare such that the maximum weekly expenditure on care for adults under 65 would be no more than the net weekly cost of a care home placement. After examining the authority's conduct, the Court held that a proper consultation had been undertaken, and that, under the policy adopted, each case would depend upon its circumstances. In exercising its discretion, the local authority would be required to take into account its own policy objectives of giving disabled persons control and choice over their care, encouraging independent living, and having fewer individuals

---

[88] On this point, in *R* v *Gloucestershire County Council, ex p Barry* [1997] AC 584 (HL), it was held that a chronically sick and disabled person's need for services could not sensibly be assessed without some regard to the cost of providing them. Although this decision depended to some extent on the distinction between statutory duties and powers that permeate the legislation, which fragmentation supplies the backdrop to the Care Act 2014, it has been consistently followed, and still represents the law; but see Lady Hale JSC's criticism in her minority opinion in the otherwise concordant case of *McDonald* v *Kensington and Chelsea Royal London BC* [2011] 4 All ER 881 (SC). For comment on the first case, see Lord Browne-Wilkinson in *R* v *East Sussex County Council, ex p Tandy* [1998] AC 714.

[89] *R* v *Sefton MBC, ex p Help the Aged* [1997] 4 All ER 532 (CA).

[90] *R* v *Birmingham City Council, ex p Mohammed* [1998] 3 All ER 788 (payment of disabled facilities grant under s 23 of the Housing Grants, Construction and Regeneration Act 1996).

[91] *R (otao Chavda)* v *London Borough of Harrow* (2007) 100 BMLR 27. It has also been held that the authority is entitled to apply a resource allocation system on which to assess the extent of financial relief payable in lieu of provision of services: *R (otao KM)* v *Cambridgeshire County Council* (2012) 126 BMLR 186 (SC). For guidance see Department of Health, *Prioritising Need in the Context of Putting People First: A Whole System Approach to Eligibility for Social Care* (2010).

[92] *R (Haggerty and Others)* v *St Helens Borough Council* (2003) 74 BMLR 33, is an interesting case in that a claim under Art 8 of the Human Rights Act 1998, Sch 2 was rejected on the grounds that 'the financial resources of the council were an important element to be considered in the balancing exercise required in the application of article 8(2)'. Art 8, however, is engaged in the provision of care within limits: *McDonald*, n 88.

[93] (2013) EWHC 2490 (Admin).

in residential care. It also held that the potential negative impact of the policy on those with protected characteristics was clear, but there was ample documentation on how the policy sought to deal with those potential effects.[94]

12.26 We have already noted (paras 12.15–12.18) the concerns which arose around the operation of s 47 of the National Assistance Act 1948, and of the unsatisfactory elements of the other legislative means to achieve its ends in practice. Of course, s 47, which was repealed in Scotland by way of the Adult Support and Protection (Scotland) Act 2007,[95] has now been repealed in England and Wales by virtue of the Care Act 2014, which states that the local authority, where it has reasonable cause to suspect:

- that an adult has needs for care and support; and
- is at risk of or is experiencing abuse or neglect; and
- as a result of those needs is unable to protect himself or herself against the risk or abuse or neglect,

must make inquiries to satisfy its suspicion, and, through its Safeguarding Adults Board—which it is obliged to establish under s 43—must take such steps as are necessary to protect the person and any property that might be in danger.[96] As with many of the other reforms set in motion by the Care Act 2014, we will have to wait and see if this approach proves more fair and transparent than the previous regime.[97]

THE ELDER INCAPAX

LEGISLATIVE DEVELOPMENT AND DISTINCTIONS

12.27 Much of the previous discussion around liberty related to the senescent—or compromised—rather than to the incapacitated old person. It is a legal axiom that an adult is to be regarded as competent unless she can be shown to be incompetent,[98] and it is with the latter that we are now concerned. Until comparatively recently, the legal protection of persons who are vulnerable by reason of being unable to manage their own welfare has been grounded upon a hotchpotch of mental health and social security law which is not easy to assimilate. Moreover, the Mental Health Acts relate to a very particular group

---

[94] Needless to say, efforts are also underway to identify new cost-effective care measures that keep the elderly in their home, such as use of personalised health monitoring technologies: E Palm, 'A Declaration of Healthy Dependence: The Case of Home Care' (2014) 22 Health Care Analysis 385.

[95] See ss 1 and 3. The major practical effect is that removal for the benefit of the neighbours is now no longer possible in Scotland other than under the mental health legislation.

[96] Care Act, ss 42–7 and Sch 2. And under s 42(3), abuse includes 'financial abuse'. A review of home care services found that, in addition to inconsistent support and lack of staff training, there were failures on the part of staff to report safeguarding concerns in line with already existing policies, and both out-of-date procedures and staff not understanding safeguarding or whistleblowing procedures: CQC, *Not just a number: Home care inspection programme* (2013).

[97] Though we note that it is already being criticised for not taking the opportunity to fully realise the right to live independently and in the community as articulated in Art 19 ECHR: T Collingbourne, 'The Care Act 2014: A missed opportunity?' (2014) 20(3) Web JCLI. And note the NICE, *Draft Guideline: Social care for older people with complex care needs and multiple long-term conditions* (2015), which states, at 3, that, 'despite recent policy focusing on integrated health and social care services, some people are still being treated as a collection of conditions or symptoms, rather than as a whole person'. The Draft Guideline was open for consultation in the summer of 2015 and is due for release in its final form in November 2015.

[98] Mental Capacity Act 2005, s 1(1).

of persons—those thought to be suffering from a recognised mental disorder—and their terms leave therapeutic vacuums that are often difficult to fill. As a result, legislation has now been passed in both England and Scotland that is specifically aimed at protecting those who have lost, or are losing, their mental capacity but who need a more flexible form of management than is provided by the mental health legislation. Parenthetically, loss of mental capacity is not necessarily confined to the aged, and for that reason we have already considered some of the important developments (Chapter 4). Nevertheless, it is clear that, excluding those who lack capacity by reason of status, the majority of incapaces will be elderly, and we revisit the legislation here with that in mind.

12.28   The Scottish Executive led the way with the Adults with Incapacity (Scotland) Act 2000. Westminster followed with the Mental Capacity Act 2005. Both Acts begin by outlining the principles underlying the justification of intervention on behalf of an incapax. The 2005 Act centres on whether the person's 'best interests' are served by intervention. In assessing these interests, the assessor must, inter alia, consider the person's past and present wishes and feelings together with 'any other factors he would be likely to consider if he were able to do so'.[99] The 2000 Scottish Act is content to specify that any action taken must be to the benefit of the adult—adding that the benefit cannot reasonably be achieved without that intervention.[100] While deliberately avoiding the concept of best interests, the 2000 Scottish Act also appeals to the past feelings of the adult.[101] Both Acts also define incapacity in terms of an inability to make decisions, and they rely heavily on the interpretation provided in *Re C*[102] (for which see Chapter 4). This relates the inability to make decisions to defective understanding or retention or assessment of information. Additionally, a person may be incapacitated by virtue of being unable to communicate, with or without aids. The underlying cause of incapacity lies, in English terms, in an impairment of, or disturbance in the functioning of, the mind, whether permanent or temporary;[103] in Scotland it results from mental disorder or inability to communicate because of physical disability.[104] In either case, the similarity of the language used to that in the Mental Health Act 1983 and the Mental Health (Care and Treatment) (Scotland) Act 2003 leads, from the start, to some confusion as to the practical application of the mental health and the mental capacity legislation in both jurisdictions.[105] Nevertheless, it is clear that Parliament's—and the courts'—intention is to keep the two distinct.[106]

---

[99] 2005 Act, s 4(5). In addition, the views of near relatives, carers, proxy decision-makers, and, in Scotland, 'any other person appearing to have authority to intervene' must be considered—which leads to the fear that, in the absence of prioritisation, conflicting views might result in inaction. But all this is, of course, at an early stage of interventionist activity. For a recent case, see *UF* v *X County Council* (2014) 17 CCL Rep 445 (COP), [2014] EWCOP 18 (best interests engaged in transferring an elder suffering from dementia from her home to a care home).

[100] 2000 Scottish Act, s 1(2).

[101] 2000 Scottish Act, s 1(4). The marked similarity between the two Acts in this connection draws attention, once again, to the increasing conflation of the principles of 'best interests' and 'substituted judgement' in UK law. The distinction is probably one without a difference, though it could be argued that someone, say in the permanent vegetative state, could have no interests.

[102] *Re C (adult: refusal of treatment)* [1994] 1 All ER 819.   [103] 2005 Act, s 2.

[104] 2000 Scottish Act, s 1(6).

[105] It is noted, however, that mental incapacity is defined as resulting from 'mental disorder (within the meaning of the Mental Health Act)': 2005 Act, Sch 4, para 23.

[106] As to the latter, see *J* v *The Foundation Trust*, n 70, at 58–9, wherein the court said that decision-makers cannot pick and choose between the two Acts as they see fit. As to the former, nothing in the 2005 Act authorises anyone to give treatment, or to consent to treatment for a mental disorder, if, at the time, her treatment is regulated by Pt IV of the Mental Health Act 1983—that is, treatment for which the 1983 Act requires either special consent or no consent: 2005 Act, s 28. For which see Chapter 13. The types of treatment which cannot be given in Scotland are subsumed under s 48(2) of the 2000 Scottish Act, which gives the Scottish

TREATING THE INCAPAX

12.29 The basis for invoking interventionist powers—that is, for deciding under which instrument—mental health or mental capacity—the carer should proceed—is now largely resolved by the pioneering opinion in J's case;[107] each case has its own particular circumstances and the assessment of these is a matter for the specialist in mental illness. It is important to remember, however, that the choice is not necessarily open. While mental disorder might be treated under both, the use of mental capacity statutes is constrained by the term itself. The reported results are as might be imagined in such an ephemeral area; it is fair to say that some 14 per cent of cases admitted under the Mental Health Acts retain their capacity to consent,[108] and could not, therefore, be treated under the 2005 Act. We are, however, impressed by the considerable powers that the mental capacity legislation across Great Britain[109] allow to the primary health carer. It is certainly true that the person who determines the provision of treatment to an incapax is constrained by the conditions of ss 4, 5, and 6 of the 2005 Act, but, when summarised, these do no more than impose good medical practice on the practitioner. Similarly, in Scotland, once the medical practitioner primarily responsible for the treatment of an adult has certified that her patient is incapable of making decisions related to his treatment, the practitioner has a relatively free therapeutic hand for up to a year.[110] It seems probable, then, that one effect of the 2003 and 2005 Acts will be to cut down considerably the use of the mental health legislation in respect of the mentally disordered aged.[111]

12.30 Treatment of the incapax is not, however, simply a matter of the doctor's opinion. The 2000 Scottish Act allows for the appointment of a guardian or of a welfare attorney who can act on behalf of an adult who is deemed by the Sheriff to be incapable. The former has powers in relation to decisions about the patient's property and financial affairs; the latter as to his or her personal welfare.[112] The interests of the incapax are carefully protected throughout the Act and the activities of any guardian are subject to the supervision of the Public Guardian. The duties and limitations of the welfare attorney are discussed in greater detail in Chapter 4. The 2005 Act follows this format closely save that the person responsible for the incapax's affairs and welfare are combined in the *donee*—that is, the person who has been given a lasting power of attorney.[113] The limitations and restrictions

Ministers a broad-brush approach to such limitations. Paradoxically, it is this very limitation, taken in conjunction with the very similar semantics of the 1983 and 2005 Acts, which paves the way to the treatment of physical disease in those who cannot decide for themselves. Non-consensual treatment of such disease is effectively barred by the terms of s 63 of the Mental Health Act 1983, and could, until recently, be provided only under common law. The 'best interests' terms of the 2005 Act now, however, provide a statutory basis for essential treatment of anyone who is incapacitated by reason of impaired functioning of the mind—and this clearly includes not only the aged dement but also both voluntary and involuntary mental patients.

[107] N 70.

[108] G Owen, G Richardson, A David, et al., 'Mental capacity to make decisions on treatment in people admitted to psychiatric hospitals: Cross sectional study' (2008) 337 BMJ 40. The seminal case of *Re C* (n 103) is a timely reminder.

[109] The 2005 Act does not run to Northern Ireland.

[110] She cannot, however, subvert the Mental Health (Care and Treatment) (Scotland) Act 2003 by using this power to place an adult in a hospital for the treatment of mental disorder: 2000 Scottish Act, s 47(7).

[111] For a useful review, see J Dawson, 'Mental capacity and psychiatric admission' (2008) 337 BMJ 5.

[112] The 2000 Scottish Act, s 80, abolishes the appointment of a curator bonis, tutor-dative, or tutor-at-law in respect of persons over the age of 16 years. For a recent case on the replacement of a guardian, see *West Lothian Council* v *For Appointment of Guardian to JG* [2015] GWD 12-219 (Sheriff C).

[113] There may be more than one donee who can act either together or separately in respect of all or different functions (s 10(4)).

placed on the donee are spelled out in detail, and are, effectively, the same as those constraining a health care provider since the latter cannot act in a way that conflicts with the decisions of the former.[114]

12.31 Thus, the provision of health care for the incapacitated elder is treated relatively informally, albeit a trifle didactically, under the English statute. The Adults with Incapacity (Scotland) Act 2000, by contrast, sets out a more precise protocol to be followed in the event that a welfare attorney has been appointed. Treatment can go ahead if there is agreement.[115] In the event of disagreement, the doctor responsible for treatment must ask the Mental Welfare Commission to nominate a medical practitioner from their list of such referees to give an opinion as to the proposed treatment—which, in the event of approval, can go ahead irrespective of opposition from the welfare attorney. If the nominated practitioner disagrees with the doctor in charge, the latter, together with any other interested person, can appeal to the Court of Session for a ruling. The impression gained is that, where there is difficulty in relation to treatment of the incapax, the Scottish Act gives priority to professional opinion; the 2005 Act, rather, tends to assume that the donee is, in fact, the voice of the patient; accordingly, she can both give and refuse consent to treatment.[116]

12.32 Both jurisdictions allow for 'patient advocacy' on behalf of the incapacitated in the event of disputes or uncertainties arising in his management. The complex interplay between the mental incapacity and health legislations is, again, demonstrated by the fact that this appears in the mental health legislation in Scotland (2003 Scottish Act; Chapter 2) but in s 35 of the Mental Capacity Act 2005 in England;[117] however, in the latter, the advocate can only intervene when 'serious medical treatment' as yet undefined, is being considered and is outwith the conditions of Pt IV of the Mental Health Act 1983. Ultimately, the Acts lay out in detail provisions for the welfare of the incapax by way of medical and allied treatment, and the underlying principle has been to balance the paternalism that is inevitable in such a relationship against the preservation of the patient's surviving autonomy and dignity. However, a recent Scottish Law Commission report which analyses recent European, Supreme Court, and lower court decisions in relation to adults with incapacity, notes that, 'in relation to treatment for physical illness or the need to safeguard physical health as a consequence of dementia or other cognitive impairment,

[114] 2005 Act, s 6(6). When making a decision that concerns life and death, however, the proxy cannot, in considering the best interests of the subject, make a decision that is motivated by a desire to bring about his or her death (s 4(5)). It has been pointed out that this is difficult to reconcile with, say, the decision in *Bland* (for which see Chapter 15): J Coggon, 'Ignoring the moral and intellectual shape of the law after *Bland*: The unintended side-effect of a sorry compromise' (2007) 27 LS 110.

[115] Although, throughout the legislation there is a disturbingly open-ended rider to the effect that '*any person having an interest* in the personal welfare of the adult' may appeal a decision to the Court of Session (emphasis added).

[116] 2000 Scottish Act, s 11(7)(c). Although the power to refuse is limited in the case of life-saving treatment (s 11(8)). In the event of disagreement, the doctor could provide life-saving treatment pending a decision by the Court of Protection (s 6(7)). In other cases of disagreement, the donee would have unrestricted access to the court (s 50(1)); it seems that the doctor would have to apply for access which would surely be allowed (s 50(3)).

[117] We suspect that the difference may well be due to the difficulty in introducing new mental health legislation that has been experienced in England and Wales. There is a similar dichotomy in respect of the significance of advance directives.

people are being confined to hospital wards without any underlying legal process'.[118] In short, the position of the geriatric (and others) remains precarious and subject to processes that are less than transparent.

12.33 The status of any advance statement or directive made prior to incapacity merits special consideration. The 2005 Act, as already mentioned in Chapter 4, reflects the almost total obeisance to patient autonomy that is now such a feature of Westminster-driven medical jurisprudence. The terms of a 'valid'[119] advance decision to refuse treatment *must* be followed in respect of any specified procedure, and such a decision takes precedence over that of a person with lasting powers of attorney.[120] The 2000 Scottish Act is silent on the point, which is addressed, in regard to the treatment for mental disorder only, in the Mental Health (Care and Treatment) (Scotland) Act 2003. Section 276 of that Act states that the Mental Health Tribunal and the principal carer need do no more than 'have regard' to the contents of the directive, although the reasons for taking any contrary steps must be recorded. It seems, therefore, that the authority of advance directives as to treatment for conditions other than mental disorder is currently uncertain in Scotland; it is probably expressed in s 1(4) of the 2000 Scottish Act, which says that *account shall be taken* of the present and past wishes of the adult when any interventionist activity is being taken. We doubt if there is any major practical distinction between the two jurisdictions as related to medical treatment because the conditions laid down in such directives are, by their nature, generally in accord with accepted medical practices; the doctor is unlikely to wish to gainsay them unless she is swayed by conscience—in which case, the correct legal procedure would be to remit the care of the patient to a colleague who is not so constrained.

12.34 Before moving to general legal protections, we should revisit the liberty issue, and note the recent case of *Cheshire West and Chester Council* v *P*,[121] in which the Supreme Court considered the criteria for determining whether living arrangements made for mentally incapacitated persons amounted to a deprivation of same under the ECHR. In this case, P, X, and Y appealed against decisions that such arrangements—in a group home—did not amount to a deprivation of liberty. In each case, although incapacitated, they had evinced dissatisfaction with their arrangements. The Court held that it is axiomatic that people with mental and physical disabilities have the same human rights as everyone else; disability imposes on the state a duty to make reasonable accommodation to cater for their special needs. Those rights included the right to physical liberty, as guaranteed by Art 5 ECHR. In rejecting the Court of Appeal's 'relative normality' approach and allowing the appeal, the Court held that the person's compliance or lack of objection to arrangements is not relevant; the relative normality of the placement, whatever the comparison made, is not relevant; and the reason or purpose behind a particular placement is not relevant. The purpose of Art 5 is to ensure that people are not deprived of their liberty without proper safeguards, and because of the extreme vulnerability of people like P, X, and Y, a periodic independent check on whether the arrangements are

---

[118] Scottish Law Commission, *Scot Law Com No. 240: Report on Adults with Incapacity* (2014), at 31.
[119] A decision is 'valid' if the person making it has capacity, and it is in writing and is countersigned by a witness. An advance decision is, however, only applicable to life-sustaining treatment if it is verified that it is to apply even if, as a result, life is at risk (s 25(5) and (6)).
[120] 2005 Act, ss 26(1) and 25(7) respectively.   [121] [2014] UKSC 19.

in their best interests is needed. X and Y's living arrangements constituted a deprivation of liberty.

GENERAL LEGAL PROTECTIONS

12.35 In addition to considering the incapax's medical interests, the Acts collect and codify the regulatory protection of their material well-being. This is largely beyond the remit of medical ethics, but we note the following. Both the 2005 Act and the 2000 Scottish Act provide for the establishment of a Public Guardian,[122] whose function is, in essence, to supervise and administer any donees of lasting powers of attorney or guardians appointed to administer the property or financial affairs of the incapacitated adult.[123] In England, the Office of the Public Guardian is the administrative arm of the Court of Protection, which is re-established as a superior court of record under Pt 2 of the 2005 Act.[124] While it is beyond the scope of this book to discuss the function of the Court of Protection,[125] suffice to say the court has extensive powers devoted to the well-being, in all senses of the word, of the incapacitated individual. It can institute reports relevant to a person from the Public Guardian or a Court of Protection Visitor, or it can call for reports from other public bodies, and the health records of the person concerned must be made available. Applications to the court can be made without previous permission by the incapax or his representatives—including the parent of a person under 18 years of age.

12.36 Outwith these formal legal institutions, the law also takes account of particular situations involving the elderly person. Contractual capacity may be denied in England and Wales to one who cannot understand the implications of a contract, and a contract which was entered into by a person whose mind was affected by dementia may be set aside. Similarly, testamentary capacity is restricted to those who can comprehend the nature and extent of their estate and the claims which people may have upon them. In assessing such capacity, however, the law is not so much concerned to place a psychiatric label on a testator as to determine the impact which an apparent specific delusion may have on the contents of the will. The rules of testamentary capacity were, in fact, developed with the interests of others in mind.

DYING FROM OLD AGE

12.37 The use of terms such as 'senility' or 'old age' to describe the cause of death on the Certificate of Cause of Death is often, and rightly, suspect on the grounds of non-specificity; nonetheless, it has the merits of honesty in a large number of cases. In the circumstances, it is surprising how little attention is paid to the management of death from old age, which is often the last service the community can provide for its constituents. Integral to this is the ethical issue of whether or not to treat a physical disease in an old

---

[122] 2005 Act, s 57; 2000 Scottish Act, s 6.

[123] The English donee also has powers related to the incapax's welfare. The Public Guardian, accordingly, has unfettered access to health records in carrying out his or her functions (s 58(5)).

[124] The previous Court of Protection, which was an office of the Supreme Court, now ceases to exist, and the new court is no longer tied to the Mental Health Act.

[125] For powers of the previous Court of Protection, see *Re W (EEM)* [1971] Ch 123 at 143.

person; such is bound to arise and is likely to provoke serious ethical problems, not least of which is whether the patient must—or, indeed, can—give consent to bodily invasion. The issue is discussed in greater detail in the following chapter where it is concluded that a mentally disordered patient can be treated under cover of 'necessity'. But the nature of senile deterioration is such that the subject will rarely be wholly competent or wholly incompetent—comprehension may be affected, but the patient may still be capable of holding and articulating views. It follows that a generalised label of 'incompetence' is likely to be justified only in the later stages of senescence, and while a plea of necessity might well be acceptable in specific cases, a person's competence should be judged in respect of each individual decision.[126]

12.38　That having been said, it must be remembered that, although it will be concerned in the end with fatal disease, much of geriatric medicine relates to the management of incurable rather than life-threatening disease. If, then, the patient's best interests or benefit represent the therapeutic yardstick—as they must—the inner world of the geriatric must be assessed subjectively and not related to the observer's own youthful or middle-aged experience or sensibilities. The senile but otherwise physically capable person is not in pain, and, for all we know, is passing a reasonably contented life. Glib phrases such as 'pneumonia is the old man's friend' come easily to the lips and can be dangerously emollient unless they are qualified; death may certainly be a relief to the patient in severe pain or incapacity, but problems raised in the treatment, say, of intercurrent infection in the contented dement are of the same order as those faced by the mentally competent—one wonders if the more honest aphorism is not that 'pneumonia in an old man is his associates' best friend'.

12.39　We would, therefore, oppose the adoption of therapeutic regimes that are biased towards non-treatment of the elderly patient on the ground of 'quality of cognitive life'.[127] Such an approach was classically expressed by including in the hospital notes the instruction 'Do Not Resuscitate', the morality and practicality of which is discussed later.[128] Judicial reliance on good medical practice emphasises the importance of considering each patient as an individual problem—there is a case to be made for elective non-treatment of the aged, but selection must be based on the individual patient's circumstances. Guidelines for treatments are just that—they do no more than provide a useful setting in which to formulate an ethical decision; they should not be seen as instructions which transcend the realities of the particular patient's condition.[129]

12.40　The issues crystallise, for the elderly, in the allocation of resources which, as we have seen, is inevitable in an expanding medical technological environment—and forceful arguments can be deployed in favour of regarding age as a determining factor. The views

[126] See *Re C (adult: refusal of treatment)* [1994] 1 All ER 819.

[127] For a study on age-related non-treatment in the Netherlands, see S Pereira, H Pasman, et al., 'Old age and forgoing treatment: A nationwide mortality follow-back study in the Netherlands' (2015) J Med Ethics doi: 10.1136/medethics-2014-102367 (online).

[128] See Chapter 15. For an excellent and still valid legal appraisal, see J Hendrick and C Brennan, 'Do not resuscitate orders: Guidelines in practice' (1997) 6 Nottingham LJ 24. For 'consumer' views see J Eliot and I Olver, 'Choosing between life and death: Patient and family perceptions of the decision not to resuscitate the terminally ill cancer patient' (2008) 22 Bioethics 179.

[129] See General Medical Council, *Treatment and care towards the end of life: Good practice in decision making* (2010), which is concerned with justifying the trust that patients should have in their physicians by ensuring that physicians show respect for human life and health.

of Callahan, although dated, are particularly interesting.[130] Callahan saw the need for objective planning if the otherwise certain breakdown in resources is to be avoided. The aged, he said, have some claim to public funds but these are not unlimited—the goal is a balanced, affordable system of care for the elderly which admits of a good balance between length and quality of life. Effectively, we should see ageing as an inevitable part of life and accept that society discharges its principal duty to the elderly by avoiding premature death. Callahan admitted that any serious form of setting limits to treatment will be unpleasant but, since the possibilities of spending money in an attempt to turn old age into permanent middle age are unending, we should impose an age limit upon ourselves. Unsurprisingly, these views have attracted opposition[131]—the argument that we should *always* prefer a younger patient before an older one on the ground that society's net life gain is more evenly distributed is attractive but too dispassionate for comfort.

12.41 While we would agree that difficult decisions may have to be taken, we prefer the egalitarian approach which will avoid positive discrimination against the elderly—expressed as the age-indifference principle which asserts that each person is entitled to the same concern, respect, and protection of society as is accorded to any other person in the community.[132] Therapeutic decisions are intensely individual matters which cannot be covered by way of restrictive formulae; age, and the effect of age, may be one factor in the decision to treat, but it cannot be the *only* or even primary factor.[133] To quote Harris:

> All of us who wish to go on living have something that each of us values equally although for each it is different in character … This thing is of course 'the rest of our lives'. So long as we do not know the date of our deaths then for each of us the 'rest of our lives' is of indefinite duration. Whether we are 17 or 70 … so long as we each wish to live out the rest of our lives … we each suffer the same injustice if our wishes are deliberately frustrated and we are cut off prematurely.[134]

In short, the commonly voiced argument that the old person has 'had a good innings' and must make way for the young is incomplete; the retiring batsman is fully entitled to a respected rest in the pavilion. Put another way, 'there is no valid reason, either theoretical or empirical, to deny the elderly full membership of the human family'.[135]

---

[130] D Callahan, *Setting Limits* (1987). This sort of view was criticised by H Moody, 'Should we ration health care on grounds of age?' in *Ethics in an Ageing Society* (1992) ch 9. And see L Pritchard-Jones, 'Ageism and Autonomy in Health Care: Explorations Through a Relational Lens' (2014) Health Care Analysis (online). For a recent partial vindication of age rationing, see L Fleck, 'Just caring: In defense of limited age-based healthcare rationing' (2010) 19 Camb Q Hlthcare Ethics 27.

[131] The obvious difficulties of involving the law in this area are summarised by M Rivlin, 'Should age based rationing of health care be illegal?' (1999) 319 BMJ 1379.

[132] J Harris, 'The principle of age indifference' in Age Concern Millennium Paper, *Values and Attitudes in an Ageing Society* (1998). And J Harris and S Regmi, 'Ageism and equality' (2012) 38 J Med Ethics 263.

[133] Much the same view has been expressed by the authoritative NICE, *Social Value Judgements: Draft for Consultation* (2005). NICE advice in this context is, in general, given a clean bill of health: A Stevens et al., 'National Institute for Health and Clinical Excellence appraisal and ageism' (2011) J Med Ethics.

[134] J Harris, *The Value of Life* (1985) p 89.

[135] For a succinct analysis of the arguments for and against age discrimination, see S Giordano, 'Respect for equality and the treatment of the elderly: Declarations of human rights and age-based rationing' (2005) 14 Camb Q Healthcare Ethics 83. More recently, see G Bognar, 'Fair Innings' (2015) 29 Bioethics 251.

12.42 We must surely agree that explicit age-based rationing, without more, is certainly contrary to anti-discrimination legislation.[136] Such problems may, however, confront the surgeon with particular force; the application of the 'productive/non-productive test'[137] must always affect her decision whether to operate on the elderly. A negative response to advanced malignant disease may be a simple matter but the improvement in operative techniques is such that the results of elective general surgery in the aged, even of an advanced technological nature such as coronary artery replacement, may be both satisfactory and rewarding—the fact that results may be generally better in the young does not mean that the same procedure in the old is not worthwhile.[138] It has, in addition, been suggested that relatively risky surgery, offering either good health or a quick death, may be particularly attractive to the old who should not be denied the choice. In any event, it is relatively unlikely that considerations of productivity can be applied to an acute surgical emergency occurring in an elderly patient with no other mortal disease.[139] The only acceptable test is then one of feasibility—there can seldom be an ethical alternative to treatment if it can be given advantageously.[140]

12.43 The dilemma remains as to what to do in the event that a geriatric patient refuses treatment when, so close is the association between the two, that one has to ask whether it is medical or social care treatment that is being rejected; management of the latter—and even, perhaps, the former—might well be subject to judicial declaratory powers as to mental capacity.[141] There can be no doubt as to the rights of the competent adult to refuse medical treatment and these rights would include, say, opposition to enforced feeding. The difficulty here, as we have acknowledged, is that the borderline between competence and incompetence is often indistinct in old age. Court judgments or decisions on the part of those responsible are unlikely to be invoked for apparently trivial matters such as the manner of oral feeding; it is probable that many old people, no matter what their situation, are fed with a varying degree of force but the action is taken on the assumption that refusal to eat is non-volitional. The process is degrading both to the patient and to the staff, and, moreover, carries considerable medical hazard. It is, however, difficult to see the alternative to compassionate and moderate coercion in such cases.

---

[136] King's Fund, n 5. And would likely offend against s 1(3) of the Equality Act 2010. But note the legal challenges that elderly patients might face in relying on the law: B Clough and M Brazier, 'Never too old for health and human rights?' (2014) 14 Med Law Int 133.

[137] See para 18.16. Decisions to operate may be heavily influenced by the 'biological age' of the patient; operation is more likely in those capable of living independently: S Farquharson, R Gupta, et al., 'Surgical decisions in the elderly: The importance of biological age' (2001) 94 J Roy Soc Med 232. For a discussion of 'biological age', see A Ring, 'Treating cancer in older people' (2012) 345 BMJ e4954, where it is pointed out that 50 per cent of cancer diagnoses are made in persons aged 70 or more.

[138] From 2000 to 2002, coronary artery bypass surgery increased by 32 per cent in those aged 75 or over: Department of Health *Standard One—Rooting out Age Discrimination* (2004).

[139] T Hope, D Sprigings, and R Crisp, ' "Not clinically indicated": Patients' interests or resource allocation?' (1993) 306 BMJ 379.

[140] It is a matter of common observation that age forms no bar to marked improvement of life following, say, joint replacement—one of the commonest form of elective surgery in old age: A-K Nilsdotter and L Lohmander, 'Age and waiting time as predictors of outcome after total hip replacement for osteoarthritis' (2002) 41 Rheumatology 1261.

[141] Mental Capacity Act 2005, s 15. See *Re F* (2009) EWHC B30 (COP), and K Keywood, 'Vulnerable adults, mental capacity and social care refusal' (2010) 18 Med L Rev 103.

12.44 Positive refusal of treatment by the competent old person is a different matter and one
which has attracted considerable attention in US courts. There, the right to be let alone
has been described as 'the most comprehensive of rights and the right most valued by civilised men',[142] and the courts have, in general, upheld such rights. But, here, we are getting
close to the euthanasia debate which is addressed in Chapter 18. In the present context, we
need only remind ourselves of the prophetic remark that has retained its place throughout
successive editions of this book: 'Society should be wary of moving from a recognition of
an individual's right to die to a climate of enforcing a duty to die.'[143]

CONCLUSION

12.45 Despite a host of publications and policies,[144] and the adoption of the Social Care Act
2014[145]—which is only now beginning to be implemented, and will continue to do so in
stages—there remains very limited evidence of any dramatic change in the care of those
who are 'different' in that they are old, lonely, and poor. Ultimately, it may well be true
that loss of dignity in the elderly derives (still) from the way that we care for our sufferers'
senescence, rather than from its illnesses.[146] For example, the management of the some
700,000 patients who suffer from dementia has been characterised by fragmentation and
inadequate scientific evidence.[147] A five-year plan was launched in 2009 to provide an
improved holistic strategy for recognition and management of the condition,[148] but the
objectives were ambitious and it is doubtful if the proposed funding of £150 million have
achieved much when spread across the nation. Nonetheless, the government has clearly
reflected on the matter of aging and dying from old age.[149] It is working with the National
Council for Palliative Care to develop a national coalition to raise the profile of end-of-life
care, and to change attitudes towards death and dying within the community, a cornerstone of which is the Partnerships for Older People Projects (POPPs).[150] Now, while elderly

---

[142] *Griswold* v *Connecticut* 381 US 479 (1965).

[143] And merits as much—if not more—attention today as it did when it was written: M Siegler and
A Wiesbard, 'Against the emerging stream' (1985) 145 Arch Int Med 129.

[144] See Department of Health, *National Service Framework for Older People* (2001), Department of Health,
Better Health in Old Age: Report from Professor Ian Philp (2004), Department of Health, *Independence, Well-
being and Choice* (2005), and White Paper, *Caring for our future: Reforming care and support* (Cm 8378, July
2012), which was the prelude to Social Care Bill 2012.

[145] The Scottish initiative and the passing of the Mental Capacity Act 2005 are also great strides forward,
but their impact is, in essence, confined to those who are clinically mentally disabled.

[146] This memorable comment, in relation to dementia, is taken from E Murphy, 'Ethical dilemmas of
brain failure in the elderly' (1984) 288 BMJ 61.

[147] A surprisingly large proportion of challenges to NICE decisions (see Chapter 11) involve the provision
of drugs for the treatment of Alzheimer's disease.

[148] Department of Health, *Living Well with Dementia: A National Dementia Strategy* (2009). For more,
see A Burns and P Robert, 'The national dementia strategy in England' (2009) 338 BMJ 616, and Nuffield
Council on Bioethics, *Dementia: Ethical Issues* (2009).

[149] Department of Health, *End of Life Care Strategy: Promoting High Quality Care for All Adults at the
End of Life* (2008).

[150] Department of Health, *National Evaluation of Partnerships for Older People Projects: Final Report*
(2010). POPPs involved 29 discrete pilot studies, which means that an overall analysis is difficult to achieve.
It seems that an improvement in the quality of life of those involved resulted, although the report is at pains
to emphasise the importance of caution in the interpretation of any results. Nonetheless, POPPs was an
ambitious project involving integration not only of established facilities such as hospitals, care homes, community nursing services, and individual families, but also the provision of 24/7 home care services—this
being based on the probably correct supposition that the majority of persons would prefer to die at home,

care is often a dispiriting area of medical responsibility, and one which has suffered from recent economic downturns, it is possible to see the management of the aged in a rosier light than that of some years back,[151] and it may well be that we just need to be patient in allowing the 'vision' articulated in the government publications and policy to be translated into practice.

although, in practice, some 58 per cent of deaths occur in NHS hospitals, 17 per cent in care homes, 4 per cent in hospices, and only 18 per cent at home: J Riley, 'A strategy for end of life care in the UK' (2008) 337 BMJ 185. Interestingly, it was found that, for every £1 spent on POPPs, there was a corresponding saving of £1.20 on emergency bed occupancy. Our reading of the report suggests that the best results derived from facilities that are already available through the social services—the one merely extended the availability of the other—but it is encouraging to find the government persevering with practical plans for the management of the elderly.

[151] The effects of the Equality Act 2010 have yet to be seen in relation to age discrimination in medical practice.

13

MENTAL HEALTH
AND HUMAN RIGHTS

INTRODUCTION

13.01 The practice of psychiatry is one of the most controversial areas of medicine, the subject
of endless public debate and of frequent political and judicial intervention. The reasons
for this are complex. One factor, however, stands out: while treatment for physical conditions almost always depends upon the consent of the patient, the psychiatrist may often
be called upon to treat the unwilling. The associated powers may involve detention for a
considerable time, a form of disposal which is usually reserved to the judiciary in a state
governed by law. In addition, psychiatric treatment is likely to be aimed at ameliorating a
disturbance of mood or behaviour. In so doing, it sets out to alter the functioning of the
human mind and this can be seen as an interference with individual autonomy which
will be justified only in exceptional circumstances. Thus, in the view of some,[1] the powers
accorded to psychiatric medicine give rise to unnecessary and unwanted intervention in
the lives of persons whose situation, although unusual, may be tolerable from their own
point of view. Others, however, have argued that society has not been ready enough to
intervene in an area in which issues of public safety are commonly involved. The tension
between these positions has led to shifts in psychiatric and legal policy, as governments
have wrestled with conflicting demands.

THE EVOLUTION OF MENTAL HEATH LAW

13.02 In the earlier part of the twentieth century, society favoured the institutional or asylum
approach to the management of mental illness. Those diagnosed as suffering from a psychiatric illness were usually sent to 'mental hospitals' where inpatient treatment would
be provided. This system was inevitably both stigmatising and coercive, and, in the late
1950s, a fundamental change in emphasis was signalled in the United Kingdom (UK)
with the publication of the Percy Commission Report, which advocated the treatment of
psychiatric patients as far as possible on a voluntary basis. The legislation which followed
from this, the Mental Health Act 1959 and its Scottish counterpart, were seen as liberalis-
ing measures but, over the following two decades, concern grew as to the extent to which
detained patients could be compulsorily treated without any obligatory review or without

---

[1] For classic examples of radical views of mental illness and society's response to it, see T Szasz, *The
Myth of Mental Illness* (1972), and R Laing, *The Divided Self* (1965). A more recent critique is contained in C
Unsworth, *The Politics of Mental Health* (1987). And see T Mason and L Jennings, 'The Mental Health Act
and Professional Hostage Taking' (1997) 37 Med Sci & Law 58.

adequate safeguards against the abuse of medical power. The Mental Health Act 1983 and the Mental Health (Scotland) Act 1984 were intended to boost patient rights while, at the same time, allowing for compulsory detention and treatment of those who were unable or unwilling to consent to treatment. Safeguards were also introduced to ensure that certain forms of aggressive treatment, such as electro-convulsive therapy (ECT), could not be given without further consultation (see para 13.28).

13.03 Greater sensitivity to the rights of the mentally ill was accompanied by an enthusiasm for treating psychiatric patients within the community. This policy, which was founded on concern for patients and a desire to allow their re-integration, was welcomed by governments which were equally keen to contain hospital costs. The closure of psychiatric wards, however, had the effect of limiting opportunities for care and treatment while, despite the good intentions, inadequate provision was made for treatment and supervision in the community—and this, in turn, exacerbated the public's concern for its own safety. Against this background, the UK entered into a further period of legislative review and consultation at the turn of the 21st century which resulted in the Mental Health Act 2007 and its earlier counterpart, the Mental Health (Care and Treatment) (Scotland) Act 2003. Like their predecessors, these Acts demonstrate how mental health policy involves balancing patient welfare and human rights considerations as against the protection of the public.

13.04 While the Mental Welfare Commission for Scotland perseveres,[2] ensuring that the above is achieved in England and Wales is now the function of the Care Quality Commission (CQC), which is an amalgam of, inter alia, the Healthcare Commission, the Commission for Social Care Inspection, and the Mental Health Commission.[3] The CQC, through the Health and Social Care Act 2008 and associated regulations, has monitoring and enforcement powers, and, through the Care Act 2014, has a responsibility to integrate some of its diverse roles (such as those under the Optional Protocol to the Convention against Torture and other Cruel, Inhuman or Degrading Treatment or Punishment) to ensure better patient experiences and outcomes.[4] Thus, it inspects facilities and reviews mental health care delivery; it can issue recommendations and require action statements when it finds failures in local services, and it can make formal proposals to amend the MHA Code of Practice 2008.[5]

13.05 Ultimately, the imposition of a policy involves control and control cannot be achieved without a measure of compulsion. At base, therefore, the merits or demerits of mental health legislation fall to be judged by the degree of compulsion it involves and its justification. The essential aim of this chapter is to consider how the current law stands up to such an analysis. Importantly, what follows could never be regarded as a substitute for a book

---

[2] Mental Health (Care and Treatment) (Scotland) Act 2003, s 4. The general remit of both Commissions is to promote the best practice as to the functioning of the respective Acts and to advise the authorities proactively as to the general and individual welfare of persons with mental disorder.

[3] For more on the remit of the CQC and the bodies it replaced, see Department of Health, *Liberating the NHS: Report of the Arms-length Bodies Review* (2010).

[4] CQC, *Mental Health Act Annual Report 2013/14* (2015), ch 1.

[5] The scope of the CQC's functions are exemplified by a summary of its 2013/14 actions, which included 4,517 interviews of detained patients, 175 interviews of patients under a community treatment order, 13,645 patients assessed by Second Opinion Appointed Doctors, 1,227 MHA visits with reports issued to providers, 174 inspections by teams including an MHA Reviewer, 1,324 mental health ward visits, 24 community treatment order visits, 47 seclusion and long-term segregation visits, 49 MHA visits to high-security hospitals, 1,016 complaints and enquiries responded to, 240 notifications received of detained patient deaths, and 909 notifications received for patients who were absent without leave: CQC n 4, at 18.

dedicated to mental health law; we are rather concerned mainly with those aspects of the regime which may impact on the ethical practice of medicine or on the human rights of the mental patient rather than with the administrative detail.

PATERNALISM, CAPACITY, AND MENTAL HEALTH

13.06   It is axiomatic that the capacity to make decisions as to treatment by those who are mentally disordered will be compromised and medical intervention in such cases is likely to be non-consensual to a degree dependent upon the severity of the disorder. The primary motivation of management must be the welfare of the patient and it follows that the compulsory treatment of mental disorder in those who pose no threat to others must be based squarely on the notion of 'justified paternalism';[6] a paternalistic act is one which is not sought by the patient but which is provided with the intention of protecting him or her from harm. Ordinarily, paternalistic action will be suspect because it offends the principle of respect for autonomy. It may be justified, however, when the person for whose benefit the act is performed is unable to make an informed choice. The absence of rationality in such persons then warrants action that is directed towards preventing their being harmed.

13.07   In some circumstances, it may be appropriate to take the basically paternalistic route to management and apply a 'best interests' test.[7] However, legitimising blanket paternalism in this way carries the danger of licensing excessive interference in the lives of those afflicted by mental illness. Moreover, it is important to reiterate that capacity is rarely an all-or-nothing affair; we should respect the decisions of individuals that they remain capable of making despite the presence of mental illness. There must, therefore, be limits both as to the determination of incompetence and the extent of treatment. These matters have been addressed in the UK along two main legislative routes—that addressing mental ill health and that addressing mental incapacity. As to the latter, this has been by way of the Mental Capacity Act 2005 in England and Wales, and the Adults with Incapacity (Scotland) Act 2000, both discussed to some extent in Chapter 12. The two Acts reach much the same conclusions but, whereas the 2005 Act perpetuates the theme of 'best interests',[8] the Scottish Parliament was at some pains to distance itself from the concept, which was thought to have unacceptable paternalistic overtones. As a result, the 2000 Scottish Act leans towards the doctrine of 'substituted judgement'—for discussion of which, see Chapter 15.

13.08   However, a distinction must be made in law between those who have simply lost capacity to handle their own affairs and those who are suffering from a recognisable mental disorder. The latter, by reason of their illness, may not only be at risk themselves and, hence, require the protection of the state, but may also constitute a public health hazard in being a danger to others. This possibility, as already noted, is bound to invoke a

---

[6]   For the classic survey of paternalism, see A Buchanan and D Brock, *Deciding for Others: The Ethics of Surrogate Decision Making* (1990) esp ch 7.

[7]   C van Staden and C Kruger, 'Incapacity to give informed consent owing to mental disorder' (2003) 29 J Med Ethics 41.

[8]   Section 4.

measure of control, the need for which may not be appreciated by those suffering from the disorder. This, in turn, leads inevitably to compulsion, which exaggerates the element of coercion in the treatment of mental disorder[9]—and finding the correct level of compromise is the function of mental health legislation. It is interesting to note how the very complex legislation demonstrates not only the public's acceptance of the close association between mental incapacity and mental disorder,[10] but also the difficulty of making a clinical distinction—the responsible Minister rather confusingly included dementia, autism, and learning disability under the heading of 'disorder or disability of the mind'.[11] Partly as a result of this, the legislation in this particular area is not easy to follow both as to form and choice of route in its application.

THE TREATMENT FRAMEWORK

13.09 At the outset, it is important to note the background to the most recent developments. The importance of the human rights element had always been appreciated but, the Human Rights Act 1998 necessitated, for the first time, extensive revision. At the same time, the turn of the century coincided with heightened concern for public safety.[12] Two Mental Health Bills incorporating this concern were presented to the Westminster Parliament and both were rejected in the face of intense criticism.[13] It is, perhaps, the ultimate measure of the difficulties encountered in finalising its terms that the greater part of the resultant Mental Health Act 2007 consists of amendments to the 1983 Act, which, therefore, remains the substantive law. Comparable legislation has, however, been in force for some time in Scotland, where the Mental Health (Care and Treatment) (Scotland) Act 2003 repealed the Mental Health (Scotland) Act 1984. In the interests of space, we will concentrate on the English and Welsh Act save to emphasise any differences demonstrated by the Scottish Act.[14]

13.10 At base, treatment for mental illness is provided in the UK on either a voluntary or an involuntary basis. It is important to appreciate that, while statute law is primarily concerned with involuntary treatment, the great majority of mental patients are, in fact, dealt with on an informal basis under which the customary principles underlying the health carer–patient relationship will apply; current intentions throughout the UK are that voluntary treatment should continue to be the ideal, and so we start there.

[9] For which see Mental Health Act 2007, s 1. We have to admit to seeing the definition provided as being so wide as to be all-embracing—but the essential element is disorder of the mind.

[10] Note that those deprived of their liberty in this way are now under the wing of the CQC—Health and Social Care Act 2008, s 4(1)(d).

[11] Department of Health, *Written Ministerial Statement on the Government's policy in response to the judgment of the European Court of Human Rights in the case of* HL v UK *(the Bournewood judgment)*, (2006). Specifically, the place of learning disability in the definition of mental disorder now differs in the 1983 and 2005 Acts.

[12] For useful medical appraisal, see L Birmingham, 'Detaining dangerous people with mental disorders' (2002) 325 BMJ 2, and S Ulrich, M Yang, and J Coid, 'Dangerous and severe personality disorder: An investigation of the construct' (2001) 33 Int J Law Psychiatry 84.

[13] Not only from the medical profession, Z Kmietowicz, 'Rip up draft Mental Health Bill, says BMA' (2005) 330 BMJ 326, but also from politicians—the 2004 Bill was roundly criticised on human rights grounds by the scrutinising Parliamentary Committee: C Dyer, 'Draft Mental Health Bill needs major overhaul, says Committee' (2005) 330 BMJ 747.

[14] The reader requiring more is directed to the many standard works on mental health law. For Scotland, see H Patrick, *Mental Health, Incapacity and the Law in Scotland*, 2nd edn (2015).

INFORMAL TREATMENT

13.11   Informal—that is, voluntary or, perhaps better, compliant—treatment may be provided by any registered medical practitioner or, indeed, by any person provided that the provisions of the Medical Act 1983 as to professional impersonation are observed. Thus, many seriously disordered psychiatric patients are looked after in nursing homes and similar institutions without having any formal order made in respect of their care. This can include arrangements to allow patients time at home, although there are attendant concerns with respect to what this means about the duty of care both to patients and their relatives should harm arise as a direct consequence of the treatment 'regime'.[15]

13.12   The regulatory position of informal patients who, typically, lack the capacity to give a proper consent to treatment but who are, nonetheless, compliant, was fully considered by the House of Lords in *R* v *Bournewood Community and Mental Health NHS Trust, ex p L*.[16] In this case, a profoundly autistic adult was admitted for inpatient treatment following an outburst of disturbed, self-harming behaviour. He was not detained compulsorily under the Mental Health Act as he did not resist admission. Relations between the hospital and the plaintiff's carers deteriorated, with the result that an action was brought against the health trust for damages in respect of unlawful detention. The Court of Appeal allowed recovery but the House of Lords overturned this decision after hearing arguments that requiring such patients to be detained under the Act—rather than admitted informally—would pose an immense burden on existing arrangements. In effect, compulsorily detaining such patients would be a luxury which the system simply could not afford. In the result, the House ruled that informal treatment of compliant patients who were, nevertheless, incapable of consenting was justified on the principle of necessity; current legislation, it was held, did not exclude the application of common law powers in the provision of treatment to psychiatric patients.[17]

13.13   Nonetheless, it had to be admitted that patients in this category who are detained—and both Lord Nolan and Lord Steyn, dissenting, agreed with Lord Woolf in the Court of Appeal that they *are* detained—were denied the statutory protections afforded those who were treated under compulsion. An appeal to the European Court of Human Rights (ECtHR) was almost inevitable, and it was largely on these grounds that the ECtHR declared informal detention to be contrary to the European Convention on Human Rights (ECHR).[18] It held that, under the existing system, the hospital's health care professionals assumed full control of the liberty and treatment of a vulnerable incapacitated individual solely on the basis of their own clinical assessments, thus violating Art 5(1), and there was no opportunity for the detainee to have his or her case heard speedily by a court, thus compromising Art 5(4).

---

[15]   See *Rabone* v *Pennine Care NHS Trust* [2012] UKSC 2; [2012] 2 WLR 381, which addressed, inter alia, the duty of care to parents of a young woman who hanged herself while on home leave within her mental health treatment regime. It was held that there was an operational duty to protect against the risk of suicide with respect to such informal patients. The parents were awarded £5,000 each. For Scottish commentary, see D Cobb, 'The Supreme Court and the state's duty to protect vulnerable groups: the effect of *Rabone*' (2012) SLT 75.

[16]   [1998] 3 All ER 289 (HL).

[17]   For a critique of the adequacy of necessity as a protection for the vulnerable, see K Keywood, 'Detaining mentally disordered patients lacking capacity: The arbitrariness of informal detention and the common law doctrine of necessity' (2005) 13 Med L Rev 108. For a Scottish consideration of the case, see Case Comment, 'Human rights and protection of vulnerable persons – the Scottish Law Commission considers *Bournewood*' (2012) SLT 201.

[18]   *HL* v *United Kingdom* (2005) 81 BMLR 131 (ECtHR).

13.14 As a result, the government introduced an interesting compromise in that it will now be unlawful for a hospital or care home to deprive a person of his or her liberty without obtaining an authorisation from a supervisory body,[19] which, depending on who commissions the patient's treatment, may be the Primary Care Trust in which the relevant hospital is situated, or the local authority in which the patient normally resided or that in which the care home is situated.[20] An authorisation, in turn, will depend upon a number of positive assessments related to the necessary requirements for establishing lawfulness, including an independent 'best interests' assessment.[21] Thus, in *Cheshire West and Chester Council* v *P*,[22] the Supreme Court emphasised that people with mental and physical disabilities have the same human rights as everyone else, and so the state has a concomitant duty to make reasonable accommodation for individual special needs. On the facts of this case, which turned on the living arrangements for three mentally disabled individuals, it stipulated that the liberty safeguards in the Mental Capacity Act 2005 require professional assessment independent of the hospital or care home in question as to the person's capacity to make a decision about accommodation, and whether it was in their best interests to be detained. The patient's compliance or lack of objection with arrangements is not relevant, the relative normality of the placement is not relevant, and the reason or purpose behind a particular placement is not relevant; the purpose of Art 5 is to ensure that people are not deprived of their liberty without proper safeguards. Moreover, because of these patients' particular vulnerability, a periodic independent check on whether the arrangements were in their best interests is needed.

13.15 In *Secretary of State for Justice* v *RB*,[23] wherein a convicted sex offender who had previously been detained in a mental hospital was then conditionally discharged to a care home (with his own agreement as to the conditions), the Court of Appeal was careful to police the parameters of conditional discharge, even with the assent of the patient, so as not to endorse mechanisms that were tantamount to deprivation of liberty. Thus, a tribunal could not rely on an assessment of a patient's best interests if this amounted de facto to deprivation of liberty in ways not envisaged in legislation. It was held that there was no statutory authority for the arrangements at issue as the original order only authorised hospital detention. Parliament could not have intended to create circumstances potentially more restrictive of liberty than detention under the 1983 Act, as amended.

13.16 Thus, institutional treatment of mental ill health, in general, is controlled by two distinct, but complementary, jurisdictional concepts. On the one hand, we have informal treatment governed by a relatively loose code, the operation of which is now determined, at least in England, by way of the best interests of the individual patient;[24] on the other, governed by the mental health legislation, we have compulsory treatment based on a rigid set of checks and balances with the patient's ultimate fate placed in the hands of the Mental Health Tribunal. It is to this latter form of control to which we now turn.

---

[19] The conditions governing the deprivation of liberty in hospitals and homes are detailed in Mental Capacity Act 2005, Sch A1 inserted by way of the Mental Health Act 2007, Sch 7.

[20] Mental Capacity Act 2005, Sch A1, paras 180 and 182.

[21] 2005 Act, s 4A as inserted by Mental Health Act 2007, s 50. For guidance on the operation and relationship between urgent and standard authorisation to detain someone lawfully, see *A County Council* v *MB* [2010] EWHC 2508 (Fam), and N Pearce and S Jackson, 'The deprivation of liberty safeguards: Part 4: challenging authorisation' (2012) 42 Fam Law 695.

[22] [2014] UKSC 19. And see *Rochdale MBC* v *KW* [2014] EWCOP 45, which applies and interprets this case.

[23] [2011] EWCA Civ 1608; (2012) 124 BMLR 13 (CA).

[24] The functions of the supervisory body described earlier are clearly underpinned by the Mental Capacity Act 2005, s 4.

NON-CONSENSUAL AND COMPULSORY TREATMENT

Guiding Principles and Definitions

13.17 A major innovation introduced by the 2007 Act is the mandatory inclusion of principles within the MHA Code of Practice (2015) which must inform decisions as to admission to hospital and treatment. Key principles include:

(a) respect for patients' past wishes and feelings;[25]

(b) respect for diversity including, diversity of religion, culture, and sexual orientation;

(c) minimising restrictions on liberty;

(d) involving patients in the structuring of treatment appropriate to them;

(e) avoidance of unlawful discrimination;

(f) effectiveness of treatment;

(g) views of carers and other interested parties;

(h) patient well-being and safety; and

(i) public safety.[26]

13.18 However, a major concern in this area is that the boundaries of mental illness should not be drawn so widely as to embrace forms of behaviour that are no more than non-conformist. Compulsory admission must be limited to conditions which amount to a recognisable illness that can be said to compromise the mental health of the sufferer, or, as we will return to later, the safety of others. Thus, perhaps the most important distinction for those who must apply the legislation lies in the definition of mental disorder. In England and Wales, this is now defined as 'any disorder or disability of the mind',[27] a definition which is so broad as to be almost beyond restrictive interpretation. However, a person with learning disability—which means a state of arrested or incomplete development of the mind which involves significant impairment of intelligence and social functioning—shall not be considered by reason of that disability to be suffering from mental disorder or requiring treatment for mental disorder unless that disability is associated with abnormally aggressive or seriously irresponsible conduct.[28] While the Scottish definition is more specific, it is equally widely embracing,[29] so we are presented with what appears to be a distinction without a difference.

13.19 It is in the realm of exclusions that we see some possibly real differences. While the Scottish Act excludes sexual orientation, sexual deviancy, transsexualism, transvestism,

---

[25] The importance of taking this into account was emphasised in *A London Local Authority* v *JH* [2011] EWHC 2420 (Fam).

[26] 1983 Act, s 118(2B) inserted by 2007 Act, s 8. With respect to status, *R (on the application of Munjaz)* v *Mersey Care NHS Trust* [2006] 2 AC 148, per Lord Bingham, held that, while the Code is guidance, hospitals should depart from it only where cogent reasons for so doing exist, and such reasons should be recorded. See MHA Code of Practice (2015), p 12. Note that Wales has its own Code—Mental Health Act 1983: the Code of Practice for Wales (2008)—which was due for revision in 2015.

[27] 1983 Act, s 1(2) amended by the 2007 Act, s 1(2).

[28] 1983 Act, s 1(2A) and (4) inserted by 2007 Act, s 2(2) and (3). In *C* v *A Local Authority* [2011] EWHC 1539 (Admin); [2011] Med LR 415, a young adult suffering from severe autism and severe learning disabilities was caught by the definition, and its provisions could be held to apply to children's homes and schools. Accordingly, he fell to be treated as between the provisions of the 1983 Act and the 2005 Act as appropriate. It was not relevant that the compulsion element of the 1983 Act was not invoked.

[29] 2003 Act, s 328, states that mental disorder means: (a) any mental illness; (b) personality disorder; or (c) learning disability, however caused or manifested.

dependence on or use of drugs or alcohol, alarming or distressful behaviour, and impru-
dent activity as lying outside the diagnosis when present without any other evidence of
mental disorder,[30] the only similar specific exclusions to be found in the Mental Health
Act 1983, as amended, are dependence on drugs or alcohol.[31]

13.20 The two jurisdictions are virtually united in defining what constitutes 'treatment' for
mental disorder. It includes nursing, psychological intervention and specialist mental
health habilitation, rehabilitation and care, as well as medication and other forms of
treatment which might more normally be regarded as being 'medical', which are aimed
primarily at alleviating, or preventing a worsening of, the mental disorder or one or more
of its symptoms or manifestations.[32] We will see, however, that this wide definition may
be something of a two-edged sword in terms of human rights. It may well be there for the
benefit of the individual; at the same time it may be used as a sophistic means by which to
detain a person whose underlying disability is fundamentally untreatable.[33]

13.21 Two important administrative innovations involve the introduction in England and Wales
of the terms 'responsible clinician'—which gives co-equal status as to patient responsibility to clinicians other than medical practitioners—and 'approved mental health
professionals'—who can be appointed by local authorities to accomplish a range of activities under the 1983 Act.[34] The former innovation is, perhaps, the more far-reaching. The
definition of a clinician who is approved as responsible for patient care is characteristically
wide[35]—in essence, it is a person who is approved for the position by virtue of his or her
profession and of having demonstrated the necessary competence. The present approved
professions are medical practitioners, chartered psychologists, first-level nurses with special experience, occupational therapists, and social workers; the concept clearly recognises
the multidisciplinary nature of the management of mental disorder and allows for many
more professionals to take over the role of what used to be the responsible medical officer.

Processes

13.22 In the absence of criminality, which we consider later, a person can be compulsorily admitted to hospital either for 'assessment' or for 'treatment',[36] upon fulfilment of stringent
conditions.[37] Applications for admission of a person to hospital can be made by the nearest relative or an approved mental health professional to the relevant hospital managers.[38]

---

[30] 2003 Act, s 328(2).   [31] 1983 Act, s 1(3) as amended by 2007 Act, s 3.

[32] 1983 Act, ss 145(1) and (4) as amended by the 2007 Act, s 7. The 2003 Act, s 329, is very similar, although
habilitation and rehabilitation do not have to be of a specialist nature.

[33] See *A v The Scottish Ministers* 2001 SC 1 discussed at para 13.60.

[34] 1983 Act, s 114 substituted by 2007 Act, s 18. And see Mental Health (Approved Mental Health
Professionals) (Approval) (England) Regulations 2008 (SI 2008/1206), and MHA Code of Practice
(2015), ch 30.

[35] 1983 Act, s 145 inserted by 2007 Act, s 14.

[36] The 2003 Act is based on different terminology—short-term detention and compulsory treatment. The
general purpose behind both the English and Scottish Acts is very similar but their practical application is
different. As already stated, considerations of space make it impossible to consider both in depth, and we will
only refer to the Scottish Act when there is a significant difference.

[37] As an alternative, an application for guardianship—usually by the local authority—can be made under
the 1983 Act, s 7. We are not, however, considering guardianship in this chapter. On the matter of stringency
of conditions, note *D v Mental Health Tribunal for Scotland* [2014] GWD 13-246 (Sh C), wherein it was held
that the consequence of a failure to follow the statutory requirements in minutiae does not invalidate treatment orders necessary not only for the benefit of the patient but also the safety of others.

[38] Applications for admission for assessment or treatment can be made by the person's nearest relative
or an approved mental health professional. In England and Wales, the application will be to the manager

Appeals by the patient or his representative are available by way of the reconstituted Mental Health Tribunals (England and Wales), or the Sheriff Principal (Scotland);[39] further appeals to the Court of Appeal or the Court of Session are available as applicable. In addition, a Patient Advocacy Service has been established in both jurisdictions and provides access to information and legal representation.[40] There are, thus, wide provisions to protect the rights of both compulsorily detained and informal mental patients.

13.23 The criteria for an application for an *admission for assessment* by an approved mental health professional is that: (1) the patient is suffering from a mental disorder; (2) the mental disorder warrants detention in hospital for the purpose; and (3) the patient ought to be detained in the interests of his or her health or safety or for the protection of others. Such an application requires the recommendation of two registered medical practitioners. It is, then, the duty of the appropriate authority, on request,[41] to arrange for the assessment of the patient with a view to determining whether he or she should be discharged, treated as an outpatient, or admitted for treatment. Admission for assessment can only last for 28 days and there are no provisions for extension. There are intricate arrangements for notification of the determination; the approved mental health practitioner is also responsible for appointing a nominated person to represent the patient and also for ensuring that advocacy services are available.

13.24 An application for *admission for treatment* can only be made if the following grounds are sufficiently demonstrated: (1) the patient is suffering from mental disorder that makes it appropriate for him or her to be treated in hospital; (2) it is necessary for the health or safety of the patient or for the protection of other persons that he or she should receive such treatment, and it cannot be provided in the absence of detention; and (3) the appropriate medical treatment is available.[42] With respect to criterion (3), the following statutory definition is offered:

> In this Act, references to appropriate medical treatment, in relation to a person suffering from mental disorder, are references to medical treatment which is appropriate in his case, taking into account the nature and degree of the mental disorder and all other circumstances of his case.[43]

It does seem that the draughtsman was keen to cover all the bases—and probably did so successfully. The application is to be founded on the recommendation of two registered medical practitioners, one of whom is specially approved for the purpose; unless this

---

of the hospital (1983 Act, s 11); in Scotland, short-term detention can be authorised by a registered medical practitioner subject to the consent of a mental health officer (2003 Act, ss 44 and 63), and the authority will be the Mental Health Tribunal for Scotland (2003 Act, s 21).

[39] 1983 Act, s 65(1A) as substituted by the 2007 Act, s 39; 2003 Act, ss 320 and 322.

[40] For the role of Independent Mental Health Advocates see the 1983 Act, s 130A inserted by the 2007 Act, s 30(2); 2003 Act, s 259; and MHA Code of Practice (2015), ch 4. For an example of advocacy services in practice, see the work of Together: http://www.together-uk.org/our-mental-health-services/advocacy/.

[41] The request may well result from removal of a person to a place of safety under emergency regulations (1083 Act, ss 135 and 136). It is to be noted that the second doctor can be dispensed with if the application is made as an emergency. The second opinion must be provided within 72 hours if admission is to be extended (1983 Act, s 4).

[42] 1983 Act, s 3 as amended by 2007 Act, ss 1 and 4. While there is no requirement for the nearest relative to be informed and consulted when a Compulsory Treatment Order is being considered, the Code notes that consultation at an early stage with the patient and those involved in the patient's care, including family and carers, is important. The role and rights of relatives were articulated in *R (otao M) v Secretary of State for Health* [2003] EWHC 1094 (Admin).

[43] 1983 Act, s 3(4) as amended by 2007 Act, s 4(1).

practitioner fulfils the role, the other must, if practicable, have had previous acquaint-ance with the patient,[44] and, of course, there are manifold regulations governing the just practice of compulsory treatment, all with the aim of reducing the ambiguities and con-troversies associated with treatment of mental disorder.[45]

Limitations on Compulsory Treatment

13.25 While treatment for mental disorder that is given by or under the direction of the approved clinician in charge of the treatment can be given without consent,[46] there are specific limitations found in ss 57, 58, and 58A of the 1983 Act that have particular ethical and human rights connotations.[47]

13.26 Section 57 deals with very serious treatments which require the patient's consent *and* a second opinion—currently, these are surgical operations designed to destroy brain tissue or its functioning.[48] The necessary conditions for providing such treatment, which apply to *any* patient,[49] are strict:

- the patient must consent;
- an independent, specially appointed,[50] medical practitioner and two other appointed persons, not being medical practitioners, have certified as to the patient's competence;
- the medical practitioner has certified that it is appropriate that the treatment be given;
- before giving this certificate, the practitioner has consulted two other persons who have been professionally concerned with the patient's treatment, one of whom is a nurse and the other is neither a nurse nor a medical practitioner.

13.27 Section 58 relates to treatments which require consent *or* a second opinion which, subject to the Secretary of State's additional regulatory powers, involve long-term treatments—currently those given for more than three months. The requirements are either:

- that the patient has consented and that the approved clinician in charge of the man-agement[51] or an appointed medical practitioner have certified as to the patient's competence; or
- that an appointed medical practitioner has certified that the patient is either incapa-ble of understanding or has refused the treatment but that, nevertheless, it is appro-priate that it be given. Before so certifying, the practitioner must consult in the same way as when certifying under s 57.

---

[44] 1983 Act, s 12(2). In Scotland, an application for a compulsory treatment order must be made to the Mental Health Tribunal, and can only be made by a mental health officer: 2003 Act, ss 57 and 63.

[45] For more on this, see the standard works, including Department of Health, *Reference Guide to the Mental Health Act 1983* (2015).

[46] 1983 Act, s 63.

[47] The latter provision was inserted by Mental Health Act 2007, s 27. The comparable Scottish provisions are found in 2003 Act, ss 234–41.

[48] Though, in every category, the Secretary of State or other appropriate national authority can add any other forms of treatment.

[49] 1983 Act, s 56(1) as substituted by the 2007 Act, s 34(1).   [50] See 1983 Act, s 12(2).

[51] The responsible clinician or person in charge of the treatment in question are excluded as certifiers in the case of ss 57, 58, and 58A treatments in the case of incompetent or non-consensual patients.

13.28   Section 58A currently deals only with ECT which may, first, be given to consenting adults who have been certified as competent, and to children under 18 who, again, have consented to treatment and are certified as being able to understand the nature and effects of the treatment—who, in short, are *Gillick*-competent.[52] ECT can also be given to the incompetent patient given what are essentially the same safeguards as for the s 58 patient; in addition, however, the certifying practitioner must ensure that the treatment does not conflict with an advance decision which is valid and applicable or with a decision made by a donee or by the Court of Protection.[53]

13.29   As is to be expected, the competent patient is free to withdraw her consent at any time during the course of these treatments; this is empowered by s 60 of the 1983 Act, and the clinician in charge of the treatment must report the occurrence and the patient's condition to the Secretary of State.[54]

Emergency Powers

13.30   On the other side of the coin, emergency powers must be available for circumstances where strict adherence to the rules would be impracticable. Thus, s 62 of the 1983 Act authorises urgent treatment of a patient detained in hospital when it is to the patient's advantage (e.g. to save her life, prevent deterioration, or alleviate serious suffering), or, conversely, when it will prevent the patient behaving violently or being a danger to others.[55] It seems that the determination of these matters is left to professional discretion. Possibly more draconian are those sections which authorise entry to premises and removal to a place of safety of an individual who is living alone and unable to look after him- or herself.[56] In addition, a constable can remove a person to a place of safety who he reasonably suspects to be suffering from a mental disorder and is in immediate need of care; this containment is valid for a maximum of 72 hours (24 hours in Scotland) or until the person is seen by a medical practitioner and an approved mental health practitioner.[57]

Treatment in the Community

13.31   In general, the preferred option for the management of mental disorder has been to avoid compulsory detention so far as is possible; this was the purpose of the Mental Health (Patients in the Community) Act 1995, and it is the purpose of ss 17A–17G of the 1983 Act, as amended by the 2007 Act.[58] The main purpose of the new provisions is to introduce 'community treatment orders', which allow for a patient who no longer requires hospital treatment to be returned to the community while preserving the

---

[52]   See Chapter 4, paras 4.59 et seq. It is to be noted that this concession does not apply in the case of ss 57 and 58 treatments—see also s 56(5).

[53]   Mental Capacity Act 2005. In Scotland, the conditions pertaining to surgical operations are similar save that, if the patient is found to be incapable of consent, treatment may only be authorised by the Court of Session (2003 Act, ss 235 and 236). Electro-convulsive therapy (s 237) and long-term therapy—i.e., treatment given for longer than two months (s 240)—can be given to a consenting patient on the certificate of his or her responsible medical officer.

[54]   When next providing a report renewing the authority for the detention—1983 Act, s 61(1).

[55]   In Scotland, see 2003 Act, s 243. Under s 299, a nurse may, in certain well-defined circumstances, detain a patient for two hours pending medical examination.

[56]   1983 Act, s 135; 2003 Act, ss 292 and 293. The relationship between these powers and those provided under the National Assistance Act 1948, s 47 is discussed at para 12.26. Similar powers exist if the person is being ill-treated or neglected.

[57]   1983 Act, s 136; 2003 Act, s 297. For more, see Department of Health, *Reference Guide to the Mental Health Act 1983* (2015), ch 7.

[58]   See 2007 Act, ss 32 and 36.

power of recall to hospital if that is necessary;[59] whether or not such an order should be issued is, in essence, a matter of agreement between the responsible clinician and an approved mental health professional.[60] Again, this is no place to detail the conditions that are designed to safeguard the rights of the patient and the safety of society. In summary, however, the essentials are that the patient must have a disorder that requires treatment, the treatment can be given outside the hospital environment and is available, and it is necessary for the responsible clinician to retain his or her powers of recall.[61] On the other hand, the responsible clinician must consider the likelihood of, say, the patient failing to abide by the conditions as to treatment that are specified in the order—the permissible limits of which are, again, carefully defined. As with existing supervised after-care, responsibility for the patient remains with the hospital from which the patient was discharged.[62] Finally, a community treatment order ceases to be in force six months after it was made but, from then on, can be extended for periods of one year at a time.

HUMAN RIGHTS AND MENTAL DISORDER

13.32 It is clear from what has already been said that human rights form an essential element in the equation of the interests of the mentally disordered and those of the public. Any legislative response to, or judicial interpretation of, a conflict of interests has to take full account of the implications of the rights detailed in the ECHR and incorporated in the Human Rights Act 1998. And, it should be said at the outset, the ultimate administrative protection of the mental patient's human rights lies in the availability of appeal procedures against the decisions taken—often at relatively low level. This is provided by the Mental Health Tribunals of which there is one for England and another for Wales,[63] and which deal with applications by or in respect of all patients who will come under the auspices of the Mental Health Act whether by way of the medical grounds or through the courts.

13.33 As to the former, applications for review of virtually any decision made in respect of a patient subject to compulsory treatment can be made by the patient or by his or her nearest relative within a defined period which varies with the decision under review.[64] The Secretary of State can also refer a case if she thinks fit. And the manager of the hospital must refer a case of admission, guardianship, or community treatment six months after the action was taken. Applications in respect of patients subject to hospital orders can be made by the nearest relative or by the patient subject to an initial detention period of six months. Patients who are subject to restriction orders (see para 13.54) may

---

[59] This is the essential distinction from after-care supervision which the order will replace.

[60] On the information to be provided and the procedures, see C Curran, P Fennell, and S Burrows, 'Responsible authority statements for mental health tribunals' (2012) Legal Action 15. On the growing use of the CTO, see D Hewitt, 'This strange republic of the good. Community treatment orders and their conditions' (2011) J Men Health L 39.

[61] See Department of Health, *Reference Guide to the Mental Health Act 1983* (2015), ch 26.

[62] See 1983 Act, s 17A(7). But a patient can be recalled to another hospital (s 17E(3)).

[63] 1983 Act, s 65 as, now, substituted by 2007 Act, s 38. The Mental Health Tribunal for Scotland, established under the 2003 Act, s 21, operates at a different level and hears applications at first instance; appeals from the decisions of the Tribunal are heard by the Sheriff Principal.

[64] The relevant period is 14 days in the case of admission for assessment and six months in the case of treatment.

also make application at 12-monthly intervals, and the Secretary of State must do so if no application has been made within the last three years.

13.34 The Tribunal must discharge a patient liable to compulsory detention if it is not satisfied that the patient is suffering from mental disorder, or that it is necessary to detain the patient on safety grounds.[65] Indeed, the powers of the Tribunal are extensive, but it is also evident that many of its decisions stand or fall on clinical diagnoses. Psychiatrists have repeatedly, and rightly, said that they do not wish to be policemen; nonetheless, it is clear that, in this area, they have the greater responsibility for the public safety. It says an enormous amount for the profession that this function, conflicting as it may well be with their responsibility for the individual patient, is performed with the widespread approval of the community.[66]

COMPULSION AND LIBERTY

13.35 Several ECHR Articles have a direct bearing on mental health law—in particular, on the issues of detention and compulsory treatment. Arguably, the most important of these is Art 5, which sets out the right to liberty in the following terms:

> Everyone has the right to liberty and security of person. No one shall be deprived of his liberty save in the following cases and in accordance with a procedure prescribed by law.

There then follow six exceptions, the relevant one in this context being: (e) the lawful detention of persons for the prevention of the spreading of infectious diseases, of persons of unsound mind, alcoholics or drug addicts or vagrants. Clearly, then, the ECHR anticipated a margin of appreciation in respect of the management of the mentally disordered.

13.36 The leading case on the interpretation of Art 5 as it applies to compulsory psychiatric treatment is *Winterwerp* v *Netherlands*,[67] in which the ECtHR set out certain minimum conditions which must be satisfied if detention under mental health legislation is to be justified. These are:

- the patient must be 'reliably shown' by 'objective medical expertise' to be of 'unsound mind';
- the disorder must be of a nature to justify detention; and
- the disorder must persist throughout the period in which the patient is detained.

These requirements are framed in broad terms which allows for some leeway in how states may interpret them. The jurisprudence of the ECtHR has, however, established that patients should not be detained if nothing can be done for them medically—and this raises many and varied questions as to what constitutes medical assistance. In *Aerts* v *Belgium*,[68] for example, the ECtHR held that it was a breach of Art 5 to detain a mentally disordered patient in a prison, without treatment, because a hospital bed was not available. Article 5 has also been found to require timely release on recovery (even if it is reasonable to stage release in the interests of the patient or the community),[69] and to require reasonably early and frequent reviews of detention decisions.[70]

[65] 1983 Act, s 72(b).
[66] J Morrow, 'The Mental Health Tribunal for Scotland – advocating a therapeutic approach' (2011) Jur Rev 265.
[67] (1979) 2 EHRR 387. More recently, see *X* v *Finland* [2012] ECHR 1371.
[68] (1998) 29 EHRR 50; (1998) 53 BMLR 79.
[69] *Johnson* v *United Kingdom* (1999) 27 EHRR 440.   [70] *E* v *Norway* (1994) 17 EHRR 30.

13.37 Closer to home, it has been held under Art 8 (right to private and family life) that a patient cannot be detained simply on the grounds of medical necessity.[71] This establishes a presumption of non-interference with the person—and, as we will see, it requires particularly strong justification to set that presumption aside. Moreover, when Art 8(1) is taken along with Art 3 (right to be free from torture or inhuman or degrading treatment), there are human rights grounds on which to question the legitimacy of *any* compulsory treatment for mental disorder. Article 8(2) allows for exceptions to Art 8(1) on the grounds, among others, of the protection of health, but it is no longer sufficient for professionals merely to appeal to what they see as the patient's 'clinical' best interests to justify compulsory treatment; broader welfare matters must also be brought into the assessment.[72] The outcome is that detention is only lawful if there is 'appropriate treatment', but this is a term which still leaves open the door to the exercise of professional discretion.

13.38 While *Winterwerp* is the benchmark case relating to compulsory detention, the extent of the protection afforded by the ECHR—and, subsequently by the 1998 Act—in respect of non-consensual psychiatric *treatment* was most significantly addressed in *Herczegfalvy* v *Austria*.[73] That case established that treatment for a mental disorder could only be given to the incapax if (1) it was conclusively established that the subject was 'of unsound mind', and (2) not only that treatment was 'medically necessary' but also that the need had been 'convincingly shown to exist'. Once again, the ECtHR left open a number of questions that could only be resolved at national level,[74] and so followed *R (on the application of Wilkinson) v RMO, Broadmoor Hospital Authority*.[75] There the patient had been detained in a high security hospital under a hospital order and restriction order for over 30 years, having been convicted of raping a young girl. There was a difference of psychiatric opinion as to the diagnosis; most of the psychiatrists who had examined him over the years diagnosed psychopathic personality disorder, but the doctor now in charge of his case decided that treatment would be appropriate for psychotic symptoms—a form of treatment which the patient was determined to resist. It was argued for the patient that the ECHR permitted the proposed treatment in the face of refusal only where this was necessary to protect others from serious harm, or, possibly, to ensure the safety of the patient himself. Such an interpretation would seriously limit the grounds for medical intervention in such circumstances and, in the result, it was not accepted by the court.[76]

13.39 However, the judgment of Simon Brown LJ contained obiter remarks which suggest that it is 'increasingly difficult to justify' any exception to the proposition that a patient, voluntary or otherwise, should be entitled to refuse medical treatment—in short, the standard of proof as to the need for non-consensual treatment of mental disorder was outstandingly high. In order that it be compatible with Art 3 (right to be free from degrading treatment), not only must the test laid down in *Herczegfalvy* be satisfied,[77] but also

---

[71] *HL* v *United Kingdom* (2004) 81 BMLR 131. See para 12.17 for further discussion.

[72] *R* v *Bournewood Community and Mental Health NHS Trust, ex p L* [1999] 1 AC 458 at 493.

[73] (1992) 15 EHRR 437.

[74] And for the jurisprudence that developed to that point, see P Bartlett, 'A matter of necessity? Enforced treatment under the Mental Health Act' (2007) 15 Med L Rev 86.

[75] (2002) 65 BMLR 15 (CA).

[76] The courts appear very reluctant to apply Art 8 in cases such as this, generally holding that non-consensual treatment for serious disease is proportionate when it is necessary for the protection of health under Art 8(2): *R (otao PS) v G (Responsible Medical Officer)* [2003] EWHC 2335; *R (otao B) v Dr SS* [2005] EWHC 1936.

[77] In this respect, the judge is entitled to reach his or her own factual conclusions: *Wilkinson*, n 75, per Simon Brown LJ at [22].

the two limbs of the test must be read as constituting a single rather than a sequential requirement.[78] Moreover, the Court in *Wilkinson* reinforced the growing opposition to reliance on the *Bolam* test,[79] pointing out that the medical construct of *Bolam* was a necessary but insufficient evidence on which to base a treatment decision; more general conditions had to be taken into consideration.[80]

13.40 The issue also arose as to whether s 63 of the 1983 Act was compatible with the patient's ECHR rights in the changed conditions. Section 63 authorised—and still does—nonconsensual treatment provided that (1) it is not a treatment for which consent is specifically required, and (2) it is given for the mental disorder from which the patient is suffering. What *Wilkinson* did not decide was whether that applied to the disorder for which the patient was admitted or that from which he was suffering at the relevant time, an important distinction because, as Auld LJ later put it:

> the discipline of psychiatry is one which, notoriously poses particular difficulties of diagnosis and distinction between mental illness in a clinical sense and personality disorders or other failings[81]

and we have seen, and will see at several points in this book, how often a diagnosis may fluctuate between, say, schizophrenia and psychopathy.

13.41 The problem was squarely addressed in *R (on the application of B) v Ashworth Hospital Authority*,[82] a case involving a man under a restriction order who, having been assessed as suffering from mental illness, resisted a transfer to a personality disorder treatment ward.[83] Speaking for the whole House, Baroness Hale, while noting that psychiatry is not an exact science and that diagnosis is not easy or clear cut,[84] concluded that s 63 of the 1983 Act authorises:

> a patient to be treated for any mental disorder from which he is suffering, irrespective of whether this falls within the form of disorder from which he is classified as suffering in the application order or direction justifying his detention.[85]

This holistic or practical, view of psychiatric diagnosis and patient management has been followed in *R (on the application of B) v Haddock*,[86] and the problems associated with diagnosis, compulsory treatment, and standards of evidential proof are now resolved in favour of what is realistic. Indeed, now that specific psychiatric diagnoses have been replaced by the single concept of mental disorder, there really is no '*Wilkinson* question' remaining.

---

[78] See the comparable case *R (otao N) v M* (2003) 72 BMLR 81 per Dyson LJ at [19].

[79] For discussion of which, see Chapter 4.

[80] Shortly after *Wilkinson*, Lord Eassie in the Court of Session also held that non-consensual treatment under the Mental Health (Scotland) Act 1984, s 26 did not infringe Arts 6 and 8 of the ECHR. The treatment concerned was not, however, a treatment requiring a second opinion: *M, Petitioner* 2002 SCLR 1001 (OH). See also *M's Curator ad Litem* v *Mental Health Tribunal for Scotland* 2012 SC 251.

[81] *R (otao B) v Haddock* (2006) 93 BMLR 52 at [36].

[82] [2005] 2 AC 276 (HL); revsd [2003] 4 All ER 319.

[83] Note that, at that time, the distinction was statutorily significant.   [84] At para 31.

[85] At para 29. It is important to note that 'compulsory treatment' under the 1983 Act, s 63 refers only to treatment given for the mental condition itself. It is probable, however, that the back-up provided by the Mental Capacity Act 2005, s 5 and, in Scotland, s 243 of the 2003 Act now provide statutory authority for non-consensual treatment of physical conditions in the incapax which was previously covered only by the common law by way of the 'best interests' test. See *GJ* v *Foundation, Primary Care Trust, Secretary of State for Health* (2009) Case 1175458T (COP), and, for commentary, N Allen, 'The *Bournewood* gap (as amended)' (2010) 18 Med L Rev 78.

[86] N 81.

13.42 The House of Lords extended this essentially practical approach to the interplay of the Human Rights Act 1998 and mental health law in *R (on the application of MH)* v *Secretary of State for Health*.[87] This case concerned a Down's syndrome adult aged 32 whose behaviour was becoming increasingly aggressive and who was admitted for assessment under s 2 of the 1983 Act. The statutory limit of 28 days' detention became prolonged as a result of various administrative difficulties and legal manoeuvring—including a contested application to replace the patient's mother as her nearest relative.[88] The patient's mother applied for judicial review of the situation, pleading that, given that the person detained was incapable of exercising her statutory rights of appeal, s 2 of the 1983 Act was incompatible with Art 5 ECHR. The House of Lords rejected the claim, largely on the ground that Art 5(4) dictates a right 'to take proceedings' by which the lawfulness of a person's detention can be decided—if the patient is incapax, the obligation then lies on the authorities to make 'every sensible effort...to enable the patient to exercise that right'. Put another way, although the initiative may be taken by someone else, the patient's rights are the same and the Act provides ample opportunity for others to take that initiative.[89]

13.43 On further appeal to the ECtHR,[90] it was held that the following principles govern with respect to Art 5 and its application to persons of unsound mind:

- an initial period of detention may be authorised by an administrative authority as an emergency measure provided that it is of short duration and the individual is able to bring judicial proceedings speedily to challenge the lawfulness or justification of the detention;

- following the expiry of an initial period of emergency detention, a person detained for an indefinite or lengthy period is entitled, in the absence of automatic periodic review of a judicial character, to take proceedings at reasonable intervals before a court;

- the proceedings must have a judicial character and afford guarantees appropriate to the deprivation of liberty and circumstances in question;

- the proceedings need not always offer the same guarantees as those required under Art 6(1) for civil or criminal litigation, but the person should have access to a court and the opportunity to be heard;

- special procedural safeguards may be needed to protect the interests of persons who, on account of their mental disabilities, are not fully capable of acting for themselves.

---

[87] [2006] 1 AC 441 (HL); (2005) 86 BMLR 71.

[88] The nearest relative, as defined in s 26 of the 1983 Act, can act as the patient's representative in respect of admission, care, and discharge. Section 29 empowers the County Court to nominate an acting nearest relative if an application to do so is made and approved.

[89] UK detainees have the power to force a dilatory Secretary of State's hand or to challenge the lawfulness of detention by way of judicial review: *R (otao Rayner)* v *Secretary of State for the Home Office* (2008) 101 BMLR 83. A detained person lacking capacity is not barred from participating and being represented in proceedings in the Court of Protection, and need not be made a party, but the Court of Protection Rules do require urgent review: *Re X (Deprivation of Liberty)* [2014] EWCOP 37. A detention will be an unlawful deprivation of liberty when the local authority fails to take proceedings 'speedily' when their authority to act is questioned: *Hillingdon LBC* v *Neary*, [2011] EWHC 1377 (COP) (which also held that the best interests assessment had been flawed for not taking into account the wishes of the patient and the desire of the father to receive him into his care).

[90] *MH* v *United Kingdom* [2013] ECHR 1008; (2014) 58 EHRR 35.

In the result, the ECtHR found that MH's initial detention was, due to the barring order resulting from the s 29 application, without the means available to challenge its lawfulness, in breach of Art 5.

13.44 In *Nottinghamshire Healthcare NHS Trust* v *RC*,[91] a case involving a Jehovah's Witness in a secure psychiatric hospital whose personality disorders resulted in self-harm, the Trust sought declaratory orders in relation to RC's capacity and advance directive, and the lawfulness of his doctor's decision not to use his s 63 powers to enforce treatment, namely a blood transfusion. The court reiterated that competent individuals, even if detained, may freely harm or kill themselves, but mentally disordered, incapacitated, and vulnerable ones can have treatment imposed on them. One lacks capacity to make a decision if, by reason of mental disorder, they are unable to understand, retain, use or weigh information relevant to their decision, but adherence to a tenet of an accepted religion which limits one's ability to weigh a treatment cannot ground a finding of incapacity; on the evidence RC had capacity to refuse treatment and make a valid advance decision. On the final matter, it stated that a decision to impose non-consensual treatment under s 63 was susceptible to judicial review, but a decision not to impose treatment was not open to review, so the Trust was well advised to apply for declaratory relief. The wording of ss 63 and 145(4) supported a conclusion that the administration of a blood transfusion could not be 'treatment' for a personality disorder, but the act of self-harming was a symptom or manifestation of the personality disorder, and treating the wound was to treat that symptom or manifestation. Thus, a blood transfusion in such circumstances is caught by s 63. However, the doctor's decision not to use his s 63 powers was also correct given RC's capacity; the benign but paternalistic view that it is in somebody's best interests to remain alive is subservient to one's sovereignty over one's body.

FORCED FEEDING OF DETAINEES

13.45 Potential conflicts between human rights, enforced detention, and the definition of mental disorder converge in the case of compulsory feeding of prisoners, many of whom will have a background of personality disorder, but many of whom may also be acting from political motives. As a consequence of this unusual mix, the position of the doctor who wishes to save the life of a subject who is actively resisting basic care demands careful and specific assessment. Current policy is that the doctor's role is to advise the prisoner of the dangers of starvation, to have treatment and hospital facilities available, but, otherwise, to refrain from interference. While this policy accords with the Declaration of Tokyo, the doctor must at times be concerned as to whether the prisoner can form an unimpaired and rational judgement. Starvation leads to severe metabolic dysfunction and, consequently, to mental impairment. A major ethical dilemma then arises as to whether the doctor can or should adjust his or her attitude according to the subject's fluctuating physiological/mental state. This clearly smacks of 'cat-and-mouse' treatment which would seem ethically improper, not least because re-feeding after some three weeks of starvation carries a serious risk of cardiac failure.[92]

13.46 The problem might be thought to have been solved in *Secretary of State for the Home Department* v *Robb*,[93] in which Thorpe J firmly held that the right of an individual to determine his future was plain, that such right is not diminished by his status as a detained

---

[91] [2014] EWCOP 1317.   [92] M Peel, 'Hunger strikes' (1997) 315 BMJ 829.
[93] [1995] 1 All ER 677.

prisoner, and that there is no countervailing state interest. However, Kennedy has pointed out, first, that it was unusual for the case, which concerned a prisoner rather than a patient, to be considered on the basis of medical law rather than as one of human rights, and, second, that the tenor of the judgment was permissive rather than obligatory—the authorities *need* not feed, not *may* not feed.[94] There is, indeed, some evidence that judicial opinion is turning away from an absolute adherence to respect for autonomy as applied to the mentally disordered. In *Nevmerzhitsky* v *Ukraine*,[95] another case of a competent prisoner refusing food, the ECtHR held that a measure which is of therapeutic necessity cannot, in principle, be regarded as inhuman and degrading—the same could be said about force-feeding that is aimed at saving the life of a detainee. Ultimately, the matter of forcible feeding is by no means closed, and each case will be decided on its own merits.

13.47 The importance of competence had been raised in *R* v *Collins, ex p Brady*,[96] in which a restricted prisoner went on hunger strike, ostensibly in protest at an attempt to move him from his protected environment. His medical officer decided to force-feed him, which decision was judicially reviewed. The court approached the question as one of human rights the answer to which was to be judged by way of reasonableness.[97] It was adjudged that Brady's hunger strike was a symptom of his personality disorder and that, as a result, treatment of starvation was treatment of the underlying psychopathy; the decision to treat was perfectly reasonable.[98] In addition, insofar as he was unable to weigh the contending issues as to risks and needs in his own mind,[99] he was incapacitated in relation to all his decisions about food, and the doctors were legally entitled to supply medical treatment in his best interests. As an addendum, in an obiter statement, Kay J had this to say:

> It would seem to me to be a matter for deep regret if the law has developed to a point in this area where the rights of a patient count for everything and other ethical values and institutional integrity count for nothing.[100]

In other words, there are recognisable situations in which the communitarian ethos supersedes that of personal autonomy.[101] Continuing in this vein, in *An NHS Trust* v *A*,[102] a hospital sought declaratory relief empowering it to forcibly feed a detainee suffering from a delusional disorder. The court held that the patient lacked capacity, and that while artificial nutrition and hydration was not 'medical treatment' for his mental disorder, and

---

[94] I Kennedy, 'Consent: Force-feeding of prisoners' (1995) 3 Med L Rev 189.

[95] (2005) 19 BHRC 177. The same feeling comes across when reading *R (otao B)* v *Dr SS* [2006] UKHRR 432 (CA); (2006) 90 BMLR 1—a case of refusal of treatment under the 1983 Act, s 58.

[96] (2001) 58 BMLR 173, [2000] Lloyd's Rep Med 355.

[97] Which is assessed based on the principles laid down in *R* v *Ministry of Defence, ex p Smith* [1996] QB 517—a particularly high standard of 'reasonableness' is needed in cases involving fundamental human rights.

[98] Much the same reasoning has been employed in cases of anorexia nervosa, for which see Chapter 4.

[99] *Re C (adult: refusal of medical treatment)* [1994] 1 All ER 819; (1993) 15 BMLR 77.

[100] (2001) 58 BMLR 173 at 193.

[101] For guidance on considerations to be taken into account in transfer decisions, see *R (otao L)* v *West London Mental Health NHS Trust* [2012] EWHC 3200 (Admin).

[102] But also note *An NHS Foundation Trust* v *X* [2014] EWCOP 35. X, an alcoholic in end-stage renal failure who also suffered from severe anorexia nervosa, had been detained and force-fed on numerous occasions. An order was sought declaring that it was not in X's best interests to be subject to further compulsory detention and treatment for anorexia notwithstanding that it may prolong her life, and that it was in her best interests for her treating clinicians not to provide her with ANH with which she does not comply. The court found that X had capacity in relation to her treatments for alcoholism, but lacked capacity in relation to decisions relating to her anorexia. However, based on all the circumstances, it concluded that it was not in her best interests to impose treatment for it despite the imperative to prolong life.

so could not be administered under s 63 of the 1983 Act, it was in his best interests and the court retained the power under its inherent jurisdiction to order a deprivation of liberty so long as adequate reviews were available.[103]

BEHAVIOUR MODIFICATION

13.48   The focus of our discussion so far has been on treatment, the main purpose of which is to restore the patient—as far as is possible—to the pre-morbid state. Psychiatry and psychology may, however, make rather broader claims and offer to alter undesirable behaviour—an extension which, to many, may represent the ultimate intrusion on human rights. The methods used to achieve this end may be non-intrusive—involve no physical intervention—or be extremely invasive. Major ethical problems arise in either case. Are coercive techniques *ever* acceptable? To what extent has the therapist the right to impose her model of desirable behaviour on the patient? Can consent ever be given to such treatments if they are offered in the form of an inducement—for example, as an alternative to punishment? These questions are posed most dramatically in relation to neurosurgery for mental disorder (NMD),[104] and treatment for sexual offenders, both of which merit some discussion.

13.49   The essential claim of NMD is that it can change behaviour patterns in reasonably predictable ways. Modern techniques involve localised stereotactic interference with parts of the brain which influence feelings and sexuality—a process which results in destruction of brain tissue approximately the size of a garden pea. Historically, NMD has been offered for a variety of conditions, most frequently for affective illnesses, aggressive behaviour, intractable pain, and unacceptable sexual urges, but these last are not now considered legitimate indications for surgical intervention—modern practice confines the procedure to treatment of depression, obsessive compulsive disorders, and bi-polar affective disorder.[105] Any discussion of its effectiveness raises, of course, the question of the standpoint from which success is measured. It is important to distinguish the concept of *therapeutic success*—removing symptoms without incurring unacceptable side effects—from that of *improved manageability*—merely rendering the patient passive and compliant. It may constitute little more than 'neutralising' the patient, and so psychosurgery lies open to the challenge that it is primarily a method of social control.[106] It is therefore important to appreciate that, although successful surgery for mental disorder might result in significant behavioural changes, the primary aim is 'to engender a release of adaptive behaviour, not a suppression of an "undesirable" or "unwanted" behavioural repertoire'.[107]

13.50   The United Nations has resolved that NMD should never be imposed on an involuntary patient and that, otherwise, its use should be subject to informed consent by the patient.[108] But even if one accepts that the patient is capable of giving a consent which is

---

[103] For guidance on considerations to be taken into account in transfer decisions, see *West London Mental Health NHS Trust*, n 101.

[104] For debate on this, see R Persaud, D Crossley, and C Freeman, 'Should neurosurgery for mental disorder be allowed to die out?' (2003) 183 Brit J Psychiat 195.

[105] Royal College of Psychiatrists Working Group, *Neurosurgery for Mental Disorder* (2000). Neurosurgery is also offered for non-obsessive-compulsive anxiety disorders in Sweden.

[106] As an early writer on the subject put it: 'Life in "Brave New World" may be more pleasant for all, but only John the Savage is fully human': J Kleinig, *Ethical Issues in Psychosurgery* (1985).

[107] D Christmas, C Morrison, et al., 'Neurosurgery for mental disorder' (2004) 10 Adv Psychiat Treatment 189, to which we are indebted for much of the detail in this discussion.

[108] General Assembly of the United Nations, Resolution A/RES/46/119 of 17 December 1991, principle 11(14).

valid, in that it is informed and uncoerced, that fact alone may not be sufficient to justify the treatment—a maiming and irreversible operation which achieves only a doubtful therapeutic purpose could well be seen as a procedure which is unacceptable on grounds of public policy. The alternative view might well be that patients should not be denied a potentially effective treatment purely because it is hazardous or open to abuse. Such treatments should, of course, be subjected to control—preferably control which embodies an element of non-medical opinion—but they should not be excluded from the range of those available by virtue only of their nature. Indeed, some have argued that advances in technology, unmet clinical need, and neuroimaging stimulation suggest that there might be growing support to revisit psychosurgery as a more extended treatment option in the future.[109]

13.51 It has been reported that neurosurgery for mental disorder takes place at three sites in the UK (Bristol, Cardiff, and Dundee), that the CQC must authorise any interventions under the 1983 Act, and that, while 17 patients received treatment in 1997–9, only four patients were treated in 2012–13, and only five were referred in 2013–14.[110] The Mental Health (Care and Treatment) (Scotland) Act 2003 has taken the rather bold step of allowing non-consensual NMD subject to approval of each individual case by the Court of Session.[111] On the whole, we urge extreme caution.

13.52 Controversy of almost equal intensity surrounds the use of chemical methods to control the behaviour of actual or potential sex offenders. Opponents have described these procedures as 'chemical castration', and have been especially concerned about their inherently coercive nature.[112] On the other hand, it is possible to view behaviour modification of this type in a properly therapeutic light. The person troubled by sexual inclinations which he cannot control may look upon drug treatment as his only hope of a normal life in the community.[113] On this analysis, the refusal of such treatment to someone who genuinely seeks it can amount to unacceptable paternalism. Just such an instance arose in *R v Mental Health Commission, ex p X*.[114] X was a compulsive paedophile who sought medical help. Standard antiandrogen treatment was unsuccessful. He then tried a new synthetic compound (Goserelin) which was administered monthly by subcutaneous insertion of a thin implant. A satisfactory response was obtained with three insertions, but the Mental Health Commission became concerned as to the validity of his consent and withdrew its approval of the relevant certificates. X applied for judicial review—as a result of which, the Commission's decision was quashed. While some of the observations made may be seen as bordering on the casuistic, we feel that the case demonstrates that, if it is possible to do so, the courts will disapprove a bureaucratic attempt to separate a patient from the treatment he genuinely seeks, and they will support the doctors who are supplying it in good faith whenever possible.

---

[109] S Eljamel, 'Strategies for the return of behavioural surgery' (2012) 3 (Suppl 1): S34.

[110] http://www.mind.org.uk/information-support/drugs-and-treatments/neurosurgery-for-mental-disorder-nmd/#.VaetWvmPGSc.

[111] Sections 234–6. Note that the position in England and Wales is still controlled by the rigid conditions of the Mental Health Act 1983, s 57.

[112] J McMillan, 'The Kindest Cut? Surgical castration, sex offenders and coercive offers' (2014) 40 J Med Ethics 583. The unavailability of chemical castration was a key feature in the extradition case of *Antzcak v Poland* [2014] EWHC 1075.

[113] L Bomann-Larsen, 'Voluntary Rehabilitation? On Neurotechnological Behavioural Treatment, Valid Consent and (In)appropriate Offers' (2013) 6 Neuroethics 65.

[114] (1988) 9 BML R77.

MENTAL HEALTH, CRIMINALITY,
AND LIABILITY

13.53 Thus far, we have been concentrating on the management of the individual as a patient and the impact on his or her human rights. In our final section we consider the potential impact of mentally disordered individuals on the wider community, and the associated liability of those who care for them. Foremost among these individuals will be those who have transgressed the criminal law;[115] it is essential to the administration of justice that persons are not sentenced to prison when the cause of their crime lies in mental disorder. Thus, subject to appropriateness and the availability of resources, the courts may remand a person awaiting trial to hospital either to obtain a report on her mental condition or for treatment of a mental disorder.[116] In the present context, however, we are more concerned with the management of those with mental disorder following conviction for an offence that is punishable by imprisonment.

COMPULSORY TREATMENT FOLLOWING CONVICTION

13.54 In certain circumstances, and subject to the rules of fixed sentencing,[117] the courts may order hospitalisation or guardianship of a convicted criminal. The former order may be strengthened by a 'restriction order' when the patient is considered to be a serious public danger;[118] the effect of such an order is to seriously restrict the statutory rights to release and the community treatment options available to the person.[119] The court must be satisfied that the order can be effected within 28 days, but, in an emergency, the order can be varied within that period if admission to a specified hospital proves impracticable. Restriction orders are subject to annual review.[120] Prior to the 2007 amendments to the 1983 Act,[121] considerable difficulty arose due to the specificity of diagnosis that was demanded in support of the issuance of the various orders. The new, broad definition of mental disorder obviates some of these difficulties and eases the hospital's responsibilities in the event of a change in diagnosis following appropriate observation—something that is particularly common within the criminal context.[122]

---

[115] But we repeat that we cannot in a book of this type embark on a discussion of both the criminal and mental health law, and the reader is directed to the appropriate textbooks for further information.

[116] 1983 Act, ss 35 and 36.

[117] Certain provisions are specifically excluded: 1983 Act, s 37(1A), substituted by Criminal Justice Act 2003, s 304.

[118] The court may also make a hospital direction, and a comparable limitation direction, in the event that it considers making a hospital order before deciding to impose a sentence of imprisonment: 1983 Act, s 45A inserted by Crime (Sentences) Act 1997, s 46. The conditions for so doing are very similar to those governing the issue of a hospital order.

[119] 1983 Act, s 41. In particular, none of the provisions relating to the duration, renewal, and expiration of authority for compulsory detention of patients (under Part II of the Act) shall apply until the patient is discharged. And, since the discharge of a restriction order is a matter for the Secretary of State alone, this can have a massive effect on the future for the criminal patient.

[120] 1983 Act, s 41(6).

[121] Specifically the repeal of s 37(7) of the 1983 Act, which laid down strict criteria as to agreement on a precise diagnosis between certifying professionals, by s 55 of the 2007 Act.

[122] This is particularly so when distinguishing schizophrenia from psychopathy: *W v Egdell* [1990] 1 All ER 835, at [6.17 et seq]; *Reid v Secretary of State for Scotland* [1999] 2 AC 512.

The Problems of Dangerousness and Treatability

13.55 The essential prerequisites for issuing a hospital order are that the person suffers from a mental disorder the nature of which makes it appropriate for her to be detained in hospital for medical treatment, and that such treatment is available.[123] Moreover, compulsory treatment of mental disorder is justified only if the disorder is sufficiently serious to warrant treatment, and if the person's remaining untreated poses a threat to her own health or safety or to the safety of others.[124] As such, the closely related issues of 'dangerousness' and 'treatability' have been central to this area of mental health law, and were a major bone of contention in the lead up to the 2007 and 2003 Acts. And while those statutes, with their broadened definition of mental disorder, seem to have resolved many of the legal uncertainties around these issues, they remain important medico-ethical problem areas warranting review of the pre-2007 era.

13.56 To begin, the proportion of psychiatrically disturbed people likely to commit violent acts (i.e., likely to be 'dangerous') is small,[125] but such persons create substantial public concern. It is politically difficult for governments to resist pressure to make their detention easier, and yet there are serious civil libertarian concerns over the too-ready use of the restrictive powers provided by mental health laws. It is salutary to ask why public safety considerations should justify the detention of those who are mentally disordered and thought to be potentially dangerous, when those who are not mentally disordered but are perhaps equally dangerous—or are reckoned to be so on the basis of their past conduct or their disclosed intentions for the future—are not subject to preventive detention. It may well be that the prediction of dangerousness is a pragmatic and imprecise—and, perhaps, fruitless—exercise;[126] many attempts have been made to determine an objective concept of dangerousness, but none have succeeded in allaying doubts as to the strong element of subjectivity that is inherent in such judgments.[127]

13.57 It was originally feared that a broadening of the definition of mental disorder might lead to its extension to those who are little more than 'different'[128]—and this may yet be the case.[129] One Scottish judge, having listened to a description of the symptomatology of personality disorder, remarked:

> It is, to my mind, descriptive rather of a typical criminal than of a person...regarded as being possessed of diminished responsibility.[130]

---

[123] 1983 Act, s 37(2) as amended by 2007 Act, s 1(4).   [124] 1983 Act, s 3(2)(c).

[125] P Taylor and J Gunn, 'Homicides by people with mental illness: Myth and reality' (1999) 174 Brit J Psychiat 174; E Walsh, A Buchanan, and T Fahy, 'Violence and schizophrenia: Examining the evidence' (2002) 180 Brit J Psychiat 490.

[126] For a discussion of the potential effect of risk assessments on the prevention of homicide, see E Munro and J Rumgay, 'Role of risk assessments in reducing homicides by people with mental illnesses' (2000) 176 Brit J Psychiat 116.

[127] Opinions differ amongst psychiatrists as to the ethical implications of making predictions of dangerousness. Not all psychiatrists are reluctant to do so; see T Grisso and P Applebaum, 'Is it unethical to offer predictions of future violence?' (1992) 16 Law and Hum Behav 621. Some commentators believe that prognostic possibilities are improving. See, in general, J K Mason, 'The legal aspects and implications of risk assessment' (2000) 8 Med L Rev 69 and, more specifically, J McMillan, 'Dangerousness, mental disorder and responsibility' (2003) 29 J Med Ethics 232.

[128] Birmingham, n 12.

[129] Insofar as it excluded promiscuity, sexual proximity, or other moral conduct, or sexual promiscuity from the application of the Act, s 1(3) has been effectively repealed by s 3 of the 2007 Act. However, the exclusion of dependence on alcohol or drugs from the statutory definition persists. Para 25 of the Explanatory Notes to the 2007 Act is confusing on the point but the Notes do not form part of the Act. The exclusion of 'promiscuity' remains a feature of the Scottish Act.

[130] *Carraher* v *HM Advocate* 1946 JC 108 at 117, per Lord Normand.

This is an unscientific view, but it points to the difficulty which many people have with the concept—in short, how is psychopathy to be distinguished, if at all, from uncomplicated sociopathic conduct? It is open to question whether this simplifies the position from a legal standpoint or blurs an important distinction that is required in the name of justice.

13.58 In the event, as we have seen, the government reached a compromise solution in an indirect way—by broadening the definition of mental disorder and abandoning the difficult concept of 'treatability' as a condition for compulsory admission to hospital in favour of susceptibility to 'appropriate treatment' which is defined, somewhat circularly, as:

> Medical treatment which is appropriate in [the case of a person suffering from mental disorder] taking into account the nature and degree of the mental disorder and all other circumstances in his case.[131]

Given this new definition, the door is open to compulsory admission for mental conditions that are 'manageable' rather than 'treatable' (i.e., curable), and the new legislation at least removed the urgency from the long-standing debate as to whether or not personality disorder is 'treatable'.[132]

13.59 The previous regimes' impasse was first considered by the House of Lords in *Reid* v *Secretary of State for Scotland*,[133] in which it was held that an order for discharge of a restricted patient was inevitable once it was established that the patient's psychopathic condition was unlikely to respond to treatment.[134] Just such a situation occurred shortly afterwards when a dangerous psychopath was declared to be untreatable and so subject to discharge from a secure hospital.[135] The public furore which followed in Scotland resulted in the passing of the Mental Health (Public Safety and Appeals) (Scotland) Act 1999, which empowered the Sheriff to refuse an appeal for discharge from hospital by a patient who is subject to a restriction order if he is satisfied that the patient is suffering from a mental disorder 'the effect of which is such that it is necessary, *in order to protect the public from serious harm*, that the patient continue to be detained in hospital, *whether for medical treatment or not*' (emphasis added).[136]

13.60 A challenge to the 1999 Act by way of the Human Rights Act 1998 was inevitable, and, in *A* v *Scottish Ministers*,[137] the Inner House undertook a balancing exercise between, on the one hand, the government's duty under Art 2 ECHR to protect the lives of its citizens, and, on the other, the Art 5 right to liberty. In addition to giving high priority to Art 2, the House relied heavily on the derogations permitted in Art 5(1)(e)[138]—that the

---

[131] 1983 Act, s 64(3) inserted by 2007 Act, s 6(3).
[132] The problem can be summed up in that one of the criteria of illness is that it 'overlays' the normal self; this cannot be said of a personality disorder which lies at the core of 'self': G Adshead, 'Murmurs of discontent: Treatment and treatability of personality disorder' (2001) 7 Adv Psychiat Treatment 407.
[133] [1999] 2 AC 512.
[134] Thus, the House of Lords overturned the contrary judgment in *R* v *Canons Park Mental Review Tribunal, ex p A* [1994] 2 All ER 659 (CA). Both courts, however, ruled that the hospital environment did, of itself, alleviate the condition, and that the patient could be detained legitimately.
[135] *Ruddle* v *Secretary of State for Scotland* 1999 GWD 29–1395.
[136] The 1999 Act, which was always intended to be an interim measure, has now been repealed, but the power to detain a person in hospital whether or not for treatment is retained in the Mental Health (Care and Treatment) (Scotland) Act 2003, and this is so whatever the form of order to which the detainee is subject.
[137] [2000] UKHRR 439. The Inner House decision was criticised in G Laurie, 'Medical law and human rights: Passing the parcel back to the profession?' in A Boyle et al. (eds), *Human Rights and Scots Law* (2002).
[138] Following, in particular, the ECtHR in *Litwa* v *Poland* (2001) 33 EHRR 53.

detention of persons is lawful for reasons which, if used to their limits, allow the state a remarkably wide margin of appreciation. *A* and its associated cases were then taken to the Privy Council,[139] where, in dismissing the appeal, the safety of the public was considered paramount. The dictum of Lord Clyde sums up the mood well:

> In principle, it cannot be right that the public peace and safety should be subordinated to the liberty of persons whose mental states render them dangerous to society.[140]

The argument was brought to an end in the ECtHR,[141] where, after rapping the UK over the knuckles—largely on account of its procrastination in hearing cases involving human rights—the ECtIIR held that, given the high risk of the applicant reoffending, his continued detention was justified under Art 5(1)(e) of the Convention; significantly, there was no requirement under that Article that detention in a mental hospital be contingent on his mental condition being amenable to treatment.

13.61 To an extent, then, the domestic law was in limbo and several attempts were made in the UK Parliament to satisfy the 'public safety' lobby.[142] Opposition was, however, intense—largely from those medical practitioners most likely to be involved[143]—and Westminster was unwilling to follow the more robust attitudes of Holyrood. In the event, the law in England and Wales was, as we have seen, adjusted essentially by way of defining both mental disorder and medical treatment in such wide terms as to cover all eventualities.[144] Any administrative doubts as to 'treatability' are now resolved by s 72(1)(b)(i) of the 1983 Act which states that the Mental Health Tribunal:

> Shall direct the discharge of a patient if they are not satisfied that he is still suffering from a mental disorder which makes it appropriate for him to be liable to be detained in hospital for medical treatment *or* [emphasis added] That it is necessary for the health and safety of the patient or for the protection of other persons that he should receive such treatment,

the implication being that if he *is* dangerous, he can be detained given 'appropriate treatment'.

13.62 That is not to say that issues of treatability are extinct. In *Reid (Alexander Lewis) v HM Advocate*,[145] a Scottish court quashed hospital and restriction orders imposed in 1967 on the grounds that evidence existed that the accused was not suffering from and had never suffered from a mental disorder, but rather that he had a dissocial personality disorder that was untreatable. Both medical knowledge and prison standards are dynamic, which can pose challenges to those working in the area and trying to determine the appropriate

---

[139] [2003] 2 AC 602.

[140] Parenthetically, *A* appears to confirm a general impression that, in interpreting the Human Rights Act 1998, UK courts tend not to use the rights of the individual as their benchmark, but rather the reasonableness or unreasonableness of their infringement by the state.

[141] *Hutchison Reid* v *UK* (2003) 37 EHRR 9.

[142] Including, as already noted, two Mental Health Bills and an ill-fated Dangerous People with Severe Personality Disorder Bill 1999.

[143] J Coid and T Maden, 'Should psychiatrists protect the public?' (2003) 326 BMJ 406. For a major review of the problem, see P Bartlett, 'The test of compulsion in mental health law: Capacity, therapeutic benefit and dangerousness as possible criteria' (2003) 11 Med L Rev 326. See also the debate led by T Szasz, 'Psychiatry and the control of dangerousness: On the apotropaic function of the term "mental illness"' (2003) 29 J Med Ethics 227.

[144] Though it is a little difficult to understand how this can satisfy the civil libertarian advocates.

[145] [2012] HCJAC 150.

disposition of a defendant. Thus, in *R v Evans (Jaimie Angela)*,[146] the appellant, convicted of arson and sentenced to prison, sought to introduce new medical evidence in relation to the original finding that her mental illness was untreatable. Acknowledging that medical science and research had moved on since sentencing, the Court of Appeal allowed fresh medical evidence to be tendered which opined that E's psychopathy was now treatable. In the result, it issued orders that she should be detained in hospital for treatment.[147]

13.63 Recently, in *G v Scottish Ministers*,[148] the appellant, G, had been acquitted of rape by reason of insanity, and had been detained in a high-security state hospital under compulsion and restriction orders. He subsequently applied for a transfer to a medium-secure hospital, arguing that, under the legislation, if the patient did not need to be detained under conditions of special security, he should be moved unless good reasons existed to refuse. The Mental Health Tribunal declined to exercise its discretion in his favour. The Supreme Court acknowledged the scope of the Tribunal's discretion and the deference owed to it, saying that, though it had to exercise its discretion in a manner consistent with Parliament's intention, it would be wrong to say that the Tribunal could decline to make the requested order only in exceptional circumstances. The Tribunal had taken into account a wide range of matters and undertaken an appropriate balancing of 'maximum benefit' and 'least restrictive alternative', being mindful of the risk to the patient and others throughout. A formulaic rehearsal of every matter referred to in the Act was not required.

Liability for Premature Release

13.64 Of course, the person who is detained by way of either the civil or the criminal law has a right to restoration of her liberty to the extent that circumstances warrant. Not only will the medical authorities have a large say as to the circumstances justifying the patient's discharge, but, should it be conditional, they will remain responsible for her treatment; it follows that the question of responsibility for any harm to the public as a result of her release into the community is very much a matter of medical law and medical practice. The possibility of harm resulting from premature release of persons with a tendency to violence is very real and is likely to influence the clinicians who are responsible for such decisions; yet, it is equally clear that excessive caution may cause injustice to the patients themselves.

13.65 The classic litigation on the subject comes from the USA where, despite it being a case of failure to detain rather than of premature release, *Tarasoff v Regents of the University of California*,[149] remains the most significant case. Here, a patient had confessed to a therapist that he intended to harm a woman who had rejected his advances. The therapist failed to act so as to protect the woman from the danger and she was later killed by the patient. Her family then sued the therapist's employers successfully. The important feature of

[146] [2013] EWCA Crim 1193.
[147] However, note *Johnstone (John Stewart) v HM Advocate*, [2013] HCJAC 92, wherein hospital and restriction orders imposed in 1998 were challenged on the basis that modern psychiatric opinion would not regard the accused as mentally impaired such that treatment might alleviate his condition, and that the services available in prison were now such that his condition could be managed there. In declining to alter the accused's disposition, the court held that, while medical opinion might change, it could not retrospectively alter orders on the basis of changes in the practice of psychiatric assessment (i.e., the original disposition was sound on the basis of knowledge and prison services, and no miscarriage of justice occurred warranting intervention).
[148] (2014) SC 84 (UKSC), [2013] UKSC 79.
[149] 529 P 2d 55 (Cal, 1974); on appeal 551 P 2d 334 (Cal, 1976).

Tarasoff, which has been both rejected and extended in later US cases, is to be found not so much in the failure to warn as in the failure to take preventive action which was available by way of the therapist's unique power to control the patient that he held. In fact, there is evidence of increasing acceptance in the USA that the psychotherapist is entitled to disclose the facts of a 'dangerous patient' if 'disclosure to the authorities is the only means of averting the threatened harm'.[150]

13.66 Considerable strains could be forced on a national health system if it had to bear the costs of harm caused by mentally disordered persons who have not been compulsorily detained; it is, therefore, interesting to consider how the UK courts have and will react in similar circumstances. There have been a number of cases concerning the comparable responsibility of the police which provide pointers; the most important of these, insofar as it has gone to the ECtHR, is *Osman v Ferguson*.[151] Here, a known paedophile 'stalker' admitted that he might well do violence. The police took no action and he later injured a child and killed one of its parents. An action in negligence was dismissed, mainly on the ground that it would not be just, fair, or reasonable to hold that the general duty laid on the police to suppress crime includes liability to unpredictable victims of crime.

13.67 The issue arose in a medical context in *Palmer v Tees Health Authority*,[152] in which damages were sought by the mother of a child who had been abducted and murdered by a psychiatric outpatient who was, at the time, under the defendant's care. The court was reluctant to recognise the clinician's duty of care on the basis that the necessary relationship of proximity between plaintiff and defendant had not been established. Not only was the identity of the potential victim unknown to the defendant, thus ruling out proximity—and, as Stuart-Smith LJ put it in the Court of Appeal, the possibility of issuing a warning—but it was also suggested that to impose liability could lead to the practice of defensive medicine which could divert the attention of health authorities away from their primary function. In fact, it is fast becoming clear that liability for damage occasioned to another's person is the exception, not the rule, where there is a third agency responsible for the immediate cause of the damage.[153]

13.68 *Palmer,* however, does not tell us what would happen in the event of a prospective victim being identifiable. For this, we can find some, albeit rather indirect, evidence from *Clunis v Camden and Islington Health Authority*.[154] In this case, the plaintiff, a psychiatric patient suffering from a schizo-affective disorder, had been discharged into community care but had missed four appointments made for him by the doctor who was responsible for his care. He attacked and killed an innocent stranger and was convicted of manslaughter on the ground of diminished responsibility. He then sued the health authority responsible

[150] *United States v Chase* 301 F 3d 11019 (9th Circ, 2002). And see R Johnson, G Persad, and D Sisti, 'The Tarasoff Rule: The Implications of Interstate Variation and Gaps in Professional Training' (2014) 42 J Am Acad Psychiatry Law 469.

[151] [1993] 4 All ER 344 (CA); *Osman v UK* (1998) 29 EHRR 245. The ECtHR confirmed the domestic court's findings save as to freedom of access to the courts, which it felt had been compromised. See now *Barrett v Enfield London Borough Council* [2001] 2 AC 550 (HL).

[152] (1998) 45 BMLR 88 (QB); [1999] Lloyd's Rep Med 151 (CA).

[153] Paraphrasing Laws LJ in *K v Secretary of State for the Home Office* [2002] EWCA Civ 775—a very similar case to that of *Palmer.* More recently, a court refused to find a duty of care on the part of a health authority towards a bus driver for harm suffered when a detained patient on an unsupervised hospital visit outside the authority's area committed suicide under the bus: *Buck v Norfolk and Waveney Mental Health NHS Foundation Trust* [2012] Med LR 266. It was held that the victim was not proximate and had not been identifiable by the authority.

[154] [1998] QB 978; [1998] 3 All ER 180.

for his care,[155] arguing that the authority's negligent failure to assess his mental state had resulted in his suffering losses resulting from conviction and imprisonment. The Court of Appeal upheld the authority's argument that to impose liability in this case would be to allow the plaintiff to profit from his own illegal act, which is contrary to the *ex turpi causa* rule preventing a wrongdoer from claiming damages in such circumstances. More importantly, it was held that, in this instance, the psychiatrist who certified that Clunis was fit for discharge was not liable to him by way of a duty of care. The arguments were, however, largely based on the distribution of liability for after-care imposed on the health authority and the local social services authority under s 117 of the 1983 Act;[156] significantly, it was stated that the question of a common law duty persisting in such conditions was undecided—and it remains open for consideration in appropriate cases.[157]

13.69　These actions were taken in negligence and, following the success of Ms Akenzua,[158] who won a very similar case against the police but, on this occasion, taken as one of misfeasance in public office, we have debated the possibility of success were an action to be raised against a National Health Service Trust on these grounds;[159] we conclude, however, that the chances would be negligible. Indeed, the evidence from various sources strongly suggests that public policy considerations, of themselves, would inhibit a *Tarasoff*-like decision in the UK. It is probable that a duty of care to a third party would only be established if there was some pre-existing relationship between the health care professional and the victim. This has been confirmed yet again and most recently in Scotland by the Court of Session in *Thomson v Scottish Ministers*,[160] in which it was held that the Scottish prison service did not owe a duty of care to the public for prisoner action when on home leave, even when the risk was grave. There would have to be some particular risk to a party bringing an action that they did not share with other members of the general public.

CONCLUSION

13.70　As should be clear from the above, this is a dynamic area of law that remains, for many, unsatisfactory.[161] Indeed, it is currently in a state of profound flux, with accessibility of quality services and the appropriate balance between individual and public interests being central concerns. Thus, the Law Commission has undertaken an examination of

---

[155]　No person is liable in either the civil or criminal courts for actions done in pursuance of the Act unless it was done in bad faith or without reasonable care: Mental Health Act 1983, s 139(1). This limitation does not, however, apply to health authorities or National Health Service Trusts (s 139(4)). For the purposes of this section, application for judicial review does not constitute 'civil proceedings' and remains open in respect of individuals: *Ex p Waldron* [1986] QB 824, sub nom *R v Hallstrom, ex p W* [1985] 3 All ER 775 (CA). There is no requirement for the High Court to establish substantial grounds for the contention before granting leave to appeal: *Winch v Jones, Winch v Hayward* [1986] QB 296; [1985] 3 All ER 97 (CA).

[156]　The local authority can only be expected to use its 'best endeavours' to meet the conditions imposed: *R (otao W) v Doncaster Metropolitan Borough Council* [2004] LGR 743; (2004) *The Times*, 13 May.

[157]　For the extent of the duties under s 117, see *R (otao Stennett) v Manchester City Council* [2002] AC 1127; [2002] 3 WLR 584. A patient for whom after-care is essential should not be discharged unless the provision of such care is assured: *R (otao H) v Ashworth Hospital Authority* [2003] 1 WLR 127; (2003) 70 BMLR 40.

[158]　*Akenzua and Coy v Secretary of State for the Home Department* [2003] 1 All ER 35.

[159]　J K Mason and G Laurie, 'Misfeasance in public office: An emerging medical law tort?' (2003) 11 Med L Rev 194.

[160]　[2011] CSOH 90; 2012 SCLR 19.

[161]　See CQC, n 4, which at 9–12, notes recurring examples of poor information provision, poor restriction practices, incomplete reporting, and poor management.

how deprivation of liberty should be managed. It is considering inter alia whether it is right to excuse individuals of their behaviour due to mental disorders, and, if so, which disorders should be included, and it is mooting a new defence of 'not criminally responsible by reason of recognized medical condition'.[162] A report and draft Bill is expected in 2017. More imminently, as a follow-on from the McManus Review,[163] the Mental Health (Scotland) Act 2015 was just passed, though not yet given Royal Assent. It is intended to facilitate people with mental disorders to more easily and quickly access treatment by encouraging the greater integration of services and sharing of information between relevant actors. It also introduces a notification scheme for victims of mentally disordered offenders, and it creates procedures whereby they can make representations before mental health tribunals and criminal courts.

---

[162] Law Commission, *Criminal Liability: Insanity and Automatism—A Discussion Paper* (2013).
[163] J McManus et al., *Limited Review of the Mental Health (Care and Treatment) (Scotland) Act 2003: Report* (2009).

14

THE BODY AS PROPERTY

INTRODUCTION

14.01 We have thus far encountered many examples of moral, ethical, and legal recognition of the relationship between the concept of 'self' and the human body. The central position in medical law of the principle of autonomy offers the individual patient the ultimate right to control his or her body and what is done with or to it. That control is most often exercised through the concept of consent or refusal of consent to treatment. Thus, we have seen (Chapter 4) that disrespect of a refusal to surgery can result in actions in negligence or assault, and the use and storage of gametes is strictly controlled according to the written consent of the donor (Chapter 8). That said, we do not have an absolute right, either ethically or legally, to do whatever we want with our bodies—we have noted how the Human Tissue Act 2004 prohibits 'trafficking' in human material,[1] and the House of Lords has been categorical that ritual physical abuse of the body for sexual pleasure remains criminal even when undertaken with the full and informed consent of the parties.[2] The question, therefore, arises as to what limits are set on the right to control our bodies or parts thereof. In recent years, this debate has centred on the status of the body as property. This chapter will consider three aspects of that debate: (1) property in material taken from living persons; (2) property in material taken from cadavers; and (3) intellectual property in human material.[3]

THE PROPERTY DEBATE BROADLY UNDERSTOOD

14.02 Intuitively, one might naturally speak of 'my body', and infer that, because it is 'my' body, I can determine what is done to it or its parts. For most people, this feeling is bound up with the proprietary notion that, because my body is my own, I 'own' my body. Historically, however, there has been precious little support for this in either legal or ethical terms.[4] No

---

[1] Human Tissue Act 2004, s 32. The Human Tissue (Scotland) Act 2006, s 20 prohibits commercial dealing in 'any part of the human body...'.

[2] *R v Brown* [1994] 1 AC 212; [1993] 2 All ER 75.

[3] Consider the work of TISS:EU, which examined new approaches to law and ethics in property concerning, inter alia, the human genome and human tissue: http://www.tisseu.uni-hannover.de/.

[4] Indeed, the common law has long been opaque as to the actual status of body parts from a property perspective. Thus, while there is jurisprudence which suggests that regenerative body material such as hair (*R v Herbert* (1961) 25 JCL 163), blood (*R v Rothery* [1976] RTR 550), and urine (*R v Welsh* [1974] RTR 478), can be the subject of property, the House of Lords has ruled that a person does not even legally possess, let alone own, his body or an un-severed part thereof, at least for criminal purposes (*R v Bentham* [2005] UKHL 18; [2005] 1 WLR 1057). In each of the former criminal cases, the accused was convicted of theft for removing the 'property' of another without permission.

single ethical principle or imperative exists on which one can ground a property right in oneself.[5] And, it is a 'spectacular non sequitur' to deduce that, because no one can own my body, I necessarily own it myself.[6] This is in part because the very idea of property is a legal one; a construct which allows us to order our society according to a worldview which facilitates the achievement of certain social goals, such as the encouragement of commerce and the sanctioning of commodification.[7] The role of ethics lies not in grounding a property right, but in determining whether it is appropriate to commodify the human body, which has a particular moral status deserving of respect (see Chapter 1). For many, a commodity approach would lead to buying and selling body parts, and this is viewed as repugnant in that it shows a fundamental disrespect for the status of the human body.[8]

14.03   Trade in bodies, parts and products gives rise to the spectre of exploitation, which is ethically questionable because it has the potential to harm.[9] The counter to this is that while no one would sanction forced participation in the trade of human material, it is unduly paternalistic to eschew the consent of individuals who would willingly sell their tissues,[10] and such was just one of the bases on which the Human Organ Transplants Act 1989 was criticised.[11] Its prohibitory terms, however, were largely reproduced in the Human Tissue Act 2004, which is concerned not just with 'organs', but with 'controlled material', which is defined as: 'any material which (a) consists of or includes human cells, (b) is, or is intended to be removed, from the human body…, excepting (a) gametes, (b) embryos, or (c) material which is the subject of a property right because of the application of human skill'.[12] Thus the new definition is considerably wider—extending the application of the no-trade rule—although, ironically, it simultaneously recognises not only that property rights *can* accrue in human material but also that these can endure. We address the acquisition of such rights in due course, but for now question the mixed messages that

---

[5] However, for argument to this effect, see D Beyleveld and R Brownsword, *Human Dignity in Bioethics and Biolaw* (2001) ch 8, and R Hardcastle, *Law and the Human Body: Property Rights, Ownership and Control* (2007). Compare D Dickenson, *Property in the Body: Feminist Perspectives* (2007).

[6] J Harris, 'Who owns my body?' (1996) 16 OJLS 55 at 71.

[7] For a classic account, see A Honoré, 'Ownership' in A Guest (ed), *Oxford Essays in Jurisprudence* (1961) ch 5. More recently, see M Quigley, 'Property and the body: Applying Honoré' (2007) 33 J Med Ethics 631, and J Wall, 'The legal status of body parts: a framework' (2011) 31(4) Ox J Legal Studies 783.

[8] See L Skene, 'Arguments against people legally "owning" their own bodies, body parts and tissue' (2002) 2 MacQuarie LJ 165, and S Munzer, 'An uneasy case against property rights in body parts' (1994) 11 Soc Philosoph Pol 259. A good account of the relative arguments is provided by the Nuffield Council on Bioethics, *Human Bodies: Donation for Medicine and Research* (2011), which also includes examples of current commercialisation practices with respect to human material.

[9] Thus, the Medical Research Council (MRC) stated that: 'The human body and its parts shall not, as such, give rise to financial gain. Researchers may not sell for a profit samples of human biological material that they have collected as part of MRC-funded research, and research participants should never be offered any financial inducement to donate samples.' MRC, *Human Tissue and Biological Samples for Use in Research: Operational and Ethical Guidelines* (2005), Part 2. And see Article 21 of the Council of Europe Convention on Human Rights and Biomedicine (1997).

[10] M Friedlaender, 'The right to sell or buy a kidney: Are we failing our patients?' (2002) 359 Lancet 971; J Savulescu, 'Is the sale of body parts wrong?' (2003) 29 J Med Ethics 138; S Harmon, 'A Penny For Your Thoughts, A Pound For Your Flesh: Implications of Recognizing Property in Human Body Parts' (2006) 7 Med Law Int 329. For an argument that failure to recognise property can lead to exploitation, see R Rao, 'Genes and spleens: Property, contract or privacy rights in the human body?' (2007) 35 J Law, Med and Ethics 371.

[11] J Radcliffe-Richards et al., 'The case of allowing kidney sales' (1998) 351 Lancet 1950.

[12] Human Tissue Act 2004, s 32(8) and (9). The 1989 Act, s 7(2) defined 'organ' as 'any part of the human body consisting of a structured arrangement of tissues which, if wholly removed, cannot be replicated by the body'.

have been sent. The 2004 Act is the first piece of legislation to expressly recognise the potential existence of property rights in human material, although it does so merely by repeating the pre-existing common law position,[13] which we have already noted has been unclear and unsatisfactory.[14] The 1989 Act said nothing about property in organs as such, but criminalised trade in them, and this is effectively repeated in the 2004 Act; moreover, the Human Fertilisation and Embryology Act 1990, as amended, relies on the expressed written wishes of donors in controlling the use and storage of gametes—which falls short of acknowledging a property right.[15] The distinction between persons and things remain strong.[16]

14.04   The issue at the heart of this debate, of course, is that of control.[17] Property, through the bundle of rights that it confers, is a powerful control device which also carries a particular message—one of the potential for commerce and trade. To recognise a 'quasi-property' claim is to support a normatively strong connection to that item and, accordingly, to establish a strong, justiciable legal interest; by the same token, 'full' property rights will only be recognised where there is little or no prospect of exploitation or other harm, which can include the 'harm' of disrespect for the dignity of the human organism. Ultimately, then, there is a widespread ambivalence about property in the body and its parts and products.

14.05   In fact, many instruments, including the Biomedicine Convention, draw a distinction between property in the body and its parts *as such* and 'inventions' using human material (which may be subject to intellectual property rights: para 14.45 et seq).[18] Similarly, although the 2004 Act imposes a prohibition on commercial dealings in human material for transplantation,[19] it recognises property in materials in some circumstances; accordingly, it excepts from the commercial ban 'material which is the subject of property because of an application of human skill'.[20] Indeed, the 2004 Act affords a power to the Human Tissue Authority (HTA) to authorise financial returns beyond mere expenses for the handling of, or trade in, human tissues. Thus, s 32(6) allows licence terms for the transporting, removing, preparing, preserving, and storing of controlled material to include payments on a commercial basis.

14.06   The reality is that trading in bodily materials, products, or by-products inside and outside the National Health Service (NHS) is an essential part of the Service.[21] In fact, tissue

---

[13]   Human Tissue Act 2004, s 32(9).

[14]   And it is regrettable that the government did not take the opportunity to clarify the law after the extensive public consultation exercise that preceded the 2004 Act.

[15]   For discussion see J Berg, 'You say person, I say property: Does it really matter what we call an embryo?' (2004) 4 Amer J Bioethics 18; J Berg, 'Owning persons: The application of property theory to embryos and fetuses' (2005) 40 Wake Forest Law Rev 159.

[16]   For a philosophical challenge to this position, see M Quigley, 'Property in Human Biomaterials—Separating Persons and Things?' (2012) 32 Ox J Legal Studies 659–683.

[17]   These decisions should be contrasted with the French case of *Parpalaix v CECOS* JCP 1984.II.20321 in which the court ordered the return of frozen sperm to the wife of the depositor on the basis of an agreement which had been made between him and the sperm bank and his original intent. It refused, however, to go so far as to recognise any property interest in the sperm. In subsequent cases the French court struggled to find a valid basis in law for dealing with embryos and sperm, vacillating between the law of obligations, on the one hand, and the principle of 'the established family', on the other: see (1996) *La Semaine Juridique* Ed G, No 27, 22666.

[18]   See C Lenk et al. (eds), *Human Tissue Research: A European Perspective on the Ethical and Legal Challenges* (2011)

[19]   Human Tissue Act 2004, s 32.   [20]   Human Tissue Act 2004, s 32(9)(c).

[21]   Acknowledged by the Nuffield Council, n 8.

banks have proliferated in recent years in both the public and private sectors (e.g., UK Stem Cell Bank,[22] Virgin Health Bank,[23] European Bank for induced pluripotent Stem Cells[24]). Mixed messages abound, however, about the role of property and commercialisation in these endeavours. The House of Lords Select Committee on Stem Cell Research recommended establishing a UK-wide bank to facilitate sharing and help address ethical sensitivities surrounding embryonic stem cell research, but stated that 'commercial interests will have a key role to play in developing therapies and in bringing effective treatments to patients as quickly as possible, and they should be encouraged'.[25]

14.07 There is also the all-important principle of respect for autonomy and freedom of choice. Undue regulatory interference cannot be justified. So it was that the European Group on Ethics (EGE) concluded that: 'The legitimacy of commercial cord blood banks for autologous use should be questioned as they sell a service, which has presently, no real use regarding therapeutic options…the majority of the Group considers that the activities of these banks should be discouraged but that a strict ban would represent an undue restriction on the freedom of enterprise and the freedom of choice of individuals/couples.'[26] It recommended that these banks should operate under strict conditions, being the EU Cells Directive 2004.[27] In contemplation of commercial practices, the EGE said: 'When the donated cells may become part of a patent application, donors should be informed of the possibility of patenting and they are entitled to refuse such use.'[28] But what of claims of entitlement by donors? On this point the EGE reiterated its view that 'Apart from justified compensation, donors ought not to get a reward which could infringe the principle of non-commercialisation of the human body'.[29]

14.08 What is important to remember as this debate rumbles on is that there is arguably nothing inherently valuable in an appeal to property itself save when such an appeal can furnish rights or solutions to disputes which escape other legal concepts. Other devices, such as consent or contract, can be used instead of property to establish rights and resolve conflicts. Indeed, Sperling has concluded that:

> Whatever the case may be,…proprietary interest does not provide any necessary procedural advantage to claimants in the post-mortem context, and cases that deal with interference with dead bodies can be perfectly well decided and remedied without the fictional and unnecessary appeal to the right to property in the body of the deceased.[30]

---

[22] At: http://www.ukstemcellbank.org.uk/.   [23] At: http://www.virginhealthbank.com/.
[24] At: http://www.ebisc.org/.
[25] House of Lords Select Committee on Stem Cell Research, *Report of the House of Lords Select Committee on Stem Cell Research*, Session 2001–2, at 6.10.
[26] EGE, *Opinion No 19: Opinion on the Ethical Aspects of Umbilical Cord Blood Banking* (2004), paras 2.1–2.2.
[27] Directive 2004/23/EC on setting standards of quality and safety for the Donation, Procurement, Testing, Processing, Preservation, Storage and Distribution of Human Tissue and Cells (OJ L102 7.4.2004, pp 48–58). Communication from the Commission of 6 January 2010 to the Council, the European Parliament, the European Economic and Social Committee and the Committee of the Regions on the application of Directive 2004/23/EC on setting standards of quality and safety for the donation, procurement, testing, processing, preservation, storage and distribution of human tissues and cells COM(2009) 708 final indicated that implementation of the Directive was satisfactory.
[28] EGE, *Report of the European Group on Ethics on the Ethical Aspects of Human Tissue Engineered Products* (2004), at 3.
[29] Ibid, at 5.
[30] N 36, p 142. D Sperling, *Posthumous Interests: Legal and Ethical Perspectives* (2008), at 142.

Whether this is also true of property claims from living individuals remains to be seen.[31] Thus, it is with just such a critical eye that we should consider the gamut of legal solutions that are and have been employed in the medico-legal sphere.

PROPERTY IN MATERIAL
FROM LIVING HUMANS

THE EVOLUTION OF PROPERTY MODELS

14.09   To fully appreciate the ambiguity towards property and variety of responses to control of materials and products from living humans, one must appreciate the distinction between commercialisation and exploitation. It is widely assumed that the interposition of commercial interests between the source of valuable material and its user is unacceptable because it leads necessarily to exploitation.[32] Thus, our main concern about allowing both property and a free(r) trade in human material might be that it could lead to (greater) exploitation of (weaker) individuals. This is undoubtedly true, but the same might be said of those who donate materials for research or transplantation—emotional coercion can be as great or greater than economic coercion; exploitation and commerce do not necessarily go hand-in-hand. Undue coercion should always be guarded against irrespective of the context or motivation. Similarly, as we discuss in the context of surrogacy (Chapter 8), it is not necessarily exploitative *in se* to offer financial incentives or rewards to individuals to use their bodies in certain ways. As Andrews has said in the context of that debate, it may be more devaluing to persons not to recognise their worth in monetary terms for the contributions they can make to society from the use of their bodies than it is to protect them from potential predators—provided, always, that the value that they represent is not entirely reducible to those terms.[33] That something is potentially exploitative does not mean that it must always be so.

14.10   As such, some jurisdictions do grant direct recognition of property rights in human material.[34] For example, the German *Bundesgerichtshof* has ruled that excised body parts that are not intended for another (such as transplant organs), and are not for return to the individual (such as stored sperm), are subject to the normal rules of personal property.[35] Often, however, the courts appeal to property rights as a means to other legal ends. For example, in *Roche* v *Douglas*,[36] an Australian case, it was held that human tissue taken from a deceased person was 'property' for the purposes of the court rules; this allowed the

---

[31] For an argument that appeals to dignity can do the necessary work (and far better) see C Foster, 'Dignity and the use of body parts' (2012) J Med Ethics; 0:1–4. doi: 10.1136/medethics-2012-100763.

[32] For discussion see P Halewood, 'On commodification and self-ownership' (2008) 20 Yale J of Law and Humanities 131.

[33] L B Andrews, 'Beyond doctrinal boundaries: A legal framework for surrogate motherhood' (1995) 81 Virginia Law Rev 2343.

[34] For a comparative and philosophical account see Sperling, n 30.

[35] Bundesgerichtshof, 9 November 1993, BGHZ, 124, 52. See also C Lenk and K Beier, 'Is the commercialisation of human tissue and body material forbidden in the countries of the European Union?' (2012) 38 J Med Ethics 342.

[36] [2000] WAR 331 (SC). For the Australian position, see S Hilmer, 'Property in the human body: A common law approach' (2005) 2(5) J Intl Biotech Law 185, and S Brown and S-N Then, 'Commercialisation of regenerative human tissue: Regulation and reform in Australia and England, Wales and Northern Ireland' (2007) 14 J Law & Med 339.

court to claim dominion over the sample in order to authorise testing to settle a paternity dispute. Similarly, in *Bazley* v *Wesley Monash IVF Pty Ltd*,[37] and *Re Edwards*,[38] the courts held that both widows were entitled to a right to possession of the sperm of their deceased husbands by virtue of the 'work done' on extracting and storing the semen and turning it into property—thereby differentiating it from the body or a corpse per se.[39]

14.11 Older US authority set the precedent for these kind of succession cases. For example, in *Hecht* v *Kane*,[40] the Californian Court of Appeal held that a deceased man who had previously deposited sperm for the use of his partner had an interest 'in the nature of ownership' of the samples such as to render them 'property' within the meaning of the Probate Code, and, accordingly, disposable property on his death.[41] In *Davis* v *Davis*,[42] the Tennessee Supreme Court held that the embryo occupied an 'interim category' as neither 'person' nor 'property', yet which entitled it to a special respect. Although the parties were denied 'a true property interest', they retained an interest—'in the nature of ownership'—in relation to the use and disposal of their pre-embryos.[43] More recently, this position was echoed and extended by the Supreme Court of British Columbia in *JCM* v *ANA*,[44] a dispute between living parties over the disposal of sperm 'straws' obtained from a US sperm bank. On dissolution of the litigants' marriage the question arose as to the destiny of the sperm, one party wishing to obtain and use it, the other wishing its destruction. Drawing heavily from English precedent, infra, the court held that the law must keep pace with medical science and that, as a matter of fact and practice, the sperm had long since been treated as an artefact of property. As such, it belonged to both parties equally with the pragmatic solution that each should receive half to dispose of as they saw fit—or a 7/6 split of the straws in favour of the woman if there were practical difficulties. It is worth noting that the use of the sperm did not create a genetic relationship of paternity since these were anonymised donor samples. The ruling stood despite a prohibition in the Canadian Assisted Human Reproduction Act that reads: 'No person shall purchase, offer to purchase or advertise for the purchase of sperm or ova from a donor or a person acting on behalf of a donor.'[45]

14.12 Statutory attempts or proposals to embody property rights in human material have been equally equivocal. A property right in genetic samples was granted to citizens of Oregon in 1995, but after several years of intensive lobbying by the pharmaceutical industry and research institutes, a 2001 reform Bill removed this right and replaced it with more stringent privacy protection.[46] The claim was that Oregon would then have the most

---

[37] [2010] QSC 118.   [38] [2011] NSWSC 478.

[39] L Skene, 'Proprietary interests in human bodily material: *Yearworth*, recent Australian cases on stored semen and their implications' (2012) 20(2) Med L Rev 227.

[40] 16 Cal App 4th 836 (1993).

[41] On the issues from an ethical perspective, see L Cannold, 'Who owns a dead man's sperm?' (2004) 30 J Med Ethics 386.

[42] 842 SW 2d 588 (1992).

[43] Similar findings can also be found in the British Isles where, in *In the Matter of X* [2002] JRC 202, the Jersey Royal Court relied on the 'interest in the nature of ownership' on the part of a minor in respect of her aborted foetus as the reason to respect her refusal to release foetal tissue to the police which was sought in the pursuit of a prosecution for under-age intercourse against the minor's sexual partner. In the final analysis the Jersey Court of Appeal overrode the refusal in the interests of justice: [2003] JCA 050. For commentary, see, A Grubb, 'Access to fetal material: Property rights and PACE' (2003) 11 Med L Rev 142.

[44] [2012] BCSC 584.

[45] Section 7(1). The court's reasoning on this point is thin and seems to amount to no more than a reiteration of the point that the sperm had de facto been serially treated as property on the facts of the case: *JCM*, para 70.

[46] Senate Bill 114 was before the 71st Oregon Legislative Assembly (8 January–7 July 2001).

far-reaching privacy legislation of its kind in the USA to protect citizens' interests, but it is doubtful if the Oregon experiment was given sufficient time for the promise and the pitfalls of a property paradigm to be addressed and explored. Similar antipathy to property rights is found elsewhere. The Australian Law Reform Commission (ALRC) undertook a consultation on the use of human genetic material, part of which considered whether individuals should have a form of property right in their own genetic material. The ALRC pointed out that, 'The recognition or creation of donor property rights might allow donors to negotiate with researchers for the use of their genetic samples and contract to share in any resulting commercial benefits'.[47] This consultation was partly prompted by the Genetic Privacy and Anti-discrimination Bill 1998, which appeared before the Australian Parliament but was defeated. Although the Australian Bill did not go as far as to recognise a property right in samples, it did require individuals' authorisation either to waive or to receive economic benefits deriving from their samples.[48]

14.13 Of course, the matter has also been grappled with in the UK, where an important groundwork for the issues is the 1995 human tissue report of the Nuffield Council on Bioethics (NCB).[49] While this has been superseded by legal developments in many respects, it remains valuable for its treatment of the cultural and philosophical considerations, with many of the NCB's conclusions remaining as valid today as they were in 1995—for example, the medical institutional expectation is that any tissue given or taken from individuals is received free of all claims.[50] There is also some sociological evidence supporting a similar belief on the part of some sectors of the public.[51] Equally, however, there is evidence that the prospect of profit from research involving donated human material is not well met in some quarters and that research participants expect there to be some 'profit pay-off' even if this does not involve any personal return.[52]

14.14 In short, attitudes and expectations are diverse and changing, and the existence of diversity raises the spectre of conflict. The NCB recommended that any disputed claim over material should be determined with regard to the nature of the consent given to the initial procedure for removal. It was the NCB's view that it should be implied in any consent to medical treatment which involves the removal of tissue that the tissue has been abandoned by the person from whom it was removed.[53] It was recommended that tissue removed from an individual who is unable to give valid consent should not be the subject of any claim, either by the incapax or by his or her representatives.[54] A similar perspective informed the NCB's report on human bodies, where the property paradigm was not entirely eschewed but a distinction was drawn between property rights as a vehicle to recognise more deep-rooted interests in recognition and control, and property claims that are motivated by income rights.[55] The latter are rejected for their overall potential to lead to exploitation.

---

[47] ALRC, *Protection of Human Genetic Information* (Issues Paper 26, 2001) para 7.47.

[48] See Senate Legal and Constitutional Legislation Committee, *Provisions of the Genetic Privacy and Non-discrimination Bill 1998* (1999). There was also a right that records and samples be returned or destroyed.

[49] Nuffield Council on Bioethics, *Human Tissue: Ethical and Legal Issues* (1995).

[50] For an argument that recognition of property claims might encourage research participation see D Gitter, 'Ownership of human tissue: A proposal for federal recognition of human research participants' property rights in their biological material' (2004) 61 Wash & Lee L Rev 257.

[51] M Dixon-Woods et al., 'Tissue samples as "gifts" for research: A qualitative study of families and professionals' (2008) 9(2) Med L Intl 131.

[52] G Haddow, G Laurie, S Cunningham-Burley, and K G Hunter, 'Tackling community concerns about commercialisation and genetic research: A modest interdisciplinary proposal' (2007) 64 Soc Sci & Med 272.

[53] N 49, ch 9, in particular para 9.14.   [54] N 49, paras 9.15–9.17.

[55] NCB, n 8, chs 5 and 7 and especially para 7.20.

14.15 The Human Genetics Commission did not address the prospect of a property model directly before its demise in 2012; it preferred instead to fall back on the familiar consent approach.[56] Even so, one of its more Draconian recommendations did find its way into law. Section 45 of the Human Tissue Act 2004 creates an offence of non-consensual analysis of DNA.[57] A person commits an offence if he has bodily material *intending* that it be analysed without consent and that the results will be used other than for an 'excepted purpose'. Such purposes include medical diagnosis or treatment, discharging the functions of a coroner or procurator fiscal, and prevention or detection of crime.[58] Research purposes can amount to 'excepted purposes' on an order of the Secretary of State. Existing holdings of material can be used lawfully for a range of health-related purposes, including clinical audit, public health monitoring, and research. The penalty extends to up to three years in prison, a fine, or both.

POLICY CONSIDERATIONS IN THE TISSUE TRADE

14.16 Ultimately, a market in materials exists and property rights *are* generated; but in many cases property rights flow to parties other than the persons from whom the material has been taken. Why should this be so? The NCB's 1995 report was based, in the main, on the premise that people see no value in their excised body parts. This premise has long dominated, yet it has always been questionable, and is now more frequently questioned.[59] 'Value' exists in a variety of forms. Consider the emotional value which we attach to foetal tissue and the controversy which has surrounded proposed research and therapies using such tissue (Chapter 20). The advent of the biotechnological age has meant that there can be considerable economic value which accrues to biotechnological products produced using human material. To suggest that patients should be deemed to abandon their tissues, is to ignore the potential values which they may well and rightly hold in retaining control over such material. A system of consents does not permit that control to be exercised as fully as might be desirable. This is not to ignore, however, the consequentialist concerns which could flow from granting individualistic rights of property in material when the public benefit of that material is derived from its collective and aggregate value. On the other hand, there are high-profile cases across many jurisdictions which suggest that the denial of property claims can leave claimants without adequate recourse, and that law and policymakers should think again about the *no property* rule.

14.17 The case which most clearly reveals the skewed attitude of the judiciary towards these matters is *Moore* v *Regents of the University of California*.[60] Although now dated this judgment remains one of the most clearly illustrative of the issues that can arise. Moore suffered from hairy cell leukaemia and his spleen was removed at the Medical School of UCLA. His doctor, Golde, discovered that cells from the spleen had unusual and potentially beneficial properties and developed an immortal cell-line from them without his patient's knowledge or consent. Moreover, Dr Golde sought and obtained a patent over the cell-line which he subsequently sold to a drug company for US$15m—and it has been reported that the drugs and therapies which were developed from the patented product

---

[56] Human Genetics Commission, *Inside Information* (2002).
[57] This is the only provision of the legislation that also extends to Scotland.
[58] Human Tissue Act 2004, s 45 and Sch 4.
[59] For an account of the NCB's 'evolution' in thinking, see M Quigley, 'From Human Tissue to Human Bodies: donation, interventions and justified distinctions?' (2012) 7 Clin Ethics 73.
[60] 793 P 2d 479 (Cal, 1990). See also, *Brotherton* v *Cleveland* 923 F 2d 661 (6th Cir, 1991).

are now worth in excess of US$3bn.[61] Moore brought an action against the researchers, the university, and the drug company when he discovered the truth. He filed 13 causes of action in total, but those concerning property and consent are of most direct interest; he alleged *conversion*—that, as the 'owner' of the cells, his property right had been compromised by the work carried out on the cells by the defendants—and he alleged breach of fiduciary duty and lack of informed consent because he had never been told of the potential use of his cells and, correspondingly, he had never given his full and informed agreement to the initial operation.

14.18   The Californian Supreme Court upheld these two last claims but rejected the argument in conversion. The court opined that it was inappropriate to recognise property in the body, first, because no precedent could be found on which to ground such a claim and, second, because to recognise individual property rights in body parts would be to hinder medical research 'by restricting access to the necessary raw materials'—a pure utilitarian consideration. Moreover, the court was concerned that a contrary decision would '[threaten] to destroy the economic incentive to conduct important medical research' because, 'If the use of cells in research is a conversion, then with every cell sample a researcher purchases a ticket in a litigation lottery'.[62] The irony of this decision is pointed out in the dissent of Broussard J:

> the majority's analysis cannot rest on the broad proposition that a removed part is not property, but...on the proposition that a *patient* retains no ownership interest in a body part once the body part has been removed. [Emphasis added.]

Put another way, while persons are denied recognition of a property interest in excised parts of our bodies, third parties may not only gain such an interest but can go on to protect it using forms of property law such as the law of patents.

14.19   This example demonstrates precisely the type of value which individuals could retain in their excised parts. The properties of the patient's cells are a *sine qua non* of the ultimate invention. And, while no one would deny that much time and money would need to be expended in turning the natural material into a patentable product, is the view of the Supreme Court in *Moore* not something of an over-reaction to the *possible* consequences of applying property law to the human body? It is entirely reasonable to hold that some financial reward should be given to the source of the valuable sample while, at the same time, accepting that the majority of the spoils should return to those who have done the work in creating a patentable invention. It is *not* reasonable to exclude completely from the equation the one person who can make everything possible.

14.20   Policy is not always on the side of the researchers, as another US dispute demonstrated.[63] In *Greenberg et al. v Miami Children's Hospital Research Institute Inc*,[64] an action was brought by parents of children affected by a rare, fatal, and incurable genetic disorder called Canavan disease against researchers who developed and patented a test for the

[61] B Merz, 'Biotechnology: Spleen-rights' *The Economist*, 11 August 1990, p 30.
[62] For comment, see B Hoffmaster, 'Between the sacred and the profane: Bodies, property, and patents in the *Moore* case' (1992) 7 Intellect Prop J 115, and E Seeney, '*Moore* 10 years later—Still trying to fill the gap: Creating a personal property right in genetic material' (1998) 32 New Engl L Rev 1131.
[63] For an account of the US regulatory position, see R Hakimian and D Korn, 'Ownership and use of tissue specimens for research' (2004) 292 J Amer Med Ass 2500.
[64] *Greenberg et al. v Miami Children's Hospital Research Institute Inc et al.* 264 F Supp 2d 1064 (SD Fla, 2003), settled action; for comment see M Anderlik and M Rothstein, '*Canavan* decision favors researchers over families' (2003) 313 J Law, Med and Ethics 450.

disease using samples donated by the families. The defendants had worked closely with afflicted families, receiving samples and gaining access to registers containing details of other affected groups around the world. However, when the Canavan gene was eventually identified, the researchers sought a patent over it and a related test, and proceeded to restrict access to the latter save through tightly controlled exclusive licences. The plaintiffs objected and, in much the same way as happened in *Moore*, mounted an action on a number of grounds, including lack of informed consent, unjust enrichment, breach of fiduciary duty, and conversion. In this last respect, the plaintiffs claimed a property interest in their samples, the genetic information therein, and information contained in the Canavan register. Paradoxically, here, policy favoured the plaintiffs—the families wanted information about the disease and the test to be freely available, while it was the patent holders who wished to restrict access and so potentially hinder research. The case was eventually abandoned after a preliminary hearing in which the judge rejected the property claim but suggested that the argument in unjust enrichment might succeed. While the precise basis for this is unclear, the outcome reveals the continuing antipathy to property approaches to individual rights.[65]

14.21 This approach was confirmed at the federal level in *Washington University* v *Catalona et al.*,[66] wherein the US District Court was asked to declare on the ownership of samples provided by research participants enrolled in cancer research conducted by Catalona while he was employed by Washington University, Missouri.[67] Dr Catalona had written to all of his participants informing them of his move to Northwestern University, Illinois, his intention to continue his valuable cancer research, and asking that they sign an authorisation for release with respect to their samples held by the university for delivery to him. Around 6,000 participants did so but the university refused to release the samples and sought declaratory relief. As the court put it, 'the sole issue determinative of this permanent injunction; in fact in this lawsuit; is the issue of ownership'.[68] In holding for the university, the court found that exclusive possession and control had come to the university after the provision of samples; that all legal, regulatory, and compliance risks fell on the university; that the university had continually exerted its ownership claims to materials in its repository, notably through the informed consent materials, and in its intellectual property policy; that the participants had freely given consent to donate samples for research at the university; and that Dr Catalona had willingly signed up to the ownership policy of his employers.

14.22 Dr Catalona and the research participants argued, inter alia, that there had been no intent to donate the samples to the university but rather to Dr Catalona; that the participants had retained control through the 'right to discontinue participation' (which is standard in research protocols); and alternatively, that participants made a bailment of property and not a gift at all. Each claim was found to be meritless. The court held that on the evidence the intent was to donate to the university and this was made sufficiently clear in the consent forms, especially the repeated use of the university logo to indicate the body under whose auspices the work would be carried out. Second, the right

[65] For discussion see J Bovenberg, 'Inalienably yours? The new case for an inalienable property right in human biological material: Empowerment of sample donors or a recipe for a tragic anti-commons?' (2004) 1:4 SCRIPT-ed 591.

[66] 437 F Supp 2d 985 (US Dist, 2006).

[67] For comment, see L Andrews, 'Rights of donors: Who owns your body? A patient's perspective on *Washington University* v *Catalona*' (2006) 34 J Law, Med and Ethics 398.

[68] N 67, at 994.

to discontinue participation did not imply a right to continued control; rather, the court suggested that a right to withdraw is nothing more than a right not to provide any more samples. Expert testimony went as far as to suggest that researchers would be operating within the law either if they were to destroy samples after withdrawal, store them indefinitely with no further use, or anonymise samples and continue in their use.[69] The bailment claim failed because it required a continuing expectation of return of property at some time, and the court found no evidence that participants had informed the university of such an expectation, nor was such an expectation reasonable in the circumstances. Furthermore, it was relevant that the medical community has never considered the relationship between research institution and research participant to be one of bailment. The Court of Appeals for the Eight Circuit affirmed the District Court's judgment in all respects,[70] stating: 'If left unregulated and to the whims of research participants, these highly-prized biological materials would become nothing more than chattel going to the highest bidder.'[71]

14.23   What are we to make of such rulings both in principle and in practice? Clearly, certain policy preferences have held sway which are open to serious question and which require a far sounder evidence base.[72] Second, and despite initial impressions, *Catalona* might be viewed as moving the debate forward in some respects. For one thing, it proceeds on the premise of property in the samples themselves and finds evidence of a transfer of ownership, albeit not where the initial 'owners' might have wanted. Washington University won because it could show prima facie evidence of absolute possession and control of the samples, and because the participants could *not* show that they had any expectations other than outright gift. But what if it were otherwise? Has the prospect of conditional gift begun to raise its head?[73] We have argued elsewhere that recognition of a modified form of property rights for individuals in their own (excised) body parts may well be appropriate,[74] and we believe that our suggestions continue to gain ground.[75]

14.24   As a post-script, we should not be distracted from the property debate by the illusion that consent is the sole, or optimal, ethico-legal solution to the dilemmas thrown up by modern medicine, as many official bodies would have us believe.[76] A consent model

---

[69] N 67, at 999.

[70] 490 F 3d 667 (2007); US Supreme Court certiorari was denied, *Catalona* v *Washington University* 128 S Ct 1122, 169 L Ed 2d 949 (2008).

[71] N 70, at 1002. In contrast to this position, we would point once again to the irony borne out by the motives in *Greenberg* and to the mounting social science evidence that research participants do not necessarily see property as a device for selfish gain but rather as a means to engage more fully in the research enterprise, and/or to curb some of its worst commercial excesses.

[72] D Price, 'Exploitation, Akrasia and Goldilocks: How many for flesh for medical uses?' (2013) 21 Med Law Rev 519.

[73] N Kanellopoulou, 'Advocacy groups as research organisations: Novel approaches in research governance' in C Lyall, T Papaioannou, and J Smith (eds), *The Limits of Governance: The Challenges of Policy-making for the New Life Sciences* (2009).

[74] K Mason and G Laurie, 'Consent or property? Dealing with the body and its parts in the shadow of Bristol and Alder Hey' (2001) 64 MLR 711; S Harmon, 'A Penny For Your Thoughts, A Pound For Your Flesh: Implications of Recognizing Property in Human Body Parts' (2006) 7 Med Law Int 329; S Harmon, 'Semantic, Pedantic or Paradigm Shift? Recruitment, Retention and Property in Modern Population Biobanking' (2008) 16 Euro J Health Law 27. Cf, C Harrison, 'Neither *Moore* nor the market: Alternative models for compensating contributors of human tissue' (2002) 28 Am J L and Med 77.

[75] M Quigley, Propertisation and Commercialisation: On controlling the uses of human biomaterials' (2014) 77 Mod Law Rev 677; S Douglas, 'The argument for property rights in body parts: scarcity of resources' (2014) 40 J Med Ethics 23.

[76] NCB, n 49; Human Genetics Commission, n 56, at para. 5.25.

disempowers individuals to the extent that the single 'right' that it gives is a right to refuse. How does this help the person who is willing to participate in research but has qualms about the subsequent use of her samples towards undesirable ends? It does not, for her only option is to not participate.[77] A property right would offer an opportunity for an element of continuing control over samples after surrender and would allow for a legally recognised voice in how they are used.[78] The same is not true once an initial consent has been obtained, for so long as the requisite information is disclosed at the time the sample is provided, the sample source's 'rights' have been exhausted.[79]

THE UK POSITION ON MATERIAL FROM LIVING HUMANS

Property in Reproductive Material

14.25 Let us begin with the beginning of life and its elemental constituents: the gametes. Whereas once the position was that the common laws in the UK were unclear and static, recent developments suggest the opposite. We have considered the statutory provisions which apply to the obtaining, storage, and use of gametes in the UK (Chapter 8), and do not propose to revisit them here. But can common law property claims trump these regulatory provisions, or provide rights not recognised in the legislation?

14.26 In *L v The Human Fertilisation and Embryology Authority, Secretary of State for Health*,[80] the claimant sought a lawful basis to preserve, store, and use her deceased husband's sperm in circumstances where his prior written consent had not been obtained and for use of the sperm abroad if fertility services were not available in the UK. As we have seen (Chapter 8), the lawfulness of this is in serious doubt under the Human Fertilisation and Embryology Act 1990, as amended; the distinguishing feature of *L*, however, was a submission that the common law, which recognises that in certain circumstances property rights can accrue in human materials, could be a lawful basis for the claimant's proposed course of action. Although this was rejected by the court—which distinguished the existing legal authorities from the case as dealing with the position *after* authorised or unauthorised removal—the point was made nonetheless that the common law 'does not stand still'.

14.27 No better illustration of this can be found than the decision in *Yearworth v North Bristol NHS Trust*.[81] Here, the Court of Appeal acknowledged the challenge for the common law as represented by the ever-expanding frontiers of medical science. In this case six men were due to receive aggressive cancer treatment which, they were advised, might damage their fertility; accordingly each man provided sperm samples pre-treatment to the

---

[77] Nor could he seek to impose conditions on his donation as there is no obvious legal right to have those conditions respected, absent a contractual relationship—rare in this context.

[78] I Goold, 'Why does it matter how we regulate the use of human body parts? (2014) 40 J Med Ethics 3; R Nwabueze, 'Body parts in property theory: An integrated framework' (2014) 40 J Med Ethics 33.

[79] For further comments on the limits of consent in the commercialisation context, see G Laurie, 'Patents, patients and consent: Exploring the interface between regulation and innovation regimes' in J Somsen (ed), *Regulating Biotechnology* (2005). This does not take us very far with the question of disposal of the commercially valueless specimen. We suggest that a consent-based action in negligence would be available if, for example, a patient's sensibilities were outraged by his tissues being used for demonstration purposes, but this is by no means certain. Support for this can be found in the guise of *AB v Leeds Teaching Hospital NHS Trust*, discussed at para 14.41. Fortunately, the question is of no more than academic interest in the overwhelming majority of cases.

[80] [2008] EWHC 2149 (Fam); [2008] 2 FLR 1999; (2008) 104 BMLR 200.

[81] [2009] 3 WLR 118; 107 BMLR 47.

hospital's fertility clinic for possible future use. Unfortunately, the storage facility suffered a technical malfunction and the sperm perished. A range of actions was brought, including negligent loss of a chance of becoming a father, psychiatric injury, and, in one case, mental distress. Of interest here is that while the judge at first instance dismissed a claim that there had been damage to the men's 'property', this was accepted by the Court of Appeal.[82] The relevance of the property claim was twofold: (1) if it can be shown that there was damage to or loss of property through breach of a duty of care, an action would lie in negligence; (2) wrongful interference with property per se is actionable in its own right through bailment.

14.28   The Court of Appeal fully acknowledged that the law has remained 'noticeably silent' about property in parts or products of the living human body, postulating that, until recently, medical science did not endow them with any value or significance. This has changed. The court was invited to leave the matter to Parliament and to avoid piecemeal development, but it declined to do so. Rather, it began its analysis by rejecting the argument that the Human Fertilisation and Embryology Act 1990, as amended, eliminates common law rights of ownership. The court's view was that the Act must be confined to its original purposes (see Chapter 8), which are to regulate the storage and use of reproductive material outside the human body and in the hands of third parties who are subject to rigorous licensing requirements. No such licences apply to individuals with respect to their own gametes or embryos produced without artificial assistance; furthermore, the legislation requires 'informed consent' from persons with respect to their reproductive materials and a large part of this is about respecting the individual's wishes about disposition.[83] The pivotal paragraph in the ruling merits repetition in full:

> In this jurisdiction developments in medical science now require a re-analysis of the
> common law's treatment of an approach to the issue of ownership of parts or products
> of a living human body, whether for present purposes (viz. an action in negligence) *or*
> *otherwise.*[84] [Emphasis added.]

The basis of confirming ownership in the sperm for the purposes of their claims in negligence was as follows:

(i)   provenance: they alone generated the sperm from their own bodies;

(ii) purpose: the object of ejaculation was for storage with a view to future use;

(iii) control: the 1990 Act confirms a negative right to require destruction of gametes (albeit not a correlative positive right of absolute control);

(iv) exclusivity: no other person, human or corporate, has any rights over gametes held under the Act;

(v)   correlation: there was a direct link between the claims of the men to control use of their sperm and the preclusion of that use by the Trust's breach of duty.

---

[82]   The claim that damage to the sperm itself once excised from the body could nonetheless still constitute a personal injury was rejected by the court: 'To do otherwise would generate paradoxes, and yield ramifications, productive of substantial uncertainty, expensive debate and nice distinctions in an area of law which should be simple, and the principles clear', n 81, paras 19–24.

[83]   This is not to imply that those wishes have paramountcy in all cases—compare, for example, requests *not* to use gametes with requests to make *specific* uses of gametes—but this is to say little because few rights are absolute.

[84]   N 81, para 45.

14.29 This is a difficult ruling to untangle.[85] There is a complex mix of references to common law and statutory provision, and the court was emphatic to point out that its decision as to property claims must be seen as context-specific, that is, in the circumstances of a negligence action for use of materials produced and designated for future use. Thus, it might be claimed that any precedent should be confined to the facts of this case. But this sits uneasily with the pivotal paragraph quoted above, and it ignores the further cause of action considered by the court, namely, bailment. Bailment is an obligation arising from the taking of temporary possession of the goods of another and involves an assumption of responsibility for their safekeeping and return.[86] The *Yearworth* court distinguished *Catalona* as a case where the tissue was clearly donated free of all claims, whereas here there was an equally clear expectation of (and obligation to) return of the sperm.[87] Bailment can be gratuitous, as in the present case, and carries with it a duty to take reasonable care of the goods.[88] Most controversially, the court found the liability to be sui generis with the consequence that the measure of damages be more akin to breach of contract than in tort, and to include reasonably foreseeable injuries such as psychiatric injury and mental distress.

14.30 For all of its qualifications and uncertainty,[89] this decision is an important turning point in medical jurisprudence. Thus, while it lacks any consideration of the (counter) policy considerations that we have seen from the USA,[90] it signals a sea change in judicial attitude towards patients' rights. It suggests, for example, that property claims might bring a range of remedies not available through other legal routes, and it offers a degree of empowerment for patients over material taken from their bodies should they choose to exercise it.[91] *Warren v Care Fertility (Northampton) Ltd*,[92] is further evidence of this willingness to support gamete-originators' wishes, though again there was no true conflict, and the republic of science was not in jeopardy. Here, W sought a declaration that it was lawful for the sperm of her late husband, H, which had been taken prior to his failed cancer treatment, to be stored beyond the statutory period, and for her use.[93] In granting the declaration, the court noted that certain information had not been furnished to H as stipulated under the law, and that, given that there was no conflict of rights as between

---

[85] For deeper analysis see S Harmon and G Laurie, '*Yearworth v North Bristol NHS Trust*: property, principles, precedents and paradigms' (2010) 69 Cam LJ 476.

[86] *Gilchrist Watt and Sanderson Pty Ltd v York Products Pty Ltd* [1970] 1 WLR 1262.

[87] The court did not consider it necessary to address the legal basis for a property claim in bailment because it was of the view that this flowed naturally and *a fortiori* from the finding with respect to their claims in tort: N 81, para 47.

[88] *Port Swettenham Authority v T W Wu and Co (M) Sdn Bhd* [1979] AC 580.

[89] N 85, and L Rostill, 'The ownership that wasn't meant to be: *Yearworth* and property rights in human tissue' (2014) 40 J Med Ethics 14.

[90] It is easy to confirm that property rights are not absolute; what remains to be seen is how and how far limits can or will be placed on them in the name of other claims, most notably claims by scientists.

[91] And it has been applied in many jurisdictions, including Australia (*Bazley v Wesley Monash IVF Pty Ltd* [2010] QSC 118, and *Jocelyn Edwards; Re the estate of the late Mark Edwards* [2011] NSWSC 478) and Canada (*JCM v ANA* [2012] BCSC 584), the latter of which extended it to both parties in the IVF enterprise. For a Scots law perspectives, see *Holdich v Lothian Health Board* [2013] CSOH 197. And see S Farran, 'Storing sperm in Scotland: a risky business?' (2011) 19(2) ERPL 258; W McBryde, 'Contract law – a solution to delictual problems?' (2012) 8 Scots Law Times 45; also S Harmon, '*Yearworth v North Bristol NHS Trust*: A Property/Medical Case of Uncertain Significance?' (2010) 13 Med, Health Care & Phil 343.

[92] [2014] EWHC 602.

[93] The Human Fertilisation and Embryology (Statutory Storage Period for Embryos and Gametes) Regulations 2009 enable the ten-year statutory period to be extended to a maximum of 55 years, subject to certain requirements.

W and H, it should take a purposive approach to the Regulations. Parliament intended to enable a deceased man's sperm to be used by a named person, provided that it was the deceased's wish. While not all of the statutory conditions were met, the husband's intentions were known, so W's Art 8 rights should be vindicated.

Property in Embryos

14.31   When we consider the union of gametes to produce a human embryo matters become still more complicated. The moral significance of embryos has been discussed (Chapter 8) and is sufficiently disputed even before property claims are added to the frame. But embryos are used and discarded, and the law must deal with this in an appropriate fashion. The Human Fertilisation and Embryology Authority (HFEA) faces the dilemma of the disposal of embryos which are created for assisted reproduction but which are not used. As we have stated, the 1990 Act, as amended, avoids any recognition of property rights, and control over the use and disposal of frozen embryos falls to be determined by the will of the parties contributing to their formation.

14.32   However, unlike gametes, two parties provide the genetic material contained in embryos, which themselves are indivisible entities. Who, then, has the power to dispose of them? Schedule 3 to the 1990 Act provides that effective written consent must be given by each person whose gametes have contributed to the embryo.[94] In practice, this gives either contributor a veto over use of the embryo but it provides neither with positive rights of disposition—the embryos must be allowed to perish if the gamete providers cannot agree and the storage time for the embryo has exceeded the statutory limit.[95]

14.33   The regulations which govern storage of gametes and embryos have been detailed in para 8.80 where it is posited that a system that involves agreement between parties who may be in conflict is almost designed for stalemate.[96] The reader will recall that, in the paradigm case of *Evans v Amicus Healthcare Ltd and Others*,[97] the English courts stuck rigidly to the letter of the law, holding that the refusal to cooperate by the estranged partners of two women who sought possession of their frozen embryos meant that there was no other legal option but to deny access to the embryos, effectively condemning the organisms to destruction. The Grand Chamber of the European Court of Human Rights (ECtHR) rejected Ms Evans's appeal and confirmed that the UK's approach to regulation in this area, based as it is on written informed consent(s), was justifiable and not a breach of human rights.[98]

14.34   We view this system of consent with a degree of concern.[99] In the absence of any property right in embryos, the aim for which they have been created can be thwarted by the absence or withholding of consent by a potentially disinterested, bitter, or uncontactable contributor. While we do not suggest that a property system would be problem-free, we believe that to recognise a property right in embryos, which vests, in the first instance, in the woman who is to receive treatment, would go a long way to resolving the current

[94] Sch 3, para 6(3).
[95] Human Fertilisation and Embryology (Statutory Storage Period for Embryos) Regulations 1996 (SI 1996/375), reg 14(1)(c).
[96] For a challenge to the consent model, see M Parker, 'Response to Orr and Seigler—Collective intentionality and procreative desires: The permissible view on consent to posthumous conception' (2004) 30 J Med Ethics 389.
[97] [2004] 3 WLR 681; [2004] 3 All ER 1025.
[98] *Evans v United Kingdom* [2007] 1 FLR 1990; (2008) 46 EHRR 34; (2007) 95 BMLR 107.
[99] J Mason, 'Discord and disposal of embryos' (2004) 8 Edin LR 84.

controversies surrounding these issues. The ruling in *Yearworth* might provide a basis for such an argument; conflicts of claims, as between the woman and the man, are neither unique nor insurmountable.[100]

Property in the Fetus in vivo and Fetal Materials

14.35   Despite our stance on the embryo in vitro, we believe that there should be no support for extending a woman's property right to an implanted fetus. A clear moral distinction is to be made between the in vitro and in vivo human organism, not least because of the immediate potentiality of the latter to become a complete human being.[101] Over 25 years ago, the Polkinghorne Committee suggested that provision be made in any consent to fetal research procedures for the relinquishment of property rights 'if, indeed, there be any'.[102] This clearly refers to maternal rights in respect of the fetus. Times have, however, changed considerably since 1989. While the Polkinghorne Committee regarded the dissociation of the use of fetal tissues and abortion as the overriding consideration, others might now see it as anomalous if a 'profit sharing' agreement were enforceable between a biotechnological institute and the donor when the tissues of a living person were used, but the institute could escape any duty of financial recompense by using tissues from a fetus.

14.36   But what of a non-viable or stillborn fetus and/or fetal material that is discharged from the mother as the result of either a medical termination or a spontaneous miscarriage? The potentiality for viable human life has clearly ended in such a case,[103] and we must consider the possibility of property afresh. The Polkinghorne Committee refused to address this issue and instead recommended that the full and informed consent of the woman be obtained concerning the use and/or disposal of the material. While we acknowledge that, in moral terms, a dead fetus might command greater respect than fetal material *in se*, we do not consider that the recognition of a property interest in either necessarily involves such a degree of disrespect as would lead us to refuse to recognise any such interest. The potential value of any tissue is uncertain but is surely increasing, and we suggest that the mother of the dead fetus should retain any available property claim not only in respect of the fetus itself but also of its associated materials.

14.37   Of course, the matters of ownership and disposal should be approached cautiously and with sensitivity at such an emotional time. We have already mentioned the decision in *Re the Matter of X*,[104] in which the court of first instance expressly relied on the analogy of a property-type interest of the mother in her dead fetus to strengthen her claim to respect for her choices about what was done with the fetal material. While her refusal was ultimately overridden by the Jersey Court of Appeal in furtherance of the public interest in the investigation and prosecution of crime, this does not detract from the significance of the appeal to property as a *complement* to an autonomy-based interest. Here, the autonomy claim was weaker because of the mother's status as a minor. In any event, the fact that property or quasi-property rights might be trumped by stronger competing public interests should come as no surprise for the former are never absolute in any context.

[100]   M Ford, '*Evans v United Kingdom*: What implications for the jurisprudence of pregnancy?' [2008] Human Rights LR 171; M Ford, 'A property model of pregnancy' (2005) 1 Int J of Law in Context 261. See para 8.80 for the problems of non-consensual paternity.

[101]   Although the fetus is not a legal person, the concept of it being 'property' is too close to that of slavery for comfort.

[102]   *Review of the Guidance on the Research use of Fetuses and Fetal Material* (1989), at paras 20.32–20.33.

[103]   The possible exception to this is the living abortus, which we discuss in Chapter 19.

[104]   N 43.

PROPERTY IN CADAVERS
AND CADAVERIC TISSUE

14.38 For a long time the 'no property in a corpse' rule was thought to exclude all possibility of property in a dead body or its parts, at least in England and Wales.[105] In *Yearworth*,[106] the Court of Appeal speculated that the general basis for the rule might be: (i) a matter of logic;[107] (ii) a matter of religious conviction; and (iii) a matter of public health. The case of *R v Kelly*,[108] however, established that there are serious limitations to any such rule which have important consequences for the users of human tissue removed from cadavers. In *Kelly*, the question was whether it was theft for a junior technician of the Royal College of Surgeons (RCS) to remove body parts for use, and ultimate disposal, by an artist who was interested in employing them as moulds for his sculptures. The defendants relied on the 'no property' rule as their defence. The court held that the rule refers only to a corpse or its parts which remain in their natural state, but that:

> parts of a corpse are capable of being property ... if they have acquired different attributes by virtue of the application of skill, such as dissection or preservation techniques, for exhibition or teaching purposes.[109]

Here, work had indeed been done on the body parts in question such that they became specimens owned by the RCS. To remove them without authority was, therefore, theft. The court opined, however, that the 'no property' rule is so deeply entrenched in English jurisprudence that legislative action would be required for it to be changed *in se*. That having been said, the court speculated that the common law might recognise property in cadaveric parts even when those parts had not acquired different attributes, but if they had attracted a 'use or significance beyond their mere existence'.[110]

14.39 What we are not told is who would be the holder of any such right. An answer is found, however, in an earlier case approved in *Kelly*: *Dobson v North Tyneside Health Authority*.[111] In *Dobson*, the relatives of a woman who had died from brain tumours brought an action in negligence against the health authority for failure to diagnose the nature of the condition properly and in time. In order to succeed, however, it was important to establish whether the tumours were malignant or benign, and this could only be done by examining samples from the deceased's brain, which had been removed by the hospital at an autopsy directed by the coroner and subsequently disposed of.[112] The relatives therefore brought a further action against the hospital alleging that it had converted 'property' to which the relatives were entitled, and that it acted as a bailee having no right of unauthorised disposal. In rejecting these claims, the Court of Appeal held that no right of possession or ownership of the brain, or indeed of the corpse, vested in the relatives. At best, a limited

---

[105] NCB, n 49, para 10.2. There is some authority in Scotland that property can exist in a corpse, at least until it is buried or otherwise disposed of: *Dewar v HM Advocate* 1945 JC 5, at 14.

[106] N 81, para 31.

[107] If ownership did not vest in the living person, why should it do so in the dead? On connectedness between our obligations to the living and to the dead, see S McGuiness and M Brazier, 'Respecting the living means respecting the dead too' (2008) 28 OJLS 297.

[108] [1998] 3 All ER 741 (CA).   [109] N 108, at 749–50.   [110] N 108, at 750.

[111] [1996] 4 All ER 474 (CA); (1996) 33 BMLR 146.

[112] The case reports that it had been preserved in paraffin, though normal procedure would be to preserve the brain in formaldehyde and remove pieces which would be processed into small 'paraffin blocks' for examination.

possessory right to a corpse is enjoyed by the executor or administrator of a deceased person, but this right is only to possess the corpse with a view to its burial or disposal.[113] It also held that property rights could arise in respect of body parts where some work or skill differentiates the body or its parts from a corpse in its natural state. It quoted, with halting approval, the following passage from the Australian decision *Doodeward* v *Spence*,[114] which involved a dispute over the 'ownership' of a two-headed fetus:

> when a person has by lawful exercise of work or skill so dealt with a human body or part of a human body in his lawful possession that it has acquired some attributes differentiating it from a mere corpse awaiting burial, he acquires a right to retain possession of it, at least as against any person not entitled to have it delivered to him for the purposes of burial.

Two elements from this passage are worth noting. First, any property right which accrues does so to the person who does the work. Second, the property right which springs into existence is subject to the right of those with the right to possession for burial.[115] We have already seen that no possessory right for burial existed in *Dobson*. But had the brain become property? Gibson LJ did not seem to think so; the brain had not been preserved for the purposes of teaching or exhibition, nor was the case analogous to a stuffing or embalming, which displays an intention to retain the part as a specimen. The brain had been removed and preserved only under the obligation to remove material bearing on the cause of death imposed by the Coroners Rules 1984.[116] The hospital intended to abide by these rules and was at liberty to destroy the brain once the material was no longer required by the coroner.

14.40 *Dobson* is as interesting for the questions that it does not answer as it is for those that it does. For example, as to the possessory right of executors, must the body and *all* of its parts be returned? Similarly, what is the role of intention in creating property rights? Reading *Dobson* and *Kelly* in conjunction, it seems that property rights can arise if work is done on a tissue *with the intention* of retaining the sample as a specimen or for some other purpose. But just how much, or little, work needs to be done? In *Kelly*, the court indicates that dissection or preservation techniques are enough to make a sample 'property'.[117] If so, then merely to carry out an autopsy or to place a sample in formaldehyde is enough to create 'property'.[118] And, as we have seen from *Dobson*, that property belongs to he who would 'use' the goods and certainly not to the source or her significant others. Thus, if the Court of Appeal in *Kelly* is correct and the common law does one day move to the position that property rights may arise because of the 'inherent' valuable attributes in tissue samples, it is undoubtedly the case that such rights will vest in the 'discoverer' of those properties. As we have seen, the long-overdue reforms of the law relating to cadavers as embodied in the Human Tissue Act 2004 leave open the position on accrual of property rights, but also leave the common law's 'no property' rule untouched—including the attribution of property because of 'an application of human skill'. At the same time, the reforms extend the consent model by allowing third parties, such as next of kin, to

---

[113] No executor or administrator had been appointed in the present case until after the body had been disposed of.

[114] (1908) 6 CLR 406 at 414, per Griffith CJ.

[115] Recent confirmation of this right and of the *Kelly* rule can be found in *Re St Andrew's Churchyard, Alwalton* [2012] PTSR 479, para 52.

[116] Coroners Rules 1984 (SI 1984/552), r 9.   [117] N 108, at 749–50.

[118] Without wishing to labour the point, there is a world of difference between placing a brain in preservative and preparing blocks for microscopic examination; the precise conditions obtaining in *Dobson* are, therefore, of some significance.

authorise, or veto, dealings with the remains of a loved one.[119] We simply point out that consent and property are not mutually exclusive concepts; indeed, to the extent that they are both a means of furnishing respect, they should perhaps be made to work together towards a common end.[170]

14.41 Litigation brought by aggrieved parents in respect of post-mortem examinations per-formed on their dead children has shed more light on the legal position. In *AB v Leeds Teaching Hospital NHS Trust*,[121] claims were made, inter alia, in negligence for psychi-atric injury and for wrongful interference with the body—a tort not previously recog-nised in English law.[122] The premise was that inadequate care and attention was exercised when obtaining parental consent to the post-mortems and that body parts of the children should not have been retained without express authority. Gage J confirmed the 'no prop-erty in a corpse' rule, but followed *Kelly* in that parts of a body may acquire the charac-ter of property provided sufficient work and skill has been expended. In the particular case of the pathologist, it was stated: 'to dissect and fix an organ from a child's body requires work and a great deal of skill...The subsequent production of blocks and slides is also a skillful operation requiring work and expertise of trained scientists'.[123] Moreover, the court held that the post-mortem examinations were lawfully executed and therefore capable of giving rise to possessory rights on the part of the pathologists; any possessory rights of the parents for the purposes of burial could not, from a pragmatic stance, be a right to return of every part of the body after post-mortem.[124]

14.42 But what if parents make it an express stipulation of their consent to post-mortem that all body samples be returned? Here, Gage J refused to create common law torts where none existed; namely, a tort of wrongful interference with the body or of conversion in the body. Rather, he held that such matters fall to be considered as a matter of negligence: the doctor who receives such instructions from parents has a duty of care to pass these on to the pathologist; he in turn is obliged to heed such a condition lest he be found to be in breach of his own duty of care.[125]

---

[119] Human Tissue Act 2004, ss 27(4) and 54(9). For a recent case examining consent with respect to deal-ing with cadaveric material, see *CM v EJ's Executor* [2013] EWHC 1680. In that case, M, a doctor, applied for declarations that samples could lawfully be taken from J and tested for communicable diseases. While off duty, M had attempted to save J's life after she had fallen from a building. M later became anxious about the risk of infection with a blood-borne disease, so she began a course of antiretroviral medication and sought samples from J's body for testing. The coroner with custody of the body gave consent subject to M having appropriate authorisation. A distant relative advised that J's parents lived abroad and did not yet know of her death, so he gave permission for samples to be taken. The court noted the importance of consent to the legislative framework, accepted that it was not reasonably practicable to seek the parents' consent, the rela-tive was in a qualifying relationship under the Act, the coroner had agreed to the removal and testing of the material, and so the court could exercise its discretion under its inherent jurisdiction.

[120] Mason and Laurie, n 74.

[121] [2004] 2 FLR 365; [2004] 3 FCR 324. The circumstances of this case arose from the concerns generated by the practices at Alder Hey and Bristol which became the subject of two public inquiries. This also saw the establishment of the Retained Organs Commission which issued Recommendations on the Legal Status of Tissue Blocks and Slides (ROC 17/6, 2003), which, at 1, supported the suggestion that 'straightforward legal ownership was not a preferred option...tissue blocks and slides should be subject to some form of custody or stewardship'.

[122] But probably recognised in Scotland: *Pollok v Workman* [1900] 2 F 354, and *Hughes v Robertson* [1930] SC 394, discussed in N Whitty, 'Rights of Personality, Property Rights and the human body in Scots law' (2005) 9 Edin LR 194.

[123] N 121, para 148.   [124] N 121, paras 158 and 160.

[125] N 121, para 161. The court also recognised the relevance of human rights arguments to the circum-stances where body parts are retained for research purposes, viz, unauthorised retention with a view to

14.43 An alternative route is available in Scotland. *Stevens v Yorkhill NHS Trust and another*,[126] emerged out of similar post-mortem circumstances. The pursuer argued that, despite authorising a post-mortem on her daughter, it was never explained to her that this would involve removal and retention of organs, particularly the brain, and, as a result, this led to severe depression and loss of employment. The suit proceeded on two grounds: (1) that a duty of care in negligence was owed to her such that she should have been informed and provided with the opportunity to give appropriate consent to the procedure, and, separately, to the removal and storage of tissue; (2) that under Scots common law wrongful interference with a corpse was actionable in its own right as an affront to human dignity. While legal authority was sparse, there was support in the ancient *actio injuriarum* (reflecting Scots law's roots in Roman law) which allowed recovery in the terms averred and in particular for recovery for solatium (hurt to feelings as opposed to psychiatric injury). This had never been superseded by statute nor was the English ruling in *Leeds Teaching Hospital* binding on a Scottish court. That case was followed, however, with respect to the negligence claim in that it was accepted that a duty of care could be owed to the mother and its scope could include information about organ removal and retention when seeking consent to post-mortem examination. These conclusions were reached without the need to rely on a property paradigm.

14.44 Once again, we see that a range of legal devices is employed to protect the interests at stake. It is helpful, however, to consider the differences here. While recognition of a property-type claim would entitle the right-holder to control (and return) of the thing itself[127]—which is what parents have often sought in cases such as these—a negligence action is for monetary compensation and requires proof of causation of a recognised form of harm, which can be a difficult hurdle. Remedies in negligence, privacy, autonomy, or *actio injuriarum* undoubtedly serve their purpose, but a property model reveals different aspects to the rights currently enjoyed by patients and their families which cannot wholly be subsumed within other concepts or under other rights of action.

INTELLECTUAL PROPERTY IN HUMAN TISSUE

14.45 We end this chapter with a shift from real property in the excised living or cadaveric tissue itself to intellectual property (IP) in the products that are generated from that tissue with the application of knowledge and skill. IP law has had to adapt rapidly in the last few decades to meet the demands of the biotechnology industry. Astronomical sums are invested in research and development, and the pharmaceutical industry has fought hard to ensure that its products receive patent protection. This, it is thought, assures a degree of return on the investment. Legal certainty becomes particularly important at times of economic crisis. The Global Agenda Council on Biotechnology reported in 2012 that the USA spent US$22bn, that the share of biotechnology in public R&D expenditure was highest in Korea (20.4 per cent), followed by Germany (18.3 per cent)

research ends is capable of engaging the right to respect for private and family life under Art 8(1) ECHR, and that the circumstances in which this could be justified by the public authority under Art 8(2) 'will probably be rare': paras 287–300.

[126] 2007 SCLR 606; (2007) 95 BMLR 1.

[127] Absent its destruction or the operation of other supervening property rights such as commixtion, confusion, or specification (to use the Scottish terminology).

and Spain (13.3 per cent), and that, of all biotech R&D, 66 per cent is for health-related applications.[128] Crucial to continued success and growth, it is felt, is a healthy IP system, and the search for patents is central to this (which is not the same as saying that more patents means a healthier system). Thus, the House of Lords recommended that barriers to collaboration be identified and the needs for incentives addressed in order to promote translational research in the UK.[129]

HUMAN MATERIAL, MORALITY, AND IP INSTITUTIONS

14.46   A patent offers a monopoly for up to 20 years over an invention to the extent that all others can be excluded from competing in the marketplace with the same, or a substantially similar, product.[130] Strict criteria must be met to obtain protection, but once secured, a patent can protect a commercial enterprise against all comers. Patenting is not, however, a morally neutral exercise and the biotechnology industry has faced problems in obtaining protection.[131] These problems have been particularly acute in Europe and arise because biotechnology involves the manipulation of living organisms.[132] Thus, for many, to patent a biotechnological invention is to patent 'life' itself. Add to this the nature of the right that is granted—a monopoly to control access to the market—and there is a perfect recipe for ideological conflict.[133]

14.47   Standard criteria for patentability are accepted in most countries of the world.[134] While terminology varies slightly, to be patentable, an invention must: (1) be new or novel; (2) involve an 'inventive step'—in the sense that the development should not be obvious to a person skilled in the particular field; and (3) have utility or be made or used in some kind of industry. In the USA, a broad and permissive approach to these criteria is adopted, and so, in *Diamond* v *Chakrabarty*,[135] the US Supreme Court (USSC) held that 'anything under the sun that is made by man' could be patented. Similarly, when, in 1988, Harvard University sought a patent for its ONCOmouse—a mouse genetically engineered with a human cancer gene in such a way that it develops cancer as a matter of course—the US Patent and Trademark Office (USPTO) granted the patent without question.

---

[128]   See data available via the World Economic Forum: http://www.weforum.org/. And see WEF, *Global Agenda Council on Future of Chemistry, Advanced Materials and Biotechnology 2014–16*: http://www.weforum. org/content/global-agenda-council-future-chemistry-advanced-materials-and-biotechnology-2014-2016.

[129]   House of Lords Science and Technology Committee, *Genomic Medicine Second Report of 2008–9*, paras 3.51–3.54.

[130]   See G Laurie, 'Patenting and the human body' in J McHale et al. (eds), *Principles of Medical Law* (3rd edn, 2010). More generally, C Waelde, G Laurie, A Brown, et al., *Contemporary Intellectual Property: Law and Policy* (3rd edn, 2013) chs 10–12.

[131]   For a useful historical account, see Nuffield Council on Bioethics, *The Ethics of Patenting DNA* (2002) Appendix 2. For a comparative discussion, see G van Overwalle (ed), *Gene Patents and Public Health* (2007), and in the stem cell context, see A Plomer and P Torremans (eds), *Embryonic Stem Cell Patents: European Patent Law and Ethics* (2010).

[132]   S Bostyn, 'The prodigal son: The relationship between patent law and health care' (2003) 11 Med Law Rev 67.

[133]   Compare early polarised debate represented by A Wells, 'Patenting new life forms: An ecological perspective' (1994) 3 Euro Intellect Prop Rev 111, and S Crespi, 'Biotechnology patents: The wicked animal must defend itself' (1995) 9 Euro Intellect Prop Rev 431.

[134]   A degree of patent criteria harmonisation was achieved with passage of the TRIPS Agreement (Trade Related Aspects of Intellectual Property Rights) at the Uruguay Round of the General Agreement on Tariffs and Trade (GATT) in 1994. TRIPS is administered by the World Trade Organization which had 161 member countries as of 26 April 2015. Many European countries embody the terms of the European Patent Convention: see European Patent Convention (2000). In the UK, see Patents Act 1977, s 1(1).

[135]   447 US 303, 66 L Ed 2d 144 (1980).

14.48 Harvard fared less well in Europe. Although an application for a patent over ONCOmouse was filed in 1985, it was not granted until 1991,[136] and even then its validity was in constant doubt with further restrictions on its scope being imposed in 2001,[137] and 2004.[138] Thus, while the monopoly was originally granted to cover 'transgenic mammals', it was ultimately restricted to 'transgenic mice'. The problem of patent protection faced by the industry in Europe stems from the 'morality provisions' of the European Patent Convention (2000), which embodies the patent law of 38 European countries as of July 2015. Article 53 of the EPC 2000 states:

(a) inventions the commercial exploitation of which would be contrary to 'ordre public' or morality; such exploitation shall not be deemed to be so contrary merely because it is prohibited by law or regulation in some or all of the Contracting States;

(b) plant or animal varieties or essentially biological processes for the production of plants or animals; this provision shall not apply to microbiological processes or the products thereof;

The Harvard patent was challenged both on the grounds that it was inherently immoral to patent 'life' under Art 53(a), and because it was an attempt to patent an 'animal variety' under Art 53(b).[139] Yet, in *HARVARD/ONCOmouse*,[140] the Examining Division (ED) of the European Patent Office (EPO) allowed the patent because it held that the morality question is to be tested by balancing the suffering of the animal with the potential benefits to humanity. It also held that the 'invention' being claimed was a 'non-human mammal', and this was much broader than a mere 'animal variety'.[141] Neither of these interpretations was disturbed by the edicts from the Opposition Division (OD). Such linguistic gymnastics are clearly driven by policy desires to make Europe attractive to biotech investors, and this is a factor which cannot be ignored.[142]

14.49 Patents over human material have been granted for many years, with some 20 per cent of human gene DNA sequences patented by 2006, the majority in the USA.[143] As with ONCOmouse, the EPO has had to deal with moral objections to such patents. The invention in dispute in *HOWARD FLOREY/Relaxin*,[144] concerned H2 Relaxin, a protein produced naturally by women at the time of childbirth which softens the pelvis and so eases the passage of the child. Howard Florey genetically engineered this protein and sought a patent for the artificial chemical. It was argued before the OD of the EPO, first, that it would be tantamount to slavery to grant a patent for such a product, in that it involved the sale of human tissue; second, that this too was exploitative and an offence to human dignity; and, finally, that any patent over DNA is inherently immoral because DNA is 'life'. Each of these arguments was rejected by the OD, which held that there can be no question of slavery because no woman is forced to surrender material—all the subjects consented. Similarly, it was not necessarily exploitative to use human material because

---

[136] [1991] EPOR 525.

[137] A Abbott, 'Harvard squeaks through Oncomouse patent appeal' (2001) 414 Nature 241. This reduced the scope of claim from 'transgenic mammals' to 'transgenic rodents'.

[138] T315/03 *Oncomouse/Harvard*, EPO, July 2004, summary available at: http://www.european-patent-office.org.

[139] *HARVARD/ONCOmouse* [1990] EPOR 4.   [140] [1991] EPOR 525.

[141] Opposition proceedings were immediately started by 16 groups after this decision.

[142] Laws which are too strict act as a disincentive and encourage more investment in the other jurisdictions (such as the USA and Japan) where morality features much less prominently.

[143] HM Treasury, *Gowers Review of Intellectual Property* (2006) para 2.30.

[144] [1995] EPOR 541.

free and informed consent was given; the OD pointed out that human material is used in a variety of contexts without the question of exploitation arising. Finally, DNA is not 'life' but a chemical substance which carries genetic information: 'no woman is affected in any way by the present patent'.[145] The general policy of the EPO has been to interpret the exceptions to patentability narrowly and to presume that the protection criteria are satisfied unless a strong contrary case can be shown.[146]

14.50 The controversy surrounding the morality of patenting DNA and genetically engineered products has also been addressed by European law, primarily in the name of protecting the European single market. After a very difficult passage lasting ten years, a European Directive was adopted in July 1998 which attempted to clarify the legal position in respect of biotechnological patents.[147] Guidance is given on the kinds of invention which should never receive patent protection,[148] and the morality provision as defined in *ONCOmouse* is incorporated in a modified, although still relatively imprecise, form.[149] A number of Member States were reluctant to implement the Directive because of general uncertainty about its terms.[150] Once again, however, the interpretative authority in charge—this time the European Court of Justice (ECJ)—took a narrow view of the circumstances, and upheld the Directive both as to its legitimacy as an instrument of European law and as to its substantive content re European patent law.[151]

14.51 This narrowness of approach in respect of interpreting patent law has, however, most recently been challenged by the advent of human embryonic stem cell (ESC) patents.[152] While it has been possible to derive stem cells from adults for over 40 years, and from animals, including animal embryos, for almost a quarter of a century, human ESCs were only first isolated in 1998. This date is significant, being also the year when the EC Directive on the legal protection of biotechnological inventions was adopted. Accordingly, there are no specific provisions on human ESCs contained within that instrument. Nonetheless, certain key provisions of the Directive have direct application:

> *Article 5(1)*: The human body, at the various stages of its formation and development, and the simple discovery of one of its elements, including the sequence or partial sequence of a gene, cannot constitute patentable inventions.

---

[145] At 550–1.

[146] See e.g. *PLANT GENETIC SYSTEMS/Glutamine Synthetase Inhibitors* [1995] EPOR 357 and *LELAND STANFORD/Modified Animal* [2002] EPOR 2 (immuno-compromised chimera mouse was patentable—controversial technology not in itself a bar to patenting).

[147] Directive of the European Parliament and of the Council on the Legal Protection of Biotechnological Inventions, No 98/44/EC of 6 July 1998.

[148] Under Art 6 the following are unpatentable: (i) processes for cloning human beings; (ii) processes for modifying the germ line genetic identity of human beings; (iii) uses of human embryos for industrial or commercial purposes; (iv) processes for modifying the genetic identity of animals which are likely to cause them suffering without any substantial medical benefit to man or animal, and also animals resulting from such processes.

[149] Art 6 requires that a substantial medical benefit accrue to humanity or animals before the morality test will be satisfied.

[150] Eight members were referred to the ECJ in July 2003 when further negotiations with the Commission came to nothing (IP/03/911, 10 July 2003). France took over 50 months to implement the Directive, and some still question whether it has done so appropriately.

[151] *Netherlands v European Parliament* (C-377/98) [2002] All ER 97 (ECJ). Note, the Directive only harmonised the law in the 15 Member States of the European Union (now 28), but the implementing regulations of the EPC have been amended to reflect the terms of the morality provisions of the Directive to ensure consistency of approach across the 38 members of the EPO.

[152] See G Laurie, 'Patenting stem cells of human origin' [2004] European Int Prop Rev 59.

Article 6(1): Inventions shall be considered unpatentable where their commercial exploitation would be contrary to *ordre public* or morality; ... (2) the following, in particular, shall be considered unpatentable: (a) processes for cloning human beings; ... (c) uses of human embryos for industrial or commercial purposes...;

From an ethical perspective, and as we have seen (Chapter 9), research using the human embryo is problematic for a number of reasons, all of which centre around the moral status of this organism. The concern surrounding ESC technologies is that, at present, we must both use and destroy a human embryo to produce valuable embryonic stem cell cultures,[153] although alternatives are now coming into use, most notably 'induced pluripotent stem cells' (iPSCs),[154] which are produced from reprogrammed adult somatic cells, and are claimed by some to avoid the ethical dilemmas of ESCs.[155] But they are not yet viewed as the best option for developing viable therapies; embryonic stem cells remain the 'gold standard'.

14.52 Patenting has always been a central feature of stem cell research, and, by 2002, more than 2,000 applications had been lodged worldwide for stem cell technologies, 500 of which related to ESCs. And while the EGE—tasked with examining 'all ethical aspects of biotechnology'[156]—opined that certain *early stage interventions* should be excluded from protection,[157] its opinion was dealt a fatal blow by the EPO when the OD considered the opposition arguments in *EDINBURGH/Animal Transgenic Stem Cells*, which related to *animal* transgenic stem cells.[158] Concerns were raised when it was suggested that the patent might extend to human cloning because the taxonomy of 'animal' includes 'human'. The OD was called upon to interpret Art 53(a) of the EPC (which, we have seen, reflect Art 6 of the Directive), following which European patents shall not be granted for *uses of human embryos for industrial or commercial purposes*. It noted that the provision could be interpreted in two ways: *narrowly*, to mean that only commercial uses of human embryos *as such* are excluded from patentability, or *broadly*, to mean that human embryonic stem cells—which as we have noted can only be obtained by destroying an embryo—are also not patentable. The OD preferred the latter approach, arguing that since embryos *as such* are already protected by Rule 23(e) (equivalent of Art 5(1), Directive), a similar interpretation of Rule 23(d)(c) (equivalent of Art 6(2)(c), Directive) would be redundant and this could not have been the intention of the legislator. Although the EGE Opinion was considered by the OD, it was rejected *in toto* because 'classic concepts of patent law are misinterpreted and confused'.[159]

---

[153] For a moral evaluation, see J Polkinghorne, 'The person, the soul, and genetic engineering' (2004) 30 J Med Ethics 593.

[154] S Brockman-Lee, 'Embryonic stem cells in science and medicine: An invitation for dialogue' (2007) 4 *Gender Medicine* 288; L Solomon and S Brockman-Lee, 'Embryonic stem cells in science and medicine, Part II: Law, ethics, and the continuing need for dialogue' (2008) 5 Gender Medicine 3; W Deng, 'Induced pluripotent stem cells: paths to new medicines' (2010) 11 EMBO Reports 161.

[155] D Zacharias, T Nelson, et al., 'The Science and Ethics of Induced Pluripotency: What Will Become of Embryonic Stem Cells?' (2011) 86 Mayo Clinic Proceedings 634; T Ishii, R Pera, and T Greely, 'Ethical and Legal Issues Arising in Research on Inducing Human Germ Cells from Pluripotent Stem Cells' (2013) 13 Cell Stem Cell 145.

[156] See Directive, Art 7. For critical reflection, see H Busby, T Hervey, and A Mohr, 'Ethical EU law? The influence of the European Group on Ethics in Science and New Technologies' (2008) 33 Euro LR 803.

[157] EGE, *Opinion No 16: Ethical Aspects of Patenting Inventions Involving Human Stem Cells* (2002).

[158] Patent Application No. 94 913 174.2, 21 July 2002, OD.

[159] While this is not the place to engage with the relative merits of the Opinion or the views of the OD, it is pertinent to point out that it felt confident in rejecting entirely the considered views of a group of ethics experts on the essential questions and the approach to be adopted. This is in stark contrast with the earlier

14.53 The debacle continued with the Wisconsin Alumni Research Foundation (WARF) application. WARF was responsible for developing the first techniques to isolate human embryonic stem cells in 1998,[160] and holds a patent over the technology in a number of jurisdictions. In 2004, it made an application for primate embryonic stem cell cultures themselves—that is, stem cell *products*—but it also disclosed the means to make such products, as one would expect. The sole method of production of the stem cell cultures that was described involved the use, and destruction, of embryos. At the examination stage,[161] the ED held that all of the claims which could be extended to human ESCs were invalid on grounds of immorality, stating: 'The use of an embryo as starting material for the generation of a product of industrial application is considered equal to industrial use of this embryo.' The rationale here is that the claimed cultures are inseparable from the means to make them; it is, in a literal sense, necessary to 'use' embryos to create the claimed invention. The message from this ruling is that the moral concern goes beyond patenting itself, and extends to general instrumentalisation; mere involvement—use—of embryos in the research is sufficient to bar the patentability of that invention.[162]

14.54 The matter was referred to the Enlarged Board of Appeal (EBoA) in 2005, but before the EBoA could rule the then President of the EPO issued a letter commenting on the referral. In his opinion, and contrary to practice to date,[163] Art 53 should not receive a restricted or narrow interpretation:

> A presumption in favour of a narrow interpretation of exceptions would unduly limit the significance of the moral jurisdiction under Article 53(a) and Rule 23d(c) the purpose of which is the incorporation of higher ranking legal and moral principles into European patent law and would thus be in conflict with the general objective of said norms.[164]

The President attended the EBoA hearing and made representations as did many other parties;[165] the Board eventually delivered its decision in November 2008.[166] It considered the intent of the legislators of both the EPC and the Directive and concluded that this was to exclude inventions such as that in the instant case which *necessarily* involved the destruction of human embryos for the invention to be performed. The concern was to prevent misuse in the sense of commodification of human embryos and affronts to human dignity. Moreover, because such use involving destruction was an integral and essential part of the industrial or commercial exploitation of the claimed invention it was, as such, a breach of the provisions in the laws. The concern of the EBoA was not the granting of the patent per se, but rather the performance of the invention.[167]

cautious approach of the EPO, which demonstrated extreme reluctance to engage with ethical issues—indeed one ED professed no authority in this domain: *HARVARD/Oncomouse* [1990] EPOR 4.

[160] J Thomson et al., 'Embryonic stem cell lines derived from human blastocysts' (1998) 282 Science 1145.

[161] *WARF/Primate Embryonic Stem Cells*, Patent Application No. 96 903 521.1 – 2401, 13 July 2004, ED.

[162] For more on these cases and the role of the EPO, see S Harmon, 'From Engagement to Re-Engagement: The Expression of Moral Values in Patenting Proceedings, Present and Future' (2006) 31 Euro LR 642.

[163] See *HARVARD*, n 140, *PLANT GENETIC SYSTEMS*, n 146, and *CYGNUS/Diagnostic Methods* [2006] EPOR 15.

[164] President Pompidou, Comments by the President of the European Patent Office on WARF, G2/06, 28 September 2006, at 37.

[165] For an account of the arguments made see S Sterckx, 'The *WARF/Stem cells* case before the EPO Enlarged Board of Appeal' (2008) 30 Euro IP Rev 535.

[166] *WARF/Primate Embryonic Stem Cells* [2009] EPOR 15 (EBA).

[167] The *WARF* reasoning has since been applied in *TECHNION/Culturing Stem Cells*, T2221/10, 4 February 2014, BoA, and *ASTERIAS/Embryonic Stem Cells, Disclaimer*, T1441/13, [2015] EPOR 9 (BoA), wherein patents were refused because their implementation involved destruction of a human embryo, and

14.55 But there was also much which did not concern the EBoA; for example, it did not feel the need to consider the question whether the standard for morality or *ordre public* should (or could) be European; nor was it concerned with the fact that research in certain European countries involving the destruction of human embryos to obtain stem cells is permitted; nor did the EBoA consider appropriate a utilitarian approach to ask whether the wider social benefits of the invention should be balanced against the prejudice to the embryo; the legislators had spoken and the prohibition was absolute. Finally, and reflecting the spirit of the EPO President, the EBoA rejected any attempt to define 'embryo' in ways found in many domestic jurisdictions—such as the UK which has a 14-day rule (and is accordingly able to strike a balance of interests between protection of the embryo and research in the public interest)—the term 'embryo' should not be given any such restrictive meaning.[168]

14.56 An irony of this decision is that an unelected, non-democratically constituted body delivered a European-wide position on the morality of dealings with embryos where other bodies, such as the ECtHR itself, have failed, and in doing so committed a major volte face.[169] As well intended as it is, the morality provision in European patent law is over-ambitious insofar as it can never attain that which it was designed to achieve; the refusal of a patent does nothing directly to prevent the creative process from continuing. Thus, Harvard could continue to produce the mouse for sale on the open market even if it had never been given a patent—all that would be lost would be a chance to monopolise that market. The same is true of ESC technologies and the creation and destruction of embryos. If one is concerned by the acts of creation/destruction, and this must be the main concern in these cases, then attention should be turned not to the point at which patent protection is offered, but the point at which the creation takes place.[170] This cannot be done through the law of patents, but rather through other mechanisms such as regulatory schemes or authorities which monitor the industry. Making morality part of patent law does nothing to regulate the biotechnology industry, except perhaps in a very indirect way of removing an incentive; allowing patent law to drive the regulatory and innovation systems is a dangerous formula.

HUMAN MATERIAL, IP, AND THE COURTS

14.57 Notwithstanding these comments, it seems that the fate for Europe is sealed, at least for the foreseeable future, as a result of the ruling of the ECJ in *Brüstle* v *Greenpeace*.[171] This was a dispute as to the patentability of isolated and purified neural precursor cells, processes for their production from ESC, and their use for treatment of neural defects. Greenpeace sought revocation of a German patent for its alleged contravention of the domestic patent law embodying Arts 6(1) and (2) of the Biotech Directive, which—as we have seen—state that patents may not be granted for inventions whose

---

because, although SCs were taken from established and publicly available lines, they also contained unpatentable subject matter as their development involved the destruction of embryos.

[168] See P Treichel, 'G2/06 and the verdict of immorality' (2009) 40 IIC 450.

[169] For British judicial angst about not giving the exclusions too wide an interpretation, see *Research in Motion UK Ltd* v *Inpro Licensing SARL* [2006] EWHC 70 (Pat); [2006] RPC 517.

[170] This is argued more fully in G Laurie, 'Biotechnology: Facing the problems of patent law' in H MacQueen and B Bain (eds), *Innovation, Incentive and Reward: Intellectual Property Law and Policy* (1997) Hume Papers on Public Policy 46.

[171] [2012] All ER (EC) 809; [2012] 1 CMLR 41.

commercial exploitation would be contrary to *ordre public* or morality, and that, in particular, patents may not be granted for uses of human embryos for industrial or commercial purposes.

14.58 In November 2009, the *Bundesgerichtshof* (German Supreme Court) sent three questions to the ECJ for clarification, the first two of which are important for present purposes:

1. What is meant by the term 'human embryos' in Art 6(2)(c)?

2. What is meant by the expression 'uses of human embryos for industrial or commercial purposes'? Does it include any commercial exploitation within the meaning of Art 6(1), especially use for the purposes of scientific research?

Thus, the ECJ was asked to consider for the first time whether human ESC inventions are properly described as an 'embryo' for the purposes of patent law. On this question, it recognised that a 'degree of sensitivity' was merited in light of the diverse attitudes around Europe.[172] Surprisingly, however, it denied that it was being asked a moral question, preferring instead to characterise the issue as a matter of legal interpretation. As a term of art in EU law not referencing any domestic law, the ECJ was duty bound to provide an independent and uniform interpretation for Europe. It defined 'embryo' as:[173]

1. any human ovum after fertilisation;

2. any non-fertilised human ovum into which the cell nucleus from a mature human cell has been transplanted; and

3. any non-fertilised human ovum whose division and further development have been stimulated by parthenogenesis.

Although these latter entities have not been fertilised, it reasoned, they are nonetheless capable of commencing development into a human being and so must be excluded from patentability. The breadth of this conceptualisation—apparently arrived at in a morality-free zone—has been roundly criticised for its failure to take into account the underpinning value and diverse approaches to human dignity around the continent.[174]

14.59 On the second question—whether embryos used in research represent their 'industrial and commercial uses', the ECJ answered in the affirmative. Indeed, once again a broad exclusionary approach was adopted:

The fact that destruction [of the human embryo] may occur at a stage long before the implementation of the invention, as in the case of the production of embryonic stem cells from a lineage of stem cells the mere production of which implied the destruction of human embryos is, in that regard, irrelevant.[175]

The trend in Europe has, accordingly, been confirmed by the highest court. It might be too early to tell the likely or feared consequences,[176] but the economic knock-on has

---

[172] *Brüstle*, para 30.   [173] *Brüstle*, paras 30–6.

[174] See A Plomer, 'After *Brüstle*: EU Accession to the ECHR and the future of European patent law' (2012) 2 Queen Mary J IP 110, and J Mansnérus, 'Brüstle v Greenpeace: Implications for Commercialisation of Translational Stem Cell Research' (2015) 22 Euro J Health Law 141.

[175] *Brüstle*, para 49.

[176] We offer further comment here: S Harmon, G Laurie, and A Courtney, 'Dignity, Plurality and Patentability: The Unfinished Story of Brüstle v Greenpeace' (2012) 38 European Law Rev 92.

already been signalled by the European Parliamentary Committee on Legal Affairs Draft Opinion on the Horizon 2020 Programme in which it is stated:

> The rapporteur also draws attention … to a recent judgment of the Court of Justice which states that human embryonic stem cells are not patentable. If the results of research cannot be patented, this affects the profitability of research and thus the public interest in funding it.
>
> The rapporteur therefore proposes that research which either involves the destruction of human embryos or which uses human embryonic stem cells should be completely excluded from EU funding. It would thus be up to individual Member States to decide, in line with their ethical rules, whether to fund such research from their own budgets.[177]

14.60 Given the uncertainty that followed in the wake of *Brüstle*, the court in *International Stem Cell Corp* v *Comptroller General of Patents* referred a question to the ECJ,[178] namely whether unfertilised human ova whose division and further development had been stimulated by parthenogenesis, and which were incapable of developing into human beings, were 'human embryos' within the Biotech Directive and therefore excluded from patentability. In a preliminary ruling, the ECJ held that the Art 6(2)(c) exclusion in the Directive must be interpreted as meaning that unfertilised human ova whose division and further development had been stimulated by parthenogenesis, and which contained only pluripotent cells and are incapable of developing into human beings, do not constitute a 'human embryo' within the meaning of that provision, if, in the light of current scientific knowledge, it did not, in itself, have the inherent capacity of developing into a human being, this being a matter for the national court to determine.[179]

14.61 Commercial interests arguably suffered another blow in *Association for Molecular Pathology* v *Myriad Genetics, USPTO et al.*,[180] a US case wherein a group of plaintiffs alleged that Myriad's patents on two human genes associated with early onset of breast and ovarian cancer—the BRCA1 and BRCA2 genes—hampered scientific research, limited accessibility to medical care, were invalid on patent law criteria, and were unconstitutional. The patents, which cover the genes themselves (composition patents) and the processes making use of them (process patents), gave Myriad a lucrative monopoly to conduct or license medical tests relating to the genes, and Myriad has become notorious for its aggressive business model and enforcement practices, particularly within the USA. The case made its way haltingly to the USSC, which held that genes and the information that they encode are not patent eligible simply because they have been isolated from the surrounding genetic material. Overturning decades of lower court precedent, it invalidated Myriad's patents on isolated genomic human DNA on the basis that a naturally occurring DNA segment is a 'product of nature', but it upheld some of Myriad's claims directed towards complementary DNA molecules, determining that synthesising these molecules creates something new.[181] Although it has been cited and extended in two

---

[177] European Parliamentary Committee on Legal Affairs, *Draft Opinion on the proposal for a regulation establishing Horizon 2020 – the Framework Programme for Research and Innovation (2014–20)*, 2011/0401(COD), at 3.

[178] [2013] EWHC 807.

[179] *International Stem Cell Corp* v *Comptroller General of Patents* [2015] Bus LR 98 (ECJ). For comment, see E Bonadio and A Rovati, 'The Court of Justice of the European Union Clarifies When Human Embryonic Stem Cells Can Be Patented' (2015) 6 Euro J Risk Reg 293.

[180] 133 S Ct 2107 (2013).   [181] *Myriad IV*, at 2111 and 2119–20.

California district court cases,[182] and other litigation is proceeding apace,[183] the extent of the fallout from *Myriad IV* has yet to be determined, especially outside the USA.

14.62   Some insight into the problems of failing to maintain some sort of boundary between patent law and regulatory regimes can be gained by considering the possible effect of the current stem cell patent rulings on countries where SC research is both legal and encouraged. The UK is one such country that has invested heavily in the science and constructed a robust regulatory framework for embryo research administered by the HFEA. As we saw in Chapter 8, the HFEA operates a licensing system whereby research is only authorised under licence and it is a criminal offence to conduct it otherwise. The HFEA has granted licences in respect of numerous ESC research projects.[184] The ethics of embryo research and SC research were considered by a number of national bodies before legal authority was given for the work to be done. But what will be the impact of the rulings from the EPO and the ECJ in terms of patent incentives on the future of the UK's research programme? While the possibility remains for the grant of national patents only,[185] the influence of the European framework cannot be ignored. Concerns prompted a Joint Statement supporting stem cell funding in Horizon 2020 from bodies such as the Wellcome Trust, the Medical Research Council, and the European Genetic Alliances' Network in June 2012.[186]

14.63   There are numerous responses that we might have to the challenges thrown up by IP. For example, one could:

- Deny Patent Protection: But this is a generally unrealistic prospect and may be counter-productive if the venture capitalists are to be believed—they would simply cease funding the research necessary to produce the products in the first place.[187]

- Improve the Patent System: Standards of drafting patent applications could be strengthened to ensure that (1) inventions are properly described, and (2) unsustainable claims to protection are not made. This, in turn, would facilitate a more rigorous examination process that should ensure that protection is granted only to innovations that are truly inventive and which have never been made available to the public.

- Move to Open Science: Advocates of this wish to free-up the sharing of scientific and medical knowledge through various mechanisms such as the use of IP rights to require sharing rather than to police exclusivity.[188]

---

[182] *Ariosa Diagnostics Inc v Sequenom Inc*, No C 11-06391 SI, 2013 WL 5863022; *Genetic Technologies Ltd v Agilent Technologies Inc*, No CV 12-01616 RS, 2014 WL 941354.

[183] T Ingram, 'Association for Molecular Pathology v Myriad Genetics Inc: The Product of Nature Doctrine Revisited' (2014) 29 Berkeley Tech LJ 385.

[184] HFEA homepage at: http://www.hfea.gov.uk/Home.

[185] Intellectual Property Office, *Practice Note on Inventions involving Human Embryonic Stem Cells* (2012): http://www.ipo.gov.uk/p-pn-stemcells-20120517.htm.

[186] See http://www.scienceeurope.org/uploads/PublicDocumentsAndSpeeches/Joint_Statement_Stem_Cell_Research_in_Europe_2014.pdf.

[187] This consideration influenced the EGE in its report on patenting human stem cells wherein it concluded that it would not be in the public interest to exclude patent protection altogether. Instead the Group recommended more rigorous ethical evaluation of controversial patent applications, see EGE Opinion No 16, n 157 above, paras 2.1 and 2.10.

[188] See, Royal Society, *Science as an Open Enterprise* (2012), and K A Oye and R Wellhausen, 'The intellectual commons and property in synthetic biology' in M Schmidt et al. (eds), *Synthetic Biology: The Technoscience and its Societal Consequences* (2009).

We suggest that it is not so much the *existence* of IP rights that is the problem with an efficient incentive and reward system, rather the ways in which they are *exercised*. Many developments to date have failed to see or address this distinction.

14.64 So long as patents endure, and they will endure, then patent offices and courts must work together to limit the effects of overly broad patents by restricting protection to the precise contribution that an invention makes to human knowledge and no further.[189] A final novel approach—and one which brings us back to the idea of patient empowerment—is illustrated by the case of PXE International which is a patient and family support group for those affected by the genetic disorder pseudoxanthoma elasticum. The group announced in 2004 that one of its leading members had been named as a co-inventor of the gene associated with the condition together with the scientists responsible for its isolation. All rights have been assigned to PXE International, which considers itself the 'steward of the gene'. The Group entered various agreements to pursue further research and develop a diagnostic kit.[190] This is an example of interest groups working together within the patent system to pursue mutually beneficial ends. The only negative comment that could be made about the arrangement is that it is, at present, a very rare beast indeed.

CONCLUSION

14.65 It seems that whether we are dealing with living or dead human tissue, whether we are looking at humanity at the structured or the molecular level, or whether we are considering domestic or international regulation, we are faced with a schizoid approach to property rights in human material. On the one hand, there is an innate antipathy to the concept; on the other, we accept the inexorable march of 'science' knowing that, if something is there to be discovered, someone will discover it—and with little concern for the consequences—and some will want to benefit, commercially or otherwise, from that discovery. Governments may set up regulatory authorities as the significance of each scientific advance becomes apparent but they are relatively powerless in the face of global pressures. What does seem clear is that, so far as the domestic scene is concerned, our courts must appreciate that this is a field in which technology and societal attitudes are advancing and being fashioned rapidly—and the common law must keep pace and accelerate as is necessary.

---

[189] Another option is to make more use of compulsory licences, but there is a significant industry cultural resistance to this in many quarters, especially in the USA. See also van Overwalle, n 131.

[190] See the PXE website at: http://www.pxe.org.

15

MEDICAL FUTILITY

INTRODUCTION

15.01 It is probably fair to say that the health care professional will, intuitively, seek to prolong life so long as it is possible to do so. The massive technological advances of the last half-century have increased our capabilities in this respect and, perhaps because of this, we have become more and more aware that, occasionally, the preservation of life can be a negative blessing. Such an assessment may come from the patient him or herself—in which case we are in the field of euthanasia, which we discuss in Chapter 18. Alternatively, the health carers may, themselves, raise the question, not as to whether it is in the patient's interest that he or she should live or die but, rather, whether his or her death should be prolonged by medical intervention. In other words, there are times when we must ask if treatment should be considered futile and should be abandoned or not even begun—and such moments will arise with patients of any age. Even so, there are two situations in which life and death decisions become fundamental and unavoidable—when we are born and when we are dying. It is for this reason that we have divided the discussion into two sections dealing, respectively, with the beginning and the end of life; it must, at the same time, be recognised that the principles derived can be applied at any intervening time.

PART 1: THE BEGINNING OF LIFE

15.02 When the first edition of this book was written, selective non-treatment of the newborn and, most particularly, withholding the means of survival from mentally handicapped infants were burning issues; the cycle of interest has repeated itself to the present day. However, the cultural shift that has occurred is one away from medical paternalism towards parental autonomy. In the adult sphere, too, we have witnessed marked changes in judicial attitudes towards the care of patients in extreme and harrowing conditions such as persistent vegetative state or neuro-degenerative disorders. Most recently, we have witnessed the emergence of a new category of patient: the minimally conscious.

15.03 All such situations have it in common that treatment may be contraindicated on the grounds either that it is achieving no medical effect or that continued treatment can be seen as being against the patient's best interests. These can be subsumed together under the general heading of futility.[1] Simple as this analysis appears to be, attempts to reach a universally satisfactory definition of 'futility' do little more that open a Pandora's box of conflicting moral values—for it cannot be denied that it raises the curtain on what is no less than

---

[1] For updates see the Medical Futility Blog: http://medicalfutility.blogspot.co.uk/.

the first act in the wider drama of euthanasia. Thus, while we find the concept useful, albeit in a restricted way, we cannot introduce it without some consideration of its limitations.

THE CONCEPT OF MEDICAL FUTILITY

15.04 The immediate appeal of the concept of *futility* lies in its seemingly absolutist language which purports to present all parties concerned with a *fait accompli*: 'there is nothing more that can be done'. However, on closer analysis it is neither so straightforward nor is it as liberating—for health care professionals or others involved in decision-making—as this interpretation suggests.[2] Jecker and Pearlman[3] reviewed the literature and identified four major alternative definitions of futility:

    (i) treatment which was either useless or ineffective;

    (ii) that which fails to offer a minimum quality of life or a modicum of medical benefit;

    (iii) treatment that cannot possibly achieve the patient's goals; or

    (iv) treatment which does not offer a reasonable chance of survival.

15.05 This mix demonstrates very well the fundamental distinction which must be made between, on the one hand, the *effect* of a treatment—which is no more than an alteration in some bodily function—and, on the other, the *benefit* of a treatment—which is something that can be appreciated by the patient.[4] Put another way, the need is to distinguish between physiological and normative futility[5]—in which case, it is arguable that the former is to be decided on purely medical grounds while the latter involves a quality or value judgement which is the prerogative of the patient or his proxy decision-makers.[6] Against which, it has been said that medical judgements are never value-free[7] and that to abandon such judgements at the behest of the patient is to subvert the core of medical professionalism.[8] The doctor's dilemma can, perhaps, best be appreciated in terms of his or her objective. When the primary aim of the health carer is to preserve life, futility has a role to play only when life can no longer be preserved—a relatively simple concept. However, it assumes a role which is far less clear-cut when the doctor assumes the role of quality of life provider and this is particularly so when decisions are made as to life or

---

[2] See R K Mohindra, 'Medical futility: a conceptual model' (2007) 33 J Med Ethics 71. More recently, see A L Caplan, 'Little hope for medical futility' (2012) 87(11) Mayo Clin Proc 1040, and C J Misak et al., 'Medical futility: a new look at an old problem' (2014) 146(6) Chest 1667, doi: 10.1378/chest.14-0513.

[3] N S Jecker and R A Pearlman, 'Medical futility: Who decides?' (1992) 152 Arch Intern Med 1140.

[4] L J Schneiderman and N S Jecker, 'Futility in practice' (1993) 153 Arch Intern Med 437 and, more recently, J L Schneiderman, 'Defining medical futility and improving medical care' (2011) 8(2) J Bioethical Inq 123, doi: 10.1007/s11673-011-9293-3.

[5] Mohindra, n 2.

[6] The major part of an issue (1992) 20 Med Law Hlth Care was given over to the problem. See, in particular, R Cranford and L Gostin, 'Futility: A concept in search of a definition' at 307. For a review of definitions see L Schneiderman, (2011), n 4. And most recently, K M Swetz et al., 'Ten common questions (and their answers) on medical futility' (2014) 89(7) Mayo Clinic Proceedings 943, doi: 10.1016/j.mayocp.2014.02.005

[7] For recognition and engagement with this reality, see S Bailey, 'The concept of futility in health care decision making' (2004) 11 Nursing Ethics 77.

[8] J F Drane and J L Coulehan, 'The concept of futility: Patients do not have a right to demand medically useless treatment' (1993) 74 Hlth Prog 28; H Brody, 'Medical futility: A useful concept?' in M B Zucker and H D Zucker (eds), *Medical Futility* (1997) ch 1.

death. In such cases, medical intervention *may* keep the patient alive but, nonetheless, futility is advanced as a justification for allowing him or her to die. Futility then becomes not futility in the face of death but, rather, futility in the face of an unacceptable quality of life, which is a far more subjective construct, and one on which the competent patient himself will doubtless have views.[9]

15.06   Thus, the whole topic of medical futility—when seen as a concept rather than as a series of problem-solving exercises—is fraught with difficulties and contradictions.[10] It has been said that futility is not only a word which is foreign to the families of disabled neonates but it is also one which is unacceptable because of its hopelessness; its use militates against achieving a defensible societal response.[11] We have great sympathy with those who object to the concept on *semantic* and *philosophical* grounds. We much prefer to speak of non-productive treatment, which places the problem firmly in the medical field and, as a result, carries the added advantage of clarity of intention.[12] Meantime, it is suggested that non-productivity and futility can be reconciled if the latter concept is confined to Schneiderman and Jecker's summary definition:

> A treatment which cannot provide a minimum likelihood or quality of benefit should be regarded as futile and is not owed to the patient as a matter of moral duty.[13]

15.07   Schneiderman and Jecker have also reminded us that there are *positive* dangers of abuse if the term 'futile treatment' is adopted uncritically within the medical vocabulary. These include the resurgence of inappropriate paternalism, the erosion of patient autonomy, the unjustified avoidance of the duty to treat—or, we might add, the creation of an ephemeral duty *not* to treat—and the introduction of disguised and arbitrary rationing of resources.[14] Many of these pitfalls are revealed in the cases which follow.[15]

SELECTIVE NON-TREATMENT OF THE NEWBORN

15.08   It is apparent that we regard the problem of non-productive treatment as one that is common to all ages; nevertheless, selective non-treatment of the newborn retains some unique features.[16] First, it is intimately bound up with the subject of abortion—insofar as a large proportion of conditions which call for 'futile' neonatal treatments were present and were diagnosable in utero and, as such, constituted ground for legal termination of pregnancy by

---

[9] See A Lelie and M Verweij, 'Futility without dichotomy: Towards an ideal physician–patient relationship' (2003) 17 Bioethics 21.

[10] In a study from California, it was found that some 64 per cent of surrogate decision-makers distrusted the accuracy of the prediction of futility while as many as 18 per cent elected to continue treatment when the prognosis was no hope of recovery: L S Zier, J H Burack, G Micco, et al. (2009) 136 Chest 110. On the importance of specificity, see J Yagera 'The futility of arguing about medical futility in anorexia nervosa: the question is how would you handle highly specific circumstances?' (2015) 15(7) Am J Bioethics 47, doi: 10.1080/15265161.2015.1039724

[11] B Anderson and B Hall, 'Parents' perceptions of decision making for children' (1995) 23 J Law Med & Ethics 15; C Weijer and C Elliott, 'Pulling the plug on futility' (1995) 310 BMJ 683.

[12] We discuss this concept in greater detail at paras 18.12 et seq.   [13] See n 4.

[14] M Wreen, 'Medical futility and physician discretion' (2004) 30 J Med Ethics 275 and T Koch, 'Care, compassion or cost?: Redefining the basis of treatment in ethics and law' (2011) 39(2) J Law, Med and Ethics 130.

[15] See generally, R Huxtable, *Law, Ethics and Compromise at the Limits of Life: To Treat or Not to Treat?* (2013).

[16] For a view that neonates and older patients should not be treated so differently, see N Jecker, 'Medical Futility and the Death of a Child' (2011) 8 Bioethical Inquiry 133.

way of the Abortion Act 1967, s 1(1)(d). What, then, of those affected fetuses which come to full term undiagnosed? Where do public opinion and the law stand between the opposite extremes, on the one hand, of upholding a right to life and, on the other, of supporting medical assessments that intervention to sustain life is a pointless exercise? There has to be a middle road but, in the case of the neonate, we have had to find it without the aid of statute.

15.09 Second, treatment decisions taken immediately after birth concern human beings who are at the most vulnerable period of their lives—human beings, moreover, who cannot express their feelings for the present or the future and who clearly cannot have indicated their preferences to their surrogates. Parents faced with decision-making at this point might agree with their medical advisers simply because they have no evidence on which to *disagree*. The nascent personality of the child often acts like a blank page on which the court will write its own version of the child's interests in his life; by contrast, the seriously compromised adult has at least experienced enough to create his or her own biographical life, and this can lead the courts to differing interpretations of 'best interests' in the cases of adults compared to the newborn.

15.10 Whatever the age or condition of the patient, however, the 'futility' debate is, as discussed earlier, likely to be conducted at the 'quality of life' level. We have, however, not yet considered whether this is, of itself, a morally tenable level. Have we the right to place relative values on lives or is all life sacrosanct irrespective of the age or stage of development?[17]

Sanctity or Quality of Life?

15.11 The doctor's dilemma is self-evident—is she or he practising truly 'good' medicine in keeping alive a neonate who will be unable to take a place in society or who will be subject to pain and suffering throughout life? In short, is one to displace a concept of the sanctity of life based on a Hippocratic and theological foundation[18] by a standard which is, essentially, justified by a utilitarian ethos? The situation gives rise to a catalogue of questions— of which the first might well be to ask if there is, in fact, any solid basis for what has become known as the 'sanctity of life doctrine'. This seems to us to be, at least, doubtful, particularly if the doctrine is to be interpreted in terms of vitalism—or 'the sanctity of life at any price'. The Hippocratic Oath proscribes euthanasia but neither it, nor the more contemporary Declaration of Geneva impose an obligation to provide treatment at all times; rather, the emphasis is on doing no harm—an approach which clearly allows for pragmatic interpretation. A persuasive case can also be made out for there being no theological imperative to regard human life as unconditionally sacrosanct.[19]

15.12 While vitalism has been largely rejected, a modified concept of the sanctity of life is still widely endorsed. Even so, who is to determine the minimum quality of life? Whose life are we considering—the infant's, or are we also taking into account that of the parents or, indeed, the well-being of society? Do we, in fact, *want* a society in which the right to life depends upon achieving a norm that is largely measured in material terms? Should the disabled infant whose dying is needlessly prolonged be helped on its way?—and, if so, is this help to be a matter of omission or should positive steps be taken to end life? And, behind all these questions lies the Human Rights Act 1998 with its implications under

[17] J Tripp and D McGregor, 'Withholding and withdrawing life-sustaining treatment in the newborn' (2006) 91 Arch Dis Childh 67.
[18] G T Brown, 'Clarifying the concept of medical futility' (2014) 14(1) Nat Catholic Bioethics Q, 39, doi: 10.5840/ncbq201414146.
[19] K Boyd, 'Euthanasia: Back to the future' in J Keown (ed), *Euthanasia Examined* (1995) ch 7.

Art 2 (the right to life), Art 3 (the right not to be subjected to inhuman or degrading treatment), Art 8 (the right to respect for private and family life), and Art 9 (the right to freedom of thought, conscience, and religion) of the European Convention.

15.13 Inevitably, then, parents must be invited to make 'life or death' decisions on behalf of their physically or mentally challenged offspring—and they will be guided by the doctor whose advice is likely to be on the lines that consideration for the preservation of life is secondary to that of preventing suffering. Thus, we have the evidence of Dr Dunn at the trial of Dr Arthur: 'no paediatrician takes life but we do accept that allowing babies to die is in the baby's interest at times'.[20] This, of course, presupposes that there is an essential difference between activity and passivity when the same end—death—is realised by either and that, arising from this, passivity does not conflict with the doctor's duty to '... maintain the utmost respect for human life'.[21] Yet, it is clear that all such decisions rest on the premise that there is a point at which death is preferable to life; and that some person can decide that point in surrogate fashion and that it is right and proper for others to follow that judgement through.

15.14 This seems to come perilously close to breaking the law. To kill a living human being deliberately is murder and, except as to the specific crime of infanticide,[22] the age of the victim has no relevance. Killing a child by omission could be prosecuted under s 1 of the Children and Young Persons Act 1933;[23] it is more likely to be charged as manslaughter although it could be murder[24]—the paramount considerations being whether there is a duty of care and, if there is, what is the extent of that duty.[25] Self-evidently, the consultant in charge of the paediatric ward has a duty of care to his or her patients, as do the range of subordinate staff. Yet, an international study of physicians working in neonatal care units found that 70 per cent of UK neonatologists admitted to administering sedatives or analgesics to suppress pain even at the risk of death, while 4 per cent confessed to administering drugs with the express intention of ending life.[26] More recently, a Swedish study found that a majority of both physicians (56 per cent) and the general population (53 per cent) supported arguments for withdrawing ventilator treatment from neonates with sever brain damage.[27]

15.15 But what of the rights of the neonate in the equation? The newly born baby has the same legal rights to respect as has every human being. From the ethical and philosophical perspective, however, this proposition has suffered sustained attack as the definition of personhood in terms of intellect has been developed.[28] We have already observed that, if it

---

[20] *R v Arthur* (1981) 12 BMLR 1 at 18. Dr Dunn subsequently stated that he would limit withholding life-saving treatment only to three groups of neonate: those with severe malformations; those with severe hypoxic/traumatic brain damage; and those of extreme prematurity with major problems such as brain haemorrhage: P M Dunn, 'Appropriate care of the newborn: ethical dilemmas' (1993) 19 J Med Ethics 82.

[21] Declaration of Geneva (2006).   [22] Infanticide Act 1938.

[23] As amended most recently by the Serious Crime Act 2015.

[24] *R v Gibbins and Proctor* (1918) 13 Cr App R 134, CCA.

[25] *R v Stone*; *R v Dobinson* [1977] QB 354; [1977] 2 All ER 341, CA.

[26] See M Cuttini et al., 'End-of-life decisions in neonatal intensive care: physicians' self-reported practices in seven European countries' (2000) 355 Lancet 2112. Compare a US study, L Barton and J E Hodgman, 'The contribution of withholding or withdrawing care to newborn mortality' (2005) 116 Pediatrics 1487. See also the Special Issue on withholding or withdrawal of life-sustaining treatment of newborn infants (including diverse religious perspectives): (2012) 88(2) Early Human Development 65.

[27] A Rydvall et al., 'To treat or not to treat a newborn child with severe brain damage? A cross-sectional study of physicians' and the general population's perceptions of intentions' (2014) 17(1) Med Health Care Philos 81, doi: 10.1007/s11019-013-9498-9.

[28] Compare, Nuffield Council on Bioethics, *Critical Care Decisions in Fetal and Neonatal Medicine: Ethical Issues* (2006).

is valid to treat the fetus as a non-person, it is also valid as a matter of logic to invoke the same parameters to deny personhood to the neonate.[29] And as stated most recently by the High Court:

> [T]he strong presumption in favour of a course of action that will prolong life is not an irrebuttable one. This position reflects the fact that life, as precious as it is, cannot be, and indeed should not be preserved at all costs in the face of its natural conclusion.[30].

It is against this legal and ethical background that we can trace the absorption of the concept of medical futility into the medical jurisprudence of the UK as, first, related to the neonate and infant.[31]

Futility or a Duty Not to Treat?

15.16 Although *R v Arthur*[32] was, chronologically speaking, not the first instance of selective non-treatment of the newborn to come before the English courts, it was undoubtedly that which brought the whole subject before the public conscience. Insofar as it was taken through the criminal courts, it is an unsatisfactory prototype and a poor precedent; nevertheless, it remains an important landmark that continues to have resonance today.

15.17 Put briefly, the salient features of the case are that a baby was born with apparently uncomplicated Down's syndrome and was rejected by his parents. Dr Arthur, a paediatrician of high repute and impeccable professional integrity, wrote in the notes 'Parents do not wish it to survive. Nursing care only'; the baby died 69 hours later. Dr Arthur was charged with murder but, during the course of the trial, medical evidence was adduced to the effect that the child had not been physically healthy; accordingly, the charge was reduced to one of attempted murder. Dr Arthur was acquitted.

15.18 The central question raised by the trial is why, in the light of the acknowledged developments in neonatal intensive care, was Dr Arthur singled out for prosecution? In our view, the most logical answer lies in the application of a 'treatability' test. Dr Arthur's patient was in no physical pain and, so far as was known prior to autopsy, he required no treatment. Death in such circumstances depends on the withholding of nourishment and to take away such a life is to make a social rather than a medical decision—the fact that it was taken by a doctor rather than a member of the public should be irrelevant. The prosecution of Dr Arthur led to a storm of resentment on the part of the leaders of the medical profession but this was almost entirely due to a failure to appreciate that there is a world of difference between withholding treatment from a dying patient and refusing sustenance to one who shows firm evidence of a will to live.[33] Any confusion as to the doctor's role is dispersed once it is appreciated that there is a fundamental distinction to be drawn between physical defect—for which invasive treatment remains an option—and mental defect for which no curative treatment is available. The failure of the medical

---

[29] Although old, the classic text advocating this position remains H Kuhse and P Singer, *Should the Baby Live?* (1985) ch 6.

[30] *Kings College Hospital NHS Foundation Trust v Y (By Her Children's Guardian), MH* [2015] EWHC 1966 (Fam).

[31] See further, R J Boyle, R Salter, and M W Arnander, 'Ethics of refusing parental requests to withhold or withdraw treatment from their premature baby' (2004) 30 J Med Ethics 402 and H McHaffie, 'A Scottish researcher's response' (2004) 30 J Med Ethics 406. For a comparative perspective, see J Porscheidt, E Verhagen, P Sauer, and J H Huben, 'Parental involvement in end of life decisions in neonatology: Legal considerations with regard to Dutch medical practice' (2011) 11(1) Med Law Int 1.

[32] (1981) 12 BMLR 1.

[33] E.g. Editorial comment 'Paediatricians and the law' (1981) 283 BMJ 1280.

establishment in this respect is exemplified in the statement at the time of the President of the Royal College of Physicians:

> Where there is an uncomplicated Down's case and the parents do not want the child to live...I think there are circumstances where it would be ethical to put it upon a course of management that would end in its death...I say that with a child suffering from Down's and with a parental wish that it should not survive, it is ethical to terminate life.[34]

15.19 By any standards, that is a remarkable interpretation of both medical and parental responsibilities and powers. In the light of later judicial decisions, which are discussed later, it is inconceivable that Dr Arthur's regime would be acceptable today. In our view, the management pattern disclosed in *R v Arthur* is best seen as an example of the dangers of extrapolating the concept of 'futility' to one of an obligation not to treat in the face of parental pressure. The acquittal of Dr Arthur should be seen as an anachronism from those times.

Case Law Other than *Arthur*

15.20 The template for contemporary approaches was undoubtedly established in the prototype case[35] of *Re B (a minor)*,[36] the judgment in which has been said to lay down the 'bedrock proposition' in this field.[37] Thus, despite its antiquity, *Re B* still merits close consideration. In essence, B was an infant suffering from Down's syndrome complicated by intestinal obstruction of a type which would be fatal per se but which was readily amenable to surgical treatment. The parents took the view that the kindest thing in the interests of the child would be for her not to have the operation and for her to die—a decision that was later described by Dunn LJ as 'an entirely responsible one'. The infant was made a ward of court and, in the face of both judicial indecision and medical disagreement, the question 'to treat or not to treat?' came before the Court of Appeal.

15.21 The summary answer to the basic question was provided by Dunn LJ in saying, 'She should be put in the position of any other mongol child and given the opportunity to live an existence'.[38] For the major analysis, however, we must look to Templeman LJ who, adhering to the general principles relating to the affairs of minors,[39] concluded that the judge of first instance, in refusing to authorise the operation, had been too much concerned with the wishes of the parents; the duty of the court was to decide the matter in the interests of the child. In coming to the conclusion that these interests were best served by treatment, he said:

> it devolves on this court...to decide whether the life of this child is demonstrably going to be so awful that in effect the child must be condemned to die or whether the life of

[34] (1981) 12 BMLR 1 at 21–2. See also the leading contemporary article, 'After the trial at Leicester' (1981) 2 Lancet 1085. It is possible that a similar attitude persisted: Z Kmietowick, 'Down's children received "less favourable" hospital treatment' (2001) 322 BMJ 815 commenting on R Evans (chairwoman), *The Report of the Independent Inquiries into Paediatric Cardiac Services* (2001).

[35] These early cases are collected and reviewed succinctly in J Read and L Clements, 'Demonstrably awful: The right to life and the selective non-treatment of disabled babies and young children' (2004) 31 J Law & Soc 482.

[36] (1981) [1990] 3 All ER 927; [1981] 1 WLR 1421, CA.

[37] *Portsmouth Hospitals NHS Trust v Wyatt and another* [2005] 1 WLR 3995; (2005) 86 BMLR 173 at para 67.

[38] [1990] 3 All ER 930 at 931; [1981] 1 WLR 1421 at 1425.

[39] Guardianship of Minors Act 1971, s 1. See, now, Children Act 1989, s 1.

this child is still so imponderable that it would be wrong for her to be condemned to die...Faced with [the] choice, I have no doubt that it is the duty of this court to decide that the child must live,[40]

and it was this that led Lord Donaldson to look upon *Re B* as close to a binding authority for the proposition that there is a balancing exercise to be performed in assessing the course to be adopted in the best interests of such children.

15.22 Templeman LJ did, however, clearly leave the door open for an alternative decision in saying:

There may be cases...of severe proved damage where the future is so certain and where the life of the child is so bound to be full of pain and suffering that the court might be driven to a different conclusion.[41]

15.23 Thus, the court clearly accepted that there is an essential prognostic difference between mental and physical handicap and, as to the latter, laid the foundations for a quality of life therapeutic standard rather than one based on a rigid adherence to the principle of the sanctity of human life. Even so, the medical profession was now left in a cleft stick; even allowing for the fact that they relate to different jurisdictions, *Re B* and *Arthur* are virtually impossible to reconcile. This unsatisfactory situation persisted for almost a decade but was then greatly clarified in a series of cases overseen by Lord Donaldson MR.[42] The decisions in these cases relate to treatment of infants rather than of the newborn. They can, therefore, be taken as early examples of the application of medical futility across the whole span of life.

SELECTIVE NON-TREATMENT IN INFANCY

15.24 The Donaldson decisions can be viewed as establishing the framework for tackling a spectrum of cases that explores the entire gamut of variables, from the (non-)relevance of distinguishing between withholding or withdrawing treatment to the difference between letting nature take its course and intervening to cause death. The approach adopted should be contrasted with the attitude of the courts in more recent cases, as we discuss in due course.

15.25 The index case, *Re C*,[43] concerned a moribund child and the essence of the decision was that the hospital were given authority to treat her so as to allow her life to come to an end peacefully and with dignity; it was specifically said to be unnecessary to use antibiotics or to set up intravenous infusions or nasogastric feeding regimes. The decision was based on the paramountcy of her welfare, well-being, and interests.

15.26 In contrast, Baby J[44] was not dying and the case illustrates more clearly the real dilemma presented by these cases. The situation was that the brain-damaged child suffered from repetitive fits and periods of cessation of breathing for which he required ventilation. There was no doubt that he could be rescued in the probable event that he sustained

---

[40] [1990] 3 All ER 930 at 931; [1981] 1 WLR 1421 at 1424.

[41] [1990] 3 All ER 930 at 931; [1981] 1 WLR 1421 at 1424.

[42] For review of these cases, see J K Mason, 'Master of the balancers: Non-voluntary therapy under the mantle of Lord Donaldson' [1993] JR 115.

[43] *Re C (a minor) (wardship: medical treatment)* [1989] 2 All ER 782, [1990] Fam 26.

[44] *Re J (a minor) (wardship: medical treatment)* [1990] 3 All ER 930; (1992) 6 BMLR 25.

further episodes of respiratory failure but it was equally certain that he would die if the necessary treatment was withheld. The question before the court was what was to be done if he sustained a further collapse. The Court of Appeal ruled that it would not be in J's best interests to reventilate him 'unless to do so seems appropriate to the doctors caring for him given the prevailing clinical situation'.[45]

15.27 In the course of his judgment, the Master of the Rolls made several observations which we see as being of particular importance. First, he stressed that, while there was a strong presumption in favour of a course of action that will prolong life, nevertheless, the person who makes the decision must look at it from the assumed view of the patient.[46] In J's case, the quality of life, even without the added effect of further hypoxic episodes, was extremely low. Second, the court held that decision-making was a cooperative effort between the doctors and the parents—or, in the case of wardship, between the doctors and the court with the views of the parents being taken into consideration;[47] any choice must be made solely in the child's best interests. Finally—and this we see as especially significant—it was emphasised that any decision taken was one which would affect death by way of a side effect; the debate was not about terminating life but solely about whether to withhold treatment designed to prevent death from natural causes.[48]

15.28 These positions were endorsed in a further case called Re J.[49] The feature distinguishing this case from the previous two was that one of the parents disagreed with the doctors as to what should be done. J's mother attempted to enforce the intensive care of her child who had sustained severe brain damage as a result of a fall. The Court of Appeal, however, refused to entertain the suggestion that it should direct clinicians to provide treatment against their best clinical judgement:

> I agree with Lord Donaldson that I can conceive of no situation where it would be proper...to order a doctor, whether directly or indirectly, to treat a child in the manner contrary to his or her clinical judgment. I would go further. I find it difficult to conceive of a situation where it would be a proper exercise of the jurisdiction to make an order positively requiring a doctor to adopt a particular course of treatment in relation to a child.[50]

Thus, this series of cases indicates a strong judicial belief in the doctor's clinical autonomy. It also shows a very determined stance in favour of a quality of life standard which is founded on the principle of the patient's 'best interests'.

15.29 It may well be permissible to see death as a blessed relief from severe pain or unacceptable bodily invasion and, therefore, an outcome of a treatment that is in the patient's 'best

[45] [1990] 3 All ER 930 at 933; (1992) 6 BMLR 25 at 29.
[46] Lord Donaldson demonstrated a sympathy with the 'substituted judgement' test throughout this series of cases (see paras 15.30–15.31).
[47] The nurses were singled out for praise in the Court of Appeal in Re C, where there were clear indications that their views should also be considered.
[48] [1990] 3 All ER 930 at 943; (1990) 6 BMLR 25 at 40, per Taylor LJ. In Re C, the Court of Appeal would not even tolerate the expression 'treat to die'.
[49] Re J (a minor) (medical treatment) [1993] Fam 15; [1992] 4 All ER 614. For ease, we refer to this case as Re J(2). Two supportive decisions were also reached in Scotland. The determination in the fatal accident inquiry concerning the death of Rebecca Cassidy supported a decision not to treat an extremely low birthweight premature infant: see S English, 'Doctor was right not to resuscitate "unviable" baby' The Times, 27 June 1997, p 11. The decision not to provide a liver transplant for a teenage girl was accepted as good medical practice in the inquiry into the death of Michelle Paul: see G Bowditch, 'Surgeon right to refuse teenager a liver transplant', The Times, 23 July 1997, p 7.
[50] [1993] Fam 15 at 29; [1992] 4 All ER 614 at 625, per Balcombe LJ.

interests'. By contrast, the patient who has sustained brain damage of such degree as to permanently deprive him or her of sensation and cognition has, arguably, no immediate interests as between death or survival.[51]

15.30 We believe that some other test is called for in the latter circumstance and that it is there, in particular, that we can legitimately call on the concept of medical futility to guide our therapeutic programming.[52] However, as we have seen, this can conflict with the respect due to *patient* autonomy and, to avoid this, it may be preferable to rely on the principle of substituted judgement—or, in other words, to follow the regime that one assumes the patient him or herself would have opted for if given the chance.[53] The objections to such a test are discussed in greater detail later.[54] For the present, we will only observe that its acceptance relieves one of an element of hypocrisy that is inherent in the 'best interests' test. We are constantly assured that judicial treatment/non-treatment decisions are founded on the best interests of the patient alone and that the interests of the relatives, carers, and, indeed, the state are entirely secondary, if not irrelevant—yet, in all honesty, it is hard, if not impossible, to separate these extraneous interests. Substituted judgement allows us to take the latter into consideration with a relatively clear conscience. A competent patient may opt for non-treatment rather than treatment and the effects of the decision on his or her family can legitimately form part of its foundation; there is no reason why this should not be incorporated in the substituted judgement.

15.31 In fact, the English courts, in their anxiety to maintain the welfare principle, have historically tended to confuse the two tests.[55] Thus, we have, again, Lord Donaldson[56] quoting McKenzie J:[57]

> It is not appropriate for an external decision maker to apply his standards of what constitutes a liveable life... The decision can only be made in the context of the disabled person viewing the worthwhileness or otherwise of his life in its own context as a disabled person.[58]

And although it was taken as expressing the best interests of J, this is as clear a description of the principle of substituted judgement as one is likely to find. It is further reflected in the 2014 assessment by Ms Justice Russell of a 17-month-old infant with catastrophic, irreversible brain injury who stated plainly: '...I start with the presumption that Z himself would want the continuation of life and that he has shown himself to be tenacious and a real fighter with a strong survival instinct to survive as long as he has'.[59] Notwithstanding, the predominance of framing the issues in terms of an ever-burgeoning best interests test has dominated the jurisprudence throughout its development.

---

[51] Compare D Sperling, *Posthumous Interests: Legal and Ethical Perspectives* (2008) ch 1.

[52] See also P Weisleder, 'Dignified death for severely-impaired infants: Beyond the best interests standard' (2007) 22 J Child Neurol 737. The role and relevance of dignity in death has been emphasised in *King's College Hospital NHS Foundation Trust v Y (By Her Children's Guardian), MH*, n 30 above, paras 56–7.

[53] 'Donning the mental mantle of the incompetent patient': see *Superintendent of Belchertown State School v Saikewicz* 370 NE 2d 64 (Mass, 1977).

[54] See paras 15.130 et seq.

[55] We would suggest that this confusion persists in the Mental Capacity Act 2005, which we discuss in Chapters 4 and 12.

[56] In *Re J* [1990] 3 All ER 930; (1990) 6 BMLR 25.

[57] In *Re Superintendent of Family and Child Services and Dawson* (1983) 145 DLR (3d) 610.

[58] [1990] 3 All ER 930 at 936; (1990) 6 BMLR 25 at 32.

[59] *King's College Hospital NHS Foundation Trust v T, V, ZT (a child by his Children's Guardian)* [2014] EWHC 3315 (Fam).

Important Cases Post-Donaldson

15.32 *Re C (a baby)*[60] concerned a decision to withdraw ventilation from a child with the result that she would die within a couple of hours. Her medical condition was described as not being in coma but as having 'a very low awareness of anything, if at all'; Sir Stephen Brown P summed up her condition as 'almost a living death'. Applying the best interests test, he was in no doubt that it would be lawful to withdraw the particular care in this particular case. He refused, however, to make any general observations of wider application—each patient must be treated according to his or her own circumstances.

15.33 We see, then, that 'best interests' can be applied equally to cases[61] in which withdrawal of care will accelerate death; but what of circumstances where parents are strongly opposed to this route? In *Re C (a minor) (medical treatment)*,[62] the parents were orthodox Jews who firmly believed that life should always be preserved. Their child, aged 16 months, suffered from spinal muscular atrophy—a progressive condition for which it was agreed there was no curative treatment. The medical team proposed withdrawal of ventilation to see if the child could survive independently; if not, they would not re-intervene. In the event, the President relied heavily on Lord Donaldson's leading cases[63] in defining the legal limits of the doctor's duties. In particular:

> [To follow the wishes of the parents] would be tantamount to requiring the doctors to undertake a course of treatment which they are unwilling to do. The court could not consider making an order which would require them so to do.[64]

15.34 Once again, this evidences an endorsement of the strong position of the medical profession in such cases. Much the same situation underlay *A National Health Service Trust v D*[65] but the jurisprudential value of this case lies in the fact that it considered the issues from a human rights perspective. The Trust applied for a declaration with respect to a seriously disabled child that, in the event of a further cardiorespiratory arrest, it would be lawful not to resuscitate him but to initiate treatment designed to let him end his life peacefully and with dignity. Medical opinion was unanimously in favour of this approach which was strongly opposed by the parents on the ground that it was premature. Cazalet J granted the declaration on the ground that it was in the child's best interests that he be so managed; in so doing, the judge defined the following position:

> the court's prime and paramount consideration must be the best interests of the child. This of course involves ... consideration of the views of the parents concerned ... However, ... those views cannot themselves override the court's view of the ward's best interests.[66]

Thus, the courts, and not any other party, lay or professional, are the ultimate arbiters in such cases.

15.35 Cazalet J also considered the implications of compliance with the European Convention on Human Rights (ECHR) and concluded that there could be no infringement of Art 2 insofar as the order was made in the best interests of D. At the same time, he confirmed

---

[60] *Re C (a baby)* [1996] 2 FLR 43; (1996) 32 BMLR 44.

[61] We discuss these cases in greater detail in J K Mason, *The Troubled Pregnancy* (2007) ch 7.

[62] *Re C (a minor)* (1997) 40 BMLR 31.

[63] *Re J (a minor)* [1990] 3 All ER 930; (1992) 6 BMLR 25; *Re J (a minor)* [1993] Fam 15; [1992] 4 All ER 614; *Re R (a minor) (wardship: medical treatment)* [1992] Fam 11; (1991) 7 BMLR 147.

[64] (1997) 40 BMLR 31 at 37.   [65] [2000] 2 FLR 677; (2000) 55 BMLR 19.

[66] [1992] 2 FLR 667 at 686; (2000) 55 BMLR 19 at 28.

that Art 3 encompassed the right to die with dignity[67]—an increasingly commonly used phrase which seems to us to be becoming equivalent to 'without the encumbrance of invasive forms of treatment'. Thus, in the *Wyatt* case (discussed more fully below), we have Hedley J stating:

> It seems to me...that in any consideration of best interests in a person at risk of imminent death is that of securing a 'good' death. It would be absurd to try to describe that concept more fully beyond saying that everyone in this case knows what it means – not under anaesthetic, not in the course of painful and futile treatment, but peacefully in the arms of those who love her most.[68]

15.36 These rulings tend to suggest that the legal position has been well settled, but a spate of more recent cases over the timespan of the last few editions of this book casts some doubt on this assumption. The more recent series began with two cases[69] which received much public attention—those of Baby Winston-Jones[70] and Baby Wyatt, mentioned above.[71] Baby Winston-Jones was nine months old and suffered from an incurable genetic condition resulting in severe cardiorespiratory dysfunction. Baby Wyatt was 11 months old at the time of the first action. She had been born very prematurely and suffered from severe and repeated respiratory failure with associated heart and renal failure. She was blind, deaf, and could make no voluntary movements. Medical opinion was unanimous that she would have minimal cognitive function but would be able to experience the pain of any future treatment. Prognosis for 12 months' survival lay between 25 per cent and 5 per cent. In both cases, the hospitals sought a declaration that it would not be unlawful to withhold ventilation should it be needed. Both sets of parents strongly opposed the request. In the case of Baby Winston-Jones, Dame Butler-Sloss decided that it was not in his best interests to be mechanically ventilated, more or less upholding the case law that has gone before.

15.37 In similar fashion, the judge at first instance in *Wyatt* followed existing precedent declaring the proposed action of the medical team to be lawful.[72] An additional factor added to the equation, however, was the question over the 'intolerable' nature of Charlotte's existence. Charlotte's parents argued that the proper test to apply in such cases was indeed 'intolerabililty' and that this could not be said of Charlotte's life which had, meantime, shown some improvement. The Court of Appeal[73] rejected this argument, stating that, at most, 'intolerability' is only a potentially valuable guide towards the determination of best interests. Best interests must be considered broadly, encompassing, but also going beyond, medical interests and should include emotional and

---

[67] Quoting *D* v *United Kingdom* (1997) 24 EHRR 423. Cazalet J did not enlarge on his interpretation of either article.

[68] *Portsmouth NHS Trust* v *Wyatt and Wyatt, Southampton NHS Trust Intervening* [2005] 1 FLR 21, at para 28; endorsed most recently by MacDonald J in *King's College Hospital* v *Y*, n 52 above, paras 56–7.

[69] For comment see, D W Meyers, 'Wyatt and Winston-Jones: Seriously ill babies and who decides to treat or let die?' (2005) 9 Edin LR 307. See also M Brazier, 'Letting Charlotte die' (2004) 30 J Med Ethics 519.

[70] *Re Winston-Jones (a child) (medical treatment: parent's consent)* [2004] All ER (D) 313 later reported as *Re L (medical treatment: benefit)* [2005] 1 FLR 491.

[71] *Re Wyatt (a child) (medical treatment: parents' consent)* [2005] 1 FLR 21; [2004] 84 BMLR 206.

[72] The case was heard twice more in the High Court: *Portsmouth Hospitals NHS Trust* v *Wyatt* [2005] EWHC 117, *Wyatt* v *Portsmouth Hospitals NHS Trust and Wyatt (No 3)* [2005] 2 FLR 480.

[73] *Portsmouth NHS Trust* v *Wyatt* [2005] 1 WLR 3995; (2005) 86 BMLR 173.

other welfare issues: 'any criteria which seek to circumscribe the best interests tests are, we think, to be avoided'.[74]

15.38 The Court of Appeal further commented that, 'the intellectual milestones for the judge in a case such as the present are ... simple, although the ultimate decision will frequently be extremely difficult' (at para 87) and, to assist in approaching the task, the court endorsed the use of a balance sheet to weigh up the benefits and burdens in continued medical intervention.[75] This was then employed very deliberately by the court in *An NHS Trust* v *MB*[76]—a case of spinal muscular atrophy which was unique in that the parents strongly opposed the withdrawal of care while, at the same time, MB was thought to have the awareness of a normal 18-month-old child.[77] In the event, Holman J considered that it was not in his best interests that his ventilator should be removed and this was so despite the fact that the list of burdens was far longer than that of the benefits and while it was acknowledged that MB was unlikely to live more than a year.[78] In contrast, the court in *Re K (a minor)*[79] issued a declaration because on the evidence there was 'no realistic sense in which one can assign to her the simple pleasure of being alive'. In *Re OT*,[80] a trust sought emergency declarations that it was no longer under a legal duty to continue to treat a severely ill child who was suffering repeated collapses and whose medical condition was judged by all medical parties to be futile. This was opposed by the parents who wanted everything to be done to prolong his life; furthermore, they argued for a breach of their human rights and those of their child with respect to the Trust's attempt to seek emergency declarations. The court followed the by now familiar route in applying best interests and granting the declarations sought. Emergency declarations were not, in and of themselves, a breach of human rights; the parents had had plenty of time to prepare a case as the dispute with the Trust unfolded. The balance of benefits and burdens supported the declarations granted.

15.39 There was, then, by this juncture in the development of the jurisprudence sufficient cases from which to divine a pattern of judicial decision-making. Holman J, in *MB*,[81] thought that these could be summarised in ten propositions which it will be helpful to repeat— although in the interests of space this is in the form of paraphrase:

  (i) the court must arbitrate on a treatment decision and exercise its own independent and objective judgement when asked to do so by one or both parties;

  (ii) this right and power only arises because the patient lacks the capacity to make a personal decision;

  (iii) substituted judgement has no place in decision-making, nor does the court decide on the reasonableness of the doctors' or parents' decisions;

  (iv) the matter must be decided on the basis of an objective approach or test;

---

[74] At para 88. For comment see A Morris, 'Selective treatment of irreversibly impaired infants: decision-making at the threshold' (2009) 17(3) Med L Rev 347 and R Heywood, 'Parents and medical professionals: conflict, cooperation, and best interests' (2012) 20(1) Med L Rev 29.

[75] See *Re A (Male Sterilisation)* [2000] 1 FLR 549.

[76] [2006] 2 FLR 319; [2006] Lloyd's Rep Med 323.

[77] Thus, it can be looked on as equivalent to the adult cases of progressive neuromuscular disease discussed in Chapter 18.

[78] This emphasises the, perhaps, obvious point that a balance sheet of this type cannot be interpreted on a purely 'mathematical head-count'.

[79] [2006] 2 FLR 883; (2006) 99 BMLR 98.   [80] [2009] EWHC 633 (Fam).

[81] N 76 at para 16.

(v) that test is the best interests of the patient—best interests being used in the widest sense;

(vi) the court must do its best to balance all the conflicting considerations in a particular case and see where the final balance of the best interests lies;

(vii) considerable weight must be attached to the prolongation of life but the principle is not absolute and may be outweighed if the pleasures and the quality of life are sufficiently small and the pain and suffering or other burdens of living are sufficiently great;

(viii) the principal authority for these considerations lies in the words of Lord Donaldson in *Re J (a minor) (wardship: medical treatment)*;[82]

(ix) all these cases are very fact specific;

(x) the views and opinions of both the doctors and the parents must be carefully considered. The parents' *wishes*, however, are wholly irrelevant to consideration of the objective best interests of the child save to the extent that they may illuminate the quality and value to the child of the child–parent relationship.

15.40 The approach now seems well settled, although the cases now proceed not in the vain of establishing any novel legal precedent, but in the case-by-case exercise of (moral?) judgement in very tragic circumstances. *NHS Trust v Baby X*[83] is a clear example of this. The parents were diametrically opposed to the care team in their view as to what counted as their son's best interests: they wanted ventilation continued while the carers were of the firm view that this should be removed in favour of palliative care only. In the event, the judge came down on the side of the carers, if it is even appropriate to talk of sides. More recent decisions follow a very similar approach taking into account an increasing array of very detailed considerations. Thus, chronologically, we have *An NHS Foundation Trust v AB* in which the court authorised withdrawal of respiratory support from a one-year-old boy with an incurable neurodevelopmental disorder and whose decline was inevitable.[84] The court applied the ten-point test above and relied upon professional guidance (see below). It did, however, concede to the parental argument that 'bagging'—as opposed to re-intubation—should occur if required within the first 24 hours after withdrawal to allow him to spend final quality time with the family. In *King's College Hospital NHS Foundation Trust v T*, the court found that '... mechanical ventilation is only just sustaining life with no other benefit'.[85] Taking an holistic view of best interests and including full account of the views of the parents, the court opined—on balance—that not only was withdrawal lawful but that continuation would likely lead to more pain, suffering, and deterioration. Finally, in *King's College Hospital NHS Foundation Trust v Y (By Her Children's Guardian), MH*, the High Court was called upon to deal with an 'Out of Hours' emergency application concerning intubation and invasive ventilation of a seven-year-old child.[86] While clearly not a neonate case, the same legal principles were applied and the balance sheet approach adopted. In acknowledging the care and reluctance of the father in being unwilling to accede to the medical opinion supporting non-intervention, the Court nonetheless declared such a course to be lawful considering both the dis-benefit of prolonging the child in a persistent vegetative state

---

[82] [1991] Fam 33 at 46.
[83] [2012] EWHC 2188 (Fam); (2012) 127 BMLR 188; [2012] Fam Law 1331.
[84] [2014] EWHC 1031 (Fam); [2014] Fam Law 969.
[85] [2014] EWHC 3315 (Fam); (2015) 143 BMLR 202; [2014] Fam Law 1678.
[86] [2015] EWHC 1966 (Fam).

and the positive benefit of allowing the parents to be physically closer to her in her final hours than would be possible if intubation were to occur.

15.41 These judgments are each an example of the real task at hand in such cases: not a formulaic application of legal rules but a delicate weighing of evidence and experience which could so easily go either way. A further fundamental tension is, however, revealed—that is, what will a court do if it prefers the parents' assessment of the child's interests? We have no authority that indicates that a court will *require doctors to treat* against their better judgement; indeed, as we have seen, this has been expressly rejected by the Court of Appeal on several occasions. At most, it is likely that a court will declare it to be part of the attending doctor's continuing duty of care to his patient to refer him or her to a colleague who is prepared to follow the parents' wishes.

15.42 Of growing import too seems to be the position of guidance from professional bodies. For example, the Royal College of Paediatrics and Child Health has produced guidance over the last two decades, the most recent edition of which appeared in March 2015.[87] In a veritable *tour de force* of the legal, ethical, and professional considerations, perhaps of most pertinence to the current discussion is this passage on the interaction between professionals and parents:

> Good practice requires ongoing discussion between relevant parties to resolve disagreements. Clarification of the facts, by obtaining second medical opinions or clarification and analysis of the ethical issues involved by clinical ethics services and others, may be helpful, as may the use of mediation techniques. Wherever possible these should be used before referral to court is made. If a matter is referred to court, the court will wish to know what attempts have been made—and by whom—to resolve conflicts.[88]

Such guidelines do not have the force of law but, as this quote suggests, their observance will go a long way to protecting the decision-makers while, equally, non-observance will reflect adversely on the person who fails to follow them. Accordingly, professional guidelines have profound significance in sensitive therapeutic fields and numerous documents relating to paediatric practice are now available.[89] The Royal College of Paediatrics and Child Health goes as far as to outline five situations where the withholding or withdrawal of curative medical treatment might be considered:

(i) children with advanced progressive incurable disease;

(ii) children whose death is expected in the foreseeable future;

(iii) children in whom there is a risk of death from a sudden acute crisis in the condition;

---

[87] Royal College of Paediatrics and Child Health, *Making Decisions to Limit Treatment in Life-limiting and Life-threatening Conditions in Children: A Framework for Practice* (2015), available at: http://www.rcpch.ac.uk/what-we-do/ethics/ethics. For comment, see V Larcher et al., 'Making decisions to limit treatment in life-limiting and life-threatening conditions in children: a framework for practice' (2015) 100 Arch Dis Child Suppl 2, doi: 10.1136/archdischild-2014-306666.

[88] N 86 above, Larcher (2015), at s 9.

[89] See Royal College of Paediatrics and Child Health, *Withholding or Withdrawing Life Saving Treatment in Children: A Framework for Practice* (2nd edn, 2004), and the update V Larcher et al., 'Making decisions to limit treatment in life-limiting and life-threatening conditions in children: a framework for practice' (2015) Arch Dis Child 100 ss 1–23: doi: 10.1136/archdischild-2014-306666; BMA, *Withholding and Withdrawing Life-prolonging Medical Treatment: Guidance for Decision Making* (3rd edn, 2007); and GMC, *Withholding Treatment and Withdrawing Care Towards the End of Life-prolonging Treatments: Good Practice in Decision-making* (2002, 2006), paras 67–77.

  (iv) children in whom sudden catastrophic events have produced a life-threatening situation; and

  (v) children in whom the prospect of survival is small, for example, some extremely premature infants.

In situations that do not fit these five categories, or where there is dissent or uncertainty about the degree of future impairment, the child's life should be safeguarded in the best possible way.

15.43 The guidelines from the British Medical Association (BMA) in 2007 are more general and, effectively, set the ethical framework within which to work. The basic presumption is that life-prolonging treatment should be initiated where there is reasonable uncertainty as to its benefit. On the other hand, best interests are not necessarily synonymous with prolongation of life and there are circumstances in which active intervention would be inappropriate. These are:

  • that the child has no potential to develop awareness;

  • that he or she will be unable to interact or to achieve the capacity for self-directed action; or

  • that the child will suffer severe unavoidable pain and distress.[90]

15.44 The BMA firmly believes that parents are generally the best judges of their young children's, and the family's, interests; doctors take the lead in judging the clinical factors and parents the lead in determining best interests more generally. In our opinion, however, statements such as this are easier to make than to interpret. While those with parental responsibility have the legal power to give or withhold consent to treatment for a child, this is always provided they are not acting against his or her best interests. We are, then, reaching a 'catch-22' position—having allocated responsibility for determination of the child's best interests, we are now subjecting that determination to a further assessment by an undefined authority. Indeed, the most controversial aspect of the BMA's guidelines lies in the statement:

> Where there is genuine uncertainty about which treatment option would be of most clinical benefit to the child or young person, parents are usually best placed and equipped to weigh the evidence and apply it to their child's own circumstances.[91]

This being followed by the caveat:

> The authority of parents to make decisions is not unlimited... Their authority is likely to be curtailed where the decision made would be contrary to the patient's interests. This might be the case where, for example, the treatment refused would provide a clear benefit to the child or young person, where the statistical chance of recovery is good or where the severity of the condition is not sufficient to justify withholding or withdrawing life-prolonging treatment.[92]

---

[90] BMA, *Withholding and Withdrawing Life-prolonging Medical Treatment*, n 89, p 106.
[91] BMA, *Withholding and Withdrawing Life-prolonging Medical Treatment*, n 89, p 98. Subject to the proviso that a responsible clinician cannot be compelled to provide treatment with which he or she disagrees.
[92] BMA, *Withholding and Withdrawing Life-prolonging Medical Treatment*, n 89, p 98.

Put another way, this means that there is no bright line to be drawn between 'general' and medical best interests—and the great majority of non-treatment decisions result from full discussion between doctors and parents.[93]

15.45   This also returns us to the crucial role of the law and more particularly the courts. Indeed, it should be noted that many of the more recent cases have come to court because human rights law now requires that all disputes over the care of a child be referred to the court as ultimate arbiter. Thus, in *Glass v United Kingdom*,[94] a case in which there was violent dissension between the parents and the doctors as to the treatment of their brain damaged son, the European Court of Human Rights (ECtHR) considered that treating a child against the wishes of his mother constituted an interference with his bodily integrity and, hence, a breach of Art 8; however, the primary reason why Art 8(2) was not engaged lay in the fact that the case was not taken to the court when the dispute developed. Accordingly, non-pecuniary damages of €10,000 were awarded.

15.46   While all the cases cited could be subsumed under the rubric of medical futility, we see them as illustrating a relatively steady—and significant—extension of the conditions that render non-treatment lawful.[95] Two common threads can be identified. On the one hand, the courts are unlikely ever to order doctors to provide treatment against their better judgement—especially for those who are severely brain damaged. As a corollary, it is clear that, no matter what may be the practical clinical situation, parents and other guardians have no *legal* right to insist on treatment that the doctors can justifiably regard as being inappropriate. This, however, depends upon the weight of the medical opinion expressed. It is true that all life and death decisions—and the applications themselves—have been based on a 'best interests' test, but the facts of each successive case also point to an incremental erosion of the pure concept of 'sanctity of life'—is it not, in fact, possible to discern the glimmers of a legal recognition of the 'personhood' construct?[96] The courts are disposed, for example, to make interim orders to allow families to come to terms with the futility of a situation and allowing gradual removal of care.[97] We can see, too, that as case law has become established there is no clear bright line between withholding and withdrawing care when the end result is the same.[98] This has been endorsed by the Nuffield Council on Bioethics as an ethically appropriate stance.[99]

15.47   Finally, a few additional cases illustrate vividly the difficulties surrounding the whole concept of futility as often coming down to an inherently subjective matter between parties. For example, continued treatment was futile from the perspective of the doctors

---

[93] For a full empirical study of how decisions are made in practice, see H E McHaffie, I A Laing, M Parker, and J McMillan, 'Deciding for imperilled newborns: Medical authority or parental autonomy?' (2001) 27 J Med Ethics 104.

[94] *Glass* v *United Kingdom* [2004] 1 FLR 1019; (2004) 77 BMLR 120.

[95] See also *Re B (a child) (medical treatment)* [2009] 1 FLR 1264 (no obligation to provide invasive treatment should it be required in a 22-month-old child unlikely to survive beyond the age of five years).

[96] D Wilkinson, 'Is it in the best interests of an intellectually disabled infant to die?' (2006) 32 J Med Ethics 454.

[97] *An NHS Foundation Trust* v *R* [2013] EWHC 2340 (Fam); [2014] 2 FLR 955; [2014] Fam Law 294.

[98] For an attempt at an argument to develop clear thresholds, see D J Wilkinson, 'A life worth giving? The threshold for permissible withdrawal of life support from disabled new born infants' (2011) 11(2) Am J of Bioethics 20. See also, D Wilkinson and J Savulescu, 'Disability, discrimination and death: is it justified to ration life saving treatment for disabled newborn infants?' (2014) 32(1–2) Monash Bioethics Rev 43, doi: 10.1007/s40592-014-0002-y.

[99] N 28, para 2.33. See also Lord Lowry in *Airedale NHS Trust* v *Bland* [1993] AC 789 at 875.

in *Re K*[100]—parental agreement—and *Re OT*[101]—parental dispute—and this, in our view, might well constitute the preferred justification of withdrawal of *medical* treatment. But, if a procedure is to be regarded as objectively futile, it must be wholly devoid of utility and, certainly, the 'futile' treatment of many of these minors was of major utility to their parents. In other words, there is a practical as well as a theoretical distinction to be made between futile treatment and *medically* futile treatment. The doctor is entitled to assess the latter and to argue in favour of its non-provision or withdrawal.[102] But, in the end, to do so is no more than a powerful contribution to the overall assessment of the former—which goes some way to supporting Sir Stephen Brown P in his resistance to generalising in this field.[103]

Conjoined Twins

15.48 Many of the cases of 'futile' medical treatment that have been considered by the courts relate to the withholding or withdrawal of mechanical means to oxygenate the tissues. Perhaps the most controversial case that has arisen in recent decades concerned the management of conjoined twins.[104] One of the twins, Mary, was so disabled as to be incapable of an independent existence. Thus, it was possible to regard separation from her sister, Jodie, as akin to disconnecting her source of oxygen—or life support machine—when its continued use was medically futile.[105] We can pre-empt discussion of the case by quoting Walker LJ:

> If Mary had been born separated from Jodie but with the defective brain and heart and lungs which she has, and if her life were being supported, not by Jodie but by mechanical means, it would be right to withdraw that artificial life-support system and allow Mary to die.[106]

It is for this reason that we have chosen to discuss the case, which has multiple facets,[107] at this particular point.

15.49 In brief, *Re A (children) (conjoined twins: surgical separation)* concerned conjoined twins, one of whom, Jodie, had a normal heart and lungs. Mary, by contrast, had no functioning heart and her lungs were unusable; her tissues were oxygenated only because she shared a common aorta and venous return with her sister. Mary would die immediately were the twins to be separated whereas, in such circumstances, Jodie would be expected to live a near normal life; both would die in a matter of months if no action was taken. Since it was

---

[100] *Re K (a child) (withdrawal of treatment)* (2006) 99 BMLR 98; compare, in particular, *Re MB*, n 76.

[101] *Re OT* [2009] EWHC 633 (Fam). A claim that emergency application for a declaration constituted a breach of Art 8 of the Convention was rejected.

[102] DJC Wilkinson and J Savulescu, 'Knowing when to stop: futility in the intensive care unit' (2011) 24(2) Curr Opin Anaesthesiol 160 for a review of US cases.

[103] *Re C (a baby)* (1996) 32 BMLR 44. See also Waite LJ, 'All these cases depend on their own facts and render generalisations... wholly out of place' in *Re T (a minor) (wardship: medical treatment)* [1997] 1 All ER 906 at 917; (1996) 35 BMLR 63 at 75. The Ethics Committee of the British Medical Association (BMA) has published comprehensive guidelines covering all age groups: Withholding and Withdrawing Life Prolonging Medical Treatment (3rd edn, 2007). See more recently BMA Ethics Department, *Medical Ethics Today* (3rd edn, 2013).

[104] *Re A (children) (conjoined twins: surgical separation)* [2001] Fam 147; (2001) BMLR 1, CA.

[105] This reconstruction was not, however, accepted by the majority of the court.

[106] (2001) 57 BMLR 1 at 109.

[107] An entire issue of the Medical Law Review (2001) 9, no 3 was devoted to the case on which there is now a massive bibliography.

never disputed that the twins constituted two living individuals,[108] the medical alternatives were stark. Either the hospital could do nothing and accept 'the will of God' that both would die—which was the parents' strong preference and which would have been legally 'acceptable' practice[109]—or they could be separated, in which case, Mary's life of a few months would be sacrificed so as to ensure Jodie's survival.

15.50 It would be convenient to be able to see this as a purely moral problem. In practice, however, the undoubtedly far from satisfactory ruling of the Court of Appeal[110] was, throughout, overshadowed by considerations of the criminal law—before any decision involving the death of Mary could be accepted, it had to be cleansed of a suspicion of murder. A number of strategies were deployed to this end. These included self-defence or its support on behalf of Jodie, the necessity of avoiding an inevitable wrong,[111] and absence of intention to kill. At least one of these factors was sufficient to convince all three judges of the lawfulness of the operation and it is beyond the scope of this book to argue these uncertain areas of the criminal law.

15.51 But, even when the problem of criminality is settled,[112] the case raises ethical questions of equivalent complexity. Fundamental to these is the problem of what constitutes 'best interests' in this and comparable cases. Here, Johnson J, at first instance, and Walker LJ on appeal were happy in the notion that it was not in Mary's best interests to be maintained alive—this being based on the quality of life she could anticipate. Other members of the Court of Appeal, however, could not accept this—Ward LJ holding that separation would bring her life to a close before it had run its natural span without providing any countervailing advantage. Thus, the difference of opinion clearly highlighted the distinction to be drawn between the concepts of the sanctity and the quality of life to which we have already drawn attention. The further distinction between commission and omission, or between activity and passivity, in end of life decision-making is closely bound to this fundamental issue. We discuss the question of whether there is an *ethical* distinction to be made elsewhere (see paras 18.43 et seq); whatever the answer may be, there certainly is an important *legal* difference which we address more fully in Chapter 18. Suffice it to say, here, that, having accepted that Mary was receiving no treatment which could be withdrawn in passive fashion, the Court of Appeal in *Re A* concluded that the operation to separate the twins constituted an assault on Mary. Thus, it was a positive action that would end her life and, as such, was dangerously close to, if not actually, crossing the Rubicon of euthanasia—a journey that the court was unwilling to make.[113] Third, *Re A* reopens the controversy surrounding the moral doctrine of double effect and its associated concept of intent (for which, see Chapter 18). The case particularly asks whether the 'good' effect—in this instance, Jodie's long-term survival—can be justified if the 'bad'

---

[108] Though it is possible to see them as an integrated 'item' sharing common assets: B Hewson, 'Killing off Mary: Was the Court of Appeal right?' (2001) 9 Med L Rev 281.

[109] Per Ward LJ at BMLR 36. This was also the preferred option of R Gillon, 'Imposed separation of conjoined twins—moral hubris by the English courts?' (2001) 27 J Med Ethics 3 and H Watt, 'Conjoined twins: separation as mutilation' (2001) 9 Med L Rev 237.

[110] For a powerful step-by-step criticism, see J McEwan, 'Murder by design: the "feel-good factor" and the criminal law' (2001) 9 Med L Rev 246.

[111] The reasoning, which precluded a defence of necessity in *R v Dudley and Stephens* (1884) 14 QBD 273, was specifically rejected in *Re A*.

[112] And a case can be made out that it was not: S Uniacke. 'Was Mary's death murder?' (2001) 9 Med L Rev 208. See also C Davis, 'Conjoined twins that can be victims of homicide' (2011) 19(3) Med L Rev 430.

[113] Johnson J in the High Court was prepared to equate cutting off Mary's oxygen supply with withdrawing food from those in coma—see discussion of *Bland* at paras 15.82 et seq—which can be regarded as an omission; the Court of Appeal rejected this unanimously.

accompaniment is at the expense of *another* non-consensual party as represented here by Mary's premature death. In the event, only Walker LJ was prepared to hold that Mary's death could be seen as an unintentional result of Jodie's survival. Given the proportionality provided by Mary's negligible advantage, if any, in remaining alive, it is difficult to see why the majority of the court rejected a not unreasonable escape route from a hideous moral dilemma.[114]

15.52 We have previously suggested that many of these difficulties could have been avoided by accepting Mary as a stillbirth which, it seems, would have been possible given that she never had any lung function.[115] To do so would also have limited the effect of the ruling in *Re A* to separation of a stillbirth which would be completely lawful; as things stand, many are concerned at the potential effect of the decision on the law of murder. Nonetheless, the court rejected this solution unanimously and we suspect that this may have been because of the somewhat conflicting way in which much of the relevant medical evidence was presented. Walker LJ, for example, quoted the leading surgeon as saying; 'Mary was not stillborn but she could not be resuscitated and was not viable'[116] which, by *Rance* standards, seems to be something of a contradiction in terms.[117] Ward LJ was content to quote the then Brooke J's definition of live birth in *Rance* and to comment, 'I think I can guarantee that when my Lord said that, he did not relate his observations to Siamese twins'—which is scarcely a robust rejection of our hypothesis.

15.53 The Court of Appeal was, then, left to solve the almost insoluble and, in the end, very nearly acknowledged that. Faced with alternatives that could never satisfy everyone, it relied on a balancing act—which decision, it asked, contained the less wrong? The court decided unanimously in favour of separation—with the proviso that the authority of the case was confined by its very unique circumstances—and, in strict utilitarian terms, this has to be seen as correct; one cannot be so certain when speaking deontologically.[118]

15.54 A final comment on the ethical components of *Re A* relates, once again, to the question of parental rights and responsibilities in such cases. The Court of Appeal took full cognisance of the parents' wishes yet barely questioned its own right to have the final say and to focus exclusively on the welfare principle.[119] Looked at dispassionately, the reasons given by the parents for their opposition to the operation—including deeply held religious convictions and the anticipated difficulties in maintaining a family unity that would be imposed by a disabled child—are, essentially, based on parental interests. Whether or not one agrees with the logic of the decision, it was based on wide-ranging analysis and careful thought rather than on custom, and this must have been to the 'better' interests of the children; as Freeman put it, 'there are more important rights to confer upon children than the right to autonomous parents'.[120] Against this, one must also quote Harris: 'This is a

---

[114] See, e.g., Uniacke, n 112. Though, as the other members of the court noted, it is not certain that double effect will always survive following *R v Woollin* [1999] 1 AC 82; [1998] 4 All ER 103. Effectively, this says that a 'bad' result cannot be seen as unintentional if it was inevitable. For a discussion in the medical context see, *R v D* [2004] EWCA Crim 1391.

[115] J K Mason, 'Conjoined twins: a diagnostic conundrum' (2001) 5 Edin LR 226.

[116] (2001) 57 BMLR 1 at 105.

[117] *Rance v Mid-Downs Health Authority* [1991] 1 QB 587; [1991] 1 All ER 801 discussed at para 9.101.

[118] The popular press recently reported on the life of the surviving twin, see *The Daily Mail*, 'Separated twin is now living a full life, says judge who ordered the operation that killed her conjoined sister', 4 October 2014, available at: http://www.dailymail.co.uk/news/article-2780371/Separated-twin-living-life-says-judge-ordered-operation-killed-conjoined-sister.html.

[119] A point more recently applied in *An NHS Trust v B* [2014] EWHC 3486 (Fam).

[120] M Freeman, 'Whose life is it anyway?' (2001) 9 Med L Rev 259.

finely balanced judgement, but perhaps just because it is, the justification for overturning the choice of the parents is absent.'[121] It is perhaps a sobering thought that a case which provoked so much controversy and which could have a profound influence on the law might never have been heard had the twins not been in the care of an authority that was anxious to proceed in circumstances where many might not have done so.

IS THE TREATMENT OF INFANTS A SEPARATE ISSUE?

15.55 There are at least two good reasons for isolating the issues in early life from those in adulthood or those which are essentially perimortal. In the first place, decisions in the first situation rest almost entirely on prognosis, which is no more than another term for expressing an informed guess as to the future. This may, in any event, be difficult and, while we know that we are dealing with only short-term survival at the end of life, this is not the case at birth—we may be confident of what will be the state of affairs next week but we cannot say the same about the next decade. Moreover, the neonate is not passing from a settled norm into a progressively less satisfactory condition; he is developing in a sub-optimal milieu which is his norm—can one say with any certainty that the Down's syndrome child, who has never known anything different, is dissatisfied with his existence within himself? Thus, we would take issue with the reasoning of Professor Williams, who wrote: 'If a wicked fairy told me she was about to transform me into a Down's baby and would I prefer to die I should certainly answer yes',[122] because this is not the question being asked of the infant. The better view is that of Lord Donaldson—that the starting point in analysing the disabled person's condition is not what might have been but what is.[123]

15.56 The second major distinction between life and death decisions at the extremes of life is that, while the adult sufferer is likely to be able to express an opinion or, save in a few cases, to have previously intimated his wishes, there is no way in which the neonate can consent to treatment, suffering, or death. Consent must be parental and one then asks where, in fact, do lie the parents' rights that it is feared will be usurped by the courts? The only lawful action of a parent is that of a 'reasonable parent' and this person is duty-bound to act in his or her child's own best interests.

15.57 In this respect, we have seen that the English courts are resolute in distinguishing between non-treatment and euthanasia[124] and that a fundamental distinction is to be made between, on the one hand, infants with pure mental defects and, at the other extreme, those with severe physical incapacity resulting, for example, from neural tube defects. Treatment of the latter is a matter of careful medical management which must incorporate an element of selection.[125] Many such disabled children will inevitably die and many

---

[121] J Harris, 'Human beings, persons and conjoined twins: An ethical analysis of the judgment in *Re A*' (2001) 9 Med L Rev 221.

[122] G Williams, 'Down's syndrome and the duty to preserve life' (1981) 131 NLJ 1020.

[123] In *Re J (a minor) (wardship: medical treatment)* [1990] 3 All ER 930 at 936; (1990) 6 BMLR 25 at 32, paraphrasing McKenzie J.

[124] The distinction is amplified in the Netherlands where specific conditions legitimising neonatal euthanasia have been promulgated in the Groningen protocol. See B A Manninen, 'A case for justified non-voluntary active euthanasia: Exploring the ethics of the Groningen protocol' (2006) 32 J Med Ethics 643. For an assessment of its impact after five years, see A A E Verhagen, 'The Groningen Protocol for newborn euthanasia; which way did the slippery slope tilt?' (2013) 39 J Med Ethics 293, doi: 10.1136/medethics-2013-101402.

[125] For an early philosophical assessment, see J Harris, 'Ethical problems in the management of some severely handicapped children' (1981) 7 J Med Ethics 117. Results from the coalface are reported by I M Balfour-Lynn and R C Tasker, 'Futility and death in paediatric medical intensive care' (1996) 22 J Med Ethics 279.

should be allowed to do so; the principle of 'allowing nature to take its course' on the basis of a shared decision between doctor and parents is acceptable in both a moral and legal sense provided that the decision is taken in the best interests of the child.[126] By contrast, if the mentally disabled child is not to live, it must be responsibly guided towards a dignified death. There is no non-treatment for the anatomically normal Down's baby because it needs no treatment and failure to feed in the latter instance can only be categorised as neonaticide—that is, *killing* of the neonate—which brings us back to the question whether there is, in fact, any true difference between non-treatment and euthanasia. Kuhse,[127] in the early stages of the debate, argued most persuasively that there is no moral or legal distinction to be drawn between activity and passivity in this area of medical practice. Were this to be accepted, we would, at the same time, have to approve the spectre of the paediatrician armed with a lethal syringe—and the concept is quite unacceptable. As we discuss later in relation to the permanent vegetative state, it is hard to assail the logic which says that a quick death is preferable to one which depends upon the vagaries of nature; nevertheless, we believe that natural death is the only acceptable concomitant of a decision not to treat a severely physically defective infant—and we also believe that food and water should be provided for any child which is capable of taking nourishment by mouth. In so saying, we admit to being guided, to a very considerable extent, by moral intuition alone—as a well-respected medical philosopher once put it, 'We are, here, noting a deep human inhibition which it might be unwise to tamper with in the name of logic'.[128]

15.58 Advances in modern medical expertise have, at the same time, brought their own problems to the neonatal period. It is increasingly possible to maintain and rear premature infants of low birthweight and evidence is accumulating that a number of such children are disadvantaged to an extent which is inversely proportionate to their birthweight.[129] The discussion of selective non-treatment is, accordingly, being extended to include attitudes to intensive care of the premature infant.[130] It is trite medicine to say that premature births should be prevented by improved antenatal care. For those cases where this fails or is not possible, however, the dilemma remains over intervention or non-intervention and when and how this might happen. The difficulty of a decision to act is that, while resuscitation may be successful, the end result may be a severely handicapped survivor; and this is not even to mention the resource implications of such a decision.

15.59 The Nuffield Council on Bioethics directly addressed these questions in its 2006 report and offered proposed guidelines for deciding to institute intensive care.[131]

> The important threshold is 25 weeks. Above this age, the recommendation is that intensive care should be initiated unless there is evidence of 'severe abnormality incompatible

---

[126] D D Raphael, 'Handicapped infants: Medical ethics and the law' (1988) 14 J Med Ethics 5 was one of the first to point to the conceptual difficulty in attributing any interest in death—'the most you can say is that someone would prefer to die'.

[127] H Kuhse, 'A modern myth. That letting die is not the intentional causation of death: Some reflections on the trial and acquittal of Dr Leonard Arthur' (1984) 1 J Appl Philos 21.

[128] R S Downie, 'Modern paediatric practice: An ethical overview' (1989) in J K Mason (ed), *Paediatric Forensic Medicine and Pathology* (1989) ch 31, p 488.

[129] R J Boyle, R Salter, and M W Arnander, 'Ethics of refusing parental requests to withhold or withdraw treatment from their premature baby' (2004) 30 J Med Ethics 402 and H McHaffie, 'A Scottish researcher's response' (2004) 30 J Med Ethics 406. In the US, see M S Webb et al., 'Ethical issues related to caring for low birth weight infants' (2014) 21(6) Nursing Ethics 731, doi: 10.1177/0969733013513919.

[130] For a review of the US experience, see A W DeTora and C L Cummings, 'Ethics and the law: practical applications in the neonatal Intensive Care Unit' (2015) 16(7) Neoreviews e384, doi: 10.1542/neo.16-7-e384.

[131] N 28, paras 9.16–9.17.

with any significant period of survival'. Below 25 weeks a series of further thresholds are proposed down to 22 weeks where the suggestion is that no resuscitation should be attempted (save as part of a clinical research study). The interim period should be handled sensitively and after full discussion with the parents; the recommendation is that parental wishes should normally be followed if these favour intervention unless there is clear evidence that this is against the child's best interests.

CONFLICTS OF VIEWS

15.60   The mass of judicial opinion that has now accumulated has certainly done much to define parental powers in this area and, as a result, no one would now deny that the parents' views should carry great weight—but, at the same time, they cannot be fully determinative.[132] Moreover, common attitudes to the management of disabled infants are based on the assumption of marital harmony, in that they relate so firmly to the wishes of 'the parents'—what if there is disagreement? Fortunately, the situation must arise only rarely. For such occasions, there are always the courts—but who is to say that judges qua judges are uniquely suited to decide controversial questions of the value of infant life?[133] It is essential that the medical and legal professions—as well as society at large—should make sure of the lines they intend to draw in the face of potential conflict, whether this be inter-professional, inter-parental, or between the parents and the professional carers themselves.[134]

15.61   *Re T (a minor) (wardship: medical treatment)*[135] is of considerable interest not only as an example of parental views winning out against overwhelming medical opinion, but also for the fact that the parents supported non-intervention in this case when there was much that could be done to save their child's life. Here, the child, curiously designated as C, was born with biliary atresia—a condition likely to be fatal within two-and-a-half years in the absence of transplantation therapy. Remedial surgery at the age of three-and-a-half weeks produced no improvement but medical opinion was unanimous in believing that the chances of a successful transplant were good and that the operation was in C's best interests. This included the opinion of a consultant engaged on behalf of the mother who opposed a further operation on the grounds of the pain and suffering C had sustained following the first procedure and who even took her child abroad where there were no facilities for a liver transplant. The child's local authority then raised the matter as a special issue under the terms of s 100(3) of the Children Act 1989. As a result, the trial judge

---

[132] We also emphasise that the 'medical' view is not necessarily the same as the 'doctor's' view. There is increasing acceptance that the care of the disabled neonate should be based on a team approach—it is the nurses, not the doctors, who will bear the brunt of non-treatment decisions. This point was well taken in the judgment in *Re C (a minor) (wardship: medical treatment)* [1990] Fam 26; [1989] 2 All ER 782. See also policies and standards from the American Academy of Pediatrics, 'Patient- and Family-Centered Care and the Pediatrician's Role' (2012) 129(2) Pediatrics 394, doi: 10.1542/peds.2011-3084, and the Royal College of Paediatrics and Child Health, *Facing the Future: Together for Child Health* (2015), available at: http://www.rcpch.ac.uk/sites/default/files/page/Facing%20the%20Future%20Together%20for%20Child%20Health%20final%20web%20version.pdf.

[133] See Walker LJ in *Re A (children) (conjoined twins: surgical separation)* (2000) 57 BMLR 1 at 16, quoting Scalia J in *Cruzan v Director, Missouri Department of Health* (1990) 497 US 261 at 294.

[134] K Savell, 'Confronting death in legal disputes about treatment limitation in children' (2011) 8 *Bioethical Inquiry* 363.

[135] [1997] 1 WLR 242; [1997] 1 All ER 906; (1996) 35 BMLR 63. For discussion, see M Fox and J McHale, 'In whose best interests?' (1997) 60 MLR 700; A Bainham, 'Do babies have rights?' (1997) 56 CLR 48; A Grubb, 'Commentary' (1997) 4 Med L Rev 315.

found that the mother's conduct was not that of a reasonable parent and directed that C be admitted to a hospital that was prepared to undertake a transplant operation.

15.62 The Court of Appeal, however, unanimously reversed this decision, largely on the grounds that the judge had failed to give adequate weight in the necessary balancing exercise to the objections of the parents—which, it was said, were supported by qualities of devotion, commitment, love, and reason. These included an assessment of the pain and suffering likely to be imposed by a second major operation and of the chances and consequences of failure. In addition, the court agreed with one expert opinion that passing back responsibility for parental care to the mother and expecting her to provide the essential commitment to the child after the operation in the face of her opposition was, in itself, fraught with danger for the child. 'How would the mother cope with having to remain in England?' asked Butler-Sloss LJ. The mother and the child were one for the purposes of the case and the decision of the court to assent to the operation jointly affected the mother and son and also the father. Waite LJ went so far as to hold that the child's subsequent development could be injuriously affected if his day-to-day care depended upon the commitment of a mother who had suffered the turmoil of her child being compelled against her will to undergo a major operation 'against which her own medical and maternal judgement wholeheartedly rebelled'.[136] The appeal was upheld and the orders of the trial judge, to the effect that surgery should be performed notwithstanding the refusal of the mother to consent, were set aside.

15.63 *Re T* raises a number of questions—both general and particular. It is, first, reasonable to question whether it is right to place discussion of the case within a section devoted to medical futility. Our view is that it represents one side of the wide concept—albeit the rather unusual reverse in which the parents, on behalf of their child, are claiming treatment to be futile insofar as it is, on balance and in their view, offering minimal benefit. It will be seen that we reject this prognostic assessment and it may be that the importance of the case lies in providing a measure of how far the concept of futility can be stretched without incursion into areas such as euthanasia—it is possible, but it is certainly not easy, to accommodate phrases such as, 'the prospect of forcing the devoted mother of this young baby to the consequences of this major invasive surgery'[137] within the envelope of the child's unaffected best interests. Equally to the point, one has to ask if the decision in *Re T* does, in fact, represent a watershed in the medico-legal symbiosis that has developed in this area. C's parents were described as health professionals; their status is unstated but the Court of Appeal was clearly impressed by their understanding of the situation—so much so that, at times, the mother's views appear to take on the significance of another expert medical opinion. Moreover, previous court decisions represent not so much a judicial submission to the medical will as, rather, a reluctance to impose a duty to treat on unwilling doctors. *Re T* was an antithetical proposition, the end result of which was to place an embargo on treatment which at least some experts were willing to provide. It may not, therefore, be a decision taken against the stream.

15.64 Whether it was a 'good' decision in medical jurisprudential terms is, again, questionable. Despite the protestations of all three judges, and despite the court's repeated assurance as to the responsibility and devotion of the parents, an unavoidable impression remains that their interests weighed heavily in the balance at the expense of the paramountcy of

---

136 [1997] 1 All ER 906 at 917; (1996) 35 BMLR 63 at 75.
137 *Re T* [1997] 1 All ER 906 at 916; (1996) 35 BMLR 63 at 74, per Butler-Sloss LJ.

those of the child. Certainly, there is great good sense in the opinion of the trial judge. There are few fields of modern medicine in which progress is as fast as it is in transplantation therapy. It is at least possible that additional technology would become available during the several years of good-quality life available within the current state of the art; not only might these then be extended beyond current expectation but, in the interim, the mother's attitude might well change. It is hard to dismiss such gains as *medically* futile objectives

15.65 *Re T* remains something of an aberration to this day. The more likely approach of the courts is probably reflected in the decision in *The NHS Trust v A (a child) and Others*.[138] This case was very similar to *Re T* in that the child was suffering from a life-threatening condition and a medical intervention was possible which the parents refused. This was a bone marrow transplant with a 50 per cent chance of normal life. For religious reasons, the parents preferred to hope for a miracle than subject their child to the painful and protracted medical regime. The court, however, preferred the medical view and deemed religious views to be irrelevant (as has always been the tendency in the UK courts). It was accepted, however, that the outcome might have favoured the parental preference if the facts had been different—for example, if life expectancy had been short or there would still have been serious impairment after intervention. However, this is in no way to suggest that the courts will dismiss lightly the views or preferences of parents, as many cases of judicial angst demonstrate very well.[139]

FUTILITY OR SCARCITY OF RESOURCES?

15.66 We have suggested already that the concept of futility carries with it the real danger that it can be used as a portal of entry to disguised and arbitrary rationing of resources. This may well be so but, before accepting this as wholly pejorative, it is well to note the underlying practicalities.

15.67 In the first place, the one necessarily follows the other. Thus, if one patient is removed from futile treatment, that resource automatically becomes available to another for whom it will be useful—but the motive behind the exchange remains subject to interpretation. Second, given that resources are not infinite, therapeutic merit is a good candidate for the most acceptable basis for their distribution; as we discuss in Chapter 11, the 'first come, first served' regime fails in principle because it dictates the provision of treatment in medically futile circumstances. Third, the law clearly accepts that resource allocation forms a proper part of medical decision-making. Thus, we have Balcombe LJ:

> making an order which may have the effect of compelling a doctor or health authority to make available scarce resources...to a particular child...might require the health authority to put J on a ventilator in an intensive care unit, and thereby possibly to deny the benefit of those limited resources to a child who was much more likely than J to benefit from them.[140]

[138] [2008] 1 FLR 70; (2007) 98 BMLR 141.

[139] As a small set of examples, see *Re LA (medical treatment)* [2010] 2 FLR 1203; [2010] Fam Law 1064; [2011] Fam Law 789 (court refusing to intervene in local authority care proceedings); *An NHS Trust v KH* [2013] 1 FLR 1471; [2013] Med LR 70; [2013] Fam Law 34 (parents who lack capacity can still make important input as a matter of legal principle); and *King's College Hospital NHS Foundation Trust v H* [2015] EWHC 1966 (Fam) (further reflection by court on its interpretation of parental wishes and modification of judgement).

[140] *Re J (a minor) (wardship: medical treatment)* [1993] Fam 15 at 30; (1992) 9 BMLR 10 at 20.

15.68 Nonetheless, the seeds of conflict are there to be sown and are well illustrated in *R v Cambridge Health Authority, ex p B*,[141] which concerned a ten-year-old child who had been suffering from lymphoma since the age of five. By the time of the action, she had received two courses of chemotherapy and had undergone whole body irradiation and received a bone marrow transplant before she suffered a further relapse. At this point, her doctors determined that no further treatment could usefully be given and estimated her life expectancy as between six and eight weeks. Her father had, meantime, obtained a second opinion from the USA which, effectively, suggested that further treatment carried an 18 per cent chance of a full cure. Doctors who were prepared to continue treatment in the UK regarded this as unduly optimistic and set the chance of success at anything between 10 per cent and 2.25 per cent—which was, of course, to be set against the risk to the patient's life and the distress associated with the proposed treatment; due to a shortage of beds, this would have to be carried out in the private sector and the cost was estimated to be in the region of £75,000. Taking into account the judgement of their own clinicians, the nature of the treatment, and its chances of success, the health authority declined to provide the funding, giving as its reasons, first, that the treatment would not be in B's best interests and, second, that the expenditure of so much money with so little prospect of success was an ineffective use of their limited resources bearing in mind the present and future needs of other patients. The father sought judicial review of this decision.

15.69 In the High Court hearing, Laws J began his determination with the words, 'Of all human rights, most people would accord the most precious place to the right to life itself'. Even if this is true, which it probably is, we doubt if it follows that there is a rights-based entitlement to any particular treatment; the 'right to life' in this context means no more than the right not to have one's life taken away and this right is in no sense infringed if it is agreed that the available treatment is either futile or against the patient's best interests. In confronting such criticism, Laws J opined that, in contrast to the position in criminal law, public law allowed no difference of principle between act and omission and, accordingly, the decision of the health authority assaulted the child's right to life. He then considered the justification for such an assault and concluded that, while the doctors could rightly assess the chances of success of the proposed treatment and its objective disadvantages in terms of risk and suffering, the assessment of the patient's best interests was not, in the end, a medical question at all. Rather, it was a matter to be decided by the child's father acting as a surrogate responsible for her overall care. Thus, in the end, the issue turned on the provision of funds—and the learned judge considered that, when the question was whether the life of a ten-year-old might be saved, by however slim a chance, the authority should do more than 'toll the bell of tight resources'. In conclusion, while admitting that there might still be cogent reasons for withholding funding which had not been explored, Laws J ordered that the authority's decision be reconsidered in the light of his judgment.

15.70 Almost predictably in the light of previous decisions in which the allocation of resources formed a part,[142] the Court of Appeal reversed this order emphasising, in general, that its function was to rule upon the lawfulness of decisions—not to express opinions as to the merits of medical judgement. In particular, the Court rejected the suggestion that the wishes of the parents had been inadequately considered; in fact, the authority was under

---

[141] (1995) 25 BMLR 5, QBD; revsd [1995] 2 All ER 129; (1995) 23 BMLR 1, CA.
[142] See paras 11.07 et seq.

great pressure from the parents and had taken its decision in response to that pressure. Second, Sir Thomas Bingham MR considered that, by any showing, the treatment was at the frontier of medical science. Third, he held:

> I have no doubt that in a perfect world any treatment which a patient... sought would be provided if doctors were willing to give it, no matter how much it cost... It would, however, be shutting one's eyes to the real world if the court were to proceed on the basis that we do live in such a world.[143]

And, further, the court cannot make a judgement as to how a limited budget is to be best allocated. In the end, it was open to the health authority to reach the decision they had already reached. We should, as a coda, note that B's treatment was ultimately funded from both private and public sources; she died 14 months after the hearing. All the doctors involved agreed that B's life under treatment was likely to be oppressive; can one say that the gain of a year of such life negates the imprint of medical futility?—it is an arguable point but we have our doubts.

15.71   The case of Child B provided the perfect setting for 'shroud-waving' in the popular press; an in-depth analysis of the media coverage shows the extent of the pressures exerted.[144] It was, of course, unfortunate that clinical and economic considerations became entwined and, inevitably, the press saw the issue almost exclusively in financial terms; the situation was, however, bound to arise as the funding for what are known as 'extra-contractual referrals'—or the purchase of medical services outside the particular health authority— is subject to special regulation. But was *Ex p B* an attempt to impose resource rationing under the cloak of medical futility? We think not. An authority must abide by the decisions of its expert advisers who were unanimous that the suggested treatment was contraindicated. In the circumstances, the authority might well have been regarded as behaving unreasonably if it *had* persisted with treatment. At the most, its attitude could be seen as part of the now familiar balancing exercise; we will never know what would have been the decision had the proposed regime not been quite so extravagant of public money—or, on the other side of the coin, had not involved quite such risk and discomfort to the patient.

15.72   *Re T* and *Ex p B* may seem to be at odds, in that the Court of Appeal recognised the interests of the parents as having a high priority in the former and rejected them in the latter. The cynic might say that this is simply a matter of health care economics. The alternative and, in our view, better approach is to see the two decisions as consistent. We do not disguise our suspicions as to the correctness of that taken in *Re T*. The fact remains that the court conducted a balancing act in both cases and, rightly or wrongly, concluded that the risks and suffering involved in treatment outweighed the chances of success. Certainly, the decisive evidence came from opposing corners but, at the end of the day, the lesson is that the courts will not impose what they, having heard the medical evidence, regard as medically futile—or, better, non-productive—treatment of children whose management is in dispute. Although they were stated in a rather different context, the words of Sir Thomas Bingham MR provide the foundation for our current jurisprudence:

> the decision of a devoted and responsible parent should be treated with respect... But the role of the court is to exercise an independent and objective judgment. If that judgment is

---

[143]   (1995) 23 BMLR 1 at 8–9.

[144]   V A Entwistle, I S Watt, R Bradbury, and L J Pehl, 'Media coverage of the *Child B* case' (1996) 312 BMJ 1587.

in accord with that of the devoted and responsible parent, well and good. If it is not, then it is the duty of the court, after giving due weight to the view of the devoted and responsible parent, to give effect to its own judgment. That is what it is there for.[145]

15.73   But what is to guide the court in its decisions? Concepts such as 'futility' and 'best interests' have strong normative appeal but, as we, hopefully, have shown, the search for objectivity in their application may itself be a futile exercise. The reality is that decision-makers are involved in a value-laden process, and this is no less true when the decision is taken in a court rather than at the patient's bedside. Often, the values to which we appeal are merely implicit in our decisions, and courts often take refuge in legal constructs which may reveal little about the underlying reasons for a particular outcome. But a trend has emerged in recent years whereby the courts have been more willing to state clearly which values inform their decisions.[146] Nowhere is this illustrated more clearly than in *R (on the application of Burke) v General Medical Council*[147] and consideration of this case provides us with the perfect bridge between our discussions of futility at the beginning and at the end of life.

PART 2: THE END OF LIFE

15.74   Mr Burke suffered from the degenerative disease cerebellar ataxia which would eventually leave him unable to communicate while still retaining his mind. Essentially, he challenged guidance issued by the GMC that it would be within the bounds of good medical practice to withhold or withdraw artificial nutrition and hydration (ANH) when the conditions were considered to be so severe and the prognosis so poor that providing ANH would be too burdensome for the patient in relation to the possible benefits. Mr Burke did not want ANH to be removed in any circumstances, no matter his state of health. For him, ANH would never be futile and it would be in his own best interests to continue to receive such care even when nothing else could be done for him medically and when the sole function of that care would be to keep his body alive. In a controversial ruling, the court of first instance held that: (i) the Guidelines concentrated too much on the right of the competent patient to refuse treatment rather than to require treatment; (ii) they did not stipulate that a doctor who did not wish to follow the patient's wishes must continue to treat until a doctor who was willing to do so was found; (iii) they failed to acknowledge a very strong presumption in favour of prolonging life; and (iv) that the standard of best interests was that of intolerability as judged from the patient's own perspective. Article 8 of the European Convention implied that it was for the competent patient, not the doctor, to decide what treatment should be given to achieve what the patient thought was conducive to his or her dignity. However, there would be no breach of Arts 2, 3, or 8 if ANH was withdrawn when it was serving absolutely no purpose and was, indeed, futile, but this would not be the case in Mr Burke's envisaged circumstances.

15.75   Munby J's analysis was based on ethical principles for which he found support in human rights law. Thus, prominence was given to *sanctity of life* (protected by Art 2 of the European

---

[145]   In *Re Z (a minor) (freedom of publication)* [1997] Fam 1 at 32; [1995] 4 All ER 961 at 986.
[146]   See R Huxtable, 'Autonomy, best interests and the public interest: treatment, non-treatment and the values of medical law' (2014) 22(4) Med Law Rev 459, doi: 10.1093/medlaw/fwt035.
[147]   [2004] EWHC 1879; [2004] 3 FCR 579, reversed [2005] 3 WLR 1132; [2005] 2 FLR 1223.

Convention), *dignity* (which underpins the entire human rights Convention but is most clearly seen in Art 3), and *autonomy* or *self-determination* (which the Strasbourg Court and its domestic counterparts are in the process of 'interpreting out' of Art 8). Munby J rated dignity highly[148] as a fundamental recognition of our humanity and a recognition, in particular, of a person's interest in the manner of his or her death. It is, as a result, surprising how little attention was paid to its meaning by both the Court of Appeal and the European Court.

15.76   Dignity is one of those concepts that are widely embraced but are, at the same time, not easily defined. It can, of course, be seen from a subjective or objective perspective, and both feature in Munby J's analysis. On the one hand, they divide along the categories of competency. At first instance it was held that it is for the patient to *determine*—and we should note with care the use of this expression—what treatment *should* or should not be given in order to achieve what the patient believes conducive to his dignity and in order to avoid what the patient would find stressing'.[149] Where the patient is incompetent, best interests applies, and the dignity test is what 'right-thinking persons' would consider undignified in such circumstances. As statements go, this is singularly lacking in definition and it is even less easy to express what is meant by the term 'protection of human dignity'. Dupré has suggested two useful approaches.[150] First, that dignity can be conflated with personality—or, respect for dignity is, in effect, respect for the uniqueness, or the moral integrity, of the individual person. Second, she suggests that the 'right to life' can be seen as more than a conflict between life and death and, rather, as a right to a dignified or a 'good' life. The difficulty is that, in either case, the ethical principle of respect for dignity can conflict with those of the sanctity of life and of self-determination and it is this which led to the rejection of Munby J's analysis by the superior courts.

15.77   The Court of Appeal overruled Munby J while endorsing the position that to remove ANH from a competent patient who wished it would be a breach of his or her human rights (Arts 2, 3, and 8), and an affront to his or her dignity, subject to one possible caveat (see later). By far the more interesting feature of the court's ruling, however, is its attitude towards the management of incompetent patients. Once again, in *Burke*, we find it falling back on the best interests test and the point is made that it can be lawful to withdraw ANH if its provision is judged not to meet this test—any doctor in doubt should seek a court declaration but he or she is not obliged by law to do so. Finally, on the scope of rights of the competent patient, the Court of Appeal stated obiter that his views will not be *determinative* in the last stages of life if the continuation of ANH might hasten death because no patient can require a doctor to treat against his best clinical judgement.[151]

15.78   We have suggested already that the concept of medical futility can be applied as a continuum from the neonate to the terminally ill. Even so, the underlying reasons for, and the management of, non-treatment will vary according to age. Thus, non-treatment in infancy has been, at least in part, a matter of the management of physical disability. But

---

[148]   Quoting his judgment in *R (on the application of A, B, X and Y) v East Sussex County Council and the Disability Rights Commission (No 2)* [2003] EWHC 167 (Admin) at [86].

[149]   *Burke*, para 15.74 above, para 130.

[150]   C Dupré, 'Human dignity and the withdrawal of medical treatment: A missed opportunity?' (2006) 6 EHRL Rev 678.

[151]   For critical reflection on this ruling, see H Biggs, 'Taking account of the views of the patient, but only if the clinician (and the court) agrees—*R (Burke) v General Medical Council*' (2007) 19(2) Child and Fam LQ 225. See also, D Gurnham, 'Losing the wood for the trees: *Burke* and the Court of Appeal' (2006) 14 Med L Rev 253.

this has been morally permissible only because treatment of itself would result in an intol-erable life which it would be inhumane to enforce on the child who would, at the same time, die naturally if he or she were untreated. Such conditions are uncommon in adult life and, when they do occur—as, for example, in accidental quadriplegia—their manage-ment is more allied to euthanasia or assisted suicide[152] than to selective non-treatment.

15.79 Disability due to brain damage is, however, common to both infancy and adulthood and we have seen that, while the courts will not tolerate the deliberate shortening of life, they are fully prepared to accede to non-treatment of associated lethal disease in the severely brain damaged child—and to base this on an undeniably 'quality of life' standard as meas-ured by a 'best interests' test. It is of some interest to speculate on why it is that this has been accepted relatively easily in the case of children while the legal attitude to the man-agement of the brain-damaged adult has taken so long to mature and has done so amid so much controversy. Is it that we give greater weight to life that has 'been lived' than to life which has no past? Do we see a sustainable distinction between starting on a life with handicap and continuing life in a disabled state? Are we less concerned with any residual cognitive ability in the infant than we are with comparable but expressible brain activity in the adult? And are we frightened of an ever-widening definition of what is perceived as intolerable in the adult? Whatever the possible distinctions, in all cases the courts are clear that they will not order a clinician to treat against his or her considered professional opinion; moreover, the courts will not allow argument about possible benefits to a patient be used to pressure health professionals and health authorities into continuing interven-tions that professionals consider to be futile. Thus in *AVS* v *An NHS Foundation Trust*,[153] the Court of Appeal made it very clear that it would not entertain hypothetical arguments about possible benefits and future health carers' willingness to provide treatment in the case of a severely affected patient with Creutzfeldt Jakob's disease. The brother of the patient was unable to produce evidence refuting the unanimous opinion of his brother's carers that it would be futile to replace a failed pump delivering a compound which had failed to produce results over the previous two years. The court therefore refused any declaration along the lines that *if* a willing professional could be found the pump should be replaced. The Court of Protection has since further confirmed that:

> In determining whether treatment would be in a patient's best interests, the court ha[s] to consider whether it would be futile in the sense of being ineffective or of no benefit to the patient. The treatment [does] not have to be likely to cure or palliate the under-lying condition or return the patient to full or reasonable health, rather it should be capable of allowing the resumption of a quality of life which the patient would regard as worthwhile.[154]

15.80 Another common feature of the cases is that we are constantly assured that we are *not* practising euthanasia in allowing such persons to die. Thus, we have Hoffmann LJ saying:

> This is not a case about euthanasia because it does not involve any external agency of death. It is about whether, and how, the patient should be allowed to die.[155]

---

[152] See also the case of Daniel James which did not come to trial but was discussed in *R (on the application of Purdy)* v *DPP* [2009] UKHL 45.

[153] [2011] EWCA Civ 7. For comment see G Douglas, 'Vulnerable adult: medical treatment' (2011) 41(apr) Fam Law 363.

[154] *United Lincolnshire Hospitals NHS Trust* v *N* [2014] EWCOP 16; [2014] COPLR 660; (2014) 140 BMLR 204.

[155] In *Airedale NHS Trust* v *Bland* [1993] 1 All ER 821 at 856; (1993) 12 BMLR 64 at 101, CA.

15.81 It is for this reason that we have detached the management of the brain-damaged adult—and, particularly, the adult in the permanent vegetative state—from our discussion of euthanasia. Legally—if less certainly logically—it sits easier under the heading of 'futile treatment'; as Lord Goff put it in the House of Lords in *Bland*, 'it is the futility of the treatment [of Anthony Bland] which justifies its termination'.[156]

THE PATIENT IN THE PERMANENT VEGETATIVE STATE

15.82 It is common knowledge that the cells of the body depend upon oxygen for their survival; it is also well understood that the cells of the brain are the most sensitive to oxygen lack. But, taking this one step further, we must also note that the brain itself is not uniformly sensitive to hypoxia.[157] In clinical terms, this means that depriving the brain of oxygen can result in anything from mild intellectual deterioration to death and, since the brain cells, once destroyed, cannot be replaced, the outcome is determined almost exclusively by how rapidly normal oxygenation can be established. Thus, whatever the cause, hypoxic *anatomic damage* to the brain is irreversible—but further damage can be prevented if an efficient oxygen supply is restored. In such a situation, therefore, one can speak of *degrees* of brain damage and resultant coma but not of *stages* of coma because, once the oxygen supply is restored, the condition is static.

15.83 Simplistically, the brain can be divided into three main areas: the cortex, which is responsible for our human intellectual existence and is the least able to withstand oxygen deficiency; the thalamus, which roughly regulates our animal existence; and the brain stem, which controls our purely vegetative functions including breathing. It follows that, at one end of the scale, oxygen lack will affect the cognitive brain while leaving the remainder functional; how much consciousness or cognitive ability is retained then depends on the degree of permanent *cortical* damage. At the other extreme, the brain stem is least affected by hypoxia; if it is so damaged, it can be assumed, as near certainly as is possible, that the rest of the brain is damaged to a similar or greater extent;[158] we are then left with *brain stem death* which is incompatible with life as it is generally understood and will be discussed under 'Concepts of Death' in Chapter 16.

15.84 Localised cerebral damage can be due to physical, structural injury or to localised cerebral hypoxia due, in turn, to swelling of the brain resulting from such injury. It can, however, be simply a part—albeit, probably the most significant part—of whole body hypoxia. Conditions producing such generalised lack of arterial oxygen may be natural—for example, heart failure or severe internal haemorrhage—or unnatural, of which drug overdose or a reduced oxygen intake, due, for instance, to a poorly given anaesthetic, are probably the most important in the present context. Violence may be such as to reduce the chest movement—as in conditions of overcrowding—or, more likely, will cause 'surgical shock', in which a lowered blood pressure results in inadequate oxygen perfusion of the tissues.

---

[156] [1993] 1 All ER 821 at 870; (1993) 12 BMLR 64 at 116.

[157] The relative term 'hypoxia' is used advisedly to emphasise that oxygen lack need not be absolute—'anoxia'—in order to cause brain damage.

[158] Lesions which affect the lower brain and leave the cortex intact are the result of local vascular damage—not of generalised hypoxia.

15.85 The clinical condition of a person whose cortical brain has been damaged but who has been re-oxygenated will vary with the degree of hypoxic insult sustained. Four degrees of coma were recognised by the early French writers:[159] *coma vigile*, which represents no more than a blurring of consciousness and intellect; *coma type* and *coma carus*, which are characterised by increasing loss of relative functions followed by vegetative functions; and, finally, *coma depassé*—something beyond coma in which all functions are lost and the patient can only be maintained by artificial means.

15.86 Thus, while all appropriate cases may properly be given intensive care for the purposes of diagnosis and assessment, it would be well-nigh impossible to justify the initiation of long-term treatment for a patient who was likely to retain no cortical and only minimal thalamic function. The identification of such a case presents a formidable technical dilemma because some *functional* or *physiological* damage may be recoverable while some 'dormant' brain cells may have survived to become activated later. This potential for evidence of clinical recovery underlies the distinction between a persistent and a permanent stage of cerebral dysfunction; it also accounts, at least in part, for the fact that recovery of brain function is more likely when it has been lost as a result of direct head injury than when a comparable loss is due to pure hypoxic damage.[160] Yet, further, it helps to explain the more recent emergence of an additional (legal) category of patient: the minimally conscious. Medical science, once again, presents the law with a seemingly infinitely granular spectrum of human experiences and catastrophes that require responsible management.[161]

15.87 At one extreme end of such a spectrum sits the wholly decorticated patient who falls into the category originally defined by Jennett and Plum[162] as the persistent vegetative state. Such a person will have periods of wakefulness but is, nevertheless, permanently unconscious; the state has been described as eyes-open unconsciousness. Thus, it is clear that a human who has lost cortical function has, simultaneously, lost his human personality but, insofar as he is capable of oxygenating his tissues naturally and without mechanical support—that is, his cardiorespiratory system is intact and functional—he is equally certainly not dead. Nonetheless, the patient then has no consciousness and the awesome nature of the condition is summed up in the phrase: 'Consciousness is the most critical moral, legal, and constitutional standard, not for human life itself, but for human personhood'[163]—the unconscious or comatose patient is incapable of fulfilling his human function in a way which transcends the loss of any other capacity; it follows that the whole status of the person in a position of persistent unconsciousness is in doubt.

[159] P Mollard and M Goulon, 'Le coma depassé' (1959) 101 Rev Neurol 3.

[160] R S Howard and D H Miller 'The persistent vegetative state' (1995) 310 BMJ 341.

[161] Compare, J T Giacino et al., 'Disorders of consciousness after acquired brain injury: the state of the science' (2014) 10 Nature Reviews Neuro 99, doi: 10.1038/nrneurol.2013.279, and S Nettleton, J Kitzinger, and C Kitzinger, 'A diagnostic illusory? The case of distinguishing between "vegetative" and "minimally conscious" states' (2014) 116 Soc Sci and Med 134.

[162] B Jennett and F Plum, 'Persistent vegetative state after brain damage' (1972) 1 Lancet 734 and, later, B Jennett, *The Vegetative State: Medical Facts, Ethical and Legal Dilemmas* (2002). For a revisitation of Jennett's contribution, see K von Wild et al., 'The vegetative state—a syndrome in search of a name' (2012) 5(1) J Med Life 3. For the legal vagaries of diagnosis, see C Dyer, 'Court case adjourned after diagnosis of persistent vegetative state changes' (2012) 345 (aug) e 5803, doi: 10.1136/bmj.e5803.

[163] R E Cranford and D R Smith, 'Consciousness: The most critical moral (constitutional) standard for human personhood' (1987) 13 Am J Law Med 233.

15.88 It is notoriously difficult to identify a satisfactory definition of the persistent vegetative state. The distinguishing features include an irregular but cyclic state of circadian sleeping and waking unaccompanied by any behaviourally detectable expression of self-awareness, specific recognition of external stimuli, or consistent evidence of attention or inattention or learned responses.[164] It is important to note that patients in this state, while generally being in a spastic condition, are not immobile and, to a varying extent, retain both cranial nerve and spinal reflexes, including those related to visual and auditory stimuli. Again, this reflects the degree of brain damage; we can, therefore, speak in terms of degrees of consciousness (or vegetativeness), although it requires skilled neurological expertise to distinguish retained—or recovered—cortical function from sub-cortical reflex activity. As we see later, the law is now responding to these shades of grey matter in recognising patients who are 'near permanent vegetative state (PVS)' or 'minimally conscious',[165] suggesting a gamut of possible experiences and diagnoses. In addition, the concept has its built-in semantic difficulties, the most urgent of which lies in the word 'persistent'. A persistent state is one which persists until it is relieved—from which it follows that the diagnosis of the persistent vegetative state envisages a potential for recovery; this was the understanding of those who coined the term.[166] It is, in our opinion, essential that discussion—and any legislation based upon it—should be devoted to the management of the *permanent* vegetative state.[167] Even then, the difficulties are not all eliminated. Permanence is a presumption rather than a certainty; whether or not that presumption is acceptable depends on empirical evidence which must, also, bow to practicality. Thus, the Multi-society Task Force in America defined the persistent vegetative state as a vegetative state present one month after acute traumatic or non-traumatic brain injury; it concluded that a permanent state can be assumed if the patient has been vegetative for one year.[168] But to say that a state is permanent if it has been present for a year[169] involves a balancing act between reasonableness and certainty. The compromise, no matter how high is the degree of clinical certainty, is unlikely to satisfy everyone and the possibility of exceptions to the rule cannot be denied; nevertheless, the advantages of establishing a cut-off point outweigh the disadvantages of prolonging the decision indefinitely. Of equal

---

[164] Multi-society Task Force on PVS, 'Medical aspects of the persistent vegetative state' (1994) 330 New Engl J Med 1499 (Pt 1), 1572 (Pt 2). See more recently, D Tarquini et al., 'Persistent vegetative state: an ethical appraisal' (2012) 33(3) Neurol Sci 695, and FE Pisa et al., 'The prevalence of vegetative and minimally conscious states: a systematic review and methodological appraisal' (2014) 29(4) J Head Trauma Rehab e23, doi: 10.1097/HTR.0b013e3182a4469f.

[165] See the minimally conscious state as involved in the case *W (by her litigation friend B) v M (by her litigation friend, the Official Solicitor) and Others* [2011] EWHC 2443 (Fam) described as being a state of awareness above that of the vegetative state but for which diagnosis was a heavily specialised and problematic area, and one which had come to attention in the years since *Bland*.

[166] See S Laureys, M-E Faymonville, and J Berre, 'Permanent vegetative state and persistent vegetative state are not interchangeable terms' (2000) 321 BMJ letters, 17 October.

[167] See, especially, Royal College of Physicians, *The Vegetative State: Guidance on Diagnosis and Management* (2003). Note that this is a restatement of the guidance originally provided in 1996. The key requirements for the diagnosis are: (i) there must be no evidence of self or environment awareness at any time; (ii) there must be no response to visual, auditory, tactile, or noxious stimuli of a kind suggesting volition or conscious purpose; (iii) and no evidence of language comprehension or meaningful expression (at para 2.2.1).

[168] See n 164.

[169] Historically agreed by the BMA: *BMA Guidelines on Treatment of Patients in Persistent Vegetative State* (2007) and by the Working Party of the Royal College of Physicians, 'The Permanent Vegetative State—Review by a Working Group Convened by the Royal College of Physicians and Endorsed by the Conference of Medical Royal Colleges and their Faculties of the United Kingdom' (1996) 30 J R Coll Physicians Lond 119 (revised 2003). See now: Royal College of Physicians, *Prolonged Disorders of*

importance is the fact that, as we have already noted, the word 'vegetative' fails to define the degree of brain damage involved. Therapeutic decisions in PVS thus depend not only on its permanence but also on the definition of vegetativeness which must, to an extent, involve a value judgement.[170] Disputes by experts over diagnosis can lead to adjournment and delay in legal proceedings.[171]

15.89 Emerging medical understanding also requires that guidelines be kept under constant review. Thus while the current Royal College of Physicians guidelines from 2013 retain reference to 'vegetative state' and 'minimally conscious state' '... as there are clear definitions for them and both the public and commissioners generally know what they mean...', it is also stated that '... [i]f and when a more acceptable, internationally agreed term emerges, this will be adopted in future iterations of these guidelines'.[172]

15.90 Having reached a diagnosis, however, we are left with what may well be regarded as the ultimate tragedy in human life—a human being who is alive in the cardiovascular sense in that he or she can breathe and maintain a heart beat, and who, at the same time, has no contact with the outside world and will never have such contact again. We discuss the concept of neocortical death later.[173] At this point we need only say that it has no place in the jurisprudence of the UK. The law as to killing is unaffected by the mental state of the victim—dements and aments are still protected insofar as the term 'reasonable being' implies no more than 'human being'—and persons in PVS still represent 'persons in being'. They present an additional jurisprudential difficulty in that, being unconscious, they are free from pain—or, at least, from treatable pain; the doctrine of 'double effect'[174] cannot, therefore, be applied within their management—and, in this respect, it is to be noted that, absent an intercurrent infection or similar complication, well-managed PVS patients have a life expectancy that is to be measured in years. We have spent some time on the definitional difficulties of the condition because, without an understanding of them, it is impossible to appreciate the distinctions which have been made in the various cases that have come before the courts over the years and the reasons underlying decisions that may appear contradictory given that all those that we discuss have it in common that the courts were being invited to pronounce on the lawfulness of withdrawing physiological support from severely brain damaged adult patients.

THE ENGLISH CASES

15.91 The first, and outstandingly most important, case in which the matter was addressed in the UK was *Airedale NHS Trust* v *Bland*.[175] Anthony Bland was crushed in a football stadium in April 1989 and sustained severe anoxic brain damage; as a result, he lapsed into PVS. There was no improvement in his condition by September 1992 and, at that time, the hospital sought a declaration[176] to the effect that they might lawfully discontinue all

Consciousness: National Clinical Guidelines (2013), available at: https://www.rcplondon.ac.uk/guidelines-policy/prolonged-disorders-consciousness-national-clinical-guidelines.

[170] A M Owen, 'Detecting awareness in the vegetative state' (2006) 3131 Science 1402.

[171] C Dyer, 'Court case adjourned after diagnosis of persistent vegetative state changes' (2012) 345 BMJ e5803.

[172] N 169 (2013), p.3.   [173] See Chapter 16.   [174] For which, see para 18.34.

[175] [1993] 1 All ER 821; (1993) 12 BMLR 64, Fam Div, CA, HL.

[176] The English courts were initially in something of a dilemma in such cases since their authority under the *parens patriae* jurisdiction was removed by way of the Mental Health Act 1959 and revocation of the last warrant under the Sign Manual. The court could no longer give effective consent to medical treatment

life-sustaining treatment and medical support measures, including ventilation, nutrition, and hydration by artificial means; that any subsequent treatment given should be for the sole purpose of enabling him to end his life in dignity and free from pain and suffering; that, if death should then occur, its cause should be attributed to the natural and other causes of his present state; and that none of those concerned should, as a result, be subject to any civil or criminal liability. This declaration—save for the final clause, which was considered inappropriate[177]—was granted in the Family Division essentially on the grounds that it was in AD's best interests to do so; the court considered there was overwhelming evidence that the provision of artificial feeding by means of a nasogastric tube was 'medical treatment' and that its discontinuance was in accord with good medical practice. An appeal was unanimously dismissed in the Court of Appeal. From three exceptionally well-considered opinions, we extract only that of Hoffmann LJ:

> This is not an area in which any difference can be allowed to exist between what is legal and what is morally right. The decision of the court should be able to carry conviction with the ordinary person as being based not merely on legal precedent but also upon acceptable ethical values.[178]

And, later:

> In my view the choice the law makes must reassure people that the courts do have full respect for life, but that they do not pursue the principle to the point at which it has become almost empty of any real content and when it involves the sacrifice of other important values such as human dignity and freedom of choice. I think that such reassurance can be provided by a decision, properly explained, to allow Anthony Bland to die.[179]

15.92 The inherent difficulty of the declarator procedure is that it is concerned only with the *lawfulness* of an action[180] and, when the *Bland* case came to the House of Lords, Lord Browne-Wilkinson and Lord Mustill were at particular pains to emphasise that the ethical issues should be considered and legislated for by Parliament:

> is this a matter which lies outside the legitimate development of the law by judges and requires society, through the democratic expression of its views in Parliament, to reach its decisions on the underlying moral and practical problems and then reflect those decisions in legislation? I have no doubt that it is for Parliament, not the courts, to decide the broader issues which this case raises.[181]

15.93 It was, therefore, not surprising that, although the House could not entirely avoid addressing the ethical and moral problems involved, it did so to a lesser extent than did the Court of Appeal. In this respect, the fundamental conflict lies in the inevitable

---

on behalf of a mentally incompetent adult unless that treatment is directed to the cause of the incompetence. Procedural matters were addressed by the establishment of the Court of Protection under the Mental Capacity Act 2005.

[177] This problem was considered in greater detail in the comparable Scottish case *Law Hospital NHS Trust v Lord Advocate* 1996 SLT 848; (1996) 39 BMLR 166, for which see paras 15.121 et seq.

[178] [1993] 1 All ER 821 at 850; (1993) 12 BMLR 64 at 95.

[179] [1993] 1 All ER 821 at 855; (1993) 12 BMLR 64 at 100.

[180] See early analysis in J Bridgeman, 'Declared innocent?' (1995) 3 Med L Rev 117 and more recently C Constable, 'Withdrawal of artificial nutrition and hydration for patients in a permanent vegetative state: changing tack' (2012) 26(3) Bioethics 157. For recent criticism, S Halliday, A Formby, and S Cookson, 'An assessment of the court's role in the withdrawal of clinically assisted nutrition and hydration from patients in the permanent vegetative state' (2015) Med Law Rev, doi: 10.1093/medlaw/fwv026.

[181] [1993] 1 All ER 821 at 878; (1993) 12 BMLR 64 at 124, per Lord Browne-Wilkinson.

distortion of the principle of the sanctity of life which would result from a decision to terminate the care on which life depended.[182] The majority of the House was able to dispose of this on the ground that the principle was certainly not absolute. Moreover, since the right to refuse treatment—including life-sustaining treatment—is now firmly part of common law and medical ethics, the principle of the sanctity of life must yield to that of the right to self-determination and, of the many lines of argument considered, it is this which seems to us to bind all five Law Lords most closely together. As Lord Goff put it,[183] the right to self-determination should not be eclipsed by the fact of incompetence—it must always be present. This also forms the basis of Lord Mustill's reasoning, which is summarised later and which, essentially, justifies the withdrawal or withholding of treatment. We are less happy with the alternative view taken, in particular, by Lord Lowry and Lord Browne-Wilkinson. In essence, this also started from the premise that non-voluntary treatment was lawful only so long as it was justified by necessity; but, once necessity could no longer be claimed—by reason of the futility of treatment—further invasion of the patient's body constituted either the crime of battery or the tort of trespass. On this view, any potential medical offence lies not in *withholding* treatment but in *continuing* it to no purpose. This argument seems to us to be dangerously open-ended in relation to conditions less clear-cut than PVS. It was this situation which Lord Mustill was clearly anxious to avoid and his concern was later borne out in guidance from the BMA which proposed extending the PVS ruling to other incapacitated patients.[184]

15.94 The greater part of the opinions in *Bland* was concerned for the doctors' position vis-à-vis the criminal law. First, it was essential to elide the possibility of murder by classifying removal of support as an omission rather than as a positive act.[185] There was wide agreement that, while there was no moral or logical difference, a distinction was certainly to be made in law. The House came to a unanimous conclusion that discontinuance of nasogastric feeding was an omission; their Lordships achieved this in various ways but, in general, it was considered impossible to distinguish between withdrawal of and not starting tube feeding—and the latter was clearly an omission. Next, the problem of the duty of care had to be addressed. Lord Mustill's argument can be summarised:

(i) treatment of the incompetent is governed by necessity and necessity is, in turn, defined in terms of the patient's best interests;

(ii) once there is no hope of recovery, any interest in being kept alive disappears and, with it, the justification for invasive therapy also disappears;

(iii) in the absence of necessity, there can be no duty to act and, in the absence of a duty, there can be no criminality in an omission.

15.95 This, however, leads to what was, perhaps, the major hurdle—can feeding be regarded as medical treatment and, therefore, a fit subject for medical decision-making, or is it always such a fundamental duty that it can never be wilfully withheld? The Lords in *Bland* had rather more trouble with this than have had their counterparts in the USA.[186] Eventually,

---

[182] For major discussion, see J Keown, 'Restoring moral and intellectual shape to the law after *Bland*' (1997) 113 LQR 481. Singer, at one extreme, saw the decision as an explicit rejection of the sanctity of life principle: P Singer, *Rethinking Life and Death* (1994), p 75.

[183] [1993] 1 All ER 821 at 866; (1993) 12 BMLR 64 at 112.

[184] BMA, *Withholding and Withdrawing Life-Prolonging Medical Treatment: Guidance for Decision Makers* (3rd edn, 2007).

[185] For further discussion of which, see Chapter 18.   [186] See paras 15.128 et seq.

however, a consensus was reached that nasogastric feeding at least formed part of the general medical management.[187] While it is certainly more difficult to see nasogastric feeding as medical treatment than it is to accept gastrostomy feeding as such, we do not share some of the academic distrust of the concept that has been expressed.[188]

15.96 At the end of the day, the House of Lords was able to justify its unanimous decision on the basis of the patient's best interests. All the opinions stressed that it was not a matter of it being in the best interests of the patient to die but, rather, that it was not in his best interests to treat him so as to prolong his life in circumstances where 'no affirmative benefit' could be derived from the treatment.[189] We confess to some difficulty in accepting a 'best interests' test in these circumstances and we return to the matter later. For the present, we point out that its application dictates the concurrent acceptance of 'good medical practice' as the yardstick of assessment. This led the House of Lords to conclude that the *Bolam* test[190]—that the doctor's decision should be judged against one which would be taken by a responsible and competent body of relevant professional opinion—applied in the management of PVS. This gives considerable discretion to the medical profession to decide what amounts to the patient's best interests by reference to its own standards[191] and, in deciding that artificial feeding was, at least, an integral part of medical treatment, the House of Lords opened the door to the health carers to withdraw alimentation. Nevertheless, the requirement to seek court approval in every case was maintained[192]—subject to the hope that the restriction might be rescinded in the future—and there was, in fact, a strong undercurrent to the effect that the decision was specific to *Bland* rather than a general statement on the removal of alimentation from brain damaged persons.

English Cases Post-*Bland*

15.97 Consideration of the later cases suggests that the previous note of caution may not have been misplaced. Almost exactly a year later, we had the case of *Frenchay Healthcare NHS Trust* v *S*.[193] This concerned a young man who had been in apparent PVS for two-and-a-half years as a result of a drug overdose. When it was discovered that his gastrostomy tube had become detached, a declaration was sought that the hospital could lawfully refrain from renewing or continuing alimentary and other life-sustaining measures and could

---

[187] The Australian courts have approached the question from a different and interesting angle. In *Gardner: re BWV* [2003] VSC 173 the central legal issue was whether the provision of ANH was 'medical treatment' (which can be refused under the Victorian Medical Treatment Act 1988, s 3) or 'palliative care' (which cannot be rejected by way of an advance statement). It was held that the provision of ANH was medical treatment. Similarly, the Supreme Court of Canada confirmed in *Cuthbertson* v *Rasouli* [2013] SCC 53 that withdrawal and withholding of life support constitutes 'treatment' under the Ontario Health Care Consent Act 1996. This, in turn, required consent from the patient or their proxy decision-maker in order to be legal.

[188] See, e.g., J M Finnis, '*Bland*: Crossing the Rubicon?' (1993) 109 LQR 329.

[189] [1993] 1 All ER 821 at 883; (1993) 12 BMLR 64 at 130, per Lord Browne-Wilkinson. See also [1993] 1 All ER 821 at 865; (1993) 12 BMLR 64 at 115.

[190] *Bolam* v *Friern Hospital Management Committee* [1957] 1 WLR 582; (1957) 1 BMLR 1.

[191] See [1993] 1 All ER 821 at 883; (1993) 12 BMLR 64 at 130, per Lord Browne-Wilkinson: 'on an application to the court for a declaration that the discontinuance of medical care will be lawful, the courts *only* concern will be to be satisfied that the doctor's decision to discontinue is in accordance with a respectable body of medical opinion and that it is reasonable' (emphasis added).

[192] Practice Note [1996] 4 All ER 766; (1996) 34 BMLR 20, and see now Practice Note (Official Solicitor: Declaratory Proceedings: Medical and Welfare Decisions for Adults who Lack Capacity) [2006] 2 FLR 373.

[193] [1994] 2 All ER 403; (1994) 17 BMLR 156, CA.

restrict any medical treatment to that which would allow him to die peacefully and with the greatest dignity. The declaration was granted and the decision was upheld on appeal.

15.98 *Frenchay* v *S* differed from *Bland* in a fundamental respect—that, although the prospect had been mooted, the actual decision to discontinue treatment was not a considered one but was one forced by events. As a corollary, the judicial inquiry was certainly hurried and this was the factor which most concerned Waite LJ in the Court of Appeal. The decision has also been subject to academic criticism on these grounds.[194] More importantly, Sir Thomas Bingham MR considered it plain that the evidence in *Frenchay* was neither as emphatic nor as unanimous as that in *Bland*'s case.[195] We must also consider the potential results of failing to make or countermanding the declaration sought—either the doctors would have been forced into an operation which was, in the opinion of the consultant in charge, of no benefit to the patient and which possibly verged on criminal intervention or they would have had to do nothing and take their chance with the law.

15.99 Sir Thomas accepted such medical opinion as was provided but was, himself, conscious of a qualitative difference between the two cases. The question thus arises as to whether *Frenchay* represents a 'slippery slope' on which we could descend from PVS to little more than physical or mental disability when assuming that the patient's 'best interests' lie in non-treatment; alternatively, is it a judicial effort to homogenise non-treatment decisions—during which process, PVS becomes merely the end-point for decision-making rather than a condition to be considered on its own? We discuss in due course the difficulties in harmonising the 'specific-case' stance adopted in *Bland* with the relatively open-ended direction as to withholding 'futile' treatment that was provided in *Re J*.[196] Meantime, perhaps the main inference to be drawn is that each case is special and must be judged on its own facts.[197]

15.100 Later English cases have been reported only spasmodically. We comment briefly on some of these mainly to indicate the quality of the evidence that was available.

15.101 *Re C*[198] concerned a 27-year-old man who had been in PVS for four years following an anaesthetic disaster. Clinically, the case was of great severity and the judge appears to have accepted without demur the evidence provided by the relatives as to the likely wishes of the patient.

15.102 *Re G*[199] related to a young man whose brain damage, sustained in a motorcycle accident, was intensified by a later anoxic episode. The case was of particular interest in that there was some dispute amongst the relatives as to the course to be adopted. Sir Stephen Brown P concluded that the dissenting views of the patient's mother should not be allowed to

---

[194] See, e.g., A Grubb, 'Commentary' (1994) 2 Med L Rev 206.

[195] [1994] 2 All ER 403 at 411; (1994) 17 BMLR 156 at 163.

[196] *Re J (a minor) (wardship: medical treatment)* [1990] 3 All ER 930; (1990) 6 BMLR 25.

[197] A point which was emphasised in *Bland* and also in the even more doubtful Irish case of *In the matter of a Ward* (1995) 2 ILRM 401. Precisely the same result was achieved in this case although the reasoning was complicated by considerations of Irish constitutional law. For discussion, see J K Mason and G T Laurie, 'The management of the persistent vegetative state in the British Isles' [1996] JR 263; J Keown, 'Life and death in Dublin' [1996] CLJ 6.

[198] The importance of continued post-mortem anonymity was considered in *Re C (adult patient: restriction of publicity after death)* [1996] 2 FLR 251 and see Practice Direction [2002] 1 WLR 325. For professional guidance to this effect, see GMC, *Confidentiality* (2009). This guidance was under review at the time of writing, see http://www.gmc-uk.org/guidance/news_consultation/25893.asp.

[199] [1995] 3 Med L Rev 80. In passing, it was held that the public interest in these cases determined that they should be heard in open court: *Re G (adult patient: publicity)* [1995] 2 FLR 528.

operate as a veto when his best interests—as defined by the surgeon in charge—favoured removal of nutrition. The scene was thus set for the comments of Lord Goff in *Bland*[200] to the effect that the attitudes of relatives, while due great respect, should not be determinative to be followed in the event of conflict.

15.103 *Swindon and Marlborough NHS Trust v S*[201] was unique among reported cases in being concerned with a patient who was being nursed at home. Rather, as in *Frenchay*, however, the issue was forced by blockage of the gastrostomy tube; further treatment would, therefore, have involved hospitalisation. Ward J held that, given the certain diagnosis of PVS, to discontinue life-sustaining measures would be in accordance with good medical practice as recognised and approved within the medical profession. Once again, as in *Re G*, the court firmly adopted *Bolam* as the benchmark—there is a strong suggestion that good medical practice is being seen as a test of lawfulness.[202]

15.104 There was no doubt as to the diagnosis in any of these three cases. *Re D*,[203] however, concerned a 28-year-old woman who had sustained very severe brain damage following a head injury some six years before. Again, an emergency arose when her gastrostomy tube became displaced. All medical opinion was to the effect that D was totally unaware of anything or anyone but she did not fully satisfy the conditions laid down by the Royal College of Physicians for the diagnosis of PVS.[204] The President of the Family Division regarded her as suffering 'a living death' and was unable to accept that, because she did not fulfil one of the diagnostic criteria, she was not in a PVS. He, therefore, did not believe he was extending the range of cases in which a declaration as to the removal of feeding and hydration might properly be considered. It was appropriate and in her best interests to make such a declaration.

15.105 *Re H*[205] involved a 43-year-old woman who had existed for three years in a severely brain-damaged state following a vehicular accident. She, too, was agreed to be wholly and unalterably unaware of herself or her environment but, equally, it was agreed that she did not fit squarely within one of the College of Physicians' diagnostic criteria. Sir Stephen Brown P thought that, in this instance, 'it may be that a precise label is not of significant importance'. Indeed, the whole area is prey to semantic juggling—one expert, while agreeing that the case did not fit the criteria for PVS, nevertheless thought that H was in a vegetative state which was permanent. The court reiterated that, while it was aware of the consequences that would follow the suspension of treatment, it did not in any sense sanction anything which is *aimed* at terminating life:

> The sanctity of life is of vital importance. It is not, however, paramount and...I am satisfied that it is in the best interests of this patient that the life sustaining treatment...should be brought to a conclusion.[206]

15.106 Thus, while all these cases show distinctive variations, they also have common features on which the jurisprudence has been, and is being, built. The first is that, the precedents having been set, the baseline lies in the confirmed diagnosis of PVS. Once that is made,

---

[200] [1993] 1 All ER 821 at 872; (1993) 12 BMLR 64 at 118.   [201] [1995] 3 Med LR 84.

[202] It does not follow that medical opinion in a case must be unanimous. So long as there is a high degree of probability that medical evidence supported withdrawal of treatment in the patient's best interests then the court would be entitled to support it: see *An NHS Trust v X* [2005] EWCA Civ 1145; [2006] Lloyd's Rep Med 29.

[203] (1997) 38 BMLR 1.   [204] See n 169.   [205] *Re H (adult: incompetent)* (1997) 38 BMLR 11.

[206] (1997) 38 BMLR 11 at 16.

the conclusion follows automatically that the patient's best interests dictate the termination of assisted feeding and, indeed, there may well be an obligation on the doctor to discontinue treatment.[207] Second, and following from this, the Official Solicitor has been loath to oppose any applications for withdrawal of support once the diagnosis is confirmed. Complete medicalisation of treatment decisions in the condition may, then, still be accepted. This having been said, a Practice Direction makes it clear that, at present, court approval should be sought in almost all cases where removal of feeding and hydration is contemplated.[208] The court is charged with weighing the advantages and disadvantages for the patient of removal in light of the available medical evidence, although it is difficult to see how any conclusion other than withdrawal could be reached when faced with a good faith assessment of medical futility by the care team. We say this in light of recent developments which—contrary to the expectations of some—demonstrate that the provisions of the Human Rights Act 1998 make virtually no difference to the position of patients in PVS.

15.107 In *NHS Trust A v Mrs M, NHS Trust B v Mrs H*,[209] declarators of legality were sought on the proposed withdrawal of feeding and hydration from two patients in PVS. In authorising this the High Court not only endorsed the pre-existing position under *Bland*, but went further in testing this precedent against possible human rights objections under the 1998 Act, namely Art 2 (right to life), Art 3 (prohibition of cruel and inhuman treatment), and Art 8 (right to respect for private life). Rather than considering the particularised reasoning of Butler-Sloss P in respect of each of these provisions,[210] a few points of principle and policy should be noted.

15.108 The court clearly adopted a *good faith* approach to the issue, focusing on the fact that, because a 'responsible body of medical opinion' has reached a conclusion as to futility, there is little more to be said on the matter. This, however, makes professionalism rather than principle the measure of patient protection. We have already shown that medical professionals are qualified only to comment on the medical futility of any proposed course of action and that the court retains, for itself, the ultimate role as arbiter of best interests.[211]

15.109 Second, in examining the content of the human rights laid before it, the court fixed on the principle of respect for personal autonomy and concluded that, because the PVS patient could not consent to continued intervention, to continue to intervene against his or her best interests—as determined by (medically qualified) others—would *violate* protection under Art 8. This, however, turns self-determination on its head. Indeed, why is this a relevant consideration in the context of someone who cannot meaningfully experience or exercise this state? It is precisely because the patient cannot do so that 'best interests' enters the equation. The error lies in the failure to appreciate that it is *respect* for the human being that is required, not only (or necessarily) respect for her 'right to choose'.

---

[207] Following the argument put forward by Grubb in 'Commentary' [1995] 3 Med L Rev 83, 85. This seems to have been confirmed by Baker J in *W (by her litigation friend B)*, n 165, para 35.

[208] Practice Note (Official Solicitor: Declaratory Proceedings: Medical and Welfare Decisions for Adults Who Lack Capacity) [2006] 2 FLR 373.

[209] [2001] 2 WLR 942; (2001) 58 BMLR 87.

[210] For such an analysis, see A R MacLean, 'Crossing the Rubicon on the human rights ferry' (2001) 64 MLR 775.

[211] As we discuss further in Chapters 4 and 12.

15.110 The court also relied upon the incapacity of these patients to restrict their rights in another respect. It held that, because PVS patients are insensate and cannot appreciate their state of being, it is not cruel and degrading to subject them to the vagaries of withdrawal of feeding and hydration—thus adopting the excessively narrow interpretation of Art 3 that a victim must be able to experience the inhuman treatment before a violation will occur.[212] This, however, is a distorted view of European jurisprudence which has held only that a victim's own subjective reactions to treatment can impact on the question of whether violation has occurred.[213] In no way does it follow, however, that subjectivity is a pre-requisite to violation.[214]

15.111 We see Lord Mustill's fears as to extending the precedent in *Bland* to other, non-PVS, cases being realised in the next English case to be considered. In *Re G (adult incompetent: withdrawal of treatment)*,[215] the patient was a 45-year-old woman who had suffered serious anoxic brain damage after inhaling her own vomitus following surgery. She had been kept alive for nine months by means of ANH when the NHS Trust responsible for her care brought the matter to court for a declaration of legality as to the withdrawal of her means of artificial sustenance. G's family supported the application, stating that she would not have wished to remain in such a state. One expert witness was enough to convince the court that there was no reasonable prospect of her ever recovering and that she should be allowed to 'die with dignity'. Moreover, it was held not to be inconsistent with her human right to life that a decision be made to discontinue treatment, despite her inability to give a valid consent to its withdrawal. A declaration to this effect was granted.

15.112 We view this decision with a degree of concern. It comes very close to the controversial guidance of the BMA, already mentioned, which suggests that an assessment of futility leading to the withdrawal of feeding and hydration may be appropriate for patients with dementia or for those who have suffered serious stroke.[216] This is highly problematic as we have argued elsewhere,[217] not least because the heavy and continuing emphasis placed on medical assessment rather than on a robust and principled approach to individualised human and patients' rights may mean that an expansionist development of clinical discretion is inevitable.

15.113 A further ruling from the Court of Appeal reflects our views and concerns, but at the same time it reveals the tragedy of so many of these cases which often feel like lose–lose scenarios. *W Healthcare NHS Trust v H and Another*[218] concerned KH who had suffered from multiple sclerosis for 30 years. She had required artificial feeding for five years and needed 24-hour nursing care to survive. She could scarcely speak and recognised nobody; she was, however, conscious and sentient. Her feeding tube had fallen out and her health carers wished to replace it. The family was opposed to this and appealed the trial judge's

---

[212] Art 3 states: 'No one shall be subjected to torture or to inhuman or degrading treatment or punishment.'

[213] *Campbell and Cosans v United Kingdom* (1983) 7 EHRR 165, para 28.

[214] Inability or awareness to feel pain in PVS or in a minimally conscious state has been challenged: M Boly et al., 'Perception of pain in the minimally conscious state with PET activation: An observational study' (2008) 7(11) Lancet Neuro 1013.

[215] (2002) 65 BMLR 6.

[216] BMA, *Withholding and Withdrawing Life-prolonging Medical Treatment*, n 89. See also GMC, *Withholding and Withdrawing Life-prolonging Treatments: Good Practice in Decision-making* (2002, 2006) paras 22–4.

[217] See G T Laurie and J K Mason, 'Negative treatment of vulnerable patients: Euthanasia by any other name?' [2000] JR 159.

[218] [2004] EWCA Civ 1324; [2005] 1 WLR 834.

opinion in favour of continued treatment. The Court of Appeal upheld the trial judge's ruling that KH should continue to be fed while expressing the deepest of sympathy for her and her family. The court stated that three tests have to be applied in cases such as this. First, is the patient capable of taking an informed decision herself? There was no doubt as to the negative response in the instant case. Second, is there a valid advance statement or directive which covers the present circumstances? We discuss this matter more fully in Chapter 4; in KH's case there was insufficient evidence of what she would have wanted to justify relying on an advanced refusal. Finally, if neither test applies, what is in the patient's best interests? It is important to note, as the court itself does, that the legal test in the UK is not substituted judgement, which we explore at paras 15.131 et seq. Thus, the court could not rely on the strong evidence from the family that KH would not have wanted to continue living in this undignified state to refuse on her behalf. The onerous task for the court was to ask, 'What is in the patient's best interests given that the decision not to feed would effectively mean that the patient would starve to death?' Unlike the PVS cases, KH would have some level of awareness of the process. Brooke LJ emphasised the high value that English law places on life and stated:

> The Court cannot in effect sanction the death by starvation of a patient who is not in a PVS state other than with their clear and informed consent or where their condition is so intolerable as to be beyond doubt...I cannot say that life-prolonging treatment...would provide no benefit...death by this route would...be even less dignified than the death which she will more probably face at some time in the more distant future.[219]

15.114   As to the process of establishing overall best interests, the Court of Appeal approved Thorpe LJ's suggested 'balance sheet' of pros and cons which, as we have seen, has also been approved in the context of neonates (para 15.38). In contrast to those cases, however, *KH* appears to endorse intolerability as the touchstone for measuring best interests. Are the streams of case law at odds? The Court of Appeal in *Wyatt* accepted that intolerability could be a useful signpost on the route towards best interests but was emphatic that the two should not be equiparated. The net result for neonates is that it can be deemed not to be in their best interests to be treated *even if* their life is not yet intolerable. *KH* would seem to suggest a higher threshold for adults. This might be an echo once again of the strains of the personhood argument, whereby a sentient adult with a lived life may be held in higher regard than a newborn with little or no experiential existence. Later cases adopt a more straightforward application of the best interests test, as conventionally understood.[220]

15.115   More recent decisions have considered the legal position regarding withholding of ANH from patients who are now seen as 'minimally conscious'.[221] We have discussed these cases at paras 4.41 et seq and need only highlight the themes pertinent to assessments of futility here. In *M (Adult Patient) (Minimally Conscious State: Withdrawal of Treatment)*,[222] (M) had previously been diagnosed as being in a vegetative state but this was revised to a diagnosis of minimally conscious state (MCS). Her family wished ANH to be removed but the health care team did not. This was the first case of MCS to be brought before the English courts. In the event, the court endorsed the balance sheet approach to best

---

[219]   [2004] EWCA Civ 1324; [2005] 1 WLR 834, para 22.

[220]   *Gloucestershire Clinical Commissioning Group v AB* [2014] EWCOP 49; (2015) 142 BMLR 242

[221]   For a working definition of this concept, see the Royal College of Physicians (2013), n 169 above. R Heywood, 'Moving on from *Bland*: the evolution of the law and minimally conscious patients' (2014) 22(4) Med L Rev 548.

[222]   [2012] 1 WLR 1653; [2012] 1 All ER 1313. For further discussion, see V Sachdeva and C Butler-Cole, 'Best interests and the minimally conscious state: the case of M' (2012) 2(1) Edler LJ 65.

interests, specifically stating that cases of PVS fell in favour of withdrawal of treatment every time (para 35) whereas MCS will depend on all facts and evidence. Technology had changed over the years and it was evident that patients who were minimally conscious could be aware of pain and of the withdrawal of ANH. On balance, and despite strong evidence of the patient's own prior views, it was held to be in M's best interests to continue treatment. Sanctity of life was confirmed as the fundamental starting position, M had some positive experiences and it was accordingly determined not to be in her best interests to withdraw care. Equally, in *An NHS Trust* v *D*,[223] the patient suffered irreparable brain damage and the question arose about the cessation of ANH. This was also rejected despite the existence of a signed letter which included, inter alia, the very clear statement: '... I refuse any medical treatment of an invasive nature (including but not restrictive to placing a feeding tube in my stomach) if said procedure is only for the purpose of extending a reduced quality of life'. This, however, still didn't meet the requirements under the Mental Capacity Act for want of a witness and a specific statement that the decision should apply to the specific treatment. In the end, the judge preferred the preservation of life.

15.116 Four recent examples illustrate the direction of travel of the jurisprudence. In *An NHS Trust* v *L*[224] patient L was initially determined to be in PVS following a cardiac arrest which resulted in 'devastating neurological injury', but was later reassessed as in minimally conscious state at a very low level of the spectrum. Medical opinion suggested a less than one per cent chance of recovering capacity as defined by the Mental Capacity Act 2005. The medical team sought a declaration of lawfulness with respect to no further intervention in the event of further deterioration. The family objected, taking an essentially vitalistic position and arguing that L would have wanted to be kept alive. In making the declaration on non-intervention the court laid down two important principles: (i) family and patient views are but one element in the balancing exercise required by law, and (ii) while a court is entitled to disagree with unanimous clinical evidence it could not require professionals to treat against their better judgement.[225] In *United Lincolnshire Hospitals NHS Trust* v *N*[226] the legal question was the permissibility of withholding intravenous fluids from a patient in MCS. In declaring this lawful, the court reiterated the previous point about non-compunction of medical staff, now buoyed by confirmation of the point from the Supreme Court.[227] Moreover, in determining whether treatment would be in a patient's best interests, the court had to consider whether it would be futile to continue in the sense of being ineffective or, of no benefit to, the patient. The court clarified that the treatment did not have to be likely to cure or palliate the underlying condition or return the patient to full or reasonable health; rather it should be capable of allowing the recovery of a quality of life 'which the patient would regard as worthwhile'. The evidence in the present case overwhelmingly supported non-intervention. In *Sheffield Teaching Hospitals NHS Foundation Trust* v *TH*[228] the court faced the detailed issue of the *management* of non-intervention, that is, even if it is lawful to withhold or withdraw treatment is there nonetheless an enduring obligation to treat supervening conditions,

---

[223] [2012] EWHC 885 (COP).   [224] [2013] EWHC 4313 (Fam); (2014) 137 BMLR 141.

[225] This re-enforces the point made in *Re J (a minor)*, n 196 above, and followed *An NHS Trust* v *MB* [2006] EWHC 507 (Fam), [2006] 2 FLR 319, para 116.

[226] [2014] EWCOP 16; [2014] COPLR 660; (2014) 140 BMLR 204.

[227] *Aintree University Hospitals NHS Foundation Trust* v *James* [2013] UKSC 67, [2014] AC 591, discussed further below at para 15.119.

[228] [2014] EWCOP 4.

such as infection? In the event, the court adjourned in this decision for a full assessment of the facts, reminding all parties that the law now requires an holistic evaluation and this had not been forthcoming.[229] Moreover, and tellingly: ' "[w]ishes" and "best interests" were never to be conflated, being separate matters that might ultimately weigh on different sides of the balance sheet'.[230] Finally, on whether treatment with antibiotics was in the patient's best interests was always a case-dependent matter. In this case evidence supported the view that relatively minor infections would be treated with a short course of antibiotics to maintain the patient's general comfort, but it was not in his interests to treat overwhelming infections such as pneumonia or septicaemia with antibiotics. Whether an infection was mild or overwhelming was a matter of clinical judgment, dependent in turn on the invasiveness of any medical response.

15.117   Finally, in *St George's Healthcare NHS Trust* v *P*[231] we find an example of a MCS patient in which the court held that it was in the patient's best interest for renal replacement therapy to continue. After an initial diagnosis of PVS, family video led to a reassessment of P's condition and re-diagnosis as MCS. Applying a strict level of scrutiny to the evidence as a whole and beginning with the presumption in favour of life, the court found almost no evidence to rebut the presumption that it was in P's best interests to be treated. Indeed, there was contrary evidence that it could extend life a further four years, that he gained benefit from his family's love and affection, that the treatment was not unduly burdensome and had a prospect of success, and he did not seem to be in pain. The court was at pains to emphasise the absolute necessity for a structured assessment in all such cases *before* any application to the court. As it said: '[w]ithout a rigorous evidential analysis, real mistakes could be made'.

15.118   We thus see, perhaps, two streams of futile cases emerging in these catastrophic cases. It is important to recognise the role of the Official Solicitor's Practice Note of 2006 in all of this.[232] An application to court should always be sought before withdrawal of ANH from patients in PVS and, now, a range of treatments from patients with minimally conscious patients as well;[233] in most circumstances, for PVS this will be little more than a confirmatory exercise in respect of the diagnosis from which a declarator of legality of withdrawal should follow.[234] The same will not be true in MCS cases. Indeed, the cases will often overlap in the sense that medical evidence can change circumstances, as a number of the above cases worryingly demonstrate. In *An NHS Trust* v *J*[235] a challenge by the Official Solicitor was successful based on evidence in the literature of a possible beneficial effect of a drug called Zolpidem on the condition of some PVS patients. The request was to delay the declaration for three days to try this, albeit unproved, intervention. It was accepted that if there was no improvement within three days withdrawal could proceed. The stay was granted by the court but there was no improvement. Still, the need for 'structured assessment' must clearly be the guiding parameter in all of these cases.

---

[229] Per *Aintree*, para 15.119.   [230] N 228, above, paras 31, 35–9, 53–6.   [231] [2015] EWCOP 42.
[232] Practice Note (Official Solicitor: Declaratory Proceedings: Medical and Welfare Decisions for Adults who Lack Capacity) [2006] 2 FLR 373.
[233] *W* v *M* [2012] 1 All ER 1313; (2011) 122 BMLR 67. The Court of Protection re-emphasised that all cases involving the PVS and, now, the MCS should be referred to the Court (COP Practice Direction 9E, para 5).
[234] Practice Note (Official Solicitor: Declaratory Proceedings: Medical and Welfare Decisions for Adults who Lack Capacity) [2006] 2 FLR 373, Appendix 2.
[235] [2006] EWHC 3152 (Fam); (2007) 94 BMLR 15.

15.119 The question indeed arises as to whether it is helpful or defensible to continue to treat these kinds of cases as distinct in legal and ethical terms. What began as a seemingly aberrational and tragic set of circumstances for the House of Lords in *Bland* more than 20 years ago has become a staple for many of the courts today: the consideration of what is futile treatment and how this is to be accommodated within the best interests test. The most recent ruling from the Supreme Court on precisely these questions lights the way forward. *Aintree University Hospitals NHS Foundation Trust v James and Others*[236] was the first case to reach the Supreme Court on the meaning of 'best interests' under s 1(5) of the Mental Capacity Act 2005. It concerned a patient who had suffered a serious of debilitating physical and mental onslaughts leaving him in a decidedly grey area of the spectrum of mental capacity. Thus while the trial judge had accepted him as being in MCS, the Supreme Court seemed to accept the view that 'Mr James's current level of awareness when not in a medical crisis "might more accurately be described [as] very limited rather than minimal" '.[237] This is important for it suggests that the ruling that follows is not dependent on the attachment of such particular labels. The case came to the Supreme Court because the judge at first instance and the Court of Appeal had adopted different approaches in their assessment of best interests and the patient's widow appealed. As to the ruling itself, the legal question was by now the standard one: is it lawful to withhold treatment from a patient without capacity such that this might lead to their death? The unanimous medical view was one of futility, while the family took the opposite position that he gained benefit from seeing family and friends, had overcome all infections to date, and had been determined to beat the cancer which was the instant cause of his ultimate condition. Although the patient had died by the time the case reached the Supreme Court, the ruling was considered and handed down for the important points of law and principle that it confirms. In summary these are:

- When dealing with the incapacitated patient, the court has no more powers than the patient would have if he had capacity; thus the court cannot demand or require a particular form of treatment (para 18).

- The correct formulation of the question is not whether it is lawful to withhold treatment, but rather whether it is lawful to give it in the patient's best interests. If the treatment is not in the patient's best interests then the court cannot lawfully consent to it (para 22).

- The case of *Bland* (and PVS in general) is particular because there is no benefit at all to be gained by intervention; in all other cases the approach should be ' . . . in considering the best interests of this particular patient at this particular time, decision-makers must look at his welfare in the widest sense, not just medical but social and psychological; they must consider the nature of the medical treatment in question, what it involves and its prospects of success; they must consider what the outcome of that treatment for the patient is likely to be; they must try and put themselves in the place of the individual patient and ask what his attitude to the treatment is or would be likely to be; and they must consult others who are looking after him or interested in his welfare, in particular for their view of what his attitude would be' (para 39).

---

[236] [2013] UKSC 67; [2014] AC 591.
[237] Para 6.

- Accordingly, 'futile' should be seen as meaning ineffective or no benefit to the patient. 'Benefit', however, must be considered relative to the patient's welfare in the widest sense: 'recovery does not mean a return to full health, but the resumption of a quality of life which Mr James would regard as worthwhile' (paras 40–5).

15.120   The appeal was then dismissed. The case is important for a number of reasons. First, in terms of precedent it drew liberally on the range of judgments we have discussed thus far with respect to neonates, PVS, and MCS patients. The ruling applies across the board. Equally, however, it appears that PVS cases remain distinct as examples of patients for whom intervention represents no benefit whatsoever and therefore no balance exercise is required.[238] Equally, such a conclusion is not restricted to that class of patient, only to those for whom benefit cannot be found. In all other cases, the balance sheet must be deployed. Moreover, and most tellingly, the assessment must be recognised for the moveable target that it is, and the bull's eye must be seen determinedly from the patient's perspective and from the circumstances in which they now find themselves.[239]

THE POSITION IN SCOTLAND

15.121   The outcome of a case similar to *Bland* was awaited with some interest in Scotland, accentuated in part by some very real jurisdictional variations between the two countries. The difficulty of deciding what were, essentially, criminal matters in a civil court was common to both jurisdictions. The House of Lords, while being unanimously wary on the point,[240] was quite prepared to accept a fait accompli: 'This appeal', said Lord Mustill, 'has reached this House, and your Lordships must decide it'. There was, however, no certainty that such pragmatism would be available to the Scottish courts. On the other hand, the English court in *Bland* was undoubtedly hampered by the absence of any residual powers of *parens patriae* and, again, the issue was in some doubt in Scotland. This, then, was the uncertain position when Scotland's first PVS case came to the Inner House of the Court of Session by way of *Law Hospital NHS Trust v Lord Advocate*,[241] in which authority was sought by relatives of a middle-aged woman in PVS (Mrs Johnstone), and by the hospital treating her, to discontinue feeding.

15.122   In the event, the Inner House confirmed that it was not competent to issue a declarator to the effect that a proposed course of action was or was not criminal—it could, however, authorise a declaration in the knowledge that it would not bar proceedings in the High Court but in the hope that it would, in practice, ensure that no prosecution was undertaken there.[242] The court did, however, find that, in contrast to the position in England, the *parens patriae* jurisdiction survived in Scotland and that any authority thus given

---

[238]   The case against reliance on 'best interests' in the context of PVS is argued by A J Fenwick, 'Applying best interests to persistent vegetative state—A principled distortion?' (1998) 24 J Med Ethics 86. An alternative view is given in the same issue: R Gillon, 'Persistent vegetative state, withdrawal of artificial nutrition and hydration, and the patient's "best interests"' (1998) 24 J Med Ethics 75.

[239]   For comment, see I Wise, 'Withdrawal and withholding of medical treatment for patients lacking capacity who are in critical condition—reflections on the judgment of the Supreme Court in Aintree University Hospitals NHS Foundation Trust v James' (2014) 82(4) Med Leg J 144 and B Clough, ' "People like that": realising the social model in mental capacity jurisprudence' (2015) 23(1) Med L Rev 53.

[240]   See [1993] 1 All ER 821 at 864–5, 876, 880, 886–7, (1993) 12 BMLR 64 at 110, 122, 127, 133–4, per Lord Goff, Lord Lowry, Lord Browne-Wilkinson, and Lord Mustill respectively.

[241]   *Law Hospital NHS Trust v Lord Advocate* 1996 SLT 848, (1996) 39 BMLR 166. The case was reported by Lord Cameron from the Outer House to the Inner House without any preliminary judgment.

[242]   1996 SLT 848 at 855; (1996) 39 BMLR 166 at 176, per Lord President Hope.

would have the same effect in law as if consent had been given by the patient. The court, in deciding as to the withdrawal of treatment, could act on its own initiative and would do so in the future.

15.123 The Inner House considered the numerous rulings that had been reached in several common law jurisdictions as to the correct test for exercising the power of consent or refusal of treatment on behalf of incompetents and concluded that the common denominator is that the decision should be taken in the patient's best interests. It followed that if, as in Mrs Johnstone's case, treatment could be of no benefit, then there were no longer any best interests to be served by continuing it.[243] Accordingly, the Lord Ordinary was authorised to provide a declarator to the effect that removal of life-sustaining treatment from Mrs Johnstone would not be unlawful in respect of its civil law consequences.[244]

15.124 The Lord President also remarked that nothing in his opinion was intended to suggest that an application must be made in every case where it is intended to withdraw treatment:

> The decision as to whether an application is necessary must rest in each case with those who will be responsible for carrying that intention into effect, having regard in particular ... to any statements of policy which may, in the light of this case, be issued by the Lord Advocate.[245]

15.125 And it is here that we run into some difficulties following a statement by the Lord Advocate[246] to the effect that the policy of the Crown Office will be that no criminal prosecution will follow a decision to withdraw feeding but that this is subject to authority to do so having first been obtained by way of the civil law. This appears to pre-empt the direction by the Inner House. However, the Lord Advocate did not say he *would* prosecute in any case that was not so authorised and he went on to say, admittedly in an unofficial ambience:

> In Scotland, a decision to withdraw treatment in any case cannot be *guaranteed* immunity from [prosecution] unless the withdrawal has first been authorised by the Court of Session.[247] [Emphasis added.]

Thus, both the Lord President and the Lord Advocate of the time agreed that decisions could be made on medical grounds and independently of the courts—but neither gave any guidance as to when it would be either necessary or unnecessary to seek judicial approval. The latter concluded in his paper: 'it is for doctors and relatives involved in such tragic situations to decide which course of action they wish to adopt'.

15.126 We would hope, and expect, that good common sense would prevail but, meanwhile, we suggest that not many doctors will be prepared to trust to chance that they have 'got it right'. It is reasonable to expect the criminal law to set out the boundaries of impermissible conduct in advance. Vagueness in criminal law offends the widely recognised

---

[243] 1996 SLT 848 at 859; (1996) 39 BMLR 166 at 182–4, per Lord Hope.
[244] It is clear that such a complex manoeuvre will be unnecessary in the future when the Inner House will use its *parens patriae* powers but it was convenient to use it in the instant case. See *Law Hospital NHS Trust v Lord Advocate (No 2)* 1996 SLT 869; (1996) 39 BMLR 166 at 197.
[245] 1996 SLT 848 at 860; (1996) 39 BMLR 166 at 184.
[246] J Robertson, 'Policy on right to die welcomed' *The Scotsman*, 12 April 1996, p 1.
[247] Lord Mackay of Drumadoon, 'Decision on the persistent vegetative state: *Law Hospital*' (1996), paper presented at the Symposium on Medical Ethics and Legal Medicine, Royal College of Physicians and Surgeons of Glasgow, 26 April 1996.

principle of legal certainty, which requires that crimes should be clearly defined. The situation has now arisen where the doctor may be required to second-guess the criminal law—a position that is hardly defensible.

15.127 This common law position remains unchanged after the passing of the Adults with Incapacity (Scotland) Act 2000. The Act allows for the appointment of a welfare guardian to act on behalf of the incompetent patient[248] but it is determinedly not concerned with any form of 'negative treatment'; that is, treatment which results in the death of the patient. Indeed, the Scottish Executive made it very clear that withdrawal or withholding decisions are outside the remit of the legislation.[249] However, we have argued elsewhere[250] that it will be impossible to maintain a clear distinction between positive and negative treatment decisions involving incapable adults, not least because the courts will invariably become involved in settling disputes as to the best thing to do under the Act: to treat or not to treat? Thus, although the powers of a proxy decision-maker under s 50 do not include a 'right' to refuse as such,[251] his or her 'right' to a second opinion challenging a medical decision to continue intervention, and ultimately the 'right' to appeal to the court, will necessarily mean that a jurisprudence relating to negative treatment will develop around this recent legislation. There have, however, been no further cases on which to test this hypothesis.

THE US POSITION

15.128 The tragic case of Terri Schiavo was played out in the US courts and legislatures and merits mention if only as an indication of how other jurisdictions approach these sensitive issues. Previous editions of this book have included a discussion of the legal position in the USA in respect of the PVS patient, but increasingly this is not of major concern to the British reader, as this is one of numerous areas in which the UK courts are forging a particularly independent path. Mrs Schiavo's case reveals how varied the paths can be. The fundamental distinction between the US and UK jurisdictions lies in the test by which to justify termination of treatment which, we have seen, is firmly held to be that of the best interests of the patient in the UK. By contrast, the substituted judgement test—in which the surrogate makes his or her best approximation of what management schedule the patient would have wanted—is a prominent standard in the USA but this is adopted only if the subjective test, which is based on what wishes the patient actually expressed, is not available. In Terri Schiavo's case, her husband was appointed as guardian and, so, surrogate decision-maker in respect of his wife's care. Mrs Schiavo had been in PVS since 1990 and her husband sought to discontinue her feeding and hydration some ten years after her accident. An Order was made to this effect in 2003 by the Florida Circuit Court after an appeal court had rejected Mrs Schiavo's parents' objection to the withdrawal.[252] The ongoing dispute eventually embroiled both the state legislature and the Governor himself, who issued an Executive Order that the patient's feeding tube should be reinstated. That Order was subsequently declared to be unconstitutional by the Florida Supreme Court,[253] and, ultimately, the matter went to the US Senate, after four requests for appeal were denied by

---

[248] And replaced the office of tutor dative which was abolished by s 80.
[249] Scottish Executive Policy Memorandum, 8 October 1999.   [250] Laurie and Mason, n 217.
[251] See further Chapter 14.   [252] *Schindler* v *Schiavo* 851 So 2d 182 (Fla 2d DCA, 2003).
[253] *Bush* v *Schiavo*, Supreme Court of Florida, 23 September 2004, No SC04–925.

the Supreme Court.[254] In a highly unusual move, the Senate passed legislation—tailored directly to Mrs Schiavo's circumstances—giving authority to re-hear the case to the federal courts. Notwithstanding, the authority to remove her ANH was upheld[255] and Mrs Schiavo died on 31 March 2005.[256]

15.129 Such political and legislative machinations simply do not form part of the British system moreover they are doubtless motivated in large part by the wider pro-life movement that is active in the USA. To this extent, there is little that we can learn from Mrs Schiavo's case save, perhaps, that, no matter what test is to be applied in deciding what is 'best' done for the patient, every effort should be made from the earliest stages to reach consensus.

ARE WE BEING HONEST?

15.130 An alternative, and perhaps radical, approach to the whole problem of the management of PVS and other cases involving ANH is to look the truth in the eye and admit that the deliberate removal of sustenance from a patient is indistinguishable from euthanasia. While this would remove a great deal of what must be regarded as paralogical argument, it would, of course, also involve a complete change of direction in the current jurisprudence—a change on which the courts would be reluctant to embark without the support of the legislature. Nonetheless, we should not shrink from considering the proposition.[257]

15.131 The fears of the judiciary and of many ethicists are summed up by Lord Goff in *Bland*, who declined to allow active steps to bring about death in PVS patients because this would be to authorise euthanasia and, 'once euthanasia is recognised as lawful in these circumstances, it is difficult to see any logical basis for excluding it in others'.[258] We question this view, first, on the ground that, if the concept of substituted judgement is accepted, removal of sustenance from PVS patients equates, at most, to passive, voluntary euthanasia which is already practised widely under one name or another. PVS cases occupy a unique niche in the spectrum of euthanasia. All higher brain function has been permanently lost; there is no awareness and no sensation. There is no alternative of palliative care because there are no senses to palliate—as Lord Goff put it, 'there is no weighing operation to be performed'. This has now been confirmed by the Supreme Court in *Aintree*.[259] Only the vestiges of the person remain as the breathing body. Put another way, the patient is truly 'dead to the world' and, once his or her close relatives have come to terms with the situation, it is futile to maintain that respiration.

15.132 All this, however, depends upon the certainty of definition and diagnosis. Anthony Bland's and Mrs Johnstone's conditions were unequivocal and the House of Lords distinguished *Bland* from other 'quality of life' cases such as *Re J*.[260] The two cases have very different ratios. In the former, a wholly insensate patient was deemed to have no interest in continued treatment which could, therefore, be discontinued as being futile. In the

[254] 125 S Ct 1692 (2005).   [255] *Schindler v Schiavo* 404 F 3d 1282 and 403 F 3d 1289 (2005).
[256] See L Shepherd, 'In respect of people living in a permanent vegetative state—And allowing them to die' (2006) 16 Health Matrix 631.
[257] K Savell, 'A jurisprudence of ambivalence: Three legal fictions concerning death and dying' (2011) 17(1) Cultural Studies Rev 5.
[258] [1993] 1 All ER 821 at 867; (1993) 12 BMLR 64 at 113.   [259] See para 15.119 et seq, above.
[260] [1990] 3 All ER 930; (1990) 6 BMLR 25, discussed at paras 15.28 et seq.

latter, it was accepted that some benefit could be derived from treatment of a patient who was not insensate but it was held that non-treatment was to be preferred when any supposed benefit was weighed against other considerations such as pain and suffering. S,[261] Re D,[262] Re H,[263] Re G,[264] and NHS Trust v X,[265] in particular, demonstrate a shift in thinking from that adopted in *Bland* towards that involved in *Re J* and one wonders if this is not something of a move towards acceptance of active euthanasia; the cases provide the most impressive example to date of the willingness of the British courts to take 'quality of life' decisions and, in our view, represent a significant step in this area of law. Equally, the MCS cases reaffirm the fundamental importance of the sanctity of life and the role of the balance sheet approach. Equally, we have *W Healthcare NHS Trust* where the Court of Appeal placed considerable weight on the impact of the dying process on the sentient patient: only intolerability of living would justify a course of action that would hasten death. At the end of the day, all the cases discussed represent variations on what is meant by 'best interests'; the fundamental question is, then, whether the jump from 'no interests' to 'a balance of interests' is acceptable in the management of the vegetative state or other chronically incapacitated states or whether it represents a quantum leap onto the slippery slope of ending 'valueless lives'. A particularly interesting variation is to be found in *An NHS Trust v J*,[266] which we have already mentioned above. Stripped to its essentials, it seems that the judicial decision was founded largely on the ground that the treatment option proposed could do J no harm. It has been suggested that, in this case, the 'best interests' test was converted to a 'not against the interests' test.[267] But, the recent decision by the Supreme Court in *Aintree* has cemented the role of best interests quite firmly as the central consideration at both common law and under statute. Moreover, it centres our attention on the presumption in favour of life and the idea that 'benefit' is an eternally context-specific notion to be assessed only from the patient's perspective.

15.133 It has to be remembered that all the post-*Bland* cases have been scrupulously examined and all were supported not only by respected medical opinion but also by the Official Solicitor. All the patients were, by any standards, existing in appalling conditions and we have the gravest doubts as to whether the failure of a single arbitrary clinical test should be allowed to distinguish them in any significant way—and it is at least arguable that the near-vegetative state is a more horrifying condition than is PVS itself.[268] We have long submitted that the approach adopted by the courts in the seminal case of *Re J*[269] could properly be applied to the withdrawal of feeding (or other vital treatment) from severely damaged adult patients. *Re J* and its allied cases went a long way to medicalising the whole approach to termination of treatment decisions and, provided medical authority is tempered by the sensitive handling of close relatives, there seems to be no fundamental reason why it should not be applied irrespective of age—and this now seems to be the broad direction of travel of the case law. If this is indeed so, the courts might then be involved only in those cases in which there is serious dispute between or within the health caring and family groups. Public acceptance of this approach will greatly eased by

[261] *Swindon and Marlborough NHS Trust v S* [1995] 3 Med LR 84.   [262] (1997) 38 BMLR 1.
[263] (1997) 38 BMLR 1, 11.   [264] (2001) 65 BMLR 6.   [265] [2006] Lloyd's Rep Med 29.
[266] [2006] EWHC 3152 (Fam).
[267] P Lewis, 'Withdrawal of treatment from a patient in a permanent vegetative state: Judicial involvement and innovative "treatment"' (2007) 15 Med L Rev 392.
[268] R Cranford, 'Misdiagnosing the persistent vegetative state' (1996) 313 BMJ 5.
[269] *Re J (a minor) (wardship: medical treatment)* [1990] 399 All ER 930; (1992) 6 BMLR 25.

an open acceptance by the medical profession of the futility of treatment of patients. This is already the position advocated by the BMA in respect of patients with severe dementia or who have suffered catastrophic stroke.[270]

15.134 Inevitably, one is reminded of the calls in the House of Lords and the Court of Session for parliamentary intervention—and, while this has its attractions, the proposal is not of unquestionable merit. To legislate for PVS alone would be to concentrate on its particular clinical status and to segregate it from the general euthanasia debate—which is as it should be.[271] Other advantages of legislation could be that the limits of PVS were statutorily determined[272] and that a clear framework could be devised within which doctors withdrawing treatment could be seen to be acting lawfully without the need for routine approval by a court. A line could thus be drawn between unequivocal and doubtful cases and a barrier placed at the edge of any developing slippery slope. On the other hand, legislation of this type could be seen as disadvantageous in that it would be restrictive—while withdrawal of support from the *Bland*-type patient would be permissible, non-treatment options might be barred in many cases of brain damage in which only minimal cognitive function remained.[273] To many, this would represent the primary function of the legislation; to others, it might seem an unacceptable price to pay for the loss of individual judgement—as we have already suggested, generalisations are difficult to apply in a medical context. It might, therefore, be thought preferable to introduce purely enabling legislation or to amend the provisions of the Mental Capacity Act 2005 now that the Supreme Court has considered its terms in the context of futile treatment.

15.135 The argument is one of long standing and is likely to continue. Meantime, we suggest that there is one step on the path to honesty that we could take without giving offence. In their anxiety to avoid conflating the final management of PVS with euthanasia, the courts in England, Scotland, and the Republic of Ireland have been at pains to emphasise that the cause of death in PVS cases is the original injury.[274] But, while it is true to say that this was the ultimate cause of death, the proximate cause, given that the patient has survived for a minimum of a year, must be the results of starvation—otherwise, there would be no death and, hence, no cause of death. There would be no difficulty in certifying death as being due to:

    (i)   inanition due to lawful removal of life support due to

    (ii)   severe brain damage due to

    (iii) cerebral hypoxia.

This concession to transparency would, we feel, actually help to defuse the emotionalism that surrounds the ultimate management of PVS and other patients with disorders of consciousness. A further purely practical advantage would be that the mortality statistics would be maintained correctly—and it would be possible to discover how often such decisions are made.

---

[270] BMA, *Withdrawing and Withholding Treatment*, n 89.

[271] J K Mason and D Mulligan, 'Euthanasia by stages' (1996) 347 Lancet 810.

[272] Perhaps based on the guidelines of the Royal College of Physicians, n 169.

[273] See paras 15.88 et seq.

[274] F Miller, R Truog, and D Brock, 'Moral fictions and medical ethics' (201) 24(9) Bioethics 453 argue that the distinction between euthanasia and withdrawal of treatment is based upon legal fictions motivated by moral reasons to uphold the view that physicians do not/should not bring about their patient's death.

'DO NOT RESUSCITATE' ORDERS

15.136 The last aspect of medical futility that falls to be discussed is the so-called 'do not resuscitate' (DNR) order.[275] There can be no doubt that it is often undesirable, effectively, to prolong the process of dying—irrespective of the competence of the patient at the time. Nevertheless, in extending the concept of non-treatment to the incapacitated rather than the incompetent, it is possible that our attitudes are being moulded overly in favour of death, rather than treatment, as a management option.[276] Moreover, we have to ask ourselves whether the DNR option is a valid example of an exercise of the principle of futility—there is a physical and moral divide between the PVS patient and the patient who is reaching the end of life in a natural fashion, albeit often in a state of diminished competence. Where one places the DNR order is a matter of ethical importance[277] and it has now been confirmed as a matter of human rights that there is a presumption in favour of patient involvement about DNR notices on medical files.[278] After much consideration, however, we doubt if it is correctly sited under 'futility' and will discuss the matter under the heading of euthanasia.[279]

CONCLUSION

15.137 This chapter has chartered the changing role of the concept of futility from absolute medical benchmark through to its deployment in a range of tragic and complex legal cases. We have identified not only the importance of challenging any assumptions about what references to futility might mean, but also witnessed the myriad ways in which the concept has found appeal. As to the law, we have seen parallel developments in the jurisprudence, involving an increasingly strong message that the deployment of best interests must be on a case-by-case basis, while at the same time we have observed the courts bringing diverse groups of cases into line under this rubric. A common message for medics, ethicists, and lawyers alike is that the loose use of 'futility' is no longer defensible. Law, ethics, and medical practice are increasingly in alignment on the need for robust and careful reflection on what futility actually means in any given context and for each particular patient.

---

[275] C Santonocito et al., 'Do-not-resuscitate order: a view throughout the world' (2012) Sep 13 J Crit Care. doi: 10.1016/j.jcrc.2012.07.005. [Epub ahead of print.]

[276] E Gedge, M Giacomini, and D Cook, 'Withholding and withdrawing life support in critical care settings: Ethical issues concerning consent' (2007) 33 J Med Ethics 215.

[277] See E P Cherniack, 'Increasing use of DNR orders in the elderly worldwide: Whose choice is it?' (2002) 28 J Med Ethics 303 and P Biegler, 'Should patient consent be required to write a do not resuscitate order?' (2003) 29 J Med Ethics 359.

[278] *R (on the application of Tracey) v Cambridge University Hospitals NHS Foundation Trust* [2014] 3 WLR 1054; [2015] 1 All ER 450; [2014] Med LR 273; (2014) 138 BMLR 1.

[279] See Chapter 18.

16

THE DIAGNOSIS OF DEATH

16.01 Death is defined in the *Oxford English Dictionary* as 'the end of life; the permanent cessation of the vital functions of a person'. *Steadman's Medical Dictionary* adds to this 'in multicellular organisms, death is a gradual process at the cellular level with tissues varying in their ability to withstand deprivation of oxygen'. That being the case, we are presented with an immediate definitional dilemma: in speaking of 'death', are we referring to cellular or to somatic death—that is, death of the individual components of the body or death of the persona? The former is a matter of biology; the latter borders on the metaphysical—and the distinction is fundamental to our concepts of death.[1]

CONCEPTS OF DEATH

16.02 There is, therefore, a potential conflict between layman and doctor. To the former, a person is either alive or dead, and this is generally based on the appearances in a fait accompli. The doctor, by contrast, is involved in death as a process and his or her dilemma lies in the search for a definable end-point. The diagnostic criteria for both somatic and cellular death are satisfied by the *ultimate* conclusion that death is 'a permanent state of tissue anoxia'. Clearly, however, this is unsatisfactory in a practical situation. First, it begs the question of what is permanent and, logically, this is one that can only be answered in retrospect—any other approach is by way of surmise. Second, and following on from this, the degree of certainty within that surmise is time-dependent—the longer the delay, the more sure one can be that re-oxygenation is impossible. None of which helps the grieving relative and, in addition, there are many times when, for both medical and social reasons, we *need* to know the earliest point at which we can say that life is extinct. As a result, and as we will see, the majority of modern discussion of death is concerned with whether, and to what extent, we can pre-empt the ultimate truism and declare the *person* to be dead.

16.03 Once more, we must revert to fundamentals and note that tissue anoxia arises in two ways—either respiration ceases, in which case there is a failure to harvest oxygen, or the heart fails, when oxygen is no longer distributed to the tissues—and this is true no matter what the *mode* of death. The vast majority of deaths are, however, natural and anticipated. In these circumstances, it is astonishing how often the moment of 'death of the person' is perfectly clear. It is generally possible to tell immediately when a loved one or a carefully observed patient 'dies'.[2] In everyday terms, the patient has 'breathed his or her last' and

---

[1] For a fuller discussion, see J K Mason, 'Death' In A Grubb, J Laing, and J McHale (eds), *Principles of Medical Law* (3rd edn, 2010) ch 20.

[2] The words 'carefully observed' deserve emphasis. The distinction between death and 'suspended animation' may be difficult to make *post facto* in some circumstances—e.g. in cases of drug overdose or hypothermia.

the heart stops beating; this is 'somatic' death.[3] But, as we have noted, the individual cells of the body are not dead; depending on their specialised needs or characteristics, they will continue to function until their residual oxygen is exhausted. Thus, the assumption that a person whose cardiorespiratory system has failed is dead is open to question, and this conundrum lies at the heart of the current *philosophical* conflict as to the meaning of 'dead'—the counter-argument to the simple 'stopped breathing' definition being that you cannot say that a body is dead when many of the bodily functions which contribute to the 'integrative function' of the body are still operating.[4]

16.04 With one exception, we find this aspect of the argument comparatively unimportant in a practical sense—the great majority of the functions cited in evidence are, at base, chemical reactions which, given a supply of oxygen and additional biochemical support, could continue independently and, at least theoretically, indefinitely.[5] The exception is, however, of major importance and rests on the disquieting realisation that even *brain cells*, together with cognitive ability, will withstand anoxia for a time, albeit for only a few minutes—from which it follows that we should treat the patient who has sustained irreversible cardiorespiratory failure as dying rather than dead, for the true agonal period in classical natural death is that which lies between cardiac and cerebral failure. We do not know how long this period lasts—indeed, it must vary with the individual— but it may be the most profound period of a person's existence and, thereby, deserving the greatest respect. It is, therefore, surprising to find that, at least in the USA, there is no standard imposed delay between cessation of cardiorespiratory function and the declaration of death—the Institute of Medicine suggests five minutes[6] but it seems it can be anything from ten minutes[7] to being discounted altogether.[8] It is at least possible that such discrepancies are founded on misconceptions. Those who support the shorter times do so on the assumption that death may be defined as the irreversible failure of the cardiorespiratory system only when the heart beat has stopped for such a period as precludes the possibility of cardiac autoresuscitation—and this could well be five minutes.[9] But the fact that the heart is irreversibly dead does not mean that the persona, as represented by cerebral function, is also dead; a longer period is needed before

---

[3] Even so, some jurisdictions demand visible evidence of pooling, or non-circulation, of the blood—so-called hypostasis—before death is finally certified. For possible sets of criteria, see D Gardiner, S Shemmie, et al., 'International perspective on diagnosis of death' (2012) 108 Brit J Anaesth i14.

[4] A useful analysis of the philosophical argument is to be found in W Chiong, 'Brain death without definitions' (2005) 35 Hastings Center Rep 30. Ultimately, the author concluded that 'death eludes definition'. The reader will have to decide whether this is a disappointing conclusion or an inevitable acceptance of the facts. For further discussion, see para 16.20.

[5] D A Shewmon, 'Chronic "brain death": Meta-analysis and conceptual consequences' (1998) 51 *Neurology* 1538. The additional biochemical support is an important qualification—we will see later that maintaining a functional body on a ventilator is a skilled art.

[6] As reported in an extremely critical article by J Menikoff, 'Doubts about death: The silence of the Institute of Medicine' (1998) 26 J Law Med Ethics 157. The author implies that the better limit would be 15 minutes. Members of the Institute of Medicine's Committee on Non-Heart-Beating Organ Transplantation refute his criticisms in a follow-up article at p 166.

[7] Derived from the Maastricht Workshop: G Koostra, 'The asystolic or non-heart-beating donor' (1997) 63 Transplantation 917.

[8] J M DuBois, 'Non-heart-beating organ donation: A defense of the required determination of death' (1999) 27 J Law Med Ethics 126. Or a matter of seconds: M M Brouek, C Mashburn, et al., 'Pediatric heart transplantation after declaration of cardiocirculatory death' (2008) 359 New Engl J Med 709.

[9] Note that this ideal is unattainable in the case of heart transplants: R M Veatch, 'Transplanting hearts after death measured by cardiac criteria: The challenge to the dead donor rule' (2010) 35 J Med Philos 313.

hypoxic death of the brain cells—and, with it, a total loss of mind—can be assumed.[10] In our view, the process of 'dying' should not be regarded as complete until some 15 minutes have elapsed since cessation of cardiac and pulmonary function—and, in parentheses, we believe that this should be a matter of hospital routine independent of the transplant programme.[11] Quite apart from the profound significance this should have on our management of 'death', it is of major significance in transplantation therapy[12] and we return to the concept in Chapter 17.

16.05 But what of our original concern as to the permanence of tissue anoxia? What if the person's 'death' is unheralded and unexpected? It is common knowledge that an apparently permanent cessation of the respiration or blood flow can, in many instances, be challenged by physical or mechanical intervention. Thus, sudden heart failure may, in suitable cases, be reversed by electrical stimulation (cardioversion) or by cardiac massage coupled, perhaps, with artificial respiration or ventilation. But, while the patient has been 'saved from the dead', the process of cellular death has been initiated by the temporary failure of oxygen distribution and, again, this has both biological and philosophical connotations. As to the former, the majority of organs will recover from such an insult but the cells of the brain are outstandingly the most sensitive in the body to oxygen deprivation and, moreover, they are irreplaceable. Thus, a situation may arise whereby the body as a whole is brought back to life but where it is now controlled by a brain which is damaged to an uncertain, yet permanent, degree. The decision to restore an interrupted cardiac function is not, therefore, a simple choice between the good (life) and the bad (death). It imposes the serious and urgent problems independent of the *diagnosis* of death which we have already discussed in Chapter 15 and which, in that context, confirm our view, already expressed, that cardiorespiratory failure should have been apparent for at least 15 minutes before being regarded as permanent.[13]

16.06 But of perhaps greater importance in the present context, it draws attention, once again, to the place of the brain in both our interpretation of and the diagnosis of death—and does so in introducing the particularly contentious concept of 'higher brain' or 'cognitive brain' death. This proposition invites the equiparation of permanent loss of personality with no longer being alive[14] and that, as a consequence, the decorticated patient should be regarded as dead.[15] Put another way, the suggestion is that the 'dead' can be seen as two entities—those who are dead in the traditional sense and those who can *be treated* as being dead.[16] Such an attitude may be tenable in a general discussion on euthanasia

---

[10] See generally J Borgigin et al., 'Surge of neurophysiological coherence and connectivity in the dying brain' (2013) 110 PNAS 14432.

[11] We are certainly not alone in our concern, although the reasoning may differ. See S K Shah, R D Truog, and F G Miller, 'Death and legal fictions' (2011) 37 J Med Ethics 719.

[12] And particularly on the practice of so-called 'non-heart beating' donation (DCD).

[13] While, at the same time, justifying the abandonment of attempts at cardioversion. The definitive report on the subject: Academy of Royal Medical Colleges, *A Code of Practice for the Diagnosis and Confirmation of Death* (2008) indicates that a period of five minutes following cardiorespiratory arrest and the absence of pupillary reflexes will be sufficient to determine permanent failure. This does not, however, necessarily imply total absence of cerebral function.

[14] An extensive review of the various theorists is: R M Veatch, 'The death of whole-brain death: The plague of the disaggregators, somaticists and mentalists' (2005) 30 J Med Philos 353.

[15] For an early exposition, see D R Smith, 'Legal recognition of neocortical death' (1986) 71 Cornell L Rev 850. For continuation, see R M Veatch, 'The impending collapse of the whole-brain definition of death' (1993) Hastings Center Reports 23, no 4, 18. And M Angell, 'After *Quinlan*: The dilemma of the persistent vegetative state' (1994) 330 New Engl J Med 1524.

[16] See R M Veatch, 'The dead donor rule: True by definition' (2003) 3 Amer J Bioethics 10.

but, when related to the definition of death, it can only confuse the issue and enhance the already strong public apprehension of premature disposal of the body.[17] What, one wonders, would be the public's answer to the question, 'Should a non-cognitive, decorticated person with continuing cardiopulmonary function be buried?'[18] Death, in our view, must remain an absolute; there is no place in medical jurisprudence for conditional phrases such as 'at death's door' or 'as good as dead'. The definition of death has not—or should not have—changed;[19] and, if we are to alter our diagnostic *methods*, the diagnosis must be as sure as it was when we were using the heart and lungs as its sole parameters. For our part, we would settle the question on the basis that 'cognitive death' does not satisfy the criteria for tissue anoxia and is not, therefore 'death'.[20] It does not follow, however, that the decorticated patient should, or will, continue to be treated in the same way as any other patient for, as we have seen in Chapter 15, a diagnosis of permanent vegetative state (PVS) may be a trigger for a process of management that will lead, ultimately, to the patient's death. Our point here, however, is that 'cognitive death' and 'absolute death' should never be treated as one and the same.

16.07   The introduction of cognitive death, however, leads to a consideration of where lies the 'life force' or, perhaps, the human *anima*? Does it exist in the heart or in the brain? This promotes further consideration of the role, not only of the heart and lungs, but also of the brain, in the diagnosis of death and it is to that which we now turn.

THE TRIADIC APPROACH TO DEATH

16.08   The mechanisms underlying acute heart failure and respiratory failure need to be distinguished. Given an adequate oxygen supply, the heart will continue to beat independently of higher control—it did, for instance, often beat for some 20 minutes following the broken neck of judicial hanging; the cause of acute, natural cardiac failure, therefore, lies within the heart itself whether this be anatomically or biochemically mediated. Respiration, on the other hand, is controlled by the respiratory centre—a nervous 'battery' situated in the brain stem—and, in practice, acute respiratory failure of the type which is important in the present context is almost invariably the result of central damage, that is, damage to the brain stem.[21] Oxygenation of the tissues, or cellular life, is, thus, based on a servo-type mechanism: the heart depends for its own tissue oxygen on the lungs which, in turn, are useless without the distributive function of the heart. Together they supply oxygen to the brain which, therefore, cannot function in the absence of competent heart and lungs—yet the lungs, themselves, depend upon a functioning brain stem. We will see that the only segment of this triad which cannot be substituted is the brain. There are, therefore, strong logical arguments for defining death in terms of death of the brain rather than in the generally accepted terms of cardiorespiratory failure; indeed, Pallis taught that all death is,

[17]   R J Devettere, 'Neocortical death and human death' (1990) 18 Law Med Hlth Care 96. This paper summarises the views of others in the field. More recently, J Fisher, 'Re-examining death: Against a higher brain criterion' (1999) 25 J Med Ethics 473.

[18]   D J Powner, B M Ackerman, and A Grenvik, 'Medical diagnosis of death in adults: Historical contributions to current controversies' (1996) 348 Lancet 1219.

[19]   As Veatch, n 14, would have us do.

[20]   For discussion of the ontological status of the PVS patient, see S Holland, C Kitzinger, and J Kitzinger, 'Death, treatment decisions and the permanent vegetative state: evidence from families and experts' (2014) 17 Med Health Care Philos 413.

[21]   Now that acute anterior poliomyelitis ('infantile paralysis') has been virtually eradicated, there are very few extra-cerebral causes of acute respiratory failure that cannot be corrected by the ventilator.

and always has been, brain stem death and that circulatory arrest just happens to be the commonest way to bring such death about.[22]

16.09 We prefer, however, to visualise the brain, the heart, and the lungs as forming a 'cycle of life' which can be broken at any point, looked at in this way, there is no need to speak of two *types* of death—that is, cardiorespiratory death or brain death; it is simply that different criteria, and different tests, can be used for identifying that the cycle has been broken.[23] And it cannot be over-emphasised that this is a *basic* premise having no necessary association with the justification of beating heart organ donation. Be that as it may, it is, nonetheless, also clear that we *must* turn to the brain when the natural functional condition of the lungs—or, occasionally, of the heart—is obscured by the intervention of a machine. Before doing so, however, we must divert into a semantic problem that we see as fundamental to the issue.

'Brain Death' and 'Death of the Brain'

16.10 This lies in the distinction between brain death per se and death of the brain as a diagnostic tool[24] and we cannot overstress the importance we attach to distinguishing between the two. The latter is a purely factual, pathological concept which can be vouched for by scientific tests or, ultimately, by anatomical inspection—it requires no philosophical sustenance. The former is a matter of interpretation—if the brain is dead, is the person dead? Clearly, this semantic distinction lies at the heart of the current surge in distrust of the acceptance of death of the individual on the basis of the death of his or her brain, a distrust which, in turn, derives from ambivalence as to the source of 'life'—does it lie, practically, in the heart as the provider of oxygen or metaphysically in the brain as the provider of personhood?

16.11 Thus, we believe that the term 'brain death' as applied to the person is a misconception which serves only to confuse the issue. It implies that there is a distinction to be made between 'brain death' and 'cardiac death' of the individual whereas the common and overriding feature of both is 'death'.[25] The true distinction can be sought either in the diagnostic methodology or, given the fact that a choice of diagnostic approaches must be made—as when the individual is undergoing intensive care—whether one believes that the source of life has been extinguished. For all these reasons, we believe that the term 'brain death' should be abandoned unless it is qualified as to its meaning.[26] Even so, the term is now too widely accepted to be abandoned and we will continue to employ it in the way that is generally understood.

16.12 The principle behind using cerebral competence as a measure of death was unintentionally confused semantically by the foundation Harvard group, who introduced the descriptive term 'irreversible coma'.[27] One's first reaction would be to equate such a condition

---

[22] C Pallis, 'Return to Elsinore' (1990) 16 J Med Ethics 10. And D Gardiner, S Shemmie, et al., 'International perspective on diagnosis of death' (2012) 108 Br J Anaesthesia i14.

[23] This was much the view taken by the original US President's Commission for the Study of Ethical Problems in Medicine, *Defining Death: Medical, Legal and Ethical Issues in the Definition of Death* (1981) and was confirmed by the President's Council on Bioethics, *Controversies in the Determination of Death* (2008).

[24] For an in-depth analysis, see W Chiong, 'Brain death without definitions' (2005) 35(6) Hastings Center Rep 20.

[25] S Laureys, 'Death, unconsciousness and the brain' (2005) 6 Nat Rev Neurosci 899.

[26] The US Council on Bioethics suggested the use of 'total brain failure' for this reason.

[27] H K Beecher (chairman), 'A definition of irreversible coma: Report of the ad hoc Committee of the Harvard Medical School to examine the definition of brain death' (1968) 205 JAMA 337.

with PVS—or decorticated—patient which we have discussed previously, or with an even lesser degree of cerebral failure.[28] It is, however, clear that the committee was describing what other Americans and, later, the British Royal Colleges dubbed 'brain death'[29] and even this term is capable of misinterpretation—in particular, it can be taken as including 'partial brain death'. A remediable alternative is to speak in terms of 'brain stem death'—a term which derives from an assumption that integrated life is impossible in the absence of a functioning brain stem.[30]

16.13   To do so, however, introduces the need to harmonise such differences as there may be between 'brain stem death' and 'whole-brain death'[31]—in essence, we must justify our belief that the terms are, in fact, synonymous. The only unnatural ways in which death or destruction of the brain stem can reasonably be expected in the presence of a normal cerebrum are accidents involving the cervical spine and spinal cord, judicial hanging, or beheading—only the first of which is germane to the present discussion. Natural diseases in the form of destructive primary lesions of the brain stem—generally in the form of haemorrhage, thrombosis, or embolism—which do not simultaneously affect the rest of the brain are rare and are either partial in type or, more commonly, rapidly fatal; in the event of survival, the resulting 'locked in' syndrome, characterised by quadriplegia and inability to speak but with preservation of consciousness and some eye movements, is a terrifying example but its existence is well appreciated by neurologists.[32]

16.14   Fatal damage to the whole brain commonly occurs in two main ways. The brain may be damaged by direct violence which, in turn, may result in either haemorrhage[33] or brain swelling—so-called diffuse axonal injury. The consequence is that the expanding brain is trapped within a rigid skull; the brain stem may then be compressed within the membranes which separate the brain from the spinal cord—and this may well be the major cause of death following head injury. The important practical point is that brain damage following direct violence may be selective rather than generalised and it is for this reason that establishing the permanence of brain damage may be more difficult when associated with violence than in the second main reason for destruction of cerebral tissue—that is, diffuse cerebral hypoxia.[34]

16.15   Whole body hypoxia is the second—and, arguably, the more important—cause of brain death. In this way, it represents the ultimate degree of cerebral hypoxic damage, the causes and degrees of which have been discussed in Chapter 15. Given that the brain is the organ in the body that is the most sensitive to oxygen lack and given that the brain stem is that part of the brain that is most resistant to hypoxia, it is difficult in the extreme

---

[28]   The authoritative report in the United Kingdom (UK) emphasises the distinction to be made between coma and PVS: Report of a Working Party of the Royal College of Physicians, *The Vegetative State* (2003). Coma classically presents as eyes-closed unconsciousness and sleep-wake cycles are absent.

[29]   Conference of Medical Royal Colleges and their Faculties in the UK, 'Diagnosis of Brain Death' [1976] 2 BMJ 1187.

[30]   The terminology was originally introduced by A Mohandas and S N Chou, 'Brain death: A clinical and pathological study' (1971) 35 J Neurosurg 211.

[31]   C Pallis, *ABC of Brain Stem Death* (1983).

[32]   For a thorough review: E Smith and M Delargy, 'Locked-in syndrome' (2005) 330 BMJ 406. *Vadera* v *Shaw* (1999) 45 BMLR 162 provides a tragic example.

[33]   Intra-cranial haemorrhage may, of course, arise naturally and one form—spontaneous sub-arachnoid haemorrhage—occurs in young, otherwise fit persons. *An NHS Trust* v *J* (2007) 94 BMLR 15 is a good example of a case which came to court. Such cases, therefore, are important non-accidental deaths which fulfil all the criteria for organ donation (see Chapter 17).

[34]   Royal College of Physicians, n 28, para 2.8.

to conceive of a generalised, fundamentally hypoxic condition destroying the brain stem while sparing the highly specialised tissue of the cerebral cortex. We believe, in common with authoritative medical and legal[35] UK opinion, that the terms most used to define the irreversible cessation of all brain function, 'brain stem death' and 'whole-brain death', can properly be regarded as synonymous in both practice and theory—in effect, the former is a convenient marker of the latter. But, since the tests devised for the diagnosis of brain death—including those in use in countries where the law speaks in terms of 'death of the whole brain'[36]—are, essentially, tests of brain stem function, the former term is to be preferred and is now in general use in the UK. Indeed, the Academy of Royal Medical Colleges states quite baldly:

> cessation of the integrative function of the brain-stem equates with the death of the individual and allows the medical practitioner to diagnose death.[37]

16.16   We do, however, accept that many misconceptions are founded on misunderstanding of the British standards for the diagnosis of brain stem death. These include three equally important phases. First, there is the exclusion of coma being due to reversible causes including drug overdose, hypothermia, and metabolic disorders while, at the same time, making a *positive* diagnosis of the disorder which has caused the brain damage and ensuring not only that it was *capable* of causing brain stem death but also that it is irremediable. Second, there is the carrying out of a number of tests specifically designed to demonstrate destruction of the several components of the brain stem—thus confirming death of the respiratory centre. Third, there is a carefully controlled system whereby a patient's inability to breathe spontaneously is proved—including tests specifically designed to demonstrate the effects of carbon dioxide tension in the blood-stream. These tests *must* be repeated although the recommendations as to the time interval are, of necessity, somewhat open.

16.17   These criteria have been criticised on the grounds that the patient is 'being asked to prove he is alive' rather than that the physician is proving death. Positive tests, such as an electroencephalogram (EEG) or an angiogram—by which cessation of the blood flow in the brain can be visualised[38]—are, therefore, often sought and one or other is, indeed, mandatory in some countries of the European Union.[39] It is hard to believe that an EEG, which measures the surface electrical activity of the cerebral cortex, would be positive in the presence of properly performed confirmatory tests for brain stem death but there is no reason why such a test should not be added if it would serve to allay any fears among the next of kin as to the certainty of death.

16.18   There is little doubt that any residual public misgiving would be lessened if the purposes of defining brain stem death were more fully understood. Certainly, it is a valuable tool

---

[35] *Re A* (1992) 3 Med L R 303, discussed at para 16.23. For Northern Ireland, see *Re T C (a minor)* 1994 2 Med L Rev 376. There seem to be no comparable decisions in Scotland although, should the question be raised, there is no doubt that *Re A* would be followed.

[36] E.g. the USA and Australia (see para 16.33). Which is not to deny that the term does nothing to satisfy those who cannot accept that a person whose cardiorespiratory system is maintained by mechanical means is dead—and, certainly, there are still many who cannot: M Potts and D W Evans, 'Does it matter that organ donors are not dead? Ethical and policy implications' (2005) 31 J Med Ethics 406; S K Shah, 'Piercing the veil: The limits of brain death as a legal fiction' (2015) 48 U Mich J L Reform 301.

[37] N 13 at 2.1.

[38] It may be useful when coma from other causes is a possibility: A I Qureshi et al., 'Computed tomographic angiography for diagnosis of brain death' (2004) 62 Neurology 652.

[39] G Citerio et al., 'Variability in brain death determination in Europe: Looking for a solution' (2014) 21 Neurocrit Care 376.

in the provision of high-quality organs for transplantation (see Chapter 17) but this is only part of the story.[40] The major purpose of the procedure was originally to establish a consensus by which patients who can no longer benefit from ventilator support can be removed from intensive care. This option is essential if the patient is to die with dignity, if the relatives are to be spared wholly unnecessary suffering, and if resources, both mechanical and human, are to be properly apportioned. It follows that there is a need for the concept of brain stem death irrespective of the transplant programme and this would persist even in the event that the requirement for human organs was dissipated; for example, by advances in regenerative medicine.[41] Meantime, it is essential that the diagnosis of death does not become confused with the application of an 'organ procurement model'. Accepting brain stem death is not a way of 'hurrying death along'; rather, the ventilator allows the pace of investigation, assessment, and prognosis to be slackened; when it comes to the point, the diagnosis of brain stem death is, in the great majority of cases, only confirming what is clear from clinical observation—that the patient is dead.

16.19   Nonetheless, there are still those who will not accept irreversible failure of the brain as a stand-alone indicator of death of the individual. The attack is, essentially, along two lines. First there are those who believe that the word 'dead' should be reserved for those whose heart has stopped beating, the underlying philosophy being, in effect, that loss of brain function should be regarded as the onset and loss of cardiac function as the termination of the process of death.[42] Clearly, such a formula can apply only when the patient is maintained on a ventilator and, even within that limited parameter, it positively excludes cardiac transplantation as an ethically acceptable procedure. More worryingly, it lends support to suspicions that different concepts of death are being used by the profession and the public and that special criteria apply in association with transplantation.[43] Understanding, or its lack, lies at the root of the problem. Yet, by simply calling for, rather, better 'education' of the public, we not only ignore the intense moral and philosophical issues involved but we also minimise the importance of religious and cultural traditions.[44] Transplant operations involving brain-dead donors have been legalised only since 1997 in Japan and a major reason for this must lie in the unique attitudes to death and to the unity of the family that are widely held in that country.[45] The Western critic should be

---

[40]   For a historical analysis, see C Machado, J Korein, Y Ferrer, et al., 'The concept of brain death did not evolve to benefit organ transplants' (2007) 33 J Med Ethics 197.

[41]   Thus, we would disagree with R D Truog, 'Brain death—too flawed to endure, too ingrained to abandon' (2007) 35 J Law Med Ethics 273.

[42]   Such a view was originally put forward by the influential Danish Council for Medical Ethics. See B A Rix, 'Danish Ethics Council rejects brain death as the criterion of death' (1990) 16 J Med Ethics 5.

[43]   I H Kerridge, P Saul, M Lowe, et al., 'Death, dying and donation: Organ transplantation and the diagnosis of death' (2002) 28 J Med Ethics 89. See also R D Truog and W M Robinson, 'Role of brain death and the dead-donor rule in the ethics of organ transplantation' (2003) 31 Crit Care Med 2391. These authors maintain that those who are brain dead are not 'dead' in the accepted meaning of the term. Nevertheless, they believe that they, and others in the 'near death' situation, should be legally available as organ donors—a proposal that only compounds the confusion and which has been criticised: Potts and Evans, n 36.

[44]   See a debate led by D Inwald, I Jakobovits, and A Petros, 'Brain stem death: Managing care when accepted medical guidelines and religious beliefs are in conflict' (2000) 320 BMJ 1266.

[45]   Current Japanese law is that the individual can choose the definition of death that is to be applied in his or her particular case—though even that is dependent on family agreement: A Bagheri, 'Individual choice in the definition of death' (2007) 33 J Med Ethics 146. The author suggested that the Japanese model could be adopted globally. For discussion of a similar approach under certain US state laws, see: J M Luce, 'The uncommon case of Jahi McMath' (2015) 147 Chest 1144.

wary before suggesting that centuries of cultural tradition should be swept aside in the name of modern medical technology.[46]

16.20 The second, and more recent, critical format is far more subtle and rests on the philosophical argument as to the integrative function of an organism as a whole and, following on from this, questions the role of the brain as a controller of the person's integrative unity. Acceptance of this central position of the brain, it is said, is integral to accepting the concept of brain death and underlies the opinions of both the President's Council in the USA[47] and the authoritative Academy of Royal Medical Colleges in the UK.[48] Increasingly, however, this view is being regarded as flawed[49] largely on the grounds that life is a holistic phenomenon and that many bodily functions continue in the face of total brain failure; the brain is not the 'central integrator' of the organism and some other measure of death must be found.[50] This critique seems to us to be applicable to both cerebral and cardiac diagnoses of death and very nearly demanding total cellular death before the body is declared dead—a requirement that, if applied, would lose contact with reality. We believe that the case for death of the brain as a measure of somatic death is made out—at least within the confines of the intensive care unit.[51]

16.21 Many of the arguments put forward against the acceptance of 'brain death' are intensely philosophical and can be criticised on the grounds that they pay insufficient attention to the cultural changes imposed by modern medical science. Perhaps we *are* 'fiddling with definitions' and should, rather, concentrate on what it is or is not ethical to do with a dying or a dead body. Some time ago, Gillett[52] proposed the convention that we do not and cannot require to prolong a life that will never again be engaged with the world; that we require a decent end to that life; and that we require that human remains should be treated with respect—why, otherwise, are we faced with the persistent 6 per cent of close kin who will veto the wishes of their deceased relatives in respect of organ donation? As part of the policy to assuage their concerns, current advice is that the diagnosis of brain stem death should be made by two doctors with specialist expertise, one of whom, at least, should be a consultant; neither may be associated with a relevant transplant team. Interestingly, the 'two doctor' protocol is satisfied if one observes the other and the positions may be reversed for the mandatory second examination.[53] Even so, while the vast majority of practitioners would abide by authoritative guidelines, there is no definitive UK law on the point. The World Health Organization (WHO) has attempted to produce harmonised standards for the determination of brain death, but has encountered considerable barriers to achieving international consensus.[54]

---

[46] The Muslim Law Council also accepts brain stem death as a proper definition of death: V Choo, 'UK Shariah Council approves organ transplants' (1995) 346 Lancet 303. But see the literature review by A C Miller, A Ziad-Miller, and E M Elamin, 'Brain death and Islam: The interface of religion, culture, history, law, and modern medicine' (2014) 146 Chest 1092.

[47] N 23.   [48] Academy of Royal Medical Colleges, n 13

[49] See, for example A Joffe, 'Are the recent defences of the brain death concept adequate?' (2010) 24 Bioethics 47; S K Shah and F Miller, 'Can we handle the truth? Legal fictions in the determination of brain death' (2010) 36 Amer J Law Med 540.

[50] D A Shewmon, 'Brain death: Can it be resuscitated?' (2009) Hastings Center Reports 18; A Thomas, 'Continuing the definition of death debate' (2012) 26 Bioethics 101.

[51] For full discussion, see F Miller, R Truog, and D Brock, 'The dead donor rule: Can it withstand critical scrutiny?' (2010) 35 J Med Philos 299.

[52] G Gillett, 'Fiddling and clarity' (1987) 13 J Med Ethics 23.

[53] N 13 at 6.3. The majority of European countries demand that the diagnosis be made either by two doctors or by a specialist practitioner.

[54] J L Bernat, 'Is international consensus on brain death achievable?' (2015) Neurology doi: http://dx.doi.org/10.1212/WNL.0000000000001552.

THE MEDICO-LEGAL EFFECTS OF APPLYING
BRAIN STEM DEATH CRITERIA

THE CRIMINAL LAW

16.22 The application of brain stem death criteria has obvious implications as to causation in cases of unlawful killing—who has killed the victim if he or she is removed from intensive care? Any difficulties disperse once it is conceded that brain stem death means death of the person.[55] It is then clear that the effect of treatment has been no more than to delay the inevitable result of the initial insult to the brain and there is no break in the chain of causation. This was first accepted in the UK many years ago in two leading cases to which we return in Chapter 18. Thus, in Scotland, it was held:

> Once the initial reckless act causing injury has been committed, the natural consequence which the perpetrator must accept is that the victim's future depended on a number of circumstances, including whether any particular treatment was available and, if it was available, whether it was medically reasonable and justifiable to attempt it and to continue it.[56]

The later English decision was fully confirmatory:

> Where a medical practitioner, using generally acceptable methods, came to the conclusion that the patient was for all practical purposes dead and that such vital functions as remained were being maintained solely by mechanical means, and accordingly discontinued treatment, that did not break the chain of causation between the initial injury and the death.[57]

These very early decisions are tending to confuse 'brain death' with 'irrecoverable hypoxic brain damage'. However, both were really examples of the latter, and it is clear that the law would never regard a doctor who removed a brain stem dead patient from the ventilator in good faith as being, thereby, responsible for his death.

THE CIVIL LAW

16.23 Although it is doubtful if it is needed for clarification, there is more recent case law which confirms the medical view that persons whose brain stems are dead are, themselves, dead. In the unusual case of *Re A*[58]—in which the parents of a child sought to have him retained on a ventilator for medico-legal reasons—the judge made a declaration that A, who had been certified as brain stem dead, was dead for all legal as well as all medical purposes and that a doctor who disconnected the apparatus was not acting unlawfully; the fact of death was emphasised when the judge held that he had no inherent jurisdiction over a dead child who could not be made a ward of court for the same reason. It is important to remember the limits of *Re A*; Johnson J did *not*, as is often suggested hold that the legal definition of death in England and Wales was couched in brain stem death terms. What he *did* do was to confirm that, in the appropriate circumstances, a person could be declared dead purely on the ground that the brain stem was dead. A major significant result of *Re A* is that it disposes of the brain stem/whole-brain argument in the UK.

---

[55] See the original statement by the Conference of Royal Medical Colleges and their Faculties in the United Kingdom, 'Diagnosis of Death' [1979] 1 BMJ 332.

[56] *Finlayson* v *HM Advocate* 1978 SLT 60 at 61, per Lord Emslie LJ-G.

[57] *R* v *Malcherek; R* v *Steel* [1981] 2 All ER 422 at 428–9, CA, per Lord Lane LCJ.

[58] N 35. See also *Re TC*, n 35.

16.24 The major legal problem still outstanding relates to the precise time that death occurs in such circumstances; there are several issues which depend upon that determination, and it is surprising that none appears to have been brought to the courts.

16.25 Lawyers are inclined to dismiss the problem of when death occurs on the assumption that the time of death can be equated to the time the diagnosis is made or to the time the ventilator support is removed. But a moment's reflection makes it clear that the diagnosis of death by way of the brainstem, and the consequent ending of treatment, must be retrospective—death has already occurred and the precise time at which it occurred is unknown and unknowable. Moreover, the choice of the time at which the necessary tests are undertaken is as likely to be based on convenience as on anything else. It is difficult to see how the doctor can conscientiously certify the 'date and time of death'—which is not the same as the 'date and time of death certification'—but it is easy to think of occasions on which he might be called upon to do so urgently.

16.26 One very real difficulty lay in the 'year and a day' rule, under which death could not be attributed to murder, manslaughter, infanticide, or suicide if it occurred more than a year and a day after the precipitating cause. This rule was repealed by the Law Reform (Year and a Day Rule) Act 1996—a statute which was introduced for the specific reason that ventilator support can often be continued indefinitely; as a result, the time when 'death on the ventilator' occurs is largely in the hands of the intensive care team.

16.27 The most intractable resulting issue seems to be that related to succession and the possibility of disputed survival. What is to be said as to the deaths of a husband and wife who are injured in the same accident, who are both ventilated, and who are both declared brainstem dead? One thing is certain—survivorship cannot be judged on the basis of the technical diagnosis because the order in which death is determined could well be purely arbitrary. It is essential to hold on to the premise that 'brainstem dead' patients are certified as being *already* dead. It would be wholly illogical to vary one's criteria to accommodate a specific situation—alternative methods in diagnosis are acceptable but double standards of death are not.[59] The rules of succession are bound by statute[60] and, accordingly, this is one aspect of brainstem death which could be subject to legislative action. It seems to us that a positive solution to 'ventilated commorientes' is currently impossible; but a negative direction on the lines that evidence as to the time of removal of ventilator support cannot, by itself, be regarded as sufficient to rebut the statutory presumptions might, at least, be equitable and, at the same time, relieve the doctor of one more moral problem.

POST-MORTEM PREGNANCY

16.28 In recent years, doctors and the public have been confronted by the picture of brain-dead women being retained on support for the sole purpose of bringing a fetus to viability.[61] A plethora of moral problems then arise, the answers to which, if there are any, depend,

---

[59] See Mason, n 1 at 1143–4.

[60] Law of Property Act 1925, s 184; Succession (Scotland) Act 1964, s 31 which excludes spouses and civil partners from the general rule.

[61] For thorough discussions, see N S Peart, A V Campbell, A R Manara, et al., 'Maintaining a pregnancy following loss of capacity' (2000) 8 Med L Rev 275; D Sperling, 'Maternal brain death' (2004) Amer J Law & Med 453; the monograph by Sperling, *Management of Post-mortem Pregnancy: Legal and Philosophical Aspects* (2006) and, A Gregorian, 'Post mortem pregnancy: A proposed methodology ...' (2010) 19 Ann Hlth Law 4011 discussing a US case decided as early as 1986.

first, on the gestational age of the fetus and, second, on whether the individual woman has or has not expressed her wishes or intentions while alive. A recent case concerned an Irish 26-year old (NP) who was 15 weeks pregnant at the time it was determined she had suffered brain death.[62] NP's father (the plaintiff) was informed that, for legal reasons relating to the protection of the unborn child in Ireland, NP would be supported by mechanical ventilation, nasogastric feeding, and other measures in an attempt to deliver her unborn child. The plaintiff viewed these measures as unreasonable and requested they be discontinued. The High Court of Ireland agreed, having heard unanimous medical evidence establishing the rapidly deteriorating condition of NP's body and the virtually non-existent prospects of a successful delivery of a live baby.

16.29   In the absence of any indication as to the woman's wishes the inclination is to say that to maintain her as an oxygenated cadaver would be an unacceptable invasion of a dying person's dignity and privacy. On the other hand, it would certainly not be unreasonable to hold that a viable fetus constitutes a living patient who should be treated in his or her best interests.

16.30   Although some would regard it as the determinant criterion,[63] the situation is not greatly eased if the woman has expressed her intentions. Suppose she wishes to be ventilated for the sake of her fetus—does the doctor *have* to follow such a choice? Or what if the woman has expressed a wish not to be maintained after death and the fetus is viable?[64]

16.31   Fortunately, the conditions envisaged must be rare—Souza et al.'s researches indicate that there may be some 1,060 pregnant women who sustain brain death on an annual global basis.[65] We suggest that, should the issue arise, it would be a matter to be decided by discussion between the doctor responsible for intensive care and, perhaps ideally, the person or persons likely to be responsible for the welfare of the living child—although the Mental Capacity Act 2005, s 9 might well be invoked so as to involve the donee of the woman's power of attorney. In the event of disagreement, the case would be a matter for the Court of Protection or the Sheriff Court in Scotland.

THE CASE FOR LEGISLATION

16.32   Post-mortem pregnancy is, however, another modern development which contributes to a latent unease as to the diagnosis of death. It is because of this persistency that the case for a modern *statutory* definition of death has been widely canvassed and is applied in many jurisdictions.

16.33   The main difficulty in framing legislation is to allow for all *modes* of death—from the elementarily obvious and natural to the complex ventilator case; it would be absurd to demand that criteria designed for the latter be applied to the former. As a result, most statutes, either existing or proposed, have applied some form of dual

---

[62] *P.P.* v *Health Service Executive* [2014] IEHC 622.   [63] E.g. Gregorian, n 61.

[64] It is just conceivable that failure to rescue a viable fetus could come within the ambit of the Infant Life (Preservation) Act 1929.

[65] J P Souza, A Oliveira-Neto, F G Surita, et al., 'The prolongation of somatic support in a pregnant woman with brain-death at 26 weeks of gestation' (2006) 113 Brit J Obs Gynaec Hlth 3. This report covers virtually all the ethical issues involved, in addition to demonstrating the massive effort involved. A 40-year-old woman who was 25 weeks pregnant was maintained for three weeks after which a healthy live-born child was delivered.

criteria of proof of death.[66] A typical expression is to be found in the US Uniform Determination of Death Act 1980,[67] which reads:

1. An individual who has sustained either: (a) irreversible cessation of circulatory and respiratory functions; or (b) irreversible cessation of all functions of the entire brain, including the brain stem; is dead.

2. A determination of death must be made in accordance with accepted medical standards.

And, as an example of Commonwealth legislation, we quote the Human Tissue Act 1982 (Victoria), s 41:

A person has died when there has occurred:

(a) Irreversible cessation of the circulation of the blood in the body of the person, or

(b) Irreversible cessation of all functions of the brain of the person.

There are similar provisions in the Human Tissue Act 1983 (NSW), s 33.

16.34 But, in essence, all these measures do is to spell out good medical practice within a legal framework—and many would feel this to be unnecessary. They lay down no specific methods, these being relegated to codes of practice—and this, we believe, is rightly so. We would certainly agree with the great majority of commentators that any statutory definition of death must be limited to an enabling concept. Medical facilities and expertise alter and do so faster than can the law; it is, therefore, essential that the evaluation of diagnostic techniques remains in the hands of the medical profession. In fact, the ethical, philosophical, and social problems inherent in the definition of death seem to have been largely solved in recent years;[68] definitive legislation might do little more than reanimate concerns which have, at least to a large extent, been put to rest and might, as a result, be self-defeating. The stethoscope and the CT scanner have it in common that both depend upon the expertise of their user—no Act of Parliament can alter that basic fact.

---

[66] See A M Capron, 'Brain death—Well settled yet still unsettled' (2001) 344 New Engl J Med 1244.

[67] 12 Uniform Laws Annotated (ULA) 589 (West 1993 and West Supp 1997).

[68] There can be few opinions expressed more uncompromisingly than that of the Academy of Medical Royal Colleges, n 13.

17

THE DONATION OF
ORGANS AND
TRANSPLANTATION

INTRODUCTION

17.01   The juxtaposition of chapters on the diagnosis of death and on transplantation of organs should not be taken to indicate that they are *necessarily* associated.[1] It is again emphasised that the concept of brainstem death is equally important to neurosurgeons, who can, as a result, allow their hopeless patients to die in peace, and to the relatives, who can now accept the fact of death in a ventilated body with good conscience. Nevertheless, and despite the introduction of new techniques, maximisation of saving lives by way of organ transplantation depends upon the acceptance of the concept of brainstem death; furthermore, the two conditions are closely linked in the public mind. This is, therefore, an appropriate point at which to discuss the ethics and legality of a procedure which, although firmly established as accepted and often optimal medical treatment, still provokes some public disquiet. Further, given that the donation of tissues which can be replaced rapidly, such as blood and bone marrow, presents few technical or ethical problems—the latter include commercialism and, at a rather more esoteric level, the deliberate production of 'saviour siblings' (discussed in Chapter 8), we are concerned here with non-regenerative tissues.

TECHNICAL CRITERIA FOR TRANSPLANTATION

BIOLOGICAL ELEMENTS OF TRANSPLANTATION

17.02   Aside from the technical expertise required, there are three major biological hurdles to be overcome in successful transplantation therapy: (1) ensuring that the donated organs are healthy; (2) preserving the viability of those organs in the period between their becoming available and their reception; and (3) neutralising the 'tissue immunity' reaction.

17.03   It is axiomatic that an organ intended as a replacement for a diseased tissue must, itself, be 'normal'. The practical result is that donors must either be living or dead as a result of trauma or from a natural disease which has no effect on the donated tissue. Arbitrary age limits for donation have been abandoned in favour of a policy of assessing the health of

---

[1]   For a brief analysis, see C Machado, 'A definition of human death should not be related to organ transplants' (2003) 29 J Med Ethics 201. See also Academy of Medical Royal Colleges, *A Code of Practice for the Diagnosis and Confirmation of Death* (2008) para 1.

the potential donor and using or rejecting the available tissues on the basis of the recipient's likely survival benefit.[2]

17.04 Viability, or continued functionality, of the donated organ is the essential element for success, and it is the assurance of viability which combines most clearly the technical and ethical problems of transplantation surgery. As has been discussed (Chapter 16), the cells of the body will deteriorate when deprived of oxygen; the process of deterioration can be slowed by chilling the organ, the survival of which then depends on the 'warm anoxic time'—that is, the interval between cessation of the circulation and chilling of the specimen. In practical terms, it becomes increasingly pointless to transplant a kidney after more than one hour's warm anoxia. Even so, the acceptable *cold* anoxic time is also finite and varies with the tissue involved—not only as regards its metabolic activity but also as to the urgency with which it must assume full function after transplantation. In general, hearts and lungs can be used up to four hours after harvesting, livers up to 8–12 hours, and kidneys can be maintained in vitro for more than 24 hours.[3]

17.05 A tissue immunity reaction results from the recognition by the body of antigenically foreign material which it will then reject with a degree of determination that depends, to a large extent, on *how* different is the donated tissue from that of the recipient. From this point of view, we can distinguish three main forms of transplantation: (1) autotransplantation, or re-siting portions of the same body, which is limited to skin or bone grafting and poses only the difficulties of highly complex surgery (and is of no concern in the present context); (2) homotransplantation, or allografting, which involves the transfer of viable tissue from one human being to another; and (3) heterotransplantation, or xenotransplantation—the transplantation of tissues from one species to another, a still highly experimental treatment which is of minimal but growing practical significance at present.

HOMOTRANSPLANTATION

17.06 Despite dealing with tissues from the same species, an immunity problem exists because, for practical purposes, no two persons other than monovular twins are genetically identical; the body can still recognise, and will reject, tissues of the same species which are 'non-self'.[4] This intra-species immune reaction can, however, be suppressed,[5] and the general principle is that such suppression will be effective—and will have less adverse side effects—in proportion to the genetic similarity of donor and recipient. Thus, sibling donation will be especially satisfactory, and intrafamilial exchanges in general are likely to show less antigenic discrepancies than are those between strangers. Other variables, however, complicate the picture. Immunosuppression is non-specific; therefore, while the

---

[2] Since the risk of graft failure is considerably greater using donors over 60 or with other well-defined conditions, the balancing exercise can be complex: R Merion, V Ashby, et al., 'Deceased donor characteristics and the survival benefit of kidney transplantation' (2005) 241 J Amer Med Ass 2726.

[3] The Human Tissue Act 2004, s 43, and the Human Tissue (Scotland) Act 2006, s 13, specifically allow for the preservation of parts intended for transplantation and the retention of the body for that purpose. Cold perfusion of the whole body or of individual organs is now common practice.

[4] The alternative—where the transplanted material attacks the host—is a difficulty of bone marrow transplantation.

[5] This is a reason for banking one's own stem cells, which one would have thought to be a vision of the future. However, a bronchial transplant using an airway modified from the patient's derived mucosal cells, and which does not require immunosuppressant drugs, has been successful: P Macchiarini et al., 'Clinical transplantation of a tissue-engineered airway' (2008) 372 Lancet 2023.

graft rejection process is being controlled, other desirable immune mechanisms—such as the body's defence against microbiological invasion—are also affected. Thus, micro-organisms that are normally resisted will be increasingly able to establish themselves in the vulnerable body—the most significant of these being viruses that are responsible for certain forms of malignant disease of the lymphoid system. Thus, although newer agents allow for increased selectivity and 'tailoring' to the needs of the individual patient,[6] the continued improvement of transplantation therapy is not simply a matter of discovering more powerful immunosuppressants.

17.07 As to the source of homotransplants, suitable organs can be provided by living or dead donors. Living donation offers many technical advantages—tissue compatibility can be measured at leisure, the operation can be elective, and the warm anoxic time can approach zero.[7] In theory, potential cadaver donors are widely available. In practice, however, the recovery of cadaveric organs is often capricious, and both donor and recipient operations must take on the character of emergency surgery. The recognition of brainstem death opened the way to what is now the standard variation on cadaver donation—'controlled donation after brain death' (or the 'beating heart' donor)—which bridges the gap between the living and the conventionally dead, and which carries with it many of the advantages of both types of donor. The legal and ethical limitations of all three methods must be considered, and will be after a brief comment on xenotransplantation.

XENOTRANSPLANTATION

17.08 In xenografts (or xenotransplantation), the immune reaction is of a different order from that seen in the allograft, and is known as 'hyperacute rejection'.[8] Nonetheless, although it is not yet a practical solution, xenotransplantation has moved closer to realisation in the last two decades.[9] The increasing sophistication of immunosuppressant drugs and techniques—in particular, those involving genetic replacement whereby transgenic animals, modified so as to contain human genetic material, are produced and, thus, take xenografting (or transplantation) closer to allografting—are changing the scene to the extent that a man has survived for 70 days following the transplantation of a baboon's liver.[10] Indeed, rapid advances precipitated precautionary governmental action which culminated in the establishment, in the United Kingdom (UK), of a Xenotransplantation Interim Regulatory Authority (UKXIRA), which was charged with overseeing the development

---

[6] P Andrews, 'Recent developments: Renal transplantation' (2002) 324 BMJ 530.

[7] The number of variables surrounding each case are such that 'statistics' comparing, say, the survival rates following living and cadaver donations are virtually meaningless—the major factor probably being the existing health of the recipients. What matters in the present context is the *graft* survival rate and, here, a probably representative US five-year survival rate is 68 per cent of grafts from cadavers and 81 per cent from living donors: United Network of Organ Sharing, *Report for 1996 to 2006* (2007).

[8] Although note that reactions will be quantifiably different when involving 'concordant species' (such as primates) as opposed to 'discordant species' (those widely separated, as in pig-to-man transplants). As to the latter, see B Ekser, P Rigotti, et al., 'Xenotransplantation of solid organs in the pig-to-primate model' (2009) 21 Trans Immunology 87.

[9] For the state of the art, Council of Europe, *Report on the State of the Art in the Field of Xenotransplantation*, CDBI/CDSP-XENO (2003) 1, B Jansen and J Simon (eds), *Xenotransplantation*, vol 2 (2008), D Shaw, W Dondorp, and G de Wert, 'Using non-human primates to benefit humans: research and organ transplantation' (2014) 17 Med Health Care Phil 573.

[10] T Starzl, J Fung, et al., 'Baboon-to-human liver transplantation' (1993) 341 Lancet 65. We remain unconvinced that such a result should be classified as a success. For analysis from the USA, see J Kress, 'Xenotransplantation: Ethics and Economics' (1998) 53 Food Drug LJ 353.

of xenotransplantation and its coordination pending the introduction of legislation. One of the first actions of the UKXIRA was to declare a moratorium on human clinical trials of xenografting pending further research. UKXIRA was, however, disbanded in 2006 and control of the procedure is now directed along two lines—clinical trials come within the ambit of the Medicines and Healthcare Products Regulatory Agency (MHRA), while review of the ethical implications is vested in local research ethics committees (RECs). Experimental treatments are assessed by the Clinical Governance Committees of individual National Health Service (NHS) Trusts.[11] The absence of a central agency to regulate a procedure that stimulates a host of ethical and practical problems is to be regretted.[12]

17.09 As to the practical problems, in addition to those related to the individual case, the community-based possibility of transmitting animal micro-organisms—in particular, viruses—to humans, and of their becoming adapted to the new environment, and of consequent human-to-human spread, is very real and constitutes what is probably the main reason why xenotransplantation is suspect.[13] A corollary to this, which crosses the ethical/practical boundary, is that donor animals would have to be reared in 'pathogen-free' environments which are hard, if not impossible, to define and maintain and which would also involve much animal suffering—and the morality of xenotransplantation depends on there being a positive balance in favour of human advantage over animal disadvantage.[14] Even if we agree that it is acceptable to use animals in this way, one must ask, 'What sort of animals?' Clearly, tissue rejection would be minimised if non-human primates were used. It is, however, widely accepted that primates have special characteristics which exclude them as organ donors.[15] Current interest, therefore, centres on the pig—an animal which has no antigenic but, nonetheless, remarkable physiological affinities with humans. Modern molecular biological techniques have already produced transgenic pigs in which at least one of the mechanisms leading to graft rejection appears to have been eliminated; there is little doubt that clinical trials using such tissues and organs are on the horizon.[16]

17.10 All of this, like so many 'advances', raises both intuitive and philosophical doubts. While the subject—which should include an analysis of speciesism and a comprehensive

---

[11] S McLean and L Williamson, 'The demise of UKXIRA and the regulation of solid-organ transplantation in the UK' (2007) 33 J Med Ethics 373.

[12] For a searching look at the problem, see L Williamson, M Fox, and S McLean, 'The regulation of xenotransplantation after UKXIRA: Legal and ethical issues' (2007) 34 J Law & Soc 441.

[13] See Nuffield Council on Bioethics, *Animal-to-Animal Transplants* (1996) ch 6, F Bach, A Ivinson, and C Weeramantry, 'Ethical and legal issues in technology: Xenotransplantation' (2001) 27 Amer J L Med 283, and, for a review of the conflicts involved—and a very firm rejection of clinical xenotransplantation in light of uncertainty as to the risks to the public—see S Fovargue and S Ost, 'When should precaution prevail? Interests in (public) health, the risk of harm and xenotransplantation' (2010) 18 Med L Rev 302. Note, however, that pretreated pigs' heart valves have been used for some time without apparent harm: A Moza, H Mertcsching, et al., 'Heart valves from pigs and the porcine endogenous retrovirus' (2001) 121 J Thorac Cardiovasc Surg 697.

[14] That such a balance exists was accepted by both Advisory Group on the Ethics of Transplantation of Animal Tissue into Humans (1996), and the Nuffield Council, n 13. For a US perspective, see M Anderson, 'Xenotransplantation: A bioethical evaluation' (2006) 32 J Med Ethics 205. And see D Shaw, W Dondorp, et al., 'Creating human organs in chimaera pigs: An ethical source of immunocompatible organs?' (2014) J Med Ethics Online.

[15] While stating this firmly, the Advisory Group considered that primates could, in strictly circumscribed conditions, be used for research into xenotransplantation. They would, of course, be protected by the Animals (Scientific Procedures) Act 1986.

[16] Department of Health, *Xenotransplantation Guidance* (2006) stated that no xeno-trials were ongoing in the UK at the time, and no animal-to-human transplants have ever been performed in the UK.

consideration of the ill-effects on human society—is too wide to be tackled here, we might make just a few passing observations. First, the morality of maintaining and breeding animals for the express purpose of substituting human body parts should be assessed;[17] it is not wholly unreal to foresee human organs being replaced by those of animals as they fail in sequence; we are then left with the unedifying picture of replacement therapy being continued until the irreplaceable and paradigmatic human organ, the brain, wears out. Since no health service could contain the costs of such a programme, longevity would become the prerogative of the rich; the structure of human society could be altered dramatically. Second, we might ask if xenotransplantation can be accommodated within our existing medical jurisprudence: *Can* a person properly consent to a journey into such uncharted territory, and how is such a paragon to be selected?[18] Writing from within the strongly consent-orientated Canadian jurisdiction, Caulfield and Robertson have pointed out that the need for continued surveillance and mandatory autopsy following xenografting must lead to concepts of 'contracts to undergo treatment' rather than consent to do so.[19] Third, is the public not entitled to dissent from a programme which undoubtedly poses a potential threat to its well-being?[20] And, given that one accepts some form of 'group consent', can the group constituency be anything less than global?[21] For all these, and other, reasons, we subscribe to an overall distrust of xenotransplantation.

17.11 It is to be noted that, although no human xenografts have, as yet, been performed in the UK, current government policy on the subject appears to be cautious, but encouraging.[22] Even so, we fancy that the great majority of commentators would prefer to see improvements in the existing homotransplantation programme rather than the development of xenotransplantation, and the remainder of this chapter is devoted to organ replacement as it is generally understood.

THE LIVING DONOR

THE REGIME BROADLY UNDERSTOOD

17.12 The legal regulation of living donations (of non-regenerative tissue) in the UK lies in both common and statute law. As to the former, the starting point must be the principle that consent to being killed or seriously injured does not obviate a charge of unlawfully

---

[17] For an analysis, see M Fox and J McHale, 'Xenotransplantation: The ethical and legal ramifications' (1998) 6 Med L Rev 42. We also wonder at what stage of modification does a transgenic pig become human? For current technical capabilities, see H Matsunari et al., 'Blastocyst complementation generates exogenic pancreas in vivo in apancreatoc cloned pigs' (2013) 110 PNAS 4557.

[18] S Fovargue, ' "Oh pick me, pick me"—Selecting participants for xenotransplant clinical trials' (2007) 15 Med L Rev 176.

[19] T Caulfield and G Robertson, 'Xenotransplantation: Consent, public health and Charter issues' (2001) 5 Med L Internat 81. See also, S Fovargue, 'Consenting to bio-risk: Xenotransplantation and the law' (2005) 25 LS 404; J Hughes, 'Justice and third party risks: The ethics of xenotransplantation' (2007) 24 J Appl Philosoph 151.

[20] This line of argument is well expressed by M A Clark, 'This little piggy went to market: The xenotransplantation and xenozoonose debate' (1999) 27 J Law Med Ethics 137. The paper should, however, be read in conjunction with its sibling written by a member of the Food and Drug Administration's (FDA) Subcommittee on Xenotransplantation: H Y H Vanderpool, 'Commentary: A critique of Clark's frightening xenotransplantation scenario' (1999) 27 J Law Med Ethics 153.

[21] It is widely agreed that the risk/benefit divide between the poor and the rich is disproportionate: R Sparrow, 'Xenotransplantation, consent and international justice' (2009) 9 Developing World Bioethics 119.

[22] Department of Health, n 16.

inflicting such injury. Living transplantation of a heart is thus precluded. This, of course, is the extreme case and, beyond it, legality would depend upon the presumed risk/benefit ratio involved—and assessment of this is difficult because the technological boundaries of medicine are always expanding and the expertise of various centres are not uniform. Thus, in recent years, the use of partial liver transplants and lung lobe transplants have increased and expanded;[23] in fact, since they can regenerate both anatomically and functionally, it may be that live liver and lung donation is more akin to bone marrow donation.[24] Given that the relative risks and benefits of a given procedure are both assessable and acceptable, the common law legality and the morality of live organ donation is now settled; consent to a surgical operation which is, in itself, non-therapeutic will be valid so long as the consequent infliction of injury can be shown not to be against the public interest.[25] This calculus is not uncomplicated, however, for the incidence of disease is also changing.[26] As such, misgivings cannot be ignored.

17.13   The statutory regulation of live donation in the UK was originally sited in the Human Organs Transplant Act 1989, which had, essentially, two purposes—to prohibit a transplant operation between living persons who were not genetically related unless it was undertaken with the agreement of the Unrelated Live Transplant Regulatory Authority (ULTRA),[27] and to prohibit any payment for organs (more on which later). The 1989 Act was repealed by the Human Tissue Act 2004 and the Human Tissue (Scotland) Act 2006, both of which deal with transplantation in broad terms,[28] and manage the practice through regulations and a statutory Code of Practice,[29] which is adopted and periodically

[23]   On liver donation, see A Marcos, R Fisher et al., 'Right lobe living donor liver transplantation' (1999) 68 Transplantation 798; V Fournier, N Foureur, and E Rari, 'The ethics of living donation for liver transplants: Beyond donor autonomy' (2013) 16 Med Health Care Phil 45; E Thomas, S Bramhall, et al., 'Live liver donation, ethics and practitioners' (2014) 40 J Med Ethics 157. On lung donation, see M Hodson, 'Transplantation using lung lobes from living donors' (2000) 26 J Med Ethics 419. Liver segments are particularly useful in paediatric care, where it is easier to achieve the necessary amount of therapeutic tissue in adult-to-child transplants. Two lung lobe donors are needed to treat a single patient. For liver and lung donation rates and transplantation levels, see NHS Blood and Transplant, *Organ Donation and Transplantation Activity Report 2014/15* (2015).

[24]   The Human Tissue Act 2004 defines 'transplantable material' as an organ *or part of an organ* listed in the Human Tissue Act 2004 (Persons who Lack Capacity to Consent and Transplants) Regulations 2006 (SI 2006/1659), reg 9, if the organ is to be used for the same purpose as the entire organ in the human body.

[25]   *A-G's Reference (No 6 of 1980)* [1981] QB 715. Figures from the US suggest that the comparable figure for *early* death following live liver donation is 1.7 per 1,000 operations: A Muzaale, N Dagher, et al., 'Estimates of early death, acute liver failure and long-term mortality among live liver donors' (2012) 142 Gastroenterology 273.

[26]   On this, see W Glannon, 'Underestimating the risk in living kidney donation' (2008) 34 J Med Ethics 127, wherein the author questioned the balance of benefit in live kidney donation and pointed to the increase in diabetes—and, hence, to the increase in late-onset renal disease—in recent years. F Delmonico, 'A report of the Amsterdam Forum on the care of the live kidney donor' (2005) 79 Transplantation (Supp 6) S53, reports that 56 of 50,000 previous donors in the USA were ultimately listed for transplant therapy themselves. A Cronin, 'Allowing autonomous agents freedom' (2008) 34 J Med Ethics 129, conversely, mounts a powerful support for the current risk/benefit consensus.

[27]   ULTRA was dissolved by the 2004 Act, and its functions were taken over by the Human Tissue Authority—established by s 13—including the overseeing of live transplantation in Scotland (under the 2006 Scottish Act, s 54).

[28]   2004 Act, ss 33–4.

[29]   See the Human Tissue Act 2004 (Persons who Lack Capacity to Consent and Transplants) Regulations 2006 (SI 2006/1659), Pt 3, in England and Wales, and the Human Organ and Tissue Live Transplants (Scotland) Regulations 2006 (SSI 2006/390). And see HTA Code of Practice 2: Donation of Solid Organs for Transplantation (2014), which applies only in part to Scotland. The HTA is also the UK's Competent Authority for implementing EU Directive 2010/53/EU on the standards of quality and safety of human

updated by the Human Tissue Authority (HTA).[30] Transplantations in Wales are additionally governed by the Human Transplantation (Wales) Act 2013, which makes it a duty of Welsh Ministers to promote transplantation medicine,[31] and which erects an opt-out system for Wales.[32] Consent to the removal of organs from living donors is covered by the common law and the Mental Capacity Act 2005.

17.14 Both regimes preserve offences if a live organ transplant is performed other than in accordance with the regulations.[33] Similarly, like their predecessor, they seem to be more concerned with family loyalties than immunological realities when it comes to donation; not only do the recent regulations make no mention of genetic compatibility, but also the Code of Practice retains donation types termed 'genetically related' and 'emotionally related'.[34] Undirected live donation (most usually of kidneys), sometimes referred to as 'altruistic donation', however, merits particular notice.[35] In addition to donations where the donor has no knowledge of the recipient, it includes paired and pooled donations.[36] To some, it may represent a significant means of improving the supply of therapeutic organs—a problem which we discuss later; to others, it may be a Pandora's box full of moral pitfalls, largely related to a potential 'free market'. This is reflected by the requirement that *all* undirected live donations must be approved by an HTA panel.[37] In any event, all living donations are subject to strong regulation, with strict rules as to the consent of the donor, the counselling of both parties, and the absence of commercial transactions.[38]

17.15 The clinician responsible for the donor must refer the matter to the HTA, which, before making a decision, must consider reports from independent qualified persons who have interviewed both the donor and the recipient,[39] and the regulations specify points which must be covered. The donation must be approved by a panel of at least three members of the HTA if the donor is an adult who lacks capacity or a child, or when the donation is paired, pooled, or non-directed and altruistic.[40] These rules, other than those associated with non-payment, are waived in the event that the donation is part of the treatment of the donor[41]—a circumstance which arises most commonly in what is known as the 'domino transplant'. Thus, in the treatment of cystic fibrosis by cadaver donation, for example, it is clinically more satisfactory to use a heart/lung preparation obtained from the dead donor than to implant a lung alone; this leaves the live recipient's heart available for donation in what will almost certainly be a non-related context.

---

organs intended for transplantation, which was transposed into UK law via the Quality and Safety of Organs Intended for Transplantation Regulations 2012 (SSI 2012/1501).

[30] Established under the 2004 Act, Pt 2.   [31] 2013 Act, s 2.

[32] 2013 Act, s 4. The HTA has prepared a draft Code of Practice for the Human Transplantation (Wales) Act 2013 (2014), which will come into effect in December 2015.

[33] 2004 Act, s 33; 2006 Act, s 17.

[34] HTA Code of Practice 2 (2014), para 29. Thus, the discouragement of inter-spousal donations, and donation by 'in-laws' or godparents is now no more than a matter of history.

[35] For a helpful review by a previous member of ULTRA, see S Roff, 'Self-interest, self-abnegation and self-esteem: Towards a new moral economy of non-directed kidney donation' (2007) 33 J Med Ethics 437. See also NHSBT, *Living Donor Kidney Transplantation 2020: A UK Strategy* (2014).

[36] HTA Code of Practice 2 (2014), para 29.

[37] Detailed regulations for undirected altruistic live donation are provided in the HTA Code of Practice 2 (2014), paras 31–43.

[38] HTA Code of Practice 2 (2014), paras 36–8.   [39] SI 2006/1659, reg 11.

[40] SI 2006/1659, reg 12. A paired donation occurs when a donor (D) donates to another person who is not genetically related and another person donates to a genetic relation of D. A pooled donation is, essentially, a paired donation involving more than one pair.

[41] SI 2006/1659, reg 10(2).

17.16 The coming into force of the 2004 Act, coupled with a change in government and NHS policy, has led to rising donation and transplantation levels in the UK. In 1994, the living donation rate was 7 per cent; the comparable figures in 2004/5 and 2009/10 were 39 per cent and 52 per cent respectively.[42] However, in 2014/15, there was a slight decline in the number of both living and deceased donors compared to the previous year, with a 5 per cent reduction in the number of patients receiving a transplant, all of which the NHS Blood and Transport (NHSBT) is now trying understand and reverse.[43]

CATEGORIES OF LIVING DONORS

17.17 It should be clear that the foregoing discussion refers to donation by (competent) adults; living donation by others, however, raises a number of additional thorny issues.

Minors as Donors

17.18 The donation of organs by children is required surprisingly often, and the advantages of live donation will apply here as much as they will in the adult situation. The legality of such operations on children below the age of 16 is clearly compatible with the 2004 Act—albeit subject to severe regulation. When, and how the opportunity should be taken within the regulatory bounds are, however, matters to be decided on the basis of medical ethics and practice rather than the law, and are best addressed from that viewpoint. As discussed (Chapter 4), consent to an operation on a minor below the age of 16 years should normally be obtained from the parents, subject only to the possible *Gillick*-rights of the child.[44] Valid parental consent, however, refers to treatment for the advantage of the child; troublesome questions arise in relation to procedures which are not calculated to be to the child's benefit. Does parental consent in such circumstances constitute an abuse of parental power?[45]

17.19 It is arguable that the principle that a minor—or an incompetent adult—cannot legally be subjected to any procedure which is not to her advantage is not an absolute one. Thus, it is possible that a court might consider the donation of an organ to be not only in the public interest, but also in the interest of the minor donor who will almost certainly be a sibling of the recipient. In such circumstances, it might be supposed that it is in the interests of the minor that a member of her family should be saved rather than die. This line

---

[42] NHSBT, *Transplant Activity in the UK, 2010–2011* (2011). Similar trends are noticed worldwide. For US figures, see OPTN/SRTR, 'Special Issue: OPTN/SRTR 2013 Annual Data Report' (2015) 15 Am J Transplantation S2. The very high proportion of live transplants in Scandinavian countries is notable. Live donation is the preferred method in some societies—e.g., in Japan, where the concept of brainstem death has only recently become acceptable, some 70 per cent of donations were of live type. Virtually all transplants in India are 'live', but this is probably an administrative rather than cultural consequence: A Singh, P Srivatsava, and A Kumar, 'Current status of transplant coordination and organ donation' (1998) 30 Transplant Proc 3627.

[43] NHSBT, n 42, Foreword. See also NHSBT, *Saving and Improving Lives: Strategic Plan 2015–20* (2015). For Scotland's strategy, see Scottish Government, *A Donation and Transplantation Plan for Scotland 2013–2020* (2013), which indicates that it will monitor developments in Wales before taking steps to introduce an opt-out system in Scotland.

[44] It is very reasonably arguable that the Family Law Reform Act 1969, s 8 has no application to non-therapeutic procedures. The statutory position in Scotland under the Age of Legal Capacity (Scotland) Act 1991, s 2(4) is unclear but donation is not positively excluded as being within the 'understanding' minor's remit.

[45] Many of the arguments surrounding the production of 'saviour siblings' (for which, see Chapter 8) might be deployed.

of argument was successfully pursued in the index US decision in *Strunk* v *Strunk*.[46] In this case, the donor, who, although adult, had a mental age of six, was chosen to donate a kidney to his critically ill brother. The court concluded that it would be in the donor's best interests for his brother's life to be saved given the evidence of the close relationship which they shared. Consequently, the operation was allowed although the donor was not in a position to give consent. *Strunk*, however, never had an easy ride, and may not represent the general rule in the USA.[47] Indeed, it may be that no general rule can be anticipated, and each case, whether in the consulting room or the court, will stand on its own merits.

17.20 In practice, while donation of regenerative tissue is permissible under stringent conditions, most jurisdictions are reluctant to allow the taking of non-regenerative tissues from minors.[48] A blanket ban on the use of minors as organ donors has been advocated by the World Health Organization (WHO),[49] and the Council of Europe's Protocol on Transplantation (2002) envisages donation involving a live incompetent as being permissible only between siblings.[50] Certainly, there are powerful reasons why limits should be placed on the use of children as tissue donors, and very great caution should be exercised in the case of young children in whom there is unlikely to be any significant understanding of what the donation entails both at the time and, most significantly, in the future. Moreover, circumstances alter cases. As we have already intimated, it might be regarded as ethically acceptable for a minor to be used as a donor within the family circle; generosity towards a brother or sister is to be encouraged and may even be regarded as a social duty.[51] Should one, however, apply the same rule where the prospective recipient is a distant cousin?[52] It is always possible that the illness of the cousin will be as distressing to

---

[46] 445 SW 2d 145 (Ky, 1969).

[47] It was followed in *Hart* v *Brown* 289 A 2d 386 (Conn, 1972) (identical twins) and *Little* v *Little* 576 SW 2d 493 (Tex, 1979) (14-year-old incompetent), but rejected in *Re Richardson* 284 So 2d 185 (La, 1973) (17-year-old incompetent), *Re Guardianship of Pescinski* 226 NW 2d 180 (Wis, 1975) (adult incompetent), and *Curran* v *Bosze* 566 NE 2d 1319 (Ill, 1990) (bone marrow transplant between three-year-old twins). Despite attempts to apply a substituted judgement test, all the relevant cases have been decided on the basis of the donor's best interests.

[48] See, e.g., France: Law no 2004–800 of 6 August 2004 maintaining Arts L1231–1 (adults) and L1231–2 and L1241–3 (minors) of the Public Health Code. Scandinavia seems to provide exceptions to the rule in Europe: donation of organs by minors is permissible, subject to varying regulation, in Denmark (Law no 402 of 13 June 1990), Norway (Law no 6 of 9 February 1973), and Sweden (Transplantation Law no 190 of 15 May 1975). Interestingly, none of the Australian states allows live organ donation by a minor. For the current situation in the USA, see L Ross and J Thistlethwaite, 'Minors as living solid-organ donors' (2008) 122 Pediatrics 454; basically, the American Academy of Pediatrics will countenance immediate familial donation by minors subject to five conditions among which benefit to both donor and donee is prominent. Thus, an overriding importance of psychological benefit to the donor is acknowledged.

[49] WHO, *Guiding Principles on Human Organ Transplantation* (1994), principle 4.

[50] Council of Europe, Additional Protocol to the Convention on Human Rights and Biomedicine on Transplantation of Human Organs and Tissues of Human Origin (2002), Art 14(2). The Convention has still not been ratified by the UK.

[51] L Ross, 'Moral grounding for the participation of children as organ donors' (1993) 21 J Law Med & Ethics 251, introduces the interesting concept of the family as an autonomous unit which can aspire to a collective purpose. Intrafamilial donation by a child advances the family's interests, which is a means of promoting the child's own interests. Nonetheless, the author was extremely wary of exposing minors to risks they do not understand.

[52] Very useful examples are to be found in Australian cases: *Re Inaya (special medical procedure)* [2007] Fam CA 658 (treatment of cousin), and *In the Marriage of GWW and CMW* (1997) 21 Fam LR 612 (aunt), in both of which a bone marrow transplant was authorised: S Then, 'The legality of tissue transplants for the benefit of family members in the UK and Australia' (2008) 10 Med Law Internat 23.

the minor as would be the illness of a sibling. Nevertheless, a policy of limiting approved donation by minors to the immediate family has the attraction of certainty.

17.21   Statute law in the UK is either non-directive or silent on the matter. Section 33 of the 2004 Act criminalises the use of bone marrow and peripheral blood stem cells only, in the present context, in the case of a child who is not competent.[53] Overall, however, transplantable material, which includes organs, can be used in the case of a child provided that the decision is taken by a panel of at least three members of the HTA.[54] Clearly, then, there is no blanket prohibition on organ donation by minors; decisions are made on a case-by-case basis. Indeed, in *Re Y*,[55] an English case involving bone marrow transplantation, the procedure was authorised between siblings largely on the ground that, absent treatment for the lymphomatous child, the mother would have less time to devote to the incapax; the procedure was, accordingly, in the best interests of the donor.[56]

17.22   But what of the minor's rights to refuse to receive a transplant? We discuss the cases of *Re M (child: refusal of medical treatment)*[57]—in which the child's refusal was overturned—and that of Hannah Jones[58]—in which refusal was accepted—in Chapter 4. Here, it need only be said that the cases are not incompatible so long as the debate is confined to whether or not life-saving treatment should ever be withheld from a *Gillick*-competent child in the absence of a court hearing. In our view, it is wrong to think in terms of the Trust attempting to force Hannah into accepting a heart transplant; the better question is whether or not it should have insisted that a judicial opinion be obtained on the matter. The details of the case are, however, now irrelevant as Hannah changed her mind and was successfully treated.[59]

PVS Patients as Donors

17.23   The current pressure to accept cognitive death as equivalent to somatic death[60] demands a brief word on the permanent vegetative state (PVS). It is, perhaps, necessary to do no more than recapitulate our view that, tragic as their state may be, persons in PVS are existing by means of their own cardiovascular system and are not dead. There can surely be no question of using them as non-voluntary donors whether or not to do so would limit their existence.[61] It is of collateral interest that the British Medical Association (BMA) does not mention the possibility in its latest wide-ranging review of organ procurement.[62] Very little is, however, certain in the medico-ethical field and an authoritative paper published

---

[53]   Human Tissue Act 2004 (Persons who Lack Capacity to Consent and Transplants) 2006 (SI 2006/1659, reg 10(3), subject to disapplication by reg 11.

[54]   Ibid, reg 12(2).   [55]   [1997] Fam 110, (1996) 35 BMLR 111.

[56]   The result of the legislative position, and precedent represented by *Re Y*, mean that the somewhat confusing obiter observations made by the Master of the Rolls in the otherwise significant case of *Re W (a minor) (medical treatment)* [1992] 4 All ER 627 (CA), are now irrelevant save as to confirming that the *Gillick*-competent minor has a right to refuse to donate. For a critique of the current approach to minors, see L Cherkassky, 'Children and the doctrine of substituted judgment' (2014) 14 Med Law In 213.

[57]   [1999] 2 FLR 1097; (2000) 52 BMLR 124.

[58]   S de Bruxelles, 'Girl wins fight to turn down transplant' *The Times*, 11 November 2008, p 3. See also C Dyer, 'Trust decides against action to force girl to undergo transplant' (2008) 337 BMJ 1132.

[59]   R Smith, 'I'm feeling brilliant ...' *Mirror News*, 17 August 2009.   [60]   See para 16.06.

[61]   Yet, it has been found that 65 per cent of US physicians would regard it as ethical to do so once the diagnosis has been made: K Payne et al., 'Physicians' attitudes about the care of patients in the persistent vegetative state; A national survey' (1996) 125 Ann Imt Med.

[62]   British Medical Association, *Building on Progress: Where Next for Organ Donation Policy in the UK?* (2012).

on behalf of an International Forum for Transplant Ethics inferred that to exempt PVS patients from the normal legal prohibitions against 'killing' would be humanitarian in that it would obviate the futile use of resources and would release organs that were suitable for transplantation.[63] We have already implied our strong antipathy to such a policy. To confuse the concept of brainstem death and to associate PVS with transplantation could only fan any embers of public distrust for 'premature grave robbing' which still remain. Burke and Hare attracted much sympathy in their role of exhumers; it was when they became pre-emptive that they fell from grace!

Donors as Vendors

17.24   The commercialisation of transplant surgery remains one of the most divisive issues in the context of living organ donation. Its acceptability involves a complex amalgam of public policy and the validation of individual consent in exceptional circumstances. On the latter score alone, it is to be distinguished from payment for cadaver organs—a matter which is better considered as an aspect of the availability of organs rather than of ethical principle. Inevitably, a British view on donation for recompense must be coloured by one's experience of the NHS. Within that framework—and given that live donation of kidneys is accepted medical practice—it is difficult to visualise the sale of organs as other than a way for the rich to obtain priority care. But it is only fair to remark that those working in a health care system that is governed by a market economy could reasonably see the situation as one in which an anxious buyer meets a willing seller. It is not easy to occupy an objective middle ground.

17.25   The problem presented acutely in England in 1989. It transpired that impoverished Turkish donors were being recruited and paid to donate their kidneys to genetically and ethnically unrelated recipients; there were wide-ranging repercussions at both legislative and professional levels, and these themselves provoked further ethical debate. The legislative response was a rushed Human Organ Transplants Act 1989 (now repealed as noted in para 17.13 et seq.). Both the 2004 and 2006 Acts prohibit commercial dealings, other than the provision of legitimate expenses, in the supply of human material for the purpose of transplantation both by the living and the dead.[64] Clearly, the legislative intention is to distinguish altruism from commercialism and to approve the former while condemning the latter.[65] Thus, the giving or receiving of reward for the supply of, or offer to supply, any 'controlled material' or of advertising to that effect remain criminal offences throughout the UK.[66] Live transplantation of 'transplantable material' is controlled by s 33 of the 2004 Act, which makes it an offence either to remove and/or to implant any transplantable material from a living person unless regulations provide otherwise.[67] The regulations dictate that each case of live donation must be decided by

---

[63] R Hoffenberg, M Lock, et al., 'Should organs from patients in permanent vegetative state be used for transplantation?' (1997) 350 Lancet 1320. There are probably around 100 potential donors in the UK.

[64] 2004 Act, s 32; 2006 Act, s 17(3). For cadaver donation, s 32(10), discussed infra.

[65] For some observations about altruism, see G Moorlock, J Ives, and H Draper, 'Altruism in organ donation: An unnecessary requirement?' (2014) 40 J Med Ethics 134.

[66] Controlled material is defined in the 2004 Act (s 32(8) and (9)) as any material which consists of or includes human cells, is removed, or intended to be removed, from a human body and is intended to be used for the purpose of transplantation; it excludes gametes, embryos, and 'material which is the subject of property because of an application of human skill'. For discussion on the last, see Chapter 14. Gametes and embryos are covered by the Human Fertilisation and Embryology Act 1990.

[67] Transplantable material is defined in reg 9, SI 2006/1659, and, in addition to organs, includes the face and limbs.

the HTA, which must, in turn, be assured that consent has been given and, most firmly, that no reward is involved in the procedure.[68]

17.26 The total ban on reward for the provision of transplantable material from living donors is widely accepted within the Western world,[69] and is governed by the consent doctrine in that it is assumed that a free, uncoerced consent is impossible in the face of financial inducement. Of course, one might ask why is it ethical to receive financial reward for participation in a research programme and not for organ donation when both have therapeutic success as the end-point?[70] It is undeniable that, in accepting these restrictions on the individual's autonomy, one is, simultaneously, accepting a degree of paternalism which could be regarded as unjustifiable.[71] Is it impossible that a commercial donor could make her decision in a reasoned manner and on her own altruistic grounds?[72] And who, in the quest for unfettered consent, is to distinguish between external financial pressure and moral pressure exerted within the family?[73] It is at least arguable that, in closing the door on the use of an inessential part of one's body for gain, Parliament is striking at the individual publican's autonomy in favour of the corporate pharisee's inner virtue.

17.27 As a result, a significant underswell of opposition to the 'no reward' imperative has developed,[74] and it has to be admitted that the philosophical discourse has been fuelled by pragmatic concern over the general shortage of organs for therapeutic use.[75] The considerable force of the counter-argument cannot be denied and can be précised by a caution that we should not deny treatment to those suffering based merely on feelings of disgust.[76] Against

---

[68] Reg 11(3). Para 47 of the HTA Code of Practice 2 (2014) states that a person commits an offence if they: '1. give, offer or receive any type of reward for the supply or offer of supply of any organ or part organ; 2. look for a person willing to supply any organ or part organ for reward; 3. offer to supply any organ or part organ for reward; 4. initiate or negotiate any arrangement involving the giving of a reward for the supply of, or for an offer to supply, any organ or part organ; 5. take part in the management or control of any type of group whose activities consist of or include the initiation or negotiation of such arrangements; 6. cause to be published or distributed, or knowingly publish or distribute, an advertisement inviting people to supply, or offering to supply, any organ or part organ for reward, or indicate that the advertiser is willing to initiate or negotiate any such arrangements'. There are also rigid safeguards as to the provision and substance of counselling—e.g. coercion of any sort must be excluded.

[69] Though not universal: J Chapman, 'Should we pay donors to increase the supply of organs for transplantation? No' (2008) 336 BMJ 1343.

[70] We are unconvinced by the philosophical argument that the wrong lies in the invasion of bodily integrity—a wrong which is offset by the good of altruism but which finds no such exculpation in the commercial situation: S Wilkinson and E Garrard, 'Bodily integrity and the sale of human organs' (1996) 22 J Med Ethics 334. The money that accrues can always be put to good use.

[71] A point made by J Savulescu, 'Is the sale of body parts wrong?' (2003) 29 J Med Ethics 138.

[72] One of the Turkish donors intended to devote the proceeds to the medical treatment of his daughter: see J Harvey, 'Paying organ donors' (1990) 16 J Med Ethics 117.

[73] For an interesting review of the subtle intrafamilial pressures that can be exerted, see N Biller-Andorno and H Schauenburg, 'It's only love? ... ' (2001) 27 J Med Ethics 16.

[74] See the powerful argument mounted by A Daar, 'Paid organ donation—the grey basket concept' (1998) 24 J Med Ethics 365—among other writings by the same author.

[75] This two-pronged argument has been expressed by L de Castro, 'Commodification and exploitation: Arguments in favour of compensated organ donation' (2003) 29 J Med Ethics 142. J Radcliffe-Richards, 'Commentary: An ethical market in human organs' (2003) 29 J Med Ethics 139, points out that, so long as it is accepted that the sale of organs would improve their availability, it is difficult to justify restriction. It is unlikely that public or political opinion could be altered to that extent.

[76] J Radcliffe-Richards, A Daar, et al., 'The case for allowing kidney sales' (1998) 351 Lancet 1950. Note that the possibility of payment for organs is still alive in the USA: A Friedman, 'Payment for living organ donation should be legalised' (2006) 333 BMJ 746; A Matas, 'Should we pay donors to increase the supply of organs for transplantation? Yes' (2008) 336 BMJ 1342.

this, it will be said that to allow payment would be to open up a traffic in organs and there is little doubt that this threat is real.[77] However, it is difficult to see why the danger could not be obviated by legalising paid donations only by way, say, of the HTA;[78] this would, at the same time, exclude what is probably the main cause of distaste for rewarded donation—that is, the involvement of the commercial middleman. There is some empirical evidence that public opposition to payment is not as strong as might be supposed—between 40 per cent and 50 per cent may find the practice permissible,[79] and it has been noted that, 'As long as there are adequate safeguards, any ethical or legal fastidiousness demanding that donation be only gratuitous could condemn the sick'.[80]

17.28 The overriding practical difficulty lies in the fact that it is now almost impossible to confine a market in organs to one jurisdiction. Networks for their commercial provision already exist; clearly any restrictions on the practice must be international if they are to be effective and, in this respect, the fact that the recorded antipathy reflects a Western view merits repetition. It is at least arguable that, in a country such as India, where there is no cadaver transplant programme and where long-term dialysis is impracticable, paid organ donation may be not only ethical but also desirable.[81] As has been said,[82] the ethical distinction between allowing one poor and needy citizen to run the risk of brain damage in the boxing ring and denying another the right to sell a kidney may be hard to define—and the point being made seems easy to accept. That is, until one reads of the reality of the situation in the investigative news media;[83] it is then that one begins to appreciate the extent of the evil that is inherent in commercial trafficking in live human body parts. It is still possible to argue that: 'Commercialisation should be curbed not by depriving a needy person of his genuine requirements but by making the enforcement agencies efficient.'[84] This has remained an unattainable dream.

THE CADAVERIC DONOR

EVOLUTION OF THE REGIME

17.29 A person has very limited rights as to the future disposal of his or her dead body in common law, and the wishes of the executors would normally be supported rather than those

---

[77] See Joint Council of Europe/UN Study, *Trafficking in organs, tissues and cells and trafficking in human beings for the purpose of the removal of organs* (2009), ch 3.
[78] The Manchester School has consistently supported a similar initiative: J Harris and C Erin, 'An ethically defensible market in organs' (2002) 325 BMJ 114; C Erin and J Harris, 'An ethical market in human organs' (2003) 29 J Med Ethics 137. And see also Friedman, n 76.
[79] A Guttmann and R Guttmann, 'Attitudes of health care professionals and the public towards the sale of kidneys for transplantation' (1993) 19 J Med Ethics 148.
[80] I Davies, 'Live donation of human body parts: A case for negotiability?' (1991) 59 Med-Leg J 100. And see this debate: N Scheper-Hughes, 'The ultimate commodity' (2005) 366 Lancet 1350 (in opposition); J Taylor, 'A "queen of hearts" trial of organ markets: Why Scheper-Hughes's objections to markets in human organs fail' (2007) 33 J Med Ethics 201.
[81] The Indian government has outlawed payment for organs since 1994, but the ban is not watertight and the demand is relentless: Singh, Srivatsava, and Kumar, n 42; G Novelli, M Rossi, et al., 'Is legalizing the organ market possible? (2007) 39 Transplant Proc 1743.
[82] J Bignall, 'Kidneys: Buy or die' (1993) 342 Lancet 45.
[83] There are a vast number of articles. We were impressed by L Rohter, 'Tracing a kidney's path of poverty and hope' *New York Times*, 27 May 2004, p 1. The Philippines is the latest jurisdiction to ban foreigners receiving organs from local inhabitants ((2008) 336 BMJ 1036).
[84] R Kishore, 'Human organs, scarcities, and sale: Morality revisited' (2005) 31 J Med Ethics 362.

of the deceased in the event of conflict. Statute law has, however, largely replaced common law, and the collection and use of cadaver organs and tissues has been regulated in the UK since 1961. Revision of the Human Tissue Act 1961 was undertaken as a result of widespread breaches of the law (see Chapter 14), resulting in the Human Tissue Act 2004 and the Human Tissue (Scotland) Act 2006. And changes in public attitudes towards the intrinsic value of human remains is reflected in the fact that the two-page 1961 Act was replaced by Acts bearing 61 and 62 sections respectively.

17.30 While the two Acts share many common features,[85] the most important conceptual difference is that the 2004 Act is dominated by the concept of 'appropriate consent' to the use of tissues, while the 2006 Act speaks in terms of 'authorisation' for removal and use of tissues from the cadaver.[86] While it could be said that this is a distinction without a difference, the latter is the semantic preference in the context of a dead principal. More importantly, the 2006 Act refers to transplantation in detail which is lacking in its counterpart—and perhaps one of the more contentious details is that a child aged 12 or over is empowered by statute to authorise the use of his body parts after death. In the end, however, it has to be noted that the provisions of the two Acts are so similar that the Scottish Ministers may call upon other UK bodies—in particular, the HTA—for assistance in many functions, which is important for the coordination of transplant services across the UK.[87]

17.31 The rather loose wording of the 1961 Act gave rise to difficulties in relation to 'lawful possession' of a dead body and the role of the deceased's relatives in its disposal, and its absence of enumerated sanctions despite defining criminal activity in respect of dealings with the dead body. These and other deficiencies have been redressed in the 2004 and 2006 Acts. However, the problem of civil liability for transgression of the statute is still in doubt. The most relevant case, *AB v Leeds Teaching Hospital NHS Trust*,[88] was concerned with the use of post-mortem tissues other than for transplantation; the case was argued in tort and the Human Tissue Act was not addressed directly. Although Gage J held that the tort of wrongful interference with the body was unrecognised in English law, there seems no reason why an action for nervous shock should not be available to a close relative who was confronted with what he regarded as a mutilated corpse and who thought that the conditions governing information and consent had not been met. Success in such actions is notoriously difficult to achieve, but an action for 'affront to feelings'—*actio injuriarum*—has succeeded in Scotland.[89]

---

[85] Once again, in the interest of space, we will concentrate on the English/Welsh Act but highlight those aspects of the Scottish Act which differ significantly from the former. A major difference of form only is that, whereas the Anatomy Act 1984—which is limited to dissection of the body in a School of Anatomy—is repealed in England/Wales and incorporated into the 2004 Act, it is retained in amended form in Scotland, where the 2006 Act takes precedence when authority for study derives from both (s 53). However, donation of the body for anatomical dissection raises few ethical problems and the remnants of the Anatomy Act 1984 are not considered further in this chapter. Note that the Corneal Grafting Act 1986 is repealed in both jurisdictions.
[86] See S McLean (chair), *Independent Review Group on Retention of Organs at Post-mortem Final Report* (2001) s 1, para 17. For comment see M Brazier, 'Retained organs, ethics and humanity' (2002) 22 LS 551, and S Harmon and A McMahon, 'Banking (on) the Brain: From Consent to Authorisation and the Transformative Potential of Solidarity' (2014) 22 Med Law Rev 572.
[87] 2006 Act, s 54. See Organ Donation Taskforce, *Organs for Transplants* (2008). The HTA is, in fact, responsible for all living transplants in Scotland.
[88] [2004] 2 FLR 365; (2004) 77 BMLR 145.
[89] *Stevens v Yorkhill NHS Trust* 2007 SCLR 606; (2007) 95 BMLR 1. For the rationale, see N Whitty, 'Rights of personality, property rights and the human body in Scots law' (2005) 9 Edin LR 194.

17.32 The 2004 Act was rushed into service as a result of the widespread unauthorised retention of tissues following post-mortem examination. Although the 1961 Act covered post-mortem examinations (s 2), it did so only as an aside, its main purpose being to regulate transplantation therapy. Legislative reform on the basis of offences related to the autopsy room was, therefore, in the nature of the tail wagging the dog; indeed, other than in respect of trafficking, the therapeutic use of cadaver organs is scarcely mentioned in the 2004 Act—transplantation is no more than one of 12 'scheduled purposes' for the use of human tissues with which the Act is concerned.[90] As a result, the regulation of transplantation in England and Wales is now dominated by the rubric of consent. In essence, the 2004 Act states that the use of a body or removed organs of a deceased person for transplantation is lawful if done with 'appropriate consent'.[91] Appropriate consent to donation, in the case of an adult, means his or her consent.[92] In the absence of an advance directive, consent may be given or withheld by a person or persons nominated under s 4 by a living adult to act in his or her interests after death.[93] If neither of these options is available, authority is vested in a person who stood in a qualifying relationship to the deceased.[94] The consent of a child to organ donation after death is valid, but in its absence, authority to consent passes to the person who has parental responsibility or, failing that, to a person in a qualifying relationship to him or her.[95] Finally, transplantation now comes under the aegis of the HTA, which is, essentially, the 'strategic' regulator of human tissue use for scheduled purposes as defined in the 2004 Act; the 'tactical' problems as to the distribution of such tissues are, in general, devolved.[96] The HTA must ensure that a relevant Code of Practice is in place,[97] and transplant surgeons are excluded from the need to have a licence to operate.[98]

17.33 Initially, one might regret that, insofar as the therapeutic use of tissues is so far separated in the public mind from activities such as research and education, the opportunity was not taken to legislate for the first time on a distinct conceptual plane. Nonetheless, it seems that the practice of transplantation therapy is relatively undisturbed in ethical terms; at the same time, the 2004 Act seems to have had little practical effect on the procurement of organs (see paras 17.44 et seq). On this issue, it is to be noted that the power of the 'person lawfully in possession of the body' (most likely the hospital) is retained to a limited extent in that, given that parts of a body lying within the hospital or similar institution may be suitable for transplantation, the management may take minimally invasive steps to preserve the parts and to retain the body for the purposes of transplantation until it is established that consent has not been, and will not be, given.[99]

---

[90] Sch 1, Pts 1 and 2.   [91] Section 1(1)(b) and (c).

[92] Section 3(6)(a) does not stipulate consent in writing.

[93] An appointment, if made orally, is valid only if it is made before two witnesses together (s 4(4)). A written appointment must be attested by at least one witness or may be part of a will (s 4(5)).

[94] The ranking of qualifying relationships is set out in s 27(4).

[95] Section 2. The overriding powers of the Coroner in respect of bodies subject to his or her authority are preserved in s 11.

[96] UK Transplant, which provided central support for and coordination of transplant services throughout the UK, has now merged with the National Blood Authority in England to become NHS Blood and Transplant: see National Blood Authority and United Kingdom Transplant (Abolition) Order 2005 (SI 2005/2532).

[97] Section 26(2)(h).   [98] Section 16(2)(c).

[99] Section 43. See para 17.37 et seq, for the relevance of this in the context of the non-heart beating donor.

CATEGORIES OF CADAVERIC DONORS

Beating Heart Donors

17.34 The success in the early days of organ transplantation was blighted by the inevitable warm anoxic time imposed between the diagnosis of death and the revascularisation of the donated organ. This dilemma is, itself, a product of a 'dead donor rule' and the assessment of death by way of the irrevocable failure of the cardiorespiratory system. In practice, however, the major proportion of cadaver-donated material will come from patients who have been maintained on ventilator support and in whom, as discussed (Chapter 16), it will be appropriate to reach a diagnosis of death by means of brain-stem criteria after which ventilation can be continued after death.[100] In this way, despite the considerable expertise required, the ideal characteristics of the living donor can be achieved in a cadaver.[101]

17.35 Why, then, is there any residual antipathy to a well-established procedure? Much must stem from an inherent revulsion at performing what is a lethal operation amid the conditions pertaining to a living patient, but this is irrational once the concept of brain stem death has been accepted—any emotional bias should be directed towards the recipients. Perhaps the major problem lies in the fact that there are still those who, in all good conscience, cannot accept the technical criteria advocated for the diagnosis of brain stem death—doubts which affect both doctors and relatives; some surgeons, while accepting a ventilated donor, will still not operate until the patient is disconnected from the machine and shows a flat electrocardiogram. At least the paradox in s 1(4) of the 1961 Act, whereby the diagnostic team and those responsible for organ removal were kept separate, yet the surgeon undertaking a beating heart donation had to 'satisfy himself by personal examination of the body that life was extinct', is now rectified in that the doctor may be satisfied that another registered medical practitioner is so satisfied.[102]

17.36 What is certain is that relatives should be given every possible assistance in understanding the transplantation programme and the concepts of death that underpin its functioning. It is clearly preferable that this should be provided by professional advisers independent of the principals concerned, and this is a major part of the services provided by transplant coordination teams that are now widely established.[103] We believe that it is such sympathetic contact that lies at the heart of any improvement in the gap between the needed and available number of transplantable organs.[104]

Non-Heart Beating Donors

17.37 An alternative or complementary approach to reducing the 'wastage' of organs would be to encourage the use of the brain stem and cardiorespiratory definitions of death in

---

[100] Although it is to be noted that less than 1 per cent of *all* deaths are of this type.

[101] And the procedure is essential to some operations—e.g. heart transplants. For ethical discussion, see R Veatch, 'Transplanting heart after death measured by cardiac criteria: The challenge to the dead donor rule' (2010) 35 J Med Philosoph 313.

[102] 2006 Act, s 11(4)(a). There is no comparable amendment in the 2004 Act. We believe that it should be legally necessary that a death certificate is signed before a donor operation is undertaken.

[103] Some 100 donor transplant coordination teams are working within NHS Trusts and more are in the pipeline: Organ Donation Taskforce, n 87, at para 17.47.

[104] Religious understanding is also important in a multicultural society: the Muslim Law Council's fatwa of 1996 approved transplantation (non-unanimously); Judaism is generally supportive of the saving of life, but this involves some unorthodoxy; Hinduism and Buddhism are positively supportive; Sikhs have no objection: S Hollins, *Religions, Culture and Healthcare* (2006).

parallel.[105] To do so takes us into—or back to—the realm of what has been called non-heart beating donation but is now referred to as donation after circulatory death (DCD).[106] Such donors derive from so-called 'controlled ventilation' and can become available in four main ways:[107]

- In the first, mechanical support is removed from a 'brain dead' ventilated patient whose heart will then cease to function as a result of hypoxia. This is little more than a matter of raising public confidence in current practice, and many surgeons adopt the procedure as a precautionary routine.

- Difficulties arise when the above practice is extended into the second and far more dubious variant that is known as 'controlled non-heart beating donation'.[108] In this format, those ventilated patients who still have brain activity but have no hope of recovery are essentially 'groomed' or prepared as potential donors *before* removal of intensive care facilities.[109] We doubt if any possible increase in donors is justified by the evident erosion of the principle that a person should not be used as a 'means to an end'—indeed, the legality of DCD is dictated by the 'best interests' of the donor.[110]

- Third, suitable patients who have died suddenly from whatever cause and who have not been ventilated can act as donors.[111] This process raises a number of practical questions which we discuss later—even so, it is reported that significant improvement in the supply of organs has been achieved through the use of so-called 'donation after circulatory death'.[112]

- Finally, recourse may be had to what is known as 'elective ventilation' with a view to use as a donor; this involves patients who, at the time of 'election', are not dead on any definition, but it introduces particular problems and we turn to it again below.

17.38   Several questions arise in relation to donation following circulatory death. First, *some* degree of organ deterioration during the warm anoxic period is inevitable; one must then ask if the use of a 'second-best' organ is better than no transplant, and, collaterally, whether it is an either ethically or legally appropriate procedure. As to the former, there is little doubt that transplantation is almost always the preferred treatment of end-stage

[105] This approach is adopted in the US Uniform Determination of Death Act discussed in Chapter 16.

[106] We doubt if such policy is any improvement insofar as the terms 'donation after circulatory death' (DCD) and 'donation after brain death' (DBD) serve to perpetuate the misconception that there are two types of *death*: M Bell, 'Non-heart beating donation: Old procurement strategy—New ethical problems' (2003) 29 J Med Ethics 176, and, N Zamperetti, R Bellomo, and C Ronco, 'Defining death in non-heart-beating organ donors' (2003) 29 J Med Ethics 182, which is, perhaps, more disturbing.

[107] A classification of non-heart beating donors was proposed in what became known as the 'Maastricht Workshop': G Koostra, J Daemon, and A Oomen, 'Categories of non-heart-beating donors' (1995) 27 Transplantation Proc 2893.

[108] It is increasingly and rightly held that such procedures are based, at best, on moral fictions: F Miller, R Truog, and D Brock, 'The dead donor rule: Can it withstand critical scrutiny?' (2010) 35 J Med Philosoph 299.

[109] E.g. by way of in vivo heparinisation designed to ensure the blood in the donated organ does not clot—a capacity that the living patient might well want to preserve. It might well be unlawful to do so: Department of Health, *Legal Issues Relevant to Non-heartbeating Organ Donation* (2009), at 6.14.

[110] See ibid. A major paper on the subject comes from Sweden: K Zeiler, E Furberg, et al., 'The ethics of non-heart beating donation: How new technology can change the ethical landscape' (2008) 34 J Med Ethics 526.

[111] G Kootstra, R Wijnen, et al., 'Twenty per cent more kidneys through a non-heart beating program' (1991) 23 Transplant Proc 910.

[112] Organ Donation Taskforce, n 87, para 2.3. The Report is, however, at pains to emphasise the need for confidence in the way death is diagnosed (at para 2.8).

renal failure so long as the organ has a reasonable chance of survival; nevertheless, a discussion of any likely shortcomings in the procedure would be an essential part of the consent process. As to the latter, the current attitude of transplant surgeons would be essential to the resolution of any dispute related to negligence; the *Bolam* principle (discussed in Chapter 5) would undoubtedly apply both as to disclosure of information and the operative technique.

17.39 More importantly, however, in returning to the original techniques which used unventilated, non-heart beating donors, we have come full circle; we are reanimating the 'race against time to save a life', and the pressures to reduce the warm anoxic time are even greater than they were now that we are fully aware of the advantages of the beating heart donation. Several techniques—among which, cold perfusion of the whole body or of the organs in situ are the most commonly used—are available to reduce the effects of anoxia but conditions often dictate that these are put to use without the consent of the appropriate person. Section 43 of the 2004 Act, which allows the institutional authorities to take steps to preserve parts of the body for use for transplantation, renders this lawful, but it limits non-consensual interference to the minimal and least invasive steps *necessary for the purpose*; subject to the 'good medical practice' test. Even so, this clearly allows for the use of procedures which are undeniably invasive.

17.40 Rapid response lies at the heart of controlled non-heart beating donation.[113] This being so, major significance attaches to what can be regarded as the true 'agonal period'—that is, the period between the beginning and the end of the somatic death process to which we have alluded in Chapter 16. In our view, in natural circumstances, this is limited by, on the former hand, irrevocable cardiorespiratory failure and, on the latter, irrevocable failure of cerebral cortical function. We are certainly not alone in our concern over both the ethics and practicalities of non-heart beating donation as currently practised,[114] with a particular challenge being its accommodation within the legal imperative that the management of an incapacitated patient must be directed to that patient's 'best interests'.[115] Nonetheless, it has long been a target treatment option,[116] and efforts have been made to justify it ethically.[117]

17.41 The 'agonal period' assumes equal practical importance in the even more controversial suggested extension of non-heart beating donation—that is, the practice of 'elective ventilation'.[118] Essentially, the concept involves extending the sources of donors so as to include the medical wards. Deeply comatose patients dying from strokes or other cerebral medical conditions are transferred to the intensive care unit and supported until brain stem death supervenes and organ retrieval can be arranged. The procedure was pioneered in

---

[113] For an outline of the technique, see S Ridley, S Bonner, et al., 'UK guidance for non-heart-beating donation' (2005) 95 Brit J Anaesthetics 592.

[114] For a consideration of the debate, see M Bell, 'Non-heart beating organ donation: Clinical process and fundamental issues' (2005) 94 Brit J Anaesthesia 474.

[115] An argument can be mounted that controlled non-heart beating donation can be justified within the wider definition of best interests articulated in *Re A (medical treatment: male sterilisation)* [2000] 1 FLR 549—J Coggon, M Brazier, et al., 'Best interests and potential organ donors' (2008) 336 BMJ 1346—but it is not very convincing. See also A McGee and B White, 'Is providing elective ventilation in the best interest of donors? (2013) 39 J Med Ethics 135.

[116] DH Consultation Document, *Organ and Tissue Transplantation: A Plan for the Future* (2001), para 48.

[117] P De Lora and A Blanco, 'Dignifying death and the morality of elective ventilation' (2013) 39 J Med Ethics 145; G Gillett, 'Honouring the donor: In death and in life' (2013) 39 J Med Ethics 149.

[118] It is to be noted that this source of organs was not considered by the Maastricht Workshop.

Exeter,[119] where a rigid protocol was drawn up before the work began. However, the procedure raised a number of legal and ethical difficulties additional to those in 'controlled' ventilation discussed earlier. Foremost among these is, perhaps, the role of the patient's relatives or representative. Section 4(1) of the 2004 Act allows for the appointment of a nominated representative to act *after* the appointer's death, and s 3(6) provides authority for qualified relatives to act on behalf of a *dead* person; we doubt if the Act adds anything to their existing powers in respect of *treatment* decisions. Removing a patient from the calm of a medical ward to the activity of the intensive care unit (ICU) can hardly be seen as being in her best medical interests,[120] and it is unlikely that the patient's relatives have any common law power to consent to the procedure. Even were this to be seen as no more than a legal quibble, the ethical question remains as to whether it is right to alter radically the mode of death, and, perhaps, to prolong the dying process, purely for the benefit of others. In the event, it was fairly rapidly agreed that the procedure involved an abuse of the 'best interests' test and that it was unlawful given the regulations in force,[121] and it has been discontinued since 1995.

17.42   Despite its obvious potential advantages to the organ harvest, we believe that elective ventilation carries a stigmatic impression that death is being presumed and it is certain that this form of organ husbandry must be very carefully controlled if a return to a public fear of 'pre-empted death' is to be avoided. Even so, this may well be a minority opinion in the face of the search for more donors, and there have been important developments in the field. First, the BMA believe that the subject should be reopened.[122] Second, the National Institute for Health and Care Excellence (NICE) appears to have changed its stance so as to include possible guidelines for changes to the role of intensive care facilities designed to facilitate practices similar to elective ventilation.[123]

17.43   It is clear that the issue of organ availability must extend from the purely numerical to considerations of organ quality, and in that context we are now faced with the concept of 'preconditioning organs'. In essence, positive efforts to ensure the highest quality of donated organs—or to extend the useable range of those which are of doubtful quality—can be pharmacologically or physically based, the latter involving some highly invasive techniques such as the induction of whole body hyperthermia. The procedure introduces a litany of ethical problems peculiar to itself and there is 'a clear need to establish an ethical consensus on the acceptability of such treatments and the responsibilities of those involved in their administration'.[124] For our part, we see preconditioning as a classic area in which it is vital to maintain the distinction between the dying patient and

---

[119] T Feest, H Riad, et al., 'Protocol for increasing organ donation after cerebrovascular deaths in a District General Hospital' (1990) 335 Lancet 1133. M Salih, I Harvey, et al., 'Potential availability of cadaver organs for transplantation' (1991) 302 BMJ 1053, suggested that, if one included potential medical donors aged 50–69, the protocol would have provided a harvest of 36 kidneys per million population annually, which approached the estimated need.

[120] Though a case can be made out for it if a wider interpretation of best interests—as expressed in *Re A (Medical treatment: male sterilisation)* [2000] 1 FLR 549—is adopted: J Hogan, M Brazier, et al., 'Best interests and potential organ donors' (2008) 336 BMJ 1346.

[121] NHS Executive, *Identification of Potential Donors of Organs for Transplantation* (1994) HSG (94) 41.

[122] See BMA, n 62, s 5. Interestingly, the BMA also appears willing to accept organs of 'higher risk' category of several types—such as the donor's age and previous health—in its search for an extended donor pool.

[123] P Watkinson, S McKechnie, et al., 'Actively delaying death to increase organ donation' (2012) 344 BMJ 9. The authors also stress the ethical 'trade-off' involved.

[124] S McNally, E Harrison, and S Wigmore, 'Ethical considerations in the application of preconditioning to solid organ transplantation' (2005) 31 J Med Ethics 631 at 633.

the potential donor—for possible combinations such as elective ventilation and preconditioning raise disturbing spectres.[125]

PROCUREMENT OF CADAVERIC ORGANS

Major Challenges

17.44   It remains trite to say that organ procurement is in an unsatisfactory state in the UK.
Some 50 per cent of cadaver organs derive from fit young adults who die as a result of
trauma,[126] and many thousands of patients eligible for transplantation are persistently
awaiting transplants of all types—and numbers will inevitably increase in the absence
of some radical action. This is, at base, because nearly half the potential donors fail to
become actual donors and it is this deficit in procurement which needs to be corrected. To
this end, there are essentially two avenues to explore: (1) law reform; and (2) professional
and public attitudinal change.[127]

17.45   As to the former, it is clear that a main source of cadaver organs under the current regime
results from a system of 'contracting in' to the transplant service, something which
requires a conscious effort that many healthy persons—particularly young persons—
find difficult to make.[128] It is widely suggested that the Acts could profitably be altered
so as to adopt a 'contracting out' position—that is, one in which consent to donation is
presumed unless it is specifically withheld.[129] Such a presumption operates in several
European countries, although with varying rigidity.[130] A power of veto is still sometimes
vested in the next of kin (Italy and Spain), the sensitivities of relatives are sometimes
deeply respected (Belgium), and sometimes held at a bare minimum (Austria, where the
cadaver kidney donor rate is among the highest of the leading 'transplant countries').[131]
Thus, a case for 'presumed consent' can be made out, and whether one adopts a 'hard
opt-out' or 'soft opt-out' system, it is everywhere recognised that the interests of the

---

[125] In essence, this encapsulates the concerns expressed by D Gardiner and R Sparrow, 'Not dead
yet: Controlled non-heart beating donation, consent and the dead donor rule' (2010) 19 Camb Q Healthcare
Ethics 17. The authors make the interesting point that any ante-mortem procedure which presupposes post-
mortem donation contravenes any dead donor rule.

[126] Many of the data quoted below have been extracted from BMA, n 62.

[127] We are not, here, considering a third option—mandatory choice—under which it would be compulsory, in some way, to express one's intention. In essence, this is the Dutch model (see n 128) on a compulsory
rather than a voluntary basis. We cannot see this as being either practical or acceptable in the UK at present.

[128] Even so, it does not seem to deter them in the Netherlands where what is possibly the most advanced
and comprehensive legislation is to be found. Under the Organ Donation (*Wet op de Orgaandonatie*) Act
1998, everyone over the age of 18 is invited to register with a central registry. The individual can register one
of four options as to post-mortem donation—a consent to donate any or specified organs, a refusal to donate,
delegation of consent to the next of kin, or delegation to a nominated person. The choice may be altered at
any time. Access to the Central Register is available on a 24/7 basis. Living donation of organs and bone marrow is also covered by the Act. The Act is fully acceptable on ethical grounds insofar as a coercive element is
avoided by providing an equal opportunity to consent or refuse.

[129] C Erin and J Harris, 'Presumed consent or contracting out' (1999) 25 J Med Ethics 365 maintain that
there is a distinction to be made between the two concepts—'presumed' consent, they say, is, in fact, no consent. For ourselves, we see the difference as little more than a semantic nuance—there is a faintly distasteful
sense of dominance in a 'presumption' which is avoided in a 'contract'—but the end result is the same and
we read the two phrases as synonymous.

[130] For a review of the European scene, see, inter alia, S Gevers, A Janssen, and R Friele, 'Consent systems
for post mortem donation of organs in Europe' (2004) 11 Euro J Health Law 126.

[131] B New et al., *A Question of Give and Take: Supply of Organs for Transplantation* (1994).

next of kin cannot be wholly ignored. In the UK, whatever framework might eventually prevail, it is near certain that organs would not be retrieved if the appropriate relatives objected.[132]

17.46   In this respect, the 2004 Act maintains the status quo insofar as s 3(6)(a) defines 'appropriate consent' to the use of the body for a purpose specified in Sch 1 in the case of an adult as the deceased's consent if a decision of his or hers was in force immediately before he or she died; but, in the absence of such a decision, consent by his or her appointed person or a qualified relative becomes 'appropriate'. This seems clear until we accept that, on purely 'social' grounds, very few, if any, transplant surgeons would act on the authority of a donor card against the wishes of the deceased's close relatives.[133] In short, although the 2004 Act is couched in terms of consent, it is, in practice, still strongly influenced by veto insofar as both the donor and the surviving relatives can frustrate the other's wish to donate—the former by way of statute, the latter by custom.[134] While it is possible to argue that this is acceptable, it is hard to see that it produces the best effects.[135]

17.47   Whether a firmer attitude would result in significantly more donations is uncertain. It has been suggested that a change from an explicit consent to a presumed consent model would result in a 25–30 per cent increase in donations rates.[136] But are such international studies comparing like with like? Spain, Croatia, and Portugal have the most successful programmes in Europe, but many factors other than the law—which still includes an opportunity for familial veto—are involved.[137] The UK has been wary of forcing through legislation which strikes at the heart of autonomy. Thus, the government established an Organ Donation Taskforce in 2006 which reported on improving the availability of organs,[138] and rejected the introduction of statutory presumed consent on the ground that there is insufficient evidence on which to embark on a major medico-ethical adventure.[139] Despite this,

---

[132] John Harris seems to be the major critic of the rule in the UK. See, in general, 'Law and regulation of retained organs: the ethical issues' (2002) 22 LS 527.

[133] Whether the consequent denial of a deceased's last autonomous act represents good medical ethical practice is another question. We have already noted that the Act is mainly concerned with disposal of body parts other than with transplantation.

[134] For the current approach, see HTA Code of Practice 2 (2014), deceased organ donation section, specifically para 102. The hierarchal dictate in the 2004 Act, s 27 applies only to consent.

[135] See S Harmon and A McMahon, n 86, and T Wilkinson, 'Individual and family consent to organ and tissue donation: Is the current position coherent?' (2005) 31 J Med Ethics 587.

[136] A Abadie and S Gay, 'The impact of presumed consent legislation on cadaveric organ donation: a cross country study' (2006) 25 J Hlth Econ 599. It is arguable, albeit involving an element of sophistry, that the introduction of an opt-out rule obviates the need to 'presume' consent: B Saunders, 'Opt-out organ donation without presumptions' (2012) 38 J Med Ethics 69. We believe that a contracting-out system is meaningless without, at the same time, 'presuming' consent.

[137] M Quigley, M Brazier, et al., 'The organs crisis and the Spanish model: Theoretical versus pragmatic considerations' (2008) 34 J Med Ethics 223. Indeed, it has been suggested that Spain demonstrates that it is possible to have the highest rates of organ donation *without* recourse to presumed consent: J Fabre, P Murphy, and R Matesanz,'Presumed consent: A distraction in the quest for increasing rates of organ donation' (2010) 341 BMJ c4973.

[138] Organ Donation Taskforce, n 87, which offered various recommendations, 11 of which the government accepted, the basic one being the establishment of a UK-wide Organ Donation Organisation. There is evidence that a 25 per cent increase had been achieved between 2007 and 2012: S Mayor, 'Elective ventilation in brain dead patients "is needed to increase organ donation" ' (2012) 344 BMJ 6.

[139] Organ Donation Taskforce, *Independent Report: The Potential Impact of an Opt-out System for Organ Donation in the UK* (2008). For a criticism of the Taskforce decision, see R Rieu, 'The potential impact of an opt-out system for organ donation in the UK' (2010) 36 J Med Ethics 534.

as noted, Wales has indeed recently introduced a soft opt-out system;[140] it has yet to be seen how it will perform as against the rest of the UK, which retains explicit consent-based systems. What is clear is that the law must evince clarity in its position one way or the other.[141]

17.48 Antipathy to or apathy in seeking the cooperation of relatives may be a further important factor in the shortfall in organ harvesting. This has led to a movement in favour of introducing a system of 'required request' for organ donation—a format which imposes a legal obligation on doctors to seek permission from the relatives for the removal of tissues from suitable dead persons. This is now the subject of federal law in the USA,[142] and was, in the 1980s, the subject of considerable debate in the UK. However, it undoubtedly compromises the clinical autonomy of the medical staff concerned, and may be superfluous given the role imposed on transplant coordinators and their teams. However, there is at least tentative evidence from Scotland that the public would accept change of the type envisaged—including some elements of financial gain,[143] but the difficulty remains that this is an area where one can manipulate the statistics—and choice of statistics—to support one's view.[144]

17.49 We are still left with the view that the interests of the donor and the recipient are so disproportionate as to render 'consent' by or on behalf of the former an invalid determinant of the outcome.[145] The maximum at stake in respect of the donor is a potential emotional disturbance for her relatives; for the recipient, the issue is one of life. As a result, it could be held to be morally impermissible to pit the one against the other.[146] The difficulty about such an argument is that it dictates a novel approach to possessory rights in the cadaver— essentially that, in some way, the dead body falls to the custody of the state.[147] While Harris has suggested that people presented with a fait accompli would soon get used to the idea, so contrary is it to the current doctrine of autonomy that it seems extremely unlikely. Moreover, we should not ignore the very real emotional—and religious—concern that many feel for the respect due to the remains of their loved ones.[148] Nonetheless, a strong case can be made for regarding cadaver organs as a community asset that should not be

---

[140] Human Transplantation (Wales) Act 2013. For a proactive analysis of such an Act, see L Cherkassky, 'Presumed consent to organ donation: Is the duty finally upon us?' (2010) 17 Euro J Hlth Law 149.

[141] For what can happen when there is a lack of clarity around consent and procurement, see *Elberte* v *Latvia* (2015) 61 EHRR 7, wherein a widow complained that Latvia had violated her Arts 3 and 8 European Convention on Human Rights (ECHR) rights by taking tissue from her deceased husband without her consent or knowledge. The European Court of Human Rights (ECtHR) found an interference with her Art 8 rights in the manner of the taking, which was arbitrary and for which the law did not satisfactorily protect against.

[142] US Public Law 99–509 9318.

[143] G Haddow, '"Because you're worth it": The taking and selling of transplantable organs' (2006) 32 J Med Ethics 324.

[144] F Bilgel, 'The impact of presumed consent laws and institutions on deceased organ donation' (2012) 13 Euro J Hlth Econ 29.

[145] And are supported in this by K O'Donovan and R Gilbar, 'The loved ones: Families, intimates and patient autonomy' (2003) 23 LS 332.

[146] H E Emson, 'It is immoral to require consent for cadaver organ donation' (2003) 29 J Med Ethics 125.

[147] This has been justified by seeing the human body—as opposed to the human spirit—as 'on extended loan from the biomass to the individual of which it forms a part': ibid, 125–6. Harris needs no such ecological support, rather seeing organ donation as no more than an example of a 'small but significant class of public goods, participation in which [should be] mandatory': J Harris, 'Organ procurement: Dead interests, living needs' (2003) 29 J Med Ethics 130.

[148] For very sensitive expressions of this side of the argument, see M Brazier, 'Retained organs: Ethics and humanity' (2002) 22 LS 550, and, more recently, S McGuinness and M Brazier, 'Respecting the living means respecting the dead too' (2008) 28 OJLS 297.

allowed to go to waste.[149] Obviously, finding the right balance is particularly challenging in the field of transplantation therapy.

Payment for Organs and Tissue

17.50 Any discussion on the availability of organs must take into account the possibility of their provision on a commercial basis. We have already discussed the ethics of donation for reward by the living. Financial reward for the donation of cadaver organs, however, has different roots, and is essentially directed to the enticement of the next of kin. Put this way, the proposition can be seen as appealing to the less-than-humane instincts of vulnerable persons and as something which the medical profession should avoid. And the possibility exists of commercialisation undermining the 'spiritual structure'[150] of transplantation medicine, which contributes to this phenomenon persisting as a matter of debate.

17.51 Opposition to direct payment for organs is deeply entrenched,[151] but manoeuvres to avoid or circumvent the inherent ethical restrictions are widely canvassed. These include wholesale supply to kidney banks rather than to individuals, standardised cash awards— or 'designated compensation' in various forms such as payment of donors' funeral expenses[152]—and an 'insurance policy' in the form of preferred status on the recipient waiting list, the latter which was, perhaps surprisingly, found to be the top-ranked option in a major survey in the USA.[153] Indeed, it has been suggested that those in the transplant field have wrongly adhered to certain moral values which are not necessarily accepted by those at the giving and receiving ends of the process.[154]

17.52 This is not to say that we approve of commercial traffic in human cadaveric organs—in fact, we find payment for the organs of the dead far less easy to justify than payment to the living donor. Assuming, however, that the process was strictly controlled—say, through the HTA—and supposing that it *succeeded* in providing life-saving treatment for those dying on the waiting list, we wonder if the public would not see reward for donation of cadaver organs in a less unfavourable light than appears at present.[155] There is, indeed,

---

[149] See also: C Hamer and M Rivlin, 'A stronger policy of organs from cadaveric donors: Some ethical considerations' (2003) 29 J Med Ethics 196. Harris's counter-argument is, however, very telling.

[150] See F Rapaport, 'Progress in organ procurement: The non-heart-beating cadaver and other issues in transplantation' (1991) 23 Transplant Proc 2699, for concerns which remain relevant.

[151] The Council of Europe recently released a statement reaffirming its abhorrence of organ sales: Council of Europe, *Statement by the Committee of Ministers on the prohibition of any form of commercialisation of human organs*, Adopted by the Committee of Ministers on 9 July 2014 at the 1205th meeting of the Ministers' Deputies.

[152] This was, in fact, the preferred option of the Nuffield Council working party chaired by Dame Strathern: Nuffield Council on Bioethics, *Human Bodies: Donation for Medicine and Research* (2011).

[153] D Kittur, M Hogan, et al., 'Incentives for organ donation?' (1991) 338 Lancet 1441. For a discussion of some options in a different context, see S Harmon, J Bai, and C Wang, 'Organ Transplantation in China and Beyond: Addressing the "Access Gap" ' (2010) 10 Medical Law International 191.

[154] T Peters, 'Life or death: The issue of payment for cadaveric organ donation' (1991) 265 J Amer Med Ass 1302. For criticism of his arguments, see E Pellegrino, 'Families' self-interest and the cadaver's organs: What price consent?' (1991) 265 J Amer Med Ass 1305. For support of payments for cadaveric organs from an unlikely source, see G Smith, 'Market and non-market mechanisms for procuring human and cadaveric organs: When the price is right' (1993) 1 Med Law Internat 17. The citations are old but are representative of the arguments that surrounded evolving policy.

[155] A suggestion that this might apply in some Commonwealth jurisdictions is to be found in W Potts, 'Increasing the supply of transplant organs by way of financial incentives' (2005) 31 Monash U L Rev 212.

evidence that the debate may be reopening in the altered environment of the twenty-first century—and we suggest that this might well be advantageous.[156]

Conditional Donation of Organs and Tissue

17.53 It is possible that the impersonality of donation as currently practised may exert a negative influence on a deceased's relatives—more organs might be donated if they were allowed more control of their intended use. Thus, the possibility exists that a form of conditional donation might succeed where failure is, consciously or subconsciously, due to the present requirement for open-ended consent. Discussion of this possibility was stifled by the fact that the first publicised offer was based on ethnic conditions—and racial discrimination is considered unacceptable in a modern pluralistic society.[157] The original panel set up by the government to report on the case rejected decision-making on the particularities of individual cases, and condemned all conditional donation as being contrary to the principles of altruism;[158] this remains established policy for transplantation programmes, but, just as there are many faces of discrimination, so are there also many measures of altruism. Conditional donation may have its difficulties and contradictions, but a blanket rejection of any motive to donate an organ other than indifference as to the outcome might well be perverse;[159] the resolution of the paradox seems to lie in a collateral resolution of the questions surrounding the ownership of body parts.[160] Certainly, it is not easy to understand the logic behind a policy whereby directed donation of organs from the living is actively promoted while its post-mortem counterpart is rejected out of hand.[161]

17.54 The matter has been re-addressed by a more recent government working party.[162] In brief, the obligatory conditions under which the transplant authorities *may consider* authorising a directed donation include:

- a consent to unconditional donation is extant;
- the parties are related either genetically, socially, or by way of friendship;
- the proposed recipient is in clinical need of a transplant and there are no persons registered in the urgent heart scheme or on the super-urgent liver list who would otherwise be eligible for the graft; and
- there is evidence, even if no more than the opinion of relatives, that the deceased would have wished to be a living donor.

---

[156] Is there, for instance, a moral distinction to be made between offering money and offering a tax-break? For discussion of this, see E Petersen and K Lippert-Rasmussen, 'Ethics, organ donation and tax: A proposal' (2012) 38 J Med Ethics 451. The latter might appeal to those who see cadaver organs as a part of the community heritage.

[157] But 'the burden of proof appears to rest with the state to justify limiting such choices'—D Price, *Human Tissue in Transplantation and Research* (2010) at 281.

[158] Department of Health, *An Investigation into Conditional Organ Donation* (2000).

[159] T Wilkinson, 'What's not wrong with conditional organ donation?' (2003) 29 J Med Ethics 163.

[160] A Cronin and D Price, 'Directed donation: Is the donor the owner?' (2008) 3 Clin Ethics 127. And, from the US, R Truog, 'Are organs personal property or a societal resource?' (2005) 5 Amer J Bioethics 14.

[161] See the remarkable 2008 case of Laura Ashworth discussed in detail by A Cronin and J Douglas, 'Directed and conditional deceased donor organ donations: Laws and misconceptions' (2010) 18 Med Law Rev 275. The authors also argue, tellingly, that deceased conditional organ donation is not unlawful under the Human Tissue Act 2004 but is a policy matter that has achieved legal status through usage. The situation is governed in Scotland by the Human Tissue (Scotland) Act 2006, s 49.

[162] Department of Health, *Requested Allocation of a Deceased Donor Organ* (2010).

It is difficult to see that this extremely restrictive protocol does much to solve the most pressing needs for reform. It will, however, be noted that unsatisfactory cases such as that of Laura Ashworth[163] would not *necessarily* occur today.

THE FETUS OR NEONATE DONOR

DONATIONS FOR INFANTS

17.55 Transplantation therapy in infancy is now a standard part of paediatric surgery. Suitable organs, such as the liver, may become available from other neonates suffering from fatal conditions; such opportunities are rare but no new issues are then involved because the infant is subject to specific and general conditions of the relevant Human Tissue Acts. This, however, is not always so in the case of the fetus who may be involved as an organ donor at maturity or as a cell donor at an early stage of development.

17.56 In the former circumstance, the fetal organs must be both mature and viable if they are to be used to good purpose. One potential source of mature organs is the stillbirth which, by definition, must be of more than 24 weeks' gestation.[164] Equally by definition, however, the stillbirth must neither have breathed nor shown any other sign of life once separated from its mother. It follows that its organs must have been anoxic for an uncertain, but almost certainly significant, time; the chances of their being viable in the sense of being transplantable are, therefore, very slight and, save in exceptional circumstances, the still-birth can be ignored as a possible source of *organs*.

17.57 It follows that the 'fetal' donor must be alive when born and we are, in fact, considering the neonate as a donor. Nonetheless, it is convenient to retain the term 'fetal donor' in order to distinguish him or her from the neonate that has been under treatment for a significant time. The 'live fetal' donor might derive from a therapeutic abortion—a possibility which is rendered more real by the Abortion Act 1967, as amended, which permits an abortion on the grounds of fetal abnormality without limit of gestational age, and absolves the doctor from liability under the Infant Life (Preservation) Act 1929 when terminating a pregnancy within the provisions of the 1967 Act. The use of a living abortus as a transplant donor would be constrained by the terms of the Polkinghorne Report, and is best regarded as an aspect of fetal research.[165] Ultimately, therefore, discussion of the fetal organ donor is limited in practice to that of the anencephalic fetus.

17.58 As the status of the decorticated neonate has been considered (Chapter 16), it need only be said here that maintenance treatment of the infant who exists only by virtue of a residual brain stem is, perhaps, the quintessential example of medical futility.[166] On the other hand, the anencephalic is, by existing standards, legally a 'creature in being' to whom the rules of homicide apply. Thus, the anencephalic neonate must be allowed a natural death which, save in exceptional circumstances, will occur within about one week.[167] Two major difficulties arise from this—first, the diagnosis of death, and, second,

---

[163] N 161.   [164] Still-Birth (Definition) Act 1992.   [165] For which see Chapter 20.

[166] The early US case, *In the matter of Baby K* 16 F 3d (4th Cir, 1994) remains a seminal illustration of the court's dilemmas when confronted with the equitable definition of 'futility'—cf, the very comparable UK case of *Baby B* (para 15.67).

[167] Paradoxically, an exception arose in the case of *Baby K*, who survived for over two years.

the unpalatable corollary that the *dead* neonate or abortus must be reanimated if it is to provide undamaged organs. As to the former, the Royal Colleges and their Faculties in the UK concluded that:

> ... organs for transplantation can be removed from anencephalic infants when two doctors who are not members of the transplant team agree that spontaneous respiration has ceased.[168]

17.59 On the face of things, this seems to be doing no more than restating a diagnostic test for death which has been, and still is, the norm—moreover, the test is equally applicable to fetuses who have been fatally brain damaged during delivery and who might, exceptionally, be considered as donors. More importantly, perhaps, it pre-empts suggestions that anencephaly per se should carry a presumption of death—for the surviving anencephalic neonate is in the same position as is the adult in the PVS.[169] It is, therefore, both unnecessary and impracticable to attempt to introduce a brain death standard. There is, however, a further practical difficulty in that fetal tissues, particularly the heart, are extremely sensitive to 'warm anoxia'—the best results from the small number of cases reported are said to have come from those infants who were placed on life support and the organs used as soon as possible without regard to the existence of brain stem activity.[170] The time required to satisfy the Royal Colleges' criterion of cessation of respiration may, therefore, dictate an unacceptable deterioration in the quality of the donor organs which, ideally, should be recovered from a 'beating heart' donor. But this practice depends, as we have seen, on the acceptance of 'brain stem death', and the transplant surgeon is left with a well-nigh insoluble and circular dilemma.

17.60 Attempts to redefine death in the anencephalic as a state of 'brain absence' or to regard such a neonate as 'not being a reasonable creature in being' seem to us to be examples of dubious semantic juggling; the same applies to the more extreme suggestion that the definition of death should be extended so as to include anencephalics as a group[171]—as McCullagh has observed:

> Classification as 'dead' will not cause an anencephalic who is breathing to cease doing so ... One would require also to accept the burial of a spontaneously breathing patient.[172]

The more honest approach is to accept that the legality and morality of anencephalic donations are matters for concern, and that it is probable that their eventual solution will be founded on strongly utilitarian rather than strict deontological principles. The implicit result of using the Royal Colleges' criteria is that anencephalic donation must involve some form of 'reanimation ventilation'. This inevitably introduces moral qualms—not the least being that the period of 'deanimation' will be unacceptably short—and, eventually, one has to ask whether the manifest invasion of normal ethical standards can be justified by the results.

[168] Working Party of the Conference of Medical Royal Colleges and their Faculties in the United Kingdom, *Report on Organ Transplantation in Neonates* (1988).
[169] See Chapter 16.
[170] The Medical Task Force on Anencephaly, 'The infant with anencephaly' (1990) 322 New Engl J Med 669.
[171] For review, see W May, 'Brain death: Anencephalics and aborted fetuses' (1990) 22 Transplant Proc 885.
[172] P McCullagh, *Brain Dead, Brain Absent, Brain Donors* (1993), p 168.

17.61   The very low numbers of potential neonate donors and the presumed poor quality of organs combined with low therapeutic success rates,[173] were all considered in what appears to be the only extant judicial consideration of the status of the anencephalic—at least in the anglophone jurisdictions.[174] T was born anencephalic, and, during her life of nine days, her parents sought to have her declared dead so that her organs could be used to save other lives. The circuit court judge held that she was not brain dead, but nevertheless gave permission for a kidney to be removed on the grounds that this was not harming her. This ruling was upheld in the District Court of Appeal, but, despite the fact that the baby was now dead, the Supreme Court of Florida accepted the case as one which 'raised a question of great public importance requiring immediate resolution'. Much of the Court's deliberation concerned the common and statute law of Florida, but questions of principle were also addressed.

17.62   Having established that T was legally alive at the relevant time, the parents' request that an additional common law standard of death should be applied to anencephalics was considered in the light of current technology. It was held that:

> We acknowledge the possibility that some infants' lives might be saved by using organs from anencephalics who do not meet the traditional definition of 'death' we affirm today. But weighed against this is the utter lack of consensus, and the questions about the overall utility of such organ donations. The scales clearly tip in favor of not extending the common law in this instance.[175]

17.63   Thus, the essential ethical problem is to decide whether the utilitarian advantages stemming from anencephalic organ donation are sufficient to offset the deontological doubts raised by the procedure. A 'cost–benefit' analysis inclines us to the view that the price is too high, but at least one recent study suggested that some 60 organs might be made available annually in the UK if this were practised, and so a reconsideration of current guidelines might be justified.[176] The question remains whether a woman can properly choose to carry an affected baby close to term purely to provide transplantable organs. Such a programme appears, at first sight, to be unethical on the ground that a human being is being used as a means. Yet, to prevent it could be seen as unreasonable paternalism. A veto not only *might* deprive potential recipients of life, but also strike a blow at a woman's right to control her body. A total ban on what may be a truly altruistic endeavour may be unjustified—but one wonders how many paediatric transplant surgeons would volunteer for a leading part in such a scenario.

DONATIONS FOR THE AGED

17.64   Before leaving the troubled (and troubling) waters of neonate donation, a few observations are warranted on fetal brain transplantation. Normal adult nerve cells cannot replicate, whereas fetal cells are actively growing and multiplying; theoretically, therefore, an implanted fetal nerve cell will grow and provide a source of important cellular metabolites that are often deficient in the aged. The use of fetal neural tissue for the

---

[173] See n 171, J Salaman, 'Anencephalic organ donors' (1989) 298 BMJ 622, and, for the US situation, D Shewmon, A Capron, et al., 'The use of anencephalic infants as organ sources' (1989) 261 J Amer Med Ass 1773.

[174] *Re TACP* 609 So 2d 588 (Fla, 1992).

[175] Ibid, at 595.

[176] E Charles, A Scales, and J Brierley, 'The potential for neonatal organ donation in a children's hospital' (2014) 99 ADC Fetal Neonatal Ed F225.

treatment of idiopathic Parkinsonism in the elderly—and its extension to the treatment of other degenerative diseases of the ageing brain—was once a burning issue. Much of the urgency has been dispelled with a moratorium on clinical trials. Moreover, enthusiasm for the procedure has been, to a large extent, diverted to the quest for stem cell therapy (for which, see Chapter 7). The procedure raises a number of legal and ethical problems which serve to illustrate the basis for the current hostility to the programme.

17.65 In contrast to fetal organs, fetal brain cells must be immature and are ideally harvested at 10–14 weeks' gestation. Thus, the first problem is that the process is inextricably linked to abortion. Effectively, then, anyone who is morally opposed to intrusive termination of pregnancy must also be opposed to fetal brain cell therapy. Second, it is obvious that the individual brain cells must be viable in themselves; can it then be said that the fetus is dead when subjected to surgery? True, a 10–14-week-old fetus is not viable and it follows that it is born dead, but it is still very difficult to assert that it is 'brain dead'. Third, we cannot overlook the revulsion with which most people view any form of tampering with the brain and, particularly, the idea of 'brain transplants'. As a consequence, the BMA's recommendation that nervous tissue should only be used for transplantation in the form of isolated neurones or tissue fragments should be endorsed.[177] Finally, there is some moral repugnance to the use of tissues from the very young to sustain the aged. This is unfair insofar as the aged are just as entitled to available treatment as any other group, but we must ensure that it is true treatment designed to ameliorate specific disease processes rather than old age itself; as is the case in xenotransplantation, it is important that we do not seek to foist the role of Mephistopheles upon the neurosurgeon.[178]

RECONSTRUCTIVE TRANSPLANTS

17.66 The concept of reconstructive or cosmetic transplantation in the form of limbs, or, at the extreme, facial transplants is now with us, but we doubt if there is, at present, sufficient practical need—or space—for major consideration of the topic. It will likely grow in importance as surgical technology advances, and it carries with it a number of novel ethical problems, so a few words are warranted. An organ, according to the *Concise Oxford English Dictionary*, is 'part of an organism that is typically self-contained and has a specific vital function'. It is, therefore, essentially mechanistic in function; in practice, it will almost always be invisible and its appearance will have no significance. The limbs, however, are not only visible, but also they have expressivist functions. The face additionally contributes heavily to the identity of the subject, and has significance not only for the individuals concerned but also for those in contact with them—and it is a significance which lives on indefinitely. The nature of the relationship between the donor, the recipient, and third parties is, therefore, not only wider but is also far more personal than it is in the case of organ donation.[179]

---

[177] Medical Ethics, 'Transplantation of fetal material' (1988) 296 BMJ 1410.

[178] For an excellent review of the agonies of a Research Review Committee, see A MacDonald, 'Foetal neuroendocrine transplantation for Parkinson's disease: An Institutional Review Board faces the ethical dilemma' (1990) 22 Transplant Proc 1030.

[179] See J Swindell, 'Facial allograft transplantation, personal identity and subjectivity' (2007) 33 J Med Ethics 449.

17.67 These considerations, including the viability of consent to an experimental procedure (Chapter 19) have been studied in depth from the medico-legal and ethical aspects by Freeman and Jaoudé,[180] who conclude that, while the problems for the recipient, particularly those of a psychological nature, have been well recognised, those besetting the donor's family and the disfigured community may have been underestimated. Others, however, believe that the more technical problems surrounding long-term immunosuppression are of greater importance.[181] For our part, we feel that there is insufficient evidence on which to base an opinion; even so, there is no doubt that the procedure is being utilised in the UK, the USA, and France, and we would therefore probably agree that, rather than considering why facial transplants cannot be justified, we should be seeking to justify why they should not be done.[182]

CONCLUSION

17.68 Logistical improvements apart, it is probable that, for the foreseeable future, UK transplantation policy will depend upon continuing and increasing public engagement. One still has to wonder at the basic reasons underlying the obdurate refusal of a significant proportion—currently some 6 per cent—of relatives to consent to the harvesting of organs even when the deceased is carrying a donor card. We suggest that misunderstanding of the modern concepts of death is probably the main factor, and it is probable that the increasing availability of dedicated transplant coordinators armed with a specific remit may provide the most effective corrective measure—it will, at the very least, ensure that more qualifying relatives are *asked* to consent. We also believe that the best strategy for counsellors lies in encouraging multiple organ donors. It is not easy to enthuse about a treatment whereby one family's joy at the donation is often necessarily balanced against another's tragedy, but the public's imagination might well be fired were it better appreciated that one regrettable death can salvage four or more lives. The suggestion in *A Plan for the Future* that coordinators should be encouraged to keep the donor family informed as to the outcome would do much to improve the sense of community involvement in what is, essentially, a community project.[183]

---

[180] M Freeman and P Jaoudé, 'Justifying surgery's last taboo: The ethics of face transplants' (2007) 33 J Med Ethics 76.

[181] P Butler, A Clarke, and S Hettiaratchy, 'Facial transplantation' (2005) 331 BMJ 1349.

[182] Ibid.

[183] We also believe that the community spirit would be fostered, and consent obtained more regularly, were hospitals to erect memorial screens in the form of 'rolls of honour' immortalising the names of post-mortem donors.

18

EUTHANASIA AND ASSISTANCE IN DYING

INTRODUCTION

18.01 Across successive editions of this book, assisted death and euthanasia have remained among the most hotly debated topics in the medico-legal curriculum, driven in large part by seemingly never-ending judicial and legislative activity. At the same time, they give rise to serious confusion which, in our view, can be laid at the door of definition. Whether it be by design or popular misconception, a pattern has developed that admits two definitions of euthanasia which are quite distinct. Thus, the *Oxford English Dictionary*'s definition is: 'a gentle and easy death, the bringing about of this, especially in the case of incurable and painful disease'.[1] Put this way, virtually any action or omission be it therapeutic or non-therapeutic, which uses 'assisted dying' as a means of relief from suffering, can be regarded as a form of euthanasia. The *Concise OED*, however, offers: 'the painless killing of a patient suffering from an incurable disease or in an irreversible coma' which, in introducing the dual concepts of intention and activity, clearly restricts the definition of euthanasia so as to correspond to what is popularly known as 'mercy killing'.[2] There are alternative specific descriptive terms for all other forms of 'assisted dying' and we believe that generalisations such as 'passive euthanasia' (see para 18.15) are, essentially, contradictions in terms which confuse the issue and which would be better discarded. We admit, however, that they are widely used and cannot be ignored.

18.02 We have already considered these principles in the context of the infant or young child; here it is proposed to discuss the subject only in relation to the adult patient. The reasons for dissociating the two are several. Unlike the infant, the adult patient may well be able to express his or her wishes as to the quality of his or her own life. Absent this, those

---

[1] See E Jackson and J Keown, *Debating Euthanasia* (2012) at 1. This is a most valuable modern source for the topic but the literature on moral status of euthanasia and of its legal implications is, of course, vast. A useful starting point is R Dworkin, *Life's Dominion: An Argument About Abortion and Euthanasia* (1993). The fundamental issue of the moral status of human life is considered by M A Warren, *Moral Status* (1997) and by J Finnis, 'A philosophical case against euthanasia' in J Keown (ed), *Euthanasia Examined* (1995) pp 23–35. See also, J McMahon, *The Ethics of Killing: Killing at the Margins of Life* (2002) and T E Quill and G E Miller, *Palliative Care and Ethics* (2014). Works concerned with specifically legal issues include: M Otlowski, *Voluntary Euthanasia and the Common Law* (2001) and H Biggs, *Euthanasia, Death with Dignity and the Law* (2001). John Keown is a consistent critic of the legalisation of euthanasia: see his *Euthanasia, Ethics and Public Policy: An Argument against Legalisation* (2002). For a cogent repudiation of our views, see L Doyal, 'The futility of opposing the legalisation of non-voluntary and voluntary euthanasia' in S A M McLean (ed), *First Do No Harm* (2006). For a specialist approach, see S Ost, 'Euthanasia and the defence of necessity: Advocating a more appropriate legal response' [2005] Crim LR 355.

[2] The use of the word 'patient' does not limit the actor to the subject's medical attendant.

responsible for the patient's management have a background of previous abilities and aspirations from which to measure the extent of any shortfall; clinical decisions can be based on history rather than on clairvoyance.

18.03   Antipathy to the premature termination of life can be based on fundamental and deeply held convictions which have a variety of different roots. Historically, prohibition against so doing have, most often, been expressed in religious terms, human life being seen as a gift over which we may have stewardship but no final control; the sanctity of life is, however, still accorded particular weight even in societies in which religious morality has been dethroned.[3] This is reflected in the human rights debate, where the right to life is embodied in Art 2 of the European Convention on Human Rights (ECHR). This provides that 'everyone's right to life shall be protected by law' and, more significantly in the present context, has been interpreted in the European courts as *not* including a right to death at one's choosing.[4] Perhaps more urgently, there is a strong public interest in protecting the interests of the vulnerable,[5] of whom those suffering from extreme disability or intense pain form a quintessential group. Most jurisdictions now admit that such persons can attempt to commit suicide without attracting the attention of the criminal law and do this on the ground that the right to self-determination is among the most fundamental of all human rights. Far fewer jurisdictions allow for lawful assistance to achieve this end. The door is thereby opened to a debate on whether some forms of assistance in achieving premature death might constitute morally acceptable practices.

A CLASSIFICATION OF ASSISTED DYING

18.04   It will be clear from the foregoing that we use the term assisted dying deliberately so as to emphasise that we regard euthanasia as a far narrower concept than is often implied in the use of the term. Nevertheless, it is still common usage to extend the boundaries of 'euthanasia' so as to include all forms of assisted dying and to formulate these in terms of the circumstance in which death occurs. Thus, on the one hand, 'euthanasia' can be considered from the patient's point of view and divided into voluntary, non-voluntary, and involuntary categories depending on whether the patient seeks death, is unable to express an opinion on the matter, or is ignored in the decision-making process. Alternatively, one can consider the status of the actor who helps to bring about death: 'Is his or her role in the process one of passivity or activity?'—or, put another way, 'Is death achieved by way of omission or of commission?' Terms like 'active voluntary euthanasia', therefore, identify the respective positions of the parties involved in assisted dying; in this particular example, the doctor is 'active' in the process and the patient is 'voluntary'—that is, compliant in the act. In this simplistic fashion, we can identify six classic different forms in which life might be terminated prematurely. Even so, we still have to feed in the ambience in which that might be done: the patient may be capax or incapax,[6] with or without prior expressed

---

[3] A Danyliv and C O'Neill, 'Attitudes towards legalising physician provided euthanasia in Britain: The role of religion over time' (2015) 128 Soc Sci and Med 52, doi: 10.1016/j.socscimed.2014.12.030.

[4] See *Pretty* v *UK* (2002) 35 EHRR 1; (2002) 66 BMLR 147 at 40.

[5] Now recognised in the Safeguarding Vulnerable Groups Act 2006. For a discussion of the developing notion of the 'vulnerable' autonomous person at common law, see G Laurie and J K Mason, 'Trust or contract: how far does the contemporary doctor–patient relationship protect and promote autonomy?' in P R Ferguson and G T Laurie (eds), *Inspiring a Medico-Legal Revolution: Essays in Honour of Sheila McLean* (2015) ch 5.

[6] On the interface between suicide, mental disorder and best interests, see G Richardson, 'Mental capacity in the shadow of suicide: what can the law do?' (2013) 9(1) Intl J Law in Context 87.

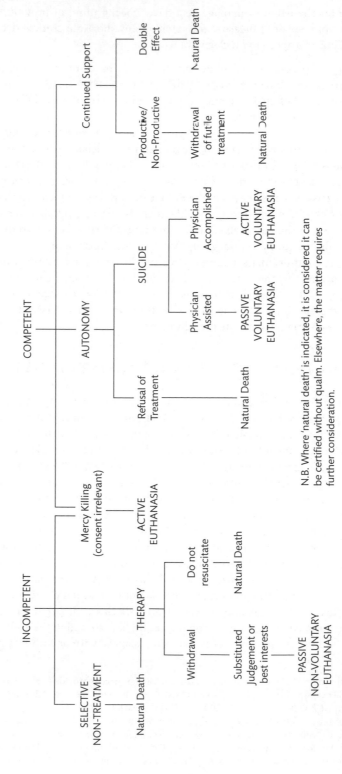

Figure 18.1 Ending life—A Suggested Outline

wishes; in addition, he or she may be terminally or incurably but non-fatally ill. Moreover, the role of the actor is not as simple as has been suggested—activity can be involved at any point on the spectrum that runs from counselling to perpetration. We have attempted to illustrate this mosaic in Figure 18.1, which also incorporates the alternative interpretative categories outlined earlier and to which we will return. It is basically structured on the degree of co-operation by the patient—in other words, on a consent model.[7]

HEALTH CARERS—A DISTINCT GROUP?

18.05 To act with the *intention* of ending a person's life in the absence of either a personal or proxy consent to do so ought, prima facie, to attract the attention of the criminal law. Clearly, any person in contact with the subject can be the actor in such circumstances and perhaps the most common examples are those of 'mercy killing' by relatives or, surprisingly often, professional carers. Motive, however, is irrelevant in the criminal jurisdictions of the United Kingdom (UK), and the English Court of Appeal[8] and the Supreme Court[9] have made it very clear that 'mercy killing' remains murder. This book, however, is concerned with *medical* law and ethics[10] and, for the greater part of the discussion, we confine ourselves to assisted death in the context of the doctor–patient relationship.[11] The isolation of health carers is conceptually important. Whereas prosecutory compassion towards the caring relative can only be justified as an example of legal pragmatism, a professional relationship[12] forecloses an emotional bond and, at the same time, opens up the whole field of what constitutes good medical practice. It also introduces us, at this early point, to the concept of the 'slippery slope'—that is, to the proposition that, once an exception to the moral norm is accepted, it will, inevitably, lead to further erosion of the modified norm and to the perpetuation of other manifestly unacceptable circumstances. This is an aspect of moral reasoning which has attracted much comment, and we return to it later in the more appropriate context of voluntary shortening of life. For the present, we do no more than remark that it is not difficult to see an incremental continuum between the typical cases of Dr Moor, who treated his dying patient by way of an easeful death, Dr Adams, who extended this to a number of elderly patients who were in pain but not dying, and Dr Shipman, who embellished the plot to include, perhaps, hundreds of such patients. It is this potential movement from the best to the worst of intentions which pervades the whole topic of assistance in dying

---

[7] A basic problem with our plan is that it is, in reality, cylindrical—i.e. decisions as to discontinuance of medical support can be made in respect of both competent and incompetent patients. It is, however, very difficult to illustrate this in a flat page illustration.

[8] *R v Inglis* [2011] 1 WLR 1110; (2010) 117 BMLR 65, CA: 'A belief that he or she was acting out of mercy... does not and cannot constitute any defence to the charge of murder' per Judge CJ at [50]. For critical commentary, D Thomas and A Ashworth, 'Sentencing: murder – mercy killing' (2011) 3 Crim LR 243.

[9] *Nicklinson v Ministry of Justice* [2014] UKSC 38; [2015] AC 657; [2014] 3 WLR 200, para 17.

[10] Though an interesting article questions whether end of life decisions are properly located in medical law: J Coggon, 'Assisted dying and the context of debate: "medical law" v "End-of-life law"' (2010) 18 Med L Rev 541.

[11] It is arguable that doctors are distinguished in law by reason of their group identity. The position of nurses is, in many ways, equivocal but we have no space for a digression—for which, see G Birchley, 'Angels of Mercy? The legal and professional implications of withdrawal of life sustaining treatment by nurses in England and Wales' (2012) 20 Med L Rev 337.

[12] It is to be noted that the fact that he or she was acting as a carer is one of the 16 factors which would favour the prosecution of a person suspected of assisting a suicide. See n 182 and associated text.

and, while terminating life in an involuntary context represents only a small part of the subject, it, nonetheless, tends to provide the focal point of the debate.

18.06   Criminal cases are rarely reported unless they demonstrate some specific point of law. Even so, it is surprising how few relevant trials of doctors[13] there have been—and this despite the number of them worldwide who claim to have taken part in some form of premature termination of life.[14] The great majority of the few who have come to trial in these circumstances have been accused of no more than using therapeutic drugs in overdose and all the relevant verdicts have indicated the reluctance of British juries to convict a medical practitioner of a serious crime when the charge arises from what they see as the doctor's considered medical judgement.

18.07   This attitude of the courts is typified in the case of Dr Moor. This GP, who admitted in the course of a public debate to having used painkillers to bring about the easy deaths of patients, was charged with the murder of a terminally ill patient into whom he was alleged to have injected a lethal dose of diamorphine. The judge left the jury in no doubt as to his own view of the matter, saying:

> You have heard that this defendant is a man of excellent character, not just in the sense that he has no previous convictions but how witnesses have spoken of his many admirable qualities. You may consider it a great irony that a doctor who goes out of his way to care for [the deceased] ends up facing the charge that he does.[15]

The jury responded by acquitting Dr Moor within an hour.

18.08   Dr Adams' far earlier, and seminal, case[16] was different because the patient involved was one amongst several of his who were incurably but not terminally ill; it is thought that he treated her with increasing doses of opiates, and, following her death, he was tried for murder. He was nonetheless acquitted. In the course of his summing up, Devlin J said: 'The doctor is entitled to relieve pain and suffering even if the measures he takes may incidentally shorten life', which is a clear direction leaving little in the way of doubt for the jury. The key word here, however, is 'incidental', meaning, most obviously, 'non-intentional'. It is, also, an early example of the invocation of the ethical doctrine of double effect, and which has been reiterated mostly recently by the Supreme Court in *Nicklinson* v *Ministry of Justice*.[17] We discuss both the concept and the case at paras 18.59 ff.

18.09   This brings us to the case of Dr Martin which can be seen as a bridge between Dr Moor and Dr Shipman. Dr Martin was tried in 2005 for the murder of three patients whose lives he admitted having shortened by excessive doses of analgesics.[18] He was acquitted but was struck off the medical register in 2010 for 'despicable and dangerous conduct' in relation

---

[13]   We are being deliberately selective here. Other health care professionals, such as care home nurses, may be much more akin to close relatives.

[14]   And not only in the UK. See, e.g., C Zinn, who reported that 'A third of surgeons in New South Wales admit to euthanasia' (2001) 323 BMJ 1268. For a more recent account of Australian practice and a comparative analysis, see B White and L Willmott, *How Should Australia Regulate Voluntary Euthanasia and Assisted Suicide?* (2012).

[15]   C Dyer, 'British GP cleared of murder charge' (1999) 318 BMJ 1306. For discussion, see R Gillon and L Doyal, 'When doctors might kill their patients' (1999) 318 BMJ 1431.

[16]   Unreported, see H Palmer, 'Dr Adams' trial for murder' [1957] Crim LR 365.

[17]   N 9 above, para 18: '… a doctor commits no offence when treating a patient in a way which hastens death, if the purpose of the treatment is to relieve pain and suffering (the so-called "double effect")'.

[18]   The case seems to be totally unreported save by way of press interviews: N Bunyan, 'Murder case GP: I helped patients die' (2010) *Daily Telegraph*, 18 June.

to 18 patients. The paucity of information leaves various unanswered questions: was he pre-empting the future by pleading euthanasia—by way of necessity—as a defence to murder, or was he relying on an *Adams*-type defence?

18.10   Finally, and at the extreme end of this particular spectrum, it is trite to remark that involuntary euthanasia performed by a doctor leaves him or her as guilty of unlawful killing as anyone else who deliberately takes human life. Dr Shipman, who was—and, it is to be hoped, will always be—the most infamous contemporary example, was convicted in 2000 of the murder of 15 patients—an example of serial killing which has cast a long shadow over the medical profession in the UK.[19] He was, of course, quite different from other doctors who may have risked prosecution to end what they saw as the unbearable suffering of terminally ill patients; he killed patients for reasons which are not altogether apparent but which may have been connected with a pathological desire to exercise control over life and death. The case seriously dented trust in the medical profession and has been widely used as an argument against lifting the current strict prohibitions on the taking of life.[20]

18.11   The critical distinction to be derived from this series of cases lies in whether it is possible to 'medicalise' the deaths. At one end, we have dying patients undergoing treatment for serious pain; as we will see later, we can then see death as a concomitant of necessary pain relief and the courts have been consistently prepared to apply the doctrine of necessity in such circumstances.[21] Dr Shipman's patients, however, were in no more discomfort than merited a visit to the doctor's surgery; medicalisation of their deaths by way of an overdose of opiates was impossible and the jury had no difficulty in regarding the case as one of multiple murder. The importance of the distinction will be re-examined in later sections of the chapter.

NON-VOLUNTARY TERMINATION OF LIFE

18.12   A person who is incapacitated by virtue either of status or of disability is, nevertheless, indisputably a creature in being. It follows that anything that has been said in respect of involuntary termination of life and the criminal law applies when the subject is incapacitated. Almost by definition, the incapax who is considered a candidate for an easeful passing will be under medical care and, given their increasing ability to maintain life in adverse conditions, doctors will be increasingly forced into considering death as a desirable therapeutic option. We have addressed this dilemma to a degree under the heading of 'futility' and with particular reference to the case of Tony Bland. It was, however, repeatedly stressed by the courts that *Bland*[22] was not concerned with euthanasia. In the

---

[19] The Shipman Inquiry, chaired by Dame Janet Smith, resulted in a series of reports culminating in the Final Report (27 January, 2005), all available at: http://webarchive.nationalarchives.gov.uk/20090808154959; http://www.the-shipman-inquiry.org.uk/home.asp. The final number of patients killed by Dr Shipman will probably never be known. The Inquiry, however, was exceptionally far ranging and addressed not only operational matters that may have contributed to the tragedy but also included inquiry into death and cremation certification, the use and monitoring of controlled drugs, single-practitioner practices, and professional monitoring and disciplinary systems.

[20] H G Kinnell, 'Serial homicide by doctors: Shipman in perspective' (2000) 321 BMJ 1594. It is to be noted that Lady Smith (n 23) did not consider that proposed safeguards went far enough: C Dyer, 'Reform of death certificate system doesn't go far enough, says judge' (2009) 338 BMJ 435.

[21] Although Dr Adams' case was by no means clear-cut. Lord Devlin later voiced serious doubts as to the result: P Devlin, *Easing the Passing: The Trial of Dr Bodkin Adams* (1986).

[22] *Airedale NHS Trust v Bland* [1993] AC 789, confirmed by the Supreme Court in *Nicklinson* v *Ministry of Justice*, n 9 above, paras 18, 22–6.

present context, we have, therefore, to revisit that scenario from what is almost the opposite direction—that is, on the proposition that death is in the patient's best interests and can, consequently, be pursued on the ground of good medical practice.

18.13 *Bland*, however, also tells us forcibly that, currently, it is unlawful to kill a person by means of a positive action whatever may be one's intentions. It follows that termination of the life of an incapacitated patient can only be lawful if it is, first, achieved by way of a failure to act and, second, that this can be justified on a 'best interests' basis.[23] What one regards as euthanasia and what as medical care of the dying depends not only on whether one is speaking in legal, moral, or medical terms but also on personal preference or prejudice. As to the latter, we have tended to use the death certificate as our benchmark—or, put simply, if death can be certified as being due to natural causes with a clear conscience, it is not euthanasia. Even so, recognisable sub-categories exist even within this limited framework. Thus, for example, treatment can be withdrawn, or not undertaken, either because it is non-productive or because its continuance results in an unacceptable quality of life.[24]

18.14 The former, as discussed in Chapter 15, is an undisputed matter of *medical* futility; the latter has, also, been addressed with particular reference to *Bland*. However, although its specificity has been eroded over the years, *Bland* remains a very particular case which cannot be extrapolated without good reason. It does, however, help in the present context by way of the obiter remarks of Lord Keith:

> In general it would not be lawful for a medical practitioner who assumed responsibility for the care of an unconscious patient simply to give up treatment in circumstances where continuance of it would confer some benefit on the patient. On the other hand, a medical practitioner is under no duty to treat such a patient where a large body of informed and responsible medical opinion is to the effect that no benefit at all would be conferred by continuance.[25]

Clearly, therefore, the same will apply, though perhaps in greater degree, when the patient's quality of life is so bad that he or she is positively *disadvantaged* by its preservation.[26] In either case, we are in the realm of what is, in our view unhelpfully, often referred to as passive non-voluntary euthanasia.

18.15 We have already remarked on how blurred are the boundaries of 'passive euthanasia' and on the subjective nature of its definition. In our view, 'pure' passive euthanasia should be limited as a term to those relatively rare management decisions involving non-voluntary patients who have retained some cortical activity but are unable to make competent decisions and who, at the same time, are not known to have previously expressed

---

[23] We return to the more general discussion of the moral distinction between activity and passivity at para 18.42.

[24] For a critical examination of the problems of classification of assisted death, see S A M McLean and S J Elliston, 'Death, decision making and the law' [2004] JR 265. And, more recently, A McGee, 'Ending the life of the act/omission dispute: causation in withholding and withdrawing life-sustaining measures' (2011) 31 LS 467.

[25] [1993] 1 All ER 821 at 890; (1992) 12 BMLR 64 at 137.

[26] It is to be noted that a failure to provide treatment in the patient's best interests does not contravene the ECHR: *An NHS Trust v D* [2000] 2 FLR 677; (2000) 55 BMLR 19; *NHS Trust A v M, NHS Trust B v H* [2001] Fam 348; (2001) 58 BMLR 87.

an unequivocal preference as to treatment in the prevailing conditions.[27] Possibly the only apposite example prior to the enactment of the Mental Capacity Act 2005 lies in *W Healthcare NHS Trust* v *H*, which we have discussed at para 15.113. The principles and difficulties encountered in the management of such cases post the 2005 Act have now been considered by the Supreme Court in *Aintree University Hospitals NHS Foundation Trust* v *James and Others*[28] where, again in the absence of better subjective evidence, the importance of preserving life was regarded as the defining premise for all management of such patients. The legal question is not whether it would be lawful to withhold treatment but whether it would be in the patient's best interests to provide it. If it is not, then it is a priori unlawful. The 'balance sheet' approach to the assessment of best interests[29] is now an integral element of the UK jurisdiction and serves as a basis for the use of so-called 'passive non-voluntary euthanasia'.

ELECTIVE NON-TREATMENT

18.16 While only a very small number of physicians would actively strive to end the life of a patient, elective non-treatment is practised fairly widely. The question of whether this constitutes good medical practice has tended to focus on the distinction between what were, at one time, known as ordinary and extraordinary treatments[30] and there is a general consensus, now established in both legal and medical opinion, that the doctor need not resort to heroic methods to prolong the life—or, perhaps better, to prolong the dying—of his or her patient. The ordinary/extraordinary distinction is, however, intensely subjective in the making and we would prefer to contrast medically productive and non-productive treatments—the test being whether a particular treatment is doing the *condition* any good. Factors such as the physical and psychological pain involved in the treatment, its claim on scarce resources, and the general prospects for the patient and his or her family may all be taken into account in deciding whether a treatment is productive.[31] Clearly, then, non-productivity and medical futility have much in common as treatment standards and, as we have already discussed in Chapter 15, the arguments for and against their adoption are very similar. Here we focus on particular instances of decision-making which remain ethically and legally controversial or which illustrate some of the reasoning which brings them within acceptable parameters.

---

[27] We draw the attention of the reader at this juncture to the case of Mr Burke, discussed at para 15.74. Here the Court of Appeal made it clear that it would not be lawful to withdraw feeding and hydration from a patient while he or she remained conscious and competent and when he or she had previously expressed a wish that it be provided. Once capacity is permanently lost, however, existing authority suggests it would be lawful to remove such care, notwithstanding the prior wishes of the patient.

[28] [2013] UKSC 67; [2014] AC 591.

[29] See *An NHS Trust* v *MB* [2006] 2 FLR 319 and discussion of benefits and burdens in *Aintree*, n 28 above.

[30] The principle has been widely attributed to the directive issued by Pope Pius XII in (1957) 49 Acta Apostolicae Sedis 1027:

Man has a right and a duty in case of severe illness to take the necessary steps to preserve life and health. That duty ... devolves from charity as ordained by the Creator, from social justice and even from strict law. But he is obliged at all times to employ only ordinary means ... that is to say those means which do not impose an extraordinary burden on himself or others.

[31] Considerations of cost and of the distribution of other resources cannot be ignored here, although they must be secondary to the well-being and the dignity of the patient. At least two speeches in *Bland* confirmed that resources might be a legitimate concern of the clinician: [1993] 1 All ER 821 at 879, 893; (1992) 12 BMLR 64 at 125, 140, per Lord Browne-Wilkinson and Lord Mustill.

Disconnecting the Ventilator

18.17 Discontinuance of ventilation is such a classic example of elective non-treatment that, although the principles remain unaffected in this situation, we feel it is helpful to consider it as a separate entity. We introduce the discussion by reference to a New Zealand case which we still regard as being most usefully illustrative.[32] *Auckland Area Health Board* concerned a patient, L, who was suffering from a progressive neurological disease (for which, see para 18.69) and was incapable of expressing his wishes. His existence depended on artificial ventilation and the question put to the High Court was in the rather stark terms: 'Would the doctors' action in withdrawing ventilator support make them guilty of homicide?'[33] Thomas J approached this issue by asking whether a doctor is obliged to continue treatment which has no therapeutic or medical benefit notwithstanding that the withdrawal of the treatment may result in the clinical death of the patient. He commented that all natural life has ceased in such a case; it was the *manifestations* of life which were maintained artificially and which were brought to an end by the doctors' intervention. He proceeded on the twin principles of humanity and common sense and concluded that life support provided *only* for the purpose of deferring certain death could not be regarded as a necessity of life; moreover, doctors have a lawful excuse to discontinue treatment when there is no medical justification for continuing that medical assistance. Withdrawal of treatment would not be unlawful if it was carried out within the accepted confines of 'good medical practice'—or adhering to a procedure which provided safeguards against the possibility of individual error. Within this scenario, withdrawal of life support would not be the cause of death *as a matter of* law—and this would concur with the common-sense perception.

18.18 Thomas J's admirable analysis attracted particularly favourable comment in the House of Lords in *Bland*. In our view it is important from the perspective of medical jurisprudence in that the judge was able to medicalise the dilemma fully and thus avoid what is, in our view, the near sophistry of the 'best interests' test. More importantly, perhaps, it is a self-supporting analysis which does not depend upon the *Bolam* test—a stratagem employed in *Bland* which we have always regarded as misplaced.

18.19 On a global scale, *Auckland Area Health Board* was, to an extent, treading old ground. It was, as we have noted, concerned with the exclusion of criminality and this had been settled many years before in the USA in the historic case of *Quinlan*.[34] So far as the UK is concerned, this matter was disposed of in the closely related Scottish case of *Finlayson*[35] and its English counterpart of *Malcherek*,[36] both of which have been discussed in relation to causation in Chapter 16. Although *Finlayson* was not cited in *Malcherek*, the two decisions have remarkable similarities in that, in excluding criminality, the judges, first, relied on the concept of good medical practice and, second, declined to define death. This latter omission might, at first glance, be interpreted as vacillation on the part of the law; in fact, it reinforces the former principle in leaving the *clinical* decision firmly in the hands of the clinician.[37]

---

[32] *Auckland Area Health Board v A-G* [1993] 1 NZLR 235; [1993] 4 Med LR 239.

[33] Crimes Act 1961, ss 151(1) and 164, NZ. A Death with Dignity Bill was narrowly defeated in 2003.

[34] *Re Quinlan* 355 A 2d 664 (NJ, 1976).   [35] *Finlayson v HM Advocate* 1978 SLT (Notes) 60.

[36] *R v Malcherek* [1981] 2 All ER 422; [1981] 1 WLR 690, CA (*R v Steel* was heard simultaneously on appeal).

[37] For a helpful clinical discussion of the interplay of the principles involved, see S H Chotirmall et al., 'Extubation versus tacheostomy in withdrawal of treatment—ethical, clinical, and legal perspectives' (2010) 25 J Crit Care 360.e1.

18.20 These principles would apply in the civil courts[38] but we would now have to feed in the effects of the Mental Capacity Act 2005[39] and the Human Rights Act 1998. There is no reason why the latter should affect the common law approach. The relevant 'right' here lies in not having one's life taken away other than in 'super-*Wednesbury*'[40] terms of reasonableness—and these will be satisfied by 'good medical practice'.[41]

18.21 It is to be noted, in parentheses, that the courts have been anxious to ensure that the cause of death be attributed to natural disease in all these cases of non-voluntary assistance in dying.[42] We suggest, and have argued already in respect of the permanent vegetative state (PVS),[43] that the cause of death following withdrawal of any form of life support should depend on whether the support was removed before or after brain stem death has occurred. If the person is dead at that time, the cause of death is clearly the original anoxic or other insult sustained by the brain. When, however, a treatment is discontinued solely by reason of its futility, there is nothing to be lost—and much to be gained by way of intellectual honesty—in attributing death, correctly, to 'Lawful withdrawal of life support systems which were necessitated by [the disease]'; currently, however, there is no precedent for such a practice.

18.22 It is almost trite to say that the ethical difficulties concerning the removal of mechanical respiratory support from those who can no longer benefit originate from the *provision* of that support—the primary decision is more important than those which follow as a consequence of that action.[44] The vast majority, perhaps all, of patients with severe brain damage must be offered intensive care when they are admitted to hospital. The doctor presented with such an emergency has virtually no choice of initiative action. He is dealing with a suddenly disabled patient and he must provide support because he cannot know whether an individual patient is going to respond either physically or emotionally to heroic treatment. Recourse to the ventilator is automatic even if for no purposes other than facilitating diagnosis and assessment; in such circumstances there is no legal or ethical objection to regarding the ventilator as merely a part of the diagnostic machinery nor to dispensing with it once a diagnosis of irretrievable functional brain loss has been made. But a decision to *treat*—as opposed to assess—is within the doctor's clinical choice and carries with it the inescapable consequence that, at some time and for some reason, the treatment must be withdrawn. The critical point for applying the productive/non-productive ethical test is, as we have already indicated, at the beginning. Can the doctor, then, decide to or accede to a later request to remove support?

18.23 Other than considerations of resource availability[45]—for which see Chapter 11—any such decisions will be based on clinical or technical grounds alone. Even so, the responsible

---

[38] And note that 'it is for the court [not the doctor], ultimately, to judge in a case of this sort what is in best interests of the patient'—see *An NHS Trust v A (sub nom An NHS Trust v X)* [2005] EWCA 1145 per Waller LJ at 83. For an infant case illustrating the continuum of thinking, see *NHS Trust v Baby X* (2012) 127 BMLR 188.

[39] For which, see Chapters 12 and 13.

[40] *R v Ministry of Defence, ex p Smith* [1996] QB 517; [1996] 1 All ER 257.

[41] And, in the event of disagreement with, say, relatives, the responsible NHS Trust would almost certainly seek the assistance of the Court of Protection.

[42] It is notable that this is embodied in the law of Washington State Death with Dignity Act 2009, s 4(2); there is no such stipulation in the corresponding Act, s 127.815§3.01(2)—see paras 18.95 ff).

[43] See Chapter 15.

[44] For pioneer views, see I M Kennedy, 'Switching off life support machines: the legal implications' [1977] Crim LR 443.

[45] There are now sufficient obiter statements from a variety of English cases to allow one to say with confidence that the courts will be sympathetic to resource-based management arguments. See Balcombe LJ in

doctor must be able to counter the proposition that his or her action represents euthanasia and is, consequently, unlawful.[46] To this end, it has been suggested that switching off a mechanical support is an omission and is, therefore, both morally and legally acceptable. In fact, this is, in our opinion, untenable in practical terms. It would be an omission not to switch *on* the emergency supply in the event of a central power failure; that is easily distinguished from a deliberate, premeditated decision to remove the power—one has to *act* to turn off the television and the same must apply to the respirator. Kennedy[47] has pointed out that a well-wisher disconnecting a conscious patient from a respirator would be guilty of homicide or perhaps of abetting suicide—and, in the USA, Mr Linares was, at least, brought before a grand jury for so doing.[48] The difference adduced by Lord Goff in *Bland*[49] was that, whereas the doctor was allowing the patient to die from his pre-existing condition, the interloper was actively intervening to stop the doctor from prolonging the patient's life. *Bland*, in fact, very nearly solves the problem—albeit indirectly. Thus, if, as was decided, the withdrawal of nasogastric feeding is an omission, it is but a short step to conclude that withdrawal of respiratory support is, likewise, an omission—and Lord Browne-Wilkinson, for one, was happy to see them as similar. The analogy admittedly involves some elasticity of conscience. So, while Lord Browne-Wilkinson further concluded that a nasogastric tube did nothing, of itself, to sustain life and that its removal could not be said to cause death, it is difficult to say the same of the ventilator of which the air-bag is an integral part. The main practical difference between the two must lie in the immediacy and the certainty of death when the respirator is turned off; the care team is, effectively, being asked to suffocate their patient.[50]

18.24 The acid test for the removal of a patient from intensive care rests on a simple alternative—either he is dead or he is not dead. Given that brain stem death has been diagnosed,[51] continued treatment is no more than treatment of a corpse; it would be positively immoral to continue other than to serve the purpose of beating heart organ donation or, conceivably, of post-mortem parturition (for which, see para 16.28 et seq).[52] It may also be proper to discontinue artificial ventilation even if death is not diagnosed. The closely allied considerations of productive/non-productive treatment and of 'death with dignity', untrammelled by tubes and wires, may be sufficient to justify withdrawal of treatment on moral grounds. The doctor may, however, rely on the purely clinical consideration that the treatment is doing, and will do, no good. One of two things may follow withdrawal of ventilator support—the patient will either continue to breathe of his own accord or he will go into respiratory failure. In the former case, the patient has reverted to a state of irreversible coma, the management of which has already been discussed. No moral or legal problem arises in the latter situation; the outcome will have resulted from a clinical decision taken in good faith and after due deliberation based on a productive/non-productive treatment test. Absent an advance directive—for which see para 18.49—consent of the

Re J (a minor) (wardship: medical treatment) [1993] Fam 15 at 30; (1992) 9 BMLR 10 at 20, discussed previously at para 15.28.

[46] For recent support of the distinction, see A McGhee, 'Me and my body: The relevance of the distinction for the difference between withdrawing life support and euthanasia' (2011) 39 J Law Med Ethics 671.

[47] N 44.

[48] 'Grand Jury Rejects Murder Count: Teary Father Not Charged in Death of Comatose Boy', *Los Angeles Times*, 19 May 1989.

[49] [1993] 1 All ER 821 at 867–8; (1992) 12 BMLR 64 at 113–14.

[50] It is very difficult to avoid the corollary—that Bland's carers were being asked to starve him to death. The answer lies in the immediacy of an asphyxial death.

[51] For full discussion see Chapter 16.   [52] *Re A* [1992] 3 Med LR 303.

next of kin, or review by the Court of Protection, would, as we have already discussed, be desirable but not essential in confirming its lawfulness. Lawfulness is, rather, determined by the benchmark of best interests: is it in the patient's best interests to continue with any particular intervention? If it is not, it must be withdrawn because continuation itself in such cases becomes illegal.[53] This consideration must therefore run the entire course of the management of patients in such extreme circumstances.

Artificial Feeding and Hydration as an Aspect of Non-treatment

18.25 Artificial feeding and hydration has been confirmed in law to be part of treatment as determined in *Bland,* discussed in Chapter 15. The *definition* of artificial nutrition and hydration (ANH)—was not, however, addressed in either *Bland* or *Re R (adult: medical treatment)*[54]—or in any of the other relevant British cases.[55] As Strong[56] pointed out many years ago, when we speak of providing nourishment, we are referring to a continuum that runs from natural breastfeeding through feeding by mouth to seriously invasive procedures which may even entail surgical operation. Once discomfort and danger are introduced, so too is balancing the advantages and disadvantages—or, in practice, applying a productive/non-productive treatment test.[57] The fundamental question is, therefore, at what *stage* does the act of feeding become medical treatment?

18.26 Increasing invasiveness carries increasing risk—it, therefore, seems logical to classify anything which involves invasion as medical treatment. At the other end of the scale, it is difficult to conceive of purely natural feeding as treatment and, so far as we are aware, no court in either the Commonwealth or the USA has ever suggested that normal feeding could properly be withheld on clinical grounds from someone able to accept it. Nonetheless, even this distinction is over-simplistic. At one extreme, spoon-feeding of a reluctant ament can be regarded as invasive and, accordingly, as medical treatment; at the other, the instillation of fluid through a tube can be seen as simple care involving no risk—but it can be done only as a *result* of invasion. An all-embracing definitional solution seems impossible. We can only look to a minimum standard and suggest that any form of feeding which requires some *medical* training and expertise can be considered medical treatment and, accordingly, may properly be subject to elective provision. By contrast, the provision of food and water by normal means may be seen as no more, or less, than an example of kindness and humanity.[58]

The 'Do Not Attempt Resuscitation' Order

18.27 There can be no doubt that it is often undesirable, effectively, to prolong the process of dying—particularly as it so often involves the use of extraordinary treatment as described earlier. This, then, is the underlying principle of the 'do not attempt resuscitation' (or

---

[53] *Aintree,* n 28 above.   [54] [1996] 2 FLR 99; (1996) 7 Med L Rev 401.

[55] The Supreme Court of Victoria held in *Gardner; re BWV* [2003] VSC 173 that artificial nutrition and hydration by means of a percutaneous endoscopic gastrostomy (PEG) was a 'medical procedure' because it depends on 'protocols, skills and care which draw from, and depend upon, medical knowledge'; the practice itself, then, was deemed 'medical treatment' for the purposes of the Medical Treatment Act 1988. The Supreme Court of Canada in *Cuthbertson* v *Rasouli* [2013] SCC 53 held that *withdrawal* of care, including ANH, was also 'treatment' under the Ontario Health Care Consent Act 1996 such that it required consent from the patient or proxy decision-maker.

[56] C Strong, 'Can fluids and electrolytes be "extraordinary treatment"?' (1981) 7 J Med Ethics 83.

[57] The complication rate of intravenous hyperalimentation may approach 50 per cent.

[58] *Airedale NHS Trust* v *Bland* [1993] 1 All ER 821 at 856; (1992) 12 BMLR 64 at 101, per Hoffmann LJ.

DNAR) order[59] whereby a pre-emptive decision is taken not to attempt resuscitation of a moribund patient in the event of cardio-pulmonary collapse.[60] The problem—which, essentially, involves a specific form of elective non-treatment, with or without the backing of an advance directive—is to establish an acceptable general policy in an area that is so susceptible to subjective judgements and the DNAR order has been the subject of a vast literature.[61] The scale of the 'problem' is far from trivial. It has been estimated that:

> 68% of the population die in hospital and 80% of these die with DNACPR notices in place ... [therefore] in relation to more than 50% of the population, a decision is taken in advance of their deaths that, if they are subject to a cardio-pulmonary arrest, they will not receive cardiopulmonary resuscitation ('CPR').[62]

There is little doubt that DNAR orders are issued more often and more freely in older patients; irrespective of the diagnosis and prognosis—DNAR orders were written in five major US medical centres for 22 per cent of patients under 54 years old, rising to 56 per cent for those aged more than 85.[63] Insofar as the elderly have had more time to acquire those conditions that will attract legitimate DNARs, this is an expected outcome. Nonetheless, it is, in our opinion, particularly important to ensure that junior doctors in the prime of life are trained to understand the needs of the elderly disabled and we discuss this in detail in Chapter 12.

18.28   The British Medical Association (BMA), the Resuscitation Council, and the Royal College of Nursing have issued guidelines in a combined document on the subject in which they stress that, while the basic principles are the same for all patients, it is essential that CPR decisions are made on an individual basis.[64]

18.29   In essence, the guidelines emphasise that an informed, non-coerced, advance directive[65] must be respected and that, in the absence of such information, the presumption should be in favour of attempting resuscitation. An advance decision that CPR will not be attempted must be made in the light of the likely outcome, the patient's ascertainable wishes, and his or her human rights; adequate communication in respect of a decision is all-important, but information should not be forced on patients who are unwilling to receive it. Recording of all steps in the process is crucial. The key question is whether CPR will provide any benefit to the patient but the wishes of one who wants to be resuscitated irrespective of the prognosis should be respected.[66] The views of the relatives of

---

[59]   Sometimes shortened to DNR ('do not resuscitate') but, as the survival rate is only some 15–20 per cent, DNAR is more logical.

[60]   Hence, the frequent synonym 'cardiopulmonary resuscitation' or CPR.

[61]   Good overviews are to be found in J Wilson, 'To what extent should patients be included in decisions regarding their resuscitation status?' (2008) 34 J Med Ethics 353; Z Fritz and J Fuld, 'Ethical issues surrounding do not attempt resuscitation orders: Decisions, discussions and deleterious effects' (2010) 36 J Med Ethics 593. Compare: Z Fritz and J P Fuld, 'Development of the Universal Form Of Treatment Options (UFTO) as an alternative to Do Not Attempt Cardiopulmonary Resuscitation (DNACPR) orders: a cross-disciplinary approach' (2015) 21(1) J Eval Clin Pract 109, doi: 10.1111/jep.12256.

[62]   R (on the application of Tracey) v Cambridge University Hospitals NHS Foundation Trust [2014] 3 WLR 1054; [2015] 1 All ER 450; [2014] Med LR 273; (2014) 138 BMLR 1, para 2.

[63]   R B Hakim, J M Teno, F E Harrell, et al., 'Factors associated with do-not-resuscitate orders: Patients' preferences, prognoses, and physicians' judgments' (1996) 125 Ann Int Med 284.

[64]   BMA, the Resuscitation Council, and the Royal College of Nursing Decisions Relating to Cardiopulmonary Resuscitation (3rd edn, 2014), available at: https://www.resus.org.uk/dnacpr/decisions-relating-to-cpr/.

[65]   For which see para 18.49.

[66]   Subject to the proviso that the doctor cannot be required to provide treatment against his or her clinical judgement: See Burke, n 134.

incompetent adults must be taken into account but it should be made clear that, unless they have been appointed as welfare attorneys, their role is to help rather than to be the decision takers.[67] The guidelines remind the reader that different legal regimes apply to adults compared with children, and as between jurisdictions; for example, while the guiding parameter in England and Wales in 'best interests', in Scotland it is the need to produce 'patient benefit'.[68] It is appropriate to consider making a DNAR order when attempted CPR will almost certainly not restart the patient's heart, when there is no benefit in so doing, or when the expected benefits are outweighed by the burdens. Decisions must always be made on an individual basis—blanket policies are unethical and, in the light of the Human Rights Act 1998, probably would not withstand the scrutiny of judicial review. The guidelines also stress the importance of adequate documentation of the decisions and of how they were reached.[69]

18.30 Well meaning though such guidelines may be, it is clear that they conceal a hornet's nest of moral dilemmas. Exclusion from resuscitation in British hospitals is most likely in patients with a current diagnosis of malignancy, dementia, or pneumonia or with a past or present history of stroke. But to what extent does a DNAR order serve as a marker for limiting other forms of care?[70] At what stage of the disease is the patient with cancer to be regarded as not to be salvaged? How are we to assess what is the patient's idea of an acceptable quality of life? To what extent is dementia a contraindication imposed for the benefit of the carers?[71] Perhaps most importantly—who is to make the decisions and how deeply involved should the patient be in the process?

18.31 This last question, and its recent resolution by the Court of Appeal, has been a key driver in the production of the latest version of the guidelines which now reflect the ruling in *R (on the application of Tracey) v Cambridge University Hospitals NHS Foundation Trust*.[72] In this judicial review a husband objected to the policy by which a DNAR order was applied to his wife by the hospital in which she was receiving care. The argument was that the hospital policy was in breach of patients' Art 8 human rights under the ECHR, among other things, (i) for inadequate provision to consult patients and their families, (ii) for failure to notify in the event of imposition of an order or to make the policy available, (iii) for failure to provide a second opinion, and (iv) for failure to have a policy that was clear and unambiguous. The action was also brought against the Secretary of State for failing to produce national guidelines that would require all relevant public bodies to address such matters. In holding that questions of DNAR engage citizens' Art 8 human rights, the Court of Appeal upheld the claimant's arguments in part, viz, there is a legal presumption that patients be involved in DNAR decisions unless there are convincing reasons not to involve them. Moreover, DNAR policies should be clear, unambiguous

---

[67] The 'proxy' terms of the Adults with Incapacity (Scotland) Act 2000 and the Mental Capacity Act 2005 must be honoured.

[68] Scottish Executive Health Department, *Resuscitation policy* (HDL (2000) 22). NHS Scotland, *Do Not Attempt Cardiopulmonary Resuscitation (DNACPR) Integrated Adult Policy* (2010), available at: http://www.scotland.gov.uk/Resource/Doc/312784/0098903.pdf. A review of the Scottish position is due to be published in September 2015.

[69] Advice from the GMC is to be found in its directive *Treatment and Care at the End of Life: Good Practice in Decision Making* (2011), pp 60–6 which follows much the same lines.

[70] M Stewart and C Baldry, 'The over interpretation of DNAR' (2011) 16 Clin Governance 119.

[71] See *Re D (medical treatment)* (1998) 41 BMLR 81; [1998] 2 FCR 178, in which treatment was lawfully suspended in a man whose long-standing mental disability made it impossible for him to commit himself to cooperate in his haemodialysis.

[72] [2014] 3 WLR 1054; [2015] 1 All ER 450; [2014] Med LR 273; (2014) 138 BMLR 1.

and readily accessible. However, the courts should be reluctant to dictate other matters of good clinical practice, such as whether there should be a second opinion. Equally, the Court declined to hold that the Secretary of State was remiss in not requiring national guidelines. The most important aspect of the case is that there is now a legal presumption that patients should be involved in these decisions. Only if medical staff can show clearly and convincingly that this would not be appropriate can this be avoided. Such circumstances might be, for example, if it is thought that the patient would suffer physical or psychological harm. Interestingly, it would not be a justification for the clinician to say nothing simply because the clinician believes that the CPR itself would be futile.[73] The patient is entitled to know such an assessment has been made.

18.32 There have been few other cases involving DNAR orders that have come before the courts. One is the significant case of *Re R*,[74] which concerned a 23-year-old man who could not sit up, chew food, or communicate in any formal way. He was probably blind and deaf and other physiological disabilities indicated that his condition was appalling. Nevertheless, he could not be regarded as being in the permanent vegetative state. A DNAR order in the event of cardiac arrest was signed by the consultant psychiatrist and agreed by the patient's mother. However, a member of the staff at the day centre at which he was treated arranged for an application for judicial review of the order. The health authority then sought a declaration that it would be lawful to withhold life-sustaining treatment—which included resuscitation and ventilation, nutrition and hydration by artificial means, and the administration of antibiotics—and to treat the patient so that he suffered minimum distress until his natural death. The application was later amended so as to exclude withholding of nutrition and hydration—and, in fact, it was proposed to perform a non-voluntary gastrostomy. At the hearing, all the medical witnesses expressed the view that CPR would not be appropriate in R's case, this being largely on the ground that it was unlikely to be successful. Withholding antibiotics was considered as a separate issue and was recommended—but only subject to the approval of the patient's general practitioner and to the consent of one or both parents. In granting the declaration as sought, the President, Sir Stephen Brown, repeated that there was no question of the court being asked to approve a course aimed at terminating life or accelerating death. In tying *Re R* to *Re J*,[75] however, the President clearly accepted that a 'quality of life' standard could be used when making such decisions in the case of adults as well as of children—this is a notable feature of several of Sir Stephen's end-of-life decisions discussed in Chapter 15. *Re R* also strongly indicated that non-treatment decisions in the case of the incapacitated should normally be taken by health professionals in concert with people close to the patient; it is only in the event of serious challenge to the clinical opinion that court intervention will be required. The case of *Tracey*, above, now makes clear the human rights dimensions of such cases and emphasises the importance of such an inclusive approach. But how far have human rights really changed the dynamics that are in play? A very recent decision helps us to answer this question. In *County Durham & Darlington NHS Foundation Trust v PP*[76] Mr Justice Cobb was asked to declare on the legality of the management of an incompetent and very frail patient, notably the continuation of AHN and the imposition of a DNR despite the objections of the family. The case is a consideration of best interests under the Mental Capacity Act 2005, and contains very graphic details of the potential

---

[73] N 72 above, para 55.
[74] *Re R (adult: medical treatment)* (1996) 31 BMLR 127; [1996] 2 FLR 99.
[75] *Re J (a minor) (wardship: medical treatment)* [1991] Fam 33; (1990) 6 BMLR 25. See Taylor LJ at BMLR 42.
[76] [2014] EWCOP 9.

negative effects of attempting CPR on such a patient. The ruling was handed down within ten days of *Tracey* and does not benefit from its analysis. Notwithstanding, the case illustrates all too clearly the genuine ethical dilemmas that DNAR raises: the family initially agreed to, then rejected, the DNAR order. The medical staff are at considerable pains to stress the deleterious effects of CPR. In the end, following *Aintree*, the matter came down to a balance of considerations rather than any trump human rights card. While fully acknowledging the views of the family, Cobb J held: '[t]hat attempts at resuscitation in the event of either a cardiac or respiratory arrest are likely to cause harm to P, which may have terminal or other deleterious consequences, such that it would not now be in her interests that they be attempted'.

18.33   In the last decade, there has been a steady increase in the development of 'care pathways'.[77] These are directed to the care of those who are estimated to have only hours or days of life remaining and are based on multidisciplinary assessment of the individual's needs in order to achieve a dignified death that is as comfortable as possible. A key feature of the plan is open and extensive consultation with the patient and his or her relatives—and it is failure in this respect that is probably at the heart of the several, largely ill-informed, criticisms that have been levelled at the process recently.[78] These led, in turn to a review of the 'Liverpool Care Pathway (LCP)', as the prototype model is popularly known, which reported in 2013.[79] It produced 44 recommendations, many of which were couched in the language of 'deep concern' and set against evidence of poor treatment that the Panel found to 'abound'. The tenor of required reforms is set by the report's title: 'More Care, Less Pathway'. The key point was that the LCP should be phased out to be replaced by local actions implementing the recommendations.[80] For our part, this is a classic example of theory and practice failing to meet. In its well-conceived origins we see the LCP as little more than structured good palliative care and, as such, is a matter of clinical judgement that is beyond the scope of this book—its sponsors are at pains to emphasise that it is *not* euthanasia in any of its forms.[81]

THE PRINCIPLE OF 'DOUBLE EFFECT'

18.34   Thus far we have discussed the relationship between medical treatment and assistance in dying as a matter of *failure* to treat. Can we reach a similar position in respect of deliberate *over*treatment? The most apposite discussion in this respect in the present context will centre on the philosophical concept of 'double effect'.[82] The principle can

[77] Marie Curie Palliative Care Institute, *What is the Liverpool Care Pathway for the Dying Patient?* (April, 2010).

[78] It is understood that the right to such consultation will be addressed in the coming amendments to the *NHS Constitution*.

[79] Independent Review of the Liverpool Care Pathway, *More Care, Less Pathway: A Review of the Liverpool Care Pathway* (2013), available at: https://www.gov.uk/government/uploads/system/uploads/attachment_data/file/212450/Liverpool_Care_Pathway.pdf.

[80] Scotland decided to phase out the LCP by December 2014, see Scottish Government, *Caring for people in the last days and hours of life – National Statement* (2014), available at: http://www.gov.scot/Resource/0046/00466482.pdf.

[81] Interestingly, the protocol does not include recourse to terminal deep sedation (see para 18.38).

[82] For a wide-ranging analysis of double effect, and, indeed of the whole euthanasia debate, see D Price, 'What shape to euthanasia after Bland? Historical, contemporary and futuristic paradigms' (2009) 125 LQR 142. The author, essentially, supports a pragmatic approach to the resolution of the problems. See also, D Mapel, 'Revising the doctrine of double effect' (2001) 18 J Appl Philos 257. For a valuable critique, and a plea for recognition of the limited relevance of the rule in assisted death, see J A Billings, 'Double effect: A useful rule that cannot justify hastening death' (2011) 37 J Med Ethics 437.

be applied to consensual as well as non-voluntary treatment but it is most appropriately subsumed under the latter heading.

18.35 We have seen that the law condemns active euthanasia on the ground of intent. The terminally or incurably ill are, however, beyond curative therapy by definition, and their management becomes a matter of the relief of suffering. Achieving this may, inevitably, involve some risk to life—but it is the patient's comfort, not his or her premature death, which is the intended therapeutic outcome. Thus, in the present context, the principle of double effect can be visualised as one allowing that an action which has a good objective may be performed despite the fact that the objective can only be achieved at the expense of a coincident harmful effect. This analysis has, however, to be qualified—the action itself must be either good or morally indifferent, the good effect must not be produced by means of the ill-effect, and there must be a proportionate reason for allowing the expected ill to occur.[83] It is implicit in this doctrine that the good effect must outweigh the bad and this may involve a value judgement. Thus, it might well be ethically right to administer pain-killing drugs in such dosage as simultaneously shortens the life of a terminally ill patient; it would not be justifiable to give the same dose to a young man with identical pain who stood a reasonable chance of recovery.

18.36 The seminal case in the UK is that of *R v Adams*, already briefly mentioned.[84] It is nonetheless worth reiterating in this particular context the dictum of Devlin J, quoted there: 'The doctor is entitled to relieve pain and suffering even if the measures he takes may incidentally shorten life' and, at the same time, noting that it was not universally approved. Twenty years after the *Adams* verdict, Lord Edmund Davies commented: 'Killing both pain and patient may be good morals but it is far from certain that it is good law.'[85] Nonetheless, Williams[86] found the proposition easily justified by necessity. The potential conflict has, however, now been at least partially resolved. Devlin J's direction was followed in *R v Cox*[87] and the charge to the jury in the latter case was cited with approval by the House of Lords in *Bland*, where we have Lord Goff:

> [It is] the established rule that a doctor may, when caring for a patient who is, for example, dying of cancer, lawfully administer painkilling drugs despite the fact that he knows that an incidental effect of that application will be to abbreviate the patient's life ... Such a decision may properly be made as part of the care of the living patient, in his best interests; and, on this basis, the treatment will be lawful.[88]

18.37 And this would hold whether one cares to justify the management regime under the essentially moral doctrine of double effect or under the legal principle of necessity.[89] However, since the judgment in *Bland*, the House of Lords has pronounced on the meaning of 'intention' in the case of *R v Woollin*,[90] in which it was directed that a consequence could be said to be intentional if the actor was 'virtually certain' that it would arise. In the Court of Appeal decision in *Re A (children) (conjoined twins: surgical separation)*,[91] Ward LJ said that it could be difficult to reconcile the doctrine of double effect with *Woollin* but, nonetheless, he could 'readily see' how the doctrine would work in cases where painkillers are administered to

---

[83] J Keown, *Euthanasia, Ethics and Public Policy* (2002). It will be seen that Dr Cox (see n 208 and associated text) would have failed on at least two counts to establish a 'double effect' justification for his action.

[84] H Palmer, 'Dr Adams' trial for murder' [1957] Crim LR 365.

[85] 'On dying and dying well—Legal aspects' (1977) 70 Proc Roy Soc Med 73.

[86] G Williams, *Textbook of Criminal Law* (2nd edn, 1983) p 416.   [87] (1992) 12 BMLR 38.

[88] [1993] 1 All ER 821 at 868; (1993) 12 BMLR 64 at 114.   [89] See Ost, n 1.

[90] [1999] 1 AC 82; [1998] 4 All ER 103.   [91] [2001] Fam 147; [2000] 4 All ER 961.

deal with acute pain.[92] Essentially, then, *Woollin* crystallises a major objection to the use of the 'doctrine' in courts of law—that is, the difficulties juries may face in applying the intention/foresight distinction which has been regarded as the 'core requirement' of double effect.[93] We have long argued that a way would be found to preserve the 'safety valve' of double effect when the matter comes to be specifically argued. It has been said:

> Clinicians have an unarticulated, intuitive grasp of the rule of double effect in almost all their therapeutic interventions,[94]

and it seems that the same can be said of the judiciary.[95] The Supreme Court has most recently and unquestioningly endorsed the role of the double effect in law in *Nicklinson* v *Ministry of Justice*,[96] citing Lord Goff in *Bland*.[97]

Terminal Sedation

18.38 The concept of terminal sedation is difficult to accommodate within the structure of this chapter.[98] The concept is unusual and is defined by Williams as, 'the administration of a sedating drug for the purpose of relieving suffering by diminishing consciousness at the end of life'. This is a reasonably innocuous goal that seems to be plausibly justified under a modified principle of double effect. McStay, however, speaks of the 'induction of an unconscious state' and adds 'which is frequently accompanied by the withdrawal of any life-sustaining intervention, such as hydration and nutrition'. Insofar as it implies an intention to hasten death, McStay's interpretation, in our view, introduces a far less easily acceptable motive but one which is, at the same time, becoming acceptable under the guise of 'early' terminal sedation.[99] Confusion is compounded when the potential uses of terminal sedation are considered. These include:

(i) to produce unconsciousness before the removal of artificial life support;

(ii) to relieve physical pain where other options have failed; and

(iii) to relieve non-physical suffering,

a catalogue which many would see as a steadily increasing resort to euphemism.[100]

---

[92] For a major analysis of the effect of *Woollin* on the management of terminal illness, see A McGee, 'Finding a way through the ethical and legal maze: withdrawal of medical treatment and euthanasia' (2005) 13 Med L Rev 357. The author concluded that whilst certain foreseeability and intent may coincide they do not always do so and, therefore, they are not identical.

[93] See a most authoritative critique by C Foster, J Herring, K Melham, and T Hope, 'The double effect effect' (2011) 20 Camb Q Healthc Ethics 56. Even so, the authors somewhat grudgingly conclude: '[The doctrine] is still useful in solving the ethical and legal conundrums thrown up by medical advance'.

[94] D P Sulmasy and E D Pellagrino, 'The rule of double effect: Clearing up the double talk' (1999) 159 Arch Intern Med 545, cf, CD Douglas, I H Kerridge, and R A Ankeny, 'Double meanings will not save the principle of double effect' (2014) 39(3) J Med Philos 304, doi: 10.1093/jmp/jhu011.

[95] D Price, n 82 at 146–7 points out that to deny the legality of double effect in the present context is going a long way towards denying the legality of any medical procedure which may cause harm.

[96] N 9 above, 18.   [97] *Bland*, n 22 above, [1993] AC 789, at p 867.

[98] For an excellent review, see G Williams, 'The principle of double effect and terminal sedation' (2001) 9 Med L Rev 41. The US scene was initially described by R McStay, 'Terminal sedation: Palliative care for intractable pain, post *Glucksberg* and *Quill*' (2003) 29 Amer J Law Med 45 and is updated here: Y Kamisar, 'Are the distinctions drawn in the debate about end-of-life decision making "principled"? If not, how much does it matter?' (2012) 40(1) J Law Med and Ethics 66.

[99] For intuitive concern, see V Cellarius, 'Terminal sedation and the "imminence condition"' (2008) 34 J Med Ethics 69.

[100] A very cautious leading article in the BMJ deprecates the imprecision of the taxonomy employed in the area: S A Murray, K Boyd, and I Byock, 'Continuous deep sedation in patients nearing death' (2008) 336 BMJ 781.

18.39 We have already discussed the application of the 'slippery slope' philosophy to the management of the terminally ill patient and terminal sedation provides a vivid example. Seen as palliative treatment for those whose death is imminent and whose dying is painful, terminal sedation could be accommodated within the acceptable processes of good medical practice—as defined by double effect.[101] We now, however, have to contend with so-called 'early terminal sedation' which involves patients whose death is not imminent and even those who are competent to take part in decision-making. In such cases we have clearly moved into the fields of assisted suicide and euthanasia and, for these reasons, Cellarius has suggested that early terminal sedation should be regarded as a distinct legal and ethical entity.[102] We do not agree. We see the procedure as euthanasia hiding under emollient terminology[103] which can do little other than still further confuse the taxonomy of assisted dying.

18.40 To the best of our knowledge, the legality of early terminal sedation has not been addressed directly in the UK courts, at least with respect to adults. It was announced in 2007 that a Mrs Taylor was bringing an action to test the legality of the procedure but the case never came to fruition.[104] As for infants, the recent rulings by Mr J Macdonald indicate that end-of-life sedation can be accommodated within the best interests test. In *King's College Hospital NHS Foundation Trust* v *Y (By Her Children's Guardian), MH*,[105] the judge ruled with respect to a seven-year-old child (Y) with spinal muscular atrophy that:

> … in the event that Y became severely distressed and / or was in pain due to further deterioration of her medical condition, it was lawful and in her best interests for her to receive pain medication (such as morphine) *and / or sedation* (such as Midazolam) for the purpose of relieving her pain and or distress, accepting that, *in an end of life situation*, such medications may reduce her respiratory drive and might therefore shorten her life (as a consequence and not as an aim). [emphasis added]

This was upheld in a second hearing and in the face of (initial) parental objection. The significance of the ruling is potentially profound given that, as we have seen in Chapter 15, the application of the legal principles of best interests are now largely the same as between neonates, children, and adults. While each case must be decided on its own terms, the role for sedation at the end of life appears to have found a legal foothold.

18.41 In other jurisdictions there is some evidence of escalation of the practice. For example, an assessment from the Netherlands[106] indicates that, while the number of people dying as a result of euthanasia fell by 1,175 between 2001 and 2005, there was a simultaneous rise of 1,200 deaths following terminal sedation. Since the study was largely based on a review of death certificates, one cannot but suspect that practitioners have found the latter to represent the easier medico-legal option.[107] A more recent comparison of the Netherlands and

---

[101] See further J Lombard, 'Sedation of the terminally ill patient: the role of the doctrine of double effect' (2015) 21(1) Med Leg J Ireland 22.

[102] V Celarius, 'Early terminal sedation is a distinct entity' (2011) 25 Bioethics 46.

[103] Nevertheless, the US Supreme Court has been interpreted as approving the practice in *Washington* v *Glucksberg* 521 US 702 (1997) and *Vacco* v *Quill* 521 US 793 (1997).

[104] C Dyer, 'Dying woman seeks backing to hasten death' (2007) 334 BMJ 329.

[105] [2015] EWHC 1966 (Fam), to be read in conjunction with the earlier ruling at [2015] EWHC 1920 (Fam).

[106] Where, almost inevitably, terminal sedation and the withdrawal of ANH are distinguished from euthanasia on the ground that the former are normal medical treatment: T Sheldon, ' "Terminal sedation" different from euthanasia, Dutch ministers agree' (2003) 327 BMJ 465. Indeed, it is now increasingly regarded as part of regular medical practice. See J Rietjens, J van Delden, B Onwuteaka-Philipsen, et al., 'Continuous deep sedation for patients nearing death in the Netherlands: descriptive study' (2008) 336 BMJ 810.

[107] See Murray et al., n 100 for similar doubts. The total number of such deaths was 11,200.

the USA has revealed potentially important cultural differences and attitudes towards the practice. [108] For example, these included differences as to whether sedation hastens death (and is therefore justifiable) and also relating to the stage at which discussions are initiated with patients and/or families (the USA being generally later).[109] The broad conclusion of the study is one with which it is difficult to disagree: more research is required into the effect and effectiveness of sedation at the end of life.

THE CAPABLE PATIENT

ACTIVITY AND PASSIVITY IN ASSISTED DYING

18.42   Those concerned to legalise the termination of life on medical grounds have tended to concentrate on what is generally known as voluntary euthanasia. This form of words implies, first, that the patient is competent and, further, that he or she specifically requests that his or her life be ended. The patient can, therefore, be seen as expressing his or her autonomy—a seminal proposition to which we will return later. Within this framework, a patient's wishes may be effected either actively or passively. This distinction—or whether there is, indeed, any true distinction—is one of the most hotly contested issues in the euthanasia debate and one which can be addressed on either the legal or the moral plane.

18.43   As to the latter, criticism of what is generally known as the act/omission distinction has been intense and sustained over recent decades. Numerous philosophical commentators[110]—and occasionally judges[111]—have expressed disquiet over the drawing of a sharp distinction between act and omission for the purposes of attributing liability for the consequences. One reason for arguing against the distinction is that it tolerates inconsistency and may merge into moral cowardice. On this view, a doctor who knows that his or her failure to treat will result in death should accept the same responsibility for that death as if he or she had brought it about through a positive act.[112] In spite of this, there remain grounds for making this distinction in relation to assistance in dying to alleviate suffering, even if its validity is rightly doubted in other fields. But how, then, can this be justified?

18.44   One response is to say that the distinction reflects a widely held moral intuition which, even if it involves inconsistency, allows for the practical conduct of day-to-day moral life. Morality, like the law, needs to be rooted in daily experience. Doctors who, say, observe a 'DNR' order are entitled to the comfort of thinking they are not actually killing the patient. A sophisticated morality will recognise such ordinary human needs. As one commentator put it at the height of the debate: 'Our gut intuition tells us that there is a difference between active and passive euthanasia and we are not going to be browbeaten into changing our minds by mere logic'[113]—and it is not beyond the capacity of moral philosophy to

---

[108] J A C Rietjens et al., 'Approaches to suffering at the end of life: the use of sedation in the USA and Netherlands' (2014) 40 J Med Ethics 235, doi: 10.1136/medethics-2012-100561.

[109] For a more cautious response to the evidence, see C Douglas, 'Moral concerns with sedation at the end of life' (2014) 40 J Med Ethics 241, doi: 10.1136/medethics-2012-101024.

[110] For a wide-ranging analysis, see L Doyal, 'The futility of opposing the legalisation of non-voluntary and voluntary euthanasia' in S A M McLean (ed), *First Do No Harm* (2006) ch 29.

[111] See, e.g., Lord Mustill in *Bland*, n 22.

[112] Strongly argued by E Jackson, 'Whose death is it anyway? Euthanasia and the medical profession' (2004) 57 CLP 414.

[113] T B Brewin, 'Voluntary euthanasia' (1986) 1 Lancet 1085. See also D P Sulmany, 'Killing and allowing to die: another look' (1998) 26 J Law Med & Ethics 55.

support this: 'We cannot capture our moral judgments by appeal to argument alone ... in the area of dying; intuitions and conceptions formed by actual experience must be given weight.'[114] A second possible response would be consequentialist in nature. The act/omission distinction plays an important role in the preservation of a near-absolute prohibition of killing. The weakening of this prohibition could have the effect of blunting the respect which we accord to human life. The combination of these two approaches is sufficient to tip the scales in favour of retaining the distinction.[115]

18.45 The legal position is, at least in one sense, clear. We can return to *Bland*, per Lord Mustill:[116]

> The English criminal law ... draws a sharp distinction between acts and omissions. If an act resulting in death is done without lawful excuse and with intent to kill it is murder. But an omission to act with the same result and with the same intent is in general no offence at all.

So far, so good, but Lord Mustill rightly went on to say:[117]

> There is one important general exception at common law, namely that a person may be criminally liable for the consequences of an omission if he stands in such a relation to the victim that he is under a duty to act.

18.46 The illogicality of this distinction has more recently been acknowledged by the Supreme Court which at the same time offered a pragmatic justification for this now well-entrenched legal position:

> While Lord Goff, Lord Browne-Wilkinson and Lord Mustill were all concerned about the artificiality of such a sharp legal distinction between acts and omissions in this context, they also saw the need for a line to be drawn, and the need for the law in this sensitive area to be clear.[118]

This clarity extends, then, also to the doctor who fails to provide, or who withdraws, treatment from a patient under his or her care: she or he cannot hide behind the general cover that there is no legal duty to rescue in the jurisprudence of the UK. There must be a justifiable reason for inaction and there is no doubt that, in the case of the competent patient, this is determined or, better, dictated by the patient's autonomy, however this is expressed—thus raising the collateral problems of distinguishing refusal of treatment from suicide and, more importantly in the present context, between suicide and physician assisted suicide.

DYING AS AN EXPRESSION OF PATIENT AUTONOMY

Refusal of Treatment

18.47 We have discussed refusal of treatment already under the heading of 'consent'. Here, we need only point out the obvious that consent to, or refusal of, treatment is a matter for

---

[114] G Gillett, 'Euthanasia, letting die and the pause' (1988) 14 J Med Ethics 61. This attitude was challenged by M Parker, 'Moral intuition, good deaths and ordinary medical practitioners' (1990) 16 J Med Ethics 28.
[115] The contrary argument has been put succinctly in an authoritative editorial article by L Doyal and L Doyal, 'Why active euthanasia and physician assisted suicide should be legalised' (2001) 323 BMJ 1079.
[116] [1993] 1 All ER 821 at 890; (1992) 12 BMLR 64 at 137.   [117] At BMLR 137.
[118] *Nicklinson* v *Ministry of Justice*, n 9 above, para 18 quoting their Lordships in *Bland* [1993] AC 789 at pp 865, 885, and 887 respectively.

the patient alone and this holds true even in the life or death situation. The doctor is now bound, both legally and professionally, to accept a refusal—provided, of course, that it is competently expressed. Indeed, the General Medical Council (GMC) has gone so far as to state that a doctor who fails to respect the wishes of a competent patient is in danger of being found unfit to practise.[119] The rationale for this is to be found in *Re T* where we have Lord Donaldson:

> This appeal is not in truth about 'the right to die'. There is no suggestion that Miss T wants to die … This appeal is about the 'right to choose how to live'. This is quite different, even if the choice, when made, may make an early death more likely.[120]

In our view, medical jurisprudence would, in general, do well to reflect on the extensive moral steps which are being taken when it accepts the cult of self-determination as its dominant principle.[121] Nonetheless, that caveat being admitted, respect for personal autonomy is now firmly established in the modern community ethos and is reflected legally in the offence of battery—the concept of (informed) refusal has now achieved the same standing as that of (informed) consent,[122] supported by common law[123] and shored up by human rights.[124] The conflict between personal autonomy and the public interest in protecting vulnerable groups has been well illustrated, for example, in the cases of Mrs Pretty[125] and Mr Nicklinson.[126] Meantime, the principles involved, and the complex association between refusal of treatment and suicide, are perfectly illustrated in that of Ms B.[127]

18.48   Ms B's case has already been described at para 4.42 and, for present purposes, we need only insert an *aide-memoire* to the effect that she was suffering from progressive paralysis, was maintained by the use of a ventilator, had already effected an advance directive (see para 18.49), and had repeatedly asked that she be disconnected from her machine. The clinicians refused to do so and Ms B then sought a declaration that the treatment she was being given was an unlawful trespass. Butler-Sloss LJ made it clear that the court

---

[119]   GMC, *Treatment and Care Towards the End of Life* (2010), para 68.

[120]   *Re T (adult: refusal of medical treatment)* [1992] 4 All ER 649 at 652; (1992) 9 BMLR 46 at 49. And see Mental Capacity Act 2005 and associated Code of Practice (2014), available at: https://www.gov.uk/government/publications/mental-capacity-act-code-of-practice.

[121]   For a searching analysis, see O O'Neill, *Autonomy and Trust in Bioethics* (2002). See also the Israeli Patients' Rights Act 1996 which, inter alia, permits a right to informed consent but, on communitarian grounds, refers refusals to a committee. On the seeming growth in importance of autonomy in the UK, see G Laurie, 'The autonomy of others: Reflections on the rise and rise of patient choice in contemporary medical law' in S A M McLean (ed), *First Do No Harm: Law, Ethics and Healthcare* (2006) ch 9.

[122]   This is argued in a wide-ranging article by E Wicks, 'The right to refuse medical treatment under the European Convention on Human Rights' (2001) 9 Med L Rev 17 who states: 'There can be no doubt that a right to refuse medical treatment is implicit within the Convention's text' (at 40). To the same effect, the Council of Europe's Convention on Human Rights and Biomedicine provides in Art 5 that any intervention in the health field may only be carried out if the patient gives a free and informed consent.

[123]   *St George's Healthcare NHS Trust v S, R v Collins, ex p S* [1998] 3 WLR 936, [1998] 3 All ER 673 is a strong authority in the UK although the case of Ms B, is the most important in the present context.

[124]   Sch 1 to the Human Rights Act 1998. For a positive judicial statement, see *Pretty v United Kingdom* [2002] 2 FLR 45; (2002) 66 BMLR 147 at para 63.

[125]   Para 18.59. For an easy appreciation of the varied views on the application of Art 8 to assisted dying, see the Court of Appeal in *R (on the application of Debbie Purdy) v DPP* [2009] EWCA 92, paras 32–46.

[126]   Para 18.58.

[127]   *Ms B v An NHS Hospital Trust* [2002] 2 All ER 449; (2002) 65 BMLR149. A very similar case had been heard before but had received little attention: *Re AK (adult patient) (medical treatment: consent)* [2001] 1 FLR 129; (2001) 58 BMLR 151.

was concerned solely with the patient's legal capacity to accept or refuse treatment[128]—and she emphasised the importance of a competent patient's free choice by imposing nominal damages of £100 against the hospital for their unlawful trespass. Seldom can the proposition that the competent adult may reject treatment, even if this will result in death, have been expressed so forcibly while, at the same time, demonstrating the limitation of the *doctors'* autonomy that is inherent in the doctrine. The frank admission by the responsible doctors that they could not bring themselves to take the step of withdrawing ventilation from a viable patient is a striking and significant aspect of the case. In the event, another hospital was found that was willing to do so.[129] The doctors' testimony serves as a reminder of the difficulties which medical staff may experience if they are expected to act contrary to their impulses to preserve life rather than to extinguish it. Even so, there is now such a mass of legal and professional medical precedent as to ensure that refusal of treatment is compatible with the law—requiring *some* medical professionals to be complicit in bringing about death—that this case shows how difficult it may be to distinguish refusal of treatment from suicide or, more significantly, from assisted suicide.

The Advance Directive

18.49 Refusal of treatment is on-going until it is rescinded,[130] and the situation can be seen as being even less straightforward when a patient seeks to refuse in advance and to prescribe the manner of their death in circumstances that are, as yet, unforeseen let alone realised. We are then into the field of the advance directive, the essential feature of which being that it should have been expressed while competent.[131] The status of the advance directive[132] or decision is, therefore, rightly discussed at this point under the umbrella heading of the capable patient. In theory, the principle of the advance directive is simple and is now enshrined in statute[133]—the individual executes a document expressing his or her wishes as to treatment of a specific condition in the event of being disabled from doing so if the condition arises in the future; the physician acts upon it when the occasion arises. While the advance directive commonly expresses a refusal of treatment, it may, equally, express the wish that life-prolonging measures be maintained—though it cannot, of course, *require* that such treatment be given.[134] Looked at in this way, the advance directive becomes an aspect of the right to choose

[128] The matter is discussed in detail in Chapter 4. Effectively a medical assessment of 'best interests' is applicable only when the patient is incompetent. Guidelines were given in *Ms B* but originated in *St George's Healthcare NHS Trust* v *S* [1999] Fam 26.

[129] Ms B died some four weeks later.

[130] Moreover, a refusal can take the form of a declaration of intention never to consent in the future: *Re C (adult: refusal of medical treatment)* [1994] 1 All ER 819, sub nom *Re C (mental patient: medical treatment)* (1993) 15 BMLR 77 at 82. However, Munby J has held that any condition purporting to make an advance directive irrevocable is contrary to public policy and void: *HE* v *A Hospital NHS Trust* [2003] 2 FLR 408; [2003] Fam Law 733. What if a new and effective treatment has evolved meantime?—see M Brazier and E Cave, *Medicine, Patients and the Law* (5th edn, 2011) at 163.

[131] The question of the capacity to refuse is dealt with in Chapters 4 and 13.

[132] Increasingly referred to as advance decisions—including within the Mental Capacity Act 2005. We believe 'directive' to be more descriptively accurate but the two terms should be regarded as interchangeable within this text.

[133] Mental Capacity Act 2005, ss 25–7. For an assessment of the implementation of these provisions, see R Heywood, 'Revisiting advance decision making under the Mental Capacity Act 2005: a tale of mixed messages' (2015) 23(1) Med L Rev 81.

[134] *R (on the application of Burke)* v *General Medical Council* [2006] QB 273; (2005) 85 BMLR 1, CA.

rather than the right to die.[135] Nevertheless, it is only *refusal* that has binding, legal significance and this note is confined to that aspect.

18.50 However, while the theory may be simple, practice has its complications which give rise to criticism. Perhaps the main concern lies in the fact that it is extremely difficult to devise an intelligible document which will be unambiguous in all circumstances; who, for example, is to define words such as 'severe', 'advanced', or 'comparable gravity'? Moreover, the 2005 Act itself lays down conditions which do not make the drafting of the directive any easier. Thus, it will not have effect if:

a) the treatment in question is not the treatment specified in the advance decision;

b) any circumstances specified in the advance decision are absent;

c) there are reasonable grounds for believing that circumstances exist which the person did not anticipate at the time of his advance decision and which would have affected his advance decision had he anticipated them,[136]

and the decision must be recorded in writing, and witnessed, if it involves refusal of life-sustaining treatment.[137] As we discuss at paras 4.44–4.49 there is now a worrying trend that failure to comply with these statutory provisions can undermine the role of prior wishes of a patient in end of life decisions whereby the courts are increasingly relying on sanctity of life as the rigid benchmark from which it is all the more difficult to depart. See, for example, in *Sheffield Teaching Hospitals NHS Foundation Trust* v *TH*,[138] where the evidence did not support an argument than a valid advance decision was in place. Instead, the court took an holistic view of the patient's best interests, taking into account the repeated and strong wishes of the patient to refuse. This resulted in a declaration that ongoing treatment should not occur save in the case of antibiotic treatment of minor infections to maintain the patient's comfort. Importantly, the court made it clear that 'wishes' and 'best interests' are not to be conflated.

18.51 Equally importantly, there is likely to be persistent concern that the patient has, during the critical phase, changed his or her mind; Dworkin, in his classic *Life's Dominion*,[139] points out that the person who drafts a 'living will' and the incompetent who benefits from it are, effectively, different persons and the one need not necessarily be empowered to speak for the other. Given these imponderables, the doctor's dilemma is summed up in the words of Lord Donaldson:

> what the doctors *cannot* do is to conclude that, if the patient still had the necessary capacity in the changed situation [he being now unable to communicate], he would have reversed his decision ... what they *can* do is to consider whether at the time the decision was made it was intended by the patient to apply in the changed situation,[140]

---

[135] An elegantly neutral consideration of advance directives is to be found in A Sommerville, 'Are advance directives really the answer? And what was the question?' in S A M McLean (ed), *Death, Dying and the Law* (1996).

[136] Section 25(4).

[137] Note that the decision is binding on health carers in England and Wales but is only of evidentiary value in Scotland (Adults with Incapacity (Scotland) Act 2000, s 1(4)(a)). Note also that the regulations surrounding advance decisions remain unchanged albeit that the decision is suicidal in nature; S A M McLean, 'Live and let die' (2009) 339 BMJ b4112.

[138] [2014] EWCOP 4.   [139] R Dworkin, *Life's Dominion* (1993).

[140] In *Re T (adult: refusal of medical treatment)* [1993] Fam 95 at 115; (1992) 9 BMLR 46 at 60.

from which it is clear that the concerned doctor cannot ignore an advance decision;[141] what he or she can do is to challenge its *validity*—and, in view of the subjective nature of much of ss 24–6, this is likely to be comparatively easy.[142] It has been suggested that, should there be conflict as to the validity or scope of an advance directive, the wording of the Act is biased in favour of the preservation of life[143]—a position that is understandable to the extent that an error leading to death cannot be rectified while one resulting in survival can always be corrected by reversion to the status quo.[144] Be that as it may, the trend seems to be towards viewing the 2005 Act as the only way to express an advance refusal and as such risks undermining the all-important value of patient self-determination, especially if many patients are likely to be unfamiliar with its terms. The concerns about and objections to advance directives discussed persist as yet another example of the difficulties of attempting to generalise in an intensely private arena.[145] Guidance as to the format for recording advance decisions was provided in *X Primary Care Trust* v *XB*,[146] including that: (i) procedures should be in place for investigating uncertainties around advance decisions and treating this as a matter of urgency; (ii) procedures should follow the Code of Practice and, ideally, advance decisions should be discussed with a health care professional (but this is not mandatory); (iii) advance decisions cannot refuse actions to keep a person comfortable (albeit that refusals can lead to death); and (iv) the court queried whether a 'valid until' clause should be included as a matter of course since each care plan should be patient-specific.[147]

SUICIDE AND ASSISTED SUICIDE

18.52 If a patient is permitted to put his or her life at risk in a negative way by refusing treatment, it is logical to suppose that he or she should be entitled to do so in a positive way and, as is well known, suicide is not a criminal offence in the UK[148] nor is it, so far as we know, in any part of the developed world. Whether this implies a legal right to end one's life is debatable but we are not, here, concerned with the morality of suicide per se. Our interest for present purposes lies in the residual offence of counselling, procuring, aiding, and abetting suicide which remains an offence in England and Wales by virtue of s 2(1) of the Suicide Act 1961.[149] In passing, it may be mentioned that there is some doubt as to whether an offence of abetting suicide exists in Scotland, where the Suicide

---

[141] See *Re AK (adult patient) (medical treatment: consent)* [2001] 1 FLR129; (2001) 58 BMLR 151. The case concerned a 19-year-old man with motor neurone disease who wished nutrition and hydration to be discontinued two weeks after he lost all capacity to communicate.

[142] Note also that withdrawal (as opposed to alteration) of an advance decision as to life-sustaining treatment need not be in writing (2005 Act, s 24(4)) which makes its discovery even more dependent on the enthusiasm of outsiders.

[143] Based on the different wording of s 26(2) and (3): S Michalowski, 'Advance refusals of life-sustaining medical treatment: the relativity of an absolute right' (2005) 68 MLR 958. The same author makes a further strong plea for inviolability of treatment refusal in 'Trial and error at the end of life—no harm done?' (2007) 27 OJLS 257.

[144] For judicial support for this, albeit when there was also a question of mental disorder, see: *Nottinghamshire Healthcare NHS Trust* v *RC* [2014] EWCOP 1317; [2014] COPLR 468; [2014] Med LR 260; (2014) 138 BMLR 147.

[145] For a helpful appraisal, see D Shaw, 'A direct advance on advance directives' (2012) 26 Bioethics 267.

[146] [2012] EWHC 1390 (Fam); (2012) 127 BMLR 122.

[147] See further, C Johnston, 'Advance decision making – rhetoric or reality?' (2014) 34(3) Legal Studies 497.

[148] Suicide Act 1961, s 1.

[149] The section is modified by the Coroners and Justice Act 2009, s 59. The changes are, however, for the purpose of clarification rather than of significant substance.

Act never applied—it is difficult to imagine a common law offence of abetting an act which is not, itself, a crime.[150] That said, recent evidence to the Scottish Parliament has revealed that 'will almost always be in the public interest to prosecute someone who has caused the death of another'. Normally, the charge will be murder whether there is 'wicked intention to kill'. In all other cases it would be culpable homicide. Worryingly, however, no specific guidance has yet been published by the Crown Office and Procurator Fiscal Service (COPFS) in Scotland.[151] Notwithstanding, the discussion will continue with a focus on England and Wales, where s 2 of the 1961 Act presumably identifies a specific, stand-alone form of homicide, we must consider the relationship of outside agencies to the would-be suicide and, particularly, the standing of the doctor in that context.

18.53 Both situations give rise to difficulty. As to the former, we will see later that the problem lies in establishing the extent of the culpability of the agent who is often a relative. As to the latter, the would-be suicide will be anxious to determine the least painful and most effective way of dying but may be hampered by ignorance; as a subset of this, he or she, being a patient, may be physically incapable of effecting death and we isolate this very specific situation under the heading of progressive neuromuscular disease. In any event, the would-be suicide may need aid, at least in the form of counselling, while, at the same time, a doctor may firmly believe death to be in his or her patient's best interests. The law as it stands, therefore, leads to a professional, moral, and/or legal impasse—as much of the recent judicial activity suggests, and we discuss this below. We propose to deal, first, with the general effect of s 2(1) and, then, to consider the role of the physician as a separate set of circumstances.

SECTION 2(1) REVISITED

18.54 It is not easy to classify the case law satisfactorily—in particular, it is in the nature of things that the majority of cases involve neuromuscular disease; it is, perhaps, somewhat artificial to devote a distinct section to that heading. Nevertheless, we will take the case of Mrs Pretty,[152] whose application was, ultimately, heard in the European Court of Human Rights (ECtHR), as our landmark example of judicial attitudes to assisted suicide. Often, wrongly in our view, referred to as active voluntary euthanasia, Mrs Pretty, who suffered from motor neurone disease and was just able to communicate, sought the assurance of the Director of Public Prosecutions (DPP) that he would not bring charges against her husband under s 2(1) of the Suicide Act if the latter took steps to end her life at her own request but by an unspecified method.[153] The DPP declined to give this assurance, saying

---

[150] The topic has been assessed by P R Ferguson, 'Killing "without getting into trouble?": Assisted suicide and Scots criminal law' (1998) 2 Edin LR 288. For a recent discussion with the Health and Sport Committee of the Scottish Parliament, see *Stage 1 Report on Assisted Suicide (Scotland) Bill* (SP Paper 712 6th Report, Session 4, 2015), paras 18–27, available at: http://www.scottish.parliament.uk/S4_HealthandSportCommittee/Reports/her15-06w.pdf.

[151] The absence of clear and transparent guidance arguably leave Scotland open to a human rights challenge, as per the *Purdy* case, discussed below at n 176 and associated text. Cf, C O'Sullivan, 'Mens rea, motive and assisted suicide: does the DPP's policy go too far?' (2015) 35(1) Legal Studies 96.

[152] *R (on the application of Pretty) v DPP* [2002] 1 AC 800; [2002] 1 All ER 1; (2002) 63 BMLR 1, HL.

[153] In effect, Mrs Pretty's application could have included anything up to and including a preleptic amnesty for murder. It is impossible to believe that the DPP could ever have given such an undertaking. Moreover, Mrs Pretty could never have accomplished her suicide alone, and the option of assisted suicide was never available. These issues do not seem to have been considered in any of the judgments.

that it was improper for him to decline in advance to prosecute a breach of the criminal law.[154] This refusal was challenged by Mrs Pretty, by way of judicial review, on the ground that the decision infringed rights which were protected under the Human Rights Act 1998.

18.55 Mrs Pretty based her claim on five Articles in the ECHR: Art 2 (the right to life), Art 3 (the prohibition of torture and cruel and degrading treatment); Art 8 (the right to respect for private life); Art 9 (the right to freedom of thought, conscience, and religion); and Art 14 (the prohibition of discrimination). Although the Court was clearly sympathetic to her plight, none of these Articles was deemed to be grounds on which to base a right to assistance with suicide. The Court rejected the argument that Art 2 created a right of self-determination in relation to life and death, holding that the right was clearly concerned with preventing the unjustified taking of life. The appellant's argument in respect of Art 3 was that there was an obligation on the part of the state to provide assistance in the prevention of suffering—a positive rather than a negative duty. This was rejected by the Court, which held that the state in this case was not in breach of its duty to prevent the infliction of suffering—Mrs Pretty's suffering resulted from a disease rather than from the act of any person.

18.56 In hindsight, it will be seen that the only Article which merited serious consideration was Art 8. However, the House of Lords did not consider a prohibition of assistance in suicide to engage autonomy for the purposes of that Article. The right of autonomy protected by the Article was the right to exercise autonomy while living one's life, and, as pointed out by Lord Bingham, there was nothing in the Article to suggest that it has any bearing on the choice to live no longer.[155] This narrow interpretation is open to criticism in that the concept of autonomy, as it is generally understood, includes decisions about dying.[156] Dying is a part of life and it is difficult to imagine how at least some decisions about the nature of one's death could be seen to have nothing to do with the exercise of self-determination.[157] The European Court[158] did, in fact, later appreciate the force of this argument holding that Art 8 is indeed engaged by these decisions. This then put the onus on the UK to justify its legal position and it fell to the Court to consider whether interference on the part of the state was justified under Art 8(2) which lists a number of exceptions that could be regarded as 'necessary in a democratic society'. In the event, the ECtHR agreed with the House of Lords in finding that the 'blanket' application of s 2(1) of the Suicide Act 1961 infringed none of the five Articles considered. In particular, Art 2 imposed a duty on the state to protect life and there was no implication that this created a right to die;[159] the prohibition of assisted suicide was accepted as necessary and not disproportionate to

---

[154] It was also constitutionally impossible—Lord Bingham in the House of Lords drew attention to the Bill of Rights 1688 which denies the Crown and its servants any power to alter laws without the consent of Parliament ((2002) 63 BMLR 1 at 44).

[155] (2002) 63 BMLR 1 at 39.

[156] This aspect of the case has been emphasised by many writers. See, e.g., H Biggs, 'A Pretty fine line: death, autonomy and letting it B' (2003) 11 Feminist LS 291 who maintained that *Pretty* and *Mrs B* are on a par. Lady Hale has, herself, discussed the problems in a non-judicial capacity: B Hale, 'A Pretty pass: when is there a right to die?' (2003) 32 CLWR 1.

[157] Mrs Pretty's case is well argued by R English, 'No rights to last rites' (2001) 151 NLJ 1844. See also K M Boyd, 'Mrs Pretty and Ms B' (2002) 28 J Med Ethics 211; A Pedain, 'The human rights dimension of the Diane Pretty case' (2003) 62 CLJ 181.

[158] *Pretty v United Kingdom* (2002) 35 EHRR 1; (2002) 66 BMLR 147.

[159] Parenthetically, the Supreme Court of Ireland has also held that a right to life does not imply a 'right to die' under the Irish Constitution in *Fleming v Ireland and Others* [2013] IESC 19. The Court did point out, however, that this would not preclude the Irish Parliament (*Oireachtas*) from legislating of assisted suicide so long as it took account of the constitutional obligation of the state to protect the right to life.

the need to protect the state's vulnerable citizens (Art 8); and that to distinguish between those who could and those who physically could not commit suicide—and, thus, to avoid any supposed discrimination against the latter contrary to Art 14—would be to undermine the protection of life that the 1961 Act was designed to safeguard.

18.57   Both the House of Lords and the ECtHR appreciated, and were much influenced by, the fear that permitting assisted dying would open the door to abuse of the sick and the elderly, an attitude that was summed up well by Lord Bingham when quoting with approval the conclusions of the House of Lords Select Committee on Medical Ethics:

> The message which society sends to vulnerable and disadvantaged people should not, however obliquely, encourage them to seek death, but should assure them of our care and support in life.[160]

18.58   Be that as it may, it is the basis for one of the main criticisms of the *Pretty* decision in that it could be held that the interests of the individual are being sacrificed in order to establish an important social policy; it is, at least, arguable that it is morally unacceptable to allow this and, more tangibly, that such a policy is a clear infringement of the subject's basic human rights. Trenchant legal criticism was also levelled at the Suicide Act itself,[161] particularly at s 2(4)—'no proceedings shall be instituted for an offence under this section except by or with the consent of the Director of Public Prosecutions'. Tur discussed the meaning of this and pointed out that it can either be definitional—that is, there is no crime in the absence of the DPP's consent—or it is dispensing—that is, it is always a crime but the DPP can dispense with prosecution in suitable cases. The judges in Mrs Pretty's case assumed the latter—as, we fancy, would most people—but, since the circumstances can only be assessed *after* the event, a dispensation is likely to lead to inconsistency and uncertainty—which is something the law should avoid.

18.59   Mrs Pretty was, effectively, seeking to legalise euthanasia—or, as we have seen, murder. Her case went unchallenged, as might well be expected, until a further high profile case was heard in 2012.[162] Mr Nicklinson was in the disastrous state of the 'locked in syndrome'; he was totally paralysed but, nevertheless, retained his cognitive faculties, being able to communicate by blinking his eyes and through sophisticated computer software. His case differed from that of Mrs Pretty insofar as his plea was limited to a declaration that it would not be unlawful, on the grounds of necessity, for his doctor to terminate his life. In short, he was asking for what, in our terminology, passes for physician accomplished suicide—a process which is close to euthanasia but which is, at the same time, to be distinguished from physician assisted suicide (for which, see para 18.68). Charles J, noting that the status of necessity as a potential defence against a charge of murder or assisting suicide was unclear, allowed the case to go to judicial review in that the Human Rights Act 1998, Art 8 was arguably engaged.

18.60   Predictably, however, the Divisional Court refused the application.[163] The grounds were several and covered a wide number of issues. In summary, it was determined, first, that any change in the law on euthanasia was a matter for Parliament; second that euthanasia was equivalent to murder and there was no defence available on the basis of lack of

[160] Per Lord Bingham (2002) 63 BMLR 1 at 42.
[161] R H S Tur, 'Legislative technique and human rights: the sad case of assisted suicide' [2003] Crim LR 3.
[162] *Nicklinson v Ministry of Justice*, QBD [2012] HRLR 16; (2012) 124 BMLR 191.
[163] *R (on the application of Nicklinson) v Ministry of Justice, R (on the application of AM v DPP and Others* [2012] 3 FCR 233; (2012) 127 BMLR 107, AM's action was basically on the lines of a combination of that brought by Mrs Pretty with unknown persons substituted for her husband and Ms Purdy. It was rejected as requiring more of the DPP than was in the officer's power.

causation, lack of intention or quasi-self-defence—the Court was unwilling to entertain a defence of necessity which should be employed with great caution; and, third, while Art 8 of the 1998 Act was certainly engaged in death decisions, a considerable margin of appreciation was available to individual jurisdictions and a blanket ban on assisted death was not incompatible with the Article.[164] Mr Nicklinson died from unassociated natural causes a week after the ruling, and despite this, his family was given leave to appeal which in the years since the last edition of this book eventually reached the Supreme Court.

18.61 *Nicklinson* v *Ministry of Justice*, heard before a bench of nine Lordships[165] of the Supreme Court, is a spaghettification of appeals and cross-appeals arising from the fact that Mr Nicklinson had not been alone in his original arguments about the legality of assisted suicide, and because the DPP was implicated by the Court of Appeal ruling to the effect that she was required to clarify (yet further) her prosecution policy on assisted suicide. The DPP cross-appealed against this last point and the Nicklinson family continued to argue for the illegality of the 1961 Act. They were co-joined by Mr Lamb who also argued that the law should be changed to allow him assistance in dying, and by an appellant known as Martin who was arguing for clearer DPP policy guidelines. On this last point the Supreme Court declined to rule that the DPP should amend her policy and her appeal was accordingly successful. The law requires that any such policy be clear and transparent but it would be inappropriate for the courts to dictate its terms.[166] In something of an aside, however, the Court noted that in evidence it had transpired that the current terms of the policy did not fully reflect the DPP's views. She was accordingly invited to reflect on the terms and to amend them accordingly without any order being made to this effect. This judicial slight of hand might also be seen to typify the majority's opinion of the appellants' arguments with respect to s 2 of the Suicide Act 1961. In sum, these can be subsumed under the umbrella of a human rights challenge to the effect that the 'blanket ban' nature of the statutory provisions took the UK outside of its margin of appreciation under the ECHR. While the majority of the Court rejected this argument, it took the opportunity to point out the significant interference with Art 8 rights that the law represented. Moreover, it called into question the defensibility of the UK's position with respect to the robustness of the arguments for maintaining the status quo. Most significantly, it signalled that a court would be justified in making a declaration of incompatibility with the ECHR, albeit that it was not so minded to do so at this time. Rather, Parliament was to be 'given the opportunity' to consider the position in light of this ruling.[167] Only Lord Kerr and Lady Hale were minded to make the declaration in the instant appeal, while Lord Clarke and Lord Sumption would intervene only if Parliament chose not to debate the issue. This remarkable 'non-decision' is as clear a message as it is possible for a court to send a legislature that circumstances must change, and we discuss the recent parliamentary events at paras 18.100 ff below. Nonetheless, we are compelled to comment on the unsatisfactory cat-and-mouse nature of these developments.[168] The institutions of the state

---

[164] Quoting *Haas* v *Switzerland* (2011) 53 EHRR 33.

[165] More accurately, eight Lordships and President Lady Hale.

[166] Interestingly, evidence from the DPP revealed only one (successful) prosecution under s 2 of the 1961 Act; moreover, no person had been prosecuted who provided assistance to the 215 people from the UK who had used the services of the Swiss Dignitas clinic in the period from 1998 to 2011.

[167] A point repeated at paras 113, 116, 118, 190, 197, and 204.

[168] For other comments, see J Finnis, 'A British "Convention right" to assistance in suicide?' (2015) 131 Law Q Rev 1, E Wicks, 'The Supreme Court judgment in Nicklinson: one step forward on assisted dying: two steps back on human rights' (2015) 23(1) Med L Rev 144, and A Mullock, 'The Supreme Court decision in Nicklinson: human rights, criminal wrongs and the dilemma of death' (2015) 31(1) Prof Neg 18.

are failing their citizens in not grasping the moral nettle on this issue. They are coming perilously close to an abrogation of constitutional responsibility. The initial *Nicklinson* decision had been described as 'the death of humanity',[169] but the outcome of the appeals process[170] can, nevertheless, be one that ought now to catalyse parliamentary action in the field.

Assisted Suicide and Tourism

18.62 Assisting a suicide will only be unlawful under the Suicide Act 1961, s 2(1) if it is conducted on a basis of immediacy and intent—the impersonal distribution of advice or information will not attract legal sanction.[171] In the circumstances envisaged here, however, the relationship will, more probably, be intimate and clearly distinguishable as such. There is now unfettered movement in search of medical interventions throughout the European Union (EU) and there is, of course, no reason why a person should not make his or her private arrangements for medical care in any part of the Union[172] or, indeed, in the rest of the world. Such arrangements may include seeking assistance with suicide which is now legally available in a number of jurisdictions (see paras 18.87 et seq). As a result, an ongoing issue has arisen in the shape of providing assistance to the suicide-seeker in making travel arrangements and the like; this becomes particularly acute when EU citizens claim access to cross-border health care services because such claims cut into sensitive Member State policy fields.[173]

18.63 The lawfulness of associating assisted travel with assisted dying was first tested as a specific issue in *Re Z (Local Authority: Duty)*,[174] in which a local authority sought to continue an interim injunction preventing a husband from taking his wife to Switzerland so that she might avail herself of the assisted suicide procedures available in that country. Mrs Z was suffering from cerebellar ataxia, an incurable and irreversible condition that left her physically incapable of fending for herself. The local authority had initially sought the injunction both to protect Mrs Z as someone it saw as vulnerable and because, in its opinion, Mr Z was committing a criminal offence. At the substantive hearing, Hedley J refused the request. He held that the powers and responsibilities of an authority in such cases were to investigate and to protect incompetent individuals and/or those subject to undue influence. Any suspicion of criminality should be reported to the appropriate authorities; given that the criminal prosecution service had been informed, and that Mrs Z was competent, the authority's duties did not extend any further. It was explicitly stated that the case 'afforded no basis for trying to ascertain the court's views about the rights or wrongs of suicide, assisted or otherwise'. The legal point was simply that competent persons are entitled to make their own decisions and that they—and those who

---

[169] S Burns, 'The death of humanity?' (2012) 162 NLJ 1146.

[170] As we go to press it has been reported that the ECtHR has found inadmissible the subsequent applications from Mr Nicklinson's widow and Mr Lamb. The decision is final: *Nicklinson and Lamb* v *the United Kingdom* (Application nos 2478/15 and 1787/15, 16 July 2015). Nicklinson failed because he failed to show new substantive issues since *Pretty* and because his argument was asking too much of the courts within the constitutional order; Lamb failed to exhaust domestic remedies relative to the particular basis of the appeal. Martin sought judicial review of GMC guidance arguing that it breached his human rights in failing to provide him with sufficient advice in how to take his own life. This was dismissed by the High Court on 20 July 2015, *R (on the Application of AM)* v *General Medical Council* [2015] All ER (D) 208 (Jul). We understand that an appeal is to be lodged.

[171] *Attorney-General* v *Able* [1984] QB 795; [1984] 1 All ER 277.

[172] Joined Cases 286/82 and 26/83, *Luisi and Carbone* v *Ministero del Tesoro* [1984] ECR 377.

[173] See further N Nic Shuibhne, 'Margins of appreciation: national values, fundamental rights and EC free movement law' (2009) 34 EL Rev 230.

[174] [2005] 1 WLR 959; [2005] 1 FLR 740.

assist them—bear the responsibility for any decisions so taken. Thus, Mrs Z's case, while interesting to the private lawyer, gave us very little insight into the relevant medical law.[175]

18.64 This aspect of s 2(4) was ultimately addressed in a very similar and now infamous action by Ms Purdy[176] who was concerned for the legal position of her husband should he accompany her to a jurisdiction where she could be lawfully assisted to die. In effect, Ms Purdy sought to fill the vacuum left by the evasive result of Mrs Z's case. Essentially, Ms Purdy argued that the Act engaged her rights under Art 8(1) of the 1998 Act but that the state's licence to derogate from that Article 'in accordance with the law' under Art 8(2) could not apply in the absence of a specific public policy as to when the DPP would or would not exercise his discretion as to prosecution. The Divisional Court, in the end, followed the House of Lords' ruling in *Pretty* that Art 8 was, effectively, unconcerned in cases of assisted suicide. However, even if that not been the case, the court held that the general provisions of administrative law and the guidance given to Crown Prosecutors in the Code of Practice to the Prosecution of Offenders Act 1985 were sufficiently clear to satisfy the requirement that the DPP, in using his discretion, was acting 'in accordance with the law' (at para 82)—and an appeal to the Court of Appeal was rejected on essentially the same grounds.[177]

18.65 Ms Purdy's case was, therefore, a matter of administrative law but with direct impact on medical law as a matter of transparency of policies impacting on individual autonomy.[178] There was no gainsaying the fact that some 100 persons had previously left the UK for suicide in Switzerland and none of their fellow travellers had been prosecuted.[179] The DPP, therefore, took the opportunity to clarify the law in this area by reference to one of these.[180] In brief, he concluded that, even though there might be sufficient evidence on which to mount a prosecution in such cases—including, in particular, evidence of help to travel to a receptive clinic—there were, equally, times when it would not be in the public interest to do so. The conditions which militated against prosecution in the case under consideration included the facts that the abettors, in this case, the dead boy's parents, had not attempted to influence him to commit suicide, there was evidence of his intention to commit suicide were he able to do so, the action taken by the family was at the more remote end of the possible spectrum of assistance, and their son's death, rather than offering any benefit to the potential accused, actually caused them profound distress. The DPP was adamant that cases will differ on their facts and that a generalisation is impossible; what his statement did, however, was to outline an envelope of conditions within which prosecution will *not* proceed—which seemed to be as helpful a contribution to the debate as was possible in the circumstances. It is also noteworthy that the Lord Chief Justice made it as clear as he could that the courts would be less than enthusiastic in their response were a prosecution to be mounted in conditions such as those envisaged in *Purdy*.[181]

18.66 Ms Purdy's case, however, proceeded rapidly to the House of Lords (as it then was) where the main thrust of the opinion was to direct the DPP to formulate an offence-specific

---

[175] For a brief analysis, see B Mahendra, 'Assisted suicide: the law upheld' (2004) NLJ 1848.

[176] *R (on the application of Debbie Purdy) v DPP* [2008] EWHC 2565 (QB); (2008) 104 BMLR 28.

[177] [2009] EWCA Civ 92; (2009) 106 BMLR 170.

[178] For our brief analysis, see J K Mason, 'Unalike as two peas: *R (on the application of Purdy) v DPP*' (2009) 13 Edin LR 298.

[179] See the more recent figures reported at n 166 above.

[180] K Starmer, *Decision on Prosecution—The Death by Suicide of Daniel James* (2008) Crown Prosecution Service, 9 December.

[181] (2009) 106 BMLR 170 at [80].

policy identifying the factors to be taken into consideration in deciding whether to prosecute in circumstances such as those exemplified by Ms Purdy's condition[182]—which, in
view of the action already taken, was scarcely a seismic contribution to the assisted-dying
debate. The House of Lords' decision did, however, include two results that are of general
significance. First, it confirmed that Art 8 of the European Convention *is* engaged in decisions related to death and to assisted dying in particular; indeed, the whole tenor of the
debate points to the logic of legislating in the field by way of human rights rather than the
criminal law.[183] Second, it made clear that, as a matter of human rights, we are entitled to
clarity in the application of the law—a matter which may have far-reaching consequences
in other areas where discretion can be exercised.

18.67   The decision in *Purdy* opened rather than closed the book on judicial involved in public
policies in this field. It was further questioned before the Supreme Court in *Nicklinson*, as
we have seen in para 18.61. The particular additional objection was that the policy should
be clearer with respect to alerting responsible people to know that they could assist someone to day through the services of Dignitas without risk of prosecution. However, the
Court categorically declined to interfere on the content of the policy, stating:

> The purpose of the DPP publishing a code or policy is not to enable those who wish to
> commit a crime to know in advance whether they will get away with it. It is to ensure
> that, as far as is possible in practice and appropriate in principle, the DPP's policy is pub-
> licly available so that everyone knows what it is, and can see whether it is being applied
> consistently.[184]

In any event, most would surely agree that it would be undesirable, indeed unacceptable,
to give carte blanche to the self-appointed 'mercy killer'[185] and it has been pointed out that
any proposal for relaxing s 2(1) would have to accept that only help provided by medically
qualified persons could be lawful.[186] This suggests that legitimising physician-assisted
suicide might be an acceptable halfway house.

PHYSICIAN-ASSISTED SUICIDE

18.68   The classic case of physician-assisted suicide (PAS) involves the doctor in no more than
providing the means of ending life—most commonly by the provision or prescription of
the necessary drugs. The patient him- or herself will complete the act which can, then, be
properly described as an act of suicide, albeit assisted. Given this scenario, the doctor is the
passive agent in the assisted-dying relationship. We regard it as essential to the euthanasia
debate to accept that PAS is what it says—suicide, not homicide. This concept is important
in that it contrasts vividly with the situation in which the patient physically cannot, or

---

[182] *R (on the application of Purdy)* v *DPP* [2009] UKHL 45, [2009] 3 WLR 403 per Lord Hope at [56].
For the current DPP policy, see Crown Prosecution Service, Policy for Prosecutors in Respect of *Cases of
Encouraging or Assisting Suicide* (2010, updated 2014), available at: http://www.cps.gov.uk/publications/
prosecution/assisted_suicide_policy.html.

[183] In which case, Art 8(2) also has effect and is significant in Scotland despite the differences in the
law on suicide across the Border. For discussion, see S A M McLean, C Connelly, and J K Mason, 'Purdy in
Scotland: we hear, but should we listen?' [2009] J R 265.

[184] *Nicklinson*, n 9 above, para 141.

[185] Lord Falconer withdrew a proposed amendment to the Coroners and Justice Bill which would have
legitimised assisted suicide by way of assisted travel in the light of the *Purdy* decision.

[186] D Morris, 'Assisted suicide under the European Convention on Human Rights: A critique' (2003) 1
EHRLR 65.

prefers not to, perform this final task and in which the doctor, in person and on request, administers the *coup de grâce*; we are, then, in the realm of physician-accomplished suicide or active voluntary euthanasia as has been discussed earlier—this, arguably, is in a different legal ambience. The difficulty is that such distinctions will not always be so simple. Take, for example, the doctor who responds to a request to disconnect the ventilator in a case of progressive neurological disease—is this to be classed as refusal of treatment by the patient or as assisted suicide or even as physician-accomplished suicide? And what of the paralysed patient who wishes to die but is receiving no treatment that can be refused—is the ending of that life a matter of assisting suicide or of active euthanasia? Or, what is the position of the doctor who performs the venepuncture and then holds the syringe while the patient presses the plunger?[187] Hard as one may try to represent them, there are no bright dividing lines between refusal of treatment, suicide, assisted suicide, physician accomplished suicide, and euthanasia. Yet, clearly, there *are* distinctions to be made even if these be intuitive. Thus, we have Lord Donaldson saying:

> On other occasions, however, the difference may be obvious. In respect of assisted suicide and euthanasia, for example, it is not difficult to see a practical difference between the classic ploy of 'leaving the pills' and undertaking a lethal injection—and it is this sort of comparison that most people have in mind when addressing the subject.[188]

Again, we have the Court in the US case of *Vacco v Quill*:[189]

> [The] distinction between assisting suicide and withdrawing life-sustaining treatment in hopeless cases is logical, widely recognized and endorsed by the medical profession and by legal tradition,

and we only wish it *were* always so. The dilemma is, however, particularly well expressed in the specific context of the management of progressive neurological disease—a matter which is further characterised as unique in that, in the majority of cases, recourse to the ploy of 'double effect' is not an available management option.

Progressive (or Incurable) Neurological Disease

18.69 Insofar as the right of the competent adult to refuse life-saving treatment is now universally established and that the legal right to control one's body has found expression in the decriminalising of suicide, it is but a short step to holding that to refuse assistance in dying to a person who is incapable of ending his or her own life is an affront to that person's rights of autonomy.[190] It is important, though, to isolate two separate issues. One is the right to reject treatment, even if one is incapable of physically resisting the imposition

---

[187] These examples are taken from D W Meyers and J K Mason, 'Physician assisted suicide: A second view from mid-Atlantic' (1999) 28 Anglo-Am L Rev 265 in which the comparative Anglo-American scene at the time is discussed in detail.

[188] For early commentary, see L R Churchill and N M P King, 'Physician assisted suicide, euthanasia, or withdrawal of treatment' (1997) 315 BMJ 137 and more recently D Orentlicher, 'The alleged distinction between euthanasia and the withdrawal of life-sustaining treatment: conceptually incoherent and impossible to maintain' (2012) 1998(3) Uni Illinois L Rev 837.

[189] 117 S Ct 2293 (1997).

[190] The issue was first raised in the UK in the *Linsell* case, in which a patient in the terminal stages of motor neurone disease sought a declaration that her doctor would not be prosecuted if he administered potentially lethal doses of analgesics when her condition deteriorated. The patient withdrew her application when she heard that a substantial body of medical opinion had endorsed her doctor's planned palliative management regime, which meant that no ruling was required: E Wilkins, 'Dying woman granted wish for dignified end' *The Times*, 29 October 1997, p 3.

of treatment. The second is more controversial and involves an attempt to assert a legal right to assistance in suicide.[191]

The right to refuse treatment

18.70 The *general* right to refuse treatment is discussed in detail at para 18.47. Here, we are concerned only with that right when it applies to the extreme examples of progressive or incurable neurological disease.[192] The application of the right in these circumstances was first upheld in the very significant Canadian decision in *Nancy B v Hôtel-Dieu de Québec*.[193] Nancy, who suffered from the Guillain-Barré syndrome, was existing by virtue of ventilation; she sought to have her ventilator disconnected and was supported in this by her family and the hospital. In making the required order, Dufour J called upon the Civil Code of Lower Canada, which held:

> 19.1 No person may be made to undergo care of any nature whether for examination, specimen taking, removal of tissue treatment or any other act, except with his consent,

and concluded that this encompassed ventilation. He proceeded:

> What Nancy B is seeking ... is ... that nature may take its course; that she be freed from the slavery of a machine as her life depends on it. In order to do this, as she is unable to do it herself, she needs the help of a third person. Then, it is the disease which will take its natural course.

As a result, the person responsible for the actual cessation of treatment would not violate the criminal law in so doing. At the same time, however, the judge ruled that, not only would it not be homicide, nor would it be suicide nor assisted suicide.

18.71 *Nancy B* was followed in England by the equally important case of *Ms B v An NHS Hospital Trust*, which we have already considered at para 18.48. It need only be reiterated here to drive home the lesson that the competent adult may reject treatment even if it will result in death. But, as we have already discussed, the case also vividly demonstrates the limitation of the *doctors'* autonomy that is imposed by the doctrine.

18.72 There is, of course, also abundant evidence that removal of life support mechanisms at the request of the patient may well be obligatory in the USA. Thus, in *Farrell*,[194] a motor neurone disease case, not only was a request for disconnection from the ventilator agreed, but the right to professional assistance during the agonal phase was upheld. An equally emphatic case arose in California, where the health care team was instructed to provide full facilities in order to ease the patient's dying.[195] It is thus clear that the US

---

[191] For a very comprehensive review of such cases, see J H Veldink, J H J Wokke, G van der Wal, et al., 'Euthanasia and physician-assisted suicide among patients with amyotrophic lateral sclerosis in the Netherlands' (2002) 346 New Engl J Med 1638 and, most recently, S Connolly, M Galvin, and O Hardiman, 'End-of-life management in patients with amyotrophic lateral sclerosis' (2015) 14 The Lancet Neurology 435.

[192] The distinction is more than pedantic. Progressive disease (see Mrs Pretty, n 152) will ultimately kill the patient; those with incurable disease (as exemplified by Mr Nicklinson, Mr Lamb, and Martin, n 9) may be kept alive for years. The medico-legal management of the two is not, therefore, interchangeable. It has been reported that Mr Nicklinson eventually refused food in an effort to end his own life: BBC News, 'Right-to-die man Tony Nicklinson dead after refusing food', 22 August 2012, available at: http://www.bbc.co.uk/news/uk-england-19341722.

[193] (1992) 86 DLR (4th) 385; (1992) 15 BMLR 95.

[194] *Re Kathleen Farrell* 529 A 2d 404 (NJ, 1987).

[195] *Bouvia v Superior Court of Los Angeles County* 179 Cal App 3d 1127 (1986).

jurisdictions recognise a practical as well as a theoretical distinction between refusal of treatment and assisted suicide.[196]

Assistance with suicide

18.73 The second issue—that of whether there is a legal right to assistance with suicide in the case of a person who cannot exercise his or her own discretion—was considered initially and extensively by the Supreme Court of Canada in *Rodriguez v A-G of British Columbia*.[197] The arguments in Ms Rodriguez's case, which concerned the setting up of a mechanism she could use to end her life should she become paralysed as a result of her motor neurone disease, were, in the main, based on Canadian constitutional law and, in particular, related to possible conflicts between the Canadian Charter of Rights and Freedoms and the Criminal Code; these are issues specific to Canadian law, but they have become relevant to UK law since the passage of the Human Rights Act 1998. It was held by a majority of 5:4 that, while the patient's autonomy was at stake in such cases, the deprivation of rights consequent on the refusal of such a request was not contrary to the principles of fundamental justice, which required a fair balance to be struck between the interests of the state and those of the individual; neither were the liberty and security of the person compromised—one reason being that the provisions in s 241 of the Criminal Code[198] prohibiting assisted suicide were there as a *protection* for the terminally ill who were particularly vulnerable as to their lives and their will to live.[199] This has strong flavours of the ECtHR ruling in *Pretty*.[200] However, when we fast-forward to 2015 and the most recent decision of the Canadian Supreme Court, we see a very different constitutional stance being taken in *Carter v Canada (Attorney General)*.[201] After being diagnosed with a fatal neurodegenerative disease in 2009, T brought this case challenging the constitutionality of the Criminal Code; she was joined, among others, by two parties who had accompanied their mother to Switzerland to complete her own assisted suicide. In a landmark decision the Supreme Court held, unanimously, that the existing legal prohibition of assisted suicide now unjustifiably infringed on citizens' Charter Rights— notably, s 7 'life, liberty, and security of the person'. Accordingly, the criminal provisions are of 'no force or effect' in prohibiting PAS for a competent adult so long as two criteria are satisfied: (i) the person validly consents to termination of their life, and (ii) they are suffering from a 'grievous and irremediable medical condition (including an illness, disease or disability) that causes enduring suffering that is intolerable to the individual in the circumstances of his or her condition'.[202] However, given the historic nature of the ruling the Court suspended its declaration for 12 months to allow the federal and provincial governments to respond, should they wish to do so.

18.74 This momentous decision is notable in many respects. First, note the *volte face* of the Supreme Court with respect to the relative weight to be given to individual autonomy as opposed to a protectionist stance by the state. The current Court's concern was that total prohibition on PAS 'catches people outside this class [vulnerable persons]' and 'sweeps conduct into its ambit that is unrelated to the law's objective'.[203] In other words, this was 'grossly disproportionate', particularly relative to a dearth of evidence that vulnerable persons are disproportionately affected in countries where PAS already exists. Second,

---

[196] See *Vacco v Quill* 117 S Ct 2293; 521 US 793 (1997).
[197] *Rodriguez v A-G of British Columbia* (1993) 107 DLR (4th) 342; (1993) 50 BMLR 1.
[198] Criminal Code of Canada, RSC (1985), C–46, s 241.
[199] (1993) 107 DLR (4th) 342 at 410, per Sopinka J.   [200] N 158 above.   [201] [2015] SCC 5.
[202] N 201 above, paras 68, 127, and 147.   [203] N 201 above, para 86.

note the terms in which the ruling is couched: 'grievous and irremediable' ... 'suffering that is intolerable'. This does not make terminal illness a threshold for qualification, and this is at odds to how much of the debate is conducted elsewhere. Finally, the Court felt able to revisit *Rodriguez*, and to invite the lower court to do so, for what is—to all extents and purposes—a fundamental shift in social circumstances. These shifts are both ideological and empirical. On the facts presented, for example, the trial court had found 'no evidence from permissive jurisdictions that people with disabilities are at heightened risk of accessing physician-assisted dying'; 'no evidence of inordinate impact on socially vulnerable populations in the permissive jurisdictions' and 'no compelling evidence that a permissive regime in Canada would result in a "practical slippery slope" '.[204] All of this was accepted by the Supreme Court and the ball now sits firmly in the court of the legislatures (pun intended).[205]

18.75   Many will posit that the developments in Canada are themselves a clear manifestation of the 'slippery slope' phenomenon, but we see it as a logical result—once you accept physician assisted suicide, you *must* accept physician-accomplished suicide in cases of neuromuscular incapacity. For patients in the UK who find themselves in the difficult circumstances such as those that affected Mrs Pretty and Ms Purdy, who clearly require some assistance in dying, this may be the only viable argument to raise. That is, however, a very special situation which can be considered as such without loss of intellectual honesty; for the time being, at least, we leave it on one side[206] and concentrate on the scenario that is generally accepted as representing euthanasia.

THE DOCTOR AS THE AGENT OF DEATH

18.76   Thus far, we have been, at least, moderately successful in finding alternative ideations to those commonly used in association with assisted dying and, in doing so, we have been able to subsume these within recognised medical jurisprudential bounds—and this is, in the main, because the management of dying is an integral part of medical practice. Such recourse is, however, scarcely available when the patient's request is not so much 'help me with my dying' but, rather 'help me to escape an intolerable life'—and that is the essence of voluntary euthanasia. We have, then, entered a new legal arena in that we have introduced an element of criminality to the doctor's role and, insofar as consent is no defence against the offence of inflicting severe injury. These were, in fact, precisely to two legal issues that had to be addressed by the Supreme Court of Canada in *Carter*. They remain an obstacle in most other jurisdictions and the matter therefore remains that of the relationship between euthanasia and murder. This was unequivocally restated in *Bland*, where we have Lord Mustill:

> that 'mercy killing' by active means is murder ... has never so far as I know been doubted. The fact that the doctor's motives are kindly will for some, although not for all, transform the moral quality of his act, but this makes no difference in law. It is intent to kill or cause

[204] N 198 above, para 107.

[205] For comment, see S Palmer ' "The choice is cruel": Assisted suicide and the Charter of Rights in Canada' (2015) 74 Cam LJ 191, doi: 10.1017/S0008197315000471, and A Attaran, 'Unanimity on death with dignity—legalizing physician-assisted dying in Canada' (2015) 372 N Engl J Med 2080-2082, doi: 10.1056/NEJMp1502442.

[206] Remembering, of course, that the UK's attitude to neurological disease is established in *Pretty*, *Purdy*, and *Nicklinson* which we have discussed in detail earlier.

grievous bodily harm which constitutes the mens rea of murder, and the reason why the intent was formed makes no difference at all.[207]

Even so, instinct—and, perhaps most appositely, instinct as demonstrated by jury verdicts—tells us that there is a further distinction to be made between assistance per formed in response to terminal illness as opposed to the management of chronic, non-fatal illness, a distinction which we have not, as yet, needed to make. Let us consider the UK case law.

Homicide or Humanity?

18.77 The above scenario was the problem when Dr Cox was charged with the attempted murder of Mrs Boyes, his patient of 13 years' standing.[208] Mrs Boyes' rheumatoid arthritis was not, of itself, a fatal condition, but it caused intense pain and distress leading her to express a wish to die; she was, indeed, already categorised as 'not for resuscitation'.[209] At trial, it was admitted that Dr Cox injected her with two ampoules of potassium chloride, which is known to be potently cardiotoxic but, at the same time, is a substance having no analgesic value—and this is one factor which distinguished Dr Cox's case.[210] The issue at trial was, therefore, reduced to that of intent—did Dr Cox *intend* to kill his patient[211] or did he hope to grant her a short pain-free period during the process of dying? As Ognall J put it at the outset of his summing up:

> If he injected her with potassium chloride with the primary purpose of killing her, of hastening her death, he is guilty of the offence charged.[212]

And later:

> If a doctor genuinely believes that a certain course is beneficial to his patient, either thera-peutically or analgesically, then even though he recognises that that course carries with it a risk to life, he is fully entitled, nonetheless, to pursue it. If in those circumstances the patient dies, nobody could possibly suggest that in that situation the doctor was guilty of murder or attempted murder.[213]

18.78 So, what distinguished Dr Cox from Dr Moor, Dr Martin, and Dr Munro[214] whose cases we have discussed above? Obviously, we can never know the precise reason for a jury verdict but we can extract some factors which they may have found important—even if only sub-liminally. First, Mrs Boyes was incurably but not terminally ill. It is interesting that very few of the vast majority of sporadic attempts to legalise 'euthanasia' in the UK has attempted to go beyond the confines of terminal disease (compare now the Canadian position).[215]

---

[207] *Airedale NHS Trust* v *Bland* [1993] 1 All ER 821 at 890; (1993) 12 BMLR 64 at 137.

[208] *R* v *Cox* (1992) 12 BMLR 38. Dr Cox was charged with attempted murder, presumably because Mrs Boyes had been cremated before her death was regarded as suspicious. Any arguments as to the cause of death would, therefore, have been speculative.

[209] For which see para 18.27 ff.

[210] Another trial concerned with voluntary euthanasia by way of injection of potassium chloride and lignocaine was aborted when the prosecution offered no evidence: *R* v *Lodwig* (1990) *The Times*, 16 March.

[211] Whether it was 'an act of mercy' was a matter only for the judge in sentencing, motive being irrelevant to the jury.

[212] *R* v *Cox* (1992) 12 BMLR 38 at 39.   [213] (1992) 12 BMLR 38 at 41.

[214] For a particularly helpful review of Dr Munro's case and its comparison with that of Dr Cox, see J Goodman, 'The case of *Dr Munro*: Are there lessons to be learnt?' (2010) 18 Med L Rev 564.

[215] Cf, the Assisted Suicide (Scotland) Bill 2013 [which included eligibility criteria relating to condition either 'terminal' or 'life-shortening'], and Lord Falconer's Assisted Dying Bill 2014 [applying to 'terminally ill' defined as has been 'an inevitably progressive condition which cannot be reversed by treatment' and

There may well be an intuitive distinction to be made on a 'sanctity of life' basis.[216] Second, Dr Cox injected a non-therapeutic substance and it is reasonable to assume that, while public opinion in the UK will give great latitude to the medical profession in its fight against suffering, it is not yet prepared to accept the use of a substance which has no analgesic effect and is known to be lethal when injected in concentrated form. Third, and as a direct result of this, he was unable to plead 'double effect' or necessity.

18.79 Dr Cox's case contained all the necessary elements of the classic murder case: intention to bring about death, direct action precipitating that death, and the absence of any defence or excuse based on the medical use of the drug. Even so, sympathy for Dr Cox was widespread.[217] No immediate custodial sentence was imposed; the GMC was content to admonish him on the grounds that, although his actions had fallen short of the high standards which the medical profession must uphold, he clearly acted in good faith; and the responsible regional health authority offered continued employment subject only to certain restrictions.[218] We believe that the jury decision was certainly right in law[219] but that such public dissatisfaction ultimately stems from distrust of the law's determination to dissociate motive from intent when faced with unlawful killing[220]—Dr Cox was certainly not a murderer as the word is commonly interpreted.[221]

18.80 Jackson summarised some of the resultant anomalies in a particularly powerful article.[222] She pointed out that the absolute prohibition of physician accomplished active euthanasia is in direct contradiction to the current movement towards the interests of the individual patient as the driving force in medicine; she concluded that the only logical reason for prohibiting doctors from complying with their patients' requests for euthanasia lies in the protection of an abstract idea as to the proper role of the medical profession[223]—and this she saw as being deeply anachronistic. Nonetheless, for reasons which appear elsewhere

'as a consequence the person is reasonably expected to die within six months']. This last definition is also thought to be at the heart of the Rob Marris Private Member's Assisted Dying Bill introduced in June 2015 [not published at time of writing]. Further details here: http://services.parliament.uk/bills/2015-16/assisted-dyingno2.html.

[216] Although, logically, one might ask why one's life expectancy should affect one's relief from 'intolerable' suffering.

[217] It had been reported that 11 per cent of doctors in the USA who were closely associated with relevant cases had received requests for a lethal injection and 4.7 per cent had complied with the request at least once: D E Meier, C-A Emmons, S Wallenstein, et al., 'A national survey of physician-assisted suicide and euthanasia in the United States' (1998) 338 New Engl J Med 1193. See also, R McCormack, M Clifford, and M Conroy, 'Attitudes of UK doctors towards euthanasia and physician-assisted suicide: A systematic literature review' (2012) 26(1) Pall Med 23, doi: 10.1177/0269216310397688, and J R Voorhees et al., 'Discussing physician-assisted dying: physicians' experiences in the United States and the Netherlands' (2014) 54(5) The Gerontologist (2014) 808, doi: 10.1093/geront/gnt087.

[218] C Dyer, 'GMC tempers justice with mercy in Cox case' (1992) 305 BMJ 1311.

[219] And that, therefore, Dr Adams' acquittal was dubious. Note, also, that, once motive is removed from the equation Dr Cox's and Dr Shipman's cases are legally compatible.

[220] This view is central to the persuasive argument in K Boyd, 'Euthanasia: Back to the future' in J Keown (ed), Euthanasia Examined (1995) ch 7.

[221] The French courts have also battled with cases similar to that of Dr Cox—the general impression being they will go to some lengths to avoid criminalising physician-accomplished euthanasia: P Lewis, 'Assisted dying in France. The evolution of assisted dying in France: A third way? (2006) 14 Med L Rev 44.

[222] E Jackson, 'Whose death is it anyway? Euthanasia and the medical profession' (2004) 57 CLP 415.

[223] A case can be made for hiving off a 'duty' to provide euthanasia to specialists in the care of the terminally ill—innovatively referred to as 'telostricians': R Crisp, 'A good death: Who best to bring it?' (1987) 1 Bioethics 74. For a recent view as to the propriety of physician involvement, see H McLachlan, 'Assisted suicide and the killing of people? Maybe: Physician-assisted suicide and the killing of patients? No' (2010) 36 J Med Ethics 306.

in this chapter, we cannot accept that individual doctors and their patients should be given free rein in this field absent specific legislation—the ghost of Dr Shipman lingers on. Moreover, any such legislation must, itself, be subject to the closest of scrutiny and subject to constant review.

Assistance or Accomplishment?

18.81 We have already mentioned the logical difficulty in maintaining a distinction between physician-assisted and physician-accomplished suicide in relation to the management of progressive neuromuscular disease. Much the same problem arises in the more common ambience of the management of, say, terminal malignant disease where, again, one has to balance the logical consequential association of the two concepts against the practical fear of the 'slippery slope'. Using the traditional terminology, one can identify a clear cascade from passive voluntary euthanasia (PAS) through active voluntary euthanasia (physician-accomplished suicide) to active non-voluntary—or true—euthanasia. At the time of writing, debate in the UK at the parliamentary levels has been confined to the legalisation of the first of these and the chances of legislation which legalises the last being accepted in the UK are currently remote.[224] Indeed, it was concern about involvement of health care professionals in such processes that led the proponents of the recent (failed) Scottish Assisted Suicide Bill to put forward a new role of 'licensed facilitator' rather than morally implicate members of the medical professions.[225] Opposition might be very much less were it possible to legislate for PAS alone—an electorate that could not accept the doctor as an executioner might be less hostile to a doctor who could be regarded as a friend when one was in need. The problem is, then, in two parts—first, is there any moral difference between physician-assisted and physician-accomplished suicide by which to justify the rigid legal distinction and, second, if there is, is it possible to legislate so as to accommodate the former without incorporating the latter and, thereby, further compromising our obligations to the vulnerable.

18.82 We will return to the problem of legislation later. As to the moral position, there is some evidence that, whatever their reasons, both doctors and the public will accept that there is a distinction to be made. In a major survey undertaken in Scotland towards the turn of the last century, McLean and Britton[226] found that, given a change in the law, 43 per cent of doctors across the UK would opt for the legalisation of PAS—defined as the patient's action leading to his or her own death—and 19 per cent for active euthanasia in which the actions of other persons lead to death; the high proportion of undecided respondents (38 per cent) should be noted. As opposed to this, 42 per cent of Scottish people would accept voluntary euthanasia—where the doctor performs the final act—while only 28 per cent would opt for suicide with assistance from the physician. It is difficult to avoid the conclusion that, in this very sensitive situation, most people would wish to pass the ultimate responsibility to others.

18.83 The results obtained from public opinion polls are always subject to varied interpretation—indeed, the public itself can appear confused.[227] Thus, in McLean and Britton's survey,

---

[224] House of Lords, *Report of the Select Committee on Medical Ethics* (HL Paper 21-1, 1994)—which, admittedly, would have no truck with PAS either. The government supported this aspect of the report: 'The Government can see no basis for permitting assisted suicide. Such a change would be open to abuse and put the lives of the weak and vulnerable at risk' (Cmnd 2553, May 1994). For recent attempts, see paras 18.100 ff below.

[225] See the report of the Health and Sport Committee, n 150 above, paras 232–56.

[226] S A M McLean and A Britton, *Sometimes a Small Victory* (1996).

[227] For a more recent overview including an assessment of various public surveys, see House of Lords Select Committee on the Assisted Dying for the Terminally Ill Bill, *Assisted Dying for the Terminally Ill Bill—First Report* (2005) ch 6 (Public Opinion).

67 per cent thought that human beings should have the right to choose when to die (with 20 per cent opposed) but only 55 per cent (with 30 per cent opposed) agreed that PAS should be legalised in Great Britain.[228] More recent studies offer a different picture. For example, the Royal College of General Practitioners surveyed its members in 2013 with the result that a strong majority favoured continued opposition to a change in the law (77 per cent, being 234 people), while a further 18 per cent supported a move to a position of 'neutrality' and only wishing to see the College move to a position of neutrality, and only 5 per cent in favour of a change in the law.[229] The BMA, for its part, has been unflinching in its institutional opposition to legal reform.[230] The GMC has taken note of its members concerns not to leave patients feeling abandoned at the end of life, and has issued guidance accordingly while remaining opposed to a change in the law.[231] In contrast, organisations such as the Campaign for Dignity in Dying has reported up to 82 per cent of support from polled members of the public with respect to the introduction of a law on assisted dying for terminally ill adults.[232] This figure reflects Seale's 2009 study,[233] where 82 per cent of the population were found to favour legislation allowing doctors to end the lives of terminally ill patients on request; only 62 per cent, however, approved PAS, thus confirming our views on accepting responsibility expressed earlier. Interestingly, the doctors in Seale's study appeared unconcerned to make a distinction—34 per cent were in favour of legislating for voluntary euthanasia and 35 per cent for PAS.[234] And what of communities likely to potentially benefit or be adversely affected by such a law in terms of their medical conditions? A 2015 briefing on the proposed Scottish Bill brought together evidence from a range of surveys.[235] Importantly, it noted:

[A] 2012 British Social Attitudes Survey, 80% of those with a disability supported a change in the law to allow a doctor to end the life of a person with a painful incurable disease if they requested it. This was slightly lower than for respondents without a disability (81%).[236] However, a more recent survey for SCOPE found that 62% of disabled people were worried

---

[228] It was stated in *Compassion in Dying* v *State of Washington* 79 Fed 3d 790 (1996) that US opinion polls show majorities of between 64 per cent and 73 per cent in favour of PAS. In a study involving oncologists and oncology patients, the latter were consistently more in favour of PAS than were their physicians: E J Emanuel, D L Fairclough, E R Daniels, and B R Clarridge, 'Euthanasia and physician-assisted suicide: Attitudes and experiences of oncology patients, oncologists, and the public' (1996) 347 Lancet 1805.

[229] Full survey results available here: http://www.rcgp.org.uk/policy/rcgp-policy-areas/assisted-dying.aspx.

[230] The BMA policy of 2006 currently represents the considered view, see http://bma.org.uk/practical-support-at-work/ethics/bma-policy-assisted-dying, last accessed 10 December 2015. Note, however, in 2015 and at the time of writing, the BMA is conducting a series of deliberative exercises on members' views, see BMA, End of life care and physician-assisted dying project (2015), available at: http://bma.org.uk/working-for-change/improving-and-protecting-health/end-of-life-care.

[231] See GMC, Treatment and Care Towards the End of Life: Good Practice in Decision Making (2010), and When a Patient Seeks Advice or Information about Assistance to Die (2013), both available at: http://www.gmc-uk.org/guidance/news_consultation/14344.asp.

[232] Campaign for Dignity in Dying, see http://www.dignityindying.org.uk/. See also, C Seale, 'Legalisation of euthanasia or physician-assisted suicide: Survey of doctors' attitudes' (2009) 23 Palliat Med 205.

[233] C Seale, 'Legalisation of euthanasia or physician-assisted suicide: Survey of doctors' attitudes' (2009) 23 Palliat Med 205.

[234] These figures are for patients with lethal disease. Professional support for euthanasia dropped to 18 per cent and to 24 per cent in the case of incurable and painful illness. Similarly, support for either from the general public dropped to less than 50 per cent in the latter situation.

[235] Scottish Parliament Information Centre, *Briefing: Assisted Suicide (Scotland) Bill* (2015), available at: http://www.scottish.parliament.uk/ResearchBriefingsAndFactsheets/S4/SB_15-02_Assisted_Suicide_Scotland_Bill.pdf.

[236] NatCen Social Research. (2015) Personal Communication with NatCen.

that a change in the law to permit assisted suicide would put pressure on people with a disability to end their lives prematurely. 55% also believed that the current legal status of assisted suicide protects vulnerable people from pressure to end their lives.[237]

18.84 Whatever one is to make of these figures, it is interesting to note that the majority of Western anglophone medical 'establishments'—as represented by their national associations—are, at best, ambivalent on the issues.[238] Nor, one feels, should moral questions be determined on the basis of straw polls.[239] The fact that a majority believes that something is right does not *make it* morally right; those who argue that public (or, indeed, professional) acceptance of PAS justifies its legalisation might consider whether, say, consistency requires them to support the morality of the death penalty in communities in which it is widely endorsed.

18.85 At the end of the day, there may be strong pragmatic reasons for the view that the medical profession simply should not involve itself in actions which confuse its role. In this respect, the classic words of Capron still merit preservation:[240]

> I never want to have to wonder whether the physician coming into my hospital room is wearing the white coat (or the green scrubs) of a healer, concerned only to relieve my pain and restore me to health, or the black hood of the executioner. Trust between patient and physician is simply too important and too fragile to be subjected to this unnecessary strain.

18.86 This concern over trust has been the subject of close scrutiny. Emanuel and his colleagues found, in their survey of cancer patients and members of the public in general, that 19 per cent of the former and 26.5 per cent of the latter would change doctors if their doctor spoke to them about euthanasia or PAS.[241] Trust is, however, only one of many considerations which are exposed in Capron's comment. In addition, there are the familiar issues of coercion and abuse, both of which may serve to render decisions to end life less than fully voluntary, as, indeed, may confusion. While the courts have traditionally expressed concerns about potential coercion of the vulnerable patient, we must consider to the moral or legal coercion of a system that puts the medical professions at the heart of assisted dying. It is to a consideration of the practical aspects of these practices that we now turn, first learning lessons from jurisdictions that have grasped the proverbial nettle.

ASSISTED DYING IN PRACTICE

THE DUTCH EXPERIENCE

18.87 The focal area for much debate and evidence gathering still lies in the Netherlands, where medically practised assisted dying became lawful in November 2000. This ended the previous halfway house arrangement in Dutch law under which euthanasia[242] remained

---

[237] Citing SCOPE (2014), Majority of people fear change to assisted suicide law. Available at: http://www.scope.org.uk/media/press-releases/july-2014/assisted-suicide-law.

[238] American Medical Association, 'Decisions near the end of life' (1992) 267 JAMA 2229; updated 1996: see C-G McDaniel, 'US doctors reaffirm opposition to euthanasia' (1996) 313 BMJ 11.

[239] This was largely the view of the House of Lords Select Committee on the 2004 Bill, para 18.84.

[240] A M Capron, 'Legal and ethical problems in decisions for death' (1986) 14 Law Med Hlth Care 141.

[241] Emanuel et al., n 228.

[242] Understood as the deliberate termination of a patient's life by a physician acting on the patient's request. Much of our authority for what follows in this section derives from a Canadian government publication:

illegal but, at the same time, doctors who accelerated their patients' deaths would not be prosecuted provided they complied with certain requirements. These have now been consolidated in the Termination of Life on Request and Assisted Suicide (Review Procedures) Act, effective since 1 April 2002 and which amends Art 293 of the Penal Code of the Netherlands, so as to read:

(1) A person who terminates the life of another person at that other person's express and earnest request is liable to a term of imprisonment of not more than twelve years or a fine of the fifth category.

(2) The offence referred to in the first paragraph shall not be punishable if it has been committed by a physician who has met the requirements of due care [referred to in Article 2 of this law] ... and who informs the municipal autopsist of this ...

18.88 The concept of due care is defined in the legislation as requiring the doctor to believe that the patient's request was 'voluntary and well considered' and that the patient's suffering was 'lasting and unbearable'. For his part the patient, having been informed about his situation, must believe that there is no other reasonable solution. The doctor must also have consulted an independent physician who has seen the patient and has given a written opinion on compliance with the due conditions.[243] In addition to setting out these criteria for the administration of euthanasia, the Act provides for the reporting of instances of euthanasia to regional review committees, which have power to refer non-compliance cases to the public prosecutor.[244] The Dutch legislation allows for prior consent, thus recognising the validity of advance decisions. A written declaration of this nature has the effect of a concrete request for euthanasia which may be exercised when the patient is no longer capable of expressing his or her will. One consequence of this is that a patient who does not have the capacity to object, but who may, in fact, not now want to die, could be killed by a doctor who, possessing an earlier written authorisation, decides that it would be better for the patient to do so.

18.89 The scale of the practice of euthanasia in the Netherlands is disputed, although most studies suggest that it is extensive. Some 2.8 per cent of deaths in the Netherlands in 2001 resulted from assistance; these involved approximately 3,500 cases of euthanasia and 300 of assisted suicide—figures which were fairly representative of the previous decade.[245] There was, however, a marked drop in absolute numbers (2,325 and 100 respectively) and

M Tiedemann and D Valiquet, 'Euthanasia and assisted suicide: international experiences' No. 91–9E (2008). More recently see, P Lewis and I Black, 'The Effectiveness of Legal Safeguards in Jurisdictions that Allow Assisted Dying (2012), available at: http://www.commissiononassisteddying.co.uk/wp-content/uploads/2012/01/Penney-Lewis-briefing-paper.pdf, and N Steck et al., 'Euthanasia and assisted suicide in selected European countries and US States: systematic literature review' (2013) 51(10) Med Care 938, doi: 10.1097/MLR.0b013e3182a0f427.

[243] Art 2(1).
[244] Controversially, the Netherlands Act provides for the carrying out of euthanasia on minors (Art 2(3) and (4)). Children between 12 and 16 who are deemed to have a 'reasonable understanding' (the statute's language) of their interests may give consent to euthanasia, provided that their decision is agreed to by parents. Children aged 16 and 17 may opt for euthanasia, but this may only be carried out if the parents (or those exercising parental authority) have been involved in the decision process.
[245] This high incidence might, in itself, give rise to concern. The House of Lords, for example, estimated that, if the Dutch model were to be implemented in Britain, it could lead to 13,000 deaths a year. This is to be compared with 650 deaths per year if the Oregon model were adopted (see para 18.95): House of Lords Select Committee on the Assisted Dying for the Terminally Ill Bill, *Assisted Dying for the Terminally Ill Bill—First Report* (2005), para 243.

in the proportion of deaths (1.8 per cent) in 2005.[246] The authors of the official evaluation[247] suggested a number of reasons for this—including a marked improvement in facilities for palliative terminal care in recent years. Importantly, however, they pointed to a change in attitudes to the pharmacological action of drugs—notably, a reluctance to attribute life-shortening properties to morphine and other opiates.[248] Thus, 'it is rather a question of a different appreciation of physicians of their own actions than an actual change in behaviour'.[249] Although the doubts as to the reporting integrity of physicians[250] seemed, at one time, to have been largely dispelled (about 80 per cent of cases were reported in 2005 as compared with 54 per cent in 2001), there is still a strong element of subjectivity in reporting which makes analysis of the figures still very difficult.[251] Figures for the decade after both the Netherlands and Belgium had legalised assisted dying showed that more than 5,000 people had died from euthanasia or assisted suicide in countries which by then allowed the practices.[252] This might provide grounds for asserting that it becomes far more difficult to control the practices once an absolute prohibition against killing is removed—and leads us back to the infamous practical slippery slope which, in effect, postulates that you cannot legislate for limited euthanasia because it will be impossible to prevent people breaching the rules.[253]

18.90 There are certainly indications that there is a slippery slope in the Netherlands. A 2014 publication suggests that deaths per 1,000 due to euthanasia rose from 10 in 2003 to 28.2 in 2012.[254] In our view, this is better seen as an example of its logical format[255] which, in essence warns us that, if a logical case can be made for a movement from position A1 to position A2, then the same logic can, and will, enable us to move from position A2 to A3. Indeed, opponents of the Netherlands model have consistently expressed concern that the grounds for its exercise will inevitably become more trivial until what matters is not the grounds for wanting to die, but the want itself.[256] Such concerns do not appear ill-founded when one reads that a Dutch psychiatrist was found to be medically justified in assisting the suicide of a physically healthy woman who was depressed.[257] This is

[246] But the figures are relatively meaningless—by 2010 the annual total had risen to 3,136, which represents a swing of some 19 per cent over the previous year.

[247] Evaluation of the Euthanasia Act, May 2007, available at: http://www.minvws.nl/en/themes/euthanasia/.

[248] More disturbingly, 7.1 per cent of all deaths were attributed to continuous deep sedation.

[249] See, now, T Smets et al., 'Reporting of euthanasia in medical practice in Flanders, Belgium: Cross sectional analysis of reported and unreported cases' (2010) 341 BMJ c5174.

[250] P J van der Maas, G van der Wal, I Haverkate, et al., 'Euthanasia, physician-assisted suicide, and other medical practices involving the end of life in the Netherlands, 1990–1995' (1996) 335 New Engl J Med 1699.

[251] Smets et al., n 249 report that only 50 per cent of euthanasia cases are now reported. This swing of the pendulum seems a characteristic of the Netherlands' experience (see n 246).

[252] C Gamondi et al., 'Legalisation of assisted suicide: a safeguard to euthanasia?' (2014) 384(9938) Lancet 127, doi: http://dx.doi.org/10.1016/S0140-6736(14)61154-5.

[253] S Smith, 'Evidence for the practical slippery slope in the debate on physician-assisted suicide and euthanasia' (2005) 13 Med L Rev 17 and, in particular, Keown (2002) n 1.

[254] Gamondi, n 252 above, Fig 1.

[255] For discussion of the distinction between slippery slopes, see Keown, n 1; S W Smith, 'Fallacies of the logical slippery slope in the debate on physician-assisted suicide and euthanasia' (2005) 13 Med L Rev 234.

[256] Concern becomes even more real when one reads a heading: 'Dutch euthanasia law should apply to patients "suffering through living" report says'—T Sheldon (2005) 330 BMJ 61. For an example of the pressures, see S Ost and A Mullock, 'Pushing the boundaries of lawful assisted dying in the Netherlands: existential suffering and lay assistance' (2011) 18 Euro J Hlth L 163.

[257] 'Mercy-killing doctor freed' The Scotsman, 22 April 1993, p 8. See also T Sheldon, 'Dutch approve euthanasia for a patient with Alzheimer's disease' (2005) 330 BMJ 1041.

precisely the situation foreseen by those who oppose legalising the termination of life and, for example, the Dutch Commission for the Acceptability of Life Terminating Action has recommended that, in some circumstances, the life of a patient suffering from severe dementia without serious physical symptoms might be terminated with or without he or she having executed an advance directive on the point.[258]

18.91 Whether this is a cause for concern depends, of course, on whether you believe the resulting position to be morally less acceptable than the original. The slippery slope is a subjective concept and we admit that we are among those who fear its influence in the context of voluntary euthanasia. There are, of course, those who would deny the very existence of such slopes[259] and we, ourselves, would not accept the proposition that, once a decision of doubtful morality has been taken, the erection of a slippery slope is *inevitable*. We would rather see the analogy as a descending lift which stops at various landings. Using this model, we are no longer slipping but, rather, getting off at, and standing on, new platforms each of which represents a new moral threshold from which to assess the next call for an incremental shift—and this is what is happening. We suggest that the Dutch experience should be taken as an object lesson rather than as a paradigm.[260]

18.92 A major difficulty in assessing the Dutch experience lies in definition and this probably derives from their use of the term 'medical decisions concerning the end of life' (MDEL).[261] MDEL includes a wide spectrum of activity ranging from manifest euthanasia, through the concept of 'double effect',[262] to the most controversial, and hard to unravel, group involving termination of life without an explicit request. Griffiths extrapolated the available data to suggest that, on these grounds, an MDEL is the immediate cause of death in more than half the deaths in the Netherlands due to chronic disease.[263]

THE EXTENDED EUROPEAN EXPERIENCE

18.93 The pioneering legislation in the Netherlands has not led to a large number of other jurisdictions following suit.[264] Nevertheless, it has now spread to the other members of Benelux.[265] A similar measure was introduced in Belgium in 2002,[266] a parliamentary action which probably reflected what was, anyway, happening in practice.[267] Curiously, the Act made no mention of PAS, leaving that practice in legal limbo[268]—the probability

[258] H Hellema, 'Dutch doctors support life termination in dementia' (1993) 306 BMJ 1364.

[259] See, e.g., D Enoch, 'Once you start using slippery slope arguments, you're on a very slippery slope' (2001) 211 OJLS 629; R S Downie and K C Calman, *Healthy Respect: Ethics in Health Care* (2nd edn, 2001).

[260] See J Griffiths et al., *Euthanasia and Law in Europe* (2008) and Lewis and Black (2012), n 242, above.

[261] Griffiths, n 260, suggests that this would be better expressed as 'medical procedures that shorten life'.

[262] See paras 18.34 ff.

[263] See also, M L Rurup et al., 'The first five years of euthanasia legislation in Belgium and the Netherlands: Description and comparison of cases' (2012) 26(1) Pall Med 43, doi: 10.1177/0269216311413836.

[264] For debate on the ambivalence of opinion in the Council of Europe see J Keown, 'Mr Marty's muddle: A superficial and selective case for euthanasia in Europe' (2006) 32 J Med Ethics 29 and the associated commentary by G Widdershaven at 34.

[265] A whole issue of the European Journal of Health Law is devoted to the specific issue of PAS: G Laurie, 'Physician assisted suicide in Europe: Some lessons and trends' (2005) 12 Euro J Hlth Law 5.

[266] Act on Euthanasia of 28 May 2002.

[267] In 2000, it was revealed that the incidence of euthanasia in the Flemish-speaking part of the country was similar to that revealed in the earlier Netherlands studies: L Deliens, F Mortier, J Bilsen, et al., 'End of life decisions in medical practice in Flanders, Belgium: A nationwide survey' (2000) 356 Lancet 1806.

[268] H Nys, 'Physician assisted suicide in Belgian law' (2005) 12 Euro J Health L 39.

is that it is subsumed under the doubtful umbrella of euthanasia. The Grand Duchy of Luxembourg followed suit in 2008—albeit only after narrowly escaping a constitutional crisis in so doing. The Benelux countries have now introduced legislation which standardises the use of advance directives but have retained individual regulation of euthanasia; surprisingly, there is no suggestion of introducing residency requirements for availability. The largest controversy to arise since the last edition of this book has been the acceptance into law of euthanasia for minors in Belgium (although note the existing provisions in the Netherlands). The significant difference is that Belgium imposes no cut-off age limit (while the Dutch rule is 12 years of age). The criteria to qualify in Belgium require that the child be terminally ill, in unbearable pain, make repeated requests, and be assessed by two doctors and a psychiatrist or psychologist. Their legal representatives must also consent. To many this is a step too far, especially given the potential coercion that severe suffering can bring.[269] To others it is but a logical extension of recognising autonomy in human beings and addressing their suffering according to their own will.[270]

18.94 Assisted suicide was decriminalised in Switzerland in 1942 (Art 115 of the Swiss Penal Code).[271] The essential element of the law is the motive of the assisting person; there is no criminality provided that the assistance is a selfless act—that is, without personal motive.[272] This provision is not directed only to the medical profession. The position of the 'mercy killer' is, however, different because direct assistance to die in these circumstances remains liable to prosecution in the absence of a genuine 'suicide'. The overall result is that what was once a trickle of terminally ill patients in search of an 'easy death' into Switzerland from more conservative countries has now become something of a stream that may grow substantially in future years if other jurisdictions maintain their stati quo.[273] It has been reported by Dignitas, for example, that between 1998 and 2013, the clinic assisted 244 Britons to die. The organisation Dignity in Dying has estimated this is the equivalent of one Briton using the service every two weeks.[274]

THE CHANGING LANDSCAPE IN NORTH AMERICA

18.95 We have argued that there *are* good moral and practical grounds for dissociating PAS from euthanasia—indeed, we will suggest later that it may be the solution to a social dilemma—and there is legislative precedent for so doing. Having seen an initiative

---

[269] A M Siegel et al., 'Pediatric euthanasia in Belgium: disturbing developments' (2014) 311(19) J Am Med Assoc 1963, doi: 10.1001/jama.2014.4257.

[270] For discussion, see L Bovens, 'Child euthanasia: should we just not talk about it?' (2015) J Med Ethics. First online, doi: 10.1136/medethics-2014-102329.

[271] O Guillod and A Schmidt, 'Assisted suicide under Swiss law' (2005) 12 Euro J Health L 23. It is to be noted that voluntary euthanasia is still unlawful although there is no minimum penalty for killing on compassionate grounds. For a review of the Swiss situation, see S Fischer, C A Huber, R M Imhof, et al., 'Suicide assisted by two Swiss right-to-die organisations' (2008) 34 J Med Ethics 810. For empirical determinants suggesting gender disparity and increased access dependent on social circumstances, see N Steck et al., 'Suicide assisted by two Swiss right-to-die organisations: a population based cohort study' (2014) Intl J Epidemiol, first published online, doi: 10.1093/ije/dyu010.

[272] This even extends, theoretically, to assistance borne out of indifference; i.e., when the party assisting the suicide has neither a selfish nor a selfless motive.

[273] Note that, while active euthanasia is covered in Benelux, only assisted suicide is lawful in Switzerland. For a comparison with the German position, see K Becker-Schwarze, 'Legal restrictions of physician assisted suicide' (2005) 12 Euro J Health L 9. And between the Netherlands and Oregon: F Pakes, 'The legalization of euthanasia and assisted suicide: A tale of two cities' (2005) 33 Int J Soc L 71.

[274] This is reported by the Scottish Parliament Briefing, n 301, p 15.

designed to decriminalise active voluntary euthanasia fail in California,[275] Oregon introduced its Death with Dignity Act in 1994, which concerned assisted suicide only. After a
series of stays on constitutional grounds, the measure was enacted by a majority of 60:40
in 1997.[276] Under the Oregon Act, it is lawful for a doctor to prescribe a lethal dosage of a
drug for a patient who wishes to end his or her life, but not to involve him- or herself in the
suicidal act. The patient must make the request voluntarily and must be competent and
be suffering from a terminal illness. Critics of the law have pointed out that it empowers
the physician to determine matters such as competence and voluntariness, and it has been
suggested that it naively accepts medical reassurances of compliance with the requirements.[277] The fact that Oregon's Medicaid Plan, which provides medical cover for indigent
patients, will pay for PAS while excluding several other treatments is of particular interest. Those who believe that financial pressure has the potential to encourage dispirited
and vulnerable people to take a convenient way out, will take their own interpretation
of the figures that suggest that in 1998 the law accounted for 0.05 per cent of all deaths
in Oregon (5.5 per 10,000), while by 2014, this had risen to 0.21 per cent of all deaths
(31 per 10,000 deaths).[278]. The Act's passage into law, moreover, was not the end of the
issue. A number of challenges were mounted, including the introduction into Congress of
the proposed Pain Relief Promotion Act 1999, which would have directly banned the use
of controlled drugs to end life, even where it was legal under assisted-suicide legislation.[279]
The failure of this Bill did not deter the US government from further attempts to prevent
assisted suicide through the use of drug administration regulations but, ultimately, the
Supreme Court found the actions of the Attorney General to be unconstitutional and the
Act remains unscathed.[280]

18.96 As something of an envoi to the Oregon position, it is, perhaps, worth noting how often
and with what success the Act has been used in recent years. In 2008, 60 Oregonians
died under the Act and the total since it was introduced is 859 (to 2014). Interestingly,
the disparity between those prescribed a legal dose and those dying in the same year—
admittedly, not necessarily a direct correlation—has remained fairly steady. Thus, while
there were 24 prescriptions and 16 deaths in 1998 (67 per cent), and 65/45 in 2006 (the
mid-point), this can be contrasted with 155 prescriptions and 105 deaths in 2014 (67 per
cent). The pattern is similar across the range of years. An obvious, tentative conclusion is
that the receipt of the prescription itself might restore a degree of dignity and control to
people's lives without the need to follow through on the final act.

18.97 It is undeniable, however, that the number of deaths each year has risen fairly steadily
from 16 in 1998 to 105 in 2014. So far as is known, there has been only one Oregonian

---

[275] A further Act—the Compassionate Choices Act 2005 (AB 654)—failed in the Judiciary Committee. It
was, however, revived in 2007, passed the Judiciary Committee, but was then put on hold.

[276] The US Supreme Court has decreed that statutes which prohibit assisted suicide—which are in force in
34 states—are not unconstitutional; the arguments are, however, essentially based on US constitutional law
and have very little relevance outside the USA: *Vacco* v *Quill* 117 S Ct 2293, 521 US 793 (1997); *Washington* v
Glucksberg 117 S Ct 2258 (1997).

[277] S R Martyn and H J Bourguignon, 'Now is the moment to reflect: two years of experience with Oregon's
physician-assisted suicide law' (2000) 8 Elder LJ 1.

[278] Oregon Public Health Division, Annual Report (2015), available at: http://public.health.oregon.gov/
ProviderPartnerResources/EvaluationResearch/DeathwithDignityAct/Documents/year17.pdf.

[279] D Orentlicher, 'The Pain Relief Promotion Act of 1999' (2000) 283 JAMA 255.

[280] *Gonzales* v *Oregon* 546 US 243 (2006). The case was formerly known as *Oregon* v *Ashcroft* 368 F 3d 1118
(2004); the 9th Circuit Court of Appeals upheld the validity of the Oregon law in 2004.

failure in a man who woke up three days after taking his drug.[281] These figures, however, serve to illustrate—as in the case of the Dutch experience—how difficult it is to maintain strict objectivity in statistical analysis. A deeply sceptical review[282] suggests that any data which depend upon self-reporting are likely to be based on under-reporting—for instance, the reported occurrence of 17 complications of PAS in nine years must be an underestimate. The author also draws attention to the strong influence which professional organisations will have on the implementation of statutes.[283] In the end, individual readers must judge the significance of the figures for themselves.[284]

18.98 It may be significant that a number of other US states have followed Oregon. Having once rejected the proposition, the state of Washington implemented legal provisions in much the same terms as Oregon and by a very similar majority (59:41).[285] A major feature of both legislations is that depression must be excluded as an influence on choice before a person can be lawfully assisted to die. It seems to us to be arguable that a person would not wish to die *unless* he or she was depressed and the distinguishing diagnosis must be difficult to make[286]—we are reminded of the scepticism famously expressed by Szasz.[287] Other states to implement laws more recently include Montana[288] and Vermont,[289] and most recently the Canadian province of Quebec has also followed suit.[290] In all of these jurisdictions, including those discussed previously, medical practitioners play a central role. With the exception of Switzerland, they must determine a person's capacity and eligibility under the law, ensure that any consent is valid, and be present at the time of death (although this is not so in Oregon). Even in Switzerland, doctors are implicated because only they can prescribe the necessary legal substances.[291]

18.99 This growing band of jurisdictions has it in common that they embrace the concept of autonomous power at the end of life while, at the same time, distancing themselves from approving suicide. The whole thrust of the Washington Death with Dignity Act

[281] D Colburn, 'Fewer turn to assisted suicide' *The Oregonian*, 11 March 2005. But the dangers associated with 'undercover' PAS (in Australia) are stressed in R S Magnusson, 'Euthanasia: Above ground, below ground' (2004) 30 J Med Ethics 441. The author argues that legalising PAS may be a safer option than prohibition.

[282] W E Hiscox, 'Physician-assisted suicide in Oregon: The "death with dignity" data' (2007) 8 Med L Internat 197.

[283] In 2002, 33 out of the 42 reported cases were 'orchestrated' by the organisation 'Compassion in Dying'.

[284] As an example, compare two papers on the same topic: M P Battin, A van der Heide, et al., 'Legal physician-assisted dying in Oregon and the Netherlands: Evidence concerning the impact on patients in "vulnerable" groups' (2007) 33 J Med Ethics 591 and I G Finlay and R George, 'Legal physician-assisted suicide in Oregon and The Netherlands: Evidence concerning the impact on patients in vulnerable groups— another perspective on Oregon's data' (2011) 37 J Med Ethics 171. One might almost wonder if the authors were looking at the same data!

[285] Initiative 1000. For a brief description, see C Dyer, 'Washington state legalises physician assisted suicide' (2008) 337 BMJ 1133. The closeness of the judicial and political differences has been a feature of the US debate as a whole.

[286] For research, see L Ganzini, E R Goy, and S K Dobscha, 'Prevalence of depression and anxiety in patients requesting physicians' aid in dying: Cross sectional survey' (2008) 337 BMJ 1682.

[287] E.g. T Szasz, 'Diagnoses are not diseases' (1991) 338 Lancet 1574.

[288] Montana joined the permissive group via judicial edict rather than legislation—a process that the European jurisdictions have been at pains to avoid. See Supreme Court of Montana, *Baxter v Montana* (2009) P 3d WL5155363 (Mont., 2009).

[289] See the Patient Choice and Control at End of Life Act 2013.

[290] CBC News, 'Quebec passes landmark end-of-life care bill', 5 June 2014, available at: http://www.cbc.ca/news/canada/montreal/quebec-passes-landmark-end-of-life-care-bill-1.2665834.

[291] For discussion and challenge on these matters see *Haas v Switzerland* (2011) 23 EHRR 53; [2011] ECHR 2422.

was directed to the terminally ill patient requesting medication that he or she 'may self-administer so as to end his or her life in a humane and dignified manner'. Moreover, it insists that actions taken in accordance with the Act 'do not for any purpose, constitute suicide, assisted suicide, mercy killing or homicide under the law'. Nonetheless, it seems clear that the movement towards legalising assisted dying is gaining momentum on a global scale while, at the same time, opposition remains fierce. As a result, and apparently against the European trend, there is no move in the UK to extend assistance in dying beyond assistance in suicide—and there are very good reasons why we should clearly define this particular Rubicon as marking the boundary between what is lawful and what is not.

THE POSITION IN THE UK

18.100 As we have already intimated, the euthanasia debate will not go away and is still alive in the UK. Lord Joffe introduced two Bills to the House of Lords in 2003 and 2004 respectively, the second of which—the Assisted Dying for the Terminally Ill Bill—became the subject of a House of Lords Select Committee report. In essence, the Bill was designed to provide legal authority for a terminally ill and mentally competent adult to request, and be provided with, either PAS or what should be called physician-accomplished suicide. The qualifying criteria included the need for there to be 'unbearable suffering' (defined as 'suffering whether by reason of pain or otherwise which the patient finds so severe as to be unacceptable and results from the patient's terminal illness'); the provision of adequate information and counselling (including the offer of palliative care, where appropriate); repeated informed requests to die from the patient; a written declaration to this effect from the patient in front of two witnesses; a 14-day waiting period; and a final verification of consent. A conscience clause for professional staff was also included with an attendant obligation to refer the patient to another colleague in the event of its being invoked. While the primary aim of the Bill was to legalise PAS, it also sought to provide for active euthanasia in cases where someone—such as an individual in the circumstances of Diane Pretty—is not physically able to take their own life.[292]

18.101 The Bill fell with the dissolution of Parliament for the May 2005 elections, and, among the recommendations of the Select Committee in its report,[293] was one that an early opportunity be taken to debate the report in the House of Lords in the new parliamentary session. Beyond this, the Committee recommended that any future Bill should consider a number of matters, including: (i) a clear distinction between assisted suicide and active euthanasia; (ii) a better articulation of a doctor's powers and responsibility under the legislation; (iii) the need for concepts such as 'terminal illness' and 'competence' to reflect current clinical practice; (iv) consideration of replacement of the criterion of 'unbearable suffering' with notions of 'unrelievable' or 'intractable' suffering; and (v) the abandonment of an obligation on the conscientious objector to refer a patient to a willing colleague. Evidence of public views on euthanasia was largely dismissed as being inconclusive and unrepresentative, but the important point to note is the discernible, albeit subtle, shift in the attitude of the House towards it being more open to the arguments of the Bill's

---

[292] For a very critical—perhaps over-critical—analysis of the Bill, see J Keown, 'Physician-assisted suicide: Lord Joffe's slippery Bill' (2007) 15 Med L Rev 126.

[293] Select Committee on the Assisted Dying for the Terminally Ill Bill, *Assisted Dying for the Terminally Ill Bill—First Report* (2005).

supporters since the last time it considered such issues.[294] Even so, when the Bill was rein-troduced, the House of Lords again shied away from parliamentary responsibility and, by means of what was, in effect, a technical ruse, the Bill was again rejected.

18.102   Since then, Lord Falconer's Bill has come and gone in the interim period between edi-tions of this book. Based on the Oregon model and following the steer given about by the Parliamentary Committee, the Bill proposed that terminally ill adults could lawfully request and receive assistance in dying from registered medical practitioners who would be exempt from the criminal provisions of the Suicide Act 1961 by the insertion of a new clause, thus:

> 2C Assisted dying – Sections 2, 2A and 2B shall not apply to any person in respect of the provision of assistance to another person in accordance with that Act.

18.103   To comply with the Assisted Dying law medical practitioners would have to (i) be satisfied that the person met the definition of 'terminally ill', and two practitioners who required to be so satisfied, (ii) determine that the person had capacity and a 'clear and settled inten-tion to end his or her own life', (iii) establish valid consent, free from coercion, and (iv) be satisfied that the person had been apprised of all alternative options. As well as having oversight of prescription of the lethal substances, an 'assisting health professional' must remain with the person either until they take the dose or decide not to do so. Thus, in myriad ways the medical professions are, once again, morally and practically entangled in proposals to change the law in England and Wales. Lord Falconer's Bill failed for want of parliamentary time, but its has been resurrected more or less wholesale by a Private Member's Bill brought by Rob Marris MP, tabled in June 2015 and due a first reading in September 2015.[295] We can only wait to witness its fate, but the heavy reliance of the medi-cal professions will surely be a considerable point of moral and professional tension.[296] One advance that did occur during the Falconer debates, however, was the unanimous vote in the House of Lords on an amendment brought by Lord Pannick to require judicial confirmation in the High Court that a terminally ill person has reached 'a voluntary, clear, settled and informed' decision. This might be seen to be akin to the judicial over-sight of withdrawal/withholding decisions with respect to patients with severe disorders of consciousness (see Chapter 15).

18.104   Attention to these matters has also been strong in Scotland in recent years. After a failed Oregon-type consultation in 2005, Margo MacDonald MSP formulated an End of Life Choices (Scotland) Bill,[297] which, after some difficulty, was presented to the Scottish Parliament. The Bill was poorly drafted and aimed far higher than its contemporaries—in effect, it sought to legalise active euthanasia while, at the same time, virtually demedi-calising the process. In our view, it had no chance of success and it was duly rejected by the Scottish Parliament.[298] Ms MacDonald secured sufficient votes in September 2012 to

---

[294]   House of Lords, *Report of the Select Committee on Medical Ethics*, HL Paper 21–1 (1994).
[295]   This occurs as we go to press and there is, as yet, no public version of the Marris Bill. Reports suggest, however, that it is another attempt at passing Lord Falconer's provisions.
[296]   See, Commission on Assisted Dying, 'The Current Legal Status of Assisted Dying is Inadequate and Incoherent …' (2012), chaired by Lord Falconer and which led to his Bill. This report considers various mod-els for the UK, concluding that a 'medical oversight model' was preferable. Available at: http://www.demos.co.uk/files/476_CoAD_FinalReport_158x240_I_web_single-NEW_.pdf?1328113363.
[297]   The Bill was later renamed the End of Life Assistance (Scotland) Bill.
[298]   For our full analysis, see G Laurie and J K Mason, 'Assisted dying or euthanasia? Comments on the End of Life Assistance (Scotland) Bill' (2010) 14 Edin LR 493.

permit her to reintroduce a Bill in Holyrood in 2013 as the Assisted Suicide (Scotland) Bill. Sadly, Ms McDonald died early in the progress of her Bill, and this was taken up by Patrick Harvey MSP. It was evident that considerable lessons had been learned from the previous experience. Of note, and in contrast the common features in other laws and proposals, were two features of the Scottish Bill. First, it purported to offer lawful assistance to persons with '… an illness or progressive condition that is terminal *or life-shortening*'. This might have been inspired by Ms McDonald's own circumstances as a Parkinson's disease patient, but in legal terms it potentially opened the scope of the putative law considerably. It would not be as narrow as the English counterpart nor, indeed, like Oregon on which much inspiration had been drawn. Second, and in response to the concerns of many sectors of the medical professions, the Bill proposed a role for 'Licensed Facilitators' whose role would be: 'to provide such practical assistance as the person reasonably requests and to provide comfort and reassurance. They could also be present with the person at the time they committed suicide and they would be responsible for recovering any unused drugs, substances …'. This too is a major departure from other medically based models.[299] Note, however, the implication of doctors remained albeit more removed. Thus, it would still be the case that two doctors would require to certify capacity and the eligibility criteria. They would, nonetheless, be far more removed from the final act. In the event, the Bill fell before the Scottish Parliament on 27 May 2015, but not before robust consideration by the Health and Sport Committee.[300] The supporting documentation are an excellent resource for those interested in the moral and political nuances of this field,[301] not least how the same 'evidence' can be presented differently by different sides of the debate.[302]

CONCLUSION

18.105 Whatever the future may hold for assisted suicide in the UK, it is certain that changes will come about only as a result of extensive argument and with little chance of consensus. One wonders, then, is legislation needed and, if it is, does it have to be as complex and meticulous as is evidenced by recent developments? It will be clear that, throughout this discussion, we have tended to the view that there is little need for legislation in respect of the incurably or terminally ill adult patient; the great majority of life or death decisions can be—and are—based on good medical practice which is contained by relatively clear legal and moral guidelines; when put to the test, the euthanasia calculus needs to be enlisted only in the cases of 'mercy killing' and physician-assisted or physician-accomplished suicide. We doubt if there is serious, extensive support for the first of these in the UK. The movement in favour of formally legalising voluntary euthanasia and PAS is, however, strong and the autonomy-based arguments advanced by its supporters merit

[299] For an assessment of the role of various actors, see A McCann, 'Comparing the law and governance of assisted dying in four European nations' (2015) 2(1) Euro J Comp Law & Gov 37, doi: 10.1163/22134514-00201003.

[300] It is interesting to note in passing that the Committee decided not to make any particular recommendation to Parliament!

[301] For a summary of the Scottish Bill and how it fits in the assisted dying landscape as of January 2015, see Scottish Parliament Information Centre, SPICe Briefing: Assisted Suicide (Scotland) Bill, (2015), available at: http://www.scottish.parliament.uk/ResearchBriefingsAndFactsheets/S4/SB_15-02_Assisted_Suicide_Scotland_Bill.pdf.

[302] Most resources can be found here: http://www.scottish.parliament.uk/parliamentarybusiness/Bills/69604.aspx.

a response. As will be apparent from our discussion earlier, we believe that there are persuasive reasons for rejecting the legalisation of voluntary euthanasia, not the least of these being the extent to which the policy of euthanasia in the Netherlands has been adequately policed and progressively more widely interpreted. The uncertainty of the common law has been used as a justification for change in the law, and although this has been clarified greatly in cases such as *Pretty, Ms B*, and *Purdy*, the most recent decision by the Supreme Court in *Nicklinson* is the clearest possible message that the courts support further clarity but remain reluctant to take this upon themselves. And yet, the example of the Supreme Court of Canada shows a boldness and subtly of spirit that is able to avoid blanket categories of lawful/unlawful or autonomous/vulnerable as the means by which to police and promote the needs of a very wide range of citizens in our society. Even if most of the medical circumstances that people experience at the ends of their lives are not clearly covered by most of the law, there remain a few—but no less important—groups of people for whom this is not true. The law and its institutions are required to deliver justice also to these citizens.

18.106   For us, the key concerns are those of 'which groups' and 'which professionals' are to benefit from, or be implicated, in any legal change. It might well be argued that it is illogical, in principle, to restrict any proposal to terminal disease; we must, however, bow to pragmatism when facing the challenges of drafting a proposal that has any chance of seeing the light of day. Equally, legal reform need not be revolutionary and completed overnight. Initial eligibility could be given to the terminally ill on the understanding that any legislation would be kept under rigorous review—both as to whether it was being abused and as to whether it should be extended in the name of fairness. It is essential to accommodate the management of what is the burning question of the present-day debate—that is, the patient with intractable neuromuscular disease as exemplified by Mrs Pretty and Mr Nicklinson, lest we risk allowing our judicial system to be driven purely by pragmatism at the expense of core principles and values. Indeed, a case can be made out for advocating an independent legislative approach to such cases. As for professionals, we find much merit in the Scottish concept of the 'licensed facilitator' coupled with a robust legally recognised conscience clause. No one, not least a medical professional, should be required to take any part in the cessation of the life of another person. Equally, the ethical imperative of 'First, do no harm' can reasonably be interpreted by many as assisting in the ultimate relief of suffering for those who have chosen this for themselves.

19

BIOMEDICAL HUMAN RESEARCH AND EXPERIMENTATION

INTRODUCTION

19.01   At one time, biomedical research using human subjects proceeded almost as a routine. Researchers justified their activities as benefiting mankind, subjects were generally happy to oblige or be reasonably recompensed, and research was a manageable volume. Attitudes and conditions have changed in large part as a result of: (1) reactions against paternalistic medicine fuelled by an increasing concern for the rights of the individual; (2) the scope, power and volume of investigations expanding greatly—there has been an explosion not only in the production of new therapeutic agents but also in control of their distribution; and (3) revulsion towards the appalling depths which were plumbed in the genocidal era of WWII when much valuable information was gathered at the cost of immense suffering.[1] Support for the research code-making that followed the war was not universal, however, and the end of the Soviet era in Eastern Europe exposed evidence that medical science in the USSR and its satellite countries had not met the ethical standards expected of it.[2] Many East European countries joined the European Union (EU) in 2004, thus obliging them to meet the evolving legal and ethical standards within the EU—and this continues to present a challenge for many.

19.02   At base, modern ethical codes appreciate the need for human research, and accept that it can often only be accomplished at the expense of some of the participants' rights to self-determination. It is, however, universally accepted that the propriety of this sacrifice depends, in the first instance, upon the grant of 'informed' consent—which we have discussed (Chapter 4)—and that specific provision for minors and mentally incompetent subjects are needed. Further, interpretation of the doctor's classic ethical position must be flexible. The Hippocratic Oath states, 'I will follow that regimen which ... I consider for the benefit of my patients and abstain from whatever is deleterious and mischievous'. The absolutist could say that this precludes all experimentation on patients, yet it is clear that progress in medicine depends upon some form of trial in which the trialist is uncertain

---

[1] The awareness of what had happened in the Nazi Germany and Imperial Japan labs fortified a determination that medical research should never again be tainted by such callous disregard for individual rights, and it is this determination which led to the adoption of international codes on research ethics.

[2] Z Szawarski, 'Research ethics in Eastern Europe' (1992) 82 Bull Med Ethics 13. In Poland, a code of medical ethics was introduced which, in a remarkable 1992 judgment of the Polish Constitutional Court, was held to outrank contradictory provisions of the law. The English text of this code was published in (1992) 82 Bull Med Ethics 13; the decision of the Constitutional Court is discussed by E Zielinska at p 25 of the same issue.

of the result—the so-called position of equipoise.[3] In allowing his patients to be involved, the primary clinical carer commits himself to accepting a similar, more dubious, role. The commonest strategy adopted is that of the randomised control trial (RCT), which, in turn, provides the paradigm representation of the ethical problems in research. A balance determined by the interests of all the parties involved must be sought if the research is to be regarded as acceptable,[4] and we discuss that balance at length in the course of this chapter.

THE EVOLUTION OF RULE-MAKING

19.03 The first internationally accepted ethical code was the Nuremberg Code, which was a direct consequence of the war crimes trials.[5] It was important, however, that the medical profession should publicly endorse the principles expressed in its ten clauses, so the Declaration of Helsinki—drawn up by the World Medical Association in 1964 and revised many times since—was subsequently adopted.[6] Many national authorities have attempted to explain or expand upon the basic principles established at Nuremberg, and important examples include the comprehensive set of guidelines issued by the Medical Research Council (MRC),[7] and the Wellcome Trust,[8] both leading funders of research in the United Kingdom (UK).

19.04 In the European context, the Council of Europe's Additional Protocol to the Convention on Human Rights and Biomedicine, which specifically relates to biomedical research, was opened for signature in January 2005. It sets out the broad principles which govern research on human subjects—under which such research is justified only if there is no alternative of comparable effectiveness.[9] Of greater immediate importance—at least in terms of the UK—is the fact that the provisions of the EU Directive on the conditions under which research into medicinal products is to be conducted are now implemented in domestic law.[10] Its emphasis is on good clinical practice which is defined as:

> a set of internationally recognised ethical and scientific quality requirements which must be observed for designing, conducting, recording and reporting clinical trials that involve

---

[3] F Miller and S Joffe, 'Equipoise and the dilemma of randomized clinical trials' (2011) 364 New Eng J Med 476.

[4] For a simplified overview, see S Edwards, R Lilford, and J Hewison, 'The ethics of randomised control trials from the perspectives of patients, the public, and healthcare professionals' (1998) 317 BMJ 1209.

[5] For a discussion of the problem of the significance of Nuremberg, see G Annas and M Grodin (eds), *The Nazi Doctors and the Nuremberg Code: Human Rights in Human Experimentation* (1992).

[6] The latest version of the Declaration was agreed at the 64th WMA General Assembly, Fortaleza, Brazil, October 2013.

[7] The MRC produced some guidelines—Annual Report of the MRC, *Responsibility in Investigations on Human Subjects* (1962–3)—before the Helsinki Declaration. Since then, a stream of guidance has flowed from the MRC, including *Good Research Practice* (2000), *Human Tissue and Biological Samples for Use in Research—Operational and Ethical Guidelines* (2001/2005), *Position Statement on Research Regulation and Ethics* (2005), *Regulation and Biomedical Research* (2009), and *Good Research Practice: Principles and Guidelines* (2012). See http://www.mrc.ac.uk.

[8] See *Guidelines on Good Research Practice* (2002/2005) and *Statement on the Handling of Allegations of Research Misconduct* (2002/2005), both available at: http://www.wellcome.ac.uk.

[9] Additional Protocol to the Convention on Human Rights and Biomedicine Concerning Biomedical Research (2005), Art 5, available at: http://conventions.coe.int/. Note that the Convention has not been ratified by the UK.

[10] Directive 2001/20/EC of 4 April 2001 relating to the implementation of good clinical practice in the conduct of clinical trials on medicinal products for human use, was implemented in the UK by the Medicines for Human Use (Clinical Trials) Regulations 2004 (SI 2004/1031), as amended by SIs 2006/1928, 2006/2984, and 2008/941.

the participation of human subjects. Compliance with this good practice provides assurance that the rights, safety and well-being of trial subjects are protected, and that the results of the clinical trial are credible.[11]

The Directive applies only to the conduct of clinical trials;[12] other forms of research are unaffected.[13] Thus, the obligation on Member States to change their laws in conformity with the Directive relates only to clinical trials of an investigational medicinal product (CTIMPs). That having been said, the Directive's fundamental principles and its requirements for structural and regulatory changes to systems of research governance led the British government to overhaul its system of research regulation. It did not take the opportunity, however, to ensure that CTIMPs and other types of research are subject to the same provisions.[14]

19.05   Perhaps unsurprisingly, various standard and novel interventions are now regulated at the European level. Space does not permit a thorough review of these regimes, but it should be noted that many of these instruments are under review or revision.[15] Our focus will be on clinical trials, the regime for which remains in a state of flux; the European Commission advanced a proposal for a Regulation in this area in July 2012,[16] and the Regulation, adopted in 2014, will take effect on 28 May 2016.[17] The 2014 Regulation articulates the general principle that a clinical trial may be held only if: (1) the rights, safety, dignity and well-being of participants are protected and prevail over all other interests; and (2) it is designed to generate reliable and robust

---

[11] 2001 Directive, Art 1(2). A Toolkit is available to help researchers and others navigate the complex regulatory landscape: see http://www.ct-toolkit.ac.uk/.

[12] It does not apply to non-interventional trials which are, essentially, trials in which the recipient of the medicinal product is being treated in the normal way without assignment to treatment by way of an advance protocol. It has been joined by Directive 2005/28/EC of 8 April 2005 laying down principles and detailed guidelines for good clinical practice as regards investigational medicinal products for human use, as well as the requirements for authorisation of the manufacturing or importation of such products.

[13] For standards applicable in other research and clinical contexts, see: Regulations (EC) No 1901/2006 and 1902/2006 of the European Parliament and of the Council of 12 December 2006 on medicinal products for paediatric use; Regulation (EC) No 1394/2007 of the European Parliament and of the Council of 13 November 2007 on advanced therapy medicinal products and amending Directive 2001/83/EC and Regulation (EC) No 726/2004; Directive 90/385/EEC relating to active implantable medical devices; Directive 93/42/EEC concerning medical devices; and Directive 98/79/EC on in vitro diagnostic medical devices specified in Directive 2007/47/EC. The latter instruments were transposed into UK law by the Medical Devices Amendment Regulations (SI 2008/2936).

[14] For criticism, see J McHale, 'Law, regulation and public health research: A case for fundamental reform?' (2010) 63 Current Legal Prob 475, and E Jackson, *Law and the Regulation of Medicines* (2012).

[15] New Regulations have been proposed, for example, for medical devices. See the Proposal for a Regulation of the European Parliament and of the Council on medical devices, and amending Directive 2001/83/EC, Regulation (EC) No 178/2002 and Regulation (EC) No 1223/2009 and the Proposal for a Regulation of the European Parliament and of the Council on in vitro diagnostic medical devices, 26 September 2012.

[16] Proposal for a Regulation of the European Parliament and of the Council on clinical trials on medicinal products for human use, and repealing Directive 2001/20/EC, 17 July 2012, COM(2012) 369 final.

[17] Regulation (EU) No 536/2014 of the European Parliament and of the Council of 16 April 2014 on clinical trials on medicinal products for human use, and repealing Directive 2001/20/EC. The main difference between a Directive and a Regulation is that while Member States have some latitude with implementation of a Directive, a Regulation is directly applicable in all Member States without need for implementation. The concern has been that while the Directive ensured safety, it resulted in a 25 per cent drop in clinical trials in Europe: R Smyth, 'Regulation and governance of clinical research in the UK' (2011) 342 BMJ d238.

data.[18] And the new instrument aims to streamline authorisation and reporting procedures.[19]

19.06 As can be seen, the field is now littered with actors, instruments, and amendments; while the European Commission provides the secretariat for the Forum for National Ethics Councils around Europe as part of the international endeavour to coordinate ethical reflection in medical research and to raise and maintain common standards,[20] the field remains complex and fragmented. The Commission's current objective is to develop a framework for Responsible Research and Innovation (RRI) designed 'to better align both the process and its outcomes, with the values, needs and expectations of European society'.[21] Indeed, and again as should be obvious, medical research governance, particularly its international element, has been something of a growth industry. One of the ironies of this is that there may now be so many instruments, regulations, and guides that the system itself is standing in the way of good ethical research.[22] In this chapter, we consider the prevailing (and highly dynamic) regime that has evolved. But first, a definition of the subject.

CONDUCTING MEDICAL RESEARCH

CORE DEFINITIONS AND DISTINCTIONS

19.07 While research and experimentation are commonly used interchangeably, we believe there is a distinction to be made. Research implies a predetermined protocol with a clearly defined end-point. Experimentation involves a more speculative, ad hoc approach to an individual subject. The distinction is significant in that an experiment may be modified to take into account the individual's response; a research programme, however, ties the researcher to a particular course of action until such time as its general ineffectiveness is satisfactorily demonstrated.[23] Moreover, while the aim of experimentation is usually linked to the interests of the subject upon whom the experiment is being conducted—for example, the deployment of a last-chance experimental technique to improve the patient's diminishing health—the overall objective of research is to acquire generalisable knowledge which, by and large, has nothing directly to do with the health state or interests of the research participants.[24]

---

[18] 2014 Regulation, Art 3.

[19] And are in keeping with the UK Academy of Medical Sciences' stinging 2011 critique of the burden of research regulation, which led to the establishment of the new Health Research Authority in the same year, with a remit of tackling the 'burden' challenge in particular: AMS, *A New Pathway for the Regulation and Governance of Health Research* (2011). For more on the HRA, see http://www.hra.nhs.uk/.

[20] See the EU's Science and Society in Europe website: http://ec.europa.eu/research/science-society/.

[21] H Sutcliffe, A Report on Responsible Research and Innovation (2011). RRI consists of six elements: (1) engagement; (2) gender equality; (3) science education; (4) ethics; (5) open access; and (6) governance.

[22] Note that the list of relevant legislation, regulation, and standards in the UK runs to almost 50 pages! Department of Health, *Research Governance Framework for Health and Social Care* (2nd edn, 2005, Annex 2008). For criticism of the regime, see B Perks, 'New regulations urged for UK health research' (2011) 17 Nature Med 142.

[23] For an excellent discussion which is not dated by its age, see B Dickens, 'What is a medical experiment?' (1975) 113 Can Med Assoc J 635.

[24] The latest version of the Department of Health research governance framework defines research as: 'the attempt to derive generalisable new knowledge by addressing clearly defined questions with systematic and rigorous methods': Department of Health, n 22, at 3.

19.08 Medical research is a global, multibillion dollar industry involving funders and researchers from public, commercial, and joint enterprises. Research can be broadly categorised as *therapeutic*, which is aimed at improved treatment for the class of patients from which participants have been drawn, and as *non-therapeutic*, which is aimed at furthering scientific knowledge which may, eventually, have a wider application than patient care.[25] This distinction makes little conceptual difference to the general requirements for ethical research. The mere fact that the research participant, being a patient at the time, may receive benefit does not mean that the programme can be undertaken unregulated by research codes—indeed, the fact that a relatively vulnerable group is involved emphasises the care with which the project should be monitored.[26] Only the degree of risk to be permitted in proportion to the expected outcome is affected by the nature of the research.

19.09 It follows from this classification that research participants may be of four general types: individual patients; a group of patients suffering from one particular condition; patients who have no association with the disease or process under review but who are readily available; and, finally, healthy volunteers—a heterogeneous group which is of importance because it may involve other 'captive' populations, including the researchers themselves. It is also important to bear in mind that we can participate in medical research without our even knowing it if our medical data are accessed and used in population-based studies. While our physical integrity is not compromised in such cases, there can be a serious risk to our personal privacy, so this research must also be subject to ethical oversight and control.[27]

19.10 The logical implication of these categories of participants is that researchers should also be categorised. Thus, the individual patient is under the care of a doctor. Any experimental procedure or treatment is, therefore, performed on a care-associated basis, and while there may be difficulties in a hospital setting where 'care' is very much a team concept, the essential doctor–patient relationship is, and should be, maintained. But it cannot be said with reference to any of the other types of research participant that 'the health of my patient [and the singular noun is to be noted] is my first consideration'; consequently, the researchers should not normally include the patients' physicians. Even so, doctors must be involved whenever human participants are subject to medical research; the danger of non-medical researchers being non-comprehension of their participants' reactions. Thus, excluding doctors would only be acceptable in the event that the researchers were their own experimental subjects. This categorisation of relationship is also important for the kinds of obligations owed between the parties, and, ultimately, the parameters of any liability. The 'pure' researcher–participant relationship is of a different nature to the doctor–patient relationship, and the standard of care owed in each will vary and depend on circumstances. Matters are complicated if these categories become blurred, but the best baseline rule should be that any clinical or quasi-clinical aspect of the relationship should be conducted according to the ethical principle, '*First Do No Harm*'.[28]

---

[25] The eminent researcher, Doll, rightly pointed out that there are other forms of research available that do not involve actual human subjects—e.g. research by questionnaire, study of records, etc.: R Doll, 'Research will be impeded' (2001) 323 BMJ 1421.

[26] Edwards et al., n 4, observe that a high proportion of participants in a research programme enter because they think they have something to gain—and this is tied to the question of how much they actually understand when consenting.

[27] The same is true of tissue samples removed from us, e.g. perhaps a biopsy has been removed during surgery and then retained for research purposes. For an excellent account of the issues see W Lowrance, *Access to Collections of Data and Materials for Health Research* (2006).

[28] B Sachs, 'The exceptional ethics of the investigator–subject relationship' (2010) 35 J Med Phil 64.

19.11 In *Walker-Smith* v *GMC*,[29] the court acknowledged the grey area between medical practice and research and suggested that the distinction is largely a matter of intent on the
part of the responsible professional. Quoting the Royal College of Physicians, it was said:

> The definition of research continues to present difficulties, particularly with regard to
> the distinction between medical practice and medical research. The distinction derives
> from the intent. In medical practice the sole intention is to benefit the individual patient
> consulting the clinician, not to gain knowledge of general benefit, though such knowl-
> edge may incidentally emerge from the clinical experience gained. In medical research
> the primary intention is to advance knowledge so that patients in general may benefit;
> the individual patient may or may not benefit directly. Thus, when a clinician departs in a
> significant way from standard or accepted practice entirely for the benefit of a particular
> individual patient, and with consent, the innovation need not constitute research, though
> it may be described as an experiment in the sense that it is novel and un-validated.[30]

The importance of this legal statement lies in its regulatory implications. It suggests that
it might fall largely to the medical profession to determine which regulatory regime—
treatment or research—will govern their interventions with vulnerable patients. From
the objective perspective, however, the overarching concern will be the nature and degree
of any harms to which the person is likely to be subjected.

THE RISKS INVOLVED

19.12 All research involves some risk, and it is the art of good investigation to minimise that
risk. Having said that, the Declaration of Helsinki,[31] the Additional Protocol (2005),[32] and
the EU Directive and 2014 Regulation,[33] all offer guidance. A risk–benefit analysis must
be undertaken in each case and patients may be involved only when the benefit to them
clearly outweighs the inconvenience, discomfort, or possible harm which the protocol
may impose. The Royal College of Physicians distinguished between research involving
'less than minimal risk' and that involving 'minimal risk'.[34] The former is the risk of the
sort involved in giving a sample of urine or a single venous sample in an adult; the latter arises where there is a reasonable chance of a mild reaction—such as a headache or
a feeling of lethargy—or where there is a remote chance of serious injury or death. The
College took the view that, if the level rises above that of minimal risk, patients should be
involved only if:

  (i)   the risk is still small in comparison with that already incurred by the patient as a
        consequence of the disease itself;
  (ii) the disease is a serious one;
  (iii) the knowledge gained from the research is likely to be of great practical benefit;
  (iv) there is no other means of obtaining that knowledge; and
  (v)   the patient gives a fully informed consent,

[29] [2012] EWHC 503 (Admin).
[30] *Walker-Smith*, at paras 11–12. For commentary, see P Case, 'Treading the line between clinical research
and therapy' (2012) 28 Prof Negl 224.
[31] Paras 16–18.   [32] Arts 6, 13, 15, 16, 17, and 21.
[33] Especially, Arts 3(2), 4, and 5 of the Directive, and Arts 6(1)(b) and 10 of the 2014 Regulation.
[34] Royal College of Physicians, *Research Involving Patients* (1990). See also Royal College of Physicians,
Guidelines on the Practice of Ethics Committees in Medical Research with Human Participants (4th edn, 2007).

and these still represent the views expressed in the very large number of comparable documents that have been produced since this report was published.

19.13 The question of whether healthy volunteers may ever be exposed to serious risks in the course of medical research is problematic. Paragraph 18 of the Declaration of Helsinki states that every study involving human subjects must be preceded by careful assessment of predictable risks and burdens to the individuals and communities involved in the research in comparison with foreseeable benefits to them, and to other individuals or communities affected by the condition under investigation. At first blush it is difficult to see what benefits are involved in medical research that involves healthy volunteers, beyond perhaps the satisfaction of helping others. Certainly, a project would have to be of exceptional importance before a substantial risk to healthy volunteers would be acceptable. On the face of things, the Additional Protocol (2005) allows more discretion in Art 6's direction in that research that does not have the potential to produce results of direct benefit to the health of the research participant may only be authorised if it 'entails no more than acceptable risk and acceptable burden for the research participant'; the emphasis appears to be more on risk taking than on assessment of risk, but both are subjective exercises. What, for example, is one to say of the use of volunteers in potentially harmful research into the development of vaccines against diseases that may affect the community? One can interpolate a further question—at what stage does a prophylactic exercise directed against an unknown hazard become, or cease to be, a research project?[35] The ethics depend on an uncertain amalgam of necessity, altruism, and courage, the contribution of each being difficult to quantify.

19.14 There will clearly be differing views as to which risks are justifiable; it is equally clear that there will be those who would accept risks of a very high order on communitarian grounds, and it is questionable whether they should be prevented from so doing. There are legal limits to the extent to which consent decriminalises the infliction of harm,[36] and it is interesting to speculate how far the consent of a volunteer to a dangerous medical experiment would serve as a defence to a charge of assault or homicide.[37] It may be that the interests of others are necessarily also in play. As we discuss in Chapter 17, the unknown risks of retro viruses spreading to the human population through xenotransplants would be reason enough to refuse all volunteers willing to make a personal sacrifice. When the threat of harm is only at the individual level, however, the choice to volunteer may be cast as one of the ultimate expressions of personal autonomy and pure altruism, and the rejection of such selfless acts becomes far more difficult to justify (certainly on a felicific calculus).[38]

19.15 All of this was made tragically real in March 2006 when six healthy volunteers at Northwick Park Hospital suffered extremely serious adverse reactions, including multiple organ failure, after participating in a first-in-man clinical trial of TGN412 (a new anti-inflammatory drug). The reactions were swift and entirely unanticipated and sent

---

[35] For an interesting discussion of the development and use of a vaccine designed to protect against biological warfare, see T Gibson, 'A shot in the arm for the military: Consent to immunisation against biological warfare agents' (2002) 5 Med L Internat 161.

[36] *A-G's Reference (No 6 of 1980)* [1981] 2 All ER 1057 (CA); *Smart v HM Advocate* 1975 SLT 65; *R v Brown* [1994] 1 AC 212.

[37] It is to be noted, however, that no such charges were brought in something of a cause célèbre at a noted US hospital: J Savulescu and M Spriggs, 'The hexamethonium asthma study and the death of a normal volunteer in research' (2002) 28 J Med Ethics 3.

[38] For discussion see T Hope and J McMillan, 'Challenge studies of human volunteers: Ethical issues' (2004) 30 J Med Ethics 110.

shock waves through the research community.[39] An Expert Scientific Group was set up to determine what went wrong and what lessons could be learned from the incident. Its report included 22 recommendations, many of which were focused on the establishment of a clearer evidence-base of risk before the transition to humans, and the vital importance of communication between researchers and regulatory authorities and between authorities on a worldwide basis.

19.16   Ultimately, as to the running of risk, researchers should err on the side of caution; if different methods/sources indicate different estimates of a safe dose in humans then the lowest value should be taken as a starting point.[40] The bottom line is that the decision to conduct a first-in-man trial in healthy volunteers or volunteer patients should be carefully considered and fully justified, taking into account all factors relevant to the safety of the subjects and the value of the scientific information that is likely to be obtained.[41] However, it is important to acknowledge that risk—voluntarily assumed or otherwise—is but one element of the overall regulation of ethical research.

GOVERNANCE OF THE UNDERTAKING

19.17   Approaches to research governance in many jurisdictions have been haphazard. In the UK, the first formal guidance on ethical review was only issued by the Department of Health in 1991,[42] and there was no legislation on human subject research until the adoption of the 2004 Regulations. Responsibility for governance has been divided between England, Scotland, Northern Ireland, and Wales, with responsibility for the English system falling initially to the Central Office for Research Ethics Committees (COREC), then to the National Patient Safety Agency (from 1 April 2005),[43] and most recently to the NHS Commissioning Board Special Health Authority (from 1 June 2012). The UK Ethics Committee Authority (UKECA), now under the Health Research Authority (HRA), has the task of establishing, recognising, and monitoring local research ethics committees so as to ensure compliance with the 2004 Regulations.[44] And, while the 2004 Regulations relate only to CTIMPs, it is the intention of the Department of Health that their terms will be treated as covering all types of work carried out by research ethics committees (RECs). This leaves us with the rather odd legal position whereby the work of some RECs is covered by legal provisions (and the rules of liability), and that of others is governed by the stated will of a government department.

19.18   While the EU's 2014 Regulation applies throughout the UK, the various Departments of Health have issued Research Governance *Frameworks* which set out principles for good research governance applicable to all research conducted within the remit of their respective jurisdictions.[45] The 2005 Framework lays out principles, requirements, and standards for acceptable research, mechanisms to meet these criteria, methods for monitoring

---

[39] P Ferguson, 'Clinical trials and healthy volunteers' (2008) Med L Rev 23.

[40] Cf, T Beauchamp, 'Why our conceptions of research and practice may not serve the best interests of patients and subjects' (2011) 269 J Internal Med 383.

[41] Department of Health, *Expert Scientific Group on Phase One Clinical Trials: Final Report* (2006).

[42] Department of Health, *Local Research Ethics Committees*, HSG (91)5. While NHS-based local research ethics committees have been around in one form or another since 1975, they did not enjoy statutory authority, and oversight of their working practices was patchy. For more, see M Brazier and E Cave, *Medicine, Patients and the Law* (5th edn, 2011). Prior to this, examples of research ethics committees can be found dating back to the 1960s, but their constitution and use were sporadic and lacking centralised control.

[43] See: http://www.npsa.nhs.uk.   [44] See Part II of the 2004 Regulations.

[45] Department of Health, n 22, Scottish Executive Health Department, *Research Governance Framework for Health and Community Care* (2006); Department of Health, Social Services and Public Safety, *Research*

compliance, and issues concerning the proper protection of research participants and the wider public. It points out that good health and social care research is a multidisciplinary affair, covering areas as diverse as ethics, science, information, health, safety and employment, finance, and intellectual property. Here, we concentrate on the ethical dimension.

19.19 Given the crucially important nature of the ethical and personal issues at stake, the Department of Health requires that research involving patients, their organs, tissues, or data must undergo prior independent scrutiny to ensure that ethical standards are met. Indeed, it is now a criminal offence to commence a CTIMP without such prior approval.[46] The 2005 Framework makes it clear that consent is the lynchpin to ethically acceptable research, and it goes on to state that additional legal requirements may come into play depending on the type of research proposed or the state of the research subject. Thus, research on those of reduced capacity may implicate the Mental Capacity Act 2005, and research using human material may engage the Human Tissue Act 2004. The reader is referred to the relevant chapters where these instruments are examined in more detail. We discuss the particular elements of consent to research in due course. The 2005 Framework's Annex (2008) details the full range of relevant legal provisions and regulations with respect to each area of research.

19.20 Responsibility and accountability have become the watchwords of the modern research governance culture. The 2001 Directive requires that a 'sponsor' now be named in each ethical review application, the sponsor being the body/person(s) with overall legal responsibility for the various elements of the conduct and management of the research, and the 2014 Regulation preserves this condition.[47] The Department of Health has rolled this out for all research undertaken in the context of the NHS or social care services in England. The framework also spends considerable time outlining the respective duties of those involved in research, such as researchers themselves, funders, care professionals, and research participants. Finally, the framework points to the need for adequate monitoring systems to ensure compliance with the framework, and the 2014 Regulation confirms the European Medicines Agency (EMA) as the body responsible for receiving clinical trial reports.[48] This is a legal obligation in respect of CTIMPs, but, once again, the Department of Health's policy is that appropriate systems of surveillance and reporting will be developed in respect of *all* NHS research.

RESEARCH ETHICS COMMITTEES

19.21 As is perhaps clear from the above, ethics committees are central to the research governance framework, but it is important to distinguish two major types. Institutional ethics committees, commonly known as Institutional Review Boards (IRBs), have functions that extend beyond research and includes therapeutic and prognostic decision-making. Common in the USA where they wield considerable power, they are being increasingly introduced elsewhere as an aid to ethical decision-making in a clinical setting. A number of IRBs, or variations on them, have been established in the UK following a pioneer effort in 1993,[49] and there are now more than 70 'clinical ethics' committees established in NHS

Governance Framework for Health and Social Care in Northern Ireland (2006); National Assembly for Wales, *Research Governance Framework for Health and Social Care in Wales* (2009).

[46] 2004 Regulations, reg 49. [47] 2014 Regulation, Arts 5 and 45.
[48] 2014 Regulation, Chapter VII, and the ICH Guidelines are specifically referenced.
[49] Editorial, 'UK's first hospital ethics committee' (1993) 90 Bull Med Ethics 5, reported the establishment of an ethics committee within an NHS trust hospital in north-west London.

hospital trusts—their role, however, differs from one institution to another.[50] Beyond this clinical setting, many private and public institutions establish ethics committees to vet research being carried out under their name; examples include private research establishments, universities, and the MRC.

19.22 RECs, such as are set up within the NHS under the auspices of the Department of Health, are of a different genre. Official Local Research Ethical Committees (LRECs) are established by health authorities to scrutinise research projects involving patients from within the specific authority. Where research involves patients/persons from a number of authorities (or, indeed, from abroad), then ethical clearance was formally required from a Multi-Centre Research Ethics Committee (MREC); these were established for the first time in 1997. The composition of RECs in the UK, along with matters of procedure, are regulated by guidelines issued by the Department of Health.[51] Matters are overseen by the National Research Ethics Service (NRES),[52] now under the auspices of the HRA— charged with delivering effective and proportionate governance.[53]

19.23 Under the *Governance Arrangements for Research Ethics Committees: A Harmonised Edition* (2011), if REC review is required, then research may not begin until a favourable REC opinion has been obtained. Each REC should include both sexes and a range of ages, with representation from hospital staff, general practitioners, and a sufficiently broad range of expertise so that the scientific and methodological aspects of proposals can be reconciled with the ethical implications. A quorum consists of at least seven members, and the REC must not normally exceed 18 members. It can, when indicated, seek the advice of specialist referees. At least one-third of the membership must be lay members and at least half of these must be people who have never been associated with the health or social services and have never undertaken research. The inclusion of 'average citizens' might be seen as a necessary political gesture, but lay members may be better placed than professionals to appreciate the effects of different treatments on the day-to-day lives of patients, and their inclusion may therefore have practical advantages. One such member must be present in a quorum, as must one expert member. REC members must undergo training.

19.24 The HRA has issued Standard Operating Procedures (SOPs),[54] which outline the kinds of factors to be considered by RECs. In the main, the considerations are very similar as between CTIMPs and other forms of research, although notable differences include (1) that approval for CTIMPs must also be given by the Medicines and Healthcare Products Regulatory Agency (MHRA), (2) sites to be used to conduct the trials must be subject to inspection and approval, and (3) an obligation of *pharmacovigilance* is imposed throughout the trial, such that any Suspected Unexpected Serious Adverse Reactions (SUSARs)[55]

---

[50] D Sokol, 'The unpalatable truth about ethics committees' (2009) 339 BMJ 891, outlines some of the anticipated difficulties with the concept of clinical ethics committees.

[51] See Department of Health, *Governance Arrangements for Research Ethics Committees: A Harmonised Edition* (2011), available at: https://www.gov.uk/government/publications/health-research-ethics-committees-governance-arrangements.

[52] http://www.nres.nhs.uk/.

[53] See Health Research Authority Regulations (SI 2011/2341) and Health Research Authority (Amendment) Regulations (SI 2012/1108).

[54] See NRES, *Standard Operating Procedures for Research Ethics Committees*, v 6.1 (2015), which should be read in conjunction with reg 15 of the 2004 Regulations, which themselves outline the considerations a REC must undertake in preparing its opinion.

[55] The SOPs follow the 2004 Regulations in defining 'Suspected Serious Adverse Reaction'. An 'adverse reaction' is any untoward and unintended response in a subject to an investigational medicinal

must be notified to the REC in accordance with European Commission guidance. More extensive and effective monitoring procedures are now in place, and chief investigators are expected to inform the REC of any Serious Adverse Events (SAEs) [56] within 15 days of it coming to their attention. The SOPs now also provide for ethical review and governance of research involving databases and human tissue, and they provide for communication with other regulators and review bodies.[57]

19.25 While as a strict matter of law the SOPs only carry weight in respect of CTIMPs, there are several reasons why undertaking medical research is effectively impossible without following them and receiving the necessary approvals. To begin with, it is not possible to use NHS patients or resources for an unapproved project.[58] Funding is also likely to be denied unless a REC's imprimatur is obtained, and the results of unapproved research are unlikely to be accepted for publication by reputable scientific journals. There are further pragmatic grounds compelling compliance with the guidelines, which clearly represent 'good professional practice'; for example, appeal to *Bolam* principles would be virtually unavailable in the event of misadventure associated with unapproved research—the *Bolitho* limitations (see para 5.42) would almost certainly apply.

19.26 The decisions of ethics committees are subject to judicial review;[59] in the same way, a researcher frustrated by a REC could pursue a remedy by that route. Appeal mechanisms are also in place.[60] The aggrieved research participant may also seek redress, most obviously through an action against the researcher.[61] Indeed, there is an obligation, as part of the ethical approval mechanism, to ensure that adequate compensation measures are available (see later). Beyond this, however, it could be argued that a relationship exists between the REC member and the research participant which is of sufficient proximity to give rise to a duty of care and that this might, in theory, lead to civil liability in a case where a REC member has failed to exercise due care in the scrutiny of a research proposal. This, however, has never been tested in court. Furthermore, the guidelines make it clear that the appointing Authority will take full responsibility for all the actions of members in the course of carrying out their duties other than those involving bad faith, wilful

product which is related to any dose administered to that subject. An adverse reaction is 'serious' if it: (a) results in death; (b) is life-threatening; (c) requires hospitalisation or prolongation of existing hospitalisation; (d) results in persistent or significant disability or incapacity; or (e) consists of a congenital anomaly or birth defect. An adverse reaction is 'unexpected' if its nature and severity are not consistent with the information about the medicinal product in question set out: (a) in the case of a product with a marketing authorisation, in the summary of product characteristics for that product; (b) in the case of any other investigational medicinal product; and (c) in the investigator's brochure relating to the trial in question.

[56] The 2004 Regulations define an SAE as an untoward occurrence that: (i) results in death; (ii) is life-threatening; (iii) requires hospitalisation or prolongation of existing hospitalisation; (iv) results in persistent or significant disability or incapacity; (v) consists of a congenital anomaly or birth defect; or (vi) is otherwise considered medically significant by the investigator.

[57] Sections 11, 12, and 14 respectively.

[58] The body conducting research is encouraged to submit its proposals to an LREC even when there is no NHS involvement.

[59] *R v Ethical Committee of St Mary's Hospital (Manchester), ex p H (or Harriott)* [1988] 1 FLR 512.

[60] See SOPs, s 8, n 58.

[61] Those injured in the course of pharmaceutical trials may be compensated by the company sponsoring the trial, as recommended by the Association of the British Pharmaceutical Industry in its *Clinical Trial Compensation Guidelines* (1991, as amended).

default, or gross negligence.[62] The precise meaning of the last term in the context of an indemnity is uncertain.[63]

RANDOMISED CONTROLLED TRIALS

RANDOMISATION

19.27 Biomedical research almost inevitably involves an RCT at some point.[64] The principle of RCTs is simple—in order to decide whether a new drug or treatment is better than an existing one, or is preferable to none at all, the new treatment is given to a group of patients or healthy volunteers and not given to another group as similar to the first as can be obtained. The subtleties of experimental design are critical to the success of the project because a badly conceived trial is fundamentally unethical, but even the best-designed RCT has its built-in moral problem: on the one hand, a relatively untried treatment which may do harm is being given to one group while, on the other, a treatment which may be of considerable benefit is being withheld from another. In one view, this is unacceptable on the grounds that it is ethically objectionable to withhold a treatment which it is believed would be beneficial to a patient; the doctor must do her best for the patient but the problem is to know what is best, and, in particular, to know whether the patient's recovery is being hindered by the restraints of the research protocol.[65] The first essential for any RCT is, therefore, that it must provide its answer as rapidly as possible and it must be terminable as soon as an adverse effect becomes apparent (though statisticians may insist on evidence from many more cases—and possibly observed for longer—than physicians may feel is necessary).

19.28 When, then, should RCTs stop? At what point does the clinician say that the evidence of benefit is sufficient to justify the conclusion that a treatment does indeed do good? Conversely, at what point does the apparent emergence of an adverse effect dictate that the project be abandoned? The patient involved in such a trial will have been informed that he is possibly being denied a potential benefit—yet his consent will have been based on his trust that there is genuine scientific uncertainty. Once this uncertainty is resolved to the extent of a belief (on a balance of probabilities) that the treatment offers clinical benefit, then it becomes questionable whether it can still be denied to some in a continuing quest for statistical significance.[66] In deciding this question, it is important that the researcher

---

[62] In this regard, see *Noordeen* v *Hill & Anor* [2012] EWHC 2847 (QB), wherein a surgeon initiated proceedings against a REC member, and it was accepted that the Health Research Agency, as the body responsible for RECs, should be joined as a party given its responsibility for any costs which may be ordered against the member.

[63] Accountability prior to the recent guidelines was considered in a major review: J McHale, 'Guidelines for medical research—Some ethical and legal problems' (1993) 1 Med L Rev 160.

[64] Indeed, it was the ubiquity and particularity of this type of research that led to the adoption of the Clinical Trials Directive in 2001. Other forms of trials, which are beyond the scope of this book, can be used and may be preferable on ethical grounds. For a full description, see A Avins, 'Can unequal be more fair? Ethics, subject allocation, and randomised clinical trials' (1998) 24 J Med Ethics 401.

[65] The practical anxiety was outlined in simple terms in F Verdú–Pascual and A Castelló–Ponce, 'Randomised clinical trials: A source of ethical dilemmas' (2001) 27 J Med Ethics 177—and the statisticians put the counter–argument: J Hilden and A Gammelgaard, 'Premature stopping and informed consent in AMI trials' (2002) 28 J Med Ethics 188. For sceptical views on the value of RCTs, see J Grossman and J Mackenzie, 'The randomized controlled trial: Gold standard or merely standard?' (2005) 48 Perspectives in Bio and Med 516.

[66] For an analysis, see N Johnson, R Lilford, and W Brazier, 'At what level of collective equipoise does a clinical trial become ethical?' (1991) 17 J Med Ethics 30. The standards of proof have been compared to the

bears in mind the fundamental precept which governs ethical medical research—that one does not use patients as a means to a scientific end, but rather treats them as an end in themselves. Even so, the practical dilemma remains—the clinically orientated researcher stands to see his subsequent report criticised for want of scientific support while the more scientifically minded one sleeps uneasily because he worries that his research has reached an inadequate conclusion. Well-designed trials should include plans for periodic analysis; there is also a good case to be made for an independent observer, or the REC, being responsible for monitoring the trial from this angle.[67]

19.29 The regulatory framework must be assessed against these ethical parameters. We have already seen, for example, that before initiating a CTIMP, the sponsor(s) must obtain both a positive endorsement from a REC,[68] and a Clinical Trial Authorisation (CTA) from the MHRA.[69] It is a criminal offence to do otherwise.[70] Monitoring research sites is part of the review process,[71] but, in general, a REC is not responsible in law for proactively monitoring research.[72] It does, however, have a duty to keep its favourable ethical opinion under review throughout the trial, especially in light of progress reports provided by the researchers, which are due annually.[73] A REC can review its favourable ethical opinion of a research project at any time,[74] and the REC may review its ethical opinion in light of concerns or challenges raised by patients, service users, carers, members of the public or patient organisations, researchers etc. where these present relevant new information not originally considered by the REC and related to any of the following: (a) the social or scientific value, or scientific design and conduct of the study; (b) risks to the safety or physical or mental integrity of participants; (c) the competence or conduct of the sponsor or investigator(s); (d) the feasibility of the study; (e) the adequacy of the site or facilities; and (f) suspension or termination of regulatory approval for the study.[75]

19.30 The principle of randomisation lies at the heart of clinical trials, and the ethical problems associated with them. It is almost impossible for health professionals not to have some preference when there is a choice of treatments.[76] For this reason, many doctors having care—especially primary care—of patients distrust the RCT, many for fear that the doctor–patient relationship will be jeopardised, and many for concerns

different standards applied in the civil and criminal courts: Editorial, 'On stopping a trial before its time' (1993) 342 Lancet 1311. For an argument that medical ethics in the clinical and research contexts should not be conflated and that equipoise does precisely that, see F Miller, 'Dispensing with equipoise' (2011) 342 Am J Med Sci 276.

[67] E Pickworth, 'Should local research ethics committees monitor research they have approved?' (2000) 26 J Med Ethics 330. The author thinks not—mainly on the grounds that they could not accommodate the extra workload but also because it would introduce an element of policing into what is an advisory role. The Declaration of Helsinki, however, acknowledges a REC's right to do so (at para 15). More compelling still, the UK SOPs make express provision for this (s 9).

[68] The 2004 Regulations require that ethical review must normally occur within 60 days of receipt of an application: 2004 Regulations, reg 15. Article 25 of the 2014 Regulation from the EU stipulates what information must be provided to the review body.

[69] SOPs, para 14.6.　　[70] 2004 Regulations, reg 49.　　[71] SOPs, s 5.

[72] See SOPs, s 10, for operational policy on research monitoring.

[73] However, in the event of a SUSAR (see earlier for definition), the sponsor's obligation to report is enhanced: SOPs, paras 10.20–10.36.

[74] SOPs, paras 10.105–10.106.

[75] SOPs, paras 10.105–10.114, especially para 10.107. For suspensions of non-CTIMPs, see SOPs, paras 10.115–10.135.

[76] True 'equipoise' may be impossible to attain for many reasons; at best, it will be unusual. Perhaps we should be looking for genuine disagreement among experts rather than genuine uncertainty.

around informed consent (discussed later).[77] Suffice to say, the consent process has a profound effect on the patient's participation—refusal may be on simple utilitarian grounds, but is equally liable to stem from confusion. No RCT can be ethical unless the professionals genuinely disagree as to which treatment yields the best results. Given that the doctors are unsure, it may be difficult for the patient to solve what appears to be an insoluble problem. The result of the cumulative adverse factors is that accrual rates to important trials can be low—it was reported, for example, that a fundamental research project intended to identify the best treatment for early breast cancer had to be closed after a very low recruitment because the insistence on full informed consent frightened off both surgeons and patients.[78] Researchers, therefore, use devices which circumvent the confrontation between clinicians and patient, and most of these involve some form of pre-selection—or 'pre-randomisation'—prior to discussion of treatment.[79] There are specific ethical and practical objections to such manoeuvres, but it seems morally doubtful to use what is essentially a ruse to obviate an agreed ethical practice which is an integral part of the basic principles not only of the Declaration of Helsinki but also of all modern directives and guidelines. One must not, however, lose sight of the contrary view, namely that this is the penalty we have to accept if we wish to avoid a return to the dark ages when treatment was not determined by the scientific method.[80]

19.31 One further feature deserves mention before we leave the subject of randomisation— that is the 'double-blind' technique. This form of research, which is virtually confined to drug trials, attempts to reduce subjectivity in assessment by keeping the assigned therapeutic groups secret not only from the patients but also from the physicians involved. This dictates that the patient's doctor cannot be the researcher; it also makes it implicit that the ethical justification of the trial is agreed by the 'caring' physicians involved, for they must have perfect equipoise if they are to join in the trial, and at the same time provide what is, to their mind, the 'best treatment' for their patients. This leads to some form of conscious pre-selection in that it may be, for example, necessary to exclude patients on the ground of the severity of their disease; the trial then becomes limited to establishing the effectiveness of a treatment for the milder forms of the disease and loses much of its validity. We find it hard to ethically justify many aspects of the 'double-blind' trial.[81]

---

[77] Edwards et al., n 4, refer to three trials in which 47 per cent of doctors concerned thought that few patients knew they were taking part in a controlled experiment, even though they had given written consent. The problem of consent may be particularly acute where the participants in an RCT are illiterate or where they do not share the scientific view of the researcher: M Barry and M Molyneux, 'Ethical dilemmas in malaria drug and vaccine trials: A bioethical perspective' (1992) 18 J Med Ethics 189. See also, M Angell, 'Investigators' responsibilities for human subjects in developing countries' (2000) 342 New Engl J Med 967, and Nuffield Council on Bioethics, *The Ethics of Research Related to Healthcare in Developing Countries* (2005).

[78] M Baum, K Zilkha, and J Houghton, 'Ethics of clinical research: Lessons for the future' (1989) 299 BMJ 251.

[79] For a simple explanation of pre-randomisation, see D Torgerson and M Roland, 'What is Zelen's design?' (1998) 316 BMJ 606. See also D Hunter, 'We could be heroes: ethical issues with the pre-recruitment of research participants' (2015) 41 J Med Ethics 557.

[80] Baum et al., n 78. For a defence of 'scientific medicine' see R Tallis, *Hippocratic Oaths* (2004).

[81] And regulatory authorities also take a cautious approach: the EU recommends that, normally, reports of SUSARs should mean that trials be unblended; the UK adopts a partial unblinding position: see SOPs, para 10.36.

GROUPS AND INDUCEMENTS

19.32 Research participants may be 'healthy volunteers',[82] or they may be 'patients',[83] and within these broad categories they may belong to specific groups, several of which are recognised by the regulatory framework, namely adults with capacity, adults without capacity, minors, and pregnant and breastfeeding women.[84]

19.33 There may be clear advantages to using healthy volunteers but, by definition, their involvement must be limited to non-therapeutic research. It can be argued that their use is, a priori, unjustifiable, but we prefer the view that people have a right to exercise altruistic impulses, particularly in a society in which free health care is extended to all. Nonetheless, considerable caution is needed, particularly as to the repetitive volunteer who is prone to exploitation even if the researchers are unconscious of this. Motivation of the ever-ready volunteer takes several forms, some good and others less so, and, among these, the problem of recompense looms large. The 2014 Regulation states that a clinical trial can only be conducted where, inter alia, no undue influence, including that of a financial nature, is exerted on subjects to so participate.[85] It is probable that, given modern social conditions, few suitable volunteers would come forward in the absence of some inducement, but large payments are clearly unethical, so a reasonable balance must be set—if for no other reason than to satisfy the needs of randomisation.[86]

19.34 Generally, approaches to payment are cautious. The Royal College of Physicians has acknowledged the use of payments under certain circumstances,[87] but even then 'payments should not be for under-going risk, and payments should not be such as to persuade patients to volunteer against their better judgement'. The Additional Protocol to the Biomedicine Convention stipulates that the ethics committee must be satisfied that no undue influence, including that of a financial nature, will be exerted on persons to participate in research. In this respect, particular attention must be given to 'vulnerable or dependent persons.'[88] The Nuffield Council offered a taxonomy that distinguishes between (1) payment, (2) recompense (to include compensation and reimbursement), (3) reward (including remuneration), and (4) purchase.[89] Their intervention ladder then

---

[82] And their use is not precluded by the Declaration of Helsinki (2013). See para 12.

[83] Medical research may be combined with medical care: Declaration of Helsinki (2013), paras 12 and 14. We doubt if this could be extended to using patients as if they were healthy; we believe that the use of persons who are already under stress, and who probably have a sense of obligation to the doctors, must bring such research close to unethical practice. In any event, non-therapeutic research in patients should be confined to a type which adds no extra burden—for example, through the use of existing blood samples. For what is, perhaps, the greatest example of the dangers of using patients in this way, see *Hyman* v *Jewish Chronic Disease Hospital* 206 NE 2d 338 (1965), where a group of hospital patients were injected with cancer cells as an active control for a group of cancer patients who were similarly treated.

[84] 2014 Regulation, Arts 28–33. And each group has specific limitations and consent requirements.

[85] 2014 Regulation, Arts 28(1)(h), 31(1)(d), 32(1)(d), and 33(d). The 2001 Directive proscribes incentives and financial inducements other than compensation in respect of minors (Art 4(d)) and incapacitated adults (Art 5(d)), and these are repeated in Parts 4 and 5 of Sch 1 to the 2004 Regulations. Otherwise, the matter would be considered by the responsible REC.

[86] Cf, E Jones and K Liddell, 'Should healthy volunteers in clinical trials be paid according to risk? Yes' (2009) 339 BMJ 4142.

[87] The Royal College of Physicians described payments to patients as 'generally undesirable' but occasionally acceptable in the case of long and tedious studies: Royal College of Physicians, *Research Involving Patients* (1990).

[88] Additional Protocol on Biomedical Research (2005), Art 12.

[89] Nuffield Council on Bioethics, *Human bodies: Donation for Medicine and Research*, (2011) para 2.44.

maps different kinds of financial involvement to the altruistic nature (or otherwise) of acts involving donation or participation in research. This signals the ethical significance of exchanges and transaction practices, leading possibly to a 'red flag' in cases tantamount to coercion. In the final analysis, however, they conclude that payment to healthy volunteers for first-in-human trials should be retained as ethically justified.[90]

19.35   The topic of inducement reintroduces the problem of populations who are special because of their easy access, malleability, etc. Students, particularly medical students, provide an example about whom there is little difficulty; they are of an age to make legally valid decisions, they may well have an active interest in the trial, and most educational establishments have very stringently controlling ethics committees to protect against repetitive use. Much the same could be said for the armed forces, who may be particularly vulnerable to improper research in war or when war threatens—even in 1990, non-consensual trials were allowed on US troops engaged in the Gulf War,[91] and we have already mentioned the use of experimental vaccines.[92] The use of prisoners is particularly controversial, and exposes a range of ethical issues.[93] It is often felt that some advantage, even if only imagined, must accrue to the prisoner participant. Others feel that advantage may be so great as to induce the prisoner to volunteer for research which involves greater discomfort or risk than would be accepted by a free person, and which may compromise his inalienable right to withdraw from the trial.[94] And, of course, prisoners could well resent protective attitudes on the grounds that it is their right to dispose of their bodies and to take such risks as they please. This could be the subject of lengthy debate but we suggest that the conditions in today's prisons are such that any process which provides some relief deserves a sympathetic evaluation, and many prisoners might be benefited through helping society.[95] Having said that, research on prisoners should be particularly rigidly controlled by RECs which should always contain lay members with experience in criminology.[96] Nowhere is it more important to observe the maxim 'the aims do not justify the means—the method must be judged in its own right'.

19.36   When comparing treatments, however, the use of patients is necessary. This is what the Declaration of Helsinki means by medical research combined with professional care, which is admissible 'only to the extent that this is justified by its potential preventive, diagnostic or therapeutic value, and if the physician has good reason to believe that participation … will not adversely affect the health of the patients who serve as research

---

[90]   See also L Stunkel and C Grady, 'More than the money: A review of the literature examining healthy volunteer motivations' (2011) 32 Contemp Clin Trials 342.

[91]   G Annas and M Grodin, 'Treating the troops: Commentary' (1991) 21 Hastings Center Rep (2) 24.

[92]   For ethical review of research involving soldiers, see SOPs, paras 1.30–1.32.

[93]   Article 20 of the Additional Protocol on Biomedical Research (2005) states: 'Where the law allows research on persons deprived of liberty, such persons may participate in a research project in which the results do not have the potential to produce direct benefit to their health only if the following additional conditions are met: (a) research of comparable effectiveness cannot be carried out without the participation of persons deprived of liberty; (b) the research has the aim of contributing to the ultimate attainment of results capable of conferring benefit to persons deprived of liberty, and (c) the research entails only minimal risk and minimal burden.'

[94]   For a comparison of the European model of regulation for research with prisoners and the American model, see B Elger and A Spaulding, 'Research on prisoners – a comparison between the IOM committee recommendations (2006) and European Regulations' (2010) 24 Bioethics 1.

[95]   For more, see A Charles, A Rid, et al., 'Prisoners as research participants: Current practice and attitudes in the UK' (2014) J Med Ethics Online.

[96]   For the approach to research involving prisoners, see SOPs, s 1, Table B, and the provisions on Flagged RECs.

subjects'.[97] A clinical trial is rarely undertaken unless there is good reason to suppose that one therapy will show an advantage over others, and particularly over those currently accepted as the best available. The advantage need not be direct; it could be collateral in that the results of the method were not better but were achieved with less disfigurement or fewer side effects. Anticipation of advantage is generally based on laboratory, or, where appropriate, animal experimentation, and while the view is occasionally expressed that the latter is less moral than is human biomedical research, it is still generally acceptable given that the conditions are controlled. The corollary, as we have already emphasised, is that an untried method must be immediately withdrawn if it is found to be positively deleterious, and the patients involved must be transferred, whenever possible, to an alternative regime. As already noted, there is a legal obligation to report early terminations of clinical trials to both the REC and the MHRA with full explanation for the decision.[98]

19.37 The results of trials involving innovative therapies may, however, take a considerable time to filter through and, by then, there may be no turning back. A clear example was provided by the study of the use of folic acid supplements in order to reduce the incidence of neural tube defects in infants. Two pilot studies were undertaken; both showed an apparent marked reduction in recurrence rates in affected families but neither stood up to statistical analysis. The problem then arose as to whether the study should be continued, and, if so, whether the clinical impression was sufficient to render the use of placebos unethical. It was decided that the matter was so important that a major RCT was indicated, the intent being to study at least 2,000 pregnancies. In the event, after more than seven years, sufficient information had been gained from 1,195 informative pregnancies. Thus, the trial could then be ended, it being clear that folic acid supplements had no adverse effects but had a significant protective effect as regards fetal neural tube defect.[99]

USE OF PLACEBOS

19.38 A placebo is an inert substance without pharmacological action. But in humans the mere taking of a substance in a clinical or quasi-clinical setting may lead to subjective, or symptomatic, improvement; this is the 'placebo effect', which must be considered whenever a new drug or procedure is on trial. On the other hand, the trial drug may do more harm than inactivity; but, for psychological reasons, inactivity must involve apparent activity if the two regimens are to be properly compared. In either case, the controlled giving of a placebo necessarily involves the deception of patients and this raises some complex issues.

19.39 The extreme position is that placebos offend against the fundamental rightness of fidelity.[100] If there is patient resistance to the use of such controls, this should not be regarded as an excuse for further deception but rather as an indication that such experiments are unacceptable to society. To this one could reply that a poor experiment is a

---

[97] Declaration of Helsinki (2013), para 14.

[98] 2004 Regulations, reg 31.

[99] MRC Vitamin Study Research Group, 'Prevention of neural tube defects: Results of the Medical Research Council vitamin study' (1991) 338 Lancet 131.

[100] For a seminal analysis, see B Simmons, 'Problems in deceptive medical procedures: An ethical and legal analysis of the administration of placebos' (1978) 4 J Med Ethics 172. More recently, see A Dowrick and M Bhandari, 'Ethical issues in the design of randomized trials: to sham or not to sham?' (2012) 94 Suppl 1 J Bone Joint Surg Am 7, and D Resnik and F Miller, 'The ethics of sham surgery on research subjects with cognitive impairments that affect decision-making capacity' (2010) 31 Contemp Clin Trials 407.

worse affront to society and that the simple expedient is to leave out those who object—little is lost other than perhaps absolute numbers, and, as previously discussed, experimental volunteers are, by nature, already a selected group.

19.40   More practical objections are based on the effect of the experiment on patient care; the circumstances in which it is ethical to deprive a patient of treatment must be strictly regulated. It would, for example, be improper to use placebo controls when pain is a feature of the condition under treatment, despite the fact that some patients might derive benefit; many painkillers are available and can be used as reference substances. The basic circumstances in which placebo trials are ethical and (arguably) necessary include, first, when there is no alternative to the experimental treatment available—such as in the treatment of degenerative neural disease, though even here *some* form of pharmacologically active substance might well be thought preferable—and, second, when the effect of adding a new treatment to an established one is under study. In the majority of instances, however, the purpose of their use is to analyse the effect of a treatment on subjective symptoms rather than on organic disease.[101]

19.41   The 2013 version of the Declaration of Helsinki has raised some interesting additional points around the use of placebos. Paragraph 33 states that the benefits, risks, burdens, and effectiveness of a new intervention must be tested against those of the best-proven intervention(s), except in the following circumstances:

   • where no proven intervention exists, the use of placebo, or no intervention, is acceptable; or

   • where for compelling and scientifically sound methodological reasons the use of any intervention less effective than the best proven one, the use of placebo, or no intervention is necessary to determine the efficacy or safety of an intervention; and

   • the patients who receive any intervention less effective than the best proven one, placebo, or no intervention will not be subject to additional risks of serious or irreversible harm as a result of not receiving the best proven intervention.

It concludes that 'extreme care must be taken to avoid abuse of this option'.

19.42   This may seem trite and fairly easily accommodated within an ethical spectrum,[102] but we have now been confronted with the extension of the placebo concept into surgery—and especially, although not exclusively, into surgery for those conditions in which symptoms and signs become intermingled.[103] Essentially, we have here a RCT in which some

---

[101]   For further criticism, see K Rothman and K Michels, 'The continuing unethical use of placebo controls' (1994) 331 New Engl J Med 384. A cautious but relatively benign attitude, which, to an extent, parallels our views, is adopted by P De Deyn and R D'Hooge, 'Placebos in clinical practice and research' (1996) 22 J Med Ethics 140. Cf, A Barnhill, 'What it takes to defend deceptive placebo use' (2011) 21 Kennedy Inst Ethics J 219.

[102]   Although see C Lenk and N Hoppe, 'Research governance in placebo-controlled trials. Is the EMA/ICH position consistent in itself and in accordance with the declaration of Helsinki?' (2014) 14 Med Law Int 114, who argue that existing guidance from both the EMA and the ICH is unsuitable, and that placebo-controlled trials urgently need more appropriate regulation.

[103]   The paradigmatic example is the use of fetal brain implants in the treatment of Parkinsonism (see para 17.64). For more, see: W Dekkers and G Boer, 'Sham neurosurgery in patients with Parkinson's disease: Is it morally acceptable?' (2001) 27 J Med Ethics 151; P Clark, 'Placebo surgery for Parkinson's disease: Do the benefits outweigh the risks?' (2002) 30 J Law Med Ethics 58; W Galpern et al., 'Sham neurosurgical procedures in clinical trials for neurodegenerative diseases: scientific and ethical considerations' (2012) 11 Lancet Neurol 643.

patients are implanted but in which the control group's brains are untouched. Space does not permit further discussion, but, on top of the philosophical difficulties involved in the acceptance of medicinal placebo therapy, we must now impose deceptive target imaging by way of magnetic resonance imaging, an anaesthetic, a scalp incision, and at least a token hole in the skull on a person who is to receive no additional therapy. Justification of the programme on utilitarian grounds is possible, but is certainly not easy.

EXPERIMENTAL TREATMENT

19.43 Early in the chapter, we distinguished between research and experimentation—the latter being regarded as involving ad hoc and untried treatment applied to an individual with little more scientific basis other than expediency. It follows that we see medical experiments—as opposed to research—on human beings as being morally justified only in extreme conditions. Nonetheless, in practice, the Declaration of Helsinki supports the concept of experimental treatment.[104]

19.44 Unfortunately, the status of the experimental therapist has been uncertain since 1797 when Dr Baker was pilloried for introducing what remains the standard treatment for limb fractures.[105] The innovative doctor cannot depend upon *Bolam* if things go wrong since, by definition, no supportive body of medical opinion is available—the pioneer therefore seems alone in many senses. Perhaps a more accurate measure of how the pioneer will be judged, however, is to be found in the earlier Scottish case of *Hunter* v *Hanley*,[106] which was accepted in *Bolam* as laying down the correct test for assessing medical conduct which departs from the norm. As Lord Clyde stated, a mere deviation from ordinary professional practice is not necessarily evidence of negligence; indeed it would be disastrous if this were so, for all inducement to progress in medical science would be destroyed. He went so far as to remark that, 'Even a substantial deviation from normal practice may be warranted by the particular circumstances'. If there *is* to be liability for deviation, it must be shown that:

1. there is a usual and normal practice;

2. practice was not adopted; and

3. the course that was adopted was one which no professional of ordinary skill would have taken had he been acting with ordinary care.

This is nothing more than an alternative formulation of the reasonableness test, and the sum and substance of the legal position, then, is that it will be for the court to ask in the circumstances of each case—drawing on medical opinion as it thinks fit—whether the deviation from established practice was reasonable for the patient at hand.[107]

---

[104] See para 37, which states: 'In the treatment of an individual patient, where proven interventions do not exist or other known interventions have been ineffective, the physician, after seeking expert advice, with informed consent from the patient or a legally authorised representative, may use an unproven intervention if in the physician's judgement it offers hope of saving life, re-establishing health or alleviating suffering. This intervention should subsequently be made the object of research, designed to evaluate its safety and efficacy. In all cases, new information must be recorded and, where appropriate, made publicly available.'

[105] *Slater* v *Baker and Stapleton* (1797) 95 ER 860.   [106] 1955 SC 200; 1955 SLT 213.

[107] An excellent illustration is provided by *Hepworth* v *Kerr* [1995] 6 Med LR 139, in which an anaesthetist was found negligent for using an unnecessary and unvalidated hypotensive technique to provide a blood-free operating area. The patient sustained neurological damage.

19.45 The patient who has no other hope is surely entitled to grasp an outside chance and, given the fact that he believes it to be a genuine chance, the doctor is entitled, and perhaps obligated, to provide it. He must, however, *believe* that there is a chance—he cannot provide, nor can the patient consent to, treatment that is expected to result in serious bodily harm or death.[108] In this respect, the ruling in *Bolitho* (see Chapter 5) may be to the doctor's advantage; given the conditions envisaged, it could be relatively easy in the event of an action in negligence to convince a court that his decision was logical *in all the circumstances* of the case. In any event, and as specified in para 37 of the Declaration of Helsinki, the informed consent of the patient is of paramount importance, not only in the context of experimentation but for all forms of research, and we return to this universally accepted precept in due course. But even where informed consent is not possible, highly experimental treatment may be legal in the right circumstances. As we have seen many times, in the absence of consent, the law in the UK falls back on the patient's 'best interests', and we have also noted the tendency of the courts to rely on the *Bolam* standard to help determine what those interests might be.

19.46 The joined cases of *Simms v Simms; A v A and another*,[109] which involved two teenagers in the advanced stages of variant Creutzfeldt-Jakob disease (vCJD), demonstrate how far the concept of best interests can be extended into the realm of unproven experiment. Both sets of parents sought declaratory relief to confirm that it would be lawful to undertake a highly experimental course of 'treatment' which had never been tested in humans, about which the risks and benefits were unknown, but which had shown some marginal varying success in mice, rats, and dogs in Japan (although higher doses in dogs often caused severe reactions and death). The 'last chance' nature of the case permeates the judgment—it was accepted by all that the children would not recover. Notwithstanding, the President of the Family Division, Lady Butler-Sloss, sought to apply the best interests test and held that this justified the attempt in light of medical evidence whereby no witness was willing to rule out the *possibility* that some benefit might accrue. She added further qualifiers, namely that, since the disease was progressive and fatal, and because there was no alternative treatment, and so long as there were no significant risks of increasing the suffering of the patient, then it would not be unlawful to attempt the treatment (even when the risks and benefits were largely unknown). Finally, she held that because there was some medical evidence that did not rule out a chance of benefit, she was content to assume that the *Bolam* test had been complied with. Tellingly, and echoing the words of Lord Clyde, she stressed that the *Bolam* test 'ought not to be allowed to inhibit medical progress';[110] in the circumstances there was a responsible body of sufficient expertise to satisfy its terms. In the end, it is difficult to tell what sort of guidance is offered by *Simms*; the extreme and rare nature of the circumstances set it apart and suggest that both the parents and the President must have felt that 'doing something' was far better than 'doing nothing', a perfectly natural human response to tragic circumstances.[111]

---

[108] *A-G's Reference (No 6 of 1980)* [1981] 2 All ER 1057 (CA).

[109] [2003] 1 All ER 669; [2003] 1 FCR 361.

[110] Ibid, para 48. Note that the President followed her own ruling in similar cases: *An NHS Trust v HM* [2004] Lloyd's Rep Med 207; *EP v Trusts A, B & C* [2004] Lloyd's Rep Med 211.

[111] Something of an interesting contrast can be seen in *Re MM (a child) (medical treatment)* [2000] 1 FLR 224, wherein the court upheld the decision of a child's doctors to abandon what they regarded as foreign experimental treatment in favour of their own approach. See further Chapter 20. *Walker-Smith v GMC*, n 30, confirms a reliance on the medical profession's own attitudes towards conduct in cases in the liminal spaces between research and therapy.

19.47   Ultimately, the balance between progress and patient interests remains a fine one and not easily struck, though efforts are underway to offer some guidance. Lord Saatchi introduced the Medical Innovation Bill 2014, which was passed by the Lords, sent to the House of Commons, halted by the then Minister of Health, and then ran out of time as a result of a general election. It has resurfaced as the Access to Medical Treatments (Innovation) Bill 2015–16, a Private Member's Bill introduced in the House of Commons and expected to have its second reading debate in October 2015.[112] While the official text is not yet available, the purpose of the new Bill is to encourage responsible innovation in medical treatment, and it is expected to follow its predecessor in stipulating that it is not negligent for a doctor to depart from the existing range of accepted medical treatments if the decision to do so is taken 'responsibly'.[113]

RESEARCH AND INFORMED CONSENT

PRACTICAL CHALLENGES WITH CONSENT

19.48   The 'ideal' ethical research programme is one that can be based on free, autonomous participation by the subject, and this, in turn, depends upon 'informed consent', the nature of which has been discussed (Chapter 4). The principles in relation to research and experimentation are similar to those governing therapy; most commentators would, however, hold that the patient's rights are, if anything, greater in the former situation than they are in the sphere of pure patient management. The standard of information provided must certainly be that of the 'reasonable participant'—if not that of the actual participant—rather than that of the 'reasonable doctor'.[114] Even so, there are many and varied difficulties which make it almost impossible to lay down hard and fast rules— these include the essential need for some measure of ignorance in the trial, the seriousness of the condition being treated, the psychology of individual patients, and the like. The complexity is such that some confrontation between the back-room and the coalface is almost inevitable.[115]

---

[112]   See http://services.parliament.uk/bills/2015-16/accesstomedicaltreatmentsinnovation.html.

[113]   Under the original Bill, the taking of a 'responsible decision' required the doctor to (a) obtain the views of one or more appropriately qualified doctors in relation to the proposed treatment, (b) take full account of the views so obtained (and in a way in which a responsible doctor would be expected to take account of such views), (c) obtain any consents required by law to the carrying out of the proposed treatment, (d) consider (i) any opinions or requests expressed by or in relation to the patient, (ii) the risks and benefits that are, or can reasonably be expected to be, associated with the proposed treatment, the treatments that fall within the existing range of accepted medical treatments for the condition, and not carrying out any of those treatments, and (iii) any other matter that it is necessary for the doctor to consider in order to reach a clinical judgement, (e) comply with any professional requirements as to registration of the treatment under the provisions of this Act with a scheme for capturing the results of innovative treatment (including positive and negative results and information about small-scale treatments and patients' experiences), and (f) take such other steps as are necessary to secure that the decision is made in a way which is accountable and transparent. For the text of the original Bill, see http://www.publications.parliament.uk/pa/bills/cbill/2014-2015/0162/15162.pdf.

[114]   For a short resumé of the debate, see L Doyal and J Tobias, 'Informed consent in medical research' (1998) 316 BMJ 1000. Much of the current discussion centres on the ethics of publication; this is inevitable as research without publication is so much wasted effort. For an argument that respect for autonomy does not necessarily demand reliance on consent, see T Walker, 'Respecting autonomy without disclosing information' (2013) 27 Bioethics 388.

[115]   In Editorial, 'Medical ethics: Should medicine turn the other cheek?' (1990) 336 Lancet 846, it was argued that 'the central dogma [of professional medical ethicists] seems to be that whatever is done for

19.49 It is widely agreed that the participant's consent must be based on four main lines of explanation: (1) the purpose of the research; (2) the benefits to the subject and society; (3) the risks involved; and (4) the alternatives open to the participant. But many questions arise. Who is to impart the information—the participant's physician or the researcher? Should the participant have the benefit of a 'friend' to interpret for him? Should there be confirmation of the consent procedure? It has been fairly widely mooted that, in fact, informed consent is a double-edged weapon—token consent may take the place of the genuine and relieve the researcher of responsibility. Might it not be better to burden the investigator with full responsibility rather than provide such a shield? Many of the US states have enacted 'informed consent statutes', some of which lay down specific disclosure requirements for particular procedures. In the same spirit, US courts, dealing with claims of inadequate information to research subjects, have tended to stress that there is a considerably higher burden of disclosure in cases involving non-therapeutic research than in therapeutic cases,[116] a view shared by a Canadian court in *Halushka* v *University of Saskatchewan*.[117] The difficulties are highlighted in 'care associated' research when, effectively, the doctrine of informed consent implies that the participant has to choose for herself whether to accept an experimental treatment or to be randomised in a comparative therapeutic trial. The philosophical basis of personal autonomy is perfectly clear, but is the ideal end attainable in practice? Ought a patient to be told of a 'last chance' effort? Is the medically naive prospective participant capable of giving consent as required? Can he be expected to understand the risks when the medical profession itself is divided?

19.50 A real problem here is that doubts as to participants' ability to understand complex medical information can very easily result in the striking of an unacceptably paternalistic attitude—sometimes with shocking consequences. Such a situation arose in New Zealand's Auckland cervical cancer campaign,[118] in which a senior doctor, believing that cancer in situ would not spread, was strongly of the view that some women with abnormal cervical smear tests were best left untreated. These patients were denied treatment over a period of 15–20 years without being told that they were, in effect, involved in a therapeutic experiment. The doctor in charge of the experimental research believed honestly and firmly in his hypothesis, but his failure to obtain consent was severely criticised both by medical colleagues and the judicial inquiry that investigated the matter; the impact on medicine there and beyond has been profound.[119] A further complicating factor arises when the risks are simply unknown. A case in point is the prospect of xenotransplantation trials and the unknown risks of animal-to-human transmission of pathogens. What is the participant to be told in such cases?[120] An added complication, which cannot be

the sake of medical science is alien to the treatment of the individual, and should therefore be labelled an "experiment", necessitating informed consent by the patient and adjudication by an ethics committee'.

[116] E.g. *Whitlock* v *Duke University* 637 F Supp 1463 (NC, 1986); affd 829 F 2d 1340 (1987).

[117] (1965) 53 DLR (2d) 436 (Sask CA). See also K Morin, 'The standard of disclosure in human subject experimentation' (1998) 19 J Leg Med 157.

[118] Judge S Cartwright, *The Report of the Cervical Cancer Enquiry* (1988); discussed by A Campbell, 'An "unfortunate experiment"' (1989) 3 Bioethics 59.

[119] C Paul, 'The New Zealand cancer study: Could it happen again?' (1988) 297 BMJ 533; P McNeill, 'The implications for Australia of the New Zealand report of the cervical cancer inquiry: No cause for complacency' (1989) 150 Med J Austral 264; G Gillett, 'NZ medicine after Cartwright' (1990) 300 BMJ 893.

[120] S Fovargue, ' "Oh pick me, pick me"—Selecting participants for xenotransplant clinical trials' (2007) Med L Rev 176.

resolved by consent alone, is whether the risks to the wider society of such trials are appreciated and can be mitigated.[121]

19.51 Many of these ethical concerns were addressed by the 2001 Directive, the UK's 2004 Regulations,[122] and guidance from NRES on its interpretation,[123] and are similarly addressed by the EU's 2014 Regulation, Art 29(2) of which states:

> Information given to the subject or, where the subject is not able to give informed consent, his or her legally designated representative for the purposes of obtaining his or her informed consent shall:
>
> (a) enable the subject or his or her legally designated representative to understand:
>> (i) the nature, objectives, benefits, implications, risks and inconveniences of the clinical trial;
>> (ii) the subject's rights and guarantees regarding his or her protection, in particular his or her right to refuse to participate and the right to withdraw from the clinical trial at any time without any resulting detriment and without having to provide any justification;
>> (iii) the conditions under which the clinical trial is to be conducted, including the expected duration of the subject's participation in the clinical trial; and
>> (iv) the possible treatment alternatives, including the follow-up measures if the participation of the subject in the clinical trial is discontinued;
>
> (b) be kept comprehensive, concise, clear, relevant, and understandable to a layperson;
>
> (c) be provided in a prior interview with a member of the investigating team who is appropriately qualified according to the law of the Member State concerned;
>
> (d) include information about the applicable damage compensation system referred to in Article 76(1); and
>
> (e) include the EU trial number and information about the availability of the clinical trial results in accordance with paragraph 6.

Article 29 goes on to state that the information must be given to the participant in writing, and her understanding of the information is to be confirmed at interview—an inherent limitation in the previous provisions being that the subject was to be given 'the opportunity to understand' what they are consenting to, with little obligation on the part of investigators to inquire as to whether any degree of actual understanding had been reached.[124]

---

[121] For an argument about proceeding with a staggered risk plan for vulnerable groups involved in research, see F Singh et al., 'Ethical implications for clinical practice and future research in "at risk" individuals' (2012) 18 Curr Pharm Des 606.

[122] Schedule 1, Pt 3 to the 2004 Regulations provides that the subject must: (1) have an interview with the investigator (or a member of his team) and be given the opportunity to understand the nature, objectives, risks and inconveniences of the trial; (2) be informed of his right to withdraw from the trial at any time without detriment; (3) be provided with a contact point where he can obtain more information about the trial; and (4) give his informed consent (or not). On this last point, the Regulations state that a person gives 'informed consent' to participate only if his decision (a) is given freely after that person is informed of the nature, significance, implications and risks of the trial; and (b) either (i) is evidenced in writing, dated and signed, or otherwise marked, by that person so as to indicate his consent, or (ii) if the person is unable to sign or to mark a document so as to indicate his consent, is given orally in the presence of at least one witness and recorded in writing.

[123] NRES, *Information Paper on Informed Consent in Clinical Trials of Investigational Medicinal Products*, v 3 (2008).

[124] The problem of 'understanding' also arises in the purely clinical context: see *Al Hamwi v Johnston* [2005] Lloyd's Rep Med 309, para 10.48.

19.52 Before leaving this topic, we should note that there have been growing arguments that consent—or the consent process—should be adapted to reflect the risks associated with the research, with less rigorous standards being applied to low-risk research.[125] Further, there remain unresolved problems associated with the use and status of consent forms, the latter of which remains unclear in the UK. It has been argued that greater attention must be paid within research governance frameworks to the research relationship and the preservation of trust through ongoing communication and consent as a relational process.[126]

RESEARCH AND THE INCOMPETENT

19.53 On one view, research (and experimentation) involving incapacitated persons should not be ruled out entirely because to do so would not only deprive them of an opportunity to engage in community-oriented beneficial activities to which they might have consented if able, but it would also mean that much research into the conditions from which these people suffer would simply be impossible.[127] In both circumstances, it is strongly arguable that a complete ban is unethical. By the same token, the extreme vulnerability of incapacitated persons requires that special care is taken to protect them and their interests. In short, difficult ethical and legal problems arise in respect of those patients who cannot give a valid consent to participation in clinical research by virtue of their mental condition. Such patients might be used in research provided certain safeguards were erected; these would be designed so as to ensure that they are not subjected to appreciable risk or inconvenience and would include the agreement of relatives and/or that of some independent supervisory party. The required approval of an independent authority would cover those instances in which it was suspected that uncaring relatives had been thoughtless.[128]

19.54 The Additional Protocol on Biomedical Research (2005) has addressed the matter of the incompetent research subject, stating that research can be undertaken if: (1) the results of the research have the potential to produce real and direct benefit to his or her health; (2) research of comparable effectiveness cannot be carried out on competent individuals; (3) the research subject has been informed of his or her rights and the safeguards prescribed by law for his or her protection, unless this person is not in a state to receive the information; (4) the necessary authorisation has been given specifically and in writing by the legal representative or an authority, person or body provided for by law, and taking into account the person's previously expressed wishes or objections; and (5) the person concerned does not object.[129] Exceptionally, where condition (1) is not satisfied, research may be authorised if it has the aim of contributing 'to the ultimate attainment of results capable of conferring benefit to the person concerned or to other persons in the same age category or afflicted with the same disease or disorder or having the same condition' provided, at the same time, that the research entails only minimal risk and minimal

---

[125] D Bromwich and A Rid, 'Can informed consent to research be adapted to risk?' (2015) 41 J Med Ethics 521.

[126] G Laurie and E Postan, 'Rhetoric or Reality: What is the legal status of the consent form in health-related research?' (2013) 21 Medi L Rev 371.

[127] This was expressly recognised in *Simms v Simms*, n 109, para 57.

[128] Almost precisely the same arguments can be made in respect of minors, but we deal with their particular circumstances in the following chapter. For an argument that advance directives should be persuasive, see T Buller, 'Advance consent, critical interests and dementia research' (2014) J Med Ethics Online.

[129] Additional Protocol, Art 15. And see the Declaration of Helsinki, paras 28–30.

burden for the individual concerned. It is this latter criterion, not the ultimate value of the research, that constitutes the benchmark.[130]

19.55   While the UK has not yet ratified the Biomedicine Convention (1997) nor signed the Additional Protocol (2005), the requirements of the prevailing regulatory framework reflect many of the terms of the Protocol. Moreover, they seek to apply both a principled and pragmatic approach to clinical trials involving incapacitated persons. As to principles, the Regulations provide in Sch 1, Pt 5 that the following underpin research involving the incompetent: (1) informed consent given by a legal representative to an incapacitated adult in a clinical trial shall represent that adult's presumed will, (2) the clinical trial has been designed to minimise pain, discomfort, fear, and any other foreseeable risk in relation to the disease and the cognitive abilities of the patient, (3) the risk threshold and the degree of distress have to be specially defined and constantly monitored and, (4) the interests of the patient always prevail over those of science and society. The Regulations also lay down some 11 conditions for lawful research. In these, the subject's legal representative is central, and the same provisions regarding research involving competent persons apply equally to the representative of the incapax.

19.56   The provisions of the Mental Capacity Act 2005 also address research involving incapable adults, but these explicitly exclude subjects involved in clinical trials (governed by the 2004 Regulations).[131] Briefly, the approach taken is that intrusive research is illegal unless the elements of the Act are complied with. The requirements are very similar save that, specifically, non-paid carers must be consulted as to the incapax's past (and likely present) views or wishes in respect of the research. Any indication, past or present, from the subject himself that he does not wish to participate must be respected. Importantly, however, and in contrast to the 2004 Regulations, the role of the carer is not to give or withhold their consent but rather 'to advise' on whether the incapacitated person should take part in the research. The REC is the final approval authority.

19.57   The situation in Scotland in respect of research involving incompetent adults has been clear since the enforcement of the Adults with Incapacity (Scotland) Act 2000.[132] The necessary conditions almost exactly parallel those laid down in the Additional Protocol (2005) save that, in addition, authority for surrogate consent is specifically vested in a person appointed as the incapax's guardian or welfare attorney;[133] where there is no appointed guardian or welfare attorney, power to consent lies with the subject's nearest relatives who have authority to act for the incapax in the order that they appear in the list that is now provided in the Mental Health (Care and Treatment) (Scotland) Act 2003.[134]

19.58   The 2004 Regulations and Scottish legislation have been revised to allow incapacitated adults into trials in emergency situations.[135] The problem is that time may not permit the

---

[130] See A Friedman, E Robbins, and D Wendler, 'Which benefits of research participation count as "direct" ' (2012) 26 Bioethics 60.

[131] Mental Capacity Act 2005, ss 30–4. The 2004 Regulations also apply to Scotland.

[132] Section 51, as amended.

[133] See too Scottish Government, *Adults with Incapacity (Scotland) Act 2000: Code of Practice (Third Edition): For Practitioners Authorised to Carry Out Medical Treatment or Research Under Part 5 of the Act* (2010). Note the legal designation of a particular REC to oversee research with this group of participants: The Adults with Incapacity (Ethics Committee) (Scotland) Regulations 2002 (SSI 2002/190).

[134] Section 254(1)(b). The position in England can be discerned from the NRES guidance on consent in clinical trials which similarly details a 'hierarchy of consent' for legal representatives: NRES, n 123, paras 19–29.

[135] The Medicines for Human Use (Clinical Trials) Amendment (No 2) Regulations 2006 (SI 2006/2984).

written consent of the appropriate person to be sought in circumstances where treatment to be given to an incapacitated adult as part of a trial must be given urgently. An incapacitated person can now be entered into a trial without the prior informed consent of a legal representative if, having regard to the nature of the trial and the particular circumstances of the case, it is necessary to take action for the purpose of the trial as a matter of urgency, but it is not reasonably practicable to obtain informed consent prior to entering the subject, and the action to be taken is carried out in accordance with a procedure approved by the REC. Consent must, however, be sought either from the participant him- or herself (if sufficiently competent) or the legal representative as soon as is practicable thereafter. If such consent is not forthcoming, the participant must be withdrawn from the trial.

THE UNETHICAL RESEARCHER

19.59 All that has gone before has assumed that the researcher is acting in good faith with the interests of the profession and of the public at heart—and that includes assumption of the public-spirited objective of research, which is to produce generalisable knowledge to improve human health. Occasionally, however, concerns arise about non-intentional conduct of researchers which falls short of acceptable ethical standards, and, worse, intentional conduct which ignores such standards, such as fraudulent behaviour and/or the publication of fraudulent studies.[136] A 2012 survey involving all 2,047 biomedical and life-science research articles that had been retracted by PubMed suggests that 67.4 per cent of these were due to misconduct, including fraud or suspected fraud (43.4 per cent), duplicate publication (14.2 per cent), and plagiarism (9.8 per cent). Only 21.3 per cent of retractions pertained to error.[137]

19.60 Doctors and researchers are under ongoing pressure, competitiveness is common, and the potential for lucrative commercial deals can all serve as temptations to act unethically.[138] Even in the academic setting, those who publish attract more funding than those who do not, publishing impacts heavily on advancement, and academic impact is facilitated by 'being first', which can encourage premature reporting.[139] All of this can lead to 'sloppy science' and/or deliberate falsification of results or suppression of truth, a critical danger being that the public, fed by the media, may be led to believe in therapeutic claims which

[136] S Lock, F Wells, and M Farthing (eds), *Fraud and Misconduct in Biomedical Research* (4th edn, 2008).

[137] F Fang, R Steen, and A Casadevall, 'Misconduct accounts for the majority of retracted scientific publications' (2012) 109 Proc Natl Acad Sci USA 17028. An earlier international survey of biostatisticians working with medical researchers revealed that 51 per cent of respondents were aware of fraudulent projects, including the fabrication or falsification of data, deceptive research design and reporting, and deliberate suppression of 'unfavourable' results: J Ranstain, M Bayse, et al., 'Fraud in medical research: An international survey of biostatisticians' (2000) 21 Controlled Trials 415. See also R Steen, 'Retractions in the scientific literature: Is the incidence of research fraud increasing?' (2011) 37 J Med Ethics 249. Some high-profile examples of falsification of results from the late 1980s and early 1990s are reported in J Smith, 'Preventing fraud' (1991) 302 BMJ 362.

[138] For concerns and approaches to encouraging an improved research culture, see Nuffield Council on Bioethics, *The Culture of Scientific Research in the UK* (2014).

[139] On publication, note *Queen May University of London v Information Commissioner* (2013) 133 BMLR 210, wherein the University appealed against a decision of the Information Commissioner ordering the disclosure of information concerning a trial to examine the efficacy and safety of the prevailing treatment for chronic fatigue syndrome. The appeal tribunal held that some papers had been published by the appellant, which intended to publish further in a peer-reviewed paper. As the timescale offered was reasonable, it was reasonable to withhold the information until publication, and earlier disclosure would not be in the public interest.

are unsupported by the data, or they may be subjected to valueless or dangerous treatments. A further pressure is generated by the sometimes very different interests that are often asked to work in cooperation. While research, as we have suggested, has a very public ethos and objective, private interests are invariably at stake, and not all of them can be reconciled with the greater public good. In this respect, we must differentiate between two sets of actors—the researchers and their funders. Researchers and funders must have a financial relationship, and clearly both the medical profession and society have a right to know how far this extends. Additionally, funders may have an interest in keeping unfavourable results out of the public domain. While this may not amount to outright public deception, there may be many reasons for a commercial enterprise to wish to protect its financial interests by questioning or disputing the value of research that goes against those interests.

19.61   The above pitfalls and challenges are well illustrated by some cases. The first, now somewhat dated, relates to the drug Debendox, which was withdrawn after Dr William McBride claimed that the drug could cause deformities in a small proportion of the children of those women who took it. An inquiry by the New South Wales Medical Tribunal concluded that McBride claimed statistically significant results where none existed.[140] McBride was reported as saying that he had changed his data in 'the long-term interests of humanity'.[141] A more recent case is the claim by Dr Andrew Wakefield that the MMR vaccine is linked to autism in children.[142] His initial publication prompted strong challenges on both scientific and ethical grounds.[143] The main ethical allegation was that of conflict of interest: Wakefield, the principal investigator in the MMR study, had not disclosed that, at the time of the research, he had been paid £55,000 by the Legal Aid Board to advise on whether the families of some of the children in the study might be able to sue for vaccine damage. A third case exemplifies starkly the potential conflict between funder and researcher. The Olivieri affair, which inspired an entire edition of the *Journal of Medical Ethics*,[144] concerned a triangular relationship between Dr Olivieri, haematologist and professor at the University of Toronto, the University as her employer, and Apotex Inc, which agreed to fund trials on a new treatment of thalassemia to be conducted by Dr Olivieri. Importantly, Apotex also entered discussions with the University about a substantial donation by the company.[145] When Dr Olivieri became concerned about some trial results and the safety of her patients, and wanted to act on these concerns (inter alia, by informing the patients), she received warnings from Apotex alleging a potential breach of the confidentiality clause of her contract. For its part, the University offered Dr Olivieri little support, and, it is alleged, constructively dismissed her over the dispute. The affair resulted in a Task Force to examine conflict of interests and freedom of research in Canada, and Dr Olivieri has since published numerous articles disputing the claims of Apotex as to the safety of their treatment. This case in particular highlights the

---

[140] M Ragg, 'Australia: McBride guilty of scientific fraud' (1993) 341 Lancet 550.

[141] N Swan, 'Australian doctor admits fraud' (1991) 302 BMJ 1421.

[142] A Wakefield et al., 'Ileal–lymphoid–nodular hyperplasia, non-specific colitis, and pervasive development disorder in children' (1998) 351 Lancet 637. This case is discussed from a public health perspective in Chapter 2.

[143] See K Madsen et al., 'A population-based study of measles, mumps and rubella vaccination and autism' (2002) 347 New Eng J Med 1477, for the former, and the campaign by *Sunday Times* journalist Brian Deer (at: http://briandeer.com/mmr-lancet.htm) for the latter.

[144] 'The Olivieri symposium' (2004) 30 J Med Ethics.

[145] For a notable British example, consider the case of Nottingham University which accepted almost £4m from British American Tobacco to fund its International Centre for Corporate Social Responsibility. For strong critique see S Chapman and S Shatenstein, 'The ethics of the cash register: Taking tobacco research dollars' (2001) 10 Tob Control 1.

importance of publishing all kinds of results—both the positive and the negative—and draws attention to the need to address squarely the interests of those involved in public/private partnerships in research.[146]

19.62   Of course, the existence of the problems exposed by these cases is appreciated within the medical and publishing world.[147] The Committee on Publication Ethics (COPE) was founded in 1997 by journal editors as a medium through which to address their growing concern.[148] COPE maintains a register of all cases reported to it since its inception, as well as a range of guidance.[149] In 2006, the UK Research Integrity Office (UKRIO) was formed as an independent advisory body hosted by Universities UK. It exists to promote good practice in addressing misconduct in research, and it has the support of government, research funders, and the industry regulators. While it has no statutory basis or disciplinary teeth, it has produced a Code of Practice which is meant to provide greater clarity for researchers rather than merely adding to the already considerable morass of instruments with little practical effect.[150] More recently, the International Committee of Medical Journal Editors (ICMJE) articulated standards which demand, inter alia, extensive disclosure of competing interests before research results can be published.[151] The combined effect of these organisations and their guidance is that it should not be possible to publish one's research in a reputable medical journal unless the required details are provided.

19.63   Beyond these mechanisms, which are aimed at avoiding and reducing misconduct, the fraudulent researcher faces a variety of sanctions. First, there are powerful professional disciplinary procedures that can effectively end a scientific career,[152] and cases are regularly investigated by the Association of British Pharmaceutical Industries and the General Medical Council (GMC).[153] Indeed, Wakefield's fitness to practise medicine in the light of the allegations surrounding his MMR study was the subject of the longest-running disciplinary case of the GMC, and it ran at considerable cost both to Wakefield and the GMC itself.[154] The researcher may also be criminally liable for fraudulently obtaining research funds, and civilly liable for any loss incurred by drug manufacturers. With respect to the

---

[146] The Royal Society has emphasised the importance of openness in science publishing, including the publication of negative results, for it is also an ethical imperative to avoid unnecessary repeat research on matters which have already been demonstrated to be fruitless avenues: Royal Society, Science as an Open Enterprise (2012). See also, R Lehman and E Loder, 'Missing clinical trial data: A threat to the integrity of evidence based medicine' (2012) 344 BMJ d8158.

[147] Medico-Legal Investigations Ltd was set up in 1996 to investigate allegations of fraud and research misconduct and to assist in the bringing of criminal and professional disciplinary proceedings and is now supported by the Association of the British Pharmaceutical Industry: http://www.medicolegal-investigations.com/. And see M Tobin, 'Reporting research, retraction of results and responsibility' (2000) 162 Amer J Respir Crit Care Med 773.

[148] This site—http://publicationethics.org/—offers many case studies detailing research and publication dilemmas together with advice on how they should be addressed.

[149] COPE, Code of Conduct and Best Practice Guidelines for Journal Editors (2011); COPE, Code of Conduct for Journal Publishers (2011).

[150] UKRIO, Code of Practice for Research: Promoting Good Practice and Preventing Misconduct (2009), which also now has a web-based version.

[151] ICMJE, Recommendations for the Conduct, Reporting, Editing, and Publication of Scholarly Work in Medical Journals (2014). This document replaces the ICMJE's Uniform Requirements for Manuscripts (2010). The reporting form is posted on http://www.icmje.org/urm_main.html. See also J Drazen et al., 'Disclosure of competing interests' (2009) 339 BMJ 874.

[152] The penalties for scientific fraud include being struck off the register for misconduct: C Dyer, 'Doctor admits research fraud' (1998) 316 BMJ 647.

[153] R Jones, 'Research misconduct' (2002) 19 Fam Pract 123.

[154] D Rose, 'Case against Dr Andrew Wakefield, who linked MMR and autism, to cost over £1m' The Times, 16 March 2009. And see Walker-Smith v GMC, n 30.

criminal law, it is an offence to provide a REC with false or misleading information in a research application relating to a CTIMP.[155] And the SOPs make it clear that a REC must report evidence of fraud or misconduct to its appointing authority and the NRES, as well as to the MHRA when the research relates to clinical trials.[156] These bodies then decide on what further action to pursue; RECs should not undertake their own investigations, but they can review and suspend their prior favourable opinion in light of an allegation of misconduct.

19.64 The considerable increase in research regulation activity—and bureaucracy—in the West has driven some researchers to pursue their work elsewhere, most notably to developing countries where research populations may be more accessible and programmes are subject to less intense scrutiny.[157] Notwithstanding this, the ethical imperatives surrounding research involving human beings remain, in essence, universal; the lack of local regulation is no excuse for not respecting ethical fundamentals,[158] which clearly erect a hierarchy of values in this context: (i) the interests of the patient always prevail over those of science and society; and (ii) freedom of research must be preserved.[159] Concerns have been expressed that these fundamentals, and the regulatory machinery that has built up around them, are not being properly taught in the medical curriculum.[160]

19.65 Before leaving this issue, we should offer a word on experimentation. We have already referred to the fact that it can be difficult distinguishing courageous innovation from unethical experimentation—and, human nature being what it is, the answer often depends on the outcome. The case which remains most vividly in the memory is that in which a baboon's heart was transplanted into a neonate with congenital heart disease.[161] Aside from the fact that the parents of the child were unmarried minors, raising concerns about their ability to give 'informed consent' in the true sense, concerns were expressed that no true belief of benefit to the child could be held. A consultant summed up the procedure as follows:

> I think this xenograft is premature because I am not aware of any finding in the clinical literature that suggests anything but the prevailing rule—the human body will reject a transplanted animal organ. Baby Fae will reject her baboon heart within the next week or two, and cyclosporine will not prevent it.[162]

Most would agree with this assessment—Baby Fae actually survived for two-and-a-half weeks—but the procedure had been approved by the university's IRB and there was some further professional support for the operation. Nevertheless, it does appear to be an example of premature experimental treatment which fails the test of a reasonable chance.

---

[155] SOPs, paras 10.88–10.90, and 2004 Regulations, reg 49.

[156] SOPs, paras 10.76–10.90. For standards and procedures relating to non-CTIMPs, see SOPs, paras 10.115–10.130.

[157] D Cyranoski, 'Chinese clinical trials: Consenting adults? Not necessarily…' (2005) 435 Nature 138.

[158] Nuffield Council on Bioethics, *The Ethics of Research Relating to Healthcare in Developing Countries* (2002) and the follow-up discussion paper from March 2005, both available at: http://www.nuffieldbioethics.org.

[159] In this respect the Additional Protocol (2005), the 2001 EU Directive and its domestic manifestations, and the 2014 Regulation are all in agreement.

[160] B Stankovic and M Stankovic, 'Educating about biomedical research ethics' (2014) 17 Med Health Care & Phil 542.

[161] L Hubband, 'The Baby Fae case' (1987) 6 Med Law 385.

[162] Details taken from H Schwartz, 'Bioethical and legal considerations in increasing the supply of transplantable organs: From UAGA to "Baby Fae" ' (1985) 10 Amer J Law Med 397.

19.66 We are left with the complex problem of whether information gained from frankly immoral research should be used for the general good—the classic examples being data obtained in the concentration camps of WWII. The arguments are finely balanced. In the end, we subscribe to the view that the fact that children do not, say, now die from certain forms of hypothermia is best regarded as a monument to those who suffered and died to make it possible; if the material is used, they will, at least, not have done so in vain.

COMPENSATION FOR PERSONAL INJURY IN RESEARCH

19.67 The research volunteer who is injured in the course of medical research may resort to a claim for compensation under the law of tort. Such a route, of course, may prove to be difficult: researchers may have taken every precaution to avoid injury and there may therefore be no evidence of negligence. Although the odds against a plaintiff in such actions may not be as long as they once were, the research subject could still be in an uncertain situation, and it is, no doubt, for this reason that all modern governance frameworks on the management of research projects emphasise the importance of compulsory protection of subjects against the possibility of mishap. Thus, the 2001 Directive states that a clinical trial may only be undertaken if, inter alia, provision has been made for insurance or indemnity to cover the liability of the investigator and sponsor,[163] while, before approving a proposal, UK RECs must be adequately reassured as to the insurance and indemnity arrangements for treatment and compensation in the event of injury, disablement, or death of a research participant attributable to participation in the research.[164] Of course, none of this guarantees the research subject adequate compensation should anything go wrong, and we suspect that most commentators would favour a form of no-fault compensation, but the answer lies in the hands of government.[165]

RESEARCH INVOLVING HUMAN TISSUE AND PERSONAL DATA

19.68 The discussion thus far has proceeded on the assumption that research or experimentation will involve some direct intrusion into the physical integrity of the research subject—some form of bodily touching. This is by no means necessary for many forms of research, particularly epidemiological, which can be conducted without any need to involve the subject directly. Patient data and samples taken or given previously for unrelated purposes

---

[163] 2001 Directive, Art 3(2)(f). And see 2014 Regulation, Art 76.

[164] SOPs, para 3.48 and Annex G. As to what constitutes 'reassurance', the SOPs state that, in the case of NHS-sponsored research, NHS indemnity will be conferred after a favourable ethical opinion from the REC and once final management permission is given for the research. Non-NHS sponsors must provide evidence of adequate insurance cover with details of the extent of cover and the source of funds: SOPs, Annex G, paras 2 and 7. When the research relates to commercially sponsored CTIMPs or new medical devices, compensation may be available under schemes administered by the Association of the British Pharmaceutical Industry (ABPI) or Association of British Healthcare Industries (ABHI). If so, the REC should receive sufficient details of the form of indemnity to be deployed: SOPs, Annex G, para 8.

[165] S Devaney, 'Rewards and incentives for the provision of human tissue for research' (2014) 40 J Med Ethics 48, offers some views on the consequences of comprehensive compensation programmes.

(such as treatment) are a source of potentially valuable medical research. On one view, the use of data in patient records or archived samples subjects the patient to no further discomfort, and it could be thought reasonable to pursue research in the name of the 'public good'. By the same token, there is a clear element of potential invasion of the patient's privacy in 'finding out things' about him without his consent, not to mention the sense of indignation, or even outrage, that can be generated at the idea of using these 'personal' rudiments—again, without the proper authority to do so. It was precisely this reaction that provoked the investigations at Bristol and Alder Hey into the retention of body parts for 'research purposes' that we have discussed already (Chapter 17).

19.69   The challenges here are manifold, not least because the 'call for consent' is not always realisable, nor is it necessarily desirable in some cases. For example, if a researcher wishes to examine tissue samples gathered many decades previously, is it reasonable to expect her to attempt to obtain consent from all the persons from whom the samples were taken—persons who may have moved, married, or died years before? The cost implications alone may make any such study non-viable ab initio.[166] Another example relates to longitudinal studies, that is, those that propose to study subjects over many years and usually by ongoing review of their medical records. Given that research generates new knowledge by its very nature, is it reasonable to require researchers to revisit subjects on a regular basis in order to obtain re-consent in the light of developments in the research?

19.70   A crude analysis of these examples might cast the core issue as one of pitting cost and convenience against consent. This would misconstrue the dilemma, which, in fact, arises from trying to force the issues into the consent paradigm—that is, from the belief that consent is 'the' answer to (all) ethical concerns.[167] It must be remembered, however, that consent itself is a means to an end and that the real aim is to respect persons and their interests. Consent is but one means by which to achieve this. In this vein, the MRC has stated that 'existing holdings' of tissue samples can be used for research even in the absence of consent provided the legal requirements are followed, the proposed use of samples (without consent) can be justified, use would be considered ethical and reasonable, the confidentiality of all donors and their associated health and research information is maintained, and an NHS REC has decided that use without consent is appropriate.[168] By the same token, the MRC reinforces the point that, in the first instance, the possibility of later research should be explained and appropriate consent obtained.[169]

19.71   This still leaves the problem of what is meant by 'appropriate consent', especially in the context of long-term studies.[170] Here, the MRC has stated that 'broad consent' is

---

[166] P Furness and M Nicholson, 'Obtaining explicit consent for the use of archival tissue samples: practical issues' (2004) 30 J Med Ethics 561.

[167] O Corrigan, 'Empty ethics: The problem with informed consent' (2003) 25 Sociology of Health and Illness 768; G Laurie and E Postan, 'Rhetoric or reality: What is the legal status of the consent form in health-related research?' (2012) 21 Med L Rev 371.

[168] MRC, *Human Tissue and Biological Samples for Use in Research: Operational and Ethical Guidelines* (2014), at 10. The MRC proposes two approaches to 'reasonableness': (1) Would a reasonable person have refused to allow their samples to be used if you had asked them? (2) Would a reasonable person be distressed if they discovered that their samples had been used without their consent? For commentary, see W Lowrance, *Access to Collections of Data and Materials for Health Research* (2006), and W Lowrance, *Privacy, Confidentiality and Health Research* (2012).

[169] MRC Guidelines, at 10.

[170] This is, of course, the language of the Human Tissue Act 2004. For guidance from the Human Tissue Authority, see *Code of Practice 9: Research* (2009).

an acceptable concept whereby it is consent to future medical research projects which would have to be approved by a properly constituted research ethics committee.[171] Thus, we can see how the protectionist role of the REC can be employed to circumvent some of the thornier issues surrounding specific consent. The SOPs for RECs details the considerations and special procedures for approval of research involving databases and human tissue.[172] Once a Research Tissue Bank (RTB) is reviewed and approved, there is no further requirement to apply for ethical approval by individual research sites or centres involved in the collection, storage, or use of tissue in the bank.[173] Thus, the lives of researchers are made a lot easier and the burden of regulation is reduced. In particular, it is not necessary to seek re-consent from individuals who have provided tissue for the bank so long as the uses are within the broad purposes for which the RTB was approved.[174]

19.72   Nevertheless, consent remains the primary policy device in legitimating medical research involving both samples and data. This is seen in both pieces of legislation governing research in these areas, these being the Data Protection Act 1998 and the Human Tissue Act 2004. Having said this, it is to be noted that neither Act requires consent in all circumstances, and both fall back on anonymisation as a way of permitting research in the absence of consent.[175] Anonymisation is essentially a means by which to protect research subjects' privacy interests,[176] and justification lies in the ill-defined notion of the public interest.[177] But the problems continue because of the not infrequent loss of useful data that accompanies anonymisation. Some forms of research simply cannot succeed in the absence of access to data from which individual subjects can be identified.[178] These problems are addressed (in England and Wales) in ss 251–2 of the National Health Service Act 2006, as amended, the provisions of which allow the Secretary of State to make regulations permitting uses of (identifiable) patient data, inter alia, in the public interest; the approval processes are carried out by

---

[171] MRC Guidelines, at 11. To be read with MRC, *Good Research: Principles and Guidelines* (2012). Considerable assistance can be gained from the MRC, *Data and Tissues Toolkit*: http://www.dt-toolkit. ac.uk/home.cfm.

[172] SOPs, ss 11 and 12 respectively.

[173] RTBs are defined as 'a collection of human tissue or other biological material, which is stored for potential research use beyond the life of a specific project with ethical approval or for which ethical approval is pending': SOPs, para 12.19.

[174] For critique, see J McHale, 'Accountability, governance and biobanks: The ethics and governance committee as guardian or toothless tiger?' (2011) 19 Health Care Analysis 231.

[175] The provisions of the 1998 Act do not apply to anonymised data; the Human Tissue Act 2004, s 1(9) is authority for conducting research on anonymised samples without consent (although suitable ethical approval is required). In neither case must the data or sample be 'irrreversibly anonymised'; i.e., that a link between the data and a person can never again be made.

[176] For a discussion of anonymisation in the common law context, see Chapter 6 and the case of *R v Department of Health, ex p Source Informatics Ltd* [2001] 1 All ER 786 (CA). Further guidance is available from the Information Commissioner's Office, *Anonymisation: Managing Data Protection Risk – Code of Practice* (2012). For comment see M Taylor, 'Health research, data protection and the public interest in notification' (2011) 19 Med L Rev 267.

[177] For more on public interest and the concept of solidarity, see B Prainsack and A Buyx, 'A solidarity-based approach to the governance of research biobanks' (2013) 21 Med L Rev 71, and S Harmon and A McMahon, 'Banking (on) the brain: From consent to authorisation and the transformative potential of solidarity' (2014) 22 Med L Rev 572.

[178] And, of course, no system can deliver a guarantee of absolute protection: see I Brown et al., 'Research regulation: Limits of anonymisation in NHS data systems' (2011) 342 BMJ d973.

the Health Research Authority's Confidentiality Advisory Group (CAG), which has offered detailed guidance on seeking approvals for the conduct of research using confidential data without consent.[179] A similar, but still ad hoc, approval system operates in Scotland through the Privacy Advisory Committee which advises NHS Scotland and the National Registers Scotland (NRS) and operates under the auspices of NHS National Services Scotland.[180]

NEW APPROACHES TO RESEARCH GOVERNANCE

19.73 The plethora of legal instruments and official guidance which has invaded the sphere of medical research sadly does little to improve the most important relationship in the entire research enterprise—namely, that between researcher and research participant. For the researcher, the foregoing discussion must seem like a bureaucratic nightmare from which she can only hope to wake unaffected.[181] For the participant, the net result of all this 'protection' may simply be that there is more paperwork to read and sign. But, as the complexities of conducting research have increased, so too has sensitivity to the related ethical and social issues been heightened. A major driver behind the establishment of the HRA was to deliver 'proportionate governance'.[182] And there are now examples of research endeavours which are not content simply to follow the prescribed regulatory path, but which rather seek to adopt a 'Regulation-Plus' or 'Ethics-Plus' approach that engages more directly and more fully with the ethical, legal, and social issues (ELSIs) at stake. Several examples illustrate the point.

19.74 UK Biobank is funded by the Wellcome Trust and the MRC to develop a resource that will facilitate research into the relationship between genetics and environment in the development of human disease.[183] The project has recruited 500,000 plus healthy participants aged 40–69 and will follow them and their health status through the final stages of their lives. Recruitment involved taking blood samples from participants and securing ongoing access to and scrutiny of their medical records and other health-related records. The 'up-front' approach adopted by the funders towards the attendant ELSI is of interest from the regulatory perspective. An Interim Advisory Group on Ethics and Governance was established at the same time as the research protocol was

---

[179] See http://www.hra.nhs.uk/resources/confidentiality-advisory-group/. For the HRA's online tool, see http://www.hra-decisiontools.org.uk/CAG/. And see HRA, *Principles of Advice: Exploring the concepts of 'Public Interest' and 'Reasonably Practicable'* (2012), and HRA, *Managing non-response: Establishing the ICO and CAG position* (2012). For a comparative review, see L Briceño Moraia, J Kaye, A Tasse, et al., 'A comparative analysis of the requirement for the use of data in biobanks based in Finland, Germany, the Netherlands, Norway and the United Kingdom' (2014) 14 Med L Int 187.

[180] See Privacy Advisory Committee, at http://www.isdscotland.org/isd/2466.html. A similar body exists in Northern Ireland.

[181] See J Peto, O Fletcher, and C Gilham, 'Data Protection, Informed Consent, and Research' (2004) 328 BMJ 1029.

[182] See Health Research Authority Regulations (SI 2011/2341) and Health Research Authority (Amendment) Regulations (SI 2012/1108).

[183] See http://www.ukbiobank.ac.uk.

being developed to advise the funders on *how* UK Biobank should be set up and oper-ate. All aspects of the project were considered—from consent through confidential-ity and on to commercialisation. The recommendations were then put out to public consultation and a final framework was agreed in light of the response. Central to that framework is the establishment of a permanent Ethics and Governance Council to act as a 'mirror' to UK Biobank in respect of its activities and its relationship with participants. Importantly, all of this has been done *in addition* to the ethical and legal regulatory requirements we have already discussed. Moreover, the fact that the ELSI discussion took place while the research protocol was being developed left open the possibility that one might influence the other and vice versa. This process will continue into the future. We have suggested elsewhere that this is an example of *reflexive* govern-ance by which we mean a system of mutual learning over time which does not expect all regulatory issues to be addressed prior to commencement of research.[184] Such an approach, if done well, does much to foster a productive and interactive research rela-tionship between researcher and participant, akin to a partnership, and it moves away from old ideas of the passive research 'subject'.

19.75 A similar project called Generation Scotland has evolved north of the Border.[185] It too seeks to explore the relationship between genes and environment, although the recruit-ment base is Scottish families of all ages, including those with members who are ill. Generation Scotland has also adopted a similar up-front ELSI approach with a very strong programme of research into public engagement. The aim is to respond as far as is possible to public views and concerns about the project; this extends from design of the project itself to issues such as the commercialisation of the outputs of research.[186] Ultimately, the exercise serves to reinforce one of the most crucial lessons in this field: human biomedical research is impossible without the participation and the sup-port of the public.[187]

19.76 Finally, research cannot generate valuable new knowledge without effective and effi-cient access to data while at the same time not diluting appropriate scrutiny. The key is to build systems of *proportionate* governance, and the Scottish Health Informatics Programme (SHIP) is one such example. SHIP is a Scotland-wide initiative aimed at better facilitating secondary uses of health data for research through a consortium of a diverse range of stakeholders including universities, researchers and NHS Scotland, and involving ongoing public engagement with the aim to build an infrastructure to deliver a national research facility to allow rapid and secure access to health data for research purposes. To deliver proportionate governance, SHIP has developed a unique one-stop-shop research portal for researchers to gain access to the robust health datasets held by those data controllers participating in the initiative, most notably NHS Scotland—the custodian of the richest datasets in the country. The SHIP Good Governance Framework (GGF) was designed and implemented after a survey of the

---

[184] See G Laurie, 'Reflexive governance in biobanking: on the value of policy led approaches and the need to recognise the limits of law' (2011) 130 Hum Genet 347, and G Laurie, A Bruce, and C Lyall, 'The roles of values and interests in the governance of the life sciences: Learning lessons from the "ethics+" approach of UK Biobank' in C Lyall et al. (eds), *The Limits of Governance* (2009) ch 3.

[185] Generation Scotland, at: http://www.generationscotland.org/.

[186] See G Haddow, G Laurie, et al., 'Tackling community concerns about commercialisation and genetic research: A modest interdisciplinary proposal' (2007) 64 Soc Sci and Med 272.

[187] M Pickersgill, 'Research, engagement and public bioethics: promoting socially robust science' (2011) 37 J Med Ethics 698.

existing legal landscape and national and international problems. It consists of four features:

1. an account of responsibilities of key actors and decision-makers (largely a matter of clarifying who is a data controller);
2. a capacity-building facility for researcher training and accreditation and wider awareness-raising (delivered through distance learning);
3. a statement of Principles and Best Practices to guide decision-making; and
4. a mechanism of principled proportionate governance in granting research access.[188]

Decision-makers are provided with a set of guiding principles to assist in determining whether linkage should take place and, taking into account the importance of public interest, the possible roles of consent and anonymisation and identification and mitigation of risks accordingly. Importantly, *proportionate* governance is delivered through a stratified mechanism of regulatory pathways that handle data linkage applications relative to these considerations, as seen in Figure 19.1.

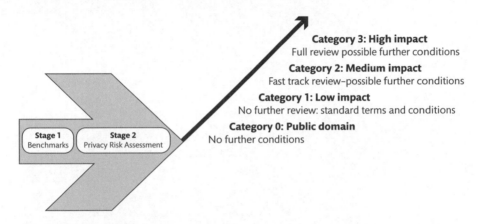

Figure 19.1 Delivering Proportionate Governance

This framework was developed through interactive design with the public and researcher communities.[189] We see, then, that when moving forward in the new research governance landscape the twin beacons of proportionality and reflexivity are key—emphasising once again the centrality of partnership in the success of the entire research enterprise.

CONCLUSION

19.77 As noted in *Richmond Pharmacology Ltd* v *Health Research Authority*,[190] health research, and clinical trials in particular, are governed by a 'complex web of regulatory provisions [from] EU Directives and domestic legislation'. Recent and ongoing efforts to reform the setting are attempting to create a more holistic framework that is more closely aligned to the concepts of proportionality and transparency such

---

[188] For further elaboration, see G Laurie and N Sethi, 'Towards principle-based approaches to governance of health-related research using personal data' (2013) 4 Euro J Risk and Reg 43.
[189] See further http://www.scot-ship.ac.uk/.   [190] [2015] EWHC 2283 (Admin).

that responsible research and innovation can be encouraged. If such can be achieved, it will not only assist researchers, but also better protect research participants, who, currently, cannot even inform themselves about all the clinical trials that are being undertaken.[191] Regulators have not yet succeeded. Indeed, the HRA, whose purpose is to facilitate this transition, was criticised in *Richmond Pharmacology* for supplying to users, via its website, material that is 'so ambiguous as to the expression of its scope as to mislead'.[192] Efforts continue.

[191] At present, only Phase II–IV trials, not Phase I trials, need be registered on the public fields of EudraCT (available at https://eudract.ema.europa.eu/), and the results of such trials are not universally accessible. The 2014 Regulation will not correct this.

[192] Para 86.

20
RESEARCH ON CHILDREN, FETUSES, AND EMBRYOS

20.01   A child is by no means a miniature version of an adult. Children respond differently to drugs, as they do to a number of other treatments, and it is impossible to say that the effect of a particular therapy on an adult will be mirrored when applied to a child. Medical research on children is, therefore, necessary before a treatment can be approved for paediatric use. As in adults, such research may entail not only therapeutic research on sick children but also essential non-therapeutic research on healthy control groups;[1] it is this non-therapeutic research which poses the most controversial ethical and legal problems.[2] These should, however, be kept in perspective. Research involving children has lowered the rate of infant mortality considerably; for example, research on vitamin A deficiency in children in developing countries has made it possible to lower mortality rates among those affected by measles.[3] Similarly, research on mother/child transmission of Human Immunodeficiency Virus (HIV) has reduced the incidence of infection in the children of infected mothers—an important matter in the control of the global pandemic. Children have as much right to participate in, and benefit from, research as their adult counterparts and some would argue that there is a moral duty to conduct such research.[4] At the same time, numerous surveys also indicate that, in practice, there is a worrying dearth of well-conducted research involving children.[5] The Royal College of Paediatrics and Child Health (RCPCH) issued a call to action in 2012 to stem a crisis in child health research.[6] It reported that '[s]ince 2000, there has been an 18% reduction in the number of university-employed child health researchers and a fall in the proportion of university employed paediatricians from 8.7% of the total consultant-level workforce in 2001 to 5.2% in 2011'.[7] Moreover, despite the fact that children make up more than 20 per cent of the United Kingdom (UK) population, less than 5 per cent of research funding goes to child health research. Most worryingly, 'the mortality rate for children under the

---

[1] Other sources reframe the two categories as research that may, or may not, offer the possibility of benefit to a particular child. See Nuffield Council on Bioethics, *Children and Clinical Research* (2015). For further general discussion, see issue 15(2) of the European Journal of Health Law (2008) and for the USA, see L F Ross, *Children in Medical Research* (2006).

[2] L Bröstrom and M Johansson, 'Involving children in non-therapeutic research: On the development argument' (2014) 17 Med Health Care Philos 53.

[3] Working Group on Women and Child Health, F Dabis, J Orne-Gliemann, F Perez et al., 'Improving child health: The role of research' (2002) 324 BMJ 1444.

[4] Canadian Paediatric Society, 'Ethical issues in health research in children' (2008) 13(8) Paediat Child Health 707. For European perspectives, see Recommendations of the Ethics Working Group of the Confederation of European Specialists in Paediatrics (CESP), *Ethical Principles and Operational Guidelines for Good Clinical Practice in Paediatric Research* (2004).

[5] R L Smyth, 'Research with children' (2001) 322 BMJ 1377.

[6] RCPCH, *Turning the Tide: Harnessing the Power of Child Health Research* (2012).   [7] Ibid.

age of five years in the UK is 30% higher than the average for Western Europe, with five excess deaths a day compared to the best performing countries'.[8] Thus, despite measures such as the introduction of European Regulation in 2006 designed to encourage more appropriately designed clinical trials of medicines intended for the treatment of children[9] and the recent launch of the UK Child Health Research Collaboration—a partnership between funders aimed at increasing and strengthening child health research[10]—much remains to be done.[11]

20.02 Such research as there is involves a variety of procedures, ranging from the completely benign—such as studies of weight and height[12]—to those that are frankly invasive. The conclusions of the Alder Hey Inquiry into the post-mortem retention of children's organs reminds us of the fact that research might still be conducted with scant regard to the rights and sensitivities of others.[13] The Court of Appeals of Maryland identified the kernel of the issue thus:

> It is not in the best interest of a specific child, in a non-therapeutic research project, to be placed in a research environment, which might possibly be, or which proves to be, hazardous to the health of the child. We have long stressed that the 'best interests of the child' is the overriding concern of this Court in matters relating to children. Whatever the interests of a parent, and whatever the interests of the general public in fostering research that might, according to a researcher's hypothesis, be for the good of all children, this Court's concern for the particular child and particular case, over-arches all other interests.[14]

20.03 We suggest that the same sentiment underlies the legal framework in the UK; notwithstanding this, there has been little judicial treatment of the topic, as we will see. Equally, the RCPCH report reminds that this important issue affects children and adults alike:

> Infants, children and young people need treatments that are developed for them, interventions that are tested in them, health services that are designed for them and policies that address their health and wellbeing. Many diseases and much ill-health in adult life have their origins in early development … Children's research offers unparalleled

---

[8] See http://www.rcpch.ac.uk/news/time-%E2%80%98turn-tide%E2%80%99-myths-child-health-research.

[9] Regulation (EC) No 1901/2006 of the European Parliament and of the Council of 12 December 2006 on medicinal products for paediatric use (amended by Regulation (EC) No 1902/2006). Also see the five-year progress report: European Commission, *Better Medicines for Children: From Concept to Reality: Progress Report on the Paediatric Regulation (EC) No 1901/2006* COM (2013) 443.

[10] http://www.rcpch.ac.uk/improving-child-health/research-and-surveillance/uk-child-health-research-collaboration/uk-child-hea.

[11] The RCPCH report in summary suggests: (i) debunk the myths surrounding clinical trials and push for the introduction of a system of 'opting out' of studies designed to reduce uncertainties in treatments, rather than 'opting in'; (ii) improve education, research training, and guidance for paediatricians: with the RCPCH pledging to improve research training for all paediatricians and clear routes into research careers; and (iii) strengthen the infrastructure for children's biomedical research in the UK by supporting the establishment of a children's trials network for non-medicines as well as medicines studies.

[12] Although see this Department of Health study *Research into Parental Attitudes Towards the Routine Measurement of Children's Height and Weight* (2007).

[13] H Bauchner and R Vinci, 'What have we learnt from the Alder Hey affair?' (2001) 322 BMJ 309, and S Dewar and P Boddington, 'Returning to the Alder Hey report and its reporting: Addressing confusions and improving inquiries' (2004) 30 J Med Ethics 463.

[14] *Grimes* v *Kennedy-Krieger Institute; Higgins* v *Kennedy-Krieger Institute* 782 A 2d 807 (2001). For critical comment, see V H Sharav, 'Children in clinical research: A conflict of moral values' (2003) 3 Am J Bioethics W12, and also M J Klag, 'A Response to "Children in Clinical Research: A Conflict of Moral Values" ' (2003) 3 Am J Bioethics W34.

opportunity to improve life-long health and turn the tide of an increasing burden of non-communicable chronic diseases, obesity, cardiovascular disease, and diabetes, which lead to premature adult death.[15]

NON-THERAPEUTIC RESEARCH ON CHILDREN

20.04 The essential difficulty with non-therapeutic research on children lies, as we have noted in the previous chapter, in the question of consent. An adult may be able to give an informed, and therefore valid, consent to participation in research—but can the same be said of a child? If a child can consent for him- or herself—that is, if his or her autonomy is sufficiently developed—then it may be acceptable, ethically at least, to allow the child to consent on his or her own behalf.[16] Indeed, the child should be consulted in any circumstances involving his or her personal integrity and, if the child's capacity is found to be such that he or she *can* consent, then the child's wishes should always be respected; but would that be enough on its own to authorise research? We will come to the legal position later, simply noting for present purposes that this is another example of where one may legitimately argue as to the role of the law in respect of the mature minor: should the law respect a child's developing autonomy in respect of *any* decision, or should it remain protective and restrictive of the child's autonomy until such time as legal adulthood is attained?[17]

20.05 And what of the child who is clearly unable to exercise his or her self-determination? Interestingly, the Declaration of Helsinki makes no specific mention of children, but it does state that in the case of research involving a 'research subject who is incompetent', the informed consent of the legally authorised representative should be procured;[18] this approach was also adopted in the guidelines on research issued by the Royal College of Paediatrics and Child Health,[19] the Medical Research Council (MRC),[20] the General Medical Council (GMC),[21] and the British Medical Association[22] and, in the USA, the

---

[15] N 6, p 16.

[16] For a range of views on the child and consent in the research context see: American Journal of Bioethics (2003) 3(4), especially D Wendler and S Shah, 'Should children decide whether they are enrolled in non-beneficial research?' (2003) 3(4) Am J Bioethics 1.

[17] The Additional Protocol on Biomedical Research (2005) to the Council of Europe Convention on Biomedicine and Human Rights (1997) states specifically in Art 15(1)(iv) that: 'The opinion of a minor shall be taken into consideration as an increasingly determining factor in proportion to age and degree of maturity'. Similarly, Art 7(a) of the UNESCO Universal Declaration on Bioethics and Human Rights provides: 'authorization for research and medical practice should be obtained in accordance with the best interest of the person concerned and in accordance with domestic law. However, the person concerned should be involved to the greatest extent possible in the decision-making process of consent, as well as that of withdrawing consent …'

[18] World Medical Association, *Ethical Principles for Medical Research Involving Human Subjects* (revised, 2008), paras 27–9.

[19] Royal College of Paediatrics and Child Health: Ethics Advisory Committee, 'Guidelines for the ethical conduct of medical research involving children' (2000) 82(2) Arch Dis Child 177; this guidance was updated in 2014: N Modi et al., 'Guidance on clinical research involving infants, children and young people: An update for researchers and research ethics committees' (2014) 99 Arch Dis Child 887.

[20] MRC, *Medical Research Involving Children* (2004). For exceptional circumstances where guardians might not be involved see para 5.5.4.

[21] GMC, *0–18 years: Guidance for All Doctors* (2007), paras 36–40 and generally, GMC, *Protecting Children and Young People: The Responsibilities of All Doctors* (2012).

[22] British Medical Association, *Consent, Rights and Choice in Healthcare for Children and Young People* (2001) and BMA, *Children and young people—a toolkit for doctors*: http://bma.org.uk/practical-support-at-work/ethics/children.

Department of Health and Human Services.[23] All of these influential bodies accept that non-therapeutic research on children is justified when it is intended to benefit other children—although it should not be carried out if it can be done equally well using adults.[24]

20.06   Parental consent may not, per se, be sufficient if proposed non-therapeutic research involves more than a minimal risk to the child—a condition which, inevitably, raises the issue of what risks are minimal. Federal Regulations in the USA have held that: 'Minimal risk means that the probability and magnitude of harm or discomfort anticipated in the research are not greater in and of themselves than those ordinarily encountered in daily life or during the performance of routine physical or psychological examinations or tests.'[25] The Institute of Medical Ethics, which studied the question in depth in the 1980s,[26] defined a minimal risk as one which carried a risk of death lower than 1:1,000,000, a risk of major complications less than 1:100,000, and a risk of minor complications of less than 1:1,000.[27] The US approach uses language; this approach uses figures. Both convey the same general message: a risk has ceased to be minimal where there is a risk that makes one stop and think.[28] In addition, the Institute thought that a child's consent should be obtained after the age of seven years. The MRC guidelines place considerable emphasis on evidence of child refusal, stating: 'A child's refusal to participate or continue in research should always be respected ... [i]f a child becomes upset by a procedure, researchers must accept this as a valid refusal.'[29] No age limit seems to be applied.

20.07   Where a child is not competent to consent or assent,[30] then obtaining parental consent is clearly important, [31] but the fact that it has been given does not, of itself, *justify* carrying out research on children. Our first concern here must be with the welfare of the child, and it need hardly be said that parental consent to something which is obviously to the detriment of the child is unacceptable, ethically and legally.[32] Parents do not have an absolute, unfettered right to regulate their children's lives; it is implicit in the modern concept of

[23] Code of Federal Regulations, Title 45: Public Welfare—Department of Health and Human Services, Pt 46—Protection of Human Subjects, Sub-part D: 45 CFR, s 46 (2009).

[24] For criticism about a lack of uniformity between guidelines, see S D Edwards and M J McNamee, 'Ethical concerns regarding guidelines for the conduct of clinical research on children' (2005) 31 J Med Ethics 351 and this is strongly echoed in the RCPCH report, n 6, paras 8.4–8.5.

[25] 45 CFR Sec 46 (102.i) (2009).

[26] Institute of Medical Ethics 'Medical research with children: Ethics, law and practice' (1986) Bull no 14, p 8. For discussion of the recommendations, see R J Robinson, 'Ethics committees and research on children' (1987) 294 BMJ 1243. See also M A Grodin, L H Glantz, and A M Dellinger, 'Children as research subjects: Science, ethics and law' (1996) 21 J Hlth Politics Policy Law 159.

[27] For a discussion of assessment of risk, see D B Resnik, 'Eliminating the daily life risks standard from the definition of minimal risk' (2005) 31 J Med Ethics 35.

[28] For guidance on minimising risks, see National Academy of the Sciences, *Ethical Conduct of Clinical Research Involving Children* (2004) and for a survey of approaches and recommendations for ways forward, A Westra et al., 'Acceptable risks and burdens for children in research without direct benefit: a systematic analysis of the decisions made by the Dutch Central Committee' (2010) 36 J Med Ethics 420.

[29] MRC, n 20, p 6.

[30] For an interesting exploration of assent in the genomics context, see S Benjamin et al., 'Engaging children in genomics research: decoding the meaning of assent in research' (2012) 14 Genetics in Med 437.

[31] For discussion of the reasons for high rates of parental refusal revealed in one survey, see K Menon and R Ward, 'A study of consent for participation in a non-therapeutic study in the paediatric intensive care population' (2014) 40 J Med Ethics 123.

[32] The converse is also true, namely, that parental objection to interventions which are deemed to be in the child's interests do not necessarily hold sway. See *Re MM (medical treatment)* [2000] 1 FLR 224; [2000]

parenthood that the aim of parental responsibilities—note not powers—is to protect and enhance the status of the child. It follows that the researcher cannot simply say, 'The parents have consented and this means that I can go ahead'; parental consent may justify the involvement of children in non-therapeutic research but it will do so only when it points to the acceptability of the research in terms of some interest of the child.

20.08 One way of assessing parental consent is to see it as a substitute for the child's own judgement which cannot, as yet, be expressed. Under this theory, parental consent does no more than voice what the child would be expected to state, had he or she the ability to do so. Acceptance of this approach salves any qualms the researcher might have—in effect, the child consents to what is done, the only complication being that this cannot be expressed personally. Critics point out that this involves a blatant fiction. It would be more honest, they argue, to accept that this constitutes non-consensual research and to admit the need to justify it on other grounds. The difficulty cannot be avoided by attempting to justify the child's involvement in terms of his 'future identification' with the decision made on his or her behalf.[33] It is difficult to see any distinction between 'identification' and 'consent' and, whatever terms one uses to imply future assent, there is no certainty that the child will, in fact, later endorse what his or her parents have decided. We have already noted, however, that the substituted judgement test has no role in UK law in respect of treatment and care; there is no reason why it should or would be any different in the context of research.

20.09 The matter may, nonetheless, be approached from an entirely different perspective—one which focuses not on any imagined consent of the child but on what is in that child's best interests. This test would allow the parents to involve the child in that which is in—or, alternatively, that which is not manifestly against—the child's best interests. The first of these would require that the non-therapeutic research secures some benefit for the child—a difficult, though not impossible, case to make.[34] A child is a member of a class within the community—the class of children—and the individual can be said to be a potential beneficiary if research will benefit the class as a whole. It is also possible to extrapolate the reasoning used to justify organ donation (see Chapter 14) and to argue that participation in research related to a disease from which, for example, a sibling is suffering will benefit the normal child—it being in his interests that his sibling should recover.

20.10 An allied benefit-based theory focuses on the altruistic nature of participation in non-therapeutic research. Here, the issue is, at base, whether parents can legitimately involve their children in projects by way of imposed selflessness. Such cooperation is undoubtedly good for the subject, but this would apply only if the child were sufficiently mature to understand the philanthropic nature of what he was doing. An older child may later derive satisfaction from the fact that he helped others when younger, but the same objection applies here as to proxy consent—how can we be sure that this is what he would feel?[35]

Fam Law 92 which, although dealing with treatment and not research per se, involved a dispute over the acceptability of risk in experimental circumstances. The court declared itself willing to override the parental objection if necessary.

[33] R B Redmon, 'How children can be respected as ends yet still be used as subjects in non-therapeutic research' (1986) 12 J Med Ethics 77.

[34] For criticism of the role of best interests in the research context, and especially as it relates to non-therapeutic research, see S Elliston, *Best Interests of the Child in Healthcare* (2007) ch 6 and B Lyons, 'Obliging Children' (2011) 19 Med Law Rev 55.

[35] For argument along these lines, see G Williams, 'Children as means and ends in large scale medical research' (2012) 26(8) Bioethics 422; Bröstrom and Johansson, n 2.

20.11 The alternative interpretation of the best interests test, which allows for measures which are not to the actual detriment of the child—or not against its interests—clearly licenses the child's involvement in non-therapeutic research so long as the risks involved are negligible.[36] This assessment gives a wider discretion to parents, who may choose to interpret their duty to society as including a duty to engage their children in pro-social activities. Such parents act within their rights, and cannot be regarded as abusing their position until such time as the child suffers actual harm or runs an appreciable risk of harm or demonstrates an unwillingness to proceed.[37]

20.12 It is now established beyond doubt that the best interests test is the legal determinant of acceptable treatment with respect to children. The extension of the test in the context of research along the lines suggested, however, would be a matter for judicial discretion; there is no ruling to date on whether the test would admit of such a generous reading. Certainly, the courts have been unsparing in recent years in fleshing out the test in respect of care, and the concept of *overall* interests has been employed time and again. We suggest that it would not be too much of a stretch of our imaginations to adopt a similar approach to child research—an approach that reflects the child's interests in his or her broader relationships with the community; this would be subject always, and of course, to a minimal, negligible, or non-existent risk to the child in question.

20.13 Thus far, we have assumed that the child in question is not of an age to give any meaningful consent. Many children of relatively tender age will be able to understand the issues involved and the question then arises as to the weight to be given to any agreement they might give. The age at which a child can appreciate the implications of what he or she is doing will obviously vary, but some generalisations may be made.[38] Children under the age of seven or eight are usually considered to be incapable of that degree of morally sophisticated thought required to make consistent altruistic decisions but, above that age, a child may be perfectly able to understand that he or she is helping doctors to cure others by taking part in the research programme.[39] A child who was not able to grasp the general idea of medical research by the age of 14 would probably be an exception today. This view is supported by a study that was designed to assess the ability of groups of nine- and 14-year-olds to make decisions relating to medical treatment. The 14-year-olds were shown to have the same general level of capacity to make this sort of decision as did adults and a surprising degree of competence was shown in the nine-year-old group.[40] The age of 14 has also been supported as an acceptable cut-off for determining the ethics of research with children involving their own consent.[41] In other camps, however, the ability of

---

[36] For further discussion, see the wide-ranging analysis by A Plomer, 'Participation of children in clinical trials: UK, European and international perspectives on consent' (2000) 5 Med L Internat 1.

[37] The test of acceptability then becomes one of the 'reasonable parent': see J K Mason, *Medico-legal Aspects of Reproduction and Parenthood* (2nd edn, 1998) pp 324 et seq.

[38] See early helpful discussion in J Berryman, 'Discussing the ethics of research on children' in J van Eys (ed), *Research on Children* (1978) p 85. See also P Alderson and J Montgomery, *Health Care Choices: Making Decisions with Children* (1996); M Paul, 'Informed consent in medical research: Children from the age of 5 should be presumed competent' (1997) 314 BMJ 1480.

[39] Cf, N Ondrusek et al., 'Empirical examination of the ability of children to consent to clinical research' (1998) 24 J Med Ethics 158.

[40] L A Weithorn and S B Campbell, 'The competency of children and adolescents to make informed treatment decisions' (1982) 53 Child Develop 285. For discussion, see R H Nicholson (ed), *Medical Research with Children* (1986) p 146.

[41] K Toner and R Schwartz, 'Why a teenager over age 14 should be able to consent, rather than merely assent, to participation as a human subject of research' (2003) 3 Am J Bioethics 38. Cf, R Ashcroft, T Goodenough, J Kent, and E Williamson, 'Children's consent to research participation: Social context and personal experience invalidate fixed cutoff rules' (2003) 3 Am J Bioethics 16.

children adequately to understand research information has been questioned—also on the basis of survey evidence—leading to a recommendation that guidance such as that discussed here should be revised so as not to place undue emphasis on child autonomy in this non-therapeutic context.[42]

20.14 The evidence may, then, be finely balanced and the ethical issues might be clarified to an extent if the law could give a clear answer to this question. Unfortunately, the law itself is uncertain in this area and this has not eased the difficulties of those involved in paediatric research. As long ago as 1962 the MRC stated that:

> in the strict view of the law, parents and guardians of minors cannot give consent on their behalf to any procedures which are of no particular benefit to them and which may carry some risk of harm.[43]

20.15 This was followed by a Department of Health circular that confirmed that interpretation in a negative way:

> Health authorities are advised that they ought not to infer [from a Royal College of Physicians' recommendation that children can be used in certain forms of research provided the consent of the guardian has been obtained] that the fact that consent has been given by the parent or guardian and that the risk involved is considered negligible will be sufficient to bring such clinical research investigation within the law as it stands.[44]

20.16 The advice of the Department of Health was roundly attacked by doctors. Lawyers were also critical of this strict view of the law, pointing out the paucity of authority on the point.[45] The position remains more or less the same to this day. In these conditions— almost amounting to a legal vacuum—the proper way of approaching the issue is to look at general legal principles governing the parent–child relationship and to infer what a court might decide if the matter were to come before it.

20.17 The judgment of the House of Lords in *Gillick* v *West Norfolk and Wisbech Area Health Authority*[46] confirmed the view that the consent of a minor to medical treatment may be adequate even without parental ratification provided that the child has sufficient understanding and intelligence to appreciate what is involved. 'Parental rights', said Lord Scarman, 'exist only so long as they are needed for the protection of the person and property of the child'. It is not certain, however, whether the *Gillick* principle, which is concerned with consent to treatment, would be applied to cases of non-therapeutic experimentation. Much would, of course, depend on the severity of the procedure—this being one of the factors to be balanced in the assessment of '*Gillick*-competence'. As to statute, it is clear that s 8 of the Family Law Reform Act 1969 refers only to diagnosis and treatment[47]—the statutory age of 16 years has, therefore, no relevance as to consent to research or experimentation. To infer from this that consent to non-therapeutic investigations is impossible below the age of majority would be, again, to accept a total embargo on paediatric research. It is not unreasonable to extrapolate Lord Donaldson's

---

[42] See also, T M Burke et al., 'Children's understanding of the risks and benefits associated with research' (2005) 31 J Med Ethics 715.

[43] *Report of the Medical Research Council for 1962–3* (Cmnd 2382) pp 21–5.

[44] Supervision of the Ethics of Clinical Research Investigations and Fetal Research HSC (5) 153.

[45] See, e.g., discussion by G Dworkin, 'Law and medical experimentation: Of embryos, children and others with limited legal capacity' (1987) 13 Monash Univ LR 189.

[46] [1986] AC 112; [1985] 3 All ER 402, HL.

[47] It is problematic as to whether this limitation applies in Scotland insofar as the Age of Legal Capacity (Scotland) Act 1991, s 2(4) refers to consent by the understanding minor to 'any surgical, medical or dental *procedure* or treatment' (emphasis added).

interpretation of the law in *Re R*[48] and to infer that anyone who can legally do so may give consent but that demurral by the minor would be a very important consideration in judging whether to carry out the research. Moreover, this would be even more significant than it would be in relation to treatment—to such an extent that it would be improbable in the extreme that a responsible doctor would ignore the minor's negative attitude.[49] The problem then becomes that of deciding whether there is any age below which a person is deemed incapable of consent and, while there is no law on the point, it would be unwise, in our opinion, for a researcher to accept the unendorsed consent of a child under the age of 16; indeed, the circumstances in which such a consent would be acceptable would be exceptional. Hazardous experimentation authorised by the consent of a minor alone might, in fact, be unlawful.[50]

20.18 To say that a procedure is legal is not to say that it is necessarily morally acceptable; furthermore, there is no reason to assume that the court, if asked, would approve an action which was unethical. The position is, therefore, still delicately balanced. Anticipating a judicial reaction is a matter for ethics committees which may assume that the court would act as a wise parent would act—giving first consideration to the child but being, at the same time, hospitable to good research.[51] Thus, the essential measure is the 'risk–benefit ratio' of the investigation—but, within this, the 'risk' factor must, without doubt, retain primary control. We also suggest that, notwithstanding what the true legal position may be, it would be, in practice, improper to proceed with research involving a child against the wishes of his or her parents. The only exception might be when that refusal was clearly unreasonable and was jeopardising an otherwise essential trial to which a child who was capable of understanding—the 'mature minor' of *Gillick*—had already consented. Such conditions must be extremely rare; in the event of their materialising, a decision to go ahead should be taken only after very careful consideration—and, probably, not even then.

20.19 It must not be thought that an ethical assessment of a project is always clear-cut. A most apposite, albeit now historic, example was an experiment in preventive medicine which entailed the deliberate infection with the virus of hepatitis of children in a home for children with serious learning difficulties. Although the chances of the children being infected naturally within six months of admission were as high as 60 per cent, the project was castigated by some writers.[52] Others disagreed with such an analysis—one of Britain's most respected paediatricians at the time described the experiment as, 'a small, carefully controlled trial for which the director also deserves a great deal of credit for his scrupulous care in securing the truly informed consent of the children's parents'.[53] The legal implications of using children as research subjects have been aired in the USA in *Grimes v Kennedy Krieger Inst Inc*,[54] a decision of the Maryland Court of Appeals. The facts of this case make disturbing reading. Families with children were encouraged to move into

---

[48] *Re R (a minor) (wardship: medical treatment)* [1992] Fam 11, (1991) 7 BMLR 147.

[49] Relevant to the assessment of competence to take one's own decisions would also be the test laid down in *Re C (adult: refusal of medical treatment)* [1994] 1 All ER 819; [1994] 1 WLR 290, for which see Chapter 4.

[50] Lord Donaldson distinguished between medical treatment and a severely damaging operation which gave no benefit to the subject: *Re W (a minor) (medical treatment)* [1992] 4 All ER 627 at 635, 639; (1992) 9 BMLR 22 at 31, 35.

[51] For an interesting comparative analysis, see C Lenk et al., 'Non-therapeutic research with minors: How do chairpersons of German research ethics committees decide?' (2004) 30 J Med Ethics 85.

[52] See, for a good review at the time, L Golman, 'The Willowbrook debate' (1973) 9 World Med (1)(79).

[53] A W Franklin, 'Research investigation on children' (1973) 1 BMJ 402 at 405.

[54] 782 A 2d 807 (2001).

houses in which only partial lead-pollution controls had been implemented. The level of lead contamination in the blood of the children living in such houses was then measured against levels in a control group living in less polluted conditions. The Court held that it would not be left to the researchers to determine what is an acceptable risk to the health of children, and that the consent of parents would not be sufficient where there was a real risk of harming the health of children.[55]

THERAPEUTIC RESEARCH ON CHILDREN

20.20 And that is an appropriate comment by which to lead us to a brief discussion of therapeutic research on children which, it might be thought, raises no more issues than does non-therapeutic research as we have discussed earlier.

20.21 A moment's thought, however, shows us that this is not true. To begin with, we cannot apply a substituted judgement test of any sort. We can make a reasonable assumption that a child would want to be cured of a disease or disability if that were possible. What we cannot know is *how* he or she would want to be cured—and we certainly cannot know if he or she would want to take a chance on a lottery choice of treatments.

20.22 As in the case of non-therapeutic research, we can appeal to the principle of respect for autonomy when the child is old enough to be capable of making a decision—although the assessment of capacity would surely have to be exceptionally rigorous in the conditions envisaged—but we have no such fall-back position in the case of the neonate or young child. The onus of consent falls squarely on the parents and we must ask if it is ever possible—or ever fair—to expect a fully informed consent as to therapeutic research from parents who are confronted by a sick, possibly dying, child. The issue thus presents starkly as one of the child's welfare or 'best interests'. The evident nature of forced choices to try almost anything in desperate circumstances is illustrated all too well in the case of *Simms* v *Simms; A* v *A and another*[56] which we discuss more fully in Chapter 19. It will be recalled that the case related to a 16-year-old and an 18-year-old, both suffering from the incurable brain disease variant Creutzfeldt-Jakob disease (vCJD). The patients could not consent for themselves and the President of the High Court applied the best interests test to authorise the application of a highly experimental treatment on the children—never before tested on humans—as a last chance therapeutic effort. The legal basis for doing so was the presence of medical evidence which agreed that there was at least a possibility that benefit might accrue.

20.23 But the application of the best interests test does still not necessarily resolve the dilemma. By definition, the doctor does not know which of the treatments on offer is the 'best' for the child—the research programme would be fundamentally unethical if he did; it follows that there is a 50 per cent chance of the decision *not* being in the child's best interests whichever choice is made—indeed, there is a 50 per cent chance of it failing a 'no detriment' test. Following this one step further, it becomes easy to conclude that therapeutic research on children can *never* be justified—or, at best, can be justified only

---

[55] For discussion, see G Johnson, 'Recent development: *Grimes* v *Kennedy Krieger Inst Inc*' (2001) 9 U Balt J Environ Law 72. And for a spirited defence: L F Ross, 'In defense of the Hopkins lead abatement studies' (2002) 30 J Law Med Ethics 50. See, too, M Spriggs, 'Canaries in the mines: Children, risk, non-therapeutic research, and justice' (2004) 30 J Med Ethics 176.

[56] [2003] 2 WLR 1465; [2003] 1 All ER 669; [2003] 1 FCR 361.

in exceptional circumstances.[57] Yet, we all know that it must be done or paediatrics will become a static subject. Allmark et al. have argued that every infant has a 'global' interest in medical progress and it is this which tips the scales in favour of ethical justification for participation in therapeutic research on children.[58] Admittedly, this carries the stamp of the advocate's last card—and it is scarcely a high trump card; nevertheless, it may well provide the escape from what is, essentially, a cul-de-sac for the utilitarian.

20.24   These problems, taken together, are sufficient to explain why paediatricians may be loath to seek parental consent to their children being involved in a dedicated programme of therapeutic research.[59] Failure to do so, however, involves following a dangerous road— consent is now accepted as providing both the key and the lock to medical interventions of any sort.[60] An example of the difficulties in defining the ethical limits of research in children was provided by the long-running investigation into the randomised controlled trial of the treatment of premature infants with breathing difficulties conducted in North Staffordshire.[61] Eighteen parents of babies involved in the study complained to the GMC that they had not been informed of the experimental nature of the treatment,[62] and as a result an official inquiry was established which was severely critical of the study from many aspects.[63] An interesting feature of this incident was the attention that it drew not only to the ethical conduct of a research project—as, for example, in obtaining informed consent—but also to the ethical component lodged in the *design* of a research project—is the design such that it will provide valid results? Clearly, this will often be controversial[64] and a main, and widely agreed, recommendation of the Griffith Report was to the effect that a new govern- ance framework should be elaborated to cover research undertaken in the National Health Service (NHS). This, as we have seen in Chapter 19, has now been instituted. The 2012 Report from the Royal College of Paediatrics and Child Health would suggest, however, that this has not improved conditions for research on children or, indeed, subjects of any age.[65]

20.25   The importance of research of all kinds is now widely accepted and incorporated into legal instruments at both the national and international levels. Thus, as already noted in the preceding chapter, we have the Additional Protocol on Biomedical Research (2005) to the Council of Europe Convention on Biomedicine and Human Rights (1997) which came into force in September 2007 and which states:

> Exceptionally and under the protective conditions prescribed by law, where the research has not the potential to produce results of direct benefit to the health of the person

[57] J Appleyard, 'Risks and benefits of research on children: Developing an ethical framework to meet children's needs' (2008) 14 C Risk 215.

[58] P Allmark, S Mason, A B Gill, and C Megone, 'Is it in a neonate's best interest to enter a randomised controlled trial?' (2001) 27 J Med Ethics 110.

[59] D S Wendler, 'Assent in paediatric research: Theoretical and practical considerations' (2006) 32 J Med Ethics 229.

[60] Further complications arise when 'incentives' are involved: R Dobson, 'Lump sums for children taking part in research may distort parents' judgment' (2002) 325 BMJ 796.

[61] M P Samuels, J Raine, T Wright, et al., 'Continuous negative extrathoracic pressure in neonatal respira- tory failure' (1996) 98 Pediatrics 1154.

[62] J Jones, 'Doctors suspended in child health inquiry' (2000) 320 BMJ 9.

[63] NHS Executive, *Report of a Review of the Research Framework in North Staffordshire Hospital NHS Trust* (R Griffiths, chair) (2000).

[64] See, e.g., E Hey and I Chalmers, 'Investigating allegations of research misconduct: The vital need for due process' (2000) 321 BMJ 752.

[65] See n 6, and also E Cave, 'Seen but not heard? Children in clinical trials' (2010) 18(1) Med L Rev 1. The RCPCH also conducted a survey in 2015 to evaluate whether any further progress has been made. The results have not been published at the time of writing: http://www.rcpch.ac.uk/participation-research.

concerned, such research may be authorised subject to the conditions laid down in [this Article] and to the following additional conditions:

(i) the research has the aim of contributing, through significant improvement in the scientific understanding of the individual's condition, disease or disorder, to the ultimate attainment of results capable of conferring benefit to the person concerned or to other persons in the same age category or afflicted with the same disease or disorder or having the same condition;

(ii) the research entails only minimal risk and minimal burden for the individual concerned; and any consideration of additional potential benefits of the research shall not be used to justify an increased level of risk or burden.

20.26   In the context of clinical trials, the 2014 EU Clinical Trial Regulation,[66] which replaces the earlier 2001 Clinical Trial Directive,[67] makes specific provision for research involving minors. Briefly, it states that research may be conducted only when a number of conditions are satisfied. With regards to study design, the clinical trial must either relate directly to a medical condition from which the minor concerned suffers or is of such a nature that it can only be carried out on minors. In addition, there should be scientific grounds for expecting that participation in the clinical trial will produce: (a) either a direct benefit for the minor concerned outweighing the risks and benefits involved; or (b) some benefit for the population represented by the minor concerned. A clinical trial should also pose only minimal risk to, and impose minimal burden on, the minor concerned in comparison with the standard treatment of the minor's condition. Other conditions pertain to consent. The researchers must obtain the informed consent of the minor's legally designated representative, and the minor must be involved in the informed consent procedure and be provided with relevant information in a way adapted to their age and mental maturity. Furthermore, the explicit wish of a minor who is capable of forming an opinion to refuse participation in, or withdraw from, the clinical trial at any time, is to be respected by the investigator.

20.27   We cannot leave the subject of research involving children without some discussion of examples of good practice. Our focus in this chapter is clearly medical research but it is important to bear in mind that children can be involved in many different kinds of investigation and, often, the ethical and legal issues will be the same or very similar.[68] Indeed, medical and social science research may well overlap, thus further complicating the governance exercise. The Children of the 90s project (aka ALSPAC) is a long-term study designed to unravel how the physical and social environments interact with genetic inheritance to affect children's health, behaviour, and development.[69] The aim is to follow children into adulthood; indeed the early recruits have now reached this stage of life. The study is particularly interesting for its active involvement of parents and children in the research design, leading to very high retention rates among family participants. As the children reached decisional maturity and the question of their voluntary, continued

---

[66] Published in the Regulation (EU) No 536/2014 of the European Parliament and of the Council of 16 April 2014 on clinical trials on medicinal products for human use, and repealing Directive 2001/20/EC. Scheduled to become applicable from May 2016.

[67] European Parliament and the Council of Europe Directive 2001/20/EC of 4 April 2001 relating to the implementation of good clinical practice in the conduct of clinical trials on medicinal products for human use. The Directive was implemented in the UK by the Medicines for Human Use (Clinical Trials) Regulations 2004 (SI 2004/1031), as amended.

[68] See, e.g., F C Manga, 'Protecting children's rights in social science research in Botswana: Some ethical and legal dilemmas' (2005) 19 Int J Law Policy Fam 102.

[69] See: http://www.alspac.bris.ac.uk.

participation arose, the project responded in 2006 by forming a Teenage Advisory Panel to help guide the project into the future. This is an excellent testing ground both to explore notions of emerging autonomy and to examine how well researchers approach these sensitive issues in partnership with research participants.

FETAL RESEARCH AND EXPERIMENTATION

20.28 Several of the legal and moral attitudes to fetal life have already been discussed. The possibilities of fetal research and experimentation, which are repugnant to many, extend the area of debate and merit further discussion.[70] Research on the fetus is of considerable importance: just as children are, medically, more than little adults so, or rather more so, are fetuses not just immature children; the environment in which they exist is wholly different and, as has already been discussed, a major proportion of morbidity of infancy is congenital in origin. Major areas of disease will never be properly understood in the absence of research on the fetus and the uterine environment.[71] Nor will the outstanding dilemma of drug therapy during pregnancy be fully resolved. Recent renewed interest in fetal cells holds some promise for wider therapeutic application.[72]

SOURCES OF FETAL MATERIAL AND THE PROBLEMS OF CONSENT

20.29 Other than those that are born alive prematurely and with which we are not currently concerned, fetuses become available for research either through spontaneous miscarriage or as a result of therapeutic abortion. It is axiomatic that any necessary consent to their use can only be given by the mother and both her attitude and that of her physicians may be different in the two scenarios.[73]

20.30 The position seems clear in the case of miscarriage. The mother is distressed and, normally, wants everything possible done for her offspring. It seems unlikely in the circumstances that a research project will be contemplated but, were it so, the informed consent of the mother would be required. The therapeutic abortion situation is rather different. In the majority of cases, the mother will have requested termination and it could be held that, in so doing, she has effectively abandoned her fetus. The Peel Committee, as the first body to conduct an in-depth examination of the issues, in 1972, made the following recommendation:

> There is no legal requirement to obtain the patient's consent for research but, equally, there is no statutory right to ignore the parent's wishes—the parent must be offered the opportunity to declare any special directions about the fetus.[74]

---

[70] See A Alghrani and M Brazier, 'What is it? Whose it? Re-positioning the fetus in the context of research?' (2011) 70(1) Cam LJ 51.

[71] See, e.g., S Rees et al., 'An adverse intrauterine environment: implications for injury and altered development of the brain' (2008) 26(1) Intl J Develop Neuroscience 3.

[72] C Holden, 'Fetal cells again?' (2009) 326(5951) Science 358; J Steenhuysen, 'Fetal tissue research declining, still important' *Reuters*, 4 August 2015.

[73] S Woods and K Taylor, 'Ethical and governance challenges in human fetal tissue research' (2008) 3 Clin Ethics 14.

[74] The Peel Committee listed 53 ways in which fetal research could be valuable at the time of its report in the early 1970s: *Report of the Committee on the Use of Fetuses and Fetal Material for Research* (1972). This quote is at para 42.

20.31 This recommendation would now be considered inadequate. The very strict rules as to consent to research on the abandoned embryo should, in theory, be extrapolated to the abandoned fetus.[75] Moreover, the Peel Report was overtaken by that of the Polkinghorne Committee[76] which detected no material distinction between the results of therapeutic or spontaneous miscarriage.[77] It was firmly recommended that positive consent be obtained from the mother before fetal tissue is used for research or treatment in either circumstance[78]—for it was thought to be too harsh a judgment to infer that she has no special relationship with her fetus that has been aborted under the terms of the Abortion Act 1967;[79] the mother was entitled, at least, to counselling on the point. The Committee also recommended that her consent should include the relinquishing of any property rights—a recommendation which has been discussed in greater detail earlier.[80] The Committee rejected the notion of any control by the father over the disposal of his child—this being on the grounds that paternal consent was not required for an abortion and that his relationship to the fetus is less intimate than is that of the mother.[81] We have already referred to the general denial of paternal interests in the fetus[82] that, in this context, we see as unreasonable. Here the intimate connection between the fetus and the woman has been broken;[83] the disposal of the fetus, then, arguably, becomes a matter in which the father should have a far greater say as compared with, for example, the decision to terminate the pregnancy. This view is not, however, reflected in the Human Tissue Authority's Code of Practice—which states that 'the needs of the woman are of paramount importance in the development of a disposal policy' following pregnancy loss.[84]

20.32 The Polkinghorne Committee was established mainly in response to concerns over fetal brain implants, and, as a consequence, one of its main concerns was that the research worker seeking consent should be wholly independent of the caring gynaecologist—every moral and public policy principle dictates that it be made absolutely clear that abortions are not being performed in order to provide research or therapeutic material; the timing of a therapeutic abortion should be subject only to considerations of care for the pregnant woman.[85]

20.33 The Human Tissue Act 2004 now governs this area; it is an ambitious piece of legislation that tries to juggle with many balls in the air at once. There are no specific provisions relating to fetal material, although undoubtedly the provisions extend to such matter since the exclusions of 'relevant material' relate only to embryos outside the human body and hair and nails from the body of a living person. The Human Tissue Authority (HTA) has the responsibility to produce Codes of Practice in respect of the Act and has, in fact, produced general guidance on the disposal of human tissues[86] and specific guidance on disposal following pregnancy loss.[87] Note, the HTA deals with issues of research separately, and

---

[75] Human Fertilisation and Embryology Act 1990 as amended, Sch 3.

[76] *Review of the Guidance on the Research Use of Fetuses and Fetal Material* (Cmnd 762).

[77] At para 2.9.   [78] At para 3.10.   [79] At para 2.8.   [80] See para 14.35.

[81] At para 6.7. For this and several other criticisms of the recommendations, see J Keown, 'The Polkinghorne Report on fetal research: Nice recommendations, shame about the reasoning' (1993) 19 J Med Ethics 114.

[82] See para 9.115.   [83] See para 14.35.

[84] HTA, *Guidance on the Disposal of Pregnancy Remains Following Pregnancy Loss or Termination* (2015), para 15. The guidance refers throughout to 'the woman', but takes into account that a woman may choose to delegate the decision to her partner, a family member, or a friend.

[85] For comment on the potential impact on women of allowing fetal research, see N Pfeffer, 'How work reconfigures an "unwanted" pregnancy into "the right tool for the job" in stem cell research' (2009) 31 *Sociology of Health & Illness* 98.

[86] HTA, *Code 5: Disposal of Human Tissue* (updated 2014).   [87] HTA, n 84.

primarily as a matter of consent, the legal position being confirmed that fetal tissue—which is defined for the purposes of the Code as being derived from pregnancy loss before 24 weeks' gestation—is regarded as the mother's tissue.[88] This brings fetal tissue firmly within the provisions of the Human Tissue Act 2004, requiring appropriate consent of the mother—and, assuming her to be still alive, only of the mother—for all of the relevant scheduled purposes in the legislation.[89] By contrast, the Code does not apply to stillbirths[90] nor to neonatal deaths, whose disposal is governed by the same provisions as apply to the deceased under the 2004 Act (see further Chapter 14). The Code notes that, in the absence of dedicated legal provisions with respect to fetal material, the relevant guidance for research on such tissue is derived from the Polkinghorne Guidelines but with one important difference. Whereas Polkinghorne recommended that women should not be told what the fetal tissue would be used for, or indeed whether it would be used at all, this is no longer lawful under the Human Tissue Act. Women must be given sufficient information to make an informed decision about the storage, use, and disposal of 'their' tissue.[91]

The Status of the Fetus

20.34   We can see, then, that, cultural and attitudinal shifts towards consent aside, the stance taken by the Polkinghorne Committee remains more or less intact. Certainly the Committee was fully alert to the fact that conditions for fetal research are not uniform and, in particular, that the fetal subject may be alive or dead—or it may be killed during the process of abortion. The living human fetus should be accorded a profound respect—a conclusion that is based upon its potential for development into a fully formed human being.[92] In so saying, the Committee clearly differentiated the dead fetus but still thought that this commanded respect. Research on the living fetus should be considered in a way broadly similar to that pertaining to children and adults and it was, therefore, recommended that it should not be undertaken if the risk to the fetus was more than minimal; research or experimentation carrying a greater risk should be limited to that which was of direct benefit to the subject. Respect for the dead fetus was recognised by the belief that research in that area should also be considered by ethics committees and this is now also subject to the HTA Codes of Practice.[93]

20.35   More recently, Alghrani and Brazier have argued that the ex utero living fetus should acquire legal personality as a baby with all of the obvious attendant consequences. This potentially profound shift would first require us to clarify the application of the current 'born alive' rule in law as the threshold for legal personhood, as well as necessitating an equally significant ethical change in our conceptualisation of what is at stake.[94]

20.36   It is now clear that 'wrongful death' in utero of the fetus that is incapable of being born alive gives rise to no action in the UK;[95] neither the dead non-viable fetus nor the stillbirth

---

[88]   HTA, *Code 1: Consent* (updated 2014), paras 171–5.   [89]   Human Tissue Act 2004, s 3.

[90]   A stillbirth is defined as a child born after the 24th week of gestation which did not breathe or show other form of life: Still-birth (Definition) Act 1992.

[91]   HTA, n 88, para 174.

[92]   At para 2.4. Note, now, how survival for 28 days bestows a new status, albeit for rules as to disposal of the corpse, HTA, *Guidance on the Disposal of Pregnancy Remains Following Pregnancy Loss or Termination* (2015), para 35.

[93]   HTA, *Code 1: Consent*, n 88.   [94]   Alghrani and Brazier, n 70.

[95]   See e.g. *Bagley* v *North Herts Health Authority* [1986] NLJ Rep 1014; *Grieve* v *Salford Health Authority* (1991) 2 Med LR 295. Actions for wrongful death of the fetus have, however, succeeded in the USA where the large majority of states recognise an action for the death of a viable fetus: see *Santana* v *Zilog Inc* 95 F 3d 780 (1996).

has any right of action of itself and the only redress available to the parents for the loss of the fetus as a result of negligence rests on the grounds of distress, inconvenience, and the like.[96] If the child were born disabled, it would clearly have a right of action against a research worker whose defence, assuming causation to have been proved, would depend on a standard of reasonable care having been observed (see further Chapter 10).

20.37 But what if the fetus should die? The fetus not being a legal person, there is no offence of feticide as such; but, should the fetus die prior to or during a resultant miscarriage, an offence may lie under s 58 of the Offences Against the Person Act 1861 or under s 1 of the Infant Life (Preservation) Act 1929 if the subject were capable of being born alive. Both these sections, however, include a requirement of intent, in the former to procure a miscarriage and in the second to destroy life. To prove an offence, it would then be necessary to show that the action amounted to constructive intent—that is, something was done when it was known that fetal death was a very high probability—and this seems a very doubtful proposition. It is, however, quite clear that intentional or reckless intra-uterine injury which results in neonatal death can attract a charge of manslaughter or of culpable homicide;[97] it is at least likely that disregard of the recommendations of the Polkinghorne Committee would give rise to an inference of recklessness. We do, however, see such eventualities as being extremely rare.

THE PRE-VIABLE FETUS

20.38 It is, perhaps, the pre-viable fetus that attracts most emotion in the general issue of fetal research. Pre-viability implies that the fetus as a whole is incapable of a separate existence but that, nevertheless, there are signs of life in some organs. There can be no doubt that this is the fetal state which offers the greatest research potential; it is also true that the time available for such research is limited and so, therefore, is the opportunity for abuse. But, again, one must ask—is this, morally speaking, a human organism[98] with at least some of the rights of a human being? And, moreover, do we know that it has no feeling and is incapable of experiencing pain and suffering?[99] The Polkinghorne Committee was unable to discern any relevant ethical distinction between the pre-viable and the viable fetus—thereby diverging from the Peel Report—and we have argued in Chapter 9 to the same end.

20.39 We suggest that the criminal law is inadequate in this area. It is doubtful whether the Abortion Act 1967 would be a sufficient safeguard in the event of an extension of techniques being coupled with a deterioration in professional standards; it might then be necessary to invent an offence of feticide.[100] The moral dilemma is clear from the questions posed earlier and, equally, turns on the definition of 'life'. We suggest that the moral

[96] Non-compliance with the terms of the Human Tissue Act 2004 with respect to obtaining the appropriate consent and non-licensed storage and use of tissue will also give rise to criminal sanction.
[97] *Kwok Chak Ming* v R [1963] HKLR 349; *McCluskey* v *HM Advocate* 1989 SLT 175; *A-G's Reference (No 3 of 1994)* [1996] QB 581; [1996] 2 All ER 10.
[98] See *A-G's Reference*, n 97.
[99] The problem of fetal experience of pain seems unresolved and one wonders if it is capable of resolution. The majority opinion seems to be that fetuses of less than 24 weeks' gestation feel no pain. For discussion, see S W G Derbyshire (2006) 332 BMJ 909. Cf, J Hopkins Tanne, 'Nebraska prohibits abortion after 20 weeks because of fetal pain' (2010) 340 BMJ c2091.
[100] Although the attitude of the European Court of Human Rights (ECtHR) to the clinical lapses demonstrated in *Vo* v *France* [2004] 2 FCR 577; (2004) 79 BMLR 71 makes this unlikely—even allowing for a distinction between clinical practice and research.

problem may be resolved by considering, first, whether a placenta is present and whether there is or is not a competent fetal–maternal connection. If there is, the fetus is, subject to normality, alive and destructive research or experimentation would be morally unacceptable; they should be disallowed on these grounds alone. If, however, the pre-viable fetus is separated from its mother, it is no longer capable of an existence; it is, therefore, possible to argue that its state is one of somatic death. Experiments or research conducted on the body are, by this reasoning, conducted during the interval between somatic and ultimate cellular death which has been described in Chapter 16. Accordingly, we suggest that the processes involve neither moral nor legal culpability—although the opportunities for research within these parameters seem limited. The point is now moot in many ways, at least legally speaking, given the position adopted by the HTA; the moral qualms of many will, however, remain.[101]

THE DEAD FETUS AND FETAL MATERIALS

20.40 Much useful research can be done on fetuses which are clearly dead or are incomplete; the major debate as to the morality of such research depends on how the fetus came to be dead—any objection on principle to the use of tissue from dead fetuses is almost certainly grounded on an overall objection to abortion. Disposal of the dead fetus—as opposed to the stillbirth—is, effectively a matter of societal rather than lawful practice. We have seen that fetal tissue, whether alive or dead, is now considered to be the mother's tissue; it follows that the dead fetus of less than 24 weeks' gestation, itself, must be 'maternal tissue'.[102] The question remains as to how far does this give control to the woman over her 'own' tissue? In particular, does she own it? We have discussed the complexities of this in Chapter 14. Suffice it to say, the Polkinghorne Committee condemned out of hand the sale of fetal tissues and materials for commercial purposes; this sentiment certainly persists in Art 21 of the European Convention on Human Rights and Biomedicine, which prohibits commerce in 'the human body and its parts, as such',[103] although this makes no specific mention of the placenta, in which, there *is* a recognised commercial value. Closer to home, the Human Tissue Act 2004 imposes a prohibition on commercial dealings in human material for transplantation purposes. This is particularly pertinent given the suggested value of fetal material for a growing range of therapeutic possibilities. Only the permission of the HTA can elide the possibility of prosecution in such cases. Note, however, material that has become property because of the application of human skill—for example, through suitable preservation techniques—is excepted from this.[104] This raises the prospect that researchers, rather than the mother, might ultimately claim property rights in fetal material, albeit that failure to obtain the mother's consent to the 'work' to be done at all would serve as a complete veto.

---

[101] Alghrani and Brazier, n 70, comprehensively analyse potential liability for researchers in navigating parental consent and the legal status of non-viable fetuses which may be never the less alive when transferred to an artificial womb (ectogenesis).

[102] Leaving aside the difficulty of equating this with the House of Lords' decision in *A-G's Reference (No 3 of 1994)* (1998) AC 245.

[103] See also, Department of Health, *Human Bodies, Human Choices*, (2002), which raised the possibility of legislation specifically excluding property rights in the body of a fetus or fetal tissue.

[104] Human Tissue Act 2004, s 32(9)(c).

EMBRYOS AND EMBRYONIC
STEM CELL RESEARCH

20.41   There are two quite distinct forms of research involving human embryos. The moral debate that preceded the passage of the Human Fertilisation and Embryology Act 1990 was concerned with research on the embryo with a view to understanding embryo development, reproductive issues, and genetic disease. In more recent years this form of research has been somewhat eclipsed by enthusiasm for research into the therapeutic use of stem cells taken from embryos. In this form of research, the embryo is a potential source of material for use on others; it is not the embryo itself that is the object of interest, but rather it becomes the source of useful research material for far wider application. In this section we will consider the two forms of research separately because of their important moral and scientific distinction and despite the fact that there are, of course, moral issues which are common to both. We must also consider, for completeness, the prospect of parallel research streams that aim to produce stem cells that do not involve the use and destruction of embryos and which, it is argued, thereby avoid many of the moral pitfalls.[105]

EMBRYONIC RESEARCH

20.42   Research into human infertility and an understanding of embryonic development and implantation are inseparable. Embryonic research is also essential to the study and conquest of genetic disease. Systematic study in both these fields depends upon a supply of human embryos, for there always comes a time when animal models are inadequate for human research purposes. Essentially, there are two adoptable attitudes: either one can be totally opposed to research and experimentation on what are considered to be living human beings who cannot refuse consent to manipulation, or one can hold that the benefits to mankind are likely to be so great that the opportunity for study must be grasped if it is presented.[106] Given that the case for human research is agreed—and we believe that it must be—the problem then arises as to how the necessary material is to be obtained, generated, and used within an acceptable moral and legal framework. There are, again, two possibilities that are by no means mutually exclusive—either one can use the inevitable surplus of embryos that are produced for infertility treatments, or one can go one stage further and create embryos in vitro for the explicit purpose of using them for research. Matters have been complicated further by the prospect of, and legal acceptance of, the creation of 'admixed embryos' for research.[107] It is first necessary to look at the general proposition.

20.43   Arguments against a policy that prohibits embryo research rely, ultimately, on the view that, although the embryo may have human properties, it is not a human being invested with the same moral rights to respect as are due to other living members of the human

---

[105]   A S Carvalho and J Ramalho-Santos, 'How can ethics relate to science? The case of stem cell research' (2012) 21(6) Eur J Hum Genet 591.

[106]   N Espinoza and M Paterson, 'How to depolarise the ethical debate over human embryonic stem cell research (and other ethical debates too!)' (2012) 38(8) J Med Ethics 496.

[107]   For possible definitions of 'admixed embryo' see the Human Fertilisation and Embryology Act 1990, as amended, s 4A(6).

community.[108] This approach has a familiar ring to it; indeed, it introduces the same concepts of personhood that have been so much a part of the abortion debate. There is, however, a crucial distinction to be made between lethal embryo research and abortion. The life of the aborted fetus is extinguished because its interests are outweighed by a more powerful and tangible set of interests—namely, those of the pregnant woman. The embryo subjected to research, by contrast, dies because of the far less obvious interests of society in the pursuit of medical knowledge. The justification of feticide in abortion does not necessarily license the taking of in vitro embryonic life—and the legislative concern for the latter in the face of a liberal abortion policy may not be as unreasonable as is sometimes argued.[109]

20.44 Yet, if we consider, first, the surplus embryo, we have to ask, 'What is the alternative to embryocide?' The techniques in IVF and the welfare of the patient demand that more embryos are created than are strictly necessary; to say that all must be implanted would be to fly in the face of the reality and what is now clear Human Fertilisation and Embryology Authority (HFEA) policy. The alternatives then lie between embryocide and reduction of multiple pregnancy—of which the former is clearly the less objectionable insofar as it involves the destruction of organisms which, left to themselves, have no future. We have discussed elsewhere[110] the ethics of obtaining good from a morally poor or doubtful fait accompli. It is now the policy of many countries that the phenomenon of so-called 'surplus embryos' is an acceptable moral halfway house in justifying embryo research. Indeed, for any country that accepts and permits an active IVF programme, the dilemma of outright destruction of these human organisms or their use for wider social benefit cannot be avoided.[111]

20.45 But the legitimacy of instrumental uses of embryos in this way can only be maintained by recourse to a basic tenet of the doctrine of double effect—that the good result of variation from a principle must not be achieved by means of an inevitable ill-effect—is observed and it is this that distinguishes research on the surplus embryo from that undertaken on the embryo that has been created for the purpose; it follows that the latter needs further justification.[112] The proponents of unrestricted research would reply that it is acceptable not only because the embryo fails to satisfy the requirements of personhood (which the fetus, also, fails to satisfy) but also because, at least in its earlier stages,[113] its cells are totipotent. In other words, in the early days of development, the conceptus is not a single,

---

[108] The issue of the status of the embryo, and in particular the ethical and religious implications of using the embryo for research, are fully and clearly canvassed in the report of the US National Bioethics Advisory Commission, *Ethical Issues in Human Stem Cell Research* (1999). Little has changed since then.

[109] See e.g. Mason at n 37, p 471. Ms Evans' case (para 8.80) clearly demonstrated that neither the fetus nor the embryo in vitro has any rights under Art 2 of the European Convention on Human Rights (ECHR).

[110] See Chapter 18.

[111] See E Haimes and K Taylor, 'The contributions of empirical evidence to socio-ethical debates on fresh embryo donation for human embryonic stem cell research' (2011) 25(6) Bioethics 334; R Scott et al., 'Donation of spare fresh or frozen embryos to research: Who decides that an embryo is spare and how can we enhance the quality and protect the validity of consent?' (2012) 20(3) Med Law Rev 255; B Farsides and R Scott, 'No small matter for some: Practitioner's views on the moral status and treatment of human embryos' (2012) 20(1) Med Law Rev 90.

[112] For further discussion see T Murphy, 'Double-effect reasoning and the conception of human embryos' (2013) 39 J Med Ethics 529; K Devolder, 'Embryo deaths in reproduction and embryo research: A reply to Murphy's double effect argument' (2013) 39 J Med Ethics 533.

[113] The use of the term 'pre-embryo' is suggested for this stage of development. We feel, however, that this smacks of changing words to establish a moral bolt-hole.

identifiable individual; any of its cells can develop (technically, *differentiate*) along a number of lines, into a placenta, a hydatidiform mole, a complete human being, or, indeed, several human beings. The early embryo thus lacks the essential qualities which go to make the human individual unique and worthy of moral respect.[114] As a research tool, however, it possesses considerable qualities and potential.

20.46   The counter-assertion is, of course, that the embryo is the first stage of the human being that is born at the end of pregnancy—and that this holds from the moment of syngamy. It has been pointed out that the embryo stage is an essential part of life and that it makes no sense to argue that a person's life begins only with the appearance of the primitive streak on about the fourteenth day after conception.[115] It follows that the use of an embryo for any purpose that does not bear upon its future good constitutes a wrong; the embryo is, otherwise, being treated as a means to an end rather than as an end in itself—a process which offends a fundamental principle governing the way in which we treat other persons. To create human life in the full knowledge that it can have only the most limited future is seen by many opponents of embryo experimentation as an example of amoral exploitation and a fairly firm step on yet another slippery slope.

20.47   Between the two 'extreme' positions—that of a total rejection of embryo research on the grounds of its inescapable immorality and that of its acceptance in the case of any embryo, however derived—lies the middle view that, whereas research on surplus embryos is acceptable, the creation of embryos for that purpose is not. This latter is, in fact, expressly prohibited by Art 18 of the Council of Europe Convention on Biomedicine and Human Rights. It is a view which is held by many, but even so, it is not easy to establish a valid moral basis for the claim—because, insofar as the ultimate outcome is their destruction, the ultimate harm done to the embryos is the same in each case. A possible philosophical solution depends on distinguishing harm from wrong. No *wrong* is done to the embryo at the time it is formed with a view to implantation; a later failure to achieve that goal is due to circumstances which are, to a large extent, beyond the control of the person who has brought it into being. By contrast, the embryo which is developed with the express intention of harming it is clearly *wronged at* the moment of its formation. Thus, while the harm done to each is the same, the wrong done is of a different quality. But do those who take the middle road adopt such reasoning in reality? It seems more probable that they accept instinctively that a utilitarian argument which holds that the benefit to mankind exceeds the harm done to what are the unfortunate rejects of a legitimate therapeutic activity cannot be substantiated in the case of specially created research subjects. This problem has raised what has been, perhaps, the most difficult hurdle for the world's legislatures— and the UK Parliament is a world 'leader', if that is not an inappropriate use of the term, in having opted in favour of the similar moral status of in vitro embryos whether they be surplus or purposeful creations. The UK stands alone in Europe, save for Belgium and Sweden, in allowing the creation of embryos for the specific purpose of performing research on them.[116]

---

[114] For other scientific arguments on the status of the embryo see E Russo, 'Stem cells without embryos? New methods of generating pluripotent cells may placate critics, but may not work, say scientists', *The Scientist*, 25 March 2005, available at: http://www.the-scientist.com/?articles.view/articleNo/23306/title/Stem-cells-without-embryos-/, and for an overview of the state of the art see S Kobold et al., 'Human embryonic and induced pluripotent stem cell research trends: Complementation and diversification of the field' (2015) 4(5) Stem Cell Reports 914.

[115] A Holland, 'A fortnight of my life is missing: A discussion of the status of the pre-embryo' (1990) 7 J Appl Philos 25.

[116] European Science Foundation, *Human Stem Cell Research and Regenerative Medicine* (2013).

20.48 There may, of course, be tenable scientific reasons for creating embryos for research purposes if these new entities possess qualities not found in their foregone counterparts. Arguments in favour of embryo creation include the role that embryo research can play in providing autologous transplants, in which the embryonic material must have the same genetic profile as the future recipient of the transplant. Other examples include specific disease modelling, whereby the embryonic material is manipulated to maximise its utility for investigations into particular diseases.[117] Arguments in favour of 'admixed embryos' are far-ranging but as yet almost entirely unproven. Notwithstanding, these have led sufficient sway in the UK to reforms to the Human Fertilisation and Embryology Act 1990, such that the creation of, and research on, human admixed embryos is permissible subject to an HFEA licence. The particular parameters of the UK domestic scene merit some closer attention.

THE LEGAL RESPONSE

20.49 The entirety of legal regulation of embryo research in the UK is embodied in the Human Fertilisation and Embryology Act 1990, as amended. By virtue of this it is illegal to conduct any research on human or admixed embryos except under licence from the HFEA. The HFEA can only issue such a licence if the project is thought to be desirable for the principal purposes detailed in the Act which include increasing knowledge or developing treatments about serious disease or other serious medical conditions; promoting advances in the treatment of infertility; increasing knowledge about the causes of miscarriage; developing more effective techniques of contraception; developing methods for detecting the presence of gene, chromosome, or mitochondrion abnormalities in embryos before implantation; or increasing knowledge about the development of embryos.[118] In the absence of further regulation, no licence may authorise altering the genetic structure of a cell while it is part of an embryo[119] and, while the hamster test for the normality of human sperm is allowed, all products of such research must be destroyed not later than the two-cell stage. There are strict regulations as to the maintenance of experimental records.[120] Overall, licences cannot authorise keeping or using an embryo after the appearance of the primitive streak—taken as being not later than 14 days after the gametes were mixed—nor may any embryo be placed in any animal.[121] Most importantly, in decreeing that research may be carried out, Parliament placed no restrictions on the source of the embryos used; the HFEA has no mandate to impose an overall embargo on the creation of embryos for that specific purpose.[122] Importantly, the HFEA granted its first licence to create human embryonic stem cells using cell nuclear transfer in August 2004 and since that time there has been an explosion of interest in this branch of science and its associated ethical concerns. We now turn to a consideration of this topic.

---

[117] H Homer and M Davies, 'The science and ethics of human admixed embryos' (2009) 19 Obs Gyn Repro Med 235.

[118] 1990 Act, Sch 2, para 3A(2) as amended by Human Fertilisation and Embryology Act 2008, Sch 2, para 6.

[119] An organism formed by cell nuclear replacement is considered to be an embryo: *R (on the application of Quintavalle) v Secretary of State for Health* [2003] 2 AC 687. See, s 1(1) of the 1990 Act, as amended, and note that 'embryo' and 'human admixed embryo' are subject to distinct definition.

[120] Section 15.   [121] Section 3.

[122] An update on guidance and licences granted is available at the HFEA website: http://www.hfea.gov.uk.

EMBRYONIC STEM CELL RESEARCH

20.50 The framers of the 1990 legislation may have imagined that the issue of embryo research would no longer be controversial once Parliament had answered the fundamental moral question and a system of tight regulation was in place. If so, they were proved wrong and the decisions of the HFEA have been subject to a wide array of judicial review proceedings ever since its inception. It was partly for this reason that the 2008 reforms sought to clarify and confirm the role of the HFEA in this realm. It was perhaps with the successful production of stable cell lines from human embryonic stem cells in 1998 that the controversy moved up to yet another level.[123] Before considering the contours of the debate, however, it is valuable to cover some of the scientific ground. The adult human body is composed of 50 trillion cells of around 200 different kinds, each with a particular function, be it an eye cell, a muscle cell, a blood cell, etc. In the beginning, however, it is not so complicated. Over a matter of hours from the initial creation of the zygote, this entity divides again and again but the cells that are created at this stage have no dedicated function—they are said to be *undifferentiated*. Indeed, within this initial period of division—which lasts no more than three to four days—these undifferentiated stem cells are *totipotent*—that is, each has the capacity to become a complete and separate embryo. This quality is soon lost, however, and by days five to seven the organism has become a *blastocyst*, a ball of around 100 cells each of which is now *pluripotent*—that is, each has the capacity to develop into any of the 200 cell types that make up the human body, but it is no longer possible for them to develop into separate embryos. As time passes, the organism—which we might now wish to call an *embryo*—will continue to grow so long as it is furnished with an appropriate environment and nutrition. These are provided by implantation in the lining of the womb from which a blood supply can be drawn (occurring around day eight of development). It is arguable that it is not until this point that the organism achieves the potential for 'human life'—a distinction which is very important when considering the status of the embryo in the Petri dish. Thereafter, the embryo will continue to develop, with the first signs of a nervous system appearing at days 14 to 15 (the primitive streak). As the embryo grows, its cells slowly become more task-orientated (*differentiated*) and begin to assume their eventual role within the body. While there is no hard and fast rule, an embryo is generally referred to as a *fetus* from week eight of its development onwards.[124] Clearly, one would be holding an immensely powerful research and therapeutic resource if one could produce a pluripotent cell line—that is, a self-perpetuating line of cells that can be replicated indefinitely in the laboratory.

20.51 Stem cells can also be derived from aborted fetal germ cells—that is, the cells that would have become the sperm or egg cells. These germ cells can be cultivated into stem cells in the same way as can occur naturally in the case of embryos. They were first developed in 1998 and they can now be differentiated into an increasingly broad range of dedicated cells.[125] A final and further source of stem cells can be found in adults, but in the main these tend to be *multipotent*—that is, they can only evolve into particular kinds of cell, or *progenitor cells*, which, although they are clearly destined for a particular end, are as yet undifferentiated. Even so, it now appears that adult stem cells can differentiate into a far

---

[123] J A Thomson et al., 'Embryonic stem cell lines derived from human blastocysts' (1998) 282 Science 1145.

[124] Although it saves a lot of misapprehension if one reserves the term embryo for the pre-implantation stage of human development.

[125] See Kobold et al., n 114.

broader range of cells than was originally thought and many advances are being made towards the production of clinical grade cell lines.[126]

20.52   Most promise with embryonic stem cells lies with those extracted from the blastocyst when they have pluripotent qualities. It is important to re-emphasise that no embryo can be derived from such cells. Equally importantly, however, is the fact that the blastocyst is destroyed in this process. If one views this organism at this stage as embryonic life we have, then, the makings of a classic ethical controversy.[127]

20.53   The ethical and legal issues surrounding human stem cell research of this nature differ from those addressed in the earlier debate on embryo research in that, whereas other forms of embryo research may be intended to assist reproductive medicine and future embryos, this type involves using embryos for the benefit of society in general. This has invigorated the opposition of those who have a principled objection to any form of embryo research.[128] At the same time, arguments in favour of such research have been forcefully advanced, often on the grounds that the benefit to humanity of the resulting therapies outweighs the interests of the embryos, particularly if use is made of cells derived from embryos which were rendered surplus within the accepted IVF treatment programme.[129]

20.54   The phenomenon of induced pluripotent stem cells (iPSCs) has been heralded by some as a sufficiently scientifically robust[130] and ethically preferable route to follow in this field of research.[131] In brief, iPSCs can be created from human somatic cells, such as skin cells, without the need to use embryos.[132] Ethically speaking, it is self-evident that many of our moral concerns disappear if it is the case that we do not need to use and destroy embryos in research; unfortunately, other ethical concerns may surface to take their place, for example, the concern that viral vectors are often used in iPSCs techniques raising the prospect of transmission of carcinogenic retroviruses to mammals.[133] Such objections as exist, however, and which are based on concerns about technical limitations or scientific risks, are being overtaken quickly by developments in the field.[134] Accordingly, a strong

---

[126]   C Unger, 'Good manufacturing practice and clinical-grade human embryonic stem cell lines' (2008) Hum Mol Genet 17(R1).

[127]   We discuss the economic and intellectual property consequences of this in Europe in Chapter 14 at paras 14.45–14.64.

[128]   See C Tollefsen, 'Embryos, individuals, and persons: An argument against embryo creation and research' (2001) 18 J Appl Philosoph 65 for an expression of ethical opposition to embryo research. More generally see S Chan, J Harris, and M Quigley (eds), *Stem Cells: New Frontiers in Science and Ethics* (2012).

[129]   As discussed at para 8.75. For an argument that the surplus status of the embryo does not necessarily make stem cell research more acceptable, see J-E S Hansen, 'Embryonic stem cell production through therapeutic cloning has fewer ethical problems than stem cell harvest from surplus IVF embryos' (2002) 28 J Med Ethics 86.

[130]   K Takahashi et al., 'Induction of pluripotent stem cells from adult human fibroblasts by defined factors' (2007) 131 Cell 861 and J Yu et al., 'Induced pluripotent stem cell lines derived from human somatic cells' (2007) 318 Science 1917.

[131]   For a contrary view see M Brown, 'No ethical bypass of moral status of stem cell research' (2013) 27(1) Bioethics 12.

[132]   K Kaji et al., 'Virus-free induction of pluripotency and subsequent excision of reprogramming factors' (2009) 458(7239) Nature 771.

[133]   J R Meyer, 'The significance of induced pluripotent stem cells for basic research and clinical therapy' (2008) 34 J Med Ethics 849.

[134]   X Y Deng et al., 'Non-viral methods for generating integration-free, induced pluripotent stem cells' (2015) 10(2) Curr Stem Cell Res Ther 153.

consensus remains, in the scientific community at least, that for now all avenues of stem cell research should be followed.[135]

20.55   The value of stem cells of whatever origin is twofold. First, they can divide and multiply more or less indefinitely without differentiation and, second, they can be manipulated so as to differentiate into particular specialised cells. These qualities mean that scientists have both a potentially endless supply of raw research material and also the means to develop a number of therapeutic applications. These range from gene therapy (for which, see Chapter 7) to developments in regenerative medicine whereby diseased or damaged cells can be replaced in conditions such as diabetes, Parkinson's disease, chronic heart failure, and injuries to, or degenerative disease of, the spinal cord. As we have already discussed, one of the main drawbacks in transplantation therapy is the rejection by the body of the implanted foreign tissue. Embryonic stem cell biology has developed its own way round this problem whereby the nucleus of an embryonic cell is replaced with a nucleus taken from the cell of the prospective patient. Stem cells are then taken from the resulting embryo and tissue is grown from them which can be transplanted back to the patient without risk of rejection. The process of creating such an embryo is known as therapeutic cloning. This is quite distinct from reproductive cloning, because the embryo is not allowed to develop beyond an early point and is not implanted in a uterus.

20.56   Scientific interest in the possibilities opened by embryonic stem cell research was accompanied by intense bioethical debate in Western Europe and the USA and a resultant crisis in legal circles about the ability of existing laws to cope with eventualities. Although the Human Fertilisation and Embryology Act 1990 allowed for research on human embryos in the UK, the purposes for which such research could be carried out were, as we have seen, limited by the conditions of Sch 2, para 3(2); at the time of the advent of the science these were far more restrictive than is now the case after the 2008 reforms. Notably, the list of permitted projects did not embrace research on embryos with a view to using embryonic stem cells for therapeutic purposes; moreover, replacement of the cells of an embryo was specifically disallowed under s 3(3)(d) of the 1990 Act (now repealed). Fresh regulations were, therefore, needed before any such work could be carried out in the UK. Public debate on the issue was initiated by the appointment by the government of an expert group to advise on the ethical and scientific aspects of stem cell research. This group recommended that embryonic stem cell research should be permitted and that therapeutic cloning involving cell nuclear replacement should be allowed.[136] A similar conclusion was reached at about the same time by a group set up by the Nuffield Council on Bioethics.[137] Media interest and the concerns of various groups, such as the Roman Catholic Church, however, remain strong.[138]

20.57   The parliamentary airing of the issue resulted in the approval of additions to the regulations in Sch 2. These additions permitted embryonic research for the purpose of increasing knowledge about the development of embryos, increasing knowledge about serious disease, and enabling such knowledge to be applied in developing treatments for serious disease. The government, however, agreed to a review of these regulations by a select

---

[135] For a sceptical view, C Power and J E J Rasko, 'Will cell reprogramming resolve the embryonic stem cell controversy? A narrative review' (2011) 155 Annal of Internal Med 114.

[136] Department of Health, *Stem Cell Research: Medical Progress with Responsibility* (2000).

[137] Nuffield Council on Bioethics, *Stem Cell Therapy: A Discussion Paper* (2000).

[138] See G Watts (ed), *Hype, Hope and Hybrids: Science, Policy and Media Perspectives of the Human Fertilisation and Embryology Bill* (2009).

committee of the House of Lords which, in due course, reported in favour of the proposed additions.[139] These were reiterated and expanded in the 2008 reforms. Embryonic stem cell research for therapeutic purposes is thus now legal, and encouraged, in the UK, provided a licence is obtained from the IIFEA, the first of which, as we have seen, was granted in 2004.[140] The UK Stem Cell Bank—the world's first—was established in 2003 in order to provide quality research materials under optimal governance restrictions in this field.[141] In part, it was also established to minimise the moral impact of embryonic stem cell research on the philosophy that more sharing would lead to less destruction of early stage human life. All stem cell and tissue collections are now subject to the provisions of the EU Tissue and Cells Directive, adopted in April 2004,[142] and incorporated into domestic law.[143] While this instrument is largely concerned with matters of storage and safety, it is important to point out that earlier versions were subject to intense lobbying in the European Parliament in an attempt to use the Directive to outlaw embryo and stem cell research entirely. These attempts did not succeed—there is, in fact, probably no legal authority for the Union to so legislate—but the attempt demonstrates well the continuing controversial nature of the research.

20.58 While the UK has proved ready to facilitate stem cell research,[144] other countries have been either more cautious or, in some cases, frankly hostile to the process.[145] There is an outright ban on all forms of embryo research in some jurisdictions; a compromise has been reached in others. There has been a particularly prolonged debate in Germany, both within and outside Parliament, and the resulting compromise allows the importation, for research purposes, of embryonic stem cell lines established prior to the date of passage of the legislation. A similar compromise had been suggested in the USA, where there was overwhelming political hostility to the use of federal funds for this purpose under the Bush Administration which led to a ban on federal funding of embryonic stem cell research. Federal funding controls, however, did not preclude the carrying out of research in a strictly privately funded setting and one of the deep ironies of the US position until the Obama administrations was that it was possible to carry out even more extensive embryo research under the guise of private conduct than may be undertaken under the seemingly more liberal regime of the UK. In practice, however, major institutions were severely inhibited by federal funding restrictions. It seems to us to be rather difficult—if not impossible—to maintain a consistent ethical stance in these circumstances. It cannot

---

[139] House of Lords, *Stem Cell Research* (HL Paper 83(i), 2002).

[140] Following a public consultation, the HFEA has given advice to government in support of permitting mitochondrial replacement in treatment: http://mitochondria.hfea.gov.uk/mitochondria/. The Nuffield Council on Bioethics (NCB) has also come out in favour of exploring the techniques further, see NCB, *Novel Techniques for the Prevention of Mitochondrial DNA Disorders: An Ethical Review* (2012). We discuss this further at 7.09 et seq.

[141] See: http://www.nibsc.org/ukstemcellbank.

[142] European Directive 2004/23/EC on setting standards of quality and safety for the donation, procurement, testing, processing, preservation, storage and distribution of human tissues and cells, came into effect on 8 April 2004. See, too, Commission Directive 2006/17/EC implementing Directive 2004/23/EC of the European Parliament and of the Council as regards certain technical requirements for the donation, procurement and testing of human tissues and cells (8 February 2006).

[143] The Human Tissue (Quality and Safety for Human Application) Regulations 2007 (SI 2007/1523).

[144] See N M R Perrin, *The Global Commercialisation of UK Stem Cell Research* (2005) and on potential barriers see E Rowley and P Martin, *Barriers to the Commercialisation and Utilisation of Regenerative Medicine in the UK* (2009).

[145] L Matthiesen-Guyader (ed), *Survey on Opinion of National Ethics Committees or Similar Bodies, Public Debate and National Legislation in Relation to Human Embryonic Stem Cell Research and Use in EU Member States* (2004).

be the case that the ethics of embryonic stem cell research can fundamentally change depending on who funds the work.[146]

20.59   In the final analysis, however, we cannot divorce the ethical debate from the socio-economic imperatives that are also at stake. The realities are that many people suffering from degenerative and other conditions could stand to benefit considerably if stem cell technologies can deliver on the hype that has accompanied them.[147] The commercial benefits for countries that take the lead in such research are not far behind. Thus, whatever one might think of the ethical issues, it is undeniable that other pressures are mounting in favour of these technologies, including the development of embryonic stem cell lines. It is perhaps this, in part, which has ushered in a complete reversal of fortune for researchers in the USA with President Obama making it one of his first acts in office to lift the ban on federal funding.[148] In Europe, and as we have suggested, it is probably beyond the competency of the EU to attempt to legislate for the morality of stem cell research, although the recent decision by the European Court of Justice on the patentability of embryonic stem cell inventions might have produced the same net result.[149] Moreover, the EU can pursue aggressive economic policies in the health arena and its Regulation on advanced therapy medicinal products sends a clear message about the economic benefits to be gained from pursuit and success of research in this field.[150] This message also, of course, reflects a moral position adopted at supranational level and which has clear practical implications at national level with respect to controversial technologies such as embryonic stem cell research—and that position, at present, seems decidedly equivocal. Thus, the EU regulation establishing the parameters for funding within the Horizon 2020 Programme prohibits the financing of: 'research activities intended to create human embryos solely for the purpose of research or for stem cell procurement'.[151] Nevertheless, research on human stem cells both adult and embryonic may be financed, depending both on the contents of the scientific proposal and the legal framework of the Member States involved. This compromise position has been welcomed by many,[152] but it will contribute little towards a more harmonised approach to stem cell research in the future.

---

[146] For an overview of different positions around the globe as at 2009 see T Caulfield et al., 'International stem cell environments: A world of difference' *Nature Reports Stem Cells*, 16 April 2009: 10.1038/stemcells.2009.61.

[147] See generally F Walsh, 'Stem cell trial aims to cure blindness', *BBC News*, 29 September 2015.

[148] Presidential Documents, *Removing Barriers to Responsible Scientific Research Involving Human Stem Cells*, Executive Order 13505 of 9 March 2009.

[149] *Brüstle* v *Greenpeace* [2012] All ER (EC) 809; [2012] 1 CMLR 41. We discuss this case at paras 14.57–14.59.

[150] Regulation (EC) No 1394/2007 of the European Parliament and of the Council of 13 November 2007 on advanced therapy medicinal products and amending Directive 2001/83/EC and Regulation (EC) No 726/2004.

[151] Regulation (EU) No 1291/2013 of the European Parliament and of the Council of 11 December 2013 establishing Horizon 2020—the Framework Programme for Research and Innovation (2014–2020) and repealing Decision No 1982/2006/EC, Art 19.

[152] Though pro-life groups have sought to challenge these arrangements; see European Commission, 'European Citizens' Initiative: European Commission replies to "One of Us"' (28 May 2014) IP/14/608.

INDEX